Abnormal Child and Adolescent Psychology

SEVENTH EDITION

Abnormal Child and Adolescent Psychology

SEVENTH EDITION

RITA WICKS-NELSON

**West Virginia University Institute of Technology,
Professor Emeritus**

ALLEN C. ISRAEL

University at Albany, State University of New York

PEARSON
Prentice
Hall

UPPER SADDLE RIVER, NEW JERSEY 07458

BS

Library of Congress Cataloging-in-Publication Data

Wicks-Nelson, Rita

   Abnormal child and adolescent psychology / Rita Wicks-Nelson, Allen C. Israel.—7th ed.
   p. cm.
   Rev. ed. of: Behavior disorders of childhood. c2006.
   Includes bibliographical references and index.
   ISBN-13: 978-0-13-235978-8
   ISBN-10: 0-13-235978-2
   1. Behavior disorders in children. I. Israel, Allen C. II. Wicks-Nelson, Rita, Behavior disorders
   of childhood. III. Title.

RJ506.B44W534 2009
618.92′89—dc22

2008002456

Editorial Director: Leah Jewell
Executive Editor: Jeff Marshall
Project Manager (Editorial): LeeAnn Doherty
Editorial Assistant: Aaron Talwar
Editor in Chief, Development: Rochelle Diogenes
Pegasus Program Manager: Richard Virginia
Senior Pegasus Program Manager: Brian Hyland
Senior Marketing Manager: Kate Mitchell
Senior Managing Editor: Ann Marie McCarthy
Associate Managing Editor: Maureen Richardson
Production Liaison: Maureen Richardson
Senior Operations Specialist: Sherry Lewis
Director, Image Resource Center: Melinda Patelli
Manager, Rights & Permissions: Zina Arabia
Manager, Visual Research: Beth Boyd-Brenzel
Manager, Cover Visual Research & Permissions: Karen Sanatar
Image Permission Coordinator: Silvana Attanasio
Interior Design: Aptara, Inc.
Cover Design: Studio Indigo
Cover Illustration/Photo: Roy Gumpel; Getty Images/Photographer's Choice
Composition/Full-Service Project Management: Aptara, Inc./Shelley L. Creager
Printer/Binder: Edwards Brothers
Cover Printer: Phoenix Color Corp.

Credits and acknowledgments borrowed from other sources and reproduced, with permission, in this textbook appear on pages 513–520.

Pearson Education, Ltd.   Pearson Education Australia PTY, Limited
Pearson Education Singapore, Pte., Ltd.   Pearson Education North Asia Ltd.
Pearson Education, Canada, Ltd.   Pearson Educación de Mexico, S.A. de C.V.
Pearson Education—Japan   Pearson Education Malaysia, Pte., Ltd.
Pearson Education, Upper Saddle River, NJ

10 9 8 7 6 5 4 3 2 1

ISBN-13: 978-0-13-235978-8
ISBN-10: 0-13-235978-2

2/17/10

Brief Contents

Contents

9 Attention-Deficit Hyperactivity Disorder 232

14   Psychological Factors Affecting Medical Conditions   391

15   Evolving Concerns for Youth   413

Preface

The study of psychological problems in children and adolescents and of efforts to assist youth and their families is both challenging and exciting. This field has continued to develop at a rapid pace. In roughly one hundred years, the study of young people has moved from relative ignorance to considerable knowledge about human development in general and disordered behavior more specifically. With much yet to be learned—and the needs of youth considerable—this is an especially worthwhile endeavor. We are fortunate to have the opportunity to participate in it.

As will be obvious to those familiar with past editions of this text, its title has been changed (from *Behavior Disorders of Childhood*). The title of this seventh edition, *Abnormal Child and Adolescent Psychology*, reflects both a general shift in preferred terminology and the developmental scope of the material that has been covered in successive editions of the text.

The current edition attests to the progress that continues to be made in understanding, assessing, treating, and preventing psychopathology of youth. Designed as a relatively comprehensive introduction, the text includes central issues; theoretical and methodological foundations; and the characteristics, correlates, epidemiology, developmental course, etiology, assessment, treatment, and prevention of psychological problems of children and adolescents. As is typically the case for a work of this kind, space limitation demands some selectivity of content.

CENTRAL THEMES

At the inception of this text, we viewed certain themes as critical to the study of problems of youth. These themes have stood the test of time, have evolved, and have become more widely and subtly recognized as essential. Indeed, their early incorporation into this text undoubtedly accounts in part for its ongoing success.

First is an emphasis on the developmental psychopathology approach as a partner to the more traditional (usual) clinical/disorder approach. The developmental psychopathology perspective assumes that disorders of young people must be viewed within a developmental context. This perspective is fully articulated in early chapters of the book and guides discussion of specific disorders in subsequent chapters.

A primary assumption is the belief that the development of normal and disturbed behavior are related and are best viewed as occurring along a dynamic pathway of growth and experience, with connections to the past and to the future. One way this proposition is reflected in the text is by the consideration of disorders across childhood and into adolescence. Taking seriously the assumption that behavioral development cannot be readily parsed by age, we employ a relatively broad time frame for discussing psychological problems in young people.

A second theme woven throughout the text is the view that behavioral problems result from transactions among variables. With few—if any—exceptions, behavior stems from multiple influences and their continuous interactions. Biological structure and function, genetic transmission, cognition, emotion, social interaction and numerous aspects of the immediate and broader environment play complex roles in generating and maintaining psychological and behavioral functioning.

Following from this, a third theme emphasizes that the problems of the young are intricately tied to the social and cultural contexts in which they experience life. Children and adolescents are embedded in a circle of social and environmental influences involving family, peer, school, neighborhood, societal, and cultural circumstances. Youth bring their personal attributes to these circumstances, are affected by them, and in turn, influence other people and situations. Meaningful analysis of psychological problems thus requires the incorporation of contextual features. Such aspects as family interactions, friendships, gender, educational opportunity, poverty, ethnicity and race, and cultural values all come into play.

A fourth major theme is a bias toward the scientist-practitioner approach. Prudent and insightful thinking is required in both figuring out the puzzles of behavioral problems and applying acquired knowledge. We believe that empirical approaches and the theoretical frameworks that rely on scientific method provide the best avenue for understanding the complexity of human behavior. Research findings, a critical component of virtually all chapters of this book, thus are brought to bear on the problems experienced by youth. Facilitating the development of children and adolescents is placed front and center in this approach.

ORGANIZATION OF THE TEXT

Although we have not formally divided the chapters into broader sections, they are conceptualized as three units.

Chapters 1 through 5 present a foundation for subsequent chapters. A broad overview of the field is presented, including basic concepts, historical context, developmental influences, theoretical perspectives, research methodology, classification and diagnosis, assessment, prevention, and treatment approaches. These chapters draw heavily on the psychological literature and also recognize the multidisciplinary nature of the study and treatment of youth. We assume that readers have some background in psychology, but we have made an effort to serve those with limited background or experience.

Chapters 6 through 14 discuss major disorders. Clinical symptoms and classification, epidemiology, the developmental course of disorder, causal hypotheses, risk and protective factors, assessment, treatment, and prevention are major considerations. Discussion of classification and diagnosis draws on the current DSM-IV-TR system but includes other classification systems, as well as dimensional approaches.

- Chapter 6 (anxiety) and Chapter 7 (mood disorders) focus on internalizing disorders.
- Chapter 8 (conduct problems) and Chapter 9 (attention-deficit hyperactivity disorder) discuss externalizing disorders.

- Specific and pervasive developmental problems are presented in Chapter 10 (language and learning disorders), Chapter 11 (mental retardation), and Chapter 12 (pervasive developmental disorders and schizophrenia).
- Chapter 13 (basic physical functions) and Chapter 14 (medical conditions) focus on health- and medical-related problems.

Chapter 15 rounds out and extends what has gone before. The chapter examines evolving concerns regarding the development of youth. These focus on critical family issues, mental health services, and briefly on youth living in countries other than the United States.

The organization of individual chapters varies, of course, depending on the information and issues relevant to the specific topic. However, considerable organizational consistency exists across Chapters 6 through 14. For most disorders, classification, clinical description, epidemiology, developmental course, etiology, assessment, and treatment and prevention are discussed in that order. At the same time, flexible organization is a guiding principle so that the complexity inherent in specific chapter topics is not sacrificed.

CONTENT: HIGHLIGHTS AND UPDATES

The content of this seventh edition is updated so as to include recent research and conceptualizations. We also have been especially sensitive to specific topics that are of high current interest. Examples follow.

- Numerous developmental models of the etiology of psychopathology in general and of specific disorders are presented.
- The developmental course and outcome of major disorders are described.
- Attention is given to the role of culture, ethnicity, and race in psychopathology.
- Attention is given to the role of gender in psychopathology—both to gender differences and factors that may underlie them.
- Attention is given to neurobiological factors in the etiology of disorders, including findings from genetic and brain imaging studies.
- Efforts to prevent the development of disorder are given explicit and increased attention throughout the text.

- Examples of specific individual and family treatments are generously interwoven throughout the text.

- In updating information on pharmacological treatments, sensitivity is given to issues concerning the use of medications with children and adolescents.

- Similiar consideration is given to specific problems that are especially relevant—such as child maltreatment, substance use, eating disorders, and bullying/victimization—and to problems that appear to be increasing in prevalence—such as autism, bipolar disorder, and obesity.

FEATURES: SOME OLD, SOME NEW

As will be obvious to users of the previous edition, we have retained the basic organization of the chapters, which appears to work well. Similarly, specific features of the book continue to emphasize for students a child-oriented, applied perspective. The text is rich in case descriptions that exemplify clinical symptoms or issues. An additional feature, the Accents, draw attention to particular topics of interest, for example, fetal alcohol syndrome, fire-setting, cultural influences, and the arguable relationship of autism and vaccines. Further, the text continues to be rich in illustrations—graphs, tables, photos, drawings—without an excessiveness that can be confusing to readers.

Other features of the text are aimed at facilitating student learning and continue to be part of the text. Key Terms in each chapter appear in color in the text and also are listed at the end of the chapter. Summaries of the chapters continue to be organized according to each chapter's major heads.

The open, colorful design of the text has been enhanced. We have given thought, as we have in the past, to avoiding clutter and confusion.

The supplementary teaching and learning materials have been enhanced, as described in the following section.

SUPPLEMENTARY TEACHING AND LEARNING MATERIALS

"Speaking Out" Videos. This set of nine video segments was filmed exclusively for Prentice Hall and allows students to see first-hand accounts of real patients with various disorders. The interviews were conducted by licensed clinicians and range in length from 8 to 25 minutes. Disorders include depression with deliberate self-harm, anorexia nervosa, alcoholism, autism, ADHD, conduct disorder, anxiety disorder, oppositional defiant disorder, and learning disability. The videos are available in VHS or DVD format. The Instructor's Manual for this text includes suggestions on how to integrate these videos into your class. Ask your Prentice Hall representative.

Instructor's Manual. The Instructor's Manual with Tests created by the authors, Rita Wicks-Nelson and Allen C. Israel, has been updated. The Instructor's Manual includes chapter outlines, learning objectives, lecture and discussion suggestions, classroom activities, a list of videos and online resources, and suggestions on how to integrate the "Speaking Out" video segments into your course. You can download the Instructor's Manual from Prentice Hall's catalog (www.pearsonhighered.com).

Test Item File. The Test Item File section has been updated to include new questions on revised text material. It includes multiple choice, true/false, short answer, and essay questions with page references to the text. Each question has been categorized as factual, applied, or conceptual. You can download the Test Item File from Prentice Hall's catalog (www.pearsonhighered.com).

PowerPoints. Powerpoint presentations are provided for each chapter, with chapter outlines, key figures and tables, and other resources to enhance your lectures. You can download the Powerpoints from Prentice Hall's catalog (www.pearsonhighered.com).

CourseSmart WebBooks. This new *Pearson Choice* offers students an online subscription to *Abnormal Child and Adolescent Psychology, 7th Edition* at a 50 percent savings. With CourseSmart, students can search the text, make notes online, print out reading assignments that incorporate lecture notes, and bookmark important passages. Ask your Prentice Hall representative for details.

TestGen Testing Software. Available on Prentice Hall's Website (www.pearsonhighered.com), this test-generating software provides instructors "best in class" features in an easy-to-use program. Create tests using the TestGen Wizard and easily select questions with drag-and-drop or point-and-click functionality. Add or modify test questions using the built-in Question Editor and print tests in a variety of formats. The program comes with full technical support.

ACKNOWLEDGMENTS

The thoughtful evaluations and suggestions of the following reviewers are much appreciated: Bethann Bierer, Metro College of Denver; Richard Cavasina, California University of Pennsylvania; Kristin Christodulu, SUNY Albany; Andrea Chronis, University of Maryland; Amity Currie, Marist College; Daniel Hurley, University of Rhode Island; John Kayser, University of Denver; Charles Fernald, University of North Carolina–Charlotte; Kristi Lane, Winona State University; Brad Mossbarger, Austin Peay State University; Michael Palmer, Arizona State University; Andrea Rotzien, Grand Valley State University; Heather Snyder, Edinboro University of Pennsylvania; Vincent Stretch, University of Southern Mississippi; Barbara Weiserbs, Kingsborough Community College.

In addition, our sincere thanks are extended to Ilana Luft, Jennifer Weil Malatras, and Karen Sokolowski. Their work in locating material, and in other ways facilitating the preparation of the manuscript, was invaluable.

Also, thanks to the Prentice Hall Staff: Jeff Marshall, Executive Editor; LeeAnn Doherty, Associate Editor; Aaron Talwar, Editorial Assistant; Maureen Richardson, Associate Managing Editor; and Shelley Creager, Production Editor.

And continuing thanks to Sara and Daniel for their caring and support.

Finally, we note that the order of authorship was originally decided by a flip of the coin to reflect our equal contribution. Our continuing collaboration has been one of equality and friendship.

Rita Wicks-Nelson

Allen C. Israel

CHAPTER 1

Introduction

To be young is to bounce balls as high as the heavens, gobble up fairytales, walk tightropes without falling, love friends with glee, and peer at the wondrous future.

Oh, that I should have to experience this thing called youth—with its ignorance, uselessness, aloneness, ups and downs, and unending insecurities.

The early years of life have long been described in extremes of emotions, behaviors, and encounters. In fact, most individuals who look back on their own youth admit to some of the extremes—but also to a sizable portion of more moderate experiences. And they frequently view their youth as a special time of growth and opportunity. It is against this backdrop that we embark on the study of the psychological problems of childhood and adolescence.

This book is written for those who ask questions and who are concerned about less than optimal development of youth. It addresses definitions, characteristics, origins, development, diagnosis, prevention, and amelioration of disordered functioning. We anticipate, and hope, that you will find this field of study as satisfying as we do. It is an area of study that encompasses both humanitarian concerns for young people and scientific intrigue.

The last decades have been a particularly promising time to study behavioral and psychological disturbance. The current need for increased understanding, prevention, and treatment is substantial, and is recognized in many parts of the world. At the same time, research into psychological disturbance and human development, including that of youth, continues to grow by leaps and bounds, with contributions from many disciplines. As is usually true in science, increased knowledge and improved methods have led to new questions and paradoxes. This combination—new understandings, and new questions, and new avenues of inquiry—gives both promise and excitement to the study of the problems of young people.

Defining and Identifying Abnormality

Behavioral repertoires come in endless varieties, and many kinds of disorders are discussed in this text (see Accent: "Some Faces of Problem Behavior"). Various labels have been applied to such problems: abnormal behavior, behavioral disturbance, emotional disorder, psychological deficit, mental illness, psychopathology, maladaptive behavior, developmental disorder, and so forth. Moreover, systems have been constructed to categorize problems and to offer guidelines to p rofessionals for identifying abnormality. Underlying this effort are complex issues in defining and distinguishing psychopathology.

The criteria for abnormality are primarily based on how a person is acting or what a person is saying and only rarely include a specific known marker for disorder. Of course, most of us would agree that problems are evident when individuals do not acquire speech, are unable to feed themselves, or see and hear things that others do not. But less dramatic instances are harder to judge and a fine line can exist between what is considered disordered and what is normal. Young people of specific ages display behaviors that may or may not be considered signs of disturbance, such as noncompliance with parental rules, social withdrawal, high activity level, fear, sadness, and delayed reading skills, to name a few. Thus, we must ask, When do we consider behaviors abnormal? and How can we distinguish everyday problems from more serious indications of psychopathology? There are no simple answers to these questions, but it is informative to consider several factors that enter into judgments about psychological or behavioral disturbances.

ACCENT

Some Faces of Problem Behavior

Four-year-old **Joey** had been kicked out of preschool, where he had sat on the floor and stared, refused to talk, and hit any child who touched him. If the teacher insisted that he participate in activities, he screamed, cried, and banged his arms and legs on the floor. Similar behaviors occurred at home. Joey rarely talked or showed emotion, and he slept fitfully, banged his head against the wall, and rocked back and forth. (Adapted from Morgan, 1999, pp. 3–4)

Although **Lakeshia** was below grade level in all her second grade subjects, she did not qualify for an individualized education plan under special education laws. She had always been considered a slow learner but these difficulties had sometimes been beneath the "radar screen" of her teachers, perhaps in part because she was quiet and well-behaved. She repeated second grade and had a tutor, but by the time she was in fifth grade, Lakeshia was failing all her subjects. An evaluation indicated low-average to borderline overall intelligence and ratings of attention and learning problems in the clinically borderline range. (Adapted from Hathaway, Dooling-Litfin, & Edwards, 2006, pp. 402–405)

Eight-year-old **Joe** had a history of multiple problems. They included chronic hyperactivity, destructive behavior, short attention span, difficulty following verbal directions, low frustration tolerance, impulsiveness, disobedience, poor interpersonal relationships, fighting, lying, stealing, running away from school, and setting fires. His parents had discounted the importance of these behaviors, preferring to believe that little boys should be allowed to express themselves. Joe's behavior worsened in the second and third grades, and the school forced further evaluation. (Adapted from Rapport, 1993, pp. 284–285)

Anne had begun to worship Satan and noted that praying to Satan brought her relief from distress. Anne had dyed her hair black, dusted her face with white powder, and looked like a character in a vampire story rather than a 14-year-old. Anne reported that she had difficulty falling asleep because she worried about her grades and her parents' divorce, for which she believed she was partly responsible. She found it hard to concentrate in school, was irritable, and had lost weight. She had no energy, no longer enjoyed activities with friends, and spent most of her time in her room. Anne denied any intent or plan for suicide, involvement with cults, or drug use. (Adapted from Morgan, 1999, pp. 35–37)

ATYPICAL AND HARMFUL BEHAVIOR

Psychological problems frequently are viewed as atypical, odd, or abnormal—all of which imply that they deviate from the average. Indeed, "ab" means "away" or "from," whereas "normal" refers to the average or standard. However, being atypical in itself hardly defines psychopathology. People who display exceptionally high intelligence, social competence, or athletic skill are generally considered fortunate, and their "oddness" is looked upon with favor. The deviations we are considering, however, are assumed to be harmful in some way to the individual. The American Psychiatric Association (1994, 2000), for example, defines a disorder as a clinically significant behavioral or psychological pattern that occurs in an individual and that is associated with distress, impairment, or increased risk of death, pain, disability, or important loss of freedom.

Abnormality or psychopathology is frequently viewed as dysfunction that resides *within* an individual and interferes with adaptation, that is, with the individual fitting the circumstances of his or her life. Alternatively, disorder might be viewed as an individual's reactions to circumstances—with the interface of the individual with other people or environmental conditions. This perspective, which is closer to our own, emphasizes that behavior is inextricably linked with the larger world in which it is embedded.

DEVELOPMENTAL STANDARDS

Age, as an index of developmental level, is always important in judging behavior, but it is especially important for children and adolescents because they change so rapidly. Judgments about behavior rely on developmental norms, which describe the typical rates of growth, sequences of growth, and forms of physical skills, language, cognition, emotion, and social behavior. These serve as developmental standards from which to evaluate the possibility that "something is wrong."

Behavior can be judged as anomalous relative to these norms in a number of ways, as indicated in Table 1–1. Delayed development, or failure to keep up with typical developmental change, indicates that something is awry. Children sometimes may achieve developmental norms and then regress, or return, to behavior typically seen in younger individuals.

Several other signs are noteworthy. These include atypical frequency, intensity, or duration of behavior, as well as the display of behavior in inappropriate situations. It is not unusual for a child to display fear,

TABLE 1–1	**BEHAVIORAL INDICATORS OF DISORDERS**

Developmental delay
Developmental regression or deterioration
Extremely high or low frequency of behavior
Extremely high or low intensity of behavior
Behavioral difficulty persists over time
Behavior inappropriate to the situation
Abrupt changes in behavior
Several problem behaviors
Behavior qualitatively different from normal

for example, but fearfulness may be a problem if it occurs excessively, is extremely intense, does not weaken over time, or is shown in harmless situations. Concern might also be expressed for the youth whose behavior abruptly changes, as when an outgoing adolescent turns solitary, or when a child displays several questionable behaviors. All of these indications of disturbance are quantitative differences from developmental norms.

Yet another manifestation that may signal the need for help is the display of behaviors that appear as qualitative differences from the norm. That is, the behavior—or the sequence in which it develops—is not seen at all in normal growth. For instance, most children become socially responsive to their caretakers soon after birth, but children diagnosed as autistic display unresponsive behaviors not seen in normal development (such as lack of normal eye contact). Qualitatively different behaviors frequently indicate a pervasive problem in development.

CULTURE AND ETHNICITY

The term culture encompasses the idea that groups of people are organized in specific ways, live in specific environmental niches, and share specific behavioral standards, beliefs, values, and practices. The role of cultural norms in judging behavior was tellingly discussed many decades ago by the anthropologist Ruth Benedict. After studying widely diverse cultures, Benedict (1934) proposed that each society selects certain behaviors that are of value to it and socializes its members to act accordingly. Individuals who do not display these behaviors, for whatever reasons, are considered deviant by the society. Deviance and normality are always related to cultural standards. Accordingly, it is not surprising to find that some disorders may be culturally specific and that

The behavior that is expected of or considered appropriate for a child varies across cultures.
(Michelle D. Bridwell/PhotoEdit Inc.) (Michal Heron/Pearson Education/PH College)

subtle differences exist in the expression of disorder. It appears, for example, that anxiety is universal but is expressed more through bodily symptoms in Asian and Latino groups than in European Americans (Serafica & Vargas, 2006).

Today's cultural analyses describe the many ways in which cultures shape normal and abnormal development and conceptualize, explain, and treat psychopathology. Cultural norms have broad influence on expectations, judgments, and beliefs about the behavior of youth. Children in the United States, for example, are expected to show less self-control and less deference to adults than children in some other parts of the world (Weisz et al., 1995). Weisz and his colleagues found that teachers in Thailand reported more conduct problems among their students than teachers in the United States, but trained observers reported just the opposite for the two student groups. The researchers suggested that Thai teachers may hold students to a more demanding behavioral standard—and thus see more problems and more readily label them. In another study, Weisz and his colleagues (1988) asked parents and teachers in Thailand and the United States to read descriptions of child problems and then answer questions about them. The Thai adults were less worried about the problems than the adults in the United States, a finding that appears consistent with the teachings of

Thai Buddhism that every condition changes and that current behavior does not reflect enduring personality.

The different ways in which problem behaviors may be explained and treated was demonstrated in a study in which mothers of North African and Middle Eastern background living in Israel were interviewed about their children who were developmentally retarded (Stahl, 1991). Almost half of the mothers gave magic-religious causes for the condition. They believed in Fate, demons entering the body, an Evil Eye, and punishment from God. These mothers accordingly relied on magic-religious treatments such as burning a piece of cloth belonging to the person who cast the Evil Eye, praying, or getting help from a rabbi. All of these behaviors are in keeping with the cultural beliefs of their native countries.

The above findings suggest the need to consider ethnicity or race when assessing various aspects of abnormality. Ethnicity denotes common customs, values, language, or traits that are associated with national origin or geographic area. Race, a distinction based on physical characteristics, can also be associated with shared customs, values, and the like. Ethnic or racial groups embedded within a heterogeneous society may express psychopathology somewhat differently and hold beliefs and standards different from those of the dominant cultural group. Such

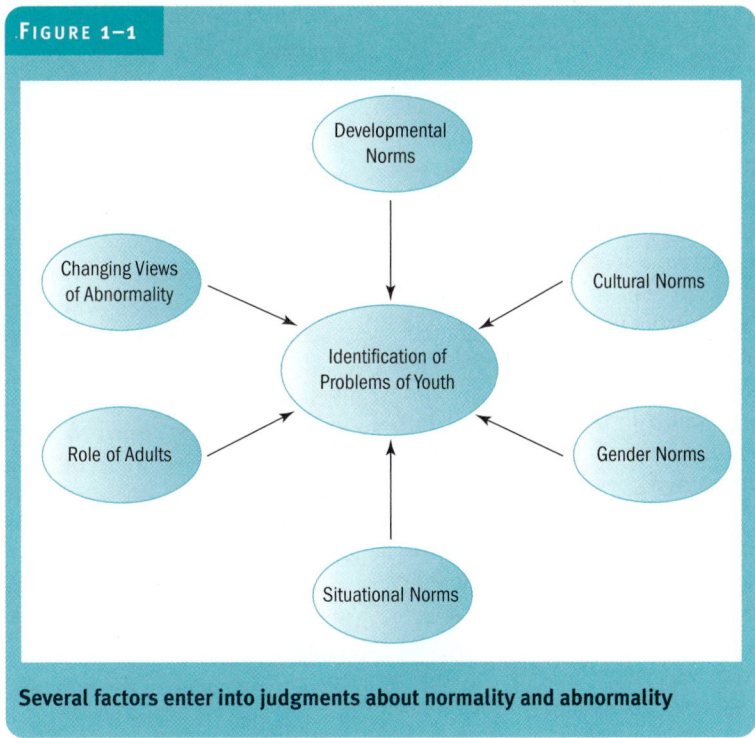

FIGURE 1–1

Several factors enter into judgments about normality and abnormality

subcultural variations have been described in the United States, as might be expected in such a heterogeneous nation (García Coll & Garrido, 2000; Yeh et al., 2004).

OTHER STANDARDS: GENDER AND SITUATIONS

Expectations based on gender also contribute to defining problem behavior. Gender norms powerfully influence development; they affect emotions, behaviors, opportunities, and choices. In most societies, males are expected to be relatively more aggressive, dominant, active, and adventurous, while females are expected to be more passive, dependent, quiet, sensitive, and emotional. These gender stereotypes play a role in judgments about normality. We would probably be less inclined to worry about the hypersensitive, shy girl and the excessively dominant boy than about their opposite-sex counterparts.

Judgments of deviance or normality of behavior also take into account situational norms—what is expected in specific settings or social situations. Energetic running may be quite acceptable on a playground but not allowed in a library. Norms for social interaction can be quite subtle; for example, how a statement is voiced can either compliment or insult another person. Individuals in all cultures are expected to learn what is acceptable and to act in certain ways in certain situations, given their age and gender. When they do not, their competence or normality may be questioned.

THE ROLE OF OTHERS

Youth, especially young children, hardly ever refer themselves for clinical evaluation, thereby declaring a problem. More likely, the feelings and beliefs of others in the immediate environment are critical in identifying problem behaviors. The labeling of a problem is likely to occur when others become concerned—for example, when parents worry about their child's social isolation or when a teacher is troubled about a child's inability to learn to read.

Referral of youth to mental health professionals thus may have as much or more to do with the characteristics of parents, teachers, or family physicians as with the young people themselves (Costello & Angold, 1995a; Verhulst & van der Ende, 1997). Indeed, disagreement often exists among adults as to whether a child or adolescent "has a problem." Although this may in part be due to different adults being exposed to different child behaviors, adult attitudes, sensitivity, tolerance, and ability to cope all play a role in identifying disorders.

CHANGING VIEWS OF ABNORMALITY

Finally, judgments about abnormality are not set in stone. Examples abound. In the 1800s, masturbation was considered a sign of disturbance or a behavior that could cause insanity (Rie, 1971). Nail biting was once seen as a sign of degeneration but is viewed as quite harmless today (Anthony, 1970). In the late 1800s, excessive intellectual activity in young women was believed by some to lead to mental problems (Silk et al., 2000). More recent years have witnessed a broader view of what is considered normal male and female development.

Many factors undoubtedly contribute to change in judgments about abnormality. Enhanced knowledge and modifications in theory have played a role. So has transition in cultural beliefs and values. For example, eating disorders, once found almost exclusively in Western societies, have increased worldwide in the past few decades, perhaps due to wider adoption of the modern Western preference for slender body size (Harkness & Super, 2000).

In summary, abnormality cannot simply be defined as an entity carried around within a person. It is most appropriately viewed as a judgment that a person's behavior, emotion, or thinking are atypical, dysfunctional, and harmful in some way—a judgment involving knowledge about development, cultural and ethnic influences, social norms, and the characteristics of the people making the judgment.

How Common Are Psychological Problems?

Determining the proportion of individuals who experience behavioral or psychological disorders suggests the extent to which prevention, treatment, and research are needed. However, prevalence depends on several factors, including the definition and kind of disorder, the method used to identify problems, and the population examined. Some investigations employ standardized scales or use formal criteria to achieve a clinical diagnosis, others look for symptoms, and still others look for functional impairment in the social environment (Bird, 1996; Crijnen, Achenbach, & Verhulst, 1997; Fombonne, 2002). Prevalence may be based on clinic or community samples.

Given all these variables, considerable variation is found in rates of problems. An extensive summary of studies reported from 1985 to 2000, which included several countries, showed that the prevalence of disorders in youths aged 4 to 18 years ranged from 5.4 to 35.5% (Fombonne, 2002). An estimate of 15 to 20% prevalence of clinic-level disorder for children and adolescents has fairly often been indicated (Costello et al., 2003; Tolan & Dodge, 2005). The American Psychological Association (2007) cites 10% of youth as having a serious mental health problem and another 10% as having mild to moderate problems.

Although research highlights the age range from childhood through adolescence, there is some information regarding infants and preschoolers. Potential problems during infancy include feeding and sleep disorders, disregulation of mood and attention, and difficulties in establishing healthy attachments to caregivers (Lyons-Ruth, Zeanah, & Benoit, 2003). A recent Danish community study of 18-month-olds found that 16 to 18% showed such disturbances (Skovgaard et al., 2007). Regarding preschoolers, a recent review indicated rates of disturbance approximating the rates observed in older children (Egger & Angold, 2006). Although investigation into very early problems has singular hindrances (e.g., the rapidity with which early behavior can change), the findings call for continued efforts to identify and understand these difficulties.

Concern has been expressed that societal change during the last few decades has resulted in an increased risk of disorders for young people. Variations across studies and methodological issues make it difficult to draw overall conclusions about secular trends (Achenbach, Dumenci, & Rescorla, 2003a; Rutter & Smith, 1995; Sourander et al., 2004). Increases may be occurring in only some kinds of disorders and for only some groups. For example, medical advances have increased the survival of infants born prematurely or with physical problems, and these infants have relatively high rates of behavioral and learning difficulties. A study in Scotland showed increases in emotional problems from 1987 to 1999 for adolescent females but not males (West & Sweeting, 2003). As shown in Figure 1–2, an investigation in the United Kingdom indicated substantial rise in conduct problems for both genders and evidence for increased emotional problems (Collishaw et al., 2004). Stress related to social factors (such as changing expectations and family divorce) and lifestyle changes (such as increased drug use) might reasonably increase the rate of psychological disorder, and this issue is receiving research attention.

Overall, despite inconsistency in the data, there is little doubt that young people have substantial needs. Yet their mental health problems too often go unrecognized in schools, primary health facilities, and other settings (Hoagwood, 2005). In addition, it is estimated that 66 to 75 percent of needy youth do not receive ad-

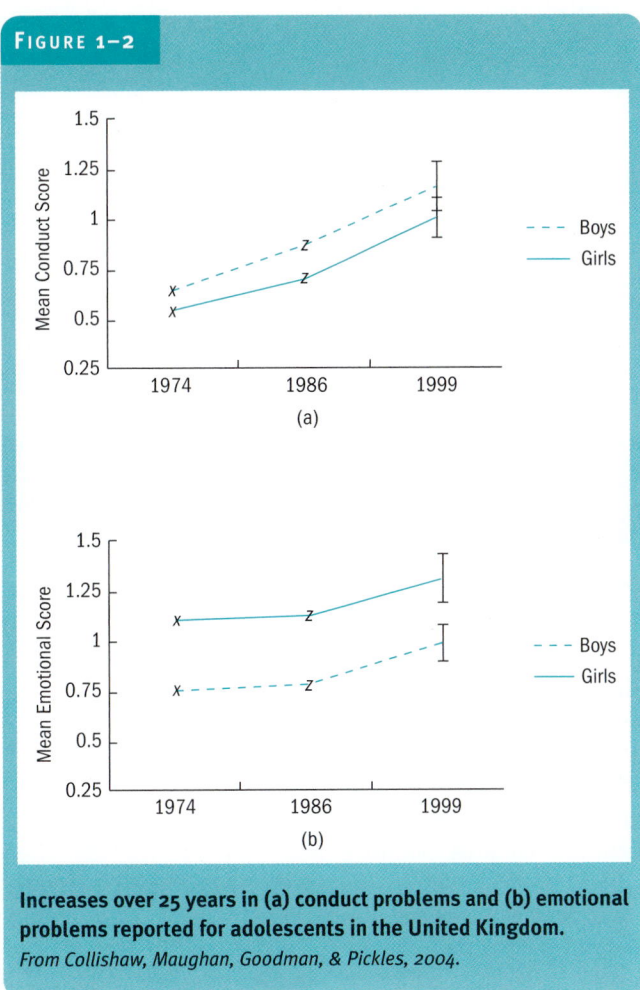

FIGURE 1-2

Increases over 25 years in (a) conduct problems and (b) emotional problems reported for adolescents in the United Kingdom.
From Collishaw, Maughan, Goodman, & Pickles, 2004.

equate treatment (Huang et al., 2005; Kestenbaum, 2000; Tolan & Dodge, 2005). Mental health services are insufficient, are less available in the communities that most need them, or lack effective coordination. Among the factors associated with lack of care are poverty, minority status, rural residence, and negative attitudes toward mental health treatment (Logan & King, 2001).

There are several reasons for concern about this situation. Surely, no one wants to see young people suffer the pain or lowered quality of life associated with psychopathology. Moreover, early disturbances can interfere with subsequent developmental processes, leading to an accumulation of problems. Mental health problems in young people adversely influence families and the broader society, as reflected in health care expenditures and other indices. Indeed, according to the World Health Organization, many of the disorders that carry the heaviest burden of adult death and disability in the developed areas of the world are related to mental

health and are often first observed in youth (Costello, Egger, & Angold, 2005).

How Are Developmental Level and Disorder Related?

Of concern to professionals and parents alike is whether and how psychological difficulties are related to developmental level. Some relationship does exist between specific problems and the age at which they usually first appear or are identified. Figure 1–3 depicts the age association for several disturbances. The reason for the link is sometimes obvious. Chronological age is correlated with developmental level that, in turn, makes some disorders more likely than others. For instance, developmental speech problems appear when children are first acquiring language skills. But other factors may be less obvious. At least for some disorders, actual onset occurs grad-

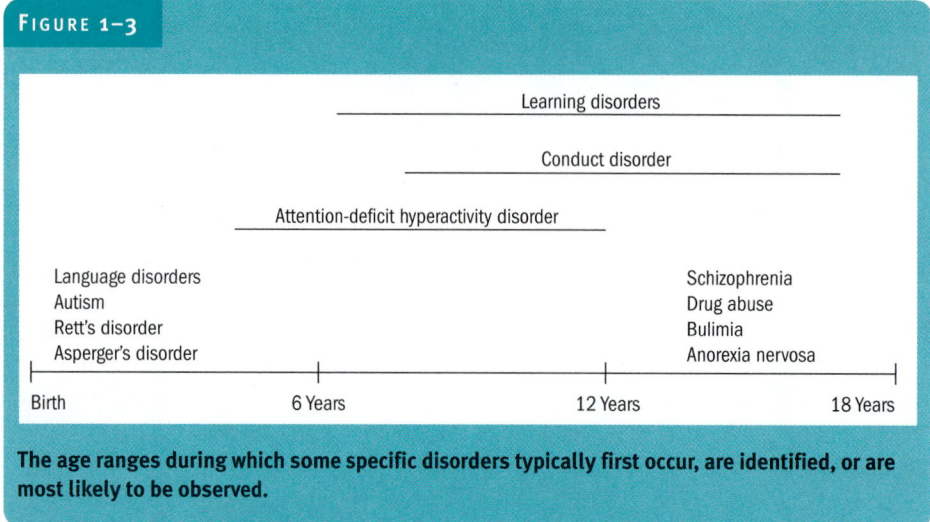

FIGURE 1–3

The age ranges during which some specific disorders typically first occur, are identified, or are most likely to be observed.

ually, with worsening of symptoms and social impairment over time (Sandberg et al., 2001). For some disorders, time of onset varies according to gender. Moreover, the time at which a disorder is said to occur may depend on extraneous circumstances. For example, although more severe cases of mental retardation are identified early in life, most are recognized during the school years when classroom demands call attention to children's abilities to learn.

Information about developmental level and disorder is helpful in several ways. Knowing the usual age of onset can point to etiology. Very early occurrence suggests genetic and/or prenatal etiology, whereas later onset directs attention to additional developmental influences. Age of onset can also tell us something about the severity or outcome of disorder. For example, typical onset of drug abuse is in adolescence;

if it occurs earlier, it is especially associated with severe drug dependency and mental problems later in life (Wills & Dishion, 2004). In addition, parents, teachers, and other adults who are aware of the usual timing of disorder may be more sensitive to the signs of specific problems in youth.

How Are Gender and Disorder Related?

For decades, the role of gender in psychopathology in the young was neglected (Crick & Zahn-Waxler, 2003). Several fascinating findings have now emerged. Consistent over the years is the finding of gender differences in the overall rates of many disturbances, with males being more frequently affected than females (Rutter & Sroufe, 2000). Table 1–2 shows

TABLE 1–2 GENDER PREVALENCE FOR SOME DISORDERS OF YOUTH

PREVALENCE HIGHER FOR MALES

Mental retardation	Rumination (an eating disorder)
Reading disabilities	Encopresis
Language disabilities	Enuresis
Autism	Tourette's disorder
Asperger's disorder	Drug abuse
Childhood disintegrative disorder	Conduct disorder
Oppositional disorder	Attention-deficit hyperactivity disorder

PREVALENCE HIGHER FOR FEMALES

Rett's disorder
Anxieties and fears
Depression
Eating disorders

Based in part on Hartung & Widiger, 1998.

the findings for several specific disorders. But the picture actually is much more complex.

Some gender differences are related to age. Males are particularly vulnerable to neurodevelopmental disorders that occur early in life, whereas females are more vulnerable to emotional problems and eating disorders that more commonly are seen at adolescence (Rutter, Caspi, & Moffitt, 2003). As shown in Figure 1–4, gender differences may exist not only in the rates of disorder but also in developmental change for externalizing problems (aggression, delinquency) and internalizing problems (anxiety, depression, withdrawal, bodily complaints). In addition, problems may be expressed differently according to gender. For example, males tend to display overt physical aggression while females are more likely to exhibit relational aggression by harmful gossip or rumor spreading (Zalecki & Hinshaw, 2004). The severity, causes, and consequences of some disorders may also vary with gender. There is still much to learn about gender differences (e.g., Dekker et al., 2007), and methodological issues must be considered.

METHODOLOGICAL ISSUES, TRUE DIFFERENCES

To some extent, reported gender differences may result from methodological practices. In the past, a bias existed for studying males, and even today mistaken inferences may be drawn from studies that exclusively focus on one gender or the other (Rutter et al., 2003). Misleading reports of gender differences also can result from females or males being more willing to report certain problems; for example, girls are more willing to speak of emotional difficulties.

Gender-specific prevalence of disorders can be an artifact of referral bias when clinical samples are studied. Clinical samples are biased toward boys, partly because help is sought for the disruptive behavior exhibited more often by boys than girls. Thus, boys with reading problems may be referred over girls with reading problems because of boys' higher rates of disruptive behaviors (Shaywitz, Fletcher, & Shaywitz, 1996). Although boys probably do have more reading problems, referral bias can give misleadingly high rates of disorder.

The bias in clinic samples may affect gender rates in another, more indirect, way (Hartung & Widiger, 1998). When more boys are seen in mental health facilities, they become the subject of more research. In turn, the disorders are described in the way boys express the symptoms, which may not be identical to the symptom picture in girls. When these descriptions (criteria) are used for identifying the disorder, fewer girls will fit the symptom picture and be identified.

Although methodological issues caution us to examine research carefully, the weight of the evidence does point to some real gender differences. To what might they be attributed? Both biological and psychosocial influences, observed prenatally onward, might reasonably underlie gender-specific psychopathology (Rutter et al., 2003; Zahn-Waxler et al., 2006). Differential biological vulnerabilities and strengths may exist. Biological differences between the sexes—in sex chromosomes, sex hormones, and

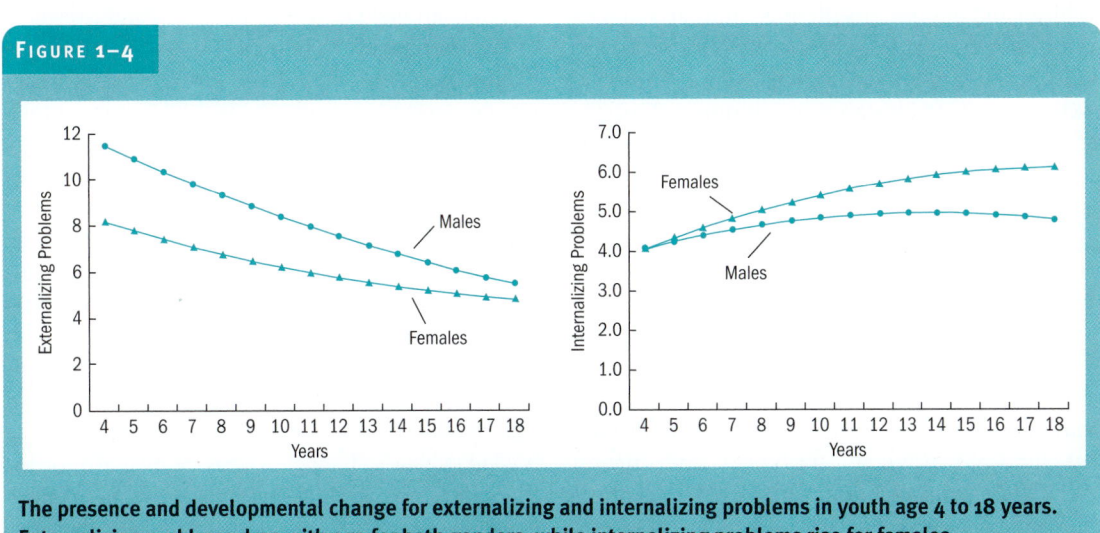

FIGURE 1–4

The presence and developmental change for externalizing and internalizing problems in youth age 4 to 18 years. Externalizing problems drop with age for both genders, while internalizing problems rise for females.
From Bongers, Koot, van der Ende, & Verhulst, 2003.

brain structure and function—play a fundamental role in gender development and differences. Biological maturity occurs later in boys, and the X and Y chromosomes are likely related to specific disorders in complicated ways. In addition, biological sex differences may exist in response to stress and in emotion, which we would expect to be relevant to psychological disturbances.

At the same time, boys and girls are differentially exposed to risk and to protective experiences associated with psychopathology. Consider the following examples. From infancy onward, boys suffer a higher rate of traumatic brain injury, which increases their risk of intellectual impairments (Anderson et al., 2001). Boys are more often physically victimized by peers, an event that is related to a variety of behavioral and emotional problems (Hanish & Guerra, 2002). Girls are more likely to have inappropriate sexual encounters. More generally, there are gender differences in friendships and interaction with parents and teachers (Rutter et al., 2003). Boys and girls also experience different sex-role expectations for how they should express emotion, control behavior, and the like. It is also worth noting that gender may affect psychological responses to circumstances, that is, to chaotic environments, family problems, and other conditions (Cicchetti & Sroufe, 2000; Leinonen, Solantaus, & Punamäki, 2003). We might expect that these gender-differentiated experiences would result in gender differences in psychopathology.

Further investigation of gender effects has the potential to inform us about the causes, prevention, and treatment of abnormal behavior. More generally, we have seen that what may appear to be simple issues regarding the psychopathology of children and adolescents often is multifaceted. Despite the complexities, progress is being made in understanding the needs of the young. This relatively recent circumstance is illuminated in the next section.

Historical Influences

Humans have long speculated on behavioral dysfunction, but early interest focused primarily on adulthood. Some analyses suggest that this was partly because children were not considered very different from adults and because they had high death rates that hindered parental attachment and interest (Ariès, 1962). However, at least by the 17th century, children were viewed as having physical, psychological, and educational needs that required nourishment, nurturance, and instruction (Pollock, 2001). By the early 18th century, they were variously seen as either stained with original sin, as innately innocent and needy of protection, or as blank slates upon which experience would write. It was not until the end of the 19th century that adolescence was conceived of as a distinct period of transition between childhood and adulthood that entails specific change, challenge, and opportunity (Demos & Demos, 1972). Differing and often conflicting views of childhood and adolescence continue to this day, undoubtedly influencing perspectives on problem behaviors and how abnormality should be treated.

PROGRESS IN THE 19TH CENTURY

The 19th century brought efforts to record the growth and abilities of the young, as well as progress in understanding disturbed development and behavior.

By this time, two explanations of adult mental illness had long been recognized: demonology and somatogenesis. Demonology is the belief that abnormal behavior results from a person's being possessed or otherwise influenced by evil spirits or demons. Both adults and youth acting in unusual, bizarre, or problematic ways were often thought to be possessed by evil spirits. Closely associated with religion, demonology tended to cast suffering individuals as wicked or evil in themselves. Although demonology is still espoused in some cultures, it is largely rejected in scientifically advanced societies.

Somatogenesis is the belief that mental disorder can be attributed to bodily malfunction or imbalance. This perspective was advocated by Hippocrates, considered the father of medicine, at a time when there was only limited knowledge in Greece and elsewhere of the workings of the human body. Although the influence of somatogenesis has waxed and waned, it has remained a hardy hypothesis. By the late 19th century, a dominant assumption regarding psychopathology was that inheritance, and degeneration that began in childhood, led to irreversible disease, which could be transmitted to the next generation (Costello & Angold, 2001). Today, due to advances in the biological sciences, somatogenesis is a dominant view that garners much enthusiasm.

Efforts to identify and classify mental illness progressed by the late 19th century. Emil Kraepelin, in 1883, published a classification system in which he tried to establish a biological basis for mental disorder. Kraepelin recognized that symptoms tended to group together—to occur in syndromes—and therefore might have a common physical cause. He viewed each

disorder as distinct from others in origin, symptoms, course, and outcome (Widiger & Clark, 2000). Eventually his work would be the basis of modern classification systems for mental disorders.

Although the study of youth generally lagged behind the study of adults, the first records of childhood disorders appeared early in the 19th century (Rie, 1971). By the end of the century, a few efforts had been made to classify children's disturbances, and causes had been proposed. Aggression, psychoses, hyperactivity, and "masturbatory insanity" in youth were all noted, with mental retardation receiving by far the most attention (Bernstein, 1996). An optimistic remedial approach to mental retardation began in Europe and spread to the United States— only to give way later to custodial institutionalization that would not be rectified for many decades.

Meanwhile, around the beginning of the 20th century, several developments began to fundamentally alter how children and adolescents were viewed, ideas about how their development might go awry, and how they might be treated (Table 1–3). Professional and scientific activities were interwoven with progressive efforts regarding young people, females, and weak and ill members of society (Silk et al., 2000).

SIGMUND FREUD AND PSYCHOANALYTIC THEORY

One of these developments was the rise of psychoanalytic theory and its associated treatment, psychoanalysis. Sigmund Freud's theory was the first modern systematic attempt to understand mental disorders in psychological terms. Indeed, it was critical to psychogenesis, the belief that mental problems are caused by psychological variables. As a young neurologist, Freud became convinced, based on his study of adults, that unconscious childhood conflicts and crises were the keys to understanding behavior.

Freud proposed three structures of the mind whose goals and tasks made conflict inevitable: the id, ego, and superego. Moreover, anxiety could be generated as a danger signal to the ego—the problem-solving part of the mind—that id impulses unacceptable to the superego were seeking to gain consciousness. Freud proposed that to protect itself from awareness of unacceptable impulses, the ego creates defense mechanisms that distort or deny the impulses. Although defense mechanisms can be adaptive, they may also generate psychological symptoms.

TABLE 1–3	SOME EARLY HISTORICAL LANDMARKS
1896	The first child clinic in the United States was established at the University of Pennsylvania by Lightner Witmer.
1905	Alfred Binet and Theophil Simon developed the first intelligence tests to identify children who could benefit from special educational efforts.
1905	Sigmund Freud's *Three Essays on the Theory of Sexuality* described a startlingly different view of childhood development.
1908	In *A Mind That Found Itself*, Clifford Beers recounted his mental breakdown and advocated an enlightened view of mental disorders, initiating the mental hygiene and child guidance movements.
1909	G. Stanley Hall invited Sigmund Freud to lecture on psychoanalysis at Clark University in Worcester, Massachusetts.
1909	William Healy and Grace Fernald established the Juvenile Psychopathic Institute in Chicago, which would become the model for the child guidance clinics.
1911	The Yale Clinic of Child Development was established for child development research under the guidance of Arnold Gesell.
1913	John B. Watson introduced behaviorism in his essay "Psychology as a Behaviorist Views It."
1917	William Healy and Augusta Bronner established the Judge Baker Guidance Center in Boston.
1922	The National Committee on Mental Hygiene and the Commonwealth Fund initiated a demonstration program of child guidance clinics.
1924	The American Orthopsychiatric Association was established.
1928–1929	Longitudinal studies of child development began at Berkeley and Fels Research Institute.
1935	Leo Kanner authored *Child Psychiatry*, the first child psychiatry text published in the United States.

ACCENT

Little Hans: A Classic Psychoanalytic Case

Freud's well-known case of "Little Hans" illustrates both the concept of symptoms arising from defense mechanisms and the phallic stage of development. Although the analysis is widely rejected today, the case served as a model for the psychoanalytic interpretation of childhood phobias (Freud, 1953/1909).

Hans was very affectionate toward his mother and enjoyed "cuddling" with her. When Hans was almost 5, he returned from a daily walk with his nursemaid frightened, crying, and wanting to cuddle with his mother. The next day, when the mother herself took him for a walk, Hans expressed a fear of being bitten by a horse, and that evening he insisted on cuddling with his mother. He cried about having to go out the next day and expressed considerable fear concerning horses.

These worsening symptoms were interpreted by Freud as reflecting the child's conflict over the sexual impulses he had toward his mother and fear of castration by his father. Hans's ego employed three defense

mechanisms to keep the unacceptable impulses unconscious or distorted. First, Hans's wish to attack his father, the rival for his mother's affection, was repressed in memory. The next step was projection of the unacceptable impulses onto the father: Hans believed that his father wished to attack him, rather than the other way around. The final step was displacement, wherein the dangerousness of the father was displaced onto a horse. According to Freud, the choice of the horse as a symbol of the father was due to numerous associations of horses with Hans's father. For example, the black muzzles and blinders of horses were viewed as symbolic of the father's mustache and eyeglasses. The fear Hans displaced onto horses permitted the child's ambivalent feelings toward his father to be resolved. He could now love his father. In addition, perceiving horses as the source of anxiety allowed Hans to avoid anxiety by simply avoiding horses (Kessler, 1966).

The psychoanalytic perspective rests on a psychosexual stage theory of development. As the child develops, the focus of psychological energy passes from one bodily zone to the next, leading the child through five fixed stages—oral, anal, phallic, latency, and genital. The first three stages involve particular crises that are crucial for later development. During the oral stage, the child must be weaned; during the anal stage, the child must be toilet trained; during the phallic stage, the child must resolve the crisis brought on by the desire to possess the opposite-sex parent (the Oedipal conflict for the boy, the Electra conflict for the girl). For Freud, the basic personality was laid down during these first three stages—by age 6 or 7—and healthy development was hindered by failure to resolve the crisis during each stage. (See Accent: "Little Hans: A Classic Psychoanalytic Case.")

In *Three Essays on the Theory of Sexuality*, published in 1905, and in his 1909 lectures at Clark University in Worcester, Massachusetts, Freud introduced his radical ideas about the importance of childhood to adult development (Evans & Koelsch, 1985; Rie, 1971). His views were controversial from the start and are criticized on several grounds. For example, they rested primarily on impressions from case stud-

ies, involved large inferences from what he observed to what he interpreted as existing, and were difficult to test. Freud's ideas nevertheless had enormous influence (Eisenberg, 2001).

Classical psychoanalytic theory has been modified by a number of workers. Some minimized sexual forces and emphasized social influences, among them Erik Erikson who proposed an influential theory of psychosocial development. Freud's daughter, Anna, elaborated his ideas and applied them to children (Fonagy & Target, 2003). By the 1930s, Freud's ideas provided a framework for conceptualizing child, adolescent, and adult behavior. They helped to establish psychiatry as a major discipline in the study and treatment of childhood disorders. In 1935, Leo Kanner authored the first child psychiatry text published in the United States.

Modification of traditional psychoanalysis has continued (Fonagy & Target, 2003; Gabbard, 2000). Some basic concepts have been altered, newer forms of therapy have evolved, and research on infant and child development has been considered. Although the overall influence of psychoanalytic theory has waned, among its many contributions are an emphasis on psychological causation, mental processes,

Both Sigmund Freud (center) and his daughter Anna Freud (foreground) were influential in the development of the psychodynamic conceptualizations of childhood disorders. *(AP Wide World Photos)*

in and I'll guarantee to take any one at random and train him to become any type of specialist I might select—doctor, lawyer, merchant, chief and yes, even beggar-man and thief, regardless of his talents, penchants, tendencies, abilities, vocations, and race of his ancestors. (Watson, 1930, p. 104)

Among the models that Watson drew on was classical conditioning, described earlier by Pavlov, whose animal studies demonstrated learning that occurred through the pairing of new with old stimuli. In addition to placing a strong emphasis on learning and environment, Watson was committed to testing ideas by experimental methods, as were other behaviorists (Horowitz, 1992).

E. L. Thorndike (1905) made an early contribution to behaviorism by formulating the Law of Effect. Simply put, this law states that behavior is shaped by its consequences. If the consequence is satisfying, the behavior will be strengthened in the future; if the consequence is unpleasant, the behavior will be weakened. Thorndike considered the Law of Effect a fundamental principle of learning and teaching; later researchers substantiated his idea. Of special note is B. F. Skinner, who is widely known for his work on operant learning—that is, for investigating and writing on the application of

John B. Watson was a highly influential figure in the application of the behavioral perspective. *(Corbis/Bettmann)*

unconscious motivation, anxiety and other emotions, infant and childhood experiences, and the child-parent relationship.

BEHAVIORISM AND SOCIAL LEARNING THEORY

In 1913, John B. Watson's essay "Psychology as a Behaviorist Views It" introduced behaviorism in the United States. Unlike Freud, Watson placed little value on describing developmental stages and on early psychological conflicts. Instead, he drew on theories of learning to emphasize that most behavior, adaptive or maladaptive, could be explained by learning experiences. Widely quoted is the following statement, which reflects his belief in the power of experience to shape children's development:

Give me a dozen healthy infants, well-formed, and my own specified world to bring them up

behavioral consequences to the shaping of behavior (Skinner, 1948; 1953; 1968). Skinner can be viewed as Watson's descendant in his emphasis on learning, the environment, and experimental methods (Horowitz, 1992).

Behaviorism, like psychoanalytic theory, thrived in the United States during the first half of the 20th century. Its impact on behavioral disorders came gradually as learning principles were applied to behavior. Albert Bandura (1977) expanded the learning approach through his study of how humans learn from others. His work on observational learning, which highlighted the social context and cognition, became a major influence (Grusec, 1992).

Learning is, of course, fundamental to human functioning, and its application to many facets of problem behavior is widespread (Jacob & Pelham, 2000). Learning approaches can improve the lives of youngsters experiencing emotional, cognitive, and social disorders. The explicit application of learning principles to the assessment and treatment of behavioral problems is referred to as behavior modification or behavior therapy. Approaches that emphasize the combination of learning principles and the social context and/or cognition are referred to as social learning or cognitive–behavioral perspectives.

MENTAL HYGIENE AND CHILD GUIDANCE MOVEMENTS

The 20th century saw another important thread being woven in different settings. Despite early interest in adult psychopathology, much remained to be done, and treatment often consisted of custodial care. The mental hygiene movement aimed to increase understanding, improve treatment, and prevent disorder from occurring at all.

In 1908, Clifford Beers wrote an account, *A Mind That Found Itself*, of the insensitive and ineffective treatment he had received as a mental patient. Beers proposed reform, and he obtained support from renowned professionals, including Adolf Meyer. Offering a "commonsense" approach to studying the patient's environment and to counseling, Meyer viewed the individual as integrated across thought, emotion, and biological functioning (Cicchetti, 2006). He also advocated a new professional role—the psychiatric social worker (Achenbach, 1982). Beers's efforts led to the establishment of the National Committee for Mental Hygiene to study mental dysfunction, support treatment, and encourage prevention.

In part because childhood experiences were viewed as influencing adult mental health, children became the focus of attention in the child guidance movement (Rie, 1971).

In 1896, at the University of Pennsylvania, Lightner Witmer had set up the first child psychology clinic in the United States (McReynolds, 1987; Ross, 1972). This clinic primarily assessed and treated children who had learning difficulties. Witmer also founded the journal *Psychological Clinic* and began a hospital school for long-term observation of children. He related psychology to education, sociology, and other disciplines.

An interdisciplinary approach was taken by psychiatrist William Healy and psychologist Grace Fernald in Chicago in 1909, when they founded the Juvenile Psychopathic Institute. The approach of this institution, which focused on delinquent children, became the model for child guidance (Santostefano, 1978). Freudian theory was integrated with educational, medical, and religious approaches in child guidance clinics (Costello & Angold, 2001). Healy and his wife, psychologist Augusta Bronner, opened the Judge Baker Guidance Center in Boston in 1917, and several other child clinics subsequently followed. The clinics began to treat cases of personality and emotional problems, and clinics flourished in the 1920s and 1930s. In 1924, the child guidance movement became formally represented in the newly formed American Orthopsychiatric Association, which today includes a variety of professionals concerned about children and adolescents.

SCIENTIFIC STUDY OF YOUTH

It was also during the early 20th century that systematic study of youth became widespread. Perhaps the most influential figure in this endeavor was G. Stanley Hall (Cravens, 1992). Among other things, he collected data on the problems of youth in order to understand mental disorder, crime, social disorder, and the like (White, 1992). Hall wrote extensively on youth, trained students who later became leaders in the field, and as president of Clark University invited Freud to lecture in 1909. He also helped establish the American Psychological Association, of which he was the first president.

At about the same time, an important event occurred in Europe: Alfred Binet and Theophil Simon were asked to design a test to identify children who were in need of special education

G. Stanley Hall contributed to the early scientific study of youth and served as the first president of the American Psychological Association.
(Corbis/Bettmann)

(Siegler, 1992). Their 1905 Binet–Simon test became the basis for the development of intelligence tests, and it encouraged efforts to measure other psychological attributes.

Another outstanding figure was Arnold Gesell, who meticulously recorded the physical, motor, and social behavior of young children in his laboratory at Yale University (Thelen & Adolph, 1992). He charted developmental norms, created and left an extensive film archive of child behavior, and was a strong advocate for optimal rearing conditions for youth.

Around 1920, child study began to benefit from several longitudinal research projects that evaluated youth as they developed over many years. Research centers existed at the universities of California, Colorado, Michigan, Minnesota, Ohio, and Washington; Fels Research Institute; Columbia Teachers College; Johns Hopkins University; and the Iowa Child Welfare Station. Knowledge about normal development began to accumulate that eventually was applied to the study of child and adolescent disorders. (See Accent: "Mrs. Hillis: Improving Corn, Hogs, and Children in Iowa.")

Current Study and Practice

Today, the study and practice of abnormal child and adolescent psychology reflect the diverse historical theories, movements, and events that were set into motion in the early decades of the 20th century. Some of the early approaches and occurrences are presently more significant than others and many new influences have come into play. Thus, both older and more recent assumptions, concepts, and knowledge give shape to a dynamic and multidisciplinary field.

The primary goals of the field are to identify, describe, and classify psychological disorder; to reveal the causes of disturbance; and to treat and prevent disorder. The approach we believe highly valuable in meeting these aims—the developmental psychopathology perspective—is discussed in chapter 2 of this text. Here, we briefly note some premises that we view as central to the field, as well as issues relevant to working with young people and their families.

- With few, if any, exceptions, psychological problems stem from multiple causes that must be reckoned with if we are truly to understand, prevent, and ameliorate such problems.

- Normal and abnormal behavior go hand in hand, and we must study one in order to understand the other.

- The complexity of human behavior calls for systematic conceptualization, observation, data collection, and hypothesis testing.

- Continued efforts are needed to construct and verify treatment and prevention programs.

- Whether they are in treatment, prevention, or research settings, young people have a right to high-quality care that is sensitive to their developmental level, family role, and societal status.

- Advocacy for the well-being of youth is appropriate, particularly because of their relative lack of maturity and social influence.

WORKING WITH YOUTH AND THEIR FAMILIES

Professionals interact with children, adolescents, and their families in many settings—research-based, medical, educational, and legal, to name a few. Substantial interaction with youth experiencing difficulties occurs in clinical settings of various sorts, and this is the focus of the present discussion.

ACCENT ● ● ● ● ●

Mrs. Hillis: Improving Corn, Hogs, and Children in Iowa

The establishment of the Iowa Child Welfare Research Station was sparked by Mrs. Cora Bussey Hillis, who demonstrated how advocacy for children can go hand in hand with advocacy for science (Cravens, 1993; Sears, 1975). Mrs. Hillis, a clubwoman married to an attorney, had considerable social and political influence. Life's tragedies, particularly the loss of three of her five children, directed and reinforced her passionate interest in child welfare.

Mrs. Hillis was aware of the much-respected agricultural station of the college in Ames, Iowa. In her mind's eye, she saw a comparable child welfare station that would be devoted to research, teaching, and dissemination of knowledge. The center would focus on problems in children's development and health. Researchers and professionals would be trained to work directly with children and parents. A body of knowledge would be constructed and disseminated to the public as rapidly as possible. Mrs. Hillis had faith that if research could "improve corn and hogs it could also improve children" (Sears, 1975, p. 17).

Working closely with Mrs. Hillis on the project was Carl Emil Seashore, a psychologist and admirer of G. Stanley Hall, who was dean of the graduate school at the State University of Iowa, in Iowa City. These two dominant, stubborn individuals did not always agree on the goals for the station, and they faced many obstacles, including difficulty in obtaining Iowa legislative support (Cravens, 1993). In 1917—after years of advocacy with women's clubs, education groups, and politicians—Mrs. Hillis achieved her dream when the Station opened at the Iowa City campus. It was a site of prolific and leading research on children's physical, mental, and social development for almost 60 years.

Interdisciplinary efforts. More than one professional is often involved in clinical activities with a young person. Among these are psychologists, psychiatrists, social workers, and special education teachers.

The majority of psychologists working with child and adolescent problems have specialized in clinical psychology; others may have specialized in school, developmental, or educational psychology. They usually hold a doctoral degree (Ph.D. or Psy.D.). Psychology has sturdy roots in the laboratory and an interest in both normal and abnormal behavior. Psychologists thus receive training in research, and have direct contact in assessing and treating individuals. Psychiatrists, on the other hand, hold a doctorate in medicine (M.D.); they are physicians who have specialized in the treatment of mental disturbance. Although psychiatrists function in ways similar to those of psychologists, they are more likely to view psychopathology as a medical dysfunction and to employ medical treatments, especially pharmacological treatments.

Social workers generally hold a master's degree (M.A.) in social work. Like psychologists and psychiatrists, they may counsel and conduct therapy, but their special focus is more broadly working with the family and other social systems in which young people are enmeshed.

Special education teachers, who usually have obtained a master's degree, emphasize the importance of providing optimal educational experiences. They are able to plan and implement individualized educational programs, thus contributing to interventions for many disorders.

Youngsters with problems also come to the attention of nurses, general physicians, teachers in regular classrooms, and workers in the legal system. Indeed, these professionals may be the first to hear about a problem. Substantial coordination among professionals and agencies is thus often necessary and valuable.

The role of parents. Professional contact with youth typically involves some, often critical, communication with families, usually with one or more parents. Families differ in their needs, including needs for support, basic education about psychopathology, and information about the availability of services. Depending on the situation, parents may play various roles in actual intervention (Kendall, 2006). As consultants, they have unique information about their child and can offer a valuable perspective of the situation. They may serve as collaborators with mental health professionals in carrying out treatment for their offspring—in effect, serving as cotherapists. When they are more

directly involved in the difficulties, parents may participate as coclients with their child or adolescent.

Unsurprisingly, parents vary in the knowledge they have about mental health and in their motivation and ability to participate. To begin with, parents seek consultation for many reasons. Most are truly concerned about the welfare of their sons and daughters, but some may primarily be motivated to ease their own worries or satisfy concerns of the school or court. Others may have inappropriate goals or believe that the outcome of treatment depends only on the mental health worker. Despite these and other issues, however, many parents form a cooperative and constructive alliance with the mental health worker, which may positively affect the outcome of intervention (Kazdin, Whitley, & Marciano, 2006).

The importance of the family is apparent in cases in which treatment is discontinued prior to successful completion. The risk of dropping out of intervention is higher among families that are at socioeconomic disadvantage (Pelkonen et al., 2000). Many other variables play a role (Armbruster & Kazdin, 1994; Kazdin et al., 1997). These include young age of mother, single parenthood, harsh child-rearing practices, parent psychopathology, and family stress. More immediate factors—such as parental belief that treatment is irrelevant or a less than satisfactory parent–therapist relationship—have also been associated with discontinuance (e.g., Hoagwood, 2005).

Whatever the situation and setting, parental involvement is usually recommended, although the type of services to families depends on whether needs are best met by education, support, skills training, cotherapy, and the like (Hoagwood, 2005). The optimal degree of parental involvement in child-centered therapy also must be evaluated. For example, relatively little parental participation may be suitable for anxious youth whose parents are overprotective (Kendall, 2006).

Working with young clients. The relative immaturity, inexperience, and vulnerability of children and adolescents require special considerations. Knowledge about and attitudes toward mental health may be quite variable. Gender differences also may exist. In a Scottish adolescent sample, Williams and Pow (2007) found negative attitudes were more common in boys, who reported less knowledge of, and less desire for, information about mental health.

Young children may lack the ability to identify problems, and they most frequently enter treatment at the suggestion or coercion of adults. Adolescents often have more input into the decision to seek clinical services, but many are sensitive about autonomy,

and this issue requires special attention (Cicchetti & Rogosch, 2002). Efforts by the mental health worker to create a therapeutic alliance with the client—that is, to forge a trusting personal bond and collaboration on the tasks of treatment—may increase the chance of a successful outcome (Green, 2006)

In working with youth, knowledge and mindfulness of normal development is essential for evaluating problems and planning intervention. An obvious example concerns training children to control their own behavior by giving themselves verbal directions in problem solving. Although such a strategy can be helpful in particular kinds of disorders, it would likely be ineffective with young children who have poorly developed verbal self-regulation skills.

Finally, youth have basic ethical rights that must be recognized and protected. Ethical standards set by the American Psychological Association (2002) address issues regarding both clinical and research activities. The guidelines concerning intervention include the rights to assent to treatment, to be informed about procedures, to participate in deciding the goals of treatment, and to receive confidential care. With young clients, developmental level enters into determining the exact ways in which these considerations play out (Behnke & Warner, 2002). We would hardly expect to employ identical guidelines for a preschooler as for a ninth grader. Nevertheless, immaturity of the child generally can demand, if anything, greater attention to ethical concerns and the child's welfare.

When they treat young people, mental health workers often face a unique mix of ethical and legal issues. Consider the following situation.

Aaron | **Clinical, Legal, and Ethical Considerations**

Mrs. Schulz, recently divorced, is seeking therapy for her 6-year-old son, Aaron. The father has shared custody and is responsible for treatment costs. He insists that Aaron is fine and does not need therapy. Mr. Schulz suggests that the problem lies with his ex-wife. The therapist, believing that Aaron requires treatment, is in a bind. Apart from legal issues of consent needed to see a child, she recognizes that proceeding without the father's consent might well lead to his undermining treatment. She must decide what is in the best interests of the child in the long run. She wishes that she had involved the father from the beginning.

Adapted from Schetky, 2000, p. 2944

In some situations, mental health workers may be called on for legal testimony, raising issues of confidentiality and potential harm to the client (Schetky, 2000). Other situations—for example, the possibility that the client may harm others or him- or herself—can demand a break in confidentiality or additional action (Oltmanns & Emery, 2007). Confidentiality is also an issue when child abuse is suspected. In all states mental health professionals must report this circumstance, whether or not it threatens the therapeutic relationship. In such instances, professionals must understand and meet legal requirements and must inform families of the kinds of things that must be reported. Ethical and legal dilemmas regarding psychological disorders are not uncommon in working with clients, but they are of special concern when they involve young people who are limited in speaking for themselves.

SUMMARY

DEFINING AND IDENTIFYING ABNORMALITY

- *Behaviors are judged as abnormal on the basis of their being atypical, harmful, and inappropriate. Standards for behavior depend on developmental, cultural, gender, and situational norms.*
- *Adult attitudes, sensitivities, and tolerance play a role in identifying disturbances in young people, and what is considered as abnormal may change over time.*

HOW COMMON ARE PSYCHOLOGICAL PROBLEMS?

- *The rates of psychopathology vary depending on several factors. The American Psychological Association estimates that 10% of youth have serious mental problems and another 10% have mild to moderate problems.*
- *Some evidence exists that rates of disorders among youth are increasing.*
- *Two thirds to three quarters of needy youth may not be receiving adequate treatment.*

HOW ARE DEVELOPMENTAL LEVEL AND DISORDER RELATED?

- *Some association exists between the onset or identification of specific disorders and age/developmental level, due in part to the timing of the child's emerging abilities and environmental demands placed on the child. Onset may occur gradually, however.*

HOW ARE GENDER AND DISORDER RELATED?

- *Gender differences occur in the rates of disorder, with boys exhibiting higher rates for many disorders. Other important differences exist, for example, in the timing, developmental change, and expression of problems.*
- *Although methodological weaknesses, including biased clinical samples, probably account in part for reported gender differences, numerous biological and psychosocial factors underlie true gender differences in psychological disorders.*

HISTORICAL INFLUENCES

- *Early interest in psychopathology focused on adults, with problems attributed to demonology or somatogenesis.*
- *The 19th century saw progress in identifying and classifying mental illness. Several childhood disorders were identified, and biological causation held sway.*
- *The early decades of the 20th century brought new knowledge and understanding through psychoanalytic theory, behaviorism and social learning theory, the mental hygiene and child guidance movements, and increased scientific study of youth.*

CURRENT STUDY AND PRACTICE

- *The current study and practice of the psychopathology of youth is shaped both by past and by more recent efforts. Emphasis is given to multiple causation, the relation between normal and abnormal behavior, scientific approaches, effective treatment and prevention, and advocacy.*
- *Working with youth often involves multidisciplinary approaches. Parents, who may play various roles in interventions, are important to its success. Regarding young clients, consideration must be given to attitudes, developmental abilities and needs, and ethical and legal requirements.*

KEY TERMS

developmental norms *(p. 3)*

culture, cultural norms *(p. 3)*

ethnicity *(p. 4)*

race *(p. 4)*

gender norms *(p. 5)*

situational norms *(p. 5)*

demonology *(p. 10)*

somatogenesis *(p. 10)*

syndromes *(p. 10)*

psychoanalytic theory *(p. 11)*

psychogenesis *(p. 11)*

id, ego, superego *(p. 11)*

defense mechanisms *(p. 11)*

psychosexual stage theory *(p. 12)*

behaviorism *(p. 13)*

classical conditioning *(p. 13)*

Law of Effect *(p. 13)*

operant learning *(p. 13)*

observational learning *(p. 14)*

behavior modification, behavior therapy *(p. 14)*

social learning perspective *(p. 14)*

cognitive–behavioral perspective *(p. 14)*

mental hygiene and child guidance movements *(p. 14)*

therapeutic alliance *(p. 17)*

2

The Developmental Psychopathology Perspective

Hardly a day passes without each of us wondering about many aspects of development and behavior. We want to know how our father manages to be consistently helpful, why a dependable classmate suddenly drops out of school, and whether a talented musician will be able to stop abusing drugs. Generally, the more usual the behavior or situation, the fewer questions we have, and the more easily answered they seem. It is the unexpected that is more likely to confound us—especially when a behavior appears to be problematic or harmful in some way.

Elizabeth   No Obvious Explanation

Elizabeth Fellows was referred to a therapist by her physician, who outlined concerns about a possible eating disorder. Elizabeth's mother, who had taken her to the physician, was worried. Not only had she heard Elizabeth vomiting in the bathroom on three occasions, but Elizabeth also had dropped all of her friends and stayed home in her bedroom. Mrs. Fellows reported that until approximately 6 months ago, Elizabeth had seemed fairly normal to her. Since then, Elizabeth had spent more and more time by herself, dropping even Katie, with whom she had been friends since kindergarten. Elizabeth had been a straight A student; now she was earning Bs and Cs. Mrs. Fellows acknowledged that 10th grade had been a difficult one, but she felt that Elizabeth's personality was changing. Mrs. Fellows was unable to remember any single event that had occurred in the past 6 months that might explain her daughter's behavior.

Adapted from Morgan, 1999, p. 46.

The ability to explain abnormality is of critical interest to those who investigate psychopathology and those who primarily treat it. Although it is possible to treat and prevent disturbances without fully understanding them, increased knowledge significantly aids these efforts. Behavioral scientists also are committed to more generally exploring an array of fundamental questions about human funtioning. In this chapter, we present a framework for conceptualizing aspects of psychological disturbances of young people.

Perspectives, Theories, Models

Much of today's understanding of both normal and abnormal behavior comes from applying the assumptions and methods of science. The writings of Thomas Kuhn (1962) and others have made us aware that science is not a completely objective endeavor. Like all of us, scientists must think about and deal with a complex world. To study and understand phenomena, scientists adopt a perspective—a view, an approach, or cognitive set. When a perspective is shared by investigators, it may be termed a paradigm. Paradigms typically include assumptions and concepts, as well as ways to evaluate these.

There are several benefits to adopting a particular view. A perspective helps make sense of the puzzling and complex universe. It guides the kinds of questions we ask, what we select for investigation, what we decide to observe and how we observe it, and how we interpret and make sense of the information we collect. The perspective that is taken strongly influences how a problem is approached, investigated, and interpreted.

There are also disadvantages in taking a perspective—mostly related to the fact that acting on a certain perspective sets some limitations. When we ask certain questions, we may preclude others. When we observe some things, we do not examine others. When we choose particular methods and instruments to detect certain phenomena, we undoubtedly miss other phenomena. We limit the ways in which we might interpret and think about new information. Taking a perspective is a trade-off—albeit one that, on balance, is more beneficial than detrimental.

THEORIES

Closely related to the process of taking a perspective—and sharing its benefits and limitations—is the process of theory construction. Simply put, a theory is a formal, integrated set of principles or propositions that explains phenomena. Because they provide concepts and formal propositions that can be tested, theories are highly valued by researchers and clinicians (Izard et al., 2002; Hinshaw, 2002).

As we saw in Chapter 1, biological, psychoanalytic, and behavior/social learning explanations of psychopathology were rooted in concepts developed in the early 20th century. Currently, numerous theories offer explanations of child and adolescent problems; they focus on emotion, self-regulation, brain functioning, higher level cognition, family interaction, and many other facets of functioning. These theories tend to apply to circumscribed areas and are referred to as microtheories. They stand in contrast to macrotheories—grand theories, such as psychoanalytic theory, that are sometimes criticized for trying and failing to explain too much or for having outlived their usefulness for generating testable hypotheses (Cicchetti & Hinshaw, 2002; Hinshaw, 2002). Microtheories are viewed as more readily proposing specific causal links among key variables, testing specific propositions, and further developing concepts based on empirical findings.

MODELS

In addition to having a theory to guide the study of psychopathology, it is often helpful to employ a model—a representation or description—of the phenomenon of study. Of particular current interest are models that encourage us to simultaneously consider the numerous factors potentially involved in psychopathology.

At the heart of interactional models is the assumption that variables interrelate to produce an outcome. One such approach, the vulnerability–stress model, conceptualizes the multiple causes of psychopathology as the working together of a vulnerability factor(s) and a stress factor(s). In this model, both vulnerability (also referred to as diathesis) and stress are necessary. They may be biological, psychological, or social factors—although vulnerability often has been considered biological and stress environmental. To take an example, a child's presumed biological vulnerability for anxiety may interact with the stress of parental divorce, resulting in problems in the child. Interactional models have contributed to our understanding of psychopathology, although they do not as easily incorporate developmental change as do transactional models.

Transactional models currently are widely employed in the study of both normal and abnormal development. The basic assumption is that development is the result of ongoing, reciprocal transactions between the individual and the environmental context. The individual is viewed as an active agent who brings a history of past experience that has shaped her or his current functioning. The environmental context is viewed as variables that are close to (proximal) or farther from (distal) the person.

Transactional models fall into the domain of systems models in that they incorporate several levels, or systems, of functioning in which development is viewed as occurring over time as the systems interact or enter into ongoing transactions with each other. An example is Gottlieb's (2003) biopsychosocial model, which integrates genetic activity, nervous system activity, behavior, and several aspects of the environment. In such a model, change at one level of functioning is assumed to influence other levels. Another example of a systems model is the ecological model, which situates the individual within a network of environmental influences and assumes transactions between the person and these influences, as well as among the several levels of the environment.

Developmental Psychopathology Perspective: An Overview

Since the 1970s, the developmental psychopathology perspective that we call upon in this text has rapidly become influential in the study of psychological disorders of youth. Central to the approach was the coming together of developmental psychology and clinical child/adolescent psychology and psychiatry (Cicchetti, 1984, 1989). Developmental psychology has traditionally taken normal development as its subject matter; it is especially focused on understanding universal principles of how people grow and change during their lifetime. The primary interest of clinical psychology and psychiatry is in identifying the symptoms of psychological disorders, understanding the causes of disorders, and alleviat-

ing the difficulties. In addition to these disciplines, contributions to developmental psychopathology come from a variety of other areas, including the biological sciences, sociology, and philosophy (Cicchetti, 2006).

Developmental psychopathology is interested in the origins and developmental course of disordered behavior, and in individual adaptation and success as well (Cummings, Davies, & Campbell, 2000; Sroufe, 1997). It is a systems framework for understanding disordered behavior in relation to normal development (Cicchetti, 2006). Rather than imposing specific theoretical explanations, it is a way of integrating various theories or approaches around a core of developmental knowledge, issues, and questions (Achenbach, 1990). As shown in Figure 2–1, these approaches—labeled microparadigms—are subsumed under developmental psychopathology.

Each microparadigm in the schema offers a view of behavioral disturbance. Each has its own assumptions, offers theoretical concepts, asks specific questions, adopts certain methods, and makes its own interpretations. Individuals working within the developmental psychopathology framework are free to adopt what they find useful from various microparadigms and reject what is not useful. For example, although psychoanalysis is often considered to have a shaky empirical base and to include explanations inconsistent with research findings (Rutter & Sroufe, 2000), psychoanalytic concepts remain important in some explanations of psychopathology.

As an integrative approach, the developmental psychopathology perspective has its own assumptions, principles, and interests. In addition to the central proposition that problem behavior can be

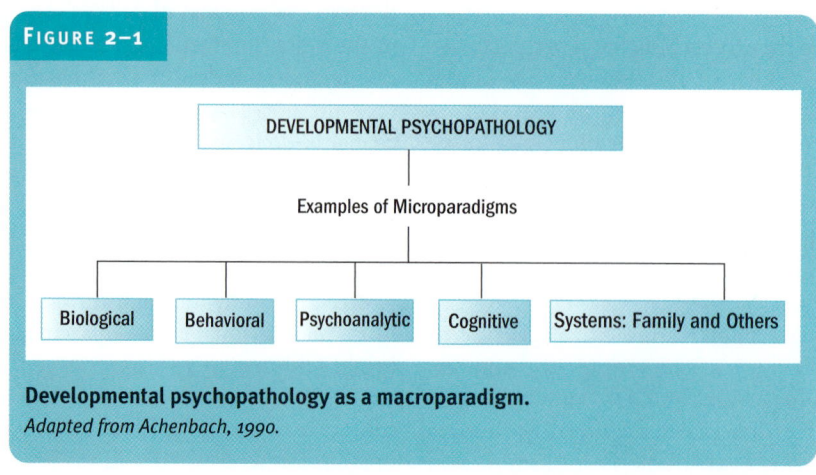

FIGURE 2–1

DEVELOPMENTAL PSYCHOPATHOLOGY

Examples of Microparadigms

Biological   Behavioral   Psychoanalytic   Cognitive   Systems: Family and Others

Developmental psychopathology as a macroparadigm.
Adapted from Achenbach, 1990.

fully understood only when normal development is considered, several other assumptions inform the developmental psychopathology perspective. We turn to these after first examining the concept of development.

Concept of Development

The concept of development can seem deceptively simple. If we were to ask strangers passing on the street to define the term *development*, many would surely offer *growth* as a synonym, with growth meaning not only bigger but also better. And most people would note that development requires time. However, any definition that stops here would fall far short of a full description of development.

Although many different depictions and explanations have been proposed, there is some consensus among theorists on the essence of development (e.g., Cummings et al., 2000; Cicchetti, 2006; Sroufe et al., 2005; Sroufe & Rutter, 1984; Hodapp, Burack, & Zigler, 1990).

- Development refers to change over the lifespan that results from ongoing transactions of an individual with biological, psychological, and sociocultural variables, which themselves are changing.

- Although quantitative change in development is noteworthy—for example, an increase in the number of a child's social interactions—qualitative change is more salient—for example, a change in the features or qualities of social interactions.

- There is a common course of early development of the biological, motor, physical, cognitive, emotional, and social systems. Within each system, early global structures and functions become more finely differentiated and also integrated. Integration occurs across systems as well so that organization and complexity are enhanced in development.

- Development proceeds in a coherent pattern, so that for each person, current functioning is connected both to past and future functioning. Development thus can be thought of as proceeding along pathways or trajectories of more or less complexity. In youth, developmental pathways are relatively open and flexible, but there is some narrowing of possibilities over time.

- Over the lifespan, developmental change may produce higher modes of functioning and the attainment of goals, but change is not inevitably positive.

Physical aging in adulthood brings decrements in functioning, and maladaptive behavior can develop at any time during the lifespan.

With the concept of development serving as a backdrop, we now turn to four overlapping issues that are central to the developmental psychopathology approach: the search for causal factors and processes, pathways of development, risk and resilience, and continuity of problems over time.

Searching for Causal Factors and Processes

There is a long history of trying to explain abnormal development in relatively simple ways. An example is the medical model. This model considers disorders to be discrete entities—things, if you will—that result from specific and limited biological causes within the individual. This explanatory approach was reinforced in the early 1900s by the realization that the microorganism that caused syphilis sometimes affected the brain, thereby causing mental disturbance. Now we realize that a single cause seldom accounts for most psychological or behavioral outcomes. (In fact, this is also true for many physical illnesses; for example, biological, psychological, and social factors appear to contribute to cardiac disease.) Thus, as is commonly acknowledged, the understanding of outcome rests on identifying multiply variables concerning both the developing person and contextual factors.

A full account of causation requires, however, more than identification of contributory factors. Developmental psychopathologists seek to understand how causal factors work together and what the underlying processes or mechanisms might be.

In conceptualizing causation, it is useful to distinguish between direct and indirect causes. When a direct effect operates, variable X leads straight to the outcome. An indirect effect is operating when variable X influences one or more other variables that, in turn, lead to the outcome. Establishing indirect effects is usually more difficult as the path of influences may be complex. Consider, for example, the reported association between parental alcohol use and children's adjustment problems. Might one or more variables underlie this link? Keller, Cummings, and Davies (2005) were interested in the possible role of marital conflict and ineffective parenting. The results of their study suggested that problem drinking led to marital conflict that, through parenting difficulties, led to child problems. These findings support the hypothesis that, given parental alcohol problems, marital conflict and ineffective parenting are mediators of child difficulties. The term mediator refers to a factor or variable that explains or brings about an outcome, more specifically, by indirect means. The identification of mediators is crucial to understanding causal processes.

So is the identification of moderators. A moderator is a variable that influences the direction or the strength of the relationships between an independent (or predictor) and a dependent (or criterion) variable. For example, suppose that boys and girls are exposed to the same treatment but that the outcome is more positive for boys than for girls. Here, it appears that gender moderates outcome. Or to take another example, if cultural context moderates the influence of an experience, outcome may differ in some way for children of different cultural backgrounds. (See Accent: "A Possible Moderating Influence of Culture.")

In examining causation, it is useful to make a distinction among necessary, sufficient, and contributing causes. A necessary cause must be present in order for the disorder to occur; a sufficient cause can, in and of itself, be responsible for the disorder. In Down syndrome, which is characterized by mental retardation, known genetic anomalies are both necessary (they must be present) and sufficient (other factors are not required). By contrast, in the debilitating disorder of schizophrenia, brain dysfunction is thought to be necessary but not sufficient. That is, brain abnormality is implicated in schizophrenia, but other factors must be present in order for the condition to arise. It is also important to recognize that contributing causes can be operating; these are not necessary or sufficient. In some disorders, several factors may contribute by adding or multiplying their effects to reach a threshold to produce the problem.

The search for causation, as we see in chapter 4, may employ various research strategies and designs. No matter what the approach, however, a strength of the developmental psychopathology perspective is its focus on understanding the mix of causal processes. We now further examine concepts and assumptions that contribute to this quest.

ACCENT

A Possible Moderating Influence of Culture

Parents in many countries report and/or endorse the use of mild physical discipline—such as spanking, slapping, grabbing, or restraining—in certain situations, although differences exist in the degree to which they use or accept such practices (Deater-Deckard, Dodge, & Sorbring, 2005; Lansford et al., 2004, 2005). In general, such punishment is correlated with aggression or acting out in childhood and later adolescence. Evidence exists, however, that this link may be moderated by the cultural context.

Lansford and her colleagues (2005) hypothesized that acting-out behavior would be reduced in cultures in which physical discipline was viewed as more normative. They assessed normativeness by three measures of parent or child perceptions of the frequency of physical discipline in the culture. The hypothesis was supported in their study of six different countries (Thailand, China, Philippines, India, Kenya, and Italy). Consonant with this finding, some research in the United States indicates that physical punishment is more normative in African American than European American families, and also that the link between physical discipline and child aggression/acting out may be weaker in African American families.

These moderating effects can be variously interpreted. For example, if parental behavior is viewed as normative, the punished child may be less likely to feel rejected, an outcome generally related to child adjustment. Or the child may be more likely to perceive physical punishment as an expression of parental authority that reflects concern for the child. Whatever underlies the moderating effect, Lansford and colleagues warn that their findings should *not* be taken as encouraging physical punishment, which was generally associated with child aggression and also with other maladjustment. The results do suggest, however, the value of examining the possible moderating role of cultural context.

"This is the path to adulthood. You're here."

Pathways of Development

The developmental psychopathology perspective assumes that abnormal behavior typically does not appear out of the blue. It emerges gradually as the child and environmental influences transact (Cummings et al., 2000). Development is characterized as involving progressive adaptations or maladaptations to changing circumstances. It can be viewed as a pathway over time, which at any point can be judged as favorable or unfavorable. Furthermore, trajectories are not cast in stone; they are viewed as open or probabilistic. New situations or circumstances, or new reactions to old circumstances, can bring about redirection.

One of the tasks of developmental psychopathology is to describe and understand pathways of adaptation and maladaptation. As a general depiction, we examine research efforts that described developmental trajectories across the adolescent years (Compas, Hinden, & Gerhardt, 1995). Figure 2–2 presents the five trajectories and briefly describes each one. Path 1 is characterized by stable good adaptation. This pathway is associated with relatively low exposure to negative circumstances, and the adolescents show positive self-worth and few problems. Path 2 indicates stable maladaptation, whereby youth who already are having problems experience adversities and inadequate resources to relieve them. The remaining paths involve significant change during adolescence. Path 3 shows maladaptation that turns into positive outcome, due at least in some cases to an environmental opportunity. Path 4 indicates an initial adaptation that, due to adversities, ends with decline. Path 5 depicts a temporary decline and a bouncing back to adaptive behavior, as might occur, for example, in experimental short-term drug abuse. An obvious aspect of these pathways is that adaptation level at any given time does not necessarily predict later functioning.

Progress is being made in understanding trajectories for several disorders, as we see in later chapters (e.g., Campbell et al., 2006; Dekker et al., 2007). Both stable and changing pathways are commonly observed.

EQUIFINALITY AND MULTIFINALITY

The transactional and probabilistic nature of developmental pathways is recognized in the principles of equifinality and multifinality. Equifinality refers to the

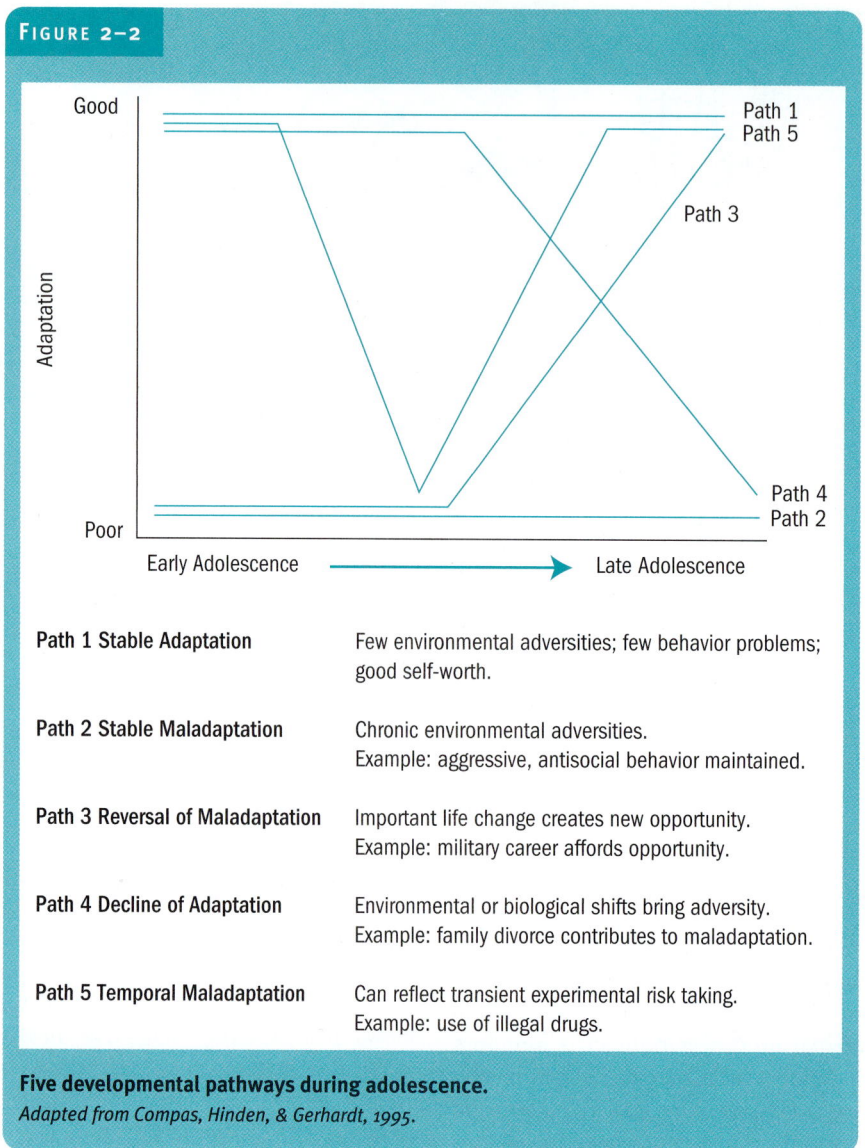

FIGURE 2–2

Path 1 Stable Adaptation
Few environmental adversities; few behavior problems; good self-worth.

Path 2 Stable Maladaptation
Chronic environmental adversities.
Example: aggressive, antisocial behavior maintained.

Path 3 Reversal of Maladaptation
Important life change creates new opportunity.
Example: military career affords opportunity.

Path 4 Decline of Adaptation
Environmental or biological shifts bring adversity.
Example: family divorce contributes to maladaptation.

Path 5 Temporal Maladaptation
Can reflect transient experimental risk taking.
Example: use of illegal drugs.

Five developmental pathways during adolescence.
Adapted from Compas, Hinden, & Gerhardt, 1995.

fact that diverse paths, or factors, can be associated with the same outcome. In other words, children can travel different pathways, or have different experiences, and yet develop the same problems (Figure 2–3.) Equifinality is observed in a number of child and adolescent disorders. A well-documented example is the finding that different pathways exist to antisocial behavior.

The second principle, multifinality, refers to the fact that an experience may function differently depending on a host of other influences that may lead to different outcomes. Simply put, children can have many of the same kinds of experience and yet end up with different problems or no difficulties at all. A well-recognized example concerns child maltreatment. Children who are abused by adults are at risk for later behavioral disturbance, but different children display different kinds of problems.

The principles of equifinality and multifinality are a reflection of a common theme in the development of behavior: Enormous complexity usually must be addressed in terms of what is likely to happen along life's pathways. In this regard, the concepts of risk and resilience contribute further to understanding the development of psychological problems.

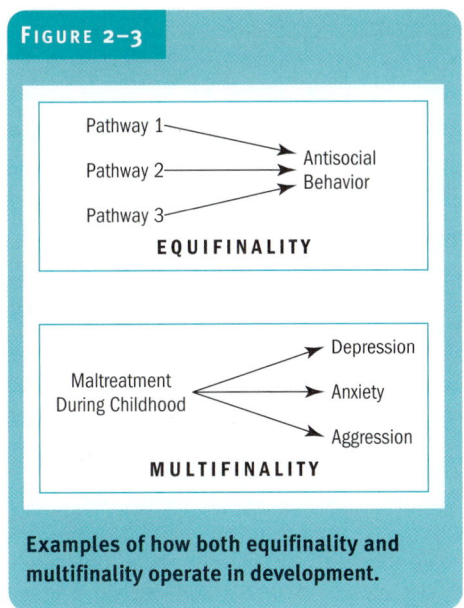

FIGURE 2-3

EQUIFINALITY

MULTIFINALITY

Examples of how both equifinality and multifinality operate in development.

Risk and Resilience

RISK FACTORS

Risk factors, or risks, are variables that precede and increase the chance of psychological impairments. Table 2–1 shows one way to organize the numerous risks that have been identified. Substantial investigation points to several important aspects of risk (Kopp, 1994; Lambert, 1988; Liaw & Brooks-Gunn, 1994; Rutter, 1987; Sameroff, 2006).

- Although a single risk factor certainly can have an impact, multiple risks are particularly detrimental; that is, their effects add or multiply. Moreover, risks tend to cluster; for instance, children at risk due to low parental education are more likely to reside in disadvantaged communities.

- The effects of many risk factors are nonspecific, a finding reflected in the principle of multifinality. However, this is not always the case; for instance, risk factors may be somewhat different for intellectual deficits than behavioral problems.

- The intensity, duration, and timing of a risk can make a difference. (See Accent: "The Timing of Risky Experiences.")

- Risk factors may be different for the onset of a disorder than for the persistence of the disorder.

- The impact of a risk factor may increase the likelihood of future risks by increasing the child's vulnerability or adversely affecting the environmental context.

A central aim of risk research is to better understand underlying processes. The distinction has been made between risks that originate in life experiences and those that reside in the youth's tendency to respond maladaptively to life events. However, it is

TABLE 2–1	**SOME DEVELOPMENTAL RISK FACTORS**
Constitutional Hereditary influences Gene abnormalities Prenatal, birth complications Postnatal disease, damage Inadequate health care, nutrition	**Intellectual and Academic** Below average intelligence Learning disability Academic failure
Family Poverty Abuse, neglect Conflict, disorganization, psychopathology, stress Large family size	**Ecological** Neighborhood disorganization, crime Racial, ethnic, gender injustice
Emotional and Interpersonal Psychological patterns such as low self-esteem, emotional immaturity, difficult temperament Social incompetence Peer rejection	**Nonnormative Stressful Life Events** Early death of a parent Outbreak of war in immediate environment

Based in part on Coie et al., 1993.

ACCENT

The Timing of Risky Experiences

An important theoretical and practical concern in developmental psychopathology is to better understand when and how experiences have different effects depending on the age or developmental level of the individual. Historically, there has been a strong interest in the proposition that early influences may be especially powerful. Among other ideas, Freud proposed that a failed infant–mother relationship carried over to later relationships, and social learning theorists suggested that early learning is especially important because it underlies later learning. Such judgments are the basis for the argument that early experiences might set later development.

Research indicates that the timing of an event can make a difference for several reasons (Rutter, 1989b, 2006). The effects of experience on the nervous system may be different depending on the nervous system's developmental status. Similarly, the effect of experience can vary with age-related psychological functioning, for example, the child's ability to think adaptively

about an adverse event. Whether an experience is normative or nonnormative may also matter. Normative events happen to most people at more or less predictable times (e.g., puberty between ages 11 and 14) whereas nonnormative events occur only to certain persons at atypical times (e.g., childhood loss of a parent). Nonnormative events are considered to be more stressful, partly because they put the individual "out of sync" with social expectations and supports.

The current view about the timing of experience holds that few, if any, events *set* an irretrievable path through life (Cicchetti & Rogosch, 2002). But the developing person may be particularly sensitive to certain experiences at certain times of life. The early years may indeed be particularly crucial in this regard. Also notable is adolescence, a transitional time characterized by remarkable physical, hormonal, psychological, and social role changes that may involve heightened strengths and vulnerabilities (Graber et al., 2004; Blakemore & Choudhury, 2006).

appropriate to view risk within a transactional model that includes both environmental circumstances and the individual. An example of this approach is shown in Figure 2–4. This conceptual model relates risky life experiences (stressors) to psychopathology (Grant

et al., 2003). The risky experiences are major or minor events that can be acute, occurring suddenly and perhaps disastrously (e.g., a damaging accident), or they can be chronic, persisting over time (e.g., poverty). The model proposes that these experiences produce a

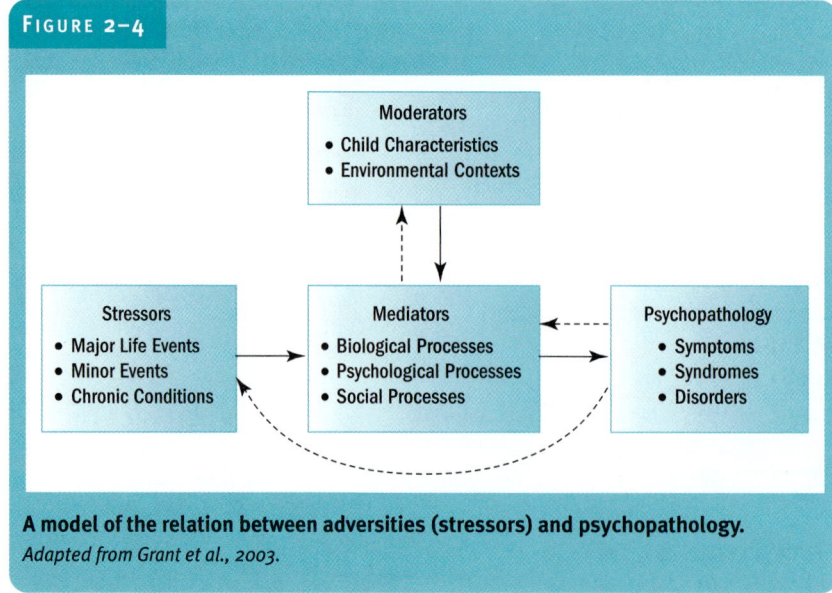

FIGURE 2–4

A model of the relation between adversities (stressors) and psychopathology.
Adapted from Grant et al., 2003.

variety of processes in the individual—biological, psychological, and social—that mediate, or lead to, psychopathology. In addition, the relationship between stressors and child mediators can be moderated by attributes of the child or the environment. For example, the child's age, gender, or sensitivity to the environment can influence the strength of this relationship. This model, which recognizes two-way influences between the components, reflects the dynamic processes of development.

RESILIENCE

Resilience is defined by relatively positive outcome in the face of significantly adverse or traumatic experiences (Luthar, 2006). In the presence of such risk, some individuals are adversely affected (are vulnerable), whereas others maintain healthy functioning (are resilient). Resilience speaks to individual differences in response to risk, in the ability to resist or overcome life's adversities (Rutter, 2006).

One of the issues regarding resilience has been how to define positive outcome (Luthar, 2006; Masten, 2001). It can be defined as the absence of psychopathology, a low level of symptoms, or adaptation beyond what would be expected in situations that overcome many individuals. It also can be defined in terms of competence regarding the developmental tasks or cultural age-expectations applied to young

people. Here, resilience is demonstrated when an individual meets major developmental tasks despite unfavorable life circumstances. Table 2–2 provides some of these widely agreed-on developmental tasks.

Three categories of protection. Why do some individuals succumb to adverse experiences, whereas others appear to rise above threat? There is a tendency to think of resilience as existing within the individual, perhaps because of the perseverance and courage that may seem to characterize children who rise above hardship. Mass media accounts of such success sometimes describe these youth as quite extraordinary, as superkids. Although the depictions may be valid, research tells us that the sources of resilience are quite variable and ordinary—a finding that Masten (2001) has captured in the term *ordinary magic*. Resilience rests on well-recognized components of both individual characteristics and environmental factors that are beneficial to most children and particularly to at-risk youth.

| Ann and Amy | The "Ordinary Magic" of Resilience |

Ann and Amy were from different family circumstances, and at 6 years of age, their functioning was dissimilar. Ann was from an affluent family background, with parents who had an intact marriage

---

TABLE 2–2   EXAMPLES OF DEVELOPMENTAL TASKS

AGE PERIOD	TASK
Infancy to preschool	Attachment to caregiver(s) Language Differentiation of self from environment Self-control and compliance
Middle childhood	School adjustment (attendance, appropriate conduct) Academic achievement (e.g., learning to read, do arithmetic) Getting along with peers (acceptance, making new friends) Rule-governed conduct (following rules of society for moral behavior and prosocial conduct)
Adolescence	Successful transition to secondary schooling Academic achievement (learning skills needed for higher education or work) Involvement in extracurricular activities (e.g., athletics, clubs) Forming close friendships within and across gender Forming a cohesive sense of self-identity

From Masten & Coatsworth, 1998.

and optimally managed both child-rearing and emotional relations with Ann. Amy, on the other hand, was from more difficult circumstances, with a single-parent father who had experienced an acrimonious divorce. During assessment at age 6, Ann was well adjusted, whereas Amy evidenced problems in the clinical range. . . . However, over the next several years, Amy was able to take advantage of her social and athletic skills to develop good social relations with classmates, and her parents (ex-spouses) learned ways to interact much more amicably as they faced custody-related decisions and problems. For example, Amy's noncustodial mother gradually came to contribute faithfully to child support, even though she had remarried and had another child. An assessment conducted when both Ann and Amy were 10 years of age indicated that Ann, whose family circumstances had continued to be stable, supportive, and positive, still scored as well-adjusted, but Amy now also scored as well-adjusted and above average in social competence.

Adapted from Cummings et al., 2000, p. 40.

One of the early notable studies of resilience was conducted with children born in 1955 on the Hawaiian island of Kauai (Werner & Smith, 1982, 2001). A high-risk group was identified on the basis of early exposure to at least four risk factors. In late adolescence, most of the high-risk children had developed behavioral and/or learning problems, but one third of the youth were successfully negotiating life. The investigators indicated that resilience originated from three broad categories: personal attributes of the youth, family characteristics, and support from outside the family. This trio of protection has been found in other research as well (Table 2–3). The three categories of factors can be thought of as countering risk factors operating in the situation. As applied to the model shown in Figure 2–4, they would be child and environmental moderators that would weaken the path to psychopathology. (As a matter of general interest, the Kauai children have now been tracked to midlife.)

Research continues to advance the concept of resilience. Whether any single variable protects an at-risk child may depend on the situation. Further, an at-risk youth may show positive outcome in some domains of functioning (e.g., emotional) and not others (e.g., academic achievement) (Luthar, 2006). Or resilience may occur in some risk situations (e.g., family conflict) and not others (e.g., peer pressure). In addition, for any individual, resilience may change over time as circumstances alter and new strengths and vulnerabilities emerge. As much as we have come to understand resilience, though, researchers note the need to further examine the role of neurobiological functioning (Curtis & Cicchetti, 2003; Luthar, 2006). For example, it would be helpful to further understand the protection offered by the ability to return to a positive emotional state after stress, which involves specific brain areas and stress hormones.

TABLE 2–3	EXAMPLES OF RESILIENCE FACTORS
Individual	Intelligence
	Easygoing, sociable nature
	Social competence
	Self-confidence
	Positive outlook
	Ability to cope with stress
Family	Parental warmth and structure
	Authoritative parenting
	Supportive extended family members
	Economic advantage
	Medical care
	Protection from violence
Extrafamiliar	Bonds to supportive teachers, clergy, peers
	Effective schools
	Connections to prosocial organizations

Based on Masten & Coatsworth, 1998; Werner & Smith, 1982, 2001.

Continuity of Disturbance

Inherent in the developmental psychopathology perspective is an interest in understanding continuity and change over time. Development is defined in terms of change, and humans certainly are malleable. But there are limits to malleability and we can expect to see both change and continuity in an individual. When someone reaches old age, the person's face is both different from and similar to its appearance at ages 10, 30, and 60. We can generally expect the same for psychological functioning.

When the issue of change or continuity is applied to the study of psychological disorders, a basic question is, Does a disorder at an earlier time in life carry over to later life? This question is important for understanding the development of disorder, and it has implications for treatment and prevention. Treatment is desirable for any disturbance that causes discomfort and maladaptation, but problems that persist warrant increased concern. Moreover, knowing that early problems predict later disturbance puts high priority on efforts to intervene early in the process.

What is known about the continuity of disorders? Although this is not an easy question to answer, some problems of youth appear notably stable, some appear relatively stable, and some are quite transitory. We cannot assume that most children will grow out of psychopathology (e.g., Visser et al., 2003). Moreover, we can expect that the expression of some disorders may change with development; that is, heterotypic continuity may occur. We would anticipate, for example, that depression in childhood would be displayed somewhat differently than in adolescence or adulthood. Other disorders may be manifested over time by a relatively stable symptom presentation; that is, a fair amount of homotypic continuity may be displayed. In any event, though, continuity can be anticipated to vary with the length of time being examined, the kinds of psychopathology or symptoms, and other variables. A host of questions can be asked about which variables predict continuity of problems. Do symptoms that are severe or pervasive, rather than mild and limited, forecast continuity? Is continuity more likely when a child simultaneously displays more than one disorder? Is gender related to continuity and, if so, with regard to all or only some disorders? Many of these questions are being addressed by researchers.

Also under investigation are the processes responsible for carrying psychopathology forward in time. Several have been demonstrated or proposed, as summarized in Figure 2–5 (Rutter, 2006; Sroufe at al., 2005). Continuity may be sustained by environmental constancy—as when poor parental care or schooling persists and continues to negatively affect development. Genetic predisposition may be involved, and early problems or experiences can affect the development of the brain and other biological systems in ways that make continuity likely. Another process concerns the construction of mental representations or views of the social environment. Even when conditions change, people tend to act in accordance with these representations, thus bringing continuity to their behavior (Sroufe at al., 2005). In addition, continuity can result from a chain of negative circumstances or interactional behavior patterns. For example, continuity may stem from children's being channeled into environments that perpetuate a maladaptive style—as when an ill-tempered boy limits opportunity by dropping out of school, thereby creating frustrating situations, to which he responds with more irritability, lack of control, and the like (Caspi, Elder, & Bem, 1987).

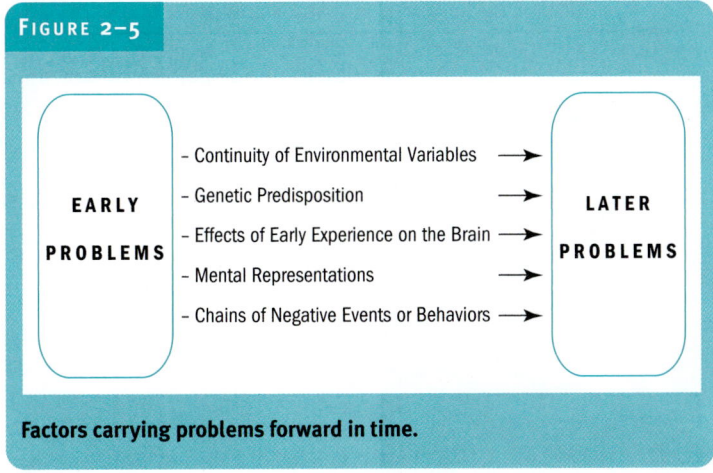

FIGURE 2–5

EARLY PROBLEMS — Continuity of Environmental Variables → — Genetic Predisposition → — Effects of Early Experience on the Brain → — Mental Representations → — Chains of Negative Events or Behaviors → LATER PROBLEMS

Factors carrying problems forward in time.

Normal Development, Problematic Outcomes

So far in this chapter, we have discussed core aspects of the developmental psychopathology perspective. We now briefly examine select areas of development in order to illustrate how normal developmental processes and less-than-optimal outcomes can go hand in hand. These areas are early attachment, temperament, emotion, and social cognitive processing. The four examples were selected to also make obvious that although it is useful to view human functioning as operating in biological, social, emotional, and cognitive domains, these domains overlap and are not independent of each other.

EARLY ATTACHMENT

Virtually all infants and their caregivers seem biologically prepared to interact in ways that foster their relationship. Most parents are remarkably sensitive in understanding and responding to their babies' signals and needs. Infants, in turn, are sensitive to parental emotional–social signals. Such synchronous interactions are the basis for the special social–emotional bond called early attachment, which develops gradually and becomes evident when the child is 7 to 9 months of age.

Recognizing that Freudian theory gave importance to the mother–child relationship, Bowlby (1969) emphasized that behaviors that facilitate attachment—smiling, crying, eye contact, proximity to caretakers, and the like—were biologically "wired" into the human species to ensure that infants would be nurtured and protected by caregivers. These behaviors

Infants and their caregivers are predisposed to interact in ways that foster attachment.

(Lisa Battaglene/Photolibrary.com)

are regarded as a component of an attachment system, which protects against high levels of threat or fear in stressful situations and also enhances the infant's exploration of novel and challenging situations (Kobak et al., 2006; Lyons-Ruth et al., 2003).

Bowlby viewed individual attachment as part of the ongoing transactions between a child and major caregivers, which help shape developmental pathways to adaptive or less adaptive outcomes. He and subsequent workers proposed that the child's attachment experiences with caregivers result in expectations, or internal models, about the caregivers' availability and responsiveness. Expectations regarding the trustworthiness of caregivers influence the child's ability to regulate emotion and cope with stress and are tied to the acquisition of a sense of confidence and self-worth—all of which are carried into future relationships and behavior.

Attachment has been studied not only in infancy but also beyond into adulthood. However, a central focus is early attachment, studied with Ainsworth's procedure, the Strange Situation. Here, a caregiver (usually the mother), the infant, and a stranger interact in a comfortable room. The caregiver leaves and returns several times on a predetermined schedule, while the child's behavior is observed in this potentially threatening situation. Initial research indicated that many infants could be categorized as displaying secure attachment or one of two types of insecure attachment (Kobak et al., 2006). Securely attached infants, when distressed by caregiver separation, seek contact with her upon her return, react positively, and use the caregiver as a secure base from which they venture forth to explore the environment. Insecurely attached infants fail to use the caregiver as a resource to cope with stress. They tend either to give fewer signals of distress and ignore the caregiver (the avoidant type) or display distress and make ineffective attempts to seek contact with the caregiver (the resistant type). The development of one pattern of attachment over another depends on child characteristics, caregiver sensitivity to the infant's needs, and the broader social context (Meins et al., 2001).

More recent research has revealed a pattern of disorganized/disoriented attachment (Green & Goldwyn, 2002; Lyons-Ruth et al., 2003). This pattern appears to reflect the lack of a consistent strategy to organize behavior under stressful situations. Infants seem apprehensive of the caregiver, and they variously display contradictory behaviors that may be misdirected and atypical (Table 2–4.) The pattern has been found at much greater frequency in high-

TABLE 2–4	SOME INDICATIONS OF DISORGANIZED/ DISORIENTED ATTACHMENT

Infant displays contradictory behaviors, such as seeking contact with the caregiver and also avoiding the caregiver.

Movements and expressions are undirected, misdirected, incomplete, or interrupted.

Movements and expressions are frozen or appear as in "slow motion."

Infant appears apprehensive regarding the caregiver.

Disorganization or disorientation is obvious in disoriented wandering, confused or dazed expression, or multiple rapid changes of affect.

Adapted from Lyons-Ruth, Zeanah, & Benoit, 2003.

risk than low-risk families (Juffer, Bakersmans-Kranenburg & van IJzendoorn, 2005). It is hypothesized that the child may experience the parent as frightening, unavailable, or threatening—and the child's behavior may become disorganized in the face of this circumstance. There is some evidence for biological vulnerability in these children.

Risk for later problems. The relationship of early attachment patterns to later behavior has been extensively investigated. Secure attachment has been associated with adaptive behavior in childhood and adolescence, such as competence and positive peer interactions (Kobak et al., 2006). In contrast, insecure attachment is linked to maladaptive behaviors—such as aggression and anxiety—particularly among children already at risk due to poverty or parent problems. In addition, early disorganized/disoriented attachment is related to future emotional and behavior problems, academic deficits, low self-esteem, poor peer interaction, unusual or bizarre classroom behavior, and dissociative behaviors (Kobak et al., 2006; Lyons-Ruth et al., 2003).

Caution is necessary, though, in interpreting these results. Not all findings demonstrate a link between early attachment and later adjustment. In addition, attachment can change from secure to insecure and vice versa, and modifications in family circumstances likely play a role (Thompson, 2000). It should also be emphasized that children who experience secure attachment may differ from those who experience insecure attachment in additional ways that affect behavior. Similarly, it may be the persistence of specific child–parent relationships, not just early attachment, that is crucial to later child adjustment (O'Connor, 2003). Despite these considerations, however, attachment theory remains a dominant approach to understanding the influence of early close relationships on later psychological development (Sroufe et al, 2005; Thompson, 2000).

TEMPERAMENT

The word temperament generally refers to basic disposition or makeup. The concept of temperament is an old one, going back to the classical Greek era. Current interest can be traced to Chess and Thomas's study of New York City children (1972; 1977). These investigators recognized environmental influences on the development of behavior, but they were struck by individual differences in how infants behaved from the first days of life. On the basis of parental interviews and actual observations, Chess and Thomas were able to demonstrate that young babies had distinct individual differences in temperament that were somewhat stable over time.

Chess and Thomas defined temperament in terms of nine dimensions of behavioral style that included reactivity to stimuli, regulation of bodily function, mood, and adaptability to change. They also identified three basic temperamental styles: easy, slow-to-warm, and difficult. The latter temperament—characterized in part by intense reactivity and negative mood—has been associated with social and psychological disturbance, but also has been defined somewhat differently across studies and garners less interest today (Rothbart & Posner, 2006; Nigg, 2006).

Chess and Thomas avoided simplistic notions about temperament and development. They suggested that early biologically based temperamental differences occur in the presence of parents who themselves differ in how they react to and manage their children. Parental responding, in turn, influences child reactions, which affects parental reactions, and so on—all of which occurs within the broader context of a changing environment. The investigators proposed that temperament is malleable and that final outcome depends on goodness-of-fit, that is, how the child's behavioral tendencies fit with parental characteristics and other environmental circumstances. The following case description demonstrates that a good match can lead to adaptation.

Carl | A Case of Goodness-of-Fit

"[Early] in life Carl had been one of our most extreme 'difficult child' temperamental types, with intense, negative reactions to new situations and slow adaptability only after many exposures. This was true whether it was the first bath or first solid foods in infancy, the beginning of nursery school and elementary school, first birthday parties, or the first shopping trip. Each experience evoked stormy responses, with loud crying and struggling to get away. However, his parents learned to anticipate Carl's reactions, knew that if they were patient, presented only one or a few new situations at a time, and gave Carl the opportunity for repeated exposure to the new, he would finally adapt positively. . . . His parents recognized that the difficulties in raising Carl were due to his temperament and not to their being 'bad parents.' The father even looked on his son's shrieking and turmoil as a sign of 'lustiness.' As a result of this positive parent–child interaction Carl never became a behavior problem even though the 'difficult' child as a group is significantly at higher risk for disturbed development."

"In his later childhood and high-school years Carl met very few new situations and developed an appropriately positive and self-confident image. However, the entry to college away from home suddenly confronted him simultaneously with a number of new situations. . . . [This] brought him for help. . . . By the end of the academic year his difficulties had disappeared. . . .He was told that similar negative reactions to the new might occur in the future. His response was, 'That's all right. I know how to handle them now.'"

Chess & Thomas, 1977, pp. 220–221.

Chess and Thomas's basic insight into temperament has stood the test of time, and more recent research has offered somewhat varied dimensions of temperament. Most accounts include aspects of approach and avoidance behaviors, positive and negative emotion, activity level, sociability, attention, or self-regulation (Compas, Connor-Smith, & Jaser, 2004; Frick, 2004; Rothbart & Posner, 2006). According to Nigg (2006), the specific attributes of temperament are encompassed by two general factors: reactivity to stimulation and self-regulation of functioning. Rothbart and Posner (2006) describe a three-factor structure, as shown in Table 2–5. Of considerable interest in this description is effortful control, a dimension that includes the ability to focus attention and inhibit behavior. Effortful control is considered crucial to healthy development and is implicated in a variety of psychological problems.

Current interest exists in exploring the relationship of temperament to psychological problems (Nigg, 2006). One perspective considers psychopathology to be an extreme of normal temperament. For example, ADHD may reflect the extreme of temperamental tendencies for impulsivity and reduced attention. Another perspective views temperament as a risk or protective factor, depending on the specific circumstance. Investigation continues into the association of different facets of temperament with difficulties such as shyness, anxiety, depression, and aggression.

EMOTION AND ITS REGULATION

Emotional reactivity and regulation are elements of temperament, but emotion is not identical to temperament and is deserving of further discussion. Three elements of emotion are widely recognized: (1) private "feelings" of sadness, joy, anger, disgust, and the like; (2) autonomic nervous system arousal and bodily reactions such as rapid heartbeat; and (3) overt behavioral expressions such as smiles, scowls, and drooping shoulders. The emotions may be viewed as relatively brief or as more general mood states that vary in intensity and that are experienced as positive or negative.

Human emotion is evident early in life: Infants express emotion and respond appropriately to the emotional expression of their caregivers (Harris, 1994; Izard et al., 2002). Two- and 3-year-olds are able to name and talk about basic emotions and exert some control over emotional expression. Ages 2 to 5 may be particularly important in the development of

TABLE 2–5	THREE-FACTOR STRUCTURE OF TEMPERAMENT
Surgency-Extraversion (positive emotionality and approach)	high-intensity pleasure high activity level smiling and laughter impulsivity not shy
Negative Affectivity	shyness discomfort fear anger-frustration sadness not easily soothed
Effortful Control	inhibitory control focusing of attention low-intensity pleasure perceptual sensitivity

From Rothbart & Posner, 2006.

connections between emotion and cognition (Izard et al., 2002). During childhood further progress is made in understanding and regulating the emotions. Although emotion has a biological basis, its development is shaped by family socialization and by the broader cultural context (Izard et al., 2006). There is evidence that family quality of care, open discussion of emotion, and modeling of emotional behavior all have influence (Eisenberg, 2006).

The emotions enter into virtually all human experience and serve several general functions (Izard et al., 2006; Lemerise & Arsenio, 2000). They play a role in communication, are involved in the development of empathy, and motivate and guide individual cognition and behavior. Unsurprisingly, emotion plays some role in psychological difficulty or maladjustment. Sadness and anger are components of depression and aggression. Undue fear and

From their facial expressions, it appears that very young children experience basic emotions such as happiness and unhappiness. The regulation of emotion is acquired gradually, and for some children much more easily than for others.
(Courtesy of L. Wicks) (Barbara Rios/Photo Researchers, Inc.)

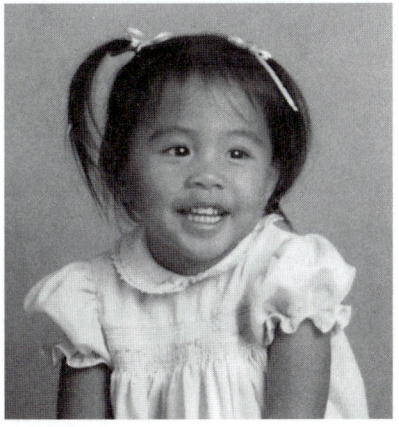 

anxiety—particularly when they endure over time—can require professional assistance. Even positive emotions can interfere with adaptive functioning; for example, the expression of joy may be excessive or inappropriate to the situation.

Understanding and regulation. The understanding of emotion is important to child competence and adjustment (Eisenberg, 2006). For example, a study by Schultz and colleagues (2001) examined emotion knowledge and social problems in 5- to 7-year-olds. Emotion knowledge was defined in terms of the children's ability to identify (1) emotional expressions on others' faces and (2) the emotion that would be experienced by a person in particular circumstances. As predicted, children who showed low levels of emotion knowledge tended to have social problems and withdrawal 2 years later. Other research demonstrates a link between the understanding of emotion and later academic or psychological problems (Fine et al., 2003; Izard et al., 2002).

Increasing evidence indicates a relationship between the complex task of emotion regulation and psychological disturbance. Individuals differ in the degree to which they react emotionally, but all must acquire the ability to regulate the emotions. This task includes learning to initiate, maintain, inhibit, or modulate the intensity of the feelings, biological responses, or expressions of emotion (Eisenberg, 2006). Emotional regulation can be viewed as overlapping with the effortful control thought to be crucial to adaptive and competent development. The importance of self-regulation was demonstrated in a study that found high levels of negative emotions combined with poor regulatory skills to be associated with both low social competence and behavioral problems. Children with good regulatory skills did not have these outcomes—regardless of whether they were high or low in emotionality (Eisenberg et al., 1997).

SOCIAL COGNITIVE PROCESSING

In contrast to feeling states that motivate and guide behavior, the cognitive domain of functioning has to do with knowing or understanding through higher order thinking processes. The role of cognition in various disorders of young people is being vigorously pursued. Here, we only consider one aspect of cognition: social cognitive processing.

Social cognitive processing has to do with thinking about the social world. It focuses on how individuals take in, understand, and interpret social situations—and how behavior is then affected (Lemerise & Arsenio, 2000). Interpretation includes thinking about the causes of the social situation, the intent of the persons in the situation, and the like. Of immediate concern to our discussion is the role that interpretation of the social situation can play in maladaptive behavior. To take an example, numerous studies indicate that children and adolescents who display more than average aggression or who have been rejected by their peers tend to interpret the behaviors of others as hostile. That is, they appear to have a bias to attribute hostility to others, especially when provoked.

It is noteworthy that although social information processing emphasizes cognition, emotion is viewed as playing an integral role (Arsenio & Lemerise, 2004; Dodge & Rabiner, 2004). Cognition and emotion may interact in various ways (cf. Lemerise & Arsenio, 2000). Poor understanding of emotion likely plays a role in misperceptions of social cues (Denham et al., 2002). Also, a youth who is already emotionally aroused may be highly prone to misperceptions. For example, the arousal of negative emotions in highly aggressive boys can increase their attribution of hostile intent to others (Orobio de Castro et al., 2003). Alternatively, the perception of hostility in others can arouse feelings of negative emotions. As these examples demonstrate, research on social cognitive processing contributes to our understanding of how thinking and emotions are united in the interchange between individuals and their environments (Rutter & Sroufe, 2000).

Cognitive processing of the social context influences much human functioning. For an everyday example, consider that children's perception of their parents' interaction with them or with each other is related to parental influence on the children (Gomez et al., 2001). Regarding psychological problems, specific beliefs and attributions about the world and the self appear to operate in depression, anxiety, and negative peer relationships, among other difficulties.

Inherent in the topics we have just examined—early attachment, temperament, emotion, and social cognition processing—is the assumption that development is rooted in both biological and experiential factors and their transactions with the child or adolescent. Influences on the development of psychopathology are further explored in chapter 3.

SUMMARY

PERSPECTIVES, THEORIES, MODELS

- *Perspectives (paradigms), theories, and models are critical to the scientific study of human development.*
- *Theories, which consist of formal propositions to explain phenomena, are highly valued because they permit the testing of hypotheses.*
- *Interactional and transactional (systems) models presume that several factors, working together, underlie pychopathology.*

DEVELOPMENTAL PSYCHOPATHOLOGY PERSPECTIVE: AN OVERVIEW

- *The developmental psychopathology perspective explores psychological disturbances with respect to several core developmental issues. It is a systems framework for organizing other perspectives or theories of psychopathology.*

CONCEPT OF DEVELOPMENT

- *Development refers to change over time resulting from transactions of an individual with biological, psychological, and sociocultural factors. It proceeds along probabilistic and coherent pathways marked by increased complexity.*

SEARCHING FOR CAUSAL FACTORS AND PROCESSES

- *A major goal of developmental psychopathology is to uncover the multiple causes of psychological disorders and underlying processes.*
- *It is important to differentiate direct and indirect influences; mediating and moderating influences; and necessary, sufficient, and contributing causes.*

PATHWAYS OF DEVELOPMENT

- *Development proceeds along complex probabilistic pathways, as reflected in the principles of equifinality and multifinality.*

RISK AND RESILIENCE

- *Risk factors increase the chance of psychopathology; many kinds have been identified. Risk is best conceptualized within a transactional model.*
- *Among important aspects of risk are the number; general or specific effects; and intensity, duration, and timing of risks.*
- *Resilience refers to a relatively positive outcome in the face of adversity. Protective factors that confer resilience on a person include individual, family, and extra-familial variables.*

CONTINUITY OF DISTURBANCE

- *Continuity of disorders over time varies, but it cannot be assumed that most children outgrow psychopathology. Both homotypic and heterotypic continuity are observed. Among the processes that underlie continuity are environmental stability, biological mechanisms, and psychological functioning.*

NORMAL DEVELOPMENT, PROBLEMATIC OUTCOMES

- *Patterns of early socioemotional attachment between children and their caregivers have been described. Secure attachment is associated with later positive outcome; insecure and disorganized/disoriented patterns are associated with unfavorable outcome.*
- *Temperament refers to biologically based, modestly stable individual styles of behaving that enter into the transactions of development. The relationship of temperament to psychopathology is being explored.*
- *Emotion is evident early in infancy and develops rapidly in childhood. Emotional reactivity, knowledge, and regulation are central in adaptive and maladaptive development.*
- *Cognitive processing of the social world is implicated in several forms of psychological problems. For example, highly aggressive children have a cognitive bias to view the world as hostile.*

KEY TERMS

paradigm *(p. 21)*

theory *(p. 21)*

microtheories, macrotheories *(p. 21)*

interactional models *(p. 21)*

vulnerability–stress model *(p. 21)*

transactional models *(p. 21)*

systems models *(p. 22)*

biopsychosocial model *(p. 22)*

ecological model *(p. 22)*

developmental psychopathology perspective *(p. 22)*

development *(p. 23)*

medical model *(p. 23)*

direct effect, indirect effect *(p. 23)*

mediator *(p. 24)*

moderator *(p. 24)*

necessary, sufficient, contributing causes *(p. 24)*

equifinality *(p. 25)*

multifinality *(p. 26)*

risk factors *(p. 27)*

resilience *(p. 29)*

developmental tasks *(p. 29)*

heterotypic continuity, homotypic continuity *(p. 31)*

attachment *(p. 32)*

secure attachment, insecure attachment *(p. 32)*

disorganized/disoriented attachment *(p. 32)*

temperament *(p. 33)*

goodness-of-fit *(p. 34)*

effortful control *(p. 34)*

emotion *(p. 34)*

social cognitive processing *(p. 36)*

CHAPTER 3

Biological and Environmental Contexts of Psychopathology

The aim of this chapter is to consider the major biological and environmental contexts of the development of psychological problems. We discuss the nervous system and brain, genetics, learning and cognition, and the social/cultural contexts of development. Basic information is provided and emphasis is placed on influences on behavioral and psychological disorders.

Brain and Nervous System

BRAIN DEVELOPMENT: BIOLOGY AND EXPERIENCE

The development of the brain and nervous system is arguably among the most fascinating of all developmental processes. Much early growth is biologically guided, but the influence of experience increases over time (Grossman et al., 2003).

The nervous system begins to develop shortly after conception when a group of cells called the neural plate thickens, folds inward, and forms the neural tube. The rapidly developing cells migrate to fixed locations. The brain contains millions of supporting cells, the glial cells, and neurons that are specialized to transmit impulses within the nervous system and to and from other body parts. These cells continue to become more complex, interconnected, and functional into the adolescent years (and to a lesser extent even later). Indeed, the brain seems to produce an excess of neurons and connections, apparently setting itself up to ensure flexibility. Different brain areas develop in spurts more rapidly than others, in a pattern that is related to functioning. Thus, areas that control voluntary movement grow substantially during the first year of life when the infant is gaining motor control, whereas the frontal part of the brain involved in complex thinking develops into the adolescent years, with spurts perhaps occurring around ages 6 and 10 and in early adolescence (Anderson et al., 2001).

The development of the nervous system has been shown to depend on the interaction of biological programming and experience. Animals given the opportunity to explore object-filled, enriched environments develop more neurons and cell connections in certain brain areas than animals reared in simple environments (Hockfield & Lombroso, 1998). Early shaping of the brain relies in part on

*"Young man, go to your room and stay there
until your cerebral cortex matures."*

the mechanism of pruning, the elimination of un-needed cells and connections. For example, brain regions important in the visual system of animals are shaped by pruning, a process that requires experience with patterned visual input (Grossman et al., 2003). Progress is being made in studying developmental change in the human brain, including both biological and environmental influences (e.g., Wallace et al., 2006).

STRUCTURE

The brain and spinal cord together form the central nervous system. The nerves outside the central nervous system that transmit messages to and from it compose the peripheral nervous system, which has two subsystems. One of these, the somatic system, involves the sensory organs and muscles and is engaged in sensing and voluntary movement. The other, the autonomic system, helps involuntary regulation of arousal and the emotions. The branches of the autonomic system either increase arousal (sympathetic system) or work to slow arousal and maintain bodily functioning (parasympathetic system). The entire nervous system communicates within itself, and is in close communication with the endocrine system, a collection of glands intricately involved in bodily functions through the release of hormones.

The brain—a wrinkled mass atop the spinal cord—has three major interconnected divisions. The hindbrain includes the pons, medulla, and cerebellum. Among other functions, the pons relays information and the medulla helps regulate heart function and breathing. The cerebellum, is involved in movement and cognitive processing. A small area called the midbrain contains fibers that connect the hindbrain and upper brain regions. It also shares with the hindbrain netlike connections, the reticular activating system, which influences arousal states such as waking and sleeping. Sometimes the midbrain and hindbrain are called the brain stem (Figure 3–1).

The third major division, the forebrain, consists chiefly of two cerebral hemispheres, the outer surface of which is referred to as the cortex. The hemispheres are connected to each other by the corpus callosum, and each hemisphere has four lobes. The cerebral hemispheres are involved in a wide variety of activities, such as sensory processing, motor control, and higher mental functioning that includes information processing, learning, and memory.

Situated below the cerebral hemispheres and deep in the brain are several subcortical structures. (They are variously said to be located in the lower forebrain or between the forebrain and the midbrain.) The thalamus is involved in processing and relaying information between the cerebral hemispheres

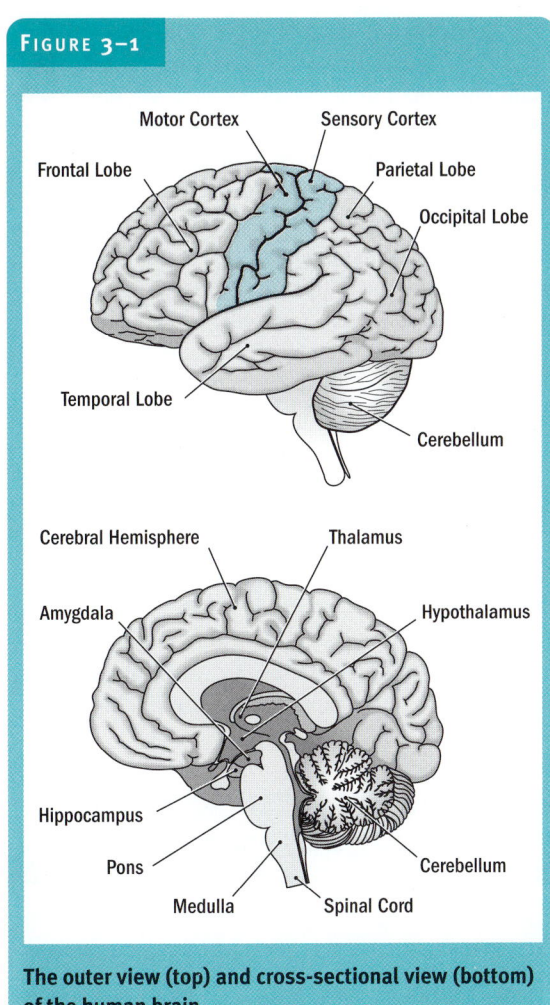

FIGURE 3–1

The outer view (top) and cross-sectional view (bottom) of the human brain.

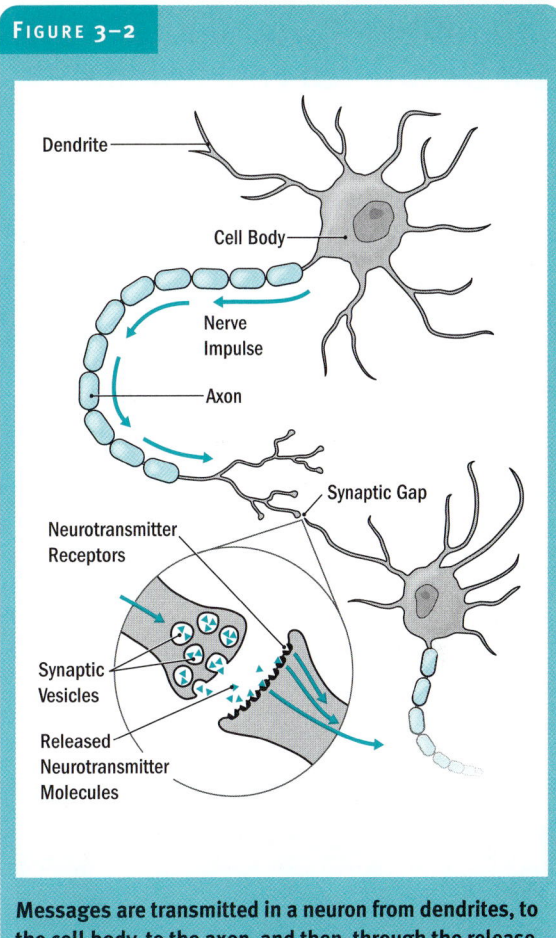

FIGURE 3–2

Messages are transmitted in a neuron from dendrites, to the cell body, to the axon, and then, through the release of neurotransmitters, across the synaptic gap to other neurons.

and other parts of the central nervous system. The hypothalamus regulates basic urges such as hunger, thirst, and sexual activity. The multistructured limbic system, which includes the hippocampus and amygdala, plays a central role in memory and emotion.

NEUROTRANSMISSION

Although neurons vary in size, shape, and chemistry, they all have three major parts: a multifunctional cell body, dendrites, and an axon. Communication between neurons occurs across a synapse, the small gap between the cells (the synaptic gap, or cleft). The dendrites of a neuron receive chemical messages from other neurons that result in an electric impulse being sent down the axon. When the impulse reaches the end of the axon, packets of chemicals—the neurotransmitters—are released. They cross the synaptic gap and are taken up by the receptor sites on the dendrites of the receiving neuron. The receiving neuron, in turn, generates new electrical impulses (Figure 3–2). Among the major neurotransmitters are dopamine, serotonin, norepinephrine, glutamate, and GABA, whose role in brain functioning is being intensely investigated.

The complexity of communication is hard even to imagine. Neurons may make thousands of connections to other neurons, and neurotransmitters may travel multiple pathways to receptor sites. Neurotransmitters can act to excite or inhibit neurons, that is, make them more or less likely to fire an impulse. Communication is far from helter-skelter, however. Brain regions work together, forming pathways, or circuits, that are associated with different neurotransmitters and functions.

Nervous System and Risk for Disordered Functioning

The nervous system is a major aspect of the constitutional factors that influence psychological functioning and behavior. Impairments can result from abnormalities of the genetic processes that guide nervous system development. In this case, dysfunction can be "wired in" from the beginning. However, harm can also be attributed to events that occur during pregnancy (prenatal), at about the time of birth (perinatal), or during later development (postnatal).

PRENATAL INFLUENCES

Poor maternal diet and health can put the developing child at risk. Research also indicates that exposure to prenatal stress can alter the fetal biological system in ways that create susceptibility to later psychological problems (Talge, Neal, Glover et al., 2007).

At one time, it was believed that the fetus was protected from most harmful substances, or teratogens, that might enter the mother's bloodstream. We now know that a variety of agents can be detrimental. Potentially harmful drugs include alcohol, tobacco, thalidomide, cocaine, heroin, and methadone. (See Accent: "Fetal Alcohol Syndrome: A Preventable Tragedy.") Radiation, environmental contaminants—such as lead, mercury, and polychlorinated biphenyls (PCBs)—and many maternal diseases—such as rubella, syphilis, gonorrhea, and AIDS—can be harmful. Teratogens are associated with malformation, functional and behavioral impairment, low birthweight, and fetal death (Hogan, 1998; Singer et al., 1997; Taylor & Rogers, 2005).

Teratogens are thought to interfere with brain cell formation and migration, as well as other developmental processes (Koger, Schettler, & Weiss, 2005). Perhaps unsurprising, the amount of exposure to a teratogen makes a difference in outcome. So does the timing of exposure during gestation. In general, specific structures and systems are most sensitive to harm when they are rapidly developing (Talge et al.,

ACCENT

Fetal Alcohol Syndrome: A Preventable Tragedy

Adverse effects from prenatal exposure to alcohol were suspected for many years before they were adequately documented. Fetal Alcohol Syndrome (FAS) is characterized by abnormal brain development and higher than average rates of numerous difficulties. The terms *alcohol-related neurodevelopmental disorder* and *alcohol-related birth defects* generally indicate less severe symptoms. Affected children are at high risk for the following attributes (American Academy of Pediatrics, 2000; Fetal Alcohol Syndrome, 2003; Fryer et al., 2007):

- Minor facial abnormalities, such as a flat upper lip and/or narrow eye openings
- Retarded growth, both prenatally and postnatally
- Neurological signs such as impaired motor skills and unusual gait
- Birth defects of the heart, kidneys, eyes, ears, and other organs
- Learning disabilities and cognitive impairments in memory, abstract thinking, comprehension, and generalization

- Hyperactivity, impulsivity, oppositional behavior, conduct disorders, and other problems

The effects of maternal alcohol use vary with several factors, including amount of alcohol exposure, timing of exposure, mother's age and health, and fetal susceptibility (American Academy of Pediatrics, 2000; Grossman et al., 2003). Not all of the children exhibit all symptoms but problems can be pervasive and can persist into adulthood. Whereas educational programs and family support can be of help, the tragedy is that FAS and related conditions are completely preventable by maternal abstinence from alcohol.

FAS occurs at an estimated 0.2 to 1.5 per 1,000 live births in the U.S. population, and the lesser symptoms perhaps three times as often (Fetal Alcohol Syndrome, 2003). Prenatal harm is much more likely when alcohol intake is large, but as little as one drink a day has been associated with infant growth retardation. (One drink is defined as 1.5 ounces of distilled alcohol, 5 ounces of wine, or 12 ounces of beer.) A safe level of maternal consumption has not been established (Taylor & Rogers, 2005).

2007). It is thought that the genetic endowment of the developing organism can act as a risk or protective factor.

Although there is no doubt that prenatal threat can be consequential, the research results must be cautiously regarded. It is, of course, unacceptable to conduct controlled experiments in which pregnant women are exposed to harmful agents. The research strategies that are feasible make it difficult to establish causality and to distinguish the impact of one teratogen from another. Teratogens tend to cluster; for example, prenatal use of illicit substances is often associated with alcohol and cigarette use (Lester, Andreozzi, & Appiah, 2006). Further, prenatal substance abuse is associated with poverty, which can influence children's development both prenatally *and* during the child's subsequent development, making it difficult to establish the timing of influence (Brown et al., 2004). Despite these hindrances, research can circumvent interpretive difficulties (D'Onofrio et al., 2003). One option is research with animals, which allows intentional exposure to teratogens and the testing of causal hypotheses—although generalizing the results to humans must be done guardedly.

PERINATAL AND POSTNATAL INFLUENCES

Developmental risks are associated with the time of birth. Excessive medication given to the mother, unusual delivery, and anoxia (lack of oxygen) can result in neurological problems in the newborn. Prematurity, low birthweight, and low birthweight relative to the length of gestation are associated with developmental problems (Saylor, Boyce, & Price, 2003). The lower the birthweight, the greater the risk. In the United States, 12% of infants are born prematurely (less than 37 weeks into gestation) and 7.5% are born with low birthweight (less than 5½ pounds) (Field, Hernandez-Reif, & Freedman, 2004). The developmental outcome for these infants depends on the interplay of biological and psychosocial factors (Werner & Smith, 2001).

Postnatal damage can result from malnutrition, accident, illness, or poisoning. For example, exposure of children to lead, even at low levels, appears to have a negative impact on brain processes involved in attention and cognitive development. In general, damage may either be localized to a specific area or more widely affect the brain.

Whenever brain damage occurs in youth, a major concern is the degree to which the resulting problems can be remediated. The plasticity, or flexibility, of the brain to recover is controversial. On the

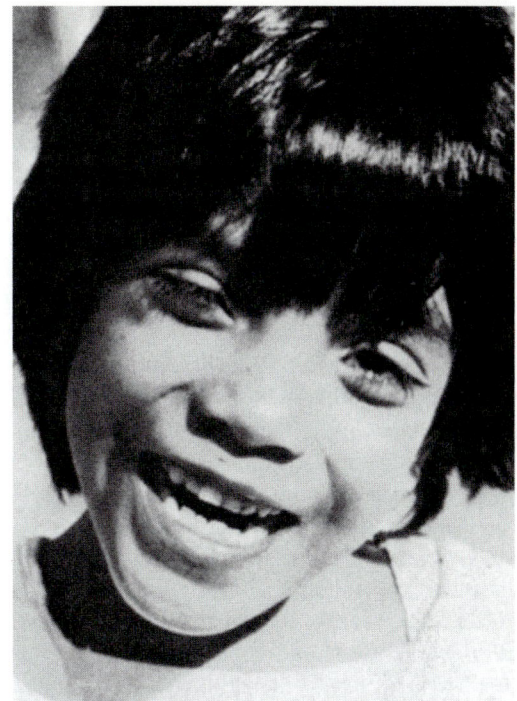

The girl pictured here is one of two daughters born to an alcoholic mother, since deceased. On the basis of history, mental deficiency, and physical findings, both daughters were diagnosed as having fetal alcohol syndrome. Several key features of the syndrome are visible in this girl, including narrow eye openings, underdeveloped-thin upper lip, flattening or absence of the usual indentation under the nose, and possible drooping of the upper eyelids.
(Courtesy of March of Dimes Birth Defects Foundation)

one hand, it is argued that the young, immature nervous system is relatively adept at restoring itself or at successfully transferring functions to undamaged brain areas (Anderson et al., 2001). On the other hand, damage to the immature brain may set up a cascade of interferences with future brain development, and deficits may become apparent over time (Limond & Leeke, 2005). The timing, extent, severity, and region of damage, as well as the kind and amount of environmental support and therapy provided, are among the factors that influence recuperation.

Genetic Context

Genetic contributions to behavioral development operate in complex ways. The basic genetic material is contained in all body cells. It consists of chromosomes containing DNA (deoxyribonucleic acid), functional segments of which are called genes. At conception, billions of chromosome combinations are possible for any one individual. Other genetic mechanisms result in even greater variability. Chromosomes may exchange genes, break and reattach to each other, and change by mutation, which is spontaneous alteration of the DNA molecule.

In some cases, early genetic processes result in obvious structural defects in the chromosomes or a lack or excess of the 23 pairs of chromosomes found in most human cells. These "errors" may be transmitted from parents, but many are not inherited. In either case, the consequence can be dire, with many of the abnormalities resulting in the death of the early-developing organism. Less severe outcomes include a variety of medical syndromes involving physical, intellectual, and psychological abnormalities. These instances are certainly of interest to mental health workers, although most individual differences relevant to psychopathology involve more subtle genetic processes, many of which implicate inheritance.

The study of genetic influences on individual differences in behavior is known as behavior genetics. Behavior genetics seeks to establish the extent of genetic influence on attributes, discover the genes involved, and understand the paths from genes to characteristics (Plomin & Crabbe, 2000). Evidence for genetic influence has been established for many attributes and psychological disorders, and progress is gradually being made in the discovery of the underlying genetic processes.

In the following discussion, we introduce some of the major methods and findings of behavior genetics with a focus on psychological disorders. Keep in mind that even today, genetic influence is often misunderstood. Genes act indirectly and in complex ways to guide the biochemistry of cells (Rutter, Moffitt, & Caspi, 2006). As applied to an individual, the term *genetic code* refers to the order in which four nucleotides (adenine, thymine, guanine, and cytosine) appear on the backbone of the DNA molecule. This sequence is the basis for the transcription, or synthesis, of messenger RNA, a molecule that carries the information to other parts of the cell, where it plays a role in the translation of the code into the manufacture of proteins (Figure 3–3). Genes that carry the code are obviously critical, and an even greater number of noncoding genes are involved in transcription and translation. In addition, only some of the coding genes in each cell are expressed, or activated, and genes can turn on and off over time. There is increasing evidence for the influence of both the internal and external environments on the processes of transcription, translation, and gene expression. As even this brief description makes clear, the path from individual genetic endowment—the genotype—to the observable characteristics of the person—the phenotype—is indirect and incredibly complex.

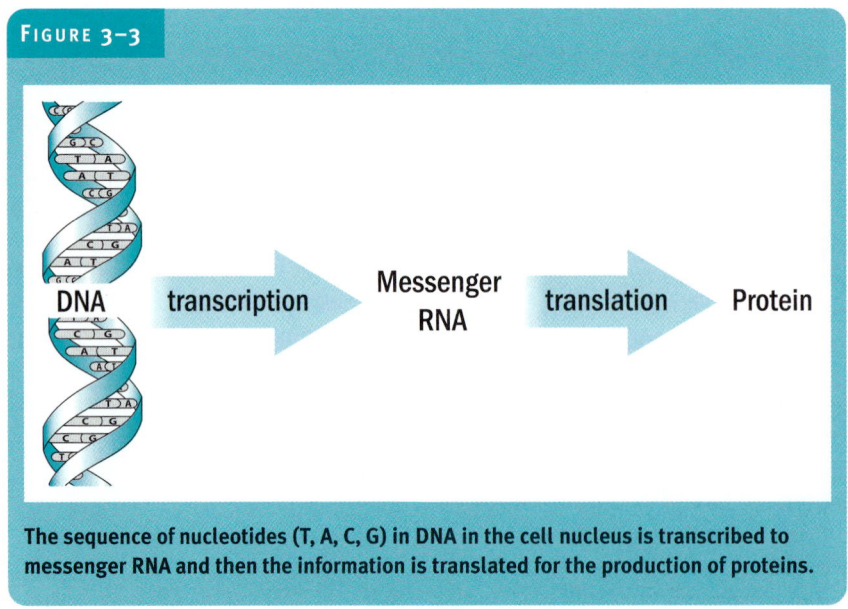

FIGURE 3–3

DNA → transcription → Messenger RNA → translation → Protein

The sequence of nucleotides (T, A, C, G) in DNA in the cell nucleus is transcribed to messenger RNA and then the information is translated for the production of proteins.

SINGLE-GENE INHERITANCE

Gregor Mendel, a monk who experimented with plants in a monastery garden in Moravia in the mid-19th century, is credited with discoveries crucial to modern genetics. Among Mendel's contributions are descriptions of the inheritance of certain characteristics that are influenced by a single gene. He correctly hypothesized that each parent carries two hereditary factors (later called genes, with each form termed an allele), but passes on only one to the offspring. He noted that one form of the gene is dominant, that is, its transmission by either parent leads to the display of the trait associated with it. The other form, the recessive, displays itself only when it is transmitted by both parents. Although we know today that single-gene inheritance is far from simple, Mendel's basic descriptions have largely stood the test of time. Dominant and recessive patterns of inheritance, as well as the sex-linked pattern described later in this text, are involved in the inheritance of many human attributes and disorders. Huntington's disease is an example of a syndrome transmitted by a dominant gene on chromosome 4; it typically shows up in adulthood, when motor problems and mental deterioration become evident. Tay-Sachs disease, transmitted recessively, causes degeneration of the nervous system and death by the age of 1 to 3 years.

In general, the effects of such single genes are quite predictable, and often result in individuals either having or not having the abnormal phenotype. One way to establish single-gene influence on a specific disorder is to identify a person with the disorder—the index case or the proband—and determine whether a known pattern of single-gene inheritance runs in the family.

MULTIPLE-GENE INHERITANCE: QUANTITATIVE METHODS

As important as single-gene effects are, multiple genes are more often implicated in complex human characteristics, such as intelligence, and in psychological disorders. Several things are notable about these genes, referred to as quantitative trait loci or QTLs (Plomin & Crabbe, 2000; Plomin, 2005). They are inherited in the usual patterns, but each has relatively small influence—which combine to create a larger effect. The genes may vary in the size of their influence and may be interchangeable in some instances. This means that any one gene may not be

sufficient or necessary for a disorder, and indeed may be carried by a person without the disorder. Multiple genes working together result in a range of phenotypes, varying from lesser to greater display of the characteristic. Multigenic influence is less predictable, or more probabilistic, than single-gene inheritance.

Research into multiple-gene influence relies on a combination of evidence from a variety of quantitative genetic methods. (See Accent: "Family, Twin, and Adoption Studies.") One goal of quantitative genetics is to assess heritability, the degree to which genetic influence accounts for variance in behavior among individuals in the population studied. Overall results suggest that with a few exceptions heritability for psychological disorders or dimensions rarely exceeds 50% and is often appreciably lower (Plomin, 1994a; Rutter, 2002). This means that substantial variation in attributes has a basis in nongenetic influences, that is, other biological and environmental influences.

Behavior genetic research does provide information about the contribution of environmental influences and how genes work together (Rutter, 2002). Both shared and nonshared environmental influences are important. Shared environmental influences refer to influences that contribute to family members developing in similar ways. Examples might be intellectual stimulation provided to the whole family or shared exposure to environmental toxins, which similarly affect siblings. Nonshared environmental influences refer to influences that are different for children growing up in the same family and result in siblings being different from each other. Examples might be the effects of differential treatment of siblings by the parents or relationships with different friends or teachers.

We should note that all behavior genetic methods have weaknesses (Rutter & Silberg, 2002). Combinations and refinement of methods, and more sophisticated quantitative analyses, seek to address many of the shortcomings of individual methods. These advances also permit evaluation of hypothetical models of genetic transmission and of the interaction of genetic and environmental influences (e.g., Harlaar et al., 2005; Rutter et al., 2006).

SEARCHING FOR GENES: MOLECULAR METHODS

Molecular genetics is a rapidly expanding field that seeks to discover the genes associated with a disorder,

ACCENT

Family, Twin, and Adoption Studies

Three basic quantitative research methods are employed with human participants: family, twin, and adoption studies (Plomin, 1994a).

Family genetic studies evaluate the likelihood of family members displaying the same or similar attributes as an index case. The aggregation, or clustering, of problems in families is assessed with regard to the degree of genetic relatedness. The average genetic relatedness is 50% for first-degree relatives (child–parents, siblings, fraternal twins), 25% for second-degree relatives (e.g., grandparents, half-siblings, uncles), and 12.5% for third-degree relatives (e.g., first cousins). If genetic influence is operating, family members who are genetically more similar to the index case should be more likely to exhibit the same or related difficulties as the proband. This pattern could also indicate family psychosocial transmission, which would similarly make close family members more alike than distant family members. However, family aggregation of an attribute is consistent with genetic influence.

The essence of twin studies is a comparison of identical twin resemblance (concordance) with fraternal twin resemblance. Identical, or monozygotic (MZ), twins have identical genes. Fraternal, or dizygotic (DZ), twins are, on average, only 50% alike genetically, just like any two siblings. Genetic influence is suggested when concordance is greater in identical twins than fraternal twins; that is, when a disorder occurs more frequently in both members of MZ twin pairs than in both members of DZ twin pairs (Edelbrock et al., 1995).

Adoption studies evaluate the relative contributions of genetics and environment by studying adopted and nonadopted individuals and their families. One strategy starts with adopted children who display a particular disorder and compares rates of that disturbance in members of the children's biological and adoptive families. Higher rates in the biological family are evidence for genetic influence. Another strategy starts with biological parents who exhibit a particular disorder and examines the rate of disturbance in their offspring adopted early in life by a nonrelated family. Rates of disorder in these children can then be contrasted with various groups (e.g., siblings who were raised by the biological parent). Also, associations between risk factors, such as family conflict, and the development of problems can be compared in adopted and nonadopted youngsters. Adoption strategies can thus help reveal complex relations between genetic and environmental influences (Braungart-Rieker et al., 1995).

---

the biochemicals coded by the genes, and how these biochemicals are involved in behavior. Research with animals is critical in these endeavors; for example, gene functioning can be "knocked out" and the effects can be studied. In research with humans, the methods of linkage analysis and association analysis are employed (Eley & Rijsdijk, 2005; Plomin & McGuffin, 2003).

The aim of linkage analysis is to reveal the location of a defective gene, that is, the specific chromosome and the place on the chromosome. This strategy takes advantage of the fact that genes on the same chromosome, especially when located close to each other, are generally transmitted to offspring together. The strategy also takes advantage of the fact that the chromosome location is known for many genetic markers (known segments of DNA that vary among individuals). Linkage analysis determines whether a specific disorder appears among family members in the same pattern as a genetic marker. If it does, it can be presumed that a gene that influences the disorder is located on the same chromosome as the marker and is close to the marker. Thus, the approximate genetic address for the disorder is revealed. Mapping the gene responsible for Huntington's disease was among the earliest successes of linkage analysis (Huntington's Disease Collaborative Research Group, 1993; Wexler, 1995). It required several years to locate and identify the defective, mutant gene on chromosome 4, and it is now possible to test individuals and to test prenatally for the gene.

Association analysis searches for genes in a different way (Plomin & McGuffin, 2003). This method tests whether a particular form of a gene (i.e., an allele) is associated with a trait or disorder in the population. Most studies compare the genetic material of persons with a specific disorder with the genetic material from a matched control group. Usually, the focus is on a particular gene—called a candidate gene—that is suspect, based on theory or past research. As an example, the DRD4 and the DAT genes have been found to be associated with attention-deficit hyperactivity disorder; both of these genes are involved in the dopamine neurotransmitter systems.

Association analysis is more suitable than linkage analysis to identify multiple genes that have relatively small influence on a disorder or trait (Plomin, 2005; Plomin & McGuffin, 2003). When such QTLs are involved, it is quite possible that only some will be revealed, at least with present research methods. However, understanding how even some of the genes operate in a disorder can contribute to understanding psychopathology and can potentially facilitate treatment and prevention.

GENE–ENVIRONMENT INTERPLAY

Although we have already noted that genetic and environmental influences work hand in hand to influence traits and behaviors, it is important to examine this interplay in greater detail. Of substantial importance are gene–environment interactions and gene–environment correlations. These occurrences have been increasingly recognized in developmental processes.

Gene–environment interaction (GxE) refers to differential sensitivity to experience due to differences in genotype (Plomin & Crabbe, 2000). An example is children whose genotype carries two recessive genes for the condition called PKU (phenylketonuria). These children, but not those who carry only one of these recessive genes, develop mental retardation when they digest certain foods. A more recently described example indicates that variations in the 5-HTT gene affect reactions to stressful life events (Caspi et al., 2003). That is, youth carrying a particular form of the gene, but not another form, were more likely to react to aversive life events so that they suffered symptoms of depression in later life (Caspi et al., 2003). These compelling examples call attention to the influence of gene–environment interaction on the development of psychopathology (Rutter et al., 2006).

Gene–environment correlation (GE) refers to genetic differences in exposure to environments. Three kinds of gene–environment correlations have been described: passive, reactive, and active. Table 3–1 defines these and provides a hypothetical example of each (Plomim, 1994b). Passive GE correlations stem from parents transmitting both their genes and gene-related rearing environments to their offspring. Reactive GE correlations reflect both the child's genetic endowment and reactions from others to the child's gene-related characteristics. Active GE correlations are based on both the child's genetic

TABLE 3–1	TYPES OF GENE–ENVIRONMENT CORRELATIONS DEMONSTRATING HOW GENETIC PREDISPOSITION AND ASPECTS OF THE ENVIRONMENT ARE LINKED

PASSIVE

A family's environment is influenced by the genetic predisposition of the parents. The child experiences this environment and *also* shares the genetic predisposition of the parents. This mechanism occurs at birth and is "passive" in the sense that the child has relatively little active input.

Example: The child who has a genetic propensity for a high activity level also experiences a high-activity family environment.

REACTIVE

A child evokes reactions from other people on the basis of her or his genetic predisposition, so that the child's genetic propensities are linked to environmental experiences.

Example: Others react to the child's gene-based high activity level.

ACTIVE

A child, particularly as he or she grows older, selects or creates environments on the basis of his or her genetic predisposition.

Example: The child with a genetic propensity for high activity level engages in activities requiring high activity rather than restrained, quiet activities such as reading.

Adapted from Plomin, 1994b.

endowment and the child's active selection of gene-related experiences. As children move through life, the impact of passive GE correlations may give way to the influences of reactive and active GE correlations. The importance of gene–environment correlations is that they inform us that a child's experiences are not independent of genetic influences. In fact, there is considerable evidence that genetic influences play a role in determining the experiences a person will have—and thus the risks and protections that will be encountered (Rutter & Silberg, 2002).

Learning and Cognition

Learning and cognition are inextricably intertwined with development. The abilities to learn and think not only become more advanced over time, but also facilitate other kinds of development as the child transacts with the environment. Our present discussion of this topic is introductory, and the vital role that learning and cognition play in psychopathology is woven throughout the text.

CLASSICAL CONDITIONING

Pavlov focused attention on the process of classical conditioning by demonstrations that hungry dogs, which normally salivate when food is present, could learn to salivate to neutral stimuli presented just prior to the presentation of food. In classical conditioning, the individual learns to respond to a stimulus that previously did not elicit the response. Many aspects of this kind of learning have been described. For example, once a new response (the conditioned response) is acquired, it can generalize to similar situations and can have far-reaching effects on emotion and behavior.

Historically, two early studies based on classical conditioning had a notable impact on the application of learning to problem behavior. (See Accent: "Albert and Peter: Two Historic Cases.") The now-famous case of little Albert was an early illustration of the conditioning of fear, the process of which is illustrated in Figure 3–4. The case of Peter demonstrated that fearful responses could be eliminated by the application of classical conditioning principles.

OPERANT LEARNING

A second basic type of learning is operant learning, which was set forth in Thorndike's Law of Effect recognizing that a positive consequence of a behavior will strengthen the behavior while a negative consequence will weaken it. The work of B. F. Skinner was especially influential. Operant, or instrumental,

ACCENT ●●●●●

Albert and Peter: Two Historic Cases

As reported by Watson and Rayner (1920), Albert, an 11-month-old child, initially showed no fear reactions to a variety of objects, including a white rat. He did, however, exhibit fear when a loud sound was produced by the striking of a steel bar. Watson and Rayner attempted to condition fear of the white rat by producing the loud clanging sound each time Albert reached for the animal. After several of these pairings, Albert reacted with crying and avoidance when the rat was presented without the noise. Thus, it appeared that fear could be learned through classical conditioning. (Needless to say, there are significant ethical difficulties in conditioning fear in children, and studies such as Watson and Rayner's are unlikely to occur today.)

The landmark study by Mary Cover Jones (1924) described the treatment of Peter, a boy nearing 3 years of age, who exhibited fear of furry objects. Jones first attempted to treat Peter by placing him in the presence of a rabbit, along with children who liked the rabbit and petted it. The treatment appeared to be working but was interrupted when Peter became ill for nearly 2 months. Just prior to his return to treatment, he was also frightened by a large dog. With Peter's fear back at its original level, Jones decided to treat Peter with a counterconditioning procedure, which involved allowing Peter to eat some of his favorite foods while the animal was moved progressively closer. In this way, the feared stimulus was associated with pleasantness. The procedure was apparently successful in reducing the boy's fears, and he was ultimately able to hold the animal by himself. Although this study has methodological weaknesses, it stimulated the development of treatments for psychological disturbance based on the principles of classical conditioning.

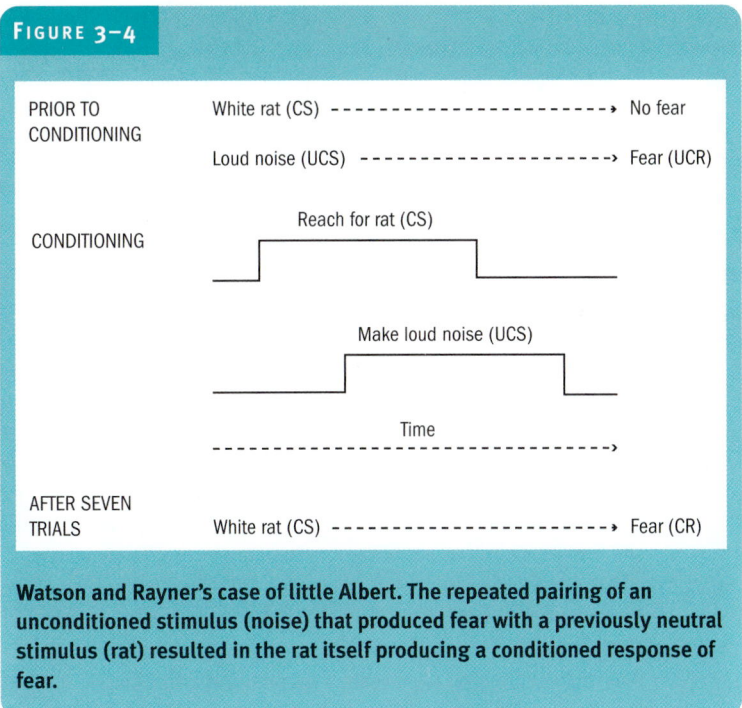

FIGURE 3-4

Watson and Rayner's case of little Albert. The repeated pairing of an unconditioned stimulus (noise) that produced fear with a previously neutral stimulus (rat) resulted in the rat itself producing a conditioned response of fear.

conditioning emphasizes the consequences of behavior. Behavior is acquired, strengthened, weakened, maintained, eliminated, or emitted in some circumstances but not in others through reinforcement, punishment, and other learning processes (Table 3–2). Operant learning is ubiquitous; through it, knowledge is acquired and adaptive and maladaptive behaviors are shaped.

The principles of operant conditioning have been applied to a broad range of behavioral problems with regard to their etiology, maintenance, and especially treatment. The specific applications of these procedures, discussed in succeeding chapters of this book, all share the assumption that problem behavior can be changed through a learning process and that the focus of treatment should be on the consequences of behavior.

OBSERVATIONAL LEARNING

Observational learning is another fundamental way through which individuals change due to experience. A wide variety of behaviors can be acquired by observing others perform them—from jumping rope, to cooperation or aggression, to social skills. As with other forms of learning, observational learning can lead to both the acquisition and the removal of problem behaviors. Early work by Bandura (1997)

and his colleagues, as well as subsequent research, demonstrated how problem behaviors may be acquired through the observation of a model.

Although observational learning may seem simple, it is actually quite complex. Children can learn new responses by watching a model; however, they are more likely to display the responses if they observe the model being reinforced for the behavior and are less likely to display them if they observe the model being punished. As with other kinds of basic learning processes, obser-vational learning can generalize. A child who observes another child being scolded for shouting may become quiet in other ways (inhibition). The observation of shooting and fighting on television may lead a child to exhibit other forms of aggression, such as verbal abuse and physical roughness (disinhibition). In neither case is the exact behavior of the model imitated; rather, a class of behaviors becomes either less likely or more likely to occur because of observation of the model.

Whether imitation is specific or generalized, complex cognitive processes are required for observational learning to occur (Bandura, 1977). The child must attend to salient features of the model's behavior, organize and encode this information, and store the information in memory. The child's imitation of the model in the near or far future depends on several factors, including recall of the

TABLE 3–2	SOME FUNDAMENTAL OPERANT CONDITIONING PROCESSES	
TERM	**DEFINITION**	**EXAMPLE**
Positive reinforcement	A stimulus is presented following a response (*contingent* upon the response), increasing the frequency of that response.	Praise following good behavior increases the likelihood of good behavior.
Negative reinforcement	A stimulus is withdrawn contingent on a response, increasing the frequency of that response.	Removal of a mother's demands following a child's tantrum increases the likelihood of tantrums.
Extinction	A weakening of a learned response is produced when the reinforcement that followed it no longer occurs.	Parents ignore bad behavior, and it decreases.
Punishment	A response is followed by either an unpleasant stimulus or the removal of a pleasant stimulus, thereby decreasing the frequency of the response.	A parent scolds a child for hitting, and the child stops hitting; food is removed from the table after a child spits, and the spitting stops.
Generalization	A response is made to a new stimulus that is different from, but similar to, the stimulus present during learning.	A child has a stern uncle with a mustache and develops fear of all men with mustaches.
Discrimination	A stimulus comes to signal that a certain response is likely to be followed by a particular consequence.	An adult's smile indicates that a child's request is likely to be granted.
Shaping	A desired behavior that is not in the child's repertoire is taught by rewarding responses that are increasingly similar to (*successive approximations* of) the desired response.	A mute child is taught to talk by initially reinforcing any sound, then a sound somewhat like a word, and so on.

information and expectation that the behavior will garner desired consequences. Thus, observational learning—and the social learning perspective associated with it—incorporates many cognitive processes.

COGNITIVE PROCESSES

Various approaches to cognition focus on how individuals mentally process information and think about the world. Briefly put, individuals perceive their experiences, construct concepts or schemas that represent experience, store information in memory, and employ their understanding to think about and act in the world. Among the many higher order mental operations involved are perception, attention, memory, and mental manipulation of information. Different facets of cognition are implicated in many different kinds of problems, such as mental retardation, specific learning disabilities, aggression, anxiety, and attention deficits, to name a few. The present discussion examines one cognitive viewpoint, the cognitive-behavioral perspective, which has contributed substantially to both understanding and treating problems of youth.

Cognitive-behavioral perspective. Among others, Kendall and his colleagues have focused not on intellectual abilities per se but on additional aspects of cognition. The cognitive-behavioral perspective incorporates cognition, behavior, emotion, and social factors (Kendall, 2006; Kendall et al., 1997b). Behaviors are assumed to be learned and maintained by the interaction of internal cognitions and emotions with external environmental events. Cognitive factors influence whether the individual pays attention to environmental events, how the person perceives events, and whether these events affect future behavior. A basic hypothesis is that maladaptive cognitions are related to maladaptive behavior. As an example of support for this assumption, maladaptive thoughts and beliefs have been found among phobic

ACCENT

Thinking about Missteps

Kendall (2006) offers an interesting—albeit less than pleasant—example of the workings of cognition. Consider, he suggests, the experience of what you would say to yourself if you stepped on something a dog had deposited on a lawn. For many people, a cognitive *structure* representing this event might automatically trigger a self-statement of dismay: Oh sh--! This statement reflects *cognitive content*. Individuals who respond thusly might then proceed to cognitively *process* the event in quite different ways, which is significant to the outcome. Some might think about social embarrassment (Did anyone see me?); others might have self-denigrating thoughts (I can't even walk!);

still others might give little attention to the experience and nonchalantly walk on. Subsequent to processing the event, individuals would draw conclusions about the event; for example, they might make causal attributions. These are cognitive *products*. Some individuals might attribute the problem to themselves (I can't do anything right!); others might blame whoever allowed the dog access to the lawn (I bet the guy knew someone would step in it!). As noted by Kendall, all of these processes are involved in a person making sense of experience. It is not so much an event itself but cognitions surrounding the event that influence the emotional and behavioral consequences for the person.

and anxious children. For instance, in test situations, children with test anxiety frequently report more off-task thoughts, more negative self-evaluations, and fewer positive self-evaluations (Ollendick & King, 1998).

Kendall and colleagues suggest one way to distinguish the complex cognitive functions that contribute to the development, maintenance, and treatment of psychopathology (Kendall, 2006; Kendall et al., 1997b). *Cognitive structures* are schema for representing information stored in memory. Constructed over time from experience, they screen new experiences and can trigger other cognitive operations. *Cognitive content* refers to the actual content of the cognitive structures stored in memory. *Cognitive processes* refer to how people perceive and interpret experience. The combination of cognitive structures, content, and processes—interacting with actual events—results in *cognitive products*. (See Accent: "Thinking about Missteps.")

Kendall (2006) also recognizes the important difference between cognitive deficiencies and cognitive distortions. *Cognitive deficiencies* refer to an absence of thinking. The lack of forethought and planning exhibited by an impulsive child is an example of cognitive deficiency. *Cognitive distortions* are inaccurate thought processes that are dysfunctional. Depressed children viewing themselves as less capable than their peers even though

others do not hold this view is an example of cognitive distortion.

Cognitive-behavioral therapy aims, through behavior-based procedures and structured sessions, to modify maladaptive cognitive structures, deficiencies, and distortions. The particular ways in which the approach both conceptualizes and treats specific disorders of youth are presented throughout this text.

Sociocultural Context: An Overview

Development, whether adaptive or maladaptive, occurs within and is influenced by an elaborate sociocultural context. Although there are various ways to conceptualize this context, ecological models have grown in importance during the last few decades. (Ecology refers to the interrelationship of organisms and their environment.)

Figure 3–5 presents one way in which youth are perceived to be embedded within, and interacting with, numerous domains of overlapping, transactional environmental influences or systems. The youth is surrounded by three contexts—family, community, and society/culture—each of which consists of structures, institutions, values, rules, relationships, and other aspects that influence development.

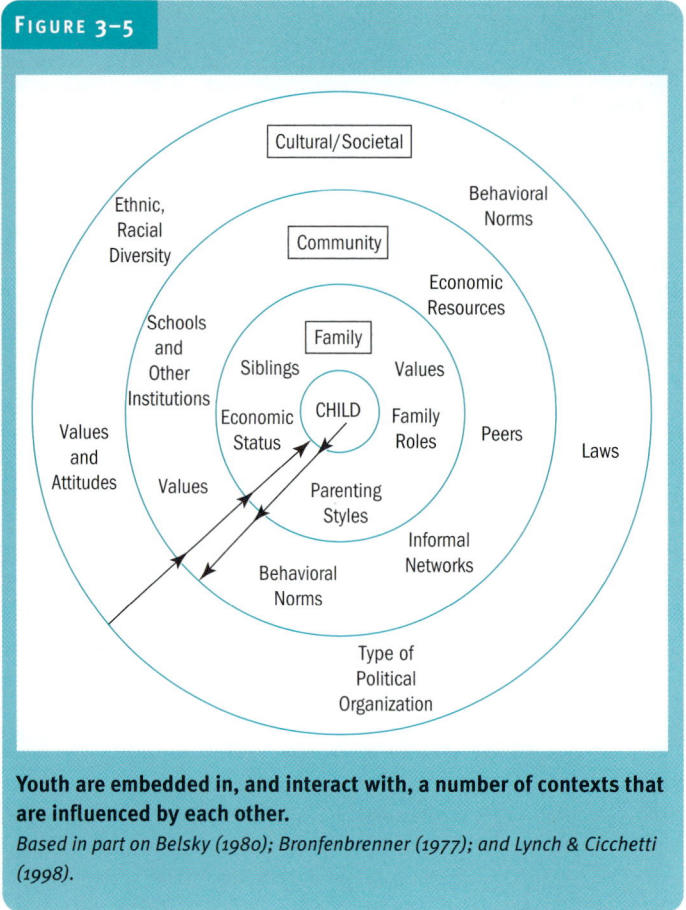

FIGURE 3-5

Youth are embedded in, and interact with, a number of contexts that are influenced by each other.
Based in part on Belsky (1980); Bronfenbrenner (1977); and Lynch & Cicchetti (1998).

The arrows in the figure emphasize the potential interactions among the systems. For example, a child both is influenced by and influences peers, who may influence and be influenced by the child's parents and the school. In general, we would expect proximal contexts—the inner circles—to have relatively more direct impact on the child than more distal contexts. It would also be anticipated that the nature and importance of any one domain would vary with the developmental level of the individual, an obvious example being an increase in peer influence from infancy into adolescence. This model serves as a backdrop for further discussion of select aspects of sociocultural influences on development.

Family Context, Maltreatment, and Divorce

For many reasons, the family has been considered a critical force in development of the young (Masten & Shaffer, 2006). Family relationships and experiences are dominant from the first days of life and endure in some way over the lifespan of most individuals. The family plays a major role in socializing the child to behave in culturally acceptable ways and in transmitting cultural values and traditions. Families are also the conduit of food, shelter, neighborhood residence, education, and other opportunities to experience the world. The family may function as a mediator or moderator in development, and provide either risk or protection.

Although many kinds of family relationships are considered influential, including sibling and grandparent interactions, the parent–child relationship is considered dominant for most youth. It is worth noting that the family is most appropriately viewed as a complex, interacting system. Not only do parents affect children and each other, but children influence parents in subtle and not-so-subtle ways. This is not to say that the parent–child relationship is symmetrical; with greater power and knowledge, parents have more opportunities to influence their offspring than the other way around (Maccoby, 1992).

Parenting Styles and Roles

Parenting styles. The quality of the relationship between parents and their offspring, beginning with early attachment, is believed to be crucial to development and adjustment. One area of influence concerns the relatively characteristic ways in which parents deal with and manage their offspring (Maccoby, 1992; Wood et al., 2003). Such parenting styles can be viewed as sets of attitudes, goals, and patterns of parenting practices that affect outcomes for children and adolescents. Analyses of parenting styles provide a general guideline for understanding families.

Two major dimensions are considered central in parent–child relationships. One dimension is degree of control; the second is degree of acceptance, or warmth. Figure 3–6 presents the four parenting styles according to these dimensions. Authoritative parenting generally is associated with the most favorable child attributes. Authoritative parents assume control; set rules and expect their children to abide by the rules; follow through with consequences; and are simultaneously warm, accepting, and considerate of the needs of their offspring. Their children, in turn, tend to be independent, socially responsible, prosocial, and self-confident. In contrast, children of authoritarian, indulgent/permissive, and neglectful parents are thought to be at greater risk for less than optimal behaviors, including aggression, withdrawal, dependence, low self-esteem, irresponsibility, antisocial behaviors, anxiety, and school problems (e.g., Steinberg et al., 1994; Wood et al., 2003).

In examining these general findings, it is worthwhile to consider three issues (Eiser et al., 2005; O'Connor et al., 2006). *First,* effective parenting involves consideration of each youth's needs, as well as developmental level. What would be controlling for one child at one developmental level would not necessarily be controlling for others. *Second,* parenting style may in part be a response to the child's characteristics as well as other relationships and circumstances in the family. *Third,* we must consider the extent to which the analysis of parenting styles holds across cultures and situations. It has been suggested, for example, that authoritative parenting may be less appropriate when local cultural values differ from those of mainstream culture in the United States, and that in the United States authoritarian parenting may protect children who are reared in disadvantaged environments.

Figure 3–6

ACCEPTANCE	CONTROL: High	CONTROL: Low
High	**Authoritative** Set and enforce standards Considerate of children's needs Encourage independence, individuality	**Indulgent/Permissive** Make few demands for mature behavior Allow children to regulate themselves Tolerate children's impulses
Low	**Authoritarian** Strictly set rules which cannot be challenged Use fairly severe punishment	**Neglectful** Uninvolved Give little time, attention, emotional commitment to children

Patterns of parental behavior.
Based in part on Maccoby & Martin, 1983.

Parental roles. Historically, the influence of mothers has received much more attention than the influence of fathers by theorists and researchers. Mothers have been considered primary in day-to-day care, management, and other aspects of child development—and have been more implicated in, and sometimes blamed for, the disturbances of their offspring. Nevertheless, recent decades have witnessed increased attention to fathers. Whereas the traditional contribution that fathers make as primary breadwinners continues to be recognized, greater emphasis is now given to fathers as providers of care and psychological support (Cabrera et al., 2000; Coley, 2001). Fathers are likely to provide somewhat different input than mothers into child development. They are more likely to encourage independence and competition, and good fathering may be especially important to the development of healthy sexual identity in daughters (Cabrera et al., 2000; Leinonen, Solantaus, & Punamäki, 2003). Paternal influences may be direct or may operate indirectly, for instance, through interaction of the father with the mother.

MALTREATMENT

Maltreatment of youth is an extreme failure to provide adequate parenting. It can also be viewed as a failure of the larger social system to provide conditions that foster adequate parenting. Such undue failure to protect the child and/or provide positive aspects of parenting might be expected to adversely affect a wide variety of developmental processes and increase the risk for a variety of problematic outcomes.

Although child maltreatment has probably existed since the beginning of civilization, recent concern is usually dated to the early 1960s (Cicchetti & Olsen, 1990). Especially influential was an article by pediatrician C. Henry Kempe and his colleagues, in which the term *battered child syndrome* was coined (Kempe et al., 1962). Their efforts were stimulated by alarm at the large number of children at pediatric clinics with nonaccidental injuries. By 1970, all 50 states had mandated the reporting of child abuse. In 1974 the U.S. Congress passed the Child Abuse Prevention and Treatment Act (Public Law 93–247) to give national focus to the problem and to prescribe actions that the states should take. Since the late 1970s, the problem has become both a major public concern and the focus of increased research and professional attention (Cicchetti & Manly, 2001).

Unfortunately, the magnitude of the problem is significant. According to a report issued by the U.S. Department of Health and Human Services (2007), in 2005 there were approximately 12 victims per 1,000 children. In addition, about 14% of victims experienced multiple types of maltreatment.

Defining maltreatment. There is agreement that child abuse and neglect are serious and prevalent problems. What is lacking is a consensus on what constitutes maltreatment. Cicchetti and Manly (2001) note that several reasons exist for the difficulty in reaching definitional consensus. Maltreatment is a legal matter defined by social agencies rather than by researchers or mental health professionals. Also, there are no clear standards for differentiating between acceptable parental disciplinary practices and maltreatment. Standards as to what is "acceptable" practice versus "maltreatment" are likely to vary across time and culture. Further, there is disagreement as to whether maltreatment should be defined in terms of the actions of the perpetrator, the effects on the child, or a combination of the two. The question of whether parental intent should be considered is a further complication. If a child is harmed but the parent did not intend to inflict harm, is the result maltreatment? In the final analysis, it may not be possible to reach agreement on a single definition that will serve all purposes. A definition that meets the needs of a research agenda may be inappropriate in a courtroom setting, and a definition that stresses overt physical symptoms may meet medical needs but minimize psychological consequences.

When most people hear the widely used term child abuse, they assume that it refers to physical assault and serious injury. However, the general legal definition of child abuse or maltreatment that has evolved over several decades includes both the commission of injuries and acts of omission, that is, failure to care for and protect (National Institute of Mental Health, 1977).

Four types of maltreatment are typically described in the literature: physical abuse, sexual abuse, neglect, and emotional abuse. The definitions of the four major types of maltreatment are presented in Table 3–3, while Figure 3–7 shows the rate of each type in the United States in 2005 (U.S. Department of Health and Human Services, 2007). Approximately 63% of victims experienced neglect, 17% experienced physical abuse, 9% were sexually abused, 7% suffered psychological maltreatment, and 2% were victims of medical

TABLE 3–3   DEFINITIONS OF THE MAJOR FORMS OF MALTREATMENT

1. **Physical abuse:** An act of commission by a caregiver that results or is likely to result in physical harm, including death of a child. Examples include kicking, biting, shaking, stabbing, or punching a child. Spanking is usually considered a disciplinary action but can be classified as abusive if the child is bruised or injured.
2. **Sexual abuse:** An act of commission, including intrusion or penetration, molestation with genital contact, or other forms of sexual acts in which children are used to provide sexual gratification for the perpetrator. This type of abuse also includes acts such as sexual exploitation and child pornography.
3. **Neglect:** An act of omission by a parent or caregiver that involves a refusal to provide, or a delay in providing, health care; failure to provide basic needs such as food, clothing, shelter, affection, and attention; inadequate supervision; or abandonment. This failure to act holds true for both physical and emotional neglect.
4. **Emotional abuse:** An act of commission or omission that includes rejecting, isolating, terrorizing, ignoring, or corrupting a child. Examples of emotional abuse are confinement; verbal abuse; withholding sleep, food, or shelter; exposing a child to domestic violence; allowing a child to engage in substance abuse or criminal activity; refusing to provide psychological care; and other inattention that results in harm or potential harm to a child. The abuse must be sustained and repetitive.

From English, 1998.

neglect. In approximately 14% of cases, other forms of maltreatment were indicated ("other" includes abandonment, threats of harm, and congenital drug addiction).

It is probably easier to detect physical abuse than other forms of maltreatment. However, the nature and severity of injuries can vary considerably. In some cases, injuries may be intentionally inflicted, but more often they result from extreme forms of discipline and physical punishment. Moreover, whereas we can define physical abuse as a separate category from other forms of maltreatment, children likely experience it in conjunction with emotional abuse and/or neglect.

In general, sexual abuse refers to sexual experiences that occur between youth and older persons

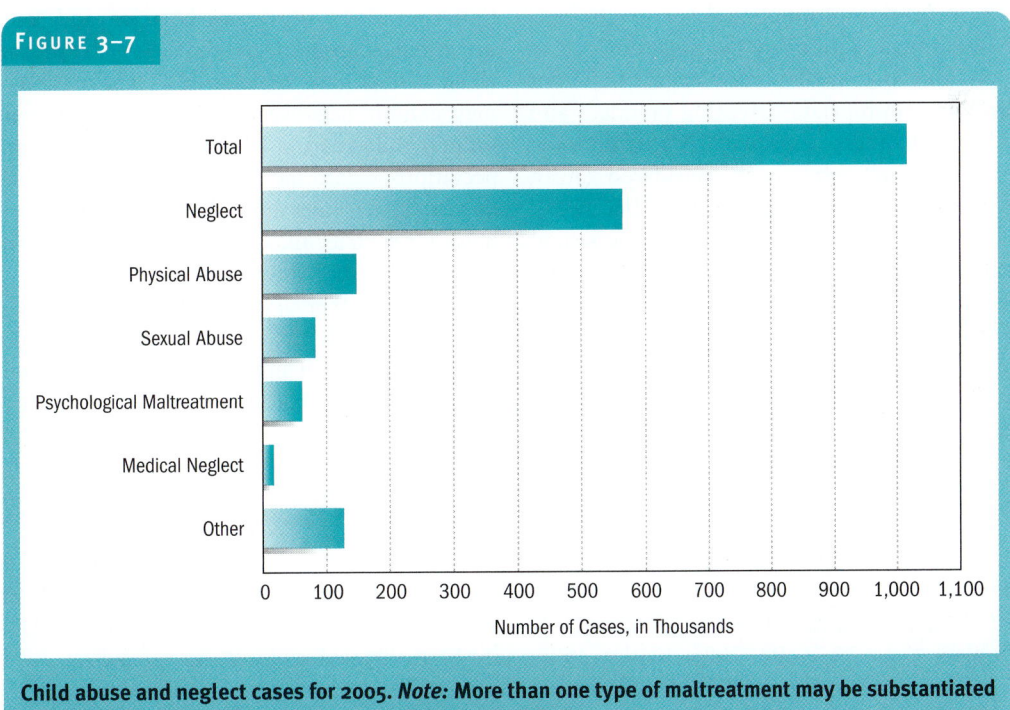

FIGURE 3–7

Number of Cases, in Thousands

Child abuse and neglect cases for 2005. *Note:* **More than one type of maltreatment may be substantiated per child. Therefore, items add up to more than the total shown.**
Adapted from U.S. Department of Health & Human Services, Child Maltreatment 2005 (Washington, DC, 2007.)

or to the sexual exploitation of the young, such as in pornographic film. Sexual abuse of girls is more common than that of boys, and cases of sexual abuse can vary with factors such as age of onset of abuse, the identity of the primary perpetrator, the number of perpetrators, the severity of the abuse, and whether the abuse was accompanied by physical violence or threats (Finkelhor, 1994; Wolfe, 2006).

Neglect, the most common form of maltreatment, refers to failure to provide for a child's basic needs. Defining a parent–child relationship as neglectful, especially in less extreme instances, clearly requires sensitivity to family and cultural values and to considerations of economic and social conditions. Neglect can involve a failure to meet physical needs—such as the need for health care or physical shelter—or it can involve abandonment or inadequate supervision. Neglect may also take the form of not meeting the youngster's educational needs by allowing repeated truancy or not attending to special education needs. The child's emotional needs may also be neglected. Emotional neglect is difficult to define, however. It may include failure to ensure adequate psychological care or failure to protect the youngster from witnessing harmful situations involving violence or substance use.

The definition of emotional (or psychological) maltreatment is probably the most difficult to agree on and the most controversial. Different standards for appropriate parenting practices and for desired outcomes are particularly at issue when psychological maltreatment is considered (Azar, Ferraro, & Breton, 1998; McGee & Wolfe, 1991). Emotional maltreatment is defined as persistent and extreme actions or neglect that thwart the child's basic emotional needs and that are damaging to the behavioral, cognitive, affective, or physical functioning of the child (Brassard, Hart, & Hardy, 2000; Cicchetti & Lynch, 1995). Emotional maltreatment can be seen both as a distinct entity and as part of all abuse and neglect (Binggeli, Hart, & Brassard, 2001).

Factors contributing to maltreatment. Conceptualizations of maltreatment recognize the complex, multiple, and interrelated determinants of the problem (Azar & Wolfe, 2006; Belsky, 1993; Cicchetti, Toth, & Maughan, 2000). The following general factors are recognized as contributing to maltreatment:

- Characteristics of the abuser
- Characteristics of the child
- Parenting practices
- Parent–child interactional processes
- Social/cultural influences

The latter category includes both the immediate social environment (e.g., family, employment, extended family, social networks) and the larger social/cultural context (e.g., poverty, societal tolerance for violence), and it appreciates the fact that maltreatment most often occurs in the context of family, social, and community deprivation.

It is impossible to even enumerate all of the specific influences that have been examined for their contribution to maltreatment. Here we highlight only some of the findings.

For the most part, parents or parent surrogates are the perpetrators of abuse. Parents who began their families at a younger age, many in their teens, are often the perpetrators (Connelly & Straus, 1992; Dixon, Hamilton-Giachritsis, & Browne, 2005). This finding may be understood, at least in part, within the context of parenting skills. Abusive parents exhibit a variety of deficits in parenting (Azar & Wolfe, 2006). They tend to engage in fewer positive interactions with their child and less interaction overall, to use more coercive and negative discipline techniques, and to use fewer explanations when disciplining their child. These parents also may exhibit negative attitudes toward parenting, limited child-rearing knowledge, inappropriate expectations regarding developmentally suitable behavior, lower tolerance for common demanding behavior such as infant crying, and misattributions of the child's motivation for misbehaving.

Several other characteristics of abusive parents have been noted, including difficulties in managing stress, difficulty in inhibiting their own impulsive behavior, social isolation from family and friends, more emotional symptoms and mood changes, and more physical health problems. High rates of substance abuse and partner violence in the home have also been reported (Wekerle et al., 2007).

It has been found that abusive parents are more likely to have experienced abuse (Kaufman & Zigler, 1987). However, it is generally agreed that the majority of maltreated children do not become abusive parents. What, then, is the link between generations? This pathway is clearly the result of a complex interaction of risk and protective factors that include characteristics of the individual, family, and social environment. For example, Dixon and colleagues (Dixon et al., 2005) found that intergenerational continuity of maltreatment was increased by the presence of poor parenting styles, parent age under 21 years, parent history of psychopathology, and residence with a violent adult.

In addition to looking at characteristics of abusing parents, professionals have asked whether certain attributes of children increase the likelihood of their being the target of maltreatment. Research suggests that children and adolescents at highest risk are those with disabilities and those who display behavioral and physical problems or interpersonal styles that adversely interact with caregiver characteristics and stress (Bonner et al., 1992; Wolfe, 2006). For example, a child's early feeding problems and irritability may place increased strain on a highly stressed parent who has limited parenting abilities. This may lead the caregiver to withdraw and become neglectful. Caregiver neglect may, in turn, lead to increases in dependent behavior and demands by the child (Wekerle & Wolfe, 2003).

Maltreatment also is influenced by the larger social context. A relationship between socioeconomic disadvantage and abuse, and particularly neglect, has been described (English, 1998). It is important to recognize, however, that the majority of families who experience disadvantage do not maltreat their offspring. Although it is hard to isolate the specific causal factors, reduced resources, stress, and other problems associated with socioeconomic disadvantage put the family and child at increased risk. The relationship of poverty and maltreatment may be due to other factors as well (Azar & Bober, 1999). For example, poor interpersonal and problem-solving skills in parents may lead both to economic disadvantage and to problematic parenting, including maltreatment. Cultural factors, too, may play a role. Korbin and colleagues (1998), for instance, found that impoverishment had a lesser impact on maltreatment in African American neighborhoods than in European American neighborhoods. This difference seemed to be mediated by the perceived quality of social connectedness found in the two kinds of neighborhoods. A sense of community, resources, and extended family may serve as protective factors against maltreatment.

Consequences of maltreatment. Basic developmental processes are disrupted by maltreatment. The social and emotional support necessary for children's successful adaptations is diminished, interfering with many areas of development. Furthermore, these youngsters may have fewer opportunities for positive experiences that may reduce the risk of maltreatment (Azar & Wolfe, 2006; Haskett et al., 2006; Salzinger et al., 2001).

Some evidence suggests that early maltreatment may be associated with neurobiological outcomes, such as dysregulation of the stress regulating system (the limbic-hypothalamic-pituitary-adrenocortical system), alteration of neurotransmitter systems, and alteration of structural and functional regions of the brain (Bremner, 2006; Cicchetti & Rogosch, 2001; Gunnar & Vazquez, 2006; Margolin & Gordis, 2000). The degree to which these neurobiological outcomes occur seems to be related to a number of factors (De Bellis, 2001), including age of onset of abuse, duration of abuse, and the presence of trauma-related psychological symptoms. There may also be gender-related differences in adverse brain development outcomes, with both boys and girls being affected but males being more vulnerable.

The effects of maltreatment are a telling example of how adverse environments may alter basic biological functioning. The neurobiological outcomes may, in turn, contribute to cognitive and psychosocial difficulties. De Bellis's (2001) developmental traumatology model describes how neurobiological outcomes may underlie the variety of negative outcomes associated with abuse and neglect. In this model, maltreatment and its effects are viewed within a broad ecological-transactional model that recognizes the effects of many other variables (Figure 3–8). For instance, the neurobiological changes resulting from the stress of maltreatment may be positively modified by subsequent supportive caregiving environments.

Given the neurobiological outcomes and the failure of parenting involved, it is unsurprising that maltreatment can result in a variety of undesirable outcomes. Children can manifest health-related difficulties (e.g., physical injury, sexually transmitted diseases) and appreciable impairments in all early developmental domains and various areas of later adjustment (Azar & Wolfe, 2006; English, 1998; Wolfe, Rawana, & Chiodo, 2006; Yates, 2004). Problems may be serious enough to meet the diagnostic criteria for a variety of psychological disorders. The impact may also be evident at different developmental stages from infancy through adolescence and into adulthood (Springer et al., 2007; Wolfe, 2006; Wolfe et al., 2006). Although this is certainly a disheartening

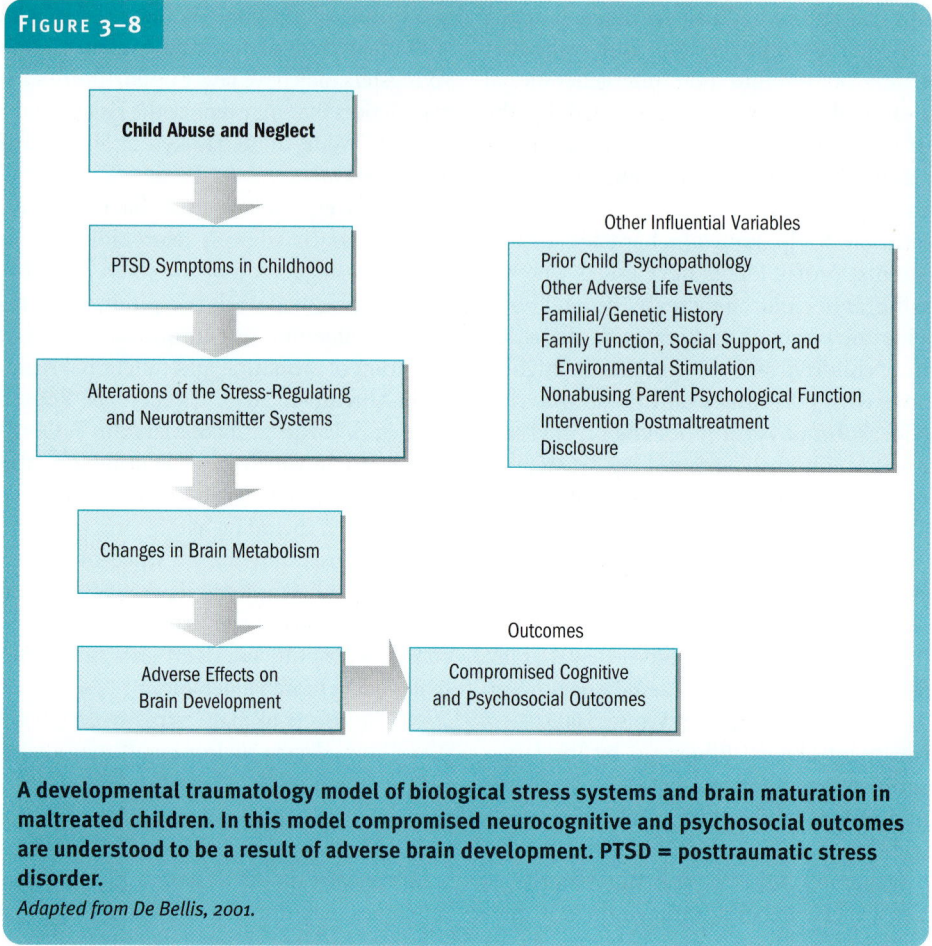

FIGURE 3–8

A developmental traumatology model of biological stress systems and brain maturation in maltreated children. In this model compromised neurocognitive and psychosocial outcomes are understood to be a result of adverse brain development. PTSD = posttraumatic stress disorder.

Adapted from De Bellis, 2001.

picture, it should be acknowledged that some maltreated children develop as competent individuals and that youths can be resilient even in the face of maltreatment (Haskett et al., 2006; McGloin & Widom, 2001).

In general, then, the impact of maltreatment is best viewed as undermining a variety of normal developmental processes affecting areas such as the development of secure attachments, cognitive functioning, self-concept, social relationships, and emotional regulation (Azar & Bober, 1999; Haskett et al., 2006; Wekerle & Wolfe, 2003). Outcomes of maltreatment are likely to be affected by many factors including the type and severity of maltreatment, developmental timing, characteristics of the youngster's family, peer relationships, and neighborhood (Finkelhor, Ormrod, & Turner, 2007; Haskett et al., 2006; Jaffee et al., 2007; Manly et al., 2001). For example, research suggests that physical abuse places children at particular risk for the

development of externalizing and antisocial behavior problems (Jaffee et al., 2004; Lau & Weisz, 2003). Given the combination of factors that causes maltreatment, effective prevention and intervention need to address many contexts—individual, familial, community, cultural, and societal—and thus include multiple components (Azar & Wolfe, 2006; Trickett et al., 1998; Wolfe, 2006). As we gain more precise understanding of the different types of maltreatment, we will be better able to shape interventions to fit specific needs.

CHANGES IN FAMILY STRUCTURE: DIVORCE

In research about the family, it has often been assumed that families consist of parents and children together in the home. In fact, families have always been more varied. Even so, by most standards, dramatic changes have occurred in family structure during the last few decades in the United States and similar countries. Many children are living in step-families of some sort. In addition, about 1.6 million youngsters live in adoptive homes, and international adoptions have become more common (U.S. Census Bureau, 2003). The percentage of single-parent families also has increased markedly during the last several decades (Figure 3–9). Single-parent families make up approximately 28% of all families with children, about one fifth of these being headed by fathers (U.S. Census Bureau, 2005). Most youth living in nontraditional homes do well, but as a group they are at risk for emotional and behavioral difficulties.

That many marriages end in divorce is well documented. The divorce rate in the United States increased dramatically in the 1960s and 1970s, reaching a peak about 1980. Although this trend has leveled off and perhaps declined modestly in recent years, it is estimated that about half of first marriages and about 60% of second marriages end in divorce (Amato & Irving, 2006; Sutton, 2003). Over one million youngsters a year may experience parental di-

vorce. However compelling, this statistic does not fully capture the problem. Many children experience considerable stress prior to the divorce. Some go through periodic separation and discord in families in which divorce petitions are filed and withdrawn. Others experience more than one divorce. Moreover, divorce and subsequent reconstitution of the family are not static events, but rather are a series of family transitions that modify the lives of children (Barber & Demo, 2006; Hetherington & Stanley-Hagan, 1999; Wallerstein, 1991).

Heightened risk. Children and adolescents from divorced and remarried families are at increased risk for developing adjustment problems (Barber & Demo, 2006; Grych & Fincham, 1999; Hetherington & Kelly, 2002; Reifman et al., 2001). Those who experience multiple divorces are at greater risk. Difficulties occur in many areas of functioning: academic, social, emotional, and behavioral. Negative consequences are most common around the period of the divorce.

There is, nonetheless, considerable variability in outcome (Fine & Harvey, 2006). Indeed, the vast

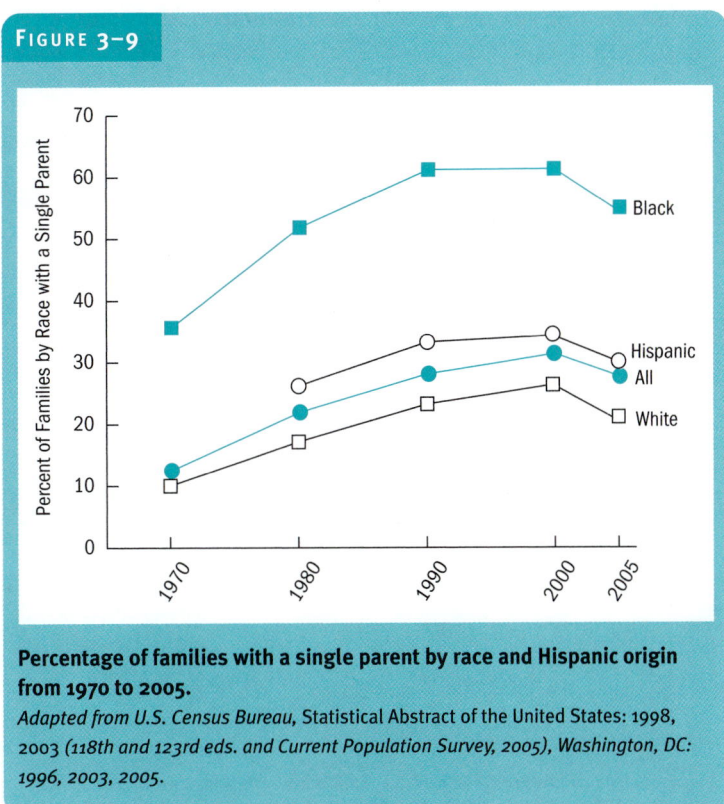

FIGURE 3–9

Percentage of families with a single parent by race and Hispanic origin from 1970 to 2005.

Adapted from U.S. Census Bureau, Statistical Abstract of the United States: 1998, 2003 (118th and 123rd eds. and Current Population Survey, 2005), Washington, DC: *1996, 2003, 2005.*

majority of children from divorced or remarried families function in the normal range, and some youth experience positive outcomes (Barber & Demo, 2006). Through divorce, some youth move out of highly conflicted and violent situations. A portion, particularly girls, may move into less stressful and more supportive circumstances. They may actually experience opportunities for the development of exceptional competencies (Fine & Harvey, 2006; Amato & Keith, 1991; Hetherington & Stanley-Hagan, 1999; Hetherington & Kelly, 2002). However, these findings should not lead us to ignore the clinical significance of the adjustment problems experienced by some young people. An important question then is: What accounts for increased risk for youth who develop adjustment difficulties and for the resilience of those who do not?

Predictors of adjustment. When considering the influence of family divorce, it is important to note that any deviation from traditional family structure has often been viewed as problematic. This perspective is, in general, not well supported. Of course, two parental figures in a good partnership generally have much to offer the child. However, the effects of family composition/parent absence are not simple and are likely modified by factors such as parent

adjustment, quality of family relationships, the child's gender, and the availability of both parents to the child (Barber & Demo, 2006; Braver, Ellman, & Fabricius, 2003; Jaffee et al., 2003). Furthermore, there are cultural and ethnic differences in how family is defined. The presence of extended family in the household, for example, is more likely among African American families than among European American families, as is an informal network of kin and friends available to function in parental roles (Emery & Kitzmann, 1995).

Hetherington and her colleagues (Hetherington, Bridges, & Insabella, 1998) suggest a model, based on a set of interrelated risks, to explain the links between divorce/remarriage and a child's adjustment. As Figure 3–10 shows, adjustment to marital transitions encompasses complex interactions among a large number of influences. To add to the complexity, while the process of family transitions is occurring, children and the developmental tasks they face are also changing (O'Connor, 2003). In addition, ethnic and cultural influences are salient in this process, although much of what we know is based on the experiences of European American families (Hetherington & Stanley-Hagan, 1999). With such complexities in mind, we turn to an examination of some of the influences likely to

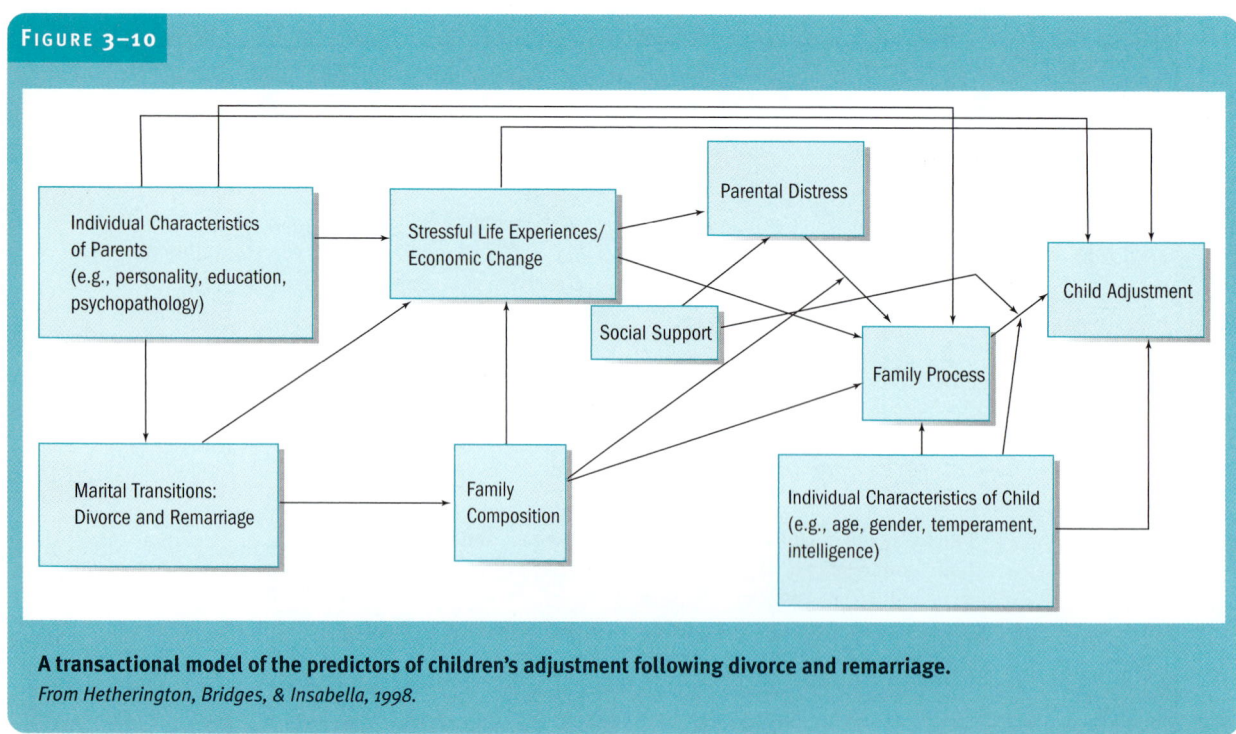

FIGURE 3–10

A transactional model of the predictors of children's adjustment following divorce and remarriage.
From Hetherington, Bridges, & Insabella, 1998.

affect the adjustment of children and adolescents to marital transitions.

A central aspect of the divorce process is the interaction among family members, particularly the ongoing relationship between the two parents. Indeed, the degree of marital discord prior to the divorce is considered to be a primary influence on the adjustment of children in the family. High levels of marital conflict—particularly marital violence—are problematic (Barber & Demo, 2006; Jaffee, Poisson, & Cunningham, 2001; Kelly, 2000). Following divorce, the ongoing relationship between the parents, between each parent and the child, and between each parent and potential stepparents or significant others contributes to complicated family transitions that affect the child (Hetherington et al., 1998).

Preexisting individual characteristics also contribute to a child's adjustment. Individual attributes of adults (e.g., antisocial behavior, depression) place some parents at risk for marital discord and multiple marital transitions—thereby increasing the risk that their children will have to deal with multiple marital changes. These and similar attributes also impact the adult's ability to parent effectively. Individual characteristics of the youth may also contribute to adjustment. Children with an easy temperament may be better able to cope with the disruptions associated with marital transitions. Those with a difficult temperament may be more likely to elicit negative responses from their stressed parents and to have greater difficulty adapting to parental negativity and marital transitions. They may be less capable of eliciting the support of other people around them (Hetherington et al., 1998). Also, a child's prior level of behavioral problems is likely to play a role in adjustment. Indeed, when prior level of adjustment is taken into account, differences between children due to marital transitions are greatly reduced.

The relationship between parental characteristics, child characteristics, and the ongoing divorce process is, however, complex. For example, the child's prior level of adjustment may have resulted in part from the marital friction that contributed to the divorce. In turn, the challenges of parenting a difficult child may have contributed to the marital difficulty and divorce. Furthermore, the parental characteristics that played a role in the divorce, as well as child behavior problems, may be influenced by common genetic contributions (Jockin, McGue, & Lykken, 1996; McGue & Lykken, 1992). Shared genes may contribute, for example, to the likelihood of parent antisocial behavior (a

risk for divorce) and acting-out problems in children and adolescents.

Gender also may affect adjustment to marital transitions. Earlier reports suggested that boys were more affected by divorce and girls by remarriage. More recent studies report less pronounced and less consistent gender differences. Improvements in research methodology may in part be responsible for this finding. So may changes in custody and visitation arrangements, which have possibly increased father involvement. The effect of gender is probably complex, depending on the aspect of adjustment studied, gender-related differences in patterns of development, pubertal timing, and other such factors (Ellis, 2004; Hetherington & Stanley-Hagan, 1999). Clearly, the role that individual characteristics play in adjustment to divorce is complicated.

Another factor that may be involved in children's adjustment is ethnic differences. For example, African American youth may benefit more from living in stepfamilies and from greater authoritarian parenting than White adolescents (Barber & Demo, 2006). It has been suggested that improved income, supervision, and role models provided by some stepfathers may be more advantageous to African American children because they are more likely to live in neighborhoods with fewer resources and social controls (McLanahan & Sandefur, 1994).

Finally, the divorce process may include changes in family circumstances that, although they are peripheral to the reasons for the marital dissolution, affect how well the family does (Amato, 2000). For example, custodial mothers and their children often experience economic decline after divorce, with many living below the poverty level. A lower standard of living and economic instability are associated with conditions that increase risk for youth, such as living in more dangerous neighborhoods and attending less adequate schools. Divorce may result in other stressful family life changes, such as more frequent moves and changes in schools. It is thought that much of the impact of these postdivorce circumstances on child adjustment is mediated by their effect on family processes (Them, Israel, Ivanova, & Chalmers, 2003). That is, economic stress and other changes can contribute to dysfunctional family relations (e.g., conflict) and interfere with effective parenting (Hetherington et al., 1998). Within this context, however, it is important to remember that positive experiences such as good parent–child communication and supportive relationships with another adult may serve as protective factors for youngsters experiencing divorce-related events (Doyle et al., 2003; Menning, 2002).

Peer Influences

The literature on development indicates the importance of peer relationships (Deater-Deckard, 2001; Hay, Payne, & Chadwick, 2004). From infancy onward, individuals relate socially to each other and as development proceeds peer relationships are likely to grow in influence. The peer group provides a unique developmental context that influences immediate and long-term social and cognitive growth (Dunn, 1996; Parker et al., 2006). Areas in which peer interactions may play a unique and/or essential role include the development of sociability, empathy, cooperation, and morality; negotiation of conflict and competition; control of aggression; and socialization of sexuality and gender roles. Peer relations may ensure the development of social competence in the face of adversity, thereby preventing or reducing the likelihood of disorder (Cicchetti, Toth, & Bush, 1988; Sroufe et al., 2000). They may also be associated with the presence of disorder.

Individual child characteristics—emotional, cognitive, and social—enter into the development of peer relationships (Hay et al., 2004). So do other social relationships. Early attachment experiences in the family are thought to be related to peer relationships and social competence (Rudolph & Asher, 2000). Parental hostility, coercion, lack of involvement, and authoritarian/restrictive styles are associated with child aggression and peer rejection (Dekovic & Janssens, 1992; Dishion, 1990). Teachers also can play a role in shaping peers' attitudes toward one another (White & Kistner, 1992), and neighborhood characteristics can influence the likelihood that a youngster will affiliate with deviant peers (Brody et al., 2001).

The multifaceted nature of peer relationships has been increasingly appreciated (Bukowski & Adams, 2005). Early research primarily focused on overall peer status, that is, on group acceptance and popularity. More recently, additional interest has been directed at particular relationships, such as that between bullies and their victims (Perren & Alsaker, 2006). The nature and role of friendship also has received greater attention (Deater-Deckard, 2001; Hartup, 1996). Having a close friend is typically viewed as a positive experience that can serve as protection against risk factors, including the effects of being rejected or neglected by classmates (Criss et al., 2002). However, friendship can encourage maladaptation (Parker et al., 2006). Discussion among friends of personal problems and the disclosure of deviant acts can increase the risk of psychological difficulties and deviant behavior. The following is a description of the role that friendship appears to have played in an unusual and unfortunate circumstance.

Peer interactions provide a unique and essential opportunity to develop certain skills.
(Courtesy of A. C. Israel)

> **Delano** **A Problematic Friendship**
>
> Delano, a 14-year-old boy, and his best friend ambushed and killed Delano's mother on her way home. In a newspaper account, the mother was said to have had "difficulties" with her son, and the family's home contained guns. Delano was described as having attention deficit disorder and learning disabilities. He had a long history of difficulties and recently had gotten into trouble with his stepbrother for wrecking a car and bringing a gun into a movie theater.
>
> Delano was described as "a lonely and unliked kid who was the frequent victim of schoolmates' taunts, jeers, and assaults. . . . He was often teased on the bus and at school because of his appearance and abilities. . . . He got teased bad. Every day he got teased. He'd get pushed around. But he couldn't really help himself. He was kind of skinny. . . . He didn't really have that many friends."
>
> There were actually two good friends. The first was relatively well adjusted, but Delano took

a gun safety course for hunting with this friend. Delano and the second youngster described themselves as the "best of friends" and spent a great deal of time together. This friend was not as well adjusted and it was this friend with whom the murder was committed. The boys admitted to planning the ambush, and it seems relatively certain that the murder would not have occurred if these two friends had not encouraged each other to do it.

Adapted from Hartup, 1996, p. 1.

One of the most commonly cited reasons for interest in children's peer relationships is the association that these relationships have with later adjustment (Parker et al., 2006; Realmuto, August, & Hektner, 2000; Woodward & Fergusson, 2000). Children who experience peer rejection, who are withdrawn and socially isolated, or who associate with deviant peers are at risk for later adjustment difficulties (Barrera, Prelow, Dumka et al., 2002; Ladd & Troop-Gordon, 2003; Laird et al., 2001; Rubin et al., 2003). Indeed, difficult peer relationships are a common reason for children's referrals to mental health centers and are reported among children with a variety of disorders (Parker et al., 2006). There is a bidirectional association of peer difficulties with adjustment problems. Not only do peer difficulties contribute to the development of behavioral disorders, but the presence of disorder adversely affects peer relationships (Achenbach & Rescorla, 2001).

How is the association of early peer problems with later psychological disturbances to be understood? It is possible that in some instances the relationship is not causal, that some unidentified general tendency underlies and independently causes both peer and other difficulties (Parker et al., 2006). When a causal link is suspect, one hypothesis is that a child's initial tendencies and social experiences enter into a negative transaction with peers that leads the child to behave in ways that perpetuate peer rejection and other difficulties.

Community and Societal Contexts

School Influences

The school is one of the most central contexts in children's lives. Although a primary function of the school is to teach intellectual skills and knowledge, schools are expected to guide additional aspects of development (Pianta, 2006). Schools help socialize youth to societal norms and values, shape motivation to achieve, and contribute to socioemotional growth and mental health. School influences operate through distal factors such as district resources and educational policy and proximal influences such as classroom climate, instruction, and social relationships.

Regarding the latter, both peer and teacher relationships are crucial in school life. Schools are the locale for important peer interactions—for supportive friendships, rejection and bullying, and social crowds and cliques. Variations in school settings undoubtedly affect peer relationships. For example, school size, division of students into educational tracts, and opportunity for informal social contact all might have influence. Further research into these and other features is needed (Pianta, 2006).

Student–teacher relationships are often critical to young people, many of whom remember in adulthood their most favored or "hated" teachers. Such relationships may play a role in positive normative development, operate as a risk factor, or serve as protection against risk. In general, close student–teacher relationships are associated with positive child outcomes, whereas conflicted relationships are linked with unfavorable school attitudes, classroom disengagement, and poor academic performance (Birch & Ladd, 1998). Student perception of teacher support, understanding, and advice is an important factor. For example, in a study that followed students from sixth through eighth grade, student perception of increasing teacher support appeared causally related to student increases in self-esteem and decreases in depression (Reddy, Rhodes, & Mulhall, 2003). Among children with emotional disturbance, confidence in teacher support may buffer vulnerability to peer conflict (Little & Kobak, 2003).

Successful completion of school is widely viewed as a contributor to positive development, but success is not realized by many youths. Low socioeconomic status, academic failure, behavioral problems, and lack of family support are among the factors associated with dropping out of school or repeating a grade level (Mattison, 2000). Of course, schools do not have control over all the determinants of student success, but particular qualities of school climate and practice foster scholastic and positive social behaviors, regardless of the characteristics of the students who attend them (Howlin, 1994; Rutter, 1983, 2000; Rutter & Maughan, 2002). In an ideal world, all children would have the opportunity to attend highly effective schools. Unfortunately, this is not the case. In the United States, where community taxes are crucial to supporting the educational system, large inequities often exist between schools attended by students from predominantly middle- and upper-class backgrounds and schools attended by children of lower social class and minority backgrounds (Lott, 2002).

SOCIOECONOMIC STATUS AND POVERTY

Socioeconomic status (SES), or social class, is determined by factors such as income, educational achievement, and occupational level, which correlate with one another. Virtually all societies are stratified according to social class, and social class is marked by differences in many facets of life—environmental conditions, social interactions, values, attitudes, expectations, and opportunities.

Although psychological problems occur in all social classes, the relatively higher risk associated with lower social class has led to an emphasis on the effects of poverty. Despite the general economic wealth of the United States, poverty is all too common among its youths. In 2005, 17.6% of youths

under age 18 were impoverished (DeNavas-Walt, Proctor, & Lee, 2006). This percentage is higher than for other age groups, a long-observed pattern. Although youth make up 25% of the U.S. population, they compose 35% of all people in poverty. We need to be mindful, too, that the risk of living in poverty is disproportionately high in female-headed households and in families of specific ethnic/racial background (Figure 3–11).

The life experiences and outcomes for poor youth are widely recognized. Poor children are more likely to have exposure to unsafe levels of lead, pesticides, air pollution, inadequate water supplies, and poor sanitation (Evans, 2004). They are more likely to live in crowded homes, with structural defects, rodent infestation, and other safety hazards. Relative to others their age, they lack learning resources such as books, appropriate toys, and computers. These youths experience increased risk for negative outcomes such as developmental delay, learning disabilities, school failure, and behavioral and psychological problems.

In discussing the impact of family income on children's achievements and verbal ability, Duncan and Brooks-Gunn (2000) pointed to the probable

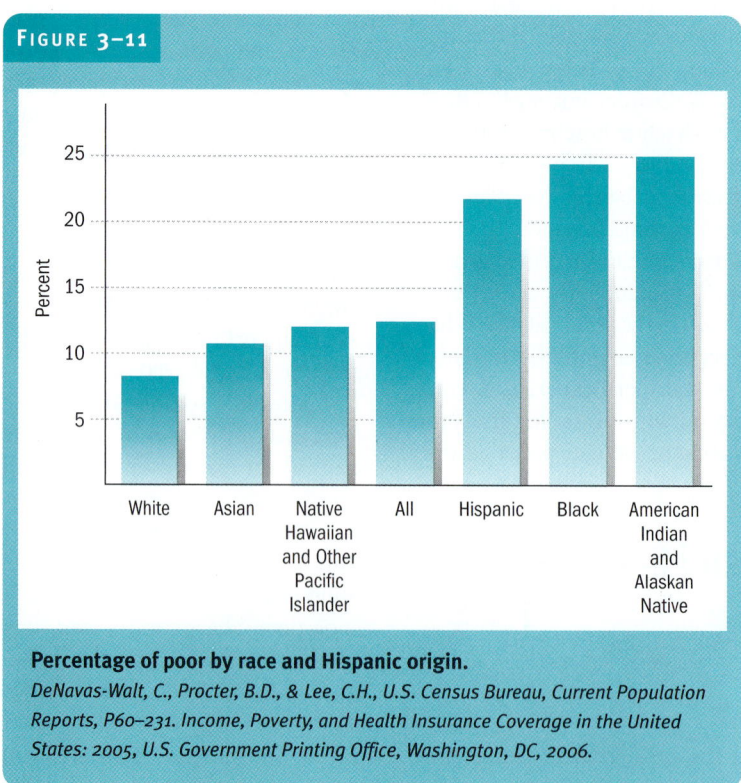

FIGURE 3–11

Percentage of poor by race and Hispanic origin.
DeNavas-Walt, C., Procter, B.D., & Lee, C.H., U.S. Census Bureau, Current Population Reports, P60–231. Income, Poverty, and Health Insurance Coverage in the United States: 2005, U.S. Government Printing Office, Washington, DC, 2006.

importance of poverty's *persistence, depth,* and *timing*. Poverty that persists over time, is severe, and occurs early in the child's life has the most negative effects. In addition, exposure to multiple risks that accumulate over time is related to developmental outcome (Evans, 2004). Figure 3–12 shows a striking difference in the number of cumulative risks experienced by poor and middle-class children in the third to fifth grade.

The family plays a crucial role in mediating the influence of poverty. Although family genetics may play some role, additional influences are involved (Evans, 2004). Parents of low SES may socialize their children to ensure acceptance by others and later job security, whereas middle-class families seem to emphasize choice, intellectual challenge, and job status for their children (Bradley & Whiteside-Mansell, 1997). Parenting in low SES homes tends to be harsher, more punitive, and less responsive (Evans, 2004) compared with that in middle-class homes, where parents spend more time and effort on and give more verbal attention to, their young children. Differences in the learning environment of the home, in turn, are related to children's development (Duncan & Brooks-Gunn, 2000). The family may mediate the effects of poverty in many other ways. The stress of being poor may

increase the likelihood of parent–child conflict, and family separation and lower marital quality are also linked to poverty (Evans, 2004). Nonetheless, we would not expect the family to be the sole mediator of poverty; peers, schools, communities, and broader cultural factors come into play.

NEIGHBORHOODS

All neighborhood/community contexts influence children and adolescents, but investigations have focused on poor urban neighborhoods. Current interest in neighborhood influences arose, in part, because poor families became increasingly clustered in urban areas during the 1970s and 1980s (Leventhal & Brooks-Gunn, 2000). Many of these communities are characterized by public housing and by a disproportionate number of families from minority ethnic/racial background. Although it would be a mistake to assume that such neighborhoods are identical, all too often they provide a recognizable developmental context that is far from optimal.

Separating neighborhood effects from family and other influences is difficult, but some evidence exists for the independent influence of neighborhoods. Leventhal and Brooks-Gunn (2000) reviewed

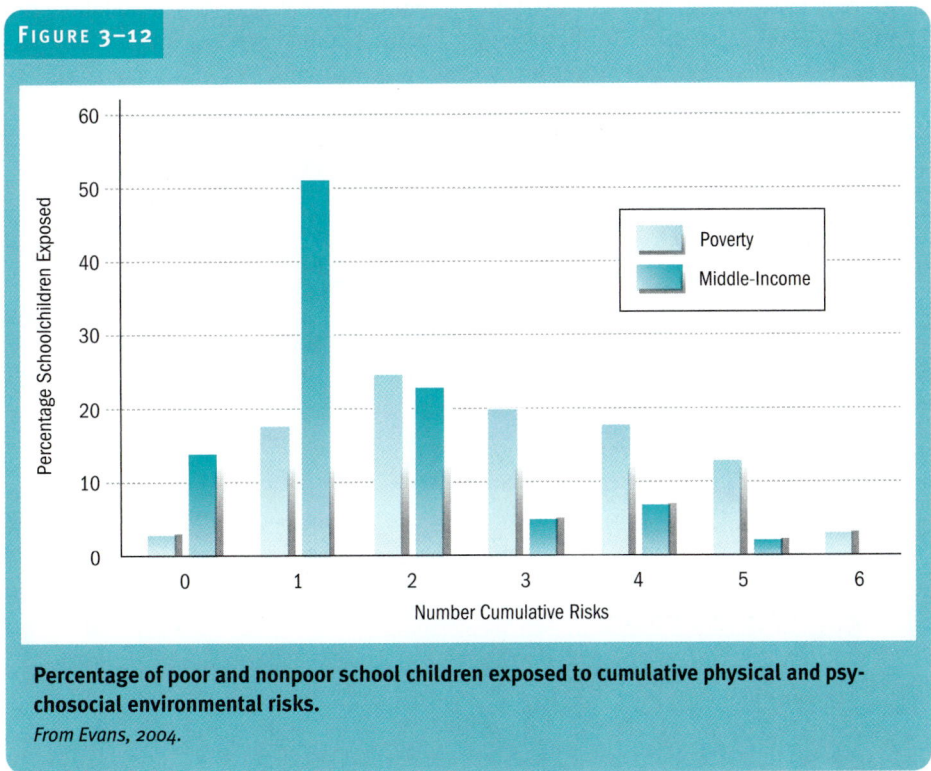

FIGURE 3–12

Percentage of poor and nonpoor school children exposed to cumulative physical and psychosocial environmental risks.

From Evans, 2004.

Very poor neighborhoods generally provide a context that is less than optimal for the development of youth.
(Stock Connection/Fotosearch.com, LLC)

findings regarding child and adolescent outcomes for academic skills, mental health, and sexuality. The most consistent finding was that living in an affluent neighborhood provided substantial benefits to youth with regard to school readiness and achievement, especially for European American youngsters. The best evidence for effects on mental health was for a stronger association between low-SES neighborhoods and acting out/aggressive behavior.

Neighborhood influence on adolescent sexual behavior varied somewhat, but low social class was related to higher levels of sexual activity. In general, the strength of community influence was in the small to moderate range.

Drawing on research findings and theoretical explanations, Leventhal and Brooks-Gunn discussed a conceptualization of the mechanisms or pathways of community influences (Figure 3–13).

- One pathway is *community resources*, which includes opportunities for learning offered in schools, libraries, and museums; quality day care; medical services; and employment.

- The second pathway focuses on *relationships*, especially within the family. It includes parents' personal characteristics; parenting styles and supervision; support networks for parents; and physical and organizational features of the home such as cleanliness, safety, and regular schedules and routines.

- The third, *community norms/collective efficacy*, refers to the extent to which communities are organized to maintain behavioral norms and order. To varying degrees formal institutions or informal networks monitor or supervise the behavior of individuals and watch physical risks that might exist. The neighborhood scrutinizes child and adolescent behavior, the availability of illegal substances, and violence, crime, and similar activities.

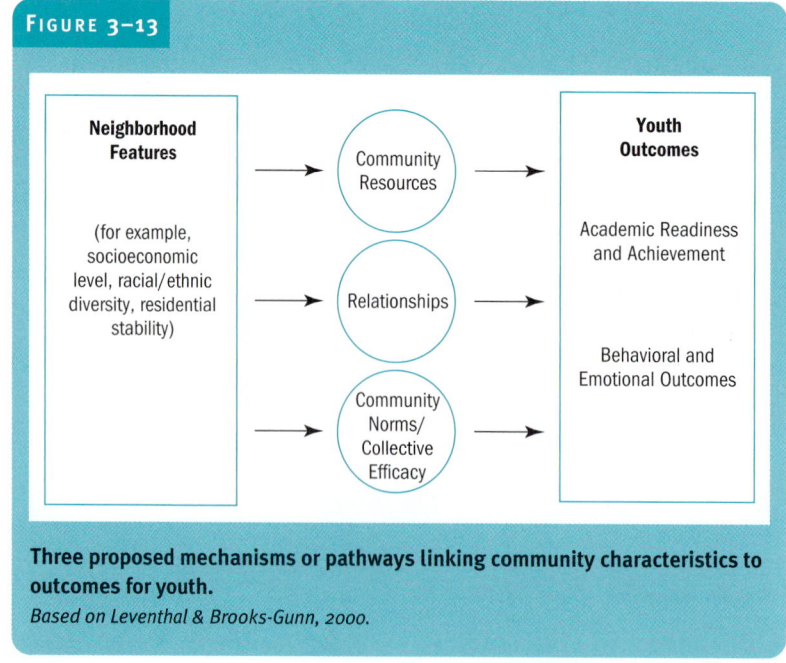

FIGURE 3–13

Three proposed mechanisms or pathways linking community characteristics to outcomes for youth.
Based on Leventhal & Brooks-Gunn, 2000.

Of these pathways, influence was clearest for norms/collective efficacy and relationships. Regarding the latter, family functioning interfaces with characteristics of the community and can act as a risk or protective influence. For example, neighborhood disadvantage is linked to children's affiliations with deviant peers and harsh or inconsistent parenting appears to encourage this association, while nurturant or involved parenting discourages it (Brody et al., 2001). Also, parents who reside in more dangerous neighborhoods tend to be more restrictive. They may cope with adverse conditions by withdrawing from them and intensely monitoring their children. Indeed, parental monitoring can provide a protective shield (Buckner, Mezzacappa, & Beardslee, 2003; Luthar & Goldstein, 2004).

Assuming that even small effects of neighborhood characteristics impact many youths, numerous studies and ameliorative efforts have been aimed at communities. An especially comprehensive approach was the federally sponsored Moving to Opportunity for Fair Housing Demonstration (MTO). Families were randomly selected to receive the opportunity to move from poor to higher SES neighborhoods and then were compared with families that were left behind. The effects of this intervention and similar programs aimed at the psychological and behavioral well-being of youth, appear complex, and some researchers are more optimistic than others regarding such community approaches to improve the lives of children (Ludwig & Mayer, 2006; Tolani & Brooks-Gunn, 2006).

CULTURE, ETHNICITY, AND MINORITY STATUS

All of the contexts we have already discussed operate within a still larger cultural context consisting of a society's beliefs and values, social structures, social roles and norms, and ways of "doing business."

Influences stemming from cultural factors may have broad positive or negative effects. For example, certain practices in the United States may inadvertently foster conduct problems in youth. A case in point concerns the exposure of youth to high levels of aggressive and violent content in media. Decades of research indicate that observing such television and film programming can increase aggression in children; more recent investigation indicates the same effect for video games (Anderson & Dill, 2007; Villani, 2001).

Risk stemming from the cultural context may be particularly high for individuals whose ethnic/racial background is other than mainstream. Indigenous groups deal with unique historical issues and matters of acculturation, that is, changes in culture resulting from cultures coming into contact with each other (Kvernmo & Heyerdahl, 1998, 2003). In many countries, indigenous groups have higher rates of psychopathology, health problems, educational disadvantages, and the like. As Figure 3–11 indicates, the U.S. poverty rate for American Indian and Alaska Native populations, averaged for the years 2003–2005, was statistically the same as for African Americans and higher than rates for other minority groups (DeNavas-Walt et al., 2006). The American Indian population has high rates of birth, unemployment, suicide, alcoholism, and death relative to the general U.S. population and in some cases to other minority groups (Spicer & Sarche, 2006; Stiffman et al., 2007). Adolescents of American Indian background have high rates of substance abuse, disruptive behavior, and incarceration in the juvenile justice system (Hawkins, Cummins, & Marlatt, 2004; Novins et al., 1999; Novins, Beals, & Mitchell, 2001).

Although minority and immigrant groups may vary from each other in many ways, they commonly face poverty, prejudice, racism, and discrimination. Devaluation by others may be perceived relatively early in life. The following is a reflection of the experiences of a 14-year-old black girl who, at a younger age, had attended school in a community of mostly white people.

Anna — Ugliness in People's Hearts

My mother pushes me and she had wanted me to get a chance at better education. Only one other student in my class was black. I was in the fifth grade, and at that age you don't understand the ugliness in people's hearts. They wouldn't play with me. I couldn't understand it. During recess I would stand there by myself beside the fence. Then one day I got a note: "Go back to Africa."

To tell the truth, it left a sadness in my heart. Now you hear them sayin' on TV, "What's the matter with these colored people? Don't they care about their children's education?" But my mother did the best for me she knew. It was not my fault that I was not accepted by those people.

Kozol, 1991, p. 35.

Prejudice and discrimination not only reduces opportunity but has other influences. For example, negative prejudgment and stereotyping of African American students may adversely affect their academic performance (Steele, 1997). Discrimination and perceived racism have been shown to be associated with symptoms such as aggression, antisocial acts, and depression in African American children and adolescents (Nyborg & Curry, 2003). More generally, prejudice may adversely affect the emotions, behavior, academic performance, and health of minority young people (Clark et al., 1999; Compas et al., 2001). Perhaps unsurprising, among the variables that may protect these youth is the degree to which they identify with their ethnic/racial group and are reared to be proud of their heritage (Caughty et al., 2002; DuBois et al., 2002).

Some investigators emphasize the need to consider the effects of the unique experiences of youth of minority ethnic and racial background on development (Garcia-Coll et al., 1996; Spencer et al., 2006).

They suggest that developmental models for nonmainstream youth include the possible influences of prejudice, discrimination, acculturation, racial socialization and identity, and cultural values. (We would add to this the need for similar consideration of other youth who, due to handicapping conditions or sexual orientation, experience more than a usual share of devaluation and prejudice.)

Finally, we should note the disadvantages often experienced by minority groups in seeking and receiving mental and other health services (e.g., Spicer & Sarche, 2006; Sue, 2003). In addition to inaccessible or inadequate services in needy communities, professionals in multicultural settings may lack the awareness, skills, and openness to others required for productive work (Fowers & Davidow, 2006). To facilitate cultural competence, the American Psychological Association (2003) has published guidelines for training, practice, and other aspects of serving multicultural communities. There is little doubt that the need is substantial.

SUMMARY

BRAIN AND NERVOUS SYSTEM

- *Early brain development depends on the interaction of biological programming and experience.*

- *The various parts of the nervous system and brain function as a whole, with specific areas playing primary roles in specific functions. Communication occurs through complex neurotransmission among neurons.*

NERVOUS SYSTEM AND RISK FOR DISORDERED FUNCTIONING

- *Damage to the brain can result from genetic, prenatal, perinatal, and postnatal events. Numerous teratogens have been identified; their prenatal effects depend on several variables. Fetal Alcohol Syndrome puts children at risk for multiple abnormalities.*

- *The capacity of young people to recover from brain damage is not easy to predict.*

GENETIC CONTEXT

- *The basic genetic material consists of chromosomal DNA residing in all body cells. Transcription and*

translation of the genetic code is affected by the internal and external environment.

- *Genetic influences on development occur through single-gene and multiple-gene processes. Such influences are studied through a variety of quantitative (family, twin, and adoption studies) and molecular (linkage and association analyses) strategies.*

- *Hereditary influences, as well as shared and nonshared environmental effects, have been demonstrated for many disorders. Less is known about the specific genes involved and how they operate.*

- *The collaboration of genetic and environmental influences is shown in gene–environment interactions and gene–environment correlations.*

LEARNING AND COGNITION

- *Learning and cognition are critical to development. Classical conditioning, operant learning, observational learning, and higher order cognitive processes play major roles in the origins and treatment of psychological disorders.*

SOCIOCULTURAL CONTEXT: AN OVERVIEW

- *The sociocultural context of development consists of overlapping, interacting domains of influences that include family, peers, community, societal, and cultural influences.*

FAMILY CONTEXT, MALTREATMENT, AND DIVORCE

- *Family interaction is complex, with fathers and mothers performing overlapping but not identical roles. Studies of parenting styles suggest that an authoritative, warm style generally fosters favorable development.*

- *Today's analyses of family life include the maltreatment of children and adolescents, the many factors that contribute to it, and its varied effects.*

- *Divorce is best conceptualized as a complex process of family transition that heightens developmental risk. Its effects depend on multiple variables.*

PEER INFLUENCES

- *Peers influence each other in many, perhaps unique, ways through friendship and other relationships. Poor peer relationships in childhood are associated with problematic behavior in childhood and later life.*

COMMUNITY AND SOCIETAL CONTEXTS

- *School resources, culture, and relationships are a central context for the development of youth. Schools teach intellectual skills and knowledge and also shape values, social and emotional behavior, motivation for learning and achievement, and mental health.*

- *Low socioeconomic status and the poverty associated with it disadvantage children in many areas of development. Poor children are exposed to multiple physical and psychosocial risks. The effects of poverty are mediated in part by family factors.*

- *Young people are influenced by the neighborhoods in which they reside. Poor neighborhoods carry risk factors that may be detrimental to academic performance, mental health, and other aspects of development. Neighborhood influences operate through community resources, family relationships, and community norms/efficacy.*

- *The broad cultural context can shape behavior in ways that are maladaptive for young people. Indigenous and minority groups often experience the risks of poverty, prejudice, and discrimination, as well as inadequate mental health care.*

KEY TERMS

● ● ● ● ● ● ● ● ● ●

neurons *(p. 39)*

central nervous system *(p. 40)*

peripheral nervous system *(p. 40)*

somatic nervous system *(p. 40)*

autonomic nervous system *(p. 40)*

endocrine system *(p. 40)*

hindbrain, midbrain, forebrain *(p. 40)*

cell body, dendrites, axons *(p. 41)*

synapse *(p. 41)*

neurotransmitter *(p. 41)*

teratogen *(p. 42)*

Fetal Alcohol Syndrome (FAS) *(p. 42)*

brain plasticity *(p. 43)*

chromosomes *(p. 44)*

DNA *(p. 44)*

genes *(p. 44)*

behavior genetics *(p. 44)*

genotype, phenotype *(p. 44)*

dominant genes, recessive genes *(p. 45)*

index case, proband *(p. 45)*

quantitative trait loci (QTL) *(p. 45)*

heritability *(p. 45)*

shared and nonshared environmental influences *(p. 45)*

family genetic studies *(p. 46)*

twin studies *(p. 46)*

monozygotic (MZ) twins *(p. 46)*

dizygotic (DZ) twins *(p. 46)*

adoption studies *(p. 46)*

linkage analysis *(p. 46)*

4

Research: Its Role and Methods

Psychology and other scientific disciplines are committed to the view that science can provide the most complete and valid information about human functioning, behavior, and development. Although common sense tells us much about behavior, science aims to go beyond common sense to systematic, reliable, and accurate knowledge. The general purpose of science is to describe and explain phenomena.

The word *science* comes from the Latin word for "knowledge," or "to know," but refers to knowledge gained by particular methods of inquiry. We might know the world from reading literature or listening to music, but we would not consider knowledge gained in this way to be scientific knowledge. Scientific understanding derives from systematic formulation of a problem, observation and collection of data, and interpretation of findings by what is considered acceptable procedures. Despite some misgivings—and even warnings of danger—about the scientific study of humans, we have come to value what science can tell us about ourselves.

Fundamentals of Research

The numerous major questions relevant to developmental psychopathology are progressively being addressed by scientific investigations (Figure 4–1). Of course, these general questions are transformed into countless more specific queries. To answer them, it is sometimes necessary only to describe phenomena. We can count the number of cases of learning disabilities and can describe the symptoms of disorders. At other times, it is necessary to determine the conditions under which a phenomenon occurs and to discover its relationship to other variables. Frequently, the quest is to determine cause-and-effect relationships.

We have noted that researchers rarely, if ever, simply pose and try to answer questions in an intellectual vacuum. They are guided by already established information, concepts, perspectives or theories, and by their own inclinations. Theoretical concepts and assumptions guide research goals, choice of variables, procedures, analyses, and conclusions. But there is always at least a

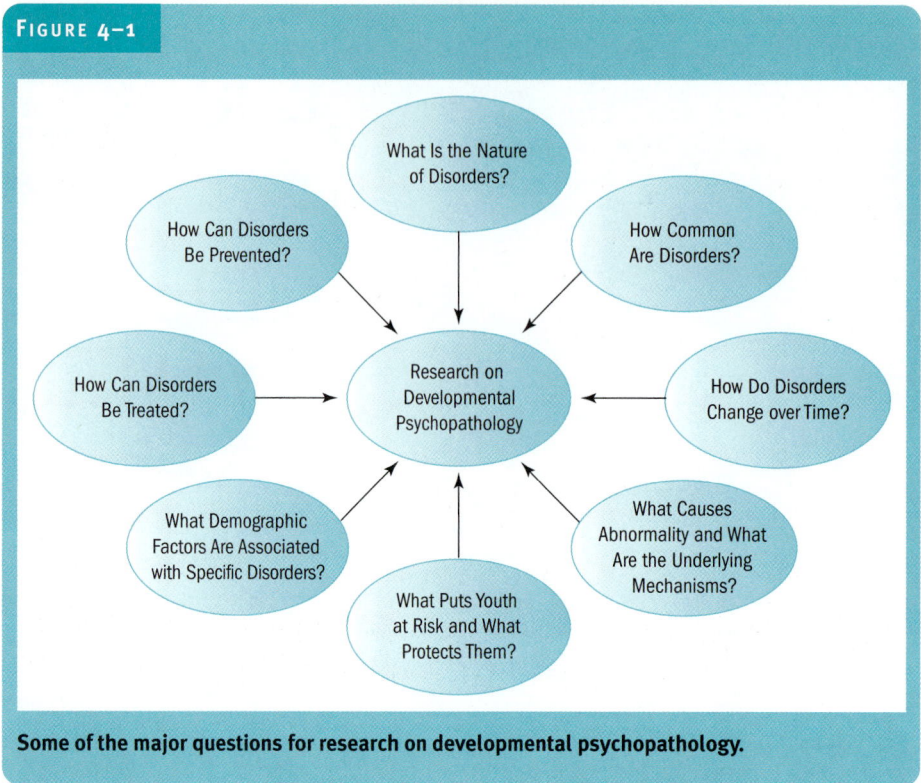

FIGURE 4-1

Some of the major questions for research on developmental psychopathology.

touch of subjectivity and creativity in the posing of research questions and in deciding how best to seek answers.

It is common to try to test specific hypotheses derived from theoretical notions. Hypothesis testing is valuable because it tends to build knowledge systematically rather than haphazardly. Any one investigation rarely proves that a hypothesis is either correct or incorrect; instead, it provides evidence for or against the hypothesis. In turn, a hypothesis that is supported serves as evidence for the accuracy and explanatory power of the underlying theory. An unsupported hypothesis, in contrast, serves to disprove, limit, or redirect the theory. Together, observations and theory advance scientific understanding.

Just as researchers ask a variety of questions and pose hypotheses, they work in a variety of settings, ranging from the natural environments of the home or community to controlled laboratory settings. Different strategies and designs are used, depending on the purposes of the research—and on ethics and practicality, too. In all cases, however, careful consideration must be given to selection of participants, observation and measurement, reliability, and validity.

SELECTION OF PARTICIPANTS

For good reason, research reports require the description of the participants and the way they were selected. This information is important in judging the adequacy of investigations and interpretations of the findings.

Investigations of development and abnormal psychology are typically interested in drawing general conclusions about a population of interest. Because it is rarely possible to study an entire population, the next best choice is to examine a representative sample. Representativeness is best achieved by random selection of participants from the population, that is, by choosing each participant by chance. Even this goal may not be feasible; for example, it is impossible to randomly select a sample from *all* preschoolers or *all* children with mental retardation. However, efforts can be made to approximate representativeness, and the extent to which it is achieved affects the interpretation of the research findings.

In the study of psychological disorders, research participants are often drawn from clinics, hospitals, and other facilities serving youths with problems. Such clinic populations are unlikely to represent the entire population of young people with disorders. They may exclude children whose families cannot afford treatment or for whom help was not sought due to denial, shame, fear, or high levels of adult tolerance. Clinic populations can also *over*represent youths who experience more serious symptoms or who act out or otherwise disturb people. Such selection bias has important implications. We have seen, for instance, how working with clinic populations rather than general populations, or boys rather than girls, might affect how disorders are defined. The characteristics of research participants and the way that participants are chosen are critical in planning and drawing conclusions from research investigations.

OBSERVATION AND MEASUREMENT

At the heart of scientific endeavors are observation and measurement, both of which can be challenging to behavioral scientists. Whereas it is relatively simple to observe and measure overt action, thought and emotion are more elusive. In any case, the scientist must provide an operational definition of the behavior or concept being studied. That is, some observable and measurable operation must be selected to define the behavior or concept. Aggression might be operationalized as the frequency with which children actually shove or threaten their playmates; depression might be operationalized by a score on a scale that measures adolescent reports of feelings of sadness and hopelessness.

In the attempt to tap all sources of information, behavioral scientists make many kinds of observations and measurements. They directly observe overt behavior in naturalistic or laboratory settings; employ standardized tests; record physiological functioning of the brain, sensory organs, or heart; ask people to report or rate their own behavior, feelings, and thoughts; and collect the reports of others about

Direct observation allows the researcher systematically to measure behavior as it is occurring.
(Courtesy of A. C. Israel)

the subject of investigation. Increasingly, highly technical genetic methods to study chromosomes and neuroscience procedures to image the brain have become additional sources of information.

Whatever the measure, it should be valid, that is, be an accurate indicator of the attribute of interest. There are several kinds of validity (Table 4–1). For instance, construct validity exists if a questionnaire about anxiety gets at what is accepted as the

TABLE 4–1	SOME TYPES OF VALIDITY PERTAINING TO MEASUREMENT
Content Validity	Refers to whether the content of a measure corresponds to the content of the attribute of interest
Construct Validity	Refers to whether a measure corresponds to the construct (concept) underlying the attribute of interest
Face Validity	Refers to whether a measure, on its surface, seems appropriate to the attribute of interest
Concurrent Validity	Refers to whether the scores on a measure correlate with scores on another acceptable measure of the attribute of interest
Predictive Validity	Refers to whether the scores on a measure predict later scores on another acceptable measure of the attribute of interest or other outcomes of interest

underlying concept or meaning of anxiety. The observations also must be reliable, that is, the data would be similar, or consistent, if measurements were taken again under similar circumstances. Numerous considerations and practices are required to ensure objective, accurate, and dependable observation and measurement. (See Accent: "The Goodness of Measurement in Research.")

RELIABILITY OF RESEARCH RESULTS

The concepts of reliability and validity apply to the results of research as well. The findings of a research study are assumed to report a "truth" about the world. The scientific method assumes that truth repeats itself, given identical or similar conditions; consequently, it can be observed again by others. Replication of findings is thus an important component of scientific work. If the same truth is not reported under similar conditions, the original finding is considered unreliable or inconsistent, and it remains questionable. The need for reliability, or repeatability, of results places a burden on researchers to be clear and concise as they conceptualize and

conduct their study, and to communicate their findings so that others may replicate and judge their work.

VALIDITY OF RESEARCH RESULTS

Whereas reliability refers to the consistency or repeatability of results, validity refers to the correctness, soundness, or appropriateness of scientific findings. The validity of research findings is a complex matter; in general, validity must be judged in terms of the purpose of the research and the way the results are used. Of major concern in many studies are internal and external validity.

The purpose of much research is to offer an explanation for phenomena. Internal validity refers to the extent to which the explanation is judged to be correct or sound. Many factors pose a threat to internal validity, depending on the methods and research designs employed (Shadish, Cook, & Campbell, 2002). Given the purpose of the research, as well as practical and ethical considerations, investigators do well to select methods and conduct research so as to maximize internal validity. In general, the extent to which

ACCENT

The Goodness of Measurement in Research

Because observations that are biased, unreliable, or invalid can be useless or misleading, investigators must always be concerned about their quality. Consider, for example, a study by Dadds and colleagues (1992), who used naturalistic observation to study childhood depression. Naturalistic observation consists of directly observing individuals in their "real world," at times simply to describe naturally occurring behavior and at other times to answer specific questions or to test hypotheses. In this study, a comparison was made of parent–child interaction in families that had a child who was referred to a clinic for depression, conduct disorder, or depression/conduct disorder. The families, and a group of nonclinic families, were videotaped during a typical evening meal.

The videotaped behavior was then independently coded by observers who were trained to use a carefully constructed observation system, the Family Observation Schedule. This instrument provided 20 categories for parent and child behaviors—among

them smiling, frowning, praising, and complaining. The reliability of measurement was then examined to determine whether the taped behaviors were coded in a consistent way by the independent coders. Such interobserver reliability is known to be generally higher when the observation schedule is optimally specific and clear. In the Dadds et al. study, interobserver reliability was checked by an additional observer, who coded one third of the tapes. The investigation also benefited from the observers' having no knowledge of each family's clinical status, that is, the problems displayed by the children. Nor did the observers know the hypotheses being tested. Such observer "blindness" decreased the chance that the observers would be biased by such information.

All of these features of the Dadds et al. investigation—a well-constructed observational measure, observer training, a check on the reliability of the coding, and blind observation—addressed important standards for measurement in research.

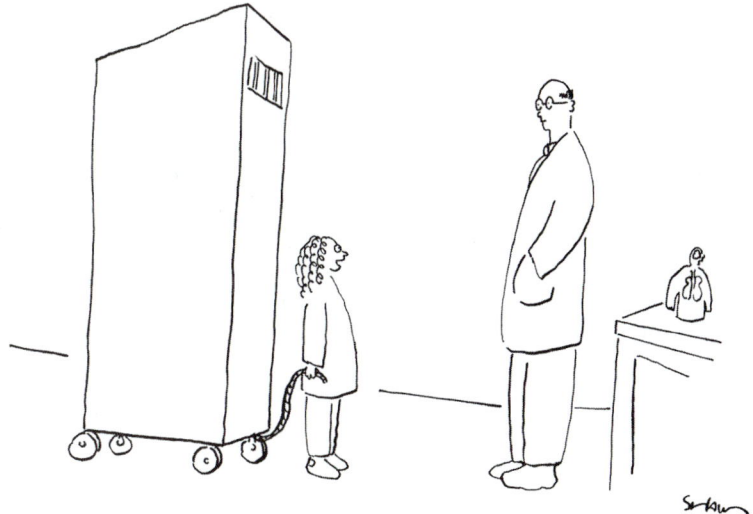

"The title of my science project is 'My Little Brother: Nature or Nurture.'"

alternative explanations can be ruled out determines the certainty that the offered explanation is valid.

External validity asks the question of generalizability, the extent to which the results of an investigation apply to other populations and situations. Researchers are virtually always interested in generalizability, but it cannot be assumed. Findings based on European American children in the United States may or may not hold for children of Mexican American ancestry; findings from research with animals may or may not apply to humans; findings from highly controlled studies conducted in controlled settings may or may not hold in real world settings. The question of generalizability is rarely, if ever, completely answered but evidence for external validity increases as various populations, settings, and methods are used.

Basic Methods of Research

There are many ways to approach and conduct research. Investigations may focus on a single person or on one or more groups of individuals. Researchers may exert comparatively more or less control over the procedures and settings. The time frame of the study may be relatively brief, or it may last several years. Nevertheless, all research methods have strengths and weaknesses, and the choice of one over another reasonably depends on the purpose and other aspects of the investigation. Moreover, conclusions are especially impressive when they are based on a convergence of findings from investigations that employ different methods.

There is no single way to conceptualize or categorize research methods. One useful distinction is between descriptive, or nonexperimental, and experimental methods. The general purpose of descriptive methods is to portray a phenomenon of interest. Observations are made and analyzed in a variety of ways. The attributes and life of a single child may be described; the behaviors of groups of adolescents who vary in some way may be compared. Frequently the relationship of two or more variables of interest is described. Nonexperimental methods are widely employed, and they may involve sophisticated correlational and multivariate statistical analysis to study complex relationships.

Experimental studies can be viewed as randomized or quasi-experimental (Shadish, Cook, & Campbell, 2002). Randomized experiments are highly esteemed because of their ability to establish cause-and-effect relationships. They require that a manipulation (A) be made, followed by an examination of the effects (B). A causal relationship exists when variation in A is related to variation in B and alternative explanations of this relationship are unlikely. Crucial to ruling out alternative explanations are random assignment of participants to the manipulation, as well as experimenter control of the procedures and extraneous factors.

Quasi-experimental studies are similar to randomized experiments in that they include a manipulation and various controls. However, participants are not randomly assigned to the manipulation. This difference reduces the confidence with which causal explanations can be made. Take, for example, a hypothetical study in which similar families of disturbed children volunteer for parent training and subsequently are compared to families who do not receive the treatment. If the training group performed better, can it be concluded that the training is effective? Perhaps the volunteer parents had better skills to begin with or were more motivated than the no-treatment parents to perform well. In fact, we cannot rule out the possibility that something besides treatment caused the effect. There are ways, however, to strengthen the argument for causation. Had each group been measured before and then after the manipulation, and had the training group made greater pre-post gains than the no-treatment group, we would have evidence for the effectiveness of the training.

With the distinctions in mind between descriptive and experimental methods, we next examine five research methods common in the study of developmental psychopathology.

CASE STUDIES

The case study is a descriptive, nonexperimental method commonly used in investigations of psychological disorders. It focuses on an individual—describing the background, present and past life circumstances, functioning, and characteristics of the person. Case studies can tell us something about the nature, course, correlates, outcomes, and possible etiology of psychological problems. In addition, they can bridge the gap that all too often exists between clinical practice and research endeavors (Kazdin, 1998).

The following is an abbreviated version of a case report of a boy who was considered at risk for a serious disorder, childhood schizophrenia.

Max | Risk for Childhood Schizophrenia

Max was a seven-year-old boy when he was first referred for psychiatric evaluation by his school principal. . . . Long-standing problems such as severe rage outbursts, loss of control, aggressive behavior, and paranoid ideation had reached crisis proportions.

Max was the product of an uncomplicated pregnancy and delivery, the only child of a professional couple. There was a history of "mental illness" in the paternal grandmother and two great aunts. Max's early development was characterized by "passivity." . . . He used a bottle until age three. Verbal development was good; he spoke full sentences at one year. Toilet training was reportedly difficult. . . .

Max was clumsy and had difficulty manipulating toys, his tricycle, and his shoelaces. When he began nursery school, he was constantly in trouble with other children. . . . Max "developed a passion for animals." . . . At age five Max acquired an imaginary companion, "Casper—the man in the wall" who was ever present. Max insisted that he could see him, although no one else could. Casper's voice, he said, often told him he was a bad boy.

Max's behavior was so unmanageable during the first and second grade he was rarely able to remain in the classroom. . . . Max described animals fighting and killing people. . . . The psychologists noted a schizoid quality because of the numerous references to people from outer space, ghosts, and martians, as well as the total absence of human subjects. . . . Despite his high intelligence (IQ 130), Max was experiencing the world as hostile and dangerous. The psychologist considered Max to be at great risk for schizophrenia, paranoid type.

Cantor & Kestenbaum, 1986, pp. 627–628.

The case study continues, telling of Max's enrollment in special schools and his psychotherapy. Parental involvement, rewards for appropriate behavior, and medication were all employed. Despite some quite disturbed behaviors, improvement occurred, and Max eventually was able to attend a university engineering program.

The primary goal of this case report was to illustrate an approach to treating children with severe disturbances and to emphasize that treatment must be tailored to each child's needs. Case studies can well meet such a goal, for one of their strengths is the power to illustrate. They can richly describe phenomena, even phenomena so rare that they would be difficult to study in other ways. They can provide hypotheses to be tested by other methods. The weaknesses of the case study concern reliability and validity. The descriptions of life events often go back in time, raising questions about their reliability and accuracy. When case studies go beyond description to interpretations, there are few guidelines to judge the validity of the interpretations. Generalization also is weak: Since only one person is examined, the findings cannot be generalized confidently to others. There are ways to increase reliability and validity in case studies, however (Kazdin, 1998). For example, the validity of treatment success in a case report can be increased by the use of objective rather than anecdotal measures of the client's behavior. Also, confidence in generalization can be improved by reports of several case studies demonstrating the same concept or outcome.

CORRELATIONAL STUDIES

Correlational studies are nonexperimental investigations that describe the relations between two or more factors without exposing the participants to a manipulation. They may be conducted in the natural environment or in the laboratory in a variety of ways, and can involve many variables in complex research designs. Statistical procedures are employed to determine the strength and nature of the relationship.

Here we only examine the basic aspects of the method. In its simplest form, the question asked is, Are factors X and Y related, and, if so, in what direction are they related, and how strongly? After the researchers select an appropriate sample, they obtain a measure of variable X and of variable Y from each participant. Statistical analysis of these two sets of scores is then performed. In this case, the Pearson product–moment coefficient, r, could be computed.

The value of Pearson r, which always ranges between $+1.00$ and -1.00, indicates the direction and the strength of the relationship.[1] Direction is indicated by the sign of the coefficient. A positive sign $(+)$ means that high scores on the X variable tend to be associated with high scores on the Y variable, and

that low scores on X tend to be related to low scores on Y. This relationship is referred to as a positive correlation (or direct correlation). A negative sign $(-)$ indicates that high scores on X tend to be related to low scores on Y, and that low scores on X tend to be related to high scores on Y. This is a negative correlation (also called an indirect, or inverse, correlation).

The strength or magnitude of a correlation is reflected in the absolute value of the coefficient. The strongest relationship is expressed by an r of $+1.00$ or -1.00. As the absolute value of the coefficient value decreases, the relationship becomes weaker. A coefficient of .00 indicates no relationship at all and the scores on one variable tell us nothing about the scores on the other variable.

Suppose that an investigator explored the association of secure attachment in infancy with childhood adjustment. For each participant, the researcher obtained a measure of secure attachment in infancy and a measure of adjustment in childhood. The hypothetical data appear in Table 4–2. Pearson r for the data was calculated, and its value is .82. How would this finding be interpreted? The positive sign indicates that children who scored higher on secure attachment tended to score higher on later adjustment. The magnitude of the coefficient indicates that the relationship is strong (since 1.00 is a perfect positive relationship).

When a correlation exists, knowing a person's score on one variable allows us to predict the person's performance on the other variable. It does not, however, permit us automatically to draw a

TABLE 4–2	DATA FROM A HYPOTHETICAL STUDY OF INFANT SECURE ATTACHMENT AND CHILDHOOD ADJUSTMENT. THE PEARSON r VALUE IS $+0.82$, WHICH INDICATES A STRONG POSITIVE RELATIONSHIP BETWEEN THE VARIABLES	
CHILD	VARIABLE X ATTACHMENT SCORE	VARIABLE Y CHILDHOOD ADJUSTMENT SCORE
Daniel	2	5
Nicky	3	4
Sara	4	12
Beth	7	16
Jessica	9	10
Alia	11	22
Brent	13	18

[1] Pearson r is one of several correlation coefficients that could be calculated, depending on the nature and complexity of the study. The general procedures and interpretations described here apply to other correlation coefficients.

cause-and-effect conclusion. One problem is that of directionality. If a positive correlation were found between parenting behaviors and child adjustment, it is possible that parenting caused child maladjustment or, alternatively, that child maladjustment caused parents to behave in a certain way. The direction of causation is unclear. The problem can sometimes be solved by examining the nature of the variables. For example, if a correlation between insecure early attachment and later childhood problems exists, it is impossible for later adjustment to cause early insecure attachment.

However, even when directionality is not a problem, a correlation may be caused by one or more unknown variables. Perhaps children's social competence is responsible for both the quality of their early attachment and their later social adjustment. To evaluate this possibility, social competence could be measured and a statistical technique could be applied to partial out, or hold constant, its effects. To the extent that the correlation remains, it is not explained by social competence. As helpful as partialing techniques are in ruling out the effects of other possible causal factors, however, an investigator can never be sure that all possible causative variables have been evaluated.

Despite the aforementioned weaknesses, correlational studies are of considerable value and are widely employed in research relevant to abnormal child and adolescent psychology. They are useful when an investigator wants to determine whether any relationships exist among variables before advancing specific hypotheses. They can be invaluable when ethical considerations preclude manipulation of the variables of interest.

In addition, techniques such as structural modeling, too complex to discuss here, permit researchers to explore complex relationships and to have more confidence in their hypotheses about cause and effect. The researcher hypothesizes specific patterns of relationships among the variables being studied. Statistical techniques are then employed to determine how well the collected data fit the model that the researcher specified. Examples of the use of this and other methods based on correlations to address questions about psychological disturbance appear throughout this text.

EXPERIMENTS OF NATURE

A notable way to examine hypotheses about relationships among variables is to employ experiments of nature, or natural experiments. Despite their name, they are not experiments and do not involve a manipulation. The condition of interest may not even be manipulable by researchers. These studies examine naturally occurring events and contrast a condi-

tion of interest with a condition in a comparison group (Shadish et al., 2002). Correlational and other statistical analyses may be used to evaluate the relationships of interest.

A noteworthy example is the investigation of the effects of institutionalization on children's development. There is a lengthy history of comparing children who reside in orphanages with children who had been adopted from orphanages or had never been institutionalized. These studies indicate an adverse effect of institutionalization on intellectual development, physical health, and an array of behaviors (MacLean, 2003). Lengthy institutionalization and poor quality of orphanages are associated with worse outcomes (Rutter, 2005; Smyke et al., 2007).

Like all research methods, experiments of nature have weaknesses and strengths (O'Connor, 2003). Regarding institutionalization, a major weakness is the potential selection bias inherent in the groups. For example, children who are adopted from orphanages may have had fewer difficulties even prior to leaving than children who remained behind. Such a selection bias makes the findings difficult to interpret. Despite weaknesses, however, natural experiments have enriched our understanding of life circumstances that cannot readily be manipulated by researchers.

RANDOMIZED EXPERIMENTS

The randomized experiment is sometimes referred to as the "true" experiment in that it is the strongest method for inferring causal links between variables. A controlled manipulation (the independent variable) is presented to participants who are randomly assigned to different conditions, or treatments. The outcome is measured (the dependent variable), and differences between experimental and control conditions are then evaluated. With the exception of the independent variable, the groups are treated as similarly as possible so that group differences can be attributed to the treatment. In addition, random assignment of participants to groups makes it likely that any differences are not caused by initial group disparity but by the manipulation itself.

To illustrate the experiment, we draw on a study of the Abecedarian Project, which asked whether at-risk children benefit from a child-centered, intellectually stimulating environment provided as part of a day care service (Campbell et al., 2001; Ramey & Campbell, 1984). Potential participants were identified through prenatal clinics and the local social service department. Families were identified as at-risk on the basis of a survey, and selected before or soon after the birth of the participant child. The investigators then paired the families according to similarity on the High Risk Index, and the children from each pair were randomly assigned to either the treatment or the control group (Ramey & Campbell, 1984).

The independent variable was the provision of the educational program. Children in the treatment group began day care by 3 months of age, and their development was tracked until they reached 54 months. The educational program included language, motor, social, and cognitive components, varying somewhat with the child's age. Control-group children did not attend the day care center and were not exposed to the educational program. Efforts were made to otherwise equate their experiences with those of the treatment group: They were given similar nutritional supplements, pediatric care, and supportive social services. The dependent variable was standardized developmental or intelligence tests administered to all the children twice annually.

The test results revealed that beginning at 18 months, children in the treatment group scored higher than children in the control group, and this difference was statistically significant.[2] Figure 4–2 shows one way of examining the findings. It indicates that at 24, 36, and 48 months, the educationally treated children were much less likely to obtain intelligence scores at or below 85 than were the control children. The researchers concluded that the educational program resulted in intellectual benefits for the treated at-risk youngsters.[3]

Is this conclusion justified; that is, does the study have internal validity? The method by which the subjects were selected and assigned makes it unlikely that the results simply reflect group differences that existed prior to the study. Moreover, efforts were made to treat the experimental and control groups similarly except for the independent variable. To the degree that this was accomplished, it can be argued that the study is internally valid and that the results are due to the treatment. With regard to this issue, caution is appropriate, however. When research is conducted in the laboratory, it is relatively easy to control the experiences of the groups. In an experiment such as Ramey and Campbell's, the degree of control and thus internal validity are less clear.

An additional issue concerns the actual collection of data. It appears that those who gave the standardized tests might have known the group to which each child had been assigned, raising the question of

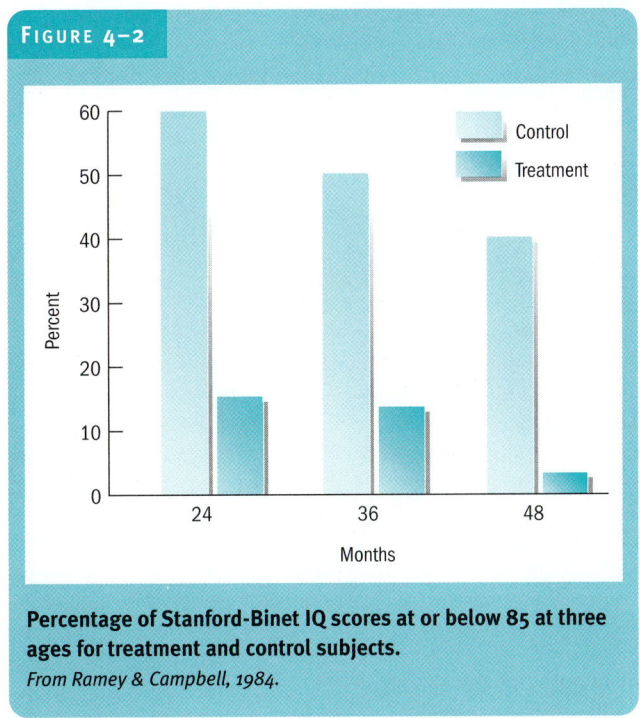

FIGURE 4–2

Percentage of Stanford-Binet IQ scores at or below 85 at three ages for treatment and control subjects.
From Ramey & Campbell, 1984.

[2] *Statistical significance concerns the probability that a finding is not due to mere chance. A common convention is that a statistically significant finding would occur by chance only 5 or less times were the study repeated 100 times. Statistical significance tests can be applied to many kinds of research methods.*

[3] *Our present purpose in discussing the Abecedarian Project is to exemplify the experiment as a research method. It is worth noting that subsequent research shows that benefits of the project were observed again several years later (Campbell & Ramey, 1994; Campbell et al., 2001).*

bias in data collection. At the same time, the individual testers had been randomly assigned to testing sessions, a procedure that could offset possible bias.

What about external validity, or generalizability, of the findings? External validity is enhanced by the intervention actually being conducted in a day care center, the setting in which the program likely would be used. In general, external validly would be anticipated to the extent that the new participants and conditions would be similar to those in the study. The positive effects of treatments may not accrue when they are employed in circumstances other than those in which they were initially demonstrated. (See Accent: "Effectiveness in Real-World Settings.")

SINGLE-CASE EXPERIMENTAL DESIGNS

Single-case experimental designs involve a manipulation with a single (or a few) participant(s). They are sometimes referred to as time-series designs because measures of the dependent variable are repeated across time periods. The designs are frequently used to evalu-

ate the effects of clinical interventions. External validity is not strong, because generalization from a single participant cannot be confidently made. It can be enhanced, however, by repeating the study with different subjects or in different settings. Internal validity may be approached with the use of specific control features.

Reversal designs. One way to control for the possibility of alternative explanations is to use the ABA reversal design. The problem behavior is carefully defined and measured across time periods, during which the subject is exposed to different conditions. During the first period (A), measures are taken of the behavior prior to any intervention. This baseline measure serves as a standard against which change can be evaluated. In the next period (B), the intervention is carried out while the behavior is measured in the identical way. The intervention is then removed; that is, there is a return to the same condition as during baseline (A).

Figure 4–3 gives a hypothetical example of the ABA design. Appropriate play behavior occurs at low

ACCENT

Effectiveness in Real-World Settings

The issue of generalizability of treatment and prevention programs receives much attention today. The important distinction is made between efficacy and effectiveness.

In recent years, progress has been made in demonstrating a causal connection between psychological and medication interventions and positive outcomes. This has been accomplished through well-conceptualized, carefully designed, and controlled research studies, conducted often in university and other research settings (American Psychological Association, 2006). When a causal connection between an intervention and a positive outcome is thusly demonstrated, the intervention is termed efficacious. Regrettably, when taken into the real world of clinical and community practice, efficacious interventions may not have the same, or even a similar, positive outcome. In other words, they may not be effective.

What factors impede the generalization of empirically tested interventions to clinical settings, and how can effectiveness be strengthened? Kamon, Tolan, and Gorman-Smith (2006) help us think about the problem. First, it may be that efficacious programs are not implemented with fidelity in real-world settings. That is, com-

ponents and procedures essential to the treatment are not understood, or not utilized, or not appropriately followed in clinical settings. It is suggested that the problem of infidelity can be overcome by increased communication between researchers and clinical workers that emphasizes training and support for adherence to the intervention protocols.

A second problem is that efficacy research may inadequately consider the characteristics of the real-world settings in which the interventions will be adopted. Cases in clinical settings may be more complex, involving multiple disorders and risks (Hibbs & Jensen, 2005). Moreover, the delivery of interventions may differ substantially in community settings; for example, delivery may be less organized or structured. In fact, studies demonstrating efficacy appear to differ in several ways from common clinical practice, including the use of more specially trained therapists (Kamon et al., 2006). To remedy the situation, it is suggested that researchers must build the characteristics of real-world settings into the designs and evaluations of interventions. Indeed, attention to this issue, and to the issue of fidelity, appears to increase generalization from research to clinical application.

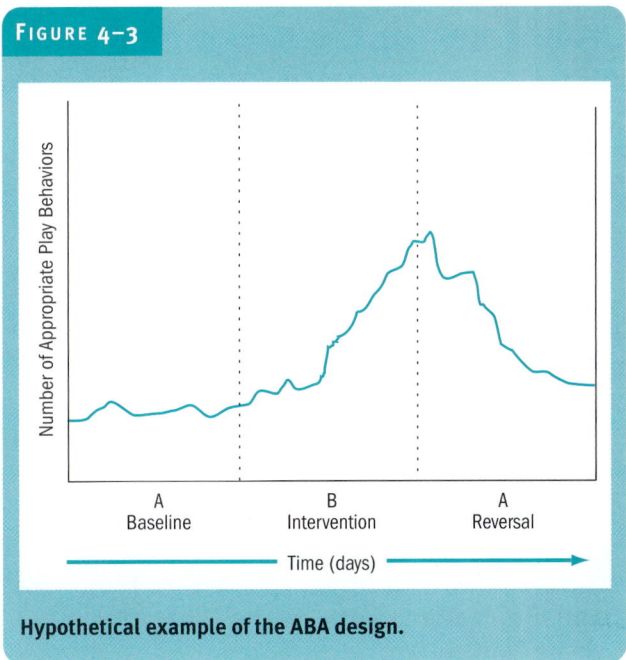

FIGURE 4-3

(y-axis) Number of Appropriate Play Behaviors

A
Baseline

B
Intervention

A
Reversal

Time (days)

Hypothetical example of the ABA design.

frequency during the baseline, increases during the treatment phase B, and decreases when the intervention is removed in the second A phase. In studies in which behavior improves during intervention, particularly if clinical treatment is the aim, a fourth period, during which the successful intervention is reintroduced, must be added. Typically the relevant behaviors show improvement again.

The ABA design is limited in that the intervention may make reversal of the targeted behavior unlikely. For example, when treatment results in increased academic skill, a child may not display decreases in the skill when intervention is removed. From a treatment standpoint, this is a positive outcome; from a research standpoint, there is no way to demonstrate that the intervention caused the positive behavior. In other instances, the researcher may hesitate to remove a manipulation once it is associated with positive change, so that a definite demonstration of its effects is lacking.

Multiple baseline designs. When reversal designs are inappropriate, alternative designs such as multiple baselines may be suitable. Multiple baselines are recorded that may represent different behaviors of a participant, the same behavior of a participant in different settings, the same behavior of a few different participants, and so on. Intervention is then presented to observe the effects on one of the baselines but not the others. If effects are found, they likely are due to intervention rather than extraneous factors.

In this way, multiple baseline designs provide some basis for internal validity.

Consider, for example, the multiple baseline design in which two behaviors by a single child are recorded across time. After baselines are established for both behaviors, the intervention is made for only one behavior. During the next phase, intervention is applied to the other behavior as well. A clinician may hypothesize, say, that a child's temper tantrums and throwing of objects are maintained by adult attention to these behaviors. Withdrawal of attention would thus be expected to reduce the behaviors. Support for the hypothesis can be seen in Figure 4–4, a hypothetical graph of the frequency of both behaviors across time periods. Because behavior change follows the pattern of the treatment procedure, it is likely that withdrawal of attention and not some other variable caused the change.

In another commonly used multiple baseline design, baselines are recorded for multiple participants, and intervention follows different time lines (Gliner, Morgan, & Harmon, 2000). In such a study, Koegel, O'Dell, and Koegel (1987) evaluated the effects of a new treatment to enhance language development in children with autism. As Figure 4–5 shows, two children began the old treatment (Teaching Method I) at the same time, and individual baselines were recorded. Child 1 then received the new treatment, and Child 2 followed several months later. Data were recorded in the clinic for two kinds of verbal imitation (the dependent variables). Similar patterns of change for

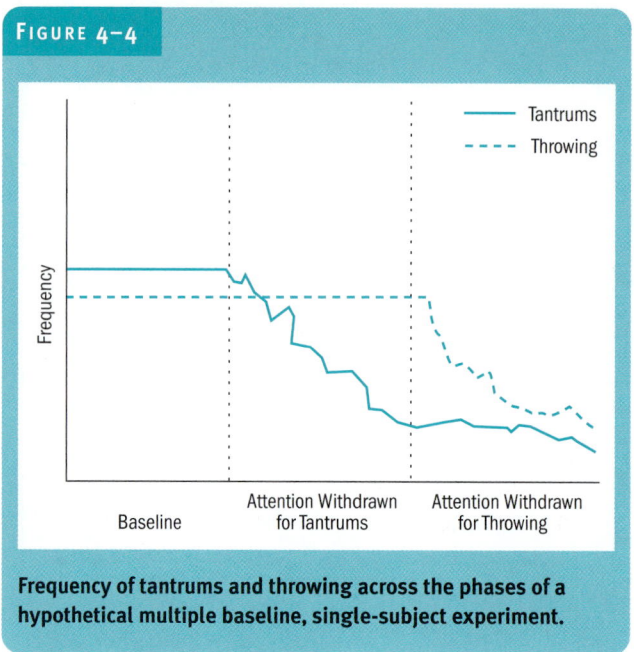

FIGURE 4–4

Frequency of tantrums and throwing across the phases of a hypothetical multiple baseline, single-subject experiment.

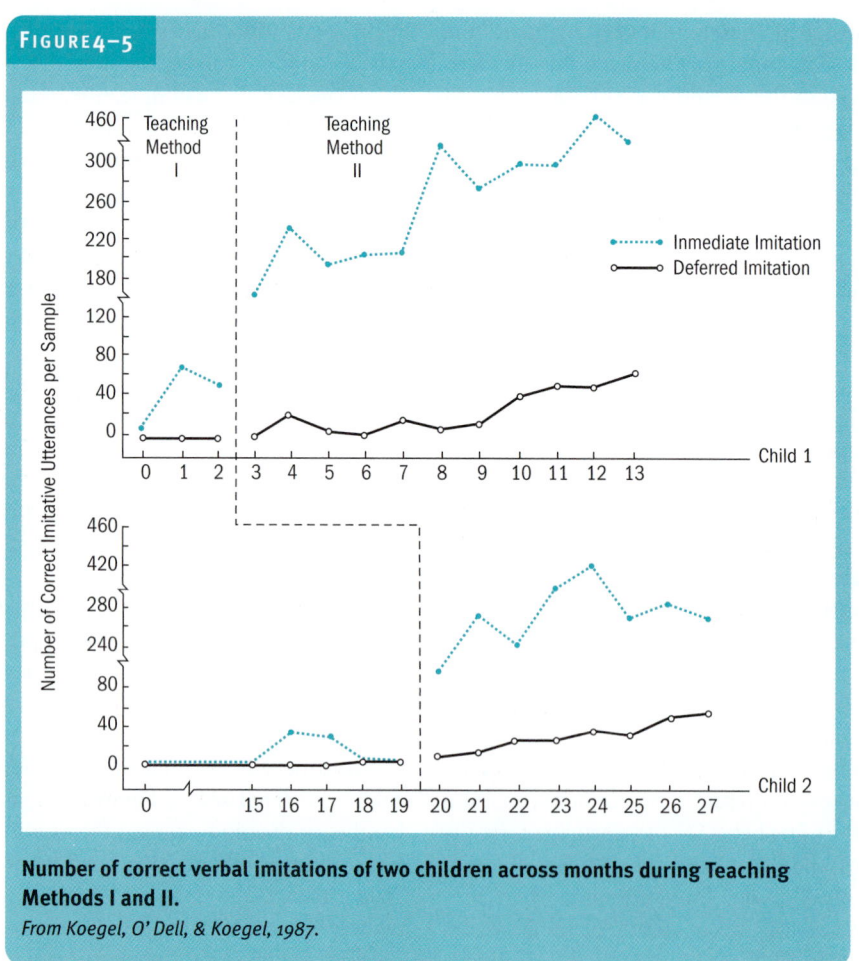

FIGURE 4–5

Number of correct verbal imitations of two children across months during Teaching Methods I and II.

From Koegel, O' Dell, & Koegel, 1987.

both children upon the introduction of the new treatment increase confidence that the treatment actually caused improvement, particularly in immediate imitation. Moreover, external validity is enhanced by the fact that the effect was observed in two individuals.

There are numerous other single-case experimental designs (Hays, 1998; Kratochwill & Levin, 1992). They all permit the researcher-clinician to test hypotheses while working with a single or a few participants and, in the case of treatment, to focus on the youth of immediate concern. Moreover, although control of extraneous factors is more easily effected in the laboratory, single-case research is relatively easy to conduct in natural environments (Morgan & Morgan, 2001). The method thus has the potential to capture actual clinic practice.

To summarize, the research methods we have discussed in this section vary in several ways, and each has weaknesses and strengths. Nonexperimental methods are appropriate for describing phenomena and are especially useful when a manipulation is not feasible. Experimental methods best meet the standards of internal validity and best permit causal inferences to be drawn. The choice of research method depends on the purpose of the investigation, as well as practical and ethical considerations. Scientific endeavors are enriched by the availability of various methods.

Time Frames in Research

In addition to the distinctions among research methods described above, investigations differ with regard to time.

CROSS-SECTIONAL RESEARCH

In this approach, participants are observed at one point in time, as if a snapshot were being taken. Group comparisons are frequently made between groups that differ in age or developmental status. For instance, aggression displayed by 8-, 10-, and 12-year-olds might be compared. Cross-sectional research is relatively inexpensive and efficient, and has contributed significantly to understanding development and psychological problems.

Nevertheless, tracing developmental change with cross-sectional research is problematic and can be misleading. If younger children display more aggression, it might be concluded that aggression decreases as children develop. But this conclusion may not be warranted. What we are seeing is an *age difference*, which is not necessarily *developmental change*.

Perhaps specific experiences of the age groups, due to societal changes over time, are responsible for the findings. The younger children might have received more reinforcement for aggression during an era characterized by greater violence and aggression.

RETROSPECTIVE LONGITUDINAL RESEARCH

Consistent with the meaning of the word *retrospective*, retrospective longitudinal research goes back in time. Adolescents may be identified on some variable of interest—such as a specific disorder—and information about their earlier characteristics and life experiences is then collected. One type of study that is frequently retrospective is the case-control study, in which a group that has been diagnosed with a disorder is compared with a group without the disorder. The purpose of this follow-back method is to seek hypotheses about the predictors or causes of the observed disturbance. In retrospective studies, caution is warranted by possible unreliability of the data because old records and memories of the past may be sketchy, biased, or mistaken. Nevertheless, the discovery of a relationship of earlier-occurring variables with the disorder can suggest risk or causal factors.

PROSPECTIVE LONGITUDINAL RESEARCH

In prospective longitudinal research, individuals are observed and then evaluated with repeated observations as time passes. In "seeing" development as it occurs, the method can uniquely answer questions about the nature and course of development. For instance, children with language disabilities can be tested at specific time intervals to discern how the deficits change as the children develop. Comparison with a group showing no language problems would be valuable. Prospective longitudinal research can be informative with regard to numerous kinds of questions. Youth who experience an early traumatic event, birth complications, or risks associated with poverty can be assessed over periods of time to determine factors related to their development. Girls and boys diagnosed with ADHD can be followed into adulthood to ascertain gender difference in outcome, if any, and the variables implicated.

This method is highly valued, but it has several drawbacks. The studies are expensive and require investigators to commit to a project for many years. Retaining participants over long periods of time may be difficult, and the loss of participants can bias the sample when dropouts are more transient, less psychologically oriented, or less healthy than those who continue. Another problem is that repeated testing of participants may make them test-wise, but attempting to control for this by changing test instruments makes it difficult to compare earlier and later findings. In addition, in planning long-term studies, researchers must take educated guesses about which variables to observe along the way, and they may miss relevant factors. For example, in discussing their 30-year longitudinal project, Sroufe and colleagues (2005) note that in hindsight they would have included measures of neurophysiological functioning that might have provided valuable information.

Finally, in interpreting longitudinal results, it is important to consider possible societal changes. If individuals were followed from birth to age 20 from 1950 to 1970, their development might be different, due to historical factors, from that of persons of the same age span followed from 1980 to 2000. The 1950–1970 group would likely have had different experiences than would the 1980–2000 group (e.g., in health care, social environments, and educational opportunity). These possible generational, or cohort, effects must be considered in interpreting longitudinal studies.

ACCELERATED LONGITUDINAL RESEARCH

To overcome some of the weaknesses of the cross-sectional and prospective longitudinal methods, researchers interested in developmental change can conduct accelerated longitudinal research, which combine the two approaches in a variety of designs.

Take, for example, a hypothetical study in which groups of children of different ages are studied over a relatively short time span. At Time I, children aged 3, 6, and 9 years are examined in a cross-sectional study. Similar examination of the same groups of children occurs again 3 years later at Time II, and again another 3 years later at Time III. Figure 4–6 depicts the study. It is clear from reading down the columns of the figure that cross-sectional comparisons can be made at three different times. In addition, as is apparent by reading from left to right across the figure, the children (A, B, and C) are studied longitudinally over a 6-year period (2000–2006). The age range in the investigation is thus 12 years (from 3 to 15 years), although the study is completed in 6 years.

Various comparisons can provide a wealth of information from such a design. To consider a possibility, if aggression were found to increase with age at Times I, II, and III (cross-sectional analyses) and also across time for each group of children (the longitudinal analyses), evidence would be strong for developmental change over the entire age range. Moreover, by comparing aggression at age 6, or 9, or 12 (as shaded in the figure), the impact of societal conditions could also be evaluated. It might be found, for example, that aggression at age 9 increased from the year 2000 to 2003 to 2006. Since only one age is involved, this increase is not developmental and likely indicates a change in societal conditions during the years under investigation. Thus, accelerated longitudinal designs can be a powerful way to separate age differences and developmental changes, while taking generational effects into consideration.

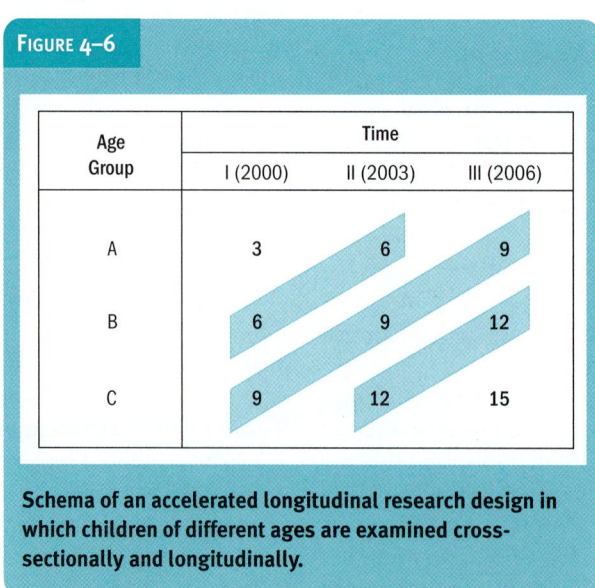

FIGURE 4–6

Age Group	Time		
	I (2000)	II (2003)	III (2006)
A	3	6	9
B	6	9	12
C	9	12	15

Schema of an accelerated longitudinal research design in which children of different ages are examined cross-sectionally and longitudinally.

Qualitative Research

Most of the research we have examined—and most research employed in studying psychopathology in youth—is quantitative. (See also Accent: "Epidemiological Research: More than Counting Noses.") Quantitative methods are essential to the empirical or positivistic paradigm that underlies much of the scientific progress made in modern times (Eisner, 2003). This perspective favors theory-guided objective measurement done by objective investigators in controlled situations.

Advocates of qualitative research point to what they see as many shortcomings of quantitative methods. They emphasize their own assumptions and values (Higgins et al., 2002; Simonton, 2003). Among these are the following:

- The qualitative approach facilitates the study of issues significant to real-world contexts.

- Events can be best understood when they are observed in natural environments rather than in contrived laboratory settings.

- Human behavior and development are best understood from a personal frame of reference when individuals have the opportunity to speak for themselves about their beliefs, attitudes, and experiences, and the meanings in their lives.

- Human experience should not be viewed in terms of separate variables but as a unified whole.

ACCENT ● ● ● ●

Epidemiological Research: More than Counting Noses

Although epidemiological research is not unique in its methods of research, its importance to the study of abnormal child and adolescent psychology warrants consideration. The approach has a basis in medicine and initially focused on investigating infectious diseases in populations. With regard to psychopathology, epidemiology can be defined as the quantitative study of the distribution and causes of disorder in human populations (Regier & Burke, 2000). Cases of disorder are identified in large populations, or representative samples of the populations, and several kinds of data about the disorders may be collected and analyzed.

One goal of epidemiology is to monitor the rates of disorders in populations, which may be measured in several ways (Table 4–3). This goal is valuable particularly because the focus on community rather than on clinical samples reduces the likelihood of selection bias. But epidemiology does much more than descriptively "count noses" (Costello, Egger, & Angold, 2005). How cases of disorder are distributed in a population provides information pertinent to risk and causation. For example, the revelation that prevalence of eating disorder increases at adolescence, especially in females, puts emphasis on causal questions regarding timing and gender. What is there about adolescence and about being female that makes a difference? Or to take another example, the lack of a correlation in population samples between autism and social class helped put to rest the belief that SES variables were important in the etiology of autism.

Although the hallmark of epidemiology is a focus on populations, assessment of individuals to determine disorder has been a central and knotty issue. Epidemiologists need to identify "cases" in large non-clinic populations. An important shift in this process has occurred. Instead of the lengthier expensive clinical interviews they once employed, researchers have increasingly used standardized structured or semi-structured interviews (Costello et al., 2005). These instruments are more efficient, many are reasonably reliable, and they facilitate comparison of the results from different investigations.

Today, epidemiology seeks to understand what groups of people are at high risk for a disorder, what factors or other dysfunctions are correlated with the disorder, what the causes and modes of transmission are, and how the disorder can be prevented or reduced. Epidemiologists interested in young people are applying the developmental perspective, for example, by measuring risk and protection and studying disorders from the time of risk to onset of disorder to outcome (Costello & Angold, 2000, 2006). In addition, epidemiology is increasingly turning to the positive aspects of health and to mental health services and policies, for example, by analyzing data on quality of life and the use of mental health services (Mezzich & Üstun, 2005). The approach is thus broadly contributing to understanding, preventing, and treating psychological problems of youth.

TABLE 4–3	SOME COMMONLY USED MEASURES IN EPIDEMIOLOGICAL RESEARCH
Prevalence	Rates of a disorder in a population at a specific point in time (e.g., total number of cases or proportion of the population)
Lifetime prevalence	Number or proportion of cases of a disorder diagnosed at any time during life
Incidence	Rates of cases of a disorder diagnosed during a specified time period

Consistent with these assumptions and values, laboratory and experimental manipulations are avoided in favor of methods such as in-depth interviews, intensive case studies, and life histories (e.g., Yow, 2005). Naturalistic observation is also important, with observations recorded in narration rather than with a restrictive coding of categories. Observer participation, in which the observer engages in and becomes a part of the setting, is valued as a way to collect credible data and to optimize understanding.

It is not unusual to collect large amounts of written data in qualitative research. Once collected, the narrative data are conceptualized, analyzed, and interpreted. This process may entail coding or categorizing statements or written observations. The categories are often viewed as arising naturally from the data rather than being based on predetermined expectations or constructed coding systems. What gets coded, how the coding is accomplished, and how data are interpreted vary with the approach and aims of the study. Quantification of data is minimal and statistical analysis has little, if any, role.

EXAMPLES OF QUALITATIVE STUDIES

Examples of topics that have been examined with qualitative methods are life experiences of individuals diagnosed in childhood as learning disabled, parents' and siblings' adjustment to having a handicapped family member, and parents' experiences regarding their child's life-threatening illness (Fiese & Bickman, 1998; Flaton, 2006; Krahn et al., 1995; McNulty, 2003).

As an example of the strategy, consider a study of parents' experiences as participants in a support program called Parent to Parent (Ainbinder et al., 1998). The specific purpose of the program was to provide support for parents who had a child with disabilities, such as mental retardation or chronic illness. Each parent was matched with a trained supporting parent who had a child with a similar disability and who provided information and emotional

support, usually by telephone. One of the ways in which the program was evaluated was through a qualitative, semistructured interview with participating parents, which explored the impact and meaning of being matched with a supportive parent. The transcribed telephone interviews were coded and categorized according to themes that emerged from the telephone conversations. Among the themes were the way the program was helpful, reasons for program failure, availability and mutuality of support, skills and information learned by the parents, and personal growth of the parents. The following examples from the parents' interviews reflect two of the themes.

Learning by the Parent. *I wanted some reassurance that [our daughter] is likely to have most of the same things everybody else has, as far as you know, going to school and having friends, going out and doing things. And [our supporting Parent's] daughter's involved in a lot of things. She's got a good life. And that gave me a great deal of hope about the future of our daughter, that she can have a good life, too. (p. 104)*

Failure of the Program. *And the other thing I've found with [the supporting parent], her baby is not doing very well sometimes. . . . She asks how my baby is and he has been doing very healthy, thank God. I don't want to say "doing great." . . . We don't share a lot about our children, actually, which is kind of what I would like. . . . I find the only time I really want to call her is if I have a problem because then I don't feel bad about saying "I have this problem and what do you think I should do?" (p. 106)*

Overall, the data indicated that talking, sharing, comparing, and learning with others who are perceived as similar can enhance coping and adaptability. The qualitative analysis of Parent to Parent provided understanding of the strengths and weaknesses of the program in a way that other data, collected from quantitative surveys, had not provided.

Weaknesses and Strengths

Like other strategies, qualitative methods have weaknesses. Sample size is often small, huge amounts of data can be difficult and costly to analyze, and questions are raised about reliability and validity. At the same time, qualitative findings can increase basic knowledge, suggest hypotheses, and illustrate and enrich quantitative findings. It also can be argued that current cultural trends are consistent with qualitative methods. The commitment to contextual research is strong, and there is high regard for applying psychological knowledge to societal problems and concerns—both of which call for research to be conducted in community and other natural settings (Fabes et al., 2000; Lerner, Fisher, & Weinberg, 2000).

Qualitative and quantitative strategies have often been viewed as adversarial (Rogers, 2000), and yet they are not necessarily at odds with each other and can be employed together. The qualitative procedures provide flexible, broad-scope investigation, whereas the quantitative procedures provide more traditional data collection and hypothesis testing. In combination, this double approach can extend the scope of the findings and each data set can serve as a check on the other, increasing confidence in the findings.

Ethical Issues

Scientific research is enormously beneficial, but it brings concerns about the welfare and rights of participants. Underlying such concerns is sensitivity to individual rights—both ethical and legal—and to past documented abuse of research participants. One well-known instance in which the problem of abuse was raised involved research into the natural course of hepatitis. From the 1950s to the 1970s, children with mental retardation who resided in the Willowbrook school in the state of New York were deliberately infected with hepatitis in order to study the disease (Glantz, 1996). Although specific instances like this of past abuse in biomedical research appear especially egregious, ethical issues in all areas require continuous attention.

For many years, government agencies and professional organizations have published ethical guidelines for research. Philosophical underpinnings were presented in the *Belmont Report: Ethical Principles and Guidelines for the Protection of Human Subjects of Research*, which led to the Code of Federal Regulations pertaining to human research participants (National Commission, 1979). The American Psychological Association's *Ethical Principles of Psychologists and Code of Conduct* addresses the multiple professional roles of psychologists, including that of the researcher (American Psychological Association, 2002). The guidelines of the Society for Research in Child Development specifically address research with youth. Table 4–4 shows an abbreviated version of these standards (two additional Principles concern scientific and personal misconduct of the researcher). There is considerable overlap in the guidelines adopted by different agencies and disciplines.

Depending on funding and the setting, research proposals may be reviewed by federally mandated Institutional Review Boards (IRBs), or by local review boards. IRBs consider such issues as the scientific soundness of the proposed research, voluntary consent of the participants, and potential harm and benefits to the participants (U.S. Department of Health and Human Services, 2005). Particular consideration is given to vulnerable persons, including youth, the mentally disabled, and the economically disadvantaged. Whether or not an official review is required, adhering to ethical standards is a mandate for all researchers. Although doing as mandated may seem quite simple, ethical concerns are often complex. The following discussion covers a few major issues.

Voluntary Informed Consent

Fundamental to most ethical guidelines is the voluntary consent of individuals to participate, given that they understand the investigation. The requirement of voluntary informed consent, which is viewed as a component of respect due all participants, often calls for written consent. Among other things, participants should know the purpose of the research, procedures, risks and benefits, and their option to refuse participation or to withdraw at any time (Richards, 2003). They should have the competence to understand the information and to judge risk and benefits. Coercion and undue influence should not be present. It is presumed that immaturity hinders children's ability to fully understand these issues and make informed decisions. Thus, until children have reached the legal age of consent, usually age 18, researchers typically require consent on their behalf from their parents or guardians.

Like some other standards, the American Psychological Association's standard dispenses with informed consent in special instances, such as research on educational curricula that would likely create no stress or harm (APA, 2002). Also like other standards, it recommends that persons not of legal age

TABLE 4–4	ETHICAL STANDARDS FOR RESEARCH WITH CHILDREN

Principle 1: Nonharmful Procedures. No research operation that may physically or psychologically harm the child should be used. The least stressful operation should be used. Doubts about harmfulness should be discussed with consultants.

Principle 2: Informed Consent. The child's consent or assent should be obtained. The child should be informed of features of the research that may affect his or her willingness to participate. When research participants are infants, their parents should be informed. If consent would make the research impossible, it may be ethically conducted under certain circumstances; judgments should be made with Institutional Review Boards.

Principle 3: Parental Consent. Informed consent of parents, guardians, and those acting in loci parentis (e.g., school superintendents) similarly should be obtained, preferably in writing.

Principle 4: Additional Consent. Informed consent should be obtained of persons, such as teachers, whose interaction with the child is the subject of the research.

Principle 5: Incentives. Incentives to participate in the research must be fair and not unduly exceed incentives the child normally experiences.

Principle 6: Deception. If deception or withholding information is considered essential, colleagues must agree with this judgment. Participants should be told later of the reason for the deception. Efforts should be made to employ deception methods that have no known negative effects.

Principle 7: Anonymity. Permission should be gained for access to institutional records, and anonymity of information should be preserved.

Principle 8: Mutual Responsibilities. There should be clear agreement as to the responsibilities of all parties in the research. The investigator must honor all promises and commitments.

Principle 9: Jeopardy. When, in the research, information comes to the investigator's attention about circumstances that may jeopardize the child's welfare, the information must be discussed with parents or guardians and experts who can arrange for assistance to the child.

Principle 10: Unforeseen Consequences. When research procedures result in unforeseen, undesirable consequences for the participant, the consequences should be corrected and the procedures redesigned.

Principle 11: Confidentiality. The identity of participants and information about them should be kept confidential. When confidentiality might be threatened, this possibility and methods to prevent it should be explained as part of the procedures of obtaining informed consent.

Principle 12: Informing the Participants. Immediately after data collection, any misconceptions that might have arisen should be clarified. General findings should be given to the participants, appropriate to their understanding. When scientific or humane reasons justify withholding information, efforts should be made to ensure that withholding has no damaging consequences.

Principle 13: Reporting Results. Investigators' words may carry unintended weight; thus, caution should be used in reporting results, giving advice, and making evaluative statements.

Principle 14: Implications of Findings. Investigators should be mindful of the social, political, and human implications of the research, and especially careful in the presentations of findings.

Summarized from the Society for Research in Child Development, 2007. http://www.srcd.org/ethicalstandards.html.

should nevertheless be asked to assent, or agree, to participate. It is suggested that adolescents be given the same information as adults and asked to sign consent forms (e.g., Ferguson, 1978; Langer, 1985). This same procedure can be used for school-age children, with information being spelled out concretely. Regarding young children, Miller (1998) suggests that the following information might appropriately be conveyed: a general idea of what will happen ("play a game"), where it will occur ("in Mr. Smith's office"), how many people will be involved ("just you and me"), how long it will take ("about 20 minutes"), whether others will do the same thing ("lots of kids from the class will be doing this"), whether a reward will be offered ("get a little prize at the end") and the opportunity to assent ("Would you like to come?"). Obviously, with infants and toddlers, informed consent is an unreasonable expectation, and parental or guardian consent is usually sufficient.

CONFIDENTIALITY

Research may involve the participants giving personal information. The principle of confidentiality assumes that they have the right to control the degree to which information can be disclosed to others. It is often necessary for the researcher to know the identity of the participant who provides specific information. However, information can be kept confidential by numbering or otherwise coding individual reports, and avoiding all names in public accounts of the research.

Several issues arise when the participants are children or adolescents (Richards, 2003). Parents, schools, and other agencies involved may be interested in the course and outcome of the research. The researcher can limit the information given to parents, as in cases in which disclosure can put the child at risk. On the other hand, in some instances, the sharing of information might potentially benefit the young person, for example, in research on adolescent use of illicit drugs. Investigators may reveal information when participants appear in danger of harming themselves or others. Participating youth, parents, and relevant agencies should understand the limits of confidentially prior to the investigation.

BALANCING IT ALL: HARM AND GOOD

A critical ethical principle is that no serious harm—physical, psychological, legal, or economic—should be done to participants. Research that, for instance, engages children in aggressive acts or exposes them to aggressive models raises questions of possible harm. Children also participate in research on the effects of medications, which can entail complex ethical dilemmas. Clearly, it is necessary to guard against the potential for harm, a principle that is referred to as nonmaleficience.

Moreover, the ethical principle of beneficience, based on respect for each individual, requires that benefits be maximized. It is not always possible for individuals to benefit personally from the research that they participate in, but a risk–benefit ratio should be considered (Hoagwood, 2003). In general, when greater benefit to the participant is likely, greater risk of harm is more acceptable. Obviously this guideline has limits in that risk of serious harm is virtually never acceptable.

In the final analysis, judgments about what is ethical often involve balancing several factors. Indeed, IRBs were instituted to aid in finding a balance between society's need for knowledge and participants' need for protection in research (Hayes, 2003). The individual's competence to understand and voluntarily consent, the risk of harm, and the possibility of benefit all play a crucial role in guiding ethical standards. Like other ethical concerns, the ethics of research can never be a completely settled matter, and ongoing discussion and tension are appropriate. Reasonable balance must be maintained, however, if beneficial research is to go forward.

When a youth participates in research, informed consent by a parent or guardian, and possibly by the youth, should usually be obtained. What constitutes informed consent by a child is a complex issue.
(Courtesy of A. C. Israel)

SUMMARY

FUNDAMENTALS OF RESEARCH

- *The aim of science is to describe phenomena and offer explanations for them.*
- *Scientific knowledge is based on systematic formulation, observation, and interpretation of findings.*
- *Hypothesis testing builds knowledge systematically and is tied to the advancement of theory.*
- *The selection of research participants is critical. Random selection best ensures that a sample represents the population from which it is drawn.*
- *Observation and measurement are accomplished in various ways in various settings. The behavior or concept being studied must be operationalized. Efforts should be made to achieve reliable (consistent) and valid (accurate) measurements.*
- *Reliability (consistency) of research results is important, as is validity (correctness) of findings. Internal validity is the degree to which alternative explanations for results can be confidently ruled out. External validity refers to generalizability of findings to other populations and settings.*

BASIC METHODS OF RESEARCH

- *Numerous research methods are employed, each suited to particular purposes and each having weaknesses and strengths. Research methods can be categorized as descriptive (nonexperimental) or experimental, the latter of which can be viewed as randomized or quasi-experimental.*
- *Case studies can provide compelling descriptions; correlational methods provide information about the relationships among variables; experiments of nature examine naturally occurring events.*
- *Randomized experiments and single-subject experiments best meet the standards for establishing causality.*

TIME FRAMES IN RESEARCH

- *The cross-sectional strategy examines groups of people at a particular point in time; it is not a strong tool for evaluating developmental change. Retrospective longitudinal research goes back in time; it can generate hypotheses. The prospective longitudinal strategy, which makes repeated observations over time, is valued for tracing development. Accelerated longitudinal designs combine the cross-sectional and prospective longitudinal approaches to permit examination of developmental change, age differences, and the influence of generational effects.*

EPIDEMIOLOGY

- *Epidemiology focuses on studying disorders in populations. It investigates the rates and distribution of disorders as well as correlates, causes, course, transmission, and interventions.*

QUALITATIVE RESEARCH

- *Qualitative research places high value on individuals' perception of their experiences in their natural environments. Data are collected through in-depth interviews, life histories, and the like. This strategy and the quantitative strategy—which values control, manipulation, and quantitative measures—are often seen as adversarial but can be complementary.*

ETHICAL ISSUES

- *Ethical issues in the conduct of research are addressed by several government agencies and professional organizations. Youth and those with mental disabilities require special protection.*
- *Central to ethical guidelines are voluntary informed consent, confidentiality, and assessment of risks and benefits to the participant.*

KEY TERMS

hypothesis testing *(p. 72)*

random selection *(p. 72)*

selection bias *(p. 73)*

operational definition *(p. 73)*

validity of measurement *(p. 73)*

reliability of measurement *(p. 74)*

internal validity *(p. 74)*

naturalistic observation *(p. 74)*

interobserver reliability *(p. 74)*

observer blindness *(p. 74)*

external validity *(p. 75)*

descriptive (nonexperimental) methods *(p. 75)*

experimental methods *(p. 75)*

randomized experiments *(p. 75)*

quasi-experimental studies *(p. 75)*

case study *(p. 76)*

correlational studies *(p. 77)*

positive correlation *(p. 77)*

negative correlation *(p. 77)*

experiments of nature *(p. 78)*

independent variable *(p. 78)*

dependent variable *(p. 78)*

statistical significance *(p. 79)*

single-case experimental designs *(p. 80)*

efficacy, effectiveness *(p. 80)*

cross-sectional research *(p. 83)*

retrospective longitudinal research *(p. 83)*

case-control study *(p. 83)*

prospective longitudinal research *(p. 83)*

generational (cohort) effects *(p. 84)*

accelerated longitudinal research *(p. 84)*

epidemiology *(p. 85)*

qualitative research *(p. 85)*

Institutional Review Boards (IRBs) *(p. 87)*

voluntary informed consent *(p. 87)*

confidentiality *(p. 89)*

nonmaleficence *(p. 89)*

beneficience *(p. 89)*

Classification, Assessment, and Intervention

Before we begin our discussion of specific problems and disorders, it is important to ask, "How are behavioral disorders of childhood and adolescence defined, grouped, evaluated, and treated?" In this chapter we will introduce the processes of classification, assessment, and intervention.

The terms *classification, taxonomy,* and *diagnosis* are used to refer to the process of description and grouping. Classification and taxonomy are the delineation of major categories or dimensions of behavioral disorders, done for either clinical or scientific purposes. Diagnosis usually refers to assigning a category of a classification system to an individual. Assessment refers to evaluating youngsters, in part to assist the processes of classification and diagnosis and in part to direct intervention. All of these entwined processes are intricately related to the clinical and scientific aspects of child and adolescent disorders.

Classification and Diagnosis

Classification systems are employed to systematically describe a phenomenon. Biologists have classification systems for living organisms, and physicians classify physical dysfunction. Similarly, systems exist to classify psychological dysfunction. These systems describe categories or dimensions of problem behaviors, emotions, and/or cognitions. A category is a discrete grouping, for example, anxiety disorder, into which an individual is judged to fit or not fit. In contrast, the term dimension implies that an attribute is continuous and can occur to various degrees. Thus, for example, a child may exhibit high, moderate, or low levels of anxiety.

Any classification system must have clearly defined categories or dimensions. In other words, the criteria for defining a category or dimension must be explicitly stated. Clear and explicit definitions allow for good communication among professionals. Also, diagnostic groupings must be clearly discriminable from one another. It must be demonstrated, too, that a category or dimension actually exist. That is, the features used to describe a category or dimension must occur together regularly, in one or more situations or as measured by one or more methods.

Classification systems must be reliable and valid. These terms were applied to research methods in chapter 4. When applied to classification or diagnosis, the terms retain the general meanings of consistency and correctness but are used in somewhat different ways.

Interrater reliability refers to whether different diagnosticians use the same category to describe a person's behavior. For example, it addresses the question, Is Maria's behavior called separation anxiety by two or more professionals who observe it? Test–retest reliability asks whether the use of a category is stable over some reasonable period of time. For example, is Sean's difficulty, originally diagnosed as oppositional–defiant disorder, diagnosed as the same disorder when he returns for a second evaluation?

There are also questions about the validity of diagnostic systems. To be valid, a diagnosis should provide us with more information than we had when we originally defined the category. Thus diagnoses should give us information about the etiology of a disorder, the course of development that the disorder is expected to take, response to treatment, or some additional clinical features of the problem. Does the diagnosis of conduct disorder, for example, tell us something about this disorder that is different from other disorders? Does the diagnosis tell us something about what causes this problem? Does it tell us what is likely to happen to youngsters who have this disorder and what treatments are likely to help? Does it tell us additional things about these young people or their backgrounds? The question of validity is thus largely one of whether we know anything we did not already know when we defined the category. Another important aspect of validity is whether our description of a disorder is accurate. Is the way we have described and classified this disorder the way it actually exists? Answering this question is often no easy matter and may require extensive clinical studies.

Finally, the clinical utility of a classification system is judged by how complete and useful it is. A diagnostic system that describes all the disorders that come to the attention of clinicians in a manner that is useful to them is more likely to be employed.

THE DSM APPROACH

The most widely used classification system in the United States is the American Psychiatric Association's Diagnostic and Statistical Manual of Mental Disorders (DSM). The Tenth Revision of the International Classification of Diseases (ICD) developed by the World Health Organization (1992) is an alternative system that is widely employed. The Diagnostic Classification of Mental Health and Developmental Disorders of Infancy and Early Childhood, Revised (DC: 0–3) is a system developed to classify mental disorders of very young children (Zero to Three, 2005). We will focus our discussion on the DSM because it is the dominant system in the United States.

The DSM is often referred to as a clinically derived classification system. Clinically derived classification systems are based on the consensus of clinicians that certain characteristics occur together. These have been described as "top down" approaches (Achenbach, 2000). Committees of experts propose concepts of disorders and then choose diagnostic criteria for defining disorders. It is from these criteria that the development of assessments and evaluations proceed.

The DSM is also a categorical approach to classification; a person either does or does not meet the criteria for a diagnosis. Thus, it is assumed that the difference between normal and pathological is one of *kind* rather than one of *degree*. This approach also suggests that distinctions can be made between *qualitatively* different types of disorders.

The DSM is an outgrowth of the original psychiatric taxonomy developed by Kraepelin in 1883. There have been a number of revisions of the DSM system. The most recent revisions are the DSM-IV and DSM-IV-TR. The DSM-IV-TR (Text Revision) was published to update information in the text material that accompanies the DSM-IV diagnostic criteria. It includes information about features that may be associated with disorders (e.g., low self-esteem) and information regarding cultural, age and gender features; probable course of the disorder; prevalence; familial patterns; and so on. This revision did not drop or add diagnostic categories, or change the diagnostic criteria for disorders (American Psychiatric Association, 2000).

Historically, the classification of abnormal behavior focused primarily on adult disorders and there was no extensive classification scheme for child and adolescent disorders (Silk et al., 2000). By the 1960s, it had become obvious that a more extensive system was needed. The DSM-II, III, and III-R expanded appreciably the number of categories specific to children and adolescents. In addition, some adult diagnoses could be used for children and adolescents. These revisions and the DSM-IV also involved some changes in the organization of particular categories (American Psychiatric Association, 1968; 1980; 1987; 1994).

The multiaxial system. The DSM is often described as a multiaxial system. Table 5–1 provides an overview of this approach. In the DSM-IV-TR, all disorders are classified in one of two major groups called axes. On Axis I, the clinician indicates any existing clinical disorder (e.g., Conduct Disorder) or other condition that may be a focus of treatment (for example, an academic problem). On Axis II, Mental Retardation or a Personality Disorder, if present, is indicated. These two axes represent the diagnostic categories that are the core of the DSM system. In addition to these two axes, it is recommended that each individual be evaluated in three other arenas, in order to create a fuller picture. Any current medical conditions that are relevant to understanding or treating the child or adolescent are indicated on Axis III. Axis IV is used to indicate any psychosocial or environmental problems that may affect diagnosis, treatment, or prognosis (e.g., death of a family member or housing problems). Axis V allows the clinician to make a numerical (0 to 100) judgment of the youngster's overall level of adaptive functioning (Global Assessment of Functioning—GAF). For example, a score of

- 100 would indicate superior functioning in a wide range of activities;

- 70 might indicate generally good functioning, but some difficulty in social or school environments;

- 50 might indicate serious impairment in social or school functioning; and

- 30 might indicate serious impairment in communication or judgment or inability to function in almost all areas.

How this multiaxial system might be used is illustrated by its application to Kevin in the following example.

Kevin   Seeking a Diagnosis

Kevin is a 9-year-old third-grader. He was brought to the clinic after his teacher repeatedly called home about his worsening behavior in school. The teacher described Kevin as likeable and friendly, but also said that, among other things, he repeatedly disrupted the class with his antics, hummed and made noises, blurted out answers, and had to be constantly reminded to stay in his seat. He was full of energy on the playground, but seemed to have few playmates and was often last to be chosen for teams. When playing games such as softball, he might be in the outfield concentrating on things in the sky or interesting pebbles on the ground. Although he seemed very bright, Kevin seldom completed his assignments in class. Despite his mother's report of considerable time and effort being spent on getting Kevin to concentrate on and complete his homework, papers sent home were seldom returned and homework was forgotten or left crumpled in his book bag.

At home Kevin is always on the go, his play is noisy and he leaves a trail of toys in his wake. Chores are left uncompleted or not done at all. Kevin's mother describes him as "the sweetest boy imaginable," but also as a "real handful." A physical examination indicates that Kevin is healthy, well nourished, and in good physical condition except for several scrapes, bruises, and healed lacerations. The only significant medical history is a broken wrist at age 3 that resulted from a fall from a high wall that Kevin had managed to climb. Kevin's birth and early development were normal, and he reached developmental milestones at a normal or early time.

To illustrate the use of the DSM-IV-TR multiaxial system, here is Kevin's diagnosis.

TABLE 5–1	THE DSM MULTIAXIAL SYSTEM
Axis I	Clinical disorders
	Other conditions that may be the focus of clinical attention
Axis II	Personality disorders
	Mental retardation
Axis III	General medical conditions
Axis IV	Psychosocial and environmental problems
Axis V	Global assessment of functioning

From American Psychiatric Association, 2000.

Axis I: Attention-Deficit Hyperactivity Disorder, Combined Type;

Academic Problem

Axis II: No diagnosis

Axis III: None

Axis IV: Impending school expulsion

Axis V: GAF = 50 (serious impairment in schoolwork, moderate impairment in social relationships)

Adapted from Frances & Ross, 2001, pp. 8–11.

The diagnostic categories. Table 5–2 presents the major DSM-IV-TR diagnostic categories described as "usually first diagnosed in infancy, childhood, or adolescence." Each category is further divided into subcategories. A clinician may give a young person any of these diagnoses or a diagnosis from elsewhere in the DSM. Some of the other diagnostic categories that might be employed for youngsters are substance use disorders, schizophrenia, mood disorders, anxiety disorders, eating disorders, and sleep disorders.

Comorbidity. One important aspect of the use of the current DSM diagnostic system is what has been termed comorbidity. This term is used to describe the situation in which youngsters meet the criteria for more than one disorder. The use of the term is controversial and some prefer the term co-occurrence (Lilienfeld, Waldman, & Israel, 1994; Widiger & Clark, 2000). Comorbidity typically implies the simultaneous existence of two or more distinct disorders in the same individual. Such co-occurrence is frequently reported (see Accent: "Co-Occurrence: A Common Circumstance") and has led some to question the DSM approach to classification. Do these youngsters have multiple distinct disorders, or are

there other ways of understanding the many difficulties that they are experiencing?

There are multiple ways to interpret the situation when a child or an adolescent meets the diagnostic criteria for more than one disorder (Angold, Costello, & Erkanli, 1999; Carson & Rutter, 1991). It may be that many disorders have mixed patterns of symptoms. For example, mood disorders may be characterized by a mixture of depression and anxiety. Another alternative is that there are shared risk factors: Some of the same risk factors lead to the problems used to define both disorders. Or perhaps the presence of one disorder creates an increased risk for developing the other disorder. A related idea is that the second problem is a later stage in a developmental progression in which earlier problems may or may not be retained, even as additional difficulties develop. For example, for some children and adolescents, a diagnosis of oppositional defiant disorder is followed by a diagnosis of conduct disorder. It has been suggested that for these youngsters the diagnoses represent a developmental pattern of a single common condition.

These are only some of the possible hypotheses to explain "comorbidity." The issues involved in understanding co-occurrence of disorders are complex, and at present the solution to this issue remains unclear. However, the frequency of co-occurrence and the conceptual issues it raises are at the heart of how we conceptualize child and adolescent psychopathology (Knapp & Jensen, 2006; Lilienfeld, 2003).

Evaluating the DSM. Over time efforts have been made to improve the DSM system. These include the more comprehensive coverage of child and adolescent disorders, the increased use of structured diagnostic rules, and attempts to draw on empirical data in a more consistent fashion (Widiger et al., 1991). However,

TABLE 5–2	THE DSM DISORDERS USUALLY FIRST DIAGNOSED IN INFANCY, CHILDHOOD, OR ADOLESCENCE
Mental Retardation	Feeding and Eating Disorders of Infancy or Early Childhood
Learning Disorders	
Motor Skills Disorders	Tic Disorder
Communication Disorders	Elimination Disorders
Pervasive Developmental Disorders (e.g., Autistic Disorder)	Other Disorders of Infancy, Childhood, or Adolescence (e.g., Separation Anxiety Disorder, Selective)
Attention-Deficit and Disruptive Behavior Disorders	Mutism

From American Psychiatric Association, 2000.

ACCENT ● ● ● ● ● ●

Co-Occurrence: A Common Circumstance

Children and adolescents who are evaluated by professionals in clinic or school settings often present with several different problems. These problems frequently fit the criteria for a number of different disorders, and thus clinicians often give these children or adolescents more than one diagnosis. How best to conceptualize these instances of co-occurrence or comorbidity is an ongoing concern. The description of Samuel that follows illustrates this common circumstance.

Samuel | A Case of Co-Occurring Disorders

Samuel, an 11-year-old child, was referred to a clinic for attempted suicide after he had consumed a mixture of medicines, prescribed to his mother, in an attempt to kill himself. Samuel had slept at home for almost two days, when he was finally awakened by his mother and brought to the hospital.

Samuel lived in an inner-city neighborhood and since second grade had been in repeated trouble for stealing and breaking into empty homes. He had academic difficulties, was assigned to a special reading class, and was truant from school on a number of occasions. His mother may have experienced several major depressive episodes, sometimes drank heavily, and may have relied on prostitution for income. Samuel's father had not been in contact with the mother since Samuel was born.

At his interview, Samuel appeared sad and cried at one point. He reported having severe "blue periods," the most recent of which had been continuous for the past month. During these periods he thought that he might be better off dead. Samuel also reported that he had recently started to wake up in the middle of the night and had been avoiding his usual neighborhood "gang."

Samuel was given a diagnosis of Major Depressive Disorder, and a diagnosis of Dysthymia (a milder but more chronic form of depression) was also considered. In addition he received a diagnosis of Conduct Disorder, Childhood Onset Type, and a diagnosis of Reading Disorder.

Adapted from Rapoport & Ismond, 1996.

substantial scientific, conceptual, and political issues remain unresolved (Carrey & Ungar, 2007; Follette & Houts, 1996; Jensen & Mrazek, 2006; Kupfer, First, & Regier, 2002; Nathan & Langenbucher, 1999). Because the DSM is currently the dominant approach to classification, it is important to mention some continuing issues and some of the concerns that have been raised regarding this system.

For example, while greater attention to the disorders of children and adolescents can be seen as a positive development, there is at the same time concern about the proliferation of categories and the very comprehensiveness of the DSM system (Houts, 2002). This raises the fundamental question (Follete & Houts, 1996; Silk et al., 2000) that perhaps we have overdefined pathological behavior—in other words, too broadly defined children's behavior as deviant (cf. Richters & Cicchetti, 1993). Designating common misbehaviors or various problems in academic skill areas such as reading and mathematics as mental disorders are examples of this concern.

One of the considerations that guided the development of the DSM is reliability. In earlier versions, disagreements between diagnosticians (interrater reliability) resulted from inadequate criteria for making a diagnosis. Thus efforts were made starting with the DSM-III to improve interrater reliability by replacing general descriptions of disorders with clearer and more delineated diagnostic criteria based on a listing of symptoms. This approach has improved communication among clinicians and researchers and has increased interclinician agreement in diagnosis. As would be expected, however, reliability still varies and may depend on the specific disorder, the nature and source of information available, other characteristics of the youngster such as gender or ethnicity, or characteristics of the clinician. Furthermore, evidence of higher levels of reliability has typically been obtained under research conditions in which diagnosticians are given special training and employ procedures different from those likely to be used in typical clinical practice (APA Working Group on Psychoactive Medications for Children and Adolescents, 2006; Nathan & Langenbucher, 1999; Pottick et al., 2007; Rapee et al., 1994).

It has been argued as well that diagnostic research has focused too heavily on reliability and clarity of communication. Although these issues are clearly important, it is also crucial for the DSM to provide an accurate representation of the nature of disorders. Whether a system is useful or helpful for clinicians, a question of utility, is different from whether it is a good description of the true nature of clinically significant differences in psychological functioning—a question of validity (Knapp & Jensen, 2006; Sonuga-Barke, 1998).

Indeed, many of the questions raised to guide the future development of classification are questions of the validity of the current system. For example, validity would be indicated if research discovered treatments or etiologies that were *specific to particular syndromes*. However, as Kupfer, First, and Regier (2002) point out, many medications have been reported as being effective in treating several DSM disorders. Similarly, with regard to etiology, research studies have challenged the assumption that separate disorders have a different underlying genetic basis. For example, it has been found that anxiety and depression may share genetic risk factors (Williamson et al., 2005).

An additional concern is that the DSM promotes a disease/medical model that emphasizes biological etiology and treatment, and that conceptualizes disorder as being within the child rather than resulting from the interaction of the child and the environment (Carrey & Ungar, 2007; Silk et al., 2000; Sonuga-Barke, 1998; Sroufe, 1997).

Concern has also been expressed regarding the DSM's relative inattention to issues of cultural context, age, and gender (Achenbach, 2000; Nathan & Langenbucher, 1999; Silk et al., 2000). The DSM-IV-TR does include, in the text that accompanies each set of diagnostic criteria, a section on "Specific Culture, Age, and Gender Features" that may alert clinicians to variations associated with culture, developmental level, and gender. Nevertheless, diagnostic criteria are largely the same for both genders and for all ages and cultures.

This approach may have important consequences. Achenbach (2000), for example, points out that if one applies a set of fixed cutpoints (number of symptoms needed for diagnosis) to diagnostic criteria, disorders may appear to have prevalence rates that vary with age and gender. The same applies to cultural differences. We could ask, however, whether these are real differences in rates of disorders. As an example, DSM-IV-TR indicates that ADHD is much more frequent in males. This gender difference in diagnosis has led the literature on ADHD to be based largely on males.

However, even nondeviant boys exhibit higher rates of behaviors characteristic of ADHD than do girls. Thus the gender difference in ADHD might be an artifact of higher base rates of these behaviors in boys. If these gender differences in base rates in the population were considered in setting diagnostic cutpoints, would gender differences in prevalence of ADHD still emerge? Similarly, reported declines in the rates of ADHD diagnoses with age may also be an artifact of the age-related decline in base rates of ADHD behaviors.

Furthermore, research suggests that the potentially complex interactions of culture, context, and behavior deserve further attention. For example, Gil and colleagues (2000) found that among U.S.-born Latino adolescent males, a greater predisposition toward alcohol involvement emerges over time as traditional values of family, cohesion, and social control deteriorate. Weisz and colleagues (2006) compared Thai and American adolescents, and found behavior problem syndromes relating to dependence and immaturity among Thai youngsters, whereas there were not comparable syndromes among American youth. The authors suggest that this is consistent with literature suggesting that Thai parenting may foster more prolonged dependence and slower psychological maturation than American parenting. It seems clear that future diagnostic and classification systems will need to pay increasing attention to issues of cultural and developmental context (Alarcon et al., 2002; Jensen & Mrazek, 2006; Pine et al., 2002; Rescorla et al., 2007).

Finally, a frequently expressed concern regarding the validity of the current DSM is its categorical approach. For example, research supported the validity of three subtypes of Attention-Deficit Hyperactivity Disorder (Lahey et al., 1994). However, Hudziak and his colleagues (1998) conducted structured diagnostic assessments of a large community sample of adolescent female twins. Their findings again supported the existence of the subtypes but suggested that the subtypes were best conceptualized as three dimensions (continuously distributed between clinical and nonclinical levels) rather than three distinct categories. Thus, is the nature of these disorders categorical (as represented in the DSM), dimensional, or both? Researchers also point out that the practice of dichotomizing continuous symptoms to form a disorder category and a nondisorder category results in reduced statistical power and may lead to misleading research outcomes. The category versus dimension question will be a central issue as systems of classification continue to be considered (Beauchaine, 2003; Doss & Weisz, 2006; Pickles & Angold, 2003; Widiger & Clark, 2000).

Many observers accept the DSM system as a dominant reality in the present zeitgeist. A classification system, like anything else, is influenced by the general social atmosphere within which it exists. With the various concerns and criticisms in mind, we turn to an alternative approach to classification.

EMPIRICAL APPROACHES TO CLASSIFICATON

The empirical approach to classification of behavioral problems is an alternative to the clinical approach to taxonomy. It is based on the use of statistical techniques to identify patterns of behavior that are interrelated. The general procedure is for a parent or some other respondent to indicate the presence or absence of specific behaviors in the youngster. The information from these responses is quantified in some way. For example, the respondent marks a "0" if the youth does not exhibit a certain characteristic, a "1" if the youth displays a moderate degree of the characteristic, and a "2" if the characteristic is clearly present. Such information is obtained for a large number of youngsters. Statistical techniques such as factor analysis are then employed, and groups of items that tend to occur together are thus identified (Achenbach, 1998). These groups are referred to as factors or clusters. The term syndrome is also often employed to describe behaviors that tend to occur together, whether they are identified by empirical or clinical judgment procedures.

Thus, rather than relying on clinicians' views about which behaviors tend to occur together, researchers can employ empirical and statistical procedures as the basis for developing a classification scheme.

Substantial evidence exists for two broadband syndromes, or general clusters of behaviors or characteristics. One of these clusters has been given the various labels of internalizing, overcontrolled, or anxiety-withdrawal. Descriptions such as anxious, shy, withdrawn, and depressed are some of the characteristics associated with this grouping. The second grouping has been variously labeled externalizing, undercontrolled, or conduct disorder. Fighting, temper tantrums, disobedience, and destructiveness are frequently associated with this pattern.

The Achenbach instruments are among the mea-sures used to derive the two broadband clusters just described. The Child Behavior Checklist (CBCL) is completed by the parents of youth 6 to 18 years of age (Achenbach & Rescorla, 2001). The Teacher Report Form (TRF) is a parallel instrument completed by teachers of youth 6 to 18 years old, and the Youth Self-Report (YSR) is completed by youths who are 11 to 18 years of age. In addition to the two broadband syndromes labeled *Internalizing* and *Externalizing,* research with these instruments has identified eight empirically defined, less general, or narrowband syndromes. These syndromes are described in Table 5–3. Every child who is evaluated receives a score on each of the syndromes, resulting in a profile of syndrome

---

TABLE 5–3	EIGHT SYNDROMES COMMON TO THE CBCL, TRF, AND YSR—WITH SAMPLE ITEMS

INTERNALIZING SYNDROMES

Anxious/Depressed	*Withdrawn/Depressed*	*Somatic Complaints*
Cries a lot	Rather be alone	Overtired
Fearful, anxious	Shy, timid	Aches, pains
Feels worthless	Withdrawn	Stomachaches

MIXED SYNDROMES

Social Problems	*Thought Problems*	*Attention Problems*
Lonely	Hears things	Can't concentrate
Gets teased	Sees things	Can't sit still
Not liked	Strange ideas	Impulsive

EXTERNALIZING SYNDROMES

Rule-Breaking Behavior	*Aggressive Behavior*	
Lacks guilt	Mean to others	
Bad friends	Destroys others' things	
Steals at home	Gets in fights	

Adapted from Achenbach & Rescorla, 2001.

scores for a particular child (see Figure 5–1; p. 104). This approach to classification evaluates each youngster on several dimensions.

Thus, this approach to classification differs from the clinical approach of the DSM in several ways. One important difference between the two approaches is how groupings are defined and formed (empirically versus clinical consensus). A second important difference is that the empirical approach to classification views problems as dimensional rather than categorical. It suggests that differences between individuals are quantitative rather than qualitative and that the difference between normal and pathological is one of degree rather than one of kind (Achenbach, 2000).

Empirically based classifications also employ data from normative samples as a frame of reference for judging the problems of an individual youngster. For the CBCL, TRF, and YSR, for example, there are two sets of norms against which to compare an individual child's or adolescent's scores. A youngster's scores can be compared with norms for nonreferred youngsters or with norms for other young people referred for mental health services. There are separate norms for each sex in particular age ranges, as rated by each type of informant. Thus, there are separate parent informant CBCL norms for boys 6 to 11, boys 12 to 18, girls 6 to 11, and girls 12 to 18, and separate similar norms for teacher and for youth informants (Achenbach & Rescorla, 2001). A youngster's scores can also be evaluated with respect to norms from multiple cultures (Achenbach & Rescorla, 2007).

To evaluate the behavior problems of an 11-year-old boy named Jason, for example, one could compare Jason's scores on the empirically based syndromes derived from his parents' reports with two sets of norms: norms of parent reports for nonreferred 11-year-old boys and norms of parent reports for clinic-referred 11-year-old boys. Scores based on Jason's teacher's TRF could be compared with two similar sets of norms of teachers' reports for 11-year-old boys. And scores based on Jason's own YSR could be compared with norms of responses of nonreferred and clinic-referred boys his age.

It is worth noting that, in addition to the dimensions/syndromes described above and outlined in Table 5–3, the Achenbach instruments can be scored to yield scales that correspond to some DSM categories (Achenbach, Dumenci, & Rescorla, 2003b; Achenbach & Rescorla, 2007). These DSM-oriented scales are one way that the two approaches might be compared.

Reliability. Reliability studies of empirically derived systems generally indicate that problem scores are quite reliable. The pattern of reliability is both interesting and informative (Achenbach & Rescorla, 2001).

Test–retest reliability correlations from two ratings by the same informant are often in the .80 and .90 ranges. So, for example, correlation for the Total Problems score on the CBCL is .94. Interrater reliability between different informants observing the child in the same situation is also quite good, although lower than for two evaluations by the same person. The mean agreement of mothers and fathers on the CBCL problem scales is .76.

Level of interrater agreement, however, is notably lower between raters who observe youth in distinctly different situations. The average correlation between parents' and teachers' Total Problem Scores, for example, is .35. Youngsters' Total Problem Scores are significantly, but modestly, related to parents' (.54) and teachers' (.21) ratings. These lower correlations may reveal something about young people's behavior, rather than just about the reliability of the approach to classification. Their behavior may have aspects that are consistent across time and situations, but it may also vary considerably with different individuals and in different situations. In addition, certain attributes may be more or less evident to different individuals or to other persons compared with the youngsters themselves (e.g., aggression versus feelings of loneliness). Such findings alert us to the possible limitations and bias of any one rater's perspective, whether this perspective is obtained by responses to a particular instrument or by clinical interview (Achenbach, McConaughy, & Howell, 1987; De Los Reyes & Kazdin, 2005; Hay et al., 1999).

Validity. The validity of empirically derived classification systems is indicated by a variety of studies. The same broadband syndromes have emerged in a variety of studies employing different instruments, different types of informants, and different samples, suggesting that the categories reflect valid distinctions (Achenbach & Rescorla, 2001). The findings show that the syndromes are valid ones because they emerge under a variety of conditions. Cross-cultural studies that find similar syndromes add further support; however, they also point to possible cultural differences in how youngsters' problems are manifested (Achenbach, Rescorla, & Ivanova, 2005; Ivanova et al., 2007a, b; Weisz et al., 2006).

Validity is also supported when differences in scores relate to other criteria. Indeed, a comparison of young people referred for outpatient mental health services with a sample of nonreferred young people matched for SES, age, and gender indicated that the clinical sample differed significantly from the nonreferred sample on all scores (Achenbach & Rescorla, 2001).

Also, differences between youngsters with high scores on different syndromes can address the validity of empirically identified syndromes. For example, comparison of young children with internalizing problems and those with externalizing problems has shown that they may differ with respect to the type of negative emotion they express and the style of emotion regulation and control that they exhibit (Eisenberg et al., 2001). Similarly, evidence suggests different correlates for the two syndromes *within* the externalizing domain (see Table 5–3). For example, research suggests that the aggressive syndrome is associated with stronger biochemical correlates and heredity, and greater developmental stability, than is the rule-breaking syndrome (Achenbach, 1998; Eley, 1997). Finally, scores on empirically derived syndromes have also been shown to predict outcomes such as future problems, use of mental health services, and police contacts (Achenbach et al., 1995; Stanger et al., 1996). Such findings support the validity of the empirical and dimensional approach to classification.

STIGMATIZATION AND THE IMPACT OF LABELS

As we have already noted, classification and diagnosis are intended to facilitate understanding and treatment of psychological problems. Although classification is intended as a scientific and clinical enterprise, it can be seen as a social process. The diagnostic label places the youngster in a subgroup of individuals and this has implications for how the young person may be viewed and treated by others. If this impact is negative, this may be due, in part, to the stigma associated with mental illness. Stigmatization refers to stereotyping, prejudice, discrimination, and self-degradation that may be associated with membership in a socially devalued group (See Accent: The Impact of Stigmatization).

Any negative impact of a diagnostic label may actually detract from the original purpose of categorizing—that of helping young people (Hinshaw, 2005). Formal classification is intended to categorize disorders, not people (American Psychiatric Association, 2000). Indeed, Dennis Cantwell, one of the creators of the current DSM approach, noted,

Any classification system classifies psychiatric disorders of childhood; it does not classify children. Thus it is correct to say, "Tommy Jones has infantile autism." It is incorrect to say "Tommy Jones, the autistic" . . . *(Cantwell, 1980, p. 350).*

It is important to be aware of the potential negative effects of the labeling process. Labels can contribute to a variety of unintended consequences. Overgeneralization is one concern. It may incorrectly be assumed that all youngsters labeled with attention-deficit hyperactivity disorder, for example, are more alike than they actually are. Such an assumption readily leads to neglect of the individual child or adolescent. Labels also may produce negative perceptions of youngsters. This is illustrated in a study by Foster and Salvia (1977). Teachers were asked to view a videotape of a boy and to rate his academic work and social behavior. The tape displayed age- and grade-appropriate behavior in all cases, but some teachers were told that the boy had a learning disability, whereas others were told that he was normal. Teachers watching the "learning disabled" boy rated him as less academically able and his behavior as more socially undesirable than did teachers watching the "normal" child.

Also, expectations regarding a youngster may be biased by the presence of a label. Others may act in a manner that is guided by such expectations, influencing the youngster to behave in a manner consistent with such expectations. The negative expectation that may be transmitted by labels is suggested by the findings of a study by Briggs and colleagues (1994). Adults read vignettes of a 6-year-old child engaged in aggressive behavior on a school playground. The stories varied regarding the family history of the child (normal, mother dying of cancer, sexually abused). After reading the vignette, the adults completed a questionnaire about their expectations regarding the behavior of the child. Results indicated that the adults had different expectations regarding the sexually abused child; for example, they believed that the sexually abused child would have more behavior problems and lesser achievement than either of the other two children.

Labels may not always produce negative expectations, however. Some suggest that labels provide an "explanation" for the child's problematic behavior. When an adult understands why the child is behaving in this manner, the adult is less likely to have negative reactions and may have more appropriate expectations for the child. That labels do not always lead to negative expectations is illustrated in a study by Wood and Valdez-Menchaca (1996). Adults interacted with four children, one of whom had previously been diagnosed with a language disorder (LD). The adults were randomly assigned to one of two conditions:

ACCENT ● ● ● ● ●

The Impact of Stigmatization

The stigma associated with mental illness is increasingly realized to be a central issue by those concerned for the well-being of children, adolescents, and their families (Hinshaw, 2005; Penn et al., 2005). Stigmatization may affect youngsters in multiple ways. It may affect both youths with a disorder and youths whose parents have a mental disorder.

Stigmatization involves stereotyping. A young person with a disorder may be viewed in terms of some negative traits or attributes, negative prejudgments, and discrimination—actions that limit the young person's rights and power. In addition, the youngster may internalize these negative evaluations and develop a negative view of his or her abilities and even him-or herself. Research suggests a number of other ways that stigmatization affects youngsters. For example, a young person with a disorder may experience a variety of negative social experiences, be denigrated, and be rejected by peers. The young person may also experience a similar impact of stigmatization in interactions with adults and even professionals. The youth's parents may be blamed for their child's difficulties. This, along with the stigma associated with the young person's disorder, may reduce the likelihood that the family will seek help.

Parental psychopathology is a risk factor for future child psychopathology. The stigma associated with mental disorders may prevent parents with a disorder from seeking help and thereby increase their children's risk. Also, the stigma associated with the parent's disorder may inhibit open family discussion and thereby further increase risk, limiting support for the children and perhaps leading them to blame themselves for their parents' or family's difficulties. Risk may also be increased if the parent and family feel the need to conceal the parent's difficulties, thereby reducing access to social support.

Understanding stigmatization and its impact is clearly a complex and difficult issue. Education regarding child psychopathology and the issue of stigmatization is clearly part of the solution. However, a broader effort is needed to overcome stigmatization. As Hinshaw (2005) has stated,

> For children and adolescents, stigma processes occur in families, schools, and communities; the notion of 'fit' between child and setting is crucial for the diagnosis of the child as mentally disturbed. Hence, community tolerance and acceptance of developmental disorders—and community facilitation of accommodation for youth with special educational needs—are essential components of fostering academic, social, and life competence. (p. 726).

The first was a nonlabel condition in which the child with LD was not identified, and the second was a label condition in which the child with LD was identified. Adults in the nonlabel group ranked the child with LD as significantly less likable, less productive, and less academically competent than the other children. Adults in the label group did not. They had observed the same inappropriate behaviors as the adults in the nonlabel group but they appeared to be more accepting of such behavior.

Finally, concern has been voiced that diagnostic labeling minimizes attention to the interpersonal and social context in which the child's behavior exists (Silk et al., 2000; Sroufe, 1997). Traditional diagnostic categories ignore the fact that a youngster's problems "belong" to at least one other person— the one who is identifying or reporting the problems (Algozzinne, 1977; Lilly, 1979). As we shall see throughout this book, there is much evidence that the way a youngster is described and viewed reflects as much on the individual doing the describing as it does on the behavior of the child or adolescent.

Many experts involved in the study and treatment of young people are concerned about potential negative consequences of diagnostic labels, and these experts advocate for various ways to reduce the possible harmful effects. Categorization, however, is embedded in our thinking and contributes to the advancement of our knowledge. Completely discarding categorization is neither desirable nor possible. Thus it is important to improve classification systems and at the same time to be sensitive to social factors inherent in the use of categories, the social status imparted by a label, and the impact of labels on the young person and the family (Adelman, 1996; Hinshaw, 2005).

Assessment

Evaluating child and adolescent problems is a complex process. By the time a young person comes to the attention of a clinician, the presenting problem is usually, if not always, multifaceted. But because assessment is the first part of any contact, the professional's knowledge of the problem is limited. Both of these factors, as well as common sense and caution, argue that the best interests of the young person are most likely served by a comprehensive assessment of multiple facets of the young person and his or her environment.

CONDUCTING A COMPREHENSIVE ASSESSMENT

Alicia An Initial Assessment

The parents of 6-year-old Alicia were seeking assistance in understanding her problems and ways to help their daughter improve her adjustment at home and school and with her peers. The parents described Alicia as impulsive, moody, and having difficulty in school. The initial information provided by the parents indicated that several male relatives on the mother's side of the family were mentally retarded and that one of these relatives had recently been diagnosed with a fragile X syndrome chromosomal disorder. The clinician hypothesized that Alicia might be a fragile X carrier because females are carriers for the defective gene associated with the syndrome. Based on initial information the clinician also hypothesized that Alicia might have ADHD and a learning disability.

Information about Alicia was gathered from several sources: the parents (interview, rating scales, daily behavioral logs, observation of parent–child interactions), the teacher (rating scales, academic performance and test scores), and Alicia herself (interview, direct observation, psychoeducational testing). Information obtained during the assessment revealed that Alicia had many characteristics of females who carry the fragile X chromosome. This was discussed with the parents and referral for a genetic evaluation revealed that this was indeed the case. The assessment also indicated that Alicia met the diagnostic criteria for ADHD and that she had a learning problem.

In addition, evaluation revealed that Alicia's parents provided a structured yet stimulating environment for her. Alicia had friends, successfully engaged in age-appropriate activities, and felt loved by her parents. She also realized that her impulsive behavior created problems for herself and her family. Positive aspects of the case were Alicia's desire to please and her good social skills, warm and loving parents, and supportive home and school environments.

The assessment led to intervention strategies that included a change in Alicia's class placement and resource support, support for the family, referral to a support group for parents of children with fragile X syndrome, behavior management techniques for the parents, and brief individual work with Alicia to help her recognize her strengths and cope with her difficulties. The clinician indicated that Alicia would likely adapt and continue to develop successfully, but further assessment and intervention might be needed as new challenges were encountered.

Adapted from Schroeder & Gordon, 2002, pp. 49–50.

As we shall see throughout our discussion, behavioral disorders in youth are complex, often encompassing a variety of components rather than a single problem behavior. Furthermore, these problems typically arise from, and are maintained by, multiple influences. Such influences include biological factors; various aspects of the youngster's behavioral, cognitive, and social functioning; and influences of the family and other social systems such as peers and school. Thus an assessment must be comprehensive in evaluating a variety of potential presenting problems, measuring a variety of aspects of youth themselves, and assessing various contexts and other individuals.

Information must be obtained from a variety of sources (e.g., the youth, parents, teachers) to assess problems that may vary by context or that may be displayed differently in the presence of different individuals. A child may behave differently at home, in school, and in playing with his or her peers. Also, observers may view the same or similar behaviors differently. A mother who is depressed and experiencing a variety of life stresses may be less able to tolerate minor deviations from expected behavior. Such differences in perception may be important both in understanding the presenting problems and in planning interventions. Assessment thus requires the use of multiple and varied methods as well as familiarity with assessment instruments for individuals of many different ages. The process requires considerable skill and sensitivity.

Assessment may be best accomplished by a team of clinicians carefully trained in the administration and interpretation of specific procedures and instruments. It is desirable for clinicians to employ evidence-based assessment—procedures for which there is empirical evidence regarding validity (Hirsch-Pasek, et al., 2005; Lilienfeld, Lynn, & Lohr, 2003; McClure, Kubiszyn, & Kaslow, 2002). As we will see later in this chapter when we discuss empirically supported treatments, such evidence-based or empirically supported practice is an ongoing goal for researchers and clinicians.

Because assessment is usually conducted immediately on contact with the young person or family, it demands special sensitivity to anxiety, fear, shyness, manipulativeness, and the like. If treatment ensues, assessment should be a continuous process, so that new information can be gleaned and the ongoing effects of treatment can be ascertained. In this way, the clinician remains open to nuances and can avoid rigid judgments about a multifaceted and complex phenomenon.

The Interview

The general clinical interview. The general clinical interview is clearly the most common method of assessment (Watkins et al., 1995). Information on all areas of functioning is obtained by interviewing the child or adolescent and various other people in the social environment.

Whether the young person will be interviewed alone will probably vary with age. An older child or adolescent generally is more capable and is more likely to provide valuable information. Nevertheless, clinicians often elect to interview even a very young child in order to obtain their own impressions. Preschool and grade school children can provide valuable information if appropriate developmental considerations are used to tailor the interview to the individual child (Bierman & Schwartz, 1986; Kamphaus & Frick, 1996). For example, an adultlike face-to-face interview may be intimidating for a young child, so a more successful technique may be to model the interview after a familiar play or school task.

Most clinicians seek information concerning the nature of the problem, past and recent history, present conditions, feelings and perceptions, attempts to solve the problem, and expectations concerning treatment. The general clinical interview is used not only to determine the nature of the presenting problem and perhaps to help formulate a diagnosis but also to gather information that allows the clinician to conceptualize the case and to plan an appropriate therapeutic intervention.

Structured diagnostic interviews. The general clinical interview is usually described as open-ended or unstructured. Because such interviews are most often conducted in the context of a therapeutic interaction and are employed along with a variety of other assessment instruments, it has been difficult to evaluate reliability and validity. Structured diagnostic interviews have arisen in part to create interviews that are likely to be more reliable. They also have been developed for the more limited purpose of deriving a diagnosis based on a particular classification scheme, such as the DSM; for use in research; or in order to screen large populations for the prevalence of disorders. These interviews can be conducted with the youth and/or parent(s). The Anxiety Disorders Interview for Children (ADIS-IV; Silverman & Albano, 1996), the Diagnostic Interview for Children and Adolescents (DICA; Reich, 2000), and the Schedule for Affective Disorders and Schizophrenia for School-Age Children (K-SADS; Ambrosini, 2000) are examples of these diagnostic interviews.

In the unstructured general clinical interview, there are no particular questions that the clinician must ask, no designated format, and no stipulated method to record information. That is not to say that there are no guidelines or agreed-on procedures for conducting an effective interview. Indeed, there is an extensive literature on effective interviewing (McConaughy, 2005; Sattler, 1998). However, unstructured interviews are intended to give the clinician great latitude. In contrast, structured diagnostic interviews consist of a set of questions that the interviewer asks the youngster. There are rules for how the interview is to be conducted, and explicit guidelines for recording and scoring the youngster's responses (McClellan & Werry, 2000).

Problem Checklists and Self-Report Instruments

Problem checklists and rating scales were described in our discussion of classification (pp. 98–100). There is a wide variety of these instruments. Some are for general use—such as the Child Behavior Checklist (Achenbach & Rescorla, 2001), the Personality Inventory for Children (Lachar & Gruber, 2001), and the Behavior Assessment System for

Children (Reynolds & Kamphaus, 2004). Others are used with particular populations. The Conners Parent Rating Scale (Conners, 2008), for instance, can be used when attention-deficit hyperactivity disorder needs to be assessed.

A considerable empirical literature suggests that these instruments may be valuable tools for clinicians and researchers (Frick & Kamphaus, 2001). In one study, the parent-reported problems and competencies of youth assessed at intake into mental health services were compared with those of demographically matched nonreferred youngsters (Achenbach & Rescorla, 2001). Checklist scores clearly discriminated between the clinic and nonreferred children regarding both behavior problems and social competencies.

A general rating scale may thus help a clinician judge the child's adjustment relative to norms for referred and nonreferred populations. This procedure can help to evaluate the appropriateness of the referral. Once a particular presenting problem is identified, the clinician might use a more specific rating scale.

Furthermore, rating scales completed by different informants may help the clinician gain a fuller appreciation of the clinical picture and of potential situational aspects of the child's problem. For example, Figure 5–1 illustrates the differences in responses of a young girl's mother and father. Differing perceptions of two informants may provide important information to a clinician. For example, the CBCL, TRF, and YSR in the Achenbach instruments make it possible to compare multiple informants' reports about the child with respect to a common set of problem items and dimensions. When two or more respondents use these instruments to describe a child or adolescent, a statistic can be computed indicating the degree of agreement. This degree of agreement for a particular youth can then be compared with the degree of agreement between comparable informants for a large representative sample. Thus it is possible to know whether the degree of agreement between Tommy's mother and his teacher is less than, similar to, or greater than the average mother–teacher agreement about boys in Tommy's age range.

FIGURE 5–1

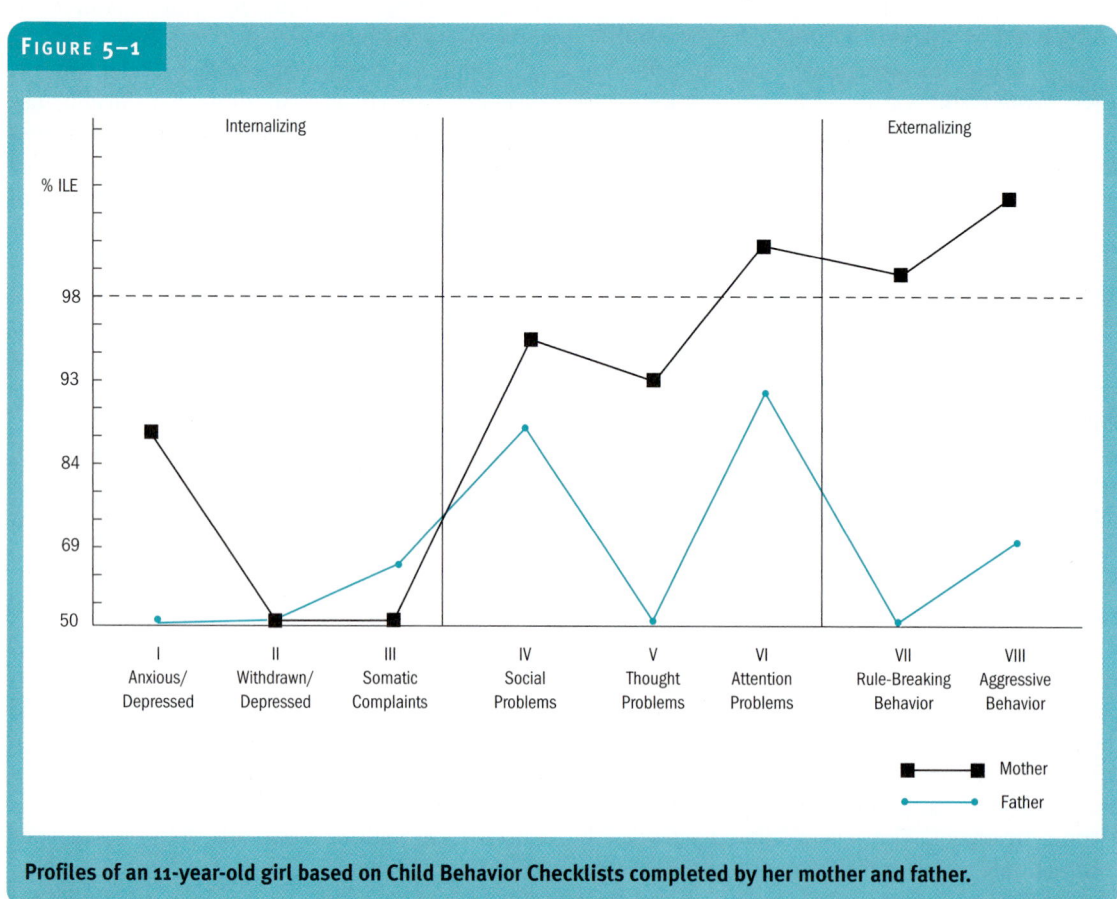

Profiles of an 11-year-old girl based on Child Behavior Checklists completed by her mother and father.

In addition, the clinician or researcher may also draw on a wide variety of self-report measures to assess the youth's own report. Here, too, there are general measures and there are also self-report measures to assess specific problems such as anxiety and depression (Kovacs, 1992, 2003; March et al., 1997). Instruments also are available to assess constructs related to adjustment such as self-control and self-concept (Connell, 1985; Harter, 1985). Many of these measures will be described in later chapters that focus on particular child and adolescent problems.

Parents and other adults may also be asked to complete self-report instruments about themselves. These instruments may assess specific problems, for example, a parent's own anxiety or depression. Or they may evaluate, a wide variety of aspects of adult functioning. For instance, the feelings, attitudes, and beliefs of adults, particularly with respect to the child or adolescent, may be assessed (e.g., the Parenting Stress Index—Abidin, 1995), or aspects of the family environment may be measured (e.g., the Family Environment Scale—Moos & Moos, 1994; and the Parent–Adolescent Relationship Questionnaire—Robin, Koepke, & Moye, 1990). Such assessment can provide important information about the social environment and factors that may contribute to problem behavior. The use of such measures acknowledges that the presenting problem is complex and exists in a social context.

OBSERVATIONAL ASSESSMENT

Early attempts to observe children's behavior used diaries or continuous observations and narrations that were deliberately nonselective (Wright, 1960). From this tradition evolved observations of a more focused, pinpointed set of behaviors that could be reliably coded by observers (Bijou et al., 1969).

More recent observational methods have most often come from workers with a behavioral/social learning perspective. Behavioral observations are frequently made in the child's natural environment, although situations are sometimes created in clinic or laboratory settings to approximate naturally occurring interactions. Observations can include reports of single, relatively simple, and discrete behaviors of the child; interactions of the child and peers; and complex systems of interactions among family members (Kolko, 1987; Israel, Pravder, & Knights, 1980; Reid, 1978). Clearly, on-

going interactions are more difficult to observe and code than are the behaviors of a single individual; however, they are likely to be theoretically and clinically relevant.

The first step in any behavioral observation system involves explicitly pinpointing and defining behaviors. Observers are trained to use the system and note whether a particular behavior or sequence of behaviors occurs. Research indicates that a number of factors affect reliability as well as validity and clinical utility of observational systems (Hops, Davis, & Longoria, 1995). For example, the complexity of the observational system and changes over time in the observers' use of the system (observer drift) are two such factors. Reactivity (a change in an individual's behavior when the individual knows that he or she is being observed) is often cited as the greatest impediment to the utility of direct observation. Careful training, periodic monitoring of observers' use of the system, and use of observers already in the situation (e.g., teachers) are some recommended ways to reduce distortions in the information obtained from direct observation.

Behavioral observations are the most direct method of assessment and require the least inference. The difficulty and expense involved in training and maintaining reliable observers is probably the primary obstacle to their common use in nonresearch contexts. Since direct observation has long been considered the hallmark of assessment from a behavioral perspective, attempts have been made to create systems that are more amenable to widespread use. Direct observation is, however, just one aspect of a multimethod approach to behavioral assessment that can include self-monitoring of behavior, interviews, ratings and checklists, and self-report instruments.

PROJECTIVE TESTS

At one time the most common form of psychological test employed to assess children was the projective test. These tests are less commonly used today, in large part because of a continuing debate regarding lack of empirical norms, reliability, and validity (Anastasi & Urbina, 1997; Kleiger, 2001; Knoff, 1998).

Projective tests were derived from the psychoanalytic notion of projection as a defense mechanism: One way the ego deals with unacceptable impulses is to project them onto some external object. It is assumed that the impulses cannot be expressed directly. Therefore, many projective tests present an ambiguous stimulus, allowing the individual to project "unacceptable" thoughts and impulses, as well as other defense mechanisms onto the stimulus. Projective tests are also used by some clinicians in a manner that involves less psychodynamic inference (Chandler, 2003). For example, the young person may see an ambiguous stimulus in terms of past experiences and present desires and thus be prompted to report these. Analyses that examine formal aspects of a test response—for example, the distance between human figures that the child draws—may also be used. Interpretations are then made on the basis of this response style rather than on the content of the response.

Projective tests may ask a child to interpret an image or to create his or her own picture. In the Rorschach test, the youngster is asked what he or she sees in each of 10 ink blots. The most commonly used methods for scoring and interpretation are based on characteristics of the response, such as the portion of the blot responded to (location), factors such as color and shading (determinants), and the nature of what is seen in the blot (content) (Exner & Weiner, 1995). The Human Figure Drawing, or Draw-a-Person test, (Koppitz, 1984; Machover, 1949)

requires the child to draw a picture of a person and then a second person of the opposite sex. The House-Tree-Person technique (Buck, 1992) asks the child to draw a house, a tree, and a person. In the Kinetic Family Drawing technique (Burns, 1987), the child is asked to draw a picture of everyone in the family, including himself or herself, "doing something." Typically the clinician then asks questions about the drawings. Murray's (1943) Thematic Apperception Test (TAT), the Children's Apperception Test (CAT) (Bellak & Bellak, 1982; Bellak & Abrams, 1997), and the Roberts Apperception Test for Children (McArthur & Roberts, 1982) provide the young person with pictures for which he or she is asked to make up a story. Figure 5–2 presents pictures similar to those used in the CAT.

INTELLECTUAL–EDUCATIONAL ASSESSMENT

The evaluation of intellectual and academic functioning is an important part of almost all clinical assessments. Intellectual functioning is a central defining feature for disorders such as mental retardation and learning disabilities, but it may also contribute to

FIGURE 5–2

Drawings similar to those employed in the CAT.

and be affected by a wide variety of behavioral problems. Compared with most other assessment instruments, tests of intellectual functioning tend to have better normative data, reliability, and validity. Although our present discussion of these instruments is brief, we will consider additional information in later chapters.

Intelligence tests. By far the most commonly employed assessment devices for evaluating intellectual functioning are tests of general intelligence. In fact, they probably are the most frequently employed assessment device other than the interview. The Stanford–Binet (Roid, 2003); the Wechsler tests—the Wechsler Preschool and Primary Scale of Intelligence (Wechsler, 2002) and the Wechsler Intelligence Scale for Children (Wechsler, 2003); and the Kaufman Assessment Battery for Children (Kaufman & Kaufman, 2004) are some of the intelligence tests widely used in clinical settings. All are individually administered and yield an intelligence (IQ) score. The average score is 100, and an individual score reflects how far above or below the average person of his or her age an individual has scored.

Intelligence tests have long been the subject of heated controversy. Critics have argued that the use of IQ scores has caused intelligence to be viewed as a real thing, a rigid and fixed attribute, rather than as a concept that is complex and subtle. Critics also claim that intelligence tests are culturally biased and have led to social injustice (cf. Kamin, 1974; Kaplan, 1985). Although intelligence tests are popular and useful in predicting a variety of outcomes, continued concern with legal, ethical, and practical issues demand that they be used cautiously, that efforts be made to improve intelligence tests, and that their usage be monitored for appropriateness (Kamphaus, 1993; Perlman & Kaufman, 1990).

Developmental scales. Assessment of intellectual functioning in very young children, and particularly in infants, requires a special kind of assessment instrument. A popular measure is the Bayley Scales of Infant and Toddler Development (Bayley, 2005). The Bayley can be used to assess children from 2 to 42 months of age and includes a Motor Scale, a Mental Scale, and a Behavior Rating Scale that assesses behavioral style (e.g., attitude, interest). Performance on developmental tests yields a developmental index rather than an intelligence score. Unlike intelligence tests, which emphasize language and abstract reasoning abilities, developmental scales emphasize sensorimotor skills and simple social skills. For example,

the Bayley examines the ability to sit, walk, place objects, attend to visual and auditory stimuli, smile, and imitate adults. Perhaps because they tap different abilities, there is only a low correlation between developmental scales, particularly when they are administered early, and measures of intellectual functioning later in childhood. Early developmental test scores may, however, be predictive of later intellectual functioning for children with serious developmental disabilities (Sattler, 1992).

Ability and achievement tests. In addition to assessing a youth's general intellectual functioning, it is often necessary or helpful to assess a child or adolescents's functioning in a particular area. Ability and achievement tests have been developed for this purpose (Katz & Slomka, 1990; Stetson & Stetson, 2001). The Wide Range Achievement Test (Wilkinson & Robertson, 2006) and the Woodcock Reading Mastery Tests (Woodcock, 1998), for example, are two measures of academic achievement that are administered to an individual youth. Tests such as the Iowa Test of Basic Skills (Hoover, Dunbar, & Frisbie, 2001) and the Stanford Achievement Test (Harcourt Assessment, 2003) are group-administered achievement tests employed in many school settings. Specific ability and achievement tests are particularly important to professionals working with children who have learning and school-related problems.

Assessment of Physical Functioning

General physical assessment. Assessment of physical functioning can provide several kinds of information valuable to understanding disordered behavior. Family and child histories and physical examinations may reveal genetic problems that are treatable by environmental manipulation. For example, phenylketonuria (PKU) is a recessive gene condition that is affected by dietary treatment. Avoidance of phenylalanine in the child's diet prevents most of the cognitive problems usually associated with the condition. In addition, diseases and defects may be diagnosed that affect important areas of functioning either directly (for example, a urinary tract infection causing problems in toilet training) or indirectly (for example, a sickly child being overprotected by parents). Also, signs of atypical or lagging physical development may be an early indication of developmental disorders that eventually influence many aspects of behavior.

Psychophysiological assessment. Changes in physiological systems are associated with both externalizing and internalizing problems (Cummings et al., 2007; Dietrich et al., 2007). Thus, psychophysiological assessments are often conducted in circumstances where a child or adolescent's arousal level is of concern. Because of the equipment that is necessary, such assessments are more common in research settings than in general clinical practice. Evaluation of heart rate, muscle tension, and respiration rate are examples of these assessments. Measures of electrical activity in the autonomic nervous system, such as skin conductance, or in the central nervous system, such as the electroencephalogram (EEG), are also often aspects of psychophysiological assessments.

Assessment of nervous system functioning. The assessment of the nervous system is important to understanding a variety of disorders such as mental retardation, autism, learning disabilities, and attention-deficit hyperactivity disorder. These assessment techniques also benefit research because they provide information regarding the mechanisms through which medications have their effects (Charney et al., 2002). Assessment of the nervous system is also an important aspect of evaluating outcomes for youngsters who experience brain injury (Yeates et al., 2007). Such assessment requires the coordinated efforts of neurologists, psychologists, and other professional workers.

NEUROLOGICAL ASSESSMENT. Neurological assessment can be achieved by a number of procedures that directly assess the integrity of the nervous system. To record an electroencephalograph (EEG) or an event-related potential (ERP), electrodes are placed on the child or adolescent's scalp that record activity of the brain cortex in general or during a time when the youth is engaged in information-processing tasks. EEG/ERP activation patterns have contributed to the understanding of brain functioning in a number of populations, including fearful and inhibited children, infants of depressed mothers, and youth with learning and language disorders, attention-deficit hyperactivity disorder, and autism (Banaschewski & Brandeis, 2007; Dawson et al., 1997; Nelson & Bloom, 1997).

Newer technologies such as brain imaging techniques have vastly improved our ability to assess brain structure and function (Eliez & Reiss, 2000; Kumra et al., 2005; Shaywitz & Shaywitz, 2003; Swain et al., 2007; Zalsman et al., 2006). For example, brain structure can be examined by computerized tomography, or the CT scan (also referred to as computerized axial tomography—CAT scan). This procedure allows tens of thousands of readings of minute variations in the density of brain tissue, measured from an X-ray source, to be computer processed to create a photographic image of a portion of the brain. The image can reveal subtle structural abnormalities of the brain.

Magnetic resonance imaging (MRI) is a noninvasive procedure that also produces images of brain structure. A large magnet and radiowaves are used to create a magnetic field around the brain. The cells in the brain respond to the radiowaves and a 3D computer image is created. Because it produces sharper images and has other advantages, the MRI has increasingly replaced CAT scans.

Other techniques help reveal brain activity. Positron emission tomography (PET) scans determine the rate of activity of different parts of the brain by assessing the use of oxygen and glucose, which fuel brain activity. The more active a particular part of the brain is, the more oxygen and glucose it uses. After a small amount of radioactive substance has been injected into the bloodstream, amounts of radiation appearing in different areas of the brain are measured while the person engages in a particular task. Many images are taken of the brain, to create a color-coded picture that indicates different levels of activity in different parts of the brain.

Functional magnetic resonance imaging (fMRI) uses the same technology as MRI and produces images by tracking subtle changes in oxygen in different parts of the brain. When particular parts of the brain are called on to perform some task, these regions receive increased blood flow and thus increased oxygen. The MRI scanner detects these changes and produces pictures of the brain that indicate areas of activity.

NEUROPSYCHOLOGICAL EVALUATIONS. Neuropsychological evaluations employ tests that primarily assess general intellectual abilities, learning, sensorimotor and perceptual skills, verbal skills, and memory. Inferences are made about brain functioning on the basis of the individual's performance on these tasks.

Neuropsychological evaluations have a number of uses (Hebben & Milberg, 2002). For example, they may be used to describe changes in psychological functioning that may arise out of alterations in the central nervous system or other disorders or conditions. They also may be used to assess changes over time and to develop a prognosis, for example, evaluating recovery from head injury (Middleton, 2001). Neuropsychological evaluations also may provide guidelines for treatment planning.

The current interest in neuropsychological evaluation is attributable, at least in part, to increased sensitivity to the needs and legal requirements of providing services to children with handicapping conditions—some of whom exhibit problems presumed to have a neurological etiology. Also, due to advances in medicine, increasing numbers of children survive known or suspected neurological trauma. The increase in survival rates of infants born prematurely is one example. Children with cancer who receive treatment that includes the injection of substances into the spinal column and radiation to the head are another example.

Neuropsychological evaluation appreciates the need for broadly based assessment (Bengtson & Boll, 2001; Hebben & Milberg, 2002). Two of the most widely used collections of instruments are the Halstead–Reitan Neuropsychological Test Battery for Children (Reitan & Wolfson, 1993) and the Luria–Nebraska Neuropsychological Battery–Children's Revision (Golden, 1987). As the term *battery* implies, these instruments consist of several subtests or scales, each intended to assess one or more abilities. The use of a broad spectrum of tests is the usual strategy employed in neuropsychological approaches to assessment (Fletcher & Taylor, 1997; Luciana, 2003). The spectrum may be fixed batteries like the examples just mentioned, or flexible batteries based on combinations of existing tests. Table 5–4 lists some of the domains that are assessed by these various tests. The importance of these various domains of functioning will become apparent as we discuss specific disorders.

Neuropsychological evaluation of children (pediatric neuropsychology) is still a relatively young field. Part of this ongoing effort is the development of instruments that derive from evolving research on cognitive development, neurological development, and brain–behavior relationships (Yeates et al., 2007). Efforts have been undertaken to compile pediatric normative data for these neuropsychological instruments (Baron, 2004). Research is also being directed toward developing strategies that more clearly specify impairment and guide rehabilitation.

Intervention: Prevention and Treatment

Intervention is an umbrella term applied to both systematic prevention and treatment of psychological difficulty. Prevention refers to interventions targeting individuals who are not yet experiencing a clinical disorder, that is, those in the general population or those at risk for disorder. For example, an eating disorder prevention program may be offered to all middle school students or for those at particular risk based on some early signs of unusual eating habits or weight concerns. On the other hand, treatment traditionally describes interventions for individuals already experiencing clinical levels of some problem (or symptoms that approach diagnostic levels). For example, youngsters who are diagnosed with Obsessive–Compulsive Disorder may receive a combination of medication and behavioral strategies to treat their problems.

Figure 5–3 illustrates one way of conceptualizing the variety of intervention strategies employed to assist youth and their families. In this model, formulated by Weisz, Sandler, Durlak, & Anton (2005), the upper semicircle contains various intervention strategies. The interventions are arrayed from the most universally applicable at the left to the most narrowly focused at the right and with prevention strategies to the left and treatment strategies to the right. The lower semicircle presents a sample of the range of potential settings in which interventions may be offered. The intervention settings are arrayed from the least restrictive on the left to the most restrictive on the right.

The concentric circles in the middle of the figure are meant to indicate the "centrality of individual strengths and supportive social connections in healthy development. . . . encircled by a cultural ring to reflect the influence of cultural and ethnic differences" (Weisz, et al. 2005, p. 631). The various intervention strategies shown in the figure are viewed as complementary to one another and in combination may be used to assist a particular youngster or population at different points in time. Multiple interventions may be delivered in the same setting, or interventions may be delivered in multiple settings.

TABLE 5–4	SOME OF THE DOMAINS EVALUATED IN NEUROPSYCHOLOGICAL ASSESSMENT

General intelligence
Memory/Learning
Language function
Attention
Motor function
Visual-motor function
Higher-order planning
Academic achievement

Adapted from Luciana, 2003.

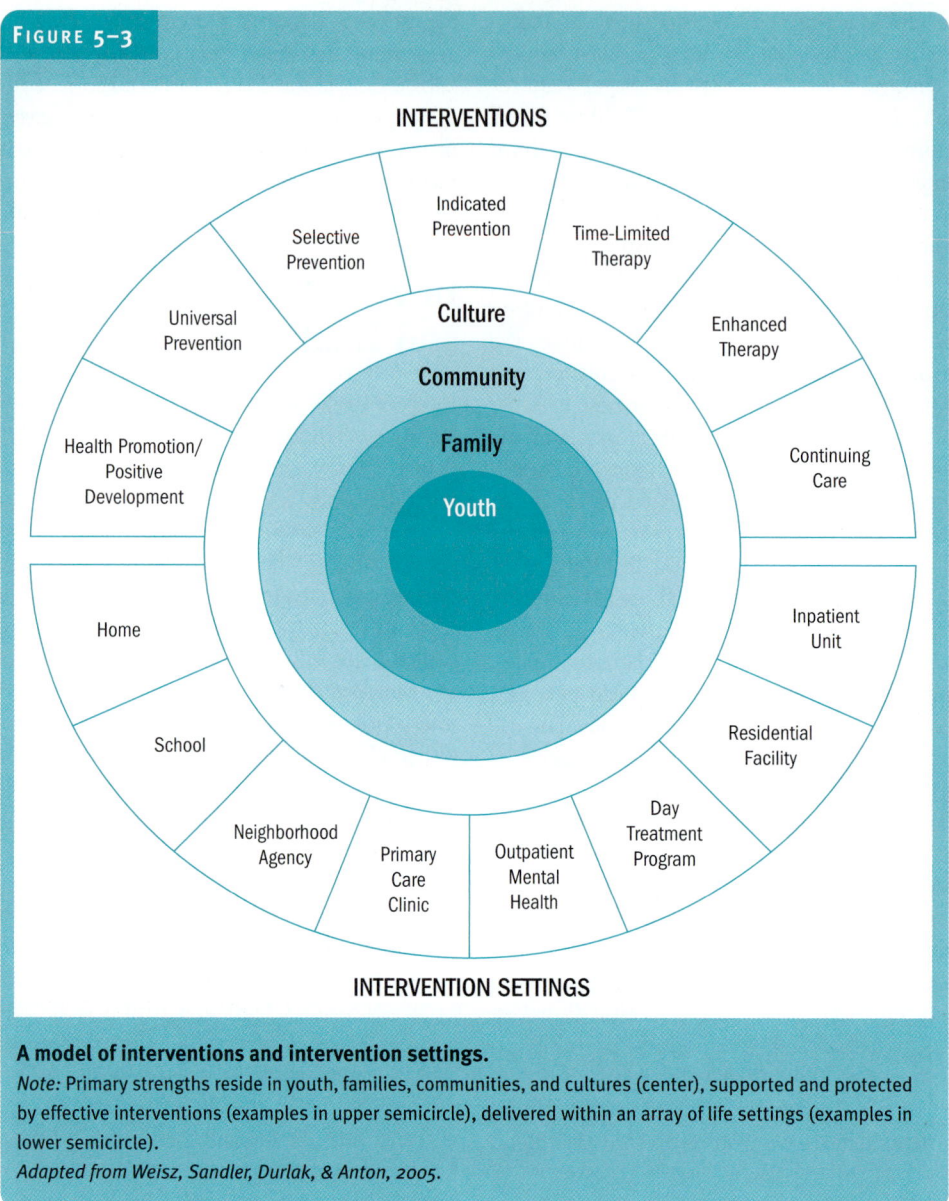

FIGURE 5-3

A model of interventions and intervention settings.

Note: Primary strengths reside in youth, families, communities, and cultures (center), supported and protected by effective interventions (examples in upper semicircle), delivered within an array of life settings (examples in lower semicircle).

Adapted from Weisz, Sandler, Durlak, & Anton, 2005.

Both prevention and treatment programs may be delivered in the home, the school, or a neighborhood agency. Treatment also may be delivered in specialized settings such as an outpatient mental health clinic. It is sometimes necessary to remove youth from their family home and provide treatment in residential settings (e.g. group homes, therapeutic camping programs, facilities that are part of the juvenile justice system) or inpatient hospital units. These settings are usually considered only for severe behavior problems. The problems may be so difficult to treat that if the youths continue to reside at home,

there is not enough contact or control for a successful outcome. Concern may also exist that youths may harm themselves or others and, therefore, that closer supervision is necessary. Children or adolescents may also be removed from the home because circumstances there are highly problematic, suggesting that successful interventions could not be achieved at home. Unfortunately, the lack of availability of alternative placements or appropriate funding can result in young people being placed in institutional settings when interventions in the home, with additional support provided to the family, or in less restrictive environments, like foster homes, might be successful. Typically, professionals strive to use interventions that allow youth to remain at home and that permit families to stay intact. On the other hand, treatment in residential settings is often undertaken when other modes of intervention have not proven successful.

As discussed in chapter 1, the beginning of the 20th century brought notable progress to the United States regarding the mental and social problems of young people. Currently, there is enthusiasm and commitment to promoting the prevention and treatment of psychological dysfunction, as well as the positive growth of children and adolescents. In this discussion we provide a general sense of what may be involved in the intervention process. In the chapters that follow, we examine various multicomponent interventions for specific disorders.

PREVENTION

In the United States, interest in prevention can be traced to the early 20th-century writings of Clifford Beers, the mental hygiene movement, and the creation of the child guidance clinics (Coie, Miller-Johnson, & Bagwell, 2000; Heller, 1996). However, progress did not come easily. Mental health professionals were trained for treatment, not prevention, and high priority was given to funding the care of individuals already experiencing mental health problems rather than to preventing future problems. Some professionals expressed doubts about the basis for prevention, since the etiology of psychological disorders is often multifactorial and difficult to establish. Moreover, specific prevention efforts—such as sex education and drug programs—were sometimes resisted by the general public because they were thought to intrude on parental prerogatives or values (Enzer & Heard, 2000).

Several arguments may be made for increasing prevention efforts. From a humanitarian viewpoint, prevention is clearly desirable because it averts discomfort and suffering. Practical considerations also argue for prevention. There are not enough (and may never be enough) professionals to treat mental disorders (Coie et al., 2000), intervention is unlikely to be available to certain groups of people, and treatment is exceedingly costly. In addition, increased understanding of risk and protective factors in psychopathology provides a firmer basis for prevention efforts. Importantly, evidence for the beneficial effects of prevention programs has been accumulating (Durlak & Wells, 1997; Evans et al., 2005; Weisz et al., 2005).

Conceptualizing prevention. Caplan is usually credited with being a catalyst for the preventive approach in mental health (Lorion, 2000). Based on the public health assumption that major diseases have been controlled only by preventive efforts, Caplan's (1964) three-prong model has served as a general framework for thinking about prevention. In this model, prevention is viewed as primary, secondary, or tertiary. *Primary prevention*, which attempts to stave off disorders in the first place, involves both general health enhancement and prevention of specific dysfunction. *Secondary prevention* is usually defined as the effort to shorten the duration of existing cases through early referral, diagnosis, and treatment. It is a "nipping in the bud" strategy. *Tertiary prevention* is an after-the-fact strategy that aims to reduce problems that are residual to disorders. It might seek to minimize the negative impact of labeling a child as learning disabled, to rehabilitate an adolescent who has suffered a severe mental disorder, or to ward off relapse after treatment.

Caplan's model and the terms he used are still employed. However, somewhat different approaches also have been put forth. Many conceptualizations tend to emphasize preventive efforts occurring prior to the full onset of disorders or problems (rather than tertiary programs). The Institute of Medicine, a part of the National Academy of Sciences, proposed three components (Munoz, Mrazek, & Haggerty, 1996), which are evident in Figure 5–3.

1. Universal prevention strategies are targeted to entire populations for which greater than average risk has not been identified in individuals. Hypothetical examples are encouraging parents to read to their children to avoid learning problems, and promoting exercise and proper diet to avoid obesity.

2. Selective prevention strategies (also called high-risk prevention strategies) are targeted to individuals who are at higher than average risk for disorder. Intervention might be directed toward individuals or subgroups with biological risks, high stress, family dysfunction, or poverty.

3. Indicated prevention strategies are targeted to high-risk individuals who show minimal symptoms or signs forecasting a disorder, or who have biological markers for a disorder but do not meet the criteria for the disorder.

It is noteworthy that the Institute of Medicine's influential model did not include efforts designed to foster wellness, that is, health promotion and positive development (Munoz et al., 1996). As exemplified in Figure 5–3, other workers include wellness in prevention and recommend fostering individual competence and self-esteem, social connections to others, security, and optimism as protection from disorder and disease (Albee, 1986, 1996; Cowen, 1991, 1994; Weissberg, Kumpfer, & Seligman, 2003). In this regard, Albee noted that many mental disorders are linked to poverty, sexism, and racism and that such social ills must be confronted. The American Psychological Association's Task Force on Prevention: Promoting Strength, Resilience, and Health in Young People endorsed the broader wellness approach (Weissberg et al., 2003).

Diversity of prevention programs. Given the several components of prevention, it is unsurprising that interventions vary tremendously in aims, focus, and setting. Programs to enhance positive development require input from fields such as human development, mental health, community planning, social policy, and the like; a developmental psychopathology approach is valuable in pointing to factors that facilitate optimal growth and resilience (Cicchetti & Rogosch, 2002). Other prevention programs for children have emphasized the modification of either the environment or children's learning or behavior and have involved mental health professionals, teachers, parents, and college students as agents of change (Durlak & Wells, 1997). In practice, however, many prevention interventions target at-risk populations, for example, children with developmental delays or single-parent families.

A distinction can be made between programs that focus on preventing a potential array of negative outcomes and programs that focus on specific symptoms of disorders. The former include, for example, interventions with economically disadvantaged children to prevent the varied cognitive, social, and emotional adversities associated with poverty (e.g., Peters, Petrunka, & Arnold, 2003). Programs focusing more on specific psychopathology include, for example, interventions for deterring the development of depression or conduct-disordered behaviors (Clarke et al., 2003; Hinshaw, 2002; Reid, Webster-Stratton, & Bayder, 2004).

TREATMENT

Clinicians are likely to be called on to treat children and adolescents whose problems are multifaceted. For example, a youth may simultaneously have problems involving anxiety and depression, social problems with peers, and academic difficulties. Indeed, it is likely that a young person will have multiple presenting problems. Furthermore, problems may vary with situations and may be more broadly defined to include other individuals. Thus clinical attention often will be directed not only to the child or adolescent but also to family members and perhaps school personnel and peers. Treatment is therefore likely to contain multiple elements that address different aspects of the clinical problem.

There are a number of ways to conceptualize treatment approaches. For example, a clinician's theoretical conceptualization of the presenting problem and of the process by which change occurs will influence how treatment is provided. Thus, a psychologist whose conceptualization of the disorder emphasizes environmental influences and contingencies is likely to consider treatments that include both the youth and significant others and that focus on modifying environmental stimuli and the consequences of behavior. Meanwhile, a psychologist whose conceptualization emphasizes cognitive processes is likely to consider interventions aimed at modifying particular cognitions, and a psychologist whose conceptualization emphasizes interpersonal processes or family dynamics is likely to consider treatments that focus on these aspects of a problem. Nevertheless, many professionals realize that psychological problems are subject to multiple influences and that treatment may involve multiple components.

As seen in Figure 5–3, treatment can also be conceptualized in terms of the length of treatment required and the number of strategies employed. Treatment may involve a limited number of sessions (e.g., 20) and a standard treatment protocol, it may be enhanced by booster sessions and supplemental strategies, or it may require a variety of strategies used in an ongoing way over an extended period.

The mode in which treatment is delivered is another aspect of treatment efforts. Treatment may be delivered in a variety of modes (e.g., individual therapy, family therapy). Indeed, clinicians may employ several different modes of treatment in a single case.

Individual and group psychotherapy. Therapists may see the young client in individual one-to-one sessions. A therapist working with a child or adolescent with an anxiety disorder may, for example, help the young person to understand the problem and teach the youth active ways of confronting and coping with the anxiety. These sessions may resemble the verbal interchanges and activities of adult sessions

The use of play as a mode of therapy is common with younger children. Play allows for the establishment of rapport, but it also provides a means of communication more age-appropriate than verbal forms of therapy. *(David Young-Wolf/PhotoEdit Inc.)*

or, particularly with young children, may employ play as the primary mode of interaction between the therapist and the child. Alternatively, various forms of individually focused treatment may be delivered in a group rather than in an individual format. The same assumptions and methods that guide individual therapies may be used. The group format may be selected in order to serve larger numbers of children and adolescents (Johnson, Rasbury, & Siegel, 1997). Another advantage of this choice is that groups offer the opportunity for socialization experiences not present in the individual mode. Group treatment also may be more appealing to young people because it is less threatening; demonstrates that peers, too, have difficulties; and often includes opportunities for activities not likely to occur in a one-to-one relationship with an adult therapist.

Play therapy. The need to alter treatment procedures to fit the young child's level of cognitive and emotional development is one factor that has produced nonverbal modes of working with children. The use of play as a therapeutic vehicle is a common mode of treatment with young children. This is consistent with the importance of play in their development (Rubin, Bukowski, & Parker, 2006). Rather than relying exclusively on abstract verbal interactions, the therapist uses play to facilitate communication. Play may also be a more familiar way for the

child to interact with an adult and may help make the child feel at ease. A therapist may use puppets and dolls, have the child draw or paint, employ specially created board games, or use children's books that tell the story of children with similar difficulties. In this manner, most practitioners use play as a part of therapy. Another option is to use play itself as a therapeutic vehicle and play therapy as a more structured and distinct approach to treatment (Ablon, 1996; Russ, 1995). The two most well-known perspectives on play therapy are derived from the psychodynamic and the client-centered perspectives.

Early psychoanalytic therapists agreed that child patients required a different mode of treatment than the highly verbal, free association mode used in adult psychoanalysis. Melanie Klein (1932) gave the child's play a prominent role in the therapeutic process and used it as the basis for psychoanalytic interpretation. In contrast, Anna Freud viewed play as only one potential mode of expression and placed less emphasis on symbolic interpretation of play. For example, she disagreed with Klein that a child opening a woman's handbag was symbolically expressing curiosity regarding the contents of the mother's womb. She suggested that, rather, the child might be responding to a previous experience in which someone brought a gift in a similar receptacle (A. Freud, 1946). The contemporary psychoanalytic position

Treatment may involve the youth, parent(s), and other family members.
(Michael Newman/PhotoEdit Inc.)

tends to favor Anna Freud's positions on play (Johnson et al., 1997).

Another major influence on the evolution of play therapy was the work of Virginia Axline, who developed her approach from the client-centered perspective associated with Carl Rogers. The basic principles outlined by Axline (1947) remain the guidelines for contemporary client-centered play therapy (Johnson et al., 1997). The therapist adjusts his or her communication style to create the appropriate accepting, permissive, and nondirective therapeutic environment. The use of play with young children helps to create such an environment.

Family therapy and parent training.

Clinicians may also work with the young person's parents or family. We will see that working with the family can take many forms. Here we highlight a few examples.

Including members of the family as part of the therapeutic process is consistent with the understanding that a clinical problem exists in a social context and that the family is a very important part of that context. Clinicians who treat adolescents with eating disorders, for example, frequently work with the entire family to change maladaptive family interaction patterns that may contribute to the development and maintenance of eating disorders (Robin, 2003; Wilfley et al., 2006). Similarly, clinicians working with youngsters who have significant conduct problems, such as juvenile offending and substance abuse, may seek to develop critical competencies and establish adaptive relationships by involving the

family as well as other social systems in the treatment process (Henggeler & Lee, 2003; McMahon, Wells, & Kotler, 2006).

Parent training is a common therapeutic tool. Many professionals have taken the position that change in the child or adolescent's behavior may best be achieved by producing changes in the way that the parents manage the young person. This viewpoint is consistent with the observation that the parent's perception, as well as the child's actual behavior, results in the child being referred for treatment. Siblings of the referred youth may have similar problems (Fagan & Najman, 2003); this is another reason that it may be helpful to work with the entire family or provide parents with a general set of parenting skills.

Parent training procedures have been applied to a wide variety of child and adolescent problems. A number of approaches have emerged, and popular books presenting these approaches appear on the shelves of bookstores everywhere. However, in terms of systematic applications and research, most work has come from the social learning/behavioral approach.

Behavioral parent training has received a great deal of clinical and research attention, and has inspired many reviews and discussions (Kazdin, 1997; McMahon et al., 2006; Webster-Stratton & Hancock, 1998). Efforts have focused on teaching parents to identify and monitor behaviors and to manage the consequences, or contingencies, that they apply to their children's behavior. Parent training approaches also include skills such as verbal communication and expression of emotion. In addition, parent training programs attempt to consider the impact of stressors such as socioeconomic disadvantage, single-parent status, social isolation, and parental depression on the effectiveness of treatment. Parent training is frequently employed as part of a multifaceted approach to treatment, and specific cultural adaptations may be implemented (Martinez & Eddy, 2005). Other components may include additional therapeutic work with the parent, direct work with the child, or work with the teacher and the school (Kazdin, 2003; Webster-Stratton & Reid, 2003).

Pharmacological treatment. Pharmacological treatments (medications) are part of the interventions employed for a variety of childhood and adolescent behavior disorders (APA, 2006; Vitiello, 2006). These treatments are often used in combination with other modes of treatment. Medications that affect mood, thought processes, or overt behavior are known as psychotropic or psychoactive, and treatment that uses medication is called psychopharmacological treatment. Two examples of some of the pharmacological agents prescribed for children and adolescents are stimulants for attention-deficit hyperactivity disorder and selective serotonin reuptake inhibitors for obsessive–compulsive disorder, depression, and anxiety disorders.

The decision whether to use psychopharmacological treatment is, in part, determined by the nature of the presenting problem. However, other considerations such as possible side effects and a family's comfort with using medication need to be considered and discussed. Racial/ethnic and income differences contribute to the rates of psychotropic medication use in young people. For example, Leslie and colleagues (2003) report that among a large sample of families receiving publicly funded services, caregivers of African American and Latino children were less likely to report use of such medication within the past year than caregivers of white children. Higher income and private insurance also were associated with a greater likelihood of psychotropic medication use.

Psychotropic drugs produce therapeutic effects by influencing the process of neurotransmission. According to Poling, Gadow, and Cleary (1991), these medications can affect neurotransmission by

- altering the body's production of a neurotransmitter
- interfering with the storage of a neurotransmitter
- altering the release of a neurotransmitter
- interfering with the inactivation of a neurotransmitter or the reuptake of a neurotransmitter, and
- interacting with receptors for a neurotransmitter.

For some psychoactive drugs, there is a specific and clearly hypothesized mechanism for action, whereas for others the specific reasons for effectiveness are unknown.

Children and adolescents have been increasingly treated with psychotropic medications. There is particular concern about the appreciable increase in treatment of children as young as 2 to 4 years of age with medications such as stimulants and antidepressants (Greenhill et al., 2003a; Zito et al., 2000). Research regarding the efficacy and safety of many of these medications for children and adolescents lags behind their use; however, research continues to address issues of safety and effectiveness (APA, 2006; Correll, 2008 Greenhill et al., 2003b; Vitiello, 2006).

EMPIRICALLY SUPPORTED INTERVENTIONS

In subsequent chapters in this text, as part of our discussion of various disorders of youth, we examine interventions for specific disorders. Interventions for which there is empirical support are emphasized—that is, prevention programs and treatments that have been deemed worthy through scientific evaluation. This approach follows from one of the themes of this text, an orientation toward empirical approaches and the methods of science.

This same emphasis, along with an increasing demand that professionals be held accountable for the effectiveness of the services they offer, was among the considerations that led professional organizations to identify such interventions. As part of this evolving effort (Chorpita, 2003; Weisz et al., 2005) several different terms, including evidence-based interventions and empirically supported interventions have been used to describe treatments for which such evidence exists. Also, criteria have been proposed to designate interventions that are evidence based or empirically supported (Chambless & Hollon, 1998; Flay et al., 2005; Ollendick, King, & Chorpita, 2006).

For example, the Society of Clinical Psychology (a division of the American Psychological Association) formed the Task Force on Promotion and Dissemination of Psychological Procedures. The task force issued a report that indicated which treatments were empirically supported, and specified the level of research necessary to establish a treatment as empirically supported (Chambless, 1996; Chambless & Hollon, 1998; Chambless et al., 1996). Three categories were noted: well-established treatments, probably efficacious treatments, and experimental treatments. The primary distinction was between *well-established* and *probably efficacious* treatments. The principal differences between the two categories are as follows:

- Well-established treatments have been shown to be superior to placebo interventions or other treatments, whereas probably efficacious treatments have been shown to be superior only to a waiting-list or no-treatment control.

- Well-established treatments have been shown to be effective in studies by at least two different teams of investigators, whereas probably efficacious treatments need not be (e.g., two studies by the same investigator are adequate).

The research for both categories must be well-controlled group or single-subject designs, and characteristics of the treatment participants (e.g., age, sex, ethnicity, diagnosis) must be clearly specified. Furthermore, treatment must have been conducted with treatment manuals, which describe precisely the treatment procedures that are followed. This method allows for the evaluation of treatment integrity—that is, the degree to which therapists in the study have followed the treatment that is described and being evaluated.

Although the evidence-based interventions movement is supported by many professionals, it is still the subject of considerable discussion and concern (Chorpita, Becker, & Daleiden, 2007). One concern is voiced by the question, "What treatment methods might clinicians use?" Perhaps there are types of therapies—from different orientations, for example—that might be effective but have yet to be tested. And what course of action is appropriate for problems for which there are no empirically supported intervention? A second concern involves the reliance on manualized treatments. Does the use of manuals mean an inflexible "cookbook" approach to treatment that ignores clinical judgment? Or can manuals be viewed as a set of careful guidelines that may be used in a clinically responsible, flexible manner? A third concern revolves around the question of the applicability and transportability of interventions from the research setting to the real world and to real-world clients (see p. 80).

Although these concerns merit consideration, our discussion throughout the remaining chapters, is sensitive to the need for interventions for which empirical evidence is strongest.

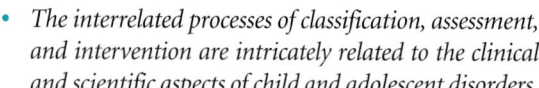

SUMMARY

- *The interrelated processes of classification, assessment, and intervention are intricately related to the clinical and scientific aspects of child and adolescent disorders.*

CLASSIFICATION AND DIAGNOSIS

- *Classification systems must have clearly defined categories or dimensions that can be discriminated from each other. Classification systems must be reliable and valid. Diagnostic systems are also judged by their clinical utility.*

- *Clinically derived classification relies on consensus among clinicians regarding disorders and their definition. The DSM, the clinically derived system most commonly employed in the United States, is a categorical approach to classification.*

- *The recent versions of the DSM include an increased number of categories and a multiaxial system to assess various aspects of functioning.*

- *The problem of comorbidity—youngsters' meeting the criteria for more than one disorder—presents particular challenges.*

- *Over time efforts have been made to improve the DSM system. The current version features greater coverage of child and adolescent disorders, more highly structured rules for diagnosis, and attempts to draw on research in a more consistent fashion.*

- *Although reliability of the DSM has been improved by more structured diagnostic rules, there is still variation across categories, and reliability may be affected by the conditions under which information is obtained and diagnoses are made. The question of validity has received considerable attention, but the validity of various aspects of the DSM system is an open question.*

- *Despite improvements, the DSM is still criticized for its relative inattention to issues of age, gender, and cultural context as well as on other clinical, scientific, ethical, social, and political grounds.*

- *Empirical approaches to classification rely on behavior checklists and statistical analyses, and tend to be associated with dimensional rather than categorical approaches to classification.*

- *Achenbach's Child Behavior Checklist, Teacher Report Form, and Youth Self-Report are examples of checklists employed in the empirical approach. There is good support for the existence of two broad syndromes—externalizing and internalizing— and support for subcategories within each general syndrome.*

- *Information from multiple informants can reveal the possible influence of situational differences on behavior and differences due to the respondent's perspective.*

- *Critics of diagnostic systems remind us of the possible dangers of labeling children and adolescents and of the potential impact of stigmatization.*

ASSESSMENT

- *Conducting a comprehensive assessment is necessary, not only for classification and diagnosis but also for planning and executing appropriate interventions. The complex process of assessment requires a multifaceted approach.*

- *The general clinical interview is the most common form of assessment. Structured interviews are often organized to provide information for a DSM diagnosis.*

- *Problem checklists can sample a wide range of behavior problems or focus on those problems particular to a specific disorder. These checklists may enable the clinician to compare a young person's behavior with appropriate norms and to examine issues such as situational aspects of a youth's behavior and the perceptions of various informants.*

- *Self-report measures are available for both the young person and the relevant adults in the child or adolescent's life. These instruments can be used to assess constructs directly related to the presenting problem (e.g., anxiety, depression) or related constructs of potential interest (e.g., self-concept, self-control, parenting stress, family environment).*

- *Observation of behavior is central to a behavioral/ social learning approach and is a direct method of assessment. The impracticality of implementing current observation systems in general clinical practice is an impediment to their widespread use.*

- *Projective tests are probably less commonly used than they once were, as a result of questions concerning their reliability and validity.*

- *Intellectual–educational assessments are conducted for a wide variety of presenting problems. These assessments evaluate general intelligence and developmental levels, as well as specific abilities and achievement. Although intelligence tests are popular, they are in many ways controversial. Given that they present a variety of concerns, they should be used cautiously.*

- *Assessment of physical functioning, especially of the nervous system, is important for many behavior problems. Methods include case histories, medical examinations, the EEG, and several newer techniques, such as the CT scan, MRI, PET scan, and fMRI. Much attention has also been given to neuropsychological testing as a means of indirectly assessing known or suspected problems in central nervous system functioning.*

INTERVENTION: PREVENTION AND TREATMENT

- *Intervention strategies can range from the most universally applicable to the most narrowly focused. Interventions may be implemented in a range of settings.*

- *The Institute of Medicine model of prevention describes three types of prevention strategies; universal, selective/high-risk, and indicated strategies. Other models include those strategies, but also add broad health promotion and wellness approaches.*

- *Treatment of children and adolescents usually includes several elements, because young people are likely to have multiple problems. Treatments are likely to include family members and may need to incorporate school personnel and peers as well.*

- *Various modes and settings for treatment of youngsters and their families are available. Psychotherapy may be conducted with a single child or adolescent or in groups. Play can be an important aspect of therapy, especially with younger clients. Treatments often include family members, focus on the family as a unit, or incorporate parent training in child management skills. Psychotropic medications have increasingly been employed in the treatment of child and adolescent disorders. Treatment may take place in a variety of settings including the clinician's office, schools, and various residential facilities.*

- *Demand for professionals to be accountable for the effectiveness of their services along with an increasing emphasis on empiricism has led professional organizations to develop interventions that are supported by research.*

KEY TERMS

classification *(p. 92)*

taxonomy *(p. 92)*

diagnosis *(p. 92)*

assessment *(p. 92)*

category *(p. 92)*

dimension *(p. 92)*

interrater reliability *(p. 93)*

test–retest reliability *(p. 93)*

validity *(p. 93)*

clinical utility *(p. 93)*

Diagnostic and Statistical Manual of Mental Disorders (DSM) *(p. 93)*

International Classification of Diseases (ICD) *(p. 93)*

Diagnostic Classification: 0–3 *(p. 93)*

clinically derived classification *(p. 93)*

categorical approach *(p. 93)*

multiaxial system *(p. 94)*

comorbidity *(p. 95)*

co-occurrence *(p. 95)*

empirical approach to classification *(p. 98)*

syndrome *(p. 98)*

broadband syndrome *(p. 98)*

internalizing syndrome/behaviors *(p. 98)*

externalizing syndrome/behaviors *(p. 98)*

narrowband syndrome *(p. 98)*

normative sample *(p. 99)*

diagnostic label *(p. 100)*

stigma *(p. 100)*

evidence-based assessment *(p. 103)*

general clinical interview *(p. 103)*

structured diagnostic interview *(p. 103)*

problem checklist *(p. 103)*

self-report measure *(p. 105)*

behavioral observation *(p. 105)*

observer drift *(p. 105)*

reactivity *(p. 105)*

projective test *(p. 105)*

intelligence (IQ) score *(p. 107)*

developmental index *(p. 107)*

ability/achievement test *(p. 107)*

psychophysiological assessment *(p. 108)*

neurological assessment *(p. 108)*

brain imaging *(p. 108)*

computerized tomography (CT) scan *(p. 108)*

computerized axial tomography (CAT) scan *(p. 108)*

magnetic resonance imaging (MRI) *(p. 108)*

positron emission tomography (PET) scan *(p. 108)*

functional magnetic resonance imaging (fMRI) *(p. 108)*

neuropsychological evaluation *(p. 108)*

pediatric neuropsychology *(p. 109)*

intervention *(p. 109)*

prevention *(p. 109)*

treatment *(p. 109)*

universal prevention strategies *(p. 111)*

selective/high-risk prevention strategies *(p. 111)*

indicated prevention strategies *(p. 111)*

play therapy *(p. 113)*

parent training *(p. 114)*

psychotropic/psychoactive *(p. 115)*

psychopharmacological treatment *(p. 115)*

evidence-based/empirically supported intervention *(p. 115)*

treatment manuals *(p. 116)*

CHAPTER 6

Anxiety Disorders

With this chapter we begin our examination of specific problems and disorders. The children and adolescents discussed in this and the next chapter are variously described as anxious, fearful, withdrawn, timid, depressed, and the like. They seem to be very unhappy and to lack self-confidence. These youngsters are often said to have emotional difficulties that they take out on themselves; thus, their problems are often termed internalizing disorders.

An Introduction to Internalizing Disorders

Empirical efforts to classify child and adolescent behavior disorders have clearly found support for a broad syndrome composed of internalizing problems (see chapter 5). Many of the problems included in clinically defined classifications would also be thought of as internalizing disorders. These problems were once broadly referred to as neuroses, a term that is now employed less frequently. More specific terms such as phobias, obsessions and compulsions, anxiety disorders, depression, and mood disorders are more likely to be used.

The relationship among more specific clinical diagnostic categories, such as the various anxiety and depressive disorders described in the DSM, is an ongoing consideration. Why is this the case? Considerable evidence indicates that a given child or adolescent often meets the criteria for more than one of the different disorders (AACAP, 2007; Angold, Costello, & Erkanli, 1999). The phenomenon of an individual's meeting the criteria for more than one disorder, which is often termed comorbidity, was discussed in chapter 5. The dilemma is an appreciable one.

It has also been suggested that what are sometimes viewed as separate disorders may be different expressions of a general disposition toward the development of internalizing difficulties. Particular environments or experiences shape this general disposition into a particular pattern of symptoms, or disorder (Williamson et al., 2005). Cultural differences may operate in this manner. Research suggests that there are no differences among cultural groups in the overall prevalence of anxiety disorders or in the temperamental qualities that may underlie the development of anxiety difficulties. However, differences in the prevalence of specific anxiety disorders and types of symptoms are reported (Austin &

Chorpita, 2004; Pina & Silverman, 2004). For example, higher rates of separation anxiety disorder and of somatic/physiological symptoms in Hispanic than in European American children have been cited (Ginsburg & Silverman, 1996; Varela et al., 2004). The strong value that Hispanic cultures place on familial interdependence (collectivism) and on empathizing with others and remaining agreeable (simpatia) has been suggested as contributing to this particular expression of anxiety by members of this cultural group.

With these considerations in mind, let us turn to an examination of internalizing disorders. In this chapter, we examine anxiety disorders, and in chapter 7, we discuss mood disorders.

DEFINING AND CLASSIFYING ANXIETY DISORDERS

What do we mean when we say that someone is anxious? Barlow (2002) suggests that,

> *anxiety seems best characterized as a future-oriented emotion, characterized by perceptions of uncontrollability and unpredictability over potentially aversive events and a rapid shift in attention to the focus of potentially dangerous events or one's own affective response to these events. (p. 104)*

Fear and anxiety have much in common, and the terms are sometimes used interchangeably. However, a distinction is made between fear as a reaction to an immediate/present threat characterized by an alarm reaction, and anxiety as a future-oriented emotion characterized by an elevated level of apprehension and lack of control. In general, anxiety and fear are viewed as a complex pattern of three types of reactions to a perceived threat (Barrios & O'Dell, 1998; Lang, 1984). This tripartite model describes overt behavioral responses (e.g., running away, trembling voice, eyes closing), cognitive responses (e.g., thoughts of being scared, self-deprecatory thoughts, images of bodily harm), and physiological responses (e.g., changes in heart rate and respiration, muscle tension, stomach upset).

In contrast to the complex combination of three components that define fear and anxiety, worry—thoughts about possible negative outcomes that are intrusive and difficult to control—is viewed as a cognitive component of anxiety (Barlow, 2002; Vasey & Daleiden, 1994).

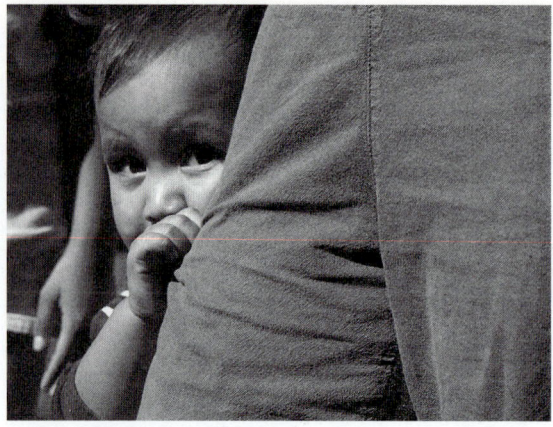

Fears and anxieties are quite common in children. It is only when these are persistent, are intense, interfere with functioning, or are developmentally inappropriate that they may require clinical attention.
(Geri Engberg/The Image Works)

One of the challenges facing clinicians is to decide whether the anxiety exhibited by a child or adolescent is normal and perhaps transitory, or atypical and persistent (Albano, Chorpita, & Barlow, 2003; Bosquet & Egeland, 2006). Anxiety is a basic human emotion. It can serve an adaptive function by alerting the youngster to novel or threatening situations. Anxiety is thus part of normal developmental processes by which the young person learns, for example, to identify and cope with arousal, develop competencies, and become more autonomous. Thus, young children learn to cope with the dark and separation, while adolescents deal with the anxieties of beginning high school and dating. What then do we know about typical fear, worry, and anxiety?

NORMAL FEARS, WORRIES, AND ANXIETIES

General prevalence. Several classic studies of general populations indicate that children exhibit a surprisingly large number of fears, worries, and anxieties (Jersild & Holmes, 1935; Lapouse and Monk, 1959; MacFarlane, Allen, & Honzik, 1954). Parents may underestimate the prevalence of fears in their children, particularly older children who are increasingly able to mask their emotions (Gullone, 2000).

Gender, age, and cultural differences. Most research suggests that girls exhibit a greater number of fears than boys. This difference is more clear in older children and less clear in preschool and elementary school children. Studies generally suggest greater fear intensity in girls as well (Gullone, 2000). Findings of gender differences probably should be interpreted with caution because gender-role expectations may, in part, be responsible for differences between boys and girls in displaying and admitting to fears (Ginsburg & Silverman, 2000).

It is commonly reported that both the number and the intensity of fears experienced by children decline with age (Gullone, 2000). Worry becomes prominent in children at about 7 years of age and becomes more complex and varied as children develop.

Certain fears appear to be more common at particular ages: for example, fear of strangers at 6 to 9 months, fear of imaginary creatures during the second year, fear of the dark among 4-year-olds, and social fears and fear of failure in older children and adolescents (Gullone, 2000; Miller, Barrett, & Hampe, 1974). Similarly, preschoolers may worry about imaginary threats, young children about their physical safety, and older children and adolescents about social situations and their competence. Thus, threats to youngsters' well-being are a prominent worry across age (Silverman, La Greca, & Wasserstein, 1995). Changes in the content of fears and worries likely reflect ongoing cognitive, social, and emotional development.

Cross-cultural examinations of common fears suggest similarities across cultures. The Fear Survey Schedule for Children (FSSC-R; Ollendick, 1983) is an inventory of fear stimuli and situations. The FSSC-R has been translated into a number of different languages. The most common fears were similar across different countries and cultures and girls were found to score higher than boys (Fonesca, Yule, & Erol, 1994).

CLASSIFICATION OF ANXIETY DISORDERS

Most authorities would not usually view age-appropriate anxieties as requiring clinical attention unless they were quite intense or continued longer than expected. However, if the fear or anxiety, even though short-lived, creates sufficient discomfort or interferes with functioning, intervention may be justified. Furthermore, anxiety disorders, if left untreated, may follow a chronic course and be associated with additional difficulties (Cartwright-Hutton, McNicol, & Doubleday, 2006; Kendall et al., 2004). How do we then define and classify disorders of childhood and adolescence in which anxiety is the principal feature? Because the DSM

approach is most commonly used, much of this chapter is organized using this system.

The DSM approach. The DSM-IV-TR describes one type of anxiety disorder that is "usually first diagnosed in infancy, childhood, or adolescence," Separation Anxiety Disorder. In addition to this disorder, a child or an adolescent can be diagnosed with many of the other anxiety disorders included in the DSM: Specific Phobia, Social Phobia, Panic Disorder, Generalized Anxiety Disorder, Obsessive–Compulsive Disorder, Posttraumatic Stress Disorder, and Acute Stress Disorder. We will define and discuss each of these disorders in our discussion of specific anxiety disorders. The definitions of most of these anxiety disorders involve similar processes such as apprehension of objects or situations, and avoidant/anxiety-reducing behaviors. They differ, largely, in terms of the content or focus of the anxiety.

The empirical approach. Empirical systems that are based on statistical procedures have also yielded subcategories related to anxiety disorders. Within the broad category of internalizing disorders, for example, Achenbach (Achenbach & Rescorla, 2001) describes an anxious/depressed syndrome (see Table 6–1). There is not, however, a separate anxiety syndrome or other narrower syndromes that correspond to the specific anxiety disorders of the DSM, suggesting that in youths, the various anxiety and depression symptoms tend to occur together. Other internalizing syndromes, such as "somatic complaints" (e.g., feeling dizzy, having stomachaches) and "withdrawn/depressed" (e.g., refusing to talk, feeling withdrawn), also contain symptoms that are likely to be related to anxiety problems.

TABLE 6–1	BEHAVIOR PROBLEMS INCLUDED IN THE ANXIOUS/DEPRESSED SYNDROME
Cries a lot	Feels too guilty
Fears	Self-conscious
Fears school	Feels hurt when criticized
Fears doing bad	
Must be perfect	Talks or thinks of suicide
Feels unloved	
Feels worthless	Anxious to please
Nervous, tense	Fears mistakes
Fearful, anxious	Worries

From Achenbach & Rescorla, 2001.

EPIDEMIOLOGY OF ANXIETY DISORDERS

Anxiety disorders are among the most common disorders experienced by children and adolescents (Costello, Egger, & Angold, 2005a). Estimates of prevalence may vary, but studies of community samples have generally reported that between 12 and 20% of school-age children and adolescents meet diagnostic criteria for one or more anxiety disorders (APA, 2006). Young people are likely to meet the criteria for more than one anxiety disorder.

Research suggests that girls are slightly more likely than boys to have an anxiety disorder (Costello, Egger, & Angold, 2005b). There appear to be no differences in prevalence of anxiety disorders in general in different ethnic groups. However, there do appear to be differences with regard to the prevalence of specific anxiety disorders (e.g. separation anxiety, social anxiety) across ethnic groups (Austin & Chorpita, 2004; Roberts, Ramsay Roberts, & Xing, 2006).

Specific Phobias

Phobias, as contrasted with developmentally appropriate fears, are of concern because they are excessive, cannot be reasoned away, are beyond voluntary control, lead to avoidance, and interfere with functioning (Miller et al., 1974). The essential feature of a specific phobia is a persistent fear of a specific object or situation that is unusual or excessive.

DIAGNOSTIC CRITERIA

The main features required for the DSM diagnosis of Specific Phobia are presented in Table 6–2. These criteria acknowledge developmental differences by noting that anxiety may be expressed differently by children and that children may not realize that their fears are unreasonable or excessive.

ACCENT

Culture, Ethnicity, and Disorder

Culture and ethnicity affect child and adolescent psychopathology in many ways. For example, certain anxiety disorders (e.g., social anxiety) may be more prevalent in certain cultures or ethnic groups. What then do prevalence findings tell us about the development of anxiety disorders?

Whether or not there are differences in prevalence, there may be cultural/ethnic differences in anxiety presentation. For example, certain symptoms (e.g., somatic symptoms) may be more common in certain cultures or ethnic groups. Also, the way in which symptoms are expressed should be considered. For example, the content of anxious cognitions may vary.

How does consideration of culture and ethnicity help us understand the development of anxiety disorders? For example, are certain risk factors more prevalent in certain groups or in the communities in which they reside? Are there cultural differences in parenting that increase the risk for, or serve as, protective factors against the development of anxiety disorders? Also, discrimination and/or the process of acculturation may be stresses that can contribute to anxiety or challenge developing coping skills.

Appreciation of the necessity for culturally sensitive assessment has increased. Instruments that were developed in one cultural context may not accurately assess anxiety in a different cultural context or ethnic group. Also, symptoms may not group into different factors in the same way for all cultural or ethnic groups. This may be due in part, as suggested above, to the differences in the ways in which anxiety presents. But this may also be due to differences in how anxiety is thought about and understood by members of different cultural groups. Language may also be an important consideration in conducting an assessment. Differences may emerge in assessment findings depending on the language employed in interviews or assessment instruments.

There has also been an increasing sensitivity to treatment issues. Adapting effective treatment programs to better fit particular cultures suggests that such adaptations may increase the effectiveness of these treatments and make them more acceptable to members of different cultural groups. It is also important to appreciate that there may be important ethnic/cultural differences in the likelihood of youngsters and their families seeking treatment. Increasing the use of and access to effective interventions serves the larger goal of helping children, adolescents, and their families.

Clearly, these considerations apply not only to anxiety disorders, but to many, if not all, of the disorders considered in future chapters.

"I'm not a scaredy-cat—I'm phobic."

In addition to these main features, the fear must produce marked distress or must interfere significantly with the youngster's normal routine, academic functioning, or social relationships. Also, the fear must have a duration of at least 6 months.

The DSM suggests that specific phobias be further subcategorized into five types: animal, natural environment (e.g., heights, storms, water), blood-injection-injury, situational (e.g., airplanes, enclosed places), and other (e.g., in children, loud sounds or costumed characters).

DESCRIPTION

Behaviorally, youngsters with specific phobias try to avoid the situation or object that they fear. For example, children who have an extreme fear of dogs may refuse to go outside. When confronted with a large dog, they

TABLE 6–2	MAJOR FEATURES FOR THE DSM DIAGNOSIS OF SPECIFIC PHOBIA

1. Marked and persistent fear that is excessive or unreasonable, cued by the presence or anticipation of a specific object or situation (e.g., flying, heights, animals, receiving an injection, seeing blood).

2. Exposure to the phobic stimulus almost invariably provokes an immediate anxiety response. **Note:** In children, this anxiety may be expressed by crying, tantrums, freezing, or clinging.

3. The person must recognize that his or her fear is excessive or unreasonable. **Note:** In children this feature may be absent.

4. The person must avoid the phobic situation(s) or must endure exposure with intense anxiety and distress.

From American Psychiatric Association, 2000.

may "freeze" or run to their parents for protection. The youngster may describe feelings of tension, panic, or disgust. The cognitive aspect of these reactions often includes thoughts of catastrophic events that may occur upon exposure to the phobic situation. Nausea, rapid heart rate, and difficulty in breathing are among the physiological reactions that may also occur. These reactions may occur even when contact with the feared situation is merely anticipated. Thus, the young person's phobia not only restricts his or her own activities, but also is likely to change the lifestyle and activities of the family as a whole.

Carlos | **A Specific Phobia**

Carlos, a 9-year-old Hispanic-American boy, presented at a child anxiety clinic with an avoidance of buttons. The problem began in kindergarten when Carlos was 5 years old. Carlos was working on an art project that involved buttons and ran out of buttons. He described being asked to come to the front of the classroom to get additional buttons from a large bowl on the teacher's desk. In reaching for the buttons, his hand slipped and all the buttons in the bowl fell on him. Carlos reported being distressed at that moment and both he and his mother report an increasing avoidance of buttons since that time. As time progressed it became more difficult for Carlos to handle buttons. Carlos also reported that he viewed buttons contacting his body as disgusting (e.g. "buttons are gross"). This led to interference in several aspects of Carlos's and his family's life such as not being able to dress himself and difficulty concentrating in school as a result of preoccupation with not touching his school uniform buttons or anything touched by his buttoned shirt.

Adapted from Silverman & Moreno, 2005, pp. 834–835.

EPIDEMIOLOGY

Specific phobias are among the most commonly diagnosed anxiety disorders in children and adolescents (Costello et al., 2005a). Although estimates vary somewhat, prevalence is generally reported as between 3 and 4% in community samples (Albano et al., 2003; Foa et al., 2005a). Specific phobias are often more prevalent in girls than in boys (Silverman & Moreno, 2005). Information regarding ethnic differences is limited, but comparisons between European—American, African-American, and Hispanic youngsters suggest more similarities than differences (Last & Perrin, 1993; Roberts et al., 2006; Silverman & Ginsberg, 1998).

Youngsters with specific phobias usually have more than one phobia and are likely to meet the criteria for other disorders. Last, Strauss, and Francis (1987) found that among clinic-referred youngsters with a primary diagnosis of specific phobia, the majority met criteria for one or more other disorders. Additional diagnoses included other anxiety disorders, depression and mood disorders, and externalizing disorders such as oppositional defiant disorder. In a community sample of adolescents, Essau and colleagues (2000) report that nearly half of the youngsters with a specific phobia met the criteria for another anxiety disorder, and depressive and somatoform disorders (physical symptoms in the absence of a known physical pathology) were also common. In addition, Verduin and Kendall (2003) report that nearly half of a clinical sample of youth whose primary diagnosis was another anxiety disorder also met the criteria for a specific phobia.

DEVELOPMENTAL COURSE

Children's phobias are commonly believed to be relatively benign, and improvement is expected over time with or without treatment. However, there is reason to question this perception and to think in terms of continuity over time (Sterba, Prinstein, & Cox, 2007; Silverman & Moreno, 2005). Findings from Essau and colleagues' (2000) sample of German adolescents, for example, suggest that, for some youngsters, phobic symptoms persist over time and are associated with impaired functioning. This finding is consistent with reports of phobic adults that suggest that specific phobias are likely to begin in childhood and may for some individuals persist into adulthood (Kendler et al., 1992b; Öst, 1987). A reasonable suggestion, therefore, is that specific phobias are likely to begin during childhood and, that for at least some individuals, they may persist over time.

Social Anxiety Disorder

DIAGNOSTIC CRITERIA

Another category of clinical level fear or phobia specified by the DSM is Social Anxiety Disorder (or Social Phobia). The essential feature of social anxiety is a marked and persistent fear of acting in an embarrassing or humiliating way in social or performance

TABLE 6–3	MAJOR FEATURES FOR THE DSM DIAGNOSIS OF SOCIAL ANXIETY DISORDER

1. A marked and persistent fear of one or more social or performance situations in which the person is exposed to unfamiliar people or to possible scrutiny by others. The individual fears that he or she will act in a way (or show anxiety symptoms) that will be humiliating or embarrassing. **Note:** In children there must be evidence of the capacity for age-appropriate social relationships with familiar people and the anxiety must occur in peer settings, not just in interaction with adults.
2. Exposure to the feared situation almost invariably provokes anxiety. **Note:** In children this anxiety may be expressed by crying, tantrums, freezing, or shrinking from social situations with unfamiliar people.
3. There must be recognition by the person that the fear is excessive or unreasonable. **Note:** This feature may be absent in children.
4. The feared situations are avoided or are endured with intense distress.

From American Psychiatric Association, 2000.

situations. The main features required for the diagnosis of social anxiety disorder are presented in Table 6–3.

As with specific phobias, these criteria acknowledge developmental differences by noting that anxiety may be expressed differently by children and that children may not realize that their fears are unreasonable or excessive. Furthermore, to distinguish social phobia from other aspects of social development, children receiving the diagnosis would be expected to display appropriate social relationships with familiar people and to experience social anxiety with peers and not just with adults.

In addition to these main features, the phobia must interfere significantly with the youngster's normal routine, academic functioning, or social relationships or must produce marked distress. Also, the phobia must have a duration of at least 6 months.

DESCRIPTION

Youngsters with social anxiety fear social activities and situations such as speaking, reading, writing or performing in public, initiating or maintaining conversations, speaking to authority figures, and interacting in informal social situations (Beidel, Turner, & Morris, 1999).

The behavioral component of this social anxiety is most frequently manifested by the avoidance of situations that involve social interactions or evaluation. Young people may avoid even everyday and seemingly mundane activities, such as eating in public. Albano, Chorpita, and Barlow (2003) describe a teenage girl who spent every lunch period in a bathroom stall in order to avoid the school cafeteria. In the cognitive realm, concerns about being embarrassed or negatively evaluated are common for these young people. They are likely to focus their thoughts on negative attributes that they perceive in themselves, to negatively evaluate their performance, and to interpret others' responses as critical or disapproving even when this is not the case. Examples of these concerns are illustrated in Table 6–4, which presents examples of items from the Social Anxiety Scale for Children-Revised (LaGreca & Stone, 1993). Somatic symptoms such as restlessness, blushing, sweating and complaints of illness and stomachaches are common physiological symptoms reported in youths with social phobias (Ginsburg, Riddle, & Davies, 2006).

Because these young people try to avoid social situations, they may miss school and may be unlikely to participate in recreational activities. For example, younger children may not attend birthday parties or participate in Scout meetings, whereas adolescents

TABLE 6–4	EXAMPLES OF ITEMS FROM THE SOCIAL ANXIETY SCALE FOR CHILDREN—REVISED

I worry about what other kids think of me.
I'm afraid that other kids will not like me.
I feel that kids are making fun of me.
I feel shy around kids I don't know.
I feel nervous when I'm around certain kids.
I feel shy even with kids I know very well.
It's hard for me to ask other kids to play with me.

By permission of author Annette M. La Greca.

ACCENT

Selective Mutism and Social Anxiety

A young kindergarten girl, Amy, does not speak in school or with her peers. She has been this way since beginning preschool. Children like Amy might be given a diagnosis of Selective Mutism.

Young people with selective mutism do not talk in specific social situations. These situations, such as the classroom or play activities, are ones in which their peers typically do talk or in which talking is important to development. Mutism occurs despite the fact that the youths speak in other situations. For example, they may speak easily with family members if no one else is present. The onset of the disorder is usually before age 5. These youths are typically described as shy, withdrawn, fearful, and clingy (American Psychiatric Association, 2000). Many of these children also display oppositional behavior (Ford et al., 1998). They may, for example, be stubborn, be disobedient, whine, or have temper tantrums.

Selective mutism is a separate DSM disorder, but some evidence suggests that it might be conceptualized as an extreme form of social anxiety (Chavira et al., 2007; Standart & Le Couteur, 2003). For example, 90 to 100% of children with selective mutism also meet diagnostic criteria for social phobia (Black & Uhde, 1995; Dummit et al., 1997). There is also some support for the idea that children with selective mutism are more socially anxious than children with social phobia who are not selectively mute. However, it remains unclear whether youths with selective mutism simply have extreme levels of a social anxiety disorder (Chavira & Stein, 2005; Yeganeh et al., 2003). Although this diagnostic distinction remains unclear, clinicians who work with young people with selective mutism may need to consider their clients' potentially severe levels of social anxiety and possible oppositional behavior in planning treatments.

---

are unlikely to attend school events, such as club meetings or dances, or to date. At least some of these young people may therefore feel lonely and have few, or low quality, friendships (Parker et al., 2006).

Youths with social phobia often report feelings of lesser self-worth, as well as of sadness and loneliness. Over time they may also experience lesser educational achievement (Ginsburg, LaGreca, & Silverman, 1998; Velting & Albano, 2001). The potential consequences for a young person are thus quite broad.

Louis | Social Phobia and Its Consequences

Louis, a 12-year-old white male, was referred by his school counselor because of periodic episodes of school refusal, social withdrawal, and excessive need for reassurance. On an almost daily basis Louis would claim he could not remain in the classroom. He would generally be sent to the nurse or counselor's office until his mother came and took him home early. Louis had few friends and rarely participated in social activities that involved other children. Louis found parties, eating in public, and using public restrooms particularly difficult. Spanish class was also particularly difficult because of regular assignments to read aloud or to carry on conversations with classmates. Louis's mother described him as always having been excessively fearful, timid, scared of everything, and needing constant reassurance. The mother herself had a history of anxiety problems, was fearful of meeting new people, and had little social contact, saying "it's basically just Louis and me." Louis received the diagnoses of Social Phobia and Generalized Anxiety Disorder.

Adapted from Silverman & Ginsburg, 1998, pp. 260–261.

EPIDEMIOLOGY

Social anxiety disorder is estimated to be present in approximately 1 to 2% of youngsters in the general community (Costello et al., 2005a), with studies employing DSM-IV criteria suggesting somewhat higher rates than earlier studies (Beidel, Morris, & Turner, 2004; Canino et al., 2004). It is also a common diagnosis in clinic populations. Last and colleagues (1992) report that 14.9% of youngsters assessed at an anxiety disorders clinic were given a primary diagnosis of social phobia, and 32.4% had a lifetime history of the disorder. On the basis of reports of youngsters seen in clinics and retrospective reports, middle to late adolescence is the typical age of onset (Chavira & Stein, 2005; Strauss & Last, 1993). This finding is consistent with the developmental considerations discussed below. Although social anxiety disorder is most frequently diagnosed in adolescents, it can occur earlier (Costello et al., 2005b; Neal & Edelmann, 2003). Prevalence probably increases with age, and the disorder may be underrecognized, particularly in adolescents (Chavira & Stein, 2005). One reason that the problem may be underrecognized is that youngsters with social phobia may minimize their problems in order to present themselves in a desirable way (DiBartolo et al., 1998). This tendency would be consistent with a concern about negative evaluation. Slightly higher rates are reported for girls, but it is not clear whether there are gender differences in the prevalence of social anxiety disorder (Chavira & Stein, 2005; Ford et al., 2003).

Most youngsters with social phobia also meet the criteria for one or more other disorders (Beidel et al., 1999; Chavira & Stein, 2005). As with Louis, another anxiety disorder is the most common additional diagnosis (Verduin & Kendall, 2003). Adolescents, in particular, may also meet the criteria for a major depressive disorder.

DEVELOPMENT COURSE

The development of social phobia can be viewed within the context of normative developmental factors (Velting & Albano, 2001). In young children between the ages of 6 months and 3 years, stranger anxiety and separation anxiety are common. The self-consciousness that is an essential part of what we mean by social phobia, however, does not develop until later. The abilities to see oneself as a social object and to feel embarrassment may emerge at about 4 or 5 years of age. Envisioning the perspective of other people and then experiencing concern over their possible negative evaluation probably do not emerge until about 8 years of age. By late childhood or early adolescence, these cognitive developmental prerequisites and the awareness that one's appearance and behavior can be the basis for others' evaluations are in place. So, for example, Westenberg and colleagues (2004) assessed fears among a sample of children and adolescents (8 to 18 years of age) from the Netherlands. Fears of social and achievement evaluation increased with age, and these age-related changes in fears were associated with level of social-cognitive maturity.

By late childhood or early adolescence, youngsters are regularly required to perform tasks that have a social-evaluative component. They are, for

Adolescence is a period during which involvement in a variety of social activities is expected. Some young people find these social demands particularly difficult.
(Penny Tweedie/Getty Images Inc.–Stone Allstock)

example, expected to speak in class, engage in group activities, and perform in athletic or musical events. Responsibility for initiating and arranging social activities is also shifting. Parents are no longer likely to be highly involved in arranging social interactions. Young adolescents also may be expected to engage in different social activities such as attending school dances and dating. The combination of these social demands and the development of self-awareness can set the stage for the emergence of social anxiety. Social anxiety disorder may be thought to evolve from anxiety that is typical in this developmental period but that is magnified for some youngsters by individual differences and social demands (Neal & Edelmann, 2003; Parker et al., 2006).

Because adolescence is a period during which social anxieties are quite common, it may be particularly difficult to distinguish between normal and abnormal social anxiety. Interpretation of severity, defined in the DSM diagnostic criteria by phrases such as "almost invariably," "marked distress," "intense anxiety," and "interferes significantly," becomes particularly important in this age group (Clark et al., 1994). The view that some level of social anxiety is common during adolescence is supported by research data (Velting & Albano, 2001). For example, Essau, Conradt, and Peterman (1999) found that approximately 51% of a community sample of youths between the ages of 12 and 17 reported at least one specific social fear. However, only some smaller proportion of youths develops more general and clinical level problems (Chavira & Stein, 2005). In a longitudinal study of a cohort of young people from New Zealand, increased anxious/withdrawn behavior at age 8 was associated with increased risk for social phobia during adolescence and young adulthood (Goodwin, Fergusson, & Horwood, 2004).

Separation Anxiety

We have chosen to describe separation anxiety followed by a discussion school refusal of because much of what has been written about the problem of school refusal and its etiology has derived from a separation anxiety perspective. In addition, given that compulsory education laws require all children to attend school, it seems likely that many children with separation anxiety would also have problems with school attendance.

DIAGNOSIS AND CLASSIFICATION

The DSM category of Separation Anxiety Disorder (SAD) is intended to describe youths who have excessive anxiety regarding their separation from a major attachment figure and/or home. Diagnostic criteria include eight symptoms involving worry or distress and related sleep and physical problems. These symptoms (Table 6–5) are associated with concerns about separation from, or worry of harm befalling, major attachment figures.

The DSM requires the presence of three or more symptoms for at least 4 weeks for a positive diagnosis. The problems must be present prior to the age of 18 and must cause significant distress or impairment in social, school, or other areas of functioning.

DESCRIPTION

Young children experiencing separation anxiety may be clingy and follow their parents around. They may express general fear or apprehension, experience nightmares, or complain of somatic symptoms (e.g., headaches, stomachaches, nausea, palpitations). Older children may complain about not feeling well, think about illness or tragedy that might befall them or their caregivers, become apathetic and depressed, and be reluctant to leave home or to participate in activities with their peers. Some young people may threaten to harm themselves. This threat is usually

Refusing to go to school and/or to be separated from parents is a common reason for referral for psychological services.
(David J. Sams/Stock Boston)

TABLE 6–5	MAJOR FEATURES FOR THE DSM DIAGNOSIS OF SEPARATION ANXIETY DISORDER

Developmentally inappropriate and excessive anxiety concerning separation from home or from those to whom the individual is attached, as evidenced by three (or more) of the following:

1. Recurrent excessive distress when separation from home or major attachment figures occurs or is anticipated
2. Persistent and excessive worry about losing, or about possible harm befalling, major attachment figures
3. Persistent and excessive worry that an untoward event will lead to separation from a major attachment figure (e.g., getting lost or being kidnapped)
4. Persistent reluctance or refusal to go to school or elsewhere because of fear of separation
5. Persistent and excessive fear or reluctance to be alone or without major attachment figures at home or to be without significant adults in other settings
6. Persistent reluctance or refusal to go to sleep without being near a major attachment figure or to sleep away from home
7. Repeated nightmares involving the theme of separation
8. Repeated complaints of physical symptoms (such as headaches, stomachaches, nausea, or vomiting) when separation from major attachment figures occurs or is anticipated

From American Psychiatric Association, 2000.

viewed as a means of escaping or avoiding separation, and serious suicidal behavior is rare.

Kenny   Separation Anxiety

Kenny, a 10-year-old boy, lived with his parents and his two half-siblings from his mother's previous marriage. He was brought to an anxiety disorders clinic by his parents because he was extremely fearful and had refused to go to school during the past several months. Kenny was also unable to be in other situations in which he was separated from his parents—such as when playing in the backyard, at Little League practice, [and] staying with a sitter. When separated from his parents, Kenny cried, had tantrums, or threatened to hurt himself (e.g., jump from the school window). Kenny also exhibited high levels of anxiety, a number of specific fears, significant depressive symptomatology (e.g., sad mood, guilt about his problems, occasional wishes to be dead, and periodic early awakening). Kenny's separation problems appeared to have begun about a year earlier when his father was having drinking problems and was away from home for prolonged periods of time. Kenny's separation problems gradually worsened over the year.

Adapted from Last, 1988, pp. 12–13.

EPIDEMIOLOGY

Estimates of the prevalence of separation anxiety disorder in community samples typically range from about 3 to 12% of young people. Among youths referred to clinics, approximately 12% to one third receive a primary diagnosis of Separation Anxiety Disorder (Canino et al., 2004; Silverman & Dick-Niederhauser, 2004; Suveg et al., 2005). Prevalence is higher in children than in adolescents, and the disorder is uncommon in older adolescents. Children and adolescents with separation anxiety disorder often also meet diagnostic criteria for other disorders. Generalized Anxiety Disorder seems to be the most common other diagnosis received (Last, Strauss, & Francis, 1987; Verduin & Kendall, 2003). The status of gender and of ethnic differences in rates of prevalence remains unclear (Ford et al., 2003; Suveg et al., 2005). Some studies report a greater prevalence of SAD among girls than among boys, but others report no gender differences. Clinical samples suggest no ethnic differences in rates, but there is some suggestion of greater rates in community samples of African American youths.

DEVELOPMENTAL COURSE

Anxiety concerning separation from a primary caregiver is part of the normal developmental process in infants. From the first year of life through the preschool years, children typically exhibit periodic distress and worry when they are separated from their parents or other individuals to whom they have an attachment. Indeed, the absence of any separation distress may indicate an insecure attachment. Even in older children, it is not uncommon for expectations, beliefs, and prior separation experiences to lead to feelings of homesickness when the children are separated from their parents (Thurber & Sigman, 1998). Such distress is viewed as problematic only when distress about separation persists beyond the expected age or is excessive.

For children with separation anxiety, symptoms often progress from milder to more severe. For example, a child's complaints of nightmares may lead to the parents allowing the child to sleep in their bed on an intermittent basis. This often rapidly progresses to the child sleeping with one or both parents on a regular basis (Albano et al., 2003). Most children appear to recover from separation anxiety disorder (Kearney et al., 2003); however, in some, the symptoms may persist and they may develop a later disorder, with depression being particularly common (Last et al., 1996). In adolescents, separation anxiety, if present, may be the precursor of more serious problems (Blagg & Yule, 1994; Tonge, 1994). There is some suggestion, based on retrospective reports of adults, that youths with separation anxiety disorder may be at particular risk for developing panic disorder or agoraphobia (anxiety about being in a situation in which escape may be difficult or embarrassing) as adults (Manicavasagar et al., 2000). However, even retrospective findings are mixed (Rabian & Silverman, 2000), and a follow-up study of young people diagnosed with separation anxiety disorder found no evidence of any such association (Aschenbrand et al., 2003). Young adults who had completed treatment for SAD when they were youths were reassessed approximately 7.5 years later in structured diagnostic interviews. Participants with a childhood diagnosis of SAD were no more likely to meet the diagnostic criteria for panic disorder or agoraphobia as young adults than were those with a childhood diagnosis of other anxiety disorders. They were, however, more likely to meet the criteria for other anxiety disorders as young adults.

School Refusal

Definition

Some children and adolescents exhibit excessive anxiety regarding school attendance. When these young people do not attend school, their condition is typically termed school refusal. School refusal is not a DSM diagnosis; however, reluctance or refusal to go to school is one of the eight symptoms listed for the DSM diagnosis of SAD, and some youths who exhibit school refusal do receive this diagnosis. However since a young person need present with only three of the eight symptoms listed in order to receive the diagnosis of SAD, not all young people with separation anxiety disorder exhibit school refusal. In addition, not all school refusers show separation anxiety (Kearney, Eisen, & Silverman, 1995; Last & Strauss, 1990). Although the most common conceptualization of school refusal attributes the problem to separation anxiety, some young people may fear a particular aspect of the school experience, in which case they might be diagnosed under the specific phobia or social phobia categories. For example, a youth may fear going to school because of anxiety regarding academic performance, evaluation, speaking in public, conflict with peers, or meeting new people.

Thus, it is best not to view all cases of school refusal as being similar or as having a single cause. Indeed, school refusal should probably be considered heterogeneous and multicausal (Suveg, Aschenbrand, & Kendell, 2005). One suggestion is that it might be more useful to classify school refusal by the function that the behavior serves—by a functional analysis—rather than by symptoms (Kearney, 2001; Kearney & Silverman, 1996). Some youths may refuse school due to negative reinforcement. These young people may avoid negative affect, such as anxiety and depression, or may escape from aversive social or evaluative situations. Alternatively, children and adolescents may refuse to go to school due to positive reinforcement. For these young people, school refusal behaviors (e.g., complaints of illness) may elicit attention from their parents. Some young people may receive positive tangible reinforcement for staying home (e.g., watching television or being served special treats). Using a functional analysis approach, treatment programs can be designed that address the functions that school refusal behavior serves for a particular young person.

Description

A certain degree of anxiety and fear about school is common for children and adolescents, but some exhibit excessive anxiety regarding school attendance. The behaviors, thoughts, and somatic complaints characteristic of separation anxiety are often part of the picture of school refusal. Young people, particularly adolescents, may also show signs of depression. They are often absent from school on a regular basis, may fall behind in the academic work, and sometimes have to repeat a grade. In addition, because they miss opportunities for social experiences, they are likely to experience difficulties with their peers as well. School refusal can be a serious problem that causes considerable distress for both the youth and his or her caregivers and that may also interfere with the young person's development. Clinical reports suggest that onset of these problems often follows some life stress, such as a death, an illness, a change of school, or a move to a new neighborhood.

School refusal is often differentiated from truancy. Truants are usually described as unlikely to be excessively anxious or fearful about attending school. They typically are absent on an intermittent basis, often without parental knowledge. The school refuser, in contrast, is usually absent for continuous extended periods, during which time the parents are aware that the youth is at home. Truants are often described as poor students who exhibit other conduct problems, such as stealing and lying. There is considerable disagreement as to whether truancy or school attendance problems associated with conduct problems and antisocial behaviors should be included in the concept of school refusal (King & Bernstein, 2001).

EPIDEMIOLOGY AND DEVELOPMENTAL COURSE

School refusal is usually estimated to occur in 1 to 2% of the general population and in about 5% of all clinic-referred cases; it is equally common in boys and girls (Elliott, 1999; King et al., 2000). It is interesting, however, that some reports suggest that as many as 69% of referrals for any kind of child phobia are for school refusal. Perhaps the percentage is so high because the problem creates considerable difficulty for parents and school personnel.

School refusal, unlike separation anxiety disorder, can be found in youths of all ages, but like separation anxiety disorder, it seems more likely to occur at major transition points. There is the suggestion that, in younger children, the problem is likely to be related to separation anxiety, but children in middle-age groups or early adolescence are likely to have complex and mixed presentations of anxiety and depressive disorders. Prognosis seems best for children under the age of 10 years, and treatment seems to be particularly difficult for older youths and those who

are also depressed (Bernstein et al., 2001; Blagg & Yule, 1994). If problems are left untreated, serious long-term consequences may result (Elliott, 1999; Suveg et al., 2005).

In working with school refusers, the majority of clinicians of all orientations stress the importance of getting the young person back to school (Blagg & Yule, 1994; King, Ollendick, & Gullone, 1990). Successful strategies take an active approach to the problem, finding a way of getting the young person back to school even if this is difficult or requires the threat of legal intervention. Applying cognitive-behavioral interventions that include exposure to fearful situations, teaching the youth coping skills, and incorporating training and advice for parents and teachers have shown promise in achieving both regular school attendance and overall improvement in functioning (King et al., 2000; Suveg et al., 2005).

Generalized Anxiety Disorder

Phobias, separation anxiety, and school refusal represent relatively focused anxiety disorders. However, anxiety is sometimes experienced in a less focused manner.

DIAGNOSTIC CRITERIA

Prior versions of the DSM employed the diagnosis of Overanxious Disorder of Childhood and Adolescence (OAD) to recognize this clinical entity. Beginning with the DSM-IV, however, this diagnosis was eliminated. Instead, children and adolescents are now considered, along with adults, under the category of Generalized Anxiety Disorder (GAD). We will use both terms here, since much of the literature has employed the term overanxious.

Generalized anxiety disorder is characterized by excessive anxiety and worry that the child or adolescent finds difficult to control. The major diagnostic features of GAD as described by the DSM are presented in Table 6–6. Some of these symptoms must be present most days for the past 6 months, and the symptoms must cause significant distress or impairment in important areas of the young person's functioning. The DSM acknowledges some developmental difference in that a child need only display one or more (contrasted with three for adults) of the six symptoms listed in part C of Table 6–6. Although GAD is the way that generalized anxiety is defined by the DSM, various questions remain about how to understand and define generalized anxiety in

TABLE 6–6	MAJOR FEATURES FOR THE DSM DIAGNOSIS OF GENERALIZED ANXIETY DISORDER

A. Excessive anxiety and worry about a number of events or activities (e.g., school performance).

B. The youth finds it difficult to control the worry.

C. The anxiety and worry are associated with one or more of the following symptoms:
   1. Restlessness or feeling on edge
   2. Being easily fatigued
   3. Difficulty concentrating
   4. Irritability
   5. Muscle tension
   6. Disturbed sleep

From American Psychiatric Association, 2000.

children and adolescents (OAD versus GAD), and how similar the symptoms of these two disorders are to those used to diagnose depression (Costello et al., 2005b; Kendall, Hedtke, & Aschenbrand, 2006).

DESCRIPTION

Clinicians frequently describe children and adolescents who worry excessively and exhibit extensive fearful behavior. These intense worries are not focused on any particular object or situation, but rather occur in regard to a number of general life circumstances and are not due to a specific recent stress. These youths seem excessively concerned with their competence and performance in a number of areas (e.g., academics, peer relations, sports) to the point of being perfectionistic and setting unreasonably high standards for themselves. They may also worry about things like family finances and natural disasters. They are often described as "little worriers." These young people repeatedly seek approval and reassurance, and exhibit nervous habits (e.g., nail biting) and sleep disturbances. Physical complaints such as headaches and stomachaches are common (Albano et al., 2003; American Psychiatric Association, 2000). The following description of John captures the clinical picture of generalized anxiety disorder.

John | Generalized Anxiety Disorder

Like his mother, John had a very low opinion of himself and his abilities . . . . and found it difficult to cope with the "scary things" inside himself. His main problem had to do with the numerous fears that he had and the panic attacks that overtook him from time to time. He was afraid of the dark, of ghosts, of monsters, of being abandoned, of being alone, of strangers, of war, of guns, of knives, of loud noises, and of snakes . . . . Like his mother again, he had many psychosomatic complaints involving his bladder, his bowels, his kidneys, his intestines, and his blood . . . . He also suffered from insomnia and would not or could not go to sleep until his mother did . . . . He was also afraid to sleep alone or to sleep without a light, and regularly wet and soiled himself. He was often afraid but could not say why and was also fearful of contact with others.

Anthony, 1981, pp. 163–164.

EPIDEMIOLOGY

Epidemiological studies of nonclinic samples suggest that generalized anxiety (overanxious) disorder is a relatively common problem. Estimates, among youth of all ages, vary from about 2 to 14% (Anderson et al., 1987; Canino et al., 2004; Cohen et al., 1993b; Costello, 1989). Generalized anxiety/overanxious disorder is probably the most common anxiety disorder among adolescents (Clark et al., 1994). Estimates of rates in the general population of adolescents range from 3.7 to 7.3% (Kashani & Orvaschel, 1990; McGee et al., 1990; Whitaker et al., 1990).

The disorder is common among youths seen in clinical settings. Keller and colleagues (1992), for example, report that 85% of the youths with an anxiety disorder were diagnosed with overanxious disorder, although other estimates are not quite this high.

The disorder is sometimes reported to be more common in girls, but there are also reports of no gender differences in prevalence. The median age of onset is estimated to be about 10 years of age. The number and intensity of symptoms seem to increase with age (Ford et al., 2003; Keller et al., 1992; Kendall et al., 2006).

Children and adolescents who meet the diagnostic criteria for GAD are likely to meet the diagnostic criteria for additional disorders (Masi et al., 2004), and rates of such co-occurrence seem higher for youths with GAD than for those with other diagnoses (Silverman & Ginsburg, 1998). Depression, separation anxiety, and phobias are common co-occurring disorders (Masi et al., 2004; Verduin & Kendall, 2003).

GAD may be overdiagnosed (American Psychiatric Association, 2000), and some have questioned whether it is a distinct disorder. What is now considered the separate disorder of GAD might instead be an indication of a general constitutional vulnerability toward anxiety or emotional reactivity (Flannery-Schroeder, 2004). It may be that professional help is sought when youngsters with this general vulnerability exhibit other anxiety or internalizing disorders (Beidel, Silverman, & Hammond-Laurence, 1996).

DEVELOPMENTAL COURSE

GAD does not seem transitory (Keller et al., 1992). Symptoms may persist for several years (Cohen, Cohen, & Brook, 1993a). Persistence may be particularly likely for those with more severe symptoms. A greater number of severe overanxious symptoms, increased impairment, and an increased risk of alcohol use have been reported among adolescents with this disorder (Clark et al., 1994; Kendall et al., 2006; Strauss, 1994).

An examination of developmental differences in co-occurring disorders provides some interesting information (Masi et al., 2004; Strauss et al., 1988). For example, although rates of co-occurrence are high for youngsters of all ages, young children seem more likely to receive a concurrent diagnosis of separation anxiety disorder, and adolescents a concurrent diagnosis of depression or social phobia. These findings may suggest a developmental difference in how generalized anxiety is experienced. Alternatively, since separation anxiety is generally more common in young children and depression and social anxiety are more common in adolescents, these

findings may also be viewed as consistent with questions, raised above, about whether GAD is a distinct disorder or an indication of a heightened general vulnerability.

Panic Attacks and Panic Disorder

Frank Panic Attacks

While falling asleep, Frank often experienced discrete episodes of his heart beating quickly, shortness of breath, tingling in his hands, and extreme fearfulness. These episodes lasted only 15 to 20 minutes, but Frank could not fall asleep in his bedroom and began sleeping on the living room couch. His father brought him back to his bed once he was asleep, but Frank was tired during the day, and his schoolwork began to deteriorate.

Adapted from Rapoport & Ismond, 1996, pp. 240–241.

Intense, discrete experiences of extreme anxiety, like Frank's, that seem to arise quickly and often, are known as panic attacks, and are another way that adolescents and children experience anxiety.

DIAGNOSTIC CRITERIA

A distinction is made between panic attacks and panic disorder.

Panic attacks. A panic attack is a discrete period of intense fear or terror that has a sudden onset and reaches a peak quickly—in 10 minutes or less. The DSM describes 13 somatic or cognitive symptoms, 4 or more of which must be present during an episode (see Table 6–7). There are three different categories of panic attacks, defined by the presence or absence of triggers. Unexpected (uncued) panic attacks occur spontaneously or "out of the blue" with no apparent situational trigger. In contrast, situationally bound (cued) panic attacks occur on almost all occasions when the person is exposed to or anticipates a feared object or situation (e.g., a dog). Situationally predisposed panic attacks occur on exposure to a situational cue, but not all the time; that is, they do not occur invariably, and they may occur following exposure rather than immediately.

TABLE 6–7	SYMPTOMS OF A PANIC ATTACK ACCORDING TO THE DSM

1. Palpitations, pounding heart, or accelerated heart rate
2. Sweating
3. Trembling or shaking
4. Sensations of shortness of breath or smothering
5. Feeling of choking
6. Chest pain or discomfort
7. Nausea or abdominal distress
8. Feeling dizzy, unsteady, lightheaded, or faint
9. Derealization (feelings of unreality) or depersonalization (feeling detached from oneself)
10. Fear of losing control or going crazy
11. Fear of dying
12. Paresthesias (numbness or tingling sensations)
13. Chills or hot flushes

From American Psychiatric Association, 2000.

Panic attacks are not themselves a disorder within the DSM system, but they may occur in the context of several different anxiety disorders.

Panic disorder. One of these disorders is panic disorder, which involves unexpected panic attacks that the person is concerned will reoccur without warning. The DSM criteria for a panic disorder are presented in Table 6–8. Panic disorder may occur with or without agoraphobia. In severe cases of panic, a youngster may remain at home or become terrified of leaving home. This agoraphobia is an attempt to avoid certain circumstances in which an uncontrollable or embarrassing attack may occur or during which help may not be available.

Although there is an established literature regarding adults, it is only relatively recently that the occurrence of panic in children and adolescents has received attention. This discrepancy was, in part, due to controversy regarding the existence of panic attacks and panic disorder in youths (Kearney & Silverman, 1992; Kearney et al., 1997; Klein et al., 1992; Suveg et al., 2005). Much of the controversy revolved around two issues.

One issue is whether young people experience both the physiological and cognitive symptoms of panic. Adults who experience panic attacks report fear of losing control, going "crazy," or dying during the attack. They also worry about future attacks. Such cognitive symptoms may not occur in children or young adolescents.

The second issue concerns whether panic is experienced by young people as spontaneous (uncued) or cued. Youths may think attacks are "out of the blue" because they may not be sufficiently aware of, or as likely to monitor, cues in their environment. Careful and detailed questioning may be needed to reveal precipitating cues. This problem is particularly acute in younger children.

TABLE 6–8	MAJOR CRITERIA FOR THE DSM DIAGNOSIS OF PANIC DISORDER

1. Recurrent unexpected Panic Attacks (see Table 6–7)
2. At least one of the attacks has been followed by 1 month (or more) of one (or more) of the following:
   a. Persistent concern about having additional attacks
   b. Worry about the implications of the attack (e.g., losing control, having a heart attack, "going crazy")
   c. A significant change in behavior related to the attacks

From American Psychiatric Association, 2000.

EPIDEMIOLOGY

Although the diagnosis of panic may be difficult, literature is accumulating to suggest the presence of panic attacks and panic disorder in adolescents and, to a lesser degree, in prepubertal children (Ollendick, Birmaher, & Mattis, 2004; Suveg et al., 2005). For example, many adults who experience panic attacks or panic disorder report that onset had occurred during adolescence or earlier.

Also, both community samples and clinic-based studies suggest that panic attacks may not be uncommon in adolescents. For example, 16% of young people between the ages of 12 and 17 in a community sample of Australian youths reported at least one full-blown panic attack in their lifetimes (King et al., 1997) and similar rates were reported in a sample of German adolescents (Essau, Conradt, & Petermann, 1999). Regarding panic disorder, the condition is rarely diagnosed prior to mid or late adolescence (Suveg et al., 2005). For example, Ford and colleagues (2003) found that while panic disorder was rarely diagnosed in younger British children, about 0.5% of youths between the ages of 13 and 15 met the criteria for panic disorder. Similar rates have been reported in a community sample of Puerto Rican, German, and U.S. youths (Canino et al., 2004; Essau et al., 1999; Whitaker et al., 1990). In clinical samples of adolescents, reported prevalence is higher—about 10 to 15% (e.g., Biederman et al., 1997; Last & Strauss, 1989). Panic attacks occur equally in boys and girls; however, panic disorder is typically reported more frequently in girls. Little information is available regarding ethnic differences (Suveg et al., 2005).

DESCRIPTION AND DEVELOPMENTAL PATTERN

Adolescents who experience panic attacks experience considerable distress and impairment. Few, however, seem to seek treatment (Ollendick et al., 2004). Studies of adolescents seen in clinics indicate that these youths evidence both the physiological and cognitive symptoms of panic. For example, Kearney and colleagues (1997) found that physiological symptoms of panic attacks were the most commonly reported symptoms, but the cognitive symptoms of fear of "going crazy" and fear of dying were also reported by 50% of youngsters.

Whether panic attacks are cued or spontaneous is less clear. Psychosocial stressors (e.g., family conflict, peer problems) were reported as possible precipitants by 26 of the 28 adolescents in this study. Some studies, however, report that for some youths, panic attacks are judged to be spontaneous. As we have mentioned, though, there is a problem in judging the spontaneous nature of panic attacks in young people.

Less is known regarding panic in younger children. Although both panic attacks and panic disorder are reported in clinical samples of children, their expression may differ somewhat from their presentation in adolescents and adults. Young children may report a general fear of becoming sick rather than describing specific physiological symptoms such as palpitations or breathlessness, or verbalizing fears of dying, going crazy, or losing control (Albano et al., 2003).

Youths with panic attacks or panic disorder who present at clinics are likely to have a family history of panic attacks or other severe anxiety symptoms. They are also likely to present with a variety of other symptoms, and the majority meet the criteria for additional diagnoses, particularly other anxiety disorders and depression (Kearney et al., 1997; Masi et al., 2000). Many of the youths with panic disorder seen in clinical settings also exhibit agoraphobia (Suveg et al., 2005). The high proportion of youth who report a history of separation anxiety led to the suggestion that separation anxiety disorder is a precursor to panic disorder. There are findings of neurophysiological signs of greater arousal among infants of mothers with panic disorder than among controls. This is consistent with the idea of an early vulnerability (Warren et al., 2003). However, it seems likely that separation anxiety disorder would be only one of many possible paths to the development of panic disorder (Hayward et al., 2004; Ollendick et al., 2004a).

Reactions to Traumatic Events

How do youngsters react to experiencing natural disasters such as hurricanes, other disasters such as fires or ships sinking, kidnapping, or the violence of a terrorist attack or war?

Trauma is usually defined as an event outside everyday experience that would be distressing to almost anyone. Early descriptions of children's exposure to trauma suggested that reactions would be relatively mild and transient, and thus these experiences were not given a great deal of attention. However, reports began to emerge of more severe and long-lasting reactions.

The investigation of 26 children kidnapped from their Chowchilla, California, school bus in 1976 is one study that influenced the understanding of children's posttraumatic responses. The children and their bus driver were held for 27 hours. At first they were driven around in darkened vans; then they were moved to a buried tractor trailer, where they remained until some of the victims dug themselves out. The child victims and at least one parent of each child were interviewed within 5 to 13 months of the kidnapping. All of the children were found to be symptomatic, with 73% showing moderately severe or severe reactions. Assessments 2 to 5 years after the kidnapping revealed that many symptoms had persisted (Terr, 1979; 1983).

DIAGNOSTIC CRITERIA FOR ACUTE AND POSTTRAUMATIC STRESS DISORDERS

Systematic study of children's reactions to trauma was also stimulated by the introduction, in the third version of the DSM, of a specific diagnosis—Posttraumatic Stress Disorder (PTSD). The current DSM criteria for PTSD (Table 6–9) require exposure to a serious traumatic event to which the child or adolescent shows an intense fearful reaction. The young person must also experience the PTSD triad of symptoms—reexperiencing, avoidance, and arousal—for more than 1 month. In addition, the disturbance must cause significant interference in important areas of the youth's functioning.

It may be necessary to pay greater attention to developmental considerations in defining posttraumatic stress disorder in children (Salmon & Bryant, 2002). Indeed, some have suggested that existing criteria are not appropriate for infants or children under age 4, and alternative criteria have been proposed (Scheeringa et al., 2003). It has also been suggested that very young children can be given the diagnosis of PTSD following exposure to a traumatic event even if they do not exhibit intense fear at the time. Furthermore, there may be differences in the number and kinds of symptoms of reexperiencing, avoidance, and arousal that young children exhibit.

The diagnostic criteria for Acute Stress Disorder (ASD) are essentially the same as those for PTSD, with two key exceptions. Perhaps the principal distinction is that ASD symptoms last for at least 2 days, but less than 4 weeks, whereas PTSD lasts for at least one month following the trauma or has a delayed onset. A young person with a significant immediate reaction to

---

TABLE 6–9	MAJOR CRITERIA FOR THE DSM DIAGNOSIS OF POSTTRAUMATIC STRESS DISORDER

A. The person has been exposed to a traumatic event that
   1. includes a threat of death, serious injury, or threat to physical integrity to the self or others; and
   2. the person's response involves fear, helplessness, or horror (in children, this reaction may be expressed instead as disorganized or agitated behavior).

B. Reexperiencing the Traumatic Event (1 or more needed for diagnosis)
   1. Recurrent distressing recollections (in young children may be trauma-related play)
   2. Recurrent distressing dreams
   3. Acting or feeling as if event were recurring
   4. Intense distress to cues that symbolize the event
   5. Physiological reactivity to cues that symbolize the event

C. Persistent Avoidance of Trauma-Related Stimuli and General Numbing (3 or more needed for diagnosis)
   1. Avoidance of trauma-related thoughts, feelings, or conversations
   2. Avoidance of activities, places, or people associated with the trauma
   3. Inability to recall important aspects of the trauma
   4. Diminished interest in significant activities
   5. Feelings of detachment from others
   6. Restricted range of affect
   7. Sense of foreshortened future

D. Persistent Symptoms of Increased Arousal (2 or more needed for diagnosis)
   1. Sleep difficulties
   2. Irritability, anger outbursts
   3. Difficulty concentrating
   4. Hypervigilance
   5. Exaggerated startle response

From American Psychiatric Association, 2000.

A number of factors influence children's reactions to a traumatic event, including aspects of the experience and the reactions of their parents and other adults.
(Segei Dolzzhenko/epa/CORBIS-NY)

a trauma may be given the diagnosis of ASD. This diagnosis may help alert adults to a youth's needs, however, it is unclear how well ASD predicts later PTSD (De Bellis & Van Dillen, 2005). The diagnosis of ASD also explicitly requires the presence of dissociative symptoms—that is, alterations in self-awareness to escape an upsetting experience. Symptoms of dissociation can be displayed as a general numbing, detachment, or "appearing in a daze," or by derealization (a marked sense of unreality), depersonalization (feeling cut off from one's feelings or environment), or dissociative amnesia (inability to recall an important aspect of the trauma). Dissociation may be present with PTSD, but it is not required for the diagnosis.

DESCRIPTION

The reactions of young people to traumatic events may vary considerably. Many exhibit symptoms without meeting the criteria for a diagnosis of PTSD, but they still experience considerable distress and interference with functioning.

Most youths become upset at reminders of the trauma, and they experience repetitive, intrusive thoughts about the event. Even children who experience mild levels of exposure to life-threatening disasters may have such thoughts. Preschool and school-age children frequently reenact aspects of the disaster in drawings, stories, and play. Initially such behavior may be part of reexperiencing symptoms, but it may become a useful part of the recovery process as well. Saylor, Powell, and Swenson (1992), for example, report that after Hurricane Hugo occurred in South Carolina, children's play progressed from blowing houses down to acting out the role of roofers during rebuilding.

Young people may also exhibit increased frequency and intensity of specific fears directly related to or associated with the traumatic experience. Thus adolescent British girls on a school trip who experienced the sinking of their cruise ship developed fears of swimming, of the dark, or of boats and other forms of transportation. These girls, however, did not show elevated levels of unrelated fears compared with schoolmates who did not go on the trip or with girls from a comparable school (Yule, Udwin, & Murdoch, 1990).

Separation difficulties and clingy, dependent behaviors are also common. These behaviors may be exhibited as reluctance to go to school or as a desire to sleep with parents. Other sleep problems, such as difficulty in getting to sleep, nightmares, and repeated dreams related to the traumatic event, are also common. A sense of vulnerability and loss of faith in the future have also been reported. In adolescents, this loss may interfere with planning for future education and careers; moreover, school performance is reported to suffer. Other commonly noted symptoms include depressed mood, loss of interest in previously enjoyed activities, irritability, and angry or aggressive outbursts. Guilt about surviving when others have died can also occur. It is also common for young people to meet the criteria for additional and multiple diagnoses (Pfefferbaum, 1997).

PTSD AND CHILD ABUSE

Child maltreatment is one form of trauma that has been viewed within the framework of PTSD. Indeed, many youngsters who experience abuse exhibit meaningful symptoms or meet the diagnostic criteria for PTSD (De Bellis & Van Dillen, 2005). In chapter 3 (p. 57) we saw that a developmental traumatology model of child maltreatment suggests that trauma-induced changes in neurobiology underlie the development of psychopathology in maltreated children (De Bellis, 2001). In this model, PTSD symptoms are considered to be the key mediator linking maltreatment and subsequent psychopathology. Accordingly, as depicted in Figure 6–1, PTSD symptoms are the initial problems that then contribute to the potential development of a wide range of behavioral and emotional problems at different times of life.

EPIDEMIOLOGY

Natural disasters, terrorism, and accidents are catastrophic events that are unpredictable in nature, making it difficult to determine the number of children and adolescents who will be exposed to traumatic events each year (Fletcher, 2003). However, we do know that young people are frequently exposed to maltreatment and are frequent victims of violent crime. Some may be at particular risk. For example, infants and younger children are at greater risk for maltreatment (Wekerle & Wolfe, 2003) and homeless adolescents are at increased risk for victimization (Stewart et al., 2004). It seems likely that an appreciable number of young people experience a traumatic event. Indeed, a survey of children and adolescents indicated that about one quarter had experienced a serious traumatic event by the age of 16 (Costello et al., 2002).

Fletcher (2003) indicates that about one third of youths exposed to traumatic events are diagnosed with PTSD—a rate slightly higher than for traumatized adults—and some findings suggest that half or more of exposed youths experience PTSD (De Bellis & Dillen, 2005). Most studies find a higher incidence of PTSD among girls. As indicated earlier, developmental differences may exist in how PTSD is expressed, particularly in very young children. Research also suggests that children, adolescents, and adults may differ with regard to some basic neurobiological responses to trauma (De Bellis, 2001; Lipschitz et al., 2003). For example, there may be differences in the response of the hypothalamic-pituitary-adrenal (HPA) axis, a critical neurohormonal regulatory system, that, under conditions of extreme stress, causes the release of neurohormones, including cortisol. The response of this system is one of the mechanisms that is thought to underlie the development of PTSD and other difficulties.

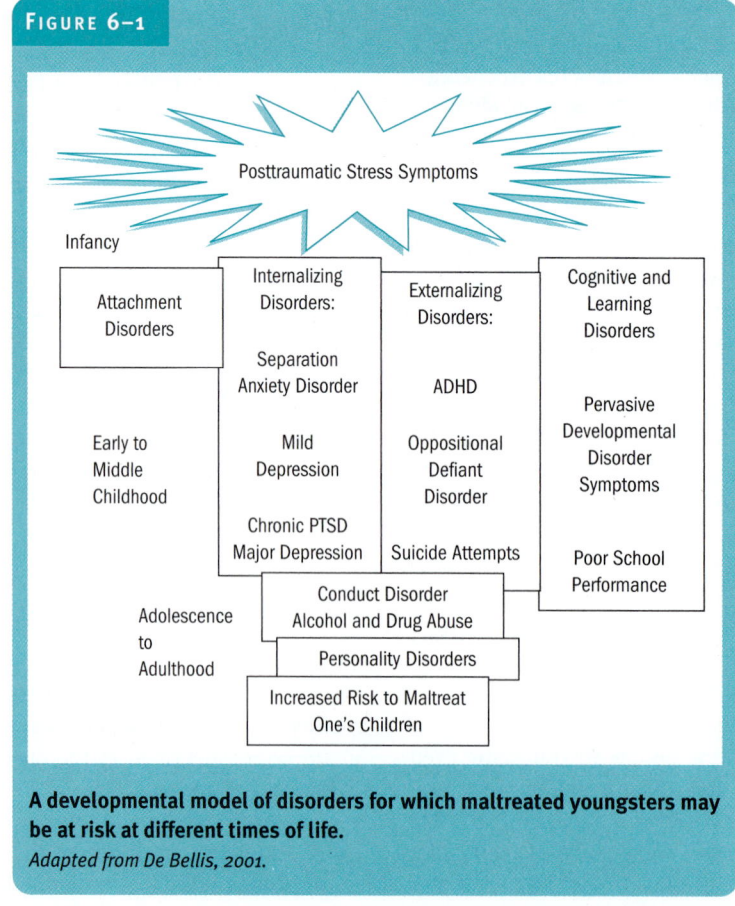

FIGURE 6–1

A developmental model of disorders for which maltreated youngsters may be at risk at different times of life.
Adapted from De Bellis, 2001.

On average, the incidence of particular PTSD symptoms appears to be above 20%. The PTSD cluster of symptoms (reexperiencing, avoidance, and arousal) has been reported in youths from a variety of different cultures (Perrin, Smith, & Yule, 2000). The most frequently occurring category of symptom is probably reexperiencing (De Bellis & Van Dillen, 2005).

Not all children and adolescents experience the same pattern or intensity of symptoms, and not all youths who experience traumas meet the criteria for PTSD. The amount of time that symptoms persist may vary, and problems may fluctuate over time. A number of factors seem to influence youths' initial reactions and the duration and severity of symptoms (La Greca, Silverman, & Wasserstein, 1998; Udwin et al., 2000).

The nature of the traumatic event may influence reactions. For example, one can group stressors into two categories: (1) acute, nonabusive stressors—nonabusive traumatic events that occur only once, like floods or accidents, and (2) chronic or abusive stressors—ongoing stressors like war or physical or sexual abuse (Fletcher, 2003). Some symptoms of PTSD appear likely to occur regardless of the type of traumatic event (e.g., trauma-related fears, difficulty sleeping). However, other symptoms vary depending on the type of trauma experienced. Also, while young people experiencing either kind of trauma appear equally likely to receive the diagnosis of PTSD, other diagnoses that they are likely to receive may vary. These differences are illustrated in Table 6–10. It may seem surprising that some symptoms or problems occur more often among young people exposed to acute, nonabusive trauma than among those exposed to chronic or abusive trauma. One possible explanation may be that children or adolescents exposed to chronic stressors come to some kind of accommodation over time with their traumas (Fletcher, 2003).

The degree of exposure to the traumatic event also appears to be an important influence. Pynoos and his colleagues (1987) studied 159 California schoolchildren who were exposed to a sniper attack on their school in which one child and a passerby were killed and 13 other children were injured. Children who were trapped on the playground showed much greater effects than those who had left the immediate vicinity of the shooting or who were not in school that day. At a 14-month follow-up among the most severely exposed children, 74% still reported moderate to severe PTSD symptoms, whereas 81% of the nonexposed children reported no PTSD (Nader et al., 1991). Although level of exposure to this life-threatening trauma was an important factor, reactions did occur among children who did not experience a high degree of exposure. Less exposed children who had a subjective experience of threat and greater knowledge of the schoolmate who was killed were more likely to have PTSD symptoms.

Individual differences that existed prior to a traumatic event (e.g., anxiety level, ethnicity) are also likely to influence the youth's reaction (La Greca et al., 1998). So, for example, a child or adolescent's prior level of general anxiety may influence her or his reaction to the traumatic event.

TABLE 6–10	RATES OF PTSD SYMPTOMS AND ASSOCIATED SYMPTOMS/DIAGNOSES IN RESPONSE TO ACUTE, NONABUSIVE STRESSORS AND CHRONIC OR ABUSIVE STRESSORS	
	TYPE OF STRESSOR	
	ACUTE-NONABUSIVE	**CHRONIC OR ABUSIVE**
DSM Symptom Cluster		
Reexperiencing	92%	86%
Avoidance/numbness	30%	54%
Overarousal	55%	71%
Associated Symptoms/Diagnoses		
PTSD	36%	36%
Generalized Anxiety	55%	26%
Separation Anxiety	45%	35%
Panic	35%	6%
Depression	10%	28%
ADHD	22%	11%

Adapted from Fletcher, 2003.

DEVELOPMENTAL COURSE AND PROGNOSIS

In general, symptoms of PTSD decline over time, but substantial numbers of children and adolescents continue to report difficulties. For example, La Greca and her colleagues (1996) examined third- through fifth-grade children during the school year after Hurricane Andrew occurred in Florida. Symptoms of avoidance and general numbing were present in about 49 percent of the children at 3 months but only about 24 percent of the children at 10 months. Similarly, the number of children with symptoms of arousal decreased from 67 to about 49 percent in the same time period. However, substantial numbers of children continued to report reexperiencing symptoms—approximately 90 percent at 3 months and 78 percent at 10 months.

Children's initial attempts at coping may also affect the course of their reactions. Children who tend to use negative coping strategies (e.g., blaming others, screaming) may be more likely to experience persistent symptoms (La Greca et al., 1996). The reactions of children and adolescents to traumatic events are also related to the reactions of their parents and others in their environment. If the parents themselves suffer severe posttraumatic stress or for

ACCENT

Terrorism and Posttraumatic Stress

On September 11, 2001, terrorists attacked New York City and Washington, DC. Many people suffered the loss of a loved one in the attack or in rescue efforts. Nearly 3,000 persons were known to be or presumed dead. Survivors, relatives, and many more were left with vivid images of planes crashing into buildings, buildings burning and falling, loss of human life, and terror and sadness on the faces of those involved. What is the impact of such events on children and adolescents?

In reaction to an earlier event, the 1995 Oklahoma City bombing, young people who lost loved ones, friends, or acquaintances, or who simply lived nearby, experienced both immediate and continuing symptoms of posttraumatic stress (Gurwitch, Kees, & Becker, 2002; Pfefferbaum et al., 1999a, 2000). Symptoms included trembling, nervousness, fear, shock, and fear that a family member or friend might be hurt. Two years following the attack, many youths in the Oklahoma City area still reported posttraumatic stress symptoms and impaired functioning at home or school. The symptoms were greatest for those who had lost an immediate family member, but many of those who had lost a more distant relative, friend, or acquaintance remained affected as well. Television exposure was a significant predictor of PTSD symptoms (Pfefferbaum et al., 1999b, 2001).

Similar reactions occurred following the September 11 attacks. The impact on families was appreciable. In New York City, many children and adolescents had a relative or friend killed or knew a teacher or coach who lost someone, and over half of families assessed reported that more than 4 hours passed between the attack and the reunion of parent and child (Stuber et al., 2002). Counseling was received by a youth in 22% of these families. In the Washington, DC, area, service use increased over the same period for the previous year (Hoge & Pavlin, 2002). Widespread and frequent media coverage also brought the trauma into many homes around the country. Many youths may have experienced stress-related symptoms and worry about safety (Saylor et al., 2003; Schuster et al., 2001; Whalen et al., 2004). Parents experiencing stress reactions were more likely to report symptoms in their child and, where youths' viewing had not been restricted, time watching TV significantly correlated with the number of reported stress symptoms (Schuster et al., 2001). Interestingly, viewing positive images (e.g., heroics and rescues) did not help—again greater viewing was associated with more child PTSD symptoms (Saylor et al., 2003).

Reactions to terrorism seem similar in many ways to reactions to other traumatic events, but there may be unique aspects (Fremont, 2004). Terrorism presents an unpredictable threat and there is extensive media coverage. There is also a profound effect on the adults and communities that typically provide support for young people. In the wake of the events of September 11, attention continues to be focused on developing successful interventions and on investigating the effects of such trauma. After the attacks, an extensive screening (CATS Consortium, 2007) in New York City indicated that as many as 75,000 young people experienced PTSD symptoms, and many reported other symptoms (e.g. depression, other anxiety disorder symptoms). However, fewer than one third of these youths sought help (Hoagwood et al., 2007).

some other reason are unable to provide an atmosphere of support and communication, their children's reactions are likely to be more severe.

Obsessive–Compulsive Disorder

DIAGNOSTIC CRITERIA

Obsessions are unwanted, repetitive, intrusive thoughts. Compulsions involve repetitive, stereotyped behaviors that the child or adolescent feels compelled to perform and that are meant to reduce anxiety or to prevent a dreaded event. Obsessive–Compulsive Disorder (OCD) involves either obsessions or compulsions, or in a majority of young people, both (March & Mulle, 1998). The definitions employed in the DSM to characterize obsessions and compulsions are presented in Table 6–11. Beyond defining the nature of obsessions and compulsions, the DSM criteria for OCD indicate that the person realizes that the thoughts and behaviors are unreasonable. This particular feature is not required for the diagnosis of OCD in children but may become part of the clinical picture in older children and adolescents. Even among very young children, odd repetitive acts may be seen as strange. However, children, as we see in the case of Stanley, may initially have their own explanations. The child may come to recognize that the ideas or behaviors involved are unreasonable but still feel the need to repeat them.

| Stanley | The Martian Rituals |

Seven-year-old Stanley indicated that he had seen a show in which Martians contacted humans by putting strange thoughts in their heads. Stanley explained his compulsion to do everything in sequences of four as a sign that he had been picked as the Martians' contact on earth. After 2 years of no contact, Stanley gave up this explanation but not his ritual.

Rapoport, 1989, p. 84.

Another criteria for the diagnosis of OCD is that the obsessions or compulsions are highly time consuming and that they interfere considerably with normal routines, academic functioning, and social relationships (Piacentini et al., 2003). The impact on Sergei's life illustrates the nature and consequences of the disorder.

| Sergei | Impairment in Functioning |

Sergei is a 17-year-old former high school student. Only a year or so ago Sergei seemed to be a normal adolescent with many talents and interests. Then, almost overnight he was transformed into a lonely outsider, excluded from social life by his psychological disabilities. Specifically, he was unable to stop washing. Haunted by the notion that he was dirty—in spite of the contrary evidence of his senses—he began to spend more and more of his time cleansing himself of imaginary dirt. At first his ritual ablutions were confined to weekends and evenings and he was able to stay in school while keeping them up, but soon they began to consume all his time, forcing him to drop out of school, a victim of his inability to feel clean enough.

Rapoport, 1989, p. 83.

| TABLE 6–11 | THE DSM DEFINITIONS OF OBSESSIONS AND COMPULSIONS |

Obsessions: Intrusive, persistent thoughts, impulses, or images that

1. cause anxiety or diistress;
2. are not simply excessive real-life worries;
3. the person attempts to ignore, suppress, or neutralize; and
4. are recognized as products of one's own mind.

Compulsions: Repetitive behaviors or mental acts that

1. the person feels driven to perform; and
2. are unrealistic attempts to prevent or reduce distress or some dreaded situation.

From American Psychiatric Association, 2000.

DESCRIPTION

Judith Rapoport and her colleagues at the National Institute for Mental Health (NIMH) conducted a series of studies that increased the attention given to obsessive–compulsive behavior in young people. Table 6–12 indicates common obsessions and compulsions among children and adolescents reported by this group and others (Henin & Kendall, 1997; Leonard et al., 2005; Rapoport, 1989).

Compulsive rituals are reported more frequently than obsessions; this finding is different from reports concerning adults, in which obsessions and compulsions are reported at fairly equivalent rates. There appear to be two broad themes to the excessive concerns and rituals: The first theme is a preoccupation with cleanliness, grooming, and averting danger, and the second theme is a pervasive doubting—not knowing when one is "right."

Childhood obsessive–compulsive disorder is often recognized only when symptoms are very severe. If a youth reaches out for help, it is frequently only after years of suffering. Young people often admit having kept their problems a secret. Among those who do seek help, many indicate that their parents were unaware of their problem. For example, diagnostic interviews conducted with a community-based sample of youths ages 9 through 17 and their mothers found that of the 35 cases of OCD identified, 4 youths were diagnosed as having OCD on the basis of the parent's report, and 32 as the result of the youth's report, but in only 1 case did the youth and parent concur (Rapoport et al., 2000).

EPIDEMIOLOGY

Obsessive–compulsive disorder is probably not as rare as was once believed (March et al., 2004; Rapoport et al., 2000). Epidemiological studies of nonreferred adolescents suggest a prevalence rate of about 1% and a lifetime prevalence rate of about 1.9% in the general adolescent population (Flament et al., 1988; Rapoport et al., 2000). Most estimates also suggest that at younger ages, boys outnumber girls, but that by adolescence, the genders are equally represented (March et al., 2004; Rapoport et al., 2000). Among a sample of 70 consecutive child and adolescent cases seen at NIMH, 7 had an onset prior to the age of 7 years, and the mean age of onset was 10 years of age. The onset of obsessive–compulsive symptoms in boys tended to be prepubertal (mean age 9), whereas in girls, the average onset was around puberty (mean age 11) (Swedo et al., 1989c). Similar age differences in onset of OCD symptoms have also been reported among community samples (Rapoport et al., 2000).

Most children and adolescents diagnosed with obsessive–compulsive disorder meet the criteria for at least one other disorder (Geller et al., 2003a; Rapoport & Inhoff-Germain, 2000). Multiple anxiety disorders, attention-deficit hyperactivity disorder, conduct and oppositional disorders, substance abuse, and depression are commonly reported (Leonard et al., 2005; Rapoport & Inhoff-Germain, 2000). Obsessive–compulsive disorder also often occurs with Tourette's syndrome (a chronic disorder with a genetic and neuroanatomical basis characterized by motor and vocal tics and related urges) or other tic disorders (Swain et al., 2007). Tics are sudden, rapid, recurrent, stereotyped motor movements or vocalizations. Children and adolescents with tics may represent a distinct subtype of OCD with regard to symptomatology and response to treatment (Leonard et al., 2005; Scahill et al., 2003; Swain et al., 2007).

TABLE 6–12   SOME COMMON OBSESSIONS AND COMPULSIONS

Obsessions
Contamination concerns (e.g. dirt, germs, environmental toxins)
Harm to self or others (e.g. death, illness, kidnapping)
Symmetry, order, exactness
Doing the right thing (scrupulosity, religious obsessions)

Compulsions
Washing, grooming
Repeating (e.g. going in and out of a door)
Checking (e.g. doors, homework)
Ordering or arranging

Keeping things in certain specific locations and order is common. It is only when these kinds of behaviors interfere with a young person's normal functioning that they should cause concern for clinicians and other adults.
(Courtesy of A. C. Israel)

DEVELOPMENTAL COURSE AND PROGNOSIS

Behavior with obsessive–compulsive qualities occurs in various stages of normal development (Evans & Leckman, 2006). For example, very young children may have bedtime and eating rituals or may require things to be "just so." Disruption of these routines often leads to distress. Also, young children are often observed to engage in repetitive play and to show a distinct preference for sameness. In his widely read book for parents, Benjamin Spock noted that mild compulsions—such as stepping over cracks in the sidewalk or touching every third picket in a fence—are quite common in 8-, 9-, and 10-year-olds (Spock & Rothenberg, 1992). Many readers of this text likely recall engaging in such behaviors. Behaviors that are common to the youth's peer group are probably best viewed as games. Only when they dominate the young person's life and interfere with normal functioning is there cause for concern. In addition, the specific content of OCD rituals generally does not resemble common developmental rituals and OCD rituals have a later stage of onset. It is not clear whether developmental rituals represent early manifestations of obsessive–compulsive disorder in some children (Evans & Leckman, 2006).

There is heterogeneity regarding the course of OCD. The disorder follows a course in which symptoms emerge and fade over time. Multiple obsessions and compulsions are usually present at any one time, and usually the symptoms change in content and intensity over time (Leonard et al., 2005; Rettew et al., 1992). Research also suggests that the disorder is likely to be chronic. Although about three quarters of

youths receiving treatment may show substantial improvement, problems persist. However, persistence may be lower than once thought (Leonard et al., 2005; Wagner et al., 2003).

Etiology of Anxiety Disorders

We have so far described several anxiety disorders. It is likely that such disturbances are influenced by multiple risk factors that interact with one another in complex ways (Barlow, 2002; Bosquet & Egeland, 2006). But risk factors and causal mechanisms are by no means clear. Much of the information that is available represents a downward extension from the adult literature.

BIOLOGICAL INFLUENCES

There is evidence for a genetic contribution to anxiety disorders. Aggregation of anxiety disorders in families is consistent with a genetic contribution. Family studies indicate that children whose parents have an anxiety disorder are at risk for developing an anxiety disorder (Beidel & Turner, 1997; Merikanges, 2005), and parents whose children have anxiety disorders are themselves likely to have anxiety disorders (Last et al., 1991). In addition, more specific examinations of the influence of inheritance (e.g., twin studies) indicate a genetic contribution (Eley et al., 2003).

Genetic influences may be expressed through differences in specific brain circuits and neurotransmitter systems. Neurotransmitters such as serotonin are thought to play a role in the development of anxiety and panic (Neumeister et al., 2004). The neurotransmitter gamma aminobutyric acid (GABA) also has received attention (Barlow, 2002). GABA is known to inhibit anxiety. Anxious individuals have low levels of GABA in particular areas of the brain. Attention also has focused on corticotrophin-releasing hormone (CRH). CRH, when released in reaction to stress or a perceived threat, has effects on other hormones and areas of the brain implicated in anxiety.

The limbic system—and the amygdala, in particular—is the portion of the brain that is most often associated with anxiety. Neuroscience research has examined processes such as attention, fear conditioning, and other emotional learning and has made use of neuroimaging techniques such as the fMRI. Findings from this research suggest that the amygdala and portions of the prefrontal cortex play a role in anxiety (McClure & Pine, 2006). Research suggests that the functioning of neurocircuits in the brains of

children and adolescents may in some ways be similar to that of adults, but that important developmental differences are likely as well.

Estimates of the degree of heritability for anxiety disorders varies. In the Virginia Twin Study of Adolescent Behavioral Development (Eaves et al., 1997), heritability estimates for anxiety tended to be lower than for other disorders; however, other findings suggest higher heritability estimates (Bolton et al., 2006). Heritability may depend on the nature of the anxiety presentation and is perhaps greatest for generalized anxiety and OCD (Eley et al.,2003). Also, some research suggests that heritability may be greatest for younger children. As children grow up, the relative contribution of genetic influences may decrease and the influence of shared family environment may increase (Boomsma, van Beijsterveldt, & Hudziak, 2005).

In sum, findings suggest that genetic factors may play a role in the development of anxiety disorders (Muris, 2006; Thapar & McGuffin, 1995). There may be different patterns of inheritance for different anxiety disorders. Alternatively, what may be inherited, rather than a specific anxiety disorder, is a general tendency, such as emotional and behavioral reactivity to stimuli (Eley et al., 2003; Muris, 2006). Furthermore, this general tendency may be a risk factor for depression as well as anxiety (Boomsma et al., 2005; Eley & Stevenson, 1999; Williamson et al., 2005). These findings also indicate a substantial contribution of environment to anxiety disorders (Eaves et al., 1997; Eley et al., 2003; Lichtenstein & Annas, 2000). Thus, there may be a general genetic risk factor for anxiety disorders and depression, and unique experiences may contribute to specific expressions of this vulnerability.

Biological influences for OCD. Many professionals have come to believe in a biological basis for obsessive–compulsive disorder (Evans & Leckman, 2006; Leonard et al., 2005). It may be particularly important to note evidence of genetic influence for obsessive–compulsive disorder. The disorder has been found to be more prevalent among youngsters with a first-degree relative with obsessive–compulsive behavior than among the general population, and many parents of youngsters with the disorder meet diagnostic criteria for OCD or exhibit obsessive–compulsive symptoms. Twin studies also suggest considerable heritability for OCD (Eley et al., 2003). In addition, a number of studies have reported that both OCD and Tourette's syndrome (or less severe tic disorders) occur in the same individuals at

higher-than-expected rates, and these studies have found a familial association between the two disorders (Spessot & Peterson, 2006; Swain et al., 2007). Research is ongoing to locate specific genes involved in OCD.

Brain imaging studies have suggested that obsessive–compulsive disorder is linked to neurobiological abnormalities of the basal ganglia, a group of brain structures lying under the cerebral cortex and several areas of the prefrontal cortex (Evans & Leckman, 2006; Leonard et al., 2005). A subset of cases of obsessive–compulsive disorder, known as PANDAS (pediatric autoimmune neuropsychiatric disorders associated with streptococcal infections), has been noted. These cases have a sudden onset or exacerbation of symptoms following infection and include tics (Leonard et al., 2005; Swain et al., 2007). They are believed to result from an autoimmune reaction produced when antibodies formed by the body against the streptococcal cells react with and cause inflammation in cells of the basal ganglia.

Temperament. The general vulnerability to anxiety discussed earlier may be associated with aspects of the child's temperament—biologically based, possibly inherited, individual differences in emotionality, behavioral style, and the like (Bousquet & Egeland, 2006; Pérez-Edgar & Fox, 2005).

An important model of the relationship of temperament and anxiety disorders has been described by Jerome Kagan and his colleagues (Kagan, 1997). Their findings are based on longitudinal research of behaviorally inhibited children, who are identified as extremely likely to withdraw from unfamiliar people or events. Of particular interest is the development of internalizing problems in these inhibited children. At 5.5 years of age, children who were originally classified as inhibited had developed more fears than had uninhibited children. Furthermore, whereas fears in uninhibited children could usually be related to a prior trauma, this was not true for the inhibited children (Kagan, Reznick, & Snidman, 1990). Other research also suggests that inhibited children are at risk for developing anxiety disorders. For example, Biederman and colleagues (1993) found that inhibited children, compared with noninhibited children, were more likely to meet the criteria for four or more disorders, for two or more anxiety disorders, and for specific anxiety disorders such as separation anxiety disorder and agoraphobia. Furthermore, the rates of anxiety disorders for inhibited children increased over the three-year period that they were followed. This and other evidence suggests that such temperamental differences are associated with increased risk

for the development of anxiety disorders during later childhood, adolescence, and young adulthood (Hirshfeld-Becker, Biederman, & Rosenbaum, 2004; Muris, 2006; Pérez-Edgar & Fox, 2005).

Gray (1987) has described a functional brain system (described further in chapter 8), part of which is a behavioral inhibition system (BIS) involving multiple areas of the brain. The BIS system is related to the emotions of fear and anxiety, and tends to inhibit action in novel or fearful situations or under conditions of punishment or nonreward. Gray's model of inhibition has also informed thinking about the contribution of temperament to the development of anxiety disorders (Chorpita, 2001; Lonigan et al., 2004).

Another approach to the contribution of temperament to anxiety disorders derives from Clark and Watson's (1991) model of emotion and the concept of negative affectivity (NA). NA is a temperamental dimension characterized by a general and persistent negative (e.g., nervous, sad, angry) mood. Research supports the hypothesis that the development of both anxiety and depression may be characterized by high levels of NA and that this may, in part, be responsible for high rates of co-occurrence of these disorders. Depression, but not anxiety, is thought to be characterized by low levels of the separate temperamental dimension of positive affectivity—pleasurable mood (Chorpita, 2002; Lonigan et al., 2004).

Negative affectivity may also combine with low levels of the temperamental factor of effortful control (EC), the ability to employ self-regulative processes (Lonigan et al., 2004). Children and adolescents with anxiety may show a bias toward attending to threatening stimuli. Anxious youths with high NA thus may attend to more negative stimuli and react more strongly to them. They would, therefore, have a need for greater EC. Thus, the combination of the temperamental qualities of low EC and high NA may contribute to the development and maintenance of anxiety and anxiety disorders.

PSYCHOSOCIAL INFLUENCES

Psychosocial influences are clearly a part of the complex interplay of risk factors that can lead to the development of anxiety disorders. Children and adolescents with a general vulnerability to anxiety may be exposed to a variety of experiences that increase their risk for anxiety disorders. For example, they may develop anxiety problems as a result of exposure to some traumatic event. As we saw earlier, exposure to traumatic events can result in posttraumatic stress reactions that may then set the stage for the development of other disorders. The reactions of parents to the trauma or to children's experience is one factor that can influence outcome. Not all children and adolescents with anxiety difficulties, however, are exposed to traumatic events. How can we understand the development of anxiety in these young people?

It has been suggested that the various psychosocial influences on the development of anxiety can be organized around the concept of a child's experiences with and perceptions of control (Chorpita & Barlow, 1998; Chorpita, 2001). The role of family and parenting in the child's development of a sense of control is a principal focus of attention.

Parents of anxious children have often been described as intrusive. Intrusive parenting is defined as excessive regulation of children's activities, overprotection, autocratic parental decision making, or instruction of children in how to think or feel (Wood et al., 2003). Such parenting behavior may affect children's sense of control/effectiveness, and their development of adaptive problem-solving and coping styles. For example, mothers and clinic-referred children with anxiety disorders were observed while completing tasks together. Mothers of these anxious children were more intrusive and more critical while working with their children than were mothers of nonclinic children (Hudson & Rapee, 2001; 2002). These influences are likely bidirectional. A child's anxious temperament may evoke an overprotective and intrusive parental response (Moore, Whaley, & Sigman, 2004).

Parents may influence the development of anxiety in several other ways (Bögels & Brechman-Toussaint, 2006; Wood et al., 2003). Children may learn to be anxious from their parents who prompt, model, and reinforce anxious behavior. Parents, who are themselves anxious, may model fearful behavior or transmit such information by telling stories of anxiety-provoking experiences. That children can learn from observing their parents' reactions is illustrated in a study of toddlers who were presented with a rubber snake or rubber spider (Gerull & Rapee, 2002). The toddlers' approach to or avoidance of these toys was measured. Toddlers whose mothers' expressions were negative toward a toy in an earlier trial were less likely to approach and more likely to show negative emotional reactions to the toy. Also, Ollendick, King, and Hamilton (1991) asked a large sample of Australian and American youngsters 9 to 14 years of age to report retrospectively on the sources of their fears.

They found that the development of highly prevalent fears was most frequently attributed to the transmission of information and modeling. A parent may also reinforce avoidant behavior once it is displayed by the child by attending to that behavior or by being oversolicitous to the child in situations that initially evoke anxious behavior.

In addition to modeling anxious behavior or relating stories of fearful and traumatic experiences, parents may influence the development of anxiety through other practices. For example, Dadds and his colleagues (1996) demonstrated that anxious children and their parents are more likely to perceive threat and therefore choose avoidant solutions to ambiguous social problems. Videotaped discussions between children 7 to 14 years old and their families revealed that parents of anxious children listened less to their children, pointed out fewer positive consequences of adaptive behavior, and were more likely to respond to a child's solutions that were avoidant. In contrast, parents of nonclinic children were more likely to listen to their children and agree with their children's plans that were not avoidant. Following the family discussion, children from both groups were asked for their plan for the situation. Anxious children offered more avoidant solutions. Parenting practices may thus contribute to the development of certain cognitive styles, for example, to the perception of situations as hostile or threatening.

The impact of parenting to the development of anxiety disorders may begin early in the caregiving process (Main, 1996). The quality of early caregiving can contribute to the development of anxious behavior, particularly among children with a fearful temperament (Fox, Hane, & Pine, 2007). For example, Hane and Fox (2006) investigated the impact of maternal care behaviors (MCB), defined by constructs such as sensitivity and intrusiveness. They found that infants receiving low-quality MCB exhibited EEG and behavioral differences, including more fearful behavior, compared with infants who received high-quality MCB.

Insecure mother–child attachments have also been shown to be a risk factor for the development of anxiety disorders (Bögels & Brechman-Toussaint, 2006). For example, Warren and colleagues (1997) reported on the adolescent outcome of a group of youths who, as infants, had been assessed using Ainsworth's Strange Situation procedure. When they were 17.5 years old, they were assessed by raters who did not know the adolescent's past attachment status. As infants, more adolescents with anxiety disorders had been classified as having anxious/resistant attachments, and more adolescents with other (nonanxiety) disorders had been classified as having avoidant attachments. Also, 28% of those who were anxiously/resistantly attached as infants developed anxiety disorders, whereas 13% who were not anxiously/resistantly attached developed anxiety disorders. Furthermore, anxious/resistant attachment was found to contribute to the development of anxiety disorders even after maternal anxiety and measures of infant temperament were accounted for. Thus, a specific kind of insecure attachment may be one of the factors that contributes to the development of anxiety disorders.

We have been discussing how families may contribute to the development of anxiety problems in children. It is important to remember that influences are likely reciprocal—that is, parents' behavior may be influenced by the anxious temperament/behavior of the child. We should also remember that families can protect children from developing these problems. Family support, for example, has been found to protect children who are exposed to traumatic circumstances (Donovan & Spence, 2000). And families may foster children's abilities to cope with potentially anxiety-provoking circumstances.

Assessment of Anxiety Disorders

A comprehensive assessment of a child or adolescent presenting with anxiety will likely involve a variety of assessment needs. Assessment strategies must be developmentally sensitive. They must address ongoing developmental changes and appreciate differences in comprehension and expressive abilities (Silverman & Ollendick, 2005). The assessment process must also allow problems of clinical concern to be differentiated from the normal fears and worries that may be common at a particular age (Kendall et al., 2000; March & Albano, 1998).

Assessment also needs to be sensitive to the needs of culturally, ethnically diverse populations (Cooley & Boyce, 2004). For example, Wren and colleagues (2007) examined the properties of a widely used rating scale for anxiety disorders in a multi-ethnic population. They found ethnic differences in the factor structure—that is, items that comprised the different anxiety factors (e.g. somatic/panic, generalized) of the scale varied by ethnicity. The variation was greatest for Hispanic children and their parents. Ethnicity also may influence the reporting of particular anxiety symptoms. For example, Pina and Silverman (2004) found that ethnicity and language choice (Spanish or English) influenced the reporting of somatic symptoms. Thus, initial and ongoing assessment presents a considerable challenge.

The child or adolescent's anxiety is not the only thing that needs to be addressed. The young person's environment will need to be assessed as well. For example, it may be desirable to assess the specific environmental events that are associated with heightened anxiety, to evaluate patterns of family interactions and communication, to assess the reactions of adults or peers to the young person's behavior, and to assess the existence of problems in other family members. The assessment of multiple aspects of the problem and the use of multiple informants, including the child or adolescent, are likely to yield valuable information.

Assessment of anxiety disorders is often guided by the tripartite model of anxiety. Thus assessment methods address one or more of the three response systems (behavioral, cognitive, physiological). Various methods of assessment exist (Greco & Morris, 2004; Silverman & Ollendick, 2005).

INTERVIEWS AND SELF-REPORT INSTRUMENTS

As is usually the case, a general clinical interview is likely to yield information that is valuable to the clinician in formulating an understanding of the case and in planning an intervention. The youth and at least one parent will typically be interviewed. Structured diagnostic interviews are available and may be employed to derive a clinical diagnosis (Silverman & Ollendick, 2005). For example, the Anxiety Disorders Interview Schedule for Children (ADIS-C/P) is a semistructured interview for the child and parent (Silverman & Albano, 1996) designed to determine the DSM anxiety diagnoses.

The most widely used method for assessing child and adolescent anxiety is self-report instruments. These measures provide reports of the behavioral, cognitive, and physiological aspects of anxiety. It is clearly important to assess symptoms from the child's or adolescent's viewpoint because it may be difficult for adults reliably to identify the existence of such discomfort. However, particularly younger children may have difficulty in labeling and communicating their subjective feelings, creating a considerable assessment challenge. Parallel measures that allow parents, teachers, and clinicians to describe the youth's anxiety also are available.

There are a number of different types of self-report measures. Some instruments allow children and adolescents to report how anxious they are in a specific situation. There are also self-report instruments that assess overall (across situations) subjective anxiety, such as the State-Trait Anxiety Inventory for Children (Spielberger, 1973) and the Revised Children's Manifest Anxiety Scale (Reynolds & Richmond, 1985), which contains items such as "I have trouble making up my mind" and "I am afraid of a lot of things." Also, the Multidimensional Anxiety Scale for Children (MASC), developed by March and his colleagues (1997), is a self-report measure that addresses the multidimensional nature of anxiety.

In addition, there are self-report instruments specifically designed to address the cognitive component of anxiety. Assessment of the cognitive component of children's anxiety has probably received less attention than it should, given that various aspects of cognitions have been implicated in the maintenance and etiology of anxiety (Kendall et al., 2000; Schniering et al., 2000). The Negative Affect Self-Statement Questionnaire (Ronan, Kendall, & Rowe, 1994) is used to assess the cognitive content associated with negative affect. A subscale for assessing anxious self-talk (e.g., "I am going to make a fool of myself") can discriminate between anxious and nonanxious children. The Coping Questionnaire-Child Version (Kendall et al., 1997a) assesses the child's ability to cope with anxiety in challenging situations. The Children's Automatic Thoughts Scale (Schniering & Rapee, 2002) assesses automatic thoughts about threats, failure, and hostility.

Some self-report instruments also exist to assess specific anxiety disorders; for example, the Revised Fear Survey Schedule for Children (Ollendick, 1983) to assess specific fears, the Social Anxiety Scales for Children and Adolescents (La Greca, 1999), and the Social Phobia and Anxiety Inventory for Children (Beidel, Turner, & Morris, 1995). The Screen for Child Anxiety Related Emotional Disorders (SCARED; Birmaher et al., 1997; 1999) assesses for the symptoms of several anxiety disorders.

Given that children and adolescents with anxiety disorders often present with a variety of other problems as well, the assessment process should include a broader exploration of problem areas. Instruments, such as the Achenbach behavior checklists, can help in describing a range of behavior problems. These instruments also provide an examination of various perspectives (the youngster, parents, teacher) on problems.

Observation of the child's behavior in the natural environment can be made as the child encounters a feared situation.
(Tony Freeman/PhotoEdit Inc.)

DIRECT OBSERVATIONS

Direct observation procedures are primarily employed for assessing the overt behavioral aspects of fears and anxieties, but may also be used to assess environmental influences that may be controlling anxiety (Dadds, Rapee, & Barrett, 1994; Silverman & Ollendick, 2005). Behavioral avoidance tests require the child or adolescent to perform a series of tasks involving the feared object or situation. Thus the young person might be asked to move closer and closer to a feared dog and then increasingly to interact with the dog.

Observations can also be made by observers in the natural environment where the fear or anxiety occurs. Alternatively, self-monitoring procedures require the youth to observe and to systematically record his or her own behavior. A daily diary of such observations may be part of an initial assessment and is also often part of treatment efforts.

PHYSIOLOGICAL RECORDINGS

As noted earlier, the physiological aspects of anxiety are included in self-report instruments. However, this component of anxiety can be more directly as-

sessed by measuring parameters such as heart rate, skin conductance, and palmar sweat. Practical difficulties often inhibit clinicians from obtaining these measures and, thus, these assessments are conducted less frequently.

Interventions for Anxiety Disorders

Interventions for anxiety in children and adolescents have a long history. However, research regarding effective treatments is less extensive than for adults. The systematic investigation of treatments for clinical-level anxiety problems and of interventions to prevent anxiety disorders has only recently received attention (D'Eramo & Francis, 2004; Feldner, Zvolensky, & Schmidt, 2004).

PSYCHOLOGICAL TREATMENTS

Much of the research on treatments for children and adolescents with anxiety disorders has supported the use of behavioral or cognitive-behavioral interventions (AACAP, 2007; APA, 2006). Several behavioral techniques for treating phobias, and cognitive-behavioral procedures for treating anxiety disorders (separation anxiety, social anxiety, generalized anxiety disorders) are considered either "well established" or "probably efficacious."

Exposure to anxiety-provoking situations is an essential element of successful fear-reduction and anxiety treatment programs (Chorpita & Southam-Gerow, 2006; Ollendick, Davis, & Muris, 2004; Silverman & Kurtines, 2005). Thus many of the behavioral treatments for phobias and components of cognitive-behavioral treatments for other anxiety disorders can be conceptualized as various ways of facilitating exposure to the relevant object or situation.

Relaxation and desensitization. Relaxation training teaches individuals to be aware of their physiological and muscular reactions to anxiety and provides them with skills to control these reactions. By tensing and relaxing various muscle groups, the person comes to sense early signs of bodily tension and to use these sensations as signals to relax. With practice the person is able to relax muscle groups in real-life situations when initial signs of tension are detected. Cue-controlled relaxation can also be taught. During muscle relaxation training, the individual is taught to subvocalize a cue word such as "calm." The cue word can be used in actual situations when anxiety is anticipated or experienced to help induce a relaxed state. Relaxation procedures are often accompanied by the incorporation of imagery—the therapist encourages the client to create vivid positive mental images designed to produce relaxation.

When relaxation training is combined with exposure to feared situations, the procedure is known as desensitization or systematic desensitization. In imaginal desensitization, a hierarchy of fear-provoking situations is constructed, and the person is asked to visualize scenes, progressing from the least to the most fear producing. These visualizations are presented as the person is engaged in relaxation. This process is repeated until the most anxiety-provoking scene can be comfortably visualized. In in vivo desensitization, the actual feared object or situation is employed rather than using visualizations.

Modeling. A commonly employed behavioral procedure is modeling. The early work of Bandura and his colleagues (e.g., Bandura & Menlove, 1968) was the impetus for subsequent research. In all modeling therapies, the youth observes another person interacting adaptively with the feared situation. The model can be live or symbolic (e.g., on film). Participant modeling, in which observation is followed by the fearful child joining the model in making gradual approaches to the feared object, is one of the most potent treatments (Ollendick et al., 2004b).

Contingency management. Modeling and systematic desensitization and its variants are treatments that were developed as ways of reducing a young person's fear or anxiety. Contingency management procedures are based on operant principles and, instead,

address the child or adolescent's avoidant/anxious behavior directly by altering the contingencies for such behavior—ensuring that positive consequences follow exposure to but not avoidance of the feared stimulus and that the young person is rewarded for improvement. These procedures are also sometimes described as reinforced practice. Contingency management or reinforced practice has been shown to be effective in treating fears and phobias and as part of the treatment for other anxiety disorders (Kendall & Suveg, 2006; Ollendick et al., 2004). Contingency management is often combined with modeling, relaxation, or desensitization procedures.

Cognitive-behavioral treatments. There is considerable support for the efficacy of cognitive-behavioral treatment programs for anxiety disorders in children and adolescents (APA, 2006; Roblek & Piacentini, 2005). These treatment programs integrate a number of behavioral and cognitive-behavioral strategies. The overall goals of these interventions are to teach the young person to

- recognize the signs of anxious arousal,
- identify the cognitive processes associated with anxious arousal, and
- employ strategies and skills for managing anxiety.

Cognitive-behavioral treatment (CBT) programs employ a variety of therapeutic strategies to achieve these goals, as shown in Table 6-13.

CBT for children with anxiety disorders is illustrated by the work of Kendall and his colleagues (Kendall, Aschenbrand, & Hudson, 2003; Kendall & Suveg, 2006). They describe a 16-week program,

TABLE 6–13	TREATMENT STRATEGIES INCLUDED IN COGNITIVE-BEHAVIORAL TREATMENTS FOR ANXIETY DISORDERS IN CHILDREN AND ADOLESCENTS

Education about anxiety and emotions
Teaching awareness of bodily reactions and physical symptoms
Recognition and modification of anxious self-talk and anxious cognitions
Relaxation procedures
Role playing and contingent reward procedures
Teaching problem-solving skills
Use of coping models
Exposure to anxiety-provoking situations
Practice in using newly acquired skills in increasingly anxiety-provoking situations
Homework assignments

Adapted from Kendall & Suveg, 2006.

which makes use of a variety of behavioral and cognitive behavioral procedures (see Table 6–13), and is divided into two segments. The first eight sessions are devoted to a progressive building of skills. During the second eight sessions, these skills are practiced in situations that expose the child to increasing levels of anxiety. The behavioral strategies include modeling, in vivo exposure, role play, relaxation training, and contingency management. The cognitive strategies include recognizing the physiological symptoms of anxiety, challenging and modifying anxious talk, developing a plan to cope with the situation, evaluating the success of coping efforts, and utilizing self-reinforcement. Throughout treatment the therapist serves as a coping model, demonstrating each of the new skills in each new situation. The following preparation of a youngster for an in vivo exposure—a visit to a mall—illustrates an exchange that might occur between a therapist and a child during Kendall's cognitive-behavioral treatment program.

Therapist: So are you feeling nervous now?

Child: I don't know. Not really.

Therapist: How would you know you were starting to get nervous?

Child: My heart would start beating faster.

Therapist: (recalling a common somatic complaint for this child) What about your breathing?

Child: I might start breathing faster.

Therapist: And what would you be thinking to yourself?

Child: I might get lost or I don't know where I am.

Therapist: And what are some things you could do if you start getting nervous?

Child: I could take deep breaths and say everything is going to be okay.

Therapist: That's good, but what if you were unsure where you were or got lost?

Child: I could ask somebody.

Therapist: Yes, you could ask somebody. Would it be a good idea to ask one of the guards or policemen? How are you feeling? Do you think you are ready to give it a try?

(Kendall & Suveg, 2006, p. 273)

The program makes use of the Coping Cat Workbook (Kendall, 1992; Kendall & Hedtke, 2006) and the acronym "FEAR" to highlight the four skills that the child learns in the program (Kendall & Suveg, 2006).

F—Feeling frightened? (recognizing bodily symptoms of anxiety)

E—Expecting bad things to happen? (recognizing anxious cognition—See Figure 6–2)

FIGURE 6–2

A therapist can use illustrations such as this to help elicit a child's anxiety-related cognitions or self-talk.

A—Attitudes and actions that can help (developing a repertoire of coping strategies)

R—Results and rewards (contingency management)

Research supports the efficacy of this approach (Kendall et al., 2003; Kendall & Suveg, 2006). For example, children diagnosed with anxiety disorders randomly assigned to a treatment condition fared better by the end of treatment than control children on a number of anxiety measures. Treated children returned, on average, to the normal range on these measures. In addition, 64 percent of the children who were treated no longer met diagnostic criteria for an anxiety disorder, compared with 5% (1 case) of the control children. Follow-up assessments, over 7 years, of young people enrolled in this program indicated that these treatment gains were maintained (Kendall et al., 2004). Other research suggests the efficacy of delivering cognitive-behavior therapy in a group rather than in an individual format (Flannery-Schroeder & Kendall, 2000; Silverman et al., 1999). Kendall's program is a child-focused program, but the contextual influences on anxiety are appreciated. Thus, parents are involved as consultants and collaborators. They attend two sessions and actively participate in a supportive role.

An Australian adaptation, referred to as the FRIENDS program, has extended the role of family involvement (Barrett, Dadds, & Rapee, 1996; Barrett & Shortt, 2003). The program has a child-focused component using the Coping Koala Group Workbook, an adaptation of Kendall's Coping Cat Workbook and program. In addition, in the family component, the child and parents are treated in small family groups. Thus, in addition to treating the child with cognitive-behavioral procedures, the program trains parents in, and allows them to and practice, child management, anxiety management, and communication and problem-solving skills to build a supportive family environment.

Research evaluations of the program indicate that the vast majority of youths, in both the child-only or child-plus-family treatments, no longer meet criteria for an anxiety disorder by the end of treatment, nor at follow-up several years later. Greater involvement of parents may be the treatment of choice for some young people. Findings from this research suggest that this may be the case for younger children and cases in which the parents themselves are highly anxious (Cobham, Dadds, & Spence, 1998; Barrett & Shortt, 2003). Other findings also suggest the value of parent participation in the treatment (Wood et al., 2006).

PHARMACOLOGICAL TREATMENTS

Several psychotropic medications are frequently suggested for treating youngsters with anxiety disorders. The evidence for efficacy is strongest for selective serotonin reuptake inhibitors (SSRIs; e.g. fluvoxamine, fluoxetine, sertraline) in treating generalized anxiety, separation anxiety, and social anxiety disorders. These disorders have clinical features in common, exhibit similar familial relationships with adult disorders, and frequently co-occur in young people (AACAP, 2007; APA, 2006). While side effects of SSRIs are typically described as mild and transitory, the FDA has issued a warning to carefully monitor youngsters on SSRIs for worsening depression or suicidality. Also, the benefit and risks of long-term use have not been studied (AACAP, 2007). Thus, in practice, the use of pharmacological treatment for anxiety in youth may not be the treatment of first choice (Gleason et al., 2007). Investigations of the comparative efficacy of CBT, SSRIs, and their combination are needed (APA, 2006).

TREATING OBSESSIVE–COMPULSIVE DISORDER

Obsessive–compulsive disorder differs in a number of ways from the other anxiety disorders we have reviewed (e.g., known and suspected etiological factors, patterns of co-occurrence). We will therefore provide a brief separate discussion of treatment for this disorder.

Two kinds of intervention, alone or in combination, seem to be the current treatments of choice for obsessive–compulsive disorder (Abramowitz, Whiteside, & Deacon, 2005; Franklin, Foa, & March, 2003; Pediatric OCD Treatment Study [POTS] Team, 2004). Cognitive-behavioral interventions are the first-line treatment of choice. Medication is the other treatment option. Various selective serotonin reuptake inhibitors (SSRIs; e.g. fluoxetine, sertraline, paroxetine, and fluvoxamine) and the serotonin reuptake inhibitor clomipramine have been demonstrated as effective pharmacological treatments, with SSRIs preferred because of their more tolerable side effects. However, the efficacy of medications is modest, a 30 to 40% reduction in OCD symptom severity. Also, the increased scrutiny regarding the safety of SSRIs suggests caution in their use (APA 2006; Geller et al., 2003b; Leonard et al., 2005; Waslick, 2006). Whether and under what circumstances to combine CBT with medication remains unclear (APA, 2006; Abramowitz et al., 2005; POTS, 2004).

CBT treatment typically involves education about OCD, training in modifying cognitions to resist obsessions and compulsions and to enhance change, and contingency management and self-reinforcement. The central aspect of cognitive-behavioral approaches, however, is exposure with response prevention (March, Franklin, & Foa, 2005). The child or adolescent is exposed to the situation that causes anxiety and the compulsive ritual is prevented by helping the youngster resist the urge to perform the ritual.

In imaginal exposure, the child is presented with a detailed and an embellished description of the feared situation for several minutes so as to create anxiety. At the same time, the child is not permitted to engage in any thoughts or behaviors to avoid the anxiety. The several-minute exposure is repeated until the anxiety is reduced to a predetermined level. The following is an example of imaginal exposure to anxiety-provoking germs.

> *You walk up to the school door and have to open the door with your hands. You forgot your gloves, so there is nothing to protect you from the germs. As you touch the handle, you feel some sticky and slimy wet stuff on your hand and your skin begins to tingle. Oh no! You've touched germs that were left there by someone and they're oozing into your skin and contaminating you with some sickness. You start to feel weak, and can feel the germs moving under your skin. You try to wipe your hands on your clothes, but it's too late. Already the germs are into your blood and moving all through your body. You feel weak and dizzy, and you can't even hold the door open. You start to feel like you're going to vomit, and you can taste some vomit coming up to your throat . . . (Albano & DiBartolo, 1997)*

In addition to, or as an alternative to, imaginal exposure, the child may be exposed to the actual anxiety-provoking situations. The involvement of the family, especially with younger children, may be an important component (Freeman et al., 2003).

PREVENTION OF ANXIETY DISORDERS

There are multiple reasons to think in terms of preventing anxiety disorders (Weisberg, Kumpfer, & Seligman, 2003). Anxiety disorders are common in childhood and adolescence. Furthermore, anxiety disorders may increase the risk for other disorders and the impact of these conditions may extend throughout the child and adolescent period and into adulthood. The development of formal and manualized prevention programs has only relatively recently begun (Foa et al., 2005b).

Indicated prevention programs target individuals who already display some symptoms but do not meet diagnostic criteria or have a mild form of the targeted problem. The content of these intervention programs is highly similar to that described in the discussion of cognitive-behavioral treatments for anxiety disorders. For example, intervention based on the FRIENDS program, described earlier, was offered to youngsters between the ages of 7 and 14 years of age and their parents. Youngsters ranged from those who did not have a disorder but showed mild anxious features to those who met the criteria for an anxiety disorder but were in the less severe range (Dadds et al., 1999). A 2-year follow-up that compared these youths with a control group that did not receive the intervention suggested that the program was useful in preventing youths with mild to moderate anxiety problems from developing more serious anxiety disorders.

A selected prevention program targets youngsters who may be at risk for a later anxiety disorder. Rapee and colleagues (2005) provided a brief (six 90-minute sessions) parent education program to parents of preschool children with high levels of withdrawn/inhibited behaviors—a risk factor for later anxiety disorders. The group sessions provided information on the nature and development of anxiety, parent management techniques (especially the role of overprotection in maintaining anxiety), principles of gradual exposure to anxiety provoking situations, and cognitive restructuring of the parents' own worries. At a 12-month follow-up, children whose parents participated in the program exhibited lower levels of anxiety diagnoses than those whose parents received no intervention.

Barrett and colleagues (2006) have described a school-based universal prevention program provided to Grade 6 (ages 10 to 11 years) and Grade 9 (ages 13 to 14 years) youth in several schools. Again, the intervention was the FRIENDS program. At the end of the intervention, and at a 36-month follow-up, participants reported significantly lower anxiety scores and were less likely to be classified as high risk than those in the control condition who did not receive the intervention. Youngsters in Grade 6 appeared to benefit more than students in Grade 9, suggesting the value of earlier intervention.

SUMMARY

AN INTRODUCTION TO INTERNALIZING DISORDERS

- There is appreciable evidence of a broad category of child and adolescent internalizing problems. Conclusions regarding more specific disorders are less certain. One issue of particular concern is the high rate of co-occurrence of multiple internalizing disorders.

DEFINING AND CLASSIFYING ANXIETY DISORDERS

- Anxiety or fear is generally viewed as a complex pattern of three response systems: overt behavioral, cognitive, and physiological responses. Anxiety is part of normal developmental processes.

- Fears are quite common in children. There seem to be age- and gender-related variations in numbers and content of fears. The most common fears seem to be similar across cultures.

- The DSM-IV-TR describes one anxiety disorder within the grouping of disorders that are "usually first evident in infancy, childhood, or adolescence": Separation Anxiety Disorder. A youngster can also receive other anxiety disorder diagnoses.

- The empirical approach to classification describes subcategories of internalizing disorders. These subcategories do not, however, suggest separate anxiety disorders and suggest that anxiety and depression tend to co-occur.

- Anxiety disorders are among the most common disorders experienced by children and adolescents.

SPECIFIC PHOBIAS

- Phobias, as distinguished from normal fears, are excessive, persistent, or nonadaptive. Specific phobias are among the most commonly diagnosed anxiety disorders in children and adolescents. They are likely to begin in childhood and may persist over time. Young people with this diagnosis, as with other anxiety disorders, frequently have co-occurring disorders.

SOCIAL ANXIETY DISORDER

- Children and adolescents with social anxiety are likely to be concerned about being embarrassed or negatively evaluated.

- Young people with selective mutism do not talk in selected social situations. This disorder may be a type of social phobia.

- Prevalence of social anxiety probably increases with age. Social anxieties are quite common during adolescence, making the interpretations of prevalence and degree of disturbance difficult.

SEPARATION ANXIETY AND SCHOOL REFUSAL

- Separation anxiety is excessive anxiety regarding separation from a major attachment figure and/or home. Separation anxiety is a common problem among children but becomes less common by adolescence.

- School refusal is anxiety that keeps a child or adolescent from attending school. This term accommodates cases of both separation anxiety and phobias related to aspects of the school situation. School refusal in adolescence is likely to be complex.

- Treatment of school refusal is most successful if it is begun early, and it probably needs to be tailored to the specific kinds of school refusal exhibited.

GENERALIZED ANXIETY DISORDER

- Children and adolescents diagnosed with generalized anxiety disorder (GAD) exhibit excessive worry and anxiety that is not focused on any particular object or situation. GAD is probably the most common anxiety disorder among adolescents. GAD is common among youngsters seen in clinical settings, and the disorder may persist. The question of overlap with other diagnoses is of concern.

PANIC ATTACKS AND PANIC DISORDER

- Panic attacks may be cued or uncued, and they may occur in the context of several anxiety disorders. Panic disorder is associated with recurrent uncued panic attacks. The presence of panic in adolescents seems likely, but the existence, particularly of uncued panic, in younger children is less clear. Family histories of panic and severe anxiety are commonly reported.

REACTIONS TO TRAUMATIC EVENTS

- The diagnosis of posttraumatic stress disorder requires reexperiencing of a traumatic event, avoidance of stimuli associated with the trauma, and symptoms of increased arousal.

- *There may be age-related differences in reactions to trauma and reactions may differ based on the nature of the traumatic event.*
- *The diagnosis of acute distress disorder may be given during the first month following the trauma. In general, symptoms decline over time, but substantial numbers of youths continue to report symptoms a long time after the trauma.*
- *Degree of exposure to the trauma, preexisting youth characteristics and coping abilities, and reactions of parents are among the influences that may determine a young person's reaction to a trauma.*

OBSESSIVE–COMPULSIVE DISORDER

- *Obsessive–compulsive disorder (OCD) is characterized by repetitive and intrusive thoughts and/or behaviors. OCD is more common than once thought and often appears to follow a chronic course.*

ETIOLOGY OF ANXIETY DISORDERS

- *The development and maintenance of anxiety disorders are influenced by multiple factors that interact in complex ways.*
- *There is a familial aggregation for anxiety disorders. Genetic factors may play a role, but for many disorders, what may be inherited is a general tendency toward emotional reactivity. Evidence for a genetic and biological basis seems strongest for obsessive–compulsive disorder and generalized anxiety disorder.*
- *A general vulnerability to anxiety may be associated with the child's temperament. The temperamental characteristic of behavioral inhibition appears to be a risk factor for the development of anxiety disorders.*
- *Psychosocial influences play a considerable role in the development of anxiety disorders. Direct exposure, imitation, information transmission, and parenting practices are some of the mechanisms of influence.*

ASSESSMENT OF ANXIETY DISORDERS

- *Assessments of anxiety should consider developmental issues and various perspectives on the young person's problem, information about a full range of problems, and information about the child or adolescent's environment should be obtained.*
- *Assessment of anxiety is typically guided by the three response systems: behaviors, cognitions, and physiological responses.*
- *Self-report instruments provide subjective reports of the various aspects of anxiety. Direct observation and behavioral approach tests assess overt behavioral aspects. Physiological recordings of anxiety are conducted less frequently.*

INTERVENTIONS FOR ANXIETY DISORDERS

- *Appreciable support exists for the effectiveness of psychological treatments for anxiety problems in youngsters. Many treatments are, at least in part, based on exposure to the feared stimulus.*
- *Procedures such as modeling, desensitization, and contingency management contribute to successful treatment. Cognitive-behavioral treatments that include a number of therapeutic strategies have proven effective in treating anxiety disorders. Pharmacotherapy, if employed, is usually an adjunct to psychological treatments.*
- *Cognitive-behavioral treatments involving exposure and response prevention and pharmacological treatment employing selective serotonin reuptake inhibitors have been shown to be effective in treating obsessive–compulsive disorder.*
- *Investigations of prevention programs, drawing on cognitive-behavioral procedures, suggest that they may be effective in preventing the development of anxiety disorders.*

KEY TERMS

internalizing disorders *(p. 119)*

anxiety *(p. 120)*

fear *(p. 120)*

worry *(p. 120)*

phobia *(p. 122)*

specific phobia *(p. 122)*

Social Anxiety Disorder (Social Phobia) *(p. 124)*

Selective Mutism *(p. 126)*

Separation Anxiety Disorder *(p. 128)*

agoraphobia *(p. 130)*

school refusal *(p. 130)*

functional analysis *(p. 130)*

truancy *(p. 131)*

Overanxious Disorder *(p. 131)*

CHAPTER 7

Mood Disorders

In this chapter we examine what are known as problems of mood or affect. Children and adolescents can experience moods that are, on the one hand, unusually elated, or on the other hand, unusually sad. When these moods are particularly extreme or persistent or when they interfere with the individual's functioning, they may be labeled as mania and depression, respectively, and they are another aspect of internalizing disorders.

Until relatively recently, mood disorders in children and adolescents had not received a great deal of attention. The increase in interest in affective problems can be traced to a number of influences. Promising developments in the identification and treatment of mood disorders in adults played a role. Also, the emergence of a number of assessment measures allowed researchers to examine the phenomenon in clinical and normal populations of youngsters. In addition, improvements in diagnostic practices have facilitated the study of mood disorders in children and adolescents. However, finding that we can apply adult diagnostic criteria to youths should not lead us to prematurely conclude that these phenomena are the same in children and adults.

When we attempt to place mood disorders in separate categories, we confront many of the same problems that we found in examining anxiety disorders. For example, children and adolescents who meet the criteria for a diagnosis of depression are often also given other diagnoses. Thus the designation of these problems as distinct entities is not without controversy. Nonetheless, examining depression and mania makes sense in terms of how the research and treatment literature is organized. In the study of mood disorders, there is a greater accumulation of literature regarding depression.

A Historical Perspective

A brief look at recent history can aid our understanding of current views of childhood depression. The dominant view in child clinical work for many years was the orthodox psychoanalytic perspective. From this perspective, depression was viewed as a phenomenon of superego and mature ego functioning (Kessler, 1988). It was argued, for example, that in depression, the superego acts as a punisher of the ego. Because a child's superego is not sufficiently developed to play this role, it was believed to be impossible for a depressive disorder to occur in children. It is not surprising, therefore, that depression in children received little attention.

A second major perspective added to the controversy regarding the existence of a distinct disorder of childhood depression. The concept of masked depression held that there was indeed a disorder of childhood depression, but that the sad mood and other features usually considered essential to the diagnosis of depression frequently were not present. It was believed that an underlying depressive disorder did exist but that it was "masked" by other problems (depressive equivalents), such as hyperactivity or delinquency. The "underlying" depression itself was not directly displayed but could be inferred by the clinician. Some professionals, indeed, suggested that masked depression was quite common and that because it was masked, childhood depression was underdiagnosed (Cytryn & McKnew, 1974; Malmquist, 1977).

The notion of masked depression was clearly problematic. There was no operational way to decide whether a particular symptom was or was not a sign of depression. Indeed, the symptoms that were suggested as masking depression included virtually the full gamut of problem behaviors in youths. The concept of masked depression was, therefore, quite controversial.

This concept was important, however. It clearly recognized depression as an important and a prevalent childhood problem. And the central notions of masked depression—that depression in children does exist and may be displayed in a variety of age-related forms different from adult depression—are still widely held. The concept that depression is manifested differently in children and adults contributed, in part, to the evolution of a developmental psychopathology perspective.

Early in the evolution of this perspective, it was suggested that behaviors that led to the diagnosis of depression (e.g., insufficient appetite, excessive reserve) might be only transitory developmental phenomena that were common among children in certain age groups (Lefkowitz & Burton, 1978). This early position drew attention to the need to differentiate transient episodes of sadness and negative affect, which may be common reactions among children, from more long-lasting expressions of such emotions. Also, the distinction between depression as a *symptom* and depression as a *syndrome* is important to consider here. One or two depressive behaviors may be viewed as typical of that developmental stage. However, it is different to suggest that a cluster of such behaviors accompanied by other problems and impaired functioning is likely to occur in a large number of children (Kovacs, 1997). The developmental perspective has become an important aspect of the study of depression (Cicchetti & Toth, 1998; Rudolph, Hammen, & Daley, 2006).

The DSM Approach to the Classification of Mood Disorders

In the DSM, depression and mania are described in the category of Mood Disorders. The diagnostic categories are the same for children, adolescents, and adults. Mood disorders are sometimes described as unipolar (one mood is experienced, typically depression) versus bipolar (both moods are experienced, depression and mania).

The DSM describes mood episodes that are not themselves diagnoses but that serve as the building blocks for the diagnosis of mood disorders. Four types of mood episodes are described. The essential characteristic of a Major Depressive Episode is a period of either depressed mood or loss of interest or pleasure in nearly all activities. The essential feature of a Manic Episode is a period of abnormally and persistently elevated, expansive, or irritable mood. A Mixed Episode includes symptoms of both Manic and Major Depressive Episodes. A Hypomanic Episode is characterized by the same symptoms as a Manic Episode, but symptoms are not as severe and do not cause impairment in functioning.

We begin our examination of mood disorders with the problem of depression, then consider mania/bipolar disorder, and conclude with a discussion of suicide.

Definition and Classification of Depression

DEFINING DEPRESSION

Understanding depression in children and adolescents is a complex task. The phenomenon itself involves a complex interplay of influences and a complex clinical presentation. In addition, there have been a variety of perspectives on depression in young people and a variety of ways in which depression has been defined.

Research findings indicate that different groups of youths may or may not be designated as depressed, depending on how depression is defined and assessed (Carlson & Cantwell, 1980; Hammen & Rudolph, 2003; Kaslow & Racusin, 1990). Such variations can lead to different conclusions regarding the causes and correlates of depression.

A study by Kazdin (1989) illustrates differences related to informants' views. DSM diagnoses of 231 consecutive child admissions to an inpatient psychiatric facility were made on the basis of direct interviews with the children and their parents. This method of diagnosing depression was compared with diagnosis based on exceeding a cutoff score on the Children's Depression Inventory (CDI). Both the children and their parents completed the CDI. In addition, children and/or their parents completed other measures to assess attributes reported to be associated with depression. Different groups of children appeared to be designated as depressed depending on the method employed. In addition, characteristics associated with depression varied depending on the method used. Some of these results are illustrated in Table 7–1. When depression was defined as a high child-reported score on the CDI, depressed children were more hopeless; had lower self-esteem; made more internal (as opposed to external) attributions regarding negative events; and, on the basis of a locus of control scale, were more likely to believe that control was due to external factors rather than to themselves. Depressed and nondepressed children defined by the other two criteria (parent CDI and DSM) did not differ from each other on these characteristics. When depression was defined by the parent CDI score, children with high depression scores exhibited more problems across a wide range of symptoms (as measured by the Child Behavior Checklist—CBCL) than those with very low depression scores. Depression as designated by the other two criteria did not appear to be associated with this wide range of problems. Thus conclusions regarding correlates of depression may be affected by the informant and method employed to designate youths as depressed.

It is not possible at this point to make definitive statements about the "correct" definition of depression. It is probably fair, however, to state that the dominant view is that child/adolescent depression is a syndrome, or disorder, and that the most often employed definitions are those offered by the DSM.

DEPRESSIVE DISORDERS: THE DSM APPROACH

Major Depressive Disorder (MDD) is the primary DSM category for defining depression. This disorder is described by the presence of one or more major depressive episodes. The symptoms required for the presence of a major depressive episode are the same for children, adolescents, and adults (with one exception), and are listed in Table 7–2. The one exception is that in children or adolescents, irritable mood can be substituted for depressed mood. Indeed, some reports suggest that a majority of depressed youths (over 80%) exhibit irritable mood (Goodyer & Cooper, 1993; Ryan et al., 1987). To diagnose a Major Depressive Episode, the DSM requires the following:

- Five or more symptoms must be present.
- One of these symptoms must be either depressed (or irritable) mood or loss of pleasure.

TABLE 7–1 MEAN CHARACTERISTIC SCORES OF DEPRESSED AND NONDEPRESSED CHILDREN AS DESIGNATED BY DIFFERENT CRITERIA FOR DEPRESSION

| | CRITERIA | | | | | |
| | CHILDREN'S DEPRESSION INVENTORY (BY CHILD) | | CHILDREN'S DEPRESSION INVENTORY (BY PARENT) | | DSM DIAGNOSIS | |
MEASURES	HIGH	LOW	HIGH	LOW	DEPRESSED	NONDEPRESSED
Hopelessness	7.3	3.3	5.3	5.0	5.4	4.8
Self-esteem	22.7	38.9	28.2	30.8	29.2	30.9
Attributions	5.4	6.5	5.8	5.8	6.0	6.0
Locus of control	9.8	6.8	8.2	8.7	7.9	8.4
Total behavior problems (CBCL)	75.8	75.3	81.6	69.0	76.5	75.0

Adapted from Kazdin, 1989.

TABLE 7–2	SYMPTOMS USED BY THE DSM TO DIAGNOSE A MAJOR DEPRESSIVE EPISODE

1. Depressed or irritable mood
2. Loss of interest or pleasure
3. Change in weight or appetite
4. Sleep problems
5. Motor agitation or retardation
6. Fatigue or loss of energy
7. Feelings of worthlessness or guilt
8. Difficulty thinking, concentrating, or making decisions
9. Thoughts of death or suicidal thoughts/behavior

From American Psychiatric Association, 2000.

- The symptoms must be present for at least 2 weeks.
- Symptoms must cause clinically significant distress or impairment in important areas of the child or adolescent's functioning (e.g., social, school).

Dysthymic Disorder is the other principal depressive disorder included in the DSM. It is essentially a disorder in which many of the symptoms of a major depressive episode are present in less severe form but are more chronic—that is, they persist for a longer period of time. Depressed mood (or in children and adolescents, irritable mood) is present for at least 1 year along with two or more of the other symptoms indicated in Table 7–3. Again, the symptoms must cause clinically significant distress or impairment. The term double depression is sometimes employed to describe instances in which both dysthymia and a major depressive episode are present. Dysthymia is typically described as developing prior to the occurrence of a major depressive episode.

TABLE 7–3	SYMPTOMS USED BY THE DSM TO DIAGNOSE DYSTHYMIC DISORDER

1. Depressed or irritable mood
2. Poor appetite or overeating
3. Sleep disturbance
4. Low energy or fatigue
5. Low self-esteem
6. Concentration or decision-making problems
7. Feelings of hopelessness

From American Psychiatric Association, 2000.

The validity of separate diagnoses of dysthymia and major depressive disorders has been questioned. There is little evidence of differences in the features or correlates of these disorders other than an earlier age of onset for dysthymia (Goodman et al., 2000).

Youngsters who are depressed can also be given the diagnosis of Adjustment Disorder with Depressed Mood. This disorder is viewed as a response to a stressor in which depressive symptoms do not meet the criteria for other depressive disorders.

As was indicated before, the view inherent in the DSM approach is that depressive disorders in children and adolescents are the same as those in adults. There is some research consistent with this perspective. However, differences have also been found and certain findings require explanation. Differences such as the gender ratio in prevalence (Dekker et al., 2007; Nolen-Hoeksema & Girgus, 1994), biological correlates (Zalsman et al., 2006), and the effectiveness of antidepressant medications (APA, 2006) are described in this chapter. Such differences are one reason why it may be premature to accept the use of the same criteria for depressive disorders across all age groups.

DEPRESSION: EMPIRICAL APPROACHES

Syndromes that involve depressive symptoms have also been identified by empirical approaches to taxonomy. This finding is illustrated by the syndromes of the Achenbach instruments (p. 98). The syndromes that include depressive symptoms that regularly occur together also include symptoms characteristic of anxiety and withdrawn behavior. Thus this research does not find a syndrome that includes symptoms of depression alone. A mixed presentation of depression and anxiety features has emerged consistently in research with children and adolescents.

How best to define and classify depression in children and adolescents remains a focus of ongoing research. One issue is determining developmentally sensitive criteria, as youths may experience depression differently at various points in development. A second issue is that depression in young people may best be conceptualized as dimensional rather than categorical (Hankin et al., 2005). Many professionals have chosen to concern themselves with children and adolescents who exhibit constellations of depressive symptoms whether or not they meet the DSM criteria for a mood disorder. This approach makes sense in that it is not clear that the cutoff set by the diagnostic criteria is the critical

Sad affect, or dysphoria, is the central characteristic of most definitions of depression.
(David Young-Wolff/PhotoEdit Inc.)

one. Many youths who fall short of meeting diagnostic criteria may still exhibit impairment in everyday functioning and be at risk for future difficulties (Georgiades et al., 2006; Lewinsohn et al., 2000).

DESCRIPTION OF DEPRESSION

In everyday usage, the term *depression* refers to the experience of a pervasive unhappy mood. This subjective experience of sadness, or dysphoria, is also a central feature of the clinical definition of depression. Descriptions of children and adolescents viewed as depressed suggest that they experience a number of other problems as well. Concern may be expressed about a youth's irritability and temper tantrums—sudden outbursts, tears, yelling, throwing things. Adults who know the child may describe loss of the experience of pleasure, social withdrawal, lowered self-esteem, inability to concentrate, and poor schoolwork as changes in the young person. Alterations of biological functions (sleeping, eating, elimination) and somatic complaints are often noted as well. The young person may also express thoughts of wishing to die.

These children and adolescents frequently experience other psychological disorders. Anxiety disorders, such as separation anxiety disorder, are probably the most commonly noted. Conduct disorder and oppositional defiant disorder also occur among depressed youth. Among depressed adolescents, alcohol and substance abuse are also common additional problems.

The case of a 15-year-old boy, Nick, illustrates many of these features as well as some of the factors that contribute to the development and course of depression.

Nick The Problems of Depression

Nick lives with his mother. His father left before Nick was born. Nick was born with a curvature of the spine as a result of which he walks awkwardly and is limited in his physical abilities. The incident that resulted in Nick being brought to the clinic was his arrest for shoplifting. . . . (His mother) reports that Nick is irritable and sullen much of the time, that they are constantly fighting and arguing. . . . Nick's outbursts have escalated recently, including occasions when he has thrown things and punched holes in walls and doors. . . .

Nick reveals that he is very unhappy, has few things in his life that give him pleasure, and feels hopeless about things improving for him. He is self-conscious about his appearance, his peers tease him and he feels that he is disliked, and he hates himself.

. . . Nick's typical day is described as: "He wakes up early in the morning after having stayed up late the night before watching television, but he lies in bed until 9:00 or 10:00 a.m. He then spends much of the day at home alone playing video games or watching television." Nick has gained considerable weight and he reports that he is having trouble controlling his appetite. . . . Nick's mother returns home from work late in the afternoon. They often argue about his having missed another day of school. They eat dinner together silently while watching television. The rest of the evening is filled with arguments. . . .

Adapted from Compas, 1997, pp. 197–198.

Epidemiology of Depression

Major depressive disorder (MDD) is by far the most prevalent form of affective disorder among children and adolescents (Lewinsohn, Rohde, & Seeley, 1998).

Among youngsters with unipolar disorders, about 80% experience MDD, 10% dysthymia without MDD, and 10% "double depression." In community surveys, overall prevalence rates for major depressive disorder are estimated to be about 12% (Costello, Egger, & Angold, 2005a). Reported rates in children range between 0.4 and 2.5%, and in adolescents between 0.4 and 8.3%. There is some debate as to whether the rate of major depression has increased in recent decades (Costello, Foley, & Angold, 2006; Evans et al., 2005a). The epidemiology of dysthymic disorder is less well studied. Prevalence rates between 0.6 and 1.7% for children and between 1.6 and 8.0% among adolescents have been reported (Birmaher et al., 1996).

Reported prevalence rates probably underestimate the scope of the problem. For example, lifetime prevalence rates, rather than prevalence rates at any one point in time, indicate that episodes of clinical depression may be quite common, particularly among adolescents. In the Oregon Adolescent Depression Project (OADP), a large prospective epidemiological study of a representative community sample of adolescents aged 14 to 18, Lewinsohn and his colleagues (1998) estimated that by age 19, approximately 28% of adolescents will have experienced an episode of major depressive disorder (35% of the females and 19% of the males). Other information suggests lifetime prevalence rates of diagnosable depressive disorders among the general population as high as 20 to 30% (Compas, Ey, & Grant, 1993; Lewinsohn et al., 1993a). This finding means that about 1 out of 4 young people in the general population experiences a depressive disorder sometime during childhood or adolescence. Even higher estimates emerge when other definitions of clinical levels of depression are employed. For example, 40 to 50% of the OADP youths scored above the criteria for depression "caseness" on a standard self-report depression questionnaire. As a comparison, 16 to 20% of adults meet "caseness" criteria.

Finally, the extent of the problem is even clearer when one includes young people who exhibit depressive symptoms but who do not meet diagnostic criteria. These youths are not included in the prevalence estimates just cited. However, such youths often exhibit impairments in their academic, social, and cognitive functioning and also are at greater risk for future disorders than are youths not exhibiting depressive symptoms (Kazdin & Marciano, 1998; Lewinsohn et al., 1998).

AGE AND GENDER

Age and gender are clearly relevant to estimates of the prevalence of depression in young people (Cyranowski et al., 2000; Harrington, 2001). Depression is less prevalent in younger children than in adolescents (Ford, Goodman, & Meltzer, 2003). Usually no gender differences are reported for children ages 6 to 12 (Angold & Rutter, 1992; Fleming, Offord, & Boyle, 1989). When differences are reported, depression is more prevalent in boys than in girls during this age period (Anderson et al., 1987). Yet among adolescents, depression is more common among girls and begins to approach the 2:1 female-to-male ratio usually reported for adults (Lewinsohn et al., 1994). This age–gender pattern is illustrated in Figure 7–1. It is worth noting that for adolescents of *both* sexes, depression is more prevalent than in younger children (Angold & Rutter, 1992; Cohen, Cohen, Kasen et al., 1993b; Lewinsohn et al., 1993a; Whitaker et al., 1990).

The OADP findings and other information (Nolen-Hoeksema & Girgus, 1994; Wade, Cairney, & Pevalin, 2002) suggest that the gender difference in major depressive disorder prevalence probably emerges between the ages of 12 and 14. Consistent with this picture are findings from the Dunedin Multidisciplinary Health and Development Study, a large epidemiological study conducted in New Zealand (Hankin et al., 1998). Rates of clinical depression (major depressive episode or dysthymic disorder) in these youths were assessed at a number of points between the ages of 11 and 21. At age 11, males showed a tendency to have higher rates of depression than females; at 13, there were no gender differences; and at ages 15, 18, and 21, females had higher rates of depression. Gender differences were greatest between 15 and 18, and rates of depression began to level off after age 18. Findings of other investigators suggest that gender differences in depression may be more pronounced among youngsters referred for mental health services than in nonreferred samples (Compas et al., 1997).

SOCIOECONOMIC, ETHNIC, AND CULTURAL CONSIDERATIONS

Lower socioeconomic status (SES) is reported to be associated with higher rates of depression. The link is probably through influences such as income, limited parental education, chronic stress, family disruption, environmental adversities, and racial/ethnic discrimination (Hammen & Rudolph, 2003;

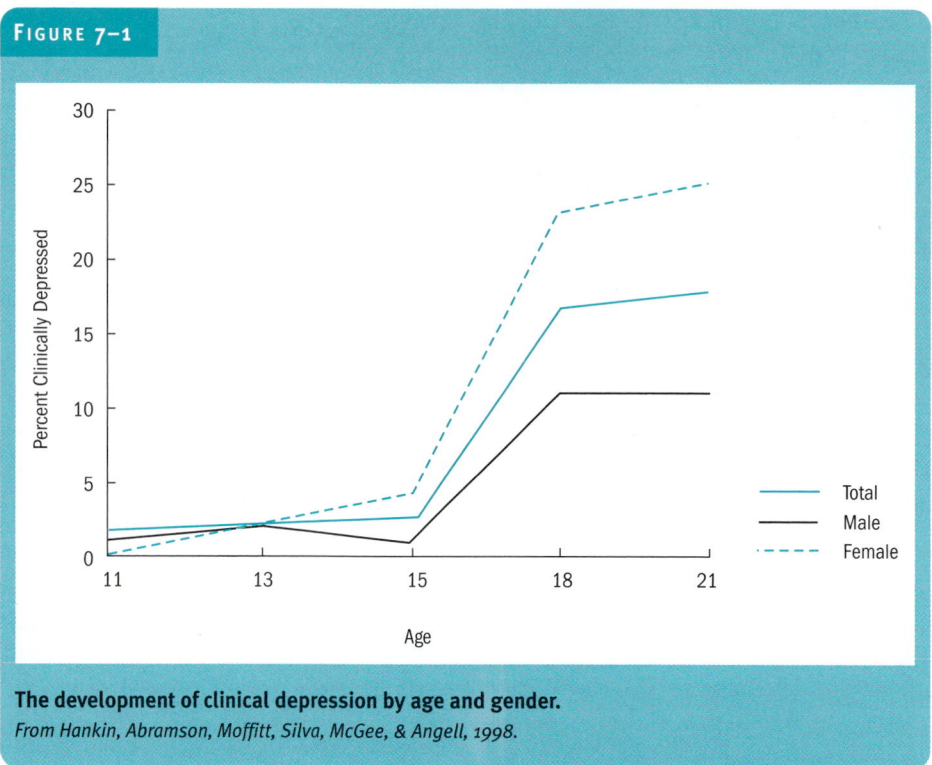

FIGURE 7–1

The development of clinical depression by age and gender.
From Hankin, Abramson, Moffitt, Silva, McGee, & Angell, 1998.

Wight, Sepúlveda, & Aneshensel, 2004). Although such SES differences may have a disproportionate impact on certain ethnic groups, there is not a great deal of information regarding racial and ethnic differences in the prevalence of depression. Comparable rates are typically reported in various ethnic groups (Canino et al., 2004; Gibbs, 2003; Hammen & Rudolph, 2003), except for a suggestion of higher rates among Mexican American children and adolescents (Organista, 2003). Although comparable rates are typically

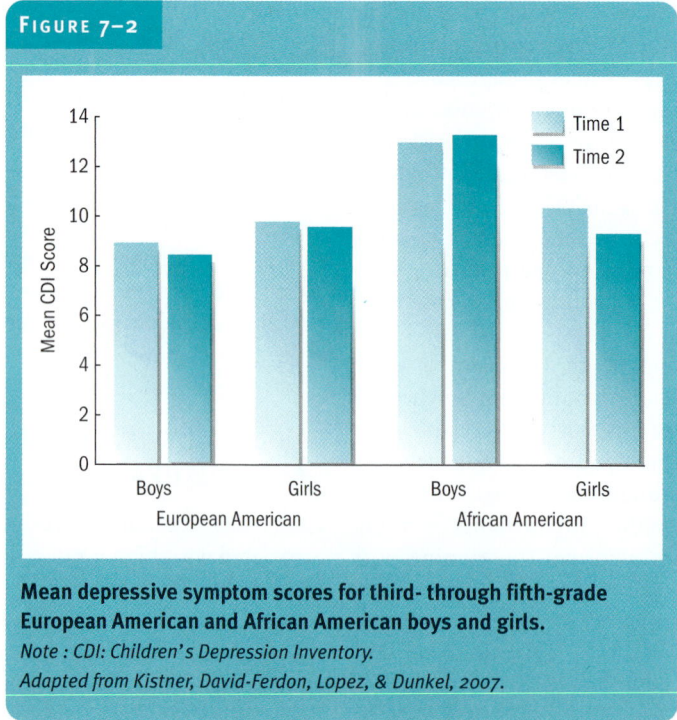

FIGURE 7–2

Mean depressive symptom scores for third- through fifth-grade European American and African American boys and girls.
Note : CDI: Children's Depression Inventory.
Adapted from Kistner, David-Ferdon, Lopez, & Dunkel, 2007.

reported for African American (AA) and European American (EA) youngsters, a comparison of youngsters in grades 3 to 5, followed over a school year, suggests an interesting ethnicity by sex interaction (Kistner et al., 2007). These findings are illustrated in Figure 7–2. AA boys reported more depressive symptoms than AA girls and EA boys and girls. Also, AA boys' depressive symptoms increased during the school year, whereas depression in the other groups decreased or remained stable. For the full sample, as well as for the AA boys, academic achievement deficits predicted increases in depressive symptoms over time.

Co-occurring Difficulties

Finally, children and adolescents who are depressed typically experience other problems as well. For example, 40 to 70% of youths diagnosed with MDD also meet the criteria for another disorder, and 20 to 50% have two or more additional disorders (Birmaher et al., 1996). The most common additional non-mood disorders are anxiety disorders, disruptive behavior disorders, and substance abuse disorders (Angold, Costello, & Erkanli, 1999; Lewinsohn et al., 1998; TADS Team, 2005).

Depression and Development

It is interesting to examine how depression is manifested and how its prevalence changes at different developmental periods. Although the diagnostic criteria in the DSM are largely the same for children, adolescents, and adults, depression may be manifested differently in these groups and, as we saw earlier in our discussion of epidemiology, there may be gender differences in developmental patterns (Compton et al., 2003; Harrington, 2001; Weiss & Garber, 2003).

Schwartz, Gladstone, and Kaslow (1998) describe the phenomenology of depression at different developmental stages. Infants and toddlers lack the cognitive and verbal abilities necessary to self-reflect and report depressive thoughts and problems. It is difficult, therefore, to know what the equivalent to adult depressive symptoms may be in this age group. Given these differences in cognitive and language abilities, and other developmental differences, it is likely that depressive behavior in this age group may be quite different than in adults. Interestingly, the description of infants separated from their primary caregivers in many ways seems similar to that of

depression (Bowlby, 1960; Spitz, 1946). These and other distressed infants, as well as infants of depressed mothers, have been observed to exhibit behaviors such as lethargy, feeding and sleep problems, irritability, sad facial expression, excessive crying, and decreased responsiveness—behaviors often associated with depression.

Depression in preschoolers is also difficult to assess. Many of the symptoms associated with later depression have been noted in children in this age group (e.g., irritability, sad facial expression, changes of mood, feeding and sleep problems, lethargy, excessive crying). Differences in cognition and language, as well as limited information, make it difficult to know how these behaviors are related to the experience of depression and depressive syndromes in older individuals and whether or not these represent stable patterns.

For the period of middle childhood (6 to 12 years), there is more evidence that a prolonged pattern of depressive symptoms may emerge. Younger children in this age group typically do not verbalize the hopelessness and self-deprecation associated with depression. However, 9- to 12-year-olds who exhibit other symptoms of depression may verbalize feelings of hopelessness and low self-esteem. Still, in youngsters in this age group, depressive symptoms may not be a distinctive syndrome but may occur with a variety of symptoms usually associated with other disorders. So, for example, as mentioned before, mixed depressed/anxious syndromes rather than separate depressed syndromes emerge in empirical taxonomies (Achenbach & Rescorla, 2001).

During the early adolescent period, the manifestation of depression is in many ways similar to the way it appears in the childhood period. Over time, however, probably in relation to shifts in biological, social, and cognitive development, depression in older adolescents starts to resemble more closely the symptoms of adult depression (Cyranowski et al., 2000). In their community sample of adolescents, Lewinsohn and his colleagues (1998) report a median age of onset for major depressive disorder at 15.5 years.

As part of their longitudinal research and their effort to examine the relationship of age of onset and familial contributions to depression, Harrington and his colleagues (1997) compared a group of prepubertal-onset depressed youngsters to a group whose onset of depression was postpubertal. Rates of depression in relatives of youths in the two groups did not differ. There were, however, other differences in the families of the two groups.

Manic disorders tended to be more common among relatives of the postpubertal-onset group, whereas there were higher rates of criminality and family discord among relatives of the prepubertal depressed youngsters. This evidence supports the view of prepubertal-onset depressive disorders as distinct from postpubertal-onset depression. In addition, continuity to major depression in adulthood was lower among prepubertal-onset youngsters than among those with postpubertal onset of depression. This finding is also consistent with viewing adolescent-onset depression as more similar to adult forms of the disorder and different from earlier onset depression.

Adolescence thus appears to be a period when depressive syndromes similar to adult depression have their onset. As noted before, there is a significant increase in the prevalence of depression in adolescence, and prevalence may reach adult levels in late adolescence (Wight et al., 2004). What, then, is the clinical course of depression during adolescence and into adulthood? How long does an episode of major depression last? Are there future episodes?

Episodes of depression in adolescents may last for an appreciable period of time and for some individuals may present a recurring problem. In the OADP community sample (Klein et al., 2001; Lewinsohn et al., 1998), the median duration of an episode of major depressive disorder was 8 weeks, with a range from 2 to 520 weeks. The mean duration of the longest episode was 6 months. Earlier onset of depression (at or before the age of 15) was associated with longer episodes. The recurrent nature of depression is illustrated by the finding that among these adolescents, 26% had a history of recurrent major depressive episodes. Kovacs (1996), in her review of studies of clinically referred youths, found a median duration of major depressive disorder episodes of seven to nine months. It was found that about 70% of these clinically referred youths had recurrences of major depressive disorder episodes when followed for 5 or more years. Thus the duration of episodes in clinical samples may be more than three times the duration in community samples, and recurrence of a major depressive episode more than twice as likely.

A sample of participants in the OADP project was interviewed after their 24th birthday. Those who prior to age 19 had met criteria for major depressive disorder or adjustment disorder with depressed mood were more likely to meet criteria for major depressive disorder during young adulthood than their peers with a nonaffective disorder or no disorder prior to

age 19 (Lewinsohn et al., 1999). In addition, follow-up studies suggest that some adolescents with major depressive disorder develop bipolar disorder within 5 years after the onset of depression, but the percentage of individuals who do so is not clear (Birmaher et al., 1996; Kovacs, 1996; Lewinsohn et al., 1999).

Etiology of Depression

Most contemporary views of depression suggest a model that integrates multiple determinants, including biological, social-psychological, family, and peer influences.

Biological Influences

Biological views of depression focus on genetic and biochemical influences. These views derive largely from adult literature (Coyle et al., 2003). There are fewer data available on children and adolescents, although more information is becoming available (Evans et al., 2005a).

Genetic influences. Genetic influences are generally thought to play a role in depression in children and adolescents (Rice, Harold, & Thapar, 2002; Zalsman, Brent, & Weersing, 2006). Support for the role of genetics in depression derives from a number of findings. For example, the data based on twin, family, and adoption studies in adults suggest a heritability component (Kendler et al., 1992a; Weissman, Kidd, & Prusoff, 1982; Wender et al., 1986). In addition, first-degree adult relatives of depressed children and adolescents have greater than expected rates of depressive disorders (Birmaher et al., 1996; Kovacs et al., 1997). Findings from twin and family designs with child and adolescent samples also suggest a genetic component for depressive symptomatology (Glowinski et al., 2003; Weissman et al., 2005). The genetic contribution may be greater for adolescent depression than for depression in prepubertal children (Scourfeld et al., 2003).

Even research that suggests heritability in depression also indicates the importance of environmental influences. For example, Eaves, Silberg & Erkanli (2003) suggest that the same genes that affect early anxiety later increase exposure to environmental influences that contribute to depression. Also Glowinski and colleagues (2003), in their study of a large sample of female adolescent twins, found evidence for genetic influences and also evidence for a large contribution of nonshared environment.

There is also the issue of what is inherited. In a family genetic study by Rende and colleagues (1993), significant genetic influence was found when the depressive symptomatology of the full sample was examined. However, surprisingly, a significant genetic influence on depression was not found if only youngsters with high levels of depression were considered. The authors suggest that one possible explanation is that genetic influence operates on personality and temperamental factors, such as emotionality and sociability, which affect the full range of depressive symptomatology. And, indeed, there is evidence that temperamental characteristics contribute to the development of depressive symptoms in children and adolescents (Compas, Connor-Smith, & Jaser, 2004). It might be reasoned that extreme depressive symptomatology may result, against this background of moderate genetic influence, from stressful life experiences.

Brain functioning and neurochemistry. It is often presumed that nervous system functioning and biochemistry play an etiological role in depression and, indeed, this may be the case. However, the study of these processes in depression is complex and difficult. Research on several fronts with adults, children, and adolescents is ongoing (Zalsman et al., 2006).

The role of neurotransmitters, such as norepinephrine, serotonin, and acetylcholine, has been a central aspect of the study of the biochemistry of depression. The impetus to study these neurotransmitters came largely from findings that the effectiveness of certain antidepressant medications with adults was related to the individuals' levels of these neurotransmitters or receptivity to them. For example, an early suggestion, the "monoamine hypothesis," proposed that low neurotransmitter levels were caused when too much neurotransmitter was reabsorbed by the neuron, or when enzymes broke down the neurotransmitter too efficiently. This process was thought to result in too low a level of neurotransmitter at the synapse to fire the next neuron. Research continues to explore the role of neurotransmitters; however, the mechanisms of action are likely to be quite complicated, rather than simply the amount of neurotransmitters available. Also, possible developmental differences in these neurotransmitter mechanisms require further exploration (Hirschfeld, 2000; Kaufman, Blumberg, & Young, 2004; Zalsman et al., 2006).

Studies of the neuroendocrine systems (connections between the brain, hormones, and various organs) add to this etiological picture. Dysregulation of the neuroendocrine systems involving the hypothalamus, pituitary gland, and the adrenal and thyroid glands is thought of as a hallmark of adult depression. These systems are also regulated by neurotransmitters. Thus the picture regarding depression is likely to be a complex one. The rapid biological changes during childhood and adolescence (e.g., hormonal activity during puberty) offer a particular challenge (Sokolov & Kutcher, 2001).

Our understanding of the neurobiology of child and adolescent depression is quite limited. Research, however, suggests that during the earlier developmental periods of childhood and adolescence, the neuroregulatory system is not equivalent to that in adulthood (Kaufman et al., 2004; Zalsman et al., 2006). Later in development (for example, in older adolescents who are more severely depressed), biological indicators may be more similar to those for depressed adults. Thus although many researchers still find evidence for a biological dysfunction in childhood depression, a simple translation of the adult findings is not sufficient.

For example, disturbances of sleep are associated with clinical levels of depression (Emslie et al., 2001). Research has indicated that EEG patterns during sleep are strong biological markers of major depressive disorders in adults (Kupfer & Reynolds, 1992; Thase, Jindal, & Howland, 2002). Many of the sleep findings reported in adults are not characteristic of children diagnosed with major depressive disorders, but some of these patterns are reported in older adolescents (Brooks-Gunn et al., 2001; Zalsman et al., 2006). For example, depressed adults have more of and different characteristics of the rapid eye movement (REM) stage of sleep. These sleep differences are not characteristic of depressed children, but some abnormalities related to REM sleep may be present in depressed adolescents.

A second example is the role of cortisol, a stress hormone produced in the adrenal glands. Adults with major depression produce excessive levels of cortisol. Similar patterns have not been observed consistently in investigations of cortisol functioning in young people (Brooks-Gunn et al., 2001; Zalsman et al., 2006). Indeed, occasionally underproduction of cortisol has been found in depressed youths (Goenjian et al., 1996). However, increased cortisol levels similar to those for depressed adults may occur among older and more severely depressed adolescents (Goodyer, Park, & Herbert, 2001; Rao et al., 1996). Also, the ratio of cortisol to dehydroepiandrosterone (DHEA), another hormone, rather than the level of cortisol levels alone, may be related to depression in children and adolescents

(Brooks-Gunn et al., 2001). Thus, again, sensitivity to developmental differences is clearly important.

Neuroimaging studies, employing brain MRI and CT scans and functional MRI, have found evidence of abnormalities in the prefrontal cortex and other areas of the brain in depressed adults. Few studies have been conducted with children and adolescents, but there is some evidence of structural abnormalities of the prefrontal cortex of depressed adolescents (Zalsman et al., 2006).

How can we understand these various findings? In general, differences in biological markers of depression might suggest that the child, adolescent, and adult disorders are different. Alternatively, such differences in biological markers may represent age-related differences in the same disorder.

SOCIAL-PSYCHOLOGICAL INFLUENCES

Despite increased interest in recent years, much of the thinking regarding influences on child and adolescent depression is still based on theories derived from work with depressed adults. We will examine several of the social-psychological influences and provide illustrations of work based on youth.

Separation and loss. A common psychological explanation of depression is that it results from separation or loss. Psychoanalytic explanations of depression, following from Freud, emphasize the notion of object loss. The loss may be real (parental death, divorce) or symbolic. Identification with and ambivalent feelings toward the lost love object are thought to result in the person's directing hostile feelings concerning the love object toward the self. Some psychodynamic writers emphasize loss of self-esteem and feelings of helplessness that result from object loss, and they minimize the importance of aggression turned inward toward the self (Kessler, 1988).

Some behaviorally oriented explanations also involve separation and loss. Both Ferster (1974) and Lewinsohn (1974) emphasized the role of inadequate positive reinforcement in the development of depression. Loss of or separation from a loved one is likely to result in a decrease in the child's sources of positive reinforcement. However, inadequate reinforcement may also result from factors such as not having adequate skills to obtain desired rewards.

Support for the theory that separation plays a role in the genesis of depression came from several different sources. For example, a fairly typical sequence of reactions of young children to prolonged separation from their parents was described by investigators (e.g., Bowlby, 1960; Spitz, 1946). In this so-called anaclitic depression, the child initially goes through a period of "protest" characterized by crying, asking for the parents, and restlessness. This is followed shortly by a period of depression and withdrawal. Most children begin to recover after several weeks.

The theme of separation-loss is a central concept in many theories of depression. The loss may be real or imagined.

(Courtesy of A. C. Israel)

The connection between loss and depression also has been examined in adult depression. For a long time, the widely held view was that early loss puts one at high risk for later depression—especially women. More recent examinations of this issue question this view, in part because most studies were plagued with methodological problems (Finkelstein, 1988; Tennant, 1988). The current view is that early loss is not in and of itself pathogenic. The link between such loss and later depression is not direct. Rather, it is hypothesized that loss, as well as other circumstances, can set in motion a chain of adverse circumstances such as lack of care, changes in family structure, and socioeconomic difficulties that put the individual at risk for later disorder (Bifulco, Harris, & Brown, 1992; Saler & Skolnick, 1992).

Much of the research on the association between loss and depression has relied on the retrospective reports of adults. However, investigation of the impact of loss on children has received some attention (Dowdney, 2000; Tremblay & Israel, 1998). For example, Sandler and his colleagues found support for a model consistent with the indirect effects of loss (West et al., 1991). In a sample of 92 families who had lost a parent within the previous 2 years, depression in children (ages 8 to 15) was not directly linked to the loss. Rather, the level of parental demoralization, family warmth, and stable positive events following the loss mediated the effects of parental death on depression in these young people. Thus, children who experience the positive aspects of these family variables are likely to be resilient following the loss of a parent (Lin et al., 2004).

Cognitive-behavioral/interpersonal perspectives.

Behavioral, cognitive, and cognitive-behavioral perspectives encompass many related and overlapping concepts (Hammen, 1992; Kaslow, Adamson, & Collins, 2000). Influences such as interpersonal skills, cognitive distortions, views of self, control beliefs, self-regulation, and stress are the focus of these perspectives. The ways in which depressed individuals relate to others and are viewed by others, and the ways that these individuals view themselves and think, are believed to contribute to how depression develops and is maintained.

Writers such as Ferster (1974) and Lewinsohn (1974) suggested that a combination of lowered activity level and inadequate interpersonal skills plays a role in the development and maintenance of depression. Interpersonal theories of depression emphasize a transactional relationship. Depressed youths both contribute and react to problematic relationships. It is suggested that depressed individuals do not elicit positive interpersonal responses from others. Indeed, there is evidence that depressed youths display deficits in social functioning, have negative interpersonal expectations and perceptions, and are viewed as less likable by others (Hammen & Rudolph, 2003; Kaslow, Brown, & Mee, 1994; Schwartz, Gladstone, & Kaslow, 1998).

A variety of cognitions may be related to depression. A learned helplessness explanation of depression (Seligman & Peterson, 1986) suggests that some individuals, as a result of their learning histories, come to perceive themselves as having little control of their environment. This learned helplessness is in turn associated with the mood and behaviors characteristic of depression. Separation may be a special case of learned helplessness: The child's fruitless attempts to bring the parent back may result in the child's thinking that personal action and positive outcome are independent of each other.

Helplessness conceptualizations emphasize how the person thinks about activity and outcome—a person's attributional or explanatory style. Depressed individuals may have an explanatory style in which they blame themselves (internal) for negative events and view the causes of events as being stable over time (stable) and applicable across situations (global). The opposite style, external-unstable-specific attributions for positive events, may also be part of this depressed style. In revisions of this perspective, the interaction of stressful life events with cognitive style is given greater emphasis (Abramson, Metalsky, & Alloy, 1989). This revision is referred to as the hopelessness theory of depression. Attributional style (a vulnerability or diathesis) acts as a moderator between negative life events that the person sees as important (a stress) and hopelessness. Hopelessness, in turn, leads to depression. Figure 7–3 illustrates how the hopelessness theory of depression views the development of depression. The theory predicts that a young person with a diathesis of a negative attributional style who is also exposed to the stress of high levels of negative life events is more likely to develop depression. A number of studies have reported maladaptive attributional styles and hopelessness in depressed youths (Kaslow et al., 2000; Schwartz et al., 2000), and the vulnerability-stress notions of hopelessness theory have received some support (Conley et al., 2001; Joiner, 2000). However, additional attention needs to be given to inconsistencies in findings, investigation of developmental patterns, exploration of potential gender differences, and a clearer articulation of the relationship of attributional style and life events (Abela, 2001; Kaslow et al., 2000).

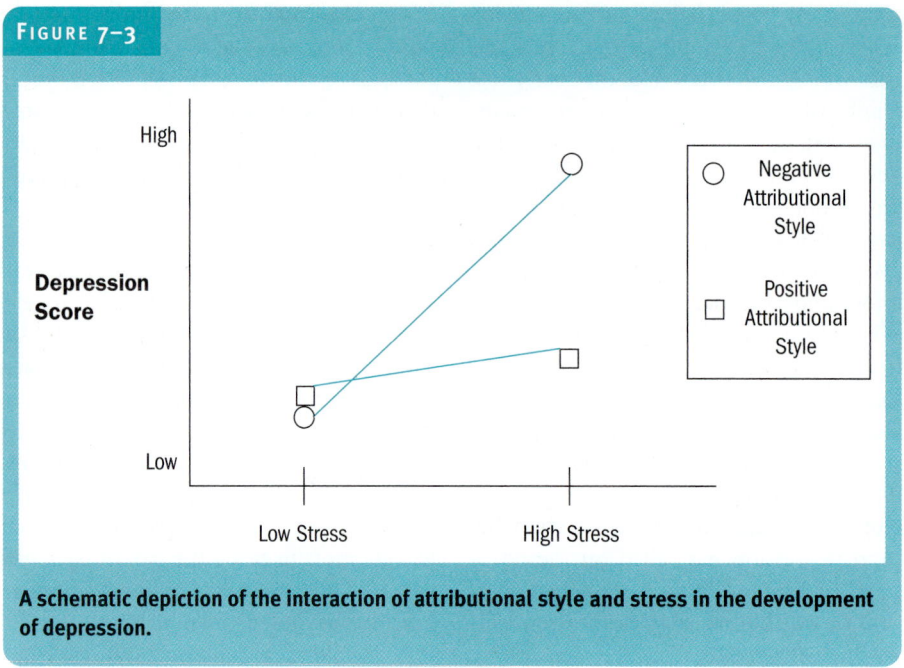

FIGURE 7-3

A schematic depiction of the interaction of attributional style and stress in the development of depression.

The role of cognitive factors in depression is also the major emphasis of other theorists. Beck (1967; 1976), for example, assumes that depression results from negative views of the self, others, and the future. Depressed individuals, Beck hypothesizes, have developed certain errors in thinking that result in their distorting even mildly annoying events into opportunities for self-blame and failure. Although findings are mixed, some research studies have found evidence in depressed youths of cognitive distortions such as those suggested by Beck's theory (Gençöz et al., 2001; Stark, Schmidt, & Joiner, 1996). Depressed youths exhibit a tendency to catastrophize, overgeneralize, personalize, and selectively attend to negative events.

The nature of the link between cognitive influences such as attributional style, hopelessness, or cognitive distortion and depression requires further clarification (Hammen & Rudolph, 2003; Kaslow et al., 2000; Rudolph et al., 2006). It is unclear whether these cognitions play a causal role in depression as an underlying vulnerability or are associated with depression in some other way—perhaps co-occurring with depression, being a consequence of depression, or being part of an ongoing reciprocal interplay with depression. Research, including cross-cultural comparisons, supports a reciprocal view of the relationship between cognitions and depression (Stewart et al., 2004).

The dimension of control, part of the helplessness perspective discussed before, has also been the focus of additional consideration. Weisz and col-leagues, for example, have found that low levels of perceived competence (the ability to perform relevant behavior) and perceived noncontingency (outcomes are not contingent on behavior) are both related to depression in children (Weisz et al., 1993b). Similarly, researchers have examined style of coping with stress as a component of the development of depression. For example, lower levels of active coping (e.g., problem solving) and greater levels of disengagement coping (e.g., avoidance) have been associated with young people's depression. Evolving models of stress and coping are likely to contribute to a greater understanding of the development of depression (Compas et al., 2004). Given the suggestion of these difficulties in depressed youths, it may be worthwhile to examine the type of coping and self-regulatory (competence) behavior evoked or encouraged by parents of depressed youths (Kaslow et al., 2000). With this observation in mind, we turn to the influences of parental depression on children and adolescents.

IMPACT OF PARENTAL DEPRESSION

A major area of research on childhood depression has been an examination of children of depressed parents. There are several reasons for the proliferation of such research. Because family aggregation of mood disorders in adults was known to exist, it was presumed that examining children of parents with mood disorders would reveal a population likely to experience childhood depression. Such a high-risk research strategy could be a more efficient means of investigating the problem than a random sampling of the population would be. In addition, such research might provide information on the continuity among child, adolescent, and adult mood disorders.

Numerous studies have found that children and adolescents from homes with a depressed parent are at increased risk for developing a psychological disorder (Beardslee, Versage, & Gladstone, 1998). A number of longitudinal studies have been particularly informative. Hammen and her colleagues (1990) compared the long-term effects of maternal depression and maternal chronic medical illness. Over the course of a 3-year period, with evaluations at 6-month intervals, children of both depressed mothers and medically ill mothers exhibited elevated rates of psychological disorder as compared with children of healthy mothers. Rates of disorder were higher for children of depressed mothers than for those with medically ill mothers.

Weissman and her colleagues (1997) followed the children of two groups of parents over a 10-year period. At the time of the follow-up, the offspring were in late adolescence or were adults. Parents and youths were assessed with a structured diagnostic interview. Youths for whom neither parent had a psychological disorder (low risk) were compared with those for whom one or both parents had a diagnosis of major depressive disorder (high risk). The youths with depressed parents had increased rates of MDD, particularly before puberty. The high-risk group also had increased rates of other disorders, including phobias and alcohol dependence. In addition, children of depressed parents experienced more serious depression than children of nondepressed parents. However, the depressed offspring of depressed parents were less likely to receive treatment than those of nondepressed parents; in fact, more than 30% never received any treatment.

Beardslee and his colleagues examined the impact of parental depression in a nonclinically referred population (Beardslee et al., 1996; 1998). Families were recruited from a large health maintenance organization. Assessments, including a structured diagnostic interview, were conducted initially and 4 years later. Families were divided into three categories: parents with no diagnosis, parents with a nonaffective disorder, and one or both parents with an affective disorder. Parental nonaffective disorder, parental MDD, and the number of diagnosed disorders that the child experienced prior to the first as-

sessment predicted whether the youngster experienced a serious affective disorder during the time between assessments.

The findings presented here suggest that the risk associated with parental depressions may not be specific. Children with a depressed parent appear to be at risk for a variety of problems, not just depression. And children of parents with other diagnoses or with chronic medical conditions may also be at risk for depression. Perhaps various disorders that youngsters experience share common risk factors, whereas some risk factors are specific to depression. It is also possible that some disruptions to effective parenting are common to parents with various disorders, whereas other disruptions are more likely to occur among parents with a particular disorder.

There may be a variety of mechanisms whereby depressive mood states in parents are associated with dysfunction in their children (Cummings, Davies, & Campbell, 2000). Shared heredity may play a role in the link between parental and child depression. Parental depression may also have an impact through a variety of nonbiological pathways. For example, parents can influence their child through parent–child interactions, through coaching and teaching practices, and by arranging their child's social environment. Before we turn to a discussion of these mechanisms, it is important to remember that influences between parent and child are likely to be bidirectional (Elgar et al., 2004). A depressed youth may, for example, generate additional stress that lessens the adult's ability to parent effectively.

Mechanisms of parental influence. As we indicated before, both depression in adults and depression in young people are associated with certain characteristic ways of thinking and cognitive styles. Depressed parents may transmit these styles to their children. Garber and Flynn (2001), for example, assessed mothers and their youngsters annually over 3 years, starting when the children were in sixth grade. A maternal history of depression was associated with lower perceived self-worth, a negative attributional style, and hopelessness among the children. Maladaptive ways of thinking may be modeled by parents and may also affect the general manner in which depressed adults parent their offspring (Nolen-Hoeksema et al., 1995).

Parental depression may result in disruption of effective parenting (Lovejoy et al., 2000). For example, the behavior of depressed parents may be accompanied by negative affect such as anger or hostility. Also, the depressed parents' absorption in their own difficulties may lead them to be withdrawn or make them inattentive to their children and unaware of their children's behavior. Monitoring of a child's behavior is a key element in effective parenting. Depressed parents may also perceive behaviors to be problematic that other parents do not. This difference in perception is important, because being able to ignore or tolerate low levels of problematic behavior is likely to lead to less family disruption. In addition, studies involving direct observation of families with a depressed parent or child indicate that interactional patterns in these families may serve to maintain the depression in the parent or child (Dadds et al., 1992; Ge et al., 1995; Hops et al., 1987). Depressed behavior by one family member may be maintained because it serves to avoid or reduce the high levels of aggression and discord that may be present in such families.

Mary | **Family Interactions and Depression**

Mary is an adolescent with considerable problems with anxiety and depression. Mary's mother was diagnosed with major depression. Her parents fought often and frequently the topic was money or problems and stresses related to her father's job. Mary's mother dealt with these difficulties by self-medicating with alcohol and developed a serious drinking problem. The conflicts, alcohol abuse, and other stresses seemed to have contributed to the development of symptoms of depression in Mary's mother. For the good of all the family members and because of her concern for her mother, Mary felt that she had to serve as a mediator for her parents' disputes and that she was responsible for alleviating her mother's sadness. Over time these family conflicts and problems contributed to Mary developing psychological difficulties of her own.

Adapted from Cummings, Davies, & Campbell, 2000, pp. 305–306.

In addition to marital discord, families with a depressed parent may exist in adverse contexts (e.g., social disadvantage/low standard of living) and may experience high levels of stressful life events (e.g., health and financial difficulties). These circumstances in turn are likely to exacerbate a parent's depressive episodes and contribute to disruptions in parenting. For example, high levels of parental stress may restrict the parent's ability to involve the child in activities outside the home and may limit the family's social networks. Thus the child may have limited opportunity to interact with other adults outside the family or to have access to other sources of social support. This deficiency may be particularly problematic in that one of the mechanisms by which depressed parents may affect the functioning of their offspring is the parents' own problems in interpersonal functioning and their perceptions of others (Hammen & Brennan, 2001).

Finally, the link between parent and child depression has been viewed in the context of attachment (Cicchetti & Toth, 1998; Elgar et al., 2004). The emotional unavailability and insensitivity that may be associated with parental depression have been shown to be strong and reliable predictors of insecure parent–child attachments. Attachment theory holds that children's internal working models or representations of the self and the social world are strongly influenced by early attachments. It is through these early relationships that the child first experiences and learns to regulate intense emotions and arousal, experiences the social world, and develops a concept of the self. In other words, working models that guide future experiences are thought to be first developed in these early attachment relationships. In children with insecure parent–child attachments, the cognitive and emotional contents of these working models have been described as remarkably similar to the cognitive and emotional patterns characteristic of depression (Cummings et al., 2000). Insecure attachments may interfere with the child's developing capacity to regulate affect and arousal and may be associated with poorer self-concept and less trust in the availability and responsiveness of the social world.

The effects of parental depression on offspring probably vary with the age and gender of the child (Hops, 1995; Lovejoy et al., 2000). Furthermore, although children of depressed parents are at increased risk for a number of difficulties, not all these children experience adverse outcomes (see the descriptions of Joe and Frank). Many form secure attachments, experience good parenting, and do not develop disorders (Beardslee et al., 1998; Brennan, Le Brocque, & Hammen, 2003).

Indeed, there may be multiple ways in which family influences serve as protective factors against the potential adverse impact of parental depression. For example, Ivanova and Israel (2006) examined the influence of family stability (defined as the predictability and consistency of family activities and routines) on adjustment in a clinical sample of children. Children's reports of family stability as measured by the Stability of Activities in the Family Environment (SAFE; Israel, Roderick, & Ivanova, 2002) significantly attenuated the impact of parental depression on child internalizing, externalizing, and total problems. That is, parental depression was associated with problems in child adjustment when family stability was low, but not when family stability was high. Figure 7–4 illustrates this protective effect of family stability on parent-reported ineternalizing problems.

Joe and Frank | Different Outcomes

Joe's father was diagnosed with major depression and his paternal grandfather also experienced episodes of depression . . . but both his parents were attentive and responsive to him. Even when Joe's father's depressive symptoms were severe, he remained attentive and emotionally warm. Joe's mother was very supportive of his father and they had a secure marriage. . . . Joe also had a close and supportive relationship with his two sisters. Joe did well in school and was popular, although he tended to be shy in large groups. He attended an excellent university, studied medicine, and became a pediatrician. Joe married, and he and his wife were happy and were attentive and responsive parents. Joe experienced periods of anxiety and occasional mild to moderate symptoms of depression. The symptoms were rarely more than subclinical and Joe never felt the need to seek therapy.

Frank's mother was diagnosed with major depressive disorder and her mother has also been depressed. His mother and father were divorced when Frank was 10. This followed many years of intense marital conflict. . . . Both parents had also been generally emotionally unresponsive toward the children, . . . and they involved Frank and his sister in their marital conflicts. . . . Frank and his sister fought with each other and were never close to each other. In preschool Frank was highly aggressive and difficult. . . . By adolescence, Frank was habitually delinquent, and he dropped out of high school. As an adult, Frank was diagnosed with a depressive disorder and his interpersonal relationships were tumultuous and typically short-lived.

Adapted from Cummings, Davies, & Campbell, 2000, pp. 299–300.

PEER RELATIONS AND DEPRESSION

Although problems with peers are common in the general population, these problems do distinguish youngsters referred to psychological services from nonreferred youths (Achenbach & Rescorla, 2001). Consistent with views that emphasize interpersonal aspects of depression, peer relation difficulties appear to contribute to the development and maintenance of depression (Goodyer, 2001; McCauley, Pavlidis, &

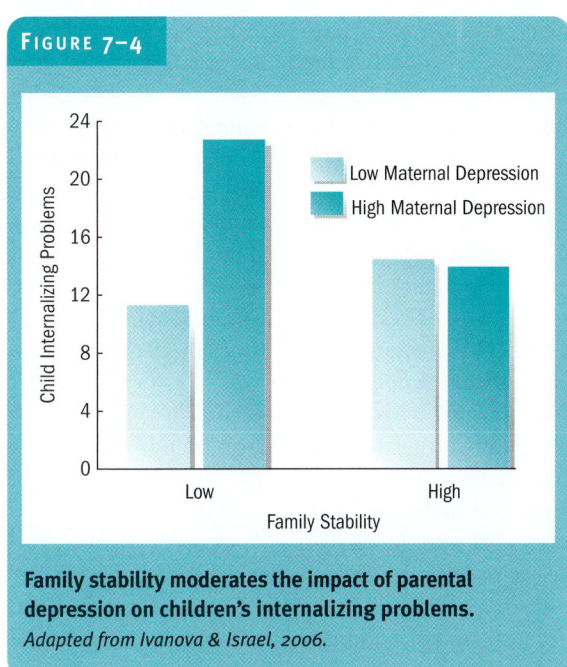

FIGURE 7–4

Child Internalizing Problems (y-axis: 0, 4, 8, 12, 16, 20, 24)

Low Maternal Depression
High Maternal Depression

Family Stability (x-axis: Low, High)

Family stability moderates the impact of parental depression on children's internalizing problems.
Adapted from Ivanova & Israel, 2006.

A withdrawn or socially isolated child may need assistance in developing appropriate social skills and in increasing peer interactions.
(Ellen B. Senisi/The Image Works)

Kendall, 2001). Peer status, for example, has been found to be associated with adjustment difficulties, including depression.

A study by Kupersmidt and Patterson (1991) illustrates the relationship between peer status and adjustment. The sociometric status of a sample of second, third, and fourth graders was assessed by asking the children to nominate their most liked and least liked peers. A peer status grouping was determined for each child. Two years later when the children were in the fourth through the sixth grade, several assessment instruments were completed, including a modified version of the Achenbach Youth Self-Report (YSR). As an index of a negative outcome, the authors examined whether a child had scores in the clinical range in one or more specific problem areas (the narrowband syndromes of the YSR). Rejected boys and girls exhibited higher than expected rates of clinical-range difficulties. Girls with neglected peer status had even higher levels of clinical-range difficulties.

The authors also examined the relationship between peer status and each of the more specific problem areas defined by the various narrowband behavior problem scores. There was no relationship between peer status and any specific behavior problem for boys. However, a finding of particular interest emerged for girls. Rejected girls were more than twice as likely to report high levels of depression than average, popular, and controversial girls. Furthermore, neglected girls were more than twice as likely as rejected girls and more than five times as likely

as the other groups of girls to report depression problems.

Peer relation difficulties may both contribute to the development and be a consequence of depression. For example, Pederson and colleagues' (2007) findings support a mediational model in which early disruptive behavior leads to subsequent peer relational difficulties during middle childhood, which, in turn, is associated with early adolescent depressive symptoms. Depression may also contribute to peer relational difficulties. Indeed, depression in young people has been found to be associated with a number of interpersonal characteristics important to peer relations and friendships. For example, depressed youngsters may perceive themselves as less interpersonally competent, have negative views of peers, have problematic social problem-solving styles, and exhibit distortions in processing of social information (Rudolph & Asher, 2000). Many of the problems in social relationships that accompany depression in young people may arise, in part, from the depressed youth's perceptions, including that others are rejecting and critical. This perception may then lead to behaviors by the depressed youngster that annoy peers, limit friendships, and result in isolation.

Assessment of Depression

The assessment of depression is likely to involve a number of strategies and to sample a broad spectrum of attributes (Stark et al., 2000; Youngstrom et al., 2004). Structured interviews may be employed to yield a DSM diagnosis, although they are more likely to be employed in research than in typical clinical settings. As we have seen, depression may manifest itself in a number of ways throughout development, and children and adolescents who experience depression are likely to exhibit other difficulties. A general clinical interview and the use of a broad assessment instrument like the Child Behavior Checklist are common. Because a variety of influences may contribute to the development of depression, it is helpful to assess the parents, family, and social environments as well as the child or adolescent.

A variety of measures that focus on depression and related constructs have been developed (Compas, 1997; Hodges, 1994; Reynolds, 1994). Of these, self-report instruments are among the most commonly employed. They are particularly important, given that many of the key problems that characterize depression, such as sadness and feelings of worthlessness, are subjective. The Children's Depression 1 (CDI) (Kovacs, 1992; 2003) is probably the most frequently used measure of this type. It is an offshoot of the Beck Depression Inventory that is commonly used for adults. The CDI asks youths to choose which of three alternatives best characterizes them during the past 2 weeks. Twenty-seven items sample affective, behavioral, and cognitive aspects of depression. Research on gender and age differences, reliability, validity, and clinically meaningful cutoff scores has been conducted for the CDI (Reynolds, 1994). The Reynolds Child Depression Scale (Reynolds, 1989) and Reynolds Adolescent Depression Scale (Reynolds, 1987; 2002) also have been reported to have good psychometric properties (Reynolds, 1994). Despite the widespread use of self-report measures, some research suggests caution in assuming equivalent measurement of depression across various racial–ethnic groups (Crockett et al., 2005).

Many self-report measures are also rephrased so that they can be completed by significant others such as the child's parents (Clarizio, 1994). Measures completed by both the child and the parent often show only low levels of correlation, and agreement may vary with the age of the youngster (Kazdin, 1994; Renouf & Kovacs, 1994). These results suggest that information provided by different sources may tap different aspects of the child's difficulties. Assessment measures can also be completed by teachers, clinicians, or other adults (Clarizio, 1994). Ratings by peers can likewise provide a unique perspective.

Measures of constructs related to depression have also been developed. For example, attributes such as self-esteem (e.g., Harter, 1985) and perceived control over events (e.g., Connell, 1985) are likely candidates for evaluation. In addition, assessing various cognitive processes such as hopelessness (Kazdin, Rodgers, & Colbus, 1986), attributional style (Seligman & Peterson, 1986), and cognitive distortions (e.g., Leitenberg, Yost, & Carroll-Wilson, 1986) have been and are likely to be helpful for both clinical and research purposes.

A number of observational measures can aid the assessment of depression in children and adolescents (Garber & Kaminski, 2000). Systematic observations of depressed youngsters interacting with others in controlled laboratory settings can potentially provide an opportunity to observe the social behavior of these youngsters with significant others. Table 7–4 lists some of the categories of behaviors that can be observed using existing systems for coding social interactions relevant to depression. Observational measures may not be used as frequently as other assessment measures because they require considerable training and coding itself is very labor intensive. There is also concern regarding the ecological validity of these observations, that is, the extent to which a brief laboratory interaction reflects real-world social interactions.

TABLE 7–4	CATEGORIES AND EXAMPLES OF DEPRESSION-RELATED BEHAVIORS THAT CAN BE OBSERVED IN SOCIAL INTERACTION TASKS

Emotions: smiling, frowning, crying, happiness, sadness, anger, fear
Affect Regulation: control or expression of affect
Problem Solving: identifying problems, proposing solutions
Nonverbal Behaviors: eye contact, posture
Conflict: noncompliance, ignoring, demanding, negotiating
Cognitive Content: criticism, praise, self-derogation
Speech: rate, volume, tone of voice, initiation
Engaged or Disengaged: enthusiasm, involvement, persistence
On or Off Task Behavior
Physical Contact: threatening, striking, affection
Symptoms: depression, irritability, psychomotor agitation or retardation, fatigue, concentration

Adapted from Garber & Kaminski, 2000.

Treatment of Depression

The treatment of depression in young people, particularly adolescents, has received increasing attention (Asarnow, Jaycox, & Tompson, 2001; Wolraich, 2003). However, less is known about the treatment of youth compared with that for adults, and treatments often are adaptations of those that seem to be successful for adults. Our discussion of treatment emphasizes pharmacological and cognitive-behavioral treatments, because these interventions, alone and in combination, have received the most research attention (Treatment for Adolescents with Depression Study [TADS], 2005).

PHARMACOLOGICAL TREATMENTS

The practice of prescribing antidepressant medication for children and adolescents is widespread (Vitiello, Zuvekas, & Norquist, 2006). However, such treatment is controversial, because the effectiveness and safety of pharmacotherapy with depressed youngsters remains unclear (APA, 2006; Moreno, Roche, & Greenhill, 2006). Tricyclic antidepressants (TCAs) such as imipramine, amitriptyline, nortriptyline, and desipramine were once widely used to treat depression in young people. But TCAs have not been demonstrated to be effective in treating depressed youth and they have many side effects. Selective serotonin reuptake inhibitors (SSRIs) such as fluoxetine and paroxetine and other second-generation antidepressants such as bupropion and venlafaxine also have been employed with depressed children and adolescents. SSRIs have fewer side effects than TCAs and are more likely to be recommended when medication is prescribed.

However, the use of such medications is, for the most part, based on limited research that does not clearly support the superiority of these antidepressant medications in either prepubertal children or adolescents (Gleason et al., 2007; Hammad, Laughren, & Racoosin, 2006; Jureidini et al., 2004). Little is known regarding long-term effectiveness. At present it is difficult to know whether or why these medications, many of which are reported effective in treating adult depression, are ineffective for youth. Differences in response to these medications may lead us to question the assumption that depression is the same across age groups. There may be neurodevelopmental, biological, psychological, and interpersonal differences in depression in children, adolescents, and adults.

Medications may ultimately prove to be effective, alone or in combination with other treatments for certain youths. However, because antidepressant medications are developed and marketed principally for adults, there are fewer well-established guidelines for their administration and less systematic data on their safety. Issues of safety and side effects are of concern because little is known regarding the long-term impact of these medications on development, particularly in young children (APA, 2006; Emslie et al., 2006; Moreno et al., 2006). Particular concern has been expressed about the possible association between SSRIs and increases in suicidal behavior (Hammad et al., 2006; Vitiello & Swedo, 2004). As mentioned in our discussion of SSRIs in the treatment of anxiety disorders, such concerns led the FDA to issue a warning about their use with children and adolescents.

Since depression is itself associated with suicide, the issue of risk and benefit from the use of SSRIs is an important one. Families and clinicians may ask: Is the risk of not employing SSRIs to treat depression in certain youth who may be at risk for suicide greater than the suicide risk associated with the use of these medications? If antidepressants are employed in treatment, the FDA recommends that the youths return to the clinician's office for more frequent visits, particularly in the early stages of treatment or dosage changes, and recommends that caregivers and clinicians be vigilant about unusual changes in behavior (U.S. Food and Drug Administration, 2007).

Combined treatments. The Treatment of Adolescent Depressions Study (TADS Team, 2004) examined the combined use of fluoxetine (an SSRI) and a form of cognitive-behavior therapy (CBT). Adolescents (ages 12 to 17) with moderate to severe major depression were randomly assigned to treatment with fluoxetine alone, CBT alone, CBT combined with fluoxetine, or placebo (pill). The TADS Team has reported that at the end of the 12-week treatment, the combined treatment produced the greatest improvement in symptoms of MDD and was superior to either treatment alone (March et al., 2006; TADS Team, 2004). While the results of this study are important, aspects of the methodology and interpretation of results have been questioned. Also, rates of remission (no longer meeting diagnostic criteria or cutoff scores) were low and many youths continued to have significant symptoms (Brent, 2006; Kennard et al., 2006).

An additional potential benefit of the combined treatment is germane to concerns about SSRIs and suicide risk. During the treatment period, suicide-related events were greatest among youths treated with fluoxetine alone (9.2%)—nearly twice as many as in the other conditions (Emslie et al., 2006). This suggests that, for youths treated with SSRIs, the combination of fluoxetine with CBT may offer some protection against suicidal events during the initial treatment period. Longer-term follow-ups are needed with regard to the effectiveness and safety of SSRIs alone or in combination. This is particularly true given that youths with the most risk for suicide were excluded from the TADS study.

PSYCHOSOCIAL TREATMENTS

Much of the literature on psychosocial interventions for depressed children and adolescents has suggested treatments based on downward extensions of interventions employed with adults. Although this is a reasonable way to begin to explore effective treatment, there are limitations to such an approach (Hammen et al., 1999; Stark, Rouse, & Kurowski, 1994). For example, the lives of depressed youths differ from those of adults. Children and adolescents have ongoing daily contact with parents that may contribute to the problem of depression. Also, youths are exposed on a daily basis to the potential negative consequences of social skill difficulties and the impact of peer relation difficulties. Adults, on the other hand, may arrange their lives to avoid familial and social contacts. The development of treatments that differ from those employed with adults and that address relevant developmental experiences of depressed children and adolescents are likely to be the most effective.

Most psychological interventions for depression in children and adolescents derive from a cognitive-behavioral perspective. Cognitive-behavioral treatments confront and modify the young person's maladaptive cognitions (e.g., problematic attributions, excessively high standards, negative self-monitoring), focus on goals such as increasing pleasurable experiences; increasing social skills; and improving communication, conflict resolution, social problem-solving, and coping skills. Several studies are described here to illustrate interventions derived from a cognitive-behavioral perspective.

Weisz and his colleagues (2003) have developed a manualized cognitive-behavioral intervention, PASCET (Primary and Secondary Control Enhanced Training), that is based on the relationship between perceived control and depression. In an initial test of this program, children in grades 3 to 6 who exhibited mild to moderate depressive symptoms were treated in small groups during school hours. The eight-session program emphasized control skills that helped identify and develop activities that the child found mood enhancing and that the child valued; that identified and modified maladaptive thoughts; that fostered cognitive techniques for mood enhancement; and that aided relaxation and positive imagery. At the end of treatment and at a 9-month follow-up, the treatment group showed significantly greater decrease in depressive symptoms than did the no-treatment control group. These results are illustrated in Figure 7–5. Weisz and colleagues have adapted this program to a primary care setting with a more

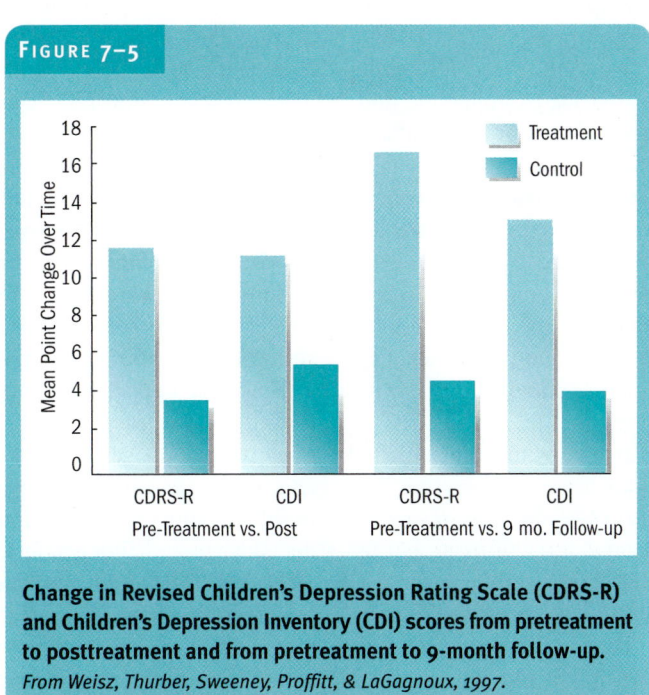

FIGURE 7–5

Change in Revised Children's Depression Rating Scale (CDRS-R) and Children's Depression Inventory (CDI) scores from pretreatment to posttreatment and from pretreatment to 9-month follow-up.
From Weisz, Thurber, Sweeney, Proffitt, & LaGagnoux, 1997.

distressed and disturbed sample of clinic-referred youth. Evaluation of this program is underway.

A cognitive-behavioral intervention known as the Adolescent Coping with Depression program, a skills-training, multicomponent intervention, has been developed by Lewinsohn, Clarke, and colleagues (Rohde et al., 2005). In an initial study (Lewinsohn et al., 1990) adolescents aged 14 to 18 who met diagnostic criteria for depression were randomly assigned to one of three conditions: adolescent-only, adolescent-and-parent, and wait-list control. Adolescents attended sixteen 2-hour sessions, twice a week, in a group or classlike setting, that focused on teaching methods of relaxation, increasing pleasant events, controlling irrational and negative thoughts, increasing social skills, and teaching conflict resolution (communication and problem-solving) skills. In the parent-involvement condition, parents met for nine weekly sessions. They were provided with information on the skills being taught to their teenagers and were taught problem-solving and conflict resolution skills.

Relative to the youths in the control group, individuals in the treatment groups improved on depression measures. For example, at the end of treatment, the recovery rate for treated adolescents was 46% whereas only 5% of the control group no longer met diagnostic criteria. The teenagers in the treatment conditions were followed for 2 years after the end of treatment, and their treatment gains were maintained. Control participants were not available for follow-up, because they were offered treatment at the end of the treatment period. A second similar study (Clarke et al., 1999) yielded comparable findings. In both studies there were few or no significant advantages for parent involvement.

Brent and colleagues (1997) compared the relative efficacy of two treatments—cognitive-behavioral therapy (CBT) and behavioral family systems therapy—with a supportive therapy condition included to control for the nonspecific effects of receiving treatment. Study participants were adolescents who met diagnostic criteria for major depressive disorder. Participants received 12 to 16 sessions of therapy over a 3- to 4-month period. Youths treated with CBT exhibited greater improvement than those in the other two conditions. The study also showed that it was necessary to improve short-term efficacy of treatment for at least some youth, as well as long-term efficacy, perhaps by longer treatment or continuing care. For example, more than half of the participants in the study required additional treatment beyond that provided. Severity of depression, the presence of co-occurring disorders, and family problems predicted the need for additional treatment. And, despite the superiority of the CBT treatment, it was not as successful for all participants. Forty percent of adolescents treated with CBT remained symptomatic at posttreatment. In addition, at 2-year follow-up there were no differences in depression between adolescents who received CBT and those in other treatment conditions (Weersing & Brent, 2003).

The effectiveness of interpersonal psychotherapy for adolescents (IPT-A), modified from interpersonal psychotherapy for depressed adults, has also been examined (Mufson et al., 2005). IPT-A is based on the premise that whatever the causes, depression is intertwined with the individual's interpersonal relationships. The therapist, through a variety of active strategies, helps the adolescent understand current interpersonal issues such as separation from parents, role transitions, romantic relationships, interpersonal deficits, peer pressure, grief, and single-parent family status. Mufson and colleagues (1999) found that adolescents diagnosed with major depressive disorder who received IPT-A showed improvement in depressive symptoms, social functioning, and problem-solving skills compared with control youths whose clinical condition was monitored. A second study by Mufson and colleagues also reported a greater reduction in depressive symptoms for IPT-A compared with a treatment control condition (Mufson et al., 2004). Rosselló and Bernal (1999) compared IPT-A with cognitive-behavioral therapy and a wait-list control in a sample of clinically depressed adolescents in Puerto Rico. Both treatment groups showed significant improvements in depressive symptoms (see Figure 7–6) and self-esteem compared with those in the control condition.

It is interesting to note that the studies by Mufson and colleagues included a large proportion of Latino youths and that Rosselló and Bernal made efforts to incorporate interpersonal aspects of Latino culture into their treatment: *personalismo*—the preference for interpersonal contacts, and *familismo*—a strong identification with and attachment to family. This was accomplished through a variety of adaptations to the treatment, such as selection of examples, sayings, and images from the adolescents' culture and context; emphasis on the interpersonal nature of the therapeutic approach; and discussion of family dependence and independence (Rosselló & Bernal, 1999; 2005). Although adolescents in both treatment groups in the Rosselló and Bernal study had comparable improvements in depression, improvement for some other outcome measures was better in the IPT-A group. The authors suggest that this may be

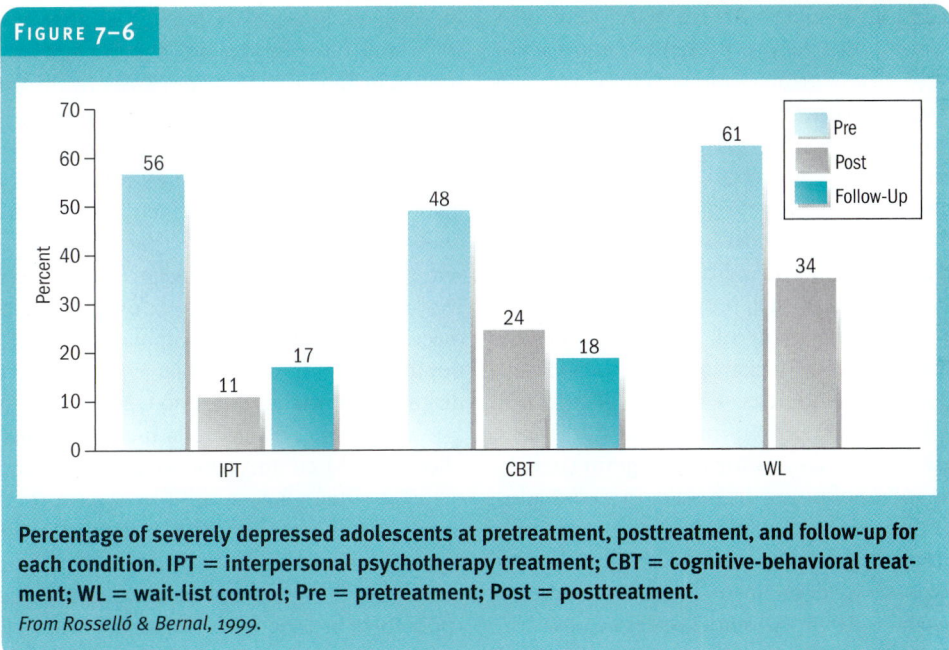

FIGURE 7–6

Percentage of severely depressed adolescents at pretreatment, posttreatment, and follow-up for each condition. IPT = interpersonal psychotherapy treatment; CBT = cognitive-behavioral treatment; WL = wait-list control; Pre = pretreatment; Post = posttreatment.
From Rosselló & Bernal, 1999.

because of the consonance of IPT-A with Puerto Rican cultural values. In a similar vein, McClure and colleagues (2005) have developed a family treatment for depressed African American adolescent girls—the Adolescent Depression Empowerment Psychosocial Treatment (ADEPT)—that includes elements of CBT, IPT-A, and family treatments that are delivered in a culturally sensitive manner. These efforts highlight the importance of evaluating the efficacy of treatments for different cultural groups (APA, 2006).

Treatments that are derived from a cognitive-behavioral perspective and treatments that address interpersonal and family aspects of depression in children and adolescents are promising. But findings are modest, particularly with regard to severely depressed youth, those with co-occurring disorders, and younger children, and with regard to long-term effectiveness (APA, 2006; Weisz, McCarty, & Valeri, 2006). Efforts to identify key elements, refine treatment, determine optimal treatment length, and generally improve the effectiveness for both psychological and pharmacological treatments are needed and are ongoing (Jensen, 2006; Stark et al., 2006).

Prevention of Depression

A number of universal depression prevention programs have been implemented and evaluated (Spence & Short, 2007). Most of these programs have been school-based and have emphasized cognitive-behavioral

procedures; a few have included components drawn from an interpersonal psychotherapy perspective. These programs are offered to all youths in a particular grade(s) at one or more schools.

For example, Spence and colleagues (Spence, Sheffield, & Donovan, 2003; 2005) evaluated a teacher-implemented, classroom-based universal intervention that taught Australian eighth graders a range of problem-solving and cognitive coping skills to deal with challenging life circumstances. Sixteen schools were randomly assigned to the intervention or a control condition. Over the time of the program, students in the intervention condition did better than those in the control condition. The positive impact of the intervention (an increase in problem-solving skills and a decrease in depression symptoms) was most evident for those students with initial high levels of depressive symptoms. However, at 1, 2, 3, and 4 year follow-ups there were no differences in depressive symptoms (or for problem-solving skills) for the students in the two conditions. A separate large-scale evaluation for ninth graders (Sheffield et al., 2006) failed to find any differences between intervention and control conditions even at the end of the program.

In general, the findings for universal prevention programs for child and adolescent depression have been modest, at best, and at long-term follow-ups effects have not been maintained. However, there is probably enough success to suggest that efforts should continue. As Spence and Short (2007) suggest, interventions may need to be longer and more intensive and, in keeping with ecological models of the etiology of depression, preventive approaches may need to place a greater emphasis on decreasing risk factors and increasing protective factors in the youth's environment.

Several of the universal programs reported greater impact for those youngsters with moderate to high initial levels of depressive symptoms. This may suggest the value of indicated prevention approaches. A number of such programs have been attempted, and, again, many of these programs are derived from a cognitive-behavioral approach (Evans et al., 2005b). The Adolescent Coping With Stress course (CWS-A) is an extension of the Adolescent Coping with Depression treatment program (p. 176) to the prevention of future depression in at-risk adolescents (Rohde et al., 2005). Adolescents in the ninth grade at three high schools who had high scores on the Center for Epidemiologic Studies Depression Scale, but who were not currently depressed based on a structured diagnostic interview, were assigned to either a 15-session, after-school, cognitive-behavioral group intervention or a usual-care control condition. At 1-year follow-up there were significantly fewer cases of either MDD or dysthymia among adolescents receiving the CWS-A intervention (14% versus 26%). Clarke and colleagues (2001) conducted a similar evaluation of the CWS-A intervention offered by a health maintenance organization (HMO). In this case the course was offered to youths with sub-syndromal levels of depression whose parents were receiving treatment for depression at the HMO. At a 15-month follow-up there were fewer new episodes of affective disorder in the CWS-A group (9%) than in the treatment-as-usual control group (29%). These and other indicated prevention programs suggest that this approach to intervention is promising and worth continued attention (Evans et al., 2005b).

Bipolar Disorder

DSM Classification of Bipolar Disorders

The other major mood disorders included in the DSM fall into the category of Bipolar Disorders. They involve the presence of mania as well as depressive symptoms. Mania is typically described as a period of abnormally elevated (euphoric) or irritable mood. Euphoric mood is characterized by features such as inflated self-esteem; high rates of activity, speech, and thinking; distractibility; and exaggerated feelings of physical and mental well-being. To meet the criteria

for a Manic Episode, mania and at least three other symptoms must be present. These symptoms are described in Table 7–5. *Bipolar I Disorder* involves a history of major depression and mania, whereas *Bipolar II Disorder* includes a history of major depression and hypomania (less severe mania). *Cyclothymic Disorder* involves chronic, but mild, fluctuations of mood that do not meet the diagnostic criteria for major depressive or manic episodes. *Bipolar Disorder Not Otherwise Specified (NOS)* is used for cases that do not meet full criteria for other bipolar diagnoses. A large number of youth with bipolar symptoms receive this diagnosis (Birmaher & Axelson, 2005).

The same DSM criteria used for adults are applied to children and adolescents. However, juvenile mania is often characterized by symptom presentations and patterns that differ from the descriptions of bipolar disorder in adults. Important developmental differences in presentation challenge clinicians to apply these criteria while being sensitive to developmental differences in expression (American Academy of Child and Adolescent Psychiatry (AACAP), 2007; Youngstrom et al., 2004). For example, in adults the clinical picture is of a cyclical disorder with acute onset of *distinct* episodes of mania and/or depression with periods of relatively good functioning between episodes. In contrast, young people are likely to exhibit very short episodes, very frequent mood shifts, mixed moods, and for at least some youths, a chronic difficulty in regulating moods.

This makes the usual "adult" distinctions a considerable challenge—defining what constitutes a manic or mood episode and describing how rapidly episodes cycle (Geller, Tillman, & Bolhofner, 2007). For example, should children who do not show episodic

TABLE 7–5	SYMPTOMS USED BY THE DSM TO DIAGNOSE A MANIC EPISODE

1. Persistent elevated, expansive, or irritable mood
2. Inflated self-esteem
3. Decreased need for sleep
4. Being more talkative than usual
5. Feeling of thoughts racing
6. Distractibility
7. Increased goal-directed activity or psychomotor agitation
8. Excessive pleasurable activity that can lead to negative consequences (e.g., buying sprees, sexual indiscretions)

From American Psychiatric Association, 2000.

mood changes, but rather exhibit what has been termed severe mood dysregulation (chronic irritability and hyperarousal) be considered one subtype of a spectrum of juvenile bipolar disorders, or should they be classified in some other way (Brotman et al., 2006)?

Also, euphoric mood is often considered the hallmark of adult mania/bipolar disorder. However, irritability is the most common mood associated with bipolar disorder in children. Thus, for a number of reasons, applying DSM-IV-TR bipolar criteria to youth is an issue of controversy and ongoing debate (Pavuluri, Birmaher & Naylor, 2005; AACAP, 2007).

Other diagnostic challenges. Young people with bipolar disorder also are likely to present with patterns of co-occurring problems and disorders (e.g., attention-deficit hyperactivity disorder) that are different from those seen in adults. For example, manic episodes and bipolar disorders in older adolescents may in some ways be similar to adult presentations. However, manic episodes in adolescents are more likely to be associated with antisocial behaviors, school truancy, academic failure, or substance use. Manic episodes in adolescents are also likely to include psychotic features. Also, bipolar disorder may initially present as depression with alterations of mood occurring only after some period of time. Another potential difficulty is discriminating between bipolar disorders and severe forms of other disorders. Manic-like behaviors are very common among children with severe forms of a variety of other disorders, including attention-deficit hyperactivity disorder and oppositional defiant disorder. Thus, diagnosing of bipolar disorder may be difficult because of confusion regarding symptoms and co-occurring disorders (Evans et al., 2005a; Tillman et al., 2003).

Finally, another challenge in diagnosing bipolar disorder in children is distinguishing symptoms of mania from typical behaviors. Kowatch and colleagues (2005) describe the strategy of FIND (frequency, intensity, number, and duration of symptoms), and thresholds for each index. This is meant to assist clinicians in judging whether behavior is a symptom of bipolar disorder rather than a manifestation of developmentally more typical behavior. Also, Geller and her colleagues (2003) have attempted to describe how various mania criteria may present in children. Table 7–6 provides

TABLE 7–6	EXAMPLES OF MANIFESTATIONS OF MANIA SYMPTOMS IN CHILDREN AND TYPICAL CHILD BEHAVIOR	
SYMPTOM	**CHILD MANIA**	**NORMAL CHILD**
Elated mood	A 9-year-old girl continually danced around the house saying "I'm high, over the mountain high." A 7-year-old boy was repeatedly taken to the principal for clowning and giggling in class (when no one else was).	A child was very excited when the family went to Disneyland on Christmas morning.
Grandiose behaviors	An 8-year-old girl set up a paper flower store in her classroom and was annoyed and refused to do class work when asked to by the teacher. A 7-year-old boy stole a go-cart. He knew it was wrong to steal, but did not believe it was wrong for him. He thought that the police were arriving to play with him.	A 7-year-old boy pretended he was a fireman, directing others and rescuing victims. In his play, he did not call the firehouse. His play was age-appropriate and not impairing.
Hypersexual behavior	An 8-year-old boy imitated a rock star—gyrating his hips and rubbing his crotch during an interview. A 9-year-old boy drew pictures of naked ladies in public and said that they were his future wife.	A 7-year-old played doctor with a same-age friend.

Adapted from Geller et al., 2003.

examples of what may be viewed as symptoms of mania in children and contrasting examples of typical child behavior. In making a diagnosis, clinicians must judge the child's behavior based on these considerations of age-appropriateness as well as appropriateness to context, and degree of impairment or interference.

DESCRIPTION OF BIPOLAR DISORDER

With the challenge of how to define and diagnose bipolar disorder in mind, descriptions of young people with bipolar disorder often describe a variety of features. Kowatch & DelBello (2006) describe manic symptoms that may be displayed by children and adolescents with bipolar disorder. These are presented in Table 7–7 and we draw on their report for our description. Children with mania may irritate those around them by being extremely happy or silly when there seems to be no reason for this euphoric mood. Adolescents may also be extremely silly or unrealistically optimistic. Irritable mood is common. A child may have many intense outbursts of anger. An adolescent may be extremely oppositional, curt, or hostile. Parents often report multiple intense mood swings daily (labile mood). Young people also report needing less sleep than usual and report having more energy than usual. Children and adolescents, when manic, may appear very restless

or driven. They also may offer grandiose views of their ability. Youths may do many things over a short period of time and, initially, be fairly productive. They may, however, become increasingly disorganized and unproductive as their mania progresses. Young people may be loud, intrusive, and difficult to interrupt. Their speech may be rapid, pressured, unintelligible, or difficult to follow, and they may report that their thoughts are racing—they can't get their ideas out fast enough. The child or adolescent may also exhibit what is often termed "flight of ideas"—changing topics rapidly in a way that is confusing to others. Even adults who are familiar with them cannot easily follow their words. When manic, youths are easily distracted. Children and adolescents with mania also may show poor judgment, becoming involved in impulsive or high-risk pleasurable behaviors (e.g. frequent fighting, alcohol or drug use, reckless driving). Some youths with bipolar disorder also may experience hallucinations and delusions (see pages 349–351).

EPIDEMIOLOGY OF BIPOLAR DISORDER

Definitional issues make accurate estimates of prevalence difficult and epidemiological data for children and adolescents is quite limited (AACAP, 2007). Bipolar disorder is thought to be relatively rare in childhood and adolescence, but its prevalence may be underestimated (Evans et al., 2005a; Youngstrom et al., 2004). Indeed, it seems that the diagnosis has become more common. Moreno and colleagues (2007) report on a national representative survey of visits to a physician's office by youths (aged 0–19 years). If one examines office visits in which the youths received a mental disorder diagnosis, one sees that the percentage of visits with a diagnosis of bipolar disorder increased from 0.42% in 1994–1995 to 6.67% in 2002–2003. This increase was larger than that among adults. Similarly, Blader and Carlson (2007) report an increase of bipolar disorder diagnoses among hospitalized youth. Between 1996 and 2004, the diagnosis rate increased from 1.4 to 7.3 per 10,000 for children and from 5.1 to 20.4 per 10,000 for adolescents.

In a community sample of adolescents aged 14 to 18 years, the lifetime prevalence of bipolar disorder was about 1% (Lewinsohn, Klein, & Seeley, 1995a). Youngstrom and Duax (2005) reported that rates of bipolar disorders among children and adolescents varied between 0 and 6% in community samples and 17 to 30% in clinical samples. It is generally

TABLE 7–7	MANIC SYMPTOMS THAT MAY BE DISPLAYED BY YOUNGSTERS WITH BIPOLAR DISORDER

Euphoric mood
Irritable mood
Mood swings
Decreased need for sleep
Unusual energy
Hyperactivity
Increased goal-directed activity
Grandiosity
Accelerated, pressured, or increased amount of speech
Racing thoughts
Flight of ideas
Distractibility
Poor judgment
Hallucinations
Delusions

Adapted from Kowatch & DelBello, 2006.

reported that females and males are equally represented and that bipolar disorder is much less prevalent in prepubertal youths than after puberty.

Similar to what we noted in our discussion of depression, in community samples of adolescents, manic-like symptoms of elevated, expansive, or irritable mood are present in adolescents who do not meet the criteria for a bipolar disorder. The youths with these subsyndromal symptoms do experience substantial impairment in functioning (Kessler et al., 2001). Indeed, some evidence suggests a bipolar spectrum, that is, a continuum extending from hypomanic personality traits to subsyndromal symptoms to mild and severe forms of the disorder rather than a categorical distinction (Lewinsohn, Seeley, & Klein, 2003; Papolos, 2003).

A number of other conditions commonly co-occur in youths diagnosed with bipolar disorder. Attention-deficit hyperactivity disorder, conduct disorder, oppositional defiant disorder, and substance abuse or dependence are among the problems commonly reported (Evans et al., 2005a; Kowatch & DelBello, 2006; Papolos, 2003). These youths also experience significant impairment in school, social, and family functioning (Lewinsohn et al., 1995a; 2003). Their families face a considerable challenge and require assistance and support that is sensitive to the child's difficulties and the family's needs (Fristad & Goldberg-Arnold, 2003). The feelings of one mother who received support through an online support group illustrate this need.

Bipolar Disorder | The Need Support for Families

One of the biggest stressors is the total isolation and lack of support. I *never* have a moment to myself. I have no friends, I have no life. I spend almost every day with a feeling of mortal terror that we will return to the horror before diagnosis and stabilization. No parent or child should ever have to experience what we and the many other parents I've met at CABF (Child and Adolescent Bipolar Foundation) have had to go through. I am tired of this life. I grieve for the loss of what I thought motherhood would be. . . . If I did not have the lifeline, I don't know what I would do some nights. I can log on after a bad day and get the support and strength to start the new day with a smile so that I can be there for my boys.

Adapted from Hellander, Sisson, & Fristad, 2003, p. 314.

DEVELOPMENTAL COURSE AND PROGNOSIS

Lewinsohn, Klein, and Seeley (1995) examined the course of bipolar disorder in a large community sample of adolescents (ages 14 to 18). The median duration of the most recent manic episode for these youngsters was 10.8 months. Among the participants in the study, youths diagnosed with bipolar disorder had experienced their first affective episode earlier (mean age = 11.75 years old) than had adolescents with a history of major depression with no periods of mania (mean age = 14.95 years old). The total amount of time spent with an affective disorder was longer for the youths with bipolar disorder as well. The estimated mean duration of affective disorder for these youths with bipolar disorder was 80.2 months compared with a mean duration of 15.7 months for youths in the OADP sample with major depressive disorder. This finding suggests that in some young people, major depressive disorder may be an early stage of bipolar disorder. The transition from MDD to bipolar disorder may be more likely to occur in youngsters with an earlier onset of depression.

Joseph | Early Bipolar Symptoms

Based on information gathered at his first hospital admission, Joseph suffered from childhood illnesses more than his eight siblings. By the time he started school at age 6 his parents described him as already having periods of being tired. Although Joseph was usually considered a "jolly boy who enjoyed himself," there were episodes of crying, irritability, and depressed moods. At school he was sometimes "extra good" and at others he "lost all interest."

By the time he was 13, the family said, "they could see it coming." Joseph began having alternating periods of "quietness and irritability." He would be at the playground ordering others around and being overly bossy at one moment and at the next he would be withdrawn, sitting quietly reading the Bible. For periods of a week or so, Joseph would sit around, tired, not talking and sometimes crying. During these times he seemed "scared."

There were rapid and extreme changes when Joseph would destroy whatever his siblings were playing with. During these times Joseph was overactive, restless, overtalkative, bold, loud, demanding, and exhibited hostile behavior and angry outbursts. The brief spells of being "quiet versus irritable" persisted through ages 13 and 14.

Joseph's symptoms and the cycling worsened dramatically at age 15 when he was first admitted to the hospital meeting the criteria for a bipolar disorder.

Adapted from Egeland, Hostetter, Pauls, & Sussex, 2000, p. 1249.

Some of the adolescents in the OADP sample who met the criteria for bipolar disorder experienced a chronic/recurrent course. Twelve percent had not remitted by age 24 (that is, they continued to meet diagnostic criteria) and of those in remission at age 18, about one quarter had another episode between the ages of 19 and 24 (Lewinsohn et al., 2003). Individuals with bipolar disorder during adolescence were far more likely to meet criteria for bipolar disorder during young adulthood than adolescents with subsyndromal bipolar disorder. Adolescents with subsyndromal bipolar disorder, however, did experience high rates of major depressive disorder during young adulthood.

Geller and colleagues (2003) studied a group of prepubertal children and early adolescents with bipolar disorder. These youths were assessed in a research setting, but received care from their own community practitioners. During a 2-year period about two thirds of these young people experienced recovery (defined as at least 8 consecutive weeks not meeting DSM criteria for mania or hypomania). A little over half of them relapsed after recovery and many continued to meet the criteria for another disorder during their recovery.

Longitudinal data are limited. However, the information that is available suggests that youngsters with bipolar disorders or symptoms might continue to display symptoms of affective and other disorders and experience considerable social and academic impairment, at least into the early adult period (Birmaher & Axelson, 2005).

RISK FACTORS AND ETIOLOGY

Information concerning risk factors for and etiology of bipolar disorders is limited. A family history of bipolar disorders is a risk factor. Children of adult bipolar patients have an increased risk for bipolar disorder and mood disorders, in general. However, it is important to note that the majority of children of bipolar adults do not have a diagnosable bipolar disorder or other mood disorder (Evans et al., 2005a).

Adult studies are consistent in showing a strong genetic component for bipolar disorders. Heritability estimates of about 80% are reported and research employing linkage analysis and other methods is underway to identify specific genes that may be involved (DePaulo, 2004; Faraone et al., 2004; Rutter et al., 1999). While research has tended to focus on issues such as describing and differentiating the disorder and on the contribution of genetics to the disorder, it is thought that environmental factors may influence the probability of an at-risk youngster developing bipolar symptoms, the degree of symptomatology, and the probability of co-occurring problems. Attention to such influences should be part of ongoing research on bipolar disorder in children and adolescents.

ASSESSMENT OF BIPOLAR DISORDER

As one might expect, the assessment of bipolar disorder in children and adolescents is less well developed than the measurement of depression. A broad spectrum of information is, again, the assessment goal (Youngstrom et al., 2004). Structured diagnostic interviews such as versions of the K-SADS, adapted to be more appropriate for use with children and adolescents, have been employed to make diagnostic decisions and to obtain additional information (Axelson et al., 2003; Geller et al., 2001). The most frequently used mania rating scales were originally developed for use with adults. The Young Mania Rating Scale (YMRS; Young et al., 1978) has been adapted for use with children and adolescents (PYMRS; Youngstrom et al., 2004). The General Behavior Inventory, designed to assess symptoms of depression, hypomania, mania, and mixed mood states has been adapted for use with children and adolescents and as a parent-report measure (Danielson et al., 2003; Youngstrom et al., 2001). Rating scales specifically designed for assessing mania in children and adolescents are being developed (Pavuluri et al., 2006).

TREATMENT OF BIPOLAR DISORDER

The treatment of bipolar disorder requires a multimodal approach to the disorder itself as well as attention to likely co-occurring difficulties and the considerable impact on family life (American Academy of Child and Adolescent Psychiatry (AACAP), 2007; James & Javaloyes, 2001). The young patient with mania may need to be admitted to a child or adolescent hospital unit so as to ensure the youngster's safety and to provide an adequately controlled environment. The choice to use an inpatient setting would be guided by the level of disturbance displayed by the youngster, the risk of harm or suicide, the level of support that the family is able to provide, and the need for medical supervision of medication.

The most common treatment for bipolar disorder is pharmacotherapy, and this is considered the first-line treatment for the disorder (AACAP, 2007). However, methodologically adequate research regarding treatment of children and adolescents is sparse (APA, 2006; Kowatch et al., 2005). It is problematic that treatments rely heavily on the adult literature, and information regarding possible side effects is lacking. Mood stabilizer (antimanic) medications such as lithium and valproate, and atypical antipsychotics (e.g. olanzapine, risperidone) are the pharmacological agents likely to be employed alone or in combination (AACAP, 2007; Evans et al., 2005c; Kowatch & DelBello, 2006). Treatment of the depressive aspects of the disorder may include the use of medications such as SSRIs. However, caution is suggested because antidepressants have been reported to destabilize the patient's mood or to incite a manic episode (AACAP, 2007; Kowatch & DelBello, 2006).

Although the primary treatment for bipolar disorder is pharmacological, education of the patient and family about the disorder is important. In addition to a psychoeducational component, individual and family therapy is often recommended. Programs designed for youngsters and their families have been developed and are undergoing evaluation (Fristad & Goldberg-Arnold, 2003; Goldberg-Arnold & Fristad, 2003; Pavuluri et al., 2004). These treatment programs include education of the youngster and family about the disorder and its treatment plus many of the cognitive-behavioral elements described in the psychosocial treatment of depression. Support groups and other forms of assistance for families, such as the website of the Child and Adolescent Bipolar Foundation (CABF) are likely to be needed as well (Hellander et al., 2003; Kowatch & DelBello, 2006). Research regarding all aspects of treatment for bipolar disorder in adolescents and children is a continuing need.

Suicide

Suicide is often mentioned in discussions of mood disorders and, in particular, depression. This association probably occurs because depression is an important risk factor for suicide, and the two problems share etiological and epidemiological patterns. However, although the two problems overlap, they are also distinct. The majority of depressed youngsters do not

attempt or commit suicide, and not every suicidal youth is depressed. Discussion of suicide includes not only concern with completed suicides, but also with attempted suicides and suicidal thoughts. There is reason to attend to this full range of suicidal behavior.

PREVALENCE OF COMPLETED SUICIDES

The rate of completed suicide is relatively low among young people compared with adults and lower for prepubertal children than for adolescents. Completed suicide by young people is nevertheless of concern. From the mid-1950s to the early 1990s the suicide rate among adolescents and young adults rose markedly. Since the mid-1990s there has been a steady decline. However, overall rates remain about twice what they were when the marked rise began and suicide is the third leading cause of death among youth (Hendin et al., 2005a; National Center for Health Statistics, 2006). The 1980 suicide rate among 15- to 19-year-olds was 8.5 per 100,000 and the 2004 rate was 8.2 per 100,000—a slight decrease. In contrast, suicides among younger children are occurring at a higher rate than two decades ago. In 1980, the suicide rate among young people between the ages of 5- and 14 was 0.4 per 100,000. Although suicides remained a relatively rare event in this age group, the 2004 rate was 0.7 youths per 100,000—an increase of 75 percent. Rates per 100,000 in 2004 of male deaths from suicides exceed those for females in both the 5- to 14-year-old (0.9 and 0.5) and 15- to 19-year-old (12.6 and 3.5) age groups. Rates are higher for White (non-Hispanic or Latino) youth than for other ethnic groups, with the exception of Native American youth (particularly males).

SUICIDAL IDEATION AND ATTEMPTS

Patty   A Suicide Attempt

Patty, a pretty 8-year-old, took an overdose of two of her mother's imipramine tablets just before going to sleep. Nobody knew about this until the next morning when Patty's mother had to wake her when she did not get up in time for school. Patty complained of a headache, dizziness, and tiredness. She was tearful and irritable and argued that her mother should "Leave me alone. I want to die." Alarmed, Patty's mother brought her to the pediatrician, who recommended that Patty be hospitalized for evaluation of suicidal behavior. . . . He believed that Patty would not be safe at home. Patty insisted that the "best thing would be for me to die."

Patty's mother told the pediatrician that the last 2 months had been very stressful for the family. She and her husband had separated and were planning to divorce. The mother described feeling very depressed and anxious over the last year. Her husband often came home drunk and would be very hostile to her and threaten her. . . .

Patty is a fine student and has many friends. . . . Patty's teacher had spoken to her mother about Patty's behavior over the previous 2 months. Patty was fidgety in class and unable to concentrate; she often day-dreamed. Her homework assignments were often not completed and her grades had dropped. Unlike her earlier behavior, Patty, in the last month, had preferred to be alone and had not joined her peers in after-school activities. She also had several arguments with her best friend.

Adapted from Pfeffer, 2000, p. 238.

If one considers the entire range of suicidal behavior, prevalence appears quite high, particularly among adolescents. Clearly, it is difficult to accurately assess the prevalence of suicidal behavior. Many attempts may go undetected and unreported, because not all cases seek medical or some therapeutic care. Also, methodological and definitional issues may limit interpretation of self-reports of suicidal ideation and attempts. Even some completed suicides may be mistakenly viewed as accidents.

Based on the national Youth Risk Behavior Survey (National Center for Health Statistics, 2006) the percentage of youths in grades 9 to 12 in the United States who seriously considered suicide significantly decreased between 1991 and 2005. However, despite some recent leveling off or decreases, during this same period, there was a significant increase in the number of young people who made an injurious suicide attempt. The information in Table 7–8 illustrates these trends. Rates of injurious suicide attempts (needing medical attention) seem particularly high among Hispanic/Latino youths. Although more young males die by suicide, females report more suicidal ideation and attempts.

A prospective longitudinal study of approximately 1,500 adolescents between 14 and 18 years of age by Lewinsohn and his colleagues (1996) also provides information about the prevalence of adolescent suicidal behavior. A total of 19.4% of these adolescents had a history of suicidal ideation. Such ideation was more prevalent in females (23.7%) than in males (14.8%). And although more frequent suicidal ideation predicted future suicide attempts, even mild and relatively infrequent suicidal thoughts increased the risk for an attempt.

Suicide attempts had occurred in 7.1% of this community sample. Females (10.1%) were more likely than males (3.8%) to attempt suicide. Suicide attempts before puberty were uncommon. The majority of attempts made by females consisted of either ingestion of harmful substances (55%) or cutting themselves (31%). Males employed a wider variety of methods—ingestion (20%), cutting (25%), gun use (15%), hanging (11%), and other methods, such

TABLE 7–8 SUICIDAL BEHAVIORS AMONG YOUNGSTERS IN GRADES 9–12				
	PERCENT WHO SERIOUSLY CONSIDERED SUICIDE			
	1991		2005	
	MALE	FEMALE	MALE	FEMALE
White (Not Hispanic or Latino)	21.7	38.6	12.4	21.5
Black or African American	13.3	29.4	7.0	17.1
Hispanic or Latino	18.0	34.6	11.9	24.2
	PERCENT YOUNGESTERS WITH INJURIOUS SUICIDE ATTEMPT			
	1991		2005	
	MALE	FEMALE	MALE	FEMALE
White (Not Hispanic or Latino)	1.0	2.3	1.5	2.7
Black or African American	0.4	2.9	1.4	2.6
Hispanic or Latino	0.5	2.7	2.8	3.7

Source: National Center for Health Statistics, 2006.

as shooting air into their veins or running into traffic (22%). Some adolescents attempted suicide more than once. The first 3 months after an attempt were a period of particularly high risk for a repeated attempt. Reattempts were made by approximately 27% of the boys and 21% of the girls during this time. The likelihood of a suicidal attempt by these youngsters remained above the rates expected in the general population for at least 2 years. At 24 months, 39% of the boys and 33% of the girls had reattempted.

Suicide attempts by adolescents and children are often conceptualized as a "cry of pain"—as expressing the thought, "I want to stop feeling pain" (De Wilde, Kienhorst, & Diekstra, 2001). Young people are often thought to be vulnerable to suicide because their problem-solving and self-regulatory skills and their abilities to cope with stressful circumstances may be limited. Some young people may be faced with circumstances that cause considerable stress that they view as beyond their control. These youths may also have limited understanding that undesirable situations can and often do change.

SUICIDE AND PSYCHOPATHOLOGY

Suicide is often thought of as a symptom of disorders such as depression. Indeed, depression is related to suicide among children and adolescents (Flisher, 1999; Lewinsohn, Rohde, & Seeley, 1996), and constructs such as hopelessness that are associated with depression have been found to predict suicidal behavior (Levy, Jurkovic, & Spiro, 1995). For example, in a longitudinal study, Kovacs, Goldston, and Gatsonis (1993) found that a significantly greater proportion of youths with depressive disorders attempted suicide than did those with other disorders. However, suicidal behavior can be associated with a variety of disorders, and suicide risk increases with the number of diagnoses. There is a significant association between bipolar disorder and risk for suicide. Also, conduct disorder and substance abuse diagnoses are common among completed suicides. Indeed, some research suggests considerable diagnostic heterogeneity among young suicide completers. Therefore, although depression is an important risk factor, the presence of a depressive disorder is neither necessary nor sufficient for the occurrence of suicidal behavior. It is probably important to be aware that some professionals indicate that the presence of problems (e.g., aggression and impulsivity in combination with or independent of depression) at levels below criteria for a diagnosis of disorder also increase the risk of suicidal behavior (Hendin et al., 2005a; King et al., 1992).

RISK FACTORS

There is no typical suicidal youth, and multiple factors likely contribute to risk for suicide (De Wilde et al., 2001; Gould et al., 2003; Hendin et al., 2005a). A history of prior suicide attempts is a strong predictor of completed suicide. However, multiple characteristics of youths themselves appear to be risk factors of suicidal behavior.

As suggested above, psychological disorders that are characterized by attributes such as depression, hopelessness, impulsivity, and aggression contribute to suicide risk. Other individual risk factors include poor interpersonal problem-solving ability and physical illness. Minority sexual orientation may be a risk factor for suicide attempts among adolescent youths. (See Accent: "Sexual Orientation and Suicide Risk.") In addition, research conducted primarily with adults suggests that biological factors such as abnormalities in serotonin function and genetic influences may possibly affect suicide risk. At present, biological findings have little impact on clinical practice (Gould et al., 2003).

A family history of suicidal behavior increases risk. Family factors (such as abuse, low parental monitoring, and poor communication) and family disruption are also frequently cited as risk factors. Although improved research is needed, it would appear that youngsters who attempt suicide are likely to grow up in families characterized by high levels of turmoil (De Wilde et al., 2001; Wagner, Silverman, & Martin, 2003). However, high levels of involvement and support from family, as well as from schools or other institutions, may serve a protective function (Gould et al., 2003; Hendin, et al., 2005a).

Other factors such as bullying, high levels of stress in school, social relations, and sociocultural influences—including the ready availability of firearms—are also thought to contribute to increased risk. Considerable concern also exists regarding contagion ("imitation" or increased suicidal behavior) following media reports or presentations of stories of youth suicide (Gould et al., 2003; Hendin et al., 2005a).

SUICIDE PREVENTION

The review by the Commission on Adolescent Suicide Prevention (Hendin et al., 2005a) suggests that attempts to prevent youth suicide are widespread. The most common programs have taken a universal prevention approach—targeting all youth in a specific setting, such as schools, regardless of individual risk. There are two types of universal prevention

ACCENT

Sexual Orientation and Suicide Risk

It is frequently suggested that suicide is more common among gay and lesbian youth than among the general adolescent population. At present, there does not appear to be evidence for a higher rate of completed suicide in these groups (American Academy of Child and Adolescent Psychiatry [AACAP], 2001; Catalan, 2000). However, the view that these young people are at increased risk for suicidal ideation and attempted suicide is widely held. Several studies of sizeable community samples suggest a two- to sevenfold increase in risk, and these youngsters also may be more likely to make suicide attempts that require medical attention (AACAP, 2001). Why might this be the case?

Research suggests that gay, lesbian, and bisexual youth are likely to report experiences that are known to be important risk factors. They may engage in early and more frequent drug and alcohol use and are more likely to be bullied and victimized at school. Many clinicians believe that the difficulties of dealing with the stigma of homosexuality and the interpersonal difficulties that this may bring might lead to depression, and there are reports of high levels of depression in such youth.

Data from the National Study of Adolescent Health (Add Health Study), a nationally representative study of U.S. adolescents, support the view that sexual orientation is a risk factor for suicidal ideation and suicide attempts, and suggest that this risk is, in part, due to known adolescent risk factors (Russell & Joyner, 2001). About 12,000 adolescents completed the survey in their homes, and information regarding the issues of sexuality and suicide was collected in a manner to minimize issues of privacy and confidentiality. Youths with a same-sex orientation (having a same-sex romantic attraction or relationship) were more likely to report suicidal thoughts and were more than twice as likely to attempt suicide as their same-sex peers. It is important to note, however, that the vast majority of youth with a same-sex sexual orientation reported no suicidal thoughts or attempts (about 85% of boys and 72% of girls). Youngsters with a same-sex orientation also scored higher on several important adolescent suicide risk factors: more alcohol abuse and depression, higher rates of suicide attempts by family members and friends, and victimization experiences.

These and other findings suggest that sexual orientation, per se, is not a risk factor for suicide attempts, but rather same-sex orientation is associated with known risk factors common to all adolescents. Indeed, the same risk factors (e.g., low self-esteem, early sexual debut, unsafe sex, substance use) are reported to be equally elevated in sexual minority and heterosexual suicide attempters (Savin-Williams & Ream, 2003). Again, it is important to remember that most youth with a same-sex orientation do not attempt suicide and are resilient in the face of considerable risk (Savin-Williams, 2001). Sexual minority youth who attempt suicide may exist in a context that amplifies the experience of other risk factors (Savin-Williams & Ream, 2003). Appreciation of this context can inform our understanding of the difficulties faced by these young people. It should also encourage us to continue to create environments in which risk will be decreased.

programs (Hendin et al., 2005c). Suicide awareness and education programs aim to increase students' awareness of, and knowledge about, suicidal behavior and to encourage them to seek help. These programs also seek to improve awareness by school staff and other adults in the community. Most awareness and education programs involve a limited number of brief sessions and are frequently part of a larger curriculum targeting high-risk behaviors. While these programs are widely applied, if and how they are effective remains unclear. For example, while many programs report increased student knowledge regarding suicide, the impact of this on suicidal behavior is unknown (Hendin et al., 2005c).

Screening programs seek to identify youth who are at risk and refer them to treatment. The assumption of such programs is that the suicidal behaviors and the psychopathology associated with suicide (e.g. depression, substance abuse) often go unnoticed and untreated. It is also assumed that identification of at-risk youth will increase the number receiving treatment and that treatment will decrease suicides. The success of such approaches relies on the availability of screening measures that are both sensitive (able to detect youth at risk for suicide) and selective (able to avoid identifying many more as at risk who are not). Timing of the screening (e.g. at the beginning of high school, before exams) may also affect the likelihood of accurate identification. It is not clear that screening programs are cost effective or that they result in high rates of follow through by those identified as at risk. Getting identified at-risk youth to follow through with treatment recommendations is clearly a complex issue—involving, for example, appropriate encouragement of youth, parental support, and availability of quality treatment services. There is no clear evidence that screening programs reduce suicide risk factors or suicidal behavior (Hendin et al., 2005c).

Selective or targeted suicide prevention programs are directed at youth who may have not yet exhibited suicidal behavior, but who are thought to be particularly vulnerable to suicide (Hendin et al., 2005b). For example, such a program might target youngsters who have recently been exposed to the

suicide of a family member or peer. The assumption of such programs is that exposed youth are at increased risk for depression, posttraumatic stress, and suicidal behavior. These programs, sometimes referred to as "postvention," are often implemented through schools and seek to support grieving youth, to identify those at risk, and to assist the community in returning to its normal functioning. Although postvention programs have proliferated, there is no systematic evidence of their effectiveness (Hendin et al., 2005b).

In general, scientifically valid evaluations have lagged behind the development and implementation of prevention programs. Much remains to be learned about youth suicide and effective intervention.

SUMMARY

- *Interest in mood disorders in young people is relatively recent. There is more information available regarding depression than mania/bipolar disorder.*

A HISTORICAL PERSPECTIVE

- *The psychoanalytic theory of depression suggested that the problem did not exist in children.*
- *The concept of masked depression, although problematic, brought greater attention to the problem and highlighted developmental issues. A developmental perspective to understanding depression has continued to evolve.*

THE DSM APPROACH TO THE CLASSIFICATION OF MOOD DISORDERS

- *In the DSM depression and mania are described in the category of Mood Disorders.*
- *The DSM describes four types of mood episodes that serve as the building blocks for the diagnosis of mood disorders.*

DEFINITION AND CLASSIFICATION OF DEPRESSION

- *The definition of depression is affected by how depression is measured and who provides information.*
- *Major Depressive Disorder, Dysthymic Disorder, and Adjustment Disorder with Depressed Mood are the DSM diagnoses typically given to depressed youths.*
- *Empirical approaches to classification suggest that children and adolescents experience syndromes that*

include a mixed presentation of depression and anxiety features.
- *Developmental differences in presentation of depression challenge the use of the same diagnostic criteria in all age groups. Whether it is best to conceptualize depression as dimensional rather than categorical is an ongoing consideration.*

EPIDEMIOLOGY OF DEPRESSION

- *Major depressive disorder is the most prevalent form of affective disorder among children and adolescents.*
- *Episodes of clinical depression are quite common among adolescents. Depression is more prevalent among adolescents than children and among girls during adolescence.*
- *Higher rates of depression are reported among low SES groups. Although comparable rates of depression are typically reported for different ethnic groups, research suggests attention to possible differences.*
- *Youngsters who are depressed are likely to experience a number of other difficulties and to meet the diagnostic criteria for a variety of other disorders.*

DEPRESSION AND DEVELOPMENT

- *How depression is manifested varies by developmental period.*
- *Episodes of depression may last for an appreciable period of time and for some youngsters may present a recurring problem.*

ETIOLOGY OF DEPRESSION

- Most contemporary views of depression in children and adolescents suggest a model that integrates multiple determinants.

- Research suggests a genetic component to depression and also considerable environmental influence.

- Research on the biochemistry of depression emphasizes the role of neurotransmitters and the neuroendocrine system. Findings suggest that during childhood and early adolescence, the biological aspects of depression differ from adult cases.

- Separation/loss has been a major theme in many theories of depression. Cognitive and behavioral theories suggest additional contributions to the development of depression, including interpersonal and cognitive aspects of functioning.

- A learned helplessness perspective suggests that a learned perception of lack of control leads to a cognitive style and behaviors characteristic of depression. Hopelessness theory emphasizes the interaction of stressful life events and cognitive style.

- Cognitive theories, such as Beck's, and self-control models of depression have also received attention.

- Maternal depression appears to be related to childhood dysfunctions, but this relationship does not seem to be either specific to childhood depression or inevitable. Various mechanisms may link maternal depression and child dysfunction.

- Interpersonal relationships with peers contribute to the development of depression, and a youngster's depression affects peers' relationships with the depressed youngster.

ASSESSMENT OF DEPRESSION

- Assessment of depression is likely to sample a broad spectrum of attributes and to involve a number of strategies. It is important to obtain information from a variety of informants and through a variety of measures.

- Structured diagnostic interviews may be employed to yield a DSM diagnosis. In addition, self-report measures are frequently employed.

- Instruments available to assess attributes associated with depression (e.g., hopelessness) and observational measures add to our ability to conduct a thorough assessment.

TREATMENT OF DEPRESSION

- The prescription of antidepressant medications to treat children and adolescents with depression is widespread and may be an important component of treatment for some youngsters. However, the use of medications continues to be controversial, because there are concerns about efficacy and safety. Selective serotonin reuptake inhibitors are most commonly employed.

- Treatments derived from behavioral and cognitive-behavioral perspectives and treatments that address interpersonal and family aspects of depression in youngsters are promising. However, continued development of treatments that are sensitive to multiple aspects of psychological, social, and family influences and to cultural differences are needed.

PREVENTION OF DEPRESSION

- A number of universal depression prevention programs have been implemented. Most have employed cognitive-behavioral procedures and some have included interpersonal components. In general, the effectiveness of universal prevention programs has been modest and not maintained over the long term.

- Indicated prevention programs, derived from a cognitive-behavioral approach, have also been implemented and appear to be effective in preventing depression in at-risk youth.

BIPOLAR DISORDER

- Bipolar disorders involve the presence of mania as well as depressive symptoms.

- The same DSM criteria used for adults are applied to children and adolescents. However, there are a number of challenges in using these criteria to diagnose children and adolescents, and behavior may vary with development.

- Definitional issues make estimates of prevalence difficult. Bipolar disorder is thought to be rare, particularly in prepubertal youngsters. However, the diagnosis has become more common.

- Evidence suggests thinking in terms of a continuum—a bipolar spectrum—rather than in categorical terms.

- Youths with bipolar disorders are likely to experience co-occurring disorders and to exhibit considerable impairment in functioning.

- *Young people who meet the criteria for bipolar disorder may experience a chronic and recurrent course of difficulties.*

- *Information concerning risk factors and etiology is limited. A family history of bipolar disorders is probably the primary risk factor and a strong genetic influence is suggested.*

- *Assessment of bipolar disorders in children and adolescents is less well developed than the measurement of depression.*

- *Treatment of bipolar disorder requires a multimodal approach. The primary treatment involves the use of pharmacological agents, particularly mood stabilizers. Research regarding all aspects of treatment for bipolar disorder in youth is needed.*

SUICIDE

- *Completed suicide is a serious concern. The range of suicidal behavior that includes suicidal thoughts and attempted suicide is more prevalent than actual, completed suicide.*

- *Suicidal behavior is related to depression but to other problems as well.*

- *Multiple complex factors contribute to suicidal behavior.*

- *Attempts to prevent youth suicide are widespread; however, the impact or success of such programs is unclear.*

KEY TERMS

masked depression *(p. 157)*

unipolar mood disorder *(p. 157)*

bipolar mood disorder *(p. 157)*

Major Depressive Episode *(p. 157)*

Manic Episode *(p. 157)*

Mixed Episode *(p. 157)*

Hypomanic Episode *(p. 157)*

Major Depressive Disorder *(p. 158)*

Dysthymic Disorder *(p.159)*

double depression *(p. 159)*

Adjustment Disorder with Depressed Mood *(p. 159)*

learned helplessness *(p. 167)*

attributional (explanatory) style *(p. 167)*

hopelessness *(p. 167)*

cognitive distortions *(p. 168)*

selective serotonin reuptake inhibitors *(p. 174)*

remission *(p. 174)*

Bipolar Disorder *(p. 178)*

Mania *(p. 178)*

euphoric mood *(p. 178)*

severe mood dysregulation *(p. 179)*

subsyndromal *(p. 181)*

contagion *(p. 185)*

CHAPTER 8

Conduct Problems

In this chapter and the next, we discuss problems often described as *externalizing*. This term denotes problems that tend to place young people in conflict with others. These behaviors are in contrast to the seemingly more inner-directed problems discussed in the two previous chapters. Various other terms also are employed to describe these types of problems—disruptive, impulsive, undercontrolled, oppositional, antisocial, conduct-disordered, and delinquent. Although there is a general understanding of this broad category, attempting to understand, define, and subcategorize such behavior is a continuing goal.

Among disruptive behavior problems, a distinction has often been made between inattention, hyperactivity, and impulsivity on the one hand, and aggression, oppositional behaviors, and more serious conduct problems on the other (Waldman, Lillienfeld, & Lahey, 1995). The behaviors in the first grouping are discussed in greater detail in the next chapter, which is devoted to attention-deficit hyperactivity disorder (ADHD). The oppositional and conduct problem behaviors of the second grouping are considered in this chapter. Young people with these problems have high rates of referral for mental

health and other social and legal services, and some portion of these youths have contributed to broad societal concern with levels of violence and crime. Conduct problems are thus the focus of considerable societal and scientific concern. We use the term *conduct problems* to refer to this group of disruptive/antisocial behavior problems. The term *conduct disorders* refers to a particular diagnostic category that falls within this domain.

Classification and Description

Disruptive behaviors are common at various stages of development. Clinicians commonly hear complaints of noncompliant, aggressive, and antisocial behavior. Parents and teachers often describe young children and adolescents who do not follow directions, do not comply with requests or seem irritable or angry. Children may engage in various forms of aggression and bullying from early school years through middle school. Many adolescents may engage in dangerous behaviors and use illegal substances. The fact that these problems are common and disruptive makes them a topic of concern for parents and for those who work with youths. They may cause considerable distress for parents and teachers, create discord among family members, or interfere with classroom functioning. Extreme and persistent forms of these behaviors cause a degree of disturbance and destruction well beyond the common experience. Thus they are of particular concern not only for the family but also for institutions such as the school and for society at large. The seeming persistence of these behaviors over time for some individuals—perhaps from early childhood through adult life—also contributes to their importance. Figure 8–1 provides an overview of types of conduct-problem behaviors that adults often describe as problematic and aversive and the DSM disorders associated with them.

DSM APPROACH: OVERVIEW

Within the section on Disorders Usually First Diagnosed in Infancy, Childhood and Adolescence, the DSM has a category of Attention-Deficit and Disruptive Behavior Disorders. This larger category includes the diagnostic categories of Attention-Deficit Hyperactivity Disorder (discussed in Chapter 9) and the diagnoses of Oppositional Defiant Disorder and Conduct Disorder, which are discussed in the present chapter.

Although our focus is children and adolescents, among Personality Disorders the DSM includes a diagnosis of Antisocial Personality Disorder (APD). This diagnosis may be applied to individuals who display a persistent pattern of aggressive and antisocial behavior after the age of 18. APD is characterized by "a pervasive pattern of disregard for and violation of the rights of others" and by multiple illegal and aggressive behaviors (American Psychiatric Association, 2000). Adults with APD may also display psychopathy—an interpersonal trait defined by characteristics such as deceitfulness, callousness, lack of remorse, and impulsivity. The diagnosis of APD requires that the pattern be present since the age of 15 with evidence that the individual did meet, or would have met, the criteria for Conduct Disorder with an onset before 15 years of age.

Later we will discuss a subgroup of youngsters who display a developmental pattern of persistent aggressive and antisocial behavior. Some of these youngsters may continue this developmental trajectory and receive the diagnosis of APD as adults. There is evidence suggesting that some of these youngsters may display the callous/unemotional traits characteristic of psychopathy (Frick, 1998a; Murrie et al., 2007). Youngsters with such traits are described as displaying shallow emotions, lacking anxiety and empathy, and feeling little or no guilt.

DSM APPROACH: OPPOSITIONAL DEFIANT DISORDER

Young children are often stubborn, do not comply with requests or directions, and in a variety of ways exhibit oppositional behavior. Not all such behavior is indicative or predictive of clinical problems (consider

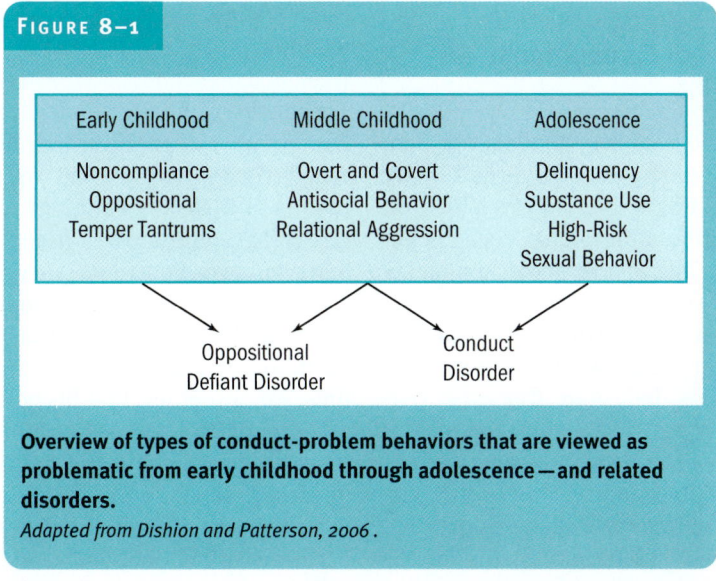

FIGURE 8–1

Early Childhood	Middle Childhood	Adolescence
Noncompliance	Overt and Covert	Delinquency
Oppositional	Antisocial Behavior	Substance Use
Temper Tantrums	Relational Aggression	High-Risk
		Sexual Behavior

Oppositional Defiant Disorder

Conduct Disorder

Overview of types of conduct-problem behaviors that are viewed as problematic from early childhood through adolescence—and related disorders.
Adapted from Dishion and Patterson, 2006.

ACCENT

Are Conduct Problems a Mental Disorder?

The diagnosis of Conduct Disorder is frequently part of the controversy over what constitutes psychopathology or mental disorder (Hinshaw & Lee, 2003; Richters & Cicchetti, 1993). Richters and Cicchetti addressed this question in part by asking if Mark Twain's characters of Tom Sawyer and Huckleberry Finn suffered from a mental disorder. As these authors point out, the two boys engaged in a sustained pattern of antisocial behavior that would warrant a diagnosis of conduct disorder—lying, stealing, aggression, truancy, running away, cruelty to animals. The boys were judged by the townspeople in social–moral terms and opinions were mixed as to whether, at heart, they were good or bad boys.

The question of what constitutes a conduct disorder is complex. One issue is whether it is appropriate to place the locus of the deviant behavior entirely within the individual and ignore the social context. As can be seen from the following excerpt the DSM acknowledges this issue:

Concerns have been raised that the Conduct Disorder diagnosis may at times be misapplied to individuals in settings where patterns of undesirable behavior are sometimes viewed as protective (e.g., in threatening, impoverished, high-crime settings). Consistent with the DSM-IV definition of mental disorder, the Conduct Disorder diagnosis should be applied only when the behavior in question is symptomatic of an underlying dysfunction within the individual and not simply a reaction to the immediate social context. (American Psychiatric Association, 2000, p. 96)

How does one determine whether a youngster's behavior is a reaction to a problematic environment or an indication of individual psychopathology? Clinicians and researchers must be sensitive and aware of both typical development and the real impact of poverty, stress, and violent communities on the development of antisocial behavior.

the following case of Henry). Indeed, appropriate and skilled assertions of autonomy may be desirable and may facilitate development (Johnston & Ohan, 1999). It is the less skilled and excessive oppositional and defiant behavior that may indicate present or future problems.

Henry | Preschool Oppositional Behavior

Mrs. Sweet reported that her 3.5-year-old son, Henry, was causing problems. She viewed Henry as a normal, active, bright boy. However, she felt the need to talk with a professional because her friends and family had made some comments about Henry's escalating disruptive behavior.

Henry was the older of two children and had a 9-month-old sister. Mrs. Sweet's responses to initial questionnaires indicated that she perceived Henry as engaging in a significant amount of disruptive behavior but the behavior was not problematic to her. The mother's log of the past week contained descriptions of inappropriate behaviors such as: "Henry hit his grandfather on the shin with a baseball bat" and "Henry scraped a knife across the kitchen wall."

Mr. Sweet did not attend the initial interview because he saw the difficulty as primarily "my wife's problem." Mrs. Sweet indicated that Henry's developmental milestones were within normal limits but that from birth Henry had been a "difficult" child. Henry spent three mornings a week at a preschool and these were problem-free. The teachers initially reported, however, that they had to be rather "firm" in their expectations. When Henry was invited to spend time with friends in their homes things went well. Difficulties were reported when friends visited him—his behavior was described as very active, getting into things that were forbidden, and in general creating chaos. Henry's father often took Henry on full-day outings and thoroughly enjoyed this time. Mr. Sweet felt that his wife should be firmer with Henry. Mrs. Sweet described the major problems as "not listening," "refusing to do as requested," and "talking back." All of these occurred primarily with her, but were beginning to occur with other people in the family.

According to Mrs. Sweet, on a typical day Henry managed routine events such as eating and bathing easily. However, when any demands were placed on him, he would refuse to comply. To avoid confrontations, Mrs. Sweet spent much of her time rearranging her schedule, but this was becoming increasingly difficult as her 9-month-old demanded more of her attention.

Henry came to a clinic-observation session wearing an army camouflage outfit, cowboy hat, and boots, and carrying two six-shooters and a toy machine gun. He greeted the clinician with "I'm going to shoot your eyes out." The clinician responded with a firm "We don't talk like that in my office." Henry quickly responded in a contrite voice, "Oh, I'm sorry." Observation of parent–child interaction indicated that Mrs. Sweet gave Henry a high rate of noncontingent positive reinforcement, placed many demands on him, and tried to get compliance through reasoning. Henry placed many demands on his mother and rarely complied with her requests. Henry and his mother seemed to enjoy playing together. Henry refused to comply with his mother's requests to pick up the toys; however, he readily complied with the clinician's requests to clean up the toys.

A recommendation was made that both parents attend classes on child development and management. Both parents and Henry were also involved in treatment sessions to increase positive parent–child interactions, to set age-appropriate limits, to increase Henry's compliance, and to determine a consistent method of discipline. This parent training program was carried out over a 6-week period with two follow-up appointments. After treatment, Henry was still described as "headstrong"; however, both parents felt that his behavior was acceptable and for the most part easily managed.

Adapted from Schroeder & Gordon, 2002, pp. 374–376.

Oppositional Defiant Disorder (ODD) is described as a pattern of negativistic, hostile, and defiant behavior that is developmentally extreme. The major criteria used to define the disorder are listed in Table 8–1. At least four of these behaviors must be present for a period of at least 6 months. To distinguish the behaviors from expected levels of opposition and assertiveness, a behavior must be judged to occur more frequently than is typical for a child of

TABLE 8–1	BEHAVIORS USED BY THE DSM TO DEFINE OPPOSITIONAL DEFIANT DISORDER

Loses temper
Argues with adults
Actively defies or refuses to comply with adult
    requests or rules
Deliberately annoys others
Blames others for own mistakes or misbehavior
Is touchy or easily annoyed
Is angry and resentful
Is spiteful or vindictive

From American Psychiatric Association, 2000.

comparable age. Furthermore, the oppositional defiant behavior must cause clinically meaningful impairment in the youngster's social or academic functioning. The following case of Jeremy illustrates the behaviors displayed by children who might receive the diagnosis of Oppositional Defiant Disorder.

Jeremy   Oppositional Defiant Disorder

Jeremy, age 9, was increasingly disobedient and difficult to manage at school. Recently he swore at a teacher and was suspended from school for several days. He also rode his bike into a store window and shattered it (once before he had broken a window when riding his bike with a friend). These and other experiences convinced his mother that she had to do something about his behavior.

Jeremy's problems had slowly escalated; however, he had been difficult to manage since nursery school. He was most likely to get into trouble when he was without close supervision. In school, Jeremy had been reprimanded for teasing, tripping, and kicking other children and calling them names. It often appeared that he was deliberately trying to annoy other children, but Jeremy always claimed that others had started the problem. Jeremy was described as bad-tempered and irritable. He did not become involved in serious fights, but occasionally had minor physical exchanges with another child. Jeremy sometimes refused to do what his teachers told him to do, arguing and giving reasons why he should not have to do his work. Despite this, his grades were good.

At home Jeremy's behavior was quite variable. On some days he was defiant and rude. Although he eventually would comply, he needed to *be told several times before he would do anything. On other days he was charming and volunteered to help, but unhelpful days predominated. Jeremy's mother reported, "The least thing upsets him, and then he shouts and screams." She described Jeremy as spiteful and mean with his younger brother.*

Jeremy completed his work and his concentration was generally good. His mother described him as "on the go all the time," but not restless. His teachers were not concerned that he was restless but were concerned about his attitude. His mother indicated that Jeremy told minor lies, but that he was truthful about important things if pressed.

Adapted from Spitzer et al., 2000, pp. 342–343.

Oppositional and noncompliant behavior is clearly a common problem, particularly during preschool age and again during adolescence (Coie & Dodge, 1998; Loeber et al., 2000). Diagnosis should therefore require high levels of such problems. Although such behavior is prevalent among nonclinic children, it is also one of the most frequently reported problems of children referred to clinics and is more common among clinic-referred children than nonreferred children (Achenbach & Rescorla, 2001; Rey, 1993). Noncompliance represents a practical problem for parents, teachers, and clinicians. Also, noncompliant, stubborn, and oppositional behavior may represent for some youngsters the earliest steps on a developmental path of persistent antisocial behavior (Hinshaw et al., 1993; Loeber et al., 1993). The appropriateness of the ODD diagnosis thus rests, on a balance between "overdiagnosing" common problems of children and adolescents as disorders, versus ignoring potential serious problems that also may be early precursors of persistent antisocial behaviors.

DSM Approach: Conduct Disorder

The diagnosis of Conduct Disorder represents more seriously aggressive and antisocial behaviors. Indeed, the violence and property destruction characteristic of many of these behaviors may considerably impact individuals, families, and communities. Nonaggressive conduct-disordered behaviors (e.g., truancy, theft) also can result in considerable harm.

The essential feature of the diagnosis is a repetitive and persistent pattern of behavior that violates both the basic rights of others and major age-appropriate societal norms. The criteria used to define the disorder are presented in Table 8–2. The diagnosis of Conduct Disorder requires that three or more of these behaviors be present during the past 12 months, with at least one of them present in the past 6 months. Also the behavior must cause clinically meaningful impairment in social or academic functioning. Two subtypes, Childhood-Onset and Adolescent-Onset, are specified on the basis of whether one or more of the criterion behaviors had an onset prior to age 10 years.

The symptoms listed in the DSM criteria for Conduct Disorder include diverse behaviors. Because only three symptoms are required for a diagnosis, the diagnosis of Conduct Disorder may represent a heterogeneous group of youths with different subtypes of conduct disorder. Such heterogeneity may be of particular concern for research investigations.

The following description of Doug illustrates many of the features that characterize children who exhibit persistent aggressive and antisocial behavior and who may receive a conduct disorder diagnosis.

TABLE 8–2   BEHAVIORS USED BY THE DSM IN DIAGNOSING CONDUCT DISORDER

AGGRESSION TOWARD PEOPLE AND ANIMALS
Bullies, threatens, or intimidates
Initiates physical fights
Has used a weapon
Is physically cruel to people
Is physically cruel to animals
Has stolen while confronting a victim
Has forced someone into sexual activity

DESTRUCTION OF PROPERTY
Has deliberately engaged in fire setting with the intention of causing serious damage
Has deliberately destroyed others' property (other than by fire setting)

DECEITFULNESS OR THEFT
Has broken into house, building, or car
Often lies to obtain goods or favors or to avoid obligations
Has stolen items of nontrivial value without confronting a victim

SERIOUS VIOLATIONS OF RULES
Stays out at night despite parental prohibitions, beginning before age 13
Has run away from home overnight at least twice (or once without returning for a lengthy period)
Is often truant from school, beginning before age 13

From American Psychiatric Association, 2000.

Doug   Early Aggressive and Antisocial Behavior

Doug, 8 years old, was brought for treatment because of his unmanageable behavior at home. The specific concern was with Doug's aggressive behavior. When Doug was angry, he would choke and hit his 18-month-old brother and constantly make verbal threats of physical aggression. Recently, Doug's behavior became more out of control, and his mother felt she was unable to cope. Apart from his aggression, Doug had played with matches and set fires over the last 3 years. These episodes included igniting fireworks in the kitchen, setting fires in trash dumpsters, and starting a fire in his bedroom, which the local fire department had to extinguish. At school his behavior had been disruptive over the last few years. His intellectual performance was within the normal range (IQ = 96), but his academic performance was barely passing. His aggressive behavior against peers and disruption of class activities led to his placement in a special class for emotionally disturbed children. Even so, his behavior was not well controlled. The school threatened expulsion if treatment was not initiated.

Doug's father frequently abused alcohol. When drunk, he would beat his wife and children. The parents separated on a number of occasions and eventually were divorced when Doug was 5 years old. After the divorce, the mother and children moved in with the maternal grandfather who also drank excessively and physically abused the children. Less than 2 years ago, the mother had another child by her former husband. With the stress of the new child, the death of her father, and Doug's continuing problems, the mother became depressed and began to drink. Although she was not employed, she spent much of her time away from the home. She would leave the children unsupervised for extended periods, with the phone number of a neighbor for the children to call if any problems arose with the baby.

Adapted from Kazdin, 1985, pp. 3–4.

EMPIRICALLY DERIVED SYNDROMES

An empirically derived syndrome involving aggressive, oppositional, destructive, and antisocial behavior has been identified in a wide variety of studies. This syndrome has been given a variety of names, including externalizing, undercontrolled, or conduct disorder. It is robust in that it emerges employing a variety of measures, reporting agents, and settings. There have been efforts to distinguish narrower groupings within this broad externalizing/conduct disorder syndrome.

Achenbach and Rescorla (2001), for example, have described two syndromes, aggressive behavior (e.g., argues a lot, destroys things, is disobedient, fights) and rule-breaking behavior (e.g., breaks rules, lies, steals, is truant), within the broader externalizing syndrome. The behaviors that are characteristic of these two syndromes are listed in Table 8–3. Children may exhibit only one or both types of problems. The validity of this distinction is supported by a variety of research findings (Achenbach & Rescorla, 2001). For example, research suggests a higher degree of heritability for the aggressive than for the rule-breaking

TABLE 8–3	BEHAVIORS FROM THE AGGRESSIVE AND RULE-BREAKING SYNDROMES	
AGGRESSIVE BEHAVIOR	**RULE-BREAKING BEHAVIOR**	
Argues a lot	Drinks alcohol	
Defiant	Lacks guilt	
Mean to others	Breaks rules	
Demands attention	Bad friends	
Destroys own things	Lies, cheats	
Destroys others' things	Prefers older kids	
Disobedient at home	Runs away	
Disobedient at school	Sets fires	
Gets in fights	Sex problems	
Attacks people	Steals at home	
Screams a lot	Swearing	
Explosive	Thinks of sex too much	
Easily frustrated	Tardy	
Stubborn, sullen	Uses tobacco	
Mood changes	Truant	
Sulks	Uses drugs	
Suspicious	Vandalism	
Teases a lot		
Temper		
Threatens others		
Loud		

Items listed are summaries of the actual content (wording) of items on the instruments. Most items are included in the Child Behavior Checklist (CBCL), Teacher Report Form (TRF), and Youth Self Report (YSR) versions of these syndromes, whereas others are specific to one or two of these instruments.
Adapted from Achenbach & Rescorla, 2001.

syndrome (Edelbrock et al., 1995). Developmental differences also exist between the two syndromes. In a longitudinal analysis, Stanger, Achenbach, and Verhulst (1997) found that the average scores of the two syndromes declined between ages 4 and 10. After age 10, however, the scores on the aggressive syndrome continued to decline, whereas scores on the delinquent syndrome (now called rule-breaking) increased. These findings are illustrated in Figure 8–2. These same authors also found that the stability (the similarity of a particular individual's behavior at two points in time)

was higher for the aggressive than for the delinquent (rule-breaking) syndrome. These and other findings suggest that it is important to distinguish between types of externalizing/conduct disorder problems.

Empirical approaches to classifying conduct disorders also suggest other ways of grouping problem behaviors within this broad category. These approaches are not mutually exclusive and indeed do overlap with the aggressive/rule-breaking distinction and with each other. Some approaches suggest a distinction based on *age of onset* (Hinshaw, Lahey, & Hart,

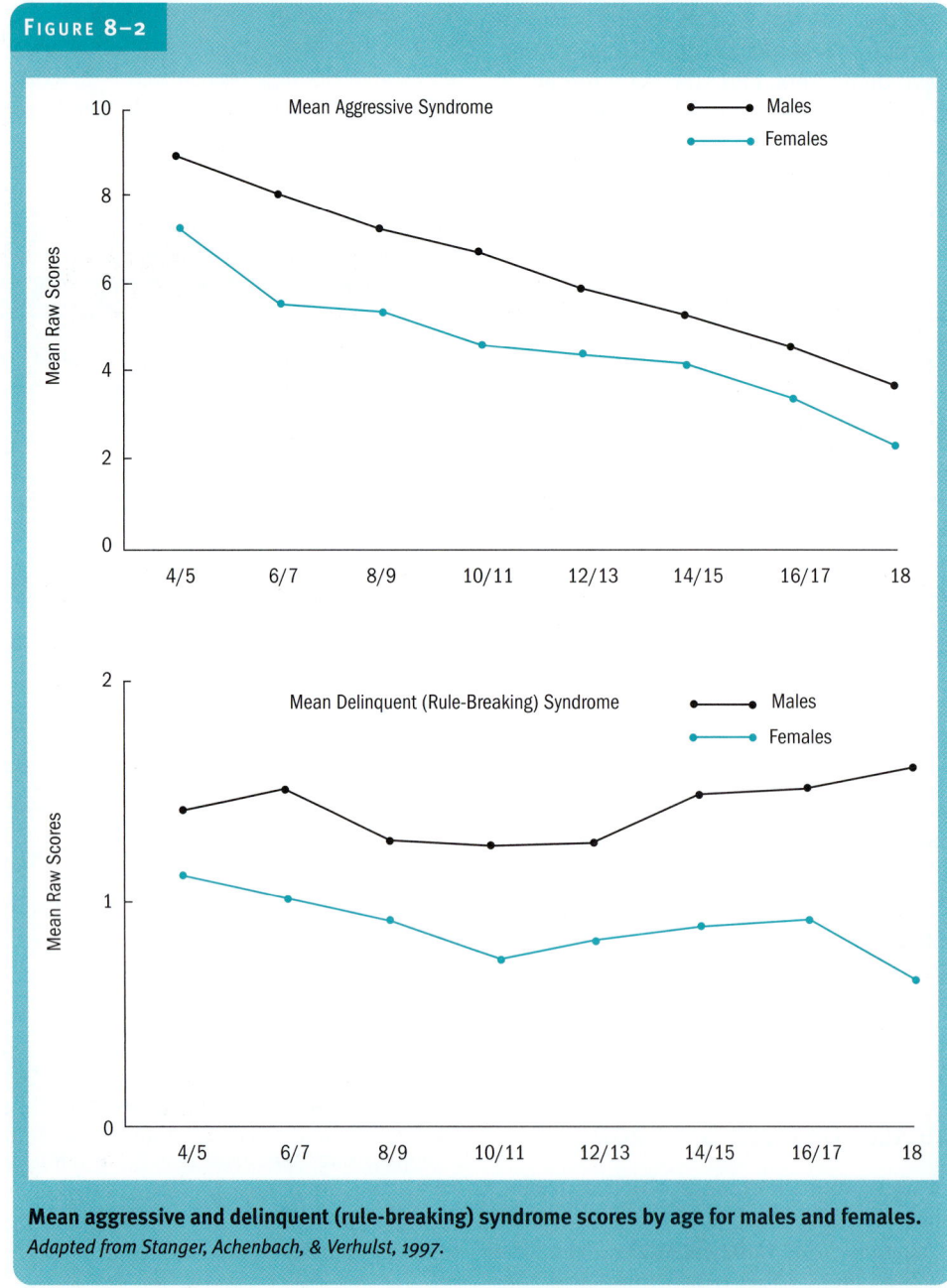

FIGURE 8–2

Mean aggressive and delinquent (rule-breaking) syndrome scores by age for males and females.
Adapted from Stanger, Achenbach, & Verhulst, 1997.

1993): a later-onset or adolescent-onset category consisting principally of nonaggressive and rule-breaking behaviors, and an early-onset category that includes these behaviors as well as aggressive behaviors. The *salient symptom* approach is based on the primary behavior problem being displayed. Distinguishing antisocial children whose primary problem is aggression from those whose primary problem is stealing is an example. It may be particularly important to single out aggressive behavior in this way. There is support for distinguishing aggression from other conduct-disordered behavior on the basis of its social impact, correlates, gender differences, and developmental course (Loeber & Stouthamer-Loeber, 1998).

Expansion of the salient symptom distinction suggests a broader distinction (Dishion & Patterson, 2006; Loeber & Schmaling, 1985) between overt, confrontational antisocial behaviors (e.g., arguing, fighting, temper tantrums), and covert, or concealed, antisocial behaviors (e.g., fire setting, lying, stealing, truancy). A further expansion suggests the grouping of conduct problems by employing two dimensions: the overt–covert distinction and a destructive–nondestructive dimension of behavior (Frick, 1998b). This approach and the clusters of behaviors based on it are illustrated in Figure 8–3. These kinds of dis-

tinctions continue to be explored in the context of an empirical and a developmental approach to understanding conduct problems.

GENDER DIFFERENCES: RELATIONAL AGGRESSION

Gender differences exist in prevalence, developmental course, and factors and processes that contribute to the development of conduct problems (Crick & Zahn-Waxler, 2003; van Lier et al., 2007b). Perhaps the most basic aspect of gender differences is the way that conduct problems are expressed in boys and girls. Much of the research on conduct disorders has been based on male samples. We saw earlier (p. 97) how focusing on one gender can influence estimates of prevalence of a disorder and how a disorder is defined.

It is frequently reported that boys exhibit significantly higher levels of aggression than do girls. Is this because girls are less aggressive? Crick and colleagues (Crick & Grotpeter, 1995; Crick & Zahn-Waxler, 2003) started with a general definition of aggression as intent to hurt or harm others. They noted that during early and middle childhood peer interactions tended to be segregated by gender. This suggested that children's aggression would focus on social issues most salient in

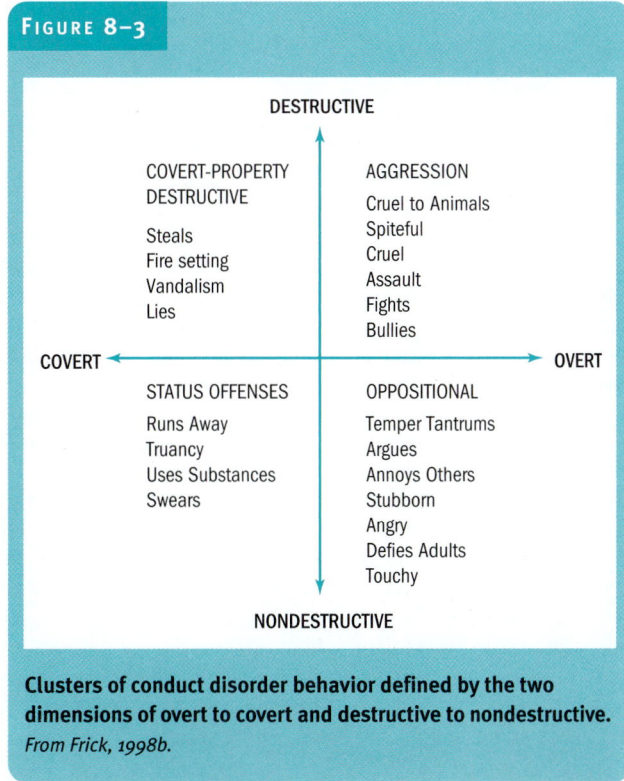

FIGURE 8–3

Clusters of conduct disorder behavior defined by the two dimensions of overt to covert and destructive to nondestructive.
From Frick, 1998b.

same-gender peer groups. In studying externalizing behaviors, aggression has generally been defined in terms of overt physical or verbal behaviors intended to hurt or harm others (e.g., hitting or pushing, threatening to beat up others). It was reasoned that this is consistent with the characteristics of instrumentality and physical dominance typical of boys during childhood. Girls, in contrast, are focused on developing close, dyadic relationships. It was thus hypothesized that girls' attempts to harm others may focus on relational issues—behaviors intended to damage another individual's feelings or friendships. Examples of such relational aggression include the following:

- purposefully leaving a child out of some play or other activity
- getting mad at another person and excluding the person from a peer group
- telling a person you will not like him or her unless he or she does what you say
- saying mean things or lying about someone so that others will not like the person (Crick & Grotpeter, 1996)

Relational aggression may fit within the realm of covert antisocial behavior (Dishion & Patterson, 2006) and is found from preschool age through adolescence (Crick, Casas, & Ku, 1999; Prinstein, Boergers, & Vernberg, 2001). Moreover, relational aggression is associated with peer rejection, depression, anxiety, and feelings of loneliness and isolation (Crick & Grotpeter, 1995; Crick, Casas, & Mosher, 1997; Crick & Nelson, 2002). Interestingly, youngsters who engage in gender nonnormative forms of aggression (i.e., overtly aggressive girls and relationally aggressive boys) exhibit more behavior problems than those who engage in gender normative aggression or are nonaggressive (Crick, 1997).

Thus, it appears important to broadly define aggression. For one thing, a sole focus on physical aggression might fail to identify aggressive girls. Crick and Grotpeter (1995) found that over 80% of aggressive girls (those who were relationally, but not physically, aggressive) would not have been identified by a definition limited to physical aggression. The concept of relational aggression challenges the view that girls are nonaggressive and

ACCENT ● ● ● ● ●

Fire Setting

Fire setting represents a behavior that would be described as covert. Although only a relatively small proportion of youths with conduct problems engage in fire setting, these youngsters are likely to display more severe conduct problems.

Juvenile fire setting accounts for the majority of arrests for arson in the United States (U.S. Bureau of the Census, 2001). It produces serious damage in terms of loss of life, injury, posttraumatic symptoms, and property damage. It is associated with serious difficulties for the youth, family, and community (Barnett & Spitzer, 1994; Kolko, 2005). Fire setters are at increased risk for later juvenile court referral and arrest for a violent crime beyond what would be predicted by the presence of conduct disorder (Becker et al., 2004).

According to Kolko (2005) there are two categories of factors that may be associated with the onset and persistence of a fire-setting problem. The first category is unusual involvement with, interest in, and/or awareness of fire. It includes playing with matches, being attracted to fire, and having limited competence regarding fire. The second domain addresses related

factors that may contribute to the development of conduct-disordered behavior in general. These factors include aspects of the youngster (e.g., aggression, impulsivity), parents (e.g., lack of involvement, poor monitoring of the child), and family (e.g., conflict, stressful life events). In this way, fire setting may be seen as part of a cluster of covert antisocial behaviors that include destruction of property, stealing, lying, and truancy. In fact, among both community and clinically referred youths, level of covert antisocial behavior predicted later fire setting (Kolko et al., 2001).

Fire setters may be exposed to a greater number and a more extreme form of the risk factors that have been described for conduct disorders in general (McCarty et al., 2005). For example, child fire setters were more likely to come from homes with marital violence and to have fathers who drank and abused pets (Becker et al., 2004). Also, Kazdin and Kolko (1986) found poorer marital adjustment and higher levels of psychological difficulties—depression in particular—among mothers of fire setters compared with mothers of non-fire setters.

suggests caution in making non-gender-specific interpretations of findings.

DELINQUENCY

In addition to empirical and DSM approaches to classifying antisocial and conduct-problem behavior, it is important to consider the notion of delinquency. The term *delinquency* is primarily a legal rather than a psychological one. As a legal term, it refers to a juvenile (usually under age 18) who has committed an index crime or a status offense. An index crime is an act that would be illegal for adults as well as for juveniles (e.g., theft, aggravated assault, rape, or murder). A status offense is an act that is illegal only for juveniles (e.g., truancy, association with "immoral" persons, violation of curfews, or incorrigibility). It is important also to make a distinction between delinquent behavior and what might be called official delinquency (delinquency that is noted on an official record).

This distinction is important because some behaviors described as delinquent are quite common. Surveys based on adolescent self-reports show that as many as 80 to 90% of youths report involvement in delinquent activity before reaching the age of 18. In contrast, if one examines official records (e.g., police, courts), a much lower rate of delinquency is suggested—15 to 35% for males and 2 to 14% for females. The estimate of rate varies with the stringency of the definition of "official record" (Moore & Arthur, 1989).

Whether an act by a juvenile gets classified as official delinquency may depend as much on the actions of others as it does on the youth's behavior. The norm violation must, of course, be noticed by someone and must be reported to a law-enforcement official. A police officer then can either arrest the youth or merely issue a warning. If the youth is arrested, he or she may or may not be brought to court. Once in juvenile court, only some individuals receive the legal designation of delinquent; others may be merely warned or released into the custody of their parents. Various definitions of delinquency can be used anywhere in this process.

As discussion so far makes clear, conduct problems encompass diverse behaviors that are viewed as disruptive and harmful to individuals engaging in them as well as to society more generally. Oppositional and conduct disorders slide into, or overlap with, several areas that are currently of particular societal concern.

VIOLENCE

The problem of youth and violence is a major concern (Margolin & Gordis, 2000; Reppucci, Woolard, & Fried, 1999). Violence is typically defined as an extreme form of physical aggression. Violence might be defined as aggressive acts that cause serious harm to others, such as aggravated assault, rape, robbery, and homicide, whereas aggression might be defined as acts that inflict less serious harm (Loeber & Stouthamer-Loeber, 1998). Thus much of what we discuss throughout this chapter regarding aggressive and conduct-problem behavior applies to violence as well. However, additional factors may influence the development of violence, and there may be different needs for the prevention and treatment of violent behavior.

When one speaks about youth violence, there are at least two concerns. First, there is the concern regarding youth as perpetrators of violent acts. Between 1985 and 1998, there was an increase of about 54% in the number of cases of violent offenses handled by juvenile courts. More recently, these rates have dropped appreciably to a level at or below what they were the 1980s. However, an appreciable number of youths are involved in violent behavior. For example, approximately 8% of murders in the United States involved a juvenile offender. Also, by age seventeen, 16% of youth report having carried a handgun and 27% reported having committed assault with the intent to seriously hurt the victim (Snyder & Sickmund, 2006).

The second concern is that young people are the most frequent victims of violence by their peers. Young people exposed to violence also are at significant risk. Part of this exposure is contact with violent peers, but youth also are exposed to violence by adults and in a number of other ways, including watching television, seeing movies, and playing video games. If one also includes in this number youths who are physically abused, who witness domestic violence, and who reside in neighborhoods with high rates of violence, the picture is even more troubling.

Young people exposed to violence, either as victims or as witnesses, are at increased risk for developing aggressive, antisocial, and other externalizing problems. But they are also at risk for developing internalizing difficulties such as anxiety, depression, and somatic symptoms (Gordis, Margolin, & John, 2001; Schwab-Stone et al., 1999). In addition, youths chronically exposed to violence may suffer abnormal neurological development and dysregulation in the biological systems that are involved in arousal and managing stress (Gordis et al., 2006). These changes can have far-reaching psychological and physical consequences (Margolin & Gordis, 2000).

There has been an increase in research related to violence and youth and a variety of governmental and professional efforts have been directed at this problem (Acosta et al., 2001; Weist & Cooley-Quille, 2001). For example, the American Psychological Association formed a special Task Force on Violence and Youth, and several organizations have taken initiatives to promote professional training in this area, to develop and disseminate position statements, and to advocate for relevant legislation.

Schools are one arena given considerable attention. Concern exists about students bringing dangerous weapons to school and about the high rate of violence in schools (Snyder & Sickmund, 2006). In the wake of several highly publicized incidents, schools and communities felt pressure to reduce the risk of violence and to protect their schoolchildren. Changes in school procedures were implemented to increase security, educational efforts were initiated to increase student awareness and to emphasize nonviolent social problem-solving strategies, and pressure

Bullying among boys is often characterized by physical aggression and intimidation.
(Michael Newman/PhotoEdit Inc.)

was exerted to provide additional services to students at risk for committing violent acts.

Although the intense media attention on dramatic school incidents increased community awareness and efforts, it probably also contributed to other actions that may be somewhat more controversial. These include the installation of metal detectors in schools, instructions by some school administrators for students to report any strange behavior by their peers, and a variety of similar policies. Although there is reason for concern about school violence, it is unclear whether there has been a drastic increase in rates of violence in schools, and some of the actions that have been taken have had negative effects on young people. It also has been noted that only a small percentage of youth violence takes place on school grounds and that the rate of violent crimes committed by youth remains low during the school day but spikes at the close of the school day (Snyder & Sickmund, 2006). School violence should therefore probably be considered and addressed with an appreciation of violence in the larger community and society. Also, programs to reduce violence in schools should do so in a manner that creates a school atmosphere that facilitates the overall development of young people while ensuring their safety.

BULLYING

Many people are familiar with the problem of bullying either through personal experience or through literature, television, or movies. Interest in this topic was generated by the work of Olweus (1993; 1994) in Scandinavia and by media attention following incidents of school violence in which bullying was implicated.

Estimates of the incidence of bullying depend on definitions employed, which probably need to consider developmental and cultural variations (Smith et al., 2002). Bullying is characterized by an imbalance of power and involves actions intended to cause fear, distress, or harm. Bullying begins to emerge in the preschool years and is common among elementary school children (Hay, Payne, & Chadwick, 2004; Schwartz et al., 1997). Data from a sample of over 15,000 youths throughout the United States suggest the scope of the problem during middle school and beyond (Nansel et al., 2001). Students in grades 6 through 10 reported involvement in bullying. About 30% reported moderate or frequent involvement (about 13% as a bully, 11% as a victim, and 6% as both). Reports of increasing use of the Internet to bully, intimidate, and embarrass

"What'll it be, Tyler—your lunch money or heaps of verbal abuse?"

victims suggest that these figures may underestimate the prevalence of bullying (David-Ferdon & Hertz, 2007).

Males were more likely than females to be involved as both perpetrators and victims, and the frequency of bullying was higher for 6th graders through 8th graders than among students in the 9th and 10th grades. Similar percentages are reported in various countries and, in general, the percentage of youngsters who report being bullied decreases with age (Kumpulainen, Räsänen, & Henttonen, 1999; Wolke et al., 2000).

Boys are exposed to more direct open attacks than are girls. Indirect bullying can occur in the form of spreading of rumors, manipulation of friendship relationships, and social isolation. This form of bullying may be harder to detect. Girls are exposed more to this subtle form of bullying than to open attacks. Boys, however, may be exposed to this indirect bullying at rates comparable to that of girls.

The typical bully is described by Olweus (1994) as being highly aggressive to both peers and adults; having a more positive attitude toward violence than students in general; being impulsive; having a strong need to dominate others; having little empathy toward victims; and, if a boy, being physically stronger than average. Not all highly aggressive youths are bullies. Differences between bullies and

other aggressive young people and the processes that underlie bullying remain to be clarified (Hay et al., 2004).

The typical victim is more anxious and insecure than other students, and is cautious, sensitive, quiet, nonaggressive, and suffering from low self-esteem. If victims are boys, they are likely to be physically weaker. This so-called submissive, nonassertive style often seems to precede being selected as a victim (Schwartz, Dodge, & Coie, 1993). Also, victims generally do not have a single good friend in their class. The protective importance of having a friend, especially a popular one, was illustrated in an interview with Eric Crouch, the 2001 Heisman Trophy winner as the outstanding college football player:

> *It was a source of pride to his mother . . . that as a popular grade school kid, Eric often befriended students whom others teased. "I talk to them, become friends with them," he would tell his mother, "and they didn't get teased anymore." (Murphy, 2001, p. 64)*

In addition to warding off victimization, support from a close friend may buffer the effects of victimization (Prinstein et al., 2001).

It is clearly important to address the bully–victim problem. Bullying may be part of a more general antisocial, conduct-disordered developmental pattern, and thus bullies are at risk for continuing behavior problems. Indeed, Olweus (1994) reports that 60 percent of boys classified as bullies in grades six through nine were convicted of at least one officially registered crime by age 24 and that 35 to 40 percent of former bullies had three or more convictions by this age, compared with only 10 percent of control boys.

The consequences for the victims of bullying also suggest the importance of intervening early. Victims experience a variety of negative outcomes, particularly depression and loneliness (Hawker & Boulton, 2000). The victims of bullying form a large group of youths whom, to a great extent, many schools may ignore, and whose parents may be relatively unaware of the problem. One can imagine the effects of going through years of school in a state of fear, anxiety, and insecurity. Some of these young people have such low self-esteem and their hope for change is so low, that they view suicide as the only possible option (Olweus, 1994). A case described by Olweus illustrates the pain that youngsters may suffer.

Henry | **A Victim of Bullying**

Henry was a quiet and sensitive 13-year-old. For several years he had been harassed and attacked occasionally by some of his classmates. . . . During the past couple of months, the attacks had become more frequent and severe.

Henry's daily life was filled with unpleasant and humiliating events. His books were pushed from his desk, his tormentors broke his pencils and threw things at him, they laughed loudly and scornfully when he occasionally responded to the teacher's questions. Even in class, he was often called by his nickname, the "Worm."

As a rule, Henry did not respond; he just sat there expressionless at his desk, passively waiting for the next attack. The teacher usually looked in another direction when the harassment went on. Several of Henry's classmates felt sorry for him but none of them made a serious attempt to defend him.

A month earlier, Henry had been coerced, with his clothes on, into a shower. His two tormentors had also threatened him several times to give them money and steal cigarettes for them. One afternoon, after having been forced to lie down in the drain of the school urinal, Henry quietly went home, found a box of sleeping pills and swallowed a handful. Henry's parents found him unconscious but alive on the sofa in the living room. A note on his desk told them that he couldn't stand the bullying any more, he felt completely worthless, and believed the world would be a better place without him.

Adapted from Olweus, 1993, pp. 49–50.

Epidemiology

Conduct problems are one of the most frequently occurring child and adolescent difficulties. Exact prevalence is difficult to establish, due to a number of methodological and definitional factors (Essau, 2003; Loeber et al., 2000). One important consideration is that diagnostic criteria for ODD and CD have changed considerably, and rates vary according to which criteria are employed. Studies of prevalence in community samples report rates between 1 and 16% for both ODD and CD (Breton et al., 1999; Costello, Egger, & Angold, 2005; Loeber et al., 2000). Median estimates are about 3% for both ODD and CD. Many estimates are based on earlier definitions. Investigations employing DSM-IV criteria report rates for ODD between about 2.3 and 5.5%, and rates for CD between about 1.5 and 2.2% in Puerto Rico, Brazil, and Great Britain (Canino et al., 2004; Fleitlich-Bilyk & Goodman, 2004; Ford et al., 2003). A retrospective report of a large nationally representative sample of U.S. adults suggests a lifetime prevalence of ODD during childhood and adolescence of 10.2% (Nock et al., 2007).

GENDER, AGE, AND CONTEXT

Conduct disorders are more commonly diagnosed in boys than in girls; a ratio of about 3:1 or 4:1 is typically cited. The DSM definition of conduct disorder, however, may emphasize "male" expressions of aggression. Thus conduct disorder may be underestimated in girls. Higher rates of ODD are also reported in boys. However, the degree of gender difference for ODD remains unclear and the applicability of the DSM criteria to girls has been questioned (Loeber et al., 2000; Maughan et al., 2004; Waschbusch & King, 2006). Gender and age differences in the prevalence of ODD and CD, based on a nationally representative sample in Great Britain (Maughan et al., 2004), are illustrated in Figure 8–4.

An increasing prevalence of conduct disorder with age is often reported for both boys and girls and there is some suggestion that, due to particular risk for

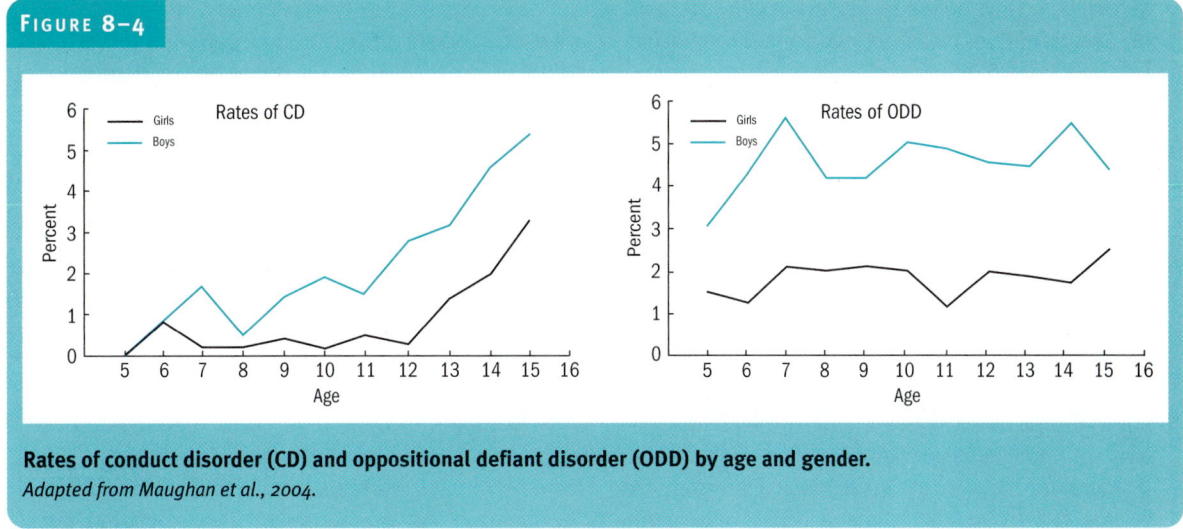

FIGURE 8-4

Rates of conduct disorder (CD) and oppositional defiant disorder (ODD) by age and gender.
Adapted from Maughan et al., 2004.

girls in the period around puberty, the gender ratio narrows temporarily in the mid-teens (Maughan et al., 2004; Moffitt et al., 2001). Some reports suggest a decline in oppositional defiant disorder with age, but findings are inconsistent (Maughan et al., 2004).

Ethnic and socioeconomic differences are often reported. However, Roberts and colleagues (2006) examined the presence of a disruptive disorder or ADHD in African American, European American, and Mexican American youth, ages 11 to 17 years, and found no differences in prevalence for the combined problem category. Contextual factors such as poverty and the stress of high-crime neighborhoods are thought to increase the risk for conduct-disordered behavior. Greater prevalence is reported in urban than in rural environments (Canino et al., 2004; Fleitlich-Bilyk & Goodman, 2004). Also, official records often indicate greater delinquency among lower class and minority youths and in neighborhoods characterized by high crime rates. Such differences may be due to selection of certain groups for prosecution, suggesting that definitions other than official records should be considered. However, estimates based on alternative methods, such as self-report, present other methodological difficulties. Although further documentation is needed, real associations between conduct-disordered behavior/delinquency and social class and neighborhoods probably do exist; however, they are probably more moderate than was once contended. The influence of these variables on child and adolescent conduct problem behavior is probably mediated by their impact on factors such as the ability of adults to parent effectively (Capaldi et al., 2002).

PATTERNS OF CO-OCCURRENCE

Children and adolescents who receive one of the disruptive disorder diagnoses also frequently experience other difficulties and receive other diagnoses (American Academy of Child and Adolescent Psychiatry, 2007b). In considering the issue of the overlap between the ODD and CD diagnoses, the DSM-IV acknowledges that oppositional defiant behavior is a common precursor of the childhood-onset type of Conduct Disorder and stipulates that a child or adolescent cannot receive both diagnoses (American Psychiatric Association, 2000). If the criteria for both Conduct Disorder and Oppositional Defiant Disorder are met, only the Conduct Disorder diagnosis is given.

Most youths who receive the diagnosis of CD do meet the criteria for ODD. In the Developmental Trends Study of clinic-referred boys 7 to 12 years old, 96% of those who met criteria for CD also met criteria for ODD. The reported average age of onset was about 6 years for ODD and about 9 years for CD, suggesting that among boys with conduct disorder, this disorder is preceded by behaviors characteristic of oppositional defiant disorder and that these behaviors are "retained" as additional antisocial behaviors emerge. On the other hand, ODD does not always result in CD. Of the boys with ODD (but no CD) at the initial assessment, 75% had not progressed to CD 2 years later. About half of the boys with ODD at Year 1 continued to meet the criteria for ODD at Year 3, and about one quarter no longer met the criteria for ODD. Thus, although most cases of conduct disorder meet the criteria for oppositional defiant disorder, most youngsters with oppositional defiant behaviors do not progress to a conduct disorder (American Psychiatric Association, 2000; Hinshaw, Lahey, & Hart, 1993).

There is also considerable co-occurrence of oppositional defiant disorder and conduct disorder with attention-deficit hyperactivity disorder (Waschbusch, 2002). Among children diagnosed with ADHD, it is estimated that between 35 and 70% develop ODD, and between 30 and 50% develop CD (Johnston & Ohan, 1999). When these disorders co-occur, ADHD seems to precede the development of the other disorders. It might be speculated that the impulsivity, inattention, and overactivity of ADHD present a particular parenting challenge. When parents' skills are limited, a pattern of noncompliant and aversive parent–child interactions may be set in motion (Patterson, DeGarmo, & Knutson, 2000). The challenges of parenting an ADHD child may thus play a role in the early onset of ODD behaviors and may continue over the course of development to maintain and exacerbate ODD/CD behaviors. Parent–child relationships are only one of the potential mechanisms whereby the presence of ADHD may increase the risk for ODD/CD. However, findings from a twin study suggest that although ADHD, ODD, and CD are each influenced by genetic and environmental factors, the covariation of the three disorders seems to be primarily influenced by shared environmental factors (Burt et al., 2001). Such a finding is consistent with the potential contribution of parenting. Whatever factors contribute to the co-occurrence of these disorders, ADHD appears to be one possible path toward more persistent and more severe conduct disorders (Fergusson & Horwood, 1998; Hinshaw & Lee, 2003; Loeber et al., 2000).

In addition, youths with disruptive behavior disorders commonly experience a variety of other difficulties. The co-occurrence with substance use was mentioned earlier. In addition, young aggressive children are frequently rejected by their peers (Newcomb, Bukowsi, & Pattee, 1993). Youths with persistent conduct problems are also frequently described as having certain neurocognitive impairments and lower school achievement (Caspi & Moffitt, 1995; Maguin & Loeber, 1996; Moffitt et al., 2001). Verbal and language deficits, in particular, have been reported among community and clinical samples, as well as deficits in executive functions (higher order cognitive functions that play a role in information processing and problem solving) (Gilmour et al., 2004; Moffitt et al., 2001). How such difficulties and conduct disorders relate to each other is a complex issue. In what ways do cognitive and language difficulties contribute to the development of conduct disorders? What is the relationship among these deficits, conduct disorder, and poor academic performance? To what extent are some of these deficiencies related to ADHD—are they characteristic of only the subset of youths with conduct disorder who also have ADHD? These and other questions remain unresolved.

Internalizing disorders also occur at higher than expected rates among youths with disruptive disorders, particularly conduct disorder (Loeber & Keenan, 1994; Loeber et al., 2000). Indeed, there is some suggestion that early co-occurrence of conduct and internalizing problems is associated with particularly high risk for negative long-term outcomes (Sourander et al., 2007).

Estimates of the rate of co-occurrence of conduct problems and anxiety disorders vary widely from 19 to 53% (Nottelmann & Jensen, 1995). Also, the literature on the nature of the association between anxiety and conduct problems is unclear and often contradictory (Hinshaw & Lee, 2003; Rutter, Giller, & Hagell, 1998). A central question is whether anxiety increases or decreases the risk for conduct disordered behavior. Gender and age differences may affect the risk (Hinshaw, Lahey, & Hart, 1993). In any event, the co-occurrence of anxiety and conduct problems is likely to be due to multiple influences (Gregory, Eley, & Plomin, 2004).

The co-occurrence of depression and conduct disorder is also clearly appreciable and in community samples has been estimated at 12 to 25% (Angold, Costello, & Erkanli, 1999; Loeber & Keenan, 1994; Nottelmann & Jensen, 1995). Among a community sample of older adolescents, Lewinsohn, Rohde, and Seeley (1995) found that a major depressive disorder co-occurred in 38% of youngsters with a disruptive behavior disorder (CD, ODD, or ADHD). In clinical samples, approximately 33% of children and adolescents have a co-occurrence of conduct and depressive disorders (Dishion, French, & Patterson, 1995). In both community and clinic populations, boys show greater co-occurrence than girls (Dishion et al., 1995; Lewinsohn et al., 1995b). Numerous factors may help account for the frequent co-occurrence of conduct problems and depression. The developmental sequence of the two disorders needs further clarification and may differ for boys and girls (Loeber et al., 2000; Wiesner, 2003). It may be that one disorder creates a risk for the other. For example, frequent failures and conflict experiences may contribute to depression in youngsters with conduct problems, or depression may be expressed as irritable, angry, antisocial behavior. Alternatively, the disorders may co-occur because of shared etiology including genetic and environmental influences.

Developmental Course

STABILITY OF CONDUCT PROBLEMS

An important aspect of conduct problems is their reported stability over time (Loeber et al., 2000; Raine et al., 2005; Stanger et al., 1996; Tolan & Thomas, 1995; Tremblay et al., 2004). Considerable evidence exists that the presence of early conduct-disordered behavior is related to the development of later aggressive and antisocial behavior and to a range of adverse psychological and social-emotional outcomes (Brame, Nagin, & Tremblay, 2001; Caspi, Elder, & Bem, 1987; Hafner, Quast, & Shea, 1975; Loeber & Farrington, 2000; Robins et al., 1971).

However, the question of the stability or continuity of antisocial/conduct-disordered behavior is a complex one (Loeber & Stouthamer-Loeber, 1998; Maughan & Rutter, 1998). It appears that some but not all youngsters continue to exhibit aggressive and antisocial behavior (NICHD Early Child Care Research Network, 2004b). Although change can occur at any time, decreases may particularly occur during preschool age and adolescence. The challenges are to describe patterns of both continuity and discontinuity, characterize shifts in the form that antisocial behaviors may take, and identify variables that influence that course of antisocial behavior over time.

AGE OF ONSET

Many studies have found that early age of onset is related to more serious and persistent antisocial behavior (Babinski, Hartsough, & Lambert, 1999; Fergusson & Woodward, 2000; Loeber & Farrington, 2000; Tolan & Thomas, 1995). A number of authors have proposed two distinct developmental patterns leading toward antisocial behavior, one with a childhood onset and the other with a late/adolescent onset (Hinshaw et al., 1993; Moffitt, 1993a, 2006).

Childhood onset. The childhood-onset developmental pattern fits with the notion of the stability of conduct-disordered behavior. Indeed, Moffitt (1993a, 2006) terms this pattern "life-course persistent antisocial behavior." Retrospective studies of antisocial adults are consistent with this picture of stable conduct-disordered behavior. It must be remembered, however, that a substantial number of children with an early onset of antisocial behavior do not persist on this pathway. The early-onset pathway is less common than the adolescent-onset pattern, with estimates of about 3 to 5% in the general population (Hinshaw et al., 1993; Moffitt, 1993a). Youngsters following this

pattern are also more likely from preschool on to exhibit other problems, such as attention-deficit hyperactivity disorder, neurobiological, and neurocognitive deficits, and academic difficulties (Raine et al., 2005; van Goozen et al., 2007). These early difficulties may be the starting point for one developmental pathway characterized by early onset and by persistent disruptive and antisocial behavior during childhood and adolescence. For some this pathway may lead to Antisocial Personality Disorder and other negative outcomes in adulthood (Fergusson, Horwood, & Ridder, 2005; Maughan & Rutter, 1998; Moffitt et al., 2002).

Even though there is stability of problematic behavior for some youngsters with an early onset, antisocial behaviors exhibit qualitative change in the course of development. Hinshaw and colleagues (1993) describe the features of this heterotypic continuity of antisocial behavior:

> *The preschooler who throws temper tantrums and stubbornly refuses to follow adult instructions becomes the child who also initiates fights with other children and lies to the teacher. Later, the same youth begins to vandalize the school, torture animals, break into homes, steal costly items, and abuse alcohol. As a young adult, he or she forces sex on acquaintances, writes bad checks, and has a chaotic employment and marital history. (p. 36)*

Some individuals with a difficult temperament may have an even earlier onset: during infancy. But research to fill in the gap prior to 3 years of age is needed (Frick & Morris, 2004; Moffitt, 2006).

Adolescent onset. An adolescent-onset developmental pattern is illustrated in the Dunedin Multidisciplinary Health and Development Study (McGee et al., 1992). Prospective examination of a birth cohort of New Zealand youths revealed a large increase in the prevalence of nonaggressive conduct problems but no increase in aggressive behavior at age 15 compared with age 11. These young people were clearly exhibiting problem behavior; for example, they were as likely to be arrested for delinquent offenses as were childhood-onset delinquents. However, their offenses were less aggressive than those of childhood-onset delinquents. The majority of females were adolescent-onset cases, while males composed most of the conduct disorder cases at age 11. This rather common emergence during adolescence of nonaggressive antisocial behavior is contrasted to early-onset antisocial behavior.

The adolescent-onset pattern is the more common developmental pathway. Individuals who exhibit this pattern show little oppositional or antisocial behavior during childhood. During adolescence, they begin to engage in illegal activities, and although most exhibit only isolated antisocial acts, some engage in enough antisocial behavior to qualify for a diagnosis of conduct disorder. However, the antisocial behaviors are less likely to persist beyond adolescence and thus are sometimes termed *adolescent-limited* (Moffitt, 1993a, 2006). Some of the youths do continue to have difficulties later in life. Experiences such as incarceration or disruption in education may contribute to more negative outcomes. However, these difficulties may not be as severe as the outcomes for the life-course-persistent individuals (Moffitt et al., 2002). It is important to determine which individuals discontinue and which persist or escalate their antisocial behavior as they enter adulthood, and to identify what accounts for these differences over time (Moffitt, 2006; White, Bates, & Buyske, 2001).

DEVELOPMENTAL PATHS

In addition to groupings of individuals by age of onset, much attention also has been given to the conceptualization of developmental progressions of conduct problems (e.g., Dodge, 2000; Farrington, 1986; Loeber et al., 1993; Patterson, DeBaryshe, & Ramsey, 1989). Loeber (1988) proposed a model that illustrates some of the attributes that might characterize the developmental course of conduct disorders within individuals. The model suggests that at each level, less serious behaviors precede more serious ones but that only some individuals progress to the next step. Progression on a developmental path is characterized by increasing diversification of antisocial behaviors. Children and adolescents who progress show new antisocial

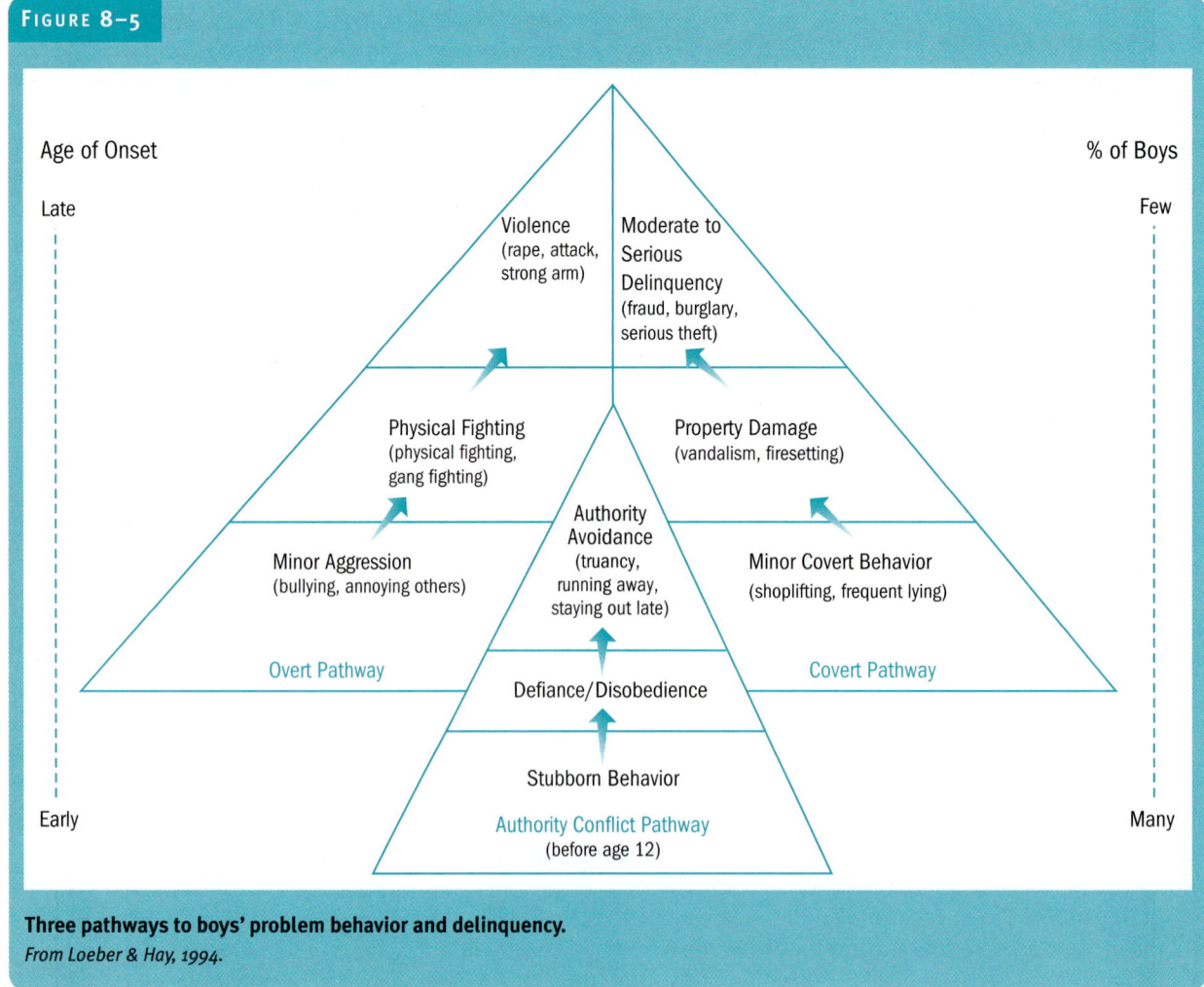

FIGURE 8–5

Three pathways to boys' problem behavior and delinquency.
From Loeber & Hay, 1994.

behaviors and may retain their previous behaviors rather than replacing them. Individuals may differ in their rate of progression.

Loeber's three-pathway model. Loeber and colleagues (1993) suggested a model that conceptualized antisocial behavior along multiple pathways. On the basis of a longitudinal study of inner-city youths, and following from distinctions between conduct problem behaviors described earlier, Loeber proposed a triple-pathway model (see Figure 8–5):

- an overt pathway starting with minor aggression, followed by physical fighting, followed by violence;

- a covert pathway starting with minor covert behaviors, followed by property damage, and then moderate to serious delinquency; and

- an authority conflict pathway prior to age 12, consisting of a sequence of stubborn behavior, defiance, and authority avoidance.

Individuals may progress along one or more of these pathways. As illustrated in Figure 8–5, entry into the authority conflict pathway typically begins earlier than entry into the other two pathways, and not all individuals who exhibit early behaviors on a particular pathway progress through the subsequent stages. The percentage of youngsters exhibiting behaviors characteristic of later stages of a pathway is less than those exhibiting earlier behaviors.

Investigators continue their efforts to describe the developmental pathways of antisocial, conduct-disordered behavior. At the same time, they also seek to identify the influences that first put youngsters on those pathways and that determine whether the antisocial behavior will continue or desist.

Etiology

The development of conduct problems is likely to involve the complex interplay of a variety of influences (Dishion & Patterson, 2006; Hill, 2002; Rutter, 2003). Table 8–4, adapted from Loeber and Farrington (2000), provides a list of categories and examples of empirically validated risk factors for childhood aggression and later delinquency. Although such listings are informative, how the various influences come together in the development of conduct problems is quite complex. In our description we present influences in separate sections, but it is important to remember that causal explanations typically involve transactional influences and multiple variations in the association of influences. Each set of influences may directly and/or indirectly

TABLE 8–4	RISK FACTORS FOR CHILD AGGRESSION AND LATER SERIOUS AND VIOLENT JUVENILE OFFENDING

CHILD FACTORS

Impulsive behavior
Hyperactivity (when co-occurring with disruptive behavior)
Early aggression
Early-onset disruptive behavior

FAMILY FACTORS

Parental antisocial behavior
Parents' poor child-rearing practices
Parental neglect and abuse
Maternal depression
Low socioeconomic status

SCHOOL FACTORS

Association with deviant siblings and peers
Rejection by peers

NEIGHBORHOOD AND SOCIETAL FACTORS

Neighborhood disadvantage and poverty
Disorganized neighborhood
Availability of weapons
Media portrayal of violence

Adapted from Loeber & Farrington, 2000.

affect the development of antisocial behavior. While our emphasis will be on intrapersonal and relationship influences, the larger contexts in which these occur should not be ignored (Dishion & Patterson, 2006).

THE SOCIOECONOMIC CONTEXT

Multiple findings suggest the importance of the larger social context. For example, the impact of poverty on oppositional and conduct problems has been demonstrated among several ethnic groups (Costello et al., 2003; Macmillan, McMorris, & Kruttschnitt, 2004) (see Accent: Moving Out of Poverty). Other influences that are associated with poverty, such as neighborhood context, also have received attention. Ingoldsby & Shaw (2002) examine the risk associated with residing in a disadvantaged community. Such neighborhoods are defined by a lack of economic and other resources, social disorganization, and racial division and tension. These factors are likely to increase the risk of exposure to neighborhood violence and involvement with neighborhood-based deviant peer groups, and thus lead to increased risk for early-onset antisocial behavior. Perceived discrimination has also

ACCENT ● ● ● ● ●

Moving Out of Poverty

Costello and colleagues (2003) report on what might be described as a natural experiment (see pg. 78) that addresses the impact of poverty on conduct problems. The Great Smoky Mountains Study investigated the development of mental disorder and the need for mental health services for youth in North Carolina. Over several years data were collected from a sample of children, 25% of whom were American Indian. In the middle of the 8-year study, a casino opened on the Indian reservation that equally raised the income of all the American Indian families. This allowed a comparison of children whose families moved out of poverty, remained poor, or were never poor. Youngsters whose families moved out of poverty showed a

significant decrease in symptoms, whereas no change occurred for the other children. The ex-poor children now exhibited nearly the same low rate of disorder as the never-poor, which was lower than that of the persistently poor. The effect was quite specific to oppositional and conduct problems rather than anxiety and depression. Further analysis suggested that the lessening of problems could be attributed to the family's having increased time to adequately supervise their offspring. An important aspect of this study is that the move out of poverty was not caused by characteristics of the families or the child—and so the findings could more clearly be attributed to the move from poverty itself.

been found to amplify the effect of ecological risks for African American youth (Brody et al., 2006). Socioeconomic and other disadvantages likely reflect a process in which adverse individual, family, school, and peer factors combine to increase a young person's chance of developing conduct problems (Chung & Steinberg, 2006; Fergusson, Swain-Campbell, & Horwood, 2004). It is also likely that positive family, peer and school influences can moderate the effects of disadvantage (Brody et al., 2006).

AGGRESSION AS A LEARNED BEHAVIOR

Aggression is a central part of the definition of conduct-disordered behavior and a common difficulty among nonreferred children. Children clearly may learn to be aggressive by being rewarded for such behavior (Patterson, 1976). Also, children may learn through imitation of aggressive models. They vicariously learn new and novel aggressive responses. Exposure to aggressive models also makes aggressive responses already in the child's repertoire more likely to occur—that is, disinhibition of aggression may occur. In addition, young people may acquire general "scripts" for aggressive/hostile interpersonal behavior.

Children and adolescents certainly have ample opportunity to observe aggressive models. Parents who engage in physical aggression toward their spouses or who physically punish their children serve as models for aggressive behavior. In fact, children

exhibiting excessive aggressive or antisocial behaviors are likely to have siblings, parents, and even grandparents with histories of conduct problems and records of aggressive and criminal behavior (Farrington, 1995; Huesmann et al., 1984; Waschbusch, 2002) and to have observed especially high rates of aggressive behavior in their homes (Kashani et al., 1992; Margolin, 1998; Patterson, DeBaryshe, & Ramsey, 1989). Aggression is also ubiquitous in television programs and in other media (Anderson et al., 2003; Bushman & Anderson, 2001).

FAMILY INFLUENCES

The family environment can play an important role in the development of conduct-disordered behaviors. As indicated before, a high incidence of deviant or criminal behavior has been reported in families of youths with conduct problems. Longitudinal studies, in fact, suggest that such behavior is stable across generations (D'Onofrio et al., 2007; Glueck & Glueck, 1968; Huesmann et al., 1984). It seems, then, that conduct-disordered children may be part of a deviant family system. Numerous family variables have been implicated, including low family socioeconomic status, large family size, marital disruption, poor-quality parenting, parental abuse and neglect, and parental psychopathology (Dishion & Patterson, 2006; Patterson, Reid, & Dishion, 1992; Waschbusch, 2002). We highlight a few of these influences.

A child may engage in aversive behaviors in order to get something that he or she wants. If the parent repeatedly gives in, this capitulation may contribute to coercive patterns of interaction in the family.
(Dennis MacDonald/PhotoEdit Inc.)

Parent–child interactions and noncompliance.

The manner in which parents interact with their children contributes to the genesis of conduct-disordered behavior. Defiant, stubborn, and noncompliant behaviors are often among the first problems to develop in children. Given that these occur in both clinic and nonclinic families, what factors might account for the greater rates in some families? One possible factor is suggested by evidence that parents differ in both the number and the types of commands that they give. Parents of clinic-referred children issue more commands, questions, and criticisms. Also, prohibitions and commands that are presented in an unclear, angry, humiliating, or nagging manner are less likely to result in child compliance (Dumas & Lechowicz, 1989; Forehand et al., 1975; Kuczynski & Kochanska, 1995). Consequences that parents deliver also affect the child's noncompliant behavior (Brinkmeyer & Eyberg, 2003; Forehand & McMahon, 1981). A combination of negative consequences (time-out) for noncompliant behavior and rewards and attention for appropriate behavior seems to be related to increased levels of compliance.

The work of Patterson and his colleagues.

Gerald Patterson and his colleagues have created the Oregon Model—a developmental intervention model for families with aggressive antisocial children—based on a social learning perspective (Patterson et al., 1975; Patterson et al., 1992; Reid, Patterson, & Snyder, 2002). Although this approach recognizes that characteristics of the child may play a role, the emphasis is on the social context.

> *If we are to change aggressive childhood behavior, we must change the environment in which the child lives. If we are to understand and predict future aggression, our primary measures will be of the social environment that is teaching and maintaining these deviant behaviors. The problem lies in the social environment. If you wish to change the child, you must systematically alter the environment in which he or she lives. (Patterson, Reid, & Eddy, 2002, p. 21)*

Patterson developed what he refers to as coercion theory to explain how a problematic pattern of behavior develops. Observations of referred families suggested that acts of physical aggression were not isolated behaviors. On the contrary, such acts tended to occur along with a wide range of noxious behaviors that were used to control family members in a process labeled as coercion. How and why does this process of coercion develop?

One factor is parents who lack adequate family management skills. According to Patterson (1976; Patterson et al., 1992), parental deficits in child management lead to increasingly coercive interactions within the family. Central to this process are the notions of negative reinforcement and the reinforcement trap. Here is an example:

- A mother gives in to her child's tantrums in the supermarket and buys him a candy bar.
- The short-term consequence is that things are more pleasant for both parties:
  - The child has used an aversive event (tantrum) to achieve the desired goal (candy bar).
  - The mother's giving in has terminated an aversive event (tantrum and embarrassment) for her.
- Parents pay for short-term gains, however, with long-term consequences:
  - Although the mother received some immediate relief, she has increased the probability that her child will employ tantrums in the future.
  - The mother has also received negative reinforcement that increases the likelihood that she will give in to future tantrums.

In addition to this negative reinforcement trap, coercive behavior may also be increased by direct positive reinforcement. Aggressive behavior, especially in boys, may meet with social approval.

The concept of reciprocity adds to our understanding of how aggression and coercion may be learned and sustained. Children as young as nursery school age can learn in a short time that attacking another person in response to some intrusion can terminate that intrusion. In addition, the victim of the attack may learn from the experience and may become more likely to initiate attacks in the future. But the eventual victim of escalating coercion also provides a negative reinforcer by giving in, thereby increasing the likelihood that the "winner" will start future coercions at higher levels of intensity and thus will get the victim to give in more quickly.

This process is exacerbated by the ineffectiveness of punishment. In families with problems, punishment does not suppress coercive behavior but may serve to increase it. The ineffectiveness of punishment may be due to the strong reinforcement history for coercive behavior and to inconsistent use of punishment in these families (Patterson, 1982).

The description of a coercive process and ineffective parenting has served as the basis for Patterson's intervention project and for his evolving developmental model (Patterson et al., 1992; Patterson et al., 2002). In addition to describing the "training" of antisocial behavior in the home, the Oregon Model describes a relationship between antisocial behavior in boys and poor peer relationships and other adverse outcomes (Dishion & Patterson, 2006; Snyder, 2002). It is suggested that ineffective parenting produces the coercive, noncompliant core of antisocial behavior, which in turn leads to these other disruptions. Furthermore, it is hypothesized that each of these outcomes serves as a precursor to subsequent drift into deviant peer groups.

The perspective of Patterson and his coworkers has expanded to include a wide array of variables that affect the family process and many problems known to be associated with antisocial behavior (Dishion & Patterson, 2006). At the core of this complex theoretical model is the parent training model (Figure 8–6) that has proven to be so robust that Patterson and his colleagues call it basic black; "it is simple, elegant and seems appropriate for more than one setting" (Patterson et al., 1992, p. 62).

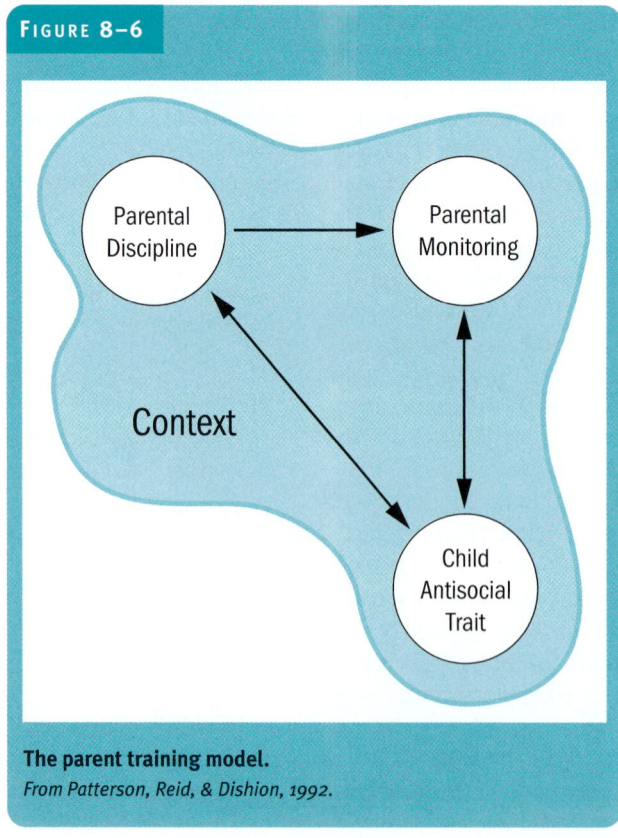

FIGURE 8–6

The parent training model.
From Patterson, Reid, & Dishion, 1992.

Parental discipline and parental monitoring both contribute to, and are influenced by, the child's antisocial behavior. Parental discipline is defined by an interrelated set of skills: accurately tracking and classifying problem behaviors, ignoring trivial coercive events, and using effective consequences when necessary to back up demands and requests. Compared with other parents, parents of problem children have been found to be overinclusive in the behaviors that they classify as deviant. Thus these parents differ in how they track and classify problem behavior. These parents also "natter" (nag, scold irritably) in response to low levels of coercive behavior or to behavior that other parents see as neutral and are able to ignore. Parents of antisocial children fail to back up their commands when the child does not comply, and they also fail to reward compliance when it does occur.

Parental monitoring of child behavior is also important to prevent the development and persistence over time of antisocial behavior. The amount of time a child spends unsupervised by parents increases with age. The amount of unsupervised time also is positively correlated with antisocial behavior. Patterson described treatment families as having little information about their children's whereabouts, whom the children were with, what they were doing, or when they would be home. This situation probably arises from a variety of considerations, including the repeated failures that these parents experienced

in controlling their children even when difficulties occurred right in front of them. Also, requesting information would likely lead to a series of confrontations that the parents preferred to avoid. These parents did not expect to receive positive responses to their involvement either from their own children or from social agencies such as schools (Patterson et al., 1992).

Extrafamilial influences and parental psychopathology. The question of why some families and not others exhibit inept management practices has received some attention. Patterson (Patterson et al., 1992) posits that any number of variables may account for changes over time in family management skills. The handing down of faulty parenting practices from one generation to the next, in part, explains the problematic parenting characteristics of antisocial families. Also, Patterson's own findings and those of other investigators support the relationship between extrafamilial stressors (e.g., daily hassles, negative life events, financial problems, family health problems) and parenting practices (Capaldi et al., 2002; Dishion & Patterson, 2006; Wahler & Dumas, 1989). Social disadvantage and living in neighborhoods that require a very high level of parenting skills also place some families at risk. Finally, various forms of parental psychopathology are associated with poor parenting practices. Parents who themselves have antisocial

Marital discord and aggression between parents can contribute to the development of conduct-disordered behavior in children.
(Johathan Nourak/PhotoEdit Inc.)

difficulties may be particularly likely to have parenting practices (e.g., inconsistent discipline, low parental involvement) associated with the development of conduct-disordered behavior (Capaldi et al., 2002). Also, heavy drinking by parents may lower their threshold for reacting adversely to their child's behavior and also may be associated with inept monitoring of the child and less parental involvement (El-Sheikh & Flanagan, 2001; Lahey et al., 1999; West & Prinz, 1987). Figure 8–7 illustrates a model of how a variety of influences may disrupt effective parenting and lead to child antisocial behavior.

Marital discord. Parental conflict and divorce are common in homes of children and adolescents with conduct problems (Cummings, Davies, & Campbell, 2000; O'Leary & Emery, 1985). The conflict leading to and surrounding the divorce are principal influences in this relationship, and divorces characterized by less conflict and greater cooperation are associated with fewer problems in children (Amato & Keith, 1991; Hetherington, Bridges, & Insabella, 1998). If aggression between the parents is also present, childhood disorder seems even more likely than would be expected on the basis of marital discord alone (Cummings, Goeke-Morey, & Papp, 2004; Jaffee, Poisson, & Cunningham, 2001; Jouriles, Murphy, & O'Leary, 1989). The relationship between marital

conflict and conduct disorders can be explained in a number of ways. Parents who engage in a great deal of marital conflict or aggression may serve as models for their children. The stress of marital discord may also interfere with parenting practices and the ability to monitor the child's behavior. Hostility and anger may also affect the child's emotion regulation development and thereby contribute to conduct problems. The relationship between discord and conduct problems may also operate in the opposite causal direction; that is, the child's disruptive behavior may contribute to marital discord.

Also, both child conduct problems and marital discord may be related to a "third variable," such as parental antisocial disorder (Lahey et al., 1988). Indeed, there are high rates of antisocial personality disorder (APD) among parents of conduct-disordered youths, and APD is associated with high rates of marital instability (Frick, 1994).

The relationship between marital conflict and child adjustment is likely to be complex and change over time. It is important to remember that these problems exist in a larger context (Davies & Cummings, 2006). It may be that a high level of environmental risk (related to family and community/neighborhood factors such as socioeconomic difficulties and high-crime neighborhoods) directly affects the youth and is also experienced by the parents, contributing to both marital and parenting difficulties (Herrenkohl et al., 2001;

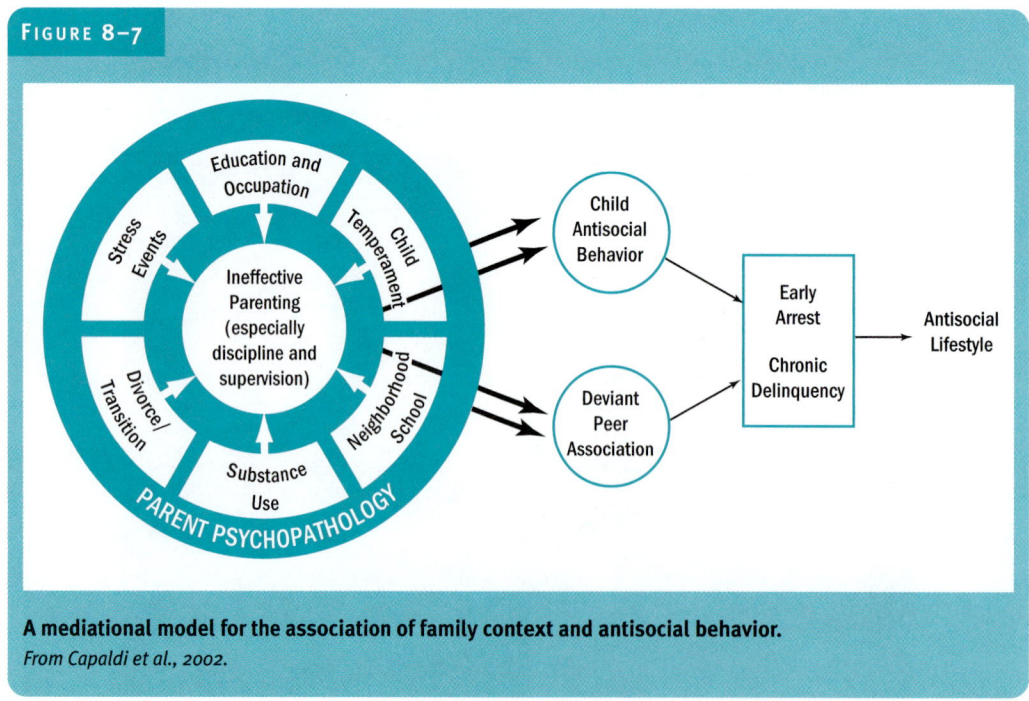

FIGURE 8–7

A mediational model for the association of family context and antisocial behavior.
From Capaldi et al., 2002.

ACCENT

Maltreatment and Conduct Problems

Early maltreatment, particularly physical abuse, is a risk factor for serious conduct problems (Lansford et al., 2002; Wekerle & Wolfe, 2003). Physically maltreated youngsters often display high levels of hostility and aggression and have frequent angry outbursts. These youngsters have higher than expected rates of conduct and oppositional defiant disorders.

Various mechanisms probably account for the association between maltreatment and conduct problems. As might be expected, persistent maltreatment may be particularly detrimental. For example, Bolger and Patterson (2001) found that chronically maltreated children were more likely to be aggressive and

rejected by peers. A suggested mechanism for this maltreatment-aggression-peer rejection pattern is the coercive interactional style the child has learned in the family of origin.

Physical maltreatment may also contribute to learning of problematic cognitive/social information-processing patterns. Indeed, the relationship between early maltreatment and later aggressive behavior is, in part, mediated by these biased social information-processing patterns (Dodge, 2003). Thus, physical maltreatment may, in part, contribute to conduct problems through the development of problematic peer relationship and cognitive processes.

Luthar, 1999; Paschall & Hubbard, 1998; Richards et al., 2004; Wahler & Dumas, 1989).

PEER RELATIONS

Peer relations are part of the complex interplay of influences that contribute to the development of conduct problems (Hay et al., 2004). Parents are often concerned that their children are being influenced by peers whose behavior they view as "bad" or "dangerous." Such concern may be reasonable. Early exposure to aggressive peers may be one factor in the early initiation of aggressive and antisocial behavior, and later association with deviant peers can contribute to the maintenance and escalation of such behavior (Fergusson & Horwood, 1998; Laird et al., 2001; Snyder, 2002).

Difficulties in interpersonal relations have repeatedly been found among youngsters with conduct problems (Lochman, Whidby, & FitzGerald, 2000). Peers often reject children who display disruptive and aggressive behavior (Bierman, 2004; Coie, Belding, & Underwood, 1988). Rejected aggressive children suffer immediate social consequences and are at risk for negative long-term outcomes such as delinquency, adult criminality, educational failure, and adult psychological maladjustment (Laird et al., 2001; Parker & Asher, 1987; Rudolph & Asher, 2000).

Not all aggressive youths are rejected, however, and those who are may not be without friends. Beginning in childhood and accelerating in adolescence,

conduct-disordered and delinquent youngsters may have friends who also engage in aggressive and antisocial behaviors. The case of Delano, described in an earlier chapter (p. 62), is a dramatic example of this. Research shows that the interactions and influences that characterize these deviant peer associations play a role in the initiation, maintenance, and acceleration of antisocial behavior (Dishion & Patterson, 2006). For example, Fergusson and Horwood (1998) reported on the linkages between early conduct problems and outcomes at age 18 in a group of New Zealand children studied longitudinally since birth. They found that conduct problems at age 8 were associated with poorer outcomes, such as leaving school by age 18 without appropriate educational qualifications and a period of 3 months or more of unemployment. One of the factors that mediated the relationship between early aggression and later poor outcomes was peer affiliations. Adolescents who between the ages of 14 and 16 reported having friends who were delinquent or who used illegal substances were at greater risk for later negative outcomes.

Peer influences are not independent of other contextual factors (Dishion & Patterson, 2006). For example, in their longitudinal study of New Zealand youngsters, Fergusson and Horwood (1999) found that family variables such as parental conflict, parental history of drug abuse and criminal behavior, and problematic early mother–child interactions were predictive of affiliation with deviant peers at age 15. Cultural and community influences come into play as well. Brody and colleagues (2001) found, in a sample of African American children, that difficulty with deviant peers was less likely if parents were nurturing and involved, but more likely if parenting was harsh and inconsistent. Furthermore, affiliation with deviant peers was less likely in neighborhoods with collective socialization practices (e.g., adults who were willing to monitor and supervise youths from their own and other families). Community economic disadvantage also was associated with greater likelihood of deviant peer affiliation, and the benefits of nurturant/involved parenting and collective socialization were most pronounced for youngsters from the most disadvantaged neighborhoods.

COGNITIVE–EMOTIONAL INFLUENCES

Consider the adolescent boy who is walking down the street and is approached by a group of peers who begin to call him names, laugh, and tease him. Some boys respond to this situation by getting angry, escalating the conflict, and perhaps reacting violently, whereas other boys are able to deflect attention to another topic, ignore it, laugh, make light of the teasing, or firmly ask that the teasing stop. The cognitive and emotional processes that occur during this situation constitute proximal mechanisms for aggressive behavior. (Dodge, 2000, p. 448)

Examining how children and adolescents think and feel about social situations is part of understanding conduct problems. For example, they may attribute hostility to another child's actions or may fail to take another person's perspective, fail to use social problem-solving skills, fail to think before they act, or, in general, fail to use self-regulation skills to control their emotions and behavior. These social-cognitive-emotional processes are part of the development and persistence of aggressive and antisocial behavior (Dodge, 2000; Lochman et al., 2000). Specific social information-processing patterns such as a focus on the positive aspects of aggression and a lack of responsiveness to emotional stimuli may be characteristic of youngsters with the callous/unemotional traits described earlier (Pardini, Lochman, & Frick, 2003; Loney et al., 2003).

The model articulated by Dodge and his colleagues illustrates how one might address social–emotional cognitions (Crick & Dodge, 1994; Dodge, 2003). The model suggests that cognitive processing begins with encoding (looking for and attending to)

and then interpreting social and emotional cues. The next steps include searching for possible alternative responses, selecting a specific response, and finally enacting the selected response. Investigations reveal that youths with conduct problems have poorer social problem-solving skills and display cognitive deficits and distortions in various parts of this process (Fontaine, Burks, & Dodge, 2002). For example, aggressive youths use fewer social cues and misattribute hostile intent to their peers' neutral actions. They also generate fewer responses and ones that are less likely to be effectively assertive and more likely to be aggressive solutions. They may also expect that aggressive responses will lead to positive outcomes. Furthermore, they may be more likely to perceive and label the arousal they experience in conflict situations as anger rather than other emotions. These reactions to internal arousal may contribute to further distortion and restricted problem solving (Lochman et al., 2000). Problematic social-cognitive-emotional processes may start quite early in life and be part of the stability of early-onset conduct-disordered behavior (Coy et al., 2001).

Dodge and his colleagues (Dodge, 1991; Schwartz et al., 1998) distinguish between two types of aggressive behavior: reactive aggression and proactive aggression. Reactive aggression is an angry ("hot-blooded") retaliatory response to a perceived provocation or frustration. Proactive aggression, in contrast, is generally not associated with anger and is characterized by deliberate aversive behaviors (starting fights, bullying, teasing) that are oriented to specific goals or supported by positive environmental outcomes. These different types of aggression are associated with different social-cognitive deficiencies (Schippell et al., 2003). Reactively aggressive youths display deficiencies in early stages of the social-cognitive process; for example, they underutilize social cues and attribute hostile intent to others. Proactively aggressive youths display deficiencies in later stages of the process; they are likely to positively evaluate aggressive solutions and to expect that they will lead to positive outcomes. The two types of aggression also seem to be related to different outcomes. Reactively aggressive boys displayed higher rates of other problems and had an earlier onset of such difficulties than proactively aggressive boys (Dodge et al., 1997). Reactively aggressive boys also seem more likely to be the targets of negative peer attitudes and behaviors (Schwartz et al., 1998).

A study by Brendgen and colleagues (2001) further illustrates the value of the reactive–proactive distinction. This study also reminds us, once again, of the interrelatedness of influences. A sample of Caucasian, French-speaking boys from low socioeconomic neighborhoods in Montreal, Canada, were categorized at 13 years of age as either nonaggressive, proactive–aggressive, reactive–aggressive, or both proactive– and reactive–aggressive. The boys, at 16–17 years of age, were asked to report on their delinquency-related physical violence (e.g., beat up other boys, used a weapon in a fight) and on their physical violence against a dating partner. In general, proactive aggression was associated with greater delinquency-related violence, and reactive aggression with greater dating violence. However, the relationship between proactive aggression and delinquency-related violence was moderated by level of parental supervision. The relationship was strong for boys who had experienced low levels of parental supervision during their early adolescent years, but the relationship was weak for boys who had experienced higher levels of parental supervision during this period. Similarly, the relationship between reactive aggression and dating violence was mediated by level of maternal warmth and caregiving. The relationship was strong for boys who had experienced low levels of maternal warmth and caregiving during their development, but this relationship was weak among boys who had experienced higher levels of maternal warmth and caregiving. Thus, although development of proactive and reactive aggression may be influenced by social–cognitive style, the developmental course of such behavior seems to be affected by styles of parenting.

Biological Influences

Contemporary discussions of the role of biological influences emphasize transactions among multiple biological and nonbiological influences (Lahey & Waldman, 2003; Susman, 1993).

Genetics. That aggressive, antisocial, and other conduct-related behaviors run in families, within and across generations, suggests the potential importance of genetic influences. Indeed, there appears to be moderate genetic influence on antisocial behavior. However, there is also the suggestion of a lesser genetic component for adolescent delinquency than for adult criminal behavior. How might this difference be explained? The childhood-onset versus adolescent-limited distinction discussed earlier may be germane. Conduct-disordered behavior and delinquent behavior are quite common during adolescence, and in many cases, they do not persist into adulthood. It

might, therefore, be reasonable to hypothesize an increased genetic component in antisocial behavior that is more aggressive and that persists from childhood into adult life (Eley, Lichtenstein, & Moffitt, 2003; Moffitt, 2006; Taylor, Iacono, & McGue, 2000).

Findings from a number of longitudinal behavior genetic studies of children and adolescents suggest a genetic component to conduct-disordered/externalizing behavior (Deater-Deckard et al., 1997; Eaves et al., 1997; Hewitt, et al., 1997). However, considerable variability in findings emerged, depending on the informant (e.g., mother or father) and the source of information (e.g. interview versus questionnaire). This research also suggested support for the effects of shared environment. Thus, conclusions regarding the nature of genetic contributions to antisocial/conduct-disordered behavior must be made with caution. Also, what may be inherited are certain characteristics, for example, body build, sensitivity to alcohol, or temperamental qualities such as irritability, impulsivity, and sensation seeking. The hypothesis that such qualities make an individual prone to antisocial behavior in response to environmental pressures seems reasonable (Frick & Morris, 2004).

Although genetic influences may play some role, they are likely to be indirect and interact in complex ways with environmental influences, such as social conditions, family variables, and certain social learning experiences in determining etiology (Rhee & Waldman, 2003; Rutter et al., 1999). For example, the contribution of maltreatment to the presence of conduct disorder in a sample of 5-year-old twins and their families suggests a gene–environment interaction (Jaffee et al., 2005). The presence of maltreatment increased the probability of a CD diagnosis by 2% among children at low genetic risk for CD and 24% among children at high genetic risk. Similarly, a gene–environment interaction is suggested in the work of van Lier and colleagues (2007a). Their research, on a sample of 6-year-old twins, examined the contribution of affiliation with aggressive friends to level of aggression. As illustrated in Figure 8–8, affiliation with aggressive peers was a risk factor for aggression. However, the contribution of having an aggressive friend was greatest for those children who were already at high genetic risk for aggression.

Neurophysiological influences. Psychophysiological variables have been frequently hypothesized to be related to antisocial behavior. Support for this notion comes from studies that find differences between

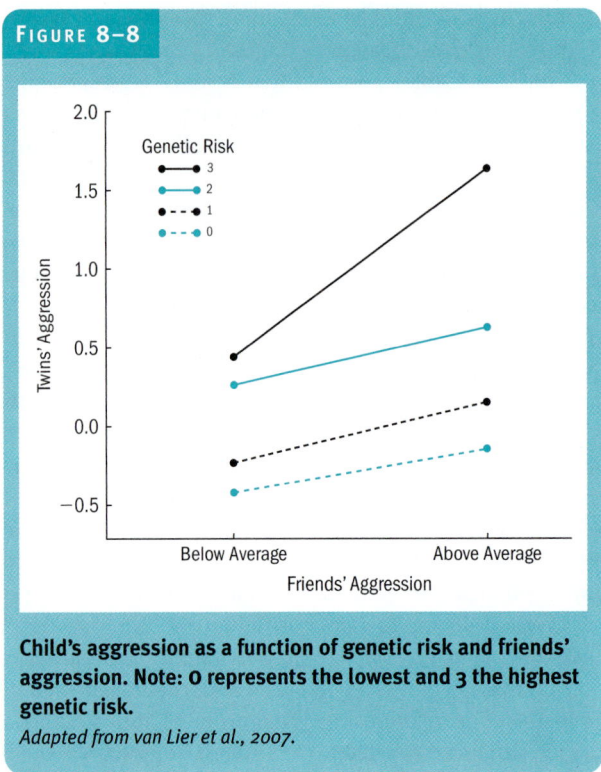

FIGURE 8-8

Child's aggression as a function of genetic risk and friends' aggression. Note: 0 represents the lowest and 3 the highest genetic risk.

Adapted from van Lier et al., 2007.

delinquent or conduct-disordered youths and control youths on psychophysiological measures such as electrodermal response (skin conductance) and heart rate (Beauchaine et al., 2001).

Quay (1993) hypothesized a biological foundation for aggressive, life-course persistent conduct disorders. This hypothesis is based on Gray's (1987) theory of brain systems: a behavioral inhibition system (BIS) and a behavioral activation (or approach) system (BAS) that have distinct neuroanatomical and neurotransmitter systems. The BIS is related to the emotions of fear and anxiety, and tends to inhibit action in novel or fearful situations or under conditions of punishment or nonreward. The BAS tends to activate behavior in the presence of reinforcement; it is associated with reward seeking and pleasurable emotions. An imbalance between the two systems is hypothesized to create a predisposition that in combination with adverse environmental circumstances produces behavior problems. Quay (1993) suggested that an underactive behavioral inhibition system (BIS) combined with an overactive reward system (BAS) may be implicated in the genesis of persistent aggressive conduct disorders.

There is an alternative model of how the two systems may operate. In this view, conduct-disordered, aggressive behavior results from an underactive BAS system in combination with an underactive BIS system (Beauchaine et al., 2001). Conduct-disordered and aggressive behavior represent a form of sensation seeking in response to chronic underarousal created by an underactive BAS system. Youths characterized as conduct-disordered also have low levels of inhibition and engage in aggressive and other antisocial behaviors to achieve satisfactory reward states and positive arousal.

A third system described by Gray (1987) might also be involved in conduct disorders. The fight/flight system (F/F) also involves distinct brain and autonomic nervous system functioning. It is proposed to mediate defensive reactions under conditions of frustration, punishment, or pain. Thus, stimuli that are viewed as threatening would activate the F/F system. Certain youths, such as those with conduct-disordered behavior, may have a reduced threshold for F/F responding, whereas youths with higher thresholds may possess characteristics such as social competence and empathy toward others in distress. In general, the BIS and BAS are viewed as motivational, whereas the F/F system is viewed as an emotion regulation system (Beauchaine et al., 2001).

Neuropsychological deficits. The idea that brain dysfunction is among the causes of antisocial behavior is not new, but the scientific investigation of such influence is relatively recent. The frontal lobes, in particular, may play a role, through deficits in verbal and executive functions (e.g., sustaining attention, abstract reasoning, goal formation, planning, self-awareness) (Ishikawa & Raine, 2003; Moffitt, 1993b; Nigg & Huang-Pollock, 2003).

Neuropsychological measures have been found to be related to indications of poor outcomes, such as early onset and stability of conduct disorder, aggressiveness, and attention-deficit hyperactivity disorder symptoms. Moffitt (1993b, 2006) proposed a developmental model that hypothesizes early insults to the infant nervous system due to factors such as prenatal or postnatal exposure to toxic agents. Compromised neurological functioning affects a variety of areas, including temperament. This effect, in turn, may set in motion a chain of problematic parent–child interactions, particularly under conditions of family adversity. Conduct disorder is thus viewed as evolving from early individual differences in neuropsychological functioning that may be perpetuated and exacerbated by transactions with the social environment. Neuropsychological conceptualizations of conduct disorder development may not apply to all conduct-disordered youngsters, and additional research and refinements of methodological and theoretical concepts are needed (Ishikawa & Raine, 2003, Moffitt, 2006).

Before turning to our discussion of assessment and intervention for conduct problems, we examine the problem of substance use.

Substance Use

Adolescent substance use is an important clinical and public health problem. The use of alcohol and other drugs is common among adolescents and preadolescents (National Institute on Drug Abuse, 2006). Some youths engage in substance use, but do not display antisocial behavior. The use of alcohol and other drugs, however, can be part of the constellation of antisocial and rule-breaking behaviors exhibited by conduct-disordered youths. There is widespread concern regarding illegal (illicit) drugs such as marijuana, cocaine, ecstasy, hallucinogens (e.g., LSD), and heroin. There also is concern regarding use of licit drugs (drugs that are legal for adults or by prescription) and other substances. Alcohol, nicotine, psychoactive medications (e.g., stimulants, sedatives), over-the-counter medications (e.g., sleep aids and weight reduction aids), steroids, and inhalants (e.g., glue, paint thinner) are readily accessible and potentially harmful. They may play a role in starting some young people on a course of long-term and increased substance use (Flory et al., 2004; Georgiades & Boyle, 2007; Mayes & Suchman, 2006).

CLASSIFICATION AND DESCRIPTION

Many adolescents experiment with substance use. One definition of a substance use problem views any use of alcohol or other substance by a minor as abuse since such use is illegal. However, those working with young people typically try to distinguish between patterns of experimentation or lesser use that are developmentally normative and patterns that may have serious short- and long-term consequences (Monti, Colby, & O'Leary, 2001).

The DSM substance use disorders are often employed to diagnose maladaptive use of alcohol or other drugs by adolescents. Substance dependence refers to a maladaptive pattern of substance use that continues for at least 12 months. Dependence includes symptoms of *tolerance* (needing increased amounts of the substance to achieve the same sensations), *withdrawal* (unpleasant feelings upon discontinuation), and *psychological dependence* (compulsive use). Symptoms of tolerance and withdrawal indicate a physiological dependence. However, the diagnosis may be given in the absence of physiological dependence. Substance abuse indicates maladaptive use, which recurs over a 12-month period and leads to one or more repeated harmful consequences. If the individual meets the criteria for dependence for a substance, then a diagnosis of substance abuse would not also be given. For both diagnoses, the DSM criteria for adolescents are the same as those for adults. However, these criteria have not been established as appropriate for adolescents (AACAP, 2005; Chassin et al., 2003).

Rodney **Alcohol and Nicotine Use**

"It was so hard to start, I had no idea it would be harder to stop." Rodney, age 17, didn't recall much about the motorcycle accident that had put him in the hospital. It involved quite a few brandy Alexanders and too little about hanging onto the passenger bar of the motorcycle. He was clear-headed enough to realize that he badly needed a cigarette.

By the time Rodney was 12, he was already attending high school classes, had won several statewide scholastic contests, and had appeared twice on a popular TV quiz show. When he was 14, his parents reluctantly let him accept a scholarship to a small but prestigious liberal arts college. "Of course I was the smallest one there . . . I'm sure I started smoking and drinking to compensate for my size."

Six months into college, Rodney was smoking a pack and a half a day. When studying for exams (he often felt he wasn't "measuring up"), he found himself lighting one cigarette from another, going through several packs in a day this way—far more than he meant to. The following year, he read the Surgeon General's report on smoking and saw a video about lung cancer ("in living—no dying—color"). He swore he would never smoke again, but he noticed that he became restless, depressed, and "so irritable my roommate begged me to light up again." Over the next year he had tried twice more to quit.

Rodney's parents were hardworking churchgoers who had never touched a drop of alcohol. Both had been appalled at what alcohol had done to their own fathers. Several times in the last few months, when he was so badly hung over he couldn't attend classes, Rodney had vaguely wondered whether he was about to follow in his grandfathers' unsteady footsteps.

When Rodney first awakened after the accident he had pins through his femur and a terrific hangover. Now, 2 days later, his vital signs were stable and normal except for a pulse of only 56. "I don't suppose you could smuggle in some nicotine gum?" Rodney asked.

Adapted from Morrison & Anders, 1999, pp. 286–287.

EPIDEMIOLOGY

According to the Monitoring the Future (MTF) study (Johnston et al., 2007)—a long-term study of American adolescents that annually surveys large samples of 8th, 10th and 12th graders—there has been a stabilization or decline in substance use among young people in recent years. For example, illicit drug use has declined more than 20% since the peak years in the late 1990s. However, approximately 26% of 8th graders, 36% of 10th graders, and 48% of 12th graders have used an illicit substance. Marijuana is the most widely used illicit drug.

The use of legal drugs is also reason for concern. Alcohol, which is the most widely used substance among all age groups, including young people (U.S. Bureau of the Census, 2003), remains in widespread use, according to the MTF study. Of particular concern is the finding that 30% of 12th graders, 19% of 10th graders, and 6% of 8th graders report having been drunk at least once in the previous month.

It is suggested that increases and decreases in the use of particular drugs are due to shifts in the perceived benefits and perceived risks that young people come to associate with each drug. The concern is that rumor of the supposed benefits spreads faster than information about adverse consequences.

Findings regarding gender, ethnic, and SES differences in substance use are not consistent. Issues of how substance use is defined, how epidemiological information is obtained, and which substances are studied probably contribute to different conclusions. Most findings suggest greater illicit drug use among males. It is often assumed that substance use problems are more prevalent among certain ethnic groups such as African Americans, American Indians, and Latino/Hispanic youngsters, than they are among European American youngsters. However, African American youth are often reported to have lower rates of substance use than European American and other ethnic groups (Mayes & Suchman, 2006; Roberts, Roberts, & Xing, 2006). Here, too, findings are inconsistent (Gibbs, 2003; LaFromboise & Dizon, 2003; Organista, 2003). One limitation of available information may be that many findings are derived from school-based studies. The differential school drop-out rates among ethnic groups may make it difficult to obtain an accurate picture regarding prevalence.

Adolescents with abuse or dependence problems typically display a number of other difficulties (Armstrong & Costello, 2002; Georgiades & Boyle, 2007; Roberts, Roberts, & Xing, 2007). Many use multiple drugs. Academic and family difficulties are common, as are delinquent behaviors. As indicated earlier, substance use is often conceptualized as a later-occurring part of a constellation of conduct problem behaviors. It is not surprising, therefore, that young people who use drugs often meet the criteria for externalizing/disruptive behavior disorders (ODD, CD) in particular. Mood and anxiety disorders also are frequently associated with substance use problems.

ETIOLOGY AND DEVELOPMENTAL COURSE

Researchers and clinicians agree that multiple risk factors and multiple etiological pathways influence whether young people begin and maintain substance use (Mayes & Suchman, 2006). Cavell, Ennett, and Meehan (2001) have described various risk and protective factors thought to be involved in these developmental pathways. These factors overlap considerably with the factors that influence the development of conduct problems in general. Here we draw on Cavell and colleagues' (2001) conceptualization to provide examples of risk and protective factors.

Individual differences, in temperament, self-regulation, and problem-solving, for example, are implicated in the onset and escalation of substance use. Genetics, as well as environmental influences, play a role (Mayes & Suchman, 2006; Wills & Dishion, 2004). Cognitive-affective components—attitudes, expectations, intentions, and beliefs about control—are prominent in conceptualizations of adolescent substance use. For instance, the anticipation of positive or negative consequences for drinking is an important proximal influence on alcohol use. The importance of expectancy regarding the effects of alcohol is illustrated in a study of the development of drinking behavior (Smith & Goldman, 1994; Smith et al., 1995). Over a 2-year period during which many of the youngsters first began to drink, expectations that drinking would facilitate social interactions predicted initiation into drinking. Those who expected social facilitation also drank more over the 2-year period, and future expectations regarding the effects of drinking became more positive. A youth's attitudes towards school and the future may also be an influence on beginning to use drugs and alcohol.

Young people who have been physically or sexually assaulted or who have witnessed violence also appear to be at increased risk for substance abuse (Kilpatrick et al., 2000). Other individual characteristics, including the presence of early conduct problems, aggression, and genetic endowment that predisposes an individual toward substance use, may also influence initiation into and the course of substance use.

Families are an important influence on adolescent substance use patterns. Aspects of parent–child relationships such as less secure attachment, high level of family conflict, and ineffectiveness of parenting skills have been linked to adolescent substance use. Also, social learning theory explanations have drawn attention to the role of modeling of behavior and attitudes. Because parents and older siblings are potential models for such behavior, the child of a parent who is an alcoholic or a substance abuser may be at particular risk (Chassin et al., 1996). Research by Hops and his colleagues (Hops et al., 2000), for example, indicates that when parents or older siblings use tobacco, alcohol, or marijuana, adolescents are more likely to initiate use of these substances. More than the specific behavior observed is affected by modeling. The adolescent may also initiate the use of other substances that serve a similar function (e.g., escape, perceived facilitation of social interactions). Furthermore, the attitude displayed by the parent can affect the young person's behavior. Adolescents are more likely to use substances when they perceive less parental disapproval for use (Chassin et al., 1998).

Peer factors are considered among the strongest influences on adolescent substance use (Dishion & Owen, 2002; Dishion & Patterson, 2006). Perceived peer substance use and perceived peer approval have been shown to be important factors. Social learning theory explanations suggest that adolescents who interact with substance-using peer models and who expect positive consequences from substance use will initiate and continue substance use. However, it is difficult to establish direct peer influence. To begin with, adolescent substance users tend to choose friends who use drugs. Also, research findings are based on adolescents' perceptions of their peers' behavior, and such perceptions may be affected by the bias to see one's own choices as common (Cavell et al., 2001).

School, neighborhood, community, and societal influences are likely to contribute to adolescent substance use. Poor academic performance and low involvement in school activities, for example, have been linked to substance use. In contrast, schools that foster a sense of commitment and community

Association with a peer group that supports the use of alcohol and other drugs may be a contributing influence to the development of substance use and abuse.
(Michelle D. Bridwell/PhotoEdit Inc.)

have lower rates of use. Although some information suggests that low-income and high-risk neighborhoods are associated with greater adolescent substance use, findings are mixed. Some studies suggest higher rates of initial experimentation in more affluent and suburban neighborhoods (Cavell et al., 2001; Luthar & D'Avanzo, 1999). Apart from difference in rate of use, the risks associated with substance experimentation may be greater for youths who reside in poorer neighborhoods, particularly if other members of their families also use or abuse substances (Luthar & Cushing, 1999). Larger social and cultural influences, such as availability of drugs and social norms regarding drug use, also contribute to the likelihood and degree of youths' substance use. Clearly, continuing research on these influences is needed. Figure 8–9 illustrates one model of how multiple influences may contribute to the initiation of substance use.

A variety of theories and conceptualizations have been suggested as ways of explaining how risk and protective factors contribute to the development of substance use. Social learning theory, as we have seen, emphasizes processes such as imitation, expectancy, and consequences. We will briefly examine a selection of other theoretical and conceptual models.

One particular model views adolescence as a period of transition that is marked by attempts to engage in certain behaviors deemed appropriate for adults but not for adolescents (e.g., Jessor & Jessor, 1977). Use of alcohol is an example of such a behavior. Individual differences and environmental variables are assumed to affect the rate at which an individual makes the transition to adulthood and thereby the age of onset of these behaviors. There may be developmental changes in neurocircuitry during adolescence that make this a period of greater

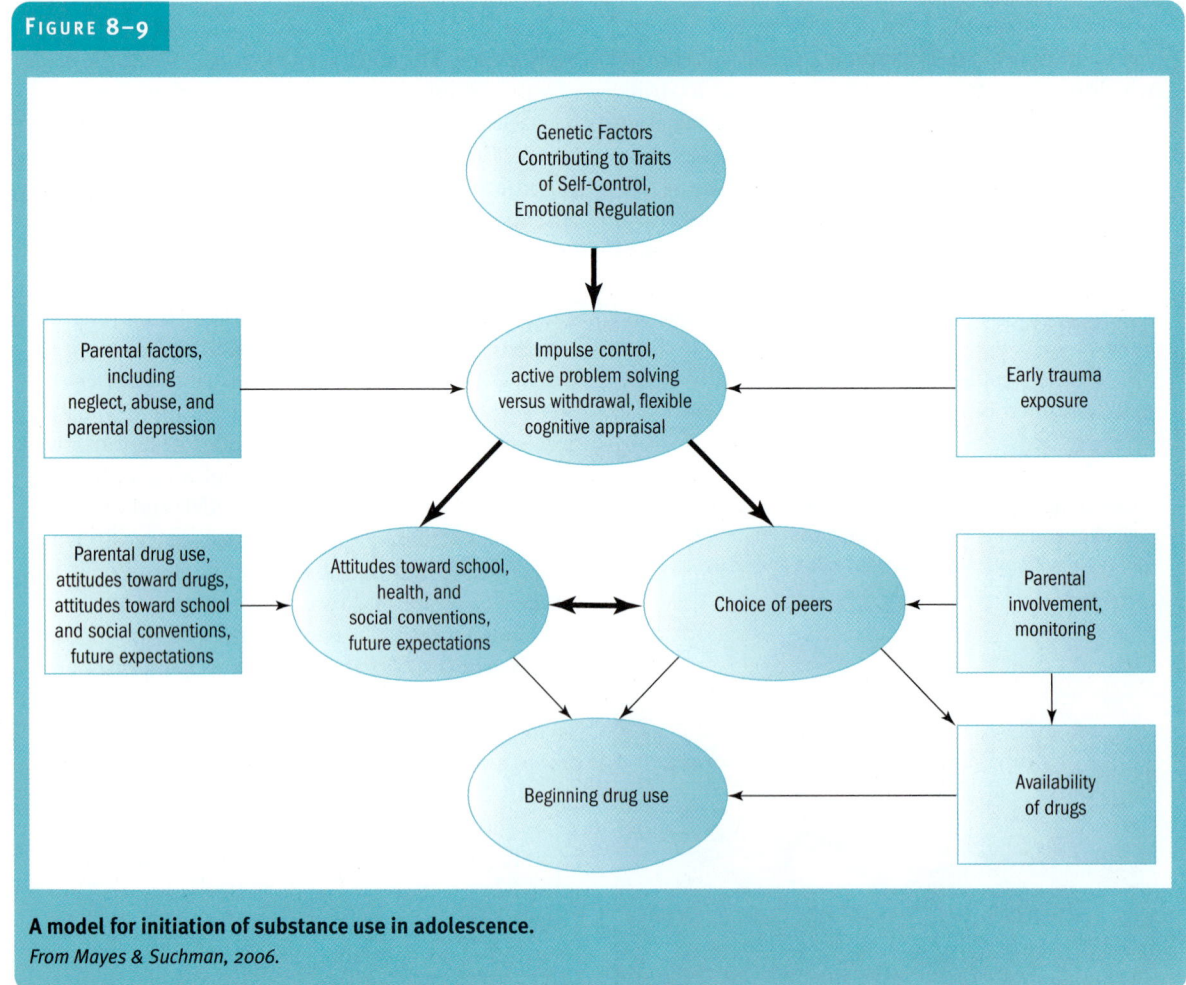

FIGURE 8–9

A model for initiation of substance use in adolescence.
From Mayes & Suchman, 2006.

vulnerability for experimentation with substances and substance use disorders (Chambers, Taylor, & Potenza, 2003).

Adolescent substance use has also been viewed within the context of a stress and coping model (Wills & Filer, 1996). Young people facing greater negative life events and perceived stress, and/or those with elevated physiological responses to stress, may be more likely to use alcohol and other substances (Chassin et al., 2003). Substance use serves a coping function for the adolescent, or at least it is perceived to do so. Whereas some young people employ a variety of adaptive-active coping mechanisms (e.g., seeking information, considering alternatives, taking direct action), others rely more heavily on the use of avoidant coping mechanisms (e.g., distraction, social withdrawal, wishful thinking) and use alcohol and other substances to deal with stress.

As we noted, young people frequently use more than one substance. One way of explaining this trend, as we have seen, is imitation of substance-using models. Another explanation posits a developmental sequence. The so-called gateway theory suggests that legal drugs such as alcohol and tobacco are entry-level drugs that precede the use of illicit drugs. It is highly unusual for a nonuser to go directly to the use of illegal drugs. Participation in one stage increases the likelihood of participation in the next stage; however, only a subgroup at each stage progresses to the next level. The earlier the young person begins one stage, the greater is the likelihood that he or she will progress to other drug use (Mayes & Suchman, 2006). Also, heavier use at any stage seems to be associated with "progress" to the next stage. Findings that alcohol and drug use are beginning early are particularly disturbing in the context of a developmental stage model.

Clearly, no single factor or theory can easily explain which youths start or persist in problematic substance use (Mayes & Suchman, 2006; Zucker, 2006). Explanations must include an array of variables—biological, psychological, and social—that interactively affect development over time (Cicchetti & Luthar, 1999; Glantz & Leshner, 2000). It seems clear, however, that early conduct problems are associated with later substance use (Lynskey & Fergusson, 1995).

Assessment

As is the case for most child and adolescent problems, assessment of conduct problems is likely to be a complex and multifaceted process. In the following sections we describe the primary procedures likely to be used by clinicians working to assess these children and adolescents. However, it should be recognized that the assessment process may also include evaluation of other aspects of the presenting problems; others' problems, attitudes, and skills (e.g., parenting); and ongoing life stresses (Frick & Loney, 2000; Lochman et al., 2000).

INTERVIEWS

A general clinical interview with the parents and older children and adolescents themselves is typically part of the assessment process. An interview with younger children may not be as easily conducted or may not be a reliable source of information; however, the opportunity to interact with the young child may be helpful to the clinician. An interview with the entire family and with the teacher or school personnel may also provide valuable information. Structured interviews can help provide a comprehensive understanding of problems and their context, and can also help determine a diagnosis.

BEHAVIOR RATING SCALES

Among general rating scales useful for assessing conduct problems are the Achenbach instruments (Achenbach & Rescorla, 2001) and the Behavioral Assessment System for Children (BASC; Reynolds & Kamphaus, 2004). They allow evaluation of a broad array of problems through the reports of multiple informants. Also useful are behavior rating scales that focus specifically on conduct problems and disruptive behavior. The Conners' Parent and Teacher Rating Scales (Conners, 2008), the Eyberg Child Behavior Inventory (ECBI), and the Sutter-Eyberg Student Behavior Inventory (SESBI) are examples (Eyberg & Pincus, 1999).

The Self-Report Delinquency Scale (SRD; Elliott, Huizinga, & Ageton, 1985) is a widely used youth self-report measure of conduct problems. Consisting of items derived from the Uniform Crime Reports and including index offenses (e.g., theft, aggravated assault), other delinquent behaviors, and drug use, it is intended for use with youngsters 11 to 19 years old. Self-report measures are less commonly used with younger children because these children may not be capable of reporting conduct problems accurately.

BEHAVIORAL OBSERVATIONS

There are a large number of behavioral observation systems designed for use in clinic, home, and school settings (McMahon & Estes, 1997; Foster & Robin,

1997). Behavioral observations are a desirable part of the assessment process because they avoid the potential bias of reports based on interviews and questionnaires.

The Behavioral Coding System (Forehand & McMahon, 1981) and the Dyadic Parent–Child Interaction Coding System II (Eyberg et al., 2005) are two similar observational systems for assessing parent–child interactions in the clinic. Both observe the parent and the child in situations that vary from free-play and child-directed activities to adult-directed activities, and both focus on parental commands (antecedents) and consequences for child compliance or noncompliance. The Interpersonal Process Code (Rusby, Estes, & Dishion, 1991) is another observational system that is an outgrowth of observational systems developed by Patterson and his colleagues.

The observational systems just described have also been used in home settings, and these and other systems have been employed in schools (e.g., The Fast Track School Observation Program; Conduct Problems Prevention Research Group, 1992). Practicing clinicians seldom use the systems because they are complex and require extensive periods of training and trained observers. The observations themselves are lengthy, and it is challenging to coordinate with times when relevant behaviors are occurring in homes or schools. An alternative to using trained observers in the home or other natural environments is to train adults in the child's environment to record and observe certain behaviors. An advantage of this approach is the opportunity to observe and record behaviors that occur at low rates (e.g., stealing or fire setting) and that would likely be missed by trained observers making occasional visits.

Intervention

Because of the challenges posed by children and adolescents with conduct problems and the impact they have on others, many different interventions have been attempted. Only a portion of these has received a careful empirical evaluation of their effectiveness. Here we will briefly describe some of the interventions that research suggests are supported or promising (Brestan & Eyberg, 1998; Christophersen & Mortweet, 2001; Kazdin, 1997; McMahon, Wells, & Kotler, 2006).

PHARMACOLOGICAL INTERVENTION

There is a paucity of well-controlled research regarding the use of medication in treating opposi-

tional defiant disorder or conduct disorder. It is important to remember that many youngsters with these disorders show symptoms of or meet the diagnostic criteria for attention-deficit hyperactivity disorder. There is considerable support for pharmacological interventions for ADHD (American Academy of Child and Adolescent Psychiatry (AACAP), 2007a). Thus children and adolescents who also present with this co-occurrence may benefit from the use of medications such as stimulants. However, from a research perspective, evaluations of pharmacological treatments for ODD or CD would need to ensure that the medication's effectiveness was not due to the presence of ADHD symptoms in the population studied. Much of the available research can be critiqued for failing to control adequately for such considerations.

Mood stabilizers are the category of medication most likely to be considered in treating extreme aggressive and conduct-disordered behaviors (McLeer & Wills, 2000; Riddle, Kastelic, & Frosch, 2001). Research support is limited, however (APA, 2006). Given a broad uneasiness regarding increased use of psychoactive medications with children, especially since there is limited or no proof of their effectiveness in young people, there is concern regarding the use of such medications (Coyle, 2000; Gleason et al., 2007; Zito et al., 2000). When psychoactive medication is employed in the treatment of aggressive conduct-disordered youngsters, it should be part of a multimodal treatment approach that includes parent training and other psychological interventions (AACAP, 2007b).

PARENT TRAINING

Parent training is among the most successful approaches to reducing aggressive, noncompliant, and antisocial behaviors in youth (Brestan & Eyberg, 1998; Kazdin, 1997; Maughan et al., 2005; Nock, 2003). Parent training programs have a number of features in common (see Table 8–5).

Some parent training programs have focused on oppositional and defiant behavior. There are ethical issues involved in reducing such noncompliance in children. Compliance is not always a positive behavior, and the child's ability to say "no" to certain requests may be desirable either to train or to retain (Dix et al., 2007). In this regard, it is important to assure that parents do not expect perfect compliance, which is neither the norm nor highly desirable in our society. A perfectly quiet, docile child should not be the treatment goal.

TABLE 8–5	COMMON FEATURES OF PARENT TRAINING PROGRAMS

- Treatments are conducted primarily with the parents.
  - The therapist teaches the parents to alter interactions with their child so as to increase prosocial behavior and to decrease deviant behavior.
  - Young children may be brought into sessions to train both the parents and the child in how to interact. Older youths may participate in negotiating and developing behavior change programs.
- New ways of identifying, defining, and observing behavior problems are taught.
- Social learning principles and procedures that follow from them are taught (e.g., social reinforcement, points for prosocial behavior, time out from reinforcement, loss of privileges).
- Treatment sessions are an opportunity to see how techniques are implemented and to practice using techniques. Behavior change programs implemented in the home are reviewed.
- The child's functioning in school is usually incorporated into treatment.
  - Parent-managed reinforcement programs for school and school-related behavior are often part of the behavior-change program.
  - If possible, the teacher plays a role in monitoring behavior and providing consequences.

Adapted from Kazdin, 1997.

The program developed by Forehand and his colleagues illustrates successful parent training that focuses on noncompliant behavior (Forehand & McMahon, 1981; McMahon & Forehand, 2003). Parents of noncompliant children (ages 4 to 7 years) were taught to give direct, concise commands, allow the child sufficient time to comply, reward compliance with contingent attention, and apply negative consequences for noncompliance. Successful treatment of noncompliance also seems to reduce other problem behaviors, such as tantrums, aggression, and crying (Wells, Forehand, & Griest, 1980). Furthermore, at follow-up, treated children were not different from nonclinic community children across multiple areas such as academic performance, relationships with parents, and adjustment (Long et al., 1994). An additional benefit appeared to be that untreated siblings increased their compliance, and it seems likely that this outcome was due, at least in part, to the mother's use of her improved skills with the untreated child (Humphreys et al., 1978).

Attention to the effective use of parent commands to increase compliance and decrease inappropriate behavior is also part of the parent–child interaction therapy (PCIT) program developed by Eyberg and her colleagues (Brinkmeyer & Eyberg, 2003; Querido & Eyberg, 2005). This program seeks to enhance parent–child attachment and to improve the poor behavior management skills of the parent. Here we highlight the portion of the program that teaches parents to use effective commands (Querido, Bearss, & Eyberg, 2002). The rules for effective use of commands that parents are taught (along with examples) are presented in Table 8–6.

As we have seen, Patterson's conceptualization of the development of antisocial behavior evolved in the context of treating these children and their families. The importance of parenting skills in Patterson's formulation led to the development of a treatment program that focused on improving these skills (Patterson et al., 1975; Patterson et al., 1992; Reid et al., 2002). The program teaches parents to pinpoint problems, to observe and record behavior, to more effectively use social and nonsocial reinforcers for appropriate or prosocial behavior, and to more effectively withdraw reinforcers for undesirable behavior. Each family attends clinic and home sessions and has regular phone contact with a therapist, who helps develop interventions for particular targeted behaviors and who models desired parenting skills. Problematic behaviors in the school setting are also targeted, and interventions involve both the parents and school personnel.

Webster-Stratton and her colleagues (2005; Webster-Stratton & Reid, 2003) have developed a multifaceted treatment program for young children (ages 2 to 8 years) with conduct problems, including oppositional defiant and conduct disorder, known as the Incredible Years Training Series. One component of the program is a standard package of videotaped programs of modeled parenting skills. These videos, which contain a large number of vignettes of about 2 minutes each, include examples of parents interacting with their children in both appropriate and inappropriate ways. The videos are shown to groups of parents, and following each vignette, there is a therapist-led discussion of the relevant interactions. Parents are also given homework assignments that allow them to practice parenting skills at home with their children.

The treatment program has been evaluated in a number of studies in which it has been compared with various control conditions (Webster-Stratton &

TABLE 8–6	RULES FOR EFFECTIVE COMMANDS FROM THE PCIT PROGRAM
RULE	**EXAMPLE**
Be *direct* rather than indirect.	Please hand me the block. *Instead of* Will you hand me the block?
State command *positively*.	Come sit beside me. *Instead of* Don't run around the room!
Give commands *one at a time*.	Put your shirt in the hamper. *Instead of* Clean your room.
Be *specific* rather than vague.	Get down off the chair. *Instead of* Be careful.
Be *age appropriate*.	Draw a square. *Instead of* Draw a hexagon.
Be *polite and respectful*.	Please hand me the block. *Instead of* Hand me that block this instant!
Explain commands *before* they are given or *after* they are obeyed.	Go wash your hands. *After the child obeys* It is good to be all clean when you go to school.
Use commands only when necessary or appropriate.	*(As child is running around)* Please sit in this chair. (Good time) *But not* Please hand me glass from the counter. (Not good time)

Adapted from Querido, Bearss, & Eyberg, 2002.

Reid, 2005). Parents completing the program have rated their children as having fewer problems than have control parents and rated themselves as having better attitudes and more confidence regarding their parenting role. Observations in the home have also shown these parents to have better parenting skills and their children to have greater reductions in problem behavior. These improvements were maintained at 1- and 3-year follow-up evaluations. Webster-Stratton (Webster-Stratton, 2005) has also expanded the program to include additional components that enhance parents' interpersonal skills and the social support that the family receives (AD-VANCE), improve the child's social problem-solving skills (Dinosaur Curriculum), promote parental involvement in school and academic activities (School), and train teachers in effective classroom management strategies (Teacher).

COGNITIVE PROBLEM-SOLVING SKILLS TRAINING

Parent training approaches focus on family aspects of conduct-disordered behavior. Other treatments focus more specifically on aspects of the youth's functioning. Among these are ones that derive from the interpersonal and social-cognitive aspects of conduct-disordered behavior. These interventions address social-cognitive deficiencies and distortions as part of the intervention (Lochman et al., 2006). Such problem-solving skills training programs share a number of features (see Table 8–7).

Webster-Stratton and colleagues' cognitive-behavioral, social skills, problem-solving, and anger management training program (Dinosaur Curriculum part of the Incredible Years series) is an example of interventions that address such deficits and skills

TABLE 8–7	COMMON FEATURES OF PROBLEM-SOLVING SKILLS TRAINING PROGRAMS

- The emphasis is on the thought processes involved in the child's approach to interpersonal situations.
  - In step-by-step approaches, the child is taught to solve interpersonal problems.
  - The child makes statements to himself or herself that direct attention to the aspects of problems that lead to effective solutions.
- Solutions (behaviors) that are selected are important as well.
  - Prosocial behaviors are fostered (e.g., through modeling, direct reinforcement).
- Structured tasks like games, academic activities, and stories are used to teach cognitive problem-solving skills.
  - As treatment progresses, these skills are increasingly applied to real-life situations.
- Therapists usually play an active role. They
  - model cognitive processes by making verbal self-statements,
  - apply a sequence of statements to problems,
  - provide cues to prompt appropriate skills, and
  - apply feedback and praise for correct skills.
- Treatment usually combines several different procedures, including modeling and practice, role playing, and consequences for the skills displayed.

Adapted from Kazdin, 1997.

(Webster-Stratton, 2005). Children ages 4 to 8 years with early-onset conduct problems receive the treatment in small groups. The program addresses interpersonal difficulties typically encountered by young children who have conduct problems. With therapist guidance, the children are taught to cope with such situations through a variety of techniques. Videotaped vignettes of children in stressful situations are viewed and discussed, and acceptable solutions and coping skills are practiced. The intervention is made developmentally appropriate and includes the use of materials such as child-size puppets, coloring books, cartoons, stickers, and prizes to enhance learning. Strategies to ensure generalization to other settings are included in the children's sessions. Also, parents and teachers, who are involved through receiving regular letters, are asked to reinforce the targeted skills whenever they notice the child using them at home or at school and to complete weekly good-behavior charts. As compared with a waiting-list group of children, at posttreatment those in the treatment program exhibited significantly fewer aggressive, noncompliant, and other externalizing problems at home and school, more prosocial behavior with peers, and more positive conflict management strategies. Most of the posttreatment changes were maintained at a 1-year follow-up.

Combined treatments. Kazdin and his colleagues (Kazdin, 2005) have demonstrated the potential benefit of combining parent training and cognitive problem-solving skills training in treating children with conduct problems. A combination of cognitive problem-solving skills training (PSST) and parent management training (PMT), similar to the procedures described before, proved superior to either treatment alone for children 7 years of age and older. (PMT alone is offered for children up to 6 years of age.) Treatment led to significant improvements in the youths' functioning at home, at school, and in the community, immediately after treatment and at a 1-year follow-up, as well as to improvements in parental stress and functioning. In addition, the combined treatments resulted in a greater proportion of the youths falling within normative levels of functioning. Also, adding a treatment component that addresses parent sources of stress improved outcomes for the child. These findings, along with the multicomponent Webster-Stratton program described earlier, suggest the value of interventions that address the multiple influences operating in conduct-disordered youth and their families. Treatment components may be combined depending on the nature and pervasiveness of the youth and family's problems.

FUNCTIONAL FAMILY THERAPY

The kinds of interventions described as successful with younger conduct-disordered children, such as parent training, may be less successful with adolescents and chronic juvenile delinquents (Kazdin, 1993; McMahon & Wells, 1998). An option for these individuals may be Functional Family Therapy (FFT), a treatment program developed by Alexander and his colleagues that integrates behavioral-social learning, cognitive-behavioral, and family systems perspectives (Alexander et al., 1998; Alexander & Sexton, 2002). Specific interventions drawn from parent management training are included. Treatment, however, also focuses on the cognitive, affective, and interpersonal processes of the family system. The goals of therapy are to engage and motivate the family for positive change, improve the communication skills of the family; modify cognitive sets, expectations, attitudes, and affective reactions; and establish new interpretations and meanings of behavior.

Treatment sessions focus on directly altering various patterns in the family. Therapists employ a variety of techniques: modeling, prompting, shaping and rehearsing effective communication skills, and providing feedback and reinforcement for positive changes. In addition, contracts are created to establish reciprocal patterns of positive reinforcement. For example, a contract regarding a privilege for a certain family member also specifies that person's responsibilities for securing those privileges and provides bonuses for all parties for compliance with the contract.

The treatment program has been demonstrated to improve the interactions of families, to lower rates of recidivism, to lower rates of court referrals for siblings of initially referred delinquents, and to be cost-effective (Aos, Miller, & Drake, 2006; Barton et al., 1985; Klein, Alexander, & Parsons, 1977).

COMMUNITY-BASED PROGRAMS

Placing severely conduct-disordered or delinquent youth in institutions that are a part of the criminal justice system is a frequently considered alternative. Concerns exist regarding the effectiveness of such interventions and the impact of placement in such institutions that exposes young people to a subculture in which deviant behaviors may be learned and reinforced. These concerns and the success of some community-based programs have led to the search for effective alternatives to institutionalization.

The Teaching Family Model (TFM) developed at Achievement Place is an oft-cited example of a community-based program for delinquent youth and an example of behaviorally based (largely operant) interventions (Fixsen, Wolf, & Phillips, 1973; Phillips, 1968). Adolescents who were declared delinquent or dependent neglect cases lived in a house with two trained teaching parents. The youths attended school during the day and also had regular work responsibilities. The academic problems, aggression, and other norm-violating behaviors exhibited by these adolescents were viewed as an expression of failures of past environments to teach appropriate behaviors. Accordingly, these deficits were corrected through modeling, practice, instruction, and feedback. The program centered on a token economy in which points and praise were gained for appropriate behaviors and were lost for inappropriate behaviors. Points could be used to purchase a variety of privileges that were otherwise unavailable. If a resident met a certain level of performance, the right to go on a merit system and thus avoid the point system could be purchased. This process was seen as providing a transition to usual sources of natural reinforcement and feedback, such as praise, status, and satisfaction. The goal was gradually to transfer a youth who was able to perform adequately on merit to his or her natural home. The teaching parents helped the natural parents or guardians to structure a program to maintain gains made at Achievement Place.

Both the program's developers and independent investigators evaluated the effectiveness of TFM (Kirigin, 1996; Weinrott, Jones, & Howard, 1982). These evaluations suggested that the TFM approach was more effective than comparison programs while the adolescents were involved in the group home setting. However, once they left this setting, differences disappeared.

Difficulties in transitions back to the youths' own families and failure to achieve long-term effectiveness are common in all interventions with delinquent populations. Given this consideration, the developers of TFM suggested a "long-term supportive family model" in which specially trained foster parents would provide care for a single adolescent into early adulthood (Wolf, Braukmann, & Ramp, 1987). Multidimensional treatment foster care (MTFC) interventions have been developed (Chamberlain & Smith, 2003). Like the TFM approach, many of these programs are based on behavioral-social learning theory, place youth in family-like settings, and intervene with problem behaviors in a natural setting. However, one or perhaps two young people, rather than a group of youths, are placed in a specialized foster care home. This decision is consistent with literature suggesting possible negative effects of interventions that permit these youths to associate with peers with similar antisocial histories (Dishion & Dodge, 2005). Foster parents are trained in behavior management skills and are provided with supervision and support by program staff. Explicit behavioral goals are set, and a systematic program including a point system is employed. The youth's school is also involved. Individual weekly sessions with a therapist that emphasize building skills are also provided for the youth. During the MTFC stay, staff work with the youth's parents or other aftercare personnel to prepare them (and the young person) for reunification. Research indicates that participants in the MTFC program were less likely to engage in delinquent activities and at 4 years postdischarge had fewer arrests (Chamberlain, Fisher, & Moore, 2002; Chamberlain & Smith, 2003). MTFC programs have been developed for both boys and girls and have been found to be cost effective (Aos et al., 2006; Leve, Chamberlain, & Reid, 2005).

MULTISYSTEMIC THERAPY

Interventions with antisocial youth are likely to require the cooperation of multiple human service agencies. Often it is difficult to coordinate services, and individualizing such efforts to fit the needs of youngsters and their families is even more challenging.

Maggie   The Need for Multiple Services

Maggie is a 13-year-old white seventh-grader who lives with her unemployed, crack-addicted mother, mother's live-in boyfriend, two sisters (ages 10 and 8), and a daughter of one of her mother's crack-addicted friends. Maggie was referred because she was physically violent at home (e.g., she was arrested several times for assaulting family members), at school (e.g., she beat a classmate with a stick and threatened to kill a teacher), and in the neighborhood (e.g., she was arrested twice for assaulting residents of her housing development). Many of Maggie's aggressive actions followed all-night binges by her mother. Maggie, who primarily associates with delinquent peers, was placed in a special class, and was recommended for expulsion from school. The family resides in a high-crime neighborhood, and the only source of income is welfare benefits.

Adapted from Henggeler et al., 1998, p. 23.

Multisystemic Therapy (MST; Henggeler & Lee, 2003) is a family- and community-based approach. The young person is considered to exist within a number of systems, including family, peers, school, neighborhood, and community. MST uses treatment strategies derived from family systems therapy and from behavior therapy to treat adolescents with serious difficulties and their families. The approach seeks to preserve the family and to maintain the youths in their homes. MST addresses not only the family system but also skills of the youth and extrafamilial influences, such as peers, school, and neighborhood. Family sessions, which are conducted in the home and community settings, are flexible and individualized for each family.

A report on a comparison of MST to the usual services offered to serious juvenile offenders and their families illustrates this approach (Henggeler, Melton, & Smith, 1992). These youths were at imminent risk for out-of-home placement. They averaged 3.5 previous arrests, 54% had at least one arrest for a violent crime, and 71% had been incarcerated previously for at least 3 weeks. The findings of this study (illustrated in Figure 8–10) indicate that MST was significantly more effective than the usual services. In addition, families receiving the MST intervention reported increased family cohesion, whereas reported cohesion decreased in the other families. Also, aggression with peers decreased for MST youths but remained the same for the youths receiving usual services. Several other reports indicate the usefulness of MST with a variety of populations, including youth presenting for psychiatric emergencies, and suggest the long-term effectiveness and cost effectiveness of this approach (Aos et al., 2006; Curtis, Ronan, & Borduin, 2004; Henggeler & Lee, 2003).

PREVENTION

The difficulties in treating adolescents with serious and persistent conduct disorders, the multidetermined nature of antisocial behavior, and the potential stability of conduct-disordered behavior certainly suggest that efforts should be directed at early, multifaceted, flexible, and ongoing interventions for some youngsters. Here we offer some examples of efforts at early intervention.

Interventions that provide treatment to families of young children with oppositional defiant behavior or early signs of aggression or similar programs also might be considered as prevention strategies. Successful treatment can reduce early

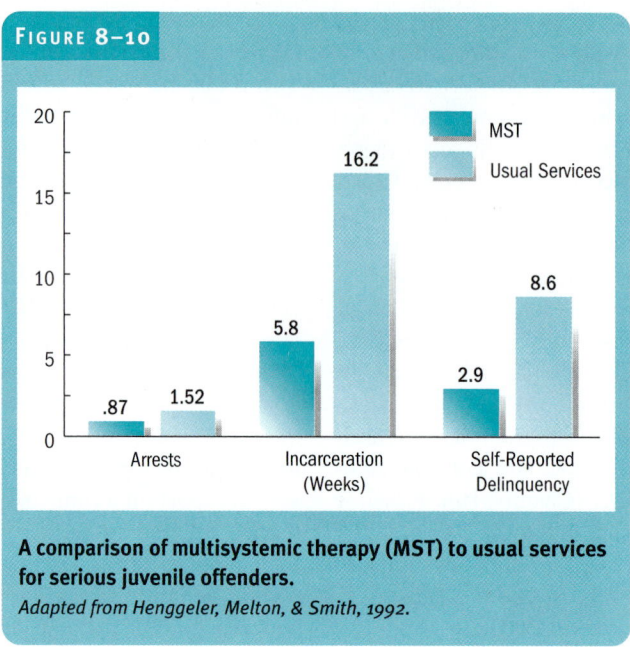

FIGURE 8–10

A comparison of multisystemic therapy (MST) to usual services for serious juvenile offenders.
Adapted from Henggeler, Melton, & Smith, 1992.

aspects of the development of conduct-disordered behavior. Also, improvement of parenting skills and family interactions, for example, can reduce risk factors and provide protective influences associated with the developmental progression of conduct problems. Thus, interventions that target preschool and early elementary-age children and their families can be considered treatment for existing conduct problems and prevention of later conduct disorders.

Beyond this conceptual overlap, some of the treatment programs described earlier have been employed as prevention programs. For example, Webster-Stratton (2005) and her colleagues evaluated The Incredible Years program as a prevention program. The BASIC parent program was provided to Head Start families in some randomly selected centers in addition to the regular Head Start program. Compared with control families at centers that received regular Head Start offerings, participating mothers improved their parenting skills. Their children exhibited significantly less misbehavior and more positive affect compared to control children whose behavior remained unchanged. In addition, teachers reported increased involvement by program parents, whereas reports indicated that control parents' involvement remained the same. One year later, in kindergarten, improvements in parenting behavior and in child behavior and affect were maintained. Webster-Stratton (2005) has reported that the program is effective with African American, Asian, Caucasian and Hispanic Head Start families. Also, other investigators have employed the program as a prevention program with Hispanic families and low-income African American mothers and their toddlers (Brotman et al., 2003; Gross et al., 2003).

There also are ongoing selective prevention trials focused on conduct problems that provide comprehensive intervention over a long period of time. For example, the Fast Track project (Conduct Problems Prevention Research Group, 1992, 2002b) is a multisite collaborative project that is following a large high-risk sample of children identified as displaying high rates of conduct problems during kindergarten as well as a representative sample of children from the same schools. Half of the children in the high-risk sample participated in an intensive and long-term intervention. This is consistent with the need to provide multiple interventions over an extended period of development for some early-onset conduct-problem youngsters. The program targets the behaviors, skills, and other risk factors involved in the development of the early-onset pathway of conduct problems. Intervention components include parent training, social-cognitive skills training, attention to peer affiliation, academic tutoring, home visits, and teacher-based classroom intervention. Evaluations of the effects of the intervention have been encouraging and have provided information regarding the variables that mediate change in conduct problems (Conduct Problems

Prevention Research Group, 1999, 2002a, 2004; Erath et al., 2006; Milan et al., 2006).

There is a need for programs that offer differing "levels" of intervention based upon the needs of the youth and family and that appreciate that youths' problems are embedded in multiple environments (Dishion & Stormshak, 2007). The Adolescents Transition Program (ATP; Dishion & Kavanagh, 2002) is one example. ATP is a family-based intervention that is embedded in the school setting and that has the goal of reducing adolescent problem behavior. It offers three levels of service to families. A Family Resource Center in the school facilitates parent–school collaboration and provides information and education to parents. This is a universal intervention. The Family Check-Up is a selected intervention offered to families identified as having an at-risk youth. This brief intervention provides an assessment, attempts to maintain current positive parenting, and encourages change of problematic parenting practices. An indicated level of intervention is available to families of youth with ongoing conduct problems. A number of professional interventions, similar to those described in the discussion of treatment programs, are offered to these families. ATP has been shown to be helpful in addressing conduct problems (Dishion & Stormshak, 2007). For example, parent contact with the Family Resource Center was related to decreases in the growth of problem behavior, particularly for at-risk youth, and a decline in relationships with deviant peers (Stormshak et al., 2005).

SUMMARY

CLASSIFICATION AND DESCRIPTION

- *Aggression, oppositional behavior, and other antisocial behaviors are among the most common problems of referred youths, as well as of young people in the general population.*

- *The DSM contains a grouping of disorders that includes Oppositional Defiant Disorder (ODD) and Conduct Disorder (CD), along with Attention-Deficit Hyperactivity Disorder (ADHD).*

- *ODD is described as a pattern of negativistic, hostile, and defiant behavior. CD is described as a repetitive and persistent pattern of behavior that violates both the basic rights of others and societal norms. Two subtypes, childhood-onset and adolescent-onset, are indicated.*

- *Empirical approaches have consistently identified a syndrome of aggressive, oppositional, antisocial behaviors. Two narrow syndromes within this broad externalizing syndrome have been designated as aggressive behavior and rule-breaking behavior.*

- *Other ways of distinguishing among groupings of conduct problems, such as age of onset, an overt versus covert distinction, and a further destructive–nondestructive distinction, have also been suggested.*

- *There are gender differences in prevalence, developmental course, and etiological influences of conduct problems. In part, such differences may be related to how aggression is expressed. The concept of relational aggression has contributed to understanding gender differences.*

- *Fire setting is a covert behavior that may occur among youths with severe conduct problems.*

- *Delinquency is primarily a legal term rather than a psychological term. Some behaviors described as delinquent are quite common.*

- *The high rates of violent behavior among young people have led to action on multiple fronts, particularly in schools.*

- *It is important to address bullying since bullying may be part of a more general antisocial developmental pattern. The victims of bullying also are at considerable risk.*

EPIDEMIOLOGY

- *Conduct problems are one of the most frequent occurring child and adolescent difficulties.*

- *Conduct disorder and oppositional defiant disorder are more commonly diagnosed in boys.*

- *An increasing prevalence of conduct disorder with age is often reported. The pattern for oppositional defiant disorder is less clear.*

- *Contextual factors such as poverty and the stress of high-crime neighborhoods are thought to increase the risk for conduct problems.*

- *An important question is whether oppositional defiant disorder is a precursor of conduct disorder.*

- *Youngsters who receive the diagnoses ODD or CD are likely to experience other difficulties. In particular, there is a high rate of co-occurrence of ODD and CD with ADHD. ADHD appears to be a risk factor for the other two disorders.*

DEVELOPMENTAL COURSE

- *An important aspect of conduct problems is their reported stability over time. However, the issue of stability is a complex one.*

- *Age of onset is an important aspect of the development of conduct problems. A childhood-onset or life-course persistent pathway is of great concern. An adolescent-onset path is more common, and antisocial behavior among such youths may be less likely to persist beyond adolescence.*

- *Conduct-disordered behavior has been conceptualized in terms of developmental progressions or paths. Pathways characterized by overt, covert, and authority conflict behaviors have been described.*

ETIOLOGY

- *Conduct problems likely develop through a complex interaction of influences.*

- *Influences from the socioeconomic context, such as poverty, neighborhood disadvantage, and related stress, affect the development of conduct-disordered behavior.*

- *Aggression and other conduct-disordered behavior can be learned through imitation.*

- *Family variables also are an important influence on the development of conduct-disordered behavior. Important mechanisms through which family influence occurs are parental involvement and parenting practices. The work of Patterson and his colleagues has contributed to our knowledge in this area.*

- *Stresses on the family, the parents' own psychological difficulties, marital discord, and child maltreatment affect both the likelihood of a child developing conduct problems and the course of the behavior.*

- *Peer relations both contribute to and are affected by conduct problems. Aggressive youngsters are often rejected by their peers, with both immediate and long-term consequences. However, these youngsters may not be without friends and the influence of bad companions is a concern.*

- *Cognitive-emotional characteristics of the youngster, such as social information-processing skills and interpersonal problem-solving skills, also contribute to the development and persistence of conduct-disordered behavior.*

- *Biological influences, such as genetic, neurophysiological, and neuropsychological influences, may also play a role.*

SUBSTANCE USE

- *The use of alcohol and drugs may be a part of a pattern of antisocial and rule-breaking behavior. Substance dependence and substance abuse are the DSM diagnoses related to substance use problems. The high rate of substance use by young people is a widespread concern. A variety of theories, models, and risk factors have been suggested to explain substance use.*

ASSESSMENT

- *Assessment of conduct problems is likely to be complex and multifaceted. Interviews, behavior rating scales, and behavioral observations are employed.*

INTERVENTION

- *Support for the use of pharmacological interventions is best for the use of stimulants with those ODD/CD youngsters who also exhibit symptoms of ADHD.*

- *Parent training is among the most successful approaches. Interventions employing cognitive problem-solving skills training focus on aspects of the youth's functioning. Treatment programs that combine these approaches and address multiple influences have been developed.*

- *Functional Family Therapy integrates cognitive-behavioral and family systems approaches.*

- *Community-based programs include the Teaching Family Model and Multidimensional Treatment Foster Care. Multisystemic Therapy is a systems-based intervention that attempts to keep the youngsters in their homes. It addresses the youth's functioning withing various systems such as family, peers, school, neighborhood, and community.*

- *Interventions that provide treatment to families of young children with oppositional defiant behavior or early signs of aggression might be considered prevention strategies.*

- *Indeed, some treatment programs for young children have been employed as prevention programs.*

- *Other selected prevention programs provide comprehensive interventions over long periods of time for at-risk youths. There are also programs that offer different "levels" of intervention based on the needs of the youth and family.*

KEY TERMS

Antisocial Personality Disorder *(p. 191)*

psychopathy *(p. 191)*

callous/unemotional traits *(p. 191)*

Oppositional Defiant Disorder *(p. 193)*

Conduct Disorder *(p. 194)*

aggressive behavior syndrome *(p. 195)*

rule-breaking behavior syndrome *(p. 195)*

overt conduct problems *(p. 197)*

covert conduct problems *(p. 197)*

destructive–nondestructive conduct problems *(p. 197)*

relational aggression *(p. 198)*

delinquency *(p. 199)*

violence *(p. 199)*

bullying *(p. 200)*

childhood-onset developmental pattern *(p. 205)*

adolescent-onset developmental pattern *(p. 205)*

coercion *(p. 209)*

negative reinforcement *(p. 209)*

reinforcement trap *(p. 209)*

discipline *(p. 211)*

monitoring *(p. 211)*

reactive aggression *(p. 214)*

proactive aggression *(p. 214)*

behavioral inhibition system *(p. 216)*

behavioral activation system *(p. 216)*

fight/flight system *(p. 216)*

illicit drugs *(p. 217)*

licit drugs *(p. 217)*

substance dependence *(p. 217)*

substance abuse *(p. 217)*

parent training *(p. 222)*

token economy *(p. 226)*

CHAPTER 9

Attention-Deficit Hyperactivity Disorder

[Cory's] mother, Mrs. Conner, called the therapist's office in tears. . . . [Cory's] teacher, Ms. Hall, had recommended that [he] be immediately placed on Ritalin, as his hyperactivity was disturbing the class. . . . Mrs. Conner reported that [Cory] was an active child who was always running around the house and crashing into the furniture. She stated that he had walked early, at ten months, and had been keeping her running ever since. . . .

Mr. Conner . . . believed that [Cory] was being allowed to disrupt class and the teachers just didn't punish him. . . . He went on to report that if he had acted the way [Cory] was acting in school he would have "gotten a beating." . . .

[Cory] reported that he knew his parents and his teacher were mad at him for being "so bad." (Morgan, 1999, pp. 6–8)

The presenting problems for children who receive the diagnosis of attention-deficit hyperactivity disorder (ADHD) are recognized in both dimensional and categorical classifications of behavioral disorders. Only a few disturbances of youth have garnered as much public interest and

have been so surrounded by debate as ADHD. Controversy especially has focused on both the nature of ADHD and the pharmacological treatment that was widely introduced in the late 1960s.

Evolving Ideas about ADHD

What we now refer to as ADHD has traveled a winding path of definitions (Barkley, 2003; Milich, Balentine, & Lynam, 2001). One early account of the disorder was given by the English physician George Still, who described a group of boys with a "defect in moral control" as inattentive, impulsive, overactive, lawless, and aggressive, among other things. In the United States, epidemics of encephalitis in 1917–1918 aroused interest in patients who suffered this brain infection and who were left with similar attributes. A comparable clinical picture also was noted in children who had suffered head injury, birth trauma, and exposure to infections and toxins.

By the late 1950s, emphasis was given to overactivity or motor restlessness in these children, and the terms *hyperkinesis*, *hyperkinetic syndrome*, and *hyperactive child syndrome* were variously applied. In time, hyperactivity was downgraded in importance, and attention deficits took center stage. The shift was reflected in the DSM-III (1980), which recognized attention deficit disorder (ADD) either *with* hyperactivity or *without* hyperactivity.

More change was yet to come. In the DSM-III-R (1987), the disorder was relabeled Attention Deficit Hyperactivity Disorder. Children received the diagnosis if they showed 8 or more of 14 items, which could be different mixes of inattention, hyperactivity, and impulsivity. That is, the disorder was viewed as unidimensional, so that any mix of symptoms met the criteria. Nevertheless, the relationship of these three primary features of ADHD was unsettled. Were they part of a single dimension? Or co-occurring but independent of each other? Were two of them alike but different from the third? In fact, the unidimensional view fell by the wayside when factor analytic research designed to better understand the nature of ADHD suggested that the disorder consists of two dimensions: (1) inattention and (2) hyperactivity–impulsivity.

DSM Classification and Diagnosis

This finding became the foundation of the present conceptualization, first presented in the DSM-IV (1994), and labeled Attention-Deficit/Hyperactivity Disorder. The two factors of inattention and hyperactivity-impulsivity compose three subtypes: Predominantly Inattentive Type (ADHD-I), Predominantly Hyperactive–Impulsive Type (ADHD-HI), and a Combined Type (ADHD–C). The major symptoms and criteria for the subtypes of ADHD appear in Table 9–1.

Diagnosis of ADHD demands the presence of some symptoms before age 7, and display of symptoms for at least 6 months. Because all the criterion behaviors are observed to some degree in normal children and may vary with developmental level, diagnosis is given only when symptoms are at odds with developmental level. There also must be clear evidence of impaired social, academic, or occupational functioning. In addition, symptoms must be pervasive; that is, they must occur in at least two settings (e.g., home and school).

Some concern has been expressed about this conceptualization of attention-deficit hyperactivity disorder. The criterion of pervasiveness raised the question of whether cases with relatively mild symptoms go unidentified (August & Garfinkel, 1993). Then, too, although the age criterion of symptom presence before age 7 appears appropriate for most

TABLE 9–1	THE DSM SYMPTOMS OF ATTENTION-DEFICIT/ HYPERACTIVITY DISORDER

A. Symptoms of Inattention

Fails to attend to details or makes careless mistakes in schoolwork or other activities.
Has difficulty in sustaining attention.
Does not seem to listen when spoken to.
Does not follow through on instructions or duties.
Has difficulty organizing tasks and activities.
Avoids or dislikes tasks requiring sustained mental effort.
Often loses things necessary for tasks or activities.
Is distracted by extraneous stimuli.
Is forgetful in daily activities.

B. Symptoms of Hyperactivity–Impulsivity

Hyperactivity

Fidgets with hands or feet or squirms.
Leaves seat inappropriately.
Runs about or climbs inappropriately (in adolescents or adults, may only be feelings of restlessness).
Has difficulty playing quietly or in quiet activities.
Is often "on the go" as if "driven by a motor."
Talks incessantly.

Impulsivity

Blurts out answers before questions are completed.
Has difficulty awaiting turn.
Interrupts or intrudes on others.

Requirements for Diagnosis

ADHD Predominantly Inattentive Type: Six or more symptoms of A
ADHD Predominantly Hyperactive–Impulsive Type: Six or more symptoms of B
ADHD Combined Type: Six or more symptoms of both A and B

From American Psychiatric Association, 2000.

cases of ADHD, it may not apply to all children and especially to those who display only inattention (Willoughby et al., 2000). In addition, the symptom list does not appear to be a good fit with the behaviors of older youths with ADHD. Perhaps even more fundamental, questions have been raised about the subtypes of ADHD. We discuss some of these issues after we look at the core features of ADHD and difficulties that are secondarily associated with the disorder. We use the general label attention-deficit hyperactivity disorder (ADHD) to refer to youth diagnosed with the disorder.

Description: Core Features

INATTENTION

Adults who come into contact with children with ADHD report various signs of inattention. These children do not stick to a task but skip rapidly from one activity to another, do not attend to what is said to them, are easily distracted, daydream, or lose things. One seemingly baffling aspect of the disorder is that the children appear unable to focus and concentrate at some times, but at other times they are able to sit for hours drawing or building with blocks. In fact, attention is situational; it can appear normal when the child is interested or otherwise motivated but problematic when the task is boring, routine, or repetitive.

Although the reports of adults provide reasonably good global descriptions of ADHD, formal observation and controlled research have been conducted to validate and elucidate attention deficits. Children and adolescents with ADHD do pay less attention to their work than children with learning disabilities or normal controls (Barkley, 2006f). In the laboratory, children with ADHD do less well than control children on many tasks that demand attention.

However, attention has many components and is conceptualized in different ways (Nigg, Hinshaw, & Huang-Pollock, 2006; Rothbart & Posner, 2006). Different components, or abilities, develop over different periods and are linked to different brain structures or systems. A distinction is often made between more automatic, early-developing attention and that which develops later and is more voluntary and immersed in higher order cognition. It is not entirely clear which deficits exist in ADHD.

For example, the ability to automatically orient to sensory stimuli (e.g., the onset of a light) does not appear to be deficient. On the other hand, selective attention deficits are found, although not always (Brodeur & Pond, 2001; Lorch et al., 2000; Huang-Pollock, Nigg, & Carr, 2005). Selective attention is the ability to focus on relevant stimuli and not be distracted by irrelevant stimuli. For children with ADHD, distraction appears more likely when tasks are boring or difficult or when irrelevant stimuli are novel or salient.

Sustained attention—paying attention to a task over a period of time—also has been examined. One of the ways in which it has been evaluated is through continuous performance tests (CPTs). Several versions exist but the fundamental task is for the person to push a button to identify a target whenever it comes on a screen, such as a letter within a series of letters (e.g., *t* must be identified each time it follows *m*). Errors can be made by not reacting to the target and by reacting to nontarget stimuli. Children with ADHD often make more of both errors and are slower in responding than normal children and children with other diagnoses (Epstein et al., 2003; Losier, McGrath, & Klein, 1996; Taylor, 1995). However, sustained attention deficits do not specifically define ADHD, because they often occur in other disorders (Swaab-Barneveld et al., 2000). Also, a true deficit in sustained attention would lead to a worsening of performance as the length of the task increases, a condition that only sometimes holds for ADHD.

There is much current interest in the role that attention might play in the regulation of behavior and emotion. It is hypothesized that an executive attention network, involving anterior structures of the brain, modulates the activation of other brain networks (Rothbart & Posner, 2006). Executive attention is thought to be important in tasks requiring the individual, for example, to monitor conflicting stimuli or to suppress a response. Since the regulation of behavior is central in ADHD, this area warrants further study.

HYPERACTIVITY AND IMPULSIVITY

Hyperactivity. Children with ADHD are described as always on the run, driven by a motor, restless, fidgety, and unable to sit still (Barkley, 2006f). These children may display gross bodily movements and talk excessively to themselves or others. In the classroom, they are out of their seats, moving their arms and legs, engaging in things irrelevant to the task at hand, or talking to others.

Although much of the information about activity problems comes from parent and teacher reports, more objective assessment can be made with direct observations and with actigraphs. The latter are small devices worn by the child to measure movement. Objective measures indicate the excessive movement of children with ADHD, as well as variation across youngsters and situations. In one study, actigraph recording showed no differences in the morning between non-ADHD and ADHD youngsters, but in the afternoon non-ADHD youngsters became less active and ADHD youngsters became more active (Figure 9–1). Another study that recorded movement continuously for

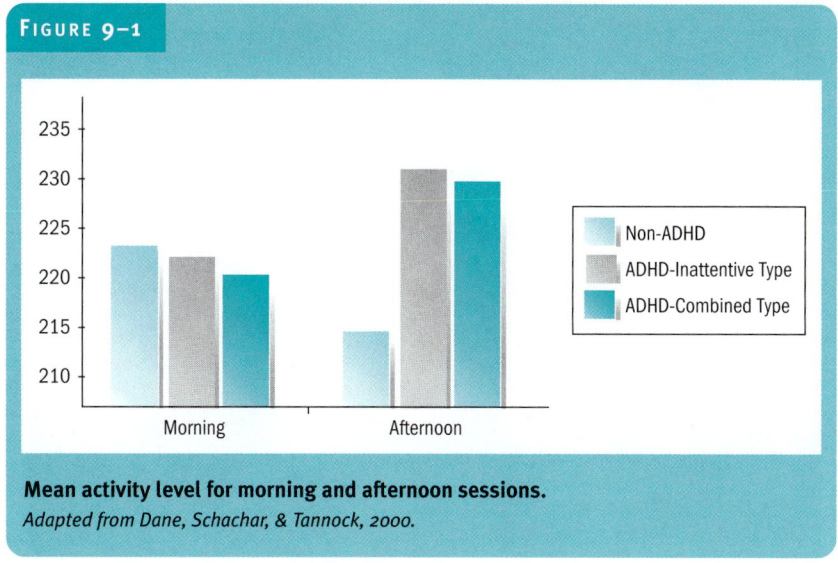

FIGURE 9–1

Mean activity level for morning and afternoon sessions.
Adapted from Dane, Schachar, & Tannock, 2000.

1 week showed that boys with hyperactivity were more active than controls during school reading and mathematics but not physical education and lunch/recess (Porrino et al., 1983). In general, motor excess and restlessness are more likely to occur in highly structured situations that demand children to sit still and regulate their behavior in the face of little reinforcement.

Impulsivity. The essence of impulsivity is a deficiency in inhibiting behavior, holding back, or controlling behavior, which appears as "acting without thinking." The child may interrupt others, cut in line in front of others, or heedlessly engage in dangerous behaviors. Activities that require patience or restraint are not well accomplished. The child's impulsivity often leads others to judge the child as careless, irresponsible, immature, lazy, or rude (Barkley, 1998).

In the laboratory, impulsivity has been assessed in different ways. Variations of the stop task are widely used (Nigg, 2001). For example, stimuli—say the letter X and the letter O—are presented on a screen, and the child is told to press one of two keys depending on which stimulus is presented. Key presses are to be withheld on a minority of trials when a special signal (a tone) comes on, so that the child must sometimes rapidly inhibit (stop) the response. Deficits on the stop task have been shown in several studies with ADHD children (Oosterlaan, Logan, & Sergeant, 1998). This finding, in conjunction with other research, makes clear that problems with inhibition of motor responses are an important aspect of attention-deficit hyperactivity disorder.

Description: Secondary Features

In addition to the core problems of ADHD, youth with the disorder experience more than their share of difficulties in diverse areas of functioning. The findings are disproportionately based on school-age children displaying the combined subtype of ADHD, and the extent to which they apply to preschoolers and adolescents, or youth exhibiting other subtypes of ADHD, requires further investigation.

MOTOR SKILLS

Motor incoordination may affect about half of children with ADHD, a figure that exceeds that for normal children (Barkley, 2006a). The difficulties are shown in clumsiness, delay in motor milestones, poor performance in sports, and the like. The child may show neurological soft signs and various tests indicate deficits in fine motor coordination and timing. Children with ADHD appear especially affected when the tasks involve complex movement and sequencing, which suggests that higher order control processes such as organization and regulation of behavior are affected (Kalff et al., 2003).

INTELLIGENCE, ACADEMIC ACHIEVEMENT

As a group, children with ADHD perform somewhat lower on intelligence tests than normal control groups, an estimated average of 9 points (Barkley, 2006a).

Although roughhouse play is a part of typical childhood activities, the child with ADHD often displays excessively energetic and undercontrolled behavior.
(Jennie Woodcock/Corbis/Bettmann)

They exhibit a range of general intelligence, though, including into the gifted range (Antshel et al., 2007). Many have specific learning disabilities in reading, mathematics, and other academic areas, which are not due to lowered intelligence (a topic discussed later in the chapter).

Reduced academic achievement is prominent among youth with ADHD (Frazier et al., 2007). Preacademic skill deficits have been shown in preschoolers with ADHD (DuPaul et al., 2001), and academic problems may be obvious in the first few years of school (Lahey et al., 1998). Failure is indicated by low achievement test scores, low school grades, being held back in grade, and placement in special education classes. As many as 56% of children need academic tutoring, 30% may repeat a grade, and 30 to 40% may experience at least one special education placement (Barkley, 2006a). Moreover, from 10 to 35% may fail to graduate high school.

Cognition: Executive Functions

Children with ADHD exhibit deficits on numerous experimental and neuropsychological tasks that are interpreted as difficulties in executive functions (Hinshaw et al., 2002; Nigg et al., 2006; Pennington & Ozonoff, 1996). Executive functions refer to several cognitive processes necessary for goal-directed behavior (Clark, Prior, & Kinsella, 2002). Executive functions are involved in planning and organizing actions and in self-regulation. Among other processes, they include working memory, verbal self-regulation, inhibition of behavior, regulation of emotion, and motor control. These higher order processes are associated with the frontal areas of the brain and their connections.

Adaptive Functioning

Relative to their level of general intelligence, children with ADHD have been shown to have deficiencies in many domains of everyday adaptive behavior. The discrepancy appears larger than for normal children and for select other disorders (Barkley, 2006a). Deficits in self-care and independence are sometimes at the level that would be expected with much greater intellectual impairment (Hinshaw, 1998). Many of the children engage in behavior more immature than what their abilities seem to warrant, and require greater monitoring by adults than what might be anticipated.

Although a failure to learn everyday skills may occur, failure to *perform* known skills might well be more crucial (Barkley et al., 2002). Indeed, because ADHD involves deficits in executive functions, which aid in the performance of goal-directed behavior, ADHD might best be seen as a disorder of "doing" rather than of "knowing" (Clark, Prior, & Kinsella, 2002).

"You're so organized!"

SOCIAL BEHAVIOR AND RELATIONSHIPS

Social difficulties, which are reported in a high proportion of cases of ADHD, may be an important reason for adults to seek professional help for children with ADHD. It is unsurprising that children who are distractible, excessively active, inappropriately talkative, intrusive, and disorganized garner negative reactions from others. When this profile is combined with the noncompliance and aggression sometimes linked to ADHD, the social difficulties may be particularly detrimental.

Various explanations have been offered for these social problems. The youngsters may only inadequately process social-emotional cues (Cadesky, Mota, & Schachar, 2000). Or they may know what is appropriate but be unable to enact the proper behavior, especially when excited or irritated. They sometimes may have social goals that could be expected to create problems; for example, they may prefer fun to the extent that they are willing to break rules (Melnick & Hinshaw, 1996). It is also relevant that children with ADHD-C have a positive bias regarding their social competence, behavioral conduct, and academic competence (Gerdes, Hoza, & Pelham, 2003; Hoza et al., 2004). They are unaware of their negative impact on others, rate their relationships as overly positive, and overestimate the degree to which they are liked and accepted.

Peer and teacher relations. Given all this, it is not surprising that children with ADHD have trouble making and keeping friends; they frequently are disliked and rejected by peers. Very rapidly, after only a few social exchanges, peers may view the child with ADHD as disruptive and unpredictable and react

with rejection and withdrawal (de Boo & Prins, 2007). Whereas negative reactions apply more strongly to children who are impulsive and hyperactive, those with only attention problems tend to be ignored or neglected (Hinshaw, 1998; Hinshaw, 2002b). Problems in child peer relationships can carry over to adolescence or appear for the first time in adolescence (Bagwell, et al., 2001).

Distractible, disruptive school behaviors can be exhibited very early (Campbell, 2002). In one study, preschool teachers rated young children with ADHD as having more problem behavior and less social skill than typical children (DuPaul et al., 2001). In another study, teachers of young children associated all subtypes of ADHD with less cooperation and fewer other positive behaviors, and they associated hyperactivity–impulsivity with disruptive and less self-controlled behavior (Lahey et al., 1998). Teachers tend to be directive and controlling when interacting with children with ADHD.

Family relations. ADHD clearly takes a toll on family interaction. In general, there is considerable parent–child conflict, with parents being less rewarding and more negative and directive (Barkley, 2006d). Negative exchanges may occur as early as the child's preschool years (DuPaul et al., 2001), and this time period is perhaps especially stressful for parents. Mother–child relations appear more difficult than father–child interactions, although the latter are still affected (Barkley, 2006d). Evidence exists that mothers give more commands and rewards to sons than daughters, and that interactions are more emotional and rancorous. Negative interactions do appear to stem from the child's behavior, with conflicts strongly associated with the child's being oppositional. Families with adolescents who have ADHD and ODD appear to have more than the usual number of arguments, negative communications, and hostility (Edwards et al., 2001).

Broader family malfunctioning associated with ADHD undoubtedly plays a role in child–parent relationships. Family difficulties include parenting stress, lowered sense of parenting competence, decreased contact with extended family, increased alcohol use, and increased rates of marital conflict, separation, and divorce (Barkley, 2006d). Parents of youth with ADHD are themselves at genetic risk for a variety of problems, including the symptoms of ADHD. A negative family profile is especially associated with the child's being oppositional or displaying conduct problems.

HEALTH, SLEEP, ACCIDENTS

There are many reports of general or specific health problems associated with ADHD, including allergies and asthma, but the data are inconsistent and do not allow clear conclusions (Barkley, 2006a).

It is not unusual for parents to report sleep difficulties in a substantial number of children with ADHD. The problems involve inability to fall asleep, night awakening, fewer hours of sleep, and involuntary movements during sleep (e.g., teeth grinding, leg restlessness). However, objective laboratory studies of overnight sleep are inconsistent regarding physiological differences in sleep (e.g., Barkley, 2006a; Kirov et al., 2007). Moreover, it is suggested that sleep difficulties may be due to co-occurring symptoms, such as anxiety and depression. Treatment with stimulant medication may also interfere with sleep.

Relatively well documented is that children with ADHD suffer more accidental injury than those without ADHD. A comprehensive review cited 57% of the children as "accident prone," and noted that 15% had at least four or more serious injuries such as broken bones, head lacerations, bruises, lost teeth, and poisonings (Barkley, 2006a). What accounts for these risks? Inattention and impulsivity have been related to unintentional injury (Rowe, Simonoff, & Silberg, 2007). According to parents, children with ADHD are inattentive in risky situations and unmindful of the consequences of their actions. Also noteworthy are motor incoordination, defiant and aggressive behavior associated with ADHD, and inadequate parental monitoring. Some of these factors are involved in the difficulties displayed by adolescents with ADHD regarding automobile-related behaviors (See Accent: "Autos, Adolescence, and ADHD.")

ACCENT ● ● ● ● ●

Autos, Adolescence, and ADHD

Most adolescents in the United States look forward to the time they can drive an automobile and they highly value the activity. Parents often look upon the advent as a mixed blessing at best, as the beginning of new worries about accidents, injuries, and other problems.

Parents of adolescents with ADHD appear to have good reason for concern. Several studies give evidence, through self-report and official records, that these youth are at heightened risk for

- repeated traffic citations, especially for speeding,
- repeated and more severe vehicular crashes,
- suspension of driving licenses, and
- illegal driving prior to obtaining a license (Barkley, 2006a).

In young drivers with ADHD, there is some evidence of inattention, distractibility, and problems in inhibition (Barkley, 2006a). In a study of young adults who had scored high on ADHD symptoms during adolescence, inattention was still linked to serious motor accidents after other influential factors, such as conduct problems and relatively little driving experience, were accounted for (Woodward, Fergusson, & Horwood, 2000).

A limited number of investigations have found differences in ratings of actual driving habits, that is, in safely maneuvering and otherwise managing the vehicle. Both adolescents and young adult drivers with ADHD rated themselves as using poorer driving behaviors, and they were similarly rated by others who knew them well (Barkley, 2006a). Interestingly, one investigation showed no differences in knowledge about driving, whereas a larger study indicated less knowledge about driving laws and rules of the road but not about aspects such as driving procedures and driving risks. It is interesting to speculate on whether driving supports the idea that ADHD is more a problem of performance than of knowledge.

DSM Subtypes

We have seen that the DSM recognizes three subtypes of ADHD: Predominantly Inattentive (ADHD-I), Predominantly Hyperactive–Impulsive (ADHD-HI), and the combination of these symptoms (ADHD-C). Many investigations, including studies in different countries, generally validate and support the usefulness of these subtypes (Gadow et al., 2000; Gomez et al., 1999; Graetz et al., 2001; Hudziak et al., 1998; Lahey et al., 1994). Symptoms tend to cluster according to these subtypes, and other characteristics differentiate the three groups. Nonetheless, the subtypes have not been equally studied and important questions are raised about them.

Research on ADHD-HI is relatively scant, and this subtype is minimally discussed in the chapter. It has been suggested that ADHD-HI is an early developmental stage of ADHD-C (Barkley, 2006f). In some cases, what seems to be ADHD-HI in preschoolers might better be considered as oppositional defiant behaviors, which may or may not fade.

Interest in the inattentive subtype (ADHD-I) has existed for many years. Recall, if you will, that the DSM had once recognized a category of attention deficit disorder without hyperactivity. It is, nevertheless, the combined subtype (ADHD-C) that has most often been described and investigated. The following case description illustrates ADHD-C, exhibited in a child of almost 7 years of age. The presence of inattention, hyperactivity, and impulsivity are obvious.

| **Jimmy** | **Combined Subtype of ADHD** |

Jimmy was not seen as a "bad" child by his parents; he was not oppositional, aggressive, stubborn, or ill-tempered. But he was in constant motion, and often wandered off, sometimes getting into dangerous situations such as running into the road without looking. Jimmy seemed eager to please his parents, but frequently did not follow through on their requests. It seemed that Jimmy was sidetracked by other things he found more interesting. His parents adopted an active style of dealing with him—monitoring him, reminding him, using immediate reinforcement and punishment.

When Jimmy was enrolled in preschool, his inattentive, overactive, and impulsive behaviors led his parents to withdraw him from one program and his being asked to leave a second program. Among the difficulties were talking during quiet times, lack of interest in group activities, distracting others, and engaging in too much imaginative play. Similar kinds of behaviors were reported in kindergarten, where he had problems focusing attention, being too active, and being unable to work independently. An evaluation at that time showed Jimmy to have high average intelligence but achieving at somewhat lower levels.

By first grade, Jimmy's impulsivity began to interfere with his social relationships. He was described as immature and silly. His peers complained of his bothering them, grabbing them, and pulling them, and although Jimmy was friendly he was unable to maintain friendships. His behavior, more acceptable at early ages, was no longer accepted by peers. The coach noted an inability to participate in organized sports and that Jimmy was off-task and silly. Teachers too had complaints: Jimmy did not follow directions or complete academic tasks on time, and he was disruptive due to excessive activity and noise making. He had fallen behind in reading and writing skills.

From Hathaway, Dooling-Litfin, & Edwards, 2006, pp. 390–391.

The description of Jimmy's behavior can be compared to a depiction of a boy who received the diagnosis of ADHD-I. It is important to note that research with inattentive children has sometimes found a factor referred to as sluggish cognitive tempo. Children displaying a sluggish cognitive tempo tend to be lethargic, prone to daydreams, confused, and more socially withdrawn (Hartman et al., 2004; Milich et al., 2001). These behaviors do not appear on the DSM list of symptoms for attention-deficit hyperactivity disorder. The following portrayal of Tim shows inattention problems and sluggish cognitive tempo. It is a very different clinical picture than that of the restless, on-the-go, and disruptive behaviors of the child with hyperactive and impulsive behaviors.

| **Tim** | **Predominantly Inattentive Subtype of ADHD** |

Tim was a quiet, somewhat introverted child who was not noticeable in a crowd. His early development was unremarkable, and he was not a behavior problem.

In elementary school, Tim's behavior and academic performance were adequate. But he did not volunteer information, often appeared in a daze, and often did not catch what teachers said when they called upon him. He had no problem in reading words but had difficulty staying with a train of thought, which created comprehension problems. Approaching third grade, with new demands for independent schoolwork, Tim began to have increased difficulties, including completing his work on time. The school determined that he was not eligible for special services, but school personnel commented on his attention lapses, poor focusing, being "spacey," and getting lost in daydreams. His grades in middle school became less consistent, ranging from Bs to Ds, and productivity declined further in seventh and eighth grades. Tim's attention problems and poor study habits took a larger toll in high school, and he was transferred to a vocational high school in eleventh grade.

Despite academic problems, Tim made and kept friends, although he was reserved and indifferent to organized recreational activities. His academic performance was a source of conflict with his mother, who reported that Tim was often irritable, talked back, and blamed others for his mistakes. He was, however, cooperative in other ways, for example, in completing home chores. Based on assessment when he was almost 18 years of age, Tim was described as presumably of average intelligence, with a chronic history of inattentiveness, distractibility, and underachievement.

From Hathaway, Dooling-Litfin, & Edwards, 2006, pp. 410–411.

For subtypes of a disorder to be valid, they must be different not only in symptoms but also in other important features. Children with ADHD-I are thought to be distinct from those with ADHD-C in several ways (Bauermeister et al., 2005; Faraone et al., 1998; Milich et al., 2001). Age of onset appears to be later, and girls with ADHD may be more likely to be diagnosed with the inattentive subtype than other subtypes (Zalecki & Hinshaw, 2004). ADHD-I children appear more passive and shy; they engage in less fighting and aggression. ADHD-I also is less associated with externalizing disorders and perhaps more strongly linked with internalizing symptoms. Unsurprising then, inattentive children are less rejected by their peers, although they may be isolated. Limited evidence also exists for differences in brain functioning (evoked potentials) between the inattentive and combined groups (Smith, Johnstone, & Barry, 2003).

Although these differences are viewed as supporting ADHD-I as a valid subtype of ADHD, the matter is not completely settled (Huang-Pollock, Nigg, & Carr, 2005). Differences often have not been found on neuropsychological testing and laboratory

studies of inattention and impulsivity (Hinshaw, 2001; Lahey, 2001; Nigg et al., 2002; Pelham, 2001). The findings, mixed at best, suggest to some that the subtypes are not distinct and that ADHD-I may instead be a milder version of ADHD-C.

With an eye toward this debate, Nigg (2006) and colleagues compared the families of children with different ADHD subtypes with control families. Compared with controls, children with ADHD-I did not have elevated family rates of ADHD-C. But children with ADHD-C did have an elevated likelihood of having relatives with ADHD-I. It was suggested that children with ADHD-I actually include both (1) those who compose a partially or wholly distinct subtype and (2) those who have a milder version of the ADHD-C subtype.

In addition, some researchers have proposed that inattentive children fall into either a group described by the DSM-IV inattention symptoms *or* a group characterized by dreamy, sluggish cognitive tempo. The latter group might represent a unique subtype of ADHD, or perhaps even a distinct disorder (Barkley, 2006d; Milich et al., 2001; Todd et al., 2005). It is suggested that sluggish cognitive tempo may involve deficits in selective attention and slow cognitive processing, in contrast to an inability to inhibit behavior that characterizes hyperactivity–impulsivity. Clearly, there is a need for further study of children showing sluggish cognitive tempo and, more generally, of the nature of attention-deficit hyperactivity disorder and its subtypes.

ADHD and Comorbid Disorders

A remarkable fact about ADHD, especially ADHD-C, is the degree to which it coexists with other disorders. As is usually the case, rates of co-occurrence depend on the samples, measures, the specific disorders, and the like. Comorbidity is higher in clinic than in community samples, with more of the referred youngsters likely than not to have another disorder (Costin et al., 2002) and a sizable number exhibiting two or more disorders. Comorbidity generally is related to greater impairment and developmental risk.

LEARNING DISABILITIES

Reports of the rates of learning disabilities (LD) in youth with ADHD vary enormously (Smith & Adams, 2006). An overall range of 15 to 40% has been suggested (Rucklidge & Tannock, 2002; Schachar & Tannock, 2002). Perhaps unsurprisingly, children with ADHD and LD are at greater risk for academic impairment than children with only ADHD (Smith & Adams, 2006). Although the relationship between ADHD and learning problems is not well understood, some evidence exists that ADHD leads to reading disabilities rather than the other way around, and that inattention is more crucially involved than hyperactivity in these reading problems (e.g., Stevenson et al., 2005). Shared genetic influence is implicated in the relationship of ADHD to reading disabilities, as well as to spelling disabilities (Stevenson et al., 2005; Trzesniewski et al, 2006). Research into the specific underlying genes is ongoing (Gaván et al., 2005).

EXTERNALIZING DISORDERS

As mentioned in Chapter 8, ADHD, Oppositional Defiant Disorder (ODD), and Conduct Disorder (CD) are considered together in the DSM-IV as Attention-Deficit and Disruptive Behavior Disorders. Researchers once wondered whether these disorders were actually only one common disorder. Epidemiological and clinic studies made it clear, however, that the disorders have distinct symptom clusters and other distinct features (Hinshaw & Lee, 2003; Nadder et al., 2001; Waschbusch, 2002). ADHD generally is more strongly associated with cognitive impairment and neurodevelopmental abnormalities. CD and ODD are more strongly related to adverse family factors and psychosocial disadvantage (Waschbusch, 2002).

ADHD can lead to ODD that in turn can lead to CD, and the symptoms of ODD and CD frequently co-occur. Substantial percentages of children and adolescents with ADHD develop ODD alone or with CD (Barkley, 2006d). Children who receive the diagnosis of either ADHD or CD are over ten times more likely to get the other diagnosis (Angold, Costello, & Erklani, 1999).

The co-occurrence of ADHD symptoms and conduct/oppositional symptoms in clinic and nonreferred groups has been extensively investigated. Compared with children with only ADHD, those with the combination appear more disturbed and impaired, both in ADHD symptoms and conduct problems (Barkley, 1998; Jensen, Martin, & Cantwell, 1997; Waschbusch, 2002). This general finding holds for preschoolers as well (Gadow & Nolan, 2002). Importantly, behavioral difficulties appear earlier in children with the combined profile, problems are likely to persist, and outcome is more negative. Other differences are noteworthy. ADHD with co-occurring conduct poblems is generally more strongly associ-

ated with coercive parent–child interactions, parental psychiatric symptoms and substance abuse, and disadvantaged social class (e.g., Hinshaw & Lee, 2003; Waschbusch, 2002). The several differences between ADHD and ADHD plus conduct problems have led to the suggestion that the combined condition may best be viewed as a subcategory of ADHD (Jensen, et al., 1997). Regardless of this issue, however, it is clear is that knowing whether a youth with ADHD also has conduct problems tells us much about the youth.

ANXIETY

It is estimated that, on average, about 25 to 35% of youths with ADHD, either in clinic or in community samples, have anxiety disorders (Barkley, 2006d; Jensen et al., 1997; Manassis, Tannock, & Barbosa, 2000). The presence of one disorder triples the odds of having the other disorder. Many questions remain about such co-occurrence, however. Some, but not all, data suggest that these children are less hyperactive and impulsive than children with ADHD who do not have anxiety disorders, and they may display fewer conduct problems and higher levels of inattention. The presence of anxiety with ADHD may be associated with some differences in performance on cognitive tasks, and differential response to interventions has inconsistently been shown (Manassis et al., 2000, Hechtman, 2005). The combined profile also shows greater persistence of ADHD symptoms but, interestingly, little risk for anxiety in adolescence and early adulthood (Barkley, 2006d).

MOOD DISORDERS

The co-occurrence of ADHD with mild depressive symptoms and major depression is found at varying rates in children and adolescents and in clinic and community samples (Barkley, 2003; Biederman, Faraone, Mick et al., 1996). Perhaps 25 to 30% of ADHD cases on average have major depression. Given one disorder the odds of having the other disorder ranges from 3.5 to 8.4 (Angold et al, 1999). ADHD plus depression frequently results in poorer outcome than either disorder alone (Barkley, 2006d). Interestingly, the overly positive perception of their own competence that some children with ADHD have appears to be absent in the presence of co-occurring depression (Hoza et al., 2004).

The association of ADHD with depression is probably complex. For example, one study of youths attending clinics suggested that ADHD led to ODD

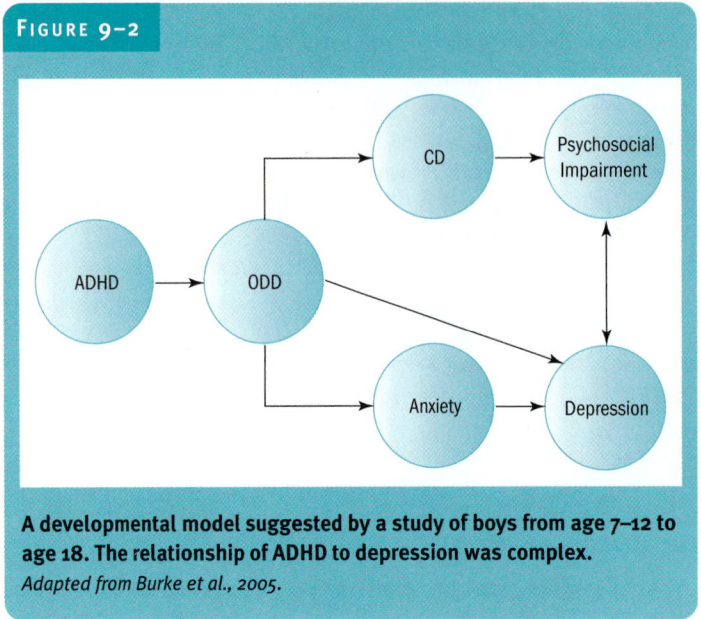

FIGURE 9–2

A developmental model suggested by a study of boys from age 7–12 to age 18. The relationship of ADHD to depression was complex.
Adapted from Burke et al., 2005.

and then to various paths to depression (Burke et al., 2005). (See Figure 9–2.) ADHD and major depression may share familial etiological factors (Barkley, 2006d). The co-occurrence of ADHD with depression in youths is associated with greater family stress and pathology, as well as with an increased risk of family members having both disorders.

The co-occurrence of ADHD and bipolar disorder has been reported in the range of 10 to 20% (Barkley, 2003), but such co-occurrence is controversial (Barkley, 2006d; Hechtman, 2005). The controversy stems from problems in identifying childhood bipolar disorder (see pp. 178–180) and from the similarity of symptoms for diagnosing mania and ADHD. Limited information does suggest that the diagnosis of childhood bipolar disorder may substantially increase the concurrent diagnosis of ADHD, but that youths with ADHD are not generally at risk for bipolar disorder. There is still much to learn about this and other co-occurring conditions.

Epidemiology

Prevalence of ADHD in U.S. school-age children has been estimated as 3 to 7% (American Psychiatric Association, 2000), although some recent epidemiological data suggest the upper ceiling may be somewhat higher (Pliszka et al., 2007). It is difficult to draw many overall conclusions about the rates of the DSM subtypes from the mixed methods and data. In clinic studies, ADHD-C is most common.

There is a large overall variation in reported rates. The distinction must be made between clinically diagnosed ADHD and designations based on parent or teacher ratings of symptoms that meet a specific criterion. Rates are typically higher in the latter kind of reports, and can reach over 20% (e.g., Nolan, Gadow, & Sprafkin, 2001). In fact, this difference might be expected because the method usually does not include criteria employed for clinical diagnosis such as age of onset, pervasiveness of symptoms, and functional impairment.

In general, less is known about prevalence in the preschool and adolescent years than in childhood. However, a decline in diagnosed ADHD from childhood to adolescence is widely observed. The disorder may indeed be less common in the teenage years, but it is also possible that diagnostic items for ADHD do not adequately describe how the disorder may be manifested in adolescence (Nigg et al., 2006).

GENDER

Gender difference in prevalence is strikingly consistent. Two to 9 boys for every girl receive the diagnosis, depending on the type of ADHD and the setting (American Psychiatric Association, 2000). The average gender ratio in community samples is 3.4 boys to 1 girl, and it is higher in clinic samples (Barkley, 2006f).

Gender differences in clinic samples probably reflect a referral bias due to boys' greater aggression and antisocial behavior. Prevalence may also be affected by the fact that the diagnostic criteria are biased toward behaviors observed more in males—such as running, climbing, and leaving one's seat in the classroom. It is interesting that when boys, but not girls, exhibit oppositional defiant behaviors, teachers may overidentify ADHD symptoms—which could inflate rates for boys (Jackson & King, 2004). These factors, or some more fundamental gender difference, may be linked with the finding that some girls display the symptoms of ADHD but at levels that do not meet the DSM-IV criteria (Waschbusch & King, 2006).

A related but more general question is whether ADHD is manifested differently in boys than in girls. An early meta-analysis of research indicated that girls with the disorder were less hyperactive, displayed fewer externalizing symptoms, and had lower intelligence (Gaub & Carlson, 1997). No gender differences were found for level of impulsiveness, academic performance, social functioning, fine motor control, or family factors such as parental depression and education. Subsequent reviews were both consistent and inconsistent with these findings and with one another. What appears to be emerging, particularly from population rather than clinic samples, is that comparisons of girls and boys reveal more similarities than differences (Bauermeister et al., 2005; Hinshaw, 2002b, Hinshaw, et al., 2002). Still, girls with ADHD may show lower levels of ADHD symptoms, conduct disturbance, or intelligence (Barkley, 2006f), and gender differences could depend on the subtypes of ADHD (Bauermeister et al., 2005).

Social Class and Culture

The relationship of prevalence and social class is unclear. ADHD does appear in all social classes and higher rates are sometimes associated with lower SES (Barkley, 2006f). The symptoms of ADHD are observed in many countries (Hechtman, 2005), which report similar gender ratios and an association of ADHD with learning and conduct problems (Whalen & Henker, 1998). But prevalence is quite variable across cultures. This may be due, of course, to differences in sampling, the way that ADHD is defined, who does the observing, and cultural values.

Developmental Course and Prognosis

The importance of studying attention-deficit hyperactivity disorder across developmental levels has become increasingly clear. Because ADHD is believed to emerge by age 7, examination of the earlier years of life can be critical to understanding the origin of the disorder. At the same time, children do not necessarily "outgrow" ADHD, as was once believed, so the developmental course of ADHD can be understood only by observing the persistence of symptoms into adolescence and adulthood.

Infancy and the Preschool Years

It is believed that at least some cases of ADHD begin in infancy, but this possibility is not easily established. How would ADHD manifest itself so early in life? It is reasonable that temperamental differences in activity level, distractibility, and the like might forecast ADHD, at least in part. Sanson and colleagues (1993) reported that a group of children who were hyperactive and aggressive at age 8 had displayed early difficult temperament, and by age 3 to 4 had been more active and less cooperative and manageable than normal children. It is hypothesized that temperamental tendencies for emotional reactivity and poor self-regulation may be precursors of later ADHD (Nigg, Goldsmith, & Sachek, 2004).

Behaviors that are symptomatic of attention-deficit hyperactivity disorder are commonly reported in preschoolers. Campbell's (2002) study of hard-to-manage preschoolers indicates that problems often lessened, but that for some children symptoms persisted and could meet the criteria for ADHD in childhood. Continuance of problems was related to higher level of initial symptoms, negative mother–child interaction, more family adversity, and more signs of conduct problems.

Shaw, Lacourse, and Nagin (2005) followed a community sample of boys from low-income families from age 1.5 to 10 years. Based on multiple measures, four developmental paths were suggested for ADHD symptoms. Figure 9–3 shows these trajectories and the percentage of children associated with each of them. Although generalization from this study must be made cautiously, the general findings parallel a study of older children. In general, it appears that most children do not show increasing rates of symptoms when followed from age 2 into childhood, but that a relatively small percentage displays chronically high levels of symptoms.

Childhood

Most cases of ADHD are referred between the ages of 6 and 12—probably in part due to school demands that children pay attention, follow rules, get along

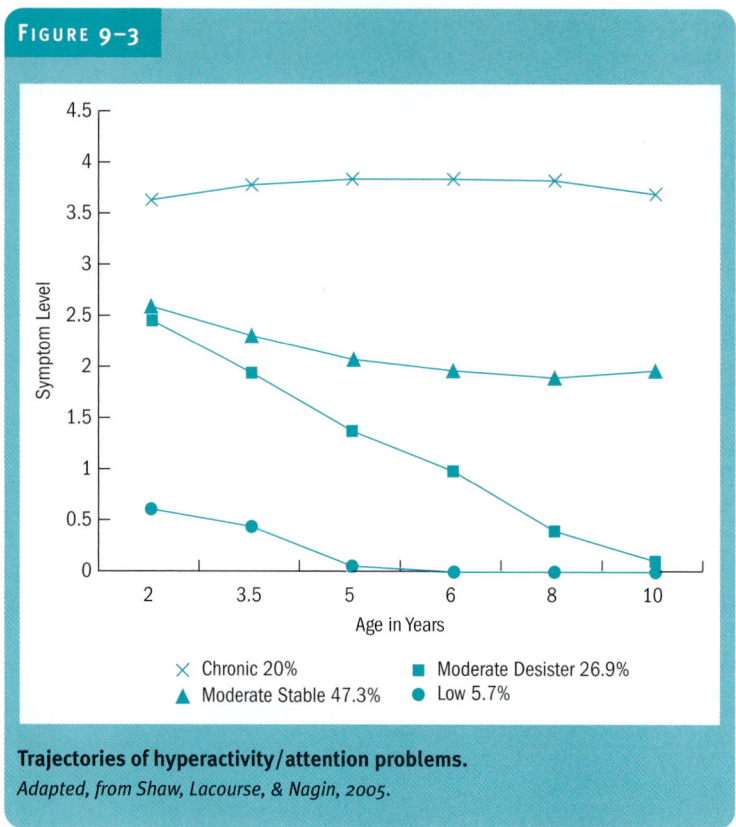

FIGURE 9–3

Trajectories of hyperactivity/attention problems.
Adapted, from Shaw, Lacourse, & Nagin, 2005.

with others, and otherwise regulate their own behavior (Campbell, 2000; Hechtman, 2005). These are the years that have been well described and documented, and during which inattention may become obvious. Among these children self-regulation and self-organization are problematic, social relationships can be far from satisfactory, peer rejection becomes obvious, and poor academic achievement is observed. Clinical-level oppositional behaviors, conduct problems, and internalizing symptoms also can become apparent in some children.

ADOLESCENCE AND ADULTHOOD

In adolescence, the core symptoms of ADHD—especially hyperactive–impulsive behaviors—may decrease in a substantial number of cases, and the diagnosis of ADHD may no longer apply. Still, the disorder can persist, with estimates ranging widely from about 40 to 80% of affected youth (Smith et al., 2006; Hansen, Weiss, & Last, 1999; Willoughby, 2003). Two aspects of symptom manifestation are noteworthy: (1) even when diagnostic criteria are not met, some adolescents may experience the core manifestations of ADHD to some degree and (2) heterotypic continuity of symp-

toms is likely. That is, the core symptoms may carry over in somewhat different forms; for example, overactive running about in childhood may later become manifest as inability to relax (Willoughby, 2003).

Several longitudinal studies of the outcome of childhood ADHD leave no doubt that the disorder puts these children at risk for a variety of other problems in adolescence. These include poor school achievement, reading problems, conduct disorder, antisocial behavior, drug use or abuse, social problems, accidents, teenage pregnancy, and internalizing problems (Fischer et al., 1993; McGee et al., 2002; Slomkowski, Klein, & Mannuzza, 1995; Smith et al., 2006). Issues that often challenge family relationships in adolescence—noncompliance to rules and conflicts over curfews and schoolwork—may be particularly prominent (Robin, 2006).

Based on the relatively few studies that followed ADHD into the adult years, it appears that substantial percentages of youth still display some core deficits and/or impaired social relationships, depression, low self-concept, antisocial behavior and personality, drug use, and educational and occupational disadvantage (Mannuzza et al., 1993; 1998; Smith et al., 2006; Weiss & Hechtman, 1986). More recently, interest has grown in adults who for the first time are identified with the symptoms of ADHD and retrospectively report a history of childhood ADHD symptoms (Barkley, 1998: Ernst et al., 2003). Of course, the question of reliability must be raised regarding such retrospective reports, and caution must be taken in generalizing from adult ADHD to child ADHD. Nonetheless, these cases of adult ADHD do suggest that the disorder can be a chronic, lifelong condition.

VARIATION AND PREDICTION OF OUTCOME

In examining developmental data for ADHD, it is important to consider the overall picture. *First*, the percentage of children who continue to have difficulties varies a good deal over studies, which may reflect true sample differences or methodological factors. *Second*, the core symptoms of ADHD, especially hyperactivity–impulsivity, appear to lessen with development. *Third*, many associated problems can exist into later years, although the trend is for difficulties to weaken over time. *Fourth*, ADHD comorbid with conduct problems is especially associated with poorer outcomes. *Fifth*, heterogeneity exists in developmental course and outcome; some children overcome earlier problems and are reasonably well adjusted in adulthood, whereas others show various kinds and degrees of problems. This latter fact prompts the question, What variables predict outcome?

Many predictors of adolescent and adult problems have been identified (Table 9–2). However, the picture is a complex one. Risk factors may be related to outcome for some subtypes of ADHD and not others. For example, early age of onset may predict worse outcome for ADHD-C than for ADHD-I (Willoughby

et al., 2000). Risks also appear different for different areas of functioning (Campbell, 1995; Fergusson, Lynskey, & Horwood, 1997; Lambert, 1988; McGee et al., 2002). Poor educational outcome appears especially associated with early deficits in attention, intelligence, and academic skill, as well as with some child-rearing practices. In contrast, the continuance of antisocial behavior is especially associated with family disturbance and the child's aggression and conduct problems. In the latter case, it appears that early ADHD symptoms combined with adverse parent–child interactions and/or other family adversities put the child on an early path to oppositional behavior and subsequent conduct disorder—which leads to persistent antisocial behavior (Loeber et al., 1995; Patterson, DeGarmo, & Knutson, 2000). Genetic influences may also play a role here.

Theories of ADHD

Various cognitive or neuropsychological accounts of ADHD have been offered. They have emphasized attention, arousal, response to reward, time perception, working memory, inhibition, executive functions, or self-regulation (Nigg et al., 2006; Rapport et al., 2001). These accounts, which tend to be conceptually related, vary in how comprehensive they are, and frequently reference brain functioning. Our discussion highlights a few of the central ideas from the voluminous research literature.

AROUSAL LEVEL

Arousal refers to alertness or the intensity or speed of reaction to stimuli, which can be measured in several ways. The regulation of arousal is an important component of functioning. Although children with ADHD may exhibit over- or underarousal, there is more evidence for the latter (Nigg et al., 2006). For example, these children show slow reaction on different laboratory tasks and underarousal of brain response. Low arousal is one component of the cognitive-energetic model of ADHD, which more broadly addresses the inability of children with ADHD to apply effort and activate cognitive resources towards task completion (Sergeant, 2000).

SENSITIVITY TO REWARD

Unusual sensitivity to reinforcement has been inconsistently noted in children with ADHD. For example, they have been shown to do poorly under partial schedules of reinforcement and otherwise low incentives (e.g., Slusarek et al., 2001). Also

TABLE 9–2	SOME VARIABLES THAT MAY PREDICT ADOLESCENT AND ADULT OUTCOMES OF CHILDHOOD ADHD

Age of onset
Severity of symptoms
Aggression; conduct problems
Academic performance
General Intelligence
Family adversities
Parents' ADHD and psychiatric disorder
Parents' child-rearing practice; parent–child interaction
Genetic factors

notable is an atypically high preference for immediate reward over delayed reward (Tripp & Alsop, 2001). A recent study suggested that children with ADHD may have abnormal cardiac responses to reward and punishment (Luman et al., 2007). These findings can be interpreted as abnormality in the reward system, which may lead to differences in responding to the usual contingencies involved in paying attention, staying on task, following rules, and the like.

AVERSION TO DELAY

Sonuga-Barke and colleagues have proposed that one path to ADHD involves an aversion to delay. In general, delay aversion would be manifested by attempts to avoid or escape delay (Sonuga-Barke et al., 2004). Thus, the preference that children with ADHD show for immediate over delayed reward may have more to do with avoiding delay than with the reward itself (Sonuga-Barke, 1994). It is argued that in situations where delay cannot be escaped or avoided, children will attend to aspects of the environment that help "speed up" the perception of time. Antrop and colleagues (2000) evaluated this

idea by observing children with and without ADHD when they had to wait in a room with little available stimulation. On some measures, the children with ADHD engaged in more activity, presumably to lessen a subjective sense of delay. In another study, Sonuga-Barke and colleagues (2004) found support for the prediction that children with ADHD would be more sensitive to environmental cues for delay because delay has particular emotional or motivational significance for them.

INHIBITION AND EXECUTIVE FUNCTIONS

As already noted, children with ADHD exhibit deficits in executive functions, the higher-order skills required for planning, organizing, and implementing goal-directed behavior. One component of executive functions is the ability to inhibit responses. Deficits in inhibition, which are well documented in ADHD, hold a central place in explaining the disorder.

Barkley's model. Barkley's (1998; 2006b) multifaceted model, which applies only to the hyperactivity–impulsivity aspects of ADHD, gives response inhibition a central role in the disorder. As Figure 9–4

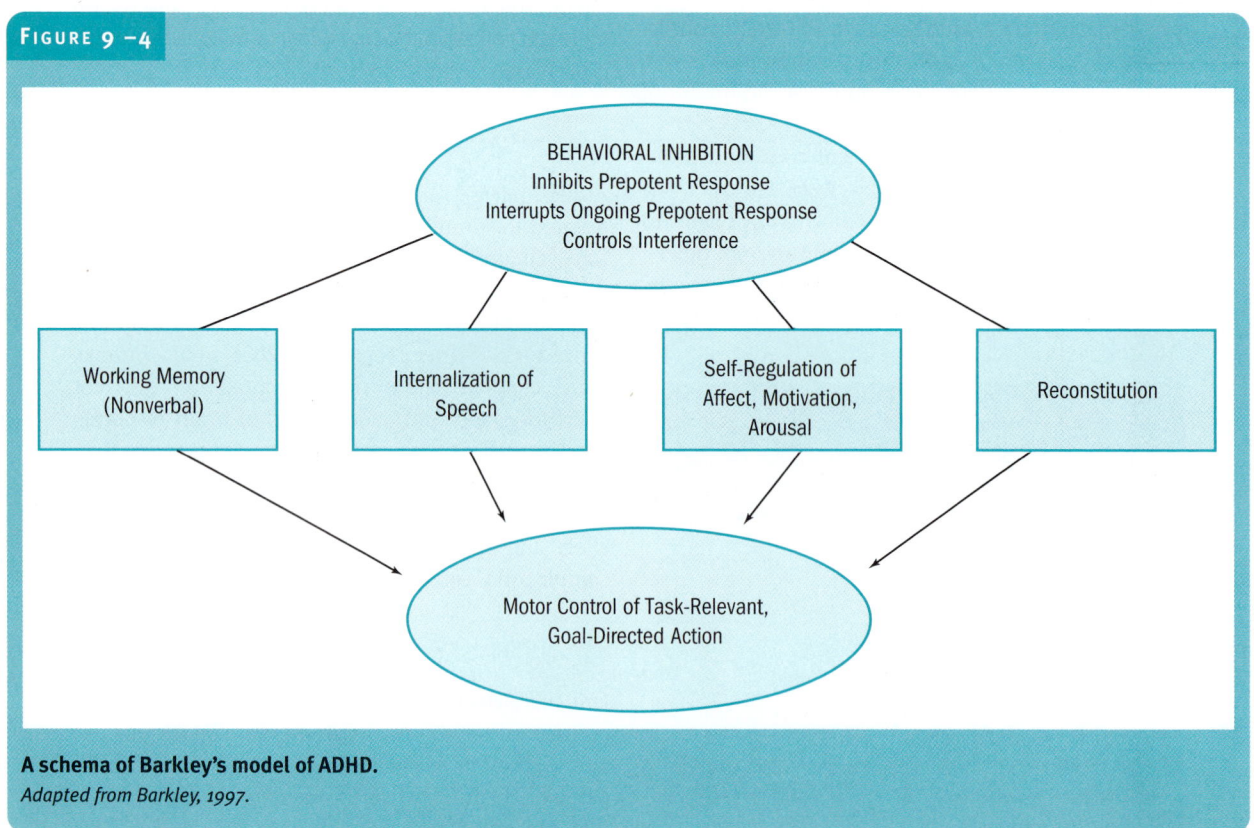

FIGURE 9 –4

A schema of Barkley's model of ADHD.
Adapted from Barkley, 1997.

indicates, behavioral inhibition is viewed as critical to the performance of four other executive functions that influence the motor control of behavior.

Behavioral inhibition is viewed as consisting of three abilities. *First* is the ability to inhibit prepotent responses, that is, responses that are likely to be reinforced or have a history of reinforcement. This ability may be the most impaired in ADHD. *Second* is the ability to interrupt responses that are already underway and proving ineffective. This allows a span of time during which the executive functions can be employed for self-regulation. The *third* inhibitory ability then comes into play, which is the ability to inhibit competing stimuli—to protect the operation of the executive functions from interference. It can be thought of as freedom from distraction. By preventing prepotent responses, stopping ineffective responses, and hindering distraction, behavioral inhibition sets the occasion for self-regulation, which involves executive functions.

The model incorporates four executive functions, briefly noted below, each of which has several elements.

- Nonverbal working memory is part of the memory system that allows the person to hold information in mind, or "on-line," that will be used to control a subsequent response. It involves representations of sensory-motor action, and the ability to bring to mind images of past sensory events.
- Internalization of speech can be thought of as verbal working memory. It allows the person to mentally reflect on rules and instructions that have been internalized to guide behavior.
- Self-regulation of affect, motivation, and arousal involves processes that allow the person to modulate emotion and motivation. It might involve, for example, a delay or lessening of anger that modifies motivation and arousal.
- Reconstitution allows the person to analyze and synthesize, to break down and recombine nonverbal and verbal units. It allows the construction of novel, creative behaviors or sequences of behaviors.

These four executive functions provide the means for the individual to self-regulate his or her behavior. A child is able to engage in task relevant, goal-directed, flexible behavior. In contrast, when inhibition is disordered, these executive functions—and thus self-regulation and adaptability—are adversely affected.

DUAL-PATHWAY MODEL

Relatively strong support exists for the involvement of inhibition and the executive functions in ADHD. Nonetheless, some researchers suggest two independent pathways in the development of the disorder (Sonuga-Barke, Dalen, and Remington, 2003). One pathway is mediated by executive deficits and the other by delay aversion. Somewhat different brain circuitry is thought to underlie these pathways. There is some evidence for the dual-pathway model (Martell, Nikolas, & Nigg, 2007; Thorell, 2007). Executive function deficits appear related to the symptoms of inattention, whereas delay aversion appears related to hyperactivity–impulsivity. The roles that various cognitive or neuropsychological mechanisms play in ADHD and their relationship to underlying biological and environmental etiologies await further investigation.

Etiology

Brain damage or injury was once considered the primary cause of ADHD. When it became evident that brain damage could not be identified in most children with the disorder, it was assumed that some undetectable "minimal brain dysfunction" existed. By the late 1950s and early 1960s, the need for better empirical evidence was recognized. Today, substantial evidence implicates brain dysfunction. Even so, many questions remain regarding etiology.

BRAIN STRUCTURE AND FUNCTION

Numerous brain systems or structures are implicated in ADHD, including the frontal lobe and underlying regions, parietal lobe, temporal lobe, corpus callosum, and cerebellum. For example, reduced brain volume has been found in these structures (Durston et al., 2004; Sowell et al., 2003), and increased gray and decreased white tissue have been observed in several regions.

Interest has focused particularly on the frontal lobes and connections to the striatal region, and the research findings are compelling (Figure 9–5). For one thing, frontal lobe functioning and damage are associated with the core symptoms of ADHD, inhibition, working memory, other executive functions, and higher order motor control (Casey et al., 1997; Semrud-Clikeman et al., 2000). In addition,

FIGURE 9-5

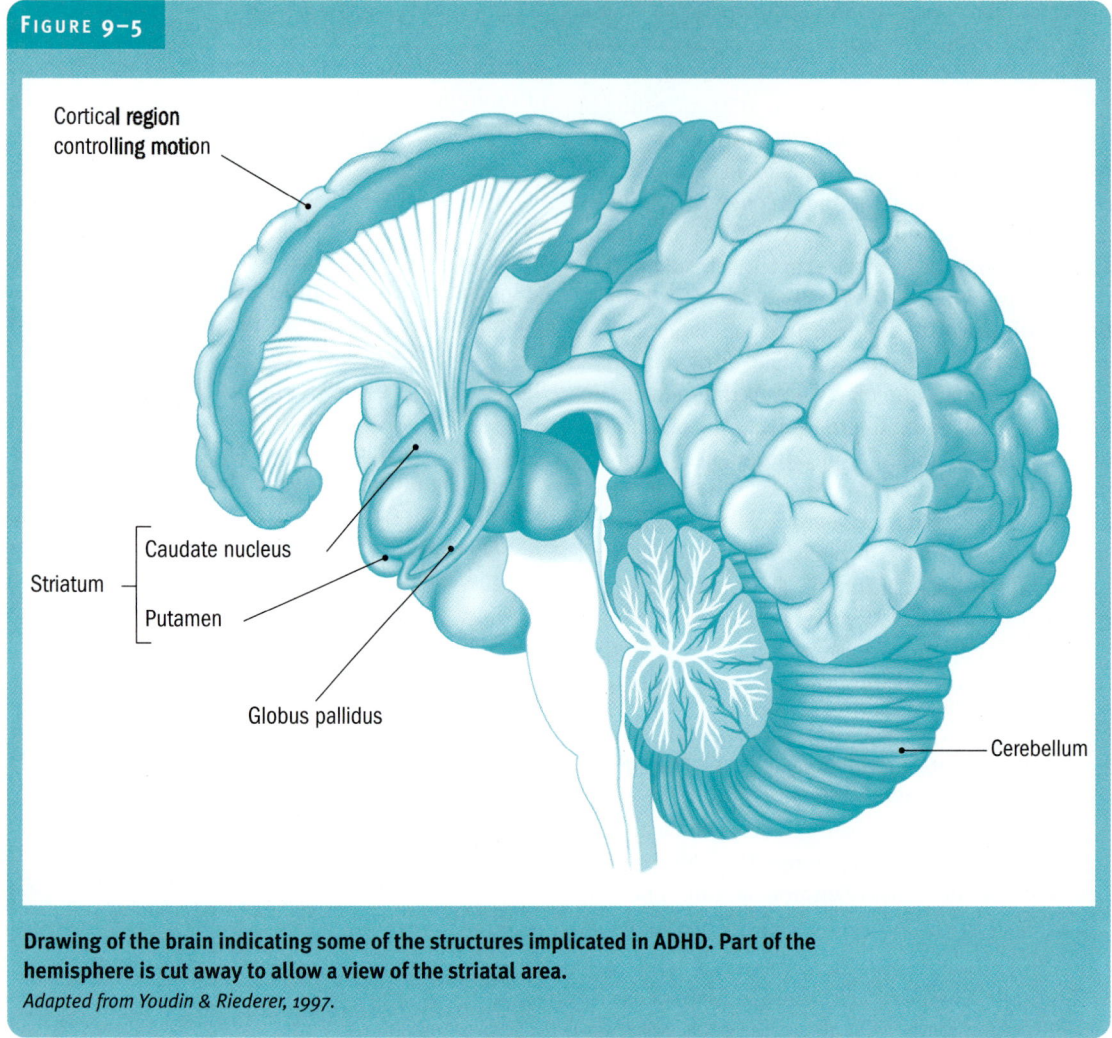

Cortical **region** controlling **motion**

Striatum
Caudate nucleus
Putamen

Globus pallidus

Cerebellum

Drawing of the brain indicating some of the structures implicated in ADHD. Part of the hemisphere is cut away to allow a view of the striatal area.
Adapted from Youdin & Riederer, 1997.

smaller-than-average size of the right frontal area, the caudate nucleus, and the globus pallidus is associated with ADHD (Barkley, 2006e; Tannock, 1998; Yeo et al., 2003). Also, various brain scans and electrophysiological measures indicate that youth with ADHD have decreased blood flow, decreased glucose utilization, and slow brain waves—all signs of underactivity—in the frontal areas and pathways connected to the striatal areas and the cerebellum (Dickstein et al., 2006; Rapport & Chung, 2000).

Another focus of neurobiological research is the biochemistry of the brain. Several neurotransmitters may be involved in ADHD but the best evidence implicates deficiencies in dopamine and norepinephrine, which are important in the functioning of the frontal and related areas of the brain

(Biederman & Spencer, 2000; Smith et al., 2006). Consistent with this finding, stimulant medications used to treat ADHD block the reuptake of dopamine and norepinephrine into the presynaptic membrane of neurons, making them more available in synapses.

Several conclusions can be drawn from investigations of the brain. *First*, although abnormalities in the frontal and striatal regions appear central, other areas are involved, including frontal-cerebellum networks (Durston et al., 2007). *Second*, underarousal of the brain is implicated. *Third*, dopamine and norepinephrine deficiency are implicated. *Fourth*, ADHD is undoubtedly a heterogeneous disorder with various disturbances in brain regions or networks involved in the regulation of attention and behavior. *Fifth*, despite having significant evidence, we still do not completely understand the neurological factors involved in ADHD.

GENETIC INFLUENCES

Numerous studies indicate that the families of children with ADHD have higher rates of psychopathology, including ADHD, than would be expected (Barkley, 2006e; Tannock, 1998). Between 10 and 35% of first-degree family members are likely to have ADHD. Children of parents with ADHD are also at high risk for the disorder. Family aggregation studies also suggest genetic influence on the co-occurrence of ADHD with other disorders. Further, limited research shows reduced brain size in the unaffected siblings of children with ADHD (Durston et al., 2004), and lowered frontal area activity in parents who themselves had displayed symptoms of hyperactivity (Hechtman, 1991; Taylor, 1994; Zametkin & Rapoport, 1986).

Twin studies provide even clearer evidence of inheritance. The average heritability across studies is about .80 (Smith et al., 2006). Heritability has been documented across a variety of measures, informants, and populations.

Finally, molecular association studies of ADHD or its symptoms implicate several genes with small effects; that is, quantitative trait loci (QTLs). Most studied are the DRD4 gene and the DAT1 gene, both of which are involved with dopamine (Plomin, 2005). Although there is considerable evidence for their association with ADHD, this association is not always found. A suggested reason for this mixed result is that ADHD may consist of many subtypes with different underlying genes (Todd et al., 2005).

BIRTH COMPLICATIONS AND PRENATAL INFLUENCES

Some studies indicate a higher risk for ADHD among children who suffered injury at birth and had low birthweight (Smith et al., 2006). Also implicated is small body size and head circumference at birth, which appear not accounted for by factors such as length of pregnancy, mother's use of alcohol and tobacco, and family income (Lahti et al., 2006).

Prenatal conditions are inconsistently associated with symptoms of ADHD or diagnosed ADHD. Despite difficulty in establishing causation from prenatal factors, it does appear that prenatal tobacco smoking and alcohol consumption can be hazardous (Rodriguez & Bohlin, 2005; Linnet et al., 2003; Vuijk et al., 2006). A large population study conducted in Finland showed that maternal smoking was associated with hyperactivity after adjustment for several other variables (Kotimaa et al., 2003). In an extensive U.S. study that followed women from pregnancy to the time their offspring were 14 years old, prenatal alcohol use was linked to activity level, attention deficits, and difficulties in organizing tasks in the youths (Streissguth et al., 1995). Animal studies showing adverse effects on the brains of offspring due to prenatal maternal alcohol and nicotine exposure are consistent with reported size reduction of the neuronal networks involved in ADHD (Mick et al., 2002).

DIET AND LEAD

For many years there was interest in the possible etiological role of diet and exposure to lead. One controversial idea was that foods containing artificial dyes and flavors, certain preservatives, and naturally occurring salicylates (for example, in tomatoes and cucumbers) were related to hyperactivity. Subsequent research did not support the claim, (Harley & Matthews, 1980; Spring, Chiodo, & Bowen, 1987). Similarly, meta-analysis of research showed that neither behavior nor cognitive functioning of children with ADHD was affected by sugar intake (Wolraich, Wilson, & White, 1995). Thus, diet does not appear to play a strong, if any, role.

That lead should be suspected of causing ADHD is not unreasonable, as high levels of lead exposure have been associated with serious deficits in biological functioning, cognition, and behavior (Tesman & Hills, 1994). Low levels of exposure over long periods of time also can adversely affect children. Several studies have examined the correlation of lead levels with attention and activity level. Lead levels of blood typically have been examined and also occasionally the amount of lead in the dentine of children's deciduous ("baby") teeth. Major studies sensitive to methodological issues have found significant but small links (Fergusson, Horwood, & Lynskey, 1993; Silva et al., 1988; Thomson et al., 1989). Even in children with high lead levels, it is estimated that lead accounts for no more than 4% of the variance of ADHD symptoms (Barkley, 2006e). This does not imply that caution should be thrown to the wind, nor that lead does not have other negative effects on children. Caution demands the protection of children from lead-based paints, toys, automobile emissions, leaded crystal and ceramic dishes, and solder on old copper pipes.

PSYCHOSOCIAL INFLUENCES

Few researchers and clinicians believe that psychosocial factors are a primary cause of ADHD, but the symptoms of the disorder are malleable to environmental influences. Psychosocial factors are likely to affect the severity, continuity, and nature of the symptoms, as well as associated and co-occurring disturbances. Some investigators note the possible interplay of psychosocial variables with genetic influence (Schachar & Tannock, 2002). For example, a child and parent may share a genotype that readily leads to impulsive, disorganized behavior (Nigg, 2006). The parent's behavior may affect the child's development of self-regulation, and the child's behavior may elicit ineffective parenting. Genetic influence is operating but is mediated through the family environment.

Unsurprisingly, family factors are among the psychosocial variables thought to be especially influential. Numerous family correlates of children's ADHD have been described, including family adversity such as economic disadvantage, family conflict and separation, and poor mental health and coping (Goodman & Stevenson, 1989; McGee et al., 2002). Nigg and Hinshaw (1998) observed that boys who had ADHD with or without antisocial behavior were more likely to have mothers with a history of depression and/or anxiety and fathers with a childhood history of ADHD. Tully and colleagues (2004) examined ADHD symptoms displayed by 5-year-old twins who had been born with low birthweight; they found that maternal warmth had a moderating effect on ratings of symptoms. Overall, there is evidence that ADHD in children can affect parent behavior and that parent behavior can influence the nature and perhaps development of ADHD (Johnston & Mash, 2001). Still, family influence needs to be regarded cautiously, as findings have been inconsistent and relatively little is known about how the family psychosocial environment interacts with genetic influences and child characteristics to shape ADHD.

Teacher behavior might play a role in shaping a child's attentiveness and impulsivity. How a classroom is organized and how activities are structured can influence a child's behavior and academic achievement, perhaps especially a child predisposed to ADHD (Pfiffner, Barkley, & DuPaul, 2006). This does not imply that teacher behavior causes ADHD but that it may affect its manifestation and outcome.

Overall, after much research, the cause of ADHD remains uncertain although genetic influence is likely. Progress is being made in unraveling genetic contributions, in understanding how brain functioning is related to the symptoms of the disorder, and in recognizing how psychosocial influences may shape and maintain the problem behaviors.

Assessment

Whether the purpose of assessment is identification of ADHD, planning for treatment, or both, several aspects of the disorder serve as useful guidelines (Barkley, 1990; 1997; Hinshaw & Erhardt, 1993; Pliszka et al., 2007).

- Because ADHD is best conceptualized as a biopsychosocial disorder, assessment must be broad-based.

- Because ADHD is developmental, a developmental history is important and assessment will vary somewhat with developmental level.

- Because ADHD is pervasive and may manifest itself differently in different settings, information specific to the settings should be obtained.

- Because ADHD has high rates of co-occurrence with other psychological disorders, assessment requires careful distinction from other disorders.

The following discussion emphasizes the psychological and social factors most pertinent to assessment, and draws heavily on Barkley and Edwards (2006) and Pliszka and colleagues (2007).

INTERVIEWS

ADHD is most often assessed early in life, so parents are critical in the interview process. Information needs to be obtained about the child's specific problems and impairments, strengths, developmental and medical history, academic achievement, and peer relationships. Direct and systematic questions about family stress and relationships are recommended because these are central in the child's social ecology and have implications for treatment. A semistructured interview combined with a standardized structured interview (e.g., The Diagnostic Interview for Children and Adolescents) offers a reliable and efficient way to collect a wealth of information (Barkley & Edwards, 2006).

It is also important to assess specific parent–child interactions, not only for diagnosis but also for treatment planning. It is useful to pose specific questions, directing attention to specific situations relevant to the child's problems and how they are managed. Questions may be asked about what the child does, how the parents respond, and how often problems occur in specific situations such as mealtimes, when the father is at home, and when the child is asked to complete chores.

The youth being assessed should also be interviewed. With younger children, the interview may simply be a time for getting acquainted, establishing rapport, and observing the child's appearance, language, interpersonal skills, and the like (Barkley & Edwards, 2006). Such observations must be interpreted cautiously, however, because children with ADHD may act more appropriately during office visits than they do in other settings. Discussion with older children and adolescents can include their views on their problems, school performance, peer relationships, the way they see their family functioning, what they think would make life better, and the like. Although the report of youth with ADHD may reflect a positive bias toward their symptoms, a private interview permits the reporting of problems or issues they may not want to discuss in the presence of parents (Pliszka et al., 2007). Interviews need to be adapted to the child's developmental status, of course, and with children it is beneficial to approach issues as they might see them (Table 9–3).

Teacher interviews can address difficulties in the school setting that may not be validly assessed by parents (Mitsis et al., 2000). A direct interview is valuable, with a focus on learning and academic problems and on peer interaction. In addition, information can be obtained about parent–school interaction and cooperation, as well as school services. Some youth with ADHD have rights to special evaluation and educational services. (Indeed, many of these children receive special education services under the Individuals with Disabilities Education Act, often under the categories of learning disabilities or behavior/emotional disturbance. (See page 290 for relevant discussion.)

RATING SCALES

Parent and teacher rating scales and checklists, which are popular tools for assessing ADHD, can provide a great deal of information with relatively little time and effort. Many of the scales are reliable and valid, are consistent with the DSM conceptualization of ADHD, and can contribute to clinic and research efforts (Collett, Ohan, & Myers, 2003). Some of these tools are broad in scope and identify not only ADHD but also its co-occurrence with other disorders. Scales with a narrower focus are useful in assessing specific aspects of ADHD.

An example of a widely employed scale is the Conners' Rating Scales (Conners, 2008). Both parent and teacher scales exist in long and abbreviated forms. Table 9–4 shows the subscales for the long form of the parent scale. The ADHD Index is

---

TABLE 9–3	IT IS BENEFICIAL TO POSE INTERVIEW QUESTIONS THAT CONSIDER THE CHILD'S PERSPECTIVE. THESE EXAMPLES TARGET THE CHILD'S SCHOOL EXPERIENCE.

- "Do you ever find that you've been sitting in class, and all of a sudden you realize your teacher has been talking and you have no idea what she's [or he's] talking about?"
- "Does it ever seem ro take you longer to get your work done compared to other kids?"
- "Do you think your work is messier than other kids' work?"
- "Do you have trouble keeping track of things you need for school?"
- "Do you have trouble finishing your homework?"
- "Does your teacher ever have to speak to you because you're talking when you're not supposed to be talking, or fooling around when you're supposed to be working?"

From Barkley & Edwards, 2006.

TABLE 9–4	SUBSCALES OF THE LONG FORM OF THE PARENT VERSION OF THE CONNERS' RATING SCALES

Oppositional
Cognitive Problems/Inattention
Hyperactivity
ADHD Index
Anxious—Shy
Perfectionism
Social Problems
DSM-IV Symptom Subscales
Conners' Global Index
Psychosomatic

Conners, 2008.

designed to rapidly identify those at risk for ADHD, and can be used to monitor the effectiveness of treatment. The Conners' Global Index also is designed to be sensitive to treatment effects. The teacher version has comparable subscales. Normative data for each of the parent and teacher scales are presented for boys and girls of different ages from age 6 to 18 years. In addition to the parent and teacher scales, there is a long and short form of a Self-Report Scale for youth age 8 to 18. Normative data are available for the self-report versions.

DIRECT OBSERVATION

Direct observation of youth in natural settings can be extremely useful because the behavioral manifestations of ADHD are relatively situational. Home and school observations for initial observation can be well worth the time they require, and observations to target behaviors for intervention can be critical to successful treatment (Jacob & Pelham, 2000). Signs of the core features of ADHD are of utmost importance, of course, but so also are indications of noncompliance, aggression, attention-seeking, and other characteristics of social interactions and relationships. Several observational coding systems for ADHD are available.

OTHER PROCEDURES

Additional assessment methods are often useful and/or necessary. Standardized tests of intelligence, academic achievement, and adaptive behavior can be helpful, particularly in clarifying issues pertaining to academic functioning.

Various kinds of procedures to specifically evaluate inattention and impulsivity have been developed. For example, the Conners' Continuous Performance Test II requires the client to press a computer key at the sight of any letter except X in the middle of the screen (Epstein et al., 2003; CPT II, 2004). Designed for children 6 years and over, the degree to which this 14-minute test differentiates ADHD requires further study (Gordon, Barkley, & Lovett, 2006). Other neuropsychological tests aimed at evaluating, for example, response inhibition and executive functions, are useful in research but are not recommended for assessment at this time.

Medical evaluation does not usually identify ADHD but when medical factors are suspect it can provide information potentially useful in treatment or in understanding the disorder. Such assessment reasonably includes a neurological examination, but neurological tests such as the EEG and brain scans are not generally recommended for children because they do not validly distinguish ADHD and may present safety issues (Pliszka et al., 2007).

Intervention

PREVENTION

It is reasonable to assume that prenatal care might have some impact on preventing ADHD from occurring at all. Nevertheless, the most effective efforts are likely to be directed at both early treatment of symptoms and minimizing secondary problems that interfere with healthy development. As we have seen, the primary symptoms of ADHD not only have immediate, negative impacts on several domains of functioning, but may set into motion an array of continuing problems. Symptoms appear to lessen over time for many children but other difficulties may be left in their wake. It is important that these be considered in prevention. For example, academic tutoring may avert the school problems many children with ADHD experience. Another example is training parents to manage their child with disruptive behaviors in order to prevent further development of noncompliant or oppositional child behaviors, which could put the child at risk for ODD and CD (Anastopoulos, Rhoads, & Farley, 2006).

PHARMACOLOGICAL TREATMENT

Many treatment approaches exist for ADHD, including social skills training, cognitive-behavioral training, and individual counseling. By far the most widely employed—and judged as evidence-based, short-term treatment—are stimulant medications, behaviorally oriented interventions, and a combination of these two approaches (American Psychological Association, 2006). Our discussion begins with pharmacological treatment.

A report by Bradley in 1937 is usually cited as the first treatment of childhood behavioral disorders with stimulant medication (Greenhill et al., 2002). Many pharmacological agents have been used for ADHD since then, but stimulant medications are the treatment of choice. Stimulants are the most frequently prescribed psychotropic medications for children, primarily for ADHD, and they are increasingly prescribed for preschoolers, adolescents, and adults (Connor, 2006; Wolraich, 2003). Extensive randomized, controlled research on effectiveness and side effects has been conducted.

The stimulants affect dopamine and norepinephrine neural networks that traverse areas of the brain implicated in ADHD (Biederman & Spencer, 2000; DuPaul, Barkley, & Connor, 1998). Most often used are methylphenidate, dextroamphetamine, and the combination of dextroamphetamine and amphetamine. (See Table 9–5.) The effects of many stimulants are rapid but wear off within a few hours, and they are often given two or three times a day. However, effective slower release preparations (Concerta and Adderall XR) can be taken only once daily, and a methylphenidate adhesive patch is available (Faraone & Giefer, 2007).

Although much controversy surrounds the use of stimulants, it is not, in the view of most professionals, due to the failure of these medications to rapidly alleviate the primary deficits of ADHD. Approximately 75% of medicated children show increased attention and reduced impulsivity and activity level (Connor, 2006). In addition to alleviating the core symptoms of ADHD, stimulants can reduce co-occurring aggressive, noncompliant, oppositional behaviors. The strongest effects have been documented for measures of attention, distractibility, and impulsivity and for social and classroom behavior (Wolraich, 2003). Perhaps not surprisingly, parents and teachers interact more positively with children who are benefiting from medication (Chronis et al., 2003).

Most research has been conducted with school-age children, but some recent studies have included preschoolers and adolescents. Due largely to an increase in medication use with preschoolers, the National Institutes of Mental Health funded a multi-site, randomized study of 3- to 5.5-year-olds. Significant decreases were found for ADHD symptoms, although the effects were smaller than for school-age children (Greenhill et al., 2006). Stimulants also benefit adolescents, although the response rate may be somewhat less than for children (Connor, 2006). Overall, then, an impressive amount of data support the claim for effectiveness of stimulants across settings, measures, and ages. Nevertheless, several concerns are expressed about pharmacological treatment of ADHD.

Concerns about stimulants. One concern about stimulant medication for ADHD is its limitations. The primary symptoms of ADHD are not alleviated in 10 to 20% of children (Anastopoulos et al., 2006) and perhaps a larger percentage of preschoolers. When symptoms are alleviated, behavior is comparable to that of typical children in only about 50% of cases. Moreover, medication has only a small to modest effect on academic production and achievement (Schachar & Tannock, 2002; Wolraich, 2003). In addition, long-term effects have not been well documented, and it appears that effects dissipate when the drug is no longer taken (Klein et al., 2004; Pfiffner et al., 2006).

A second concern about stimulant treatment is possible adverse biological side effects. Moderate side effects occur in 4 to 10% of cases (Greenhill et al., 2002), although preschoolers may experience somewhat more difficulties than older children. Sleep problems, decreased appetite, stomach pain, headaches, irritability, and jitteriness have all been reported. The effects are often mild to moderate and may diminish in 2 or 3 weeks, or after a reduction in dosage. Suppression of growth has long been a concern and this issue is not completely settled (Pliszka et al., 2007). Small decreases in growth have sometimes been reported, although growth suppression may weaken over time. So far no relationship with adult height or weight is documented. Also sometimes reported is an initiation or a worsening of motor and vocal tics in some children, but recent studies challenge this finding (Gadow et al., 2007; Pliszka et al., 2007).

In general, when stimulants are prescribed and used appropriately, they are considered relatively safe drugs for most youth. This does not mean, of course, that the need for monitoring should be taken lightly. Individuals vary in their responses to different dosages

---

TABLE 9–5	MEDICATIONS MOST COMMONLY USED TO TREAT ADHD

Medications of First Choice

Stimulants
    Methylphenidate (Ritalin; Concerta)
    Dextroamphetamine (Dexedrine)
    Combined Amphetamine and Dextroamphetamine
        (Adderall; Adderall XR)
Specific Norepinephrine Reuptake Inhibitors
    Atomoxetine (Strattera)

Second-Line Medications of Choice

Antidepressants
    Bupropion
    Tricyclics (Imipramine; Desipramine)
Antihypertensives
    Clonidine
    Guanfacine

and different stimulants. In fact, there are warnings about the use of Adderall XR in youths with underlying heart defects (Handen & Gilchrist, 2006), and the stimulant pemoline is associated with liver failure and death (Wolraich, 2003). Monitoring and reasonable caution are always appropriate.

A third concern about childhood stimulant use is the possibility that it increases the risk for later alcohol and substance use or abuse. About the same number of studies indicate no risk, increased risk, and reduced risk (American Psychological Association, 2006). In a recent community study in which increased drug use was not found in adolescents with ADHD, increased use was found in those with ADHD and co-occurring externalizing disorder (August et al., 2006). A related issue that warrants a watchful eye is the illicit use of the stimulants themselves. It is recommended that stimulants should not be prescribed if there is any known or suspected drug use (Connor, 2006).

In addition to the concerns already discussed, critics have argued that medication is too readily prescribed. Some believe that it is overused because it is a "quick fix" for the schools and for some parents. In fact, prescription of stimulant medications has risen over time (Greenhill et al., 2002), and use with preschoolers is striking (Zito et al., 2000). Perhaps increases can partly be attributed to public acceptance of medication, increased prescribing to girls and adolescents, and use of medication for longer treatment time (Reich, Huang, & Todd, 2006).

While the issue of excessive medication use calls for monitoring, so does inappropriate prescription practices. For example, in a survey of four communities, only one-eighth of children meeting the criteria for ADHD received adequate intervention with stimulants, whereas another survey found that 72% of the children receiving stimulants failed to meet the ADHD criteria (Greenhill et al., 2002). Reich and colleagues (2006) found that 59% of boys and 46% of girls who met the criteria for ADHD received medication; 35% receiving stimulant medication did not meet the diagnostic criteria, although they had symptoms of ADHD. There are reasons for choosing or rejecting medication as part of a treatment plan, but careful consideration needs to be involved.

Concern about the use and misuse of medication for ADHD has at times led to heated controversy that was fed by media coverage in major magazines and on television. Media attention that serves to educate is beneficial, of course. Unfortunately, concerns about medications have sometimes been expressed in emotionally charged, exaggerated—and perhaps harmful—ways by parents, professionals, and organized groups (Barkley, 1998; Swanson et al., 1995). Extreme emotional reaction and exaggeration are rarely helpful, but professionals who recognize the benefits of stimulants also point to their limitations and warn against their misuse or overuse.

BEHAVIORALLY ORIENTED TREATMENT

Behaviorally oriented interventions for ADHD employ the usual behavioral strategies. Emphasis is placed on the consequences of behavior, with reinforcers including tokens or points that can be exchanged for a variety of rewards and social consequences such as praise. Negative consequences are often used as well, in which the child loses opportunity for reinforcers (time out) or must give up privileges or earned reinforcers (response cost). Compared to pharmacological treatment, behaviorally oriented approaches put more emphasis on improving key functional domains, such as social relationships and school performance. Most interventions are conducted in the school or home, with parents or teachers working directly with the child. Parent training programs are designed to optimize parents' management of their child with ADHD.

Parent training (PT). Parent training is a commonly employed treatment for ADHD (Schachar & Tannock, 2002). Managing a child with ADHD can be stressful for families, and parents tend to become exhausted and overly directive. They may also begin to view themselves as lacking the normal skills of parenting (Anastopoulos, Smith, & Wien, 1998). These facts coupled with the obvious influence that parents have on their children's behavior make families a natural focus of intervention. Still, PT may not always be a treatment of choice (Anastopoulos et al., 2006). It is most suitable for children ages 4 to 12, and for families in which the child's ADHD appears as a basis of family difficulty. PT may not be suitable when parents are experiencing excessively high levels of stress due to marital conflicts or other circumstances.

Although parent training programs vary somewhat, they share the goal of teaching child management techniques (Anastopoulos & Farley, 2003). As an example, we briefly examine an intervention that emphasizes the management of the core symptoms of ADHD and noncompliance and defiance in children between 4 and 12 years of age. This focus is consistent with the view that ADHD involves a deficit in behavioral inhibition and risk for conduct disturbances.

TABLE 9–6	STEPS IN THE PARENT TRAINING INTERVENTION DESCRIBED BY ANASTOPOULOS, RHOADS, AND FARLEY

1. Program overview and overview of ADHD
2. Discussing parent–child relationships, principles of behavioral management
3. Improving parent skills in using positive attention ("catching the child being good")
4. Extending positive attention; teaching how to give commands
5. Establishing a home token/point system
6. Adding response cost to child management
7. Teaching the use of time-out for more serious child misbehavior
8. Managing behavior in public places, such as grocery stores and church
9. Handling school issues (e.g., daily report card); preparing for termination of PT
10. Booster session to review child status and troubleshoot problems

Adapted from Anastopoulos, Rhoads, & Farley, 2006.

Appropriate parental management of child behavior is viewed as bringing the child's behavior under increased parental control, facilitating the child's awareness of behavioral consequences, preventing the development of comorbid conditions, and alleviating parental stress.

The treatment program consists of 10 components that are covered in 8 to 12 sessions with an individual family or groups of families. As Table 9–6 indicates, in addition to training in behavioral management, the sessions include information to increase understanding of ADHD, discussion of special and future problems, consideration of the child's school situation, and a booster session for review and troubleshooting.

In families in which the child's behavior is oppositional and disruptive, PT can improve parenting skills and child behavior and, to a lesser extent, reduce ADHD symptoms (American Psychological Association, 2006). More is known about the effects on school-age children, but similar changes have been found in preschoolers and adolescents. PT appears to be one of the most validated treatments for children with ADHD who display oppositional, defiant behavior.

Classroom management. School-based behavioral intervention is effective in addressing inattention, disruptive behavior, and academic performance. Most commonly the teacher administers contingency management intervention, and typically receives training and consultation from a mental health specialist (Jacob & Pelham, 2000). Procedures usually include token reinforcement, time out, and response cost. Contingency contracting, in which the child and the teacher sign a written agreement specifying how the child will behave and the contingencies that will accrue, can be helpful (Table 9–7). Often essential is a daily report card sent to parents that reflects the child's performance regarding targeted behaviors. The report card serves as feedback to the child, informs the parents so that they can reward the child for progress, and promotes communication between the teacher and the parents.

There is some evidence that children with different subtypes of ADHD might profit from different kinds of teacher strategies (Pfiffner et al., 2006). For example, those with ADHD-I might especially benefit from interventions that accommodate a slow work

TABLE 9–7	HYPOTHETICAL CHILD–TEACHER CONTINGENCY CONTRACT

I agree to do the following:
1. Take my seat by 8:10 every morning.
2. Remain in my seat unless Ms. Duffin gives permission to me or the class to leave seats.
3. Not interrupt other students when they are speaking.
4. Complete morning written work as assigned before lunch break.
5. Complete afternoon written work as assigned before gym or recess In the afternoon.

I agree that when I do the above, I will:
 . . . earn extra time In the computer corner
 . . . earn extra time to do artwork
 . . . earn extra checkmarks that I can trade for art supplies.

I agree that if I do not do 1–5 above each day, I will:
 . . . not be able to participate in recess activities.

Based on DuPaul, Guevrement, & Barkley, 1991.

style. However, the targeting of behaviors on an individual basis is a key to success. Effective targeting should include the following areas.

- Skills and behaviors that replace the specific problems should be emphasized. A child with organizational problems needs to be taught how to use and manage desk and locker space, while a child with social deficits needs to learn appropriate interaction.

- Although on-task performance is important, broader academic performance goals need to be targeted. Amount of work completed is an important element for achievement. Young children need to strengthen basic skills (reading, writing, arithmetic) so they will not fall behind, while older students need help in additional academic areas.

- Common problem situations need to be targeted, for example, behaviors required during recess and transitions between classes or activities.

Although behavioral interventions have typically focused on managing behavior through contingency-based principles, the structure and organization of both the classroom and learning tasks may be important to children with ADHD (Pfiffner et al., 2006). Classrooms that are well organized and predictable, with attractive posters displaying rules, are generally recommended and may be especially helpful for children with ADHD. Placing the child's desk away from other children and near the teacher can reduce peer reinforcement of inappropriate behavior and also facilitate teacher monitoring and feedback. Regarding learning tasks themselves, there are several useful strategies. Among these are increasing stimulation within the task—for example, by the use of color, shape, or tape recordings—keeping the length of the task within the child's attention span, and varying the format and materials. There is evidence that allowing some task-related choice facilitates work productivity, and that computer-assisted instruction (which often includes clear rules, segmented tasks, and swift feedback) increases attention and work productivity. While many of these strategies are generally advantageous, they may be of critical help to students with ADHD. There is, however, a need for further research in this area.

Teachers are crucial, of course, in influencing the learning environment of the classroom and in implementing behavioral programs. A considerable amount of time and energy is required to effectively manage children with disabilities, as well as to collaborate with parents, administrators, and other professionals. Teachers generally appear to favor positive over negative contingencies, behavioral plus medication over medication-only approaches, and time-efficient (e.g., daily report cards) over time-consuming (e.g., response cost) techniques (Pfiffner et al., 2006; Pisecco, Huzinec & Curtis, 2001). In general, teacher knowledge, beliefs, attitudes, flexibility, tolerance for the disruptions common in ADHD, and interactional style might well

The well-being of children with ADHD is undoubtedly influenced by teachers' attitudes and abilities to manage and organize classroom activities.
(Ellen B. Senisi/The Image Works)

be important variables regarding the success of classroom-based programs (Greene, 1995).

MULTIMODAL TREATMENT

Behaviorally oriented methods can frequently help alleviate ADHD in the short term (American Psychological Association, 2006). Empirical investigations show that on-task, attentive, appropriate behaviors can be shaped and academic performance improved. However, behavioral programs often require much effort and time, can be expensive, and may provide less-than-optimal benefits. At the same time, the limitation and criticism of medication have continued to raise questions about its use for ADHD. This situation has resulted in combining behaviorally oriented and pharmacological treatments. Research on such multimodal approaches has been conducted and two major studies are noteworthy.

A major effort was initiated in 1990 at two large medical centers in Montreal and New York (Klein et al., 2004). Children age 7 to 9 years were randomly assigned to receive either (1) methylphenidate or (2) methylphenidate plus psychosocial intervention (including parent training, academic assistance, social skills training, and psychotherapy) or (3) a control treatment consisting of medication plus professional attention that avoided the components of the psychosocial intervention. The children had been diagnosed according to DSM-III-R, which allowed diagnosis based on a mix of symptoms of inattention, hyperactivity, and impulsivity. The investigators were particularly interested in enhancing the effects of medication with a relatively intense psychosocial treatment aimed at specific areas of functioning. Overall, evaluation after the 2-year project indicated improvements in several areas of behavior in all conditions but did not indicate additional benefits when psychosocial components were combined with medication (Abikoff et al., 2004a; 2004b; Hechtman et al., 2004).

MTA study. The Multimodal Treatment Assessment Study (MTA) is the largest long-term evaluation of treatment options. This six-center investigation was initiated by the National Institutes of Mental Health. Close to 600 children with ADHD-C, age 7 to 9 years, were randomly assigned to one of four treatment conditions lasting for 14 months (MTA Cooperative Group, 1999a). The treatments were as follows:

- **Medication Treatment.** Children received medication, mostly methylphenidate, with dosage carefully assigned, monitored, and adjusted at monthly sessions with the child and parents. Teacher input was also available for these sessions. Medication was given for the entire time period.

- **Behavioral Treatment.** The intensive program consisted of parent training sessions; school-based intervention including teacher consultation and a trained aide who worked with the child part-time for 60 days; and a child-focused, behaviorally oriented summer camp experience. (See Accent: "Summer Training Program.") Training gradually leveled off; by the end of the investigation parents were seen monthly or not at all.

- **Combined Treatment.** Medication and behavioral treatments were integrated.

- **Community Care Treatment.** Children in this comparison group received various routine treatments in their communities. As it turned out, 67% were on medication, with dosage levels lower than for the medication treatment group. The children were seen only once or twice by a physician, and there was no teacher contact for feedback.

Initial evaluations of the MTA study were conducted before, during, and at the end of the 14 months. Numerous measures were taken of core ADHD symptoms, associated problems, and family factors. A follow-up assessment was conducted 10 months after the termination of treatment, and again about 1 year later.

Core ADHD symptoms were reduced for children in all groups over the 14-month treatment, but the amount of improvement varied with the type of treatment (MTA Cooperative Group, 1999a; 1999b). Overall, the medication and combined treatments were superior to behavioral and community care treatments, and did not differ from each other. However, interesting differences emerged with further analyses. The findings are numerous and complex, as briefly demonstrated by specific examples:

- For several measures, the combined treatment had the greatest effect (MTA Cooperative Group, 1999a). This was true for parent ratings of their children's externalizing and internalizing symptoms, and for reading achievement.

- For children with comorbid ADHD and anxiety, behavioral treatment was as effective as the medication or the combination treatments (Rieppi et al., 2002).

- Social class moderated some of the outcomes. Families with more education benefited the most

ACCENT:

The Summer Training Program

There are many who believe that ADHD is best treated by a comprehensive approach. This view was expressed by Pelham and colleagues (2005) as they described the typical Summer Training Program (STP). The program is an intensive social learning intervention that targets the functional impairments of ADHD rather than its primary symptoms. The underlying rationale is the relative importance of functional impairments to the outcomes of attention-deficit hyperactivity disorder. Available for youths age 5 to 15, the program operates in a camp-like setting for 8 weeks from 8 AM to 5 PM on weekdays. The goals are to improve (1) peer and adult relationships, (2) academic performance, and (3) self-esteem. A parent training component is included.

The participants are placed in age-appropriate groups of about 12 youths each, overseen by five trained counselors. The group serves as a natural backdrop for working on peer and adult relationships. Social skills training is provided in 10-minute daily sessions that include modeling and role playing. Such training has received attention from behaviorally oriented therapists and is integrated into broader based interventions (American Psychological Association, 2006). In addition, there is opportunity for group problem solving.

Each day, the groups spend 3 hours in classroom sessions conducted by teachers and aides. It is recognized not only that children with ADHD often have academic problems but also that summer months without academic learning puts even normal children at risk for losing academic ground. Two hours of classroom time are devoted to individualized seatwork, cooperative reading with another student, and individualized academic skill building with a computer-based program. The third hour is devoted to art in which group projects provide an opportunity for cooperative peer interaction.

The remainder of each day is given to leisure activities in age-appropriate small group play and sports. Children receive intensive skill training and coaching. While the skills are valued in themselves, especially for children with poor motor skills, sports competence also is valued because it enhances peer status and self-esteem.

The STP treatment components include operant and cognitive-behavioral approaches, and children are assessed for medication needs. Staff members are highly trained to record a child's behavior and respond appropriately. Parents have nearly daily contact with the program, and participate in a weekly training session designed to implement at home the behavioral techniques employed in the program. Research on the nature and treatment of ADHD is an important component of the STP. A treatment manual is available, and the program has been adopted at several sites. It has been recognized by the American Psychological Association as a model intervention.

from the combined treatment, but this was not so for families with less education (Rieppi et al., 2002). Also, in poorer but not other families the use of medication was associated with decreased closeness between families and their children (MTA Cooperative Group, 1999b).

Additional findings regarding medication are interesting. The MTA study supports previous findings that lower dosage medication is used when behavioral components are part of the treatment package. In addition, the difficulties that some families have in accepting medication treatment are apparent in the MTA study. Prior to intervention, 6 percent of families refused medication, whereas virtually none refused behavioral treatment (Vitiello

et al., 2001). Moreover, MTA families expressed less satisfaction with the medication treatment than with the behavioral and the combined interventions.

POSTTREATMENT FOLLOW-UP The 10-month posttreatment assessment examined the persistence of effects of the four treatments on select measures (MTA Cooperative Group, 2004a; 2004b.) Children who had been in the medication or combined treatments still showed improvement compared with the other children regarding ADHD and oppositional defiant symptoms (but not some other problems). However, these positive effects were about 50% weaker than they had been at the end of treatment.

The second follow-up was conducted about 1 year later (Jensen et al., 2007). Most of the participants were now 11 to 13 years of age. Primary measures were taken of ADHD symptoms, ODD symptoms, reading, social skills, and overall functional impairment. There were no significant group differences on any of the measures. Figure 9–6 shows the parent and teacher ratings of ADHD symptoms over the entire period. Symptom level had decreased for all the groups throughout the period.

The investigators conducted some exploration into the reasons for the loss of benefits over time to those who had received the medication or combined treatments. This was not an easy task, because after the 14 months of treatment, the families had been on their own to provide, or not provide, various intervention options. Thus, some children who had been assigned medication during treatment no longer took it, while some who had not been assigned medication during treatment had begun to take it. Despite such complexities, there was some suggestion that decreased use of medication might have played a role in the loss of the initial benefits to children who had been in the medication or combined treatment group. However, further analysis could prove helpful.

It is perhaps unsurprising that the early benefits of medication and combined treatments were not maintained for a longer period of time. Children and families were treated for a relatively short period, and at the termination of treatment were free to make their own decisions. We know that the effects of medication are not sustained when medication is discontinued, and previous research had shown only short-term effects of behavioral and combined treatments. It does appear that ADHD more often than not requires sustained intervention. Researchers will undoubtedly further analyze the MTA study to better understand the effects of the interventions.

It is probably fair to say that at the present time, practitioners take various stances with regard to treatments. Medication is widely employed but is not given first preference by every professional and every family (Leslie et al., 2007). Many mental health professionals believe that a combination of medication and behaviorally oriented treatments is the best approach for a disorder that is as multidimensional as ADHD and carries considerable risk for comorbid disorders.

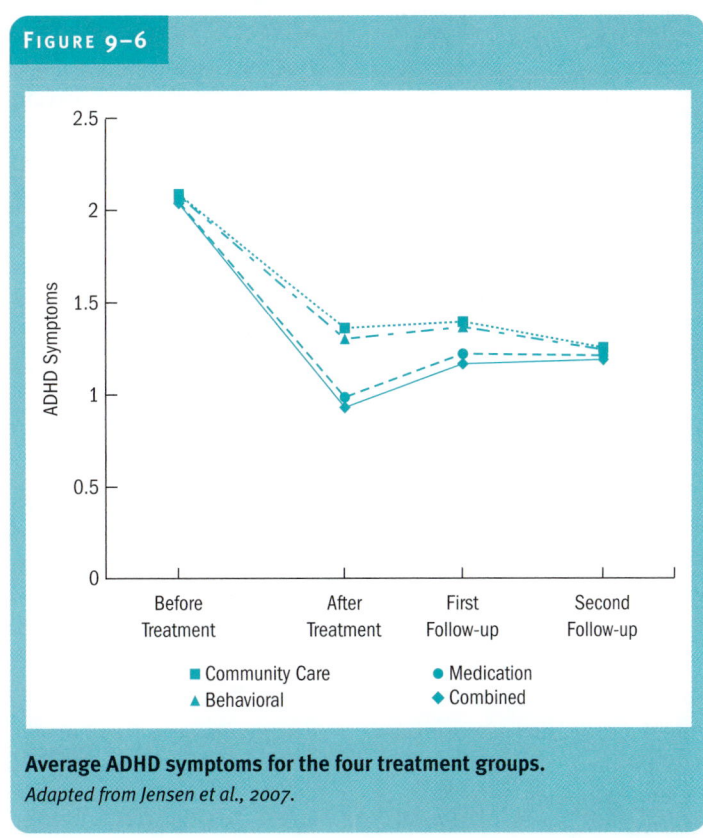

FIGURE 9–6

Average ADHD symptoms for the four treatment groups.
Adapted from Jensen et al., 2007.

SUMMARY

EVOLVING IDEAS ABOUT ADHD

- Accounts of ADHD have shifted over time regarding symptoms and their conceptualization. Two factors are now widely recognized: inattention and hyperactivity–impulsivity.

DSM CLASSIFICATION AND DIAGNOSIS

- The DSM recognizes three subtypes of ADHD: Predominately Inattentive, Predominately Hyperactive–Impulsive, and Combined.

- Diagnosis demands the presence of symptoms for at least 6 months by age 7 and impairment in at least two settings.

DESCRIPTION: CORE FEATURES

- The core problems of inattention, hyperactivity, and impulsivity are widely observed by parents, teachers, and researchers.

DESCRIPTION: SECONDARY FEATURES

- As a group, youths with ADHD display several secondary difficulties, among which are motor problems, somewhat lowered intelligence, academic failure, executive dysfunction, deficits in adaptive behavior, social and conduct problems, and higher risk for accidents.

DSM SUBTYPES

- Many differences exist between ADHD-I and ADHD-C, but questions remain about all the subtypes. Less is known about ADHD-HI.

- Some children with ADHD-I exhibit a sluggish cognitive tempo, which some investigators suggest is a unique disorder rather than a subtype of ADHD.

ADHD AND COMORBID DISORDERS

- ADHD co-occurs at high rates with learning disabilities, externalizing disorders, and internalizing disorders. Co-occurrence with conduct problems is most understood, and the combined disorder heightens the risk of negative outcomes.

EPIDEMIOLOGY

- About 3 to 7% of school-age children are estimated to have ADHD. Rates decline in adolescence. Boys are diagnosed more frequently than girls. Rates of ADHD appear somewhat higher in children of lower social class. ADHD is observed in many countries with varying prevalence.

DEVELOPMENTAL COURSE AND PROGNOSIS

- Temperamental precursors of ADHD may appear very early in life, and hyperactivity and impulsivity can be observed at preschool age. A minority of these children continues to have problems into childhood. The school environment increases demands on the child and academic, social, and conduct problems may become obvious.

- For some children, the core features of childhood ADHD continue into adolescence and, to a lesser degree, into adulthood, although hyperactivity and impulsivity appear to weaken over time. Difficulties such as poor academic achievement and antisocial behavior are observed. Continuity of problems is linked to several variables.

THEORIES OF ADHD

- Cognitive and neuropsychological theories of ADHD emphasize various deficits, such as underarousal, unusual sensitivity to reinforcement, and aversion to delay.

- Barkley's model, which applies to ADHD-C, proposes that deficits in behavioral inhibition interfere with executive functions to produce impairment in the regulation of behavior. A dual-pathway model suggests that executive dysfunction and delay aversion contribute independently to ADHD.

ETIOLOGY

- Evidence exists for structural and functional abnormalities of the brain. Several regions are implicated but especially frontal-striatal and cerebellum networks. There is evidence for underactivity, and dopamine and norepinephrine are implicated.

- Substantial genetic transmission of ADHD is indicated by family and twin studies, and a handful of genes have been identified as relevant to ADHD. Adverse birth complications, low birthweight, and prenatal alcohol and tobacco use may underlie some cases. Diet is unlikely to be a causal factor. Exposure to lead is a small, but significant, factor in some cases.

- The psychosocial environment plays a role in shaping and maintaining ADHD behaviors. Family factors are particularly important, and consideration is given to teacher behavior.

Assessment

- *The identification of ADHD requires broad-based assessment that takes into account developmental level, various settings, and co-occurrence with other disorders.*

- *A comprehensive assessment includes interviews with the youth, parents, and teachers; the administration of standardized rating scales; direct observation; intelligence and achievement testing; and consideration of medical and social factors.*

Intervention

- *Effective prevention for ADHD likely focuses on early treatment of core and major functional problems, such as social difficulties.*

- *There is substantial evidence that stimulant medication can relieve the core symptoms of ADHD in most youth. However, limitations exist and there are numerous concerns about stimulant use.*

  - *Behaviorally oriented interventions, including parent training and school-based interventions, are evidence-based treatments for ADHD.*

  - *The MTA study, the largest long-term comparison of treatments, revealed initial but waning benefits for medication and medication plus behavioral treatments.*

- *Many researchers and professionals believe that multimodal treatment of the various aspects of ADHD is most appropriate.*

Key Terms

Predominately Inattentive Type (ADHD-I) *(p. 233)*

Predominately Hyperactive-Impulsive Type (ADHD-HI) *(p. 233)*

Combined Type (ADHD-C) *(p. 233)*

continuous performance tests *(p. 234)*

stop tasks *(p. 235)*

executive functions *(p. 236)*

sluggish cognitive tempo *(p. 239)*

delay aversion *(p. 246)*

Multimodal Treatment Assessment Study (MTA) *(p. 257)*

Summer Training Program (STP) *(p. 258)*

CHAPTER 10

Language and Learning Disabilities

Specific problems that arise in the development of language and learning are discussed in this chapter. These disabilities can vary from subtle to severe, interfere with the innumerable daily needs and pleasures of communication, cast a shadow of failure and frustration over the school years, and adversely affect adult occupational life. Indeed, it can be argued that language and learning disorders have had increasing impact on individual lives because of escalating demands for certain kinds of skills and learning in our industrial and technologically sophisticated world.

Child and adolescent difficulties in language and learning are associated with many known medical, genetic, and behavioral syndromes. Such conditions are not, however, the focus of this chapter. Rather, our primary interest is in youths who display specific impairments that are out of keeping with other aspects of their development. It is assumed that disturbance occurs relatively early and is not readily explained by social factors.

Professionals from diverse disciplines have been interested in language and learning problems—notably educators, psychologists, physicians, and language specialists. Approaching their work from different perspectives, they have generated diverse, albeit often overlapping, terminology, definitions, emphases, causal theories, and treatments. This rich history is reflected throughout the present chapter.

A Bit of History: Unexpected Disabilities, Unmet Needs

Specific language and learning problems have been recognized for a long time. Two major themes have left a strong mark on the field (Lyon et al., 2006; Lyon, Fletcher, & Barnes, 2003). One is scientific and clinical interest in understanding individuals who display specific deficits that appear discrepant with their intelligence or other abilities. The other, more applied, theme is an emphasis on the need to improve services to young people exhibiting such deficits.

Curiosity about discrepant, or unexpected, lack of abilities within individuals can be traced to work in Europe in the 1800s. Consider as an example the following description of a 10-year-old boy.

Thomas   So Many Abilities

He was apparently a bright and in every respect an intelligent boy. He had been learning music for a year and had made good progress in it. . . . In all departments of his studies where the instruction was oral he had made good progress, showing that his auditory memory was good. . . . He performs simple sums quite correctly, and his progress in arithmetic has been regarded as quite satisfactory. He has no difficulty in learning to write. His visual acuity is good.

Hinshelwood, 1917, pp. 46–47.

Yet, despite the boy's successes, it was reported that he was unable to learn to read. Many similarly puzzling cases were presented by physicians, and the field developed an early medical orientation that linked specific impairments with brain abnormalities. For example, in the latter 1880s, Broca described the inability of his adult patients to express themselves verbally while maintaining the capacity to comprehend what others said. Soon after, Wernicke documented brain lesions in patients who had problems in understanding language but otherwise did not exhibit language and cognitive impairment. Each of these men traced the specific disability to an area in the brain that now carries his name. Over many years, brain damage in adults was linked to behavioral symptoms such as specific speech problems, learning difficulties, and inattention (Hammill, 1993). Similar developmental problems in youth were hypothesized to be caused by brain injury or dysfunction of some sort, perhaps too subtle to be identified.

As Table 10–1 indicates, behavioral scientists in the United States, building on the European work, began to contribute a psychological orientation to the study of learning problems (Hallahan & Mock, 2003). Although brain dysfunction was often assumed, etiology was downplayed in favor of understanding the characteristics of learners and the educational remediation of learning deficits (Lyon et al., 2003). By the mid-1900s, several kinds of interventions were recommended. Nevertheless, concern was growing that a group of children had educational needs that were not being met by the schools.

In 1963, representatives from several organizations met at a symposium sponsored by the Fund for Perceptually Handicapped Children. In his address to the participants, Samuel Kirk, a well-respected psychologist, noted that the children of their concern

TABLE 10–1	HISTORICAL OVERVIEW OF THE FIELD OF LEARNING DISABILITIES
European Foundation Period (c. 1800–1920)	European physicians and researchers explore links between brain injury and disabilities (e.g., in language and reading)
U.S. Foundation Period (c. 1920–1960)	Building on European work, psychologists, educators, and others focus on identification of disabilities and remediation in educational settings via language, perceptual, and motor approaches
Emergent Period (c. 1960–1975)	Emergence of the concept of learning disabilities (LD) Various groups offer definitions of LD Advocacy by parents and professionals for effective educational services
Solidification Period (c. 1975–1985)	Solidification of federal definition and regulations for LD Focus on empirically validated research (e.g., on memory)
Turbulent Period (c. 1985–2000)	Efforts to reach consensus on definition Dramatic growth in number of LD students Continued research; progress on etiology, intervention Continued vexing questions (e.g., about definition, special education)

Based on Hallahan & Mock, 2003.

exhibited a variety of deficiencies that were presumed to be related to neurological dysfunction—especially learning difficulties, perceptual problems, and hyperactivity. Kirk suggested and defined "learning disabilities" as a suitable term that he believed could encourage and guide the assessment and educational intervention so needed by these children. That evening the conferees organized into what is today called the Learning Disabilities Association of America (Hammill, 1993).

Kirk's presentation is recognized as a milestone in the emergence of the concept of learning disabilities (Lipka & Siegel, 2006; Lyon et al., 2006). Parents and educators henceforth played an important role in an area previously dominated by physicians and psychologists (Hallahan & Kauffman, 1978; Taylor, 1988). Parents were given hope that their children's problems were limited and treatable; teachers were relieved of the suspicion that they were to blame for student failure; concerned professionals were provided a term that could make children eligible for special services. It was recognized that youth labeled as "learning disabled" constituted a heterogeneous group.

By the late 20th century, efforts were made to reach consensus on the definitions of learning disabilities, provide special education services, and conduct research into these disabilities. The last few decades have seen progress, and the number of youth categorized as disabled has dramatically increased. Nonetheless, challenges remain regarding the definition and conceptualization of specific language and learning disabilities, as well as related issues.

Definitional Concerns

To understand the problems of definition we turn to the Education for All Handicapped Children Act of 1975 (Public Law 94-142), which has had enormous influence on the field of language and learning disorders or disabilities. A sweeping educational mandate, it has been amended several times over the years and retitled the Individuals with Disabilities Education Act (IDEA). Its definition of learning disability has had an impact on the educational system, children and families, clinicians and researchers.

Specific learning disability means a disorder in one or more of the basic psychological processes involved in understanding or in using language, spoken or written, in which the disorder may manifest itself in an imperfect ability to listen, think, speak, read, write, spell, or to do

mathematical calculations. The term includes such conditions as perceptual handicaps, brain injury, minimal brain dysfunction, dyslexia, and developmental aphasia. The term does not include children who have learning problems which are primarily the result of visual, hearing, or motor handicaps, or mental retardation, or emotional disturbance, or of environmental, cultural, or economic disadvantage. (U.S. Office of Education, 1977, p. 65083)

This is a general definition that refers to disorder in basic psychological processes, but does not identify them. Several conditions, including neurological anomalies, are referenced in a general way. The definition also lacks specific criteria for identifying disabilities. In addition, it explicitly excludes children whose disabilities are due to several factors that could be expected to cause learning problems. The exclusionary criteria have been questioned, partly because it may be difficult to distinguish underachievement due to emotional disturbance, lack of motivation, or cultural or economic disadvantage. The presence of exclusionary criteria, in combination with the lack of specific criteria to define learning disabilities, has led to the statement that learning disabilities are defined more by what they are *not* than by what they are.

Definitional concerns have resulted in different, albeit overlapping, definitions and ways to identify disabilities (Dean & Burns, 2002; Lyon et al., 2006). Definitional problems have led to different prevalence rates, incomparability of groups chosen for research purposes, and varying standards to determine whether children will receive special education services. Here, we provide a snapshot of the definitional problem by considering how learning disabilities have often been identified.

IDENTIFYING SPECIFIC DISABILITIES

A lack of agreed-upon criteria to identify learning disabilities has been a continuing problem. What criteria and methods are to be used to decide that a child's language or learning skills are below expectations? In fact, different guidelines have been offered and several methods generated. Most often they have not targeted underlying psychological processes, and they raise questions.

IQ-achievement discrepancy. A common way to identify disabilities has been by a discrepancy between the individual's intellectual ability and specific achievement level. It is assumed that if a specific disability exists, performance on measures of *general* ability (typically IQ tests) will exceed performance on achievement tests of the hypothesized *specific* impairment. Guidelines often call for the discrepancy to be severe or significant, but this has been defined somewhat differently. A discrepancy of two or more standard deviations between intelligence test scores and achievement test scores often is employed, but smaller differences have been acceptable.

Below average achievement. Another approach identifies disabilities by determining that the youth is performing below expected grade level in at least one academic area. Variations occur in the specific criterion, however. Thus, a sixth grader, for example, might be labeled with a learning disability when his or her achievement is on a fourth- *or* fifth-grade level. A general problem with this method of identification is that a large discrepancy is more serious for a younger than an older child: being 2 years behind is more serious for a third grader than for a sixth grader. The problem can be reduced by setting the criterion, for instance, at a 1-year deficiency for younger children and 2 years for older children, but judgment still must be made about the criterion for each grade level.

Poor achievement can also be identified by comparing the child's performance with those of peers of the same age on standardized tests of language, reading, writing, and arithmetic. The degree to which performance must fall below that of peers varies with school districts and researchers. The criterion is usually set in the range of one to two standard deviations below the mean on standardized tests.

The poor achievement and especially the IQ-achievement discrepancy approaches have been challenged in numerous ways (Dyck et al., 2004; Hollenbeck, 2007). For example, it is argued that intelligence tests rely strongly on language abilities, so that overall intelligence may be underestimated in children with language or learning disabilities—making a discrepancy less probable. Others have pointed out that when a discrepancy from a high IQ is identified, the "disability" might be quite different from that of a discrepancy from a much lower IQ. Still another criticism is that there is no way to discriminate between deficits of the child and of poor instruction. Serious questions also have been raised about the exclusion of children considered to be "slow learners," that is, for whom a discrepancy is not found (Stanovich, 1989; Vellutino et al., 2004). There is growing recognition that in several ways specific disabilities do not differ much from general learning

problems that do not meet discrepancy formulations (Scruggs & Mastropieri, 2002). Overall, these arguments have somewhat weakened the IQ-achievement discrepancy approach (Dean & Burns, 2002). Nonetheless, intelligence often is considered by requiring that the child with low achievement also exhibit average intelligence, or an IQ that does not fall below the score that typically defines mental retardation (about 70). The inclusion of children with both low achievement and relatively low intelligence in the group termed learning-disabled is a contentious issue (e.g., Kavale & Forness, 2003).

Response to intervention (RTI). A relatively recent innovative approach to defining disability depends on exposing children to intervention prior to diagnosing them with a disability. The approach was given impetus in the latest 2004 reauthorization of IDEA by the suggestion that educational agencies might consider the child's response to scientific, research-based intervention (Hollenbeck, 2007). The rationale is that children whose response to valid intervention is poorer than that of their peers can be identified as having a learning disability (Fuchs, Fuchs, & Hollenbeck, 2007). This approach includes all children and also allows the elimination of poor instruction as a cause of the child's performance.

The RTI approach moves children through a series of interventions of increasing intensity (Hollenbeck, 2007). A group of children—say, kindergartners—is first exposed to a specific intervention—for example, a research-based reading program—and subsequently each child's reading skills are assessed. Children with deficits next receive special, more intensive intervention, perhaps in small groups, followed by another evaluation. At this point, or perhaps after an even more intensive additional intervention, the child who has not positively responded is recognized as having a disability and is eligible for special education services.

RTI is a newly developing approach and there are many unresolved basic issues. What interventions are best employed? What criteria for determining deficits? How is RTI to be used with older students, and implemented in school classrooms? Professionals hold differing views and attitudes regarding RTI. Some view it as replacing identification of learning disabilities by IQ-achievement discrepancy; others see it as only one component of a broader evaluation. It is also seen as a strategy for prevention or intervention. In addition, not all professionals desire to move from traditional methods of identification to a new method with unanswered questions. There also is concern that including all students shifts the conceptualization of LD as a *specific* disability to a more general disability of low achievement. Clearly, there is much to be learned about RTI.

Despite the problems of definitional confusion, substantial progress has been made in understanding language and learning disabilities. We begin the following discussion with language disorders because they are likely to be identified earlier and because they are often implicated in other disabilities.

Language Disabilities

The study and treatment of language impairments has been both independent of and integrated with the study and treatment of "learning disabilities," which typically refer to reading, writing, and arithmetic. Language disabilities have historically been known as *aphasia*, a term that means loss of language due to brain damage or dysfunction. When the matter at hand is developmental disorder in youth—as it is in our discussion—aphasia is not an accurate fit, and the terms *developmental aphasia* and *developmental dysphasia* were once employed. These terms have largely given way to *specific language impairment (LI or SLI)*, *specific language disabilities*, or *language disorders*. We use these terms interchangeably.

NORMAL LANGUAGE DEVELOPMENT

An overview of normal language development serves as a framework for understanding disabilities. Language, as we usually know it, is a system of communication based on sounds that are combined into words and sentences to represent experience and carry meaning. Table 10–2 defines the basic components

TABLE 10–2	BASIC COMPONENTS OF LANGUAGE
Phonology	Sounds of a language and rules for combining them
Morphology	Formation of words, including the use of prefixes and suffixes (e.g., un, ed, s) to give meaning
Syntax	Organization of words into phrases and sentences
Semantics	Meanings in language
Pragmatics	Use of language in specific contexts

of language that must be mastered by all users of oral and written language.

Phonology has to do with the basic sounds of a language. English has 42 basic sounds, or phonemes. As a written language, it has 26 alphabet letters, which singly or in combinations are called graphemes. There is a correspondence between phonemes and graphemes. Of course, letters are combined to form words, which carry meaning. Morphology has to do with the formation of words, and syntax refers to the organization of words into phrases and sentences. Morphology and syntax are parts of grammar, the system of rules that organize a language. Thus, English speakers who follow the rules say "He dances well," not "He well dance." The rules of language help facilitate meaningful communication, which is referred to as semantics. Finally, pragmatics is the use of language in context; in social situations it includes such aspects as taking turns when speaking with another person or judging when to initiate conversation.

Superimposed on the basic components of language are reception and expression. Receptive language has to do with the comprehension of messages sent by others. Expressive language concerns the production of language, that is, sending messages. Reception is developmentally acquired earlier than expression—as anyone who tries to learn a second language quickly discovers.

Infants come into the world geared for language; their amazing capacity progresses rapidly and in sequential milestones during the first few years of life (Table 10–3). During the first year, infants can distinguish and produce sounds that are not part of the native language that surrounds them, and then this ability contracts to the sounds of their language. Thus, it appears that an innate ability to process language sounds is shaped through experience. By their first birthdays, most infants are saying a few words. Some speech sounds are more difficult than others, and individual differences in pronunciation, or articulation, become obvious. Even before this time, infants have begun to understand the communications of others.

By 2 years of age, most children have gone from saying single words, to two-word utterances, to longer strings of words set in meaningful phrases or sentences. Vocabulary increases dramatically, different parts of speech are acquired, and the ability to arrange words improves. Comprehension also grows, and parents of 3-year-olds perceive that they are talking with someone who is no longer a "baby." Indeed, infancy—a term derived from a Latin word that means "incapable of speech"—is usually said to be over at age 2. Progress continues at a rapid rate and includes

TABLE 10–3	EARLY ACQUISITION OF LANGUAGE AND COMMUNICATION	
	RECEPTION	**EXPRESSION**
Birth to 6 months	Reacts to sudden noise. Is quieted by a voice. Locates sound. Recognizes name and words like "bye-bye."	Cries. Babbles, laughs. Initiates vocal play. Vocalizes to self. Experiments with voice.
6 to 12 months	Stops activity to "no." Raises arms to "come up." Obeys simple instructions. Understands simple statements.	Makes sounds that exist in the culture's language. Combines vowel sounds. Imitates adult sounds. Says first words.
12 to 18 months	Carries out two consecutive commands. Understands new words. Listens to nursery rhymes.	Uses ten words. Requests objects by name. Connects sounds so that they flow like a sentence.
18 to 24 months	Recognizes many sounds. Understands action words like "show me."	Uses short sentences. Uses pronouns. Echoes last words of a rhyme.
24 to 36 months	Follows commands using "in," "on," "under." Follows three verbal commands given in one utterance.	Uses possessive, noun–verb combinations. Ninety percent of communications are understandable by primary caregiver.
36 to 48 months	Increases understanding of others' messages and social context of communication.	Uses increasingly complex language forms, such as conjunctions and auxiliary verbs.

Based on Bryant, 1977; Whitehurst, 1982.

pragmatics. By age 7, many of the basics of language are acquired, although language development continues into adolescence and even into adulthood.

DSM CLASSIFICATION AND DIAGNOSIS

From even a brief review of language development, it is obvious that a variety of impairments might occur; problems can exist in phonology, syntax, semantics, and so forth. It is possible, then, to classify disabilities in several ways. Although attempts to subgroup language disabilities have not been very successful, a basic distinction is often made between those who have difficulty with expressive language and those who have problems with receptive language.

Under the category of Communication Disorders, the DSM considers three disorders of primary interest to our discussion. Table 10–4 provides a summary of the diagnostic criteria for these. For Phonological Disorder to be diagnosed, a child must fail to display developmentally appropriate and dialect-appropriate speech sounds. Diagnosis of Expressive Disorder or Mixed Receptive–Expressive Disorder requires assessment with standardized, individually given language and intelligence tests. Expressive Disorder exists when language expression is inferior to the person's nonverbal intelligence and reception (comprehension) of language. The category of Mixed Receptive–Expressive Disorder reflects the fact that receptive problems do not typically occur alone. Diagnosis of this disorder requires both reception and expression of language to be below the child's nonverbal intelligence. In all cases of language disorders, impairments must be severe enough to interfere with daily functioning. Impairments cannot be accounted for by mental retardation or sensorimotor deficits, nor to insufficient environmental stimulation. (It is noteworthy that the DSM system includes impairments caused by medical, genetic, or physical conditions as well as developmental impairments of unknown cause. In this chapter, only developmental disabilities are discussed.)

TABLE 10–4	**THE DSM CRITERIA FOR THREE COMMUNICATION DISORDERS**	
PHONOLOGICAL	**EXPRESSIVE**	**RECEPTIVE–EXPRESSIVE**
A. There is failure to use developmentally appropriate and dialect-appropriate speech sounds (e.g., use of substitutions and omissions).	A. Scores from standardized measures of expressive language are substantially below scores for nonverbal intelligence and receptive language.	A. Scores from standardized measures of both receptive and expressive language are substantially below those for nonverbal intellectual capacity.

B. The difficulties interfere with academic or occupational achievement or with social communication.

C. If mental retardation, a speech-motor or sensory deficit, or environmental deprivation is present, the language difficulties are in excess of those usually associated with these problems.

From American Psychiatric Association, 2000.

DESCRIPTION

Phonological disorder. Children with this disorder have difficulty in articulating speech sounds. The course of speech sound production is generally similar to that of typical development, but it is delayed and proceeds more slowly (Johnson & Beitchman, 2005c). Children with impaired speech make incorrect speech sounds, substitute easily made sounds for more difficult ones, or omit sounds. Most youngsters display some misarticulation as they acquire the linguistic and motor skills necessary for speech, so developmental norms are crucial in diagnosis. The following case study describes severe articulation problems in a three-year-old boy.

Ramon | Phonological Disorder

Ramon was a talkative boy whose speech was virtually unintelligible despite his normal hearing and language comprehension. The rhythm and melody of his speech suggested that he was trying to produce multiword communications typical for his age. He produced only a few vowels and some early-developing consonants. Many of his spoken words were thus indistinguishable. He said *bahbah* for bottle, baby, and bubble, and used *nee* for knee, need, and Anita (his sister). Ramon also omitted consonant sounds at the end of words. On occasion, he reacted with frustration and tantrums to the difficulties in making his needs understood.

Adapted from Johnson & Beitchman, 2005c, p. 3151.

Articulation impairment is sometimes referred to as speech impairment, to differentiate it from other language disorders. (In fact, children with simple misarticulations but no other difficulties are not considered to have specific language disorder according to some definitions [Leonard, 1998].) However, problems in phonology can go beyond a simple inability to accurately produce speech sounds to a broader problem in the child's understanding of the sound structure of the language (Snowling, Bishop, & Stothard, 2000; Whitehurst & Fischel, 1994). Thus, for example, the child may have difficulty in knowing which word rhymes with another or whether "soup" or "coat" starts with the same sound as "Sam" (Bishop, 2002). Such problems have more serious developmental implications.

Expressive language disorder. This disorder involves the production of language with regard to vocabulary, grammar, and other aspects of language output. Youngsters with expressive problems may have a limited amount of speech and may speak in extremely short, simple sentences. Vocabulary may be small; critical parts of sentences may be missing; unusual word order may be displayed. Especially problematic, children may exhibit undue errors in marking word forms such as plurals or verb tense. In addition, phonological problems may be observed. However, children with expressive problems understand speech and age-level concepts, and thus they can appropriately respond to others' communications.

These characteristics are seen in the following description of Amy, a sociable, active 5-year-old with expressive language disorder (Johnson & Beitchman,

2005a). One day while Amy was playing with her friend Lisa, each girl told the story of Little Red Riding Hood to her doll.

Amy **Problems in Language Expression**

Lisa's story began: "Little Red Riding Hood was taking a basket of food to her grandmother who was sick. A bad wolf stopped Riding Hood in the forest. He tried to get the basket from her but she wouldn't give it to him."

By contrast, Amy's story demonstrated marked difficulties in verbal expression: "Riding Hood going to grandma house. Her taking food. Bad wolf in a bed. Riding Hood say, what big ears, grandma? Hear you, dear. What big eyes, grandma? See you, dear. What big mouth, grandma? Eat you all up!"

Many features of Amy's story are characteristic of expressive language disorder of children of Amy's age: short, incomplete sentences; simple sentence structure; omission of grammatical function words (e.g., is, the) and endings (e.g., possessives); problems in question formation; and incorrect use of pronouns (e.g., "her" for "she"). Nonetheless, when tested by methods that did not require verbal responding, it was clear that Amy understood the details and plot of the Riding Hood tale as well as her friend did. Amy also demonstrated adequate comprehensive skills in her kindergarten classroom, where she ably followed the teacher's verbal instructions.

Adapted from Johnson & Beitchman, 2005a, p. 3138.

Receptive–expressive language disorder. This disorder involves difficulties in comprehending the communication of others. Single words, phrases, sentences, the multiple meanings of a word, or the past tense may all be problematic. The child may fail to respond to speech, seem deaf, respond inappropriately to others' speech, or be uninterested in television. In addition, there are difficulties in expressing language shown by children with expressive disorder (Johnson & Beitchman, 2005b). Problems may occur in phonology as well—although these are not central to the disorder.

The description of a 5-year-old boy, Trang, illustrates receptive–expressive impairments. This child lived with his parents and siblings, who were proficient in both English and Vietnamese. His development in both languages was much slower than that of his siblings, and kindergarten assessment revealed impairments in both reception and expression.

Trang **Problems in Language Reception and Expression**

Trang understood a limited number of words for objects, actions, and relations. He often failed to follow classroom instructions, particularly those that involved words for time (e.g., yesterday, after, week) and space (e.g., beneath, in front of, around). His conversation with other children often broke down because he did not understand fully what they were saying, nor could he express his own ideas clearly. As a result he was not a favored playmate, and most of the children in his class ignored him. His limited interactions further reduced Trang's opportunities for improving and practicing his already weak language skills. Additional assessment, conducted with the assistance of a Vietnamese interpreter, revealed that Trang showed similar receptive and expressive language deficits in Vietnamese. His nonverbal skills, however, were generally appropriate for his age. He readily constructed intricate buildings and vehicles with small, plastic building blocks; he easily completed complex jigsaw puzzles; and he successfully solved numerical, conceptual, or analogical problems, as long as they were presented nonverbally.

Adapted from Johnson & Beitchman, 2000b, p. 2642.

When considering language disorder, it is helpful to keep in mind the considerable variation across children in the kinds and severity of problems experienced. Imagine, if you will, the difference between a child with only articulation deficits and a child who is unable to comprehend much of what is being communicated by others. Life is different too for the child who has minor articulation deficits and one whose speech can hardly be understood by others.

EPIDEMIOLOGY AND DEVELOPMENTAL COURSE

Children referred for psychiatric services have very high rates of language impairment, for example, 40 to 50% (Toppelberg et al., 2002). Limited epidemiological studies suggest overall rates of about 7% (Bishop, 2002; Tomblin, 2006). Even so, prevalence varies with age and type of disorder.

Boys are widely reported as having higher rates than girls (American Psychiatric Association, 2000). Although higher prevalence in clinic samples may reflect referral bias, this does not seem to completely account for the gender difference (Viding et al., 2004).

Higher rates also have been noted in children from low socioeconomic groups (Carroll et al., 2005; McDowell, Lonigan, & Goldstein, 2007; Toppelberg & Shapiro, 2000). What might explain this correlation? If hereditary factors play a role, family language disabilities might result in families attaining low educational and occupational status. It is also possible that poor children who use dialects different from the standard English employed in standardized assessment instruments are overidentified.

Language disorders usually appear by age 3 or 4, but mild difficulties may not be identified until later (American Psychiatric Association, 2000). Some impairments may first become apparent with the demands of schoolwork and greater complexity of language. It may be more difficult to ascertain what a child understands than to observe impairments in the expression of speech.

Studies of children and adults of various ages, followed for various periods of time, indicate that improvement can occur over time and that language abilities can reach the normal range (Leonard, 1998). However, a hierarchy of risk based on the type of disorder has been noted. Children who display only articulation problems are at lowest risk, those with expressive problems are at middle risk, and those with receptive–expressive problems are at highest risk for later language impairments (Baker & Cantwell, 1989; Rutter, Mawhood, & Howlin, 1992; Whitehurst & Fischel, 1994).

Phonological problems, especially when mild, are quite common during the preschool years, but about 75% of mild to moderate cases remit by age 6 (American Psychiatric Association, 2000). Such difficulties are rare in adolescence. Regarding expressive difficulties, some children, often referred to as "late talkers," eventually reach the normal range of language development but still fall somewhat short of most of their peers (Johnson & Beitchman, 2005a; Rescorla, 2002; Tomblin et al., 2003). However, a substantial number of children with early expressive difficulties continue to exhibit impairment. Regarding receptive–expressive difficulties, many children may never develop completely normal language and their problems may increase over time. A study that followed boys with severe receptive–expressive impairments into their early twenties found that 20% had a level of comprehension below that of 10-year-old children and about 25% had equally poor expressive skills (Mawhood, Howlin, & Rutter, 2000). Little change occurred over the next decade (Clegg et al., 2005). In general, although children diagnosed with language impairments are often said to be "delayed" in language development, many get a late start and develop more slowly, with abilities leveling off or falling behind and never catching up (Leonard, 1998; Miller & Tallal, 1995; Tallal & Benasich, 2002).

One of the burdens of language disorder is its association with poor academic progress and learning disabilities. School achievement is affected: more students are retained at grade level and fewer students attend high school (Tomblin et al., 2000). At least in part, this finding undoubtedly is due to the association of language disorders with learning disabilities (Tomblin et al., 2000; Young et al., 2002). For instance, one longitudinal study found that language-impaired children were 4.6 times as likely to have later reading disability compared to typically developing children (Table 10–5). In another study, 51% of children with language disorder had reading disability and 55% of children with reading disability had language impairment (McArthur et al., 2000). The role that language plays in reading problems is suggested by the finding

TABLE 10–5	RISK OF HAVING A LEARNING DISABILITY* AT AGE 19 IN A GROUP IDENTIFIED WITH LANGUAGE IMPAIRMENTS AT AGE 5
LEARNING DISABILITY	**RISK**
Reading	4.6
Spelling	4.1
Math	3.7
Reading + spelling	4.7
Reading + math	9.4
Spelling + math	4.4
Reading + spelling + math	7.8

*A learning disability was defined by performance below the 25th percentile on tests of reading, spelling, or math, and an IQ (verbal or performance) of at least 80.

Adapted from Young et al., 2002.

that weaknesses in early language (e.g., knowing names and sounds of letters, vocabulary, grammar) are associated with later reading problems (De-Thorne et al., 2006; Lonigan, Burgess, & Anthony, 2000; Raitano et al., 2004).

COGNITIVE DEFICITS

Children with language impairments commonly exhibit subtle, nonlinguistic cognitive deficits. Proposals have been made regarding how these deficits might contribute to language disorder (Bishop, 1992). Speed of information processing, auditory perception, and memory are among the areas examined (Leonard, 1998; Leonard et al., 2007).

One hypothesis is that a general limitation in information-processing capacity is involved in language disorder. The information-processing model assumes, among other things, that rapid handling of information facilitates processing. Limitation in speed of processing is notable in children with language disabilities (Leonard et al., 2007). They appear to respond more slowly across a variety of tasks, which suggests that a processing limitation affects performance across domains. When a particular language operation requires especially rapid processing, detrimental effects would be expected.

A second, more specific, hypothesis relates language impairments to various deficits in auditory processing (Corriveau, Pasquini, & Goswami, 2007; Leonard, 1998). Perception of brief, rapid sound is considered important in language, so a child who cannot catch rapidly flowing sound cues might well have language difficulties. Research has shown that children with language impairments do appear to have difficulty identifying very fast sounds embedded in speech (Tallal & Benasich, 2002). Moreover, infants at family risk for language/learning impairments exhibited longer processing times for auditory stimuli. Further support for the hypothesis comes from studies indicating that when sound cues in speech syllables are extended in experimental studies, speech discrimination improves.

A third proposal implicates both verbal short-term and working memory (Gathercole & Alloway, 2006). A distinction can be made between these aspects of memory. Verbal short-term memory is specialized for the temporary storage of information pertaining to language. It is thought to be involved with the sound structure, or phonology, of language. Deficits are apparent in a variety of tasks, including the immediate repetition of a string of nonwords (e.g., mep, shom) that has been said aloud. Research,

including meta-analysis, shows that children with language disabilities have deficits in nonword repetition and phonological memory (Bishop, 2002; Conti-Ramsden, 2003; Estes, Evans, & Else-Quest, 2007). It is worth noting that in typically developing children, phonological memory is related to the acquisition of speech production, vocabulary, comprehension, and the processing of syntax (Marton & Schwartz, 2003).

With regard to verbal working memory, both the storage and the processing of verbal information is involved. Working memory requires holding verbal information in mind while it is used, for example, to follow a sequence of directions or steps in mathematics. Children with language disorders do poorly on measures of complex verbal memory (Gathercole & Alloway, 2006). Such difficulty may not be an underlying cause of language problems, but it likely contributes to the reading and mathematics problems that are associated with language disabilities.

Although progress is being made in understanding subtle cognitive deficits exhibited by children with language impairments, much is yet to be investigated. Given the heterogeneity of problems, several deficits are probably involved.

Learning Disabilities: Reading, Writing, Arithmetic

The terms *learning disabilities* (LD) and *learning disorders* refer to specific developmental problems in reading, writing, and arithmetic—the "three Rs" essential to classroom learning and everyday functioning. These disorders respectively have been called *dyslexia*, *dysgraphia*, and *dyscalculia*—terms that are used less today. Although learning disabilities are often described as if they are "pure," deficits frequently occur in combinations. Most children with learning disorders have reading problems, and many have additional learning difficulties. Specific learning disabilities are recognized by the educational system and by the DSM and ICD.

DSM CLASSIFICATION AND DIAGNOSIS

Table 10–6 provides a summary of the DSM criteria for diagnosis of Reading Disorder, Disorder of Written Expression, and Mathematics Disorder. Diagnosis is based on a substantial discrepancy between how well a person performs on individually given,

TABLE 10–6	THE DSM CRITERIA FOR DISORDERS OF READING, WRITTEN EXPRESSION, AND MATHEMATICS

A. Achievement or ability, as measured by standardized tests, is substantially below that expected given the person's age, measured intelligence, and age-appropriate education.

B. The disturbance significantly interferes with academic achievement or activities of daily living that require the ability.

C. If a sensory deficit is present, the difficulties are in excess of those usually associated with the sensory deficit.

From American Psychiatric Association, 2000.

standardized achievement tests relative to the person's age, intelligence, or age-appropriate education. The disability must interfere significantly with academic achievement or daily living. It cannot be accounted for by a sensory deficit.

We discuss specific topics for each of these disorders before examining more general issues. Emphasis is placed by far on reading disabilities because of their high prevalence and because they have been most investigated.

READING DISABILITIES (RD)

Description. Reading can be defined as "the process of extracting and constructing meaning from written text for some purpose" (Vellutino et al., 2004, p. 5). It requires the ability to readily identify words in running text in order to discern the meaning of the text. Among the many skills involved in this "on-line" process are language abilities, cognitive skills, understanding of the conventions of written text (e.g., reading from left to right on a page), and a store of knowledge about the world.

An enormously complex process, reading virtually always entails instruction. When it is not mastered, children may struggle to recognize single written words or to pronounce them correctly when reading aloud, read excessively slowly or haltingly, have limited vocabulary, be able to read but not to understand what they have read, or not remember what they have read. Given these complexities, extensive efforts have been made to discover whether reading problems fall into subtypes based on reading skills or underlying cognitive deficits.

These efforts have largely failed to generate valid subtypes (Siegel, 2003; Tannock, 2005c). However, an important distinction is made between problems in word-level reading and in the comprehension of written text.

Epidemiology and developmental course. The reported prevalence of RD has varied considerably. A conservative estimate is 4 to 10% of the U.S. school-age population (Tannock, 2005c). Lyon and colleagues (2006) note that estimates historically have fallen between 10 and 15% of the U.S. school-age population. Discrepancies in reported rates are due in part to sampling differences and definitional inconsistency. For example, rates are higher in inner city samples, and when disabilities are defined by low achievement rather than by an IQ-achievement discrepancy (Tannock, 2005c).

Boys have been more often diagnosed with RD than girls, and genetics and selection bias have been proposed as explanations (Lipka & Siegel, 2006). The male to female ratio may be about 3 or 4 to 1 in clinic samples, and perhaps smaller in the general child population (Willcutt & Pennington, 2000).

Reading disorders have been identified at varying rates in many countries (Grigorenko, 2001). Further research would be useful in clarifying the degree to which this might be explained by the differing structures of different languages, societal attitudes toward reading disabilities, or methodological factors.

Disorder tends to persist during the school years into adolescence and adulthood (McGee et al., 2002; Snowling, Muter, & Carroll, 2007). Some variation is seen in outcome, however (Shaywitz et al., 2003; Williams & McGee, 1996). Some children with poor reading skills in early childhood have been reported to catch up with their peers by preadolescence or adolescence, and improvement can occur even later. General intelligence, mother's reading ability, and initial severity of reading problems may predict outcome. In addition, youths with initially severe problems are further disadvantaged by not being able to practice reading, because experience and practice with print material is considered important in improving literacy skills.

Underlying processes. Various psychological processes have been implicated in RD. Theories of visual system abnormalities were the most influential throughout the 20th century until the 1970s and 1980s (Vellutino, et al., 2004). For example, Samuel Orton, a central figure in early research on reading, erroneously noted that among other difficulties visual–perceptual deficits caused dyslexic children to reverse letters (*d* for *b; saw* for *was*) and even to write in mirror images (Vellutino, 1979). Other theorists have suggested that dyslexia is caused by visual system defects that lead to impairments in scanning, tracking, or processing visual stimuli. Currently, it is believed that perceptual processing deficits, including auditory processing, may be involved in some way in RD (Boden & Giaschi, 2007; Tannock, 2005c).

Nonetheless, the present view of reading disorder emphasizes its fundamental relationship to language impairment (Vellutino et al., 2004). A critical role is given to phonological processing, that is, using the sound structure of language to process written material. Before they can learn to read, children must realize that spoken words can be segmented into sounds, an ability referred to as phonological awareness. For instance, they must recognize that the word *sad* contains three sounds, even though *sad* is said as one unit of sound. Also necessary is phonological decoding, that is, understanding that letters (graphemes) correspond to sounds (phonemes) and being able to map letters to sounds. Much evidence supports the importance of phonological processing, particularly in early learning to read (Lipka & Siegel, 2006). Young children who are aware of the sounds of their language and who can decode letters, syllables, and single words become better readers. In contrast, phonological processing deficits are associated with difficulty in naming single words, reading, and spelling. Moreover, interventions that target phonological processing deficits improve single word identification and reading. Cross-cultural studies also point to the importance of phonological processes in the reading of alphabet-based languages other than English (Grigorenko, 2001; Paulesu et al., 2001). (For more on cross-cultural studies see Accent: "Vulnerability and Reading in Different Languages.")

ACCENT ● ● ● ● ●

Vulnerability and Reading in Different Languages

The value of cross-cultural investigation is demonstrated in studies of reading in different languages. Some of the basic findings give us food for thought.

To begin with, alphabet-based languages vary in the consistency in which letters map to sounds—German and Italian are more consistent than English and French. Reading skills are more readily acquired in the more consistent languages, and there are fewer cases of reading disorder as shown in the accurate recognition of single words (Paulesu et al., 2001; Tannock, 2005c). However, even in cultures using the more consistent languages, some individuals do not read as well as others. Interestingly, this is not very evident in phonological processing, but instead is revealed more in tests of short-term memory and rapid naming of words (Vellutino et al., 2004). It has also been shown that German-speaking children with reading problems are able to read long unfamiliar words and nonwords as well as their non-impaired peers—presumably because of the relatively consistent matching of letters and sounds. They do, however, show problems in reading in a smooth, fluent way.

Perhaps even more striking is the comparison of reading disabilities in alphabet-based languages with those in logographic languages such as Chinese, which requires knowledge and recognition of hundreds of complex visual symbols with different meanings. Research suggests that learning to read in Chinese is associated with several deficits rather than with difficulties in phonological processing. Visual skills are a stronger predictor of reading ability in Chinese than in alphabet-based languages. Moreover, brain scans indicate that functioning of a right frontal area is disrupted in impaired reading of Chinese rather than a left posterior area typically seen in impaired reading of English (Siok et al., 2004).

What can be made of these fascinating findings? For Vellutino and his colleagues (2004), the findings underscore the fact that reading disorder depends on certain innate susceptibilities interacting with environmental factors, including the language specific to the culture in which children learn to read. Some alphabet languages, such as German, may be less demanding for a vulnerable child, whereas others, such as English, may present heightened challenges. Moreover, different languages may make different demands on specific abilities. Thus, the child with a particular vulnerability may be likely to develop a reading disability in one culture but not in another.

Nevertheless, reading entails much more than phonological processing. Snowling (2000) has pointed out that decoding skills certainly aid the child in reading words that follow the usual grapheme–phoneme rules, but they do not help much for words such as *yacht* and *biscuit*. The same is true for knowing how to read the word *bow* in "The magician took a bow," and understanding *she* in "Susan gave Jane an apple and she was happy" (p. 246). Snowling, and others, emphasize that reading involves phonological, syntactic, and semantic components, and that the demands placed on these components change over time.

It is also notable that some children—perhaps 5 to 10%—who are not deficient in phonological processing have difficulties in understanding what they read (Lyon et al., 2003). These children can decode and recognize single words, but they variously exhibit small vocabulary, poor understanding of syntax, deficits in working memory, and problems in drawing inferences from text. They may often go unidentified by teachers (Nation et al., 2004). There is considerable need to better understand disabilities in comprehension, including developmental paths and intervention (Berninger et al., 2006; Lipka, Lesaux, & Siegel, 2006).

Pathways to reading. Research has contributed to knowledge about reading by studying children over several years. Here, we look at two examples.

Snowling, Gallagher, and Frith (2003) conducted three assessments of children age 3 to 8 years who were or were not at family risk for reading problems. Many more of the at-risk youngsters exhibited reading problems at age 8; they had experienced continuous language impairments as well. Other at-risk children did not meet the criteria for reading problems at age 8, although they showed poorer performance than the control group in many language and reading skills. [A follow-up at age 12–13 showed continuing problems for the impaired groups (Snowling, Muter, & Carroll, 2007).] The data collected throughout the study suggested two paths to successful reading. One path originated with children's early language skills and the other with early letter knowledge (phonological path). The investigators proposed that at-risk children only slowly developed the phonological path, but that some were protected from reading problems at age 8 because (1) they had sufficient language skills and (2) as learning to read proceeds, reading depends more on language-related skills (e.g., using the context of a sentence). The investigators recognized that language

skills are not the only factor that might protect high-risk children; others include reading instruction, children's ability to pay attention, and the practice of reading.

Employing a different research strategy, Lipka and colleagues (2006) studied the development of late-emerging reading. Although problems in the early acquisition of reading have been of great interest, it appears that reading difficulties—both word-level and comprehension difficulties—can first emerge around the fourth or fifth grade (Leach, Scarborough, & Rescorla, 2003). Using a standardized reading measure, Lipka and colleagues identified a group of fourth graders as reading disabled. The group had been drawn from a large representative sample of children who had been tested annually on several measures of reading, starting in kindergarten. These data showed that the children with reading disability in fourth grade had moved along three paths (see Figure 10–1). One path involved consistently poor reading (PR); a second path involved some fluctuation (FR). Of most interest was a path showing a more dramatic drop-off, with scores falling into the disability range only at fourth grade (LE). On the basis of the various measures available over the years, the investigators suggested that children following this late-emerging path actually (1) had not mastered early phonological processing skills, but had masked the deficit by learning to sight read many words, or (2) had only inadequately mastered phonological processing skills, so that the increased demands of fourth-grade reading had taken their toll. Noteworthy is that this late-emerging group represented 36% of the reading-disabled children and that other studies have found somewhat larger rates of children whose reading problems appear to emerge relatively late. The study by Lipka and colleagues suggests that such children may have early subtle deficits that require monitoring. Late-emerging reading problems warrant further investigation.

As is obvious by the preceding discussion, much is still unknown about reading and reading disabilities. At the same time, the importance of phonological processing in learning to read has been established.

DISABILITIES OF WRITTEN EXPRESSION

Children with disorders of written expression are the last to hand in classwork and may sit for hours over homework. Their writings may be rife with errors, be difficult to decipher, and contain disorganized content lacking in length and richness. Writing is

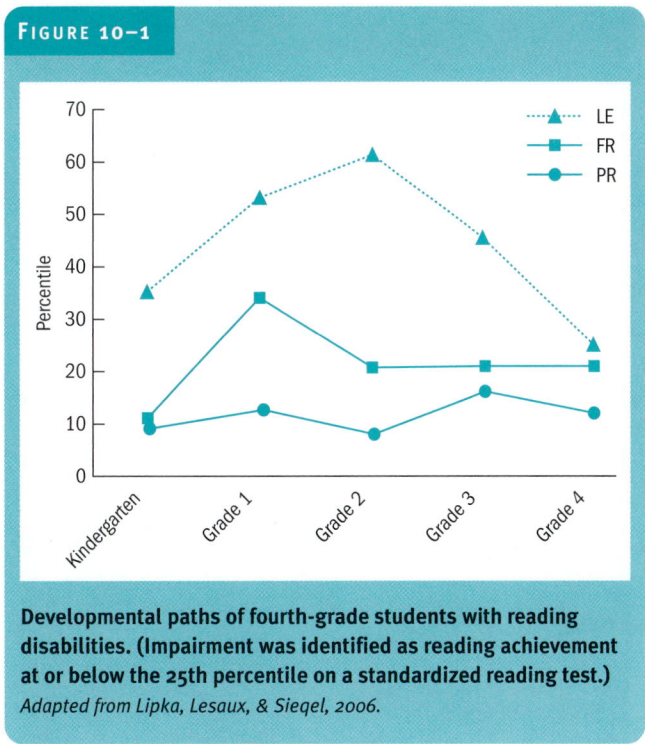

FIGURE 10–1

Developmental paths of fourth-grade students with reading disabilities. (Impairment was identified as reading achievement at or below the 25th percentile on a standardized reading test.)
Adapted from Lipka, Lesaux, & Sieqel, 2006.

multidimensional and implicates multiple language processes as well as visual–motor and other cognitive abilities (Lyon et al., 2006; Tannock, 2005a). It has been useful to make a distinction between transcription and text generation, that is, composition.

Transcription involves putting ideas into written form; it is fundamental in the early development of writing (Berninger & Amtmann, 2003). Many deficiencies are observed in poor transcription—in punctuation, capitalization, word placement—but problems in handwriting and spelling are central. Disabilities can occur in one or both of these. In typical development, smooth, rapid, and clear handwriting develops gradually and entails effort. A child with transcription problems produces letters and words on paper slowly and laboriously, and sometimes is unsuccessful at writing (Figure 10–2). Good handwriting requires not only motor skill, but also that letters be stored in working and long-term memory, planned for, and retrieved from memory. Good spelling depends, among other abilities, on understanding the connections between sounds and conventional spelling, on word recognition, and on knowledge and retrieval of learned letters/words from memory (Berninger & Amtmann, 2003; Lyon et al., 2003). The following case description of 11-year-old C.J. demonstrates some of the difficulties of

deficient transcription and also the implication it has for text generation.

C.J. Writing, Writing, All Day Long

Fifth-grader C.J.'s problems had been increasing; he exhibited deteriorating grades, failure to complete assigned schoolwork, and some inattention and oppositional behaviors. C.J.'s identical twin had an early history of language and reading problems. C.J. participated in class discussions and had no problems with reading or math computation, but his written work was putting him at risk for failing his grade level. C.J. had an increasing dislike for school, sometimes skipped classes, found writing to be extremely tedious, and expressed a desire to talk rather than write about his many ideas. "It's writing, writing all day long—even in math and science." He reported that his teacher thought he was lazy and his writing atrocious. "He slings my work back at me to do over again, gives me detention, and when I try to explain he tells me I've got a bad attitude."

An assessment with the Wide Range Achievement Test-3 revealed average to high-average reading and math performance, but significant problems in spelling. C.J. also did poorly on a

FIGURE 10-2

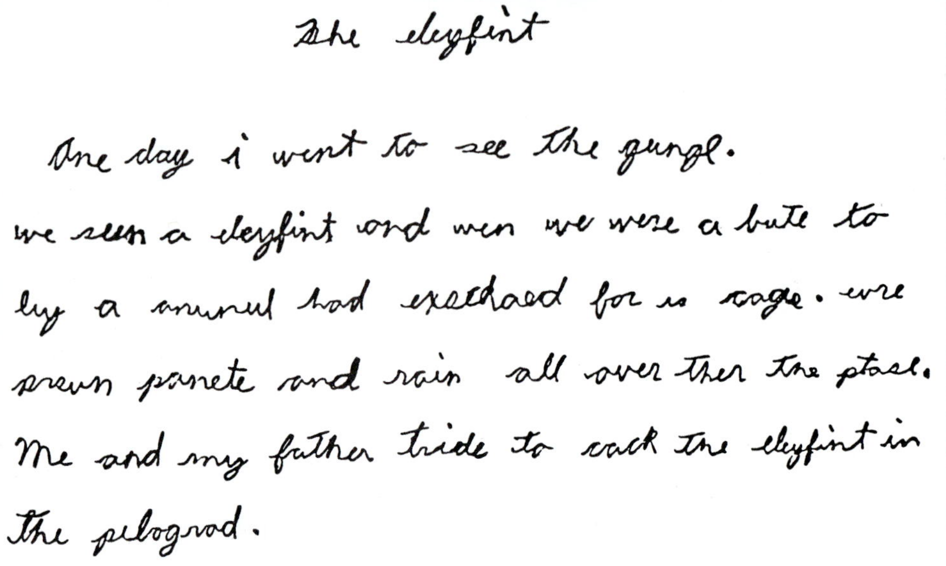

The Elephant
One day I went to see the jungle. We seen a elephant and when we were about to leave an animal escaped from his cage. Every person panicked and ran all over the place. Me and my father tried to catch the elephant in the playground.

The writing of an 11-year-old boy and the probable translation. The writing shows imagination, a rich vocabulary, and a basic grasp of storytelling. There also are misspellings of common and uncommon words, poorly formed letters, and retracing of letters that suggest difficulty in mechanics of writing.
Adapted from Taylor, 1988.

standardized test of written expression and an informal text generation task. On the latter, he produced three barely legible short sentences that lacked punctuation and capitalization but contained several spelling and grammar errors. C.J. attained average scores on a standardized oral language test but omitted sounds or syllables on a nonword test. The latter is sensitive to mild residual language impairments and written language impairments. The diagnosis of disorder of written expression was formulated by the assessment team, with no other DSM disorder.

Adapted from Tannock, 2005a, pp. 3126–3127.

Text generation (or composition) can be viewed as the creation of meaning in written form. Among other requirements it demands that the child be able to retrieve from memory words, sentence structure, and stored information about the topic of interest. Also critical are higher-order executive functions and metacognitive skills, the latter involving the person's understanding of how information gets processed (Graham & Harris, 2003; Schumaker & Deshler, 2003; Wong et al., 1997). Disabled writers lack skills in understanding the goal of their writing, developing a plan, organizing the points to be made, linking ideas, monitoring and revising their work, and the like. Many of these components apply to language and thinking more generally and are thus less specific to writing disorders than is transcription (Lyon et al., 2003). This does not mean, of course, that these skills are less important in understanding and ameliorating children's difficulties in writing. Figure 10–3 provides

FIGURE 10–3

Hokey and basketball are two sports they both have comparesions they both sports, they contrast in many ways like in hokey you use a stick and a puck, but in basketball you use one ball and your hands. They also compare in that when you play them the goal is to get the puck or basketball into a goal or net. Another contrast is that hokey is played on ice and basketball is played on courts. When you play hokey or basketball you noticed that the puck and ball both touch the ground that is another way to compare. In hokey the goal.net is placed on the ground and in basketball the net is on a backboard in the air that is another contrast. If you have ever been to a hokey or basketball game there is always quaters or periods in a game so that the players can take a break, in that way they compare. Basketball has four quarters and Hockey has three periods to a game and they are different in that way. But the best comparisions in hokey and basketball is the fans, many people love hockey and basketball that's why they are one of most played and favored sports in the world.

A compare-and-contrast essay written by an adolescent with learning disabilities.
From Wong, Butler, Ficzere, & Kuperis, 1997.

an example of the work of an adolescent assigned to write a compare-and-contrast essay. The essay is comprehensible, but demonstrates weak sentence construction, awkward phrasing, lack of paragraphing, and deficits in organization. This student's writing greatly improved through an intervention program aimed at teaching cognitive and metacognitive skills.

Epidemiology and developmental course. The prevalence of writing disorders is not definitively known. Perhaps 6 to 10% of school-age children have some form of writing disability (Lyon et al., 2003; Tannock, 2005a). Standardized tests for writing skill are limited and assessment may require analyses of a child's written work. Developmental norms are important, of course, in judging the quality of writing; for example, before age 8 or so, motor skills may not be well developed and only simple narrative can be expected (Lipka & Siegel, 2006). By second grade, though, the disorder is usually apparent (American Psychiatric Association, 2000), and referral for problems sharply increases around the

fourth grade, when school curricula demand increased writing (Berninger & Amtmann, 2003; Tannock, 2005b). Longitudinal studies of development are lacking but cross-sectional research suggests that the disorder persists for some youths.

MATHEMATICS DISABILITIES (MD)

The term *mathematics* encompasses many domains, such as the sciences of algebra, calculus, set theory, and the like (Tannock, 2005b). Mathematics disorder or disabilities is a diagnostic label that refers to one branch of mathematics, that of arithmetic abilities. Descriptions of mathematics disorder in children indicate an array of difficulties including performing simple addition and subtraction, understanding arithmetic terms and symbols, memorizing mathematical facts, and understanding spatial organization (Geary, 2003). The defining features of MD are not established, but the core deficits are thought to involve the understanding of number and the learning, representation, and retrieval of basic arithmetic facts (Cirino et al., 2007).

Early procedural and strategy impairments.
Research has emphasized basic understanding of children's early counting and arithmetic abilities (Geary, 2003; 2004; Torbeyns, Verschaffel, & Ghesquière, 2004). Even the relatively simple calculations accomplished by very young children require some understanding of number and counting. By age 5, many typically developing children understand basic principles of counting (e.g., an object in an array of objects can be counted only once), although they may have difficulties with other principles (e.g., objects in an array can be counted in any order). As they take on simple calculations, there is a gradual transition to more advanced procedures. For example, *counting all* (e.g., 2 + 3 is added by counting 1-2-3-4-5) gradually gives way to *counting on* (e.g., the child starts with 2 and then adds on 3-4-5). Counting procedures are soon represented in memory and arithmetic facts can then be called up automatically. The addition of 2 + 3 no longer requires counting: 5 is quite effortlessly and rapidly retrieved. Children with arithmetic disabilities acquire many of these procedures and strategies more slowly and employ them less frequently and with less speed and accuracy. In addition, deficits or delays exist in memory-based retrieval processes, which persist through the elementary school years. Children in third grade or above may exhibit errors in rapid retrieval of number facts (e.g., $7 \times 9 = 63$); in using addition, subtraction, multiplication, and division for more complex problems; and in employing fractions and decimals (Tannock, 2005b). Those with co-occurring reading problems are particularly susceptible to errors in arithmetic word problems and complex calculation (Cirino et al., 2007).

In examining these findings, the following are worth noting. *First*, longitudinal investigations are necessary for a more complete understanding of developmental course. *Second*, some investigators have failed to distinguish children with only mathematics disability from children who also have reading disabilities. The co-occurring condition, which may affect about 50 percent of children with mathematics disorder, is linked to more pronounced difficulties and is being further differentiated (Geary, 2004; Fuchs, Fuchs, & Prentice, 2004; Jordan, Hanich, & Kaplan, 2003). *Third*, research is needed on more complex mathematics and on possible underlying cognitive deficits, such as working memory, executive functions, and visual-spatial skills (e.g., Wilson & Swanson, 2001). *Fourth*, although there is evidence that several regions of the brain subserve different arithmetic operations, brain studies of children with

mathematics disorder are needed (Lyon et al., 2003; Tannock, 2005b). *Fifth*, although limited family and twin studies give evidence of genetic influence, the acquisition of arithmetic skills is highly sensitive to the quality of instruction in the classroom (Lyon et al, 2006; Tannock, 2005b).

Epidemiology and developmental course. There are relatively few studies of the prevalence of mathematics disabilities and they vary in how they define and measure deficits. Given this, it appears that 5 to 8% of school-age children display some form of mathematics disabilities (Geary, 2004; Lyon et al., 2003). This figure may drop to 1% when cases with co-occurring reading disabilities and ADHD are excluded (American Psychiatric Association, 2000). Gender differences have not been found in most studies.

Similarly lacking are studies of the course and persistence of mathematics disabilities. There is indication of some persistence of disabilities, however; for example, Prior and colleagues (1999) found that 57% of children with arithmetic disorder at age 7 to 8 had arithmetic problems 4 years later. Although further study is required, mathematics disabilities can be identified during the early school years and can persist into adolescence and adulthood (Lyon et al., 2003; Tannock, 2005b). Fortunately, research-based child intervention is appearing, focusing on basic skills (such as fact retrieval and procedures) and higher order skills (such as word problems) (Lyon et al., 2006).

Co-occurring Disorders

We have seen that various language and learning disabilities frequently occur together. Youth with these disabilities—in both clinic and community samples—also have a higher than average risk for other disturbances (Beitchman et al., 1996; Conti-Ramsden & Botting, 2004; Rutter, Mawhood, & Howlin, 1992).

Language impairment has been associated with externalizing and internalizing problems in youths of various ages. A recent study showed that 40% of 5-year-olds displayed withdrawn behavior, bodily symptoms, and aggressive behavior (van Daal, Verho & van Balkom, 2007). The continuity of behavioral disturbance is suggested by a longitudinal study of a community sample identified with language deficits at age 5 (Beitchman et al., 1996; 2001). A follow-up conducted at about age 19 indicated that the individuals had higher rates of anxiety disorder than a control group, and males were at risk for antisocial

ACCENT ● ● ● ● ●

Nonverbal Learning Disabilities (NVLD)

As a matter of general interest, we note a puzzling disorder to which the term "learning disabilities" is applied. A group of youths who display a unique profile of learning impairments, in which language skills are relatively intact, is said to exhibit Nonverbal Learning Disabilities (NVLD). The disorder has been given other names, including "right hemisphere deficit syndrome" and "social–emotional learning disabilities." The conceptualization of NVLD is uncertain, and it has been likened to a few different pervasive developmental and mental retardation syndromes.

Abnormal brain development or damage, involving the white matter and right hemisphere, is thought to underlie NVLD (Anderson et al., 2001; Rourke & Fuerst, 1995). Relative strengths exist in verbal abilities and relative deficits in mathematics, visual-spatial skills, and social competence. Visual memory deficits and a deficit in immediate memory for faces have been shown (Liddell & Rasmussen, 2005). Such problems are thought to be responsible for problems in interpreting other people's facial expressions, gestures, and other nonverbal signals. NVLD also is associated with the development of internalizing behavioral symptoms. Youngsters with NVLD may be identified later than children with obvious language impairments, and on the basis of social-emotional rather than cognitive problems (Anderson et al., 2001). The following is a brief description of a girl diagnosed with NVLD whose neuropsychological functioning was evaluated at ages 5 and 14.

Jenny   A Profile of NVLD

Jenny was evaluated due to learning and social problems. She reportedly had experienced some neonatal problems, relatively early development of expressive language, and somewhat slow development of motor skills. Formal evaluation showed intact intellectual and linguistic abilities with less well-developed nonverbal abilities, especially visual and visual-motor skills. She appeared disorganized and displayed difficulties on memory tasks requiring her to encode and retain material. Educational and social strategies were recommended to minimize Jenny's difficulties.

Jenny's childhood years were characterized by continual problems and intervention. Psychotherapy was discontinued when her parents felt it was unhelpful. A diagnosis of ADHD led to treatment with medication. Later occurring symptoms of obsessive–compulsive behaviors and the sensation that she was being watched led to hospitalization to determine whether Jenny suffered from a psychotic illness.

When she was 14, she underwent a second neuropsychological evaluation precipitated by depressive symptoms as well as ongoing behavioral and learning difficulties. During assessment Jenny was quiet, passive, reflective, cooperative, and anxious. Her language and literacy skills were intact, as were sustained attention and verbal learning. But many abilities were now well below average. She had particular difficulties in social comprehension, visual perception and memory, visuomotor coordination, and mathematics. A similar ongoing pattern of difficulty and decline in cognitive, academic, and social behavior has been observed in other children with NVLD.

Adapted from Anderson et al., 2001, pp. 425–432.

---

personality. Nevertheless, some investigations indicate relatively low risk and the need to consider type and severity of language disabilities (Snowling et al., 2006). Children with only articulation problems appear to show the fewest and least severe psychological difficulties (van Daal et al., 2007).

There is interesting evidence that disturbances associated with language impairments can be mediated by co-occurring reading problems, at least in older youth (Tomblin et al., 2000). Reading difficulties alone are associated with psychological problems, including anxiety (Ackerman et al., 2007; Goldston et al., 2007). A recent study of adolescents, for example, indicated that these youths had both higher risk for suicidal ideation/attempts and for school dropout, which were interrelated (Daniel et al., 2006).

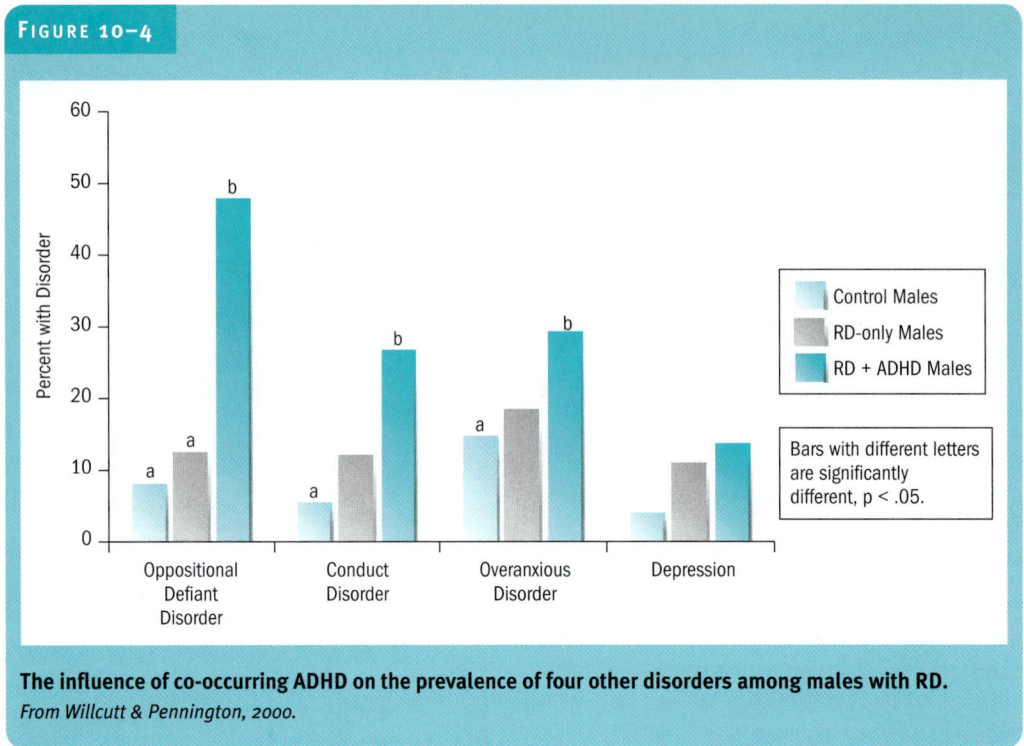

FIGURE 10-4

The influence of co-occurring ADHD on the prevalence of four other disorders among males with RD.
From Willcutt & Pennington, 2000.

Reading disabilities also have frequently been associated with conduct disturbance, particularly in boys. Several causal connections are theoretically possible, and longitudinal research has suggested an indirect path from reading disorder to later conduct problems. Early behavior problems and family factors are thought to play a role (Fergusson & Lynskey, 1997; Prior et al., 1999; Williams & McGee, 1996). A recent twin study of boys indicated that the association of reading disabilities and antisocial behavior was largely due to shared environmental factors but, importantly, that each problem had an effect on the other (Trzesniewski et al., 2006). That is, not only was genetic influence relatively small, but also reading and antisocial problems were intertwined and as one changed so did the other.

Finally the association of LD with ADHD is well established, as we saw in Chapter 9. Comorbidity is estimated at about 3.5% of the U.S. school-age population (Smith & Adams, 2006). Willcutt and colleagues (2001) compared the cognitive deficits of nonreferred twins who displayed reading disorder, ADHD, or both disorders. Reading disability was associated with deficits regarding the sounds and memory of words, ADHD with deficits in inhibition. Children who exhibited both disorders had deficits

in both areas that combined to make them the most disabled. Similar results have come from other investigations, although further research is needed on the comorbid condition. (Bental & Tirosh, 2007; Purvis & Tannock, 2000; Rucklidge & Tannock, 2002). Moreover, comorbidity of LD and ADHD is associated with heightened risk for still other disorders. Figure 10–4 demonstrates this finding in males; a somewhat different and weaker effect was found for females.

Social and Motivational Problems

Although many children and adolescents with language and learning disabilities do quite well socially, develop a positive sense of self, and maintain interest in learning, others find these areas problematic.

SOCIAL RELATIONS AND COMPETENCE

The social relations of at least some children with disabilities are less than satisfactory. Teachers associate learning disabilities with a variety of problematic behaviors (Mishna, 2003), and peers often rate children with learning disorders as less popular, more rejected, and more neglected than nondisabled youngsters (Nowicki, 2003; Ochoa & Palmer, 1995). Overall, these children may have fewer friends, lower quality of friendship, and higher levels of loneliness (Wiener & Tardif, 2004). Risk for social rejection can begin in the early school years and continue into young adulthood (Bryan, 1997).

What underlies social difficulties? There is no definitive answer to this question. Behavioral problems associated with learning disabilities, such as ADHD, may adversely affect peers (Vaughn, La Greca & Kuttler, 1999). In addition, children with learning disorders appear to have lower social competence than their nondisabled peers, which might well affect social relationships (Lipka & Siegel, 2006; Nowicki, 2003; Toro et al., 1990). They have difficulties in identifying the emotional expression of others, understanding social situations, guessing how other youngsters feel in particular situations, and solving social problems.

Whatever the underlying causes, poor social relationships and poor social skills increase risk for school alienation and dropout, loneliness, and withdrawal (Deater-Deckard, 2001; Vaughn et al., 1999). Risk for victimization or bullying by peers may also be increased (Nowicki, 2003). For example, in one study three times as many 11-year-olds with language impairments reported experiencing victimization more than once a week than did normal 11-year-olds (Conti-Ramsden & Botting, 2004).

ACADEMIC SELF-CONCEPT AND MOTIVATION

Research with normally developing youths indicates that their beliefs about prospects for achievement can influence effort and performance (Molden & Dweck, 2006). In general, viewing intelligence as malleable and effort as stimulating ability are adaptive. Moreover, responding to failure with a mastery orientation is more adaptive than responding with a helplessness orientation. Mastery is indicated by attributing failure to lack of effort or task difficulty, expecting future improvement, and maintaining problem solving and positive affect. In contrast, a helplessness orientation involves expecting failure, giving up, and demonstrating negative self-cognition and affect. Similarly, self-efficacy, beliefs about one's abilities and competence to carry out a task, is related to outcome on that task (Bandura, 1997).

Meta-analyses indicate that learning disorders are associated with a lowered sense of worth (Elbaum & Vaughn, 2003; Nowicki 2003). Some children with disabilities rate their general sense of self as relatively low and more consistently rate their academic abilities negatively (Lipka & Siegel, 2006). School experiences contribute to children's self-perceptions, and by age 4 or 5, some children are already sensitive to teacher criticism and respond to it by, for example, downgrading the quality of their work (Cutting & Dunn, 2002). Compared with

Social interaction and motivational factors play an important role in the development of learning and learning difficulties.
(Peter Skinner/Photo Research, Inc.)

typical students, those with LD report more help-lessness and lower self-efficacy even when their school grades are comparable (Lackaye et al., 2006; Núñez et al., 2005).

Given these considerations, it is easy to see that children with disabilities can enter a vicious cycle of academic failure and low motivation that works against them (Licht & Kistner, 1986). As a result of academic failure, they come to doubt their intellectual abilities and believe that their efforts to achieve are futile. Such learned helplessness exacerbates the situation as the youngsters are more likely to give up in the face of difficulty. In turn, further failure is experienced, which reinforces their belief in lack of ability and control (Figure 10–5).

Nevertheless, not all youth with disabilities adopt negative perceptions and behaviors (Núñez et al., 2005). This was demonstrated in a study of the self-perceptions of middle-school students with LD (Meltzer et al., 2004). Some of the students reported positive academic self-perceptions; others held negative self-perceptions. The former group reported expending greater effort on school-work than the latter group and employing learning strategies to bypass the effects of their impairments. Their teachers viewed them similarly, and also saw them as performing at a similar academic level as their peers without LD. This and related research suggest a need for further understanding of resilience factors regarding youths with LD.

Etiology of Language and Learning Disabilities

BRAIN ABNORMALITIES

Language and learning disabilities are associated with cerebral palsy, epilepsy, nervous system infections, head injury, prenatal alcohol use, and neurological delays and soft signs (e.g., Snowling, 1991; Taylor, 1989; Vellutino et al., 2004). Direct study of the brain indicates how it might be implicated in specific developmental disabilities. Many regions of the brain are likely to be involved in some way; for example, the cerebellum and certain visual and auditory pathways could play a role in perceptual processing in language or reading disorders (Heim & Benasich, 2006). A major focus of investigation is the left hemisphere, long considered crucial to language functions.

Brain structures. Structures of the brain have been investigated through postmortem examination and brain scans. Especially implicated is the planum temporale and the surrounding region (Hynd, Marshall, & Gonzalez, 1991; Hynd & Semrud-Clikeman, 1989a; 1989b; Peterson, 1995). This area, which roughly corresponds with Wernicke's area and is used in language, involves the upper surface of the temporal lobe extending to the lower surface of the parietal lobe. In most—but not all—adults in the general population the area is larger in the left hemisphere than the right. In persons with specific language and reading disorders, asymmetry often is absent. The right side has been found to be as large or even larger than the left, and the left temporal lobe to be smaller than normal (Eliez et al., 2000). In addition, cell abnormalities in the brain have been observed to be more common in individuals with specific disabilities. As informative and interesting as these and other structural findings are, caution is needed in drawing conclusions. Differences in the brains of adults with disabilities may not be the same as in children, research samples are often small, and findings are not completely consistent (Vellutino et al., 2004).

Brain functioning. Much attention has been given to evaluating brain activity with a variety of scanning methods as children and adults engage in language and reading tasks. Differences have been shown between impaired and nonimpaired readers in brain regions involved in language and reading (Shaywitz, 2003). (See Figure 10–6.) An area in the front of the

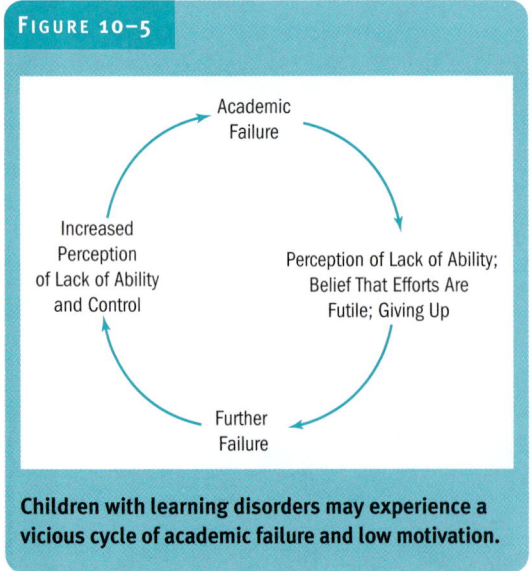

FIGURE 10–5

Academic Failure

Perception of Lack of Ability; Belief That Efforts Are Futile; Giving Up

Further Failure

Increased Perception of Lack of Ability and Control

Children with learning disorders may experience a vicious cycle of academic failure and low motivation.

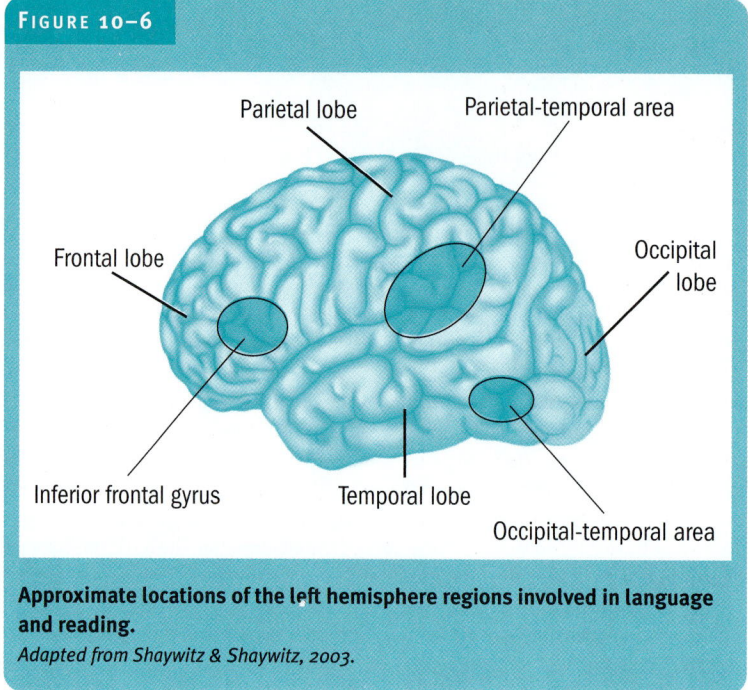

FIGURE 10–6

Parietal lobe

Parietal-temporal area

Frontal lobe

Occipital lobe

Inferior frontal gyrus

Temporal lobe

Occipital-temporal area

Approximate locations of the left hemisphere regions involved in language and reading.
Adapted from Shaywitz & Shaywitz, 2003.

brain (corresponding to Broca's area) aids in word analysis. A second area, the parietal-temporal area (including Wernicke's area) plays a central role in phonological processing, that is, in integrating the visual and sound aspects of language. A third area at the junction of the occipital and temporal lobes is especially involved in rapid word recognition; it becomes increasingly important as readers come to rely more on automatic, almost instantaneous word recognition rather than on basic phonological processes. In general, strong readers rely more on the back areas of the brain when reading, and most processing occurs on the left side.

It has been proposed that reading disorders involve faulty wiring of the system necessary for good language and reading. Several studies show that patterns of brain activation are different in children and adults with or without reading problems when they engage in various phonological and reading tasks (e.g., Cao et al., 2006). In individuals with reading disabilities, the posterior left side appears underactive and the corresponding posterior right side may be overactive (Breier et al., 2003; Shaywitz et al., 1998). There is also some evidence that the front left area of the brain may be relatively overactive, and that as children with reading disabilities get older they may increasingly employ the frontal area of the brain (Shaywitz & Shaywitz, 2003).

In examining these findings, it is helpful to recall that the brain is a dynamic network: abnormalities in one area might affect another, perhaps as an effort to compensate for what is not working properly. Shaywitz and colleagues suggest that the use of alternative routes—greater reliance on the front brain area and the right hemisphere—allows some readers to achieve accurate, although not rapid and fluent, reading (Shaywitz, 2003; Shaywitz et al., 2003).

Further research is required to better understand brain functioning in reading disorders. Meanwhile, fascinating results are coming from research that shows brain changes associated with interventions for reading and language deficits. (See Accent: "Intervention and Brain Changes")

GENETIC INFLUENCES

Genetic effects on language and learning disabilities have been investigated with the gamut of genetic methods.

Language. Specific language disorders aggregate in families, although 30 to 60% of index cases appear to be the only member of their family with a language disorder (Tallal & Benasich, 2002). High heritability has been documented in twins for articulation and

ACCENT

Intervention and Brain Changes

Simos and colleagues (2002) worked with 7- to 17-year-olds with average intelligence but severe disabilities in word recognition and phonological skills. Preintervention brain scans indicated an abnormal activation pattern for phonological tasks: little or no activation of the left posterior (parietal-temporal) region and increased activation of the corresponding region of the right brain. The youths received about 80 hours of phonological training over 8 weeks. Not only did measures of word accuracy show improvement into the normal range, but brain scans also indicated increased activation in the left posterior hemisphere relative to the corresponding right side. No changes over time were shown in activation patterns for the normal control group. Figure 10–7 exemplifies the findings in one of the treated children. Simos and colleagues (2007) subsequently reported similarly positive results in 7- to 9-year-olds who received intervention focusing on phonological processing and reading fluency.

A more extensive investigation of 6- to 9-year-olds with reading disabilities examined the outcome of a phonologically based intervention delivered at school over 8 months (Shaywitz et al., 2004). Daily 50-minute sessions progressively focused on letter-sound associations, phoneme analysis of words, timed reading of words, oral story reading, and word dictation. After intervention, the treated participants significantly improved in reading and brain activation was more in keeping with that of a nonimpaired control group. Follow-up of some of the children 1 year after intervention indicated continued improvement in the occipital-temporal region, known for its involvement with automatic word processing.

Research that documents both improvement in select language/reading skills and correlated neurobiological change suggests that psychosocial intervention can affect brain development. It holds promise of increased understanding of disabilities and of treatments for children who have difficulty in reading (Coyne et al., 2004; Hatcher et al., 2004).

FIGURE 10–7

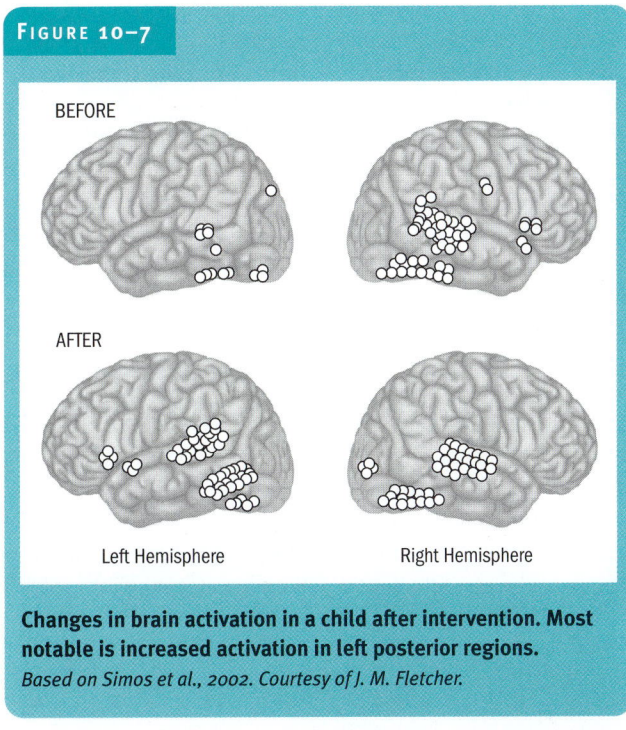

BEFORE

AFTER

Left Hemisphere   Right Hemisphere

Changes in brain activation in a child after intervention. Most notable is increased activation in left posterior regions.
Based on Simos et al., 2002. Courtesy of J. M. Fletcher.

expressive language difficulties (DeThorne et al., 2006). Concordance for disabilities is about 85% for identical twins and about 50% for fraternal pairs (Spinath et al., 2004). Molecular genetics studies have identified linkages on chromosomes 13, 16 and 19, which involve different language deficits (Johnson & Beitchman, 2005a; Plomin & McGuffin, 2003).

Reading. Parents of youth with RD have high rates of reading problems and, conversely, youth whose parents have reading difficulties are at higher risk for these problems (Carroll & Snowling, 2004; Grigorenko, 2001). Twin comparisons give evidence of genetic influence, and heritability has been estimated at about 60% (Stevenson et al., 2005). Influence on several components of reading has been shown, including on phonological processing and single-word reading. This is a particularly interesting finding given the importance of these processes in language and reading disorders.

Some progress has been made in identifying specific chromosomes that might contribute to RD. Chromosomes 6 and 15 were the first to be identified and subsequent linkage studies implicated chromosomes 18 and 2 (DeFries & Light, 1996; Grigorenko, 2001; Plomin & McGuffin, 2003).

The involvement of multiple genes in RD is supported by evidence that reading skills in children at family risk, and in the general population, appear to fall on a continuum (Pennington & Lefly, 2001; Snowling et al., 2003). Further, both general reading *ability* and *disability* are heritable and are genetically linked (Harlaar et al., 2005). These findings suggest that there is no "disease" gene for RD but rather that a number of genes work together with other risk factors to produce susceptibility to reading disorders.

The co-occurrence of language and reading difficulties raises the question of whether the disorders share a genetic predisposition. In fact, co-occurrence of these problems appears in the families of children with disabilities (Flax et al., 2003), and genetic research suggests shared genetic influence (Hohnen & Stevenson, 1999). Interestingly, several gene locations linked to RD have been linked to phonological (articulation) disorder (Smith et al., 2005).

Writing and mathematics. Genetic influence on written expression is seen with regard to spelling. Family aggregation of spelling problems has been revealed, as well as heritability in twin studies (Schulte-Körne, 2001; Tannock, 2005a). Chromosome 15 may be linked to spelling disorder.

Shalev and colleagues (2001) found that parents and siblings of probands with mathematics disabilities exhibited rates of impairment about 10 times higher than what would be expected in the general population. In addition, limited twin data indicate higher concordance for mathematics disability in identical than fraternal pairs (Lyon et al., 2003). It also appears that mathematics and reading disabilities may have a shared genetic vulnerability (Kovacs et al., 2007).

Overall, as with other disorders, evidence for genetic influences is mounting but much is yet to be learned about genetic processes involved in specific disabilities.

PSYCHOSOCIAL INFLUENCES

Genetic behavior studies point to a role for environmental influences on normal and impaired development relevant to specific disabilities (Chapman, 2000; Grigorenko, 2001). From other types of research, we know that several psychosocial variables are important in typical language development (Chapman, 2000; Weizman & Snow, 2001). Early vocabulary growth is predicted by the number or sophistication of words the child hears from its mother. And more rapid language development is predicted by, for example, the mother's elaborating on the child's speech and commenting on what the child is paying attention to. Although family variables may not be the root of language problems, they may play a role in maintaining deficits (Whitehurst & Fischel, 1994).

Stevenson and Fredman (1990) found that large family size and certain aspects of mother–child interaction were linked to reading problems, and they noted that family involvement in the child's learning may be especially influential on early reading acquisition. However, family factors are not always found (Snowling et al., 2007). On the other hand, there is evidence that children with reading disabilities shun the activity, and that the amount of reading a child does is related to reading skills. Lowered expectations of teachers and children themselves may be especially hazardous for those whose learning requires extraordinary effort.

It is also generally believed that factors such as overcrowded classrooms, math anxiety, and quality of instruction can affect the acquisition of mathematics skills (Shalev et al., 2001). Indeed, quality of educational instruction is viewed by some researchers as an important environmental influence (Snowling, 2000).

Assessing Language and Learning Disabilities

Children's language or learning problems are typically first noticed by parents or teachers, whose sensitivity to the difficulties are valuable for early intervention. (See Accent: "Clues for Identifying Reading Disorder.")

When language disorders are suspected in preschoolers, parents seek assessment from a variety of professionals. Family and child history, speech and language evaluation, assessment of verbal and nonverbal intelligence, and screening for hearing, neurological, and medical problems are generally appropriate (Bishop, 2002). Speech and language specialists can make a critical contribution in early assessment and/or later ongoing assessment necessary for intervention. A multidisciplinary team including language specialists, preschool teachers, psychologists, and physicians, among others, may be formed to plan intervention (Kirk, Gallagher, & Anastasiow, 2000). Later occurring or more subtle language problems and learning handicaps may be assessed in mental health settings, but are often evaluated in the educational system, following procedures recommended by government regulations for the assessment and education of handicapped youth.

ACCENT ● ● ● ● ●

Clues for Identifying Reading Disorder

Sally Shaywitz (2003), a neuroscientist and physician who has been in the forefront of reading disorder research, notes that parents can play an important role in identifying reading disorder. The identification requires the parents to carefully observe the child, know what to look for, and be willing to spend time listening to the child speak and read. With this in mind, Shaywitz has presented clues for recognizing that a child may need further assessment.

Clues During the Preschool Years

Delayed language

Difficulty in learning and appreciating common nursery rhymes

Mispronounced words; persistent baby talk

Difficulty in learning (and remembering) names of letters

Failure to know the letters in child's own name

Clues During Kindergarten and First Grade

Failure to understand that words can be segmented and sounded out

Inability to learn to associate letters with their appropriate sounds

Reading errors not connected to the sounds of the letters, for example, *big* is read as *goat*

Inability to read common one-syllable words or to sound out even simple words

Complaints about the difficulty of reading, or avoidance of reading

History of reading difficulties in parents or siblings

Clues from Second Grade and Beyond

Among the many clues in speaking:

mispronunciation of long, unfamiliar, or complicated words; influent speech (hesitations, pauses, use of "ums"); inability to find the exact word; inability to reply rapidly when questioned; difficulty in remembering bits of verbal information such as dates and lists.

Among the many clues in reading:

slow reading progress; difficulty in reading unfamiliar words, function words such as *that* and *in*, or multisyllable words; omitting parts of words; oral reading that is choppy, labored, or slow; avoidance of reading; reading that improves in accuracy but not in fluency; family history of reading and spelling difficulties.

In keeping with the notion that specific reading disorder is discrepant with a child's general abilities, Shaywitz recommends looking for intellectual strengths in the child, such as the ability to figure things out, an understanding of new concepts, comprehension of stories read or told by others, and good reasoning and abstraction skills.

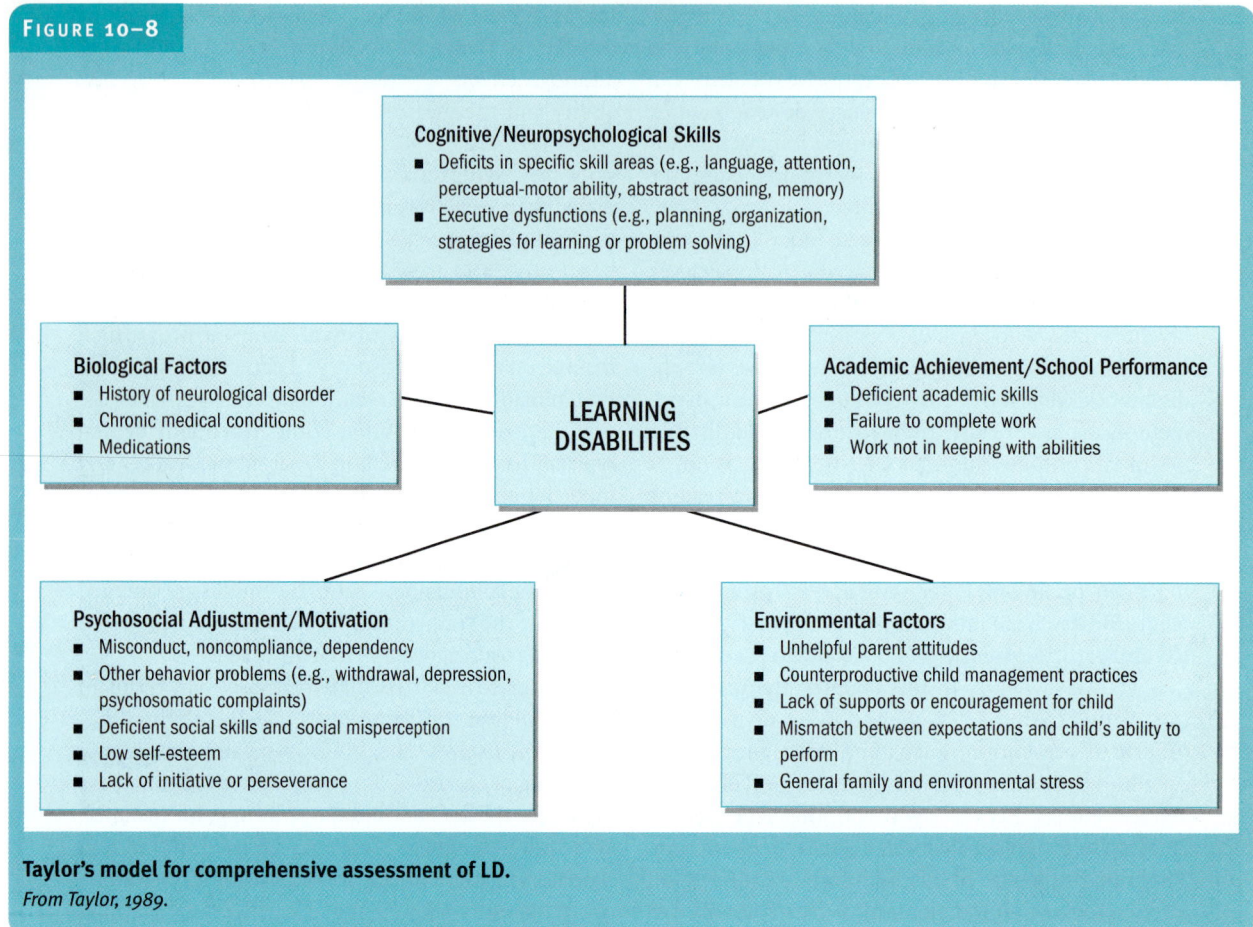

FIGURE 10–8

Cognitive/Neuropsychological Skills
- Deficits in specific skill areas (e.g., language, attention, perceptual-motor ability, abstract reasoning, memory)
- Executive dysfunctions (e.g., planning, organization, strategies for learning or problem solving)

Biological Factors
- History of neurological disorder
- Chronic medical conditions
- Medications

LEARNING DISABILITIES

Academic Achievement/School Performance
- Deficient academic skills
- Failure to complete work
- Work not in keeping with abilities

Psychosocial Adjustment/Motivation
- Misconduct, noncompliance, dependency
- Other behavior problems (e.g., withdrawal, depression, psychosomatic complaints)
- Deficient social skills and social misperception
- Low self-esteem
- Lack of initiative or perseverance

Environmental Factors
- Unhelpful parent attitudes
- Counterproductive child management practices
- Lack of supports or encouragement for child
- Mismatch between expectations and child's ability to perform
- General family and environmental stress

Taylor's model for comprehensive assessment of LD.
From Taylor, 1989.

Crucial in identifying language and learning disabilities—and understanding a child's particular deficits—are standardized tests to evaluate language, reading, spelling, and mathematics (Lipka & Siegel, 2006). Numerous tests exist to assess specific components of these domains (Beitchman & Young, 1997). Evaluations for reading, for example, might include measures of sounding out words, matching letters and sounds, and comprehending written material. It is important to evaluate both errors made by the child and evidence of strengths.

Tests of general intelligence are also valuable, and may be essential to establish an IQ-achievement discrepancy for diagnosis or requirements for special education services. Additional psychological assessment, such as of cognitive processing or motor skills, may or may not be useful, depending on the goals of assessment (Lipka & Siegel, 2006).

When it is relevant, the evaluator should also discuss the child's study habits, motivations, self-esteem, and concerns (e.g., Bryan, 1997). Because language and

learning disabilities are defined in terms of achievement and intelligence, there is probably a tendency to bypass the behavioral, social, and motivational contexts in which the child is operating. Taylor (1989) has provided a model for comprehensive assessment of disabilities that includes the child's psychological adjustment and motivation (Figure 10–8). It also takes into account environmental factors that can promote or have adverse influences on the child's functioning, such as parental attitudes and the match between the child's abilities and others' expectations.

Intervention for Language and Learning Disabilities

PREVENTION

As general rule, prevention of developmental disorders is linked to early identification and treatment. Regarding language disabilities, with the exception of severe

cases, it can be challenging to identify meaningful impairments in toddlers. Children 2 to 3 years old who are late talkers or exhibit other expressive problems can fall into the normal range of language development by early school age or they can continue to have difficulties (e.g., Rescorla, 2002). Thus, prevention requires the monitoring of early language problems.

There is considerable interest today in the prevention of learning problems. At the national level, much concern is expressed over the substantial number of youths who are not acquiring necessary academic skills. Some of these children have specific disabilities while others have more general achievement problems. We also know that untreated disabilities often continue, and that later treatment is not as successful as earlier intervention. Yet, too many reading problems go undetected until the second or third grade (Shaywitz, 2003), and referrals for learning problems too often occur only after several years of academic failure. Research is continuing into early risk factors for RD and early identification (Puolakanaho et al., 2007).

As we saw early in this chapter, the response-to-treatment approach is viewed by some as an approach to prevention. Fuchs and colleagues (2007) refer to the multiple intervention levels of RTI as prevention efforts. Recall, if you will, that RTI exposes children to progressively intense levels of instruction. The initial exposure of all children to a carefully selected intervention (curriculum) is conceptualized as primary (universal) prevention. Students who do less well than their peers at this level are considered at risk and are provided with more intense educational efforts, or secondary (selective) prevention. Those who respond poorly to this second tier of intervention are viewed as demonstrating unexpected failure and they receive comprehensive evaluation to determine the appropriateness of special education services—that is, tertiary prevention.

Although it is premature to know how RTI will fare, the approach captures the merging of prevention and treatment. Regardless of how youth are identified, early intervention tends to target basic skills, and reading programs predominate. Thus, many efforts focus on phonological processing and word-level reading.

TREATMENT FOR LANGUAGE DISABILITIES

The history and literature on treatment for language impairments, especially articulation and expressive language, differs somewhat from that for learning disabilities, and our discussion only touches briefly on

this area. Reviews and meta-analyses of interventions indicate that language development can be enhanced, although effects depend in part on the type of disability and the measures employed (Law & Garrett, 2004; Leonard, 1998). Articulation and expressive skills (e.g., syntax, vocabulary) are more easily remediated than receptive abilities. There is some evidence that both clinician- and parent-directed therapy can be effective, and a few studies found indirect benefits for child behavior and parent outcomes.

In his discussion of treatment, most of which focused on expressive disorders, Leonard (1998) noted that in many ways, interventions appear similar to the way that parents and other adults teach language to typically developing children. Operant procedures and modeling are widely used in treatment, and it is not unusual for toys and pictures to be a part of the training procedures. For example, the trainer presents language forms (e.g., plural nouns) and the child is encouraged to imitate the trainer, and/or reinforcers are given for the child's communication in natural settings.

Leonard reported that treatment can result in some children, on some tasks, closing the gap between themselves and their typically developing peers (e.g., Leonard et al., 2006). There is limited evidence for the generalization of training; for instance, an acquired language form may be used in different sentences in spontaneous speech. In addition, follow-up evaluations showed that the effects of training may endure over time. Despite these findings, though, the picture is not all positive. Language often improves but does not reach adequate levels, so that many youngsters remain socially and academically disadvantaged. Thus, both success and the need to improve treatments are evident.

TREATMENT FOR LEARNING DISABILITIES

Historically, interventions for learning disorders have reflected the multidisciplinary nature of the field. Psychologists, physicians, educators, optometrists, and communication therapists have all had a hand in treatment. In the late 1960s and 1970s, many different approaches were employed (Hammill, 1993; Lyon & Cutting, 1998). Conceptually they could be classified as medical, psychoeducational, or behavioral (see Figure 10–9).

The medical (or etiological) oriented approach viewed LD as stemming from biological pathology (Lyon et al., 2006). Deficits in underlying neurological processes were hypothesized to hinder the development of language, visual and auditory perception,

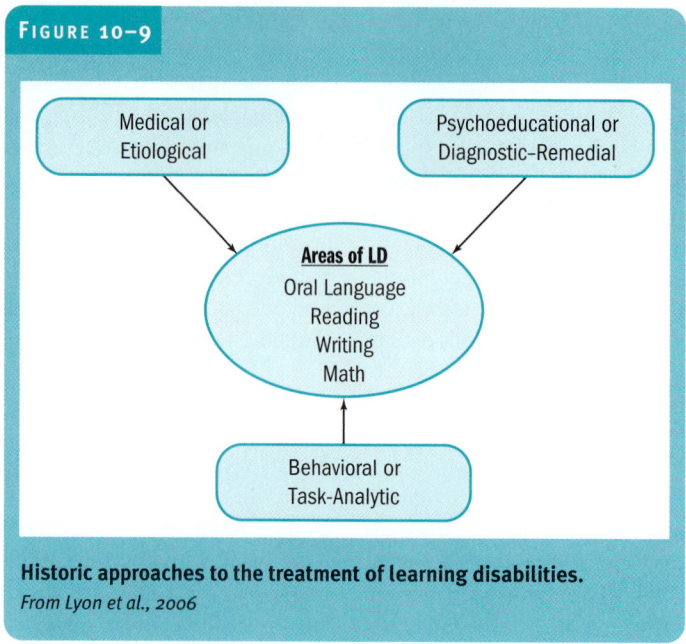

FIGURE 10–9

Historic approaches to the treatment of learning disabilities.
From Lyon et al., 2006

perceptual–motor functioning, and the like. For example, oral language problems might be viewed as the result of brain damage from anoxia, and treatment might entail exercise to stimulate the brain areas relevant to language. Nevertheless, there was little evidence to support the model and treatment methods.

Particularly prevalent was the pychoeducational (or diagnostic–remedial) approach, which targeted various perceptual and cognitive processes assumed to underlie disabilities (Hammill, 1993). Training programs that involved practice in eye–hand coordination, spatial relationships, or language were offered by educational specialists. Unlike the medical approach, the teaching of academic and information processing skills was advocated (Lyon et al., 2006). Student strengths in visual, auditory, language, and motor modalities were taken into account. Despite the popularity of these efforts, many fell by the wayside due to lack of documented success (Dean & Burns, 2002; Hammill, 1993).

In contrast to other approaches, the behavioral (or task-analytic) model made no assumptions about underlying organic pathology or information processing deficits (Lyon et al., 2006). Its aim was to improve academic or social skills through techniques based on learning principles, such as contingency management, feedback, and modeling (Lyon & Cutting, 1998).

As described by Lyon and colleagues (2006), the three historic approaches have contributed to current interventions. For example, today's neuropsychological models hark back to the early medical approach in their emphasis on the role of neurobiology. These models view student abilities in terms of underlying brain functioning, but they also incorporate the early psychoeducational approach by linking instruction to student strengths and weaknesses in cognitive processing. Given current interest in neurobiology, neurobiological models are garnering attention.

However, the strongest evidence for effective treatment is for today's task-analytic, cognitive, and cognitive-behavioral approaches. *Task-analytic methods* are represented in directive instruction that pinpoints the acquisition of needed skills and teaches to them. That is, if the child has a disability in writing, exercises and practice are provided in writing sentences and paragraphs. Among other things, direct instruction entails selecting and stating goals, presenting new material in small steps and with clear and detailed explanations, incorporating student practice and student feedback, guiding students, and monitoring student progress (Gettinger & Kohcik, 2001; Lyon & Cutting, 1998). Some direct instruction programs are highly organized and scripted regarding curriculum and teacher behavior, for example, programs developed by Engelmann and colleagues, which have proven effective for high-risk students (Adams & Carnine, 2003).

The *cognitive approach* seeks to increase student awareness of the demands of the learning task, the use of learning strategies appropriate to the task (e.g., rehearsal of material), monitoring the success of strategies, and switching strategies when necessary. Organization and strategy use are key elements.

The approach has been applied to reading comprehension, mathematics, written expression, memory skills, and study skills (Maccini & Hughes, 1997; Wong et al., 2003).

The *cognitive-behavioral approach* puts special emphasis on students directing their own learning. Students are taught to record their learning activities, assess their progress, self-reinforce their own behavior, and otherwise manage or regulate learning. The combination of cognitive and behavioral-cognitive techniques is exemplified in intervention for writing skills deficits by, among other things, instructing students how to organize the writing task, employ different strategies, and evaluate their work (Graham & Harris, 2003).

Effectiveness of intervention. There is a voluminous literature on treatment for reading, mathematics, writing, and spelling disabilities. (For a review, see Lyon et al., 2006). Our goal here is to comment on reports of the effectiveness of intervention. Reviews indicate that intervention can be ameliorative and can also fall short of ideal effectiveness.

Direct instruction (task-analytic), cognitive, and behavioral-cognitive approaches have generally been shown to be more effective than other approaches to learning disabilities (Lyon et al., 2003, 2006; Hatcher, Hulme, & Snowling, 2004; Torgesen et al., 2001). Swanson and Hoskyn conducted extensive meta-analyses of intervention. One of these contrasted 180 interventions with control comparisons (Swanson & Hoskyn, 1998). A variety of learning disabilities, including language deficits, were targeted with reading disabilities the most frequently treated. Four models were compared: Direct Instruction; Strategy Instruction (emphasizing prompts, explanations, and modeling of strategies and cognitive approaches); Combined Treatment of both Direct and Strategy Instruction; and interventions that appeared to have no components of either Direct Instruction or Strategy Instruction. The analysis showed positive effects of moderate size for Direct Instruction alone and for Strategy Instruction alone, and a larger effect for Combined Treatment. All areas of academic disabilities responded to intervention—although effects were stronger in some areas than others and varied from high to low-moderate. Another meta-analysis examined the instructional activities embedded in interventions for older children and adolescents (Swanson & Hoskyn, 2001). Particularly effective was the teaching of organizational skills and explicit practice. The latter included repeated practice, reviews, and feedback.

Swanson and Hoskyn (1998) suggested that optimal training includes both lower order (instruction at the skill level) and higher order instruction (emphasis on the knowledge base and explicit strategies). They speculated that both instructional approaches are valuable because reading, mathematics, and other academic areas involve several component processes. Overall, the possibility of substantial remediation of learning disabilities through thoughtfully designed and implemented interventions is indicated. Nevertheless, research shows that a proportion of youth do not adequately respond to any single intervention (Hatcher et al., 2006; Torgeson et al., 2001) and further effort on their behalf is required.

Special Educational Services

In the United States, educational services for persons with various kinds of disabilities have evolved dramatically over the last decades. Criticisms of services, legal decisions, and a growing social commitment to the rights of children with disabilities to appropriate education resulted in the Education for All Handicapped Children Act of 1975. Subsequent federal regulations extended opportunities and rights. Public Law 99-457 amended the Education for All Handicapped Children Act, extending provisions to developmentally delayed 3- to 5-year-olds and creating voluntary intervention for infants. The Education for All Handicapped Children Act was expanded under the title the Individuals with Disabilities Education Act (IDEA) in 1990, and IDEA was reauthorized and amended in 1997 and in 2004.

IDEA encompasses several categories for serving youth with disabilities that include speech or language impairments, learning disabilities, mental retardation, emotional disturbance, autism, and sensory and medical impairments such as blindness, deafness, and orthopedic problems. Increasing numbers of individuals have been served under IDEA. About 6.7 million persons, ages 3 to 21 years, received services in 2005–2006 (U.S. Department of Education, 2007). Forty-one percent of these had specific learning disabilities, and 22% had speech or language impairments.

The four purposes of IDEA have remained essentially unchanged over the years (U.S. Department of Education, 2000):

- To ensure that all students with disabilities obtain an appropriate free public education that emphasizes special education and related services to meet their particular needs.

- To ensure that the rights of these students and their parents are protected.

- To assist states and localities in providing education to children with disabilities.
- To assess and ensure the effectiveness of these educational efforts.

Appropriate education fundamentally means educational experiences tailored to each child's needs. An individual education plan (IEP) is constructed by a team of professionals, with parental participation, for each student receiving special education. IEPs must consider the child's present functioning, short-term and long-term educational goals, educational services to be provided, expected duration of services, procedures for evaluations, and, for older students, the transition from school to work (Mercer & Mercer, 2001). The plans must be systematically reviewed by a committee and the child's parents.

Under IDEA, students with disabilities are to be educated in the least restrictive environment, that is, with their nondisabled peers to the maximum extent appropriate. Disabled students were once viewed as a poor fit for public community schools, but mainstreaming these students in general education

classrooms became a central feature of educational placement. Then, in the late 1980s, through the Regular Education Initiative, a call went out for inclusion of students beyond mainstreaming. The premise of inclusion is that schools should be restructured to be supportive, nurturing communities that meet the needs of all students (Mercer & Mercer, 2001), with the general education teacher assuming primary responsibility for included students (Beirne-Smith et al., 2006).

In practice, consistent with the concept of appropriate education in the least restrictive environment, several options should be available for students in need of special education services. The options range from the general education classroom, with or without supplemental services, to special classes in community schools, to special day and residential schools (Figure 10–10). These settings provide increasing levels of support, and appropriate education means matching the child with the appropriate setting.

Currently, most students with LD are in general education classrooms with varying degrees of supplemental services, such as special instruction in the classroom or part-time instruction in resource

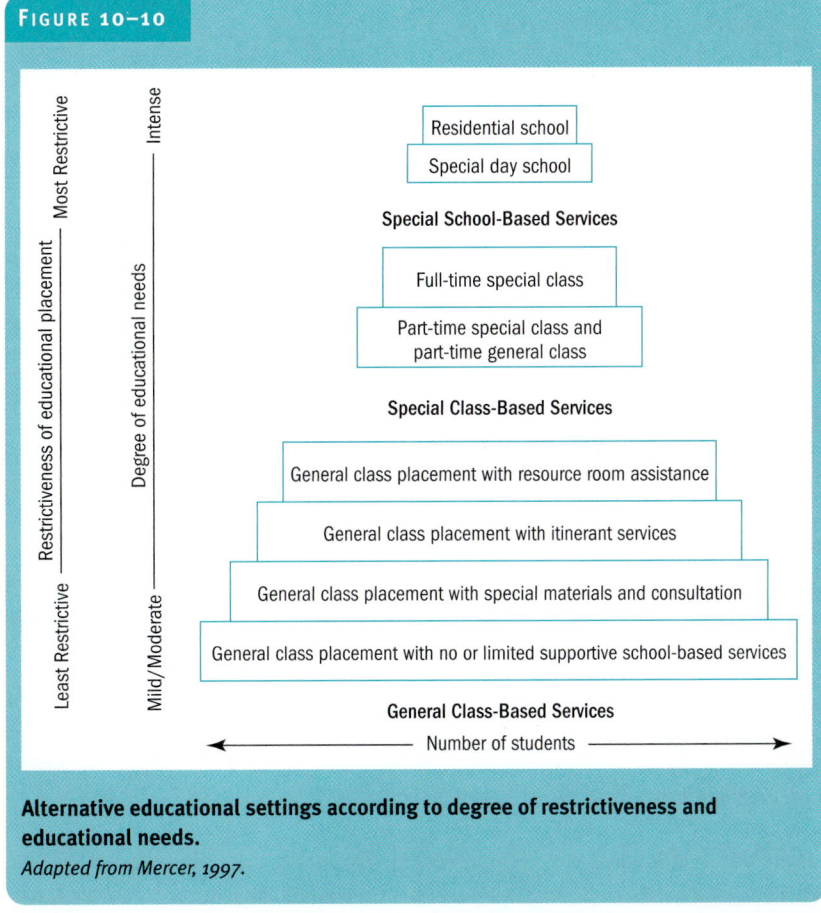

FIGURE 10–10

Alternative educational settings according to degree of restrictiveness and educational needs.
Adapted from Mercer, 1997.

rooms. However, it is likely that much variation exists across states regarding educational placement for these students (McLeskey et al., 2004).

SCHOOL PLACEMENT: BENEFITS AND CONCERNS

The issue of how best to serve students with special needs has been controversial. This is not an easy matter to settle, because research must address a variety of kinds and severity of disabilities, as well as many alternative programs. Given the complexity of the issue, a considerable amount of past research did not clearly support the once-anticipated academic and social benefits of contained special education classrooms (Howlin, 1994; Detterman & Thompson, 1997).

With the policy of inclusion came questions about its benefits or disadvantages. By the late 1990s, 75% of students with disabilities were educated in general education classrooms and the trend seems to be a hearty one (U.S. Department of Education, 2000). Inclusion nevertheless elicits both approval and criticism (Beirne-Smith et al., 2006). Advocates have pointed to research showing benefits to academic achievement and social outcomes for the included students (Hobbs & Westling, 1998; Rea, McLaughlin, & Walther-Thomas, 2002; Waldron & McLeskey, 1998). Included students have been found to do better on standardized achievement tests and in relating to others, with no greater behavioral difficulties. Outcomes for nonhandicapped students in these classrooms have also been reported as favorable (Cole, Waldron, & Majd, 2004; Staub & Peck, 1994/1995). Advocates of inclusion believe that concern is best directed not toward *whether* inclusive education should be provided but toward *how* it should be implemented to maximize its effectiveness.

In contrast, critics of inclusion point to data that do not support it, including reports of little academic advantage and lower levels of self-esteem among students with disabilities (Cole et al., 2004). It is also argued that although the inclusion policy has helped reduce discrimination and segregation of students with disabilities, it has strengthened a false belief that no student requires special consideration and that placement in special education settings is a harmful discriminatory approach (Kauffman, McGee, & Brigham, 2004). Moreover, opponents see inclusion as violating both children's rights and federal mandates for appropriate educational placement. They argue that a continuum of educational settings best serves varying student needs—and is consistent with the desires of many parents and educators (Mercer & Mercer, 2001).

Overall, research is more supportive than not for students with LD spending most of their time in general classrooms, and teachers are mostly supportive (e.g., McLesky et al., 2004). However, teachers are concerned that they lack specialized knowledge for the task, and have inadequate resources and time to implement special curricula and practices (DeSimone & Parmar, 2006). Indeed, this may often be the case.

Inclusion can be challenging in other ways. Many special education teachers, who formerly taught in relatively autonomous special classrooms, now work in collaboration with regular teachers in general classrooms (Klingner & Vaughn, 2002). The attitudes of school principals are important in implementing inclusion—and yet one study showed that most principals were uncertain of its benefits (Praisner, 2003). Parents of children with disabilities desire quality educational experiences for their children but can have concerns about their welfare, perhaps especially if the child has severe disabilities (Palmer et al., 2001).

The policy of inclusion clearly has brought benefits and has also made demands on the educational system. Both "good" and "poor" programs are being implemented (Cole et al., 2004), and schools that conduct successful programs are being recognized (Morocco et al., 2006).

SUMMARY

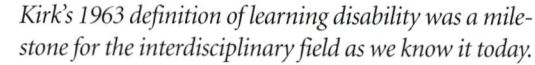

A BIT OF HISTORY: UNEXPECTED DISABILITIES, UNMET NEEDS

- *Today's field of language and learning disabilities can be traced to interest in individuals who exhibited discrepant abilities and to advocacy to improve services to them.*

- *Kirk's 1963 definition of learning disability was a milestone for the interdisciplinary field as we know it today.*

DEFINITIONAL CONCERNS

- *The influential definition of specific learning disability offered by the federal government has been criticized* on several counts and has led to variation in how specific disabilities are defined and identified.

- Specific disorders are usually identified by an IQ-achievement discrepancy or discrepancy between a youth's performance and what is normally expected in terms of grade level, age, or standardized achievement tests. Criticism of the IQ-achievement discrepancy approach has weakened it somewhat but IQ is still often considered during diagnosis.

- Response to intervention is a newly developing, multilevel approach to identifying disabilities and/or preventing them.

LANGUAGE DISABILITIES

- Language development is well underway by 2 to 3 years of age, and basic abilities are acquired by about age 7.

- As conceptualized by the DSM, specific language disorders include phonological, expressive, and receptive–expressive disorders.

- Epidemiological studies suggest a rate of about 7% for 5-year olds, but rates vary with age and type of disorder. Boys have higher rates than girls, and disability is linked to lower SES.

- Simple articulation problems often remit; outcome is more variable for early expressive problems and poorest for receptive–expressive disorder. Risks include continuing language disabilities, learning disabilities, and academic difficulties, as well as social and behavioral problems.

- Among the cognitive deficits proposed as contributing to language disorders are slow general information processing, impaired auditory processing, and verbal memory deficits.

LEARNING DISABILITIES: READING, WRITING, ARITHMETIC

- Specific reading disorder, the most common learning disability, may occur in 10 to 15% of school-age children, and rates are higher in boys. Reading problems can diminish but often tend to persist.

- Reading disabilities (RD) can be viewed in terms of word-level and comprehension problems. Perceptual deficits may be involved, but emphasis is given to the role of language. Phonological processing deficits are considered critical, especially in learning to read, but problems in other language components are implicated.

- Specific writing disorder entails deficits that affect transcription and text generation. Prevalence is

estimated at about 6 to 10% of school-age children, and many children also display reading problems. The disorder is usually apparent by second grade, referral may increase at about fourth grade, and some persistence of difficulties is noted.

- Specific mathematics disabilities include deficits in numerous skills required for arithmetic competence. Five to 8% of school-age children may be affected. Mathematics disabilities can be identified during the early school years and can persist.

CO-OCCURRING DISORDERS

- Children and adolescents with specific disabilities are at risk for both internalizing and externalizing problems, including ADHD.

NONVERBAL LEARNING DISABILITIES

- NVLD refers to a pattern of learning disabilities in which language is relatively spared but impairments exist in visual-spatial, mathematics, and social skills.

SOCIAL AND MOTIVATIONAL PROBLEMS

- A disproportionate number of students with language and learning problems are at risk for poor social relations; low social competence may be an underlying factor.

- Risk also exists for low self-concept, low academic self-perceptions, low self-efficacy, and a helplessness orientation.

ETIOLOGY OF LANGUAGE AND LEARNING DISABILITIES

- Abnormalities of brain structure, notably the planum temporale, and brain activation are associated with specific disabilities. Most centrally involved in RD are the temporal-parietal, temporal-occipital, and frontal lobes. Limited research suggests that intervention can lead to change in brain activation.

- Genetic transmission of various disabilities is documented in family and quantitative genetic studies. Progress is slowly being made in identifying specific genes. There is evidence for multiple gene effects on reading, and shared genetic influence on co-occurring language and reading difficulties.

- Family factors probably play some role in disabilities, but are not always evident. Lack of reading, poor instruction, and lowered expectations may be implicated in etiology.

ASSESSING LANGUAGE AND LEARNING DISABILITIES

- *Parents may call on a variety of professionals to assess early language disorders. Evaluation of later occurring language and learning problems is commonly conducted in educational settings.*

- *Standardized tests of language, reading, spelling, and arithmetic skills are critical in assessment. Intelligence tests can be helpful or necessary. Evaluation of cognitive and social functioning and the child's family context can provide a fuller assessment.*

INTERVENTION FOR LANGUAGE AND LEARNING DISABILITIES

- *Early identification and intervention are critical to prevention efforts. Current interest exists in the response to treatment (RTI) approach. As would be expected, early intervention focuses on basic skills, and most are directed to reading disabilities.*

- *Treatment of articulation and expressive language disorders rely strongly on operant and modeling techniques.*

- *Early treatment models of LD can be conceptualized as medical, psychoeducational, and behavioral. Current evidence supports the effectiveness of task-analytic, cognitive, and behavioral-cognitive approaches.*

- *Well-implemented interventions can be effective, for both language and learning disorders, although there is a continuing need to improve treatments.*

SPECIAL EDUCATIONAL SERVICES

- *The Individuals with Disabilities Education Act (IDEA) ensures a public education in the least restrictive environment possible to disabled students, and also safeguards the rights of families and ensures assistance in providing effective services.*

- *Of the children served by IDEA, about 41% are categorized as learning disabled and about 22% as language impaired. Most attend general education classrooms with varying degrees of supplemental supports.*

- *Some disagreement continues over the drawbacks and benefits of inclusion.*

KEY TERMS

Education for All Handicapped Children Act *(p. 264)*

Individuals with Disabilities Education Act (IDEA) *(p. 264)*

phonology *(p. 266)*

phonemes *(p. 266)*

graphemes *(p. 266)*

morphology *(p. 266)*

syntax *(p. 266)*

grammar *(p. 266)*

semantics *(p. 266)*

pragmatics *(p. 266)*

receptive language *(p. 266)*

expressive language *(p. 266)*

Phonological Disorder *(p. 267)*

Expressive Disorder *(p. 267)*

Mixed Receptive–Expressive Disorder *(p. 267)*

phonological processing *(p. 273)*

transcription (written text) *(p.275)*

text generation *(p.276)*

Nonverbal Learning Disabilities (NVLD) *(p. 279)*

individual education plan (IEP) *(p. 291)*

least restrictive environment *(p. 291)*

mainstreaming *(p. 291)*

inclusion *(p. 291)*

Mental Retardation/
Intellectual Disabilities

Mental retardation is not something you have, like blue eyes or a bad heart. Nor is it something you are, like being short or thin. It is not a medical disorder. . . . Nor is it a mental disorder. . . . Mental retardation refers to a particular state of functioning. (Luckasson et al., 1992, p. 9)

Mental retardation, or intellectual disabilities, has long been recognized, but until about 1700 it was poorly understood and scarcely viewed as different from other disorders (Reschly, 1992). By the early 1800s, the problem was understood to involve deficient intellectual functioning and handicaps in the daily tasks of living. These two features remain central, although ideas about mental retardation have evolved and are evolving even today.

Perhaps more strongly than many other disturbances, mental retardation has been seen as a trait of the individual. This perspective is largely being replaced by the view that functioning is best described as a fit between the abilities of the individual and his or her personal and social environment. Biological causation is fully recognized, but the numerous ways

in which the environment plays a role are being given more than passing attention.

The labels applied to mental retardation have also changed over time. The terms *idiot*, from the Greek meaning "ignorant person," *imbecile*, from the Latin meaning "weakness," and *moron*, meaning "foolish or having deficient judgment," were all once employed in the professional literature (Potter, 1972; Scheerenberger, 1983). These terms had been used by professionals as clinical descriptions, but they took on increasingly negative connotations, and changes in terminology were partly an attempt to substitute more positive labels. Currently, we are witnessing another transition.

After extensive consideration, the influential American Association on Mental Retardation (AAMR) has decided to drop the term mental retardation and replace it with *intellectual disabilities (ID)* (Schalock et al., 2007). The new term is seen as more consonant with the current perspective of mental retardation and as similar to terms employed in Europe. In agreement with the new term, the AAMR now calls itself the American Association on Intellectual and Developmental Disabilities (AAIDD). Recognizing this transition, we largely employ the newly adopted label, but we interchange it with *mental retardation (MR),* which appears in major classification systems and the literature, including past publications by the AAIDD.

Definition and Classification

The AAIDD Approach

We begin discussion with the definition offered by the American Association on Intellectual and Developmental Disabilities, which has led efforts to understand and ameliorate mental impairment. Founded in 1876, this organization has long provided conceptualizations of mental retardation that have often been adopted by other professional groups. In its latest manual, published in 2002, it offered the following definition:

> *Mental retardation is a disability characterized by significant limitations both in intellectual functioning and in adaptive behavior as expressed in conceptual, social, and practical adaptive skills. This disability originates before age 18. (Luckasson, et al., 2002, p. 8)*

Three criteria must be met before a person can be diagnosed with mental retardation. The *age criterion,* before 18, signifies that mental retardation is seen as a disturbance in development. Age 18 is appoximately the age at which individuals in our society assume adult roles and when crucial psychosocial development and brain development have typically occurred. *Limitation in intellectual functioning* refers to scores that are approximately two or more standard deviations below the mean on standardized general tests of intelligence, such as the Stanford–Binet and the Wechsler scales. Scores of 70 or below usually meet this criterion. *Limitation in adaptive skills* is defined as performance at least two standard deviations below the mean on standardized tests of conceptual, social, or practical skills. The requirement of *both* intellectual and adaptive behavior deficits means that individuals who fall into the retarded range on intelligence tests but otherwise get along adequately at home, school, or work do not meet the criteria for mental retardation. Nor do those with deficits in adaptive behavior who perform adequately on intelligence tests warrant the diagnosis. In addition, assessment and judgments of functional limitation must consider the contexts of the individual's life, that is, the community, cultural diversity, and the like.

The AAIDD has presented a theoretical model of mental retardation that incorporates influences, supports, and individual functioning. As indicated in Figure 11–1, five influences are mediated by supports

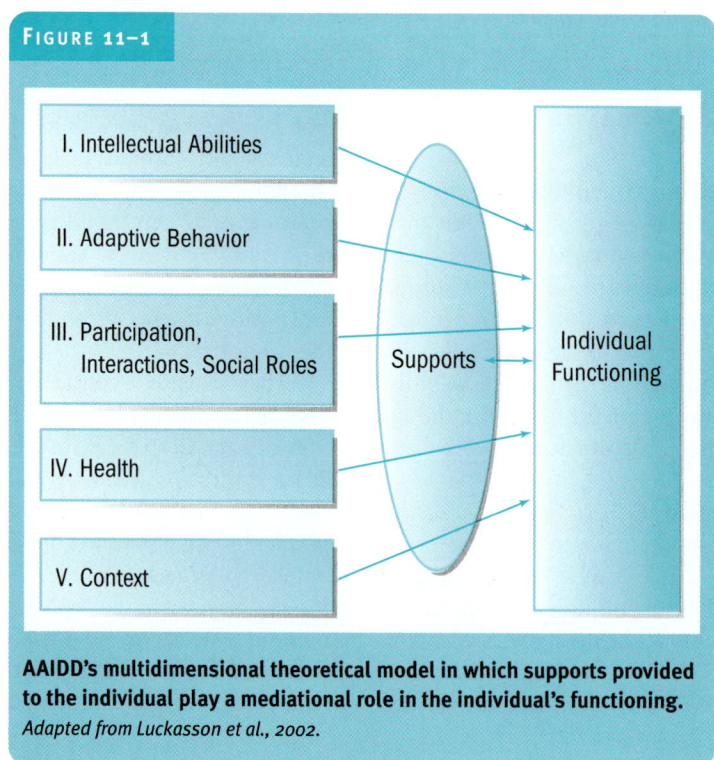

FIGURE 11–1

I. Intellectual Abilities

II. Adaptive Behavior

III. Participation, Interactions, Social Roles

IV. Health

V. Context

Supports

Individual Functioning

AAIDD's multidimensional theoretical model in which supports provided to the individual play a mediational role in the individual's functioning.
Adapted from Luckasson et al., 2002.

provided to the individual. Intellectual disabilities are not viewed as an absolute trait of the individual, and it is assumed that appropriate supports generally result in improved functioning. Moreover, children or adolescents with mental disability are viewed as complex individuals who have strengths as well as limitations.

Levels of needed supports. Because great variability exists in the abilities of people with mental retardation, it seems reasonable to use subgroupings based on the severity of intellectual impairment in intervention and research. Following this line of reasoning, the AAIDD once employed four levels of impairment: mild, moderate, severe, and profound. Individuals were assigned to a subgroup according to their intelligence test scores. This approach was widely adopted by other classification systems. Nonetheless, the AAIDD eliminated the approach in 1992 and recommended that each individual with disabilities be assessed for levels of needed environmental supports, that is, resources and strategies that will promote development and well-being. The identification and amount of supports needed are judged for nine areas, as shown in Table 11–1. This approach recognizes that needs for supports might be different in one area of functioning than another and might change over time. It also highlights the view of mental retardation as dynamically linked to the social environment rather than as a static quality of the individual.

THE DSM AND PAST APPROACHES

The DSM approach to diagnosis and classification is both similar and dissimilar to the AAIDD approach (American Psychiatric Association, 2000). Concurrent intellectual and adaptive limitations are required for diagnosis, as is onset of the disorder before age 18. The DSM requires an IQ of approximately 70 or below on standardized tests of intelligence. The criteria call for deficits in at least two areas of adaptive behavior, and the DSM notes the usefulness of tests of adaptive behavior.

The DSM departs from the AAIDD in its continued classification of individuals according to level of intelligence. (The ICD-10 does the same.) It was widely felt that the elimination of classification by IQ would leave clinicians and researchers without a reliable and meaningful way to group individuals (Baumeister & Baumeister, 2000). In fact, classification by IQ scores is customary for most researchers and many practitioners (Hodapp et al., 2006).

Table 11–2 shows the four levels of retardation employed by the DSM. About 85% of all cases are of mild retardation. Persons with mild retardation are viewed as quite different in functioning and in other important ways from persons classified at the other three levels. Thus, in practice, a distinction is commonly made between mild retardation and more severe impairment, with the IQ of about 50 marking the boundary.

It is worth noting that mild and moderate retardation were respectively labeled *educable mentally retarded* and *trainable mentally retarded* by educators in the United States based on judgment of abilities to learn. This classification provided a basis for school placement. Changes in educational policy and practices regarding exceptional students have made the classification less relevant, as educators rely less on IQ and more on functional descriptions of the child's needs (Handen & Gilchrist, 2006a).

Also noteworthy is historical change in the diagnostic criteria for mental retardation. Many professionals criticized the AAIDD in 1992 when it

TABLE 11–1	AREAS IN WHICH THE AAIDD RECOMMENDS ASSESSMENT FOR NEEDED SUPPORTS
• Human development	• Health and safety
• Teaching and education	• Behavioral
• Home living	• Social
• Community living	• Protection and advocacy
• Employment	

Luckasson et al., 2002.

TABLE 11–2	LEVELS OF MENTAL RETARDATION RECOGNIZED BY THE DSM	
LEVEL	IQ RANGE	PERCENTAGE OF MR POPULATION
Mild	50–55 to about 70	85
Moderate	35–40 to 50–55	10
Severe	20–25 to 35–40	3–4
Profound	below 20–25	1–2

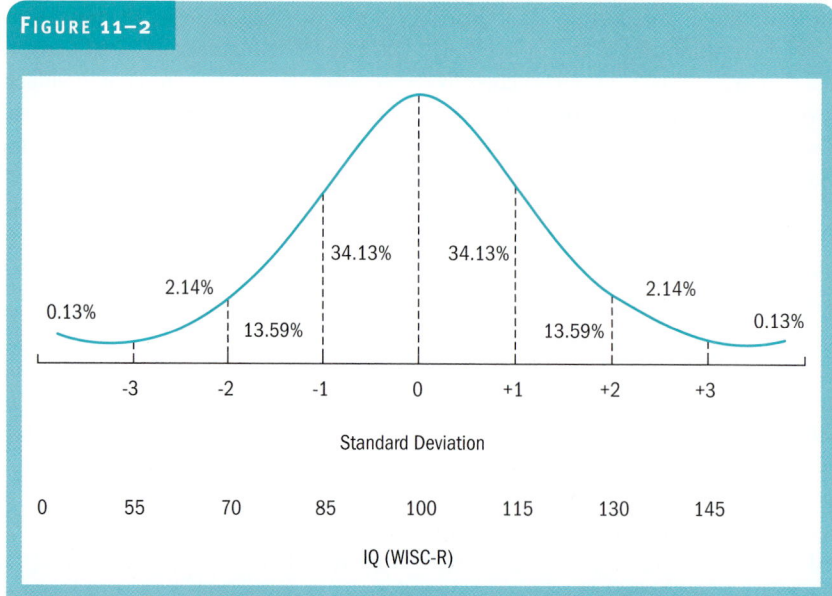

FIGURE 11–2

The distribution of scores on the WISC-R test of general intelligence fitted to the normal distribution. Standard deviation units indicate how far above or below a score is from the mean of 100. The standard deviation for the WISC-R is 15 points. When MR is defined by one or more standard deviations below the mean, approximately 16% of the population is mentally retarded. When MR is defined by two or more standard deviations below the mean, 2 to 3% of the population is mentally retarded.

recommended that 75 be considered the ceiling for the IQ criterion for diagnosis. This suggestion took into account the standard error of measurement of intelligence tests, which is about 5 points. However, this ceiling could double the number of persons being diagnosed (King, Hodapp, & Dykens, 2005), and especially affect persons from certain socially disadvantaged groups. To go back even further in time, there was concern in 1959, when the AAIDD employed a definition that allowed individuals to be diagnosed with MR when they scored one or more standard deviations below the mean on intelligence tests (Figure 11–2). Those who scored in the approximate range of 69 to 85 were labeled as retarded at the borderline level. By this definition, about 16% of the population could be diagnosed as mentally deficient. Critics argued that the criterion was unreasonable and that it disproportionately labeled some disadvantaged groups as retarded. Subsequently, the AAIDD shifted the IQ criterion. Changes in and controversy about the definition of mental retardation demonstrate the degree to which MR is a socially constructed category that has sometimes provoked heated debate.

Nature of Intelligence and Adaptive Behavior

Because measures of intelligence and adaptive behavior are central to defining intellectual disabilities, it is important to look more closely at their development and the concepts that underlie them.

MEASURED INTELLIGENCE

Tested intelligence is the most prominent criterion for mental retardation, and it is inextricably woven with retardation (Baumeister & Baumeister, 2000). As simple as the concept of intelligence seems on the surface, its meaning has raised many questions. We might agree, as have theorists, that it involves the knowledge possessed by a person, the ability to learn or think, or the capacity to adapt to new situations. Beyond these general definitions, we might run into disagreements. Theorists themselves argue, at times passionately, about the precise nature of intelligence, and they hold various perspectives on it (Anderson, 2001). We can hardly do justice to this topic, and our goal is to address issues that are most relevant to understanding intellectual disabilities.

Modern intelligence testing goes back to the work of Alfred Binet and his colleagues at the beginning of the 20th century. Their approach—the traditional psychometric approach—focused on individual differences and on the idea that underlying abilities explained differences in intellectual functioning (Beirne-Smith, Ittenbach, & Patton, 1998). Intelligence is often viewed as consisting of a general ability, called *g*, and numerous specific abilities, for example, motor and verbal abilities (Johnson et al., 2004). Intelligence is measured by the presentation of tasks that tap both general and specific abilities. This psychometric approach is sometimes described as examining the products of intellectual, or cognitive, abilities rather than the processes involved in the abilities.

In recent years, information-processing theories have come to the fore, focusing on the processes by which individuals perceive sensory stimuli, store information, manipulate information, and perhaps act on it. Different theorists have somewhat different ways of conceptualizing these processes, but in any case, intelligence is measured according to how well a person performs on processing tasks. For example, the abilities to attend to and simultaneously deal with several bits of information might be measured (Anastasi & Urbina, 1997). Information-processing approaches contribute much to the understanding of mental retardation and are increasingly integrated into the measurement of intelligence. However, it was the psychometric approach that largely shaped views of intelligence throughout most of the 20th century.

Early test construction and assumptions. When Binet and his colleague Simon were asked by school officials in Paris to find a way to identify children who needed special educational experiences, they tested students of different ages on brief tasks relevant to classroom learning. In 1905, their work resulted in the first intelligence scale, consisting of tasks that average students of various ages passed. When children were evaluated on the scale, they were assigned what would be called a mental age (MA), that is, the age corresponding to the chronological age (CA) of children whose performance they equaled. Thus a 7-year-old who passed the tests that average 7-year-olds passed was assigned an MA of 7; a 7-year-old who only passed the tests that average 5-year-olds passed obtained an MA of 5.

Binet made several assumptions about intelligence (Siegler, 1992). He believed that intelligence

encompassed many complex processes, was malleable within limits, and was influenced by the social environment. Binet argued that carefully constructed standardized tests were necessary to minimize inaccurate evaluations of children. Moreover, he and his colleagues devised methods to improve intellectual functioning, and they recommended that educational programs be fitted to each child's special needs.

Intelligence testing was brought to the United States when Henry Goddard translated and used the Binet scales with residents of the Vineland Training School in New Jersey. Then, in 1916, about 5 years after Binet's death, Lewis Terman, working at Stanford University, revised the early scales into the Stanford–Binet test. Terman adopted the idea of the intelligence quotient (IQ) as the ratio of an individual's mental age to chronological age, multiplied by 100 to avoid decimals. The ratio IQ enabled direct comparison between children of different ages. Today the major intelligence tests employ statistical comparison, so that what is often referred to as IQ is no longer a quotient, but a score that nevertheless denotes age comparison (Table 11–3).

Goddard and Terman made some markedly different assumptions from those of Binet about the nature of intelligence. They assumed that the tests measured inherited intelligence that would remain stable over the life of the individual (e.g., Cravens, 1992). They also saw the need for eugenics, the improvement of the human species by control of inheritance. These beliefs had social implications that were to generate heated debate about the assumptions and

TABLE 11–3	MEASURES RELEVANT TO TESTS OF INTELLIGENCE
CA	Chronological age.
MA	Mental age. The age score corresponding to the chronological age of children whose performance the examinee equals. For the average child, MA = CA.
IQ (ratio)	The ratio of mental age to chronological age multiplied by 100. IQ = MA/CA x 100.
IQ (deviation)	A standard score derived from statistical procedures that reflects the direction and degree to which an individual's performance deviates from the average score of the age group.

ACCENT ● ● ● ● ●

Measured Intelligence: A History of Abusive Ideas

Not long after their introduction, intelligence tests began to influence U.S. public policy, even though some tests and their administration were of questionable quality. IQ tests played a role in establishing immigration quotas for people of southern European background and in introducing laws for the sterilization of people considered mentally deficient (Strickland, 2000). In fact, "unsexing" the "unfit," which had already begun, increased during the early 1900s (Wehmeyer, 2003). Many states passed sterilization laws, and such a law was upheld in 1927 by the Supreme Court in a Virginia case, *Buck v. Bell*. California law called for the sterilization of state hospital inmates and "feeble-minded" children residing in state-run homes. Forced sterilization affected over 50,000 persons before scientists and others overtly criticized the controversial practice.

Although perhaps not as dramatic, the use of intelligence tests in the schools also has been controversial. After compulsory education laws were passed, the public schools employed intelligence tests to assess children's capacity for school learning (MacMillan & Reschly, 1997). Children of poor families and some minorities generally performed relatively poorly on the tests. In more recent times, this group included children of African American, Hispanic, and Native American background, although the confounding of social class and racial/ethnic background should be recognized. Concern was raised about test results disproportionately identifying minority and poor children as intellectually deficient—resulting in placements in special education classrooms. Critics charged that standard English tests were used with bilingual students, the content of tests did not always relate well to the students' subcultures, and the tests were not of good quality. Confrontations with the educational system ensued, some of which reached the courts (MacMillan, Keogh, & Jones, 1986). Legal outcomes often, but not always, favored plaintiffs for minority groups. The influential *Larry P. v. Riles* case, brought by black plaintiffs, resulted in restrictions on the use of intelligence tests for identifying and placing black children into special education programs in California. Overall, the educational system was required to stringently monitor the use and administration of intelligence tests.

Inherent in the early uses and abuses of tests was the assumption that measured intelligence is a stable, biologically programmed characteristic of individuals. Today's more accepted view is that intelligence tests assess important aspects of functioning that result from the interaction of heredity and environment and that at least to some degree is modifiable by environmental factors (Fagan & Holland, 2002).

uses of intelligence tests, as well as the treatment of persons with retardation. (See Accent: "Measured Intelligence: A History of Abusive Ideas.")

Stability and validity of tested intelligence.

Intrinsic to the debates about intelligence is the issue of whether measured intelligence is stable over time. Stability can be examined by studying a group of people longitudinally and correlating earlier IQ scores with later IQ scores. When such test–retest measurements are made after preschool age, a median correlation of .77 has been found (King et al., 2005). Further, the IQ scores of persons with intellectual disabilities are more stable than the IQ scores of persons with average or above scores, and the lower the score, the greater the stability. It is important to note, however, that such analyses examine groups of people and that individual scores can change, often in response to changing family situations or educational opportunities.

Another central issue about intelligence is what an IQ score tells us about a person. This is, of course, a question about the validity of intelligence tests—whether the test tells us what it is designed to tell us. If intelligence is defined as an ability that relates to school performance, evidence exists for the validity of intelligence tests. After age 5, the correlations of IQ with school grades and reading, spelling, and mathematics achievement scores are moderately high, generally in the range of .40 to .75 (Berger & Yule, 1985; Matarazzo, 1992). Measured intelligence is also related to later school completion, employment, and income (Ferguson, Horwood, & Ridder, 2005). On the other hand, IQ tests tell us less about a variety of social behaviors (e.g., social adjustment). Nevertheless, it is relevant to note that IQ scores that fall below the average range are generally better predictors of academic and nonacademic performance than those in the normal range.

Intelligence tests are an important tool, but caution is necessary in interpreting them. IQ scores are relatively stable, but they are not cast in stone. They provide important information about individual functioning but cannot tell us everything. Serious questions have been raised about the cultural bias of the tests, and about their limitations as well. Factors that might contribute to intelligence—such as motivation and social responsiveness—are not well discriminated by the tests (Scarr, 1982; Siegler, 1992), and IQ tests may not well reflect problem solving in the real world (Sternberg et al., 1995). Consider also the uncertainty of intelligence tests due to the Flynn effect, the finding that IQ scores in populations systematically improve over time as the tests become older. Periodic updating—that is, construction of new norms—resets the mean score and the test becomes more difficult (Kanaya & Ceci, 2007). Performance then drops several points on average for both typical children and those scoring in the mentally retarded range. Kanaya, Scullin, and Ceci (2003) noted that the diagnosis of mental retardation can be affected by how old the test norms are when the child is assessed. Thus, in considering whether a child meets the IQ criterion for retardation "it may not be sufficient to simply look to see whether the IQ score is below some cutoff point" (p. 790).

ADAPTIVE FUNCTIONING

Historically, the failure to socially adapt to one's environment was at the heart of the concept of mental retardation (Schalock et al., 2007). The emphasis on intelligence came later. Several decades ago, working at the Vineland Training School, Edgar Doll focused on the importance of social and personal competence in the everyday lives of persons with ID (King et al., 2005). He published a scale to measure what today is the concept of adaptive behavior. In 1959, the AAIDD first included deficits in adaptive functioning as a criterion for mental retardation.

Adaptive behavior has generally been thought of as "what people do to take care of themselves and to relate to others in daily living. . . ." (Grossman, 1983, p. 42). The ideas of personal self-help skills, social competence and social responsibility, and community

The ability to engage in routine activities and tasks substantially heightens the well-being of youth with intellectual disabilities.
(Hattie Young/Photo Researchers, Inc.)

living skills appear central in major tests of adaptive behavior (Luckasson et al., 1992; 2002). Developmental change is taken into account. Behaviors associated with sensorimotor, communication, self-help, and primary socialization skills are emphasized in early life, whereas during later childhood and adolescence, reasoning and judgments about the environment and social relationships increase in importance. When judgments of adaptation are made, they should consider the expectations of the community and sociocultural context in which the person is functioning. For example, a child may have social skill deficits in a school setting and yet meet the expectations of the neighborhood.

Adaptive behavior is viewed as overlapping with but not identical to intelligence. Research shows a positive correlation in the range of .4 to .6 between scores on adaptive behavior tests and intelligence tests (Kanaya et al., 2003). Thus, as measured intelligence decreases, individuals are more likely to have difficulties in everyday functioning, and this may be especially true for individuals with lower levels of intelligence (King et al., 2005).

Some controversy exists regarding adaptive behavior. Not all professionals are in favor of weighting adaptive behavior as heavily as intelligence in the definition of retardation (Baumeister & Baumeister, 2000). They tend to view adaptive behavior as the result or correlate of intellectual disabilities. Concern is also expressed about measuring adaptive behavior. In fact, the development of adaptive behavior scales has lagged behind that for intelligence, judgments of adaptive behavior vary with the person evaluating it, and it is unclear how many factors compose adaptive behavior.

Despite controversy, however, it is widely agreed that daily living skills are critical to the adjustment and satisfaction of youth with intellectual disabilities.

Description

Underlying ID are a heterogeneous group of known syndromes and poorly understood general conditions. In some cases, the effects are confined to mild deficits in intellectual and adaptive behavior but in others there are severe impairments in cognitive, sensory, motor, language, socioemotional, or behavioral systems. Differences in functioning can be illustrated in several ways.

One way is to examine descriptions of functioning according to levels of intelligence. Table 11–4 provides a brief description for mild, moderate, severe, and profound disability with a focus on expectations for communication skills, academic learning, and need for supervisory living arrangements. These descriptions give a sense of the enormous variability in abilities. The following provides a brief account of some problems experienced by a child diagnosed with profound mental retardation.

Annalise   Profound Intellectual Disabilities

Annalise was born after an unremarkable pregnancy. Her mother recalled significant feeding difficulties in the first few weeks of life, and Annalise's developmental milestones were delayed. She did not walk, for example, until approximately 4 years of age. Her progress was variable while she was enrolled in an early intervention program. She has essentially never been able to use spoken language.

The family reports that Annalise's medical history is extraordinarily complicated. It includes an episode of congestive heart failure, thyroid problems, diabetes, and an apparent allergy to milk. When she was 4 or 5 years of age, she became preoccupied with food, consuming everything in sight. Genetic testing for Prader–Willi syndrome was negative, but a deletion on chromosome 1 was later revealed.

Annalise has never been very sensitive to the thoughts or feelings of others, and she sometimes literally walked over other children. She has many circumscribed interests, and if allowed would watch small vignettes from Disney videos over and over again. She has been preoccupied with sorting and stacking objects, and at one time she would tantrum if not permitted to organize stones and pebbles as she passed them. Due to her preoccupation with food, the family has had to lock the refrigerator and food cabinets. They are hoping that medication will reduce Annalise's anxiety and obsessions that hinder her from fuller participation in activities.

Adapted from King et al., 2005, pp. 3084–3085.

TABLE 11–4	BRIEF DESCRIPTION OF FUNCTIONING ACCORDING TO LEVELS OF MENTAL RETARDATION

MILD RETARDATION

Usually develops social and communication skills in preschool years

Has minimal sensorimotor deficits

Can acquire about sixth-grade academic skills by late teens

Usually achieves adult vocational and social skills for self-support

May need guidance, assistance, supervised living, but often lives successfully in the community

MODERATE RETARDATION

Usually develops communication skills in early childhood

Can attend to personal care, with support

Is unlikely to progress beyond second-grade academic skills

Can benefit from social and occupational skills training and perform unskilled or semiskilled work

Can adapt to supervised community living

SEVERE RETARDATION

May learn to talk and minimally care for self at school age

Has limited ability to profit from preacademic training

In adulthood, may perform simple tasks with supervision

In most cases, can adapt to community living with family or in group homes

PROFOUND RETARDATION

In most cases, has a neurological condition

Has sensorimotor impairments in childhood

With training, may show improvement in motor, self-care, and communication skills

May do simple supervised tasks

Requires structure and constant supervision with individual caregiver for optimal development

Based on American Psychiatric Association, 2000; Singh, Oswald, & Ellis, 1998.

It is also informative to compare the developmental profiles of individual cases of children with mental disability. As an example, Figure 11–3 shows the profiles for Bob and Carol, both 10 years of age, presented by Kirk, Gallagher, & Anastasiow (2000). Bob's functioning has been judged as mildly retarded, Carol's as severely retarded. Bob's physical characteristics (height, weight, motor coordination) do not vary much from those of his typically developing peers, but his abilities in the language, academic, and social areas lag by approximately 3 years (or grade levels). In contrast, Carol is somewhat further behind her peers in physical attributes and otherwise is functioning at the 4-year-old level. It was suggested that, with appropriate support, Bob might benefit from typical academic experiences, but that Carol would require specialized training to help her develop her potential.

A third way in which the clinical picture can be filled out is by further description of the physical/medical, learning/cognitive, and social functioning of children with intellectual disabilities. Most youth with ID, particularly those with mild disability, show no unusual physical characteristics and blend into the general population. But a sizable number do show atypical appearance that ranges from minor to more obvious abnormalities. Disturbances in physical functions also occur. Up to 20% of persons with disabilities have a seizure disorder; other problems include motor difficulties, impaired eyesight or blindness, and deafness (Singh et al., 1998). Abnormalities of physical appearance and function are especially associated with the more severe levels of mental retardation, as are many medical conditions, such as cerebral palsy, epilepsy, cardiac problems, and kidney disease. The lifespan of those with ID has increased: in the United States, it rose from a mean of 25 years to 49 years between 1983 and 1997 (Lenhard et al., 2007). This is still well below the average lifespan, and it is disproportionately accounted for by high death rates at the lower levels of disabilities (Patja et al., 2000).

Investigators have described learning and cognition from various perspectives. Children with mental retardation can learn, but there is immense variability with level of disability and etiology. Early investigations of classical and operant conditioning showed that basic learning is possible at all levels of mental retardation, although special considerations are often required, particularly in cases of severe retardation. Over the years, operant learning has been of specific interest regarding treatment. New behaviors can be shaped by successive approximations; desirable behaviors can be maintained and undesirable behaviors weakened by consistent application of appropriate contingencies.

Research based on information-processing approaches, primarily with individuals with mild or moderate disability, has been fruitful in documenting numerous problems. Deficits in various abilities, including attention, working memory, the use of effective strategies to mentally organize information, monitoring one's own thinking, and generalizing learning to new situations, have been described (e.g., Tomporowski & Tinsley, 1997). Disability is not all-or-none, of course. In some youth, competence has been displayed in visual recognition memory, long-term memory on many tasks, and

FIGURE 11–3

Developmental profiles of two children with different levels of mental retardation.

From Kirk, Gallagher, & Anastasiow, 2000.

the use of rehearsal as a memory strategy (Bray, Fletcher, & Turner, 1997). The study of different syndromes of retardation is instructive in demonstrating differential cognitive strengths and weaknesses, a topic to which we later return.

Finally, large heterogeneity is observed in social skills and understanding across the range of retardation. These skills include behaviors as diverse as appropriate eye contact and facial expression, initiating greetings and interaction, reciprocal group interaction, and solving social problems (e.g., Handen & Gilchrist, 2006a). Research has emphasized the social competencies of those with mild and moderate retardation (Greenspan & Love, 1997). These youths do exhibit impairments in social cognition, as indicated in understanding social cues, social situations, and others' perspectives. However, it appears that competence can gradually improve and that skills develop in the same order as for typically developing children.

There seems little doubt that some of the social problems of children with mental retardation are attributable to the intellectual disability, language deficits, and physical/medical impairments characteristic of retardation. It would be a mistake, however, not to recognize the influence of social experience. Youth with ID tend to experience greater social isolation despite today's heightened commitment to include them in social and educational activities. It is also likely that other people, perhaps due to discomfort, behave somewhat atypically during social interactions with these youths. Thus, individuals with ID likely have insufficient opportunity to practice social interaction and observe appropriate models and social relations.

Co-occurring Disorders

The well-being and adaptation of individuals with ID are hindered by various psycholoical problems, some of which are sufficiently severe to meet the criteria for clinical diagnoses. Prevalence of diagnosed or significant problems is in the range of 30 to 50% (Handen & Gilchrist, 2006a). According to the American Psychiatric Association (2000), the rate may be three to four times the rate in the general population.

The kinds of disturbances exhibited are similar to those shown in the general population. Among the most common are attention-deficit hyperactivity disorder and oppositional/conduct problems (Handen & Gilchrist, 2006a; Hodapp et al., 2006). Anxiety, depression, aggression, obsessive–compulsive behavior, schizophrenia, autism, stereotypes, and self-injury have all been reported. Limited investigation indicates that the developmental trajectories for many problems are similar to those found for normal children (de Ruiter et al., 2007). However, the kinds of problems may differ with level of retardation. Depressive feelings, anxiety, and antisocial problems may be more common in individuals with mild disabilities, whereas psychosis and autism may be more prevalent with lower intellectual ability (Dekker & Koot, 2003b). Finally, particular problems are associated with specific syndromes of mental retardation. For example, Lesch–Nyhan syndrome is associated with self-injury and Prader–Willi syndrome with insatiable eating.

It can be difficult to accurately identify or diagnose co-occurring problems. One reason is that professionals tend to view such difficulties as an intricate part of mental retardation and thus fail to recognize them (Hodapp et al., 2006; Jopp & Keys, 2001). Such overshadowing, as it is called, has been documented among different professionals working in different settings. A second reason is that the cognitive and communication impairments of ID can make it difficult to identify problems, especially in severe retardation. This might be particularly so for symptoms requiring descriptions of internal feelings and experiences—a task that may be complicated even for youth with mild disabilities. We would expect, for example, that depressive symptoms might be challenging to assess because the youth must be able to identify and label sadness, hopelessness, and the like. Still another factor can hinder diagnosis. Although standard diagnostic criteria apply quite well when IQ is about 50 or higher, they do not apply well at lower levels of retardation (Handen, 1998).

What accounts for high rates of problems or disorders in intellectual disabilities? Neurological factors no doubt explain some disturbances and probably play a stronger role in more severe retardation. Biological causation is suggested by the association of specific genetic syndromes with specific problems (Moldavsky, Lev, & Lerman-Sagie, 2001). The stigma of retardation, lack of developmental opportunities, and low quality of living arrangements are among other possible influences (Table 11–5).

Co-occurring problems undoubtedly lower the quality of life for young people with ID and can significantly affect family interaction, school placement, and community adjustment. Fortunately, increased attention is being given to this issue.

TABLE 11–5	FACTORS THAT MAY CONTRIBUTE TO PSYCHOLOGICAL PROBLEMS IN ID

Neurobiological processes underlying mental retardation
Side effects of medication
Communication deficits
Inadequate problem-solving and coping skills
Reduced opportunity for development of social skills
Reduced opportunity for development of supportive social relationships
Stigma leading to low self-concept
Family stress
Vulnerability to exploitation and abuse

Based in part on King, Hodapp, & Dykens, 2000, 2005.

Epidemiology

The prevalence of mental retardation is variously estimated as between 1 and 3% of the general population, but it depends on the criteria used and other variables (King et al., 2005). Assuming a normal distribution of intelligence test scores and an IQ of about 70 as the criterion for ID, a rate of over 2% would be expected (Figure 11–2). In fact, a greater number of cases than predicted by the normal distribution actually cluster at the low end of performance. Nonetheless, when intellectual disabilities are defined by *both* IQ and adaptive behavior, a prevalence around 1% is suggested (American Psychiatric Association, 2000; Hodapp & Dykens, 2003). It is assumed that some individuals with mild ID as defined by IQ scores are not identified because their behavior is sufficiently adaptive in their environments.

Prevalence rates are especially interesting when age and severity of mental retardation are inspected. Rates are lower prior to school age, and the children identified tend to have moderate or lower IQ scores. It appears that the more severe cases attract more immediate attention, although not all such cases are identified this early. A dramatic shift then occurs when children enter school. Prevalence increases as more mild cases are diagnosed, apparently because the children are unable to meet the new situational demands. Rates appear to level off in adolescence and a decline occurs in adulthood. This decline may in part be due to the capacity of some adults to successfully work in unskilled jobs and otherwise function adequately, or perhaps they become less available for evaluation. At the lower levels of ID, rates may drop because of the relatively short lifespan of these individuals.

Other variables are important when prevalence is examined (Hodapp & Dykens, 2003; King, Hodapp, & Dykens, 2000). Mental retardation appears more in males than females—perhaps due to reporting bias, other environmental factors, and male vulnerability to biological influences. In fact, males are at greater risk for genetic syndromes associated with ID. In addition, children and adolescents from families of low socioioeconomic status account for a disproportionate number of cases, specifically mild cases—an important finding revisited later in the chapter.

Developmental Course and Considerations

Very different life trajectories can be anticipated for children with mental retardation. Stability of diagnosis is not inevitable and individuals with mild disability can, with appropriate training and opportunity, develop adequate intellectual or adaptive skills so that criteria for the disorder are no longer met (American Psychiatric Association, 2000). For most youths, though, ID is lifelong. Severity and cause of the disorder make a difference in course and outcome, as do factors such as associated medical problems, psychopathology, and family variables (Volkmar & Dykens, 2002).

Theorists and practitioners have been interested in developmental issues pertaining to cognition in children with intellectual disabilities relative to typical growth. Earlier research tended to focus on milder retardation for which there was no identified cause; later efforts included more severe retardation with known organic etiologies.

The *rate* of intellectual development has been of interest. Typical development is seen as occurring gradually over time throughout childhood and adolescence, with some spurts and regressions. Development is slower than usual in children with MR, but for many youth the rate of growth is fairly steady (King et al., 2005). Nonetheless, different patterns have been observed for specific syndromes, for example, a slowing after a few years of steady growth.

Another developmental consideration has to do with the *sequence* of intellectual growth. Intelligence normally develops in some orderly way. Does this course hold for retardation? Early research focused on whether youngsters with retardation followed the four stages of cognitive growth that, according to Jean Piaget, all typically developing youngsters display as they come to think in more complex ways. Research confirmed that children with intellectual disabilities generally do progress through the same Piagetian stages—and other cognitive sequences—as do nonretarded children, but do so more slowly and ultimately do not progress as far (Hodapp & Dykens, 2003; Hodapp & Zigler, 1997). The participants in early research were children with retardation for which there was no clear organic cause, but subsequent research included children with Down syndrome.

These findings have practical implications for working with youth with ID. For example, the fact that the sequence of development in mild retardation is often similar to that of typical development provides a guideline for constructing curricular materials for teaching these children.

Etiology

Although intellectual disabilities are associated with hundreds of specific medical and genetic conditions, as well as with physical and psychosocial environmental circumstances, causation is not clearly identified in an estimated 30 to 40% of individuals seen in clinical settings (American Psychiatric Association, 2000). Etiology is more likely to be puzzling in milder cases of disability.

Johnny   Unknown Cause of MR

Johnny is a 10-year-old boy with mild mental retardation. Although from birth his parents considered him somewhat "slow," Johnny was not diagnosed. . . until his early grade-school years. To this day, no clear [cause] has been provided for Johnny's mild mental retardation. As measured by the Stanford–Binet IV, his IQ is 67, with no significant difference between his verbal and perceptual processing scores. Johnny does, however, show impulsivity and problems in attending. . . . Johnny's mental retardation first became apparent at the end of the first grade. At that time, a student study team at his school worked with Johnny's classroom teacher and the resource room teacher to help Johnny improve his basic work organizational skills and increase his attention span. At his parents' request, Johnny was also evaluated for attention-deficit hyperactivity disorder by the local psychiatrist, who prescribed stimulant medication that seemed to help.

Adapted from King et al., 2000, p. 2599.

Historically the two-group approach to the etiology of ID has been influential in both theory and research (Volkmar & Dykens, 2002). Accordingly, individuals with intellectual disabilities are viewed as falling into two categories that differ in several ways. The groups, as indicated in Table 11–6 are referred to

TABLE 11–6	THE TWO-GROUP APPROACH TO MENTAL RETARDATION	
	ORGANIC	CULTURAL–FAMILIAL
	Individual shows a clear organic cause of mental retardation	Individual shows no obvious cause of retardation; sometimes another family member is also retarded
	More prevalent at moderate, severe, and profound levels of retardation	More prevalent in mild mental retardation
	Equal or near-equal rates across all ethnic and SES levels	Higher rates within minority groups and low-SES groups
	More often associated with other physical disabilities	Few associated physical or medical disabilities

Adapted from Hodapp & Dykens, 2003.

as the organic group and the cultural–familial group. Biological etiology is clear for the organic group, and in the 1960s and 1970s causation for the cultural–familial group was attributed primarily to environmental deprivation. Current knowledge and theory indicates the wisdom of viewing causation as more complex and interactive. A multicausal model underlies our discussion, but it is worthwhile to distinguish organic, multigenic, and psychosocial etiology or risks.

ORGANIC INFLUENCES

Attributing mental retardation to pathological organic factors implies that biological conditions are crucial in accounting for disordered brain function and intellectual disability. The idea that disability is caused by biological "defect" has a strong place in the history of mental retardation. In past times the argument was often based on flimsy or flawed "proof." For example, in his influential study of the Kallikak family, Goddard (1912) traced the quite distinct genealogical lines of Martin Kallikak. One line originated from Kallikak's liaison with a barmaid, the second from later marriage to a woman of "better stock." From information on several hundred of Kallikak's descendants, Goddard found a pronounced difference in the two families, namely, that the first liaison had resulted in more mental deficiency, criminality, alcoholism, and immorality. Obvious weaknesses existed in this study, most notably the questionable accuracy of the data. But the results were taken as evidence that mental retardation is an inherited biological trait—although family environment could just as well have played a role.

Today there is more valid evidence for biological risk and causation, as well as greater understanding of its nature. Zigler and his colleagues pointed to the fact that although IQ scores are said to be normally distributed in the general population, they actually fall into a distribution that resembles the normal curve except for a "bump" at the low end (Burack, 1990; Zigler, Balla, & Hodapp, 1984). This excess of low scores, they suggested, is accounted for by individuals who have suffered major biological impairment (Simonoff, Bolton, & Rutter, 1996). In fact, evidence exists for a group of individuals with more severe mental retardation, coming about equally from all social classes, that shows an excess of specific genetic abnormalities, multiple congenital anomalies, clear evidence of brain dysfunction such as cerebral palsy, and reduced life expectancy.

It is estimated that perhaps 50% of cases of ID have some known organic cause (Volkmar & Dykens, 2002). Biological risk may be based in genetic

processes, prenatal or birth variables, or postnatal circumstances.

MULTIGENIC INFLUENCES

The organic factors just discussed are assumed to cause ID through abnormal brain development or brain damage. In contrast, multigenic, or polygenic, influences derive from multiple genes (quantitative trait loci) whose effects combine to produce variation in intelligence in normal populations. Mental retardation can be viewed as representing the lower scores in this variation.

Current understanding of hereditary influences on intelligence in populations has a basis in behavior genetic research (Plomin, DeFries, & McClearn, 1990). Intelligence test performance of identical twins is more similar than that of fraternal twins; when identical twins are reared apart, similarity decreases but is still high. Studies of families and adopted children lend support to the twin findings. In general, it is estimated that about 50% of the variation in tested intelligence in populations is due to genetic transmission of multiple genes.

Research studies also suggest that the influence of multiple genes may vary with the level of retardation. Whereas pathological organic factors are more strongly associated with the more severe levels of disability, the opposite appears to hold for multigenic influences. One family study, for example, revealed that the IQs of siblings of children with severe retardation averaged 103, hinting that severe retardation did not "run in families" and that some specific organic factor had caused retardation in the affected child. In contrast, the IQs of siblings of children with mild retardation averaged 85, suggesting general family influence, perhaps multigenic inheritance, psychosocial effects, or a combination of these (Broman et al., 1987; Scott, 1994).

This is not to say, of course, that pathological organic factors never cause mild mental retardation. Indeed, we might anticipate that biological advances will reveal now-undetected organic abnormalities that contribute to mild impairments. Nevertheless, multiple factors are likely involved in the etiology of mild cases and these may include multiple genes as well as psychosocial influences (Hodapp et al., 2006).

PSYCHOSOCIAL INFLUENCES

Interest in psychosocial causation of intellectual disabilities was tied to the conceptualization of cultural–familial retardation. The terms *garden variety* and *undifferentiated* also were used, reflecting the large number of cases that were not readily distinguished from one another (Crnic, 1988). These children appeared quite normal, possessed relatively good adaptive skills, were often first identified on entering school, and as adults often blended into the general population. Their family members were frequently described in similar ways.

It has been observed for many years that mild retardation in families occurs disproportionately in the lower socioeconomic classes and in some minority groups, and could be caused by psychosocial/cultural disadvantage. Many psychosocial variables associated with low social class put children at risk—such as low parental education, particular parental attitudes, lack of social support, and stressful life events (Sameroff, 1990). The adverse effects of psychosocial variables may operate through more than one pathway. Inadequate intellectual stimulation might hinder early brain development, especially the growth of synaptic networks. Behavior and motivation conducive to success in the classroom and other learning environments may not be acquired or supported.

Specific associations have been demonstrated among social class, home environment, and children's intellectual development. One study found, for instance, that ability at age 3 was related to social class and parental practices, for example, parents interacting with and talking to their child (Hart & Risley, 1992). As a group, educationally and economically deprived parents may lack the skill, or otherwise be unable, to stimulate children's language and cognitive development. One team of investigators, that for many years was engaged in an intervention and research program for disadvantaged preschool children, proposed a model for the development of retardation that reaches across generations (Greenwood et at., 1992; 1994). In this model, because of limited parental interactions, young children begin to fall behind intellectually. When they reach school, the children's home situation combines with school practices that lead to low educational motivation, exposure,

TABLE 11–7	THE FOUR AAIDD CATEGORIES OF RISK AND ETIOLOGY PERTAINING TO INTELLECTUAL DISABILITIES			
TIMING	**BIOMEDICAL**	**SOCIAL**	**BEHAVIORAL**	**EDUCATIONAL**
Prenatal	1. Chromosomal disorders 2. Single-gene disorders 3. Syndromes 4. Metabolic disorders 5. Cerebral dysgenesis 6. Maternal illnesses 7. Parental age	1. Poverty 2. Maternal malnutrition 3. Domestic violence 4. Lack of access to prenatal care	1. Parental drug use 2. Parental alcohol use 3. Parental smoking 4. Parental immaturity	1. Parental cognitive disability without supports 2. Lack of preparation for parenthood
Perinatal	1. Prematurity 2. Birth injury 3. Neonatal disorders	1. Lack of access to birth care	1. Parental rejection of caretaking 2. Parental abandonment of child	1. Lack of medical referral for intervention services at discharge
Postnatal	1. Traumatic brain injury 2. Malnutrition 3. Meningoencephalitis 4. Seizure disorders 5. Degenerative disorders	1. Impaired child-adult relationship 2. Lack of adequate stimulation 3. Family poverty 4. Chronic illness in the family 5. Institutionalization	1. Child abuse and neglect 2. Domestic violence 3. Inadequate safety measures 4. Social deprivation 5. Difficult child behaviors	1. Impaired parenting 2. Delayed diagnosis 3. Inadequate early intervention services 4. Inadequate special-educational services 5. Inadequate family support

From Luckasson et al., 2002.

and achievement, resulting in a high rate of school dropout. In turn, when these children become parents, they are unable to contribute optimally to the cognitive growth of their offspring.

It is, nevertheless, difficult to pinpoint any one cause of intellectual disabilities in disadvantaged children. These youth are also at risk for major inherited abnormalities, prenatal and birth adversities, postnatal malnutrition and disease, and other adversities. Variation due to multiple-gene inheritance is not ruled out. Given what is known about the intricacies of development, multifactor explanations might frequently apply.

MULTIFACTOR CAUSATION

Although it is still easy to fall back on the historical tendency to view intellectual disabilites as a result of *either* biological *or* psychosocial factors, more complex explanations are now clearly recognized. The AAIDD suggests that multifactor explanations are not necessarily inconsistent with the two-group approach (Luckasson et al., 2002). In some cases, biomedical factors may predominate whereas in other cases, social, behavioral, or educational factors may predomini-

nate. But even when a known medical disorder is strongly associated with mental retardation, the level of disability may be determined, within limits, by some mix of other biological and psychosocial factors. For example, intelligence, adaptive behavior, and behavioral problems are influenced by the home and school environment in children with the genetic-based fragile X syndrome (Reiss & Dant, 2003). The AAIDD views the development of disabilities within a multiple risk model that encompasses biomedical, social, behavioral, and educational factors that can operate at different times in life (Table 11–7).

Genetic Syndromes and Behavioral Phenotypes

A major trend in the research on ID is the investigation of genetic syndromes, which allows comparison of groups of youths affected by different known organic etiology. The research can shed light on the link between genes, brain functioning, and behavior. In this discussion, we highlight four syndromes—Down, fragile X, Williams, and Prader–Willi. Table 11–8 lists

TABLE 11–8	SOME PHYSICAL ATTRIBUTES AND BEHAVIORAL PROBLEMS ASSOCIATED WITH SYNDROMES OF INTELLECTUAL DISABILITIES	
	PHYSICAL	BEHAVIORAL
Down	Upward slant and folds at corner of eyes, flat facial features, fissured tongue, broad hands and feet, poor muscle tone	Relatively good social skills and mild manner but also noncompliance, stubbornness, augumentativeness, inattention, overactivity Depression developing in adolescence and adulthood, dementia in adulthood
Fragile X	Boys tend to have velvetlike skin, double-jointed thumbs, and by adolescence long faces, large ears, oversized testicles	Inattention, hyperactivity, stereotyped movements, anxiety, social avoidance, poor peer interaction (Girls: shyness, anxiety, social avoidance) Co-occurring autism that is associated with greater developmental delay
Williams	"Elfinlike" face (e.g., small lower jaw, prominent cheeks), growth deficiency, often an aged appearance in late adolescence or early adulthood	Anxiety, fears and phobias, inattention, hyperactivity, indiscriminate and overly friendly social interaction, poor social judgment
Prader–Willi	Flat face with almond-shaped eyes and prominent forehead, small hands and feet, short underdeveloped gonads, obesity	Excessive eating and food hoarding, obsessions and compulsions, aggression, anxiety, impulsivity, tantrums

Based on Aman, Hammer, & Rojahn, 1993; Bailey et al., 2000; Capone, 2001; Hodapp, et al., 2006; Karmiloff-Smith & Thomas, 2003; King, Hodapp, & Dykens, 2005; Moldavsky et al., 2001; State, King, & Dykens, 1997; Volkmar & Dykens, 2002; Whitman, O' Callaghan, & Sommer, 1997.

some of the physical and behavioral features associated with each. The association of specific syndromes and behavior has led to the notion of behavioral phenotypes, meaning that a genetic disorder predisposes individuals to certain behaviors, some of which may change with development (Hodapp et al., 2006).

Down Syndrome

Down syndrome, the most common single disorder of mental retardation, occurs in 1 in 800 to 1,000 live births (Capone, 2001). The condition was described in 1866 by John Langdon Down, who attributed it to maternal tuberculosis. In 1959, only 3 years after human chromosomes were described, trisomy 21 was discovered in persons with Down syndrome. As shown in Figure 11–4, chromosome 21 appears in a triplet instead of a pair. Ninety-five percent of all cases are attributed to this abnormality, which is caused by failure of the chromosome pair to divide in meiosis, the process in which ova and sperm are formed. Trisomy 21 seems to occur almost randomly, is not inherited, and is mostly traced to the mother. It is related to advancing maternal age, with risk notably higher after age 40.

Although the mechanism through which the extra genes influence development is unknown, several parts of the brain are affected, with abnormalities that include reduced brain size, reduced number and density of neurons, and abnormal dendrites (Capone, 2001). Brain pathology virtually identical to the abnormal plaques and tangles found in Alzheimer's disease is observed by age 35 to 40, and the symptoms of this disease are seen in three-quarters of affected persons by the time they reach 70. There is risk of other serious health problems, such as heart defects, although life expectancy has climbed substantially in recent years (Patja et al., 2000).

Intellectual disability usually is evident during the first few years of life, and amid spurts and regressions the rate of development slows throughout childhood and adolescence (Capone, 2001). Retardation typically ranges from moderate to severe (Moldavsky et al., 2001). Unusually large declines in cognitive and adaptive functioning have inconsistently been reported in adults; these are perhaps related to the development of dementia (Hawkins et al., 2003).

The relative cognitive impairments and strengths associated with Down syndrome are becoming better understood. Most children acquire speech but it is delayed, and expressive language is more affected than comprehension. Evidence exists for deficits in verbal short-term memory and auditory processing

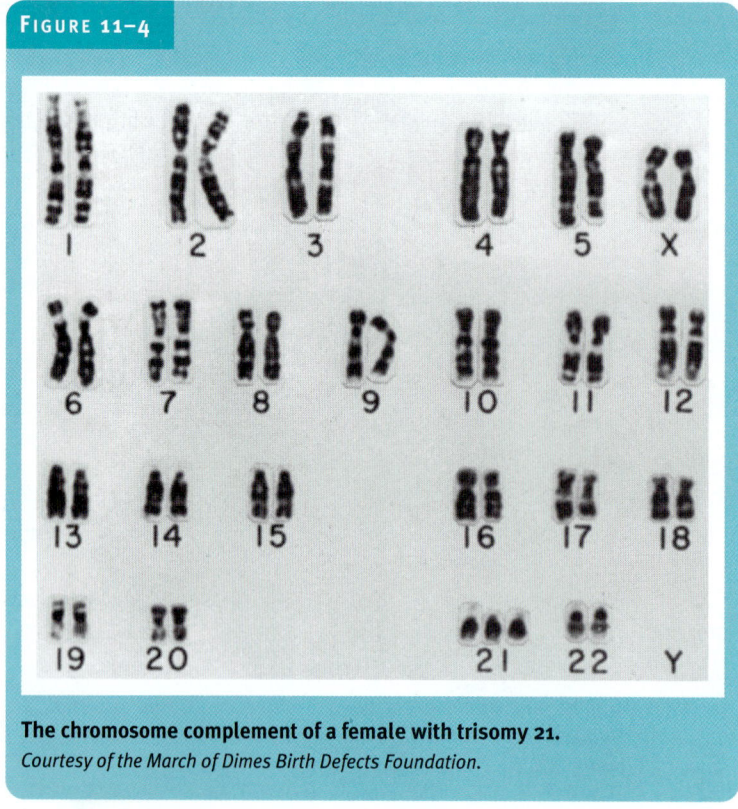

FIGURE 11–4

The chromosome complement of a female with trisomy 21.
Courtesy of the March of Dimes Birth Defects Foundation.

(Laws & Gunn, 2004). Visual–spatial abilities are relatively good.

FRAGILE X SYNDROME

First described in 1969, this syndrome is second to Down syndrome as a cause of mental retardation and is the most common inherited cause. Even so, it is likely not well known by the general public and, in fact, there may be a need for increased knowledge of both fragile X and Down syndromes on the part of practitioners (Lee et al., 2005). (See Figure 11–5.)

Fragile X syndrome occurs in 1 of 4,000 male births and 1 of 8,000 female births (Reiss & Dant, 2003). Much investigative work was necessary to track down the complex X-linked mechanism (Simonoff et al., 1996; Thapar et al., 1994). The disorder involves repeats of a mutation of a triplet of DNA nucleotides (cytosine, guanine, guanine). People in the general population have between 6 and 50 of these repeats; carriers of the syndrome have 50 to 200 repeats. When the number of repeats expands to over 200, the FMR-1 gene is not expressed and the full-blown fragile X syndrome is manifest. In this case, sons are more affected than daughters, whose second X chromosome provides some protection (King et al.,

2005). The number of repeats affects the extent of inactivation of the FMR-1 gene, interference with protein production, and symptom display. Inactivation of the FMR-1 gene is thought to adversely affect synaptic maturation and brain circuitry (Grossman et al., 2003; Reiss & Dant, 2003). Structural abnormalities have been found in several brain areas.

Nearly all males with fragile X have mental retardation, usually moderate. Most children are not identified until about age 3, although parents report earlier concerns (Bailey, Skinner, & Sparkman, 2003). Language skills develop to a level of about 4 years and then plateau. There is a predictable slowing of cognition and adaptive behavior beginning as early as age 5, with development reaching a plateau by later childhood or early adolescence (Reiss & Dant, 2003). Weaknesses are notable in visual–spatial cognition, sequential information processing, motor coordination, arithmetic, and executive functions. Verbal long-term memory and acquired information appear to be relative strengths (Volkmar & Dykens, 2002). Nowhere near as many females with fragile X syndrome display mental retardation, and when they do, it tends to be mild. Learning disabilities, behavior problems, and social impairments are common in females with one affected X chromosome.

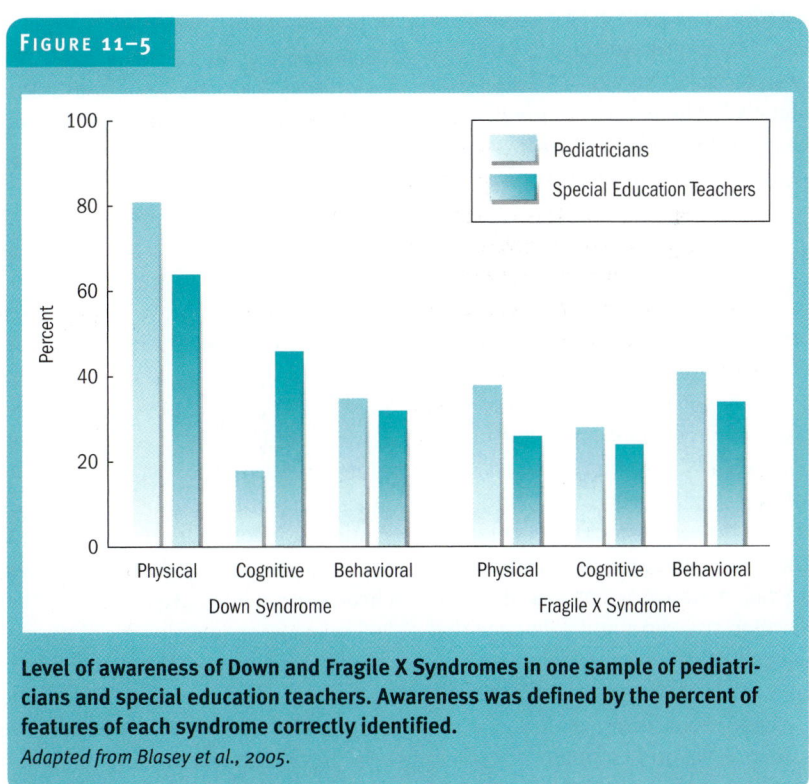

FIGURE 11–5

Level of awareness of Down and Fragile X Syndromes in one sample of pediatricians and special education teachers. Awareness was defined by the percent of features of each syndrome correctly identified.
Adapted from Blasey et al., 2005.

WILLIAMS SYNDROME

This rare syndrome, occurring in an estimated 1 case in 20,000, results from a random mutation involving small deletions of several genes on chromosome 7 (Karmiloff-Smith & Thomas, 2003). Cardiac and kidney problems, hypersensitivity to sound, and deficient depth perception are among the difficulties reported. The syndrome is typically associated with mild to moderate mental retardation, with IQs mostly in the range of 50 to 70. Brain studies have linked the disorder to both the visual system and the frontal lobe (Bower, 2004).

Most striking in Williams syndrome is the difference between visual–spatial abilities and linguistic functioning. Short-term visual–spatial memory is deficient, and visual–spatial skills are far below what would be expected in keeping with the children's mental age. Even at adolescence, there is an inability to perceive gross differences in spatial orientation and to copy simple stick figures. Individuals with Williams syndrome, however, are interested in human faces and can infer "wanting" and "thinking" from facial cues (Elgar & Campbell, 2001).

In contrast, short-term verbal memory is stronger and verbal IQ is typically significantly higher than performance IQ. Children and adults are described as having relative strengths in auditory processing and music. Despite some weaknesses in aspects of language such as syntax and reading, they display strengths in grammar and can employ a sophisticated vocabulary (Laing et al., 2001; Karmiloff-Smith & Thomas, 2003). Many of the characteristic behaviors and abilities of the syndrome are evident in the following case description.

Robert | An Example of Williams Syndrome

Robert was born after a full-term, unremarkable pregnancy. His 38-year-old mother was a music teacher, and his father was a 40-year-old science teacher. His two sisters were healthy and developing well. As a newborn, Robert was extremely fussy and later he was a picky eater. His parents thought him high-strung, and he often cried or cringed when his sisters played too loudly. Robert's milestones were slightly delayed, but a pediatrician reassured his parents that boys often showed slight delay and that Robert was a lively, social child who would catch up.

When Robert was 3 years of age, his parents insisted on an assessment. Modest delays were found in motor, linguistic, and cognitive functioning. He was described as friendly and engaging, a charming child with a cute, appealing face. Robert was enrolled in a special kindergarten and the remainder of his school years was spent in a combination of special and regular classrooms.

At age 7, Robert was assessed as having an IQ of 66, with near-normal short-term memory and expressive language and notable deficits in visual–spatial skills. He had difficulty with writing and arithmetic, loved science and music, and was amazingly conversant when he had the chance to talk with others. Indeed, his parents felt he was overly friendly and active, with passing intense interests in unusual items, such as vacuum cleaners.

During early adolescence, Robert became increasingly anxious. He developed fears of storm clouds and dogs, and refused to ride on elevators. When a sister left for college, he worried about her health and her ability to watch the weather. Despite having nightmares, occasionally pacing with worry, and complaining of stomachaches, Robert attended school, had a small group of friends from Special Olympics, sang in the high school choir, and was often selected to play the piano at school concerts. When Robert was 17 years of age, his parents happened to see a television program on Williams syndrome and were "jolted" to see the similarly between their son and the people being portrayed. Genetic testing confirmed the diagnosis. This led to Robert meeting and engaging in activities with other youth with Williams syndrome and feeling less alone. His parents found a social community with which to share their feelings and concerns.

Adapted from King et al., 2005, p. 3082.

PRADER–WILLI SYNDROME

This syndrome occurs in an estimated 1 in 15,000 births (King et al., 2005). It was first identified in 1956 and is the first human disorder to demonstrate genomic imprinting. The term refers to genes being expressed (activated) depending on whether they are inherited from the mother or father. Prader–Willi syndrome involves genes in a certain area of chromosome 15 that are normally expressed solely by the chromosome inherited from the father (Milner et al., 2005). In approximately 70% of cases of the syndrome, there is a deletion of these genes. In most remaining cases, both chromosomes 15 are inherited from the mother so that the relevant paternal genes are absent.

Intellectual functioning in this syndrome ranges from borderline to moderate levels, with an average

IQ of about 70 (Hodapp et al., 2006). Professionals have been particularly interested in the hyperphagia (excessive eating) and food hoarding that develops between ages 2 and 6, is lifelong, and is a leading cause of death. A disturbance of the brain's hypothalamus is probable. Research also has recently focused on the high rates of nonfood obsessions and compulsions exhibited in Prader–Willi syndrome, which appear during the preschool years. These include skin picking and concerns with exactness, order, cleanliness, and sameness in the environment.

Interestingly, some evidence suggests that the features of Prader–Willi syndrome may be different for the genetic subtypes (King et al., 2005; Milner et al., 2005). Cases of paternal gene deletion may show lower intelligence, especially verbal, and more frequent or severe behavioral difficulties. At the same time, the ability to solve jigsaw puzzles is high. The maternal genetic condition may show decreased performance on visual–spatial tasks, fewer facial characteristics, and a tendency for severe depressive symptoms and impairments in social interaction. Further investigation of these differences is needed

and holds promise—as does research of other syndromes—of advancing our understanding of gene-brain-behavior relationships in development.

Family Accommodations and Experiences

The birth of a child with a disability is likely to be a traumatic and sad event for a family for several reasons. Parents realize that expectations will never be fulfilled, worry about the child, and in some instances experience a stressful and frustrating diagnostic process (Bailey et al., 2003). An unusual amount of attention must be given to the intellectual and psychological needs of the youth, and often to physical needs as well. In addition, parents often confront decisions that are unique or uncommon in typical families concerning, for example, living and school arrangements, health, and future planning for lifetime care and supervision. At times, these decisions may involve especially difficult practical and ethical issues (See Accent: "Deciding What's Best for Children.")

ACCENT ●●●●●

Deciding What's Best for Children

It is not always easy for parents to make decisions about the care and management of children with disabilities, who are limited in giving their own opinions. Two quite different examples can demonstrate this point.

Since the 1970s, an unknown, probably small, number of parents have opted for reconstructive facial surgery for their children with Down syndrome (Goeke et al, 2003). The surgery most often involves multiple procedures that include tongue reduction and implants in the nose, chin, and other facial areas. The stated goals are improved physical functioning (e.g., speech, breathing) and appearance. The distinctive facial features of Down syndrome are readily recognized by the general public, and presumably act to stigmatize the child. Stigmatization, which includes devaluation of the person, prejudice, and discrimination, has long occurred with mental disorders (Hinshaw, 2005; Major & O'Brien, 2005). Reconstructive surgery for Down syndrome is in part an attempt to lessen stigmatization. Nevertheless, questions are raised about whether this goal is met, particularly in light of the pain surgery causes and possible negative psychological effects. It is also suggested that reconstructive

surgery may actually decrease the acceptance of Down syndrome.

More recently, controversy has arisen in the wake of a medical intervention to cause growth attenuation in a 6-year-old girl through high doses of estrogen and removal of the uterus and breast buds (Gunther & Diekema, 2006). The child, who is severely disabled, is cared for at home by loving parents who feared that, as she grew, they would no longer be able to provide care for her. Improved quality of life for the child was the main consideration, and the intervention was approved by a review committee. Strong criticism of the decision has been voiced, including by the AAIDD (AAIDD Position Paper, 2007). The drastic treatment is criticized as having unknown medical risk with no guarantee of avoiding eventual out-of-home care. It is contended that more stringent review was appropriate. The AAIDD also argues that growth attenuation devalues the child's humanity, has the potential for future medical abuse, and should be rejected as a treatment option. At the same time, the organization advocates for the provision of support and services to parents who shoulder the caregiving of children with extraordinary needs.

How should we think about families who have a child with retardation or other developmental disorders? Early investigations focused on determining adverse effects on family members. Today, families are viewed in a more normative way—as similar to other families coping with stress. They are seen as accommodating their lifestyles to their child's needs even as these needs and other circumstances vary over time (Seltzer et al., 2001; von Gonard et al., 2002). Moreover, joy and satisfaction are recognized as part and parcel of their experience.

Numerous influences on family coping and satisfaction exist, including child behavior problems, marital interaction, parental intellectual functioning, daily hassles, siblings' perceptions, social class variables, professional services, and social support (e.g., Atkinson et al., 1995; Sloper et al., 1991; Stoneman & Gavidia-Payne, 2006; Wolf et al., 1998). The effects of having a child with disabilities also may vary with family ethnic/racial background (Neely-Barnes & Marchenko, 2004). Differences have been reported across ethnic/racial groups in perceptions about disability and about participation in the systems that provide services. These numerous factors—child characteristics, family characteristics, and social variables—create a complex picture.

Family members likely are affected in different ways to varying degrees. Mothers may elect not to work outside the home or to work part time (Seltzer et al., 2001). When they are employed, they face greater than usual work-related stress, for example, in finding child care and services for a youngster with unique needs (Parish, 2006; Warfield, 2001). The child's behavioral problems are correlated with parental reports of stress, depression, and anxiety, and mothers may be more affected than fathers (Hastings et al., 2005). But we should not oversimplify how family members are challenged. One study showed, for instance, that mothers are more affected by the child's behavior and fathers by variables external to the child, such as unemployment and financial strain (Sloper et al., 1991). Moreover, marital partners affect each other, and mothers' distress and children's behavior problems have a bidirectional relationship (Hastings et al., 2006).

Siblings also are undoubtedly challenged by the need to accommodate the child with ID. There is evidence that siblings provide more than usual custodial care and emotional support to the child with disabilities (Hannah & Midlarsky, 2005). Siblings may have difficulties in knowing how to talk to others about their sister or brother with disabilities, and they are often socialized to anticipate caring for the child with ID in the future (Orsmond & Seltzer, 2000; Turnbull, 2004).

Youngsters with mental retardation or other developmental disabilities require and benefit from extraordinary care and nurturing from their families. The extent to which these families experience stress, adjust to high demands, and are fulfilled depends on many factors.

(Frank Siteman/Stock Boston)

REWARDS AND SATISFACTIONS

Despite the challenges of rearing a youth with developmental disabilities, many families do well and report positive aspects of their experiences. Scorgie and Sobsey (2000) investigated transformations in the lives of parents of children with disabilities. Transformations were defined as significant positive changes set into motion by a traumatic or challenging event. The parents reported learning to speak out, becoming stronger, seeing life from a new perspective, and having greater compassion. These parents recognized negative aspects of rearing a child with special needs—for example, career limitations and reduced social participation—and they emphasized the importance of balancing the challenging and positive aspects.

Siblings of a youth with disabilities can be well adjusted (Kaminsky & Dewey, 2000), and some report that their experiences led them to increased empathy, patience, acceptance of differences, ability to help others, and appreciation for health and family (Eisenberg, Baker, & Blacher, 1998). One woman, looking back on her extraordinary commitment to her brother with intellectual disabilities, noted:

> *I don't know who I would be if Danny wasn't born. He gave me from a very early age, a direction. He has taught me in his own somewhat unorthodox way about prioritizing and about what's important. . . . And he's taught me compassion and a lot about diversity. . . . Certainly, I have learned patience because he has his own time frame . . . the only thing Danny does quickly is eat . . . . I like to think that being Danny's sister has made me more empathetic. . . . (Flaton, 2006, p. 140–141)*

Fortunately, considerable recognition is now given to more complete portraits of family interaction and functioning. Family systems pespectives focus on understanding numerous family needs and facilitating family quality of life (Turnbull, 2004). Research indicates that helping families identify and obtain community resources can be especially advantageous (Handen & Gilchrist, 2006a). Among others things, these resources can provide child and family therapy, child care, economic assistance, medical and dental care, and adult education.

Assessment

Assessment for intellectual disabilities may be conducted for several purposes. An initial diagnosis of intellectual disabilities can guide parents and teachers, or allow the family to obtain school and community services. Beyond this, more specific information about the child's cognitive strengths and weaknesses can contribute to educational planning. Assessment of the youth's behavioral tendencies and problems, as well as family dynamics, may be necessary for insuring psychological well-being. Medical evaluation can shed light on current or potential health problems, and the diagnosis of a specific syndrome can be valuable in understanding health, intellectual, and behavioral issues. Here, our discussion describes some of the widely used tests to assess intelligence and adaptive behavior; later in the chapter we look at functional assessment as part of an approach to treatment.

DEVELOPMENTAL AND INTELLIGENCE TESTS

Standardized, individually given intelligence tests are central to diagnosing mental retardation. For infants, toddlers, or children with severe deficiency, developmental tests substitute for intelligence tests.

Developmental tests. Several standardized, individually given developmental scales exist. Among the most popular is the Bayley Scales of Infant Development-II, which covers age 1 month to 42 months (Bayley, 1969/1993). Performance on this test is termed developmental quotient (DQ), because it evaluates different abilities than do tests for older children. Infant scales give greater emphasis to sensorimotor functioning and less emphasis to language and abstraction. This feature may partly account for the fact that performance on infant tests is not highly correlated with later IQ in the normal population. However, developmental tests may be better predictors of mental retardation than of average or above intelligence, especially of severe retardation and when other assessment information is also considered.

Stanford–Binet intelligence scale. This test is now in its fifth edition (Roid, 2003). The previous edition was substantially reorganized, but many of its subtests were retained. Five areas are now assessed: Fluid Reasoning, Knowledge, Quantitative Reasoning, Visual–Spatial Processing, and Working Memory. The S–B includes toys and objects helpful in assessing young children, and nonverbal evaluation is possible in each cognitive area. Scores can be obtained for each of the cognitive areas; in addition, a Nonverbal, Verbal, and Full-Scale IQ can be obtained. The standardization group for the S–B fifth edition is a representative U.S. sample, ages 2 to 85 years.

Wechsler tests. These tests are immensely popular for assessing mental retardation. The Wechsler Preschool and Primary Scale of Intelligence (WPPSI-R) is designed for ages 4 to 6.5 years (Wechsler, 2002). It contains subscales that are designated as either verbal or performance tasks. Three IQ scores are calculated: Verbal IQ, Performance IQ, and Full-Scale IQ that combines the verbal and performance scores.

The Wechsler Intelligence Scale for Children–Fourth Edition (WISC-IV) is based more on cognitive models than earlier versions of this test (Wechsler, 2003). Examples of subtests are vocabulary, block design, digit span, and coding. Instead of earning a verbal and performance IQ, the child obtains four index scores: Verbal Comprehension, Perceptual Reasoning, Working Memory, and Processing Speed. A Full-Scale IQ is derived from ten core subtests included in these four indices. The WISC-IV was standardized on a sample of U.S. children ages 6 to 16.

Kaufman tests. The Kaufman Assessment Battery for Children–Second Edition (KABC-II), designed for ages 3 to 18, emphasizes cognitive processing (Kaufman & Kaufman, 2004). Five scales are offered. For example, the sequential processing/short-term memory scale requires step-by-step processing of content, whereas the simultaneous processing scale requires integrating several pieces of visual–spatial information at the same time. The KABC-II permits the evaluator to employ either four or five scales based on two different models relevant to the reason for referral or the child's background. One of the models is more applicable to the child from a mainstream language and cultural background, whereas the other may be more suitable for a child of different background. Both models result in a global intelligence score. The Kaufman tests also include the Adolescent and Adult Intelligence Test (KAIT), designed for ages 11 and up.

ASSESSING ADAPTIVE BEHAVIOR

Adaptive behavior can be assessed through interviews with families or caretakers, direct observation, and self-report in some cases. Several standardized scales have been constructed, and attention has been given to reliability and validity.

Vineland adaptive behavior scales. These scales, originated by Doll at the Vineland Training School, are available in the second edition (Sparrow, Cicchetti, & Balla, 2005). Information can be collected for individuals from birth to age 90 through semistructured interviews or rating scales with parents or caregivers. Also available is a questionnaire for teachers to assess individuals ages 3 through 21 years. The scales cover communication, daily living skills, socialization, and motor skills. In addition, the optional domain of maladaptive behavior can be used (Table 11–9). Scores from the separate domains and an overall score can be compared with scores from a normal standard group and special groups with disabilities. Research has suggested that the Vineland scales differentiate among different disorders and do measure what they are intended to measure (Balboni et al., 2001).

Adaptive behavior scales. For several years, the AAIDD has published adaptive behavior scales to be employed in the schools and community (Luckasson et al., 2002). The Adaptive Behavior Scales–School Edition (ABS-S:2) examines a wide range of behaviors that include language development, physical development, personal and community self-sufficiency, social responsibility, and adjustment. The comparison norm groups consist of public school children, ages 3 through 16, with or without disabilities. This scale is designed to guide school personnel with regard to the child. The Adaptive Behavior Scales–Residential

TABLE 11–9	DOMAINS EVALUATED BY THE VINELAND ADAPTIVE BEHAVIOR SCALES (VINELAND-II)
Communication	Receptive Expressive Written
Daily Living Skills	Personal Domestic Community
Socialization	Interpersonal Relationships Play and Leisure Time Coping Skills
Motor Skills	Fine Gross
Maladaptive Behavior (optional)	Internalizing Externalizing Other

and Community (ABS-RC:2), which taps many of the same factors as the school scale, is based on performance of persons ages 18 and over with developmental disabilities.

AAIDD's assessment for supports. AAIDD has developed guidelines for assessing each person's needs for supports (Luckasson et al., 2002). Although this is not assessment for adaptive behavior, the idea of needed support is aligned with facilitating adaptive behaior. Consistent with the AAIDD's philosophy, the aim is to provide services to improve the functional capabilities of those with ID (p. 297). The process involves identifying the areas in which support is needed, appropriate support activities, and the level of support needed in each activity. For example, an adolescent may require aid in interacting with community members or in personal hygiene. Support could be provided through simple monitoring, teaching activities, or physical supports. The level of support judged necessary could range from minimal to substantial. The AAIDD also has published the Supports Intensity Scale, based on an interview that evaluates practical support needs in 85 daily living, medical, and behavioral areas (Thompson et al., 2004). Based on norms for adults with developmental disabilities, it is appropriate for persons 16 years and over and thus has limited application to youth.

Intervention

CHANGING VIEWS, GREATER OPPORTUNITIES

Attitudes toward intellectual disabilities have reflected the general beliefs of the times and have influenced how those with retardation were treated by the societies in which they lived (Cytryn & Lourie, 1980). Modern attitudes can be traced to the late 1700s and the case of the "Wild Boy of Aveyron," otherwise known as Victor. The boy, first seen running naked through the woods, was captured and assigned to a medical officer, Jean M. Itard, at the National Institute for the Deaf and Dumb in Paris. Victor's senses were underdeveloped; his memory, attention, and reasoning were deficient; and his ability to communicate was almost nil (Itard, as cited in Harrison & McDermott, 1972). Itard attributed the boy's deficits to lack of contact with civilized people, but the treatment he designed failed and Victor remained in custodial care until his death. Despite the unfortunate outcome, Itard's effort stimulated interest in the "feebleminded" or "retarded" (Rie, 1971).

The middle to late 1800s saw a favorable climate spread across the United States. Residential schools opened to educate children with retardation and then return them to the community (Szymanski & Crocker, 1985). Unfortunately, optimism waned as increased interest in biological causation, the rise of psychoanalysis, and the misuse or misunderstanding of IQ tests strengthened the belief that persons with mental retardation could hardly be helped and were a detriment, if not a danger, to society. Widespread institutionalization and custodial care ensued, with institutions growing in number and size throughout the first half of the 20th century.

The last several decades have again witnessed more favorable attitudes, conditions, and interventions. In addition to increased knowledge and scientific advances, the 1960s brought commitment to the rights of poor, handicapped, and minority populations. Extensively adopted was the philosophy of normalization, which contends that each individual has the right to life experiences that are as normal and as least restrictive as possible. Normalization has influenced many aspects of life for people with ID, including living arrangements and worklife, educational services, and treatments.

Regarding living arrangements, at one time families were encouraged to place their children in out-of-home care (Llewellyn et al., 1999). Although some individual circumstances still warrant this arrangement, attitudes have dramatically shifted. Residence in large state institutions in the United States decreased from the late 1970s, and closures or downsizing of institutions has continued (Coucouvanis et al., 2003; Lakin et al., 2003). (See Figure 11–6.) In place are small out-of-home settings, which generally have improved the quality of life for residents (Felce, 2006). Moreover, most youth with intellectual disabilities currently live at home and to varying degrees are integrated into their neighborhoods. Because ID usually persists at some level, concern for these young people underscores the need for social and work opportunities in their adult years. Indeed, opportunity for supported employment in the community has increased over several years, although further improvement is needed (Braddock, Rizzolo, & Hemp, 2004).

When applied to intervention for mental retardation, the goal of normalization is to produce behaviors that are as normal as possible by employing methods that are as culturally normal as possible (Mesibov, 1992; Thompson & McEvoy, 1992; Wolfensberger, 1980). This applies to prevention, educational efforts, and treatment.

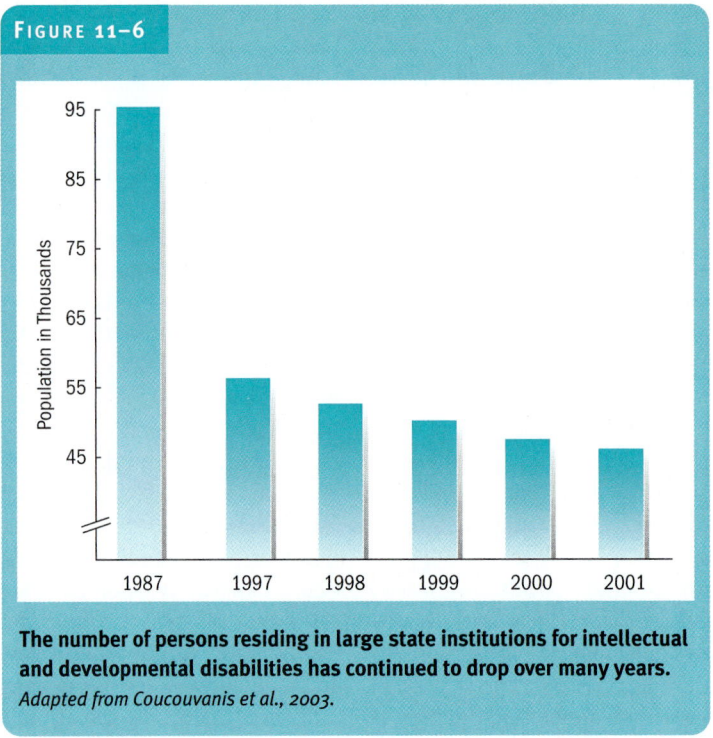

FIGURE 11–6

The number of persons residing in large state institutions for intellectual and developmental disabilities has continued to drop over many years.
Adapted from Coucouvanis et al., 2003.

PREVENTION

In keeping with the multiple risks and causes of mental retardation, prevention efforts vary substantially. Universal prevention includes prenatal care and diet, as well the avoidance of alcohol and other teratogens during pregnancy. Advances in genetics have contributed to prevention, for example, by early detection of PKU, which enables immediate dietary adjustments to reduce intellectual disabilities. Efforts continue to identify and reduce environmental chemicals that adversely affect prenatal and postnatal cognitive development.

The provision of early intervention programs that focus on at-risk infants and preschoolers is an important selective prevention effort. Many of the programs emphasize child and family needs, include several elements, and often entail an educational component. (See Accent: "Examples of Early Intervention Programs.") The federal government has been instrumental in encouraging early educational intervention through the Individuals with Disabilities Education Act (IDEA) (Beirne-Smith, Patton, & Kim, 2006). Conceptually, these programs transition to the school system, where some of the practices and policies of the educational system can be viewed as measures to prevent intellectual decline or the development of social and psychological problems.

Medical advances have lowered the death rate of premature or low birthweight infants and investigations are under way in how best to optimize development and prevent problems.
(Jonathan Nourok/PhotoEdit Inc.)

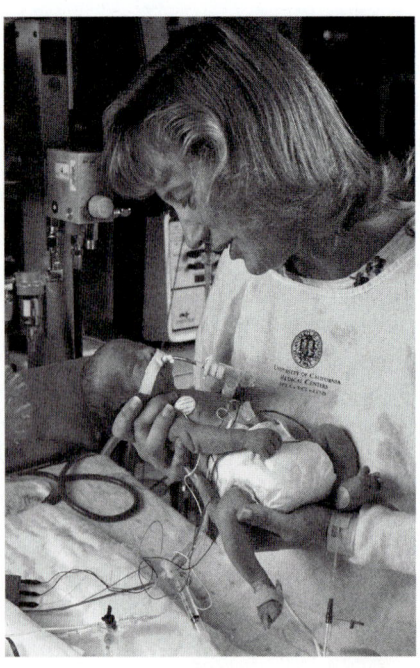

ACCENT ● ● ● ● ●

Examples of Early Intervention Programs

One type of early intervention for at-risk infants is programs to prevent or reduce adverse outcomes of low birthweight or prematurity, including developmental delay and later school failure (Field, Hernandez-Reif, & Freedman, 2004). An example is the multisite Infant Health and Development Program, a comprehensive 3-year randomized clinical trial that consisted of home visits, family education and support, and educational day care for the children (Bradley et al., 1994). Evaluation of these at-risk children at age 3 showed several positive effects, including benefits to cognitive development. At age 8, children of relatively high birthweight (2,100–2,500 grams), but not those weighing less, showed some cognitive and academic benefits (McCarton et al., 1997). At age 18, this group had better language skills and mathematics achievement, although there was no difference from controls in grade retention and special-education placement (Olds, Sadlar, & Kitzman, 2007).

In a very different type of program to prevent adverse effects of low birthweight or prematurity, newborns receive systematic bodily massage (e.g., Dieter et al., 2003; Field et al., 2004). Treated infants achieve significantly greater weight gain, earlier hospital discharge, and other positive outcomes, which may enhance parent–infant interactions and thus development. Investigations of which types of interventions are best for which at-risk infants, and of the long-term effects of the programs, are needed (Lester, Bigsby, & Miller-Loncar, 2004).

Among the most significant early intervention efforts are multipurpose programs for preschoolers designed to reduce the risks of economic disadvantage. It is assumed that early experience is vital for intellectual, as well as social, growth. Examples are the Abecedarian project (p. 78) and Head Start, which was initiated by the federal government in 1965 (Ripple & Zigler, 2003). In addition to a child educational component, Head Start includes child health care, parent education and involvement, and social services. It now serves children from birth to age 5, including those with disabilities. Over a 30-year period, the effectiveness of preschool interventions, including that of Head Start, has been studied (Guralnick, 1998; Ramey, 1999; Ramey & Ramey, 1998; St. Pierre & Layzer, 1998). Among the conclusions is that (1) children in these programs receive cognitive and social benefits and (2) it is crucial to continue educational and other supports into childhood.

As we turn to school services and treatments, the multiple needs of youth with ID must be recognized. Intervention can be as varied as medication to control seizures, programs to teach self-help or social skills, efforts to reduce maladaptive behaviors, academic classes in reading or arithmetic, and counseling. The following discussion examines, to varying degrees, educational services, behavioral intervention, pharmacological treatment, and psychotherapy.

EDUCATIONAL SERVICES

The adoption of IDEA has dramatically, if gradually, changed access to public education for persons with intellectual disabilities. It has strengthened individualized programming for children with retardation, increased parents' participation in the education of their offspring, and provided greater opportunity for alternative educational settings. Despite variation that exists across school districts and regions, more children with ID are attending local schools and joining their peers in general classrooms. The following description provides a glance into one boy's school experiences.

Brian | Life in the Mainstream

Brian is a 17-year-old boy with moderate mental retardation associated with Down syndrome. He has been mainstreamed with same-age peers throughout his schooling with the support of classroom aides. Brian, whose IQ is 53, has some difficulties with articulation, and his language consists mainly of two- to four-word sentences. Recently, he was introduced to reading and he now can read 50 sight words. Although he occasionally has difficulty managing anxiety and can be stubborn, Brian is well liked by his teachers and classmates, and his parents boast that he has been a charming, pleasant child from infancy. In addition to attending classes at the local high school, Brian is an assistant manager for the high school's cross-country team and actively participates in Special Olympics. He also spends time learning job skills in community settings.

Adapted from King et al., 2005, p. 3083–3084.

The benefits of special educational settings, mainstreaming, and inclusion have been questioned, just as they have been for other kinds of disabilities. However, students with mental retardation can be successfully integrated into community schools, and outcome is influenced more by instructional and other classroom features than by placement itself. Effective inclusion does require considerable investment of resources, time, effort, and teacher commitment (Hocutt, 1996; Beirne-Smith et al., 2006).

The inclusion of students with severe retardation—many of whom have physical disabilities and special health needs—is especially challenging. Parents of these children are not always supportive. In a study that asked parents whether full inclusion would be a "good idea," 45% answered in the negative regarding their child (Palmer et al., 2001). The most cited

Increased numbers of children with mental handicaps now are attending community schools in which they are fully or partially integrated into general education classrooms.

(Richard Hutchings/Photo Researchers, Inc.)

reason was belief that the child's impairments precluded any benefit. In the words of one parent:

My daughter is like an infant physically and a toddler emotionally, socially, intellectually ... advancing a child like my daughter along with her peer group would be isolating and inappropriate (p. 475).

The second most commonly cited reason was the belief that full inclusion would place undue burden on teachers and be detrimental to typically developing students. These parents also were concerned that their child's needs for a curriculum that emphasizes basic living skills or functional skills would not be met and also that their child might be neglected, harmed, or ridiculed.

Transition. Consistent with the philosophy of normalization is concern about what happens to youth with ID when they leave the school system. Since 1990, IDEA specifies that all children should have a transition plan as part of their Individual Education Plan (IEP) (AAIDD Fact Sheet, 2007). Members of the IEP team have the task of identifying future community work, living, and educational opportunities, as well as the skills and knowledge required by the student. Mercer and Mercer (2001) note that all successful plans must include academic programs that prepare the student for independent work or further schooling; vocational education; self-advocacy training; and collaboration among professionals, family, and potential employers. It is promising that intervention for ID has increasingly incorporated community integration across the lifespan.

BEHAVIORAL INTERVENTION AND SUPPORT

In the 1960s, advocates of behavior modification began to work in institutions that previously provided custodial care but little training or education (Whitman, Hantula, & Spence, 1990). Behavior modification gradually became dominant and was the subject of an enormous amount of research. A wide range of behaviors at all levels of handicap was targeted. Operant procedures were used to enhance adaptive skills and reduce maladaptive behavior.

Over the years, behavioral techniques have progressed. Guidelines have been established for various methods, and precision in teaching and generalization of learned skills have been advanced (Handen, 1998). An important distinction has been made between discrete trial learning and naturalistic, or incidental, learning. In discrete trial learning, the clinician selects the task to be learned and provides clear directives, prompts, and consequences for appropriate behavior. Teaching is usually conducted in a quiet place, away from distractions. In naturalistic learning the teaching situation is informal and less structured. It is more likely to be initiated by the child, amidst everyday contexts; for example, the child's request for a toy is used as an opportunity for teaching. Both discrete trial learning and naturalistic learning have been shown to be effective, and naturalistic learning is believed to be especially effective for generalization of learning.

Efforts have also been made to train those who work with youngsters with mental retardation—in the home, school, community programs, or residential placements. Courses and curricula have been developed to disseminate information to caregivers. Parent training has been shown to be effective, and parents can profit from ongoing contact with professionals (Handen, 1998). Overall, behavioral intervention has had considerable success in serving young people with ID.

Enhancing adaptive behavior. Operant techniques have been employed to enhance a variety of adaptive behaviors. These include self-help skills, imitation, language, social behavior, academic skills, and work behaviors. Here, we comment on two of these areas.

The acquisition of daily living skills is an important goal of intervention. For youths with more severe levels of retardation, it may be a central component (Beirne-Smith et al., 2006). Children and adolescents who cannot dress and feed themselves or otherwise cannot take care of their basic needs are often limited from participating in educational and social activities. Those who are unable to shop, order food in restaurants, wash their clothes, or catch a bus can hardly enjoy independence in community living. Thus self-help programs target a gamut of adaptive behaviors.

Considerable attention also has been given to facilitate social skills, mostly but not exclusively for mild and moderate retardation (e.g., Matson, LeBlanc, Weinheimer, 1999). Training has been provided in various settings and has included behavioral and cognitive-behavioral techniques such as instruction, self-instruction, modeling, role playing, and reinforcement (Hughes, 1999; Marchetti & Campbell, 1990). The presence of normally developing peers has been shown to facilitate social interaction, as have teacher encouragement and prompts (Handen & Gilchrist, 2006a). In addition to these treatments, it is recognized that everyday activities can enhance social development. For example, participation in the Special Olympics by persons with mental retardation has been linked with social competence (Dykens & Cohen, 1996).

Reducing maladaptive behavior. Self-stimulation, bizarre speech, tantrums, aggression, and self-injury are among the behaviors that interfere with social relationships, learning, and community living—and sometimes directly harm individuals with ID. A variety of techniques have been employed to reduce these behaviors, and success has been documented with single-subject research designs.

In this discussion, we emphasize self-injury because intervention for this behavior has been especially problematic. The rate of repetitious self-injurious behavior (SIB), which usually disappears in typically developing children by school age, varies, and it may be more common at the lower levels of retardation (Handen & Gilchrist, 2006a). Self-injurious behaviors differ in form—head banging, biting, hitting the self, and such—and intensity ranges from

Special Olympics is an example of community programs that attempt to normalize the lives of youth with retardation and to provide opportunities to develop social skills as well as a sense of accomplishment and self-worth.
(AP Wide World Photos)

minor to life-threatening damage. Biological or environmental factors, or their combination, may underlie the behavior (Mace et al., 1998). The association of SIB with Lesch–Nyhan and other genetic syndromes suggests an abnormal organic need for sensory stimulation that self-injurious behavior might provide. Even so, SIB is clearly influenced by environmental variables.

The history of treating SIB shows that it can be relatively difficult to change (Bregman & Gerdtz, 1997). Medications are only somewhat successful, and early behavioral interventions often failed. When self-injury threatened the child and interventions were ineffective, punishments such as squirting lemon juice into the mouth and contingent electric shock were sometimes employed. Although aversive consequences can be somewhat effective, they raise serious ethical questions and are dissonant with a respectful approach to treatment. They are not now recommended or recommended only in brief interventions for severe cases after review and consent (AAIDD/ARC Position Papers, 2007; Bregman & Gerdtz, 1997). Effective and more acceptable procedures have evolved.

POSITIVE BEHAVIOR SUPPORT. This approach, which aims to reduce problem behaviors in natural settings, relies on behavioral principles and functional assessment or analysis (Handen & Gilchrist,

2006a). It often incorporates the teaching of a new response that will substitute for the maladaptive behavior.

Among others, Newsom (1998) has discussed variables that influence maladaptive behaviors. Figure 11–7 shows a schema that can be applied to SIB. *Setting events* are background variables that can change the probability that the behavior will occur. For example, fatigue can make it more likely that the child will respond with SIB. *Antecedent stimuli* occur just prior to self-injury and precipitate the behavior. *Positive consequences* for SIB are critical in maintaining it. Self-injury can be positively reinforced with tangibles such as food and activities, or attention from caretakers as they try to verbally deter a child from engaging in self-injury. Self-injury also can be negatively reinforced. For example, when unwanted demands are made, the child may engage in self-injury, with the result that caregivers may cease to make the demands—thereby negatively reinforcing SIB. This schema of variables points to ways in which a challenging behavior can be modified. Altering the setting events and antecedent stimuli—for example, by avoiding them altogether—can prevent SIB from occurring at all. Altering reinforcement contingencies or teaching the child a behavior to substitute for the already-occurring maladaptive behavior can reduce self-injury.

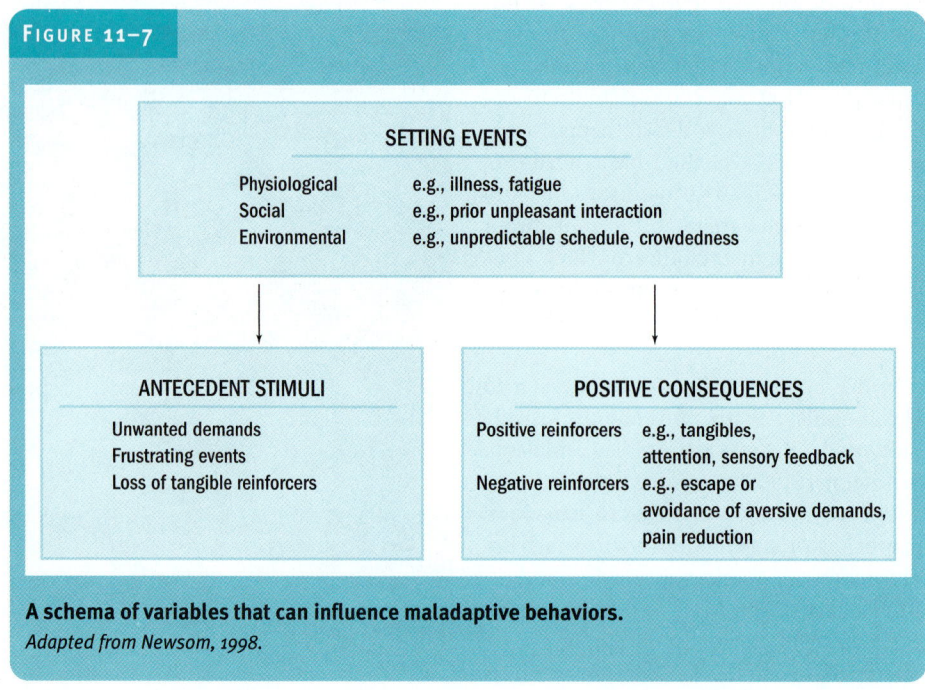

FIGURE 11–7

SETTING EVENTS

Physiological	e.g., illness, fatigue
Social	e.g., prior unpleasant interaction
Environmental	e.g., unpredictable schedule, crowdedness

ANTECEDENT STIMULI

Unwanted demands
Frustrating events
Loss of tangible reinforcers

POSITIVE CONSEQUENCES

| Positive reinforcers | e.g., tangibles, attention, sensory feedback |
| Negative reinforcers | e.g., escape or avoidance of aversive demands, pain reduction |

A schema of variables that can influence maladaptive behaviors.
Adapted from Newsom, 1998.

Importantly, specific treatment plans are based on assessing how the child is behaving in what situations, with what consequences, and perhaps with what intent. Evaluation is accomplished with a functional assessment or a functional analysis (Handen & Gilchrist, 2006a). Functional assessment acquires information from detailed interviews with adults interacting with the child and observation of the child in the natural setting. In contrast, functional analysis entails a manipulation of variables to determine their influence on the behavior. For a demonstration of its use, see Accent: "Functional Communication Training."

Research findings support the effectiveness of positive behavior support. More generally, the American Psychological Association considers behavioral interventions to be empirically validated treatment for developmental disabilities (Handen & Gilchrist, 2006a).

PHARMACOLOGICAL TREATMENT

Medications are not known to strengthen intellectual functioning in cases of retardation but are aimed at alleviating medical or psychological symptoms. One study reported that 2 to 7% of children living in the community received psychotropic drugs, and this number rose to 19 to 33% when antiseizure medications were considered (Singh et al., 1998). As might be expected, drug treatment generally increases with the number and severity of behavioral problems. And it is generally higher for those living in institutions, particularly in larger institutions or institutions with restrictive environments. Features of these institutions certainly may be partly responsible for high medication use, but individuals who are institutionalized also are more likely to have behavioral problems to begin with.

ACCENT

Functional Communication Training

Functional Communication Training aims to reduce challenging behavior by encouraging the child to substitute in its place an adaptive behavior. It is assumed that maladaptive behaviors are often used intentionally as a way to communicate needs or desires. The first step in Functional Communication Training is functional analysis; the second is to select and train a more positive way to communicate.

The approach is exemplified in the case of Matt, a 5-year-old boy who was diagnosed with moderate mental retardation and cerebral palsy (Durand, 1999). Matt lived with his parents and attended a school for students with developmental disabilities. He lacked verbal language, but he was able to point to express his desires. Matt frequently bit his hand and screamed—behaviors that had not succumbed to prior interventions. The treatment strategy had several components:

- Matt's teacher was trained to conduct the intervention in the classroom.
- The teacher determined the circumstances in which Matt most frequently engaged in self-biting and screaming. She assessed Matt's behavior by using a rating scale and also by systematically observing his behavior under four conditions: low teacher

attention during a task, low access to a preferred tangible object during a task, a more difficult task, and a control condition. This analysis showed that Matt's maladaptive behavior occurred when he was faced with a difficult task.

- Matt was trained to ask for help on difficult tasks by pressing a pad on a device, which activated a voice saying "I need help."
- The effectiveness of the training was evaluated.

The entire intervention required several weeks. The results of the functional analysis (A) and the final evaluation of Matt's behavior (B) are shown in Figure 11–8. The positive outcome is consistent with similar studies showing the effectiveness of Functional Communication Training in which youngsters are taught to communicate their desires through adaptive spoken language or with mechanical devices when needed. This particular study is interesting in that it included trips to a community store in which Matt had experienced difficulty and frustration handling money as he purchased candy. After intervention, Matt used the mechanical device to ask the shopkeeper for help in managing his money.

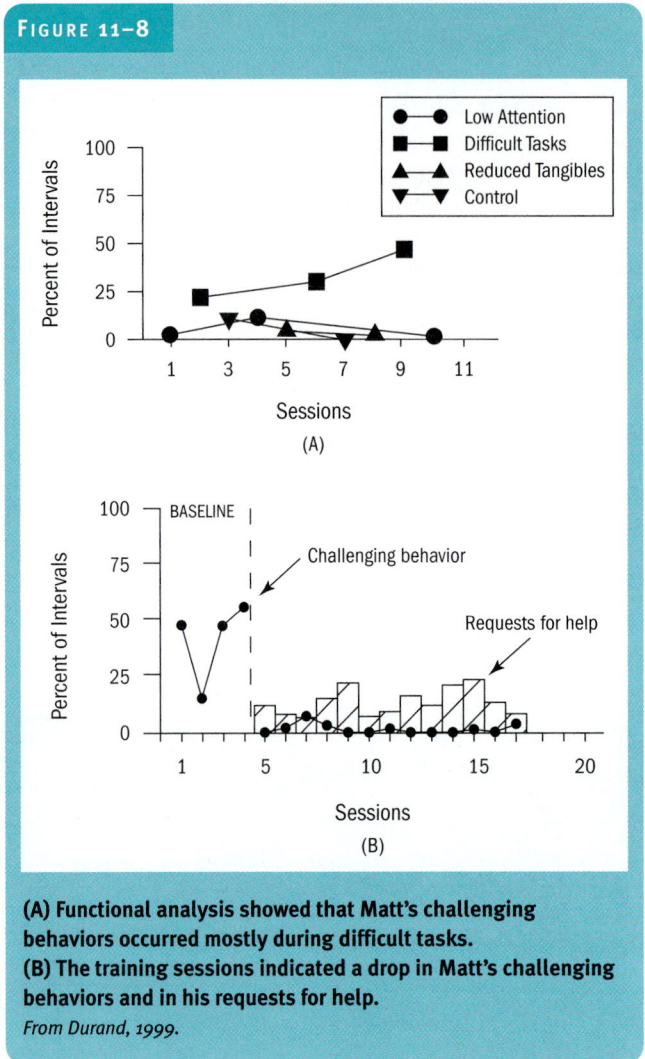

FIGURE 11–8

(A) Functional analysis showed that Matt's challenging behaviors occurred mostly during difficult tasks.
(B) The training sessions indicated a drop in Matt's challenging behaviors and in his requests for help.
From Durand, 1999.

Given the prevalence and variation of problems associated with ID, all major categories of medications have been used: stimulants, antipsychotics, antidepressants, antianxiety medications, and others. Limited evidence exists for the effectiveness of pharmacological treatment. The symptoms of ADHD, which affect perhaps 9 to 16% of children with ID, lessen with stimulant medication. However, response rates are lower than for typical cases of ADHD and negative side effects may be greater (Handen & Gilchrist, 2006b; Pearson et al., 2004). Typical antipsychotic medications have been used to treat aggression, hyperactivity, antisocial behavior, and stereotypes. More recently, the newer atypical antipsychotic medications became the treatment of choice, with some research supporting their efficacy and safety.

However, studies of effectiveness are inadequate both for youth and adults. It is clear that the manage-ment of medication for youths with ID requires special consideration. Careful monitoring is necessary because the difficulty of diagnosing comorbid psychopathology raises the issue of the appropriateness of any prescribed medication. Added to this, determining the effectiveness and side effects of drugs is challenging due to youth's limited ability to describe what they are experiencing. Possible drug interactions also require a watchful eye, particularly in cases involving medical conditions (King et al., 2000). Limited research does indicate that medication response is similar to that shown by other populations, but that fewer persons with ID benefit from medications and that negative side effects are more frequent (Handen & Gilchrist, 2006b; King et al., 2005). Moreover, concern exists over questionable practices. For example, antipsychotic medications appear to be overused or prescribed at excessively high dosages, according to studies in the United Kingdom (Hodapp et al., 2006).

PSYCHOTHERAPY

Research into the use and effectiveness of psychotherapy for individuals with ID is scant (Beail, 2003; Handen & Gilchrist, 2006a). There is some indication that professionals recommend behavioral interventions over more traditional counseling or "talking" approaches. In addition, the literature indicates disagreement on the effectiveness and usefulness of psychotherapy. Some professionals argue that it has little or no place in treating youth with intellectual disabilities (Sturmey, 2005). Others argue that it should not be precluded in the presence of mild and moderate intellectual deficits (Hurley, 2005).

It is agreed that psychotherapy techniques must be adapted to the developmental level of the child or adolescent (King et al., 2000). For instance, therapists should probably be directive and set specific goals. Language should be concrete and clear, and nonverbal techniques (e.g., play or other activities) are necessary when communication deficits exist. Short, frequent sessions also may be required.

Substantial agreement also exists that the research on psychotherapy is methodologically weak (Handen & Gilchrist, 2006a; Prout & Nowak-Drabik, 2003). There is an interest in encouraging high-quality investigation into what psychotherapy methods are effective for what kinds of problems and at what level of retardation.

SUMMARY

DEFINITION AND CLASSIFICATION

- *Mental retardation/intellectual disabilities is defined by subaverage intellectual functioning with concurrent deficits in adaptive skills manifested before age 18.*
- *The AAIDD views ID as multidimensional, with environmental supports mediating outcome.*
- *The AAIDD classifies intellectual disabilities by levels of needed supports. The DSM classifies them according to four IQ levels. About 85% of cases are of mild retardation.*

NATURE OF INTELLIGENCE AND ADAPTIVE BEHAVIOR

- *Binet and colleagues viewed intelligence as somewhat malleable and influenced by the social environment. The subsequent assumption of fixed inheritance and the misuse of intelligence tests resulted in controversies and legal battles.*
- *Measured intelligence is relatively stable for most people and correlates reasonably well with academic-related achievements. IQ scores must be interpreted with care, however.*
- *Adaptive behavior refers to domains of everyday behavior, such as self-help and social competence. It correlates with IQ, but is not the same as measured intelligence.*

DESCRIPTION

- *The abilities of young people with ID show immense variation, as exemplified by IQ levels and individual profiles of characteristics. Various levels of difficulties are manifest in physical and medical attributes, learning and cognitive ability, and social functioning.*

CO-OCCURRING DISORDERS

- *Rates of psychological problems and disorders are high in youths with ID. The kinds of problems appear similar to those in the general population, but can be difficult to identify and diagnose.*

EPIDEMIOLOGY

- *The prevalence of ID in the general population is 1 to 3%, depending on the criterion used and on sampling. Rates are disproportionately high in school-age children, males, and individuals of lower social class.*

DEVELOPMENTAL COURSE AND CONSIDERATIONS

- *The developmental course and outcome of mental retardation varies widely but most youths will require some degree of support throughout life.*
- *Compared with typically developing intelligence, the intellectual abilities of youth with ID tend to develop*

in the same sequences but at slower rates. Specific deficits may be exhibited, depending on level of retardation and/or etiology.

ETIOLOGY

- *The historic two-group approach to etiology conceptualized ID as falling into an organic or a cultural–familial group.*

- *Organic influences, which are associated with more severe retardation, can originate in genetic, prenatal, birth, or postnatal adversities.*

- *Multiple-gene effects are considered especially important in mild MR of unknown etiology, which can be viewed as representing the lower end of the distribution of intelligence in the population.*

- *Psychosocial influences, which may operate across generations of socially disadvantaged families, is also viewed as particularly relevant to milder levels of retardation.*

- *AAIDD's multiple risk model reflects the current perspective of etiology as complex and interactive.*

GENETIC SYNDROMES AND BEHAVIORAL PHENOTYPES

- *Genetic syndromes—such as Down, fragile X, Williams, and Prader–Willi—are currently receiving much research attention. Each syndrome tends to be associated with a particular physical, cognitive, and behavioral phenotype.*

FAMILY ACCOMMODATIONS AND EXPERIENCES

- *Family adjustment to having a child with ID is influenced by child characteristics, family characteristics, and social variables.*

- *Family members likely are affected differently and families experience both unique stress and rewards.*

ASSESSMENT

- *Assessment of ID is best guided by its goals. In addition to the evaluation of intelligence and adaptive behavior with standardized scales, assessment can target needed supports, co-occurring psychopathology, family functioning, and medical status.*

INTERVENTION

- *Historically, treatment for ID has varied in approach and quality. In recent decades there has been heightened concern for the rights of youth with ID, and the philosophy of normalization has taken center stage.*

- *Primary and selective prevention for ID targets prenatal care, diet, genetic conditions, environmental risks, and the risks of low birthweight and economic disadvantage.*

- *IDEA and related policies have brought increased educational integration to students with ID, although complex issues remain about school inclusion.*

- *A range of behavioral techniques are effective in strengthening appropriate skills and weakening maladaptive behaviors. Positive behavior support and functional assessment and functional analysis are effective approaches.*

- *Pharmacological treatment and psychotherapy are both in need of controlled outcome studies. The former is relatively common; it can be effective for some medical and behavioral disturbances but requires especially careful monitoring. Psychotherapy, with adaptations, arguably may be useful in mild or moderate ID.*

KEY TERMS ●●●●●●●●●

mental age *(p. 299)*

intelligence quotient *(p. 299)*

eugenics *(p. 299)*

Flynn effect *(p. 301)*

overshadowing *(p. 304)*

two-group approach *(p. 306)*

organic mental retardation *(p. 307)*

cultural–familial retardation *(p. 307)*

behavioral phenotype *(p. 310)*

normalization *(p. 317)*

discrete trial learning *(p. 321)*

naturalistic (incidental) learning *(p. 321)*

self-injurious behavior *(p. 321)*

positve behavior support *(p. 322)*

functional assessment *(p. 323)*

functional analysis *(p. 323)*

CHAPTER 12

Pervasive Developmental Disorders and Schizophrenia

The disorders discussed in this chapter are characterized by pervasive problems in social, emotional, and cognitive functioning, which have a basis in neurobiological abnormality. Development may be qualitatively different from typical development in ways that have compelled an enormous amount of interest and investigation. Pervasive developmental disorders and schizophrenia are now considered independent from each other, but they share a rich history.

A Bit of History

Although the disorders we are about to discuss have long been recognized, confusion and debate have surrounded them. Historically, these disorders were associated with adult psychoses—that is, severely disruptive disturbances implying abnormal perceptions of reality. Psychotic disturbances were noted in early 20th-century classifications of mental disorders based on Kraepelin's work. Bleuler applied the term *schizophrenias* to these disorders, which involve disturbances in reality, such as hearing voices and seeing images that do not exist. Investigators noted a small percentage of cases that had begun in childhood (Marenco & Weinberger, 2000).

Ideas about psychoses and other severe disturbances developed gradually over many years. Some investigators described groups of children with early onset of schizophrenia, and others pointed to syndromes that appeared similar, but not identical, to schizophrenia. Various diagnostic terms were applied, including *disintegrative psychoses* and *childhood psychoses*. Beginning around 1930 and for several years afterward, *childhood schizophrenia* served as a general label, while numerous subcategories were employed (Volkmar, 1987; Rutter & Schopler, 1987).

In 1943, Leo Kanner described what he called "early infantile autism," arguing that it was different from other cases of severe disturbance, which generally had later onset. One year later, Hans Asperger described a group of children whose symptoms overlapped with Kanner's cases. Although these men did not know each other—and apparently believed they were writing about different types of disturbance—today autism and Asperger syndrome are viewed as similar disorders (Frith, 2004).

By the early 1970s, data from several countries showed that severe disturbances were age related, with a relatively large number of cases appearing before age 3, remarkably low prevalence in childhood, and increased prevalence in adolescence (Kolvin, 1971). This pattern suggested that different syndromes might underlie the earlier-occurring and later-occurring disturbances. Several investigators argued that children whose problems appeared early were different from those whose problems came later, not only in behavior but also in social class, family history, and other factors (Dawson & Castelloe, 1992).

Only gradually was a distinction made between schizophrenia and a group of related disorders, today referred to as pervasive developmental disorders. Schizophrenia is a psychotic disturbance that affects a small number of children, rises in frequency in adolescence, and increases still more in early adulthood. The DSM recognizes a broad category that includes schizophrenia and applies to all age groups. Pervasive developmental disorders are early-occurring, nonpsychotic disturbances that are qualitatively deviant from a person's developmental level. The DSM includes five disorders under the category of Pervasive Developmental Disorders (PDDs). These are Autistic Disorder (autism), Asperger's Disorder, Rett's Disorder, Childhood Disintegrative Disorder, and Pervasive Developmental Disorder Not Otherwise Specified (PDD-NOS). Autism has by far been the most studied, but greater attention is now given to the other PDDs. In addition, three of the PDDs are now believed to fall into a continuum of autism: Autistic Disorder, Asperger's Disorder, and PDD-NOS. Our discussion emphasizes autism, given its dominant role, but we also address the related disorders.

Austistic Disorder

DSM Classification and Diagnosis

Kanner's early descriptions of autism noted communication deficits, good but atypical cognitive potential, and behavioral problems such as obsessiveness, repetitive actions, and unimaginative play. He emphasized, however, that the fundamental disturbance was an inability to relate to people and situations from the beginning of life. He quoted parents who referred to their disturbed children as "self-sufficient," "like in a shell," "happiest when left alone," and "acting as if people weren't there" (1973, p. 33). To this extreme disturbance in emotional contact with others, Kanner applied the term *autistic*. The following is an abbreviated description of a case presented by Kanner.

Paul | **Autistic Aloneness**

Paul was a slender, well built, attractive child, whose face looked intelligent and animated. . . . He rarely responded to any form of address, even to the calling of his name. . . . He was obviously so remote that the remarks did not reach him. He was always vivaciously occupied with something and seemed to be highly satisfied. . . . There was, on his side, no affective tie to people. He behaved as if people as such did not matter or even exist. It made no difference if one spoke to him in a friendly or harsh way. He never looked up at people's faces. When he had any dealings with persons at all, he treated them, or rather parts of them, as if they were objects.

Adapted from Kanner, 1943, reprinted, 1973, pp. 14–15.

TABLE 12–1	DSM FEATURES OF AUSTISTIC DISORDERS

A TOTAL OF SIX OR MORE FROM 1, 2, AND 3

1. Qualitative impairment in social interaction manifested by at least two of the following:
   - Impaired nonverbal behaviors
   - Failure to develop age-appropriate peer relationships
   - Lack of spontaneous sharing of enjoyment or interests
   - Lack of social or emotional reciprocity

2. Qualitative impairment in communication manifested by at least one of the following:
   - Delay or lack of spoken language
   - When speech is adequate, impairment in initiating or sustaining conversation
   - Stereotyped, repetitive, or idiosyncratic language
   - Lack of varied, age-appropriate, spontaneous make-believe or social imitative play

3. Restricted, repetitive, stereotyped patterns of behavior, interests, or activities manifested by at least one of the following:
   - Abnormal preoccupation with stereotyped and restrictive interests
   - Inflexible adherence to nonfunctional routines or rituals
   - Stereotyped and repetitive motor mannerisms
   - Persistent preoccupation with parts of objects

American Psychiatric Association, 2000.

Although not all of Kanner's observations proved accurate, most of the characteristics he described were subsequently noted by others and are central in defining the disorder. Table 12–1 shows the DSM diagnostic features for Autistic Disorder. The primary symptoms are impaired social interaction, disturbed communication, and the presence of restrictive, repetitive behaviors and interests—which are sometimes referred to as the triad of impairments. Diagnosis requires a total of at least six items, with all three features present. Onset must occur prior to age 3.

DESCRIPTION: AUTISM'S TRIAD OF IMPAIRMENTS

Descriptions of autism focus more heavily on preschool and school-age children. It is important to note, though, that these youngsters can appear quite different from each other, both in specific symptoms and in severity of problems.

Social interaction. Parental accounts and home video recordings of infants prior to their family's suspicion of problems indicate that subtle differences in social interaction can begin very early. Even before 1 year, some of the infants are less likely than comparison infants to be visually responsive, less likely to respond to their names, and more likely to show aversion to being touched by another person (Baranek, 1999; Werner et al., 2000). Older infants fail to track people visually, avoid eye contact, exhibit an "empty" gaze, fail to respond to others with emotional expression and positive affect, and show little interest in being held (e.g., Adrien et al., 1993; Stone, 1997). Figure 12–1 demonstrates this behavior with data from a laboratory study showing that 4-year-olds with autism gazed at their mothers less than children with Down syndrome and those with typical development.

Quite striking in autism are deficits in joint attention interactions, which in typical youngsters begin to develop after 6 months. These interactions involve

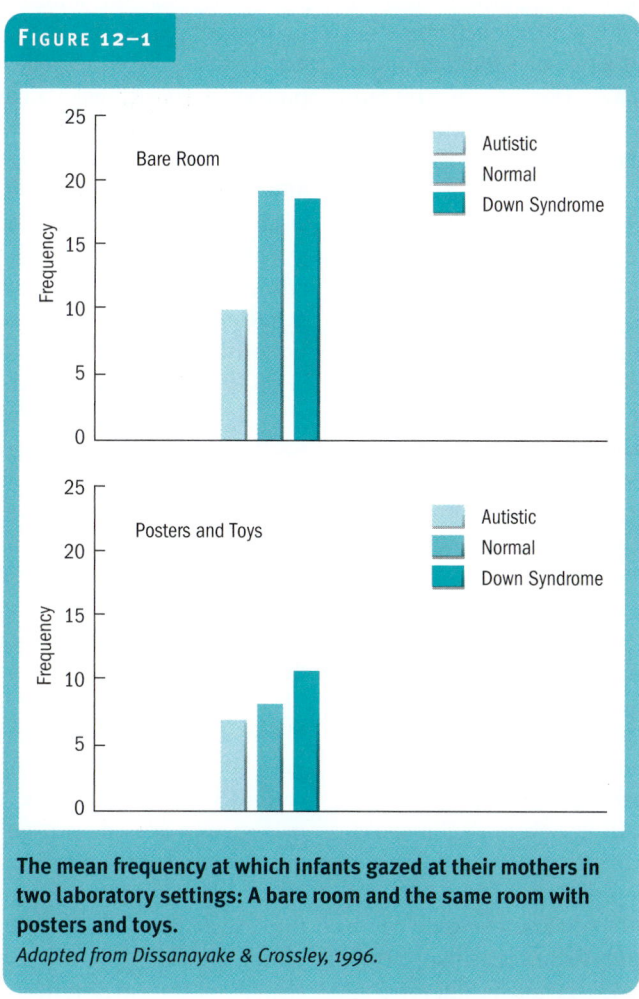

FIGURE 12–1

The mean frequency at which infants gazed at their mothers in two laboratory settings: A bare room and the same room with posters and toys.

Adapted from Dissanayake & Crossley, 1996.

gestures, such as pointing and eye contact—that is, joint visual attention—that center the child's and caregiver's attention on an object, in order to share an experience. In addition, young children with autism imitate the actions of others less than typical youngsters (Rogers et al., 2004). They appear to miss out on the mutual connection between two people and the potential it holds for learning about themselves and others.

Because such behaviors interfere with social interaction, we might expect a lack of attachment to parents. A meta-analysis showed that slightly over half of the children with autism showed secure attachment in the Strange Situation (Rutgers et al., 2004). Secure, insecure, and disorganized attachment have been demonstrated in children with autism (van IJzendoorn et al., 2007; Willemsen-Swinkels et al., 2000).

Abnormal processing of social stimuli, specifically of the face, is another component of deviant social interaction. Typical infants are attracted to the human face and rapidly recognize the faces of their mothers. Facial processing, including emotional expression, is considered crucial to development (Dawson & Toth, 2006). Children with autism often show impairment in recognizing faces, matching emotional faces, and memorizing faces. They also process faces in atypical ways (Berger, 2006). For example, they focus on the mouth rather than the eyes as typically developing children do. Or, to take another example, they have relatively little difficulty in processing photos of faces that appear upside down, whereas typical children do have difficulty with this task.

During childhood, a variety of social deficits, such as lack of understanding of social cues and inappropriate social actions, also are evident. There is a certain aloofness, disinterest, and lack of social reciprocity. The child may ignore others, fail to engage in cooperative play, or seem overly content to be alone (Volkmar et al., 1997). Even higher functioning adolescents and adults may seem "odd," have difficulty with the subtleties of social interaction, and have problems forming friendships as they move through life.

Communication. Disturbed communication—both nonverbal and verbal—is the second aspect of the triad of difficulties in autism. As we have already seen, nonverbal communication involving the face and eyes is atypical or deficient. In addition, perhaps 30% of children with autism never develop spoken language (Dawson & Troth, 2006). In those who acquire language, development is delayed and often abnormal. Babbling and verbalizations may be abnormal in tone, pitch, and rhythm (Sheinkopf et al., 2000; Tager-Flüsberg, 1993). Echolalia and pronoun reversal are commonly observed. In echolalia the person echoes back what another has said, a behavior also seen in dysfunctions such as language disorders, schizophrenia, and blindness. Pronoun reversal is more common in autism than in other disorders or normal development and may persist into adulthood. The child may refer to others as *I* or *me*, and to the self as *he, she, them,* or *you.*

Difficulties with vocabulary, syntax, comprehension, and other forms of language exist; these may resemble specific language impairments (Chapter 10) (Dawson & Toth, 2006). Perhaps most notable is deficits in pragmatics, the social use of language (Klinger et al., 2003). Conversation is characterized by irrelevant details, inappropriate shifts in topic, or disregard of the normal give-and-take of conversation—or there may be an overall failure to develop conversation. Nevertheless, within the wide range of symptoms of autism, some children do function at a higher level. They may be able to tell stories, communicate better when given prompts (Loveland & Tunali-Kotoski, 1997), and read. And some exhibit hyperlexia, a little-understood feature in which single-word reading is extraordinary but comprehension of what is read is problematic (Grigorenko, Klin, & Volkmar, 2003).

Restricted, repetitive, stereotyped behavior and interests. The third major impairment of autism is atypical and often odd behaviors, interests, and activities that are described as restricted, repetitive, and stereotyped. These encompass repetitive motor behaviors, obsession with parts of objects, preoccupation with restricted interests, and inflexible adherence to routines or rituals (Richler et al., 2007).

Repetitive, stereotyped motor behaviors include rocking; walking on the toes; whirling; and arm, hand, or finger flapping (Klinger et al., 2003). Although many of these oddities are seen in normally developing young children and in children with other disorders, they occur in autism more frequently and with greater severity (Bodfish et al., 2000; Turner, 1999). They appear to be especially common in younger children with autism and those with lower intelligence.

Also particularly characteristic of autism are higher order repetitive, obsessive activities and interests (Turner, 1999). These include unusual preoccupations with aspects of the environment. Children may seem obsessed with numbers or some object; they may compulsively collect articles or be overly absorbed in hobbies. They may adopt motor routines, such as rearranging objects, and insist on following rituals for eating and going to bed. Minor changes in the environment, such as rearrangement

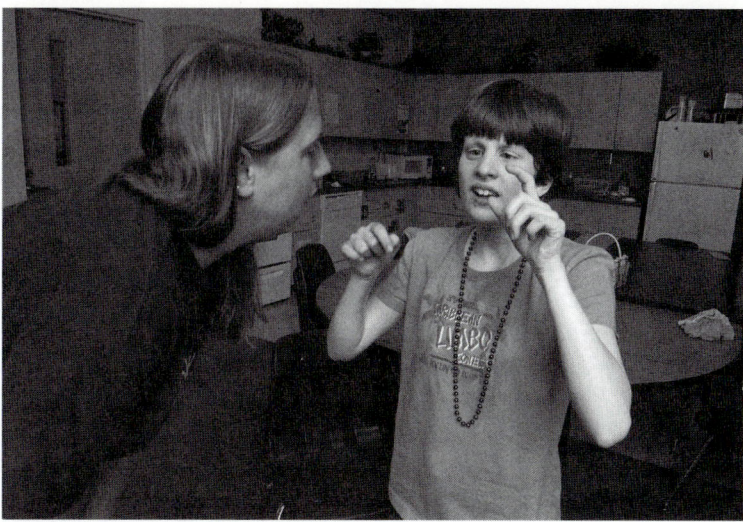

Stereotyped movements commonly occur in youth with autism.
(Robin Nelson/PhotoEdit Inc.)

of furniture or schedules, can cause them to be very upset. These obsessive behaviors may be more common in older children with autism.

DESCRIPTION: AUTISM'S ASSOCIATED IMPAIRMENTS

Although they are not necessary for the diagnosis of autism, several additional features are often associated with it and are meaningful in understanding the disorder.

Sensory/perceptual impairments. The sensory organs are intact but abnormal responses to stimuli make sensation and perception suspect. Some youth appear oversensitive to stimulation (Dawson & Toth, 2006). They may be disturbed, for example, by the sound of a vacuum cleaner or the feel of a light embrace. Sensory input may thus be disliked, feared, or avoided. But undersensitivity may be a more common problem (Rogers & Ozonoff, 2005). Children may fail to respond to sounds, verbal communications, or the sight of others. The clinical picture may be puzzling; for example, a child may seem unaware of a loud noise but fascinated by the quiet ticking of a watch (Volkmar & Klin, 2000). In some cases, a child's failure to respond to sound leads parents to think their child is deaf.

Overselectivity is also common in autism (Ploog & Kim, 2007). Children with autism may seem "stuck" on a particular stimulus while ignoring competing stimuli, which may implicate attentional processes (Landry & Bryson, 2004). Such overselectivity may be manifested in the obsessive attention paid to a toy or a piece of paper. And failure to respond to the complexity of stimuli in the environment can interfere with the child's learning. (Other anomalies involving perception and attention are documented, and we will later examine these.)

Intellectual performance. Although there is a wide range of intelligence in autism, including above average, 70 to 75% of all cases show mental retardation, with many youths exhibiting severe or profound deficiency (Joseph, Tager-Flüsberg, & Lord, 2002; Volkmar, Klin, & Schultz, 2005). The distinction is made between individuals functioning at a higher or lower level, with an IQ of about 70 being the defining score. This is an important way in which persons with autism differ, and intelligence levels are quite stable over time. Higher IQ is associated with less severe autistic symptoms, different educational needs, and greater chance of normal functioning in later life (Howlin et al., 2004; Stevens et al., 2000; Wing, 1997).

The test profiles of persons with autism generally indicate an interesting, uneven cognitive development. Deficits exist in abstract and conceptual thinking, language, and social understanding. Relative strengths appear in rote learning, rote memory, and visual–spatial skills (Happé, 1994; Volkmar & Klin, 2000). Performance scores are usually higher than verbal scores across the IQ range. This discrepancy can lessen from preschool age to adolescence in higher functioning autism, perhaps because the individuals develop better language skills (Joseph et al., 2002).

That autistic symptoms occur amidst such wide variability in general intelligence is puzzling. To make matters more perplexing, a small minority of youth exhibit so-called splinter skills—abilities much higher than expected on the basis of their general intelligence—and savant abilities that are strikingly better than among normally developing youth (Miller, 1999). (See Accent: "Savant Abilities and Autism.")

Adaptive behavior. Autism is characterized by difficulties in dealing with the comings and goings of everyday life. Performance on the Vineland Adaptive Behavior Scales shows a unique profile for persons with autism compared with typical peers matched on intelligence (Carter et al., 1998; Kraijer, 2000). Self-help and daily living skills are roughly what is expected on the basis of mental ability, communication skills fall somewhat short of this, and social skills are far below the expected level.

Other features. Although young children with autism are frequently described as physically attractive, some show minor physical anomalies. A certain gracefulness and bodily agility have been noted, but so have poor balance, uncoordinated gait, and motor awkwardness in adolescence (Molloy, Dietrich, & Bhattacharya, 2003; Volkmar & Klin, 2000). Behaviorally, these children can exhibit tantrums, aggression, hyperactivity, and self-injurious behavior, perhaps partly out of frustration and inability to communicate through language. Adolescents may experience shifts in mood, fear and anxiety, and depression. Some may also have unusual eating preferences and sleep problems, although these symptoms require further investigation (Klinger et al., 2003). None of these problems are specific to autism, of course, but they can interfere with everyday functioning and require special management.

EPIDEMIOLOGY: AN EPIDEMIC?

Over 30 epidemiological studies of autism, involving close to 5 million persons ranging in age from birth to early adulthood, were conducted in several countries from the mid-1960s to the early 2000s (Fombonne, 2003; Volkmar et al., 2004). The increase in prevalence over this time period is quite striking. Research published between 1966 and 1991 reported a median rate of 4.4 cases per 10,000; between 1992 and 2001, the rate was 12.7. A prevalence of 10 persons per 10,000 was proposed as an estimate for autism, and 27.5 per 10,000 when other pervasive developmental

ACCENT ● ● ● ●

Savant Abilities and Autism

Savant abilities are not unique to autism, but persons with autism make up a disproportionate number of persons with these abilities (Volkmar et al., 2005). Spectacular feats—usually in memory, mathematics, calendar calculations, word recognition, drawing, and music—are displayed (Miller, 1999; Heaton & Wallace, 2004). Some of these are indeed amazing (Treffert, 1988). One individual needed only 1.5 minutes to calculate the number of seconds in 70 years, 17 days, and 12 hours, even considering the effects of leap years. And one 5-year-old, despite limited language and retarded daily living skills, had perfect music pitch, a classical piano repertoire, and the ability to improvise music. Savant abilities are often associated with higher IQ levels but have been reported among individuals with IQs as low as 55 and in children whose deficits preclude testing (Miller, 1999).

There is no known explanation for these abilities, and numerous proposals have been put forth. It is unlikely that savant abilities can be simply explained by rote memory or practice, as had sometimes been suggested. Heaton and Wallace (2004) note that spectacular talents in art and music defy such simple explanations and that, moreover, savant abilities often entail the use of rule-based knowledge. For example, savant skills in calendar calculation involve the regularities that are inherent in calendars. Heaton and Wallace are inclined to believe that many of the information-processing skills found in typical functioning are present in those with autism and savant abilities. In addition, some individuals with autism tend to overfocus on detail, which may give them an advantage in acquiring basic knowledge in some domains. Savant skills do tend to be related to repetitive and obsessive behaviors, suggesting that the individual is highly interested in them and motivated to practice them (Pring, Hermelin, & Heavey, 1995). Any ultimate explanation of savant abilities is likely to involve several influences, including genetic influences (Nurmi et al., 2003).

disorders were included (Fombonne, 2003; Tanguay, 2000; Volkmar & Klin, 2000).

Nevertheless, several investigations report higher rates (Newsom & Hovanitz, 2006). A study conducted by the Centers for Disease Control and Prevention (CDC) in one metropolitan area indicated a rate of 31 per 10,000 cases of autism for children, with this figure rising to 34 for autism spectrum disorders. Studies in other countries reported similar or even higher prevalences. More recently, based on data from 14 states, the CDC reported a rate of about 67 per 10,000 eight-year-olds with autistic disorder, Asperger syndrome, or PDD-NOS (CDC Press Release, 2007). The CDC's director noted some uncertainty as to whether the data reflected an actual increase in disorder or the result of better studies.

What accounts for these high rates? Is there a true increase of disorder or are other factors at work? The following methodological and social factors are thought to play at least some role in the escalation of reported prevalence (Newsom & Hovanitz, 2006; Wazana, Bresnahan, & Kline, 2007).

- The criteria for autism have been broadened over several years. It appears that children at both higher and lower levels of functioning are more likely to be diagnosed.

- Children are being diagnosed at younger ages. In part, this is attributable to better understanding of pervasive developmental disorders and the availability of early screening and diagnostic tests.

- Increased awareness and other factors have resulted in more cases being identified. Parents are more familiar with the symptoms of the disorders, physicians are receiving better training about developmental disorders, and medical clinics for developmental disorders have increased.

- An incentive for diagnosis was provided by expanded services due to the Individuals with Disabilities Education Act (IDEA) and by eligibility for federal Supplementary Security Insurance benefits. Prior to IDEA's expanded coverage, children with PDDs were likely to receive diagnoses such as MR, LD, or emotional disturbance.

The extent to which these factors influence the prevalence of autism and related disorders is unclear. A recent investigation that estimated the impact of three methodological factors on predicted rates of autistic disorder concluded that each factor predicted some increase (Wazana et al., 2007). Efforts to clarify increases in rates are important, since any true rise in cases would pose critical questions about causation, especially whether changing environmental variables are putting children at increased risk.

Over time, one of the aspects of autism that has remained constant is gender difference. In both epidemiological and clinic studies, boys display autism more often than girls, with the ratio of 3.5–4 boys to 1 girl (Volkmar et al., 2005). Interestingly, in autism without mental retardation, the ratio of boys to girls is perhaps as high as 6:1; when intelligence is in the moderate to severe range of mental retardation, the ratio of boys to girls is as low as 1.5:1. This suggests that more severe underlying pathology is required before the disorder is expressed in girls.

Epidemiological research has largely failed to support the once-held belief that autism and social class are related. Early reports of high prevalence in the upper social classes probably resulted from nonrepresentative samples (Fombonne, 2003).

DEVELOPMENTAL COURSE AND PROGNOSIS

Although most parents of children with autism become concerned about symptoms in their infants by age 2 (see Figure 12–2), diagnosis occurs, on average, at age 5.5 years (Dawson & Toth, 2006). Some children always seemed different to their parents, others appeared to develop normally for a while and then failed to reach developmental milestones on schedule, and still others regressed and displayed qualitatively different development (Davidovitch et al., 2000). When regression was noted, it often occurred during the latter half of the second year of life. Among other behaviors, the children stopped gazing at others, orienting to their names, spontaneously imitating others, and using meaningful words (Goldberg et al., 2003; Lord, Shulman, & DiLavore, 2004). An obvious weakness of this research is reliance on retrospective reports, and the frequency of regression is not established.

Childhood often brings improvement in social, communication, and self-help skills (Piven et al., 1996; Sigman, 1998). Repetitive movements tend to lessen and obsessive interests tend to increase (Klinger et al., 2003). Lowered symptom levels may occur in adolescence, but deterioration and a variety of behavior problems, such as aggression and anxiety, are also reported (American Psychiatric Association, 2000; Spector & Volkmar, 2006).

In early adulthood, progress may be made but symptoms persist for most persons. Perhaps 15% of persons achieve independence, with successful work placement and some social life (Volkmar et al., 2005).

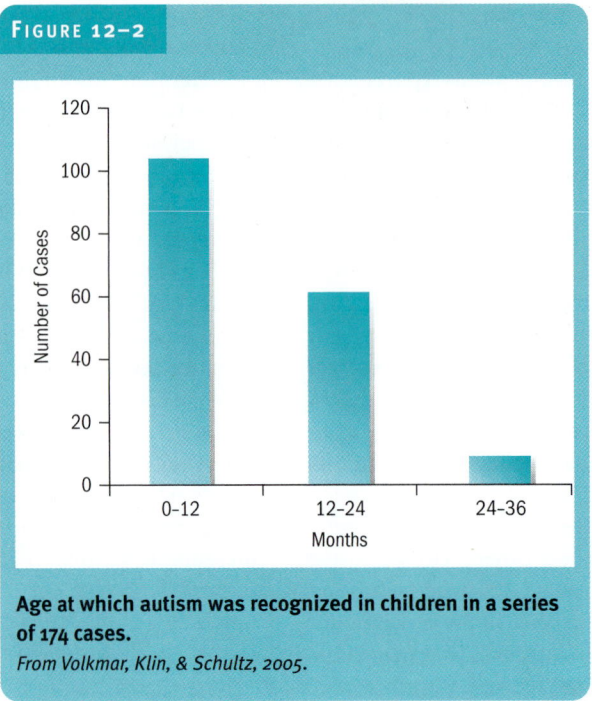

FIGURE 12–2

Age at which autism was recognized in children in a series of 174 cases.
From Volkmar, Klin, & Schultz, 2005.

Numerous studies consistently show that the long-term outcome is poor when early IQ is below 50 or when communicative language is lacking by age 5 or 6 (Howlin et al., 2004; Volkmar & Klin, 2000). A follow-up of children with IQs of at least 50 found that those with childhood IQs of 70 or above did notably better, suggesting that this IQ level is the better predictor of adult independent living (Seltzer et al., 2003). For these individuals, life may include typical achievements and rewards, although some behavioral difficulties may persist. We should also note here that more recent early interventions could be lessening the impact of autism, particularly for higher functioning youth.

Temple Grandin   A Personal Account

Temple Grandin (1997), a university professor of animal science, has written a firsthand account of autism. She attributes a good part of her success in life to educational opportunity and mentors. She was provided early structured nursery school and language training, was mainstreamed from kindergarten through sixth grade, and then attended boarding school before enrolling in a small liberal arts college. She had wise mentors: her mother and aunt, teachers, and people in industry who hired her and helped her develop her abilities.

Ms. Grandin experienced "horrible oversensitivity" to sound and touch; as a child, someone's touch brought "an overwhelming, drowning wave of stimulation." As an adult, she experiences difficulties in memory and in learning verbally. She relies heavily on images that she has stored in her mind, and she thinks in pictures. For her, concepts are visualizations of many examples. For instance, she has no general or abstract concept of a boat, just images of several boats she has seen. To think about boats, she must search her visual memory for specific boats and then find associated images. Thinking in pictures is slower than verbal thinking, but it lends itself to Ms. Grandin's occupational task of designing equipment.

Ms. Grandin reports that she has become better at handling social situations. She uses prerehearsed responses for common interactions, and she depends on logic rather than emotion when she uses these responses. Ms. Grandin characterizes her functioning by intellectual more than emotional intensity. She speaks of the motivations and balances in her life this way:

Many people with autism become disillusioned and upset because they do not fit in socially and they do not have a girlfriend or boyfriend. I have just accepted that such a relationship will not be part of my life. . . . I want to be appreciated for the work I do. I am happiest when I am doing something for fun, like designing an engineering project, or making something that makes a contribution to society.

Grandin, 1997, p. 1039.

UNDERLYING COGNITIVE DEFICITS

So far we have focused on defining the core and associated features of autism, but controlled research gives a more complete picture of the psychological deficits of autism. Investigators have asked whether particular cognitive impairments, related to brain areas thought to be important in autism, might account for the various core symptoms of autism. Three cognitive areas have been emphasized: theory of mind, central coherence, and executive functions (Volkmar et al., 2004).

Theory of mind. Evidence exists that autism and autism-like disorders entail a disturbance in the ability to mentally represent the social world. Extensively studied is theory of mind, the ability to infer mental states in others and in one's self. Having a theory of mind (ToM) means that we understand that mental states exist—that humans have desires, intentions, beliefs, feelings, and so forth—and that these mental states are connected to action. Theory of mind can be thought of as the ability to read others' minds, which guides our interaction with others. In typically development, children of 3 to 4 years usually have first-order abilities, that is, some understanding of people's private mental states (Wellman, 1993). At about age 6, children acquire second-order abilities: They can think about another person's thinking about a third person's thoughts.

Aspects of ToM have been evaluated with various tasks (Figure 12–3). The Sally–Anne test is a simple

---

FIGURE 12–3

(A)   The Sally–Anne task. The child is asked where Sally will look for the marble when she returns to the room.

Sally puts the marble in the basket, then exits the room.

Anne enters and transfers the marble to a box.

(B)   Examples of faux pas stories. The child is asked, In the story, did someone say something that he or she should not have said?

Kim helped her Mum make an apple pie for her uncle when he came to visit. She carried it out of the kitchen. "I made it just for you," said Kim. "Mmm," replied Uncle Tom. "That looks lovely. I love pies, except for apple, of course!"

James bought Richard a toy airplane for his birthday. A few months later, they were playing with it, and James accidentally dropped it. "Don't worry," said Richard. "I never liked it anyway. Someone gave it to me for my birthday."

Two theory of mind tasks.
From Baron-Cohen et al., 1999.

test to determine whether a child understands that another person can hold a false belief (Baron-Cohen, 1989). Here, the child is told that after Sally placed a marble in a basket and left the room, Anne transferred the marble to another container and exited. The child is asked where Sally will look for the marble when she returns. To demonstrate ToM, the child must understand that Sally falsely believes the marble is in the basket where she placed it, and that this belief will guide her action. This first-order task can be modified to evaluate second-order ability. In this case, when Sally leaves the room, she peeks back and sees Anne transfer the marble. The child being tested is asked, "Where does Anne think Sally will look for the marble?" The child must "read" what Anne is thinking about Sally's thoughts. There is compelling evidence that the majority of children with autism fails such first-order tests and that a greater number fails second-order tests (Baron-Cohen & Swettenham, 1997).

Because some children with autism are able to pass second-order tasks, more challenging tasks have been constructed. For example, in the faux pas test the child is told stories in which character A commits a faux pas—that is, unintentionally says something that might negatively impact character B. The child being evaluated is asked to identify the faux pas. In order to succeed on this task, the child must understand that (1) the two characters in the stories have different knowledge and that (2) the statement of character A emotionally affects character B. On this test, children with autism or a related disorder who were able to pass second-order ToM tests did less well than typically developing children (Baron-Cohen et al., 1999). The findings suggest that the faux pas test is an advanced test of ToM and that it can be difficult even for children with higher functioning autism.

The research evidence shows that ToM deficits in autism exist across different ages and can be present in higher functioning autism. Baron-Cohen and others believe that such "mind blindness" underlies many of the social and communication deficits of autism—for example, failure to understand facial expression, relate to others, acquire the pragmatics of language, and engage in pretend play (Tager-Flüsberg, 1997; Baron-Cohen & Swettenham, 1997; Waterhouse & Fein, 1997).

Weak central coherence. In normal cognition, individuals have a tendency to use context to weave together bits of information to make a whole, to give global meaning. This penchant, which is referred to as central coherence, is viewed as varying from strong to weak in the general population (Happé, Briskman, & Frith, 2001). On the basis of performance on specific visual–perceptual tasks, Frith and Happé proposed that individuals with autism are weak in central coherence; that is, they tend to focus on parts of stimuli rather than on integrating information into wholes. Simply put, they see the trees rather than the forest.

Performance on perceptual tasks has best illustrated deficits in central coherence. Children with autism generally perform better than controls on embedded figure tasks, which call for recognizing a stimulus figure that is embedded within a larger picture. In an important study, Shah and Frith (1993) investigated the quite striking superior performance that persons with autism show on the block design task of the Wechsler intelligence test. They not only perform well compared with their achievement on other IQ tasks, they outperform typically developing children and control children with mental retardation. Superior ability to break the block design into segments helps on this task (Figure 12–4).

Such findings suggest that youths with autism process information in a more analytic, less global and integrative way than do normal youths—which can lead to exceptional performance on some tasks

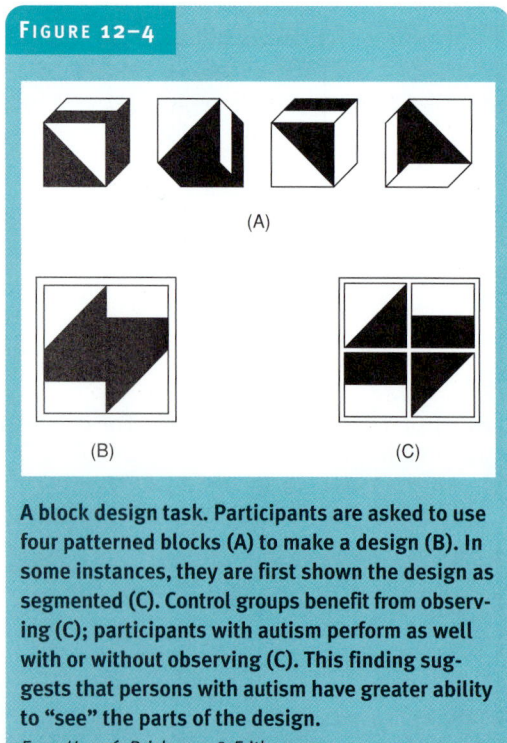

FIGURE 12–4

A block design task. Participants are asked to use four patterned blocks (A) to make a design (B). In some instances, they are first shown the design as segmented (C). Control groups benefit from observing (C); participants with autism perform as well with or without observing (C). This finding suggests that persons with autism have greater ability to "see" the parts of the design.
From Happé, Briskman, & Frith, 2001.

and poor performance on others. In fact, an interesting aspect of this research is that it offers an explanation for some perceptual strengths in autism. Further understanding of central coherence is being sought. For example, Pellicano and colleagues (2005) found that in typical preschoolers central coherence was not related to ToM but was associated with executive functions.

Executive dysfunction. Children, adolescents, and adults with autism perform more poorly than control groups on tests of executive functions (McEvoy, Rogers, & Pennington, 1993; Ozonoff, 1997; Yerys et al., 2007). This result has led to the proposal that such impairment may underlie and account for autistic symptoms. However, data have been accumulating that deficits do not exist in late preschool-age children. A recent study of toddlers (mean age 2.9 years) showed almost no differences from the performance of age-matched typical children (Yerys et al., 2007). It thus seems that executive function deficits are not primary but develop secondarily in autism.

Multiple psychological deficits. A central question regarding the research on psychological deficits is whether any single deficit can account for the symptoms of autism. In fact, each of the deficits examined above appears to account for some but not all of the symptoms (Bailey et al., 1996; Baron-Cohen & Swettenham, 1997). It is also doubtful that these deficits appear in all persons with autism, and the deficits do not seem specific to autism (Plaisted, Swettenham, & Rees, 1999; Peterson, 2004). This suggests that although they are important, they are not fundamental to the disorder. Moreover, questions are raised about the relationship of these deficits to other skills, for example, ToM deficits to language ability (Colle, Baron-Cohen, & Hill, 2007).

Due in part to these issues, researchers are extensively exploring early-occurring behaviors such as face perception, joint visual attention, and imitation (Berger, 2006; Kylliäinen & Hietanen, 2004; Volkmar et al., 2004). Many of these are thought to be involved in the development of affective social development that is so deviant in autism. To some extent, this interest harks back to a perspective that has persisted since Kanner's time—that is, to intersubjectivity, a special awareness that persons have of each other that motivates them, from the moment of birth, to communicate with the emotions and interests of others (Trevarthen & Aitken, 2001). Interestingly, it has been hypothesized that such an innate ability is related to a mirror neuron system in the brain that may allow a person to perceive another person like the self and internally experience the actions and intents of the other (Oberman & Ramachandran, 2007).

NEUROBIOLOGICAL ABNORMALITIES

Diverse evidence exists for neurobiological anomalies in autism. Neurological examinations indicate soft signs of brain dysfunction, abnormal EEGs are found, and the association with epilepsy and mental retardation suggests brain anomalies (Akshoomoff et al., 2007; Minshew, Sweeney, & Bauman, 1997; Volkmar & Klin, 2000). Various brain structures and regions have been considered with postmortem examination, brain imaging, and animal models. Most consistently studied and implicated are the temporal lobe–limbic system, the frontal lobes, and the cerebellum (Minshew et al., 1997; Pennington & Welsh, 1997; Schultz & Klin, 2002). These connected regions are part of what is sometimes referred to as the "social brain" (Frith, 2004).

An interesting finding is unusually large brain size—perhaps by 5 to 10%—in toddlers (Fombonne et al., 1999; Volkmar et al., 2004). Large brain size apparently is not present at birth, but an atypical growth spurt occurs soon afterward and then levels off (Newsom & Hovanitz, 2006). The brain reaches its maximum size by 4 to 5 years of age, much earlier than usual. It has been suggested that unguided growth produces excessive brain connections. Whatever developmental process underlies size abnormality, some evidence exists for atypical size in several brain structures.

Microscopic studies of the temporal–limbic system, frontal lobes, and cerebellum also indicate anomalies (Filipek, 1999; Tanguay, 2000). These include decreased number and size of cells, high cell density, less dendritic branching, and abnormal cell migration. There are also abnormalities in the minicolumns (a functional cell unit) of the cortex of the temporal and frontal lobes (Casanova et al., 2002). This finding points to decreased inhibition of activity, which could cause widespread cognitive and behavioral problems (Volkmar et al., 2004). Some of the microscopic studies suggest that brain anomalies may develop prenatally.

Several regions of the brain show reduced activity, most notably the frontal lobes and limbic system, particularly the amygdala (Newsom & Hovanitz, 2006). Some findings suggest abnormal activity during tasks such as face processing.

Although interest exists in the biochemical systems, consistent findings are lacking (Volkmar et al., 2004). Limited data indicate abnormalities of brain serotonin during childhood (Filipek, 1999) and of dopamine in the frontal lobes in adolescence (Ernst, 2000). The most dependable biochemical finding is high blood levels of dopamine in 25 to 50% of cases, but the significance of this is unclear (Bailey et al., 1996; Mulder et al., 2004).

Understanding of the neurobiology of autism is progressing, although a definitive portrait has not yet emerged. Given the research findings and the mix of symptoms of the disorder, it is likely that there are abnormalities of multiple brain structures, regions, or networks.

ETIOLOGY

Dominant among early etiological proposals was that parenting played a critical causative role in autism. Kanner described the typical parents of a child with autism as highly intelligent, professionally accomplished people who were preoccupied with scientific, literary, and artistic concerns, and who treated their offspring in a coldly mechanical way (1943; Kanner & Eisenberg, 1956). Inadequate, "refrigerator" parenting became implicated in causing autism, even though Kanner hypothesized an innate social deficit. Bettelheim's (1967a, 1967b) psychoanalytic theory was an especially influential psychosocial explanation (Mesibov & Van Bourgondien, 1992). Accordingly, autism was caused by parental rejection or pathology that resulted in the young child's retreating into an autistic "empty fortress." Due to lack of evidence, this approach eventually went by the wayside, and today's parents play important roles in advocacy and treatment for their children. Current interest in etiology focuses on variables that might account for neurobiological abnormalities.

Prenatal and early-life risk.
Many pregnancy and birth variables have been associated with autism and related disorders, but are often not found in specific cases (Newsom & Hovanitz, 2006). Evidence is relatively strong for such variables as bleeding in late pregnancy, blood incompatibility between the fetus and mother, prolonged or sudden labor, and oxygen requirement at birth. Seasonal birth pattern has been suspect as a risk, because time of year is associated with potentially dangerous viral infections, testosterone levels, and so forth. However, research does not indicate that youth with autism are born during any particular season of the year (Tanguay, 2000; Yeates-Frederikx et al., 2000).

Medical conditions.
Numerous medical conditions are associated with autism—epilepsy, cerebral palsy, infections such as meningitis, hearing impairment, and some genetic disorders (Bailey et al., 2000; Rutter et al., 1999; Volkmar & Klin, 2000). Such conditions appear in perhaps 10% of cases of autism and related disorders, and the association is relatively strong when mental disability is present (Johnson & Myers, 2007). About 25% of those with autism have seizure disorders (Schultz & Klin, 2002), with onset disproportionately in early childhood and adolescence (Volkmar et al., 2005). Two genetic conditions specifically associated with autism are fragile X syndrome (p. 311) and tuberose sclerosis (Volkmar et al., 2004). The latter, caused by inherited or new gene mutations, involves the growth of tumors in the brain and other organs that cause varied effects, including developmental delays, behavioral problems, and intellectual disabilities. Whether this condition or fragile X syndrome plays a causal role in autism or simply coexists with autism is unknown.

Related to medical issues is the question of a relationship between PDDs and vaccines given to prevent diseases that are otherwise unassociated with autism. This question has sparked several investigations and much controversy. (See Accent: "Do Vaccines Cause Autism?")

Genetic influence.
Major twin studies of autism document much higher concordance in monozygotic twins than in dizygotic twins (Bailey et al., 1995; Steffenburg et al., 1989). Monozygotic twins of probands have about a 60% chance of having autism, and an even greater probability of an autism-like disorder (Veenstra-vanderweele & Cook, 2003). The comparative figure for dizygotic cotwins is about 4.5%.

Family studies of autism are generally consistent with twin study findings. The rate of autism in siblings of autistic children varies from 2 to 7%, and about 8% of extended families have an additional autistic member (Bailey et al., 1996; Newsom, 1998; Rutter et al., 1999). Yet other interesting findings have emerged. *First*, a higher than expected rate of other pervasive developmental disorders is found in families. *Second*, family members exhibit impairments in social, communicative, and repetitive behaviors that are similar to autism but not severe enough for any diagnosis (Piven & Palmer, 1997;

ACCENT

Do Vaccines Cause Autism?

The controversy regarding the relationship of vaccines to PDDs originated with parents associating their children's onset of pervasive development disorders with the measles, mumps, and rubella vaccine (MMR) that the youngsters had received to prevent these disease (Wakefield et al., 1998). The parents had sought advice from gastrointestinal experts after the children had developed intestinal problems. Wakefield and colleagues hypothesized that, through a complex route involving an immune response, measles virus in the vaccine was responsible for both the intestinal illness and PDDs. Subsequently, another group of researchers proposed that an atypical autoimmune response to the vaccination affected the brain and caused autism (Newsom & Hovanitz, 2006). So far several studies have failed to find a connection between MMR and PDDs (Honda, Shimizu, & Rutter, 2005; Institute of Medicine, 2004; Taylor et al., 1999).

Concern has also been expressed that vaccines with thimerosal, a mercury-containing preservative, put children at risk for PDDs. The potential negative effects of mercury are well known, and among the arguments is

that (1) some children may be especially susceptible, and (2) the amount of thimerosal received by children has increased due to changes in recommended vaccinations. As with the MMR studies, the weight of the evidence does not appear to support a relationship between PDDs and thimerosal-containing vaccines (Costello, Foley, & Angold, 2006; Newsom & Hovanitz, 2006). Figure 12–5 shows results from a Danish study that examined the annual incidence (new cases) of autism before and after thimerosal was discontinued in vaccines.

The debate over vaccines and PDDs has become a contentious one, and mercury in vaccines has been eliminated or reduced in many countries (Kirby, 2005). Reviews by major government and professional groups in the United States have not supported the role of vaccines as causative. It is recognized that a small number of children could be unusually susceptible to MMR (Honda et al., 2005), and the effects of thimerosal are still debated (Newsom & Hovanitz, 2006). Meanwhile, parents tell of the plight of their damaged children in court, advocacy groups call for more research, and some parents may endanger their children by refusing vaccines.

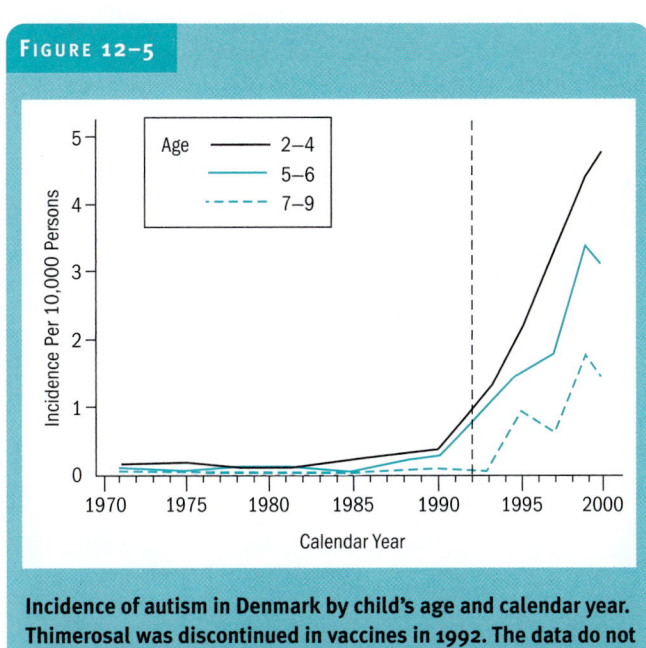

FIGURE 12–5

Incidence of autism in Denmark by child's age and calendar year. Thimerosal was discontinued in vaccines in 1992. The data do not support a correlation between autism and thimerosal-containing vaccines.

From Madsen et al., 2003.

Szatmari et al., 2000). These problems decrease as the genetic relationship becomes more distant (Pickles et al., 2000). Moreover, genetic, rather than social, influence was suggested by Szatmari and colleagues (2000) in an adoption study. They found that impairments occurred more significantly in biological than adoptive families in three major areas of function (Figure 12–6). Overall, the combined findings indicate that a broad genetic predisposition leads to autism, autism-like disorders, or milder related problems—that is, to a continuum of disorder.

The modes and mechanisms of genetic transmission are not established, but genetic heterogeneity is highly likely, and investigators favor the idea that various interacting genes best explain most cases (Rutter et al., 1999; Veenstra-vanderweele & Cook, 2003). This possibility is suggested by the continuum of disorder and the varied clinical picture. Many chromosomes are implicated, including 2, 5, 7, 15, 16, 17, and 19 (Newsom & Hovanitz, 2006). A duplication of genes in a particular region of chromosome 15 has been observed in an estimated 1 to 3% of cases of autism (Sutcliffe & Nurmi, 2003), and this region is also linked to Prader-Willi syndrome (p. 312) and other developmental disorders.

AUTISM SPECTRUM DISORDERS AND OTHER PDDS

As noted earlier, autism, Asperger's disorder and Pervasive Developmental Disorders Not Otherwise Specified (PDD-NOS) are frequently viewed as falling along a spectrum of severity of symptoms, with autism having more severe symptoms (Frith, 2004; Szatmari, 2000). This conceptualization is increasingly reflected in the literature by reference to *autism spectrum disorders.* Asperger's disorder and PDD-NOS are at times referred to as "lesser variants" of autism. The overlap of symptoms of these three disorders is obvious in the following discussion, which also describes differences between them, Rett's Disorder, and Childhood Disintegrative Disorder.

Asperger's disorder (AS). Although Asperger first wrote of this syndrome in 1944, many years passed before English-speaking professionals took notice and the diagnosis was not recognized by the DSM and ICD until the early 1990s (Klin & Volkmar, 1997). Asperger's disorder, or Asperger syndrome, is marked by qualitative deficits in social interaction and by restrictive, repetitive, stereotyped interests and behaviors. In these ways, it resembles autism. However, according to the DSM, youths with AS display no significant delay in language, cognitive development, adaptive behavior (except in the social domain), or curiosity about the environment.

Individuals with AS have difficulties in establishing friendships and other positive social bonds. They have deficits in the use of nonverbal social gestures, emotional expression, and early sharing behaviors. Social awkwardness, inappropriateness, lack of empathy, and insensitivity are apparent.

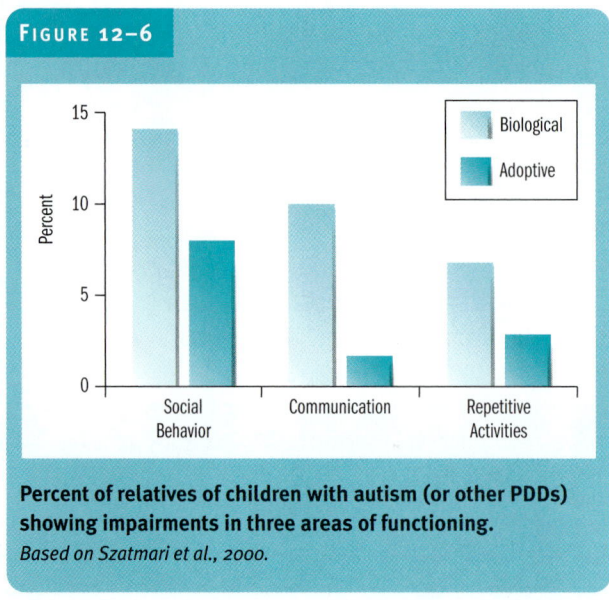

FIGURE 12–6

Percent of relatives of children with autism (or other PDDs) showing impairments in three areas of functioning.
Based on Szatmari et al., 2000.

They seem to have some interest in other people, but their lives are often marked by loneliness. Although research indicates impairment in ToM skills and the perception of complex emotions, the exact nature of their social deficits is not fully understood (Frith, 2004).

Particularly striking are obsessive and restricted interests, the focus of which seems to know few bounds; astronomy, kitchen appliances, historical events, and geographical locales are a few examples. The child may collect an inordinate number of facts and recite them in a pedantic, egocentric, long-winded style. Indeed, Asperger referred to his patients as "little professors." Adults with AS are known for their meticulous work—whether in art or science (Frith, 2004). At the same time, youths and adults often exhibit imagination, for example, in art.

Other problems not required for diagnosis have been observed. A variety of motor problems may exist, as well as behavioral problems such as noncompliance, negativism, and aggression (Miller & Ozonoff, 2000; Volkmar & Klin, 2000). Some of the difficulties of Asperger's disorder can be seen in the following description.

Robert   Asperger's Disorder

Robert's parents had no concerns about his early development. Peer interaction problems became noticeable in preschool, where he was seen as somewhat eccentric, partly due to his intense interest in astronomy. By age 10, numerous problems and concerns (e.g., visual–motor difficulties, social isolation) had led to therapy and educational accommodation.

Evaluated in his twelfth year, Robert had a verbal IQ of 150 and a performance IQ of 116. His visual–motor coordination and executive skills were far below average—indicating poor manual dexterity, slow motor function, poor visual–spatial skills, and a tendency toward getting "stuck" on a stimulus or behavior. His receptive and expressive vocabulary were excellent, but he communicated in a rather formal and pedantic style. When asked, for example, to provide another word for "thin" he offered, "dimensionally challenged."

In social interaction, Robert often failed to respond to the facial expressions and gestures of others; he avoided eye contact and appeared to look through people. He was initially reserved but appeared to become more comfortable with the evaluator, and he discussed his interest in astronomy. He engaged in a long, intense, vigorous monologue—and was insensitive to the evaluator's efforts to change the subject. He also described two children he considered friends; their relationship seemed based on their interest in computers.

Adapted from Volkmar et al., 2000.

The rate of AS is not established, although prevalence appears smaller than for autism (Fombonne, 2003). Boys are identified more often than girls, and diagnosis occurs on average much later than for autism (Dawson & Toth, 2006). Systematic study of the course and outcome of the disorder is needed, but outcome appears fair to good (Volkmar et al., 2005). Asperger himself thought that many of his patients could do reasonably well, and current clinical impressions agree that outcome can be favorable in terms of living independently, finding employment, and having a family (Frith, 2004). Social impairments, however, may persist over time.

The relationship of AS to higher functioning autism is not completely settled. Although language ability is supposed to differentiate the two syndromes, the distinction is often difficult to make. For Asperger's disorder, there are reports of later onset, more complex speech, higher verbal IQ, less severe social and communication problems, fewer motor mannerisms, and more noticeable restricted interests (Ghaziuddin et al., 2000; Miller & Ozonoff, 2000; Volkmar & Klin, 2000). Nonetheless, AS may not be *qualitatively* different than higher functioning autism in symptoms, associated features, and biological factors (Macintosh & Dissanayake, 2004). Thus, Asperger's syndrome is viewed by some as higher functioning autism. The research is not without flaws, and AS is defined somewhat differently by various clinicians and investigators (Mattila et al., 2007).

Rett's disorder. Among the ways in which Rett's disorder, or Rett's syndrone, as well as Childhood Disintegrative Disorder, differs from autism spectrum disorders is in poorer outcome. (See Table 12–2 for a comparison of PDDs.) The syndrome was described in 1966 by Andreas Rett, an Austrian physician, who noticed two young girls in his waiting room exhibiting similar hand-wringing movements. He then discovered among his patient records six more cases with similar symptoms and developmental history (Van Acker, 1977).

Children with this disorder seem to develop normally during the first months of life, and then

TABLE 12–2	COMPARISON OF PERVASIVE DEVELOPMENTAL DISORDERS (PDDs)				
FEATURE	AUTISTIC DISORDER	ASPERGER'S SYNDROME	RETT'S SYNDROME	CHILDHOOD DISINTEGRATIVE DISORDER	PERVASIVE DEVELOPMENTAL DISORDER NOT OTHERWISE SPECIFIED
Age at recognition (months)	0–36 months	Usually > 36 months	5–30 months	> 24 months	Variable
Sex ratio	Male > Female	Male >> Female	Female (?Male)	Male > Female	Male > Female
Loss of skills	Variable	Usually not	Marked	Marked	Usually not
Social skills	Very poor	Poor	Varies with age	Very poor	Variable
Communication skills	Usually poor	Fair	Very poor	Very poor	Fair to good
Circumscribed interests	Variable (mechanical)	Marked (facts)	NA	NA	Variable
Family history— similar problems	Sometimes	Frequent	Not Usually	No	Unknown
Seizure disorder	Common	Uncommon	Frequent	Common	Uncommon
Head growth decelerates	No	No	Yes	No	No
IQ range	Severe MR to normal	Mild MR to normal	Severe MR	Severe MR	Severe MR to normal
Outcome	Poor to fair	Fair to good	Very poor	Very poor	Fair to good

>> = much greater than; NA = not applicable.
From Volkmar, Klin, & Schultz, 2005.

regress and deteriorate in distinctive ways. Head growth decelerates, hand skills are lost with subsequent stereotyped hand movements, and the child walks with poorly coordinated gait. Social engagement is lost, language is severely impaired, and severe or profound retardation develops.

Brain neurons are smaller and more densely packed than normal, and there are fewer dendritic connections, especially in the motor, temporal, and hippocampal areas (Kerr, 2002). The brain stem is also implicated. Several biochemical abnormalities have been noted. In 1999, causation was linked to a gene on the X chromosome that regulates other genes; over one hundred mutations have now been described. Although a mutation may occur in either parent, it is more probable in the father, who passes it to his daughter. Indeed, Rett's disorder primarily is known in females, but there are boys with Rett's disorder or something similar to it (Volkmar et al., 2005).

The prevalence of the syndrome is not well established, although 1 in 15,000 to 22,000 has been suggested for females—with lower rates for males. The condition is categorized as a PDD due to autistic-like behaviors, particularly during the preschool years (Volkmar & Klin, 2000). The child may become somewhat more interested in social interaction during childhood and adolescence, but communicative and behavioral problems remain relatively stable while there is a progressive loss of skills.

Childhood disintegrative disorder (CDD).
Theodore Heller first described this syndrome in 1908. He termed it *dementia infantilis*, and it also has been called *Heller's syndrome* and *disintegrative psychosis* (Volkmar & Klin, 2000). According to the DSM criteria, development must be normal for at least 2 years and symptoms must be present before age 10. By this time, many acquired skills are lost. Diagnosis calls for significant loss in at least two areas of the following: language, social skills, bowel or bladder control, play, or motor skills. In addition, abnormal functioning must be present in two areas of autism's triad of disturbances. The disorder is usually associated with severe mental retardation.

Bob   Childhood Disintegrative Disorder

Bob's early history was within normal limits. By age 2, he was speaking in sentences and his development appeared to be proceeding appropriately. At 40 months he was noted to exhibit, abruptly, a period of marked behavioral regression shortly after the birth of a sibling. He lost previously acquired skills in communication and was no longer toilet trained. He became uninterested in social interaction, and various unusual self-stimulatory behaviors became evident. . . . Behaviorally, he exhibited features of autism. At follow-up at age 12 he still was not speaking, apart from an occasional single word, and was severely retarded.

Adapted from Volkmar, 1996a, pp. 496–497.

The evidence for neurological disturbance in CDD includes abnormal EEGs and seizures (Volkmar et al., 2005). CDD occurs in perhaps 1 child in 100,000 and prevalence is greater in males than females. Onset is usually between 3 and 4 years of age and may be gradual or abrupt. Impairments seem to remain fairly constant over time, although improvement may occur in a small number of cases. Evidence exists that more children with CDD than with autism are mute, display loss of self-help skills, and have IQ scores less than 40 (Volkmar & Klin, 2000). These youngsters are among the lowest functioning of children with PDDs. The regression and marked loss of skills found in CDD suggest an underlying genetic disorder (Volkmar et al., 2004).

PDD-NOS. According to the DSM, this category applies when symptoms appear related to but fail to meet the diagnostic criteria for autism and other pervasive developmental disorders. The diagnostic criteria are only generally described, with no specific items. Youths with PDD-NOS must display impaired reciprocal social interaction and *either* impaired communication *or* stereotyped behavior and interests (American Psychiatric Association, 2000). Cases of so-called atypical autism fall into the PDD-NOS category, that is, cases in which the criteria for autistic disorder are not met due to late onset, atypical symptoms, milder symptoms, or all of these.

Leslie   PDD-NOS

Leslie was a difficult baby, although her motor and communicative development seemed appropriate. She related socially and sometimes enjoyed social interaction. However, she was easily overstimulated, and appeared unusually sensitive to aspects of the environment. She sometimes flapped her hands out of excitement. When she was four years of age, Leslie's parents sought an evaluation because in nursery school she exhibited peer interaction problems and a preoccupation with adverse events. At this time, her communication and cognitive skills were in the normal range. However, she had difficulties in social interaction and a tendency to impose routines on social interaction.

Leslie attended a therapeutic nursery school and her social skills improved. She did well academically in a special kindergarten, but peer interaction problems and unusual affective response continued. As an adolescent, Leslie viewed herself as a loner who tended to enjoy solitary activities.

Adapted from Volkmar et al., 2005, p. 3181.

Aside from social interaction problems, children diagnosed with PDD-NOS exhibit a varied mix of difficulties (Volkmar et al. 2005; Sicotte & Stemberger, 1999). Differentiating PDD-NOS from other disorders can be problematic, and in some children the condition resembles autism while in others it resembles Asperger's disorder (Walker et al., 2004). Nevertheless, a study of nonverbal 2-year-olds reported clear differences between autism and PDD-NOS and short-term stability of diagnosis into the third year (Chawarska et al., 2007). These toddlers with PDD-NOS exhibited social impairments but were more likely to engage in social interaction (e.g., vocalizing, smiling, eye contact, joint attention). Research indicates that more boys than girls are diagnosed and that PDD-NOS may be more prevalent than autism. As a group, youths with PDD-NOS have better outcomes than those with autism, but this category of disorder clearly requires further investigation.

ASSESSMENT

Although assessment has focused disproportionately on autism, much of the following discussion can be applied to other PDDs.

Because autism encompasses many areas of functioning and implicates neurobiological deficits, it requires broad-based assessment (American Academy of Child and Adolescent Psychiatry, 1999; Charman & Baird, 2002). The clinician must involve the parents in order to obtain a unique picture of the child's functioning and also to lay the groundwork for possible treatment. It is also important to take a history of prenatal, birth, developmental, familial, and medical factors, as well as of any past intervention. Medical examination may be valuable in helping to identify autism, investigate its causes, and treat associated conditions such as seizures.

Psychological and behavioral evaluations typically include interviews, direct observation of the child, and psychological tests. Tests of intelligence, adaptive behavior, and language are among the useful instruments, depending on the individual case. Several instruments exist to specifically assess autistic behaviors, and others are being developed to evaluate AS. These tools are based on observation of the child and/or reports of past or present behavior. Of these, the following briefly described instruments serve somewhat different purposes or employ somewhat different approaches.

Evaluating autistic behaviors.

Early identification or screening has high priority because early intervention can be important (Charmon & Baird, 2002). Increased knowledge of early social and communication behaviors has led to efforts to identify children who may be exhibiting few blatant problems. Two examples are the Checklist for Autism in Toddlers (CHAT) and the modified M-CHAT in each, a brief set of questions is asked of parents or professionals concerning, for example, joint attention and imaginative play (Baird et al., 2000; Robins et al., 2001).

The Childhood Autism Rating Scale (CARS) is widely employed for screening children and older persons (Newsom & Hovanitz, 1997; Western Psychological Services, 2007). It consists of 15 items on which the child is rated after observation, usually by professionals. The items cover many areas of functioning, including emotional response, imitation, social relations, communication, perception, and intelligence (Schopler et al., 1980; Schopler, Reichler, & Renner, 1988). Each item is rated in terms of severity, and the sum of points determines mild to moderate or severe autism. Identification of autism highly corresponds to DSM diagnosis of the disorder (Rellini et al., 2004).

The Autism Diagnostic Interview–Revised (ADI-R) is a widely used semistructured interview conducted with parents and caregivers (Western Psychological Services, 2006). It assesses communication, social interaction, and restricted, repetitive behavior and interests in youth and adults. The ADI-R is designed to discriminate autism from other developmental disorders.

The Autism Diagnostic Observation Schedule (ADOS) consists of four modules of activities, one of which is selected as relevant to the age and language abilities of the person being evaluated (e.g., Lord et al., 2000). It is useful for a wide range of individuals. Each module creates opportunity for the person to display behaviors relevant to autism, for example, by engaging the person in play or in storytelling. A recent study of very young children showed ADOS to be sensitive to differences between autism and PDD-NOS (Chawarska et al., 2007).

PREVENTION

As with other early-onset developmental disorders with an apparent genetic and neurological etiology, universal prevention involves receiving prenatal care and improving environmental quality. Early intervention is currently the most effective selective prevention strategy for autism and related disorders.

Recognizing the importance of early intervention, the America Academy of Pediatrics recently adopted new guidelines for the early identification of children at risk for autism spectrum disorders (Johnson & Myers, 2007). Pediatricians are advised to monitor youngsters for early possible symptoms during every routine visit. Discussion with parents, direct observation of the child, and the use of screening tools such as the M-CHAT are suggested. It is recommended that a child suspected of developmental delay or risk immediately be referred for more extensive evaluation or for attendance in an early intervention program. A "wait and see" posture is to be avoided.

According to Newson & Hovanitz (2006), most early intervention programs occur in preschool settings in universities, classrooms originating from private educational organizations, or public schools. Behavioral approaches are frequently employed. The curriculum focuses on attention, imitation, language, play, and social skills. In the beginning, the emphasis is on one-to-one and small-group instruction, after which it gradually shifts to more natural classroom circumstances. These model programs can substantially improve intelligence, language, and the rate of overall development, as well as decrease autistic symptoms. Gains on standardized tests have been shown, and about half of the preschoolers proceed into regular classrooms, with or without supplementary services. A follow-up of one group of children indicated that those who had entered the program at age 4 and/or whose IQ was 59 or higher gained 26 IQ points, on average, prior to leaving the program, and they were attending public school classrooms 4 to 6 years later (Harris & Handleman, 2000). The age and intelligence of children when they enter the programs are correlated with progress.

TREATMENT

For both early and later treatments, the mainstay approaches are behavioral and educational. Pharmacological intervention has an ancillary role in treating PDDs. The vast differences in symptoms and secondary problems—and in the severity of disturbance—is a critical determinant of the goal and intensity of treatment and educational efforts.

Pharmacological treatment. Medication mostly targets problem behaviors such as aggression, self-injury, agitation, and stereotypes. The typical antipsychotic medications antagonistic to dopamine can help some youth by reducing problematic behaviors, but adverse side effects occur over time in a minority of cases (American Psychological Association, 2006). Of particular concern are side effects such as motor problems, including tremors and tardive dyskinesia (involuntary repetitive movements of the tongue, mouth, and jaw). These medications have thus been largely replaced by atypical antipsychotic medications that are antagonistic both to dopamine and serotonin and generally have fewer side effects. Risperidone has been most investigated and has been shown in controlled research to bring behavioral improvement across all ages (Arnold et al., 2003; Malone et al., 2002; Nicolson, Awad, & Sloman, 1998). A major side effect of antipsychotic medication is weight gain, which can be a serious health threat.

Stimulant medication has been shown to lessen disruptive behavior in children and adolescents (American Psychological Association, 2006). However, methylphenidate appears to have negative side effects (agitation, irritability, insomnia) for many of these children. In one study it had to be discontinued in 18% of children.

Many other classes of medications are employed, but evidence for efficacy is weak or not established. Side effects may be relatively high. Although a substantial number of children with autism spectrum disorders receive medication, much is still unknown about the effects, including long-term effects.

Behavioral intervention. Psychosocial treatments, specifically behavioral treatments, can be viewed as falling into two approaches (American Psychological Association, 2006). One approach focuses on specific targets. These may involve deficits, such as in language or social skills, or specific maladaptive behaviors, such as stereotyped behaviors or self-injury. The second approach is intensive, comprehensive treatment over a relatively long period of time that aims to improve numerous primary and secondary problems of autism.

Early behavioral intervention consisted of simple demonstrations of behavior change in children with autism (Koegel, Koegel, & McNerney, 2001; Schreibman, 2000). Subsequent efforts were made to teach a variety of adaptive behaviors and to discourage undesirable behaviors. An outstanding example of this early work was the approach taken by Lovaas and his colleagues at the University of California at Los Angeles, who were among the first to teach verbal communication to children with autism (Lovaas, Young, & Newsom, 1978; Newsom, 1998). In highly structured sessions, they used the usual tools of operant intervention, such as contingent reinforcement, prompts, shaping, modeling, and procedures to facilitate the generalization of learning.

Early behavioral efforts enjoyed success but were also challenged by failures. For instance, youngsters receiving language training often failed to initiate speech or to use speech in everyday activities (Koegel, 2000). Children who acquired responses often did not generalize the responses to different situations. Some maladaptive behaviors could only be modified using punishment, and other behaviors were hardly modifiable at all (Schreibman, 1997).

Improved behavioral procedures have brought increased success. Functional analysis of maladaptive behavior and Functional Communication Training (p. 323) have been successfully used with children with autism, including those with mental retardation. These children can acquire adaptive behaviors through both discrete trial and naturalistic learning that is more likely to generalize to other settings. In addition, the acquisition of some skills can facilitate other positive behaviors; for example, teaching children to initiate social and academic interactions may help them learn language and social skills.

These various behavioral approaches have been incorporated into strategies known as Incidental Teaching, Milieu Teaching, Pivotal Response Training, and the like (Schreibman, 2000). The approach taken in, for example, pivotal response training is to target core pivotal behaviors that, when improved, may improve other behaviors as well (Koegel et al., 2001; Koegel, Koegel, & Brookman, 2003). Because impairments in autism tend to be extensive, and because targeting each problem is extremely time consuming and expensive, pivotal response training holds promise for time-efficient and cost-effective intervention (Table 12–3).

TABLE 12–3	PROCEDURES USED IN PIVOTAL RESPONSE TRAINING TO STRENGTHEN THE CHILD'S MOTIVATION TO INITIATE AND RESPOND TO ENVIRONMENTAL STIMULI

To Increase Motivation to Respond
  Child is permitted to select activities and objects.
  Tasks are varied.
  Reinforcement is given liberally to the child's
    attempts to respond.
  Natural reinforcers are employed.
  Opportunity is given to the child to use acquired
    responses as new ones are learned.
*Child Is Taught to Respond to Multiple Cues in the
  Environment*
Child Is Taught Self-Regulation
Child Is Taught to Initiate Behavior

Based on Koegel, Koegel, & McNerney, 2001.

COMPREHENSIVE BEHAVIORAL INTERVENTION: THE YOUNG AUTISM PROJECT. Although the targeting of specific behaviors can be beneficial, early, intensive, comprehensive programs are necessary to bring about substantial improvement in the lives of children with autism. In 1970, a groundbreaking intervention was developed by Lovaas and his colleagues that aimed at multiple positive outcomes, an effort known as the Young Autism Project (Lovaas, 1987; Lovaas & Smith, 1988). Participants were children under age 4—because early age maximizes new learning—who were free of major medical problems (Lovaas & Smith, 2003). Most received 40 hours per week of one-to-one intervention with experienced behavioral therapists, with sessions tapering off near the end of the approximately 3-year program.

This program employs discrete trial learning throughout training, incidental learning after the first few months, and small group teaching in preschool during the final years (see Table 12–4). Initially, it is

TABLE 12–4	TREATMENT STAGES IN THE YOUNG AUTISM PROJECT

STAGE	LENGTH	TEACHING METHODS	GOALS (EXAMPLES)
1. Establishing a teaching relationship	~2–4 weeks	Primarily discrete trial training (DTT)	Following directions such as "sit" or "come here," reducing interfering behaviors such as tantrums
2. Teaching foundational skills	~1–4 months	Primarily DTT	Imitating gross motor actions, identifying objects, dressing, beginning play with toys
3. Beginning communication	~6+ months	DTT, incidental teaching	Imitating speech sounds, expressively labeling objects, receptively identifying actions and pictures, expanding self-help and play skills
4. Expanding communication, beginning peer interaction	~12 months	DTT, incidental teaching, dyads with typical peers	Labeling colors and shapes, beginning language concepts such as big/little and yes/no, beginning sentences such as "I see —," beginning pretend play and peer interaction
5. Advanced communication, adjusting to school	~12 months	DTT, incidental teaching, small group, regular education preschool	Conversing with others, describing objects and events, comprehending stories, understanding perspective of others, working independently, helping with chores

Adapted from Lovaas & Smith, 2003.

usually necessary to reduce maladaptive behaviors that interfere with learning, such as tantrums; to teach imitation and compliance with verbal commands; and to train basic behaviors such as dressing and playing with toys. Considerable effort is then given to language and communication skills, as well as to peer interaction and interactive play. During the last year or so, emphasis is placed on advanced communication and school adjustment. Parents are an integral part of the intervention. They attend all meetings regarding their child, work with therapists for the first 3 to 4 months implementing discrete trial learning, and subsequently use incidental learning to encourage communication, self-help, and other behaviors in everyday settings.

An initial evaluation of the Young Autism Project compared three groups. Group I had received behavioral treatment for more than 40 hours each week, Group II had received almost the same treatment but for fewer than 10 hours weekly, and Group III had received no training in the project. The groups were similar in characteristics and intervention lasted for 2 or more years. Group I children, who averaged 7 years of age, had an increase of thirty points in IQ, and significantly higher educational placement than the other two groups, which did not differ from each other. A second evaluation when Group I children averaged 13 years of age showed that they had maintained improvements over Group II youngsters (McEachin, Smith, & Lovaas, 1993). Eight of the nine Group I children who had done well at the first evaluation were holding their own in regular classrooms and approached normal functioning.

Although this study had a stronger scientific design than most treatment studies at that time (Rogers, 1998), it received some criticism (Mundy, 1993; Rogers, 1998; Schopler, Short, & Mesibov, 1989). Since then, a random-assignment outcome study has shown positive but weaker findings, perhaps due to fewer hours of treatment or lower intelligence of the children (Lovaas & Smith, 2003; Smith, Groen, & Wynn, 2000). Additional investigations document the benefits of similar behavioral programs (Newsom & Hovanitz, 2006).

The overall findings have made the behavioral approach a leading option for treatment and early intervention. Drawing on evaluations of behavioral approaches—and also of psychoeducational interventions such as TEACCH, which is discussed in the next section—Schreibman (2000) has cited the following as well-established facts:

- Intensive treatments—that is, treatments given for many hours a day and/or in many of the child's daily environments—can be extremely effective.

- Intervention when children are very young has the potential for significant gains.

- Effective treatments are associated with carefully controlled learning situations.

- Effective interventions must use techniques to promote generalization and maintenance of acquired learning (e.g., parent training, naturalistic teaching).

- When their parents are trained to be major treatment providers, children are more likely to generalize and maintain their learning.

- A great deal of variation exists in outcome; different children may benefit from different approaches.

TEACCH: comprehensive psychoeducational treatment. TEACCH, which stands for Treatment and Education of Autistic and related Communication handicapped Children, is a university-based statewide program in North Carolina mandated by law to provide services, research, and training for autism and related disorders (Schopler, 1997). The approach has evolved over 30 years as an alternative to a psychoanalytic-based approach used in the 1960s at the University of North Carolina. From the beginning, families played a critical role in developing TEACCH, and priority was given to three areas: home adjustment, education, and community adaptation. A clear philosophy and set of values emerged over the years, as shown in Table 12–5.

TABLE 12–5	SHARED VALUES OF THE TEACCH TREATMENT PROGRAM

Characteristics of autism are understood from observation rather than through professional theory.

Parent–professional collaboration is vital.

The child's adaptation is improved through teaching new skills and making environmental accommodations to deficits.

Assessment for individualized treatment occurs through formal instruments or informal observation.

Priority is given to cognitive and behavior theory.

Enhancement of skills and acceptance of deficits go hand in hand.

A holistic orientation deals with the whole situation.

Lifelong community-based services are crucial.

Based on Schopler, 1997.

TEACCH operates regional centers that provide individual assessment, training for parents to serve as cotherapists for their children, family support, employment support for older persons with autism, consultation, professional training, and collaboration with other relevant agencies. TEACCH affiliates with hundreds of North Carolina classrooms, and offers training for teachers. Students are enrolled in the classrooms after they are assessed by TEACCH and receive an individualized educational plan. Parents and professionals also collaborate on educating the wider community about autism and on developing additional community services.

TEACCH has been evaluated in various ways (Schopler, 1994, 1997; Ozonoff & Cathcart, 1998). It has been recognized for excellence and implemented across the United States and in Europe. At the same time, there are weaknesses in the outcome studies, including lack of control groups (Smith, 1999).

Educational opportunities. Autism is among the disabilities included in the Individuals with Disabilities Education Act (IDEA). Thus school districts are obliged to identify children with autism, provide services from birth, include families in evaluation and intervention, and deliver appropriate educational programs. The commitment to the least restrictive placements and school inclusion has diminished institutionalization and has increased educational opportunities for children with autism.

From limited data, it appears that some children with autism can benefit from inclusion, although the findings are mixed (White et al., 2007). There is some evidence that children with autism spectrum disorders who have lower cognitive ability are more likely to be in self-contained special education classrooms. Academically, these settings have historically been thought to offer more intensive input, but some studies indicate no differences between special education and regular classrooms. Opportunity for social interaction with typical peers may offer greater benefits by promoting social development. Factors such as adaptation of curricula, social skills training, teacher attitude, and encouragement of peer interaction are among the factors important to successful inclusion (Durand, 2001).

Perhaps unsurprising, opinions about full school inclusion run the gamut from advocacy of inclusion to arguments for more varied educational settings (Burack, Root, & Zigler, 1997). Numerous workers and professional organizations favor the philosophy of least restrictive placement, and they argue that the marked differences in abilities in persons with autism require alternative educational settings.

In the broader schemes of things, intervention efforts must focus on preparation for appropriate independent functioning and quality of life. Also critical is support to families, who experience many challenges rearing a child with disabilities (Schieve, et al. 2007). Progress is being made in improving the lives of youth with autism and related disorders and their families. In part, this is the result of both rigorous research and the commitment and advocacy of families and professionals alike.

The successful teaching of children with autism usually requires special strategies. This photograph of a seven-year-old boy with autism interacting with a classmate captures the social communication difficulties that sometimes must be overcome.

(Ellen B. Senisi/Photo Researchers, Inc.)

Schizophrenia

As we noted at the beginning of this chapter, for many years the term childhood schizophrenia was applied to heterogeneous groups of children with certain severe impairments. Even after diagnostic confusion was reduced—for example, by defining autism as a distinct disorder—a fundamental question remained: Does schizophrenia appearing in children and adolescents differ from adult schizophrenia or is it the same basic disorder manifesting itself at different times of life? By 1980, some consensus was reached that the essential features of schizophrenia hold across age, and the same basic diagnostic criteria were applied to individuals of all ages.

Although the low prevalence of childhood schizophrenia makes it difficult to study, it continues to be of interest to researchers. The study of schizophrenia in adolescents has perhaps been relatively neglected, probably because it is viewed as similar to adult schizophrenia. Our primary interest in this chapter is schizophrenia of young people, but we consider adult-onset schizophrenia when it bears on this topic. In keeping with the clinical and research literature, our discussion often distinguishes between childhood schizophrenia, with onset usually defined as before age 13, and adolescent schizophrenia.

DSM CLASSIFICATION AND DIAGNOSIS

Table 12–6 indicates the DSM major diagnostic features for schizophrenia. At least two features usually are required for at least 6 months, and one or more major areas of functioning must be below the level achieved prior to onset. For youth, this means failure to have reached normal levels of interpersonal, academic, or occupational achievement.

The first four features listed in Table 12–6, referred to as positive symptoms, indicate distortion or excess in normal functioning. Hallucinations, or erroneous perceptions, and delusions, or erroneous beliefs, are viewed as hallmarks of the psychosis of schizophrenia. Disorganized speech, which reflects thought disorder, is another critical feature. Disorganized behavior is manifested in many ways: inappropriate silliness, unexpected agitation and aggression, lack of self-care, and the like. Catatonic behaviors are motor disturbances, such as decreased or excessive motor reactivity, and rigid and strange bodily postures.

Individuals with schizophrenia also may display negative symptoms, that is, a diminution or lack of normally occurring behaviors. Thus they may exhibit little emotion (flat affect), their speech may consist of brief replies that do not seem to convey much information (alogia), or they may neither initiate nor maintain goal-directed actions (avolition).

The diagnosis of youth with schizophrenia is reasonably reliable (Hollis, 2000, 2002), but the strong reliance on positive symptoms, such as hallucinations and delusions, has implication for very young children. Early developmental level may not lend itself to these psychotic manifestations, nor to such symptoms being reported by the child or being reliably assessed. In fact, it is difficult to diagnose schizophrenia until age 7 or 8 (Gooding & Iacono, 1995). This means, of course, that if schizophrenia manifests itself very early, it is unlikely to be identified.

The DSM criteria for schizophrenia are similar to that of the ICD. Both systems also include subcategories for schizophrenia, such as paranoid and disorganized schizophrenia. However, subgroups have not been extensively applied to children. One study that identified subtypes found changes in the subtypes over time (Eggers et al., 2000).

DESCRIPTION: PRIMARY AND ASSOCIATED FEATURES

Hallucinations. Hallucinations are false perceptions that occur in the absence of identifiable stimuli. Individuals experiencing hallucinations report hearing, seeing, or smelling things that others do not hear, see, or smell. Such perceptual abnormalities can vary in content and in complexity. For example, simple hallucinations are indistinct shapes or sounds, whereas complex hallucinations are more organized, such as identifiable figures or voices (Volkmar et al., 1995).

TABLE 12–6	MAJOR DSM FEATURES OF SCHIZOPHRENIA

1. Delusions
2. Hallucinations
3. Disorganized speech (thought disorder)
4. Disorganized or catatonic behavior
5. Negative symptoms: diminished affect, speech content, or goal-directed activities

Two of the above are required for diagnosis (but only one if delusions are bizarre or hallucinations consist of a voice commenting on the person's behavior/thoughts or two voices conversing with each other).

American Psychiatric Association, 2000.

TABLE 12–7	SOME CHARACTERISTICS OF CHILDHOOD SCHIZOPHRENIA IN FOUR STUDIES					
				PERCENT OF CASES SHOWING SYMPTOMS		
	MEAN AGE	MALE: FEMALE	MEAN IQ	AUDITORY HALLUCINATIONS	VISUAL HALLUCINATIONS	DELUSIONS	THOUGHT DISORDER
Kolvin et al., 1971 N = 33	≈11.1	2.66:1	86	82	30	58	60
Green et al., 1992 N = 38	9.58	2.17:1	86	84	47	55	100
Russell et al., 1989 N = 35	9.54	2.2:1	94	80	37	63	40
Volkmar et al., 1988 N = 14	≈7.86	2.5:1	82	79	28	86	93

Adapted from Green et al., 1992; Russell et al., 1989; and Volkmar, 1991.

Table 12–7 shows some of the characteristics of four samples of children diagnosed with schizophrenia, including the hallucinations they reported. Hallucinations occurred at consistently high rates across the samples. Auditory hallucinations were the most common, and visual hallucinations were reported fairly often. Those involving touch and smell were quite rare. These findings are in keeping with studies of adolescents and adults with schizophrenia. Table 12–8 details the variety of hallucinations reported in one study of 9-year-olds, and the percentage of children who experienced each type. It was not uncommon for a single child to report several types. The following are examples of the children's accounts:

Auditory: The kitchen light said to do things and "shut up."

Command: A man's voice said "murder your step-father" and "go play outside."

Visual: A ghost with a red, burned, and scarred face was seen several times in different places.

Religious: God said, "Sorry D., but I can't help you now, I'm helping someone else."

Persecutory: Monsters said that the child is "stupid" and that they will hurt him.

Delusions. Delusions are false beliefs that are maintained even in the face of realistic contradiction. They vary in content. For example, delusions of persecution involve beliefs of impending harm from someone, whereas delusions of reference involve inaccurate beliefs that certain events or objects have particular significance. Delusions can

also be simple or complex, and fragmented or organized. As shown in Table 12–7, delusions occurred quite consistently in the majority of children diagnosed with schizophrenia. Table 12–8 shows

TABLE 12–8	PERCENTAGE OF CHILDREN WITH HALLUCINATIONS AND DELUSIONS
TYPES OF HALLUCINATIONS	**PERCENT**
Nonaffective auditory	80
Command	69
Visual	37
Conversing voices	34
Religious	34
Persecutory	26
Commenting voices	23
Tactile	17
Olfactory	6
Somatic	6
TYPES OF DELUSIONS	**PERCENT**
Persecutory	20
Somatic	20
Bizarre	17
Reference	14
Grandiose	11
Thought insertion	11
Control/influence	9
Mind reading	9
Thought broadcasting	6
Thought control	3
Religious	3

From Russell, Bott, & Sammons, 1989.

the many types of delusions reported by children, some of whom reported several types. The following are examples:

Persecutory: A child believed his father had escaped jail and was coming to kill him.

Somatic: A child believed that a boy and a girl spirit lived inside his head.

Bizarre: A boy was convinced he was a dog and growing fur. One time he refused to leave a veterinarian's office unless he got a shot.

Grandiose: A boy had the firm belief that he was different and able to kill people. He believed that when God zoomed through him, he became strong.

Thought disorder. Delusions are a disturbance in the content of thought, but the form of thinking is also distorted in schizophrenia. Thought disorder involves difficulties in organizing thoughts and is reflected in disorganized speech. There are several indications of thought disorder. The person may display loose associations, that is, jump from topic to topic with no obvious connection between topics and without awareness of the problem. Speech may be illogical, incoherent, and incomprehensible to others. It may also have impoverished content, conveying little information because it is vague, too abstract or concrete, or repetitive. It may include neologisms, made-up words that are meaningless to others. Thought disorder is suggested in this excerpt from an interview with a 7-year-old boy:

> *I used to have a Mexican dream. I was watching TV in the family room. I disappeared outside of this world and then I was in a closet. Sounds like a vacuum dream. It's a Mexican dream. When I was close to that dream earth I was turning upside down. I don't like to turn upside down. Sometimes I have Mexican dreams and vacuum dreams. It's real hard to scream in dreams. (Russell et al., 1989, p. 404)*

Thought disorder may be exhibited in high percentages of children with schizophrenia, but different studies show variation in rates (Table 12–7). Perhaps these differences are real, but they may also be due to difficulty in identifying thought disorder in children (McClellan, 2000).

Associated characteristics. Among the features associated with childhood schizophrenia are motor abnormalities that include awkwardness, delayed milestones, poor coordination, and peculiar posture (Eggers, 1978; Nicolson & Rapoport, 2000; Watkins, Asarnow, & Tanguay, 1988).

Impaired communication is common (McClellan, Werry et al., 2001). For example, when asked a question, children with schizophrenia may be less likely to give any reply, and when they do reply, they may be less likely to give information to supplement their simple answers (Abu-Akel et al., 2000). The children also use fewer conjunctions and other speech devices to connect ideas (Caplan et al., 2000). Atypical features such as echolalia and neologisms occur.

Many children with schizophrenia score in the low average range or borderline on IQ tests; perhaps 10 to 20% of cases show significant impairment (McClellan, 2005). There is some evidence for a decline in intelligence during at least the first few years after psychotic symptoms appear (Jacobsen & Rapoport, 1998).

Neuropsychological and experimental evaluations indicate specific deficits in child and adolescent schizophrenia, for example, on tasks of attention, memory, abstraction, and executive function (Cervellione et al., 2007; Kumra et al., 2000; Ross et al., 2005). These deficits are generally similar to those of adult schizophrenia (Reichenberg & Harvey, 2007), but are reported to be more severe (Frazier et al., 2007).

Emotional and social disturbances also are evident in childhood schizophrenia. Some of these difficulties indicate the flat affect and lack of social interest—the negative symptoms—that reportedly are more common in early-onset than adult schizophrenia (Hollis, 2002). Social problems include shyness, withdrawal, isolation, and ineptness (Bettes & Walker, 1987; Eggers et al., 2000; Watkins et al., 1988). In addition, inappropriate emotion, moodiness, anxiety, and depression have been reported (e.g., Green et al., 1992; Prior & Werry, 1986).

EPIDEMIOLOGY

The prevalence of schizophrenia in children is not established, but the disorder is considered rare. Schizophrenia appears in about 1% of the general population. It is estimated that no more than 1% of all these cases occur before 10 years of age, and 4% before the age of 15 (McClellan, 2005). Onset climbs during adolescence into early adulthood, and generally peaks from about age 15 to 30. Childhood schizophrenia appears more common in boys, with the sex ratio perhaps flattening out in adolescence.

Childhood schizophrenia may occur at higher rates in less educated and less professionally successful families; however, the data are mixed and may be biased by reliance on hospital samples (McClellan, Werry et al., 2001). In adulthood, schizophrenia is more prevalent in the lower socioeconomic classes and in urban settings (Brown, Bresnahan, & Susser, 2005). It also is observed in cultures all over the world, with similar symptom profiles.

DEVELOPMENTAL COURSE AND PROGNOSIS

The onset of schizophrenia in childhood is likely to be gradual, or insidious (McClellan, 2005). Nonpsychotic symptoms occur prior to psychotic symptoms and diagnosis. These early characteristics include delays and aberrations in language and in motor, sensory, and cognitive functions—as well as social withdrawal, peer difficulties, school problems, and "odd" personality (Asarnow, Tompson, & McGrath, 2004; McClellan et al., 2003; Nicolson & Rapoport, 2000). The question has been raised as to whether early symptoms should be viewed as precursors or as early manifestations of the disorder (Asarnow & Asarnow, 2003). As it is, psychotic symptoms—and thus diagnosis—become more likely at school age.

As we might expect, developmental level makes its way into children's psychotic experiences (Eggers, 1978; Russell et al., 1989). Early hallucinations are likely to include animals, toys, and monsters, and to be simple. Similarly, when delusions first appear, they are quite simple (e.g., a monster wants to kill me), and then they gradually become more elaborate, complex, abstract, and systematized. These changes are in keeping with cognitive and socioemotional development (Volkmar, 1996b).

Adolescent onset of schizophrenia seems not to be as insidious as child onset. Many diagnosed adolescents nonetheless have histories of attention, motor-perceptual, and other neurodevelopmental problems as well as worry, shyness, moodiness, and aggression. This picture seems more similar to adult-onset schizophrenia, in which there is considerable variation in the timing, severity, and nature of early features (Rossi et al., 2000). The psychotic symptoms exhibited by adolescents also are more similar to those seen in adults. For instance, persecutory and grandiose delusions are more common than in child cases, and delusions are more complex and systematized (Volkmar et al., 1995).

Further research is needed on the course and outcome of schizophrenia in youth. Much variation has been reported in the course of the disorder (Eggers et al., 2000). It does appear that, as in adult cases, some youth have a chronic condition, others experience episodes of difficulties that come and go, and still others partially or fully recover (e.g., Hollis, 2000). However, full recovery is not common. A 42-year follow-up of cases with onset by age 14 found that roughly 25% had recovered, 25% had partial recovery, and 50% had a continuing severe course (Eggers & Bunk, 1997). From other investigations, we can surmise that roughly half to three-quarters of cases may not do well (Asarnow et al., 2004; Gillberg, Hellgren, & Gillberg, 1993; Jarbin, Ott, & von Knorring, 2003; Krausz & Muller-Thomsen, 1993).

Research suggests that poor adjustment before onset, insidious onset, an extended initial psychotic episode, negative symptoms, and a longer time lapse before treatment may predict poor outcome (Hollis, 2002). In any event, though, early age of onset is associated with poor outcome, suggesting that child and adolescent schizophrenia are more ominous than adult-onset schizophrenia (Hollis, 2000; McClellan, Werry et al., 2001). In fact, various investigations report that schizophrenia diagnosed in youth shows more severe symptoms and cognitive impairments (Frazier et al., 2007). Figure 12–7 exemplifies this finding in a major study of youth 8 to 19 years of age diagnosed with schizophrenia and a related disorder (schizoaffective disorder).

Unfortunately, child and adolescent schizophrenia, as shown in a limited number of studies, carries a higher than usual risk for premature death, as does adult-onset schizophrenia (Hollis, 2002; Meltzer et al., 2003). This outcome appears to be due to a mix of causes, such as undetected medical conditions, suicide, and other violent events. The following describes a case of childhood-onset schizophrenia that terminated in tragedy.

| **Mary** | **Developmental Course of Childhood Schizophrenia** |

Mary had always been a very shy child. She would become mute at times, had severe difficulties making friends, was frequently oppositional, and had occasional enuresis. By the time she reached roughly 10 years of age, Mary showed academic difficulties in addition to continuing social isolation. She became depressed,

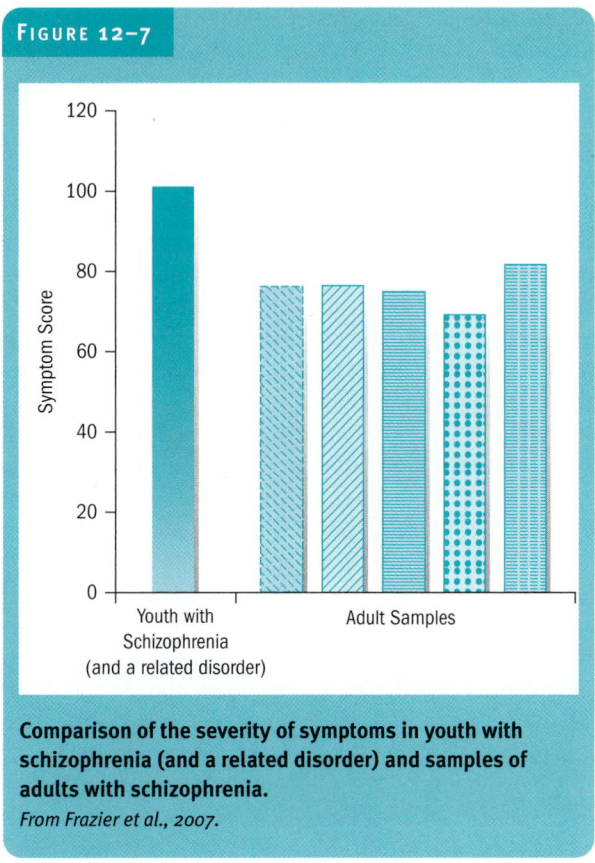

FIGURE 12–7

Comparison of the severity of symptoms in youth with schizophrenia (and a related disorder) and samples of adults with schizophrenia.
From Frazier et al., 2007.

felt that the devil was trying to make her do bad things, believed that her teacher was trying to hurt her, and was preoccupied with germs. Her behavior became increasingly disorganized. She talked of killing herself, appeared disheveled, and ran in front of a moving car in an apparent suicide attempt.

This episode precipitated an inpatient psychiatric evaluation, during which Mary continued to show bizarre behavior. . . . Although Mary's functioning improved during hospitalization and she returned to her family, throughout her childhood and adolescent years she was tormented by fears, hallucinations, the belief that others were out to get her, and occasional bouts of depression often accompanied by suicide attempts. She continued to be socially isolated and withdrawn, and to perform poorly in school. At age 17 (after several brief inpatient hospitalizations), Mary was admitted to a state hospital, where she remained until the age of 19. During this period her affect was increasingly flat, and her psychotic symptoms persisted. One week after discharge from the hospital, Mary went into her room, locked the door, and overdosed on her medications. She was found dead the next morning.

Adapted from Asarnow & Asarnow, 2003, p. 455.

NEUROBIOLOGICAL ABNORMALITIES

Nervous system anomalies have been revealed for schizophrenia. Many of the findings come from adult cases and from children at high risk who were diagnosed in adolescence or adulthood, but findings have begun to accumulate for childhood schizophrenia. The findings are notably similar across age groups.

Neurological dysfunction is suggested by general symptoms of children with schizophrenia, such as motor delay, coordination problems, and other soft neurological signs (Jacobsen & Rapoport, 1998). In addition, minor physical abnormalities—including irregularities of the face, head, hands, and feet—occur at elevated rates in schizophrenia (Brennan & Walker, 2001; Marenco & Weinberger, 2000). These suggest genetic influence and/or prenatal insult during the first and second trimesters, when the nervous system is rapidly developing.

Both brain imaging and postmortem studies show structural abnormalities of the brain across ages, although not universally (Asarnow & Asarnow, 2003; Greenstein et al., 2006). Among the most common findings are enlargement of the fluid-filled lateral ventricles and reduced volume of the brain—most consistently in the temporal–limbic (e.g., hippocampus, amygdala), frontal, and parietal areas. (See Figure 12–8.) Interestingly, the brain areas in which reduced volume appears in children with schizophrenia become more similar to the areas shown in adult schizophrenia as the children age (Greenstein et al., 2006). This is evidence of continuity of the disorder in children and adults. Volume reduction also has been found in the cerebellum. Reduced volume mostly involves gray matter, but white matter reduction has been reported (Davis et al., 2003). Reduced brain volume and enlarged ventricles have been associated with negative symptoms, poor adjustment before diagnosis, and neuropsychological deficits (Buchanan & Carpenter, 2000; Davis et al., 2003; Gur et al., 1998). Structural abnormalities of brain cells also have been noted. Neurons sometimes appear abnormal and in atypical locations. They appear densely packed, with fewer synaptic processes and connections, and altered synaptic chemistry.

Brain disturbance is demonstrated in other ways. Symptoms of schizophrenia have been associated with abnormal activity in the frontal and temporal lobes, with negative symptoms being associated with reduced frontal lobe activity (Hollis, 2002). In addition, low reactivity of the autonomic nervous system, which might involve the hippocampus, has been widely reported for a subgroup of adults with schizophrenia, and a study of children suggested similar abnormality (Jacobsen & Rapoport, 1998; Ohman & Hultman, 1998).

For many years, dopamine has been implicated in schizophrenia. Dopamine is important in several cerebral pathways, including the frontal and temporal–limbic areas. This neurotransmitter is blocked by medications that relieve psychosis, and substances that increase dopamine worsen symptoms of schizophrenia. Still, dopamine's role in schizophrenia is far from being completely understood. Numerous subtle transmitter dysfunctions might exist, including an imbalance between dopamine and other neurotransmission systems (Asarnow & Asarnow, 2003). The involvement of other neurotransmitters, such as GABA and glutamate, is of interest.

What is to be made of the various, and sometimes inconsistent, findings about the brain? Taken together, the evidence suggests that several brain areas and neurotransmitters, functioning in complex ways, are responsible for schizophrenia. Current proposals suggest that schizophrenia involves abnormalities in the connections among parts of a widely distributed network, predominately of frontal and temporal–limbic circuits (Evans et al., 2005).

ETIOLOGY

Given the evidence of brain anomalies, it is not surprising that etiological hypotheses and investigations

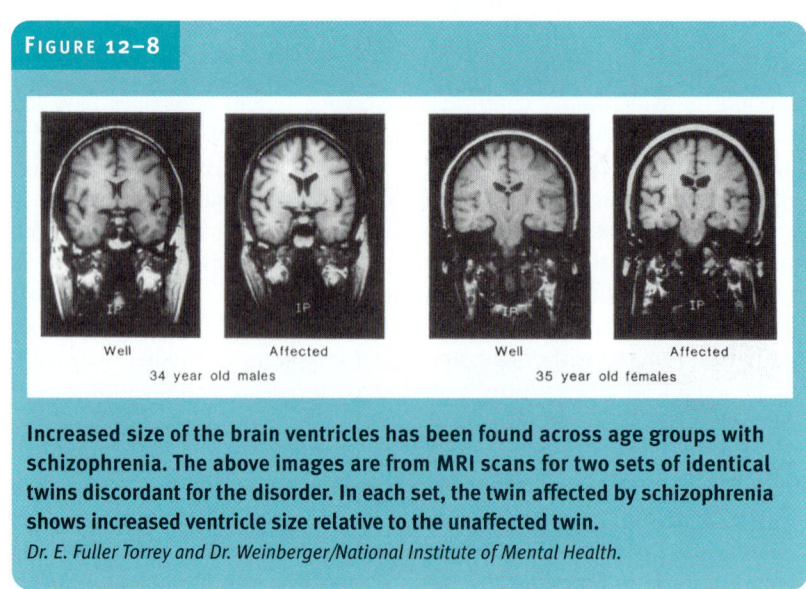

FIGURE 12–8

Well   Affected
34 year old males

Well   Affected
35 year old females

Increased size of the brain ventricles has been found across age groups with schizophrenia. The above images are from MRI scans for two sets of identical twins discordant for the disorder. In each set, the twin affected by schizophrenia shows increased ventricle size relative to the unaffected twin.
Dr. E. Fuller Torrey and Dr. Weinberger/National Institute of Mental Health.

have sought to explain the origins of these abnormalities and how they might account for schizophrenia. Most of the research applies to schizophrenia of adulthood.

Genetic factors.
Extensive research conducted in several countries on adult-onset schizophrenia indicates that risk for the disorder increases as genetic relationship to an adult proband increases (Gottesman, 1993; Mortensen et al., 1999). For example, risk is about 12% for children of a schizophrenic parent but only 2 percent for first cousins. Twin data show greater concordance in identical than fraternal twins—in the range of 45–55% versus 13–17% (Plomin & Crabbe, 2000; Evans et al., 2005). Adoption studies also point to genetic influence. Genetic vulnerability may express itself in disorders similar to but less severe than schizophrenia (e.g., schizoaffective and schizotypal disorders) and in cognitive processing deficits associated with schizophrenia (Hollis, 2002; MacDonald et al., 2003). The findings suggest the inheritance of a more general vulnerability and a spectrum of schizophrenia disorders.

A limited number of studies in which schizophrenia arose in childhood provide interesting findings. The family members of the probands were at greater risk for schizophrenia or schizophrenia-like disorders than what would be expected in the general population—and risk appeared even higher than for relatives of adult-onset probands (Hollis, 2002; Nicolson & Rapoport, 2000; Ross et al., 1999). Thus, genetic vulnerability appears to play at least as important a role in child-onset as adult-onset schizophrenia.

No single chromosome or gene with substantial effect has been found, and it is generally believed that multiple genes with small effects are involved. Although overall findings have been inconsistent, among the chromosomes implicated are number 2, 5, 6, 8, 13, 15, and 22 (Evans et al., 2005; Plomin & McGuffin, 2003). Of current interest is a gene on chromosome 15 thought to be involved in the functioning of the hippocampus and dopamine regulation. Also of interest is the COMT gene on chromosome 22; it too is implicated in dopamine regulation. A recent meta-analysis indicates the association of schizophrenia and chromosome 22 (Murphy, 2005). Interestingly, persons with velocardiofacial syndrome, which involves gene deletions on chromosome 22, are at higher risk for schizophrenia, and the syndrome has been found in about 5% of children with schizophrenia. The syndrome is characterized by physical/medical, mild learning, and psychiatric problems.

The involvement of several genes with small effects creates a complex etiological picture. It is also clear that genetic influences do not tell the entire story. How can we explain the fact that so many identical cotwins of adults with schizophrenia do not have schizophrenia? Nongenetic influences apparently play a role in producing schizophrenia. One meta-analysis of twin studies found evidence for modest shared environmental influences, which could include early exposure to toxins, infections, and prenatal influences (Sullivan, Kendler, & Neale, 2003).

Prenatal factors and pregnancy complications.
Prenatal and birth adversities are sometimes linked to child and adult schizophrenia (Asarnow & Asarnow, 2003).

Among the prenatal factors examined are infectious agents. Interesting results came from a study of Finnish women who had been exposed in pregnancy to influenza virus during an epidemic (Mednick et al., 1988). Children whose mothers had been exposed during the second trimester of pregnancy had a greater risk for eventually developing schizophrenia. Some additional studies replicated risk from influenza, but others failed to do so (Brown et al., 2005; Marenco & Weinberger, 2000). Other research has implicated exposure of the fetus to respiratory infections and rubella.

Numerous complications of pregnancy and birth have inconsistently been associated with schizophrenia, for example, bleeding during pregnancy and emergency cesarean birth (Asarnow & Asarnow, 2003; Brown et al., 2005). Birth complications, particularly those in which the infant is deprived of oxygen, have shown a stronger association with schizophrenia relative to other environmental factors (Canon & Rosso, 2002). Also reported are low birthweight and small head circumference, leading to the hypothesis that abnormal fetal growth underlies schizophrenia (Brown et al., 2005).

Weaknesses in the research on prenatal and birth complications have been recognized, although later studies appear to be methodologically stronger. It is difficult to draw firm causal conclusions in correlational designs. It is possible, for example, that genetically abnormal fetuses may cause some prenatal or perinatal complications.

Psychosocial influences.
There is reason to believe that psychosocial stress could contribute to

schizophrenia. For adult-onset schizophrenia, adverse life events (stress) have been found to increase in the weeks prior to symptom occurrence (Fowles, 1992). Also, increased stress hormones have been related to subclinical manifestations of schizophrenia (Evans et al., 2005). In addition, psychosocial stress has been linked to worsening of symptoms and relapse after improvement.

Family characteristics have long been suspected of causing schizophrenia. Indeed, the phrase "schizophrenogenic mothering" was once used to capture the idea that pathological parenting was the basic cause of the condition. There has been vacillating interest in the role of family interaction and climate.

Research has examined the possible role of communication deviance (CD), that is, distorted and vague communication that indicates dysfunctional thinking and attention. Parental CD has been linked to schizophrenia (or related disorder) in youth (Asarnow, Goldstein, & Ben-Meir, 1988; Tienari, Wynne, & Wahlberg, 2006). It is unclear how these findings should be interpreted (Asarnow & Asarnow, 2003). Are they a reflection of family stress, parental psychopathology, or additional variables? Other investigations have considered the possible influence of parental expression of criticism and hostility. Although high expressed emotion (EE) was linked to the eventual diagnosis of schizophrenia (or related disorders) in high-risk adolescents (Valone, Goldstein, & Norton, 1984), it remains doubtful that parents of children with schizophrenia are more critical than other parents (Hollis, 2002). It is worth noting, however, that in adult-onset schizophrenia, high EE is correlated with the return of symptoms after remission (Butzlaff & Hooley, 1998).

Limited research with adoptees has implicated family processes. For example, the possible influence of family climate was shown in the Finnish Adoption Study, which examined adopted children of mothers with schizophrenia or related disorders and a comparison adopted group whose mothers had no such diagnoses (Tienari et al., 1990; Tienari et al., 2006). Ratings of the functioning of the adoptive families permitted analysis of the rearing environment. The findings indicated that the genetically at-risk adoptees who later developed schizophrenia and related disorders had been reared in families with disturbed relationships. Also suggested was that low genetic risk served as protection against negative family climate.

Neurodevelopmental model. Present knowledge about schizophrenia has led to the proposal that etiology involves multiple factors. A vulnerability-stress model is often invoked as a general framework. It assumes that an organismic vulnerability, probably genetic, but possibly prenatal insult, interacts with environmental stress to produce somewhat different developmental paths and outcomes. Some individuals reach a threshold to exhibit diagnosable schizophrenic symptoms or similar but less severe symptoms, whereas others do not.

The last few decades have seen growing interest in the neurodevelopmental model of schizophrenia (Bearden et al., 2006; Weinberger & McClure, 2002). According to this model, early development of the brain goes awry, affecting critical brain circuits. (See Figure 12–9.) Early difficulties, such as motor and language problems, mark early development, and increased difficulties occur in cognitive, social, and psychological function. In most cases, the primary symptoms of the disorder are manifested when the brain further matures in adolescence or early adulthood. Investigators have pointed to numerous changes occurring in the hormonal and brain systems during adolescence that could "enable" expression of the disorder (Marenco & Weinberger, 2000). Of particular interest is that late adolescence is an important time for selective pruning of the synapses in the frontal lobes and association areas. It is hypothesized that excessive pruning at this time is related to the appearance of symptoms. Social environmental influences may also interact with biological changes.

The exact way or extent to which this model might apply to childhood schizophrenia is unclear. As we have seen, numerous similarities between early-onset and late-onset schizophrenia strongly suggest that they are not different disorders. However, childhood schizophrenia appears to involve more severe symptoms as well as a less favorable course and outcome. This suggests that greater genetic liability, or greater biological vulnerability perhaps combined with greater environmental adversity, may produce the disorder so early in life.

ASSESSMENT

The following categories can serve as a guide for comprehensive assessment for suspected child or adolescent schizophrenia (McClellan, Werry et al., 2001; Volkmar, 1996b).

- Historical information, including data on pregnancy complications, early development, age of onset, course of symptoms, and medical and family history.

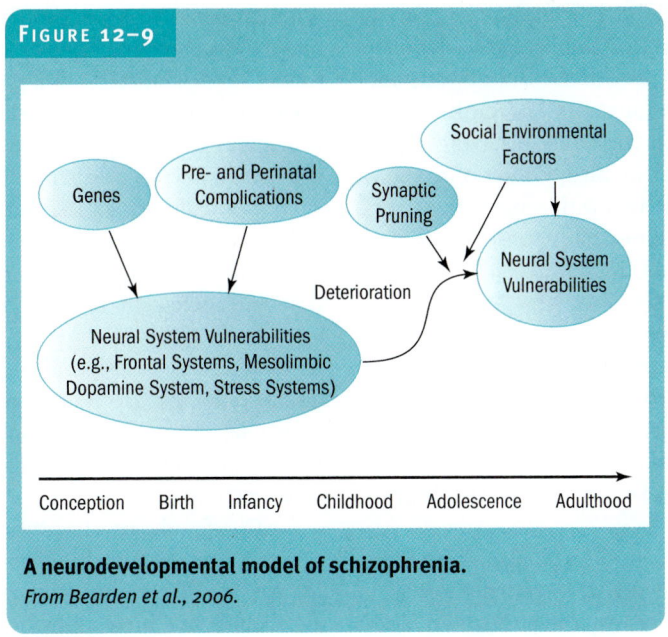

FIGURE 12-9

A neurodevelopmental model of schizophrenia.
From Bearden et al., 2006.

- Assessment for the positive and negative symptoms of schizophrenia and associated features.

- Psychological assessment that includes intelligence, communication, and adaptive skills testing.

- Physical examination, EEGs, brain scans, and laboratory tests, as needed in some cases.

- Consultation with the school and social services as necessary.

Although early identification can facilitate appropriate treatment, it presents particular challenges. The early-occurring nonpsychotic behavioral maladjustments of schizophrenia are observed in other disorders as well. In addition, children with other disorders—such as bipolar disorder and major depression—relatively often report hallucinations (Shaw & Rapoport, 2006). Indeed, children with schizophrenia may initially receive diagnoses of PDD, ADHD, mood disorders, and anxiety disorders, among others (Schaeffer & Ross, 2002).

As previously noted, it may be difficult to identify the positive symptoms of schizophrenia in children. Standardized rating scales (e.g., the Kiddie Positive and Negative Syndrome Scale) and semistructured interviews (e.g., the K-SADS, the Schedule for Affective Disorders and Schizophrenia for School-aged Children) can be helpful. However, children in nonclinic and clinic populations report seeing ghosts or shapes, hearing voices, and the like—and such hallucinations often do not indicate psychosis (McGee,

Williams, & Poulton, 2000; Mertin & Hartwig, 2004; Vickers & Garralda, 2000). Similarly, it can be difficult to tell whether bizarre ideas, obsessions, and preoccupations reported by the young should be considered psychotic delusions. This is especially true in children younger than 5 or 6, who are still limited in thinking logically and in distinguishing reality from fantasy (Volkmar et al., 1995). In addition, assessment of thought disorder has been especially difficult. It can be affected by a child's language skills, which are crucial in evaluating thinking processes. Moreover, what is considered abnormal thinking varies with developmental level (Caplan, 1994; Caplan et al., 2000).

Assessment of adolescents, especially older adolescents, is less problematic than that of children. Psychotic symptoms appear more similar to those of adult-onset schizophrenia, although they do not always indicate full-blown schizophrenia (Altman, Collins, & Mundy, 1997; Mertin & Hartwig, 2004). Psychotic symptoms at this time of life can be associated with several disorders, including substance abuse, epilepsy, and mood disorders (Calderoni et al., 2001; McClellan et al., 2003; Ulloa et al., 2000). Thus, manifestations of psychosis must be interpreted within the broader clinical presentation.

PREVENTION

Present knowledge about schizophrenia can aid prevention efforts (Evans et al., 2005). Programs to decrease prenatal and birth complications in the general population are worthwhile. Early identification and treatment are associated with fewer symptoms in the future (Hollis, 2002). Youths can be identified as at risk on the basis of having experienced adverse prenatal or birth conditions, and/or having first-degree relatives with schizophrenia or a related disorder. In addition, since onset is insidious for children and many adolescents, efforts might focus on early signs of the disorder.

Some efforts have targeted adolescents in the prodromal phase of the disorder, that is, when schizophrenic symptoms first appear (Evans et al., 2005). Components of the programs include medication, psychosocial treatment, and education for health care professionals. These efforts can at least delay the onset of psychosis.

Nevertheless, prevention is challenging because many of the early signs of schizophrenia appear in normal children or those with other disorders, and a substantial number of youths who exhibit early signs or symptoms of the disorder do not develop schizophrenia. In addition, the low prevalence of childhood schizophrenia hinders research on prevention with this age group.

TREATMENT

As with other aspects of early-occurring schizophrenia, we must generalize from what is known about treatment of adults. Treatment can vary substantially, depending on the severity of the case, whether the case is in an acute or a chronic phase, the opportunities for intervention that exist, community/family support, and the perspective of the therapist. Many children and adolescents with the disorder may live at home and attend local schools (Frazier et al., 2007). Among those with severe disturbance, some remain at home and may attend special schools; others are placed in hospitals and other residential settings for periods of time. It is believed that the best treatment strategy employs multiple methods to alleviate the multiple problems frequently encountered. Pharmacological and psychosocial interventions are the treatments of choice.

Pharmacological intervention. Traditional antipsychotic or atypical antipsychotic agents are central in treating schizophrenia (American Psychological Association, 2006). In adults, they can alleviate hallucinations, delusions, thought disturbance, and other symptoms. Limited research evidence exists for effectiveness in children. Atypical antipsychotic medications are increasingly used as they have fewer side effects, and they may act on both positive and negative symptoms (McClellan, 2005). But they, too, have some adverse side effects, such as weight gain and sedation. Clozapine, which appears especially effective for children and adolescents, carries risks for seizures and serious blood abnormalities, and thus is recommended only in cases that do not respond to other medications (Asarnow et al., 2004). Systematic studies with children and adolescents are still crucially needed.

Psychosocial intervention. Medications largely aim at reducing psychotic symptoms, whereas psychosocial treatment encompasses broader objectives. Some of these interventions are ameliorative or promising.

The family psychoeducational approach is a popular strategy for adults that is likely to be critical for youth. Today's family interventions are fueled by a collaborative philosophy in which blame is not placed on families, as it sometimes was in the past (Asarnow et al., 2004). Table 12–9 indicates some of the major components of family interventions. Behavioral approaches are important components of many interventions that target skills training, and these and cognitive–behavioral methods hold promise (Evans et al., 2005). Also promising are interventions providing support, education, and training of skills such as emotional awareness, self-monitoring, and coping during social interaction.

A comprehensive approach and a supportive environment are generally recommended for adults, although there is only limited research on this issue (American Psychological Association, 2006). For young people, the hardship of schizophrenia stems from both the disturbing symptoms and the

TABLE 12–9 MAJOR COMPONENTS OF FAMILY INTERVENTIONS FOR SCHIZOPHRENIA

Education about schizophrenia (e.g., causal hypotheses, course, treatments)
Enhancing strategies for coping with schizophrenia
Training in family communication emphasizing clarity and feedback tactics
Training in problem solving; managing everyday situations and stress
Crisis intervention during severe stress and/or signs of relapse of the disorder

Adapted from Asarnow, Tompson, & McGrath, 2004.

disruption of normal development (McClellan, Werry et al., 2001). It thus stands to reason that treatment must consider the reduction of specific symptoms and also the facilitation of psychological, social, educational, and occupational development. Treatment components may vary over time, but support is crucial across all phases of the disorder, not just during the acute phase. Since youth with schizophrenia may require relatively intensive home and community services that include the schools (Schiffman & Daleinen, 2006), systematic case management and coordination is likely to be beneficial (Asarnow et al., 2004). And as with other aspects of early-onset schizophrenia, the importance of research in advancing knowledge about the effectiveness of intervention can hardly be overstated.

SUMMARY

A BIT OF HISTORY

- *Disorders that are today known as pervasive developmental disorders and schizophrenia were historically associated with each other.*

- *The DSM classification of Pervasive Developmental Disorders includes five disorders, three of which are often referred to as the autism spectrum disorders.*

AUTISTIC DISORDER

- *The primary manifestations of autistic disorder are early-occurring impaired social interaction, impaired communication, and restricted, repetitive behaviors and interests. Associated problems include deficits in perception, intelligence, adaptive behavior, and motor skills.*

- *The prevalence of autism has dramatically increased in recent years. Methodological and social factors may at least partly account for increases. Prevalence is higher in boys and unrelated to social class.*

- *Autistic symptoms are recognized by age 2 in most infants. Symptoms can lessen throughout childhood; adolescence is marked by variable course. Perhaps 15% of youths with autism achieve independent living.*

- *Considerable research has been devoted to theory of mind, central coherence, and executive functions. Attention is now more focused on social, affective features of autism.*

- *Neurobiological research suggests that autism involves impairment in multiple brain areas or networks.*

- *The evidence for an inherited predisposition for autism—and a spectrum of autistic symptoms—is substantial. Associated medical conditions and prenatal/birth complications may play some causal role. Controversy exists over vaccines and thimerosal, but research results do not support a causal role.*

- *The pervasive developmental disorders and their relationship to one another are receiving substantial study. Autism, Asperger's disorder, and PDD-NOS are conceptualized as falling along a continuum of severity. Outcomes for Rett's disorder and Childhood Disintegrative Disorder are relatively poorer.*

- *Comprehensive assessment for autism includes evaluation for autistic symptoms, intelligence, and adaptive behavior.*

- *Behavioral and educational interventions are the mainstay of treatment and early prevention, with medication as an adjunct. Autism falls under the mandates of the Individuals with Disabilities Education Act.*

SCHIZOPHRENIA

- *The hallmarks of schizophrenia are hallucinations, delusions, thought disorder, disorganized behavior, and negative symptoms.*

- *The prevalence of schizophrenia is low in childhood and escalates in adolescence. Rates appear somewhat higher in males during childhood but the gender difference may flatten in adolescence.*

- *The onset of schizophrenia in youth often is insidious, with nonpsychotic symptoms appearing prior to psychotic symptoms. The course of schizophrenia varies, but full recovery is unlikely in most cases. Childhood schizophrenia is hypothesized to be a severe form of adult-onset schizophrenia.*

- *Neurological abnormalities in schizophrenia are evidenced in several ways. Frontal and temporal–limbic circuits and dopamine are especially implicated, and the disorder likely involves brain connectivity.*

- *Genetic influence, prenatal/birth variables, and psychosocial factors are causally implicated in schizophrenia. Multifactor vulnerability–stress and neurodevelopmental models are hypothesized.*

- *Comprehensive assessment is required for schizophrenia. It can be problematic to identify psychotic symptoms in children.*

- *Prevention of schizophrenia is challenging. Guidelines for treatment of youth are largely based on treatment of later-onset cases. A multimethod approach is recommended, which includes antipsychotic medications and psychosocial treatments.*

KEY TERMS

joint attention *(p. 329)*

echolalia *(p. 330)*

pronoun reversal *(p. 330)*

overselectivity *(p. 331)*

splinter skills/savant abilities *(p. 332)*

theory of mind *(p. 335)*

Sally–Anne test *(p. 335)*

faux pas test *(p. 336)*

central coherence *(p. 336)*

intersubjectivity *(p. 337)*

Asperger's disorder *(p. 340)*

Rett's disorder *(p. 341)*

childhood disintegrative disorder *(p. 342)*

PDD-NOS *(p. 343)*

positive symptoms *(p. 349)*

hallucinations *(p. 349)*

delusions *(p. 349)*

disorganized speech *(p. 349)*

disorganized behavior *(p. 349)*

catatonic behavior *(p. 349)*

negative symptoms *(p. 349)*

loose associations *(p. 351)*

neologisms *(p. 351)*

insidious onset *(p. 352)*

Disorders of Basic Physical Functions

In this chapter and the next we discuss problems of physical functioning and health. Because in many ways these problems represent the interface between psychology and pediatrics, the term *pediatric psychology* is often applied to this field of research and practice. For many of the problems discussed (e.g. toilet training, sleep difficulties), parents first turn to their pediatrician for help. Some problems may require collaboration between psychologists and physicians. The life-threatening starvation of adolescents with anorexia nervosa and the problem of enlarged colons in children with encopresis are two examples.

It is common for children to exhibit some difficulty in acquiring appropriate habits of elimination, sleep, and eating. Both the child's ability to master these relevant tasks and the parents' ability to train the child are important to the immediate well-being of both. Parents may be judged by themselves and others by how they manage these early child-rearing tasks. Also, how these tasks are handled can set the foundation for later interactions. Although parents solve many early difficulties themselves, they also frequently seek professional assistance (Schroeder & Gordon, 2002). This chapter examines some commonly encountered difficulties that are part of normal development. The principal focus, however, is on problems that are serious enough to be of clinical concern.

Problems of Elimination

TYPICAL ELIMINATION TRAINING

Toilet training is an important concern for parents of young children (Schroeder & Gordon, 2002). Parents may view control of elimination as a developmental milestone for the child. Furthermore, entry into day care or another program may depend on achievement of appropriate toileting. For the child, pleasing the parent, a sense of mastery, and the feeling of no longer being a "baby" may all contribute to the importance of achieving toileting control.

The usual sequence of acquisition of control over elimination is nighttime bowel control, daytime bowel control, daytime bladder control, and finally, nighttime bladder control. Although there is considerable variation as to when children are developmentally ready to achieve control over elimination, bowel and daytime bladder training usually are completed between the ages of 18 and 36 months.

Parents differ on when they feel it is appropriate to begin daytime training. Much of this decision is related to cultural values, attitudes, and real-life pressures on the parent (e.g., day care requirements, other siblings). An example of how day-to-day considerations probably affect this decision is illustrated by the advent of the disposable diaper. Ready availability of disposable diapers reduced many parents' inclinations to start training early.

There are probably several factors that contribute to successful training. Being able to determine that the child is developmentally ready to begin training is certainly important. Also, correctly judging when the child has to go to the toilet can lead to important early success experiences. Adequate preparation, such as using training pants rather than a diaper, having the child in clothes that are easy to remove, and having a child-size potty seat available are also helpful. Finally, the common practice of providing praise and concrete positive reinforcers (e.g., stickers, raisins) for appropriate toileting behavior, and doing so in a relaxed manner, has been demonstrated to be effective (Schroeder & Gordon, 2002).

ENURESIS

Jay | Enuresis and Its Consequences

Jay, a seven-year-old, had never achieved nighttime continence but had been continent during daytime for several years. He wets his bed an average of four days per week. No other significant behavior problems are present except for mild academic difficulties, and Jay's developmental history is unremarkable except for mild oxygen deprivation at birth and a delay in acquiring speech. Jay's biological father wet the bed until age nine.

Jay's mother and stepfather disagree on how they view his bedwetting. His mother feels he will grow out of it. His stepfather views Jay's bedwetting as laziness and removes privileges following episodes of enuresis. Both parents change the sheets when they are wet and attempt to restrict Jay's fluids prior to bedtime. They see the enuresis as a significant source of distress for the family and the conflict over how to handle it as exacerbating the problem.

Adapted from Ondersma & Walker, 1998, pp. 364–365.

Description and classification. The term enuresis comes from the Greek word meaning "I make water." It refers to the repeated voiding of urine during the day or night into the bed or clothes when such voiding is not due to a physical disorder (e.g., diabetes, urinary tract infection). A lack of urinary control is not usually diagnosed as enuresis prior to the age of 5, when continence might be expected. Also, a certain frequency of lack of control is required before the diagnosis of enuresis would be made, and this frequency varies with the age of the child. The DSM definition requires either a frequency of twice weekly for at least three consecutive months or wetting that is associated with clinically significant distress or impairment in important areas of functioning (American Psychiatric Association, 2000).

A distinction is often made between the more common nocturnal enuresis (nighttime bedwetting) and diurnal enuresis (daytime wetting). Enuresis is also referred to as primary if the child has never demonstrated bladder control and as secondary when the problem is preceded by a period of urinary continence. About 85% of all cases of enuresis are of the primary type (Walker, 2003).

Epidemiology. Estimates of prevalence indicate that among 5-year-olds, 7% of boys and 3% of girls exhibit enuresis and that by 10 years of age the percentages are 3 and 2, respectively. By age 18, prevalence decreases to 1% for males and less than 1% for females (Walker, 2003).

Etiology. A number of factors have been proposed as causes of enuresis, but no definitive cause has been established. At one time, enuresis was widely believed to be the result of emotional disturbance (Gerard, 1939). However, evidence does not support the view that enuresis is primarily a psychopathological disorder (Christophersen & Mortweet, 2001). When emotional difficulties are present in a child with enuresis, they most commonly are a consequence of enuresis rather than a cause. Parents of children with combined nocturnal and diurnal enuresis may be particularly likely to report psychological problems in their children (Joinson et al., 2007; Van Hoecke et al., 2006). Enuretic children, especially as they become older, are very likely to experience difficulties with peers and other family members. It would not be surprising if the child's self-image suffered (Wagner, Smith, & Norris, 1988). Also, enuresis and emotional problems may occur together because similar factors (e.g., a chaotic home environment) contribute to the development of both.

It is frequently suggested that sleep abnormalities contribute to the development of enuresis. Many adults, for example, assume that nocturnal enuresis occurs because the child is an unusually deep sleeper. Indeed, parents often spontaneously report difficulty in arousing their enuretic children during the night. However, research regarding the role of sleep and arousal is inconsistent (Mikkelsen, 2001). Wetting can occur in any of the stages of sleep, not just in deep sleep. This and other evidence raises doubts about viewing all or most cases of enuresis as a disorder of sleep arousal (Walker 2003). However, in some subgroups of youngsters, enuresis may, at least in part, be due to sleep arousal patterns.

Another biological pathway that has been suggested is a lack of normal nocturnal increases in antidiuretic hormone (ADH), which might lead to a higher production of urine. Among evidence for this hypothesis is the fact that some enuretic children respond well to an antidiuretic medication (desmopressin acetate, a hormone analog). However, evidence is not consistent and does not support low levels of ADH as the only or the primary cause of enuresis, although it may be a factor in some cases (Mikkelsen, 2001).

Family histories of youths with enuresis frequently reveal a number of relatives with the same problem. Higher rates of concordance for enuresis also have been reported among monozygotic than dizygotic twins, and multigenerational studies further support the notion of a significant genetic contribution to the disorder. Several different chromosomes have been implicated, and there may be a number of different modes of genetic transmission (Mikkelsen, 2001).

Overall, information regarding biological influences strongly suggests that at least some number of enuretic children have an organic predisposition toward enuresis (Sethi, Bhargava, & Phil, 2005). This predisposition may or may not result in the development of enuresis, depending on various experiential factors, such as parental attitude and training procedures.

The central tenet of behavioral theories of enuresis is that wetting results from a failure to learn control over reflexive wetting. Failure can result from either faulty training or other environmental influences that interfere with learning (e.g., a chaotic or stressful home environment). Many behavioral theories incorporate some maturational/physical difficulty, such as bladder capacity or arousal deficit, into their explanation.

Treatment. Prior to beginning any treatment, the child should be evaluated by a physician to rule out any medical cause for the urinary difficulties. If a parent seeks treatment for a very young child, a discussion of developmental norms may be helpful. Finally, if treatment for enuresis is to be initiated, careful preparation and parental cooperation are necessary.

A variety of pharmacological agents have been used in the treatment of enuresis. Imipramine hydrochloride (Tofranil), a tricyclic antidepressant, was at one time the most commonly employed. The effectiveness of imipramine seems to rely on the child's continuing to take the medication. Moreover, there is concern regarding possible side effects (Houts, 2003; Walker, 2003). Desmopressin acetate (DDAVP) has become the primary pharmacological treatment for enuresis, in part because it may have a lower risk of side effects than imipramine. Desmopressin was suggested as a treatment on the basis of its ability to control high urine output during sleep. Research findings suggest that DDAVP may reduce bedwetting even in cases that are difficult to treat. However, as with imipramine, relapse occurs; that is, wetting resumes if the drug is discontinued (Mikkelsen, 2001; Walker, 2003).

Behavioral treatments for nocturnal enuresis have received considerable research attention (Christophersen & Mortweet, 2001; Mellon & McGrath, 2000). The most well-known method is the urine-alarm system. This procedure was originally introduced by the German pediatrician Pflaunder in 1904 and was adapted and systematically applied by Mowrer and Mowrer (1938). Since then, the device and the procedures have been refined by a number of investigators. The basic device consists of an absorbent sheet between two foil pads. When urine is absorbed by the sheet, an electric circuit is completed which activates an alarm that sounds until it is manually turned off (see Figure 13–1). The parents are instructed to awaken the child when the alarm sounds. The child is taught to turn off the alarm and to go to the bathroom to finish voiding. The bedding is then changed, and the child returns to sleep. Usually the family keeps records of dry and wet nights, and after 14 consecutive nights of dryness, the device is removed.

Research conducted on the urine-alarm system indicates that it is successful in a clear majority of cases and that it is the treatment of choice for enuresis (APA, 2006). It is also more cost-effective than medications such as DDAVP (Houts, 2003; Mikkelsen, 2001). Treatment durations range between 5 and 12 weeks. Relapse has been reported in about 40% of cases, but reinstituting training often results

FIGURE 13–1

A urine alarm for treatment of enuresis. The child wears a urine sensor in the underclothes attached to an alarm worn on the nightclothes or wrist.

in a complete cure (Christophersen & Mortweet, 2001).

Modifications of the standard urine-alarm procedures have been introduced to reduce relapses. Full Spectrum Home Training was designed to build on initial treatment success, to reduce relapse, and to decrease the rate at which families dropped out of treatment (Houts, 2003). The procedure, which is cost-effective, is a treatment manual–guided package that includes a urine-alarm system; cleanliness training (having the child change his or her own bed and night clothes); a procedure to increase bladder capacity, which is known as retention control training; and overlearning, a process of training children to a higher criterion of successive dry nights than is usually thought to be necessary. The training program is delivered in a single 1-hour group session, and the parents and children then contract to complete the training at home with regular calls from the treatment staff as the only additional contact.

A study by Houts, Peterson, and Whelan (1986) illustrated the program's success and examined the contribution of the components to reducing relapse. Participating families received one of three treatment combinations: Group 1 received the urine-alarm system plus cleanliness training (BP), Group 2 received these two components plus retention control training (BP-RCT), and Group 3 received these three components plus overlearning (BP-RCT-OL)—the full package. A control group of children was followed over an 8-week period. No spontaneous remission of wetting occurred in control children, and they were then randomly assigned to one of the three treatment conditions. The findings of this study indicate that the three conditions were equally effective in treating enuresis. However, at a 3-month follow-up, relapse was significantly less in the BP-RCT-OL group than in the other two groups. These results suggest the importance of overlearning in preventing relapse.

ENCOPRESIS

Susan   Encopresis and Its Consequences

Susan, a six-year-old, had been soiling at least once per day since birth. The frequency of soiling had not decreased despite nearly constant attempts to convince her to use the toilet. Following careful medical examination, Susan's physician was certain that all medical causes for her condition had been ruled out. Tests, however, did reveal a considerable amount of fecal matter in her colon. During the course of the assessment, Susan's mother indicated that both she and her daughter were becoming very frustrated. It was also revealed that Susan was experiencing significant anxiety and pain with toileting. It appeared that Susan had learned to retain feces and to fear toileting following early experiences with large and painful bowel movements. The toileting problems had begun to affect Susan's social functioning and self-esteem.

Adapted from Ondersma & Walker, 1998, pp. 371–372.

Description and classification. Functional encopresis refers to the passage of feces into the clothing or other unacceptable area when this is not due to physical disorder. The diagnosis is given when this event occurs at least once a month, for at least 3 months, in a child of at least 4 years of age (American Psychiatric Association, 2000). Two subtypes of encopresis are recognized on the basis of the presence or absence of constipation. The vast majority of encopretic children are chronically constipated and are classified as having constipation with overflow incontinence (or retentive encopresis).

Epidemiology. Less writing and research have been done concerning encopresis than concerning enuresis (Christophersen & Mortweet, 2001; Mikkelsen, 2001). Estimates of prevalence range between 1.5 and 7.5% of children. Percentages appear to decrease with age, and the condition is very rare by adolescence. The problem occurs more frequently in males (Walker, 2003).

Pediatricians, who are likely to see a broad population of children, argue that the majority of children with encopresis have no associated psychopathology, a position supported by other professionals (Christophersen & Mortweet, 2001). However, because encopresis occurs during the day more often than at night, it is more socially evident than enuresis and also is more likely to carry a social stigma. Consequently, encopresis is likely to be a source of considerable distress to both parents and children, and may therefore be associated with more behavior problems. For example, in the Worcester Encopresis Study (Young et al., 1996), children with encopresis who had been referred to a pediatric gastroenterology clinic were reported to have more behavior problems and lower social competence scores than children without toileting problems. Following treatment, these children had fewer problems and improved social skills. To the extent that associated psychological difficulties do exist, they may be a consequence, rather than an antecedent, of encopresis, or both may be related to common environmental factors (e.g., stressful family circumstances).

Etilology. Most theories acknowledge that encopresis may result from a variety of causative mechanisms (McGrath, Mellon, & Murphy, 2000). Initial constipation and soiling may be influenced by factors such as diet, fluid intake, medications, environmental stresses, or inappropriate toilet training. The rectum and colon may become distended by the hard feces. The bowel then becomes incapable of responding with a normal defecation reflex to normal amounts of fecal matter.

Medical perspectives on the problem tend to stress a neurodevelopmental approach (Christophersen & Mortweet, 2001; Mikkelsen, 2001). Encopresis is viewed as more likely to occur in the presence of developmental inadequacies in the structure and functioning of the physiological and anatomical mechanisms required for bowel control. These organic inadequacies are viewed as temporary.

A behavioral perspective on encopresis stresses faulty toilet training procedures. Poor dietary choices may combine with the failure to apply appropriate training methods consistently. Some cases of encopresis may also be accounted for by avoidance conditioning principles. Avoidance of pain or fear reinforces retention. Positive consequences may also maintain soiling, and inadequate reinforcement may be given for appropriate toileting (Doleys, 1989). These various learning explanations are not incompatible with physiological explanations. For example, poor toilet training may compound insufficient physiological–neurological mechanisms.

Treatment. Most treatments for encopresis combine medical and behavioral management (McGrath et al., 2000; Mikkelsen, 2001). After the parent and the child have been educated about encopresis, the first step usually consists of an initial cleanout phase using enemas or high fiber intake to eliminate fecal impactions. Next, parents are asked to schedule regular toilet times and to use suppositories if defecation does not occur. Modifications in diet, laxatives, and stool softeners are employed to facilitate defecation. Positive consequences, such as a shared activity chosen by the child, are used to reward unassisted (no suppository) bowel movements in the toilet, as well as clean pants. If soiling occurs, children may be instructed to clean themselves and their clothes. Later in the course of training, laxatives and suppositories are withdrawn. While interventions are not as well established as for enuresis, research suggests that such treatment is highly effective and that relapse rates are low (APA, 2006; Mikkelsen, 2001). In cases where soiling is being used to manipulate the environment (e.g., being allowed to leave school, getting the mother's time and attention) additional family therapy may be indicated (Walker, 2003).

Sleep Problems

Parents commonly complain of difficulties in getting their young children to go to sleep and to sleep through the night. Nightmares are another concern that parents often report. To understand these problems, as well as more serious sleep disorders, it is necessary to understand the variations in normal sleep for children.

SLEEP DEVELOPMENT

At all ages, there is considerable individual variability in a normal sleep pattern. Furthermore, patterns of sleep change with development (Horne, 1992; Mindell & Owens, 2003). For example, the average newborn sleeps between 16 and 20 hours per day. By the time children are 1 year old, the average amount of sleep has fallen to 12 hours. The typical 6- to 12-year-old sleeps 10 to 11 hours each day. In addition to the number of hours of sleep, other aspects change as well. For example, newborns distribute their sleeping equally between day and night. Fortunately for parents, by about 3 months of age, infants have adopted the day–night pattern typical in adults, and by 18 months, sleep patterns are usually quite stable.

Within sleep periods there are two broad phases: rapid eye movement, or REM, sleep; and nonrapid eye movement, or NREM, sleep. NREM sleep is divided into four stages. Stages 3 and 4, the deepest part of sleep, are characterized by very slow waves in the EEG and are thus sometimes referred to as slow wave sleep. Throughout the night, the brain cycles through these stages of sleep. The time spent in different stages of sleep varies and changes with development. In the first year of life, for example, active REM sleep changes from about 8 hours to about half this amount, thus also reducing the proportion of time spent in REM relative to other phases of sleep. The sequencing, or pattern in which the various stages of sleep occur, also changes. The phases of sleep are intermixed in an irregular pattern in infants. However, as the child develops, regular patterns of light NREM, deep NREM, and REM sleep are gradually established.

COMMON SLEEP PROBLEMS

During the first year of life, parents' most frequent complaint is that the child does not sleep through the night. A reluctance to go to sleep and nightmares often occur during the second year, and 3- to 5-year-old children may present a variety of problems, including difficulty in going to sleep, nighttime awakenings, and nightmares. Surveys suggest that approximately one-quarter to one-third of infants and younger children experience some form of sleep problem that is disturbing to the family (Goodlin-Jones, Burnham, & Anders, 2000; Mindell, 1993). Some infants' and young children's sleep difficulties may be associated with conditions such as colic, with feeding practices, or with dietary problems such as milk intolerance.

School-age children also experience a variety of sleep problems, including bedtime resistance, delayed sleep onset, and night waking (Blader et al., 1997; Sadeh, Raviv, & Gruber, 2000). Indeed, sleep problems in older children may be underestimated, because older children are less likely to alert their parents to their difficulties (Gregory, Rijsdijk, & Eley, 2006; Owens et al., 2000). Even in adolescence, complaints

. . . And so the princess and the prince lived happily ever after. The end. Now get some sleep. We want you to be fresh as a daisy for your first day of college tomorrow."

regarding sleep are common, particularly the need for more sleep and difficulty in falling asleep. At this age, youths often experience decreasing amounts of sleep due to later bedtimes combined with earlier school start times. Indeed, Snell, Adam, & Duncan (2007) report that, on the basis of a nationally representative sample of U.S. children 3–18 years of age, total sleep time declined, particularly on weekdays, as children aged (see Figure 13–2). On weekdays, older children go to bed later and wake up earlier. The greatest decrease in sleep duration appears to occur at the time of transition from middle to high school, and there is actually an increase in sleep time as adolescents transition out of high school. Insufficient sleep may contribute to problems such as poor academic performance, anxiety, depression, and health difficulties (Buckhalt, El-Sheikh, & Keller, 2007; Fredriksen et al., 2004; Gregory et al., 2005; Snell et al., 2007).

Whether early sleep difficulties continue and/or develop into more serious sleep disorders is probably a function of a complex interplay of individual and environmental influences (Dauvilliers, Maret, & Tafti, 2005; El-Sheikh et al., 2006; Warren et al., 2006). Indeed, clear discrimination between common sleep difficulties and some sleep disorders is difficult. However, sleep problems that are frequent, persistent, and associated with other problems for the young person are considered sleep disorders. Sleep problems that do not cause the youth significant distress or do not result in impairment in important areas of functioning would not be considered a diagnosable disorder (American Psychiatric Association, 2000).

Sleep Disorders

There are many types of sleep disorders that are of concern to clinicians working with infants, children, and adolescents (Anders & Eiben, 1997; Streisand & Efron, 2003). The sleep disorders of primary concern are usually classified into two major categories: dyssomnias, or difficulties in initiating and maintaining sleep or of excessive sleepiness; and parasomnias, or disorders of arousal, partial arousal, or sleep-stage transitions (American Sleep Disorders Association, 1997).

Dyssomnias. Problems of getting to sleep and sleeping through the night, if severe and chronic enough, fall into the category of dyssomnias. These sleep and waking problems are indeed common. They frequently are viewed as manifestations of the child's neurophysiological development and therefore are expected eventually to resolve. However, child, parental, and environmental factors do play a role in a substantial number of cases. For example, when a parent rocks and soothes a young child to assist the

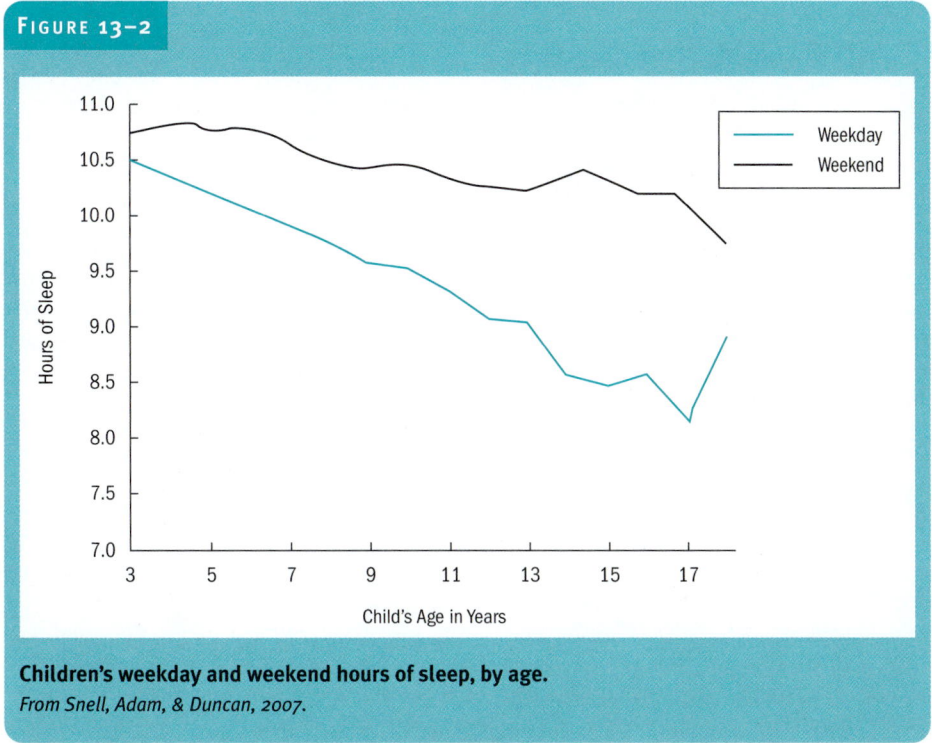

FIGURE 13–2

Children's weekday and weekend hours of sleep, by age.
From Snell, Adam, & Duncan, 2007.

child in falling asleep at night, the child may not learn to soothe herself or himself or learn to return to sleep during a normal night waking. A comparison of poor sleepers and good sleepers between 12 and 36 months of age revealed some surprising findings (Minde et al., 1993). Mothers' sleep diaries indicated more night wakings for the poor sleepers. However, filmed recordings indicated no differences in the actual number of wakings for the two groups. The poor sleepers were unable or unwilling to go back to sleep and woke their parent. In contrast, good sleepers were able to return to sleep on their own either by looking around and falling asleep or by quieting themselves, for example, by hugging a toy animal or sucking their thumbs. Whatever the cause, these problems may persist over many years, and they can result in considerable distress to the families involved (Stores, 1996).

The presence of dyssomnias may be underestimated. Young children's reports of difficulty in getting to sleep or staying asleep may be mistaken for attention seeking and the young child's level of cognitive development may not allow them to recognize a sleep problem. Also, a child may present with a variety of difficulties, and objective recording of sleep may reveal sleep problems that were not recognized by either the child or the parent (Sadeh et al., 2000). Dyssomnias may result in impairment in social, educational, or other areas of functioning. Yet the family may not be aware that sleep difficulties are contributing to these problems.

Sleep problems may be related to other problems in a number of ways. On the one hand, children's fear or worries may contribute to the development of problems in falling and staying asleep. In older children, sleep problems may be associated with worrisome cognitions—concerns about school or peers, ruminations about past or anticipated experiences, or fears. In addition, adolescents may have difficulty in establishing good sleep habits in the context of their changing lifestyles. Another reason that sleep difficulties and other problems may occur together is that they may be manifestations of a common set of etiological mechanisms such as difficult temperament, family discord, or parenting practices.

ACCENT

Sleep Apnea

Young people may experience disrupted or inadequate sleep for a number of reasons. One of these is obstructive sleep apnea (OSA), a respiratory sleep disorder characterized by repeated brief episodes of upper airway obstruction and resulting multiple transient arousals from sleep. These events result in fragmented and insufficient sleep and daytime fatigue and inattention. Mindell and Owens (2003) provide some basic information about the disorder.

Common nighttime symptoms of sleep apnea include loud snoring, pauses and difficulty in breathing, restless sleep, sweating during sleep, and bedwetting. Episodes may occur primarily during REM sleep in the later part of the night. In addition to fatigue, daytime symptoms may include mouth breathing, chronic nasal congestion or infection, and morning headaches.

Parents may be unaware of the symptoms that occur during sleep or otherwise fail to report them to their pediatricians. Instead, parents often initially complain of difficulties such as behavior problems, hyperactivity, inattentiveness and academic problems (Mulvaney et al., 2006). OSA symptoms may become evident only after the parents are directly questioned about their child's sleep. Information from interview and physical examination is important, but the only way to reliably diagnose OSA is by a sleep study, in which the youngster sleeps overnight in a laboratory. EEG and other physiological measurements are taken and the youngster's sleep is observed.

OSA is a common sleep disorder with peaks of prevalence between the ages of 2 and 6 years and in adolescence. In young children enlarged tonsils and adenoids are the most common risk factors. In adults the disorder is most commonly associated with obesity. Increasing prevalence of obesity suggests that this may become more of a relative risk for children and adolescents.

Removal of the tonsils and adenoids is the most common treatment in children, and symptom relief typically follows. Not all youngsters are candidates for such surgery, however. The use of a CPAP (continuous positive airway pressure) device can relieve apnea symptoms, but does not cure the problem. The youth wears a nasal/face mask during sleep and the device delivers pressure to keep the airways open. For young people who are obese, weight loss is recommended.

Parasomnias. Several of the childhood sleep disorders that cause concern for parents fall into the category of parasomnias. These include sleepwalking, sleep terrors, and nightmares.

SLEEPWALKING. An episode of sleepwalking (somnambulism) begins with the child's sitting upright in bed. The eyes are open but appear "unseeing." Usually the child leaves the bed and walks around, but the episode may end before the walking stage is reached. An episode may last for a few seconds or 30 minutes or longer. The child usually has no later memory of the episode. It was once believed that the sleepwalking child was exceptionally well coordinated and safe. This belief has proven to be a myth, and physical injury is a danger of the disorder.

Danielle   Sleepwalking

Danielle, 11 years old, told her mother that she thought that she was "going crazy." During the past 2 months there were several occasions when she awoke confused about where she was. Although she had gone to sleep in her own room, she awoke in other locations around the house. When she awoke in her older brother's room she felt concerned and guilty. Her younger sister reported that several times she had seen Danielle walking around the house at night like a "zombie" and not responding when she called her name. Danielle feared that she might have "amnesia" because she had no memory of anything happening during these nights. A medical history and examination revealed no history of seizures or current physical problems. Other than anxiety about her sleep problem and usual age-appropriate concerns, Danielle seemed well adjusted and she was functioning very well in school and with her family.

Adapted from Spitzer et al., 2000, pp. 337–338.

Approximately 15% of children between the ages of 5 and 12 have isolated experiences of walking in their sleep. Sleepwalking disorder, that is, persistent sleepwalking, is estimated to occur in 1 to 6% of the population. The problem usually continues for a number of years but then disappears by adolescence (American Psychiatric Association, 2000).

The vast majority of sleepwalking episodes occur in the first 1 to 3 hours following sleep onset. The fact that sleepwalking occurs during the later stages of NREM sleep (deep sleep) appears to invalidate the idea that sleepwalking is the acting out of a dream, because dreams occur in REM sleep. A characteristic EEG pattern has been found to precede each episode of sleepwalking. This EEG pattern

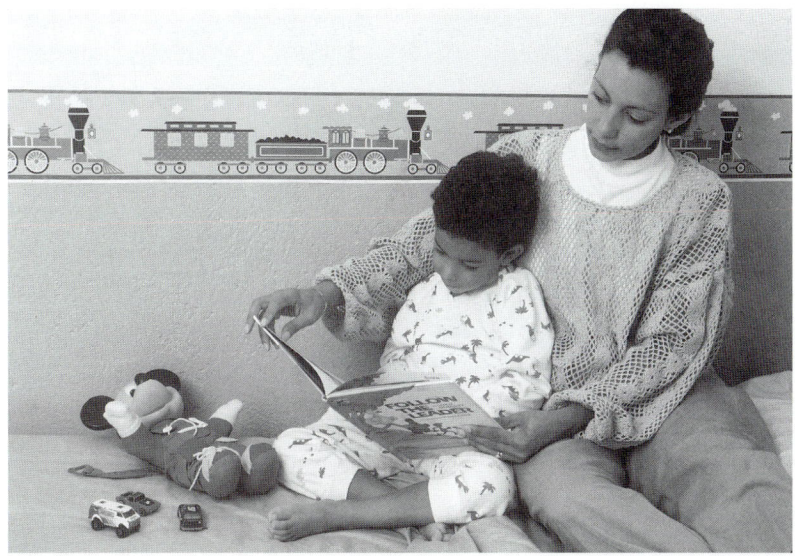

Establishing a predictable bedtime routine is helpful in reducing children's sleep problems.
(Laura Dwight/Laura Dwight Photography)

exists in 85% of all children during the first year of life but is present in only 3% of 7- to 9-year-olds. Thus, it has been suggested that central nervous system immaturity is of significance in sleepwalking disorder, and knowledge that the disorder is usually outgrown is consistent with that conceptualization. This view does not, however, rule out psychological or environmental factors. Frequency of sleepwalking has been reported to be influenced by the specific setting and by stress, fatigue, and physical illness (American Psychiatric Association, 2000; Mindell & Owens, 2003). Greater concordance rates for sleepwalking among monozygotic twins than among dizygotic twins and family patterns of sleepwalking have also been reported, leading some to propose a genetic component to the disorder. Unlike the case for adults, the presence of sleepwalking in children has not been found to be associated with psychological disturbance (Dollinger, 1986; Stores, 1996).

SLEEP TERRORS AND NIGHTMARES. Both sleep terrors and nightmares are fright reactions that occur during sleep. Sleep terrors, also known as night terrors or pavor nocturnus, are experienced by approximately 3% of children. Sleep terrors typically occur between the ages of 4 and 12 and most individuals outgrow the problem by adolescence (Mindell & Owens, 2003). Nightmares and sleep terrors are often confused, but they differ in a number of ways (see Table 13–1).

Sleep terrors occur during deep, slow-wave sleep and at a fairly constant time, usually about 2 hours into sleep. The event is quite striking in that the still-sleeping child suddenly sits upright in bed and screams. The face shows obvious distress, and there are signs of autonomic arousal, such as rapid breathing and dilated pupils. In addition, repetitive motor movements may occur, and the child appears disoriented and confused. Attempts to comfort the child are largely unsuccessful. The child usually returns to sleep without fully awakening and has little or no memory of this event the next morning. The conceptualization of the causes of sleep terrors is similar to that previously described for sleepwalking, and, indeed, they occur in the same part of the sleep cycle.

Nightmares are the other fright reaction that occurs during sleep and are common in children between the ages of 3 and 6 years (Mindell & Owens, 2003; American Sleep Disorders Association, 1997). These dreams occur during REM sleep. Parents may underestimate their children's nighttime fears. The findings illustrated in Figure 13–3 suggest that this may be particularly true for older children (Muris et al., 2001). It is frequently thought that the dreams are a direct manifestation of anxieties that the child faces. It has been suggested that children typically extinguish their fears by gradually exposing themselves during daytime hours to the feared stimulus (Kellerman, 1980). Factors such as parental protectiveness or lack of awareness of their children's fears, however, might limit the child's ability to engage in such daytime exposure or coping. In the absence of exposure and coping, anxieties and associated nightmares may continue or be exacerbated.

TABLE 13–1	CHARACTERISTICS DIFFERENTIATING NIGHTMARES AND SLEEP TERRORS	
NIGHTMARES	**SLEEP TERRORS**
Occur during REM sleep	Occur during NREM sleep
During middle and latter portions of the night	During first third of night
Verbalizations, if any, are subdued	Child wakes with cry or scream, and verbalizations usually present
Only moderate physiological arousal	Intense physiological arousal (increased heart rate, profuse sweating, pupils dilated)
Slight or no movements	Motor activity, agitation
Easy to arouse and responsive to environment	Difficult to arouse and unresponsive to environment
Episodes frequently remembered	Very limited or no memory of the episode
Quite common	Somewhat rare (1 to 6%)

Adapted from Wilson & Haynes, 1985.

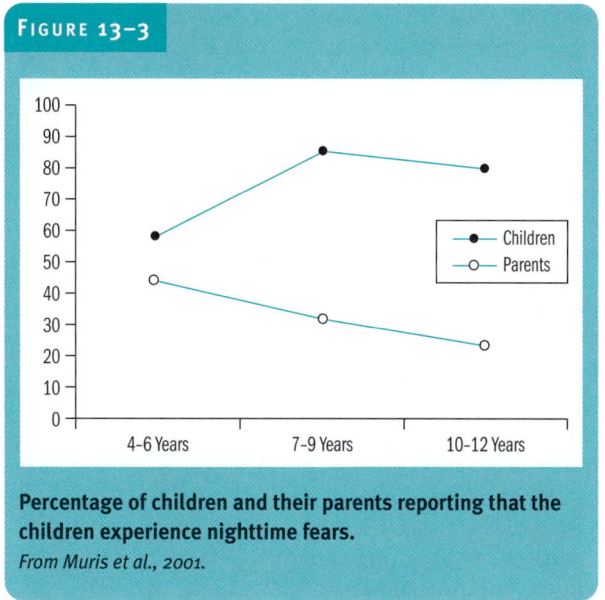

FIGURE 13–3

Percentage of children and their parents reporting that the children experience nighttime fears.

From Muris et al., 2001.

Matthew   Recurrent Nightmares

The recurrent nightmares that 11-year-old Matthew experienced led his parents to seek help. Matthew was doing well in school, was involved in many activities, and had friends. His parents described him as sensitive and serious, but quite happy. A sleep diary indicated that nightmares had occurred on 11 of 14 nights. Matthew went to sleep in his own bed, but after the nightmare slept in his parents' or older brother's bedroom. Although his parents and brother did not mind, Matthew felt it was immature to have to sleep in their rooms. Recently, Matthew had been taking longer to fall asleep at night. Matthew complained of being tired during the day and upset about having another nightmare.

The parents indicated that Matthew had experienced occasional night terrors between the ages of 4 and 6. These had begun at the time of his maternal grandfather's death and after a difficult bout with the flu and high fever. During his preschool years Matthew had at least one nightmare a week, but since then only occasional nightmares until the past month. There were no health or other problems in the family except that the paternal grandfather had experienced a heart attack 2 months earlier, but he was home and recovering.

Matthew described his life as enjoyable and stimulating, but reported a number of situations that made him very sad or angry. Several bullies on the school bus repeatedly teased and pushed younger children including his younger brother. Matthew was also having difficulty completing a particular Scout badge and he described his older brother as being particularly irritating to the entire family.

The parents and Matthew were reassured and told that he was a child with many strengths and also sensitivity to injustices and others being hurt. It was suggested that his nightmares were related to these stresses at home and at school. A brief intervention was recommended. The treatment consisted of Matthew discussing the content of his nightmares with his parents and keeping a diary of the content. Matthew was also taught relaxation techniques. The clinician and Matthew reviewed the content of the nightmares and role played responses that resulted in a victory over the scary events. There was also a focus on the events that were creating stress. Matthew and the clinician took a problem-solving approach to the bullies on the bus and the parents had the school principal investigate and intervene in the bullying incidents. The family discussed sibling squabbles and the older brother was encouraged to spend more time with his own friends.

Matthew's nightmares decreased over the next month. This coincided with Matthew's having greater control over daily events and the resolution of the bullying problem. Matthew realized that he might have occasional nightmares and that if they became recurrent he would identify and cope with stressors in his environment.

Adapted from Schroeder & Gordon, 2002, pp. 214–216.

No single theoretical framework has proven successful in explaining the development of nightmares, and explanations allowing for multiple causes (e.g., developmental, physiological, and environmental factors) are likely to have the greatest utility.

TREATING SLEEP PROBLEMS

Initiating and maintaining sleep. A number of different interventions have been demonstrated to be effective in dealing with the problems of bedtime refusal, difficulty in falling asleep, and nighttime wakings (Christophersen & Mortweet, 2001; Mindell, 1999; Sadeh, 2005).

Extinction (ignoring) procedures are based on the assumption that attention to nighttime fussing maintains children's sleep problems. Thus parents are taught to put the child to bed at a designated time and then to ignore the child until a set time the next morning. Some parents find it very stressful to ignore long periods of bedtime crying, so they may use a variant of the extinction procedure, graduated extinction, that has proven to be successful. First, parents ignore bedtime crying for an agreed-upon time for which they feel comfortable, and then over several nights, they increase the period before they check on the child.

Establishing positive bedtime routines also appears to be a promising intervention. Parents are taught to develop a consistent bedtime routine at a regularly scheduled bedtime. The routine involves calm activities that the child enjoys. Another successful procedure, scheduled awakenings, involves having the parent awaken the child and console the child approximately 15 minutes before typical spontaneous awakening. These scheduled awakenings are gradually faded out.

Finally, there is research to support the value of parent education in preventing the development and worsening of these kinds of sleep problems. Parents are provided information about sleep, the importance of routine, and the importance of putting the child to bed while partially awake so that the child can learn to go to sleep without an adult's being present.

Pharmacological agents have been among the most widely used treatments. However, good support for their effectiveness is lacking, and there is concern regarding negative side effects and recurrences of sleep disturbances with discontinuation of treatment. Given such concerns, behavioral interventions are recommended for most problems prior to the use of pharmacological treatments (e.g., Anders & Eiben, 1997; Mindell & Owens, 2003).

Parasomnias. In many cases of sleep terrors and sleepwalking, intensive treatment may not be indicated, because the episodes usually disappear spontaneously. Education and support may be sufficient. However, a number of treatments have been suggested. These include scheduled awakenings, contingency management, instructional procedures, and anxiety-reduction procedures (Christophersen & Mortweet, 2001). Durand and Mindell (1999) used a multiple baseline design to evaluate the effectiveness of scheduled awakenings for three boys, each with a several-year history of sleep terrors. During the baseline period, data on the occurrence of sleep terrors were recorded. During the intervention phase, parents were provided with an explanation of the procedures. They were instructed to awaken their son approximately 30 minutes prior to the typical sleep-terror time by lightly touching him until the child opened his eyes, and then to allow him to fall back to sleep. The scheduled awakening intervention quickly reduced the frequency of sleep terrors, and success was maintained at a 12-month follow-up.

Pharmacological treatments of sleep terror and sleepwalking have also been reported; however, the medications may actually produce effects that set the stage for recurrences of these disorders, and side effects are a concern (Shaffer & Waslick, 1996).

Consistent with the view of anxiety as the basis for nightmares, the majority of treatments for nighttime fears have involved cognitive-behavioral anxiety-reduction techniques (Gordon et al., 2007). These treatments have typically been effective, but the active components of the various treatments need to be clarified.

Problems of Feeding, Eating, and Nutrition

Establishing eating habits and food preferences is one of the primary aspects of early socialization. Mealtimes are often an occasion for family interactions and rituals, and other social interactions frequently revolve around food and eating. These and other considerations suggest the importance of food and eating-related behaviors.

COMMON EATING AND FEEDING PROBLEMS

A wide range of problems having to do with eating and feeding are commonly reported in young children

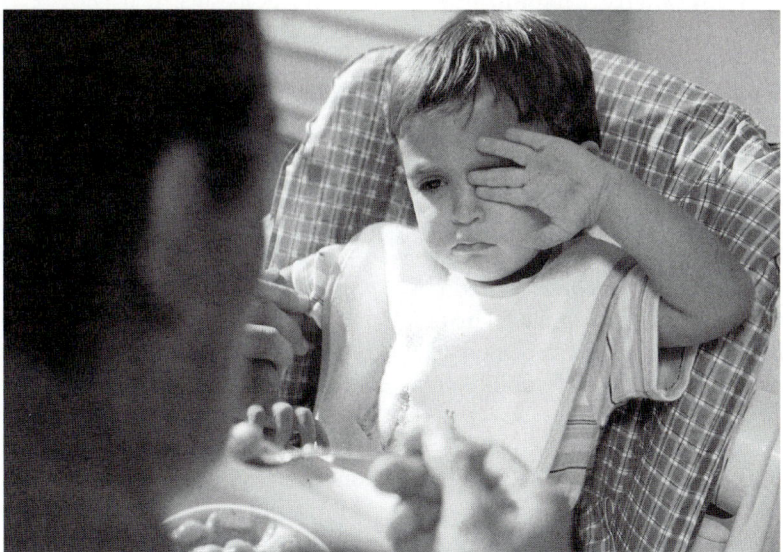

Young children often exhibit feeding and eating problems. This difficulty may result in disruption and cause their parents considerable distress.
(SuperStock, Inc.)

(Budd & Chugh, 1998). These include undereating, finicky eating, overeating, problems in chewing and swallowing, bizarre eating habits, annoying mealtime behaviors, and delays in self-feeding. Many of these problems can cause considerable concern for parents and appreciable disruption of family life. For example, Crist and Napier-Phillips (2001) indicated that over 50% of parents report one problem feeding behavior and more than 20% report multiple problems. Also, O'Brien (1996) found that approximately 30% of a sample of parents of infants and toddlers reported that their children refuse to eat the foods presented to them. Adequate nutrition and growth are clearly a concern, but restricted eating is also often accompanied by behavioral problems such as tantrums, spitting, and gagging. Severe cases of food refusal may be associated with even more difficult social and psychological problems, and may result in medical complaints and malnourishment. Indeed, some cases of failure to thrive (life-threatening weight loss or failure to gain weight) can be conceptualized as a special case of such refusal (Kelly & Heffer, 1990; Kerwin & Berkowitz, 1996). Thus some feeding and eating problems may actually endanger the physical health of the child. The disorders discussed in the following sections are some that appear in the DSM and that have attracted attention from researchers and clinicians.

Early Feeding and Eating Disorders

Rumination disorder. Rumination (or mercyism) is a syndrome characterized by the voluntary and repeated regurgitation of food or liquid in the absence of an organic cause. When infants ruminate, they appear deliberately to initiate regurgitation. The child throws his or her head back and makes chewing and swallowing movements until food is brought up. In many instances, the child initiates rumination by placing his or her fingers down the throat or by chewing on objects. The child exhibits little distress; rather, pleasure appears to result from the activity. If rumination continues, serious medical complications can result, with death being the outcome in extreme cases (American Psychiatric Association, 2000).

Rumination is most often observed in two groups, in infants and in persons with developmental disabilities. Among children who are developmentally normal, rumination usually appears during the first year of life and is thought to be a form of self-stimulation. Sensory and/or emotional deprivation are both associated with rumination. In individuals with intellectual disabilities, later onset is often observed, and the incidence of the disorder seems to increase with greater degrees of intellectual disability. In both groups, rumination appears to be more prevalent in males (Kerwin & Berkowitz, 1996; Mayes, 1992).

Management of the problem will probably involve a multidisciplinary team. Treatments emphasizing the use of social attention contingent on appropriate behavior have been successful, and there is some suggestion that with infant ruminators, improving mothers' ability to provide a nurturing and responsive environment is effective (Mayes, 1992; Nicholls, 2004). These procedures have the advantage of being easily implemented by the parents in the home and of being acceptable to them. However, controlled evaluations of interventions are needed.

Pica. *Pica* is the Latin term for magpie, a bird known for the diversity of objects that it eats. Pica is characterized by the habitual eating of substances usually considered inedible, such as paint, dirt, paper, fabric, hair, and bugs.

During the first year of life, most infants put a variety of objects into their mouths, partly as a way of exploring the environment. Within the next year, they typically learn to explore in other ways and come to discriminate between edible and inedible materials. The diagnosis of pica is therefore usually made when there is persistent consumption of inedibles beyond this age, and pica is most common in 2- and 3-year-olds.

Information regarding prevalence is limited, but pica is reported to be particularly high among individuals with developmental disabilities (American Psychiatric Association, 2000; McAlpine & Singh, 1986; Nicholls, 2004). Pica can lead to a variety of damage, including parasitic infection and intestinal obstruction due to the accumulation of hair and other materials. The disorder also appears to be related to accidental poisoning (American Psychiatric Association, 2000; Halmi, 1985).

A number of causes for pica have been postulated including parental inattention, lack of supervision, and lack of adequate stimulation (Kerwin & Berkowitz, 1996). Cultural influences such as superstitions regarding eating certain substances should also be considered (Millican & Lourie, 1970; Paniagua, 2000).

Educational approaches aimed at informing parents of the dangers of pica and at encouraging them to deter the behavior may be somewhat successful. However, it is necessary to supplement such interventions with more intensive therapeutic endeavors in some cases. Behavioral interventions that address antecedents and consequences of pica behav-

ior have been suggested (Bell & Stein, 1992; Linscheid & Rasnake, 2001).

Feeding disorder of infancy or early childhood.
The essential feature of this disorder is a persistent failure to eat adequately that results in the child's failing to gain weight or experiencing a significant weight loss. The DSM criteria for Feeding Disorder of Infancy or Early Childhood requires that this problem must be present for at least one month and not be due to a gastrointestinal or other medical condition, to other disorders (e.g., rumination disorder), or to the lack of available food (American Psychiatric Association, 2000). The problem is often discussed as one aspect of "failure to thrive," and conceptualization of these feeding problems and their treatment often are discussed as part of this larger construct.

Approximately 1 to 5% of pediatric hospital admissions are due to failure to thrive, and about one-half of these may be due to feeding disturbances. The prevalence of failure to thrive based on community samples is estimated at about 3%. Feeding disorder of infancy and early childhood appears to be equally common in males and females (American Psychiatric Association, 2000).

That an infant or a young child would cease to eat adequately is puzzling and clearly troublesome. This problem and associated malnutrition can result in disruption in multiple areas of physical, cognitive, and social-emotional development at this critical time. The young child may be irritable and difficult to console or may appear apathetic and withdrawn—characteristics that may further contribute to feeding difficulties.

Multiple causes most likely contribute to the development of feeding disorders (Benoit, 2000). The particular influences that contribute are difficult to determine, in part because it is difficult to observe the child and family prior to the development of the problem. Drotar and Robinson's (2000) review and discussion of failure to thrive suggests that one might conceptualize the development of a feeding disorder in terms of the parent's competence—defined as sensitivity to the child's developing repertoire and as communication and involvement with the child. In this conceptualization, the parent's competence is influenced by three sets of factors.

The first set is the parent's personal resources. Identification with the parental role, knowledge of effective parenting skills, and attachment and relationships with their children may be disrupted in these parents. This problem may, in part, be due to traumatic experiences in the parent's own childhood that disrupted the development of these parenting processes. Parental psychopathology, particularly depression, may also contribute to diminished parental resources.

The second set of factors is characteristics of the infant or child that may contribute to the problem by increasing the complexity of child-rearing for parents with limited personal resources. Thus factors such as low birthweight, acute physical illnesses, various disabilities, and temperamental characteristics may contribute to the development of a problem.

Finally, the family's social context is likely to interact with personal parental resources and child characteristics to affect parenting competence. Poverty or economic stress, serious parental or family conflict, the family's social networks and resources, and availability of community resources are among the contextual factors that may be implicated.

The focus of intervention has been on treating the physical/nutritional symptoms to improve growth and developmental outcome. Multidisciplinary treatments that include medical, nutritional, educational, and psychological components are typical, but controlled studies indicate mixed and often disappointing outcomes (Benoit, 2000).

OBESITY

Obesity is typically defined in terms of body mass index (BMI, weight in kilograms divided by square of height in meters). A BMI at or above the 95th percentile for age and gender is often defined as overweight.

Obesity is an important health problem and is among the most prevalent nutritional diseases in children and adolescents. An estimated 17% of U.S. children and adolescents ages 2–19 are overweight and certain ethnic/racial groups appear to be at particular risk. Mexican-American male children and adolescents, and Mexican-American and non-Hispanic black female children and adolescents, are more likely to be overweight. In addition, reports indicate that rates of child and adolescent obesity have been increasing (Center for Disease Control, 2007; Ogden et al., 2006). Data from the National Health and Nutrition Examination Survey (NHANES) illustrate this problem (Figure 13–4). Findings such as these lead the U.S. Surgeon General, the American Academy of Pediatrics, and others to call for a plan to reduce obesity (American Academy of Pediatrics, 2003; Levi, Segal, & Gadola, 2007).

Obesity in childhood is associated with numerous physical health problems, including the risk of diabetes and heart disease (Daniels, 2006; Morrison, Friedman, & Gray-McGuire, 2007). In addition, there are associations with educational, social and psychological difficulties (Puhl & Latner, 2007; Zametkin et al., 2004). For example, Geier and colleagues (2007) found that among a sample of inner-city fourth to sixth graders, overweight children were absent significantly more than normal weight children

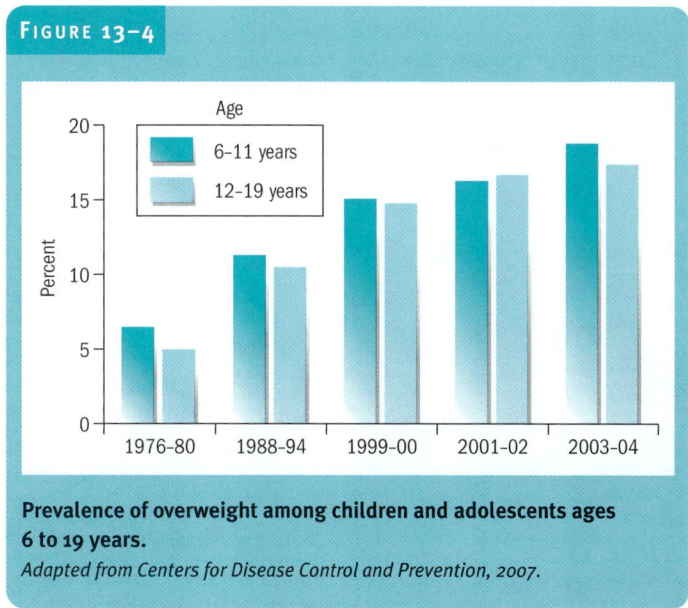

FIGURE 13–4

Prevalence of overweight among children and adolescents ages 6 to 19 years.
Adapted from Centers for Disease Control and Prevention, 2007.

even when controlling for age, gender, and race/ethnicity. Also, in a study by Israel and Shapiro (1985), the behavior problem scores of children who were enrolled in a weight-loss program were significantly higher than the norms for the general population, but significantly lower than the norms for children referred to clinics for psychological services. Clearly, the degree to which these problems contribute to or result from being overweight cannot be determined from this study.

The obese child's social interactions may be adversely affected by negative evaluations (Puhl & Latner, 2007). Because children hold negative views of obesity, children who are perceived as overweight are ranked as less liked (Latner & Stunkard, 2003). Negative attitudes toward overweight peers have been found in children as young as age 3. Overweight youths may experience social isolation, rejection and bullying (Griffiths et al., 2006). These effects appear to continue throughout development. College acceptance rates are lower for obese adolescent girls than for nonobese girls with comparable academic credentials, and discrimination and lowered expectations may continue into college (Puhl & Latner, 2007). The obese youth's self-esteem may be adversely affected by such experiences (Stern et al., 2007). However, many obese youths do not have adjustment difficulties and they may maintain their general self-esteem despite reactions to their physical appearance (Israel & Ivanova, 2002).

Etiology. The causes of obesity are certainly multiple and complex. Any explanation must include biological, psychological, and social/cultural influences (Cawley, 2006; Cope, Fernández, & Allison, 2004; Jelalian & Mehlenbeck, 2003; Sallis & Glanz, 2006).

Interventions that target obesity address both problematic food intake and inactivity.

(Tony Freeman/PhotoEdit Inc.)

Biological influences include genetic factors and the metabolic effects of dieting and exercise (Price, 1995; Saris, 1995). Leptin deficiency in severely obese children is an example of a potential mechanism (Cope et al., 2004; Montague et al., 1997). Leptin is a protein that is believed to be involved in signaling the brain to end eating; a gene identified in mice appears to control the production of leptin. Genetic contributions are likely to be complex rather than simple. Of course, biological influences are not independent of environmental influences; rather, these influences interact. So for example, leptin levels can be affected by eating styles associated with obesity (Laessle, Wurmser, & Pirke, 2000).

Psychosocial factors are also important in the development of obesity. Both logic and research suggest that the food intake and activity level of obese children are in need of change (Anderson & Butcher, 2006). Problematic food intake and inactivity are likely to be affected by family, peer, and other environmental influences and to be learned in the same manner as any other behavior (Laessle, Uhl, & Lindel, 2001; Storch et al., 2007). For example, parents influence and support weight-related behaviors (Moens, Braet, & Soetens, 2007). And children also observe and imitate the eating behavior of their parents and others around them, and are reinforced for engaging in that style of eating (Klesges & Hanson, 1988). Eating and inactivity may also become strongly associated with physical and social stimuli, so that they become almost automatic in some circumstances. Moreover, people may learn to use food to overcome stress and negative mood states, such as boredom and anxiety. The treatment of obesity that has been developed from a social learning perspective seeks to break these learned patterns and to develop more adaptive ones.

Larger cultural influences are also germane. Television provides a striking example of how the larger society might contribute to the development of weight problems. American children and adolescents have easy access to high-caloric foods, watch a great deal of television, frequently play video games, and in general lead a sedentary lifestyle (Jelalian & Mehlenbeck, 2004; Robinson & Killen, 2001). In addition to the negative effects of inactivity associated with television watching, the vast majority of food product advertisements viewed by children and adolescents are high in sugar and fat (Powell et al., 2007). Indeed, the probability of being overweight is associated with the amount of television viewing, and reduction in viewing may lead to decreases in degree of obesity (Gordon-Larsen, Adair, & Popkin, 2002; Robinson, 1999).

Sean   Obesity and Family Environment

Sean, a 10-year-old who was 50% overweight for his height and age, enrolled in a treatment program for obese children and their families. Sean's pediatrician described a history of steady, greater than expected weight gains with extreme increases in the last three years. Sean's father was normal weight, but his mother was about 40% overweight and had made numerous unsuccessful weight-loss attempts. Neither of Sean's two siblings was overweight. Sean snacked frequently on large amounts of high-calorie food, with most of his calories consumed after school while his parents were at work. His mother often found candy wrappers in Sean's room and pockets. Sean's parents reported that as Sean gained weight, his physical activity decreased and most of his leisure time was spent watching television. They were concerned with his frequent shortness of breath. Sean had no close friends and was something of a loner. He was teased about his weight at school and by his siblings. Although the parents indicated that they were committed to Sean's losing weight, there were indications of some family "sabotage." Much of the family's activities revolved around food, and food was used as a reward. Sean's father described himself as a gourmet cook, and his high-calorie, high-fat meals were "family times." Sean spent considerable time visiting his grandmother, who took pleasure in providing him with food and snacks.

Adapted from Israel & Solotar, 1988.

Behavioral treatment. Multifaceted programs that emphasize behavioral interventions and education are the most effective treatments for childhood obesity (Cooperberg & Faith, 2004; Young et al., 2007). The work of Israel and his colleagues (Israel et al., 1994; Israel & Solotar, 1988) illustrates the general approach. Children and parents attend meetings during which the following four areas are regularly addressed: *intake,* which includes nutritional information, caloric restriction, and changes in actual eating and food preparation behaviors; *activity,* which includes both specific exercise programs and increasing the energy expended in daily activities, for example, walking to a friend's house rather than being driven; *cues,* which identify the external and internal stimuli associated with excessive eating or inactivity;

and *rewards,* which provide positive consequences for progress by both the child and the parent. Homework assignments are employed to encourage the families to change their environments and to practice more appropriate behavior.

The role of parental involvement has been noted as an important element. Israel, Stolmaker, and Andrian (1985), for example, provided parents with a brief course in the general principles of child management. The parents then participated with their children in a behavioral weight-reduction program that emphasized the application of the general parenting skills to weight reduction. Another group of parents and children received only the behavioral weight-reduction program. At the end of treatment, both groups achieved a significantly greater weight loss than the control children who were not receiving treatment. One year following treatment, children whose parents had received separate child-management training had maintained their weight losses better than other treated children.

These results and others suggest the importance of changing family lifestyles and of providing parents with the skills necessary to maintain appropriate behavior once the treatment program has ended (Israel, 1988; Young et al., 2007). This is a particularly important issue in light of repeated evidence that individuals frequently regain the weight they have lost. In addition to parental involvement, the importance of increased activity, particularly when it is part of the family's lifestyle, and various other family factors have been shown to be related to treatment outcome (Epstein et al., 1995; Israel, Silverman, & Solotar, 1986).

In addition to improving parental involvement, enhancing the child's self-regulatory skills may be valuable (Israel et al., 1994). Children receiving a multidimensional treatment program, comparable to the four-area program described before, were compared with children receiving a similar intervention plus enhanced training in comprehensive self-management skills. The results of this study are presented in Figure 13–5. In the 3 years prior to treatment, children in the two conditions had shown similar patterns of increasing percentage of overweight. Both treatment conditions resulted in comparable reductions in the percentage of overweight during treatment. However, whereas children in the standard condition appeared to return to pretreatment trends in the 3 years following intervention, children in the enhanced self-regulation condition did not.

Although research supports the effectiveness of the behavioral approach to children's weight reduction

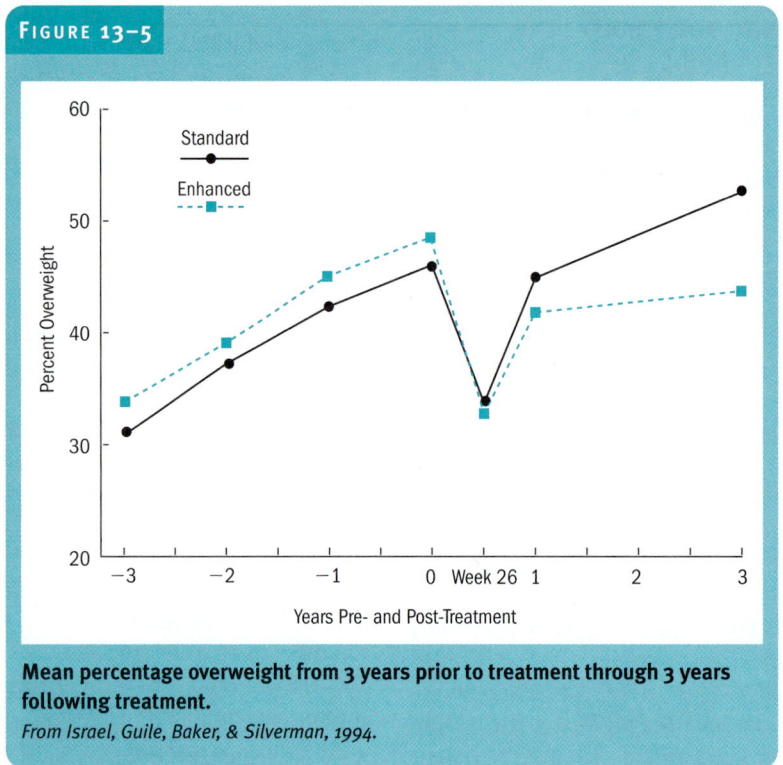

FIGURE 13–5

Mean percentage overweight from 3 years prior to treatment through 3 years following treatment.
From Israel, Guile, Baker, & Silverman, 1994.

(Cooperberg & Faith, 2004; Israel, 1990; Israel & Zimand, 1989; Young et al., 2007), there is a need for improved interventions that produce greater, more consistent, and more long-lasting weight loss and for attention to issues of setting appropriate treatment goals and tailoring interventions to particular populations (Faith et al., 2001; Israel, 1999; Jelalian et al., 2007). Prevention efforts are also needed (Stice, Shaw, & Marti, 2006). Programs targeting the general population, or high-risk groups in particular, need to be part of the effort to deal with this common problem. These programs should seek, through the media and schools, to educate youngsters and their families and to actively change harmful nutritional and activity lifestyles.

Eating Disorders: Anorexia and Bulimia Nervosa

Anorexia nervosa and bulimia nervosa are eating disorders that involve maladaptive attempts to control body weight, significant disturbances in eating behavior, and abnormal attitudes about body shape and weight. These disorders were once considered quite rare. The number of cases reported, as well as "subclinical" levels of these problems, has increased

(Lucas & Holub, 1995; Striegel-Moore & Bulik, 2007). This increase may be due to actual increases in eating disordered behavior and/or to greater awareness and reporting of these problems.

DEFINITION AND CLASSIFICATION: AN OVERVIEW

There is continuing consideration regarding the best way to define eating disorders (Wonderlich et al., 2007). Several dimensions are involved in making distinctions between eating disorders or attempting to subcategorize a particular disorder. An individual's weight status is one such consideration. A person with an eating disorder may be underweight, within the normal weight range, or overweight.

A second consideration is whether the individual engages in binge eating. A binge is defined by the DSM as (1) eating a larger amount of food during a discrete period of time (e.g., 1 hour) than most people would be expected to eat during that time and (2) feeling a lack of control of eating during this episode. However, there is some question as to whether the individual must consume a large amount of food in order for an episode to be considered a binge (Anderson & Paulosky, 2004). Some suggest that the feeling of loss of control and the violation of dietary standards are the central characteristics of a binge.

A third consideration is the method that the person uses to control her or his weight. A distinction is often made between restricting and purging strategies. The first strategy refers to severely restricting food intake and/or engaging in highly vigorous exercise. The second strategy involves purging oneself of unwanted calories through methods such as vomiting or the misuse of laxatives, diuretics, or enemas.

Weight status, the presence or absence of binge eating, and the method employed to control one's weight therefore are important considerations in thinking about eating disorders. We turn now to how these dimensions are involved in describing eating disorders.

CLASSIFICATION AND DESCRIPTION: DSM APPROACH

The DSM describes two primary eating disorder diagnoses: Anorexia Nervosa and Bulimia Nervosa. The DSM also includes a category of Eating Disorder Not Otherwise Specified (EDNOS). This diagnosis may be applied to eating disorders that would not meet the criteria for either anorexia nervosa or bulimia nervosa. One such disorder is Binge-Eating Disorder (BED). BED is characterized by recurrent binge eating; however, the individual does not engage in the inappropriate weight-control behaviors that are part of bulimia nervosa (described below). The DSM considers BED as requiring further study prior to making BED a separate diagnosis.

Anorexia nervosa. Individuals with eating disorders whose body weight is well below expected levels (15 percent below or more) are likely to be given the diagnosis of anorexia nervosa (AN). A drive for extreme thinness and a fear of gaining weight are characteristics of individuals with this diagnosis. The seriousness of extreme weight loss is illustrated by Bruch's (1979) classic description of one of her clients.

| Alma | **Like a Walking Skeleton** |

. . . she (Alma) looked like a walking skeleton, with her legs sticking out like broomsticks, every rib showing, and her shoulder blades standing up like little wings. Her mother mentioned, "When I put my arms around her I feel nothing but bones, like a frightened little bird." Alma's arms and legs were covered with soft hair, her complexion had a yellowish tint, and her dry hair hung down in strings. Most striking was the face—hollow like that of a shriveled-up old woman with a wasting disease, . . . Alma insisted that she looked fine and that there was nothing wrong with her being so skinny. "I enjoy having this disease and I want it." (pp. 2–3)

The DSM criteria employed to diagnose AN are presented in Table 13–2. The criterion of less than 85% of expected weight can be the result of the young person's refusal to gain weight or if the young person is still growing, the failure to gain enough weight to meet the 85% criterion. Some definitions have stressed that psychological variables, such as a sense of personal inadequacy, are also central to defining the disorder (Bruch, 1973; 1986; Yates, 1989).

The DSM distinguishes between two subtypes of AN on the basis of whether or not the person binges:

- *Binge-eating/purging anorexics* exhibit a persistent pattern of binge eating and purging.

- *Restricting anorexics*, on the other hand, achieve their weight loss by fasting and/or excessive exercise and do not binge eat.

Bulimia nervosa. In contrast to anorexia nervosa, individuals with eating disorders whose body weight is not below expected levels are likely to be given the diagnosis of bulimia nervosa (BN). In general, BN is characterized by recurrent binge eating. A persistent overconcern with body shape and weight is also exhibited. Such overconcern means, of course, that the

TABLE 13–2	CRITERIA USED BY THE DSM TO DIAGNOSE ANOREXIA NERVOSA

1. Body weight less than 85 percent of expected weight
2. Intense fear of gaining weight
3. Disturbance in perception of body weight and shape or denial of seriousness of low body weight
4. Absence of three consecutive menstrual cycles in postmenarcheal females

From American Psychiatric Association, 2000.

bulimic individual needs to employ some method of compensating for binge eating. The most frequently cited method is purging by vomiting or the use of laxatives.

The DSM criteria used to diagnose BN are presented in Table 13–3. To receive this diagnosis, the symptoms must not occur exclusively during episodes of anorexia nervosa—that is, a person who displays the symptoms as part of anorexia nervosa would not receive both diagnoses.

The principal consideration in describing subtypes is whether purging is employed to compensate for binge eating. Thus there are two subtypes of BN in the DSM:

- The *purging type* is one in which the person regularly induces vomiting or misuses laxatives, diuretics, or enemas.

- The *nonpurging type* is one in which the person fasts and/or exercises excessively but does not regularly purge.

EPIDEMIOLOGY

Prevalence estimates for eating disorders are largely based on samples that combine adolescents and young adults. These disorders occur predominantly in young women. The rate of occurrence in males is about one-tenth of that in females (American Psychiatric Association, 2000; Thompson & Smolak, 2001). Thus, females represent over 90% of all cases. AN is reported to occur in about 0.5% of females. BN is more commonly diagnosed, occurring in 1 to 3% of females (Gowers & Bryant-Waugh, 2004). Lewinsohn and colleagues (1993a) reported a lifetime prevalence rate for bulimia of approximately 1 to 1.5% in a random sample of high school females, and this finding

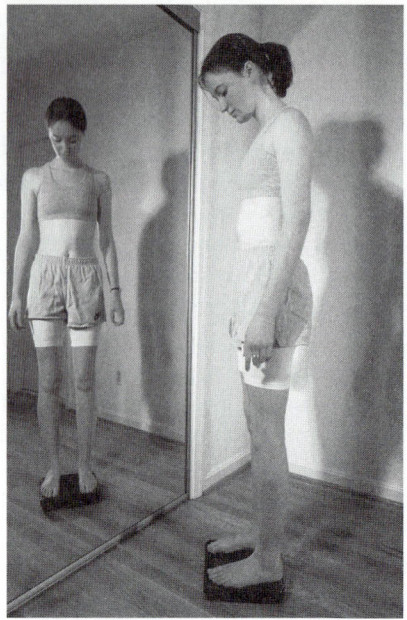

Extreme concern with weight and body shape has become common among girls and young women.
(Richard T. Nowitz/Photo Researchers, Inc.)

seems consistent with other estimates of prevalence in the general population of adolescent females (Wilson, Becker, & Heffernan, 2003).

These numbers may actually underestimate the prevalence of eating disorders, because individuals with these disorders may be overrepresented among those who do not cooperate with prevalence studies (Wilson et al., 2003). Perhaps more importantly, the stated prevalence rates are based on individuals' meeting full diagnostic criteria for AN or BN. But many other individuals exhibit various aspects of disordered eating and disturbances of body image (Ackard, Fulkerson, & Neumark-Sztainer, 2007). Of these individuals, many may meet the criteria for an Eating Disorder Not Otherwise Specified, and this diagnosis may be more common than AN or BN in young people (Walsh et al., 2005a; Wonderlich et al., 2007). These cases are also sometimes described as a "partial syndrome" or as "subclinical." Youths with a partial syndrome may experience substantial social and educational impairment. And adolescents who do not fully meet diagnostic criteria may in many ways resemble those who do and may be at considerable risk for the development of other disorders, especially depression (le Grange et al., 2004; Lewinsohn, Striegel-Moore, & Seeley, 2000; Patton et al., 1997).

Of particular interest is the finding that subclinical concerns with weight and shape and unusual

TABLE 13–3	CRITERIA USED BY THE DSM TO DIAGNOSE BULIMIA NERVOSA

1. Recurrent episodes of binge-eating
2. Recurrent inappropriate compensatory behavior to prevent weight gain
3. Occurrence of items 1 and 2 at least twice a week for 3 months
4. Self-evaluation unduly influenced by body shape and weight

From American Psychiatric Association, 2000.

eating behaviors are increasingly common among younger adolescents and even preadolescent girls. Thus, although eating disorders that meet full diagnostic criteria typically occur in late adolescence, dieting and disordered eating behaviors and attitudes are appearing in younger children (Stinton & Birch, 2005; Thompson & Smolak, 2001). These problems may be precursors of more serious eating disorders.

There is some suggestion that by the fourth and fifth grade, girls are worried about being or becoming overweight and desire to become thinner. Among middle-school children, concerns about weight remain prevalent, and more extreme weight control behaviors seem to be employed (Childress et al., 1993). Evidence suggests that extreme weight concern in these young girls is predictive of the emergence of later eating disorder symptoms and of depression, lowered self-esteem, and feelings of inadequacy and personal worthlessness (Killen et al., 1994a,b; Lewinsohn et al., 1993a; Stice & Bearman, 2001). Such feelings may, in turn, lead to increased concern with weight and shape among girls who already place great personal value on these physical attributes (Cohen-Tovee, 1993). Even at this young age concerns with weight and shape have been reported to be more prevalent among girls than boys (Shapiro, Newcomb, & Loeb, 1997; Thelen et al., 1992). However, there is also increasing concern regarding disordered eating and body dissatisfaction among young males (McCabe & Ricciardelli, 2004).

Ethnic, and cultural differences. Eating disorders are usually reported to occur predominantly in young women, particularly young white women from middle to upper class backgrounds. However, ethnic and cultural differences among adolescents require further investigation. There is probably insufficient evidence regarding ethnic minorities. Research does suggest differences among young African American, European American, and Hispanic females with regard to body dissatisfaction and inappropriate compensatory behaviors (e.g. vomiting) (Walsh et al., 2005a).

It is suggested that eating disorders are a culturally related phenomena, particularly bulimia nervosa (Keel & Klump, 2003). This would suggest that the more "Westernized" young women from other cultures become, the more likely they are to develop eating disorders. Within Western culture certain groups may be at particular risk. These include individuals involved in activities such as gymnastics, wrestling, ballet, and cheerleading in which weight-control behaviors and abnormal eating are used to enhance performance or appearance. Elite female athletes appear to be at highest risk and nonelite high school female athletes may be less likely than nonathletes to have an eating disorder or to report body dissatisfaction (Jacobi et al., 2004; Smolak, Murnen, & Ruble, 2000).

Co-occurring disorders. Eating disorders commonly co-occur with a number of other disorders (O'Brien & Vincent, 2003). Lewinsohn, Striegel-Moore, and Seeley (2000) report that in a community sample of adolescent girls, 90% of those with full syndrome eating disorders experienced one or more co-occurring disorders. Depression, anxiety disorders, substance use disorders, and personality disorders are commonly reported as co-occurring with both anorexia and bulimia nervosa (Kaye et al., 2004).

DEVELOPMENTAL COURSE AND PROGNOSIS

Anorexia nervosa. The age of onset of AN is typically during adolescence, with peaks at ages 14 and 18 (Thompson & Smolak, 2001). Cases of earlier onset are rare but do exist (Gowers & Bryant-Waugh, 2004; Lask & Bryant-Waugh, 1992). Some individuals may experience a single episode; others fluctuate between periods of restoration of normal weight and relapse (perhaps to dangerously low levels of weight that require hospitalization). Still others may gain weight but continue eating disordered behaviors that meet the criteria for BN or EDNOS (American Psychiatric Association, 2000; Walsh et al., 2005a).

Anorexia nervosa is a serious disorder, and a substantial proportion of young women with the disorder have poor outcomes (Grinspoon et al., 2000; Katzman, 2005; Steinhausen, 1997; Wentz et al., 2001). Extreme weight loss can lead to significant medical complications (e.g., anemia, hormonal changes, cardiovascular problems, dental problems, loss of bone density), and the disorder may be life-threatening. It has been reported that over 10% of cases end in death, with many of the deaths resulting from suicide (Birmingham et al., 2005; Walsh et al., 2005a).

Bulimia nervosa. The onset of BN extends from adolescence into early adulthood. Binge eating often begins during or after a period of restrictive dieting driven by extreme dissatisfaction with body shape and weight. The DSM describes the course of the disorder as either chronic or intermittent, with periods

of remission alternating with recurrences of binge eating. However, over the long term, symptoms of BN diminish in many individuals (American Psychiatric Association, 2000). Although some individuals may no longer meet the diagnostic criteria for BN, problems may persist—some individuals may meet the criteria for EDNOS, and many meet the criteria for major depressive disorder (Fairburn et al., 2000; Lewinsohn et al., 2000).

The recurrent vomiting associated with BN may result in dental problems due to the loss of tooth enamel. Other medical problems such as fluid and electrolyte disturbances may also occur, particularly among those who purge (American Psychiatric Association, 2000).

ETIOLOGY

A variety of causal mechanisms have been proposed to explain the development of eating disorders. Indeed, it is likely that AN and BN are multiply determined and result from a variety of different patterns of influences (Jacobi et al., 2004; Striegel-Moore & Bulik, 2007). Being female is probably the most reliable risk factor. Other factors, however, are needed to help explain the gender difference and the development of eating disorders. A description of some of the risk factors and influences that have been considered follows.

Cultural influences and body dissatisfaction. Any discussion of the development of eating disorders is likely to address cultural influences and gender roles for women (Smolak & Murnen, 2004; Striegel-Moore & Bulik, 2007). Our society's emphasis on and valuing of slim and young bodies, particularly for women, likely contributes to body dissatisfaction and the development of eating disorders (Mirkin, 1990;

Striegel-Moore & Bulik, 2007). For example, Dittmar, Halliwell & Ive (2006) asked the question, "Does Barbie make girls want to be thin?" Many young girls own at least one Barbie doll. Barbie is exceptionally thin and her body proportions are unattainable and unhealthy. In the study, girls ages 5 to 8 were exposed to picture-book images of either Barbie dolls, Emme dolls (body proportions of a dress size 16), or neutral stimuli without any descriptions of bodies. Girls exposed to Barbie reported lower body esteem and greater desire for a thinner body than girls in the other conditions. This was particularly true for younger girls. Girls exposed to Emme did not differ from those who viewed neutral images. Such findings raise concerns that at a very young age girls may internalize a thin ideal.

Media, peers, and families transmit these cultural messages of thinness (Dohnt & Tiggerman, 2006; Wertheim, Paxton, & Blaney, 2004). Clark & Tiggeman (2007), for example, found that, among girls in grades 4 to 7, greater exposure to television shows and magazines that emphasized appearance, and involvement in appearance conversations with peers, were related to greater body dissatisfaction. The relationship of these cultural influences to body dissatisfaction was mediated by appearance schemas— acceptance of the importance placed on appearance. (See Figure 13–6.) Additional research also points to the influence of the media and suggests that young women may unfavorably compare themselves to persons depicted in the media (Levine & Harrison, 2004; Wiseman, Sunday, & Becker, 2005). Similar concerns are increasing with regard to young men. (See Accent: "Being Buff: Weight and Shape Concerns in Young Men.") Beyond possible direct influences, body dissatisfaction also can contribute to lowered self-esteem and depressed mood (Paxton et al., 2006) which, in turn, may contribute to the development of eating disorders (Measelle, Stice, & Hogansen, 2006).

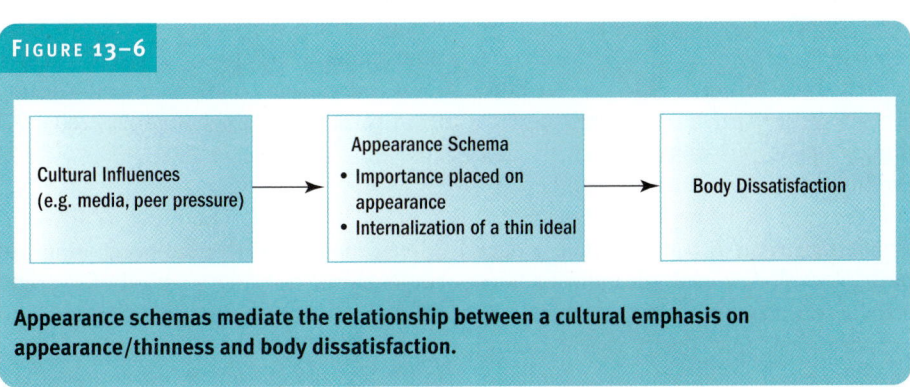

FIGURE 13–6

Cultural Influences (e.g. media, peer pressure) → Appearance Schema • Importance placed on appearance • Internalization of a thin ideal → Body Dissatisfaction

Appearance schemas mediate the relationship between a cultural emphasis on appearance/thinness and body dissatisfaction.

ACCENT

Being Buff: Weight and Shape Concerns in Young Men

Much of the literature has focused on eating-disordered behavior and weight and body image concerns in young women. This is, at least in part, due to the high rates of such difficulties among females. More recently, attention has begun to turn to young men, and whether eating, weight, and body shape concerns are underestimated in the male population. Part of what we should recognize here is a possible gender bias in how a disorder is defined. So, for example, drawing from the literature on young women, interest has largely focused on issues such as the desire for a smaller and thinner body and losing weight. Although losing weight may be a concern for some young men who are overweight, most young men do not desire a small, thin body. The ideal for many young men may be a larger or at least more muscular body. Perhaps defining body dissatisfaction and weight concerns in a different way would paint a different picture regarding body image concerns and disordered eating in young men.

Indeed, it has become accepted among researchers and others that weight and shape concerns and body dissatisfaction have become more common among males. McCabe and Ricciardelli (2004) highlighted some of the reasons for this trend. Male bodies are more often featured in popular magazines and models have become more muscular. Popular athletes, film stars, and many other male icons also have become increasingly muscular. Action figures, such as G.I. Joe, have followed the same trend and are likely to have physiques equal to or exceeding those of advanced body builders. Also, weight training has become more prevalent among young men and may be viewed as normative. Thus, similar to what young women have experienced, cultural pressures may be increasingly affecting young men.

What are the consequences of these trends? Appearance and weight have, for a long time, been considered overly important influences on young women's self-esteem. Similar concerns may be emerging as central to men's feelings of self-worth and mood (Paxton et al., 2006). Problematic eating styles may be increasing. In addition, excessive exercise and musclebuilding strategies may be escalating among young males, including the use of steroids to achieve results.

The literature is not extensive regarding disordered eating and body dissatisfaction in young men. Nonetheless, there is information that suggests the presence of eating-disordered behavior in young men. In addition, both disordered eating and the pursuit of muscularity in adolescent males seem to be influenced by similar factors. Furthermore, several factors consistently associated with disordered eating in young women (e.g., importance of appearance, body mass index, negative affect, self-esteem, perfectionism, and pressure from others to lose weight) also appear to be associated with problematic eating behaviors in young men (Ricciardelli & McCabe, 2004).

Thus, one perspective on the development of eating disorders emphasizes contemporary social influences that place too great an emphasis on physical appearance, create a "culture of thinness," and may transmit a message that personal, social, and economic opportunity are associated with appearance and a thin body (Anderson-Fye & Becker, 2004; Smith et al., 2007). It is important to understand both this exposure and the social pressure to internalize this message in order to counteract their contribution to the development of eating-disordered behavior.

Dissatisfaction with weight and body shape has come to be viewed as defining characteristic of eating disorders and as one of the early aspects of the development of such problems. Pictorial instruments that graphically assess body dissatisfaction in young children have been developed as part of a comprehensive assessment of eating disorders (Collins, 1991; Gardner, 2001; Stewart & Williamson, 2004). Use of such instruments (see Figure 13–7) has contributed to the view that body dissatisfaction and other problematic beliefs and behaviors are common and are present even in very young children.

Some authors remind us that unusual eating styles are not recent phenomena, and that historical accounts can assist us in examining our conceptualization of eating disorders (Attie & Brooks-Gunn, 1995). There was, for example, a group of women living in the High Middle Ages (13th through 16th centuries)

FIGURE 13-7

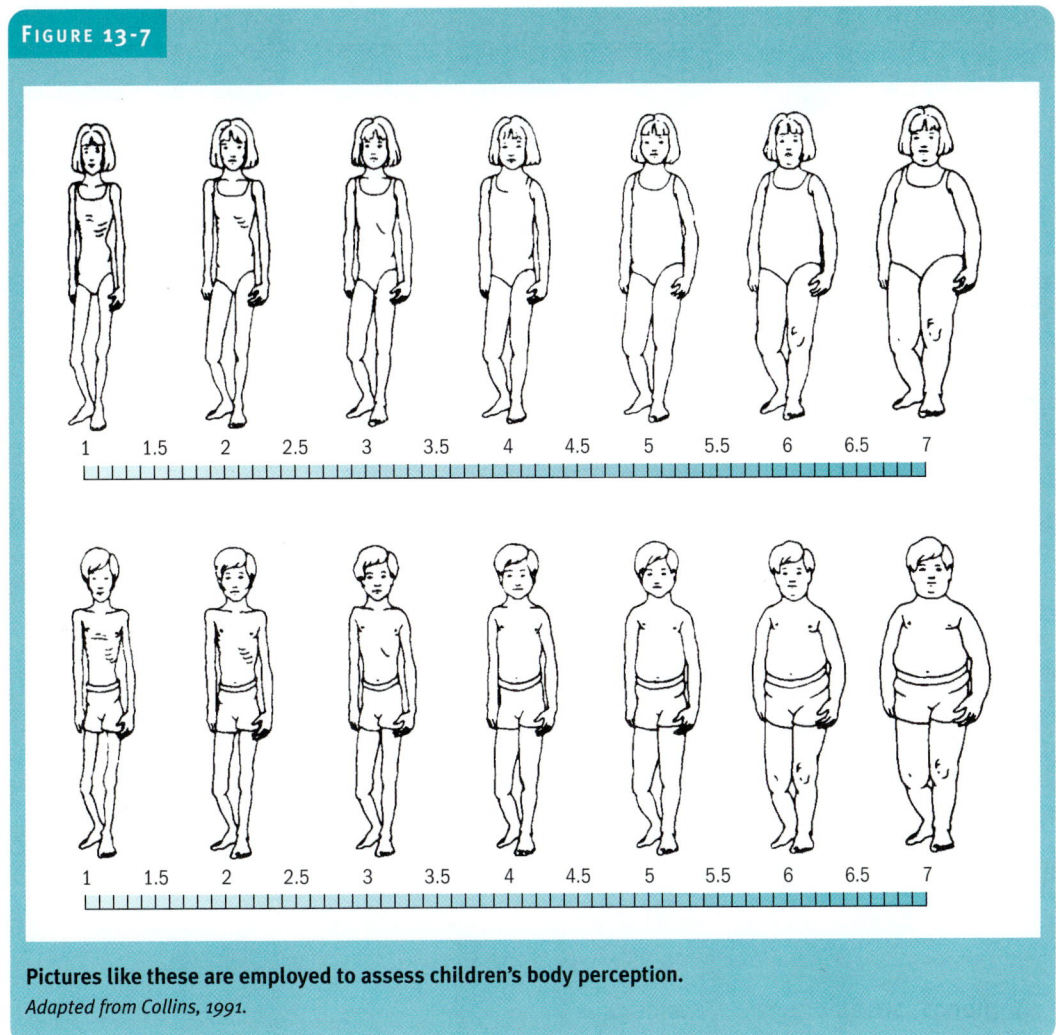

Pictures like these are employed to assess children's body perception.
Adapted from Collins, 1991.

who maintained extreme eating restrictions and what might be viewed as bizarre and pervasive behaviors and images regarding eating and food (Bell, 1985; Brumberg, 1986). Descriptions of the behavior of these women bear a remarkable similarity to contemporary eating disorders. The most interesting twist to this tale, however, is that these women were later canonized as saints. Bell (1985) chose the term "holy anorexia" to describe the condition of these women and to call attention to the cultural dimension in diagnostic efforts.

Individual risk factors. The relationship between personality traits and eating disorders has received considerable attention. For example, perfectionism (striving for unreasonably high standards and defining one's worth based on accomplishments) has been reported to be associated with eating disorders

(Bardone-Cone et al., 2007). However, research does not support viewing perfectionism and other personality traits such as obsessionality, impulsivity, restraint, and conformity as pre-existing risk factors for eating disorders. At best, the relationship between personality traits and eating disorders remains unclear. Alternatively, personality traits may be factors that affect the course of an eating disorder, or they may be consequences of an eating disorder (Wonderlich et al., 2005; Walsh et al., 2005b).

Early feeding difficulties. There may be continuities from early childhood feeding difficulties to later eating problems and disorders. Clinical reports mention early feeding difficulties in individuals with eating disorders, and there is some research support for this position. For example, Marchi and Cohen (1990) longitudinally traced maladaptive eating patterns in

a group of children. Their findings suggested that early childhood pica was a risk factor and that picky eating was a protective factor for bulimic symptoms in adolescence. On the other hand, picky eating and digestive problems in early childhood were risk factors for elevated symptoms of AN in adolescence. Kotler and colleagues (2001) found that maternal reports during early childhood of eating conflicts, struggles with food, and unpleasant meals were predictive of later AN in adolescence or young adulthood, whereas eating too little during childhood was somewhat protective regarding a future diagnosis of BN. Certainly, more research is needed; however, it may be that experiences that begin early in childhood, such as food acceptance pattern and the balance between external and self-control of eating, are important factors in shaping later eating problems (Fisher & Birch, 2001).

Weight history. Family weight history and the individual's previous weight history are frequently considered as possible risk factors. There is much debate about the idea that the self-starvation that is characteristic of AN begins as an attempt to control genuine overweight. It has been suggested that comments that the young girl is "getting plump" may stimulate normal dieting, which evolves into anorexic refusal to eat. However, the role of a personal and family history of being overweight in the development of AN remains unclear, and the frequency of dieting among adolescent girls raises the question of why some girls who begin this common social ritual persist well beyond the point of socially desired slimness.

Similar considerations have been discussed regarding BN, and there does seem to be evidence that supports personal and family history of overweight as a risk factor (Wilson et al., 2003). Some young women with such a history may become bulimic. Their problematic behaviors may begin as more typical attempts to reduce weight that could not meet the thin cultural ideal.

Research by Fairburn and his colleagues (1997) supports the role of weight history. Three groups of participants were recruited from a community sample: a group with BN, a group with other disorders (depression and anxiety), and a group of healthy controls. The groups were compared on a number of putative risk factors for BN. Whereas participants with BN experienced a significantly greater exposure to most risk factors compared with healthy controls, there were very few differences in risk exposure for the bulimia group as compared with the participants

with other disorders. A history of childhood obesity and negative self-evaluation were two of the risk factors to which the BN group experienced greater exposure. These factors thus appear to increase the risk for developing the specific disorder of BN.

Sexual abuse. Reports based on clinical cases have suggested early sexual abuse as a cause of eating disorders. Studies involving children are limited (Connors, 2001) but reviews suggest a small but significant association between childhood sexual abuse and eating-disordered behavior (Smolak & Murnen, 2002). The nature of this relationship remains unclear. However, sexual abuse would appear to be a risk factor for psychopathology in general, rather than a specific risk for the development of eating disorders (Jacobi et al., 2004; Walsh et al., 2005b). This, of course, does not mean that clinicians working with young people should not consider the occurrence of sexual abuse, which may be part of a pathway to eating disturbance for some individuals (Feldman & Meyer, 2007; Wonderlich et al., 2001).

Family influences. Historically, many explanations regarding the development of eating disorders emphasized family variables. Bruch's (1979) description of Ida is a classic example of family influences. The girl is described as the object of much family attention and control, and as trapped by a need to please. Anorexia nervosa, according to Bruch, is a desperate attempt by the child to express an individual identity.

Ida   A Sparrow in a Golden Cage

She enjoyed being home but missed the fuss they had made about her in the past, when everybody was acutely concerned about her. . . . Even as a child, Ida had considered herself not worthy of all the privileges and benefits that her family offered her, because she felt she was not brilliant enough. An image came to her, that she was like a sparrow in a golden cage, too plain and simple for the luxuries of her home, but also deprived of the freedom of doing what she truly wanted to do.

Adapted from Bruch, 1979, pp. 23–24.

It is difficult to determine whether any pattern observed in a family subsequent to the onset of a disturbance is a cause or an effect. This is especially the case in AN, in which family observations have frequently followed the young person's life-threatening refusal to eat. Families are often described as having a high incidence of weight problems, affective disorder, and alcoholism or drug abuse. Parental attitudes and beliefs concerning eating, weight, and body shape may be particularly important. Also, aspects of the family environment, such as periods of low parental contact and high parental expectations, have been suggested as risk factors (Fairburn et al., 1997). Families of young women with eating disorders have variously been described as exhibiting parental discord and as controlling, indifferent, rejecting, and overprotective (Jacobi et al., 2004). While some research does suggest that family patterns are associated with eating disorders, there is no clear support for any pattern of relationships nor any "typical eating-disordered family" (Steinberg & Phares, 2001; Walsh et al., 2005b).

Biological influences. Eating and the biological mechanisms behind it are complex; thus, numerous biological mechanisms have been studied. The onset of anorexia nervosa is most often around puberty. However, there is no definitive explanation of why puberty increases risk. The idea that early menarche is a risk factor for either anorexia or bulimia nervosa is not supported (Walsh et al., 2005b).

Research on biological influences has focused on neurobiological and genetic influences. Eating behavior can both be influenced by and effect changes in neurobiological and neuroendocrine systems, so determining causal relationships is not easy. It has been difficult to determine whether a particular biological difference found in young women with eating disorders placed them at initial risk for the disorder or resulted from change in the biological system due to disordered eating.

Research suggests differences in neurotransmitter (e.g., serotonin, norepinephrine) activity are associated with eating disorders (Jacobi et al., 2004; Kaye et al., 2005; Klump & Gobrogge, 2005). For example, serotonin plays a major role in the inhibition of feeding, and decreased serotonin activity has been observed in individuals with anorexia and bulimia nervosa—both during the illness and after recovery.

A genetic contribution to eating disorders has also been suggested (Jacobi et al., 2004; Klump & Gobrogge, 2005; Striegel-Moore & Bulik, 2007). There are higher than expected rates of eating disorders among family members of individuals with AN and BN. Twin studies also suggest a genetic component to eating disorders. However, such research is difficult to conduct for AN because the disorder has a relatively low prevalence. Despite limitations, it seems likely that additive genetic influences (cumulative impact of multiple genes) contribute to the development of AN

and BN and interact with unique (nonshared) environmental influences. The identity of particular genes and the manner in which genes contribute to eating disorders remain unclear, but the mechanisms may involve complex contributions to personal styles, such as rigidity/obsessionality or general anxiety level, or to biological processes involved in the regulation of eating behavior (Bulik, Wade, & Kendler, 2001; Klump, McGue, & Iacono, 2000).

INTERVENTION

In general, there is research support regarding interventions for BN, but far less for AN. Furthermore, interventions targeting adolescents have received limited attention and; thus, recommendations are based largely on controlled studies with adults (APA, 2006; Gowers & Bryant-Waugh, 2004; Wilson, Grilo, & Vitousek, 2007). Because eating disorders likely develop from and are maintained by a variety of influences, and because of considerable heterogeneity among individuals, interventions that address multiple influences are needed. Here we briefly highlight some approaches.

Family approaches. Family therapy for eating disorders derives from the observation by clinicians of varying persuasions that families are intimately involved in the maintenance of this behavior. Family therapy is widespread in clinical practice, but research support is more limited.

There is some support for the effectiveness of family interventions for adolescents with AN, but additional research is clearly needed (Fairburn, 2005; Lock, 2004; Robin, 2003). The Maudsley approach (Dare & Eisler, 1997; Lock & le Grange, 2005) is the best-studied family therapy. This approach avoids viewing families as pathological and blaming them for the development of AN. The position taken is that the causes of the disorder are unknown and the family is considered the most important resource for the adolescent's recovery. Treatment takes place over one year, with initial intense support of the family gradually faded over time. Treatment is broadly divided into three phases. The first phase is highly focused on the eating disorder, refeeding, and weight gain. Families are encouraged to work out for themselves the best way to refeed their anorexic child. Once the adolescent is gaining weight and eating takes place with minimal struggle, the second phase begins. Eating disorder symptoms are the main subject of sessions, but the goal is to assist the family in finding ways to return control back to the adolescent.

As this occurs other family issues can begin to be reviewed. Once the adolescent achieves a healthy weight the final phase is undertaken. General issues of adolescent development and the ways they have been affected by AN are addressed (Lock, 2004).

Two modes of family involvement have been compared: conjoint family therapy (CFT), in which the whole family is seen together, and separated family therapy (SFT), in which the same therapist sees the adolescent individually and the parents in separate sessions. Overall, CFT and SFT produced significant and comparable weight gain, improved menstrual functioning, and improved psychological functioning by the end of treatment and at a 5-year follow-up (Eisler et al., 2001, 2007). For a subset of families in which mothers were highly critical, adolescents who received SFT achieved greater weight gain during follow-up than did those who received CFT. Family involvement may have to be tailored to the family and/or adjusted over the course of treatment.

Cognitive-behavioral treatments.
Cognitive-behavioral treatment of BN has appreciable research support and is viewed by many as a treatment of choice for this disorder (Mitchell, Agras, & Wonderlich, 2007; Wilson et al., 2007). Controlled research has shown the cognitive behavioral approach to the treatment of BN to be superior to no treatment and to alternative treatments, including pharmacotherapy and a variety of other psychotherapies. However, treatment evidence is based largely on adult samples, and adaptations for adolescent populations are needed (APA, 2006; Schapman-Williams, Lock & Couturier, 2006).

Treatment involves a multifaceted program that is based on the rationale that cognitive distortions and a loss of control over eating are at the core of the disorder (Fairburn, 1997). According to this view, cognitions regarding shape and weight are the primary features of the disorder, and other features—such as dieting and self-induced vomiting—are secondary expressions of these concerns. In the initial stage of treatment, the patient is educated regarding BN, and the cognitive view of the disorder is made clear. During this early stage, behavioral techniques are also employed to reduce bingeing and compensatory behaviors (e.g., vomiting) and to establish control over eating patterns. These techniques are supplemented with cognitive restructuring techniques, and as treatment progresses, there is an increasingly cognitive focus on targeting inappropriate weight-gain concerns and on training self-control strategies for resisting binge eating. Next, additional cognitively

oriented interventions address inappropriate beliefs concerning food, eating, weight, and body image. Finally, a maintenance strategy to sustain improvements and to prevent relapses is also included.

As discussed earlier, most adolescents do not meet the diagnostic criteria for AN or BN. Their problems may be diagnosed as an Eating Disorder Not Otherwise Specified. Thus, adolescents seeking treatment may present with a wide range of eating-disorder problems. Fairburn and colleagues (Fairburn, Cooper, & Shafran, 2003) have developed a cognitive-behavioral individualized treatment program based on a "transdiagnostic" model of eating disorders. This program matches specific therapeutic interventions to the particular eating-disorder features of the adolescent, rather than providing treatment based on diagnosis.

Interpersonal psychotherapy.
Interpersonal psychotherapy (IPT) focuses on interpersonal problems involved in the development and maintenance of a disorder. Research suggests that IPT is effective in the treatment of BN in adults. This therapeutic approach does not directly target eating symptoms, but seeks to enhance interpersonal functioning and communication skills. The rationale for such an approach is based, in part, on research indicating the role of interpersonal influences (e.g., actions of peers, friends, family; comparison with others) on the development of body image and self-esteem (Tantleff-Dunn, Gokee-LaRose, & Peterson, 2004). An assessment of the individual's interpersonal history is obtained. One or more of four interpersonal problem areas are the focus of the intervention: grief, role transitions, role disputes, and interpersonal deficits. The following case of Gayle illustrates the contribution of role transitions to the development of an eating disorder.

Gayle Interpersonal Role Transitions

Gayle, an 18-year-old with bulimia, graduated from a small high school and began attending a large university far from home. Gayle was an only child, was very close to her parents, and had been part of a small circle of childhood friends. She was both excited and frightened about going away to college. Quickly she felt pressured by the need to impress others and make new friends. Gayle described herself as having been "sheltered" and "catapulted into adulthood." The therapy began by focusing on facilitating Gayle's transition to college, independence, and adulthood. As she developed a network of social support and gained confidence in her abilities to care for herself, Gayle's purging and preoccupation with her physical appearance decreased.

Adapted from Tantleff-Dunn, Gokee-LaRose, & Peterson, 2004, p. 170.

Pharmacological treatment. Although case reports suggest that different pharmacological treatments can be successful with eating-disordered patients, controlled research, particularly regarding adolescents, is either lacking or presents a somewhat more cautious picture. There seems to be little support for the effectiveness of any pharmacological approach in the treatment of AN (APA, 2006; Walsh et al., 2005c). However, antidepressant medications are commonly used, and these and other medications continue to be investigated (Attia & Schroeder, 2005). In controlled studies with adults, antidepressant medication has been reported effective for treating BN (de Zwaan et al., 2004; Walsh et al., 2005c). Effectiveness may be limited to only some patients, and medication would not appear to be the primary treatment of choice. The role of antidepressants in treating BN in adolescents remains unclear (Gowers & Bryant-Waugh, 2004; Walsh et al., 2005c). Moreover, caution is indicated regarding side effects with individuals who are already psychologically and physiologically at risk.

Prevention. There is a considerable prevalence among adolescents of eating-disordered behavior that does not meet the criteria for anorexia or bulimia nervosa or is considered "subclinical." In addition, signs of eating-disordered behavior and attitudes in younger children are frequent. Thus, there is reason to think in terms of prevention. However, empirical studies on the prevention of eating disorders are relatively limited.

Evaluations of universal prevention programs have largely focused on programs that target older youngsters (Walsh et al., 2005b). Some programs address issues related to healthy weight regulation (HWR) and focus on issues such as restrictive dieting, body image, and social and cultural influences. Other programs focus on broader issues such as self esteem and social competence (SESC) as a way to prevent the onset of eating-disordered behavior and attitudes. Evidence is limited, but does offer some suggestion regarding interventions (Walsh et al., 2005b). There are some promising findings for SESC approaches among middle-school students. For example, Steiner-Adair and colleagues (2002) employed a curriculum that taught recognition and critical evaluation of cultural messages and prejudices regarding appearance, weight, and eating, and was designed to help seventh-grade girls become more assertive and supportive of each other. Eating disorder knowledge and weight-related body esteem were significantly higher by the end of the curriculum, and remained high at a 6-month follow-up. It seems less clear whether programs using the HWR approach are of benefit for middle-school children, and universal prevention programs targeting high school students have found no significant effects on attitudes or behavior. Given these findings and limited studies it is unclear whether universal interventions are effective in preventing eating disorders.

Targeted prevention studies have primarily focused on interventions for self-selected samples of older adolescents and college students. Research suggests that these interventions may reduce risk factors for high-risk individuals, at least in the short term, but care should be taken in generalizing these findings to adolescents or younger children (Walsh et al., 2005b).

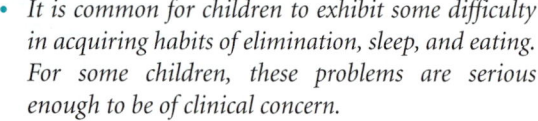

SUMMARY

- *It is common for children to exhibit some difficulty in acquiring habits of elimination, sleep, and eating. For some children, these problems are serious enough to be of clinical concern.*

PROBLEMS OF ELIMINATION

- *Toilet training is an important concern for parents of young children. Knowledge of the typical sequence of control over elimination and of appropriate*

parenting practices can contribute to successful training.

- *Enuresis and encopresis are disorders of elimination that seem best explained by a combination of biological predisposition and failure to train and/or learn bodily control.*

- *Desmopressin is the best-supported medically oriented procedure for treating enuresis. Behavioral interventions that include a urine-alarm procedure* have high success rates and low rates of remission, and they are the treatments of choice at present.

- Encopresis is probably best dealt with through a combination of medical and behavioral procedures.

SLEEP PROBLEMS

- Sleep problems are common in infants, children, and adolescents. Sleep disorders are persistent sleep difficulties that cause the child distress or interfere with other functioning.

- Difficulties in initiating and maintaining sleep (dyssomnias) may be related to neurophysiological development, but are probably also affected by environmental influences such as bedtime routines and the appropriate cues for sleep. Sleep disorders such as sleepwalking and sleep terrors (parasomnias) are probably best conceptualized as resulting from a combination of nervous system immaturity and environmental factors.

PROBLEMS OF FEEDING, EATING, AND NUTRITION

- A wide range of problems having to do with eating and feeding are commonly reported in young children. Many of these problems cause considerable concern for parents and appreciable disruption of family life.

- Some eating and feeding problems are more serious and persistent, and may actually endanger the physical health of the young person.

- The early feeding and eating disorders in the DSM are Rumination Disorder, Pica, and Feeding Disorder of Infancy or Early Childhood, which is also often discussed as failure to thrive.

- Childhood obesity is quite prevalent and an important health problem. The development of obesity is influenced by a complex interaction of biological, psychological, and socio-cultural influences.

- The learning of adaptive eating and activity patterns is the basis of behavioral treatment programs for obesity. This approach to treatment is probably the most successful. However, greater weight loss and better maintenance still need to be achieved, and priority needs to be given to prevention and early intervention.

EATING DISORDERS: ANOREXIA AND BULIMIA NERVOSA

- Weight status, the presence or absence of binge eating, and the method employed to control one's weight are important considerations in thinking about eating disorders.

- The DSM describes two primary eating disorder diagnoses: Anorexia Nervosa and Bulimia Nervosa. A category of Eating Disorder Not Otherwise Specified (EDNOS) is also included. A potential category of Binge-Eating Disorder is being studied.

- Anorexia nervosa (AN) is a serious disorder characterized by extreme weight loss, an intense fear of becoming fat, and disturbance in the perception of body weight and shape. A number of other physical and psychological problems are present as well. A distinction is made between restricting and binge-eating/purging anorexia.

- Bulimia nervosa (BN) refers to a repeated pattern of binge eating followed by some inappropriate compensatory mechanism. A distinction is made between purging and nonpurging types.

- Females represent about 90% of all cases of eating disorders (AN and BN). EDNOS may be more common than AN or BN among youngsters. Increasing prevalence of eating-disordered behavior and attitudes among young girls has been noted. There is also increased concern regarding disordered eating and body dissatisfaction in young males.

- Ethnic and cultural differences deserve further consideration and certain groups, such as some athletes and dancers, may be at particular risk.

- Depression, anxiety disorders, and substance abuse commonly co-occur with eating disorders.

- Age of onset for AN is typically during adolescence. For many individuals the disorder, or other eating problems, persists over a considerable period of time. For some, the disorder may be life threatening.

- The onset of BN extends from adolescence into early adulthood. Although symptoms diminish for many individuals, there is concern regarding persistent eating difficulties and depression.

- Explanations that incorporate multiple influences are needed to understand the development of eating disorders. Cultural influences, early feeding difficulties, weight history, family influences, and genetic and other biological influences are among the influences to consider.

- Treatments for AN and BN specific to adolescents have received limited attention, and current treatment recommendations are therefore based largely on downward extensions of studies with adults.

- The use of family therapy or family involvement in treatment is widespread in clinical practice, although further empirical support is required. The Maudsley approach to treating AN is the best-studied family therapy.

- *Cognitive-behavioral treatment is the intervention for BN for which there is the best-controlled research support. Interpersonal psychotherapy has also proven to be effective with young adults.*

- *The effectiveness of pharmacological treatments for eating disorders in adolescents is unclear.*

- *Empirical studies of prevention of eating disorders are relatively limited.*

KEY TERMS

enuresis *(p. 362)*

nocturnal enuresis *(p. 362)*

diurnal enuresis *(p. 362)*

primary enuresis *(p. 362)*

secondary enuresis *(p. 362)*

urine-alarm system *(p. 363)*

encopresis *(p. 364)*

rapid eye movement (REM) sleep *(p. 366)*

nonrapid eye movement (NREM) sleep *(p. 366)*

dyssomnias *(p. 367)*

parasomnias *(p. 367)*

obstructive sleep apnea *(p. 368)*

sleepwalking *(p. 369)*

sleep terrors *(p. 370)*

nightmares *(p. 370)*

failure to thrive *(p. 373)*

rumination *(p. 373)*

pica *(p. 374)*

Feeding Disorder of Infancy or Early Childhood *(p. 374)*

obesity *(p. 375)*

body mass index *(p. 375)*

binge *(p. 378)*

restricting *(p. 379)*

purging *(p. 379)*

Eating Disorder Not Otherwise Specified *(p. 379)*

Binge-Eating Disorder *(p. 379)*

anorexia nervosa *(p. 379)*

bulimia nervosa *(p. 379)*

CHAPTER 14

Psychological Factors Affecting Medical Conditions

In this chapter we examine how psychological factors contribute to our understanding of youngsters with chronic medical conditions. We also examine how psychological influences contribute to the delivery of effective medical treatment. In addressing these topics, we touch on issues such as the role of the family, youngsters' adaptation and adjustment to chronic conditions, and the adherence of youngsters and families to regimens recommended by health care practitioners. In order to illustrate the interfaces between psychology and medicine, we describe the application of psychology to various medical conditions such as asthma, cancer, diabetes, and HIV/AIDS. To understand the evolution of current thinking and practice, it is helpful to have some appreciation of the history of such endeavors.

Historical Context

The topics discussed in this chapter would in the past have come under the heading of psychosomatic disorders. The main focus of interest was on actual physical conditions, such as asthma, headaches, ulcers, and nausea. These disorders were known or presumed to be affected by psychological factors. The terminology for describing these disorders has undergone a number of changes in the last few decades. The term *Psychosomatic Disorders* was replaced in the DSM-II by *Psychophysiological Disorders*, and in the DSM-III and III-R with the term *Psychological Factors Affecting Physical Condition*. The term has been modified in the DSM-IV and DSM-IV-TR to Psychological Factors Affecting Medical Condition.

The uncertainty over terminology reflects a long-standing controversy over the nature of the relationship between mind and body, the psyche and the soma. During the 20th century, interest in the effects of psychological processes on the body resulted in the development of the field of psychosomatic medicine. Early investigators began to accumulate evidence and to develop theories of how psychological factors played a causative role in specific physical disorders (Alexander, 1950; Grace & Graham, 1952; Selye, 1956). As this field developed, several trends emerged. An increasing number of physical disorders were seen to be related to psychological factors. Even the common cold was thought to be affected by emotional factors. The question therefore arose as to whether it was fruitful to identify a specific group of psychosomatic disorders or whether psychological factors were operating in all physical conditions. In addition, the focus began to shift from psychogenesis, that is, psychological cause, to multicausality, the idea that social and psychological (as well as biological) factors all contribute to both health and illness at multiple points. The latter view is holistic, assuming a continuous transaction among influences.

With this shift in thinking, the field began to expand considerably. The ongoing role of social and psychological factors in the development of medical conditions, their consequences, and their treatment, and the role of those same factors in prevention and health maintenance all began to receive increased attention. In this chapter, we will examine some of the specific medical problems that have received the attention of psychologists and look at some other selected topics of interest. Our examination will allow us to illustrate the changes that have occurred and the current status and diversity of this field.

Psychological and Family Influences on Medical Conditions

In this section, we will look at information on asthma to illustrate how psychological and family variables may influence the symptoms of pediatric medical problems. This examination of asthma will allow us to see how thinking about the role of psychological variables in physical illness has changed and expanded.

 **Asthma**

| Loren | **Managing Asthma** |

Loren is a twelve-year-old boy with moderate to severe asthma. For the fourth time in a year, he was hospitalized because of asthma. At hospital rounds, Loren's physician pointed out that his asthma could be controlled if he avoided triggers of his asthma, including exercise-induced attacks, and if he complied with his medication regimen. It was also pointed out that Loren did not use his nebulizer properly. Instead of alleviating his respiratory distress, most of the medication was wasted because of inappropriate inhaler use. Lack of quick relief frustrated Loren. As a result he tended to become angry, a behavior that only exacerbated his asthma. It was decided to (1) teach Loren to identify and avoid triggers of his asthma, (2) review his medication and adjust the regimen if possible, (3) improve his compliance to his medical treatment regimen, (4) teach him how to use his nebulizer correctly, and (5) teach him skills to control his frustration.

Adapted from Creer, 1998, p. 411.

Description and prevalence. Defining and describing asthma is complex (McQuaid & Walders, 2003; National Institutes of Health, 1997). Asthma is a disorder of the respiratory system that is characterized by hyperresponsiveness of the airways to a variety of stimuli. Hyperresponsiveness results in inflammation and narrowing of air passages, and air exchange is impaired, particularly during expiration. Intermittent episodes of wheezing and shortness of breath (dyspnea) result. Within the same individual, as well as across individuals, attacks may vary in severity. Thus asthma is an illness that is quite unpredictable, a problem for both research and management of the disorder. Severe attacks, known as status asthmaticus, which are life threatening and require emergency medical treatment, are another challenge in treating asthmatic children. The fear of not being able to breathe and the danger of severe attacks are likely to create appreciable anxiety in the young person and in family members.

Asthma is a common chronic illness in young people. Approximately 10 percent of youngsters are asthmatic, and urban, minority and poor children are overrepresented (Creer, 1998; Koinis-Mitchell et al., 2007; Miller, 2000). Asthma is a potentially reversible disorder, but the impact of the disease on the young person is considerable. It can include hospitalization, emergency room use, and many lost school days (Weiss, Gergen, & Hodgson, 1992; Yeatts & Shy, 2001).

Clearly, the greatest threat is loss of life, and all measures used to treat the physical symptoms of asthma—daily medication to prevent wheezing, environmental control of potential irritants, desensitization to allergens, avoidance of infection, and emergency treatment to stop wheezing—are geared to prevent death. Although much has been done to improve treatment, increasing prevalence of asthma, as well as increases in medical costs, hospitalization, and mortality rates, are reasons for continuing concern and, again, urban poor youth are at particular risk (Bray et al., 2006; Creer, 1998; Koinis-Mitchell et al., 2007; McQuaid & Walders, 2003).

Etiology. The causes of asthma are complex, and there is a considerable history of controversy concerning etiology. Indeed, the exact cause remains unknown (Creer, 1998; McQuaid & Walders, 2003). However, it is broadly acknowledged that genetic or other factors place some youngsters at risk for developing asthma (National Institutes of Health, 1997). Some cause or a number of causes produce a hypersensitivity of the air passages. Once established, this hypersensitivity results in the youngster's responding to various irritants more easily than would a nonasthmatic individual.

Individuals with highly sensitive and labile respiratory tracts are potentially exposed to a second set of factors that influence whether asthmatic attacks occur. This second set of influences has come to be thought of as *trigger* mechanisms or *irritants*, rather than direct causes of asthma. Every child or adolescent has different triggers and triggers can differ over time for the same youngster (Creer, 1998).

Repeated respiratory infection may play a role in the development of asthma, and respiratory viral infections can set off or worsen the severity of an attack. Allergies may also be related to the development and occurrence of asthmatic attacks. A young person may have allergies to inhaled substances (such as dust, the dander of a pet, or pollen) or to ingested substances (such as milk, wheat, or chocolate). Physical factors such as cold temperatures, tobacco smoke, pungent odors, and exercise and rapid breathing may also contribute to wheezing. Furthermore, psychological stimuli and emotional upset are often considered important triggers of asthma attacks (Creer, 1998; Wood, Cheah, et al., 2007).

Psychological and family influences. Although we have come to view the causes of asthma differently, in much of the early literature asthma was viewed primarily as a disease with psychological

Parental concern over precipitating a symptomatic attack may often lead children with chronic illnesses, such as asthma, to spend appreciable time isolated from their peers.
(By permission of United States Department of Health and Human Services — Public Health Service (ADM, 77–497).)

causes. However, over time it became clear that there is little, if any, convincing evidence that psychological or family factors play a significant role as an original cause of the reduced respiratory capacity characteristic of asthma. There is, however, evidence that these factors may play an important role in precipitating or triggering asthmatic attacks in at-risk youngsters.

Like many other investigators, Purcell and his colleagues (1969)—working at the Children's Asthma Research Institute and Hospital (CARIH) in Denver—observed that some children became free of symptoms fairly soon after being sent away from their parents for treatment. Indeed, in the 1950s, "parentectomy" was suggested as the treatment of choice for some children (Peshkin, 1959). Were these effects due to changes in the emotional environment or in the physical environment?

An interesting study on separation suggested some answers to these questions (Purcell et al., 1969). Prior to the beginning of the study, parents of asthmatic children were interviewed and asked about the degree to which emotions precipitated asthmatic attacks. Children for whom emotions were important precipitants were expected to respond positively to separation from their parents (predicted positive), whereas children for whom emotions played less of a role were not expected to show improvement. For the predicted positive group, all measures of asthma improved during the separation period. The children who were not predicted to respond to separation exhibited no differences across phases on any measure.

The findings of this research study, and of others like it, led investigators to view changes in the psychological atmosphere as the basis for improvement in asthmatic symptoms. However, over time both the investigators at CARIH and other investigators came to view such findings somewhat differently. Although the magnitude of changes reported might be statistically significant, they were not clinically significant. And changes might have been due to increased compliance with prescribed medical regimens when the substitute parents moved in and the children's parents lived in a hotel. Indeed, current treatments to improve asthmatic functioning do focus on improving adherence (Lemanek, Kamps, & Chung, 2001).

This does not mean that psychological factors and family functioning play no role in asthma. There seems little doubt that these factors, in general, do play a role (Berz et al., 2007; Kaugars, Klinnert, & Bender, 2004; McQuaid & Walders, 2003; McQuaid et al., 2007). Home environment (e.g., dust, animal dander), activities of family members (e.g., smoking, outdoor activities), and stress (e.g., family fights, divorce) may act as triggers for asthmatic attacks. For example, Wood, Lim, and colleagues (2007) found, in a sample of young people aged 7 to 17 with asthma, that negative family emotional climate was associated with disease severity. These findings suggest that negative emotional climate was associated with the young person's depressive symptoms, which were associated both directly and indirectly (through emotional triggers) with the severity of the youth's asthma (see Figure 14–1).

The young person's asthma may affect the family in many ways. Parents may experience increased anxiety, lose work days because of their child's illness, and suffer high medical costs, while siblings may experience loss of attention and restrictions in choice of family activities. Also, family members likely have to assist in the management of the disease, especially for younger children. It is therefore not surprising that psychological interventions have focused on educating families about the triggers of asthma attacks, on the consequences of asthma, and on helping young people and their families manage

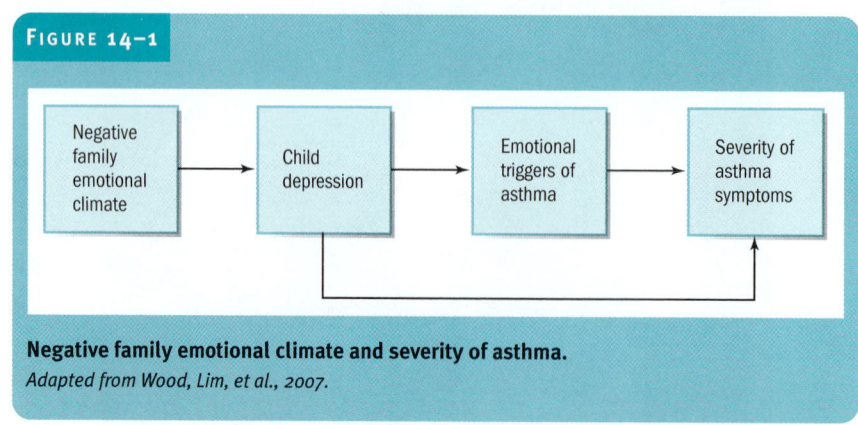

FIGURE 14–1

Negative family emotional climate and severity of asthma.
Adapted from Wood, Lim, et al., 2007.

the disease (Creer, 2000; McQuaid & Walders, 2003; McQuaid et al., 2005).

Thus, the focus on psychological and family factors has shifted from the cause of a chronic illness such as asthma to an interest in how children, parents, and family may influence the frequency and severity of the symptoms and how they can manage the disorder (Kaugars et al., 2004; Markson & Fiese, 2000; McQuaid et al., 2007; Wood, Lim, et al., 2007).

Consequences of Chronic Conditions

Another interest is the consequences of chronic medical conditions for young people and their families. The effects of any chronic illness are likely to be pervasive, particularly if the illness is life threatening. The young person is likely to experience substantial stress and anxiety. In addition, limitations due to illness often place obstacles in the way of normal development. For example, contact with peers may be limited or school attendance may be disrupted.

Of course, the family, too, needs to cope with the illness, its treatment, and its effects over long periods of time. Such long-term demands are bound to be difficult to handle, and the consistency required by treatment regimens is stressful in its own right. Thus the entire family may experience considerable anxiety and have appreciable stress placed on its daily routines.

ADJUSTMENT AND CHRONIC ILLNESS

Research on chronic illness has become a priority for pediatric psychologists (Kazak, 2002; Phelps, 2006). One frequent question is whether chronic illness leads to poor adjustment. The answer would appear to be not necessarily, but these illnesses and related life experiences probably place the young person at increased risk for adjustment problems, particularly those of an internalizing nature (LeBovidge et al., 2003; Hysing et al., 2007; McQuaid, Kopel, & Nassau, 2001; Rodenburg et al., 2005; Schwartz & Drotar, 2006). Research findings suggest that there is considerable variation in adjustment among chronically ill youths. Although the majority of young people with a chronic illness do not experience adjustment problems, subsets of more vulnerable patients do exist (Patenaude & Kupst, 2005; Schwartz & Drotar, 2006; Wallander, Thompson, & Alriksson-Schmidt, 2003).

However, measuring adjustment at any one time is unlikely to provide a complete picture. Adjustment for the young person and family members is likely to be an ongoing process, beginning at diagnosis and continuing through treatment, treatment completion, perhaps relapse, and the long-term course that is inherent in a chronic illness (Friedman, Latham, & Dahlquist, 1998; Kazak, 2005). This has led some professionals to consider a posttraumatic stress framework to understand the initial reaction to diagnosis and treatment and to adjustment over time (Bruce, 2006; Schwartz & Drotar, 2006; Stuber & Shemesh, 2006).

Adjustment to chronic illness is best thought of as a complex function of a number of variables (Phipps et al., 2005). Characteristics of the young person and family members probably contribute to the adjustment of both the young person and the family; for example, the youth's existing competencies and the types and variety of coping skills that the young person possesses are likely to be important in this process. A second category of variables is disease factors, such as severity, degree of impairment, and the functional independence of the young person. In addition, the youth's environment (e.g., family, school, health care) is likely to be a factor in variations in adjustment. An appreciation of the complexity of the problem is illustrated in the model offered by Wallander, Varni, and their colleagues (Wallander & Varni, 1998; see Figure 14–2).

In the following sections, we examine two of the categories of influences on adjustment to chronic illness: illness parameters and family functioning.

Illness parameters and adjustment. In seeking to understand the adjustment among young people with chronic illnesses, it is reasonable to ask whether aspects of the illness itself contribute to differences in adjustment. In attempting to answer this question, the severity of the illness, stress related to the illness, perceptions regarding the illness, and the degree of functional impairment produced by the illness are among the variables that have been examined. Of course, analyzing these dimensions separately is not always possible. For example, a more severe illness is likely to be related to greater restrictions in normal functioning. However, each of these variables seems important.

Certain conditions are more severe than others, but severity of illness also can vary among young people with the same condition. What, then, might be the impact of severity of the medical problem? Findings are conflicting (Miceli et al.,

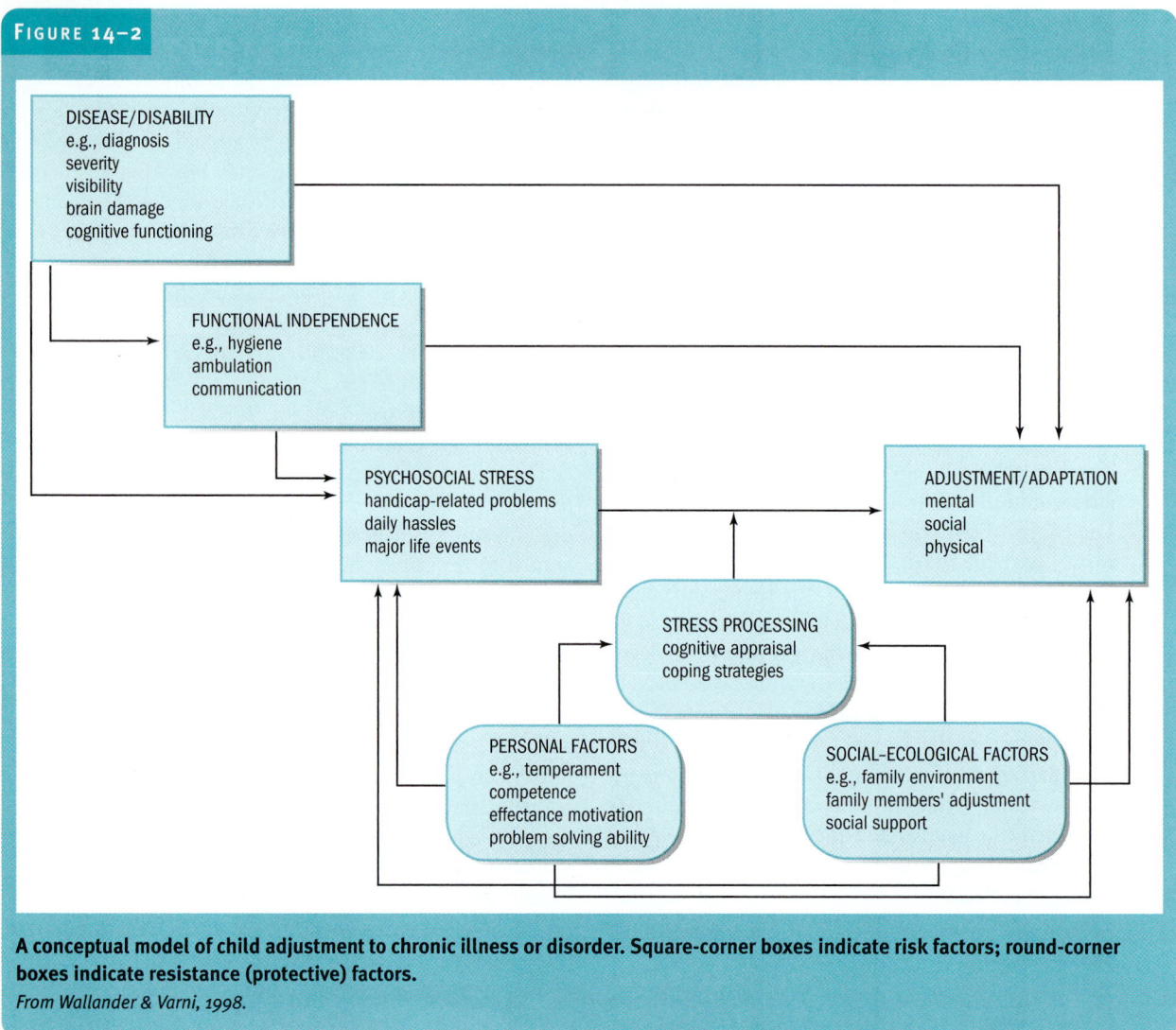

FIGURE 14–2

A conceptual model of child adjustment to chronic illness or disorder. Square-corner boxes indicate risk factors; round-corner boxes indicate resistance (protective) factors.

From Wallander & Varni, 1998.

1999), however, some research does suggest a relationship between illness severity and adjustment (Blackman & Gurka, 2007; McQuaid, Kopel, & Nassau, 2001). For example, a longitudinal examination of youths with juvenile rheumatoid arthritis (JRA) found that although there were no significant overall differences in social functioning between children with JRA and control youths, severity of disease was a risk factor. Peers' ratings of liking declined over the 2-year period for children with more severe disease compared with those with mild disease. Also, children with active disease were chosen fewer times as a best friend than children in remission (Reiter-Purtill et al., 2003). However, more severe forms of a disorder are not always associated with poorer adjustment, and relationships are likely to be complex and may rely on the youth's

and family's perceptions of the severity of the condition (Barakat, Alderfer, & Kazak, 2006; Klinnert et al., 2000; Wallander & Varni, 1998).

The young person's attitude toward the illness and the degree of stress experienced by the youth and family also may impact adjustment. For example, Le Bovidge, Lavigne & Miller (2005) examined the adjustment of young people aged 8 to 18 with chronic arthritis. Greater illness-related and non-illness-related stresses were both associated with higher levels of anxiety and depressive symptomatology and parent reports of adjustment problems. A more positive attitude toward illness, in contrast, was associated with lower levels of anxiety and depressive symptomatology. Figure 14–3 illustrates the relationship of arthritis-related stress and illness attitude to depressive symptomatolgy.

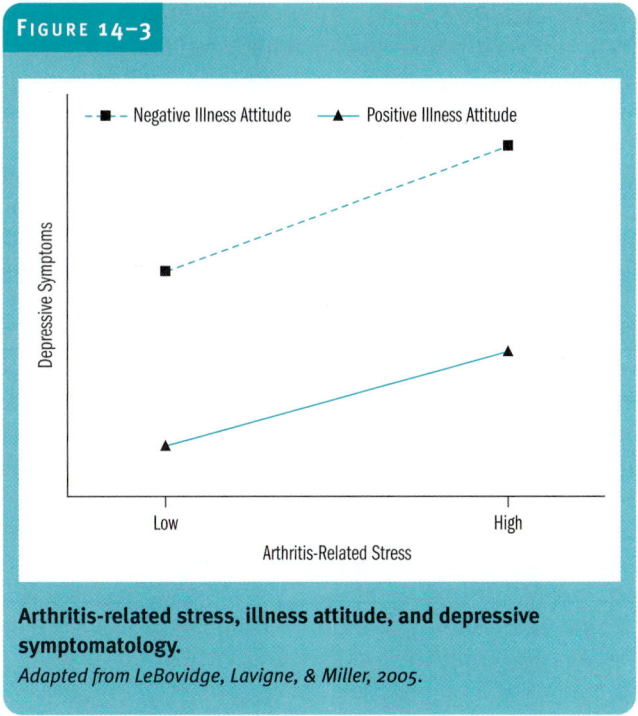

FIGURE 14–3

Arthritis-related stress, illness attitude, and depressive symptomatology.

Adapted from LeBovidge, Lavigne, & Miller, 2005.

Adjustment also may be associated with the degree of functional limitation (how restricted the youth is) due to the chronic condition (Bleil et al., 2000; Meijer et al., 2000). For example, functional limitations may affect the number of absences from school or relationships with friends. The degree to which the illness is controlled also appears to be important. Although these results suggest that anxiety, depression, and the like are outcomes of illness-related parameters, investigators acknowledge that the direction of causation is not clearly established. Anxiety, depression, and the like may contribute to illness parameters such as poor illness control, more severe illness symptoms, and greater functional limitations (Wiebe et al., 1994).

Ethically, we cannot manipulate emotional conditions or illness severity, nor can we randomly assign young people to diseases. Thus, interpreting the impact of aspects of illness is inevitably difficult. Furthermore, although illness factors may help predict adjustment, predictive ability is not very strong. Integrating illness factors into a more normative approach—one that combines these factors with the stress, risk, and resilience factors included in etiological models for young people without chronic medical disorder—is a useful approach (Soliday, Kool, & Lande, 2000). Such an approach would allow for identification of factors relatively unique to chronic

illness, as well as those common to other young people and families. Among the variables that might be the focus of such a normative approach is family functioning.

Family functioning and adjustment. It is not surprising that family functioning is related to the psychological adjustment of chronically ill children and adolescents (Kaugars et al., 2004; Power, 2006). Without denying the particular risks and stressors associated with chronic conditions, it is reasonable as a starting point to assume that some of the family influences that are related to adjustment of other children and adolescents, such as parental depression and marital conflict, are also related to the adjustment of young people with chronic illness. Indeed, this seems to be the case (Lavigne & Faier-Routman, 1993; Wood, Lim, et al., 2007).

Lisa   Diabetes Management and Family Context

Lisa is a 14-year-old with a history of insulin-dependent diabetes mellitus and a variety of behavior and health status problems. Her mother reports difficulties with Lisa's diabetes management, which have gotten worse recently, resulting in 10 hospitalizations in the past 12 months.

Lisa is the only adopted child in a family of four youngsters. She has three brothers, ages 20 years, 2 years, and 1 month. The 2-year-old was born seriously ill and required several operations, although he is now in good health. During the assessment process, Mrs. L openly expressed her hostility toward Lisa. In contrast, the oldest son is seen as perfect. Mrs. L is also exceptionally nurturing towards her two younger sons.

The births of the two younger brothers clearly changed Lisa's role in the family from youngest child and the focus of Mrs. L's nurturance to sibling caretaker. Mrs. L is feeling increasingly stressed and recently left work to care for the two boys. She is angry at her husband for his passive stance, but this remains largely unexpressed. The oldest son's decision to leave home for college leaves her without any male support. Mrs. L directs much of her anger towards Lisa. Lisa is angry also, and this is directed primarily toward her father. It is possible that she may be receiving subtle encouragement from her mother for this. At the same time, Lisa's difficulties draw her parents together. Lisa's behavior and hospitalizations also shift the family focus of attention away from her brothers and toward her.

Adapted from Johnson, 1998, pp. 428–429.

A variety of family influences known to be related to child and adolescent adjustment in general have also been investigated in populations of young people with chronic conditions (Wallander et al., 2003). Timko and her colleagues (1993), working with youths with juvenile rheumatoid arthritis, examined how parental risk and resilience factors predicted disease-related functional disabilities (e.g., ability to grip things, ability to do routine household chores), pain, and psychosocial adjustment. After the ages of the youths and initial levels of their functioning were controlled for, parents' personal strain and depressed mood and fathers' drinking were associated with poorer adjustment in the young people 4 years after initial contact. Better parental social functioning, the mothers' involvement in social activities, and the fathers' number of close relationships, on the other hand, seemed to facilitate the youths' adjustment. Given that attention has often concentrated on the contribution of maternal factors, it is interesting that the fathers' risk and resilience factors contributed to the youths' functioning and adjustment beyond what was already accounted for by maternal factors and other influences.

Illness-related and family factors may moderate or mediate each other's relationship to adjustment. Findings by Wagner and her colleagues (2003), for example, suggest that parental distress may interact with illness-related factors to affect child adjustment. Among youths with juvenile rheumatoid arthritis, the impact of parental distress was evident for those young people who perceived their illness to be more intrusive—that is, interfering with their ability to engage in activities. These young people were more depressed. In contrast, parental distress was unrelated to the depression of youths with low levels of perceived illness intrusiveness.

Bleil and her colleagues (2000) also studied the contribution of illness-related functional status and family factors. The degree to which a young person was restricted by asthma was related to symptoms of depression. This relationship, however, was mediated by the security of the relationship between the mother and youth. That is, functional status appeared to affect security of mother–child relatedness, which in turn affected the youth's level of depression.

Family variables such as conflict, control, and organization also appear to be associated with adjustment. In their comparison of diabetic youths and matched controls with acute illness, Wertlieb, Hauser, and Jacobson (1986) found that overt expression of family conflict was related to greater problem behavior in both groups. However, other factors differentiated the groups. One particularly interesting finding involved differences in attempts to control and maintain the family system. Among the acutely ill youths, a greater control orientation in the family was strongly related to a greater probability of behavior problems. In contrast, among the diabetic youth, low levels of family organization were associated with high levels of behavior problems. Families with a diabetic child have appreciable demands placed on them to organize daily routines involved in the management of the illness. Successful management of the diabetes probably requires appreciable organization and structure, as well as overtly dealing with issues of control. Structured and controlling family environments may be associated with better metabolic control of the diabetic condition. The relationship of family environment to adjustment relationships, however, is likely to be complex

(Seiffge-Krenke, 1998; Wallander et al., 2003; Weist et al., 1993).

Cohesion is another family variable that seems to be important. It is often suggested that a life-threatening illness draws family members closer together. Increased cohesion, although not a universal reaction to illness, has been observed in families coping with a variety of illnesses (Ross et al., 1993; Wood et al., 1989). Level of cohesion also is frequently associated with the adjustment of the young person and other family members (Helgeson et al., 2003; Lavigne & Faier-Routman, 1993; Sloper, 2000).

A study of adolescent cancer survivors illustrates the importance of cohesion; however, it too suggests that relationships are likely to be complex (Rait et al., 1992). Adolescents who had previously been treated for leukemia, Hodgkin's disease, or non-Hodgkin's lymphoma, and who were currently in remission, participated in the study. The participants were 12 to 19 years old at the time of the assessment. The authors hypothesized that the experience of cancer would result in greater family cohesion and that cohesion would be associated with the psychosocial adjustment of these cancer survivors.

The adolescents completed a standard measure of family adaptability and cohesion. The cancer survivors' scores did differ from a normative community group, but not in the predicted direction. The adolescents who had survived cancer described their families as less cohesive than the community sample. There was, though, the expected relationship between cohesion and adjustment. Greater cohesion was associated with better posttreatment psychological adjustment. However, an interesting complexity was suggested. Among "recent" survivors (treatment completed a year or less ago) and "long-term" survivors (treatment completed more than 5 years ago), there was a strong relationship between family cohesiveness and adjustment. For "intermediate" survivors (treatment completed between 1 and 5 years ago), however, the association between family cohesiveness and adjustment was dramatically decreased.

These findings illustrate the importance of studying adjustment as a process over time and attending to critical developmental transitions such as transition to school and to early adolescence (Helgeson et al., 2007; Holmbeck, Bruno, & Jandasek, 2006). The young person's condition may change, and the effect of the illness on the family may not be static. Furthermore, changes in the young person and in the illness may require changing styles of family involvement. Because young people with chronic illnesses have a greater chance of survival than ever before, these findings suggest the need for continued exploration of how time since treatment, current developmental level, age at diagnosis, and other variables may be related to the association of family environment and the young person's psychological adjustment.

As more children and adolescents survive chronic illnesses, the complexities of studying long-term adjustment become clear. Are perceived deficiencies (e.g., lower achievement) due to poorer adjustment or to reasonable life choices about what is important? Rather than asking about better disease adjustment, it may be more reasonable to ask how the experience of chronic illness affects individual development (Eiser, 1998).

CANCER: ADAPTING TO CHRONIC ILLNESS

Cancer has long been viewed as a fatal and little understood disease. Although this frightening image still remains, it is not as accurate as was once the case. With increasing survival rates, the emphasis has shifted from "dying from" to "living with" cancer (Eiser, 1998). It may now, for many youngsters, be more appropriate to view cancer as a chronic condition rather than a fatal disease (Cruce & Stinnett, 2006). For example, in 1960, acute lymphocytic leukemia, the most common form of childhood cancer, had a survival rate of 1% 5 years after diagnosis. By the mid-1970s, the survival rate had increased to about 49%, and by the end of the 20th century, to about 83% (Ries et al., 2001). Advances in treatment have improved the overall 5-year survival rate for childhood cancer to over 75% (National Cancer Institute, 2004).

However, treatments are often lengthy, highly invasive, stressful, and accompanied by considerable pain. Working with this population thus presents multiple and complex challenges. In addition to the initial task of helping the young person and family understand and come to accept the illness, it is important to assist them in coping with a long and stressful treatment regimen and the additional stressors that the illness and its treatment place on them. For example, advice regarding the young person's school, teacher, and peer group is likely to be important during treatment and afterward (Cruce & Stinnett, 2006). Also, concerns regarding the longer-term impact of the disease are considerable (Vannatta & Gerhardt, 2003). Potential effects are probably

Families may require continuing assistance to help them in supporting their child with cancer.
(Sean Cayton/The Image Works)

related to developmental period. For adolescents the disease may interfere with the development of autonomy as a result of increased dependence on family and medical staff, and it may impose restrictions on social life and the development of close interpersonal relationships. Adolescence also is a developmental period during which some high-risk behaviors (substance use) may be somewhat normative. Even brief involvement in such behaviors can have significant consequences for young people with cancer. Problematic outcomes, however, are not inevitable. The provision of ongoing psychosocial services to families throughout this process may buffer the impact of the cancer experience and allow these young people to develop and function much like their peers. Such support and services may also assist siblings and other family members who are affected (Dolgin et al., 2007; Kazak, 2005; Lobato & Kao, 2005; Woznick & Goodheart, 2002).

One must also be aware that the very treatments that have resulted in longer survival may contribute to long-term challenges. Advances in treatments such as chemotherapy and radiation have contributed to increased life expectancy. However, young people who have completed these treatments are at increased risk for growth and reproductive difficulties as well as cardiac, pulmonary, renal/urological, gastrointestinal, ocular, and dental problems. Cosmetic impairments and functional limitations (e.g., diminished stamina) have also been frequently noted. Some of these effects may not be apparent immediately after treatment, but may occur later among survivors, and their impact may evolve over time (Moore, 2005; Vannatta & Gerhardt, 2003). Interventions to help prevent and control negative physical outcomes are thus also suggested (Tercyak et al., 2006).

The immediate and long-term impacts on the central nervous system—of treatments such as irradiation and chemotherapy to prevent central nervous system occurrence of leukemia—are not entirely clear. However, it appears that impairment does occur in cognitive and academic functioning (Carey et al., 2007; Espy et al., 2001; Mahone et al., 2007; Moore, 2005; Raymond-Speden et al., 2000).

The shift to coping, adjusting, and adapting to cancer is clearly a more optimistic approach than in years past when survival rates were very low. However, while we continue to attempt to understand this process and assist young people and families, we must also monitor long-term outcomes and side effects of treatment. In addition, relapse remains possible, and these individuals are at increased risk for secondary cancers. Maintaining vigilance without creating additional and undue anxiety, and at the same time promoting an optimistic and adaptive attitude, presents a considerable challenge.

A similar perspective on adaptation applies to other chronic illnesses such as sickle cell disease and HIV/AIDS (see Accent: "The Impact of HIV/AIDS in Children and Adolescents") and to conditions such as head injury (Brown et al., 2006; Lewis, 2001; New, Lee, & Elliott, 2007; Wade et al., 2006). The

ACCENT ●●●●●

The Impact of HIV/AIDS in Children and Adolescents

An appreciable number of those infected with HIV and AIDS are women of childbearing age. The HIV-positive children born to these women are some of the saddest images of the AIDS story. Indeed, about 90% of young people infected with the virus acquire it through their mothers (Armstrong, Willen, & Sorgen, 2003). These babies are often very sick and frequently are given away or taken from their mothers. Many of them are taken in by foster parents who are willing to take on the challenge of caring for such a child. Fortunately, with medical advances, the number of HIV babies born to HIV-positive women has dropped dramatically over time. However, this problem remains a considerable international concern.

Although the majority of young people become infected through vertical transmission from their mothers, some, such as those with hemophilia, become infected through the blood supply. For older children and adolescents, there is also concern regarding transmission by drug use or sexual contact (Donenberg, Paikoff, & Pequegnat, 2006).

With medical advances producing greater survival rates, attention has shifted from terminal care for affected youths to management of the condition and improving quality of life (Armstrong et al., 2003).

We have known for some time that children born infected with HIV are likely to have developmental and cognitive problems. HIV progresses faster in children than in adults and is more likely to result in neurological abnormalities because of the effects of the virus on immature nervous and immune systems (Wachsler-Felder & Golden, 2002). By school age these neurological problems result in significant learning, language, and attention difficulties, and emotional and social difficulties are also evident. The impact may be greater for young people with greater compromise of their immune system (Bordeaux et al., 2003). Young people with HIV/AIDS are thus likely to have to continue to adapt to extraordinary circumstances and are also likely to present their caregivers with exceptional challenges.

It is important to remember that not all HIV-infected youths have clinically significant emotional and behavioral problems (New et al., 2007; Bachanas et al., 2001). However, among those who do, particularly those born to HIV-positive mothers, a complex set of influences is likely contributing to the difficulties (Steele, Nelson, & Cole, 2007). Clearly, some of the problems are direct outcomes of their disease (Wachsler-Felder & Golden, 2002). The medical treatments and the stress of adhering to a long-term medical regimen and a chronic illness are probably factors as well. Families also face difficult decisions regarding disclosure of the illness both to the child and others. In addition, many of these young people were born to mothers whose prenatal care was not optimal, who abused drugs when they were pregnant, or who had serious psychopathology themselves. All of these powerful influences, as well as family and environmental risks that the young people may have faced after their births, make current problematic outcomes understandable. The adaptation challenges are considerable and call for a coordinated and intensive program of assistance for these young people and their families.

consequences of the illness or condition itself as well as the impact of intensive, demanding, and long-term treatments need to be addressed in understanding adaptation to these chronic conditions over time.

Facilitating Medical Treatment

Attempts to provide psychological treatment that would improve a patient's medical condition have long been an aspect of the interface between psychology/psychiatry and medicine. The vast majority of early attempts sought to provide the patient with psychotherapy as a means of reducing physical symptoms or curing illness. Such direct assaults on illness through psychotherapy proved to be largely ineffective (Werry, 1986). More recent efforts have taken a somewhat different approach to integrating a psychological perspective into the clinically relevant, empirically supported treatment of medical problems (Beale, 2006; Drotar & Lemanek, 2001). Although a comprehensive review of these multiple efforts and strategies is beyond the scope of the present chapter, a few important illustrations follow.

ADHERENCE TO MEDICAL REGIMENS

The terms adherence and compliance describe how well a young person or family follows recommended medical treatments such as taking medications, following diets, or implementing lifestyle changes. Diabetes provides an excellent illustration of the way psychologists have increasingly attempted to understand the complex tasks encountered by families managing chronic childhood disorders (Delamater, 2000; Drotar, et al., 2000; La Greca & Bearman, 2003).

A description of diabetes. Diabetes is one of the most common chronic diseases in youngsters, affecting approximately 1.8 youths per 1,000. Type 1 (DM1), also known as insulin-dependent diabetes mellitus, is a lifelong disorder that results when the pancreas produces insufficient insulin. Daily replacement of insulin by injection is required. Because the onset of DM1 typically occurs in childhood, this form of diabetes is often referred to as a childhood or juvenile diabetes. In Type 2 diabetes (DM2), rather than insulin deficiency, insulin resistance occurs, impairing cellular uptake of insulin. DM2 was previously viewed as an adult-onset disorder; however, 10 to 20% of new cases of diabetes in youth are of this type. DM2 is disproportionately high among African American, American Indian, and Latino/Hispanic populations. DM2 may be managed by weight reduction, exercise, and careful diet. However, many young people with this form of diabetes need insulin injections (Gortmaker & Sappenfield, 1984; Sandberg & Zurenda, 2006; Wysocki, Greco, & Buckloh, 2003).

Onset of DM1 occurs most often around puberty, but can occur at any time from infancy to early adulthood. Although the exact etiology of DM1 is unclear, genetic factors appear to be involved. Both forms of diabetes increase the long-term risk for damage to the heart, kidneys, eyes, and nervous system. If the disorder is not controlled, a condition known as ketosis, or ketoacidosis, may occur. This is a very serious condition that can lead to coma and death.

The young person and family face a treatment regimen that includes dietary restrictions, daily injections of insulin, monitoring of urine, and testing of blood glucose levels (see Table 14–1). On the basis of the daily tests for level of sugar—and factors such as timing of meals, diet, exercise, physical health, and emotional state—the daily dosages of insulin must be adjusted. Even under the best of circumstances, "insulin reactions" occur often. Thus the youngster must be sensitive to the signs and symptoms of both

TABLE 14–1	SOME ACTIVITIES REQUIRED OF DIABETIC CHILDREN AND FAMILIES

Inject insulin regularly
Test blood regularly
Exercise regularly
Avoid sugar
Check for symptoms—low
Check for symptoms—high
Be careful when sick
Shower regularly
Wear diabetes ID
Watch weight
Eat meals regularly
Adjust diet to exercise
Carry sugar
Test blood as directed
Change injection site
Inject insulin as directed
Watch dietary fat
Take care of injuries
Eat regular snacks
Control emotions
Inspect feet

Adapted from Karoly & Bay, 1990.

hyperglycemia (excessively high levels of blood glucose) and hypoglycemia (excessively low blood glucose). Adverse reactions involve irritability, headache, shaking, and—if not detected early enough—unconsciousness and seizures. The fact that symptoms are different for different individuals and are subjectively experienced makes the task of identifying them complicated. Parents and youths are therefore faced with a difficult, often unpredictable, and emotion-laden therapeutic program that requires careful integration into daily life (Delamater, 2000; Johnson, 1998).

Management of the diabetic condition. The first task in treatment is for the team of professionals to gain and maintain control of the diabetic condition. As this task is achieved, insulin requirements often decrease, and the initial fears and concerns of the youngster and family are often reduced. This has come to be known as the "honeymoon period." This period of partial remission may terminate gradually and often ends about 1 to 2 years after initial diagnosis. In any case, beginning a diabetes self-management program with families during the first few months after diagnosis may avoid any deterioration in metabolic function, and early intervention with young children may help to reduce adherence problems and problems in diabetic control during later periods (Davis et al., 2001; Delamater et al., 1990). Transferring control for management of the disease from the professional to the family and child or adolescent, as well as requiring maintenance of such control over long periods of time, is one of the challenges of working with chronic illness (Meltzer et al., 2003; Palmer et al., 2004).

Adherence to the diabetic regimen. The concept of adherence is multifaceted (La Greca & Bearman, 2003; Riekert & Drotar, 2000). Appreciation of this complexity has led to the development of intervention programs that combine strategies such as education, training in self-management skills, and parent/family involvement. Such programs appear to be promising (Christophersen & Mortweet, 2001; La Greca & Bearman, 2003; Lemanek et al., 2001). The initial step in most programs is to educate the youngster and family about the disease. Although such efforts are regularly made, it cannot be assumed that, following these efforts, the family's knowledge will be adequate. Therefore, it is helpful to assess knowledge. Behavioral observation methods have been employed to assess whether the young person knows how to execute necessary skills such as urine and blood glucose testing. Questionnaires are frequently used to measure knowledge of the disease and the application of that knowledge to different situations (e.g., the role of insulin, and adjusting diet based on blood sugar readings). However, adherence is not just a matter of accurate information and knowledge; it requires that the prescribed tasks be accurately and consistently carried out.

We will highlight several important variables that are involved in adherence. Developmental level is one important variable (Iannotti & Bush, 1993; Johnson, 1993; Palmer et al., 2004). For example, children under 9 years may have difficulty accurately measuring and injecting insulin. In general, knowledge and skills seem to increase with age (Rovet & Fernandes, 1999). However, it may be unwise, even with adolescents, for parents to withdraw from participation (Holmes, 2006; McQuaid et al., 2003; Meltzer et al., 2003).

Adolescence is a period during which management of diabetes often deteriorates (Anderson et al., 2000; Johnson, 1995). The adolescent's knowledge of the disease and its management may be overestimated. Adolescents may, for instance, make errors in estimating their blood glucose levels, particularly when blood glucose levels are quite variable (Meltzer et al., 2003). Whereas increasing cognitive development potentially allows the adolescent to better understand the illness and to manage a complex routine, there are other aspects of cognition that may interfere with adherence. For example, Murphy, Thompson, and Morris (1997) found that adolescents who (1) have a negative perception of their bodies, (2) perceive little control over health when ill, and (3) have an external attributional style for negative events were at risk for poor adherence.

During this period control is often gradually transferred to the youngster, and parental participation often ceases, but total withdrawal of adult involvement may not be advisable (Holmes et al., 2006). It may be important for the parent to continue to monitor the adolescent's diabetic care behaviors (Ellis et al., 2007). Also, individual judgments of a young person's developmental readiness and the balance of child and parent involvement must be made (Hanna, DiMeglio, & Fortenberry, 2007; Wiebe et al., 2005).

For example, Palmer and colleagues (2004) studied young people between the ages of 10 and 15 who had a diagnosis of DM1 for at least 1 year. Mothers' and children's perceptions of who was responsible for various aspects of diabetes management were assessed. Measures of the youth's developmental maturity were also obtained. The youths also completed a measure of their level of self-reliance/autonomy, and their pubertal status was assessed through mothers' reports of the extent to which their child displayed specific signs of puberty. Metabolic control of the diabetes was assessed through medical records of Hba_{1c} (glycosylated hemoglobin test—reflecting average blood glucose levels). Among individuals with low levels of self-reliance/autonomy and low pubertal status, transfer of diabetes responsibility from mother to child was associated with higher Hba_{1c} values (poorer control). The effects on metabolic control of self-reliance, pubertal status, and maternal responsibility for diabetes are illustrated in Figure 14–4.

Social and emotional concerns, such as peer acceptance and greater participation in activities, also are associated with decreased adherence (Thomas, Peterson & Goldstein, 1997). Young people with diabetes may wish to avoid appearing different. The unusual behaviors required for control of their condition (e.g., injections, glucose testing), the dietary demands of eating frequently (when others are not), and the need to avoid high-fat foods and sweets (when others are eating junk food) make conformity difficult. Some of these social challenges

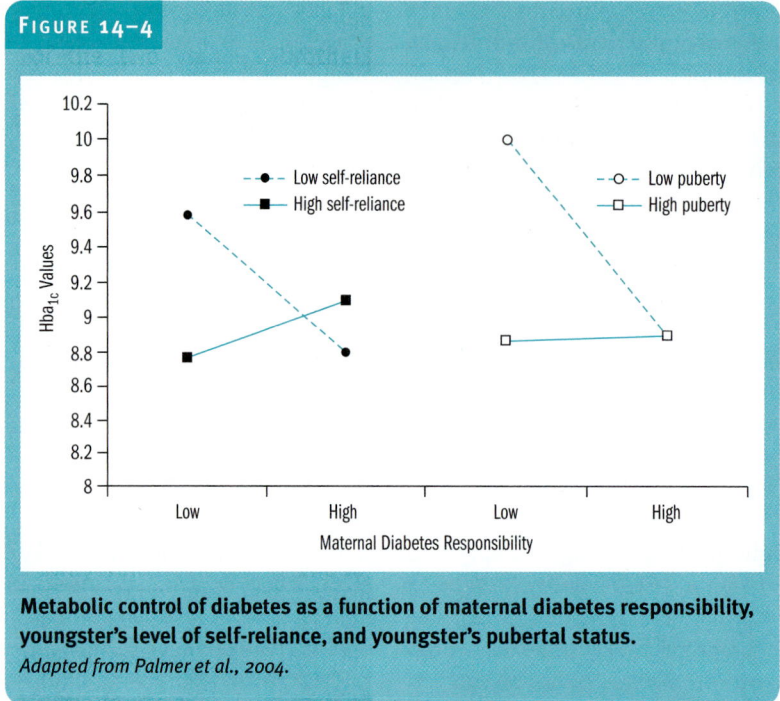

FIGURE 14–4

Metabolic control of diabetes as a function of maternal diabetes responsibility, youngster's level of self-reliance, and youngster's pubertal status.
Adapted from Palmer et al., 2004.

are illustrated in Table 14–2. These vignettes are used to assess social problem solving among diabetic youth. Conflicts with parents over issues of independence are also likely to be present. Such social and interpersonal issues most likely combine with actual physical changes, like those associated with delayed puberty, to increase management and compliance difficulties for adolescents (Brooks-Gunn, 1993; Johnson, 1998). Interventions that maintain parental involvement yet minimize parent–adolescent conflict and improve communication and problem-solving skills are needed (Anderson et al., 2000; Wysocki et al., 2003).

Many other problems regarding adherence are worthy of continued attention. For example, anticipating environmental obstacles to compliance is important. Creating interventions that help adolescents deal with peers concerning their diabetes and that facilitate appropriate peer support, for instance, may greatly facilitate compliance with recommendations (Greco et al., 2001). The realization that the immediate consequences of diabetes management are often negative, and therefore may reduce the individual's commitment to adherence, may also help to anticipate difficulties. For example, the immediate consequence of injections is discomfort, whereas the adverse effect of skipping injections is not immediate. Thus, interventions that reduce the immediate negative effects of compliance may be of value.

TABLE 14–2 | **EXAMPLES OF VIGNETTES TO EVALUATE SOCIAL PROBLEM-SOLVING IN DIABETIC YOUTH**

GLUCOSE TESTING
Your friends ask you to go to a video arcade, and it's almost time for you to test your glucose. You don't have your test materials with you, and your friends are impatient to leave. If you stop and test, they will leave without you.

DIET—SWEETS
You are invited to your best friend's birthday party, where they are going to serve cake and ice cream at a time when you are supposed to have a snack. But cake and ice cream would not fit into your diet plan at all, since you are supposed to have a snack that is low in sugar and fat.

DIET—TIME OF EATING
Your friends invite you out for dinner at your favorite restaurant, but they want to go really late, a lot later than you would normally eat.

ALCOHOL
Your friends invite you to a big party. You go there, and you find out that almost everyone is drinking beer. Your friends offer you some beer and seem to expect that you will drink it just as everyone else did.

Adapted from Thomas, Peterson, & Goldstein, 1997.

Attention to the role of the health care system and primary care providers (pediatrician, nurse) is another important aspect of the adherence process (Dunbar-Jacob, 1993; La Greca & Bearman, 2003). Changes in the health care system may have resulted in shortened medical visits and a less personal relationship with providers. These conditions may contribute to poorer communication and poorer adherence. The behavior of health care providers is important. Information provided must be sufficient and presented in a manner that allows the family to carry out complex regimens (DiMatteo, 2000; Ievers et al., 1999). Health care providers, too, must be sufficiently aware of the youngster's level of cognitive development so as to not overestimate or underestimate the youngster's understanding of the illness and treatment regimen. Providers also must assist the youngster and family in achieving a developmentally appropriate balance of responsibilities for diabetes care (Lewin et al., 2006). These issues suggest the importance of training health care providers to be sensitive to the needs of individual families and children and to improve professional–patient communication (DiMatteo, 2000; Power, 2006).

PSYCHOLOGICAL MODIFICATION OF CONDITION-RELATED PAIN

The Eastern mystic who walks on hot coals, voluntarily slows the heart, and by the power of the mind closes a wound has always fascinated inhabitants of the Western world. Fascinating, too, are the shaman's cures by removal of evil spirits, the miracles performed by faith healers, and cures of medical ailments by inert placebos (Ullmann & Krasner, 1975). These phenomena highlight in a dramatic fashion the possible role of psychological interventions in the treatment of medical disorders. Each phenomenon suggests that psychological procedures can directly affect physical functioning. The systematic and scientific study of how psychology can be used to directly treat physical symptoms such as pain has become part of the shifting emphasis in understanding mind–body relationships.

The use of relaxation and biofeedback to treat young people's headaches is one example of attempts to directly modify physical functioning through psychological interventions. Headaches are usually classified as tension, migraine, or a combination of the two. The pain and suffering that can accompany intense headaches, and the desire to avoid potential negative aspects of drug treatment led to the exploration of nonpharmacological approaches (Andrasik, Blake, & McCarran, 1986; Lofland, Sturges, & Payne, 1999).

Biofeedback refers to a procedure in which some device gives immediate feedback to the person about a particular biological function. Feedback is usually provided by a signal such as a light or tone or by some graphic display. Such feedback, some form of relaxation training or a combination of the two, seem effective in producing clinically meaningful levels of improvement in children's headaches (Burke & Andrasik, 1989; Holden, Deichmann, & Levy, 1999; Powers, Jones, & Jones, 2005; Scharff, Marcus, & Masek, 2002).

Cindy   Chronic Headache Pain

Cindy, 14 years old, attended a demanding private school. She reported that she had been experiencing daily headaches for 18 months. She described constant pain that varied in intensity but she never experienced total relief from the pain. She had carefully followed the medication and other recommendations of her neurologist, but experienced only minimal improvement. Cindy did not feel well enough to participate in social activities and had become isolated from her friends. She could not concentrate when the pain intensified and her grades had begun to suffer. Cindy also stopped participating in sports to avoid exacerbating the pain. She described experiencing fatigue and frustration and believed that she would never get rid of her headaches. Cindy received biofeedback-assisted relaxation training that incorporated guided imagery, breathing exercises, and progressive muscle relaxation. Within three sessions Cindy was able to produce dramatic changes in the physiological indices targeted by the biofeedback and reported decreased pain and anxiety while practicing the cognitive-behavioral techniques. Cindy was encouraged to use these skills at school. After six sessions, Cindy reported marked decreases in the intensity of her headaches and feelings of efficacy in coping with pain. Her headaches rarely decreased to the level of being undetectable, but the pain levels dropped to the point where she was able to resume her previous activities, and her grades improved.

Adapted from Powers, Jones, & Jones, 2005, p. 72.

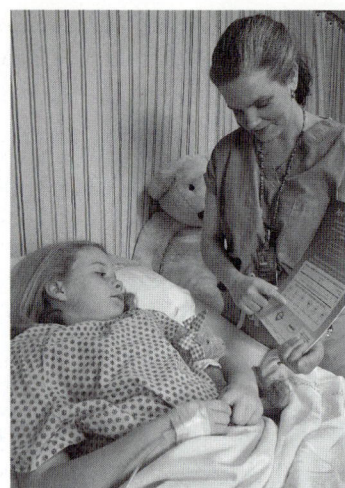

It is common for young people to exhibit distress during medical procedures. Particularly for those who must undergo frequent treatment, techniques that reduce or help control distress can facilitate good medical care.
(George Dodson/Pearson Education/ PH College)

Innovations to increase accessibility of treatments have also been explored. Connelly and colleagues (2006) developed a minimal therapist contact cognitive-behavioral treatment for recurrent pediatric headache. As an adjunct to the recommendations of their neurologist, participants received CD-ROMs containing the "Headstrong" program. Participants completed four week-long modules (education, relaxation, thought-changing, and pain behavior modification) and received weekly phone contact to answer questions. Children who received the CD-ROM program had significant improvements in their headaches beyond that of the control group who continued following their neurologists' prescriptions.

REDUCING PROCEDURE-RELATED PAIN AND DISTRESS

Developing psychologically based procedures for enhancing the effectiveness of medical treatment is another important and growing area of interest. Procedures for dealing with pain and discomfort associated with medical treatment illustrate this potentially important contribution.

Pain and distress. Despite its seeming simplicity, pain is a complex phenomenon that is difficult to assess. It is difficult, for example, to separate the pain or discomfort that the person is suffering from the anxiety that the person is experiencing while undergoing a painful medical procedure. This difficulty has led some to use the term *distress* to encompass pain, anxiety, and other negative affect (Jay, 1988; Varni, Katz, & Waldron, 1993). Whatever term is employed, three different response systems might be assessed: cognitive-affective, behavioral, and physiological (Blount, Piira, & Cohen, 2003; McCulloch & Collins, 2006).

Self-report measures of the cognitive-affective component of pain are the measures most frequently employed. This is probably an intentional choice. Because pain is a subjective experience, assessing the youth's experience of pain is important (Dahlquist & Switkin, 2003). In addition, the greater accessibility of this component and the relative ease of measurement are certainly factors. However, measurement is not without its difficulties. For example, the young person's developmental level plays a large role in selecting a self-report measure. Because older children may be able to describe pain in semantic terms, they can be assessed by means of interviews and questionnaires. For younger children, professionals rely on concrete and visual methods, such as a pain thermometer that visually represents degrees of pain in numerical terms (see Figure 14–5). In very young children who may not have the number concepts and discriminations required to use this method, different measures can be employed. For example, faces with expressions ranging from broad smiles to severe frowns, along with colors to indicate intensity of pain, may be useful. If photographs are employed, use of ethnically appropriate images may be important (Beyer & Knott, 1998; Hicks et al., 2001).

The behavioral component of children's distress (for example, behaviors that require the child to be physically restrained) can often interfere with effective medical treatment. Observational methods are often used to assess children's distress behaviors. Structured behavioral observations employing a system of defined behaviors and trained observers have been employed in a variety of contexts (Blount et al., 2003; Elliot, Jay, & Woody, 1987). Such procedures can be expensive and time consuming; an alternative is to use global ratings of the young person's distress behaviors by parents or nurses.

Assessment of the physiological aspect of pain is far less common (Christophersen & Mortweet, 2001). Melamed and Siegel's (1975) measurement of palmar sweat before and after youngsters underwent elective surgery and Jay and colleagues' (1987) monitoring of pulse rate prior to bone marrow aspiration are examples of use of physiological measures.

A child's subjective pain experience must be assessed in a developmentally appropriate manner. A pain thermometer like the one pictured is one way of concretizing differences in pain experience for young children.

However, the equipment necessary and the difficulty involved in reliably obtaining measures such as heart rate, blood pressure, and skin conductance make such measures less likely to be employed.

Helping the child cope. Procedures have been developed to assist young people in coping with the pain associated with their disease or disorder, or with the treatments they receive (Blount et al., 2003; Powers et al., 2005; Walco et al., 1999). Many of the medical procedures used to assess and treat children with chronic disorders are aversive. Well-timed preparation of the young person that contains appropriate information that he or she can understand and remember is the first step in reducing distress and in helping the young person cope (Peterson & Mori, 1988; Spafford, von Baeyer, & Hicks, 2002). The basic rationale for preparation is that unexpected stress is worse than predictable stress. From the simple statement that preparation is good follows the complex question of how this is best achieved for varying situations and for different young people. Research provides some guidelines and suggests certain procedures (Kazak, 2005; MacLaren & Cohen, 2005; Salmon, McGuigan, & Pereira, 2006).

Children's distress and experiences of pain during medical procedures are related to the behavior of their parents (Friedman et al., 1998). When parents use strategies to distract the child or to direct the child to use coping techniques, the child exhibits less distress. Parental anxiety may reduce the effectiveness of distraction techniques (Dahlquist & Pendley, 2005). Also, when parents attempt to comfort the child by reassuring statements or apologies, distress is greater (Harbeck-Weber & Peterson, 1996; Manimala et al., 2000; Salmon & Pereira, 2002).

The behavior of the medical practitioner is also likely to affect the young person. An interesting finding is that information presented in a reassuring manner may reduce child distress (Dahlquist, Power, & Carlson, 1995). It may be that young people respond differently to parents and to staff and that a combination of distraction/direction from the parents and reassurance from medical practitioners is most beneficial to the young person (Friedman et al., 1998).

Young people themselves have made some recommendations regarding coping strategies (Ross, 1988). Many of these suggestions cluster around the perception of being in control (Carpenter, 1992), and many involve the young person's controlling the environment during the aversive treatment procedure. The following comment by a 10-year-old boy undergoing emergency room burn treatment illustrates this phenomenon:

> *I said, "How about a hurting break?" and he (intern) said, "Hey, man, are you serious?" And I said, "Sure. Even when ladies are having babies they get a little rest between the bad pains." And they (the pediatric emergency room personnel) all laughed and he said, "OK, you get a 60-second break whenever you need it," and then it was much, much better, like you wouldn't believe it. (Ross, 1988, p. 5)*

Although young people may be capable of generating their own strategies for coping with pain and distress, procedures for teaching effective stress management/coping skills are also needed. Most interventions consist of a variety of coping strategies derived from behavioral and cognitive-behavioral perspectives. Table 14–3 lists some of the skills included in such programs.

The work of Jay and her colleagues on reducing the stress of youngsters undergoing bone marrow aspirations is a good example of such efforts (Jay et al., 1987; 1991; 1995). Bone marrow aspirations (BMAs) are often conducted for children and adolescents with leukemia in order to examine the marrow for evidence of cancer cells. The procedure, in which a

TABLE 14–3	SOME SKILLS TAUGHT TO ASSIST CHILDREN IN COPING WITH MEDICAL PROCEDURES

Deep breathing exercises (deep inhalation and slow exhalation)
Distraction (e.g., counting ceiling tiles, music)
Emotive imagery (reconceptualizing the setting or pain)
Relaxing imagery
Progressive muscle relaxation (relaxing muscle groups)
Modeling or active coaching of coping skills
Behavioral or imaginal rehearsal (of the medical procedures)
Rewards for using coping strategies

Adapted from Dahlquist, 1992.

large needle is inserted into the hip bone and the marrow is suctioned out, is very painful. The use of general anesthesia and intramuscular injections of sedatives are avoided because there is concern regarding substantial medical risks and side effects.

The intervention package developed by Jay and her colleagues consists of five major components: filmed modeling, breathing exercises, emotive imagery/distraction, positive incentive, and behavioral rehearsal. The intervention package is administered on the day of the scheduled BMA, about 30 to 45 minutes prior to the procedure.

In the first step, the young person is shown an 11-minute film of a same-age model undergoing BMA. The model, on a voice overlay, narrates the steps involved in the procedure, as well as his or her thoughts and feelings at crucial points. The model also exhibits positive coping behaviors and self statements. The child in the film exhibits a realistic amount of anxiety but copes with it rather than exhibiting no anxiety and distress at all. After observing the film, the patients are taught simple breathing exercises, which are intended as active attention distracters but may also promote some relaxation.

The patients are then taught imagery/distraction techniques. Emotive imagery (Lazarus & Abramavitz, 1962) is a technique in which images are used to inhibit anxiety. A child's hero images are ascertained in a discussion with the child. They are then woven into a story that elicits positive affect that is presumed to be incompatible with anxiety, that transforms the meaning of the pain, and that encourages mastery rather than avoidance of pain. One girl's emotive imagery resembled the following story:

She pretended that Wonderwoman had come to her house and asked her to be the newest member of her Superpower Team. Wonderwoman had given her special powers. These special powers made her very strong and tough so that she could stand almost anything. Wonderwoman asked her to take some tests to try out these superpowers. The tests were called bone marrow aspirations and spinal taps. These tests hurt, but with her new superpowers, she could take deep breaths and lie very still. Wonderwoman was very proud when she found out that her superpowers worked, and she made the Superpower team. (Jay et al., 1985, p. 516)

Another imagery distraction technique involves teaching the young person to form a pleasant image that is incompatible with the experience of pain (e.g., a day at the beach). The young person chooses either the emotive or the incompatible strategy and is given guidance during the bone marrow procedure to help in forming the images.

A positive incentive component of the intervention includes a trophy presented as a symbol of mastery and courage. The young person is told she can win the trophy if she does "the best that she can possibly do." The situation is structured so that every patient can be successful in getting the trophy.

There is also a behavioral rehearsal phase during which younger children "play doctor" with a doll, whereas older children are guided in conducting a "demonstration." The young people are instructed step-by-step in the administration of the BMA. As the young person goes through the procedure, the doll is instructed to lie still and do the breathing exercises and imagery.

Jay and her colleagues (1987) compared this cognitive-behavioral package with a low-risk pharmacological intervention (oral Valium) and a minimal treatment-attention control condition. Each young person experienced each of these interventions during three different BMAs. It was randomly determined which of the six possible orders of these interventions was received. When in the cognitive-behavioral intervention condition, young people had significantly lower behavioral distress, lower pain ratings, and lower pulse rates than when they were in the control condition. When young people were in the Valium condition, they showed no significant differences from the control condition except that they had lower blood pressure scores.

The findings of this study represent one example of interventions that can help young people and families cope with the distress associated with certain medical procedures. The incorporation of parents or other family members into such programs can improve the maintenance of child coping, reduce parent/family distress, and improve the cost effectiveness of interventions that otherwise might require a great deal of professional time (Powers et al., 1993; Schiff et al., 2001). Such interventions hold the promise of making delivery of effective medical treatment more likely (Blount et al., 2003).

PREPARATION FOR HOSPITALIZATION

Young people suffering from chronic illness often require periodic hospitalization to stabilize their functioning. Other young people, too, may need to enter the hospital for scheduled surgery, for some other procedure, or in an emergency. Indeed, about one-third of all young people are hospitalized at least once. Siegel and Conte (2001), writing on the history and status of hospitalization for medical care, indicated that in the mid-1950s the importance of the child's psychological reaction to early hospitalization and surgery began to be recognized. Two films by James Robertson at the Tavistock Clinic are suggested to have been instrumental in changing attitudes and practices. One film portrayed a young child's intense distress at being separated from his parents for a week while undergoing minor surgery. The other film demonstrated the positive adjustment of a young person whose mother remained with him while he was hospitalized for surgery. Also, a substantial research literature documented the stressful effects of hospitalization (Siegel & Conte, 2001). Improvements have occurred since the 1950s and 1960s, when much of this research was conducted. For example, in 1954 most New York hospitals allowed parental contact only during 2 visiting hours per week. In contrast, Roberts and Wallander (1992), describing a 1988 survey of 286 hospitals in the United States and Canada, found that 98% of the hospitals had unrestricted visiting for parents and that 94% allowed parent rooming-in.

Most hospitals now also offer prehospital preparation for both the child and the parents when admissions are planned (O'Byrne, Peterson, & Saldana, 1997; Roberts & Wallander, 1992). One well-supported method involves models who, although apprehensive, cope with the hospitalization stresses. Melamed and Siegel's (1975) film, *Ethan Has an Operation*, showed a 7-year-old boy prior to, during, and after surgery. The child narrated the story and showed realistic but adaptive reactions to the procedures. The film has been shown to be an effective means of preparation for hospitalization and surgery (Melamed & Siegel, 1980;

Peterson et al., 1984). This is but one example of the use of modeling. Other films and the use of puppets have been shown to be effective as well (Peterson et al., 1984), and interventions often combine modeling with explicit training of coping techniques. Current efforts are directed at preparation procedures that are well timed; are matched to individual characteristics of the child, parent, and family; and are cost effective. Therefore, these procedures are likely to be used (Peterson et al., 1990; Siegel & Conte, 2001; Vernon & Thompson, 1993).

Despite the improvements in hospitalization procedures, children are still faced with stressors. Spirito, Stark, and Tyc (1994), for example, found that 50% of the chronically ill young people whom they asked to name a stressor since they had been in the hospital, described a specific aspect of hospitalization (e.g., noises preventing sleep, rude staff, slow service). By way of comparison, only 33% and 17%, respectively, indicated pain-related concerns or an illness-related problem (e.g., side effects of treatment, problems or limitations caused by their illness). In contrast, the percentages of young people hospitalized for acute illness or injuries who indicated hospital-, pain-, or illness-related stressors were 39%, 51%, and 10%, respectively. This finding highlights the potential differing needs of children with prior hospitalization experiences. Hospital stressors require attention, because improvements in these areas are likely to enhance the mood state and adjustment of young people, particularly those who are chronically ill and may require frequent hospitalizations.

The Dying Child

Clearly, one of the most distressing aspects of working with severely ill children and adolescents is the prospect of death. Even though much progress has been made at increasing survival rates, the numbers still fall appreciably short of 100% (National Cancer Institute, 2004). Increased survival rates may make the death of a child even harder to bear when it does occur (Eiser, 1994). Several important and difficult questions are raised by the prospect of a dying child:

- What is the child's understanding of death?
- How can we best prepare the young person and the family?
- How do we prepare people for death while sustaining their motivation for treatment?
- Can we help the family begin to accept the child's impending death but prevent the family from prematurely distancing from the child?

ACCENT

Preventing Childhood Injury

Prevention and health maintenance is another aspect of current pediatric psychology. Prevention of injury is one example of such efforts. Many efforts to prevent injury to children are inspired by the work of Lizette Peterson (DiLillo & Tremblay, 2005).

Each year millions of children are injured. Indeed, injuries are the leading cause of death and medical visits for youths over the age of 1 in the United States (Centers for Disease Control and Prevention, 2007). Clearly, the loss of life and function is tragic, and the medical costs considerable (Deal et al., 2000; Schwebel & Gaines, 2007).

There are a number of challenges to injury prevention (Tremblay & Peterson, 1999). One obstacle is that serious injuries are often mistakenly assumed to occur infrequently and to be chance events and, thus, unavoidable. Such assumptions do not encourage an active prevention effort. Professionals therefore suggest abandoning the common term *accident* in favor of *unintentional injury*, a term that acknowledges that the event, though not deliberate, might have been avoided.

Another challenge to injury prevention described by Tremblay and Peterson (1999) is the variety of modes of injury and thus potential interventions: "A toddler mastering the operation of the gate blocking access to the swimming pool, a 7-year-old riding a bicycle without a helmet, and a 16-year-old driving with peers who ridicule him when he stays within the speed limit are all candidates for a variety of potential interventions. . . ."

A basic contribution of psychology is the perspective that there are important behavioral antecedents to injury prevention. Behaviors of young people (e.g., impulsivity, risk taking), parents (e.g., supervision, protectiveness), and peers (persuasion, modeling), and environment-based variables (e.g. chaos, hazards), can contribute to child injury and likely interact with each other (Morrongiello, 2005; Schwebel & Gaines, 2007). The risk, for example, of a child's ingesting household poisons is increased when the child is old enough to explore his or her environment but still young enough to impulsively ingest a substance, and by a setting in which poisons are accessible and constant supervision is lacking.

Prevention efforts can involve tactics directed at the entire population (multimedia campaigns), particular subsets of the population (bicycle safety programs for families with young children), or at certain milestones (yearly visits to the pediatrician). Providing education about vulnerability and the seriousness and extent of childhood injuries is part of the effort (Morrongiello & Matheis, 2007a). It is also important for parents not to rely on child-based strategies (e.g., teaching rules) prematurely or exclusively (Morrongiello, Ondejko, & Littlejohn, 2004b). They should also not be lulled into a false sense of security. For example, parents whose children use safety equipment such as bicycle helmets may allow their children to take greater risks and young people themselves may feel less vulnerable (Morrongiello & Matheis, 2007b). This may offset some of the benefits of safety instruction and equipment (DeLillo & Tremblay, 2001).

Multiple-component prevention programs aimed at modifying risk behaviors and that include contingencies and incentives for appropriate injury-prevention behavior are needed (Barton, Schwebel, & Morrongiello, 2007; Peterson, Reach, & Grabe, 2003; Schwebel et al., 2006).

- What do we do after the young person dies?
- How is the helper affected by working with the dying child?

Children's ideas about death change during development and are influenced by experiences, family attitude, and cultural factors (Candy-Gibbs, Sharp, & Petrun, 1985; Poltorak & Glazer, 2006). Cognitive development plays a role in the evolving conceptualization of death (Ferrari, 1990: Oltjenbruns, 2001). Young children may think of death as being less alive and assume it to be reversible. At about 5 years of age, an appreciation of the finality of death may be present, but death still does not seem inevitable. An understanding of death as final and inevitable and of personal mortality emerges at about age 9 or 10. Nevertheless, children may be aware of death and be worried about their fatal illness even if they do not have a fully developed concept of death. And fatally ill youths' concepts of death do not appear to be more advanced than those of physically well youth (Jay et al., 1987). Although adolescents' understanding of death may be similar to that of adults, attention to the particular aspects of this stage of development is needed (Balk & Corr, 2001; Freyer et al., 2006).

Family members, too, must certainly be made aware of the seriousness of the young person's illness (Duncan, Joselow, & Hilden, 2006; Wolfe et al., 2000b). However, an appropriate balance between acceptance of death and hope for life is probably adaptive. It is a genuine challenge to prepare parents for the death of their child, while also enabling them to help the child emotionally and to assist with the treatment regimen. This undertaking requires knowledgeable and sensitive mental health staff. As our ability to lengthen survival—and perhaps to raise hopes of some future cure—increases, the problem becomes even more difficult. Integration of support services into the total treatment program and immediate availability and access are important in delivering needed help. Once a point is reached where the child's death is likely, the focus of intervention must shift. Information and support are still needed, but the focus must change to helping the child and family to be most comfortable and to make the best use of the remaining time. Moreover, the family should not be abandoned after the young person's death. Continued assistance is needed and such support should be a part of the total treatment (Duncan et al., 2006; Friedman et al., 1998; Wolfe et al., 2000a).

Caregivers, too, are not immune to the effects of observing a dying child or adolescent. Efforts must be made to educate caregivers and to reduce the high cost of helping: the inevitable stress, the feelings of helplessness, and the likelihood of burnout (Koocher, 1980; Sahler et al., 2000). These are not trivial matters. The helpers' adjustment, their efficiency, and the potential impact of their behavior on the family and youngster are of concern (Hilden et al., 2001). In *Who's Afraid of Death on a Leukemia Ward?* (1965), Vernick and Karon offered poignant anecdotes to this effect. One anecdote describes the impact of helpers' behavior on a 9-year-old patient who, after taking a turn for the worse, received some medical treatment and began to show improvement:

One day while she was having breakfast I commented that she seemed to have gotten her old appetite back. She smiled and agreed. . . . I mentioned that it looked as if she had been through the worst of this particular siege. She nodded in agreement. I went on to say that it must have been very discouraging to feel so sick that all she could do was worry—worry about dying. She nodded affirmatively. I recognized that the whole episode must have been very frightening and that I knew it was a load off her mind to be feeling better. She let out a loud, "Whew," and went on to say that except for me, nobody really talked with her. "It was like they were getting ready for me to die." (p. 395)

Certainly, one of the most difficult decisions is what to tell the dying youth. A protective approach or "benign lying" was once advocated. The young person was not to be burdened, and a sense of normalcy and optimism was to be maintained. Most professionals now feel that this approach is not helpful and probably is doomed to failure anyway. The stress on the family of maintaining this deception is great, and the likelihood that the young person will believe the deception is questionable. In this decision, and in other aspects of working with the child and family, some balance must be struck that takes into consideration the child's developmental level, past experiences, timing, and an understanding of the family's culture and belief system (Dolgin & Jay, 1989; Oltjenbruns, 2001). An example of such a balance is illustrated in the following excerpt:

A child with a life-threatening illness should be told the name of the condition, given an accurate explanation of the nature of the illness (up to the limit of his ability to comprehend), and told that it is a serious illness of which people sometimes die. At the same time, however, the child and family can be told about treatment options and enlisted as allies to fight the disease. An atmosphere must be established in which all concerned have the opportunity to ask questions, relate fantasies, and express concerns, no matter how scary or far fetched they may seem. When the patient is feeling sick, weak, and dying, there is no need to [be reminded] of the prognosis. If a family and patient know a prognosis is poor but persist in clinging to hope, one has no right to wrest that from them. The truth, humanely tempered, is important, but we must be mindful of the patient and how [the patient's] needs are served. To tell the "whole truth" or a "white lie" for the benefit of the teller serves no one in the end. (Koocher & Sallan, 1978, p. 300)

SUMMARY

HISTORICAL CONTEXT

- *The current view that psychological factors are relevant to physical disorders in a number of different ways represents a shift from the earlier, more limited view of psychosomatic diseases caused by emotional factors.*

PSYCHOLOGICAL AND FAMILY INFLUENCES ON MEDICAL CONDITIONS

- *Current conceptualizations of the role of psychological and family factors in chronic illness are illustrated through the example of asthma. Psychological and family influences are among a variety of possible trigger mechanisms that can bring on an asthmatic episode. The child's asthma may impact other family members, and family assistance is needed in managing the medical condition.*

CONSEQUENCES OF CHRONIC CONDITIONS

- *There is likely to be considerable individual variability in how youngsters and families cope with chronic conditions. Adjustment is likely to be an ongoing process and is influenced by a number of variables.*

- *Researchers have sought to determine the impact of parameters of the illness, such as severity, and of aspects of family functioning, such as control, organization, and parental distress, on the chronically ill youth's adjustment.*

- *With increasing survival rates for young people with chronic conditions, the adaptation over time of the young person and family to the illness and its treatment are of great interest. Adaptation to cancer and HIV/AIDS are two examples.*

FACILITATING MEDICAL TREATMENT

- *Psychology can contribute to effective treatment of medical conditions in a number of ways.*

- *Medical treatment may be rendered ineffective because of difficulties that the patient and family experience in trying to adhere to prescribed treatment regimens. Attempts to improve adherence require attention to multiple dimensions such as the young person's developmental level, peer and social influences, family patterns of interaction, and the role of the health care professional.*

- *Psychological treatments (for example, relaxation and biofeedback) may modify physical functioning and the pain associated with chronic conditions. Treatment of headaches is an example of this kind of application.*

- *Psychologically based procedures may also facilitate the delivery of medical interventions. Treatment programs to reduce the pain and distress felt by young people who are undergoing medical procedures and preparation for hospitalization are examples of psychological influences enhancing medical interventions.*

- *Understanding the antecedents of unintentional injury and developing interventions to prevent such injuries is another example of ongoing efforts at the interface of psychology and medicine.*

THE DYING CHILD

- *Despite increasingly high survival rates, the prospect of death is one of the most distressing aspects of working with some chronically ill youth. Psychological contributions to helping these children, their families, and the professionals who work with them can be an aid in effective and caring treatment.*

KEY TERMS

psychosomatic disorders *(p. 391)*

Psychological Factors Affecting Medical Condition *(p. 391)*

psychosomatic medicine *(p. 391)*

functional limitation *(p. 397)*

functional disabilities *(p. 398)*

adherence to (compliance with) medical regimens *(p. 402)*

biofeedback *(p. 405)*

emotive imagery *(p. 408)*

unintentional injury *(p. 410)*

CHAPTER 15

Evolving Concerns for Youth

This final chapter addresses select current concerns for children and adolescents. It is a truism that the future of every society depends on its youth, and that the welfare of children and adolescents is tied to many factors. The lives of youth are affected by what is happening in the lives of their parents and in their communities, the value assigned to the young, the priorities given to health care and education, and a host of other factors. The economic resources of nations make a difference, so that even basic care and opportunity are problematic in developing countries. Nevertheless, because the implementation of programs devoted to youth also depends on social attitudes, care can vary enormously even when resources are adequate. Sensitive and attentive adults are looking at such influences with an eye toward better care for youth.

Progress in understanding human development also is stimulating efforts toward optimizing the potential of the young. Although knowledge about development is incomplete, we have come far from viewing children and adolescents simply as incomplete adults. Their unique needs are better known; the general course of physical, intellectual, and social growth is well on the way to being mapped; and developmental influences, including risk and protective factors, are increasingly understood. There is enthusiasm for using this knowledge to enhance development, even as we seek to better understand the experiences of young people.

In this chapter, we discuss three areas of current concerns regarding youth. Reflecting the importance of family influence woven throughout the text, we first look at family issues regarding the care of children. Next, mental health services for youth are discussed. Finally, the well-being of children and adolescents living in nations other than the United States is briefly examined.

Who Cares for Children: Family Issues

We are all aware that U.S. families have changed dramatically in the last several decades, perhaps most obviously through increased rates of divorced, single-parenting, and step-parent households. (For a review of divorce, see p. 59.) Concerns are voiced by many people about the well-being of the family. Nevertheless, scholars who have studied its history have challenged the idea that the family has decayed from some past idyllic form. They point out that there have always been various family forms and that family well-being relies less on family structure than on family attributes such as warmth, communication, and support. Recent studies indicate that such attributes benefit new family forms evolving from technologies such as in vitro fertilization and sperm and ova donation (Golombok, 2006).

It is, nonetheless, appropriate to ask questions about the impact of social change on the family and, more specifically, on who is caring for children, under what circumstances, and with what consequences. Although the scope of discussion is necessarily limited, it is our purpose to draw attention to the issue by examining maternal employment and day care for children. In addition, we look at two other areas—adoption and foster care—that directly influence the care and experiences of a large number of children.

MATERNAL EMPLOYMENT AND CHILD CARE

The increase of women in the labor force has transformed family life. In 1950, 12% of married women with a preschool child worked outside the home. In 2003, that figure was 60%—and 77% for married women with a child age 6 to 17 (U.S. Bureau of the Census, 2004). A major concern has been the effects on young children of being cared for by adults other than their parents.

Effects of nonparental care. Children of employed mothers are cared for in many different arrangements. Care is provided by relatives or nonfamily, in or out of the family home, or by nonfamily in center-based settings. Many variables are associated with the type, amount, and quality of care. Nonparental care increases notably after age 2 (Federal Interagency Forum on Child and Family Statistics, 2004). Generally, parents prefer less formal arrangements for infants under 2 years, and more formal settings, such as center-based care, for children 3 and older (McCartney, 2006). Unsurprising is that the amount of nonparental care for children, birth through 6 years of age, is greater when mothers are employed for longer hours. Family economic resources also play a role, with greater social advantage being associated with higher quality care, more hours per week in care, and the child remaining in center care for a longer period (NICHD Early Child

Care Research Network, 2006). Family ethnicity is somewhat related to care as well; for example, Latino families prefer informal arrangements.

What is known about the impact of nonparental care on young children's well-being? Decades of research on this topic have been marked by debate—sometimes rancorous—among professionals and in the public press (Belsky, 2001; Scarr, 1998). Investigators have examined cognitive and social outcomes for children and have especially considered the quality and amount of care, as well as some characteristics of the family. Interpretations of the findings have been made difficult by the correlation between family characteristics and the choice of settings and quality of care. For example, if highly competent parents are likely to select high-quality day care, the cause of positive child outcomes of day care may be unclear. For this reason, the more recent research has tended to control for the possible effects of family selection of care, as well as other factors.

Many studies indicate that the effects of early child care depend in part on the quality of day care, which is defined by several indices—such as the ratio of caregivers to children, responsive staff–child interaction, staff training, developmentally appropriate curricula, and health and safety standards (Scarr, 1998). High-quality care is positively related to the development of cognition and language for youngsters who enter day care early in life (Belsky, 2001; NICHD Early Child Care Research Network, 2006). Benefits also apply to social behavior, such as prosocial skills, albeit to a smaller extent.

The effects of the amount of day care that children receive—that is, the hours of care per week and/or the age at which children begin nonparental care—are more complex. Debate has centered on psychosocial outcomes, and some studies claim that more time in care is associated with child troublesome behavior while other studies do not show this link (Loeb et al., 2004; NICHD Early Child Care Research Network, 2003a). Overall, there may be some negative effect, with children in more care exhibiting relatively more externalizing problems. A recent report from a major study evaluating children from 4 years of age through the end of sixth grade found such an association in the early years, but the association no longer held by third grade (Belsky et al., 2007). However, greater exposure to center care was related to such problems, as reported by teachers.

The somewhat mixed research findings have led investigators to give more attention to differences in outcome that might exist for economically disadvan-

The effects of daycare on children depend, in part, on the quality of the programs, the amount of time the child spends in daycare, and the family background of the child.
(Brenda Black and Louis Toby/Black Toby Photography)

taged families. Interest in these families also increased after 1996 federal regulations put higher employment demands on women on welfare, resulting in greater employment of these women. Several studies suggest that nonmaternal care benefits children from disadvantaged homes. Loeb and colleagues (2004) found positive cognitive outcomes for children of low-income families who attended day care centers and whose mothers entered the workforce when the children were between 12 and 42 months of age. Quality of care had some influence in the expected direction. The children cared for by family members showed no cognitive effects but more behavioral problems. In another study, as shown in Figure 15–1, Canadian children from low SES families who had full-time nonmaternal care during the first year of life performed better on a receptive language task at age 4 to 5 years than children from low SES families who were in maternal care or part-time nonmaternal care; (Geoffroy et al., 2007). Still another study of low-income families found that both high quality care and more extensive time in care

FIGURE 15–1

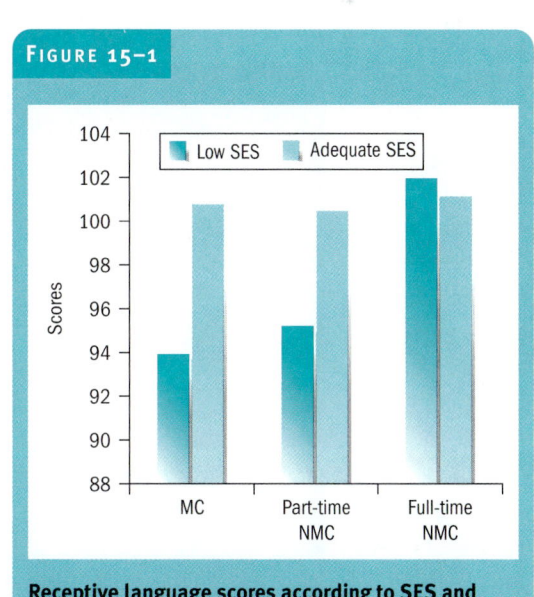

Receptive language scores according to SES and child care arrangements in the first year of life.
MC = maternal care; NMC = nonmaternal care
From Geoffroy et al., 2007.

were linked to beneficial effects on cognitive and behavioral development (Votruba-Drzal, Coley, & Chase-Lansdale, 2004). Such findings suggest that nonparental child care may serve as a protective factor for young children who experience disadvantaged family circumstances.

The larger lesson to be learned from the research on child care is that the effects of different arrangements may vary depending on the broad context of children's lives. More generally, the issue of nonparental care has implications for social policy. It is noteworthy that child care effects tend to be small to moderate in size, and weaker than the influence of parents (NICHD Early Child Care Research Network, 2006). However, these effects can be important when they involve large numbers of children and may provide benefits particularly to some disadvantaged children. In a nation that depends heavily on nonmaternal care, the availability of quality day care is not incidental to children's welfare.

Care of school-age children. Although professional debate over child care has focused on early care, concern exists for youth of school age. Some older children have no formal provisions for after-school care. These are the so-called latchkey children, or children in self-care, who must use a key to let themselves into their empty homes after school. The term self-care is typically applied to children of elementary and middle

school age, because it is usually agreed that preschool children should always have supervision and that high school students do not need the level of supervision that would be considered child care. Accurate estimates of the prevalence of self-care are hard to come by, but national surveys indicate that self-care as a primary arrangement rises dramatically from age 8 to age 12 (Federal Interagency Forum on Child and Family Statistics, 2004; Figure 15–2).

The developmental implications of self-care likely are affected by the amount of time in self-care, the child's developmental level, family influences, neighborhood characteristics, and available social supports. Studies of the impact of self-care suggest either problematic outcomes or no differences between self-care and other after-school arrangements (Vandell & Shumow, 1999). Factors such as younger age and time spent hanging out with peers rather than being at home seem to be associated with poorer outcomes for children in self-care. The negative effects of self-care may also be more evident for children from disadvantaged families.

The choice of self-care is probably determined by multiple considerations, but one factor is the availability of after-school programming. Evidence supports the benefit of quality after-school programming, including extracurricular activities (NICHD Early Child Care Research Network, 2004). For example, some developmental benefits were found when low-

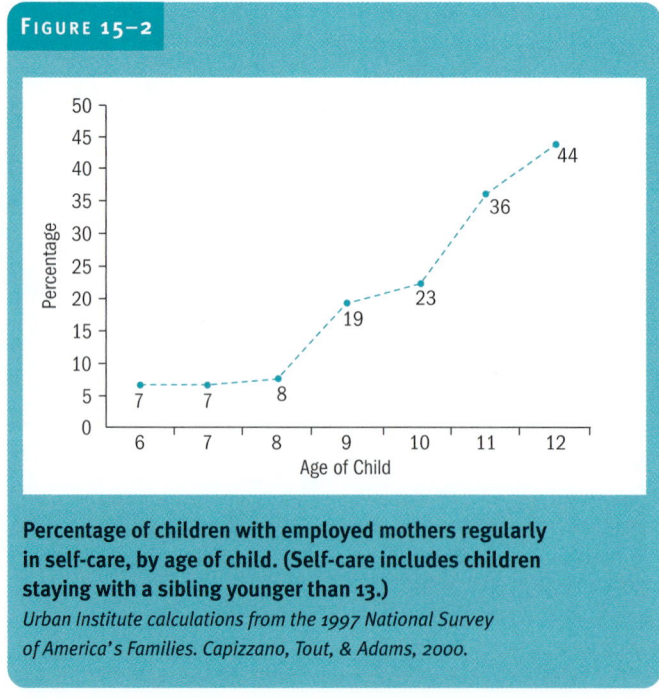

FIGURE 15–2

Percentage of children with employed mothers regularly in self-care, by age of child. (Self-care includes children staying with a sibling younger than 13.)
Urban Institute calculations from the 1997 National Survey of America's Families. Capizzano, Tout, & Adams, 2000.

income third to fifth graders attended after-school recreational and academically oriented programs rather than being in informal care with neighbors and relatives (Posner & Vandell, 1999). Structured programming may help children avoid potentially harmful situations such as exposure to deviant peers, illegal activities, or violence. In general, evidence for positive effects of after-school programs is strongest for low-income children, children in high-crime urban neighborhoods, younger children, and boys (Vandell & Shumow, 1999). Nevertheless, even supervised out-of-home programs are not necessarily beneficial. Characteristics of the programs (e.g., adult leadership, scheduled meetings) can be important in predicting positive behavioral outcomes (Coley, Morris, & Hernandez, 2004). Such considerations have led to recommendations for government and communities to address children's out-of-school time and to develop more and better-quality after-school programming (Larner, Zippiroli, & Behrman, 1999).

Self-care, even if not ideal, may still be an appropriate arrangement for some children. When self-care is employed, it is necessary to ensure that the child is adequately prepared. Peterson (1989) suggested that three major areas need to be considered in preparation: injury risk, emotional difficulties, and selection of activities. Preparation has several components, including discussion with the child and arrangements for a contact person if the child feels that help is needed. Also essential is a safe and secure environment for the youths.

ADOPTIVE FAMILIES

Our discussion so far has focused on youth living with at least one biological parent, but millions of children live in other kinds of arrangements, including adoptive families. In the United States, about 120,000 youth are adopted each year, about two-thirds of these by biologically unrelated parents and the remainder by biological kin or stepparents (Nickman et al., 2005). Most adoptions are arranged through public agencies or private agencies and attorneys. The children may not "match" their families, as when, for example, white families adopt African American children (Rushton & Minnis, 1997). Moreover, international adoptions in the United States have increased dramatically (Center for Adoption Research and Policy, 2004). Children come to their new families from countries as diverse as China, Korea, Romania, Russia, Guatemala, and the Philippines. A substantial number of these adoptions are transracial as well as transcultural.

Many children return to empty homes after school. The impact of such self-care requires further study.
(Courtesy of A. C. Israel)

Although adoption has not always been viewed positively, it is frequently seen in an affirmative way, as an alternative family structure that meets the needs of both child and parents. In the United States and similar countries, adoption most often involves middle-class couples choosing to enlarge their families and children who come from less advantaged situations. Nevertheless, there has been concern over the development of adopted children. Research has shown that adoptees are seen in disproportionate numbers at mental health clinics, and questions have been raised about whether the subgroup of children coming from disadvantaged backgrounds can overcome earlier negative experiences (van IJzendoorn & Juffer, 2006). It is recognized that unfortunate preadoptive situations exist and that children not adopted immediately can experience various kinds of hardships. Some of these youth may be affected by such factors as poor prenatal care of the mother; poor diet; living with birth families made dysfunctional by poverty, drug addiction, or psychological problems; or living in transitional settings such as orphanages or foster care settings.

What then does research tell us about the development of adopted children? In broaching this issue, it is appropriate to keep in mind that the various circumstances of adoptions can make it difficult to sort out the findings, and not all issues have been examined. Nevertheless, numerous investigations allow for some reasonably supported general conclusions.

In this discussion, we draw on the results of a series of meta-analyses of more than 270 studies of adoptions within countries and across countries (van IJzendoorn, Juffer, & Poelhuis, 2005; van IJzendoorn & Juffer, 2006). Depending on the data available in the studies, the adopted youth were compared with (1) "past peers"—the peers or siblings they left behind in institutions or their family of origin—and (2) "current peers"—unadopted peers or siblings in their current adoptive environments. More data were available for current peers than past peers. Most relevant to our discussion are the following findings:

- Adoptees surpassed their past peers on IQ and school achievement. Differences from current peers were only negligibly lower. However, more learning problems and special education referrals were reported for adoptees.

- On measures of attachment to caregivers, adoptees were more secure than past peers but less secure than current peers.

- On measures of self-esteem, adopted children showed no differences from their current peers.

- Adoptees exhibited more psychological problems than their current peers, but the differences were small. Adoptees were more often referred to mental health settings.

This large body of research indicates that adoption generally benefits children; the available data show that they surpass the peers they left behind. Moreover, most adoptees function within the normal range in intellectual and psychosocial domains, although there is risk, mostly small to moderate, for early attachment and behavioral difficulties. Many researchers note the resilience of adoptive children, particularly those who move from disadvantaged or abusive preadoptive circumstances.

Meta-analyses of research also indicate three commonly found risk factors. Generally associated with increased risk are late age of adoption, male gender, and preadoption factors such as neglect/abuse, prenatal drug exposure, behavioral problems, and foster and institutional care (e.g., Gunnar et al., 2007; Nickman, 2005; Rutter et al., 2007).

We do not wish to oversimplify the many questions that require further research regarding adoption. Does improved quality of the lives of adopted children compensate for broken bonds with birth family and in some cases with cultural roots? What coping mechanisms are employed by adopted children over what issues (Smith & Brodzinsky, 2002)? What can be done to support the adoption of older youth (Rushton & Dance, 2007)? In the final analysis, of course, these issues do not detract from the positive aspects of adoption (Miller et al., 2000). Rather, they suggest the need for research and for specific policies (e.g., early adoption) and support for adoptive families.

International and interracial adoptions, illustrated by this Western-Japanese family, can bring unique enrichments and challenges.
(Margaret Ross/Stock Boston)

FOSTER CARE

Although it is ordinarily preferable for children and adolescents to remain with their birth families, substitute care is not always avoidable. Substitute placement occurs involuntarily or voluntarily when families are unable to care for their offspring. In earlier times in the United States and other countries, these youth were placed in institutions and had few connections to their families. Concerns about harmful effects of institutionalization led to family foster care, with a major goal of returning the children to their biological families (Benoit, M. B., 2000). However, many youth remained in foster care for long periods of time, some until they reached the legal age to be independent. Although foster care certainly can have positive influences, it also can be inadequate; moreover, the rate of disruption is high, with children being moved from placement to placement (Barber, Delfabbro, & Cooper, 2001; Minty, 1999).

In an effort to improve this situation, the federal government enacted the Adoption and Safe Family Act (ASFA) in 1997 (see Figure 15–3). Among other changes brought by ASFA, the provision of a permanent home is given priority. Within a specified time each child must either be returned to the biological family or be adopted or permanently placed with a foster family, which can include relatives or legal guardians (Allen & Bissell, 2004).

The ASFA provides the states with a financial incentive for the adoption of children in temporary foster care. In some circumstances, it may be difficult to attain this goal (Becker, Jordan, & Larsen, 2007). Administrative agencies, including the courts, can be so overloaded that they are unable to operate in a competent and timely fashion. In the words of one caseworker frustrated with the system, "... the courts appear insensitive to the harm done by children's languishing in temporary homes and to the benefits of permanent families" (Wicks-Nelson & Israel, 2006, p. 438). And the task has been made more difficult by an overall increase of children and adolescents—disproportionately of minority background—in foster care, and by the experiences of these youth. Many reasons exist for public out-of-home care, among them poverty, homelessness, parental substance abuse, HIV/AIDS, domestic violence, and maternal incarceration (Bass, Shields, & Behrman, 2004; Rosenfeld et al., 1997). Children in foster care often have lived in disorganized homes, have been traumatized, have developmental and behavioral problems, and require special medical and educational care. In addition, foster parents do not always receive the support and training that are needed to facilitate the development of these youths.

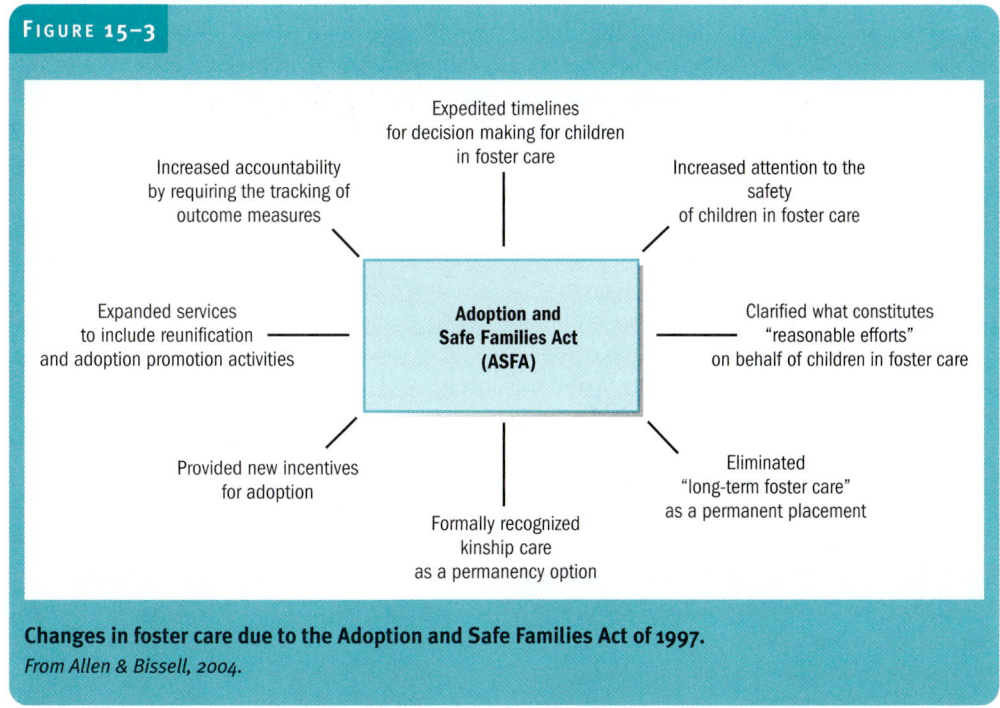

FIGURE 15–3

Expedited timelines for decision making for children in foster care

Increased accountability by requiring the tracking of outcome measures

Increased attention to the safety of children in foster care

Expanded services to include reunification and adoption promotion activities

Adoption and Safe Families Act (ASFA)

Clarified what constitutes "reasonable efforts" on behalf of children in foster care

Provided new incentives for adoption

Formally recognized kinship care as a permanency option

Eliminated "long-term foster care" as a permanent placement

Changes in foster care due to the Adoption and Safe Families Act of 1997.
From Allen & Bissell, 2004.

The foster care system is attempting to respond to these circumstances. For example, because youth in foster care are at risk for psychological problems, treatment foster care programs have been created (Benoit, M. B., 2000; Dore & Mullin, 2006; Rosenfeld et al., 1997). Prior to the child's being placed in their care, foster parents understand that the child requires mental health services and that they will serve as agents of change. Special training and help is given to foster care parents, and links are forged with community mental health services. In the Family to Family approach, communities where foster care is especially needed are targeted, and financial incentives are given to foster parents to develop a mentoring relationship with birth parents (Chipungu & Bent-Goodley, 2004). Both sets of parents ideally work with professionals to reunite birth families.

Linares and colleagues (2006) offer an example of the potential benefits of such coparenting. Parent training and coparenting training were provided to biological and foster parent pairs (primarily Latino and African American) of maltreated (primarily neglected) children between the ages of 3 and 10 years of age who had been placed in regular foster care. The Incredible Years (IY) parent training program (p. 223) was employed, based on evidence of its effectiveness in teaching parenting skills and in reducing externalizing problems, a common difficulty of children in foster care. A separate coparenting component addressed communication, conflict resolution, and cooperative parenting of the child. The program was designed to augment services already offered to families. IY and coparenting training were provided to biological/foster parent pairs, rather than separately, to facilitate cooperation and communication between families and to avoid fragmented services. There were significant differences between intervention families and families who received usual services at the end of the intervention and at a 3-month follow-up. Intervention families exhibited significant gains in both positive parenting and coparenting for both sets of parents and at the follow-up reported a trend for fewer child externalizing problems.

Another change that has occurred in foster care over the last two decades is an increase in placement of children in the homes of relatives. Some disagreement exists as to the disadvantages and benefits of this arrangement. Kin, compared with nonfamily foster parents, tend to be older and in poorer health, and to have less income; they often are grandparents (Green, 2004). The needs of these families may be greater, and they receive less service and supervision. There is also concern that birth parents will have inappropriate access to the children. At the same time, kin placements may be less disruptive and result in greater stability for the child. With decreases in the availability of nonfamily foster families, most states now view kinship foster care as a feasible and preferable option (Benoit, M. B., 2000).

Developments in the foster care system give some reason for optimism. It is important to acknowledge that most individuals working in the system are well intentioned and caring. Increased resources, innovative problem solving, more services for foster children and families, and improved coordination of services are among the recommendations for improving substitute care (Bass et al., 2004).

Mental Health Services for Youth

We now turn to a brief discussion of mental health services for youth. Over the years, many studies of mental health services have been conducted. It is widely agreed that children and adolescents are underserved (Hoagwood, 2005; Huang et al., 2005; President's New Freedom Commission on Mental Health, 2003). Two-thirds to three-fourths of youth with diagnosable disorders do not receive mental health services (Kestenbaum, 2000; Ringel & Sturm, 2001; Tolan & Dodge, 2005).

One aspect of the problem is lack of adequate funding for services to persons who need them. To various degrees, funding is provided by federal and state governments, third-party (health insurance) providers, and clients themselves. It has usually been more difficult to obtain financial coverage for mental health than other kinds of health needs. Efforts to achieve mental health parity—funding for mental health services equivalent to that for other health care services—have been pursued at state and federal levels. Escalating costs and funding patterns adversely affect both middle-class and poorer families (Kiesler, 2000).

However, the problem of adequate services is much broader than funding, and includes attitudes toward mental health care, integration of services into primary care settings, emphasis on preventive care and early intervention, and attention to cultural context (Tolan & Dodge, 2005). In addition, many families—particularly of ethnic minority background—find it difficult to access services.

Early mental health services for youth emphasized a community approach (Pumariega & Glover, 1998). Child guidance clinics provided interdisciplinary and low-cost services to children and adolescents and their families. Services subsequently became more hospital-based, and guidance and mental health clinics experienced lack of funding and support. Hospital and residential care increased during the 1970s and 1980s, partly because of increased third-party payment. Meanwhile there was a dramatic increase in the population of poor minority children who needed but could not obtain mental health services. Many of these children went into the child welfare system when their parents were unable to care for them, and many were placed in residential and detention facilities. This dire situation and growing medical costs resulted in a call for publicly funded community-based services. Today's services are delivered in various settings, including mental health clinics, psychiatric or full service hospitals, residential centers, private professional practices, child welfare and juvenile agencies, and schools (Weisz et al., 2005). It has been suggested that an emphasis should be placed on providing services in community-based settings that are frequently utilized by youngsters and their families (Tolan & Dodge, 2005).

For example, schools can play an important role in the delivery of services to the millions of enrolled students and their families (Huang et al., 2005; Romer & McIntosh, 2005; Weist, 1997). Indeed, school-based mental health services may be an especially important way in which underserved ethnic minority populations can receive care (Kataoka et al., 2007). Traditional mental health services in schools are largely limited to children enrolled in special education and a relatively small number involved in interventions with school psychologists. Yet, the school setting has clear advantages in that it is readily accessible, can provide frequent contact, and can avoid the stigma of mental health consultation. In making this point, Kestenbaum (2000) quotes a colleague who said,

I decided to adopt what I have come to refer to as the Willie Sutton Theory of Children's Mental Health. When reporters asked Willie Sutton, the notorious bank robber of the 1930s, why he robbed banks, he answered "that's where the money is." If you wanted to provide mental health services to children, I reasoned,

you had to go where the children were: in the schools. (p. 6)

Efforts to expand school services includes the entire range from prevention to treatment to posttreatment monitoring. Increases in the kinds of programs offered and improved coordination are commonly recommended (Huang et al., 2005). For example, one idea is to set up partnerships between schools and community mental health agencies. Some schools now have general health centers, and mental health services could be readily embedded in these. A call has gone out to incorporate a public health perspective with an emphasis on serving broad populations, preventing problems, strengthening positive behaviors, and conducting evaluations (Strein, Hoagwood, & Cohn, 2003; Weist & Christodulu, 2000). The model of the school as the provider of comprehensive services has also been employed (Holtzman, 1997). "Full-service schools" are the primary neighborhood institution for promoting child and family development, which includes educational, health, and mental health goals within a framework of community-based participation.

FRAGMENTATION, UTILIZATION, EVALUATION

Concerns have generally been expressed about the fragmentation of mental health services. A single family may have contact with and receive services from a variety of mental health, educational, social service, and other agencies. In recognition of the need for better coordinated services, efforts have been made to develop community-based, interagency systems of care that "wrap around" individual youth and families (Mental Health: A Report of the Surgeon General, 2001). These efforts have been aided by the federal government's Child and Adolescent Service System Program (CASSP). By providing leadership and funding to the states, CASSP has encouraged a comprehensive model of care, interagency collaboration, parental involvement, and sensitivity to the needs of minority groups (Pumariega & Glover, 1998). Other aspects of the model include treatment in the least restrictive environment, early identification of problems and intervention, and smooth transition into adult care systems when necessary. A similar approach was taken by the Comprehensive Community Mental Health Services for Children and Their Families Program; it provides financial support to the states, territories, and Indian tribal organizations to care for millions of children through a coordinated, comprehensive network of mental health and other services (Mental Health: A Report of the Surgeon General, 2001). Overall, evaluations of such systems of care indicate benefits such as reduced use of residential and out-of-state treatments, parental satisfaction with care, and improved functional behavior of the children.

Whereas fragmentation of services certainly can be problematic, so can low utilization of available services. Help-seeking behavior is likely to be complex and to vary with personal and other variables (Sears, 2004; Yeh et al., 2004). Several demographic variables predict service use (Logan & King, 2001). Caucasian families, those of higher social class, and those living in urban areas are more likely to use professional services. Ethnic minority families may be more likely to seek help from family and community contacts rather than professionals, and premature termination of services is higher for Hispanic and African American youngsters and their families (Mental Health: A Report of the Surgeon General, 2001). Also, beliefs about causes of problems in children may, in part, be responsible for differences in service utilization (Yeh et al., 2005). If programs are to successfully serve diverse ethnic/racial populations, they must incorporate cultural traditions, beliefs, and ways of interpersonal interactions.

Finally, with regard to youth services, there is a need both to continue to evaluate services and to disseminate information about effective services. It is clear that evidence-based treatment for young people can ameliorate a variety of disorders (Hibbs & Jensen, 2005; Kazdin & Weisz, 2003). Research efforts need to continue to address transporting these treatments into general clinical practice (Chorpita, Becker, & Daleiden, 2007; Weisz et al., 2005). Also, the public and families need information about children's mental health and the availability, effectiveness, and costs of care (Newman & Tejeda, 1996; Tolan & Dodge, 2005). Similarly, agencies and institutions providing services would profit from greater dissemination of information about efficacious prevention and treatment programs (Hoagwood, 2005; Rotheram-Borus & Duan, 2003).

Although mental health services are improving, continuing needs are recognized. The Subcommittee on Children and Families of the President's New Freedom Commission on Mental Health articulated 10 intercorrelated challenges to be addressed in order to achieve a stronger system of mental health care for youth and families (Huang et al.,

TABLE 15–1 VISION FOR CHILDREN'S MENTAL HEALTH SERVICES

Comprehensive home- and community-based services and supports
Family partnership and support
Culturally competent care
Individualized care
Evidence-based practice
Coordination of services, responsibility, and funding
Prevention, early identification, and early intervention
Early childhood intervention
Mental health services in schools
Accountability

Adapted from Huang et al., 2005.

2005). The aspects of this vision are listed in Table 15–1. The goal of all such efforts is effective coordinated services that can be accessed by all who need them.

Youth in the Global Society

As we turn our attention to the international scene, we note that mass transportation and communication, including the Internet, are making the functional world smaller day by day. The lives of youth are already being strongly influenced by this phenomenon, and the impact will become even more pervasive throughout the 21st century.

THIRD WORLD POVERTY AND HEALTH

Although poverty in the United States is rightly of concern, the effects of being poor are dramatically worse in developing countries. The link between poverty and bodily as well as psychological well-being is observed in various measures—nutrition, disease, lack of opportunity, and death. For example, malnutrition and specific mineral deficiencies (e.g., iron) are associated with developmental, cognitive, and behavioral risk (Chang et al., 2002; Pollitt et al., 1996). In many developing countries, malnourishment is ubiquitous.

Youth in developing countries can benefit from public health programs that include improved nutrition, prenatal care, immunization, screening for medical conditions, child safety, family planning, and the like (Rahman et al., 2000). Progress has been made on several fronts. For instance, disease has been reduced, fewer children are underweight, and more families are consuming iodine in their diets. Figure 15–4 shows the reduction that occurred from 1960 to 1998 in the mortality of children under the age of 5 years, a measure viewed as an overall indication of how well children are doing. Although these rates have continued to decline, enormous needs still exist (Progress for Children, 2007). An estimated 9.7 million children died in 2006 before their fifth birthday. Continuing efforts are required for further improvements and to maintain any gains accomplished. At the present time, huge resources and efforts are needed to deal with the HIV/AIDS epidemic. Since the late 1970s, millions of children have died of AIDS-related disease or been orphaned due to the AIDS virus (Children on the Brink, 2004).

Some international attention is being paid to psychological and behavioral problems of youth, but only relatively recently (Rahman et al., 2000). Epidemiological reports attest to a substantial rate and range of disabilities (e.g., internalizing, externalizing, mental retardation, pervasive developmental disorders). However, mental health professionals are in short, even dire, supply in some regions of the world

(Omigbodun et al., 2007). The neglect of mental health needs may be due, at least in part, to both an understandable focus on high mortality rates and a lack of awareness of the importance of mental health. Ultimately, if interventions are to be successful, local community involvement as well as standards and values are important considerations. For example, conduct "disturbance" may be viewed in some communities as a disciplinary rather than a mental health concern, and certain interventions might be more acceptable than others. Thus, as with other health programs, cultural sensitivity is critical.

EXPOSURE TO ARMED OR SOCIOPOLITICAL CONFLICT

Exposure to armed conflict or to threatening sociopolitical environments affects the development of a significant minority of young people throughout the world (Barenbaum, Ruchkin, & Schwab-Stone, 2004). Cambodian youth suffered extensive hardships and violence during the Pol Pot regime and subsequently lived in refugee camps for extended periods of time (Mollica et al., 1997; Savin et al., 1996). Youth have experienced the horrors of "ethnic cleansing" (e.g., in some African and European nations), and

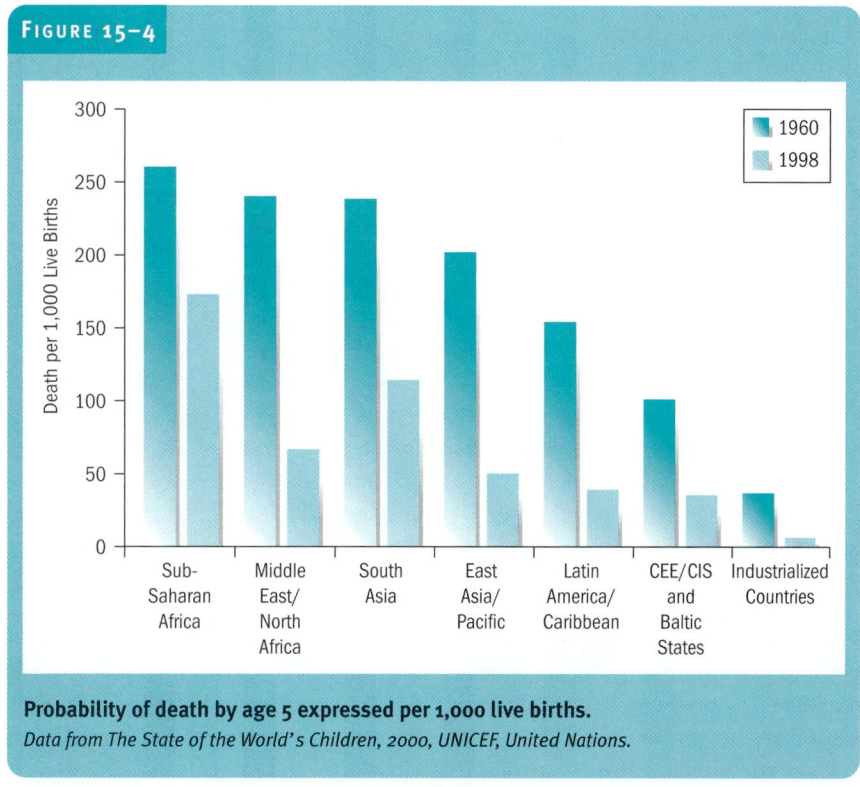

FIGURE 15–4

Probability of death by age 5 expressed per 1,000 live births.
Data from The State of the World's Children, 2000, UNICEF, United Nations.

Significant numbers of youth throughout the world are exposed to the risks of sociopolitical conflict and life in refugee camps.
(Jose Cendon/AP World Wide Photos)

many currently live in areas in which the threat of war is chronic (e.g., some nations in the Middle East). In addition to direct traumatic experiences and bodily threats to the self and loved ones, these situations can be characterized by uncertainty, temporary or permanent separation from family and community, inadequate nutrition, lack of shelter, control by the "enemy," and the like.

It is worth noting that research on the effects of war itself is not easy to accomplish. It is difficult to collect data immediately or soon after armed conflict, and longer-term outcome is confounded by less-than-optimal experiences following war. Investigations often have been conducted with immigrant groups and especially refugee groups, who may be living in camps and still experiencing trauma, loss, and poor living conditions.

Given this circumstance, rates of psychopathology vary tremendously across studies, anywhere from 22 to 94% (Barenbaum et al., 2004). A variety of problems are evident, including post traumatic stress (PTSD), depression, anxiety, somatic complaints, grief reactions, and social withdrawal. Of these, PTSD, depression, and anxiety have been most noted. PTSD appears to be more associated with war experiences, and depression with subsequent life conditions (Thabet, Abed, & Vostanis, 2004).

Psychological upset can be enduring. Young adults who as children had experienced trauma during the Pol Pot regime had a lifetime rate of PTSD of 59% (Hubbard et al., 1995). Although their experiences were probably especially horrific and threatening, other studies indicate both persistence and reduction of disorder over time. A variety of risk factors operate regarding the development of disorder (Ehntholt & Yule, 2006). These include multiple and severe traumatic experiences, lack of information about missing family members, inability to respond to new situations, separation from family, poor family cohesion or mental health, low levels of social support, and postmigration stress. But young people may exhibit remarkable resilience (Lustig et al., 2004). Coping strategies may seem quite ordinary. For example, Sudanese children living in refugee camps in Northern Uganda did what they could to cope. They sought the company of others, engaged in wishful thinking, and prayed (Paardekooper, de Jong, & Hermanns, 1999).

Efforts are underway to prevent or treat the negative effects of war-related disorders. These vary, of course, depending on the problems and situation—that is, whether young people remain in war-threatened countries, live in refugee camps, or are adjusting to resettlement in unknown communities and countries. Regarding immediate efforts to alleviate distress from war, for example, teachers in Bosnia were trained to understand the needs of students, and counseling was set up at youth clubs for adolescents and at a child–parent outpatient clinic in Bosnia (Yule, 2000). Another example is a program focusing on structured activities for 6-to-17-year-old Palestinian youth who lived in life-threatening circumstances (Loughry et al., 2006).

As a general approach to some intervention needs, a three-phase model is recommended by Ehntholt & Yule (2006). (See Figure 15–5.) Initially, it is often necessary to establish a sense of safety and trust in the youths. Although a sense of trust and safety is important in all interventions, it can be particularly difficult to establish with persons who have experienced serious threats or witnessed horrifying events. The second phase of intervention targets specific problems, for example, PTSD or depression. The third phase focuses on building for the future, and includes discussion of both practical plans and future aspirations. The model recognizes that moving back and forth between the phases is often necessary.

The more we understand about treating the victims of war and conflict—including the mediators and moderators of stress reactions and resilience—the better our chance of alleviating and preventing emotional adversity. Nevertheless, few would dispute the opinion that war "must be regarded with abhorrence in terms of its terrible human toll in human suffering, especially on its most innocent bystanders—children and adolescents" (Jensen & Shaw, 1993, p. 697).

DIVERSITY AND INTERNATIONAL COOPERATION

An obvious implication of the shrinking world is the increased need to deal well with others of different facial appearance, color, dress, custom, and belief. It is estimated that at least 5,000 ethnocultural groups exist around the world (Marsella, 1998). Furthermore, we are currently witnessing massive relocations of people into foreign countries and cultures. The challenge of adapting to ethnic and racial differences, although not new by any means, is substantial.

In the United States, the challenge of diversity has a long history. Prejudice and fears often have had adverse effects on peoples of various groups—Native Americans, African Americans, Irish, Poles, Asians,

Arabs, Latinos, Jews, and Catholics, to name a few. Being of minority status remains a risk factor for quality of life, health, and opportunity, even as the United States becomes increasingly multicultural (Hawkins, Cummins, & Marlatt, 2004; Lurie & Dubowitz, 2007; Nyborg & Curry, 2003).

As a discipline, psychology has participated in the study of issues related to diversity, although efforts have perhaps not always been as timely as could be hoped. A historic example is the work of Kenneth Clark and his colleagues that played a role in the 1957 Supreme Court decision, *Brown v. Board of Education*, which overthrew the "separate but equal" doctrine that had permitted racial segregation in the public schools (Clark, Chein, & Cook, 2004). Clark, an African American, became president of the American Psychological Association in the late 1960s (Pickren & Tomes, 2002). At about that time, the American Psychological Association became more committed to addressing problems of race and related matters. Today, concerns exist about various problems and progress of diverse cultural and racial groups living in the United States (Gibbs, Huang, & Associates, 2003; Pettigrew, 2004; Whaley & Davis, 2007).

The need also exists for increased study across cultures and the processes of international cooperation. In fact, an important outgrowth of closer communication among the peoples of the world is greater international effort to solve problems and to optimize living conditions. Over several decades, world attention has been drawn to promoting the healthy development of youth. The United Nations declared 1979 the International Year of the Child and subsequently drafted the U.N. Convention on the Rights of the Child. Among other rights, this document cites the rights of children to a family environment, an adequate standard of living, education, freedom of religion and self-expression, and rights to be free from specific harms such as abuse, torture, and exploitation (Murphy-Berman & Weisz, 1996).

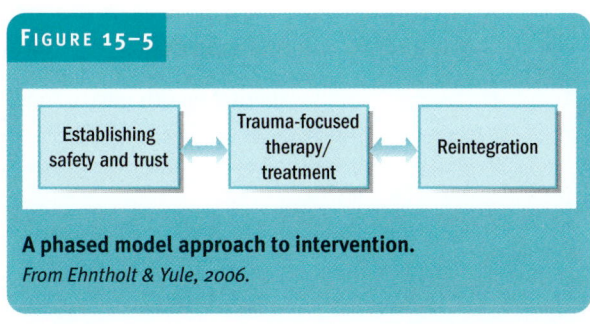

FIGURE 15–5

A phased model approach to intervention.
From Ehntholt & Yule, 2006.

The United Nations also has sponsored world summits and conferences, innumerable programs to benefit children, and the collection of data on youth to monitor progress and make recommendations.

Many other concerned organizations, both public and private, are addressing global issues such as poverty, education, infant mortality, medical and mental health needs, violence, and environmental pollution. Because these problems can have a crucial influence on the development of children and adolescents, international cooperation holds the promise of improving the lives of young people.

SUMMARY

WHO CARES FOR CHILDREN: FAMILY ISSUES

- *The effects of nonmaternal day care on young children depend on many factors. High-quality care can have beneficial effects on cognitive and behavioral development. The effects of amount of care are less clear; higher amount may be associated with externalizing problems. Children of highly disadvantaged families may particularly benefit from high quality care. The influence of day care is weaker than parental influence.*

- *The effects of self-care by older children are variable. However, supervised, high-quality out-of-school programs have been shown to be advantageous, perhaps especially for disadvantaged families.*

- *Most adopted youth function in the normal range, and adoption is beneficial to children coming from less advantaged circumstances. Adoption is associated with mild to moderate risk for behavioral and learning problems. Gender, age at adoption, and preadoption experiences are associated with outcome.*

- *Current policy regarding foster care assumes that it is temporary and that the child either will return to the birth family or will join a permanent adoptive or foster care family. Concerns are expressed about foster care and efforts are being made to address them.*

MENTAL HEALTH SERVICES FOR YOUTH

- *Mental health services for youth are inadequate, underfunded, fragmented, and underutilized by certain groups. Services are offered in various settings; the use of community-based settings, including schools, is recommended. Federally sponsored efforts encourage comprehensive, coordinated, accessible services.*

YOUTH IN THE GLOBAL SOCIETY

- *Many challenges to the development of young people are evident worldwide, such as poverty, disease, poor nutrition, and lack of mental care services. International efforts have brought improvements but enormous needs persist.*

- *Millions of children and adolescents suffer loss and physical and psychological damage from armed and sociopolitical conflicts. Interventions to alleviate and prevent war-related disorders are underway.*

- *A functionally smaller world has heightened the need for people to adapt to, and be enriched by, diversity. International cooperation holds promise for improving the lives of needy children and adolescents.*

KEY TERMS

Adoption and Safe Family Act *(p. 419)*

treatment foster care *(p. 420)*

mental health parity *(p. 420)*

Glossary

ABA (reversal) research design   Single-case experimental design in which the behavior being examined is measured during a baseline period (A), a period of manipulation (B), and a period in which the manipulation is removed (A). The manipulation (B) is reintroduced when treatment is the goal.

Accelerated longitudinal research designs   Various designs that combine the longitudinal and cross-sectional research strategies to maximize the strengths of those methods.

Acute onset   The sudden (rather than gradual) onset of a disorder.

Adaptive behavior scales   Psychological instruments that measure an individual's ability to perform in the everyday environment—for example, to wash one's hair, interact socially, and communicate.

Adoption studies   In genetic research, the comparison of adopted children with their biological and their adoptive families to determine hereditary and environmental influences on characteristics.

Affect   Emotion or mood. By extension, an affective disorder is a mood disorder such as depression or mania.

Agoraphobia   Excessive anxiety about being in a situation in which escape might be difficult or embarrassing.

Anoxia   Lack of oxygen.

Antisocial behavior   A pattern of behavior that violates widely held social norms and brings harm to others (e.g., stealing, lying).

Aphasia   Loss or impairment of language, caused by brain anomalies.

Attachment   A strong socioemotional bond between individuals. Usually discussed in terms of the child–parent or child–caretaker relationship, attachment is generally viewed as having a strong influence on a child's development.

Attention   The focusing or concentration of mental energy on an object or event. Attention has many components, which are linked to different brain regions. Attention deficits are manifested in problems such as distractibility and difficulty in sustaining effort.

Attribution (attributional style)   The way an individual thinks about or explains actions and outcomes; for example, a child's attributing his or her school failure to lack of innate intelligence.

Authoritative parenting   Style of parenting in which parents set rules and expectations for their children, follow through with consequences, and simultaneously are warm, accepting, and considerate of their children's needs. This style is thought to be associated with positive development in children.

Autoimmune disorder   A condition in which the body's immune system attacks its own healthy tissue.

Autonomic nervous system   A part of the nervous system that regulates functions usually considered involuntary, such as the operation of smooth muscles and glands. The system controls physiological changes associated with emotion. (*See* central nervous system.)

Baseline   The measured rate of a behavior before an intervention is introduced. Baseline rates of a behavior being examined can then be compared with rates measured during and following an intervention.

Behavior therapy/behavior modification   An approach to the treatment of behavior disorders that is based primarily on learning principles.

Behaviorally inhibited temperament   A temperamental tendency in which the individual is highly reactive to and stressed by unfamiliar stimuli.

Binge   A relatively brief episode of excessive consumption (e.g., of food) over which the individual feels no control.

Biofeedback   Procedures by which an individual is provided immediate information (feedback) about his or her physiological functioning (e.g., muscle tension, skin temperature). It is assumed that the individual can come to control bodily functioning through such feedback.

Case study   Method of research in which an individual case is described. The case study can be informative, but cannot be generalized with confidence to other persons or situations.

Central coherence   The tendency of individuals to weave bits of information together so as to create a whole, or global, meaning. Central coherence is contrasted with the (analytic) tendency to focus on parts of stimuli, rather than the whole.

Central nervous system   In humans, the brain and spinal cord. (*See* autonomic nervous system.)

Child guidance movement   An early to mid-20th-century effort in the United States to treat and prevent childhood mental disorders. Importance was given to the influence of family and wider social systems on the child.

Chromosome   A threadlike structure in the cell nucleus that contains the genetic code. Human cells possess 23 pairs of chromosomes, except for the ovum and sperm, which possess 23 single chromosomes.

Chromosome abnormalities   Abnormalities in the number and/or structure of the chromosomes, which can lead to fetal death or anomalies in development.

Classical conditioning A form of learning, also referred to as Pavlovian conditioning. In classical conditioning, an individual comes to respond to a stimulus (conditioned stimulus or CS) that did not previously elicit a response. Classical conditioning occurs when a CS is paired with another stimulus (the unconditioned stimulus, or UCS) that does elicit the desired response (unconditioned response, or UCR). When this response is elicited by the conditioned stimulus alone, it is called a conditioned response (CR).

Clinical significance The degree to which research findings are meaningful regarding real-life applications.

Clinical utility The adequacy of a classification system, diagnosis, or assessment instrument; judged on the basis of how fully the observed phenomena are described and how useful the descriptions are.

Coercion A process in which a noxious or aversive behavior of one person (e.g., aggression by a child) is rewarded by another person (e.g., a parent). Often applied to the development of conduct-disordered behavior.

Cognitive strategies Strategies related to information processing, memory, and the like; for example, rehearsing and categorizing information or addressing the interpretation of an experience or event.

Cohort A particular age group of individuals. A cohort may differ in life experiences and values from an age group born and raised during a different era.

Comorbidity A term used when an individual meets the criteria for more than one disorder (e.g., Attention-Deficit Hyperactivity Disorder and Oppositional Defiance Disorder). (*See* co-occurrence.)

Compulsions Behaviors the individual feels compelled to repeat over and over again, even though they appear to have no rational basis.

Computerized tomography (CT) scan A procedure that assesses the density of brain tissue and produces a photographic image of the brain. A CT scan allows investigators to directly assess abnormalities of brain structures. Also sometimes referred to as a computerized axial tomography (CAT) scan.

Concordant In genetic research, refers to individuals who are similar in particular attributes; for example, individuals may be concordant in activity level or in meeting the diagnostic criteria for a disorder.

Conditioned stimulus (CS) A neutral stimulus, which through repeated pairings with a stimulus (unconditioned stimulus) that already elicits a particular response, comes to elicit a similar response (conditioned response).

Contingency management Use of procedures that seek to modify behavior by altering the causal relationship between stimulus and response events, for example, modifying a particular outcome or consequence of a behavior.

Continuous performance test (CPT) A method for evaluating sustained attention and impulsivity. In a CPT, the individual must identify a target stimulus when it appears in a series of stimuli. Errors are made by not reacting to the target stimulus or by reacting to nontarget stimuli.

Control group In an experiment, a group of participants treated differently from the group of participants who receive the experimental manipulation. The two groups are later compared.

The purpose of a control group is to ensure that the results of the experiment can be attributed to the manipulation rather than to other variables.

Co-occurrence A term used when individuals experience the problems (symptoms) associated with more than one disorder (e.g., anxiety and depression). (*See* comorbidity.)

Correlation coefficient A number, obtained through statistical analysis, that reflects the presence or absence of a correlation and the strength and direction (positive or negative) of a correlation. Pearson *r* is a commonly used coefficient. (*See* positive correlation; negative correlation.)

Correlational research A research method aimed at establishing whether two or more variables covary, or are associated. (*See* positive correlation; negative correlation.) The establishment of a correlation permits the prediction of one variable from the other, but does not automatically establish a causal relationship.

Covert behaviors Behaviors that are not readily observable. When describing antisocial behaviors this term refers to behaviors that are concealed, such as lying, stealing, and truancy. (*See* overt behaviors.)

Critical period A relatively limited period of development during which an organism may be particularly sensitive to specific influences.

Cross-sectional research A research strategy aimed at observing and comparing different groups of participants at one point in time. Cross-sectional research is a highly practical way to gather certain kinds of information.

Cultural familial retardation A term, less popular now, referring to the majority of cases of milder mental retardation that "runs in families" and for which biological causation is not established.

Defense mechanisms In psychoanalytic theory, psychological processes that distort or deny reality so as to control anxiety. Examples are repression, projection, and reaction formation.

Deinstitutionalization The movement to place or treat people with disorders at home or in various community settings rather than in institutions.

Delinquency A legal term that refers to an illegal behavior by a person under 18. Such behavior may be illegal for an adult as well (e.g., theft) or may be illegal only when committed by a juvenile (e.g., truancy).

Delusion An idea or belief that is contrary to reality and is not widely accepted in one's culture (e.g., delusions of grandeur or of persecution).

Dependent variable In the experimental method of research, the measure of behavior that may be influenced by the manipulation (the independent variable).

Development Change in structure and function that occurs over time in living organisms. Typically viewed as change from the simple to the complex, development is the result of transactions among several variables.

Developmental level The level at which an individual is functioning with regard to physical, intellectual, or socioemotional characteristics.

Developmental psychopathology The study of behavioral disorders within the context of developmental influences.

Developmental quotient (DQ) A measure of performance on infant tests of development, paralleling the intelligence quotient (IQ) derived from intelligence tests for older children.

Diathesis   Vulnerability to a disease or disorder.

Differential reinforcement of other behaviors (DRO)   In behavior modification, application of relatively more reinforcement to desirable behaviors that are incompatible with specific undesirable behaviors.

Difficult temperament   Tendency of an individual to display negative mood, intense reactions to stimuli, irritability, and the like. A difficult temperament is a risk factor for behavior problems.

Discordant   In genetic research, refers to individuals who are dissimilar in particular attributes; for example, two individuals may be discordant in activity level or clinical diagnosis.

Discrete trial learning   Method of modifying behavior or teaching in which the clinician or teacher presents specific tasks or materials in small steps, provides clear directives or prompts, and applies consequences. The setting is structured for learning. (*See* incidental learning.)

Dizygotic (fraternal) twins   Twins resulting from two independent unions of ova and sperm that occur at approximately the same time. Dizygotic twins are genetically no more alike than are nontwin siblings.

DNA   Deoxyribonucleic acid. The chemical carrier of the genetic code, found in the chromosomes and composed of sugar, phosphates, and nucleotides. The nucleotides carry the hereditary information.

Dyslexia   General term referring to reading disorder not due to general intellectual deficiency.

Echolalia   The repetition of the speech of others, either immediately or delayed in time. A pathological speech pattern commonly found in autism and psychoses.

Education for All Handicapped Children Act of 1975   Public Law 94–142, which set influential federal guidelines for the rights of handicapped children to an appropriate public education. Reauthorized and expanded, the law is now titled the Individuals with Disabilities Education Act (IDEA).

Ego   According to psychoanalytic theory, the structure of the mind that operates predominantly at the conscious level. The ego is said to mediate between instinctual urges and reality, and is responsible for decision making.

Electroencephalograph (EEG)   A recording of the electrical activity of the brain.

Empirical   The process of verification or proof by accumulating information or data through observation or experiment (in contrast to reliance on impression or theory).

Empirically supported assessments and treatments   Assessments and interventions for which there is empirical support for their effectiveness; procedures that have been deemed worthy through scientific evaluation.

Epidemiology   The study of the occurrence and distribution of a disorder within a population. Epidemiology seeks to understand the development and etiology of disorder.

Equifinality   The concept that different factors or paths can result in the same or similar developmental outcomes. For example, somewhat different paths can lead to conduct-disordered behavior.

Etiology   The cause or origin of a disease or behavior disorder.

Eugenics   Efforts to improve human characteristics through the systematic control of reproduction and thus genetics.

Evidence-based assessments and treatments   *See* empirically supported assessments and treatments.

Executive functions   Higher order mental abilities involved in goal-directed behavior. Included among executive function are planning and organizing behavior, using short-term or working memory, inhibiting responses, and evaluating and switching strategies.

Experimental research   A research strategy that can establish causal relationships among variables. Participants are exposed to the independent variable in order to determine possible effects on the dependent variable. Comparison groups are included and procedures are carefully controlled to help rule out effects of extraneous factors.

External validity   In research, the degree to which findings of an investigation can be generalized to other populations and situations.

Externalizing disorders   Behavioral disorders in which the problems exhibited seem directed at others (e.g., aggression and lying).

Extinction   A weakening of a learned response, produced when reinforcement that followed the response no longer occurs.

Factor analysis   A statistical procedure that suggests which behaviors or characteristics tend to occur together by correlating each item with every other item and then grouping correlated items into factors.

Flynn effect   Refers to the finding that scores on general tests of intelligence tend to increase over time as the tests become older.

Fraternal twins   *See* dizygotic twins.

Functional analysis   Behavior analysis; that is, the assessment of variables that might be influencing the occurrence and maintenance of a behavior. Determining such antecedent variables and consequences for behavior can be crucial in modifying the behavior.

Functional magnetic resonance imaging (fMRI)   A noninvasive magnetic radiowave technology which produces images that indicate areas of brain activity by tracking subtle changes in oxygen in different parts of the brain. (*See* magnetic resonance imaging.)

Gene   The unit of the chromosome that carries the genetic code.

Gene–environment correlation   Correlation indicating the presence of genetic differences in exposure to environments. That is, genetic influences play a role in determining the experiences a person has. For example, a child who is genetically predisposed to be shy may be treated in certain ways by others or may elect to avoid highly social activities.

Gene–environment interaction   Differential sensitivity to experience due to differences in genotype. For example, children with recessive genes for PKU (phenylketonuria) develop intellectual disabilities when they ingest certain kinds of foods.

Generalization of learning   The process by which a response is made to a new stimulus that is different from, but similar to, the stimulus present during learning.

Genotype   The complement of genes that a person carries; the genetic endowment.

Goodness-of-fit   Degree to which an individual's attributes or behaviors match or fit the attributes or demands of the individual's environment.

Grapheme A unit of a writing system—a letter or a combination of letters—that represents the sounds of a language (the phonemes).

Hallucination A false perception (e.g., hearing a noise, seeing an object) that occurs in the absence of any apparent environmental stimulation.

Heritability The degree to which genetic influences account for variations in an attribute among individuals in a population.

Heterotypic continuity The continuity of a disorder over time in which the form of the problem behaviors changes over time. Contrasts with homotypic continuity, in which the form does not change.

High-risk prevention strategies (also called **selective prevention strategies**) Prevention strategies targeted at individuals who are at higher than average risk for disorder.

Hypothesis In science, a proposition or "educated guess" put forth for evaluation by some scientific method.

Id According to psychoanalytic theory, the structure of the mind present at birth. Said to be the source of all psychic energy, the id is held to operate entirely at the unconscious level, seeking immediate gratification of all instinctual urges, such as sexual urges.

Identical twins See monozygotic twins.

Impulsivity Acting without thinking; a failure to inhibit behavior. Some children with attention-deficit hyperactvity disorder exhibit impulsivity.

Incidence Number or proportion of persons in a population newly diagnosed with a disorder during a specific time period.

Incidental learning Method of modifying behavior or teaching in informal, natural settings. Incidental learning takes advantage of the everyday context—for example, by teaching tasks relevant to what a child is engaging in at the moment. Learning procedures, such as contingency management, are typically employed.

Inclusion The idea that all children with disabilities can best be educated, and should be included, in regular classrooms. (See Regular Education Initiative.)

Independent variable In the experimental method of research, the variable manipulated by the researcher.

Indicated prevention strategies Prevention strategies that are targeted at high-risk individuals who show minimal symptoms or early signs of a disorder, or who have biological markers for a disorder, but do not meet the criteria for the disorder.

Individual Education Plan (IEP) Detailed educational plan legally mandated for each person being served by the Individuals with Disabilities Education Act.

Individuals with Disabilities Education Act (IDEA) Current federal law ensuring the rights of handicapped persons from birth to age 21 to appropriate public education. The act ensures (1) education and services in the least restrictive setting possible, (2) parent participation in the child's education, and (3) assistance to the states in carrying out the mandates of the act. (See Education for All Handicapped Children Act of 1975.)

Information processing Complex mental processes by which the organism attends to, perceives, interprets, and stores information. (See attention, working memory, executive functions, cognitive strategies.)

Informed consent In research or treatment, the ethical and legal guideline that potential participants be reasonably informed about the research or treatment as a basis for their consent or willingness to participate.

Insidious onset Gradual, rather than sudden (acute), onset of a disorder.

Intelligence quotient (IQ), deviation A standard score, derived from statistical procedures, that reflects the direction and degree to which an individual's performance on an intelligence test deviates from the average score of the individual's age group.

Intelligence quotient (IQ), ratio The ratio of mental age (MA), derived from performance on tests of intelligence, to chronological age (CA), multiplied by 100. (IQ = MA/CA × 100).

Interactional model of development The view that development is the result of the interplay of organismic and environmental variables. (See transactional model of development.)

Internalizing disorders The large category of disorders—many of which were traditionally referred to as neuroses—in which the problems exhibited seem directed more at the self than at others, (e.g., fears, depression, and withdrawal).

Internal validity The degree to which research findings can be attributed to certain factors. Internal validity frequently concerns the degree to which the result of an experiment can be attributed to the experimental manipulation (the independent variable) rather than to extraneous factors.

Interrater reliability The extent to which different raters agree on a particular diagnosis or measurement.

In vivo A term referring to the natural context in which behavior occurs. For example, in vivo treatment is delivered in the setting in which the behavior problem occurs (e.g., the home rather than the clinic).

Joint attention interactions Behaviors, such as pointing and eye contact, that simultaneously focus the attention of two or more people on the same object or situation, presumably for sharing an experience.

Learned helplessness Passivity and a sense of lack of control over one's environment that is learned through experiences in which one's behavior was ineffective in controlling events.

Least restrictive environment Regarding education, refers to the idea that individuals with disabilities have the right to be educated with their typically developing peers to the extent that such education is maximally feasible.

Lifetime prevalence Number or proportion of persons in a population diagnosed with a disorder at any time during life.

Longitudinal research A research strategy in which the same participants are observed over a relatively long period of time, with their behavior measured at certain points in time. Longitudinal research is particularly helpful in tracing developmental change.

Magnetic resonance imaging (MRI) A noninvasive procedure that creates a magnetic field around the brain. Cells in the brain respond to the radio waves, and a three-dimensional image of the structures of the brain is created. (See functional magnetic resonance imaging.)

Mainstreaming The educational practice of placing individuals with disabilities into community schools and into the least restrictive settings appropriate to their needs. Most of the children who are mainstreamed spend the majority of their school

time in classrooms with typically developing peers, with various degrees of special support.

Maturation Changes that occur in individuals relatively independently of the environment, provided that basic conditions are satisfied. For example, most humans develop the ability to walk, given normal physical health and opportunity for movement.

Mediating influence The effect that a variable has to bring about or cause an outcome. For example, when variable *A* affects variable *M*, which, in turn, affects variable *B*, the impact of *A* on *B* is said to be mediated by *M*.

Mental age (MA) The score corresponding to the chronological age (CA) of children whose intellectual test performance the examinee equals. For the average child, MA = CA.

Mental hygiene movement An effort organized in the United States early in the 20th century to bring effective, humane treatment to the mentally ill and to prevent mental disorders. The mental hygiene movement was closely associated with the child guidance movement.

Metacognition The understanding of one's own information-processing system.

Metamemory The understanding of the working of one's memory or the strategies used to facilitate memory.

Minimal brain dysfunction (MBD) The assumption that the central nervous system or brain is functioning in a pathological way to a degree that is not clearly detectable.

Moderating influence The effect that a variable has to reduce or strengthen an outcome. For example, when the relationship of variable *A* to variable *B* depends on the level of variable *M*, *M* is said to be the moderator of the relationship of *A* to *B*.

Monozygotic (identical) twins Twins resulting from one union of an ovum and a sperm. The single zygote divides early into two, with the new zygotes having identical genes (and thus being of the same sex).

Morphology Regarding language, refers to the forms of words or the study of word formation.

Multifinality The concept that a factor may lead to different developmental outcomes. For example, child abuse may result in different kinds of behavior problems.

Multigenic influence The influences of multiple genes that combine in some way to affect an attribute or behavior. Also referred to as multiple-gene or polygenic influence.

Multiple baseline research designs Single-case experimental designs in which a manipulation is made and multiple behaviors or multiple participants are measured over time.

Mutation Spontaneous change in the genes that can be transmitted to the next generation. One of the genetic mechanisms that accounts for variation in species and individuals.

Nature vs. nurture controversy The debate about the relative influence of innate and experiential factors on the shaping of the individual. Also known as the hereditary vs. environmental debate.

Negative (inverse) correlation Correlation in which two (or more) variables covary such that high scores on one variable are associated with low scores on the other and vice versa.

Negative reinforcement The process whereby the probability or strength of a response increases because the response was followed by the removal of an aversive stimulus.

Neuropsychological assessment The use of psychological tests and behavioral measures to indirectly evaluate the functioning of the nervous system. Performance on these measures is known or presumed to reflect specific aspects of the functioning of the brain.

Neurotransmitter A chemical that carries the nerve impulse from one neuron, across the synaptic space, to another neuron. Examples of neurotransmitters are serotonin, dopamine, and norepinephrine.

Nonnormative developmental influences The effects on development which stem from events that are not necessarily unusual in themselves, but that occur only to some individuals, perhaps at unpredictable times. Examples are serious injury in childhood and the premature death of a parent. (*See* normative developmental influences.)

Nonshared environmental influence The portion of environmental influences on an attribute that is experienced by one family member, but not other members. (*See* shared environmental influence.)

Normal distribution (curve) The bell-shaped theoretical distribution or probability curve that describes the way in which many attributes (e.g., height, intelligence) occur or are assumed to occur in the population.

Normalization The philosophy that persons with disabilities have the right to experiences that are as normal as possible for the individual. (*See* mainstreaming; least restrictive environment.)

Normative developmental influences The effects on development which stem from events that happen to most individuals in some more or less predictable way. An example is puberty. (*See* nonnormative developmental influences.)

Norms Data based on information gathered from a segment of the population that represents the entire population. Norms serve as standards for evaluating individual development or functioning.

Nuclear family A family unit consisting of the father, mother, and children.

Observational learning Learning that occurs through viewing the behavior of others. Modeled behavior can be presented in live or symbolic form.

Obsessions Recurring and intrusive irrational thoughts over which the individual feels no control.

Operant learning Learning in which responses are acquired, maintained, or eliminated as the result of consequences (e.g., reinforcement, punishment) and other learning processes.

Operational criteria (definition) A specified set of observable operations that are measurable and that allow one to define some concept. For example, maternal deprivation might be defined by the amount of time the child is separated from its mother.

Overlearning The procedure whereby learning trials are continued beyond the point at which the child has satisfied the stated criteria. Overlearning is intended to increase the likelihood that the new behavior will be maintained.

Overt behaviors Behaviors that are readily observable. When describing antisocial behaviors, this term refers to behaviors that are confrontational such as physical aggression, temper tantrums, and defiance. (*See* covert behaviors.)

Panic attack A discrete period of intense apprehension, fear, or terror that has a sudden onset and reaches a peak quickly.

Paradigm A shared perspective or framework consisting of a set of assumptions and conceptions that guide the work of a group of scientists.

Partial correlation statistical procedure A statistical procedure that aids in the interpretation of a demonstrated correlation by removing the effects of one or more specific variables.

Perinatal The period at or around the time of birth.

Perspective *See* paradigm.

Phenotype Observable attributes of an individual that result from the individual's genetic endowment, developmental processes, and the transactions of these.

Phobia Anxiety about, and avoidance of, some object or situation. This reaction is judged to be excessive, overly persistent, unadaptive, or inappropriate.

Phonological awareness The understanding that spoken words can be segmented into sounds (e.g., that "cat" has three sounds) and that sounds are represented by letters or combinations of letters of the alphabet.

Phonological decoding In alphabet-based languages, mapping letters to sounds.

Phonological processing Using the sound structure of a language to process written material. Deficits in such processing are central in reading disorders.

Phonology The sounds of a language or the study of speech sounds.

Pica The habitual eating of substances, such as dirt, paper, and hair, usually considered inedible.

Placebo A treatment that alters a person's behavior because he or she expects that change will occur. Placebos are often employed as control conditions to evaluate whether a treatment being tested is effective for reasons other than the person's belief in it.

Positive (direct) correlation Correlation in which two (or more) variables covary with each other such that high scores on one variable are associated with high scores on the other variable and low scores on the one variable are associated with low scores on the other.

Positive reinforcement The process whereby the probability or strength of a response increases because the response is followed by a positive stimulus.

Positron emission tomography (PET scan) A procedure for directly assessing activity in different parts of the brain by assessing the use of oxygen and glucose that fuel brain activity.

Posttraumatic stress disorder A reaction to a trauma that is characterized by the reexperiencing of the trauma accompanied by symptoms of increased arousal and by avoidance of stimuli associated with the traumatic event.

Pragmatics (of language) The use of speech and gestures in a communicative way, considering the social context. Pragmatic skills include using appropriate gestures and language style.

Predictive validity The extent to which predictions about future behavior can be made (e.g., by knowing the individual's diagnosis or performance on some test).

Premorbid adjustment The psychological, social, or academic/vocational adjustment of a person prior to the onset of the symptoms of a disorder or its diagnosis.

Prenatal Having to do with the period of development that occurs during pregnancy or gestation.

Prevalence Number or proportion of persons in a population with a disorder at a given time.

Primary prevention The prevention of disorder(s) in the population by methods implemented before the full occurrence of the disorder(s). Primary prevention involves efforts to prevent specific disorders and to enhance general wellness.

Proband The designated individual whose relatives are assessed to determine whethar an attribute occurs in other members of the individual's family. Also called an index case.

Projection A defense mechanism whereby the ego protects against unacceptable thoughts or impulses by attributing them to another person or some object.

Projective tests Psychological tests that present ambiguous stimuli to the person. The person's response is presumed to reflect unconscious thoughts and feelings that are unacceptable to the ego and therefore cannot be expressed directly.

Pronoun reversal Deviant speech pattern in which speakers refer to themselves as "you," "she," or "he" and refer to others as "I" or "me." Often found in autism.

Prospective research designs Designs that identify participants and then follow them over time. (*See* retrospective research designs.)

Psychoactive (psychotropic) drugs Chemical substances that influence psychological processes (e.g., behavior, thinking, emotions) by their effects on nervous system functioning. Examples are stimulants and antidepressants.

Psychogenesis The view that the development of a behavior or disorder is due to psychological influences.

Psychosis A general term for severe mental disorder that affects thinking, the emotions, and other psychological systems. The hallmark of a psychosis is disturbed contact with reality.

PTSD *See* posttraumatic stress disorder.

Punishment A process whereby a response is followed by either an unpleasant stimulus or the removal of a pleasant stimulus, thereby decreasing the frequency of the response.

Qualitative research A research approach which assumes that events are best understood when they are observed in context and from a personal frame of reference. The methods employed include in-depth interviews and intensive case studies. (*See* quantitative research.)

Quantitative research A research approach that places a high value on objective quantitative measurement in a highly controlled situation, as characterized by the experiment. (*See* qualitative research.)

Random assignment In research, the assignment of individuals to different groups so that each individual has an equal chance of being assigned to any group. Such chance assignment helps make the groups comparable on factors that might influence the findings.

Recidivism The return to a previous undesirable pattern. The juvenile delinquent who again commits a crime after completing a treatment program illustrates recidivism.

Regular Education Initiative (REI) Proposal that all children with disabilities be educated in regular classrooms rather than special education settings.

Reinforcement A process whereby a stimulus that occurs contingent on a particular behavior results in an increase in the

likelihood of that behavior. (*See* positive reinforcement; negative reinforcement.)

Relapse   The reoccurrence of a problem after it has been successfully treated.

Reliability   The degree to which an observation is consistently made. The term can be applied to a test or other measurement or to a system of classification. (*See* test–retest reliability; interrater reliability.)

Resilience   The ability to overcome adversities or risk factors and function adaptively despite negative circumstances.

Response prevention   A behavioral treatment procedure in which the person is not allowed to engage in, or is discouraged from engaging in, a compulsive ritual or avoidant behavior.

Retrospective research designs   Designs that utilize information about past events; follow-back designs. (*See* prospective research designs.)

Risk   The degree to which variables (risk factors) operate to increase the chance of behavior problems.

Savant abilities   Specific and remarkable cognitive abilities (e.g., in memory or arithmetic) of individuals who otherwise exhibit intellectual disability.

Scientific method   An empirical approach to understanding phenomena. The scientific approach involves systematic formulation, observation and measurement, and interpretation of findings.

Secondary prevention   The prevention of disorders in the population by shortening the duration of existing cases through early diagnosis and treatment.

Selective prevention strategies   (*See* **high-risk prevention strategies**)

Self-injurious behavior   Repetitious action that damages the self physically, such as head banging or pulling one's own hair. Self-injurious behavior is observed especially in autism and mental retardation.

Self-monitoring   A procedure in which the individual observes and records his or her own behaviors or thoughts and the circumstances under which they occur.

Self-stimulatory behavior   Sensorimotor behavior that serves as stimulation for the person. Often refers to a pathological process, such as when an autistic child repetitiously flaps his or her hands.

Semantics   The study of meanings in language.

Separation anxiety   Childhood anxiety regarding separation from the mother or other major attachment figures.

Shared environmental influences   The portion of environmental influences on an attribute that is experienced by two or more family members. (*See* nonshared environmental influences.)

Single-case experiments   Experimental research designs employed with a single participant (or a few participants) in which a manipulation is made and measurements are taken across periods of time. (*See* ABA; multiple baseline designs.)

Socioeconomic status (SES)   Social class. Indices of SES include income, amount of education, and occupational level.

Somatogenesis   The view that development of a behavior or disorder is due to biological causes.

Stage theories of development   Theories of development which postulate that growth occurs in a recognizable order of noncontinuous stages or steps that are qualitatively different from each other. Examples are Piaget's cognitive theory and Freud's psychosexual theory.

Statistical significance   In research, the probability equal to or below which the findings obtained in a study or experiment are due merely to chance. By tradition, a finding is statistically significant when there is a 5-percent-or-less probability that it occurred by chance.

Stereotypy   A repetitive action or movement, such as hand flapping.

Stop-signal task   A method for evaluating behavioral inhibition. The individual must press a button when a target stimulus comes on a screen but must withhold this response when a special signal also comes on.

Stress   A situation or event that brings strain to the individual. Stress is considered a risk factor for behavioral and physical illness.

Superego   According to psychoanalytic theory, the structure of the mind that is the conscience or self-critical part of the individual. The superego reflects society's morals and standards as they have been learned from parents and others.

Sympathetic nervous system   A part of the autonomic nervous system that, among other things, accelerates the heart rate, increases blood glucose, inhibits intestinal activity, and, in general, seems to prepare the organism for stress or activity.

Syndrome   A group of behaviors or symptoms likely to occur together.

Syntax   The aspect of grammar that deals with the way words are put together to form phrases, clauses, and sentences.

Systematic desensitization   A behavioral treatment for anxiety. In systematic desensitization, the client visualizes a hierarchy of scenes, each of which elicits more anxiety than the previous scene. The visualizations are paired with relaxation until they no longer produce anxiety.

Systematic direct observation   Observation of specific behaviors of an individual or group of individuals in a particular setting, with the use of a specific observational code or instrument.

Temperament   Individual differences in emotionality, social responsiveness, activity level, and self-control. One's temperament is a biologically based disposition that can be transformed by experience.

Teratogens   Conditions or agents that are potentially harmful to the prenatal organism.

Tertiary prevention   The prevention of disorders in the population by reducing problems residual to disorders. An example is support groups for persons who are returning to the community after hospitalization for mental disorders.

Test–retest reliability   The degree to which a test or diagnostic system yields the same result when applied to the same individual(s) at different times.

Theory   An integrated set of propositions that explains phenomena and guides research.

Theory of mind   The ability to infer mental states (e.g., beliefs, knowledge) in others or the self.

Time-out   Behavior modification technique in which an individual displaying an undesirable behavior is removed from the immediate environment, usually by placement in an isolated room. Time-out is viewed conceptually as the elimination of positive reinforcement or as punishment.

Token economy A behavioral treatment procedure developed from operant conditioning principles. A set of behaviors is established that earns or costs reward points, given in the form of some scrip, such as poker chips. These tokens can then be exchanged for prizes, activities, or privileges.

Transactional model of development The view that development is the result of the continuous interplay of organismic and environmental variables. The transactional model of development is conceptually similar to the interactional model of development, but emphasizes the ongoing, mutual influences of factors.

Trauma An event outside of everyday experience that would be distressing to almost anyone.

Treatment foster care An effort to alleviate behavioral problems of children in foster care by working with foster parents and linking the child to the community mental health system.

Twin study In genetic research, the comparison of monozygotic twin pairs with dizygotic twin pairs to determine whether the former are more like each other than the latter. A type of research investigation frequently employed to examine the effects of hereditary and environmental variables.

Unconditioned stimulus (UCS) A stimulus that elicits a particular response prior to any conditioning trials. The loud noise that causes an infant to startle is an example of an unconditioned stimulus.

Universal prevention strategies Prevention strategies that are targeted at entire populations for which greater-than-average risk has not been identified.

Validity A term used in several different ways, all of which address issues of correctness, meaningfulness, and relevancy. (*See* internal validity; external validity; predictive validity.)

Wait-list (waiting-list) control group Group of participants in a research study who do not receive the treatment being investigated. A wait-list control group allows the investigators to compare changes in a group of individuals who received treatment with changes in a group of similar individuals who did not receive treatment. The term *wait list* is derived from the fact that those in the control group are offered treatment once the comparison is completed.

Working memory Part of the memory system that briefly holds and actively manipulates, or works on, information that it receives from the sensory systems or calls up from long-term memory. Working memory is sometimes referred to as short-term memory.

Zygote The cell mass formed by the joining of an ovum and sperm; the fertilized egg.

References

AAIDD Fact Sheet. (2007). Transition. Retrieved July 20, 2007 from http://www.aamr.org/Policies/faq-transition.shtml.

AAIDD Position Paper. (2007). Board Position Statement: Growth Attenuation. Retrieved July 20, 2007 from http://www.aamr.org/Policies/growth.shtml.

AAIDD/ARC Position Papers. (2007). Behavioral supports. Retrieved July 23, 2007 from http://www.aaidd.org/Policies/pos-beh-sppts.shtml.

Abela, J. R. Z. (2001). The hopelessness theory of depression: A test of the diathesis-stress and causal mediation components in third and seventh grade children. *Journal of Abnormal Child Psychology, 29,* 241–254.

Abidin, R. R. (1995). *Parenting Stress Index: Professional manual* (3rd ed.). Odessa, FL: Psychological Assessment Resources.

Abikoff, H., Hechtman, L., Klein, R. G., Gallagher, R., Fleiss, K., Etcovitch, J. et al. (2004a). Social functioning in children with ADHD treated with long-term methylphenidate and multimodal treatment. *Journal of the American Academy of Child and Adolescent Psychiatry, 43,* 820–829.

Abikoff, H., Hechtman, L., Klein, R. G., Weiss, G., Fleiss, K., Etcovitch, J. et al. (2004b). Symptomatic improvement in children with ADHD treated with long-term methylphenidate and multimodal psychosocial treatment. *Journal of the American Academy of Child and Adolescent Psychiatry, 43,* 802–811.

Ablon, S. L. (1996). The therapeutic action of play. *Journal of the American Academy of Child and Adolescent Psychiatry, 35,* 545–547.

Abramowitz, J. S., Whiteside, S. P., & Deacon, B. J. (2005). The effectiveness of treatment for pediatric obsessive-compulsive disorder: A meta-analysis. *Behavior Therapy, 36,* 55–63.

Abramson, L. Y., Metalsky, G. I., & Alloy, L. B. (1989). Hopelessness depression: A theory-based subtype of depression. *Psychological Bulletin, 96,* 358–372.

Abu-Akel, A., Caplan, R., Guthrie, D., & Komo, S. (2000). Childhood schizophrenia: Responsiveness to questions during conversation. *Journal of the American Academy of Child and Adolescent Psychiatry, 39,* 779–786.

Achenbach, T. M. (1982). *Developmental psychopathology.* New York: Wiley.

Achenbach, T. M. (1990). Conceptualizations of developmental psychopathology. In M. Lewis & S. M. Miller (Eds.), *Handbook of developmental psychopathology.* New York: Plenum.

Achenbach, T. M. (1998). Diagnosis, assessment, taxonomy and case formulations. In T. H. Ollendick & M. Hersen (Eds.), *Handbook of child psychopathology* (3rd ed.). New York: Plenum Press.

Achenbach, T. M. (2000). Assessment of psychopathology. In A. J. Sameroff, M. Lewis, & S. M. Miller (Eds.), *Handbook of developmental psychopathology* (2nd ed.). New York: Kluwer Academic/Plenum Publishers.

Achenbach, T. M., & Rescorla, L. A. (2001). *Manual for the ASEBA School-Age Forms & Profiles.* Burlington, VT: University of Vermont, Research Center for Children, Youth, & Families.

Achenbach, T. M., & Rescorla, L. A. (2007). *Multicultural Supplement to the Manual for the ASEBA School-Age Forms & Profiles.* Burlington, VT: University of Vermont, Research Center for Children, Youth and Families.

Achenbach, T. M., Dumenci, L., & Rescorla, L. A. (2003a). Are American children's problems getting worse? A 23-year comparison. *Journal of Abnormal Child Psychology, 31,* 1–11.

Achenbach, T. M., Dumenci, L., & Rescorla, L. A. (2003b). DSM-oriented and empirically based approaches to constructing scales from the same item pools. *Journal of Clinical Child and Adolescent Psychology, 32,* 328–340.

Achenbach, T. M., Howell, C. T., McConaughy, S. H., & Stanger, C. (1995). Six-year predictors of problems in a national sample of children and youth: II. Signs of disturbance. *Journal of the American Academy of Child and Adolescent Psychiatry, 34,* 488–498.

Achenbach, T. M., McConaughy, S. H., & Howell, C. T. (1987). Child/adolescent behavioral and emotional problems: Implications of cross-informant correlations for situational specificity. *Psychological Bulletin, 101,* 213–232.

Achenbach, T. M., Rescorla, L. A., & Ivanova, M. Y. (2005). Cross-cultural consistencies and variations in child and adolescent psychopathology. In K. F. Frisbay & C. Reynolds (Eds.), *Handbook of multicultural school psychology.* New York: John Wiley.

Ackard, D. M., Fulkerson, J. A., & Neumark-Sztainer, D. (2007). Prevalence and utility of DSM-IV eating disorder diagnostic criteria among youth. *International Journal of Eating Disorders, 40,* 409–417.

Ackerman, B. P., Izard, C. E., Kobak. R., Brown, E. D., & Smith, C. (2007). Relation between reading problems and internalizing behavior in school for preadolescent children from economically disadvantaged families. *Child Development, 78,* 581–596.

Acosta, O. M., Albus, K. E., Reynolds, M. W., Spriggs, D., & Weist, M. D. (2001). Assessing the status of research on violence-related problems among youth. *Journal of Clinical Child Psychology, 30,* 152–160.

Adams, G., & Carnine, D. (2003). Direct instruction. In H. L. Swanson, K. R. Harris, & S. Graham (Eds.), *Handbook of learning disabilities.* New York: Guilford Press.

Adelman, H. S. (1996). Appreciating the classification dilemma. In W. Stainback & S. Stainback (Eds.), *Controversial issues confronting special education: Divergent perspectives* (2nd ed.). Boston: Allyn and Bacon.

Adrien, J. L., Lenoir, P., Martineau, J., Perrot, A., Hameury, L., Larmande, C., & Sauvage, D. (1993). Blind ratings of early symptoms of autism based upon home movies. *Journal of the American Academy of Child and Adolescent Psychiatry, 32,* 617–626.

Ainbinder, J. G., Blanchard, L. W., Singer, G. H. S., Sullivan, M. E., Powers, L. K., Marquis, J. G., & Santelli, B. (1998). A qualitative study of Parent to Parent support for parents of children with special needs. *Journal of Pediatric Psychology, 23,* 99–109.

Akshoomoff, N. Farid, N., Courchesne, E., & Haas, R. (2007). Abnormalities on the neurological examination and EEG in young children with pervasive developmental disorders. *Journal of Autism and Developmental Disorders, 37,* 887–893.

Alarcón, R. D., Bell, C. C., Kirmayer, L. J., Lin, K. M., Üstün, B., & Wisner, K. L. (2002). Beyond the funhouse mirrors. Research agenda on culture and psychiatric diagnosis. In D. J. Kupfer, M. B. First, & D. A. Regier (Eds.), *A research agenda for DSM-V.* Washington, DC: American Psychiatric Association.

Albano, A. M., Chorpita, B. F., & Barlow, D. H. (2003). Childhood anxiety disorders. In E. J. Mash & R. A. Barkley (Eds.), *Child psychopathology* (2nd ed.). New York: Guilford Press.

Albano, A. M., & DiBartolo, P. M. (1997). Cognitive-behavioral treatment of obsessive-compulsive disorder and social phobia in children and adolescents. In L. VandeCreek (Ed.), *Innovations in clinical practice* (Vol. 15). Sarasota, FL: Professional Resource Exchange.

Albee, G. W. (1986). Toward a just society. Lessons from observations on the primary prevention of psychopathology. *American Psychologist, 41,* 891–898.

Albee, G. W. (1996). Revolutions and counterrevolutions in prevention. *American Psychologist, 51,* 1130–1133.

Alexander, F. (1950). *Psychosomatic medicine.* New York: W. W. Norton and Co.

Alexander, J. F., & Sexton, T. L. (2002). Functional Family Therapy (FFT): A model for treating high-risk, acting-out youth. In F. W. Kaslow (Ed.), *Comprehensive handbook of psychotherapy: Vol. 4, Integrative/eclectic.* New York: Wiley.

Alexander, J., Barton, C., Gordon, D., Grotpeter, J., Hansson, K., Harrison, R., Mears, S., Mihalic, S., Parsons, B., Pugh, C., Schulman, S., Waldron, H., & Sexton, T. (1998). *Blueprints for violence prevention: Functional family therapy.* Boulder, CO: Venture.

Algozzine, B. (1977). The emotionally disturbed child: Disturbed or disturbing? *Journal of Abnormal Child Psychology, 5,* 205–211.

Allen, M., & Bissell, M. (2004, Winter). Safety and stability for foster children: The policy context. *The Future of Children, 14,* 49–73.

Altman, H., & Collins, M., & Mundy, P. (1997). Subclinical hallucinations and delusions in nonpsychotic adolescents. *Journal of Child Psychology and Psychiatry, 38,* 413–420.

Aman, M. G., Hammer, D., & Rojahn, J. (1993). Mental retardation. In T. H. Ollendick & M. Hersen (Eds.), *Handbook of child and adolescent assessment.* Boston: Allyn & Bacon.

Amato, P. R. (2000). The consequences of divorce for adults and children. *Journal of Marriage and the Family, 62,* 1269–1287.

Amato, P. R., & Irving, S. (2006). Historical trends in divorce in the United States. In M. A. Fine & J. H. Harvey (Eds.), *Handbook of divorce and relationship dissolution.* Mahwah, NJ: Lawrence Erlbaum Associates.

Amato, P. R., & Keith, B. (1991). Parental divorce and the well-being of children: A metaanalysis. *Psychological Bulletin, 110,* 26–46.

Ambrosini, P. J. (2000). Historical development and present status of the Schedule for Affective Disorders and Schizophrenia for School-Age Children (K-SADS). *Journal of the American Academy of Child and Adolescent Psychiatry, 39,* 48–58.

American Academy of Child and Adolescent Psychiatry. (1999). Practice parameters for the assessment and treatment of children, adolescents, and adults with autism and other pervasive developmental disorders. *Journal of the American Academy of Child and Adolescent Psychiatry 38* (suppl.): 32s–54s.

American Academy of Child and Adolescent Psychiatry. (2001). Practice parameters for the assessment and treatment of children and adolescents with suicidal behavior. *Journal of the American Academy of Child and Adolescent Psychiatry, 40,* 24S–51S.

American Academy of Child and Adolescent Psychiatry. (2005). Practice parameter for the assessment and treatment of children and adolescents with substance use disorders. *Journal of the American Academy of Child and Adolescent Psychiatry, 44,* 609–621.

American Academy of Child and Adolescent Psychiatry. (2007). Practice parameters for the assessment and treatment of children and adolescents with anxiety disorders. *Journal of the American Academy of Child and Adolescent Psychiatry, 46,* 267–283.

American Academy of Child and Adolescent Psychiatry. (2007). Practice parameters for the assessment and treatment of children and adolescents with bipolar disorder. *Journal of the American Academy of Child and Adolescent Psychiatry, 46,* 107–125.

American Academy of Child and Adolescent Psychiatry. (2007a). Practice parameter for the assessment and treatment of children and adolescents with attention-deficit/hyperactivity disorder. *Journal of the American Academy of Child and Adolescent Psychiatry, 46,* 894–921.

American Academy of Child and Adolescent Psychiatry. (2007b). Practice parameter for the assessment and treatment of children and adolescents with oppositional defiant disorder. *Journal of the American Academy of Child and Adolescent Psychiatry, 46,* 126–141.

American Academy of Pediatrics. (2000). Fetal alcohol syndrome and alcohol-related neurodevelopmental disorders. *Pediatrics, 106,* 358–361.

American Academy of Pediatrics. (2003). Prevention of pediatric overweight and obesity. *Pediatrics, 112,* 424–430.

American Psychiatric Association. (1952, 1968, 1980, 1987, 1994). *Diagnostic and statistical manual of mental disorders.* Washington, DC: American Psychiatric Association.

American Psychiatric Association. (2000). *Diagnostic and statistical manual of mental disorders (4th ed.). Text Revision.* Washington, DC: American Psychiatric Association.

American Psychological Association. (2002). *Ethical principles of psychologists and code of conduct.* Washington, DC: Author.

American Psychological Association. (2003). Guidelines on multicultural education, training, research, practice, and organizational change for psychologists. *American Psychologist, 58,* 377–402.

American Psychological Association. (2007). Increasing access and coordination of quality mental health services for children and adolescents. Retrieved May 27, 2007, from http://www.apa.org/ppo/issues/tfpacoord.html

American Sleep Disorders Association. (1997). *The international classification of sleep disorders, revised: Diagnostic and coding manual.* Rochester, MN: American Sleep Disorders Association.

Anastasi, A., & Urbina, S. (1997). *Psychological testing.* Upper Saddle River, NJ: Prentice Hall.

Anastopoulos, A. D., & Farley, S. E. (2003). A cognitive-behavioral training program for parents of children with attention-deficit/hyperactivity disorder. In A. E. Kazdin & J. R. Weisz (Eds.), *Evidence-based psychotherapies for children and adolescents.* New York: Guilford Press.

Anastopoulos, A. D., Rhoads, L. H., & Farley, S. E. (2006). Counseling and training parents. In R. A. Barkley (Ed.), *Attention-deficit hyperactivity disorder. A handbook for diagnosis and treatment.* New York: The Guilford Press.

Anastopoulos, A. D., Smith, J. M., & Wien, E. E. (1998). Counseling and training parents. In R. A. Barkley, *Attention-deficit hyperactivity disorder.* New York: Guilford Press.

Anders, T. F., & Eiben, L. A. (1997). Pediatric sleep disorders: A review of the past 10 years. *Journal of the American Academy of Child and Adolescent Psychiatry, 36,* 9–20.

Anderson, B. J., Brackett, J., Ho, J., & Laffel, L. M. B. (2000). An intervention to promote family teamwork in diabetes management tasks: Relationships among parental involvement, adherence to blood glucose monitoring, and glycemic control in young adolescents with Type 1 diabetes. In D. Drotar (Ed.), *Promoting adherence to medical treatment in chronic childhood illness: Concepts, methods, and interventions.* Mahwah, NJ: Lawrence Erlbaum Associates.

Anderson, C. A., Berkowitz, L., Donnerstein, E., Huesmann, R., Johnson, J. D., Linz, D. et al. (2003). The influence of media violence on youth. *Psychological Science in the Public Interest, 4,* 81–110.

Anderson, C. A., & Dill, K. E. (2007). Video games and aggressive thoughts, feelings, and behavior in the laboratory and in life. *Journal of Personality and Social Psychology, 78,* 772–790.

Anderson, D. A., & Paulosky, C. A. (2004). Psychological assessment of eating disorders and related features. In J. K. Thompson (Ed.), *Handbook of eating disorders and obesity.* Hoboken, NJ: John Wiley.

Anderson-Fye, E. P., & Becker, A. E. (2004). Sociocultural aspects of eating disorders. In J. K. Thompson (Ed.), *Handbook of eating disorders and obesity.* Hoboken, NJ: John Wiley.

Anderson, J. C., Williams, S., McGee, R., & Silva, P. A. (1987). DSM-III disorders in preadolescent children: Prevalence in a large sample from the general population. *Archives of General Psychiatry, 44,* 69–76.

Anderson, M. (2001). Annotation: Conceptions of intelligence. *Journal of Child Psychology and Psychiatry, 42,* 287–298.

Anderson, P. M., & Butcher, K. F., (2006). Childhood obesity: Trends and potential causes. *The Future of Children, 16,* 19–45.

Anderson, V., Northam, E., Hendy, J., & Wrennall, J. (2001). *Developmental neuropsychology. A clinical approach.* Philadelphia: Taylor & Francis.

Andrasik, F., Blake, D. D., & McCarran, M. S. (1986). A biobehavioral analysis of pediatric headache. In N. A. Krasnegor, J. D. Arasteh, & M. F. Cataldo (Eds.), *Child health behavior: A behavioral pediatrics perspective.* New York: Wiley.

Angold, A., Costello, E. J., & Erkanli, A. (1999). Comorbidity. *Journal of Child Psychology and Psychiatry, 40,* 57–87.

Angold, A., & Rutter, M. (1992). Effects of age and pubertal stratus on depression in a large clinical sample. *Development and Psychopathology, 4,* 5–28.

Anthony, E. J. (1970). Behavior disorders. In P. H. Mussen (Ed.), *Carmichael's manual of child psychology,* Vol. II. New York: John Wiley.

Anthony, E. J. (1981). The psychiatric evaluation of the anxious child: Case record summarized from the clinic records. In E. J. Anthony & D. C. Gilpin (Eds.), *Three further clinical faces of childhood.* New York: S P Medical & Scientific Books.

Antrop, I., Roeyers, H., Van Oost, P., & Buysse, A. (2000). Stimulation seeking and hyperactivity in children with ADHD. *Journal of Child Psychology and Psychiatry, 41,* 225–231.

Antshel, K. M., Faraone, S. V., Stallone, K., Nave, A., Kaufman, F. A., Doyle, A. et al. (2007). Is attention deficit hyperactivity disorder a valid diagnosis in the presence of high IQ? Results from the MGH Longitudinal Family Studies of ADHD. *Journal of Child Psychology and Psychiatry, 48,* 687–694.

Aos, S., Miller, M. & Drake, E. (2006). *Evidence-based public policy options to reduce future prison construction, criminal justice costs and crime rates.* Retrieved August 2007 from http://www.wsipp.wa.gov/rptfiles/06-10-1201.pdf

APA Working Group on Psychoactive Medications for Children and Adolescents. (2006). *Report of the Working Group on Psychoactive Medications for Children and Adolescents. Psychopharmalogical, psychosocial, and combined interventions for childhood disorders: Evidence base, contextual factors, and future directions.* Washington, DC: American Psychological Association.

Ariés, P. (1962). *Centuries of childhood.* New York: Vintage Books.

Armbruster, P., & Kazdin, A. E. (1994). Attrition in child psychotherapy. In T. H. Ollendick & R. J. Prinz (Eds.), *Advances in clinical child psychology.* New York: Plenum Press.

Armstrong, F. D., Willen, E. J., & Sorgen, K. (2003). HIV and AIDS in children and adolescents. In M. C. Roberts (Eds.), *Handbook of pediatric psychology* (3rd ed.). New York: Guilford Press.

Armstrong, T. D., & Costello, E. J. (2002). Community studies of adolescent substance use, abuse, or dependence and psychiatric comorbidity. *Journal of Consulting and Clinical Psychology, 70,* 1224–1239.

Arnold, L. E., Vitiello, B., McDougle, C., Scahill, L., Shah, B., Gonzalez, M. N. et al. (2003). Parent-defined target symptoms respond to risperidone in RUPP Autism Study: Customer approach to clinical trials. *Journal of the American Academy of Child and Adolescent Psychiatry, 42,* 1443–1450.

Arsenio, W. F., & Lemerise, E. A. (2004). Aggression and moral development: Integrating social information processing and moral domain models. *Child Development, 75,* 987–1002.

Asarnow, J. R., & Asarnow, R. F. (2003). Childhood-onset schizophrenia. In E. J. Mash & R. A. Barkley (Eds.), *Child psychopathology.* New York: Guilford Press.

Asarnow, J. R., Goldstein, M. J., & Ben-Meir, S. (1988). Parental communication deviance in childhood onset schizophrenia spectrum and depressive disorders. *Journal of Child Psychology and Psychiatry, 29,* 825–838.

Asarnow, J. R., Jaycox, L. H., & Tompson, M. C. (2001). Depression in youth: Psychosocial interventions. *Journal of Clinical Child Psychology, 30,* 33–47.

Asarnow, J. R., Tompsom, M. C., & McGrath, E. P. (2004). Annotation: Childhood-onset schizophrenia: Clinical and treatment issues. *Journal of Child Psychology and Psychiatry, 45,* 180–194.

Aschenbrand, S. G., Kendall, P. C., Webb, A., Safford, S. M., & Flannery-Schroeder, E. (2003). Is childhood separation anxiety disorder a predictor of adult panic disorder and agoraphobia? A seven-year longitudinal study. *Journal of the American Academy of Child and Adolescent Psychiatry, 42,* 1478–1485.

Atkinson, L., Scott, B., Chrisholm, V., Blackwell, J., Dickens, S., Tam, F., & Goldberg, S. (1995). Cognitive coping, affective distress, and maternal sensitivity: Mothers of children with Down syndrome. *Developmental Psychology, 31,* 668–676.

Attia, E., & Schroeder, L. (2005). Pharmacologic treatment of anorexia nervosa: Where do we go from here? *International Journal of Eating Disorders, 37 (Suppl.),* 60–63.

Attie, I., & Brooks-Gunn, J. (1995). The development of eating regulation across the life span. In D. Cicchetti & D. J. Cohen (Eds.), *Developmental psychopathology* (Vol. 2: *Risk, disorder, and adaptation*). New York: John Wiley.

August, G. J., & Garfinkel, B. D. (1993). The nosology of attention-deficit hyperactivity disorder. *Journal of the American Academy of Child and Adolescent Psychiatry, 32,* 155–165.

August, G. J., Winters, K. C., Realmuto, G. M., Fahnhorst, T., Botzet, A. & Lee. S. (2006). Prospective study of adolescent drug use among community samples of ADHD and non-ADHD participants. *Journal of the American Academy of Child and Adolescent Psychiatry, 45,* 824–832.

Austin, A. A., & Chorpita, B. F. (2004). Temperament, anxiety, and depression: Comparisons across five ethnic groups of children. *Journal of Clinical Child and Adolescent Psychology, 33,* 216–226.

Axelson, D., Birmaher, B. J., Brent, D., Wassick, S., Hoover, C., Bridge, J., & Ryan, N. (2003). A preliminary study of the Kiddie Schedule for Affective Disorders and Schizophrenia for School-Age Children mania rating scale for children and adolescents. *Journal of Child and Adolescent Psychopharmacology, 13,* 463–470.

Axline, V. M. (1947). *Play therapy.* Boston: Houghton Mifflin.

Azar, S. T., & Bober, S. L. (1999). Children of abusive parents. In W. K. Silverman & T. H. Ollendick (Eds.), *Development issues in the clinical treatment of children.* Boston: Allyn & Bacon.

Azar, S. T., Ferraro, M. H., & Breton, S. J. (1998). Intra-familial child maltreatment. In T. H. Ollendick & M. Hersen (Eds.), *Handbook of child psychopathology* (3rd ed.). New York: Plenum Press.

Azar, S. T., & Wolfe, D. A. (2006). Child physical abuse and neglect. In E. J. Mash & R. A. Barkley (Eds.), *Treatment of childhood disorders,* (3rd ed.). New York: The Guilford Press.

Babinski, L. M., Hartsough, C. S., & Lambert, N. M. (1999). Childhood conduct problems, hyperactivity-impulsivity, and inattention as predictors of adult criminal activity. *Journal of Child Psychology and Psychiatry, 40,* 347–355.

Bachanas, P. J., Kullgren, K. A., Schwartz, K. S., Lanier, B., McDaniel, J. S., Smith, J., & Nesheim, S. (2001). Predictors of psychological adjustment in school-age children infected with HIV: Stress, coping, and family factors. *Journal of Pediatric Psychology, 26,* 343–352.

Bagwell, C. L., Molina, B. S. G., Pelham, W. E., & Hoza, B. (2001). Attention-deficit hyperactivity disorder and problems in peer relations: prediction from childhood to adolescence. *Journal of the American Academy of Child and Adolescent Psychiatry, 40,* 1285–1292.

Bailey, A., Le Couteur, A., Gottesman, I., Bolton, P., Simonoff, E., Yuzda, E., & Rutter, M. (1995). Autism as a strongly genetic disorder: Evidence from a British twin study. *Psychological Medicine, 25,* 63–78.

Bailey, A., Phillips, W., & Rutter, M. (1996). Autism: Towards an integration of clinical, genetic, neuropsychological, and neurobiological perspectives. *Journal of Child Psychology and Psychiatry, 37,* 89–126.

Bailey, D. B., Hatton, D. D., Mesibov, G., Ament, N., & Skinner, M. (2000). Early development, temperament, and functional impairment in autism and fragile X syndrome. *Journal of Autism and Developmental Disorders, 30,* 49–59.

Bailey, D. B., Skinner, D., & Sparkman, K. L. (2003). Discovering fragile X syndrome: Family experiences and perceptions. *Pediatrics, 111,* 407–416.

Baird, G., Charman, T., Baron-Cohen, S., Cox, A., Swettenham, J., Wheelwright, S., & Drew, A. (2000). A screening instrument for autism at 18 months of age: A 16–year follow-up study. *Journal of the American Academy of Child and Adolescent Psychiatry, 39,* 694–702.

Baker, L., & Cantwell, D. P. (1989). Specific language and learning disorders. In T. H. Ollendick & M. Hersen (Eds.), *Handbook of child psychopathology.* New York: Plenum.

Balboni, G., Pedrabissi, L., Molteni, M., & Villa, S. (2001). Discriminant validity of the Vineland Scales: Score profiles of individuals with mental retardation and a specific disorder. *American Journal of Mental Retardation, 106,* 162–172.

Balk, D. E., & Corr, C. A. (2001). Bereavement during adolescence: A review of research. In M. S. Stroebe, R. O. Hansson, W. Stroebe, & H. Schut (Eds.), *Handbook of bereavement research: Consequences, coping, and care.* Washington, DC: American Psychological Association.

Banaschewski, T., & Brandeis, D. (2007). What electrical brain activity tells us about brain function that other techniques cannot tell us — a child psychiatric perspective. *Journal of Child Psychology and Psychiatry, 48,* 415–435.

Bandura, A. (1977). *Social learning theory.* Englewood Cliffs, NJ: Prentice Hall.

Bandura, A. (1997). *Self-efficacy: The exercise of control.* New York: Freeman.

Bandura, A., & Menlove, F. L. (1968). Factors determining vicarious extinction of avoidance behavior through symbolic modeling. *Journal of Personality and Social Psychology, 8,* 99–108.

Barakat, L. P., Alderfer, M. A., & Kazak, A. E. (2006). Posttraumatic growth in adolescent survivors of cancer and their mothers and fathers. *Journal of Pediatric Psychology, 31,* 413–419.

Baranek, G. T. (1999). Autism during infancy: A retrospective video analysis of sensory-motor and social behaviors at 9–12 months of age. *Journal of Autism and Developmental Disorders, 29,* 213–224.

Barber, B. L., & Demo, D. H. (2006). The kids are alright (at least most of them): links between divorce and dissolution and child well-being. In M. A. Fine & J. H. Harvey (Eds.), *Handbook of divorce and relationship dissolution.* Mahwah, NJ: Lawrence Erlbaum Associates.

Barber, J. G., Delfabbro, P. H., & Cooper, L. L. (2001). The predictors of unsuccessful transition to foster care. *Journal of Child Psychology and Psychiatry, 42,* 785–790.

Bardone-Cone, A. M., Wonderlich, S. A., Frost, R. O., Bulik, C. M., Mitchell, J. E., Uppala, S., & Simonich, H. (2007). Perfectionism and eating disorders: Current status and future directions. *Clinical Psychology Review, 27,* 384–405.

Barenbaum, J., Ruchkin, V., & Schwab-Stone, M. (2004). The psychosocial aspects of children exposed to war: Practice and policy initiatives. *Journal of Child Psychology and Psychiatry, 45,* 41–62.

Barkley, R. A. (1990). *Attention-deficit hyperactivity disorder.* New York: Guilford.

Barkley, R. A. (1997). Attention-deficit/hyperactivity disorder. In E. J. Mash & L. G. Terdal (Eds.), *Assessment of childhood disorders.* New York: Guilford Press.

Barkley, R. A. (1998). *Attention-deficit/hyperactivity disorder.* New York: Guilford Press.

Barkley, R. A. (2003). Attention-deficit/hyperactivity disorder. In E. J. Mash & R. A. Barkley (Eds.), *Child psychopathology.* New York: Guilford Press.

Barkley, R. A. (2006a). Associated cognitive, developmental, and health problems. In R. A. Barkley (Ed.), *Attention-deficit hyperactivity disorder. A handbook for diagnosis and treatment.* New York: The Guilford Press.

Barkley, R. A. (2006b). A theory of ADHD. In R. A. Barkley (Ed.), *Attention-deficit hyperactivity disorder. A handbook for diagnosis and treatment.* New York: The Guilford Press.

Barkley, R. A. (2006c). Attention-deficit/hyperactivity disorder. In D. A. Wolfe & E. J. Mash (Eds.), *Behavioral and emotional disorders in adolescents. Nature, assessment, and treatment.* New York: The Guilford Press.

Barkley, R. A. (2006d). Comorbid disorders, social and family adjustment, and subtyping. In R. A. Barkley (Ed.), *Attention-deficit hyperactivity disorder. A handbook for diagnosis and treatment.* New York: The Guilford Press.

Barkley, R. A. (2006e). Etiologies. In R. A. Barkley (Ed.), *Attention-deficit hyperactivity disorder. A handbook for diagnosis and treatment.* New York: The Guilford Press.

Barkley, R. A. (2006f). Primary symptoms, diagnostic criteria, prevalence, and gender differences. In R. A. Barkley (Ed.), *Attention-deficit hyperactivity disorder. A handbook for diagnosis and treatment.* New York: The Guilford Press.

Barkley, R. A., & Edwards, G. (2006). Diagnostic interview, behavior rating scales, and the medical examination. In R. A. Barkley (Ed.), *Behavioral and emotional disorders in adolescents. Nature, assessment, and treatment.* New York: The Guilford Press.

Barkley, R. A., Shelton, T. L., Crosswait, C., Moorehouse, M., Fletcher, K., Barrett, S., Jenkins, L., & Metevia, L. (2002). Preschool children with disruptive behavior: Three-year outcome as a function of adaptive disability. *Development and Psychopathology, 14,* 45–67.

Barlow, D. H. (2002). *Anxiety and its disorders: The nature and treatment of anxiety and panic* (2nd ed.). New York: Guilford Press.

Barnett, W., & Spitzer, M. (1994). Pathological fire-setting 1951–1991: A review. *Medicine Science and the Law, 34,* 4–20.

Baron, I. S. (2004). *Neuropsychological evaluation of the child.* New York: Oxford University Press.

Baron-Cohen, S. (1989). The autistic child's theory of mind: A case of specific developmental delay. *Journal of Child Psychology and Psychiatry, 30,* 285–297.

Baron-Cohen, S., O'Riordan, M., Stone, V., Jones, R., & Plaisted, K. (1999). Recognition of faux pas by normally developing children and children with Asperger syndrome or high-functioning autism. *Journal of Autism and Developmental Disabilities, 29,* 407–418.

Baron-Cohen, S., & Swettenham, J. (1997). Theory of mind in autism: Its relationship to executive functions and central coherence. In D. J. Cohen & F. R. Volkmar (Eds.), *Handbook of autism and pervasive developmental disorders.* New York: John Wiley.

Barrera, M. Jr., Prelow, H. M., Dumka, L. E., Gonzales, N. A., Knight, G. P., Michaels, M. L., Roosa, M. W., & Tein, J. Y. (2002). Pathways from family economic conditions to adolescents' distress: Supportive parenting, stressors outside the family, and deviant peers. *Journal of Community Psychology, 30,* 135–152.

Barrett, P. M., Dadds, M. R., & Rapee, R. M. (1996). Family treatment of childhood anxiety: A controlled trial. *Journal of Consulting and Clinical Psychology, 64,* 333–342.

Barrett, P. M., Farrell, L. J., Ollendick, T. H., & Dadds, M. (2006). Long-term outcomes of an Australian universal prevention trial of anxiety and depression symptoms in children and youth: An evaluation of the Friends Program. *Journal of Clinical Child and Adolescent Psychology, 35,* 403–411.

Barrett, P. M., & Shortt, A. L. (2003). Parental involvement in the treatment of anxious children. In A. E. Kazdin & J. R. Weisz (Eds.), *Evidence-based psychotherapies for children and adolescents*. New York: Guilford Press.

Barrios, B. A., & O'Dell, S. L. (1998). Fears and anxieties. In E. J. Mash & R. A. Barkley (Eds.), *Treatment of childhood disorders* (2nd ed.). New York: Guilford Press.

Barton, B. K., Schwebel, D. C., & Morrongiello, B. A. (2007). Increasing children's safe pedestrian behaviors through simple skills training. *Journal of Pediatric Psychology, 32*, 475–480.

Barton, C., Alexander, J. F., Waldron, H., Turner, C. W., & Warburton, J. (1985). Generalizing treatment effects of functional family therapy: Three replications. *The American Journal of Family Therapy, 13*, 16–26.

Bass, S., Shields, M. K., & Behrman, R. E. (2004, Winter). Children, families, and foster care: Analysis and recommendations. *The Future of Children, 14*, 5–29.

Bauermeister, J. J., Matos, M., Reina, G., Salas, C. C., Martinez, J. V., Cumba, E. et al. (2005). Comparison of the DSM-IV combined and inattentive types of ADHD in a school-based sample of Latino/Hispanic children. *Journal of Child Psychology and Psychiatry, 46*, 166–179.

Baumeister, A. A., & Baumeister, A. A. (2000). Mental retardation: Causes and effects. In M. Hersen & R. T. Ammerman (Eds.), *Advanced abnormal child psychology*. Mahwah, NJ: Lawrence Erlbaum.

Bayley, N. (1969, 1993). *Bayley Scales of Infant Development: Birth to two years*. San Antonio, TX: Psychological Corporation.

Bayley, N. (2005). *Bayley Scales of Infant and Toddler Development, Third Edition (Bayley-III)*. San Antonio, TX: Harcourt Assessment.

Beail, N. (2003). What works for people with mental retardation? Critical commentary on cognitive-behavioral and psychodynamic psychotherapy research. *Mental Retardation, 41*, 468–472.

Beale, I. L. (2006). Efficacy of psychological interventions for pediatric chronic illnesses. *Journal of Pediatric Psychology, 31*, 437–451.

Bearden, C. E., Meyer, S. E., Loewy, R. L., Niendam, T. A., & Cannon, T. D. (2006). The neurodevelopmental model of schizophrenia: updated. In D. Cicchetti & D. J. Cohen (Eds.), *Developmental psychopathology. Vol. 3*. Hoboken, NJ: John Wiley & Sons.

Beardslee, W. R., Keller, M. B., Seifer, R., Lavorie, P. W., Staley, J., Podorefsky, D., & Shera, D. (1996). Prediction of adolescent affective disorder: Effects of prior parental affective disorders and child psychopathology. *Journal of the American Academy of Child and Adolescent Psychiatry, 35*, 279–288.

Beardslee, W. R., Versage, E. M., & Gladstone, T. R. G. (1998). Children of affectively ill parents: A review of the past 10 years. *Journal of the American Academy of Child and Adolescent Psychiatry, 37*, 1134–1141.

Beauchaine, T. P. (2003). Taxometrics and developmental psychopathology. *Development and Psychopathology, 15*, 501–527.

Beauchaine, T. P., Katkin, E. S., Strassberg, Z., & Snarr, J. (2001). Disinhibitory psychopathology in male adolescents: Discriminating conduct disorder from attention-deficit/hyperactivity disorder through concurrent assessment of multiple autonomic states. *Journal of Abnormal Psychology, 110*, 610–624.

Beck, A. T. (1967). *Depression: Clinical, experimental, and theoretical aspects*. New York: Harper & Row.

Beck, A. T. (1976). *Cognitive theory and emotional disorders*. New York: International Universities Press.

Becker, K. D., Stuewig, J., Herrera, V. M., & McCloskey, L. A. (2004). A study of firesetting and animal cruelty in children: Family influences and adolescent outcomes. *Journal of the American Academy of Child and Adolescent Psychiatry, 43*, 905–912.

Becker, M. A., Jordan, N., & Larsen, R. (2007). Predictors of successful permanency planning and length of stay in foster care: The role of race, diagnosis and place of residence. *Children and Youth Services Review, 29*, 1102–1113.

Behnke, S. H., & Warner, E. (2002). Confidentiality in the treatment of adolescents. *Monitor on Psychology, 33*, 44–45.

Beidel, D. C., Morris, T. L., & Turner, M. W. (2004). Social phobia. In T. L. Morris & J. S. March (Eds.), *Anxiety disorders in children and adolescents*. New York: Guilford Press.

Beidel, D. C., Silverman, W. K., & Hammond-Laurence, K. (1996). Overanxious disorder: Subsyndromal state or specific disorder? A comparison of clinic and community samples. *Journal of Clinical Child Psychology, 25*, 25–32.

Beidel, D. C., & Turner, S. M. (1997). At risk for anxiety: I. Psychopathology in the offspring of anxious parents. *Journal of the American Academy of Child and Adolescent Psychiatry, 36*, 918–924.

Beidel, D. C., Turner, S. M., & Morris, T. L. (1995). A new inventory to assess childhood social anxiety and phobia: The Social Phobia and Anxiety Inventory for Children. *Psychological Assessment, 7*, 73–79.

Beidel, D. C., Turner, S. M., & Morris, T. L. (1999). Psychopathology of childhood social phobia. *Journal of the American Academy of Child and Adolescent Psychiatry, 38*, 630–646.

Beirne-Smith, M., Ittenbach, R. F., & Patton, J. R. (1998). *Mental retardation*. Upper Saddle River, NJ: Prentice Hall.

Beirne-Smith, M., Patton, J. R., & Kim, S. H. (2006). *Mental retardation*. Upper Saddle River, NJ: Pearson.

Beitchman, J. H., Wilson, B., Brownlie, E. B., Walters, H., Inglis, A., & Lancee, W. (1996). Long-term consistency in speech/language profiles: II. behavioral, emotional, and social outcomes. *Journal of the American Academy of Child and Adolescent Psychiatry, 35*, 815–825.

Beitchman, J. H., Wilson, B., Johnson, C. J., Atkinson, L., Young, A., Adlaf, E. et al. (2001). Fourteen-year follow-up of speech/language-impaired and control children: Psychiatric outcome. *Journal of the American Academy of Child and Adolescent Psychiatry, 40*, 75–82.

Beitchman, J. H., & Young, A. R. (1997). Learning disorders with a special emphasis on reading disorders: A review of the past 10 years. *Journal of the American Academy of Child and Adolescent Psychiatry, 36*, 1020–1032.

Bell, K. E., & Stein, D. M. (1992). Behavioral treatments for pica: A review of empirical studies. *International Journal of Eating Disorders, 11*, 377–389.

Bell, R. (1985). *Holy anorexia.* Chicago: University of Chicago Press.

Bellak, L., & Abrams, D. M. (1997). *The T.A.T., C.A.T., and S.A.T. in clinical use* (6th ed.). Needham Heights, MA: Allyn and Bacon.

Bellak, L., & Bellak, S. (1982). *Children's Apperception Test (CAT).* Lutz, FL: Psychological Assessment Resources, Inc.

Belsky, J. (1980). Child maltreatment: An ecological integration. *American Psychologist, 35,* 320–335.

Belsky, J. (1993). Etiology of child maltreatment: A developmental-ecological analysis. *Psychological Bulletin, 114,* 413–434.

Belsky, J. (2001). Developmental risks (still) associated with early child care. *Journal of Child Psychology and Psychiatry, 42,* 845–859.

Belsky, J., Vandell, D. L., Burchinal, M., Clarke-Stewart, A., McCartney, K., & Owen, M. T. (2007). Are there long-term effects of early child care? *Child Development, 78,* 681–701.

Bender, L. (2003). *Bender Visual-Motor Gestalt Test, Second Edition.* San Antonio, TX: Harcourt Assessment.

Benedict, R. (1934). *Patterns of culture.* Boston: Houghton-Mifflin.

Bengtson, M. L., & Boll, T. J. (2001). Neuropsychological assessment of the child. In C. E. Walker & M. C. Roberts (Eds.), *Handbook of clinical child psychology* (3rd ed.). New York: John Wiley & Sons.

Benoit, D. (2000). Feeding disorders, failure to thrive, and obesity. In C. H. Zeanah, Jr. (Ed.), *Handbook of infant mental health* (2nd ed.). New York: Guilford Press.

Benoit, M. B. (2000). Foster care. In B. J. Sadock and V. A. Sadock (Eds.), *Comprehensive textbook of psychiatry* (Vol. II). Philadelphia: Lippincott Williams & Wilkins.

Bental, B., & Tirosh, E. (2007). The relationship between attention, executive functions, and reading domain abilities in attention deficit hyperactivity disorder and reading disorder: a comparative study. *Journal of Child Psychology and Psychiatry, 48,* 455–463.

Berger, M. (2006). A model of preverbal social development and its application to social dysfunctions in autism. *Journal of Child Psychology and Psychiatry, 47,* 338–391.

Berger, M., & Yule, W. (1985). IQ tests and assessment. In A. M. Clarke, A. D. B. Clarke, & J. M. Berg (Eds.), *Mental deficiency: The changing outlook.* New York: The Free Press.

Berninger, V. W., Abbott, R. D., Vermeulen, K. & Fulton, C. M. (2006). Paths to reading comprehension in at-risk second-grade readers. *Journal of Reading Disabilities, 39,* 334–351.

Berninger, V. W., & Amtmann, D. (2003). Preventing written expression disabilities through early and continuing assessment and intervention for handwriting and/or spelling problems: Research into practice. In H. L. Swanson, K. R. Harris, & S. Graham (Eds.), *Handbook of leaning disabilities.* New York: Guilford Press.

Bernstein, D. M. (1996). The discovery of the child: A historical perspective on child and adolescent psychiatry. In M. Lewis (Ed.), *Child and adolescent psychiatry: A comprehensive textbook.* Baltimore: Williams & Wilkins.

Bernstein, G. A., Hektner, J. M., Borchardt, C. M., & McMillan, M. H. (2001). Treatment of school refusal: One-year follow-up. *Journal of the American Academy of Child and Adolescent Psychiatry, 40,* 206–213.

Berz, J. B., Carter, A. S., Wagmiller, R. L., Horwitz, S. M., Murdock, K. K., & Briggs-Gowan, M. (2007). Prevalence and correlates of early onset asthma and wheezing in a healthy birth cohort of 2- to 3-year olds. *Journal of Pediatric Psychology, 32,* 154–166.

Bettelheim, B. (1967a). *The empty fortress.* New York: Free Press.

Bettelheim, B. (1967b, Feb. 12). *Where self begins.* New York Times.

Bettes, B. A., & Walker, E. (1987). Positive and negative symptoms in psychotic and other psychiatrically disturbed children. *Journal of Child Psychology and Psychiatry, 28,* 555–568.

Beyer, J. E., & Knott, C. (1998). Construct validity estimation for the African-American and Hispanic Oucher Scale. *Journal of Pediatric Nursing, 13,* 20–31.

Biederman, J., Faraone, S., Mick, E., Moore, P., & Lelon, E. (1996). Child Behavior Checklist findings further support comorbidity between ADHD and major depression in a referred sample. *Journal of the American Academy of Child and Adolescent Psychiatry, 35,* 734–742.

Biederman, J., Faraone, S. V., Marrs, A., Moore, P., Garcia, J., Ablon, S., et al. (1997). Panic disorder and agoraphobia in consecutively referred children and adolescents. *Journal of the American Academy of Child and Adolescent Psychiatry, 36,* 214–223.

Biederman, J., Rosenbaum, J. F., Bolduc-Murphy, E. A., Faraone, S. V., Chaloff, J., Hirshfeld, D. R., & Kagan, J. (1993). A 3–year follow-up of children with and without behavioral inhibition. *Journal of the American Academy of Child and Adolescent Psychiatry, 32,* 814–821.

Biederman, J., & Spencer, T. J. (2000). Genetics of childhood disorder: XIX. ADHD, Part 3: Is ADHD a noradrenergic disorder? *Journal of the American Academy of Child and Adolescent Psychiatry, 39,* 1330–1333.

Bierman, K. L. (2004). *Peer rejection: Developmental processes and intervention strategies.* New York: Guilford Press.

Bierman, K. L., & Schwartz, L. A. (1986). Clinical child interviews: Approaches and developmental considerations. *Journal of Child and Adolescent Psychotherapy, 3,* 267–278.

Bifulco, A., Harris, T., & Brown, G. (1992). Mourning or early inadequate care? Reexamining the relationship of maternal loss in childhood with adult depression and anxiety. *Development and Psychopathology, 4,* 433–449.

Bijou, S. W., Peterson, R. F., Harris, F. R., Allen, K. E., & Johnston, M. S. (1969). Methodology for experimental studies of young children in natural settings. *The Psychological Record, 19,* 177–210.

Binggeli, N. J., Hart, S. N., & Brassard, M. R. (2001). *Psychological maltreatment of children.* Thousand Oaks, CA: Sage Publications.

Birch, S. H., & Ladd, G. W. (1998). Children's interpersonal behavior and the teacher-child relationship. *Developmental Psychology, 34,* 934–946.

Bird, H. R. (1996). Epidemiology of childhood disorders in a cross-cultural context. *Journal of Child Psychology and Psychiatry, 37,* 35–50.

Birmaher, B., & Axelson, D. (2005). Bipolar disorder in children and adolescents. In A. Marneros & F. Goodwin (Eds.), *Bipolar disorders: Mixed states, rapid cycling, and atypical forms.* Cambridge, UK: Cambridge University Press.

Birmaher, B., Brent, D., Chiapetta, L., Bridge, J., Monga, S., & Bauger, M. (1999). Psychometric properties for the Screen for Child Anxiety Related Emotional Disorders (SCARED): A replication study. *Journal of the American Academy of Child and Adolescent Psychiatry, 38,* 1230–1236.

Birmaher, B., Khetarpal, S., Brent, D., Cully, M., Balach, L., Kaufman, J., & McKenzie Neer, S. (1997). The Screen for Child Anxiety Related Emotional Disorders (SCARED): Scale construction and psychometric characteristics. *Journal of the American Academy of Child and Adolescent Psychiatry, 36,* 545–553.

Birmaher, B., Ryan, N. D., Williamson, D. E., Brent, D. A., Kaufman, J., Dahl, R. E., Perel, J., & Nelson, B. (1996). Childhood and adolescent depression: A review of the past 10 years. Part I. *Journal of the American Academy of Child and Adolescent Psychiatry, 35,* 1427–1439.

Birmingham, C. L., Su, J., Hlynsky, J. A., Goldner, E. M., & Gao, M. (2005). The mortality rate from anorexia nervosa. *International Journal of Eating Disorders, 38,* 143–146.

Bishop, D. V. M. (1992). The underlying nature of specific language impairment. *Journal of Child Psychology and Psychiatry, 33,* 3–66.

Bishop, D. V. M. (2002). Speech and language difficulties. In M. Rutter & E. Taylor (Eds.), *Child and adolescent psychiatry,* Oxford, UK: Blackwell Publishing.

Black, B., & Uhde, T. W. (1995). Psychiatric characteristics of children with selective mutism: A pilot study. *Journal of the American Academy of Child and Adolescent Psychiatry, 34,* 847–856.

Blackman, J. A., & Gurka, M. J. (2007). Developmental and behavioral comorbidities of asthma in children. *Journal of Developmental & Behavioral Pediatrics, 28,* 92–99.

Blader, J. C., & Carlson, G. A. (2007). Increased rates of bipolar disorder diagnoses among U.S. child, adolescent, and adult inpatients, 1996–2004. *Biological Psychiatry, 62,* 107–114.

Blader, J. C., Koplewicz, H. C., Abikoff, H., & Foley, C. (1997). Sleep problems of elementary school children: A community survey. *Archives of Pediatrics and Adolescent Medicine, 151,* 473–480.

Blagg, N., & Yule, W. (1994). School refusal. In T. H. Ollendick, N. J. King, & W. Yule (Eds.), *International handbook of phobic and anxiety disorders in children and adolescents.* New York: Plenum Press.

Blakemore, S.-J., & Choudhury, S. (2006). Development of the adolescent brain: Implications for executive functions and social cognition. *Journal of Child Psychology and Psychiatry, 47,* 296–312.

Bleil, M. E., Ramesh, S., Miller, B. D., & Wood, B. L. (2000). The influence of parent-child relatedness on depressive symptoms in children with asthma: Tests of moderator and mediator models. *Journal of Pediatric Psychology, 25,* 481–491.

Blount, R. L., Piira, T., & Cohen, L. L. (2003). Management of pediatric pain and distress due to medical procedures. In M. C. Roberts (Eds.), *Handbook of pediatric psychology* (3rd ed.). New York: Guilford Press.

Boden, C., & Giaschi, D. (2007). M-stream deficits and reading-related visual processes in developmental dyslexia. *Psychological Bulletin, 133,* 346–366.

Bodfish, J. W., Symons, F. J., Parker, D. E., & Lewis, M. H. (2000). Varieties of repetitive behavior in autism: Comparisons to mental retardation. *Journal of Autism and Developmental Disorders, 30,* 237–243.

Bogels, S. M., & Brechman-Toussaint, M. L. (2006). Family issues in child anxiety: Attachment, family functioning, parental rearing and beliefs. *Clinical Psychology Review, 26,* 834–856.

Bolger, K. E., & Patterson, C. J. (2001). Developmental pathways from child maltreatment to peer rejection. *Child Development, 72,* 549–568.

Bolton, D., Eley, T. C., O'Connor, T. G., Perrin, S., Rabe-Hesketh, S., Fijsdilk, F., & Smith, P. (2006). Prevalence and genetic and environmental influences on anxiety disorders in 6-year-old twins. *Psychological Medicine, 36,* 335–344.

Bongers, I. L., Koot, H. M., van der Ende, J., & Verhulst, F. C. (2003). The normative development of child and adolescent problem behavior. *Journal of Abnormal Psychology, 112,* 179–192.

Bonner, B. L., Kaufman, K. L., Harbeck, C., & Brassard, M. R. (1992). Child maltreatment. In C. E. Walker & M. C. Roberts (Eds.), *Handbook of clinical child psychology.* New York: Wiley.

Boomsma, D. I., van Beijsterveldt, C. E. M., & Hudziak, J. J. (2005). Genetic and environmental influences on anxious/depression during childhood: A study from the Netherlands twin register. *Genes, Brain, and Behavior, 48,* 466–481.

Bordeaux, J. D., Loveland, K. A., Lachar, D., Stehbens, J., Bell, T. S., Nichols, S. et al. (2003). Hemophilia growth and development study: Caregiver report of youth and family adjustment to HIV disease and immunologic compromise. *Journal of Pediatric Psychology, 28,* 175–183.

Bosquet, M., & Egeland, B. (2006). The development and maintenance of anxiety symptoms from infancy through adolescence in a longitudinal sample. *Development and Psychopathology, 18,* 517–550.

Bower, G. (2004, Sept. 11). A very spatial brain defect. *Science-News, 166,* 165–166.

Bowlby, J. (1960). Grief and mourning in infancy and early childhood. *Psychoanalytic Study of the Child, 15,* 9–52.

Braddock, D., Rizzolo, M. C., & Hemp, R. (2004). Most employment services growth in developmental disabilities during 1988–2002 was in segregated settings. *Mental Retardation, 42,* 317–320.

Bradley, R. H., Whiteside, L., Mundfrom, D. J., Casey, P. H., Kelleher, K. J., & Pope, S. K. (1994). Contributions of early interventions and early caregiving experiences to resilience in low-birthweight, premature children living in poverty. *Journal of Clinical Child Psychology, 23,* 425–434.

Bradley, R. H., & Whiteside-Mansell, L. (1997). Children in poverty. In R. T. Ammerman & M. Hersen (Eds.), *Handbook of prevention and treatment with children and adolescents.* New York: John Wiley.

Brame, B., Nagin, D. S., & Tremblay, R. E. (2001). Developmental trajectories of physical aggression from school entry to late adolescence. *Journal of Child Psychology and Psychiatry, 42,* 503–512.

Brassard, M. R., Hart, S. N., & Hardy, D. B. (2000). Psychological and emotional abuse of children. In R. T. Ammerman & M. Hersen, (Eds.), *Case studies in family violence* (2nd ed.). New York: Kluwer Academic/Plenum Publishers.

Braungart-Rieker, J., Rende, R. D., Plomin, R., DeFries, J. C., & Fulker, D. W. (1995). Genetic mediation of longitudinal associations between family environment and childhood behavior problems. *Development and Psychopathology, 7,* 233–245.

Braver, S. L., Ellman, I. M., & Fabricius, W. V. (2003). Relocation of children after divorce and children's best interests: New evidence and legal considerations. *Journal of Family Psychology, 17,* 206–219.

Bray, M. A., Kehle, T. J., Theodore, L. A., & Peck, H. L. (2006). Respiratory impairments. In L. Phelps (Ed.), *Chronic health-related disorders in children: Collaborative medical and psychoeducational interventions.* Washington, DC: American Psychological Association.

Bray, N. W., Fletcher, K. L., & Turner, L. A. (1997). Cognitive competencies and strategy use in individuals with mental retardation. In W. E. MacLean (Ed.), *Ellis' handbook of mental deficiency, psychological theory and research.* Mahwah, NJ: Lawrence Erlbaum.

Bregman, J. D., & Gerdtz, J. (1997). Behavioral interventions. In D. J. Cohen & F. R. Volkmar (Eds.), *Handbook of autism and pervasive developmental disorders.* New York: John Wiley.

Breier, J. I., Simos, P. G., Fletcher, J. M., Castillo, E. M., Zhang, W., & Papanicolaou, A. C. (2003). Abnormal activation of temporoparietal language areas during phonetic analysis in children with dyslexia. *Neuropsychology, 17,* 610–621.

Bremner, J. D. (2006). Traumatic stress from a multiple-levels-of-analysis perspective. In D. Cicchetti & D. J. Cohen (Eds.), *Developmental psychopathology. Vol. 2. Developmental neuroscience.* (2nd ed.). Hoboken, NJ: John Wiley & Sons.

Brendgen, M., Vitaro, F., Tremblay, R. E., & Lavoie, F. (2001). Reactive and proactive aggression: Predictions to physical violence in different contexts and moderating effects of parental monitoring and caregiving behavior. *Journal of Abnormal Child Psychology, 29,* 293–304.

Brennan, P. A., Le Brocque, R., & Hammen, C. (2003). Maternal depression, parent-child relationships, and resilient outcomes in adolescence. *Journal of the American Academy of Child and Adolescent Psychiatry, 42,* 1469–1477.

Brennan, P. A., & Walker, E. F. (2001). Vulnerability to schizophrenia: Risk factors in childhood and adolescence. In R. E. Ingram & J. M. Price (Eds.), *Vulnerability to psychopathology: Risk across the lifespan.* New York: The Guilford Press.

Brent, D., Holder, D., Kolko, D., Birmaher, B., Baugher, M., Roth, C., Iyenagar, S., Johnson, B. (1997). A clinical psychotherapy trial for adolescent depression comparing cognitive, family, and supportive therapy. *Archives of General Psychiatry, 54,* 877–885.

Brent, D. A. (2006). Commentary: Glad for what TADS adds, but many TADS grads still sad. *Journal of the American Academy of Child and Adolescent Psychiatry, 45,* 1461–1464.

Brestan, E. V., & Eyberg, S. M. (1998). Effective psychosocial treatments of conduct-disordered children and adolescents: 29 years, 82 studies, and 5,272 kids. *Journal of Clinical Child Psychology, 27,* 180–189.

Breton, J.-J., Bergeron, L., Valla, J.-P., Berthiaume, C., & Gaudet, N. (1999). Quebec child mental health survey: Prevalence of DSM-III-R mental health disorders. *Journal of Child Psychology and Psychiatry, 40,* 375–384.

Briggs, K., Hubbs-Tait, L., Culp, R. E., & Morse, A. S. (1994). Sexual abuse label: Adults' expectations for children. *The American Journal of Family Therapy, 22,* 304–314.

Brinkmeyer, M. Y., & Eyberg, S. M. (2003). Parent-child interaction therapy for oppositional children. In A. E. Kazdin & J. R.

Weisz (Eds.), *Evidence-based psychotherapies for children and adolescents.* New York: Guilford Press.

Brodeur, D. A., & Pond, M. (2001). The development of selective attention in children with attention deficit hyperactivity disorder. *Journal of Abnormal Child Psychology, 29,* 229–239.

Brody, G. H., Chen, Y. F., Murry, V. M., Ge, X., Simons, R. L., Gibbons, F. X. et al. (2006). Perceived discrimination and the adjustment of African American youths: A five-year longitudinal analysis with contextual moderation effects. *Child Development, 77,* 1170–1189.

Brody, G. H., Ge, X., Conger, R., Gibbons, F. X., Murry, V. M., Gerrard, M., & Simons, R. L. (2001). The influence of neighborhood disadvantage, collective socialization, and parenting on African-American children's affiliation with deviant peers. *Child Development, 72,* 1231–1246.

Broman, S., Nichols, P. L., Shaughnessy, P., & Kennedy, W. (1987). *Retardation in young children: A developmental study of cognitive deficit.* Hillsdale, NJ: Erlbaum.

Bronfenbrenner, U. (1977). Toward an experimental ecology of human development. *American Psychologist, 32,* 320–335.

Brooks-Gunn, J. (1993). Why do adolescents have difficulty adhering to health regimes? In N. A. Krasnegor, L. Epstein, S. B. Johnson, & S. Yaffe (Eds.), *Developmental aspects of health compliance behavior.* Hillsdale, NJ: Lawrence Erlbaum Associates.

Brooks-Gunn, J., Auth, J. J., Peterson, A. C., & Compas, B. E. (2001). Physiological processes and the development of childhood and adolescent depression. In I. M. Goodyer (Ed.), *The depressed child and adolescent* (2nd ed.). Cambridge, UK: Cambridge University Press.

Brotman, L. M., Klein, R. G., Kamboukos, D., Brown, E. J., Coard, S. I., & Sosinsky, L. S. (2003). Preventive intervention for urban, low-income preschoolers at familial risk for conduct problems: A randomized pilot study. *Journal of Clinical Child and Adolescent Psychology, 32,* 246–257.

Brotman, M. A., Schmajuk, M., Rich, B. A., Dickstein, D. P., Guyer, A. E., Costello, E. J. et al. (2006). Prevalence, clinical correlates, and longitudinal course of severe mood dysregulation in children. *Biological Psychiatry, 60,* 991–997.

Brown, A. S., Bresnahan, M., & Susser, E. S. (2005). Schizophrenia: environmental epidemiology. In B. J. Sadock & V. A. Sadock (Eds.), *Comprehensive textbook of psychiatry. Vol. 1.* Philadelphia: Lippincott Williams & Wilkins.

Brown, J. V., Bakeman, R., Coles, C. D., Platzman, K. A., & Lynch, M. E. (2004). Prenatal cocaine exposure: A comparison of 2-year-old children in parental and nonparental care. *Child Development, 75,* 1282–1295.

Brown, R. T., Connelly, M., Rittle, C., & Clouse, B. (2006). A longitudinal examination predicting emergency room use in children with sickle cell disease and their caregivers. *Journal of Pediatric Psychology, 31,* 163–173.

Bruce, M. (2006). A systematic and conceptual review of posttraumatic stress in childhood cancer survivors and their parents. *Clinical Psychology Review, 26,* 233–256.

Bruch, H. (1973). *Eating disorders: Obesity, anorexia nervosa, and the person within.* New York: Basic Books.

Bruch, H. (1979). *The golden cage: The enigma of anorexia nervosa.* New York: Vintage Books.

Bruch, H. (1986). Anorexia nervosa: The therapeutic task. In K. D. Brownell & J. P. Foreyt (Eds.), *Handbook of eating disorders:*

Physiology, psychology, and treatment of obesity, anorexia, and bulimia. New York: Basic Books.

Brumberg, J. J. (1986). "Fasting girls": Reflections on writing the history of anorexia nervosa. In A. B. Smuts & J. W. Hagen (Eds.), *History and research in child development. Monographs of the Society for Research in Child Development, 50* (4–5, Serial No. 211).

Bryan, T. (1997). Assessing the personal and social status of students with learning disabilities. *Learning Disabilities Research & Practice, 12,* 63–76.

Bryant, K. (1977). Speech and language development. In M. J. Krajicek & A. I. Tearney (Eds.), *Detection of developmental problems in children.* Baltimore: University Park Press.

Buchanan, R. W., & Carpenter, W. T. (2000). Schizophrenia: introduction and overview. In B. J. Sadock & V. A. Sadock (Eds.), *Comprehensive textbook of psychiatry* (Vol. II). Philadelphia: Lippincott Williams & Wilkins.

Buck, J. N. (1992). *House-Tree-Person projective drawing technique (H-T-P): Manual and interpretive guide* (Revised by W. L. Warren). Los Angeles: Western Psychological Services.

Buckhalt, J. A., El-Sheikh, M., & Keller, P. (2007). Children's sleep and cognitive functioning: Race and socioeconomic status as moderators of effects. *Child Development, 78,* 213–231.

Buckner, J. C., Mezzacappa, E., & Beardslee, W. R. (2003). Characteristics of resilient youth living in poverty: The role of self-regulatory processes. *Development and Psychopathology, 15,* 139–162.

Budd, K. S., & Chugh, C. S. (1998). Common feeding problems in young children. In T. H. Ollendick & R. J. Prinz (Eds.), *Advances in clinical child psychology* (Vol. 20). New York: Plenum Press.

Bukowski, W. M., & Adams, R. (2005). Peer relationships and psychopathology: Markers, moderators, mediators, mechanisms, and meanings. *Journal of Clinical Child and Adolescent Psychology, 34,* 3–10.

Bulik, C. M., Wade, T. D., & Kendler, K. S. (2001). Characteristics of monozygotic twins discordant for bulimia nervosa. *International Journal of Eating Disorders, 29,* 1–10.

Burack, J. A. (1990). Differentiating mental retardation: The two-group approach and beyond. In R. M. Hodapp, J. A. Burack, & E. Zigler (Eds.), *Issues in the developmental approach to mental retardation.* New York: Cambridge University Press.

Burack, J. A., Root, R., & Zigler, E. (1997). Inclusive education for students with autism: Reviewing ideological, empirical, and community considerations. In D. J. Cohen and F. R. Volkmar (Eds.), *Handbook of autism and pervasive developmental disorders.* New York: John Wiley.

Burke, E. J., & Andrasik, F. (1989). Home vs. clinic-based biofeedback treatment for pediatric migraine: Results of treatment through one-year follow-up. *Headache, 29,* 434–440.

Burke, J. D., Loeber, R., Lahey, B. B., & Rathouz, P. J. (2005). Developmental transitions among affective and behavioral disorders in adolescent boys. *Journal of Child Psychology and Psychiatry, 46,* 1200–1210.

Burns, R.C. (1987). *Kinetic House-Tree-Person Drawings: K-H-T-P: An interpretive manual.* London: Routledge.

Burt, S. A., Krueger, R. F., McGue, M., & Iacono, W. G. (2001). Sources of covariation among attention-deficit/hyperactivity disorder, oppositional defiant disorder, and conduct disorder:

The importance of shared environment. *Journal of Abnormal Psychology, 110,* 516–525.

Bushman, B. J., & Anderson, C. A. (2001). Media violence and the American public: Scientific facts versus media misinformation. *American Psychologist, 56,* 477–489.

Butzlaff, R. L., & Hooley, J. M. (1998). Expressed emotion and psychiatric relapse. *Archives of general psychiatry, 55,* 547–552.

Cabrera, N. J., Tamis-LeMonda, C. S., Bradley, R. H., Hofferth, S., & Lamb, M. E. (2000). Fatherhood in the twenty-first century. *Child Development, 71,* 127–136.

Cadesky, E. B., Mota, V. L., & Schachar, R. J. (2000). Beyond words: How do children with ADHD and/or conduct problems process nonverbal information about affect? *Journal of the American Academy of Child and Adolescent Psychiatry, 39,* 1160–1167.

Calderoni, D., Wudarsky, M., Bhangoo, R., Dell, M. L., Nicolson, R., Hamburger, S. D. et al. (2001). Differentiating childhood-onset schizophrenia from psychotic mood disorders. *Journal of the American Academy of Child and Adolescent Psychiatry, 40,* 1190–1196.

Campbell., F. A., & Ramey, C.T. (1994). Effects of early intervention on intellectual and academic achievement: A follow-up study of children from low-income families. *Child Development, 65,* 684–698.

Campbell, F. A., Ramey, C. T., Pungello, E. P., Miller-Johnson, S., & Burchinal, M. (2001). The development of cognitive and academic abilities: Growth curves from an early childhood educational experiment. *Developmental Psychology, 37,* 231–242.

Campbell, S. B. (1995). Behavior problems in preschool children: A review of recent research. *Journal of Child Psychology and Psychiatry, 36,* 113–149.

Campbell, S. B. (2000). Attention-deficit/hyperactivity disorder. In A. J. Sameroff, M. Lewis, & S. M. Miller (Eds.), *Handbook of developmental psychopathology.* New York: Kluwer Academic/ Plenum.

Campbell, S. B. (2002). *Behavior problems in preschool children.* New York: The Guilford Press.

Campbell, S. B., Spieker, S., Burchinal, M., Poe, M. D., & the NICHD Early Child Care Research Network. (2006). Trajectories of aggression from toddlerhood to age 9 predict academic and social functioning through age 12. *Journal of Child Psychology and Psychiatry, 47,* 791–800.

Candy-Gibbs, S. E., Sharp, K. C., & Petrun, C. J. (1985). The effects of age, object, and cultural/religious background on children's concepts of death. *Omega Journal of Death and Dying, 15,* 329–346.

Canino, G., Shrout, P. E., Rugio-Stipic, M., Bird, H. R., Bravo, M., Ramirez, R. et al. (2004). The DSM-IV rates of child and adolescent disorders in Puerto Rico. *Archives of General Psychiatry, 61,* 85–93.

Cannon, T. D., & Rosso, I. M. (2002). Levels of analysis in etiological research on schizophrenia. *Development and Psychopathology, 14,* 653–666.

Cantor, S., & Kestenbaum, C. (1986). Psychotherapy with schizophrenic children. *Journal of the American Academy of Child Psychiatry, 25,* 623–630.

Cantwell, D. P. (1980). The diagnostic process and diagnostic classification in child psychiatry: DSM-III. *Journal of the American Academy of Child Psychiatry, 19,* 345–355.

Cao, F., Bitan, T., Chou, T-L., Burman, D. D., & Booth, J. R. (2006). Deficient orthographic and phonological representations in children with dyslexia revealed by brain activation patterns. *Journal of Child Psychology and Psychiatry, 47,* 1041–1050.

Capaldi, D., DeGarmo, D., Patterson, G. R., & Forgatch, M. (2002). Contextual risk across the early life span and association with antisocial behavior. In J. B. Reid, G. R. Patterson, & J. Snyder (Eds.), *Antisocial behavior in children and adolescents: A developmental analysis and model for intervention.* Washington, DC: American Psychological Association.

Capizzano, J., Tout, K., & Adams, G. (2000). Child care patterns of school-age children with employed mothers. Washington, DC: Urban Institute.

Caplan, G. (1964). *The principles of preventive psychiatry.* New York: Basic Books.

Caplan, R. (1994). Thought disorder in childhood. *Journal of the American Academy of Child and Adolescent Psychiatry, 33,* 605–615.

Caplan, R., Guthrie, D., Tang, B., Komo, S., & Asarnow, R. F. (2000). Thought disorder in childhood schizophrenia: Replication and update of concept. *Journal of the American Academy of Child and Adolescent Psychiatry, 39,* 771–778.

Capone, G. T. (2001). Down syndrome: Advances in molecular biology and the neurosciences. *Developmental and behavioral pediatrics, 22,* 40–59.

Carey, M. E., Hockenberry, J. J., Moore, I. M., Hutter, J. J., Krull, K. R., Pasvogel, A., & Kaemingk, K. L. (2007). Effect of intravenous methotrexate dose and infusion rate on neuropsychological function one year after diagnosis of acute lymphoblastic leukemia. *Journal of Pediatric Psychology, 32,* 189–193.

Carlson, G. A., & Cantwell, D. P. (1980). Unmasking masked depression in children and adolescents. *American Journal of Psychiatry, 137,* 445–449.

Carpenter, P. J. (1992). Perceived control as a predictor of distress in children undergoing invasive medical procedures. *Journal of Pediatric Psychology, 17,* 757–773.

Carrey, N., & Ungar, M. (2007). Resilience theory and the diagnostic and statistical manual: Incompatible bed fellows? *Child and Adolescent Psychiatric Clinics of North America, 16,* 497–513.

Carroll, J. M., Maughan, B., Goodman, R., & Meltzer, H. (2005). Literacy difficulties and psychiatric disorders: evidence for comorbidity. *Journal of Child Psychology and Psychiatry, 46,* 524–532.

Carroll, J. M., & Snowling, M. J. (2004). Language and phonological skills in children at high risk of reading difficulties. *Journal of Child Psychology and Psychiatry, 45,* 631–640.

Carson, C., & Rutter, M. (1991). Comorbidity in child psychopathology: Concepts, issues and research strategies. *Journal of Child Psychology and Psychiatry, 32,* 1063–1080.

Carter, A. S., Volkmar, F. R., Sparrow, S. S., Wang, J-J., Lord, C., Dawson, G. et al. (1998). The Vineland Adaptive Behavior Scales: Supplementary norms for individuals with autism. *Journal of Autism and Developmental Disorders, 28,* 287–302.

Cartwright-Hatton, S., McNicol, K., & Doubleday, F. (2006). Anxiety in a neglected population: Prevalence of anxiety disorders in pre-adolescent children. *Clinical Psychology Review, 26,* 817–833.

Casanova, M. F., Buxhoeveden, D. P., Switala, A. E., & Roy, E. (2002). Minicolumnar pathology in autism. *Neurology, 58,* 428–432.

Casey, B. J., Castellanos, F. X., Giedd, J. N., Marsh, W. L., Hamburger, S. D., Schubert, A. B., Vauss, Y. C., Vaituzis, A. C., Dickstein, D. P., Sarfatti, S. E., & Rapoport, J. L. (1997). Implication of right frontostriatal circuity in response inhibition and Attention-deficit/Hyperactivity Disorder. *Journal of the American Academy of Child and Adolescent Psychiatry, 36,* 374–383.

Caspi, A., Elder, G. H. Jr., & Bem, D. J. (1987). Moving against the world: Life-course patterns of explosive children. *Developmental Psychology, 23,* 308–313.

Caspi, A., & Moffitt, T. E. (1995). The continuity of maladaptive behavior: From description to understanding in the study of antisocial behavior. In D. Cicchetti & D. J. Cohen (Eds.), *Developmental psychopathology.* (Vol 2: Risk, disorder, and adaptation). New York: John Wiley & Sons.

Caspi, A., Sudgen, K., Moffitt, T. E., Taylor, A., Craig. I. W., Harrington, H. et al. (2003). Influence of life stress on depression: Moderation by a polymorphism in the 5–HTT gene. *Science, 301,* 386–389.

Catalan, J. (2000). Sexuality, reproductive cycle and suicidal behaviour. In K. Hawton & K. van Heeringen (Eds.), *The international handbook of suicide and attempted suicide.* Chichester, UK: John Wiley & Sons, LTD.

CATS Consortium. (2007). Implementing CBT for traumatized children and adolscents after September 11: Lessons learned from the Child and Adolescent Trauma Treatments and Services (CATS) Project. *Journal of Clinical Child Psychology, 36,* 581–592.

Caughty, M. O., O'Campo, P. J., Randolph, S. M., & Nickerson, K. (2002). The influence of racial socialization practices on the cognitive and behavioral competence of African American preschoolers. *Child Development, 73,* 1611–1625.

Cavell, T. A., Ennett, S. T., & Meehan, B. T. (2001). Preventing alcohol and substance abuse. In J. N. Hughes, A. M. La Greca, & J. C. Conoley (Eds.), *Handbook of psychological services for children and adolescents.* New York: Oxford University Press.

Cawley, J. (2006). Markets and childhood obesity policy. *The Future of Children, 16,* 69–88.

CDC Press Release (2007). *CDC releases new data on autism spectrum disorders (ASDs) from multiple communities in the United States.* Retrieved September 20, 2007 from http://www.cdc.gov/od/oc/media/pressrel/2007/r070208.htm.

Center for Adoption Research and Policy. Homepage: *Frequently asked questions.* Retrieved September, 2004 from www.centerforadoptionresearch.org.

Centers for Disease Control and Prevention. (2007). *WISQARS^{TM} Web-based Inquiry Statistics Query and Reporting System.* Retrieved September 30, 2007, from: http://www.cdc.gov/ncipc/wisqars/

Centers for Disease Control and Prevention: National Center for Health Statistics. (2007). *Prevalence of overweight among children and adolescents: United States, 2003–2004.* Retrieved September 2007, from http://www.cdc.gov/nchs/products/pubd/hestats/overweight_child_o3.htm

Cervellione, K. L., Burdick, K. E., Cottone, J. G., Rhinewine, J. P., & Kurma, S. (2007). Neurocognitive deficits in adolescents with schizophrenia: longitudinal stability and predictive utility for short-term functional outcome. *Journal of the American Academy of Child and Adolescent Psychiatry, 46,* 867–878.

Chamberlain, P., Fisher, P. A., & Moore, K. (2002). Multidimensional Treatment Foster Care: Application of the OSLC intervention model to high-risk youth and their families. In J. B. Reid, G. R. Patterson, & J. Snyder (Eds.), *Antisocial behavior in children and adolescents: A developmental analysis and model for intervention.* Washington, DC: American Psychological Association.

Chamberlain, P., & Smith, D. K. (2003). Antisocial behavior in children and adolescents: The Oregon multidimensional treatment foster care model. In A. E. Kazdin & J. R. Weisz (Eds.), *Evidence-based psychotherapies for children and adolescents.* New York: Guilford Press.

Chambers, R. A., Taylor, J. R., & Potenza, M. N. (2003). Developmental neurocircuitry of motivation in adolescence: A critical period of addiction vulnerability. *American Journal of Psychiatry, 160,* 1041–1052.

Chambless, D. L. (1996). In defense of dissemination of empirically supported psychological interventions. *Clinical Psychology: Science and Practice, 3,* 230–235.

Chambless, D. L., & Hollon, S. D. (1998). Defining empirically supported therapies. *Journal of Consulting and Clinical Psychology, 66,* 7–18.

Chambless, D. L., Sanderson, W. C., Shoham, V., Bennett Johnson, S., Pope, K. S., Crits-Cristoph, P., Baker, M., Johnson, B., Woody, S. R., Sue, S., Beutler, L., Williams, D. A., & McCurry, S. (1996). An update on empirically validated therapies. *The Clinical Psychologist, 49(2),* 5–18.

Chandler, L. A. (2003). The projective hypothesis and the development of projective techniques for children. In C. R. Reynolds & R. W. Kamphaus (Eds.), *Handbook of psychological & educational assessment of children: Personality, behavior, and context* (2nd ed.). New York: Guilford Press.

Chang, S. M., Walker, S. P., Grantham-McGregor, S., & Powell, C. A. (2002). Early childhood stunting and later behaviour and school achievement. *Journal of Child Psychology and Psychiatry, 43,* 775–783.

Chapman, R. S. (2000). Children's language learning: An interactionist perspective. *Journal of Child Psychology and Psychiatry, 4,* 33–54.

Charmon, T., & Baird, G. (2002). Practitioner review: Diagnosis of autism spectrum disorder in 2- and 3-year-old children. *Journal of Child Psychology and Psychiatry, 43,* 289–305.

Charney, D. S., Barlow, D. H., Botterman, K., Cohen, J. D., Goldman, D., Gur, R. et al. (2002). Neuroscience research agenda to guide development of a pathophysiologically based classification system. In D. J. Kupfer, M. B. First, & D. A. Regier (Eds.), *A research agenda for DSM-V.* Washington, DC: American Psychiatric Association.

Chassin, L., Curran, P. J., Hussong, A. M., & Colder, C. R. (1996). The relation of parental alcoholism to adolescent substance use: A longitudinal follow-up study. *Journal of Abnormal Psychology, 105,* 70–80.

Chassin, L., Presson, C. C., Todd, M., Rose, J., & Sherman, S. J. (1998). Maternal socialization of adolescent smoking: The intergenerational transmission of parenting and smoking. *Developmental Psychology, 34,* 1189–1201.

Chassin, L., Ritter, J., Trim, R. S., & King, K. M. (2003). Adolescent substance use disorders. In E. J. Mash & R. A. Barkley (Eds.), *Child psychopathology* (2nd ed.). New York: Guilford Press.

Chavira, D. A., & Stein, M. B. (2005). Childhood social anxiety disorder: From understanding to treatment. *Child and Adolescent Psychiatric Clinics of North America, 14,* 797–818.

Chavira, D. A., Shipon-Blum, E., Hitchcock, C., Cohan, S., & Stein, M. B. (2007). Selective mutism and social anxiety disorder: All in the family? *Journal of the American Academy of Child and Adolescent Psychiatry, 46* 1464–1472.

Chawarska, K., Klin, A., Paul, R., & Volkmar, F. (2007). Autism spectrum disorder in the second year: stability and change in syndrome expression. *Journal of Child Psychology and Psychiatry, 48,* 128–138.

Chess, S., & Thomas, A. (1972). Differences in outcome with early intervention in children with behavior disorders. In M. Roff, L. Robins, & M. Pollack (Eds.), *Life history research in psychopathology,* Vol. 2. Minneapolis: University of Minnesota Press.

Chess, S., & Thomas, A. (1977). Temperamental individuality from childhood to adolescence. *Journal of the American Academy of Child Psychiatry, 16,* 218–226.

Children on the Brink. 2004. *A joint report of new orphan estimates and a framework for action.* Retrieved September 30, 2004 from http://www.UNAIDS.org.

Childress, A. C., Brewerton, T. D., Hodges, E. L., & Jarrell, M. P. (1993). The Kids' Eating Disorders Survey (KEDS): A study of middle school students. *Journal of the American Academy of Child and Adolescent Psychiatry, 32,* 843–850.

Chipungu, S. S., & Bent-Goodley, T. B. (2004). Meeting the challenges of contemporary foster care. *The Future of Children, 14,* 75–93.

Chorpita, B. F. (2001). Control and the development of negative emotions. In M. W. Vasey & M. R. Dadds (Eds.), *The developmental psychopathology of anxiety.* New York: Oxford University Press.

Chorpita, B. F. (2002). The tripartite model and dimensions of anxiety and depression: An examination of structure in a large school sample. *Journal of Abnormal Child Psychology, 30,* 177–190.

Chorpita, B. F. (2003). The frontier of evidence-based practice. In A. E. Kazdin & J. R. Weisz (Eds.), *Evidence-based psychotherapies for children and adolescents.* New York: Guilford Press.

Chorpita, B. F., & Barlow, D. H. (1998). The development of anxiety: The role of control in the early environment. *Psychological Bulletin, 124,* 3–21.

Chorpita, B. F., Becker, K. D., & Daleiden, E. L. (2007). Understanding the common elements of evidence-based practice: Misconceptions and clinical examples. *Journal of the American Academy of Child and Adolescent Psychiatry, 46,* 647–652.

Chorpita, B. F., & Southam-Gerow, M. A. (2006). Fears and anxieties. In E. J. Mash & R. A. Barkley (Eds.), *Treatment of childhood disorders* (3rd ed.). New York: The Guilford Press.

Christophersen, E. R., & Mortweet, S. L. (2001). *Treatments that work with children: Empirically supported strategies for managing childhood problems.* Washington, DC: American Psychological Association.

Chronis, A. M., Pelham, W. E., Gnagy, E. M., Roberts, J. E., & Aronoff, H. R. (2003). The impact of late-afternoon stimulant dosing for children with ADHD on parent and parent-child domains. *Journal of Clinical Child and Adolescent Psychology, 32,* 118–126.

Chung, H. L., & Steinberg, L. (2006). Relations between neighborhood factors, parenting behaviors, peer deviance, and delinquency among serious juvenile offenders. *Developmental Psychology, 42,* 319–331.

Cicchetti, D. (1984). The emergence of developmental psychopathology. *Child Development, 55,* 1–7.

Cicchetti, D. (1989). Developmental psychology: Some thoughts on its evolution. *Development and Psychopathology, 1,* 1–3.

Cicchetti, D. (2006). Development and psychopathology. In D. Cicchetti & D. J. Cohen (Eds.). *Developmental psychopathology. Vol. 1: Theory and method.* Hoboken, NJ: John Wiley & Sons.

Cicchetti, D., & Hinshaw, S. P. (2002). Editorial: Prevention and intervention science: Contributions to developmental theory. *Development and Psychopathology, 14,* 667–671.

Cicchetti, D., & Luthar, S. S. (1999). Developmental approaches to substance use and abuse. *Development and Psychopathology, 11,* 655–656.

Cicchetti, D., & Lynch, M. (1995). Failures in the expectable environment and their impact on individual development: The case of child maltreatment. In D. Cicchetti & D. J. Cohen (Eds.), *Developmental psychopathology: Risk, disorder, and adaptation* (Vol. 2). New York: John Wiley & Sons.

Cicchetti, D., & Manly, J. T. (2001). Operationalizing child maltreatment: Developmental processes and outcomes. *Development and Psychopathology, 13,* 755–757.

Cicchetti, D., & Olsen, K. (1990). The developmental psychopathology of child maltreatment. In M. Lewis & S. M. Miller (Eds.), *Handbook of developmental psychopathology.* New York: Plenum Press.

Cicchetti, D., & Rogosch, F. A. (2001). The impact of child maltreatment and psychopathology on neuroendocrine functioning. *Development and Psychopathology, 13,* 783–804.

Cicchetti, D., & Rogosch, F. A. (2002). A developmental psychopathology perspective on adolescence. *Journal of Consulting and Clinical Psychology, 70,* 6–20.

Cicchetti, D., & Sroufe, L. A. (2000). Editorial: The past as prologue to the future: The times, they've been a-changin'. *Development and Psychopathology, 12,* 255–264.

Cicchetti, D., Toth, S., & Bush, M. (1988). Developmental psychopathology and incompetence in childhood: Suggestions for intervention. In B. B. Lahey & A. E. Kazdin (Eds.), *Advances in clinical child psychology,* Vol. 11. New York: Plenum.

Cicchetti, D., & Toth, S. L. (1998). The development of depression in children and adolescents. *American Psychologist, 53,* 221–241.

Cicchetti, D., Toth, S. L., & Maughan, A. (2000). An ecological-transactional model of child maltreatment. In A. J. Sameroff, M. Lewis, & S. M. Miller (Eds.), *Handbook of developmental psychopathology* (2nd ed.). New York: Kluwer Academic/Plenum Publishers.

Cirino, P. T., Fletcher, J. M., Ewing-Cobbs, L., Barnes, M. A., & Fuchs, L. S. (2007). Cognitive arithmetic differences in learning difficulty groups and the role of behavioral inattention. *Learning Disabilities Research & Practice, 22,* 25–35.

Clarizio, H. F. (1994). Assessment of depression in children and adolescents by parents, teachers, and peers. In W. M. Reynolds and H. F. Johnston (Eds.), *Handbook of depression in children and adolescents.* New York: Plenum Press.

Clark, C., Prior, M., & Kinsella, G. (2002). The relationship between executive function abilities, adaptive behavior, and academic achievement in children with externalizing behaviour problems. *Journal of Child Psychology and Psychiatry, 43,* 785–796.

Clark, D. B., Smith, M. G., Neighbors, B. D., Skerlec, L. M., & Randall, J. (1994). Anxiety disorders in adolescence: Characteristics, prevalence, and comorbidities. *Clinical Psychology Review, 14,* 113–137.

Clark, K. B., Chein, I., & Cook, S. W. (2004). The effects of segregation and the consequences of desegregation: A (September 1952) Social Science Statement in the *Brown v. Board of Education of Topeka* Supreme Court Case. *American Psychologist, 59,* 495–501.

Clark, L., & Tiggemann, M. (2007). Sociocultural influences and body image in 9- to 12-year-old girls: The role of appearance schemas. *Journal of Clinical Child and Adolescent Psychology, 36,* 76–86.

Clark, L. A., & Watson, D. (1991). Tripartite model of anxiety and depression: Psychometric evidence and taxonomic implications. *Journal of Abnormal Psychology, 100,* 316–336.

Clark, R., Anderson, N. B., Clark, V. R., & Williams, D. R. (1999). Racism as a stressor for African Americans. *American Psychologist, 54,* 805–816.

Clarke, G. N., Hawkins, W., Murphy, M., Sheeber, L. B., Lewinsohn, P. M. & Seeley, J. R. (1995). Targeted depression of unipolar depressive disorder in an at-risk sample of high school adolescents: A randomized trial of a group cognitive intervention. *Journal of the American Academy of Child and Adolescent Psychiatry, 34,* 312–321.

Clarke, G. N., Hornbrook, M. C., Lynch, F. L., Polen, M. R., Cale, J., O'Connor, E. et al. (2001). A randomized trial of a group cognitive intervention for preventing depression in adolescent offspring of depressed parents. *Archives of General Psychiatry, 58,* 1127–1134.

Clarke, G. N., Hornbrook, M. C., Lynch, F. L., Polen, M., Gale, J., O'Connor, E. A. et al. (2001). A randomized trial of a group cognitive intervention for preventing depression in adolescent offspring of depressed parents. *Archives of General Psychiatry, 58,* 1127–1134.

Clarke, G. N., Rhode, P., Lewinsohn, P. M., Hops, H., & Seeley, J. R. (1999). Cognitive-behavioral treatment for adolescent depression: Efficacy of acute group treatment and booster sessions. *Journal of the American Academy of Child and Adolescent Psychiatry, 38,* 272–279.

Clegg, J., Hollis, C., Mawhood, L., & Rutter, M. (2005). Developmental language disorders—a follow-up in later adult life: Cognitive, language, and psychosocial outcomes. *Journal of Child Psychology and Psychiatry, 46,* 128–149.

Cohen, P., Cohen, J., & Brook, J. (1993a). An epidemiological study of disorders in late childhood and adolescence-II. Persistence of disorders. *Journal of Child Psychology and Psychiatry, 34,* 869–877.

Cohen, P., Cohen, J., Kasen, S., Velez, C. N., Hartmark, C., Johnson, J., Rojas, M., Brook, J., & Streuning, E. L. (1993b). An epidemiological study of disorders in late childhood and adolescence-I. Age- and gender-specific prevalence. *Journal of Child Psychology and Psychiatry, 34,* 851–867.

Cohen-Tovee, E. M. (1993). Depressed mood and concern with weight and shape in normal young women. *International Journal of Eating Disorders, 14,* 223–227.

Coie, J. D., Belding, M., & Underwood, M. (1988). Aggression and peer rejection in childhood. In B. B. Lahey & A. E. Kazdin (Eds.), *Advances in clinical child psychology,* Vol. 11. New York: Plenum.

Coie, J. D., & Dodge, K. A. (1998). Aggression and antisocial behavior. In W. Damon (Series Ed.) & N. Eisenberg (Vol. Ed.), *Handbook of child psychology: Vol. 3. Social, emotional, and personality development* (5th ed.). New York: John Wiley.

Coie, J. D., Miller-Johnson, S., & Bagwell, C. (2000). Prevention science. In A. J. Sameroff, M. Lewis, & S. M. Miller (Eds.), *Handbook of developmental psychopathology.* New York: Kluwer Academic/Plenum.

Coie, J. D., Watt, N. F., West, S. G., Hawkins, J. D., Asarnow, J. R., Markman, H. J. et al. (1993). The science of prevention: A conceptual framework and some directions for a national research program. *American Psychologist, 48,* 1013–1022.

Cole, C. M., Waldron, N., & Majd, M. (2004). Academic progress of students across inclusive and traditional settings. *Mental Retardation, 42,* 136–144.

Coley, R. L. (2001). (In)visible men: Emerging research on low-income, unmarried, and minority fathers. *American Psychologist, 56,* 743–753.

Coley, R. L., Morris, J. E., & Hernandez, D. (2004). Out-of-school care and problem behavior trajectories among low-income adolescents: Individual, family, and neighborhood characteristics as added risks. *Child Development, 75,* 948–965.

Colle, L., Baron-Cohen, S., & Hill, J. (2007). Do children with autism have a theory of mind? A non-verbal test of autism vs. specific language impairment. *Journal of Autism and Developmental Disorders, 37,* 716–723.

Collett, B. R., Ohan, J., & Myers, K. M. (2003). Ten-year review of rating scales. V: Scales assessing attention-deficit/hyperactivity disorder. *Journal of the American Academy of Child and Adolescent Psychiatry, 42,* 1015–1037.

Collins, E. (1991). Body figure perceptions and preferences among preadolescent children. *International Journal of Eating Disorders, 10,* 199–208.

Collishaw, S., Maughan, B., Goodman, R., & Pickles, A. (2004). Time trends in adolescent health. *Journal of Child Psychology and Psychiatry, 45,* 1350–1362.

Compas, B. E. (1997). Depression in children and adolescents. In E. J. Mash & L. G. Terdal (Eds.), *Assessment of childhood disorders* (3rd ed.). New York: Guilford Press.

Compas, B. E., Connor-Smith, J., & Jaser, S. S. (2004). Temperament, stress reactivity, and coping: Implications for depression in childhood and adolescence. *Journal of Clinical Child and Adolescent Psychology, 33,* 21–31.

Compas, B. E., Connor-Smith, J. K., Saltzman, H., Thomsen, A. H., & Wadsworth, M. E. (2001). Coping with stress during childhood and adolescence: Problems, progress, and potential in theory and research. *Psychological Bulletin, 127,* 87–127.

Compas, B. E., Ey, S., & Grant, K. E. (1993). Taxonomy, assessment, and diagnosis of depression during adolescence. *Psychological Bulletin, 14,* 323–344.

Compas, B. E., Hinden, B. R., & Gerhardt, C. (1995). Adolescent development: Pathways and processes of risk and resilience. *Annual Review of Psychology, 46,* 265–293.

Compas, B. E., Oppedisano, G., Connor, J. K., Gerhardt, C. A., Hinden, B. R., Achenbach, T. M., & Hammen, C. (1997). Gender differences in depressive symptoms in adolescence: Comparison of national samples of clinically referred and nonreferred youths. *Journal of Consulting and Clinical Psychology, 65,* 617–626.

Compton, K., Snyder, J., Schrepferman, L., Bank, L., & Shortt, J. W. (2003). The contribution of parents and siblings to antisocial and depressive behavior in adolescents: A double jeopardy coercion model. *Development and Psychopathology, 15,* 163–182.

Conduct Problems Prevention Research Group. (1992). A developmental and clinical model for the prevention of conduct disorder: The Fast Track Program. *Development and Psychopathology, 4,* 509–527.

Conduct Problems Prevention Research Group. (1999). Initial impact of the Fast Track prevention trial for conduct problems: I. The high-risk sample. *Journal of Consulting and Clinical Psychology, 67,* 631–647.

Conduct Problems Prevention Research Group. (2002a). Evaluation of the first 3 years of the Fast Track prevention trial with children at high risk for adolescent conduct problems. *Journal of Abnormal Child Psychology, 30,* 19–36.

Conduct Problems Prevention Research Group. (2002b). The implementation of the Fast Track program: An example of large-scale prevention science efficacy trial. *Journal of Abnormal Child Psychology, 30,* 1–18.

Conduct Problems Prevention Research Group. (2004). The effects of the Fast Track program on serious problem outcomes at the end of elementary school. *Journal of Clinical Child and Adolescent Psychology, 33,* 650–661.

Conley, C. S., Haines, B. A., Hilt, L. M., & Metalsky, G. I. (2001). The Children's Attributional Style Interview: Developmental tests of cognitive diathesis-stress theories of depression. *Journal of Abnormal Child Psychology, 29,* 445–463.

Connell, J. P. (1985). A new multidimensional measure of children's perceptions of control. *Child Development, 56,* 1018–1041.

Connelly, C. D., & Straus, M. A. (1992). Mother's age and risk for physical abuse. *Child Abuse & Neglect, 16,* 709–718.

Connelly, M., Rapoff, M. A., Thompson, N., & Connelly, W. (2006). Headstrong: A pilot study of a CD-ROM intervention for recurrent pediatric headache. *Journal of Pediatric Psychology, 31,* 737–747.

Conners, C. K. (2008). *Conners' Rating Scales-3rd Edition: Conners 3 manual.* North Tonawanda, NY: Multi-Health Systems, Inc.

Connor, D. K. (2006). Stimulants. In R. A. Barkley (Ed.), *Attention-deficit hyperactivity disorder. A handbook for diagnosis and treatment.* New York: The Guilford Press.

Connors, M. E. (2001). Relationship of sexual abuse to body image and eating problems. In J. K. Thompson & L. Smolak (Eds.), *Body image, eating disorders, and obesity in youth: Assessment, prevention, and treatment.* Washington, DC: American Psychological Association.

Conti-Ramsden, G. (2003). Processing and linguistic markers in young children with specific language impairment (SLI). *Journal of Speech, Language, and Hearing Research, 46,* 1029–1037.

Conti-Ramsden, G., & Botting, N. (2004). Social difficulties and victimization in children with SLI at 11 years of age. *Journal of Speech, Language, and Hearing Research, 47,* 145–161.

Cooley, M. R., & Boyce, C. A. (2004). An introduction to assessing anxiety in child and adolescent multiethnic populations: Challenges and opportunities for enhancing knowledge and practice. *Journal of Clinical Child and Adolescent Psychology, 33,* 210–215.

Cooperberg, J., & Faith, M. S. (2004). Treatment of obesity II: Childhood and adolescent obesity. In J. K. Thompson (Ed.), *Handbook of eating disorders and obesity.* Hoboken, NJ: John Wiley.

Cope, M. B., Fernández, J. R., & Allison, D. B. (2004). Genetic and biological risk factors. In J. K. Thompson (Ed.), *Handbook of eating disorders and obesity.* Hoboken, NJ: John Wiley.

Correl, C. U. (2008). Antipsychotic use in children and adolescents: Minimizing adverse effect to maximize outcomes. *Journal of the American Academy of Child and Adolescent Psychiatry, 47,* 9–20.

Corriveau, K., Pasquini, E., & Goswami, U. (2007). Basic auditory processing skills and specific language impairment: A new look at an old hypothesis. *Journal of Speech, Language, and Hearing Research, 50,* 647–666.

Costello, E. J. (1989). Developments in child psychiatric epidemiology. *Journal of the American Academy of Child and Adolescent Psychiatry, 28,* 836–841.

Costello, E. J., & Angold, A. (1995). Developmental epidemiology. In D. Cicchetti & D. J. Cohen (Eds.), *Developmental psychopathology.* New York: John Wiley.

Costello, E. J., & Angold, A. (2001). Bad behaviour: An historic perspective on disorders of conduct. In J. Hill & B. Maughan (Eds.), *Conduct disorders in childhood and adolescence.* New York: Cambridge University Press.

Costello, E. J., & Angold., A. (2006). Developmental epidemiology. In D. Cicchetti & D. J. Cohen (Eds.), *Developmental psychopathology. Vol. 1. Theory and method.* Hoboken, NJ: John Wiley & Sons.

Costello, E. J., & Angold, A. C. (2000). Developmental epidemiology: A framework for developmental psychopathology. In A. J. Sameroff, M. Lewis, & S. M. Miller (Eds.), *Handbook of developmental psychopathology.* New York: Kluwer Academic/Plenum Publishers.

Costello, E. J., Compton, S. N., Keeler, G., & Angold, A. (2003). Relationships between poverty and psychopathology. *Journal of the American Medical Association, 290,* 2023–2029.

Costello, E. J., Egger, H., & Angold, A. (2005a). 10-Year research update review: The epidemiology of child and adolescent psychiatric disorders: I. Methods and public health burden. *Journal of the American Academy of Child and Adolescent Psychiatry, 44,* 972–986.

Costello, E. J., Egger, H. L., & Angold, A. (2005b). The developmental epidemiology of anxiety disorders: Phenomenology, prevalence, and comorbidity. *Child and Adolescent Psychiatric Clinics of North America, 14,* 631–648.

Costello, E. J., Erkanli, A., Fairbank, J. A., & Angold, A. (2002). The prevalence of potentially traumatic events in childhood and adolescence. *Journal of Traumatic Stress, 15,* 99–112.

Costello, E. J., Foley, D. L., & Angold, A. (2006). 10-year research update review: The epidemiology of child and adolescent psychiatric disorders: II. Developmental epidemiology. *Journal of the American Academy of Child and Adolescent Psychiatry, 45,* 8–25.

Costin, J., Vance, A., Barnett, R., O'Shea, M., & Luk, E. S. (2002). Attention deficit hyperactivity disorder and comorbid anxiety: Practitioner problems in treatment planning. *Child and Adolescent Mental Health, 7,* 16–24.

Coucouvanis, K., Polister, B., Prouty, R. & Lakin, K. C. (2003). Continuing reduction in populations of large state residential facilities for persons with intellectual and developmental disabilities. *Mental Retardation, 41,* 67–70.

Cowen, E. L. (1991). In pursuit of wellness. *American Psychologist, 46,* 404–408.

Cowen, E. L. (1994). The enhancement of psychological wellness: Challenges and opportunities. *American Journal of Community Psychology, 22,* 149–179.

Coy, K., Speltz, M. L., DeKlyen, M., & Jones, K. (2001). Social-cognitive processes in preschool boys with and without oppositional defiant disorder. *Journal of Abnormal Child Psychology, 29,* 107–119.

Coyle, J. T. (2000). Psychotropic drug use in very young children. *Journal of the American Medical Association, 283,* 1059–1060.

Coyle, J. T., Pine, D. S., Charney, D. S., Lewis, L., Nemeroff, C. B., Carlson, G. A. et al. (2003). Depression and Bipolar Support Alliance Consensus Development Panel. *Journal of the American Academy of Child and Adolescent Psychiatry, 42,* 1494–1503.

Coyne, M. D., Kame'enui, E. J., Simmons, D. C., & Harn, B. A. (2004). Beginning reading intervention as inoculation or insulin: First-grade reading performance of strong responders to kindergarten intervention. *Journal of Learning Disabilities, 37,* 90–104.

CPT II. (2004). *MHS 2004 catalogue.* North Tonawanda, NY.

Cravens, H. (1992). A scientific project locked in time: The Terman genetic studies of genius, 1920s–1950s. *American Psychologist, 47,* 183–189.

Cravens, H. (1993). *Before Head Start: The Iowa Station and America's children.* Chapel Hill, NC: University of North Carolina Press.

Creer, T. L. (1998). Childhood asthma. In T. H. Ollendick & M. Hersen (Eds.), *Handbook of child psychopathology* (3rd ed.). New York: Plenum Press.

Creer, T. L. (2000). Self-management and the control of chronic illness. In D. Drotar (Ed.), *Promoting adherence to medical treatment in chronic illness: Concepts, methods, and interventions.* Mahwah, NJ: Erlbaum.

Crick, N. R. (1997). Engagement in gender normative versus non-normative forms of aggression: Links to social-psychological adjustment. *Developmental Psychology, 33,* 610–617.

Crick, N. R., Casas, J. F., & Ku, H. C. (1999). Relational and physical forms of peer victimization in preschool. *Developmental Psychology, 35,* 376–385.

Crick, N. R., Casas, J. F., & Mosher, M. (1997). Relational and overt aggression in preschool. *Developmental Psychology, 33,* 579–588.

Crick, N. R., & Dodge, K. A. (1994). A review and reformulation of social information-processing mechanisms in children's social adjustment. *Psychological Bulletin, 115,* 74–101.

Crick, N. R., & Grotpeter, J. K. (1995). Relational aggression, gender, and social-psychological adjustment. *Child Development, 66,* 710–722.

Crick, N. R., & Grotpeter, J. K. (1996). Children's treatment by peers: Victims of relational and overt aggression. *Development and Psychopathology, 8,* 367–380.

Crick, N. R., & Nelson, D. A. (2002). Victimization within peer relationships and friendships: Nobody told me there'd be friends like these. *Journal of Abnormal Child Psychology, 30,* 599–607.

Crick, N. R., & Zahn-Waxler, C. (2003). The development of psychopathology in females and males: Current progress and future challenges. *Development and Psychopathology, 15,* 719–742.

Crijnen, A. A. M., Achenbach, T. M., & Verhulst, F. C. (1997). Comparisons of problems reported by parents of children in 12 cultures: Total problems, externalizing and internalizing. *American Academy of Child and Adolescent Psychiatry, 36,* 1269–1277.

Criss, M. M., Petit, G. S., Bates, J. E., Dodge, K. A., & Lapp, A. L. (2002). Family adversity, positive peer relationships, and children's externalizing behavior: A longitudinal perspective on risk and resilience. *Child Development, 73,* 1220–1237.

Crist, W., & Napier-Phillips, A. (2001). Mealtime behaviors of young children: A comparison of normative and clinical data. *Journal of Developmental and Behavioral Pediatrics, 22,* 279–286.

Crnic, K. A. (1988). Mental retardation. In E. J. Mash & L. G. Terdal (Eds.), *Behavioral assessment of childhood disorders: Selected core problems.* New York: Guilford.

Crockett, L. J., Randall, B. A., Shen, Y. L., Russell, S. T., & Driscoll, A. K. (2005). Measurement equivalence of the Center for Epidemiological Studies Depression Scale for Latino and Anglo Adolescents: A national study. *Journal of Consulting and Clinical Psychology, 73,* 47–58.

Cruce, M. K., & Stinnett, T. A. (2006). Children with cancer. In L. Phelps (Ed.), *Chronic health-related disorders in children: Collaborative medical and psychoeducational interventions.* Washington, DC: American Psychological Association.

Cummings, E. M., Davies, P. T., & Campbell, S. B. (2000). *Developmental psychopathology and family process: Theory, research, and clinical implications.* New York: The Guilford Press.

Cummings, E. M., El-Sheikh, M., Kouros, C. D., & Keller, P. S. (2007). Children's skin conductance reactivity as a mechanism of risk in the context of parental depressive symptoms. *Journal of Child Psychology and Psychiatry, 48,* 436–445.

Cummings, E. M., Goeke-Morey, M. C., Papp, L. M. (2004). Everyday marital conflict and child aggression. *Journal of Abnormal Child Psychology, 32,* 191–202.

Curtis, N. M., Ronan, K. R., & Borduin, C. M. (2004). Multisystemic treatment: A meta-analysis of outcome studies. *Journal of Family Psychology, 18,* 411–419.

Curtis, W. J., & Cicchetti, D. (2003). Moving research on resilience into the 21st century; Theoretical and methodological considerations in examining the biological contributions to resilience. *Development and Psychopathology, 15,* 773–810.

Cutting, A. L., & Dunn, J. (2002). The cost of understanding other people: Social cognition predicts young children's sensitivity to criticism. *Journal of Child Psychology and Psychiatry, 43,* 849–860.

Cyranowski, J. M., Frank, E., Young, E., & Shear, M. K. (2000). Adolescent onset of the gender difference in lifetime rates of major depression: A theoretical model. *Archives of General Psychiatry, 57,* 21–27.

Cytryn, L., & Lourie, R. S. (1980). Mental retardation. In H. I. Kaplan, A. M. Freedman, & B. J. Sadock (Eds.), *Comprehensive textbook of psychiatry/III,* Vol. 3. Baltimore: Williams & Wilkins.

Cytryn, L., & McKnew, D. (1974). Factors influencing the changing clinical expression of the depressive process in children. *American Journal of Psychiatry, 131,* 879–881.

Dadds, M. R., Barrett, P. M., Rapee, R. M., & Ryan, S. (1996). Family process and child anxiety and aggression: An observational analysis. *Journal of Abnormal Child Psychology, 24,* 715–734.

Dadds, M. R., Holland, D. E., Laurens, K. R., Mullins, M., Barrett, P. M., & Spence, S. H. (1999). Early intervention and prevention of anxiety disorders in children: Results at 2-year follow-up. *Journal of Consulting and Clinical Psychology, 67,* 145–150.

Dadds, M. R., Rapee, R. M., Barrett, P. M. (1994). Behavioral observation. In T. H. Ollendick, N. J. King, & W. Yule (Eds.), *International handbook of phobic and anxiety disorders in children and adolescents* (pp. 349–364). New York: Plenum Press.

Dadds, M. R., Sanders, M. R., Morrison, M., & Rebgetz, M. (1992). Childhood depression and conduct disorder: II. An analysis of family interaction patterns in the home. *Journal of Abnormal Psychology, 101,* 505–513.

Dahlquist, L., Power, T., & Carlson, L. (1995). Physician and parent behavior during invasive cancer procedures: A multidimensional assessment. *Journal of Pediatric Psychology, 20,* 477–490.

Dahlquist, L. M. (1992). Coping with aversive medical treatments. In A. M. La Greca, L. J. Siegel, L. J. Wallander, & C. E. Walker (Eds.), *Stress and coping in child health.* New York: Guilford.

Dahlquist, L. M., & Pendley, J. S. (2005). When distraction fails: Parental anxiety and children's responses to distraction during cancer procedures. *Journal of Pediatric Psychology, 30,* 623–628.

Dahlquist, L. M., & Switkin, M. C. (2003). Chronic and recurrent pain. In M. C. Roberts (Ed.), *Handbook of pediatric psychology* (3rd ed.). New York: Guilford Press.

Dane, A. V., Schachar, R. J., & Tannock, R. (2000). Does actigraphy differentiate ADHD subtypes in a clinical research setting? *Journal of the American Academy of Child and Adolescent Psychiatry, 39,* 752–760.

Daniel, S. S., Walsh, A. K., Goldston, D. B., Arnold, E. M., Reboussin, B. A., & Wood. F. B. (2006). Suicidality, school dropout, and reading problems among adolescents. *Journal of Learning Disabilities, 39,* 507–514.

Daniels, S. R. (2006). The consequences of childhood overweight and obesity. *The Future of Children, 16,* 47–67.

Danielson, C. K., Youngstrom, E. A., Findling, R. L., & Calabrese, J. R. (2003). Discriminative validity of the General Behavior Inventory using youth report. *Journal of Abnormal Child Psychology, 31,* 29–39.

Dare, C., & Eisler, I. (1997). Family therapy for anorexia nervosa. In D. M. Garner & P. E. Garfinkel (Eds.), *Handbook of treatment for eating disorders* (2nd ed.). New York: Guilford Press.

Dauvilliers, Y., Maret, S., & Tafti, M. (2005). Genetics of normal and pathological sleep in humans. *Sleep Medicine Review, 9,* 91–100.

David-Ferdon, C., & Hertz, M. F. (2007). Electronic media, violence, and adolescents: An emerging public health problem. *Journal of Adolescent Health, 41,* S1–S5.

Davidovitch, M., Glick, L., Holtzmam, G., Tirosh, E., & Safir, M. P. (2000). Developmental regression in autism: Maternal perception. *Journal of Autism and Developmental Disorders, 30,* 113–119.

Davies, P. T., & Cummings, E. M. (2006). Interparental discord, family process, and developmental psychopathology. In D. Cicchetti & D. J. Cohen (Eds.), *Developmental psychopathology Vol. 3: Risk, disorder, and adaptation.* (2nd ed.). Hoboken, NJ: John Wiley & sons, Inc.

Davies, R. R., & Rogers, E. S. (1985). Social skills training with persons who are mentally retarded. *Mental Retardation, 23,* 186–196.

Davis, C. L., Delamater, A. M., Shaw, K. H., La Greca, A. M., Edison, M. S., Perez-Rodriguez, J. E., & Nemery, R. (2001). Parenting styles, regimen adherence, and glycemic control in 4- to 10-year-old children with diabetes. *Journal of Pediatric Psychology, 26,* 123–129.

Davis, K. L., Stewart, D. G., Friedman, J. I., Buchsman, M., Harvey, P. D., Hof, P. R. et al. (2003). White matter changes in schizophrenia. *Archives of General Psychiatry, 60,* 443–456.

Dawson, G., & Castelloe, P. (1992). Autism. In C. E. Walker & M. C. Roberts (Eds.), *Handbook of clinical child psychology.* New York: Wiley.

Dawson, G., Frey, K., Panagiotides, H., Osterling, J., & Hessl, D. (1997). Infants of depressed mothers exhibit atypical frontal brain activity: A replication and extension of previous findings. *Journal of Child Psychology and Psychiatry, 38,* 179–186.

Dawson, G., & Toth, K. (2006). Autism spectrum disorders. In D. Cicchetti & D. J. Cohen (Eds.), *Developmental psychopathology. Vol. 3.* Hoboken, NJ: John Wiley & Sons.

De Bellis, M. D. (2001). Developmental traumatology: The psychobiological development of maltreated children and its implications for research, treatment, and policy. *Development and Psychopathology, 13,* 539–564.

De Bellis, M. D., & Van Dillen, T. (2005). Childhood post-traumatic stress disorder: An overview. *Child and Adolescent Psychiatric Clinics of North America, 14,* 745–772.

de Boo, G. M., & Prins, P. J. M. (2007). Social incompetence in children with ADHD: Possible moderators and mediators in social-skills training. *Clinical Psychology Review, 27,* 78–97.

De Los Reyes, A., & Kazdin, A. E. (2005). Informant discrepancies in the assessment of childhood psychopathology: A critical review, theoretical framework, and recommendations for further study. *Psychological Bulletin, 131,* 483–509.

de Ruiter, K. P., Dekker, M. C., Verhulse, F. C., & Koot, H. M. (2007). Developmental course of psychopathology in youths with and without intellectual disabilities. *Journal of Child Psychology and Psychiatry, 48,* 498–507.

De Wilde, E. J., Kienhorst, C. W. M., & Diekstra, R. R. W. (2001). Suicidal behaviour in adolescents. In I. M. Goodyer (Ed.), *The depressed child and adolescent* (2nd ed.). Cambridge, UK: Cambridge University Press.

de Zwaan, M., Roerig, J. L., & Mitchell, J. E. (2004). Pharmacological treatment of anorexia nervosa, bulimia nervosa, and binge eating disorder. In J. K. Thompson (Ed.), *Handbook of eating disorders and obesity.* Hoboken, NJ: John Wiley.

Deal, L. W., Gomby, D. S., Zippiroli, L., & Behrman, R. E. (2000). Unintentional injuries in childhood: Analysis and recommendations. *The Future of Children, 10(1),* 4–22.

Dean, V. J., & Burns, M. K. (2002). Inclusion of intrinsic processing difficulties in LD diagnostic models: A critical review. *Learning Disability Quarterly, 25,* 170–176.

Deater-Deckard, K. (2001). Recent research examining the role of peer relationships in the development of psychopathology. *Journal of Child Psychology and Psychiatry, 42,* 565–579.

Deater-Deckard, K., Dodge, K. A., & Sorbring, E. (2005). Cultural differences in the effects of physical punishment. In M. Rutter & M. Tienda (Eds.) *Ethnicity and causal mechanisms.* New York: Cambridge University Press.

Deater-Deckard, K., Reiss, D., Hetherington, E. M., & Plomin, R. (1997). Dimensions and disorders of adolescent adjustment: A quantitative genetic analysis of unselected samples and selected extremes. *Journal of Child Psychology and Psychiatry, 38,* 515–525.

DeFries, J. C., & Light, J. G. (1996). Twin studies of reading disability. In J. H. Beitchman, N. J. Cohen, M. M. Konstantareas, & R. Tannock (Eds.), *Language, learning, and behavior disorders.* New York: Cambridge University Press.

Dekker, M. C., Ferdinand, R. F., van Lang, N. D. J., Bongers, I. L., van der Ende, J., & Verhulst, F. C. (2007). Developmental trajectories of depressive symptoms from early childhood to late adolescence: gender differences and adult outcome. *Journal of Child Psychology and Psychiatry, 48,* 657–666.

Dekker, M. C., & Koot, H. M. (2003). DSM-IV disorders in children with borderline to moderate intellectual ability. II: Prevalence and impact. *Journal of the American Academy of Child and Adolescent Psychiatry, 42,* 915–922.

Dekovic, M., & Janssens, A. M. (1992). Parents' child-rearing style and child's sociometric status. *Developmental Psychology, 28,* 925–932.

Delamater, A. M. (2000). Critical issues in the assessment of regimen adherence in children with diabetes. In D. Drotar (Ed.), *Promoting adherence to medical treatment in chronic childhood illness: Concepts, methods, and interventions.* Mahwah, NJ: Lawrence Erlbaum Associates.

Delamater, A. M., Bubb, J., Davis, S. G., Smith, J. A., Schmidt, L., White, N. H., & Santiago, J. V. (1990). Randomized prospective study of self-management training with newly diagnosed diabetic children. *Diabetes Care, 13,* 492–498.

Demos, J., & Demos, V. (1972). Adolescence in historical perspective. In D. Rogers (Ed.), *Issues in adolescent psychology.* Englewood Cliffs, NJ: Prentice-Hall.

DeNavas-Walt, C., Procter, B. D., & Lee, C. H. (2006). Current Population Reports, P60–231, *Income, Poverty, and Health Insurance Coverage in the United States: 2005.* U.S. Government Printing Office, Washington, DC.

Denham, S. A., Caverly, S., Schmidt, M., Blair, K., DeMulder, E., Caal, S. et al. (2002). Preschool understanding of emotions: Contributions to classroom anger and aggression. *Journal of Child Psychology and Psychiatry, 43,* 901–916.

DePaulo, J. R. (2004). Genetics of bipolar disorder: Where do we stand? *American Journal of Psychiatry, 161,* 595–597.

D'Eramo, K. S., & Francis, G. (2004). Cognitive-behavioral psychotherapy. In T. L. Morris & J. S. March (Eds.), *Anxiety disorders in children and adolescents.* New York: Guilford Press.

DeSimone, J. R., & Parmar, R. S. (2006). Middle school mathematics teachers' beliefs about inclusion of students with learning disabilities. *Learning Disabilities Research & Practice, 21,* 98–110.

DeThorne, L. S., Hart, S. A., Deater-Deckard, K., Thompson, L. A., Schatschneider, C., & Davison, M. D. (2006). Children's history of speech-language difficulties: Genetic influences and associations with reading-related measures. *Journal of Speech, Language, and Hearing Research, 49,* 1280–1293.

Detterman, D. K., & Thompson, L. A. (1997). What is so special about special education? *American Psychologist, 52,* 1082–1090.

DiBartolo, P. M., Albano, A. M., Barlow, D. H., & Heimberg. R. G. (1998). Cross-informant agreement in the assessment of social phobia in youth. *Journal of Abnormal Child Psychology, 26,* 213–220.

Dickstein, S. G., Bannon, K., Castellanos, F. X. & Milham, M. P. (2006). The neural correlates of attention deficit hyperactivity disorder: an ALE meta-analysis. *Journal of Child Psychology and Psychiatry, 47,* 1051–1062.

Dieter, J. N. I., Field, T., Hernandez-Reif, M., Emory, E. K., & Redzepi, M. (2003). Stable preterm infants gain more weight and sleep less after five days of massage therapy. *Journal of Pediatric Psychology, 28,* 403–411.

Dietrich, A., Riese, H., Sondeijker, F. E. P. L., Greaves-Lord, K., van Roon, A. M., Ormel, J., (2007). Externalizing and internalizing problems in relation to autonomic function: A population-based study in preadolescents. *Journal of the American Academy of Child and Adolescent Psychiatry, 46,* 378–386.

DiLillo, D., & Tremblay, G. (2001). Maternal and child reports of behavioral compensation in response to equipment usage. *Journal of Pediatric Psychology, 26,* 175–184.

DiLillo, D., & Tremblay, G. C. (2005). Lizette Peterson: A collaboration of passion and science. *Journal of Pediatric Psychology, 30,* 533–535.

DiMatteo, M. R. (2000). Practitioner-family-patient communication in pediatric adherence: Implications for research and clinical practice. In D. Drotar (Ed.), *Promoting adherence to medical treatment in chronic childhood illness: Concepts, methods, and interventions.* Mahwah, NJ: Lawrence Erlbaum Associates.

Dishion, T. J. (1990). The family ecology of boys' relations in middle childhood. *Child Development, 61,* 874–892.

Dishion, T. J., & Dodge, K. A. (2005). Peer contagion in interventions for children and adolescents: Moving towards an understanding of the ecology and dynamics of change. *Journal of Abnormal Child Psychology, 33,* 395–400.

Dishion, T. J., French, D. C., & Patterson, G. R. (1995). The development and ecology of antisocial behavior. In D. Cicchetti & D. J. Cohen (Eds.), *Developmental psychopathology* (Vol. 2: *Risk, disorder and adaptation*). New York: John Wiley & Sons.

Dishion, T. J., & Kavanagh, K. A. (2002). The Adolescent Transitions Program: A family-centered prevention strategy for schools. In J. B. Reid, G. R. Patterson, & J. Snyder (Eds.), *Antisocial behavior in children and adolescents: A developmental analysis and model for intervention.* Washington, DC: American Psychological Association.

Dishion, T. J., & Owen, L. D. (2002). A longitudinal analysis of friendships and substance use: Bidirectional influence from adolescence into adulthood. *Developmental Psychology, 28,* 480–491.

Dishion, T. J., & Patterson, G. R. (2006). The development and ecology of antisocial behavior in children and adolescents. In D. Cicchetti & D. J. Cohen (Eds.), *Developmental psychopathology, Vol. 3: Risk, disorder, and adaptation* (2nd ed.). Hoboken, NJ: John Wiley & sons..

Dishion, T. J., & Stormshak, E. A. (2007). *Intervening in children's lives: An ecological, family-centered approach to mental health care.* Washington, DC: American Psychological Association.

Dissanayake, C., & Crossley, S. A. (1996). Proximity and sociable behaviours in autism: Evidence for attachment. *Journal of Child Psychology and Psychiatry, 37,* 149–156.

Dittmar, H., Halliwell, E., & Ive, S. (2006). Does Barbie make girls want to be thin? The effect of experimental exposure to images of dolls on the body image of 5- to 8-year-old girls. *Developmental Psychology, 42,* 283–292.

Dix, T., Stewart, A. D., Gershoff, E. T., & Day, W. H. (2007). Autonomy and children's reactions to being controlled: Evidence that both compliance and defiance may be positive markers in early development. *Child Development, 78,* 1204–1221.

Dixon, L., Hamilton-Giachritsis, C., & Browne, K. (2005). Attributions and behaviours of parents abused as children: a mediational analysis of the intergenerational continuity of child maltreatment (Part II). *Journal of Child Psychology and Psychiatry, 46,* 58–68.

Dodge, K. A. (1991). The structure and function of reactive and proactive aggression. In D. Pepler & K. Rubin (Eds.), *The development and treatment of childhood aggression.* Hillsdale, NJ: Erlbaum.

Dodge, K. A. (2000). Conduct disorder. In A. J. Sameroff, M. Lewis, & S. M. Miller (Eds.), *Handbook of developmental psychopathology* (2nd ed.). New York: Kluwer Academic/Plenum Publishers.

Dodge, K. A. (2003). Do social information-processing patterns mediate aggressive behavior? In B. B. Lahey, T. E. Moffitt, & A. Caspi (Eds.), *Causes of conduct disorder and juvenile delinquency.* New York: Guilford Press.

Dodge, K. A., Lochman, J. E., Harnish, J. D., Bates, J. E., & Pettit, G. S. (1997). Reactive and proactive aggression in school children and psychiatrically impaired chronically assaultive youth. *Journal of Abnormal Psychology, 106,* 37–51.

Dodge, K. A., & Rabiner, D. L. (2004). Returning to roots: On social information processing and moral development. *Child Development, 75,* 1003–1008.

Dohnt, H., & Tiggemann, M. (2006). The contribution of peer and media influences on the development of body satisfaction and self-esteem in young girls: A prospective study. *Developmental Psychology, 42,* 929–936.

Doleys, D. M. (1989). Enuresis and encopresis. In T. H. Ollendick & M. Hersen (Eds.), *Handbook of child psychopathology* (2nd ed.). New York: Plenum.

Dolgin, M. J., & Jay, S. M. (1989). Childhood cancer. In T. H. Ollendick & M. Hersen (Eds.), *Handbook of child psychopathology* (2nd ed.). New York: Plenum.

Dolgin, M. J., Phipps, S., Fairclough, D. L., Sahler, O. J. Z., Askins, M., Noll, R. B., et al. (2007). Trajectories of adjustment in mothers of children with newly diagnosed cancer: A natural history investigation. *Journal of Pediatric Psychology, 32,* 771–782.

Dollinger, S. J. (1986). Childhood sleep disturbances. In B. B. Lahey & A. E. Kazdin (Eds.), *Advances in clinical child psychology,* Vol. 9. New York: Plenum.

Donenberg, G. R., Paikoff, R., & Pequegnat, W. (2006). Introduction to the special section on families, youth, and HIV: Family-based intervention studies. *Journal of Pediatric Psychology, 31,* 869–873.

D'Onofrio, B. M., Slutske, W. S., Turkheimer, E., Emery, R. E., Harden, P., Heath, A. C. et al. (2007). Intergenerational transmission of childhood conduct problems: A children of twins study. *Archives of General Psychiatry, 64,* 820–829.

D'Onofrio, B. M., Turkheimer, E. M., Eaves, L. J., Cory, L. A., Berg, K., Solaas, M. H., & Emery, R. E. (2003). The role of the Children of Twins design in elucidating causal relations between parent characteristics and child outcomes. *Journal of Child Psychology and Psychiatry, 44,* 1130–1144.

Donovan, C. L., & Spence, S. H. (2000). Prevention of childhood anxiety disorders. *Clinical Psychology Review, 20,* 509–531.

Dore, M. M., & Mullin, D. (2006). Treatment foster care: Its history and current role in the foster care continuum. *Families in Society, 87,* 475–482.

Doss, A. J., & Weisz, J. R. (2006). Syndrome co-occurrence and treatment outcomes in youth mental health clinics. *Journal of Consulting and Clinical Psychology, 74,* 416–425.

Dowdney, L. (2000). Childhood bereavement following parental death. *Journal of Child Psychology and Psychiatry, 41,* 819–830.

Doyle, K. W., Wolchik, S. A., Dawson-McClure, S. R., & Sandler, I. N. (2003). Positive events as a stress buffer for children and adolescents in families in transition. *Journal of Clinical Child and Adolescent Psychology, 32,* 536–545.

Drotar, D., & Lemanek, K. (2001). Steps toward a clinically relevant science of interventions in pediatric settings: Introduction to the special issue. *Journal of Pediatric Psychology, 26,* 385–394.

Drotar, D., Riekert, K. A., Burgess, E., Levi, R., Nobile, C., Kaugars, A. S., & Walders, N. (2000). Treatment adherence in childhood chronic illness: Issues and recommendations to enhance practice, research, and training. In D. Drotar (Ed.), *Promoting adherence to medical treatment in chronic childhood illness: Concepts, methods, and interventions.* Mahwah, NJ: Lawrence Erlbaum Associates.

Drotar, D., & Robinson, J. (2000). Developmental psychopathology of failure to thrive. In A. J. Sameroff, M. Lewis, & S. M. Miller (Eds.), *Handbook of developmental psychopathology* (2nd ed.). New York: Kluwer Academic/Plenum Publishers.

DuBois, D. L., Burk-Braxton, C., Swenson, L. P., Tevendale, H. D., & Hardesty, J. L. (2002). Race and gender influences on adjustment in early adolescence: Investigation of an integrative model. *Child Development, 73,* 1573–1592.

Dumas, J. E., & Lechowicz, J. G. (1989). When do noncompliant children comply? Implications for family behavior therapy. *Child and Family Behavior Therapy, 11,* 21–38.

Dummit, E. S., Klein, R. G., Tancer, N. K., Asche, B., Martin, J., & Fairbanks, J. A. (1997). Systematic assessment of 50 children with selective mutism. *Journal of the American Academy of Child and Adolescent Psychiatry, 36,* 653–660.

Dunbar-Jacob, J. (1993). Contributions to patient adherence: Is it time to share the blame? *Health Psychology, 12,* 91–92.

Duncan, G. J., & Brooks-Gunn, J. (2000). Family poverty, welfare reform, and child development. *Child Development, 71,* 188–196.

Duncan, J., Joselow, M., & Hilden, J. M. (2006). Program interventions for children at the end of life and their siblings. *Child and Adolescent Psychiatric Clinics of North America, 15,* 739–758.

Dunn, J. (1996). Children's relationships: Bridging the divide between cognitive and social development. *Journal of Child Psychology and Psychiatry, 37,* 507–518.

DuPaul, G. J., Barkley, R. A., & Connor, D. F. (1998). Stimulants. In R. A. Barkley (Ed.), *Attention-deficit hyperactivity disorder.* New York: Guilford Press.

DuPaul, G. J., Guevrement, D. C., & Barkley, R. A. (1991). Attention-deficit hyperactivity disorder. In R. A. Barkley (Ed.), *Attention-deficit hyperactivity disorder.* New York: Guilford Press.

DuPaul, G. J., McGoey, K. E., Eckert, T. L., & VanBrakle, J. (2001). Preschool children with attention-deficit/hyperactivity disorder: Impairments in behavioral, social, and school functioning. *Journal of the American Academy of Child and Adolescent Psychiatry, 40,* 508–509.

Durand, V. M. (1999). Functional communication training using assistive devices: Recruiting natural communities of reinforcement. *Journal of Applied Behavior Analysis, 32,* 247–267.

Durand, V. M. (2001). Future directions for children and adolescents with mental retardation. *Behavior Therapy, 32,* 633–650.

Durand, V. M., & Mindell, J. A. (1999). Behavioral intervention for childhood sleep terrors. *Behavior Therapy, 30,* 705–715.

Durlak, J. A., & Wells, A. M. (1997). Primary prevention mental health programs for children and adolescents: A meta-analytic review. *American Journal of Community Psychology, 25,* 115–152.

Durston, S., Davidson, M. C., Mulder, M. J., Spicer, J. A. Galvan, A., Tottenham, N. et al. (2007). Neural and behavioral correlates of expectancy violations in attention-deficit/hyperactivity disorder. *Journal of Child Psychology and Psychiatry, 48.* 881–889.

Durston, S., Pol, H. E. H., Schnack, H. G., Buitelaar, J. K., Steenhuis, M. P., Minderaa, R. B. et al. (2004). Magnetic resonance imaging of boys with attention-deficit/hyperactivity disorder. *Journal of the American Academy of Child and Adolescent Psychiatry, 43,* 332–340.

Dyck, M. K., Hay, D., Anderson, M., Smith, L. M., Piek, J., & Hallmayer, J. (2004). Is the discrepancy criteria for defining developmental disorders valid? *Journal of Child Psychology and Psychiatry, 45,* 979–995.

Dykens, E. M., & Cohen, D. J. (1996). Effects of Special Olympics International on social competence in persons with mental retardation. *Journal of the American Academy of Child and Adolescent Psychiatry, 35,* 223–229.

Eaves, L., Silberg, J., & Erkanli, A. (2003). Resolving multiple epigenetic pathways to adolescent depression. *Journal of Child Psychology and Psychiatry, 44,* 1006–1014.

Eaves, L. J., Silberg, J. L., Meyer, J. M., Maes, H. H., Simonoff, E., Pickles, A., Rutter, M., Neale, M. C., Reynolds, C. A., Erickson, M. T., Heath, A. C., Loeber, R., Truett K. R., & Hewitt, J. K. (1997). Genetics and developmental psychopathology: 2. The main effects of genes and environment on behavioral problems in the Virginia Twin Study of Adolescent Behavioral Development. *Journal of Child Psychology and Psychiatry, 38,* 965–980.

Edelbrock, C., Rende, R., Plomin, R., & Thompson, L. A. (1995). A twin study of competence and problem behavior in childhood and early adolescence. *Journal of Child Psychology and Psychiatry, 36,* 775–785.

Edwards, G., Barkley, R. A., Laneri, M., Fletcher, K., & Metevia, L. (2001). Parent-adolescent conflict in teenagers with ADHD and ODD. *Journal of Abnormal Child Psychology, 29,* 557–573.

Egeland, J. A., Hostetter, A. M., Pauls, D. L., & Sussex, J. N. (2000). Prodromal symptoms before onset of manic-depressive disorder suggested by first hospital admission histories. *Journal of the American Academy of Child and Adolescent Psychiatry, 39,* 1245–1252.

Egger, H. L., & Angold, A. (2006). Common emotional and behavioral disorders in preschool children: presentation, nosology, and epidemiology. *Journal of Child Psychology and Psychiatry, 47,* 313–337.

Eggers, C. (1978). Course and prognosis of childhood schizophrenia. *Journal of Autism and Childhood Schizophrenia, 8,* 21–36.

Eggers, C. & Bunk, D. (1997). The longterm course of childhood-onset schizophrenia: A 42–year followup. *Schizophrenia Bulletin, 23,* 105–117.

Eggers, C., Bunk, D., & Krause, D. (2000). Schizophrenia with onset before the age of eleven: Clinical characteristics of onset and course. *Journal of Autism and Developmental Disorders, 30,* 29–38.

Ehntholt, K. A., & Yule, W. (2006). Practitioner review: assessment and treatment of refugee children and adolescents who have experienced war-related trauma. *Journal of Child Psychology and Psychiatry, 47,* 1197–1210.

Eisenberg, L. (2001). The past 50 years of child and adolescent psychiatry: A personal memoir. *Journal of the American Academy of Child and Adolescent Psychiatry, 40,* 743–748.

Eisenberg, L., Baker, B. L., & Blacher, J. (1998). Siblings with children with mental retardation living at home or in residential placement. *Journal of Child Psychology and Psychiatry, 39,* 355–363.

Eisenberg, N. (2006). Emotion-related regulation. In H. E. Fitzgerald, B. M. Lester, & B. Zukerman (Eds.), *The crisis in mental health. Critical issues and effective programs. Vol. 1.* Westport, CT: Praeger.

Eisenberg, N., Cumberland, A., Spinrad, T. L., Fabes, R. A., Shepard, S. A., Reiser, M., Murphy, B. C., Losoya, S. H., & Guthrie, I. K. (2001). The relations of regulation and emotionality to children's externalizing and internalizing problem behavior. *Child Development, 72,* 1112–1134.

Eisenberg, N. et al. (1997). Contemporaneous and longitudinal prediction of children's social functioning from regulation and emotionality. *Child Development, 68,* 642–664.

Eiser, C. (1994). The eleventh Jack Tizard Memorial Lecture. Making sense of chronic disease. *Journal of Child Psychology and Psychiatry, 35,* 1373–1389.

Eiser, C. (1998). Long-term consequences of childhood cancer. *Journal of Child Psychology and Psychiatry, 39,* 621–633.

Eiser, C., Eiser, J. R., Mayhew, A. G., & Gibson, A. T. (2005). Parenting the premature infant: Balancing vulnerability and quality of life. *Journal of Child Psychology and Psychiatry, 46,* 1169–1177.

Eisler, I., Dare, C., Hodes, M., Russell, G., Dodge, E., & le Grange, D. (2000). Family therapy for adolescent anorexia nervosa: The results of a controlled comparison of two family interventions. *Journal of Child Psychology and Psychiatry, 41,* 727–736.

Eisler, I., Simic, M., Russell, G. F. M., & Dare, C. (2007). A randomised controlled treatment trial of two forms of family therapy in adolescent anorexia nervosa: a five-year follow-up. *Journal of Child Psychology and Psychiatry, 48,* 552–560.

Elbaum, B., & Vaughn, S. (2003). Self-concept and students with learning disabilities. In H. L. Swanson, K. R. Harris, & S. Graham (Eds.), *Handbook of learning disabilities.* New York: Guilford Press.

Eley, T. C. (1997). General genes: A new theme in developmental psychopathology. *Current Directions in Psychological Science, 6,* 90–95.

Eley, T. C., Bolton, D., O'Connor, T. G., Perrin, S., Smith, P., & Plomin, R. (2003). A twin study of anxiety-related behaviours in pre-school children. *Journal of Child Psychology and Psychiatry, 44,* 945–960.

Eley, T. C., & Craig, I. W. (2005). Introductory guide to the language of molecular genetics. *Journal of Child Psychology and Psychiatry, 46,* 1039–1044.

Eley, T. C., Lichtenstein, P., & Moffitt, T. E. (2003). A longitudinal behavioral genetic analysis of the etiology of aggressive and nonaggressive antisocial behavior. *Development and Psychopathology, 15,* 383–402.

Eley, T. C., & Stevenson, J. (1999). Using genetic analyses to clarify the distinction between depressive and anxious symptoms in children. *Journal of Abnormal Child Psychology, 27,* 105–114.

Elgar, F. J., McGrath, P. J., Waschbusch, D. A., Stewart, S. H., & Curtis, L. J. (2004). Mutual influences on maternal depression and child adjustment problems. *Clinical Psychology Review, 24,* 441–459.

Elgar, K., & Campbell, R. (2001). The cognitive neuroscience of face recognition: Implications for developmental disorders. *Journal of Child Psychology and Psychiatry, 42,* 705–717.

Eliez, S., & Reiss, A. L. (2000). MRI neuroimaging of childhood psychiatric disorders: A selective review. *Journal of Child Psychology and Psychiatry, 41,* 679–694.

Eliez, S., Rumsey, J. M., Giedd, J. N., Schmitt, E. J., Padwardhan, A. J., & Reiss, A. L. (2000). Morphological alteration of temporal lobe gray matter in dyslexia: An MRI study. *Journal of Child Psychology and Psychiatry, 41,* 637–644.

Elliot, C. H., Jay, S. M., & Woody, P. (1987). An observational scale for measuring children's distress during painful medical procedures. *Journal of Pediatric Psychology, 12,* 543–551.

Elliot, D. S., Huizinga, D., & Ageton, S. S. (1985). *Explaining delinquency and drug use.* Beverly Hills, CA: Sage.

Elliott, J. G. (1999). School refusal: Issues of conceptualization, assessment, and treatment. *Journal of Child Psychology and Psychiatry, 40,* 1001–1012.

Ellis, B. J. (2004). Timing of pubertal maturation in girls: An integrated life history approach. *Psychological Bulletin, 130,* 920–958.

Ellis, D. A., Podolski, C. L., Frey, M., Naar-King, S., Wang, B., & Moltz, K. (2007). The role of parental monitoring in adolescent health outcomes: Impact on regimen adherence in youth with Type 1 diabetes. *Journal of Pediatric Psychology, 32,* 907–917.

El-Sheikh, M. & Flanagan, E. (2001). Parental problem drinking and children's adjustment: Family conflict and parental depression as mediators and moderators of risk. *Journal of Abnormal Child Psychology, 29,* 417–432.

El-Sheikh, M., Buckhalt, J. A., Acebo, C., & Mize, J. (2006). Marital conflict and disruption of children's sleep. *Child Development, 77,* 31–43.

Emery, R. E., & Kitzmann, K. M. (1995). The child in the family: Disruptions in family functions. In D. Cicchetti & D. J. Cohen

(Eds.), *Developmental psychopathology: Risk, disorder, and adaptation* (Vol. 2). New York: John Wiley & Sons.

Emslie, G., Kratochvil, C., Vitiello, B., Silva, S., Mayes, T., McNutty, S. et al., & the TADS Team. (2006). Treatment for Adolescents With Depression Study (TADS): Safety results. *Journal of the American Academy of Child and Adolescent Psychiatry, 45*, 1440–1455.

Emslie, G. J., Armitage, R., Weinberg, W. A., Rush, A. J., Mayes, T. L., & Hoffmann, R. F. (2001). Sleep polysomnography as a predictor of recurrence in children and adolescents with major depressive disorder. *International Journal of Neuropsychopharmacology, 4*, 159–168.

English, D. J. (1998). The extent and consequences of child maltreatment. *The Future of Children, 8(1)*, 39–53.

Enzer, N. B., & Heard, S. L. (2000). Psychiatric prevention in children and adolescents. In B. J. Sadock & V. A. Sadock (Eds.), *Comprehensive textbook of psychiatry* (Vol. II). Philadelphia: Lippincott Williams & Wilkins.

Epstein, J. N., Erkanli, A., Conners, C. K., Klaric, J., Costello, J. E., & Angold, A. (2003). Relations between continuous performance test performance measures and ADHD behaviors. *Journal of Clinical Child Psychology, 31*, 543–554.

Epstein, L. H., Valoski, A. M., Vara, L. S., McCurley, J., Wisniewski, L., Kalarchian, M. A., Klein, K. R., & Schrager, L. R. (1995). Effects of decreasing sedentary behavior and increasing activity on weight change in obese children. *Health Psychology, 14*, 109–115.

Erath, S. A., Bierman, K. L., & the Conduct Problems Prevention Research Group. (2006). Aggressive marital conflict, maternal harsh punishment, and child aggressive-disruptive behavior: Evidence for direct and indirect relations. *Journal of Family Psychology, 20*, 217–226.

Ernst, M. (2000). Commentary: Considerations on the characterization and treatment of self-injurious behavior. *Journal of Autism and Developmental Disorders, 30*, 447–450.

Ernst, M., Kimes, A. S., London, E. D. et al. (2003). Neural substrates of decision making in adults with attention deficit hyperactivity disorder. *American Journal of Psychiatry, 160*, 1061–1070.

Espy, K. A., Moore, I. M., Kaufmann, P. M., Kramer, J. H., Matthay, K., & Hutter, J. J. (2001). Chemotherapeutic CNS prophylaxis and neuropsychologic change in children with acute lymphoblastic leukemia: A prospective study. *Journal of Pediatric Psychology, 26*, 1–9.

Essau, C., Conradt, J., & Petermann, F. (1999). Frequency and comorbidity of social phobia and social fears in adolescents. *Behaviour Research and Therapy, 37*, 831–843.

Essau, C. A. (2003). Epidemiology and comorbidity. In C. A. Essau (Ed.), *Conduct and oppositional defiant disorders: Epidemiology, risk factors, and treatment*. Mahwah, NJ: Erlbaum.

Essau, C. A., Conradt, J., & Petermann, F. (1999). Frequency of panic attacks and panic disorder in adolescents. *Depression and Anxiety, 9*, 19–26.

Essau, C. A., Conradt, J., & Petermann, F. (2000). Frequency, comorbidity, and psychosocial impairment of specific phobia in adolescents. *Journal of Clinical Child Psychology, 29*, 221–231.

Estes, K. G., Evans, J. L., & Else-Quest, N. M. (2007). Differences in the nonword repetition performance of children with and without specific language impairment: a meta-analysis. *Journal of Speech, Language, and Hearing Research, 50*, 177–195.

Evans, D. L. and the Commission on Adolescent Depression and Bipolar Disorder. (2005a). Defining depression and bipolar disorder. In D. L. Evans, E. B. Foa, R. E. Gur, H. Hendin, C. P. O'Brien, M. E. P. Seligman, & B. T. Walsh (Eds.), *Treating and preventing adolescent mental health disorders. What we know and what we don't know: A research agenda for improving mental health of our youth*. New York: Oxford University Press.

Evans, D. L. and the Commission on Adolescent Depression and Bipolar Disorder. (2005b). Prevention of depression and bipolar disorder. In D. L. Evans, E. B. Foa, R. E. Gur, H. Hendin, C. P. O'Brien, M. E. P. Seligman, & B. T. Walsh (Eds.), *Treating and preventing adolescent mental health disorders. What we know and what we don't know: A research agenda for improving mental health of our youth*. New York: Oxford University Press.

Evans, D. L. and the Commission on Adolescent Depression and Bipolar Disorder. (2005c). Treatment of depression and bipolar disorder. In D. L. Evans, E. B. Foa, R. E. Gur, H. Hendin, C. P. O'Brien, M. E. P. Seligman, & B. T. Walsh (Eds.), *Treating and preventing adolescent mental health disorders. What we know and what we don't know: A research agenda for improving mental health of our youth*. New York: Oxford University Press.

Evans, D. L., Foa, E. B., Gur, R. E., Hendin, H., O'Brien, C. P., Seligman, M. E. P., & Walsh, B. T. (Eds.) (2005). *Treating and preventing adolescent mental health disorders. What we know and what we don't know: A research agenda for the mental health of our youth*. New York: Oxford University Press.

Evans, D. W., & Leckman, J. F. (2006). Origins of obsessive-compulsive disorder: Developmental and evolutionary perspectives. In D. Cicchetti & D. J. Cohen (Eds.), *Developmental psychopathology. Vol. 1*. (2nd ed.). Hoboken, NJ: John Wiley & Sons.

Evans, G. W. (2004). The environment of childhood poverty. *American Psychologist, 59*, 77–92.

Evans, R. B., & Koelsch, W. A. (1985). Psychoanalysis arrives in America. *American Psychologist, 40*, 942–948.

Exner, J. E., Jr., & Weiner, I. B. (1995). *The Rorschach: A comprehensive system* (Vol. 3: *Assessment of children and adolescents*) (2nd ed.). New York: Wiley.

Eyberg, S. M., Nelson, M. M., Duke, M., & Boggs, S. R. (2005). *Manual for the Dyadic Parent–child Interaction Coding System* (3rd ed.). Gainesville, FL: University of Florida.

Eyberg, S., & Pincus, D. (1999). *Eyberg Child Behavior Inventory & Sutter–Eyberg Student Behavior Inventory–Revised*. Lutz, FL: Psychological Assessment Resources.

Fabes, R. A., Martin, C. L., Hanish, L. D., & Updegraff, K. A. (2000). Criteria for evaluating the significance of developmental research in the twenty-first century: Force and counterforce. *Child Development, 71*, 212–221.

Fagan, A. A., & Najman, J. M. (2003). Association between early childhood aggression and internalizing behavior for sibling pairs. *Journal of the American Academy of Child and Adolescent Psychiatry, 42*, 1093–1100.

Fagan, J. F., & Holland, C. R. (2002). Equal opportunity and racial differences in IQ. *Intelligence, 30*, 361–387.

Fairburn, C. G. (1997). Eating disorders. In D. M. Clark & C. G. Fairburn (Eds.), *Science and practice of cognitive behaviour therapy.* Oxford: Oxford University Press.

Fairburn, C. G. (2005). Evidence-based treatment of anorexia nervosa. *International Journal of Eating Disorders, 37 (Suppl.),* 26–30.

Fairburn, C. G., Cooper, Z., Doll, H. A., Norman, P., & O'Connor, M. (2000). The natural course of bulimia nervosa and binge eating disorder in young women. *Archives of General Psychiatry, 57,* 659–665.

Fairburn, C. G., Cooper, Z., & Shafran, R. (2003). Cognitive behaviour therapy for eating disorders: A "transdiagnostic" theory and treatment. *Behaviour Research and Therapy, 43,* 509–529.

Fairburn, C. G., Welch, S. L., Doll, H. A., Davies, B. A., & O'Connor, M. E. (1997). Risk factors for bulimia nervosa: A community-based case-control study. *Archives of General Psychiatry, 54,* 509–517.

Faith, M. S., Saelens, B. E., Wilfley, D. E., & Allison, D. B. (2001). Behavioral treatment of childhood and adolescent obesity: Current status, challenges, and future directions. In J. K. Thompson & L. Smolak (Eds.), *Body image, eating disorders, and obesity in youth: Assessment, prevention, and treatment.* Washington, DC: American Psychological Association.

Faraone, S., Biederman, J., Mennin, D., Russell, R., Tsuang, M. T. (1998). Familial subtypes of attention deficit hyperactivity disorder: A follow-up study of children from antisocial-ADHD families. *Journal of Child Psychology and Psychiatry, 39,* 1045–1053.

Faraone, S. V., & Giefer, E. E. (2007). Long-term effects of methylphenidate transdermal delivery system of ADHD on growth. *Journal of the American Academy of Child and Adolescent Psychiatry, 46,* 1138–1147.

Faraone, S. V., Glatt, S. J., Su, J., & Tsuang, M. T. (2004). Three potential susceptibility loci shown by a genome-wide scan for regions influencing the age of onset of mania. *American Journal of Psychiatry, 161,* 625–630.

Farrington, D. P. (1986). Stepping stones to adult criminal careers. In D. Olweus, J. Block, & M. R. Yarrow (Eds.), *Development of antisocial behavior and prosocial behavior.* New York: Academic Press.

Farrington, D. P. (1995). The development of offending and antisocial behaviour from childhood: Key findings from the Cambridge Study in Delinquent Development. *Journal of Child Psychology and Psychiatry, 36,* 929–964.

Federal Interagency Forum on Child and Family Statistics. 2004. *America's children: Key national indicators of well-being.* Washington, DC: U.S. Government Printing Office.

Felce, D. (2006). Both accurate interpretation of deinstitutionalization and a post institutional research agenda are needed. *Mental Retardation, 44,* 375–382.

Feldman, M. B., & Meyer, I. H. (2007). Childhood abuse and eating disorders in gay and bisexual men. *International Journal of Eating Disorders, 40,* 418–423.

Feldner, M. T., Zvolensky, M. J., & Schmidt, N. B. (2004). Prevention of anxiety psychopathology: A critical review of the empirical literature. *Clinical Psychology: Science and Practice, 11,* 405–424.

Ferguson, L. R. (1978). The competence and freedom of children to make choices regarding participation in research: A statement. *Journal of Social Issues, 34,* 114–121.

Fergusson, D. M., Horwood, L. J., & Ridder, E. M. (2005). Show me the child at seven II: childhood intelligence and later outcomes in adolescence and young adulthood. *Journal of Child Psychology and Psychiatry, 46,* 850–858.

Fergusson, D. M., & Horwood, L. J. (1998). Early conduct problems and later life opportunities. *Journal of Child Psychology and Psychiatry, 39,* 1097–1108.

Fergusson, D. M., Horwood, L. J., & Lynskey, M. T. (1993). Early dentine lead levels and subsequent cognitive and behavioural development. *Journal of Child Psychology and Psychiatry, 34,* 215–227.

Fergusson, D. M., Horwood, L. J., & Ridder, E. M. (2005). Show me the child at seven: The consequences of conduct problems in childhood for psychosocial functioning in adulthood. *Journal of Child Psychology and Psychiatry, 46,* 837–849.

Fergusson, D. M., & Lynskey, M. T. (1997). Early reading difficulties and later conduct problems. *Journal of Child Psychology and Psychiatry, 38,* 899–907.

Fergusson, D. M., Lynskey, M. T., & Horwood, L. J. (1997). Attentional difficulties in middle childhood and psychosocial outcomes in young adulthood. *Journal of Child Psychology and Psychiatry, 38,* 633–644.

Fergusson, D. M., & Woodward, L. J. (2000). Educational, psychological, and sexual outcomes of girls with conduct problems in early adolescence. *Journal of Child Psychology and Psychiatry, 41,* 779–792.

Ferrari, M. (1990). Developmental issues in behavioral pediatrics. In A. M. Gross & R. S. Drabman (Eds.), *Handbook of clinical behavioral pediatrics.* New York: Plenum.

Ferster, C. B. (1974). Behavioral approaches to depression. In R. J. Friedman & M. M. Katz (Eds.), *The psychology of depression: Contemporary theory and research.* Washington, DC: Winston.

Fetal Alcohol Syndrome. (2003). Retrieved March 2004 from http://www.cdc.gov/ncbdd/fas/fasask.htm.

Field, T., Hernandez-Reif, M., & Freedman, J. (2004). Stimulation programs for preterm infants. *Social Policy Report, 18(1),* 3–19.

Fiese, B. H., & Bickman, N. L. (1998). Qualitative inquiry: An overview for pediatric psychology. *Journal of Pediatric Psychology, 23,* 79–86.

Filipek, P. A. (1999). Neuroimaging in the developmental disorders: The state of the science. *Journal of Child Psychology and Psychiatry, 40,* 113–128.

Fine, M. A., & Harvey, J. H. (2006). Divorce and relationship dissolution in the 21st century. In M. A. Fine & J. H. Harvey (Eds.), *Handbook of divorce and relationship dissolution.* Mahwah, NJ: Lawrence Erlbaum Associates.

Fine, S. E., Izard, C. E., Mostow, A. J., Trentacosta, C. J., & Ackerman, B. P. (2003). First grade emotion knowledge as a predictor of fifth grade self-reported internalizing behaviors in children from economically disadvantaged families. *Development and Psychopathology, 15,* 331–342.

Finkelhor, D. (1994). The international epidemiology of child sexual abuse. *Child Abuse & Neglect, 18,* 409–417.

Finkelhor, D., Ormrod, R. K., & Turner, H. A. (2007). Re-victimization patterns in a national longitudinal sample of children and youth. *Child Abuse & Neglect, 31,* 479–502.

Finkelstein, H. (1988). The long term effects of early parent death: A review. *Journal of Clinical Psychology, 44,* 3–9.

Fischer, M., Barkley, R. A., Fletcher, K. E., & Smallish, L. (1993). The adolescent outcome of hyperactive children: Predictors of psychiatric, academic, social, and emotional adjustment. *Journal of the American Academy of Child and Adolescent Psychiatry, 32,* 324–332.

Fisher, J. O., & Birch, L. L. (2001). Body image in children. In J. K. Thompson & L. Smolak (Eds.), *Body image, eating disorders, and obesity in youth: Assessment, prevention, and treatment.* Washington, DC: American Psychological Association.

Fixsen, D. L., Wolf, M. M., & Phillips, E. L. (1973). Achievement place: A teaching-family model of community-based group homes for youth in trouble. In L. Hammerlynck, L. Handy, and E. Mash (Eds.), *Behavior change: Methodology, concepts and practice.* Champaign, IL: Research Press.

Flament, M. F., Whitaker, A., Rapoport, J. L., Davies, M., Berg, C. Z., Kalikow, K., Sceery, W., & Shafer, D. (1988). Obsessive compulsive disorder in adolescence: An epidemiological study. *Journal of the American Academy of Child and Adolescent Psychiatry, 27,* 764–771.

Flannery-Schroeder, E. C. (2004). Generalized anxiety disorder. In T. L. Morris & J. S. March (Eds.), *Anxiety disorders in children and adolescents.* New York: Guilford Press.

Flannery-Schroeder, E. C., & Kendall, P. C. (2000). Group and individual cognitive-behavioral treatments for youth with anxiety disorders: A randomized clinical trial. *Cognitive Therapy and Research, 24,* 251–278.

Flaton, R. A. (2006). "Who would I be without Danny?" Phenomenological case study of an adult sibling. *Mental Retardation, 44,* 135–144.

Flax, J. F., Realpe-Bonilla, T., Hirsch, L. S., Brzustowicz, L. M., Bartlett, C. W., & Tallal, P. (2003). Specific language impairments in families: Evidence for co-occurrence with reading impairments. *Journal of Speech, Language, and Hearing Impairments, 46,* 530–543.

Flay, B. R., Biglan, A., Boruch, R. F., Castro, F. G., Gottfredson, D., Kellam, S. G. et al. (2005). Standards of evidence: Criteria for efficacy, effectiveness and dissemination. *Prevention Science, 6,* 151–175.

Fleitlich-Bilyk, B., & Goodman, R. (2004). Prevalence of child and adolescent psychiatric disorders in southeast Brazil. *Journal of the American Academy of Child and Adolescent Psychiatry, 43,* 727–734.

Fleming, J. E., Offord, D. R., & Boyle, M. H. (1989). Prevalence of childhood and adolescent depression in the community: Ontario Child Health Study. *British Journal of Psychiatry, 155,* 647–654.

Fletcher, J. M., & Taylor, H. G. (1997). Children with brain injury. In E. J. Mash & L. G. Terdal (Eds.), *Assessment of childhood disorders* (3rd ed.). New York: Guilford Press.

Fletcher, K. E. (2003). Childhood posttraumatic stress disorder. In E. J. Mash & R. A. Barkley (Eds.), *Child psychopathology* (2nd ed.). New York: Guilford Press.

Flisher, A. J. (1999). Mood disorder in suicidal children and adolescents: Recent developments. *Journal of Child Psychology and Psychiatry, 40,* 315–324.

Flory, K., Lynam, D., Milich, R., Leukefeld, C., & Clayton, R. (2004). Early adolescent through young adult alcohol and marijuana use

trajectories: early predictors, young adult outcomes, and predictive utility. *Development and Psychopathology, 16,* 193–213.

Foa, E. B. & Commission on Adolescent Anxiety Disorders. (2005a). Defining anxiety disorders. In D. L. Evans, E. B. Foa, R. E. Gur, H. Hendin, C. P. O'Brien, M. E. P. Seligman, & B. T. Walsh (Eds.), *Treating and preventing adolescent mental health disorders. What we know and what we don't know: A research agenda for improving mental health of our youth.* New York: Oxford University Press.

Foa, E. B. & Commission on Adolescent Anxiety Disorder (2005b). Prevention of anxiety disorders. In D. L. Evans, E. B. Foa, R. E. Gur, H. Hendin, C. P. O'Brien, M. E. P. Seligman, & B. T. Walsh (Eds.), *Treating and preventing adolescent mental health disorders. What we know and what we don't know: A research agenda for improving mental health of our youth.* New York: Oxford University Press.

Follette, W. C., & Houts, A. C. (1996). Models of scientific progress and the role of theory in taxonomy development: A case study of DSM. *Journal of Consulting and Clinical Psychology, 64,* 1120–1132.

Fombonne, E. (2002). Case identification in an epidemiological context. In M. Rutter & E. Taylor (Eds.), *Child and adolescent psychiatry.* Oxford, UK: Blackwell Publishing.

Fombonne, E. (2003). Epidemiological surveys of autism and pervasive developmental disorders: An update. *Journal of Autism and Developmental Disorders, 33,* 365–382.

Fombonne, E., Rogé, B., Claverie, J., Courty, S., & Frémolle, J. (1999). Microcephaly and macrocephaly in autism. *Journal of Autism and Developmental Disorders, 29,* 113–119.

Fonagy, P., & Target. (2003). *Psychoanalytic theories. Perspectives from developmental psychopathology.* New York: Brunner-Routledge.

Fonesca, A. C., Yule, W., & Erol, N. (1994). Cross-cultural issues. In T. H. Ollendick, N. J. King, & W. Yule (Eds.), *International handbook of phobic and anxiety disorders in children and adolescents.* New York: Plenum Press.

Fontaine, R. G., Burks, V. S., & Dodge, K. A. (2002). Response decision processes and externalizing behavior problems in adolescents. *Development and Psychopathology, 14,* 107–122.

Ford, M. A., Sladeczek, I. E., Carlson, J., & Kratochwill, T. R. (1998). Selective mutism: Phenomenological characteristics. *School Psychology Quarterly, 13,* 192–227.

Ford, T., Goodman, R., & Meltzer, H. (2003). The British child and adolescent mental health survey 1999: The prevalence of DSM-IV disorders. *Journal of the American Academy of Child and Adolescent Psychiatry, 42,* 1203–1211.

Forehand, R., King, H. E., Peed, S., & Yoder, P. (1975). Mother-child interactions: Comparisons of a noncompliant clinic group and a non-clinic group. *Behaviour Research and Therapy, 13,* 79–84.

Forehand, R., & McMahon, R. J. (1981). *Helping the noncompliant child: A clinician's guide to parent training.* New York: Guilford.

Foster, G. G., & Salvia, J. (1977). Teacher response to the label of learning disabled as a function of demand characteristics. *Exceptional Children, 43,* 533–534.

Foster, S. L., & Robin, A. L. (1997). Family conflict and communication in adolescence. In E. J. Mash & L. G. Terdal (Eds.). *Assessment of childhood disorders* (3rd ed.). New York: Guilford Press.

Fowers, B. J., & Davidow, B. J. (2006). The virtue of multiculturism. *American Psychologist, 61,* 581–594.

Fowles, D. C. (1992). Schizophrenia: Diathesis-stress revisited. *Annual Review of Psychology, 43,* 303–336.

Fox, N. A., Hane, A. A., & Pine, D. S. (2007). Plasticity for human neurocircuitry: How the environment affects gene expression. *Current Directions in Psychological Science, 16,* 1–5.

Frances, A., & Ross, R. (2001). *DSM-IV-TR case studies: A clinical guide to differential diagnosis.* Washington, DC: American Psychiatric Association.

Franklin, M., Foa, E., & March, J. S. (2003). The Pediatric Obsessive-Compulsive Disorder Treatment Study: Rationale, design, and methods. *Journal of Child and Adolescent Psychopharmacology, 13,* S39–S51.

Frazier, J. A., McClellan, J., Findling, R. L., Vitiello, B., Anderson, R., Zablotsky, B. et al. (2007). Treatment of early-onset schizophrenia spectrum disorders (TEOSS): Demographic and clinical characteristics. *Journal of the American Academy of Child and Adolescent Psychiatry, 46,* 979–988.

Frazier, T. W., Youngstrom, E. A., Glutting, J. J., & Watkins, M. W. (2007). ADHD and achievement: Meta-analysis of the child, adolescent, and adult literature and a concomitant study with college students. *Journal of Learning Disabilities, 40,* 49–65.

Fredriksen, K., Rhodes, J., Reddy, R., & Way, N. (2004). Sleepless in Chicago: Tracking the effects of adolescent sleep loss during the middle school years. *Child Development, 75,* 84–95.

Freeman, J. B., Garcia, A. M., Fucci, C., Karitani, M., Miller, L., & Leonard, H. L. (2003). Family-based treatment of early-onset obsessive-compulsive disorder. *Journal of Child and Adolescent Psychopharmacology, 13,* S71–S80.

Fremont, W. P. (2004). Childhood reactions to terrorism-induced trauma: A review of the past 10 years. *Journal of the American Academy of Child and Adolescent Psychiatry, 43,* 381–392.

Freud, A. (1946). *The psycho-analytical treatment of children.* London: Imago.

Freud, S. (1953). *Analysis of a phobia in a five-year-old boy (1909).* Standard Edition. Vol. 10. Ed. and trans. James Strachey, London: The Hogarth Press.

Freyer, D. R., Kuperberg, A., Sterken, D. J., Pastyrnak, S. L., Hudson, D., & Richards, T. (2006). Multidisciplinary care of the dying adolescent. *Child and Adolescent Psychiatric Clinics of North America, 15,* 693–715.

Frick, P. J. (1994). Family dysfunction and the disruptive disorders: A review of recent empirical findings. In T. H. Ollendick & R. J. Prinz (Eds.), *Advances in clinical child psychology.* Vol. 16. New York: Plenum Press.

Frick, P. J. (1998a). Callous-unemotional traits and conduct problems: A two-factor model of psychopathy in children. In D. J. Cooke, A. Forth, & R. D. Hare (Eds.), *Psychopathy: Theory, research, and implications for society.* Dordrecht, The Netherlands: Kluwer.

Frick, P. J. (1998b). Conduct disorders. In T. H. Ollendick & M. Hersen (Eds.), *Handbook of child psychopathology* (3rd ed.). New York: Plenum Press.

Frick, P. J. (2004). Integrating research on temperament and childhood psychopathology: Its pitfalls and promise. *Journal of Clinical Child and Adolescent Psychology, 33,* 2–7.

Frick, P. J., & Kamphaus, R. W. (2001). Standardized rating scales in the assessment of children's behavioral and emotional problems. In C. E. Walker & M. C. Roberts (Eds.), *Handbook of clinical child psychology* (3rd ed.). New York: John Wiley & Sons.

Frick, P. J., & Loney, B. R. (2000). The use of laboratory and performance-based measures in the assessment of children and adolescents with conduct disorders. *Journal of Clinical Child Psychology, 29,* 540–554.

Frick, P. J., & Morris, A. S. (2004). Temperament and developmental pathways to conduct problems. *Journal of Clinical Child and Adolescent Psychology, 33,* 54–68.

Friedman, A. G., Latham, S. A., & Dahlquist, L. M. (1998). Childhood cancer. In T. H. Ollendick & M. Hersen (Eds.), *Handbook of child psychopathology* (3rd ed.). New York: Plenum Press.

Fristad, M. A., & Goldberg-Arnold, J. S. (2003). Family interventions for early-onset bipolar disorder. In B. Geller & M. P. DelBello (Eds.), *Bipolar disorder in childhood and early adolescence.* New York: Guilford Press.

Frith, U. (2004). Emmanuel Miller lecture: Confusions and controversies about Asperger syndrome. *Journal of Child Psychology and Psychiatry, 45,* 672–686.

Fryer, S. L., McGee, C. L., Matt, G. E., Riley, E. P., & Mattson, S. N. (2007). Evaluation of psychopathological conditions in children with heavy prenatal alcohol exposure. *Pediatrics, 119,* e733–e741.

Fuchs, L. S., Fuchs, D., & Hollenbeck, K. N. (2007). Extending responsiveness to intervention to mathematics at first and third grades. *Learning Disabilities Research & Practice, 22,* 13–23.

Fuchs, L.S., Fuchs, D., & Prentice, K. (2004). Responsiveness to mathematical problem-solving instruction: Comparing students at risk of mathematics disability with and without risk of reading disability. *Journal of Learning Disabilities, 37,* 293–306.

Gabbard, G. O. (2000). Psychoanalysis and psychoanalytic psychotherapy. In B. J. Sadock & V. A. Sadock (Eds.), *Kaplan & Sadock's Comprehensive textbook of psychiatry* (Vol. II). Philadelphia: Lippincott Williams & Wilkins.

Gadow, K. D., & Nolan, E. E. (2002). Differences between preschool children with ODD, ADHD, and ODD+ADHD symptoms. *Journal of Child Psychology and Psychiatry, 43,* 191–201.

Gadow, K. D., Nolan, E. E., Litcher, L., Carlson, G. A., Panina, N., Golovakha, E. et al. (2000). Comparison of attention-deficit/hyperactivity disorder symptom subtypes in Ukrainian schoolchildren. *Journal of the American Academy of Child and Adolescent Psychiatry, 39,* 1520–1527.

Gadow, K. D., Sverd, J., Nolan, E. E., Sprafkin, J., & Schneider, J. (2007). Immediate-release methylphenidate for ADHD in children with comorbid chronic multiple tic disorder. *Journal of the American Academy of Child and Adolescent Psychiatry, 46,* 840–847.

Garber, J., & Flynn, C. (2001). Predictors of depressive cognitions in young adolescents. *Cognitive Therapy and Research, 25,* 353–376.

Garber, J., & Kaminski, K. M. (2000). Laboratory and performance-based measures of depression in children and adolescents. *Journal of Clinical Child Psychology, 29,* 509–525.

Garcia Coll, C., Crnic, K., Lamberty, G., Wasik, B. H., Jenkins, R., Garcia, H. V. et al. (1966). An integrative model for the study of developmental competencies in minority children. *Child Development, 67,* 1891–1914.

García Coll, C., & Garrido, M. (2000). Minorities in the United States: Sociocultural context for mental health and developmental psychopathology. In A. J. Sameroff, M. Lewis, & S. M. Miller (Eds.), *Handbook of developmental psychopathology.* New York: Kluwer/Plenum Publishers.

Gardner, R. M. (2001). Assessment of body image disturbance in children and adolescents. In J. K. Thompson & L. Smolak (Eds.), *Body image, eating disorders, and obesity in youth: Assessment, prevention, and treatment.* Washington, DC: American Psychological Association.

Gathercole, S. E., & Alloway, T. P. (2006). Practitioner review: Short-term and working memory impairments in neurodevelopmental disorders: Diagnosis and remedial support. *Journal of Child Psychology and Psychiatry, 47,* 4–15.

Gaub, M., & Carlson, C. L. (1997). Gender difference in ADHD: A meta-analysis and critical review. *Journal of the American Academy of Child and Adolescent Psychiatry, 36,* 1035–1045.

Gaván, J., Willcut, E. G., Fisher, S. E., Francks, C., Cardon. L. R., Olson, R. K. et al. (2005). Bivariate linkage scan for reading disability and attention-deficit/hyperactivity disorder localizes pleiotropic loci. *Journal of Child Psychology and Psychiatry, 46,* 1045–1056.

Ge, X., Conger, R. D., Lorenz, F. O., Shanahan, M., & Elder, G. H. (1995). Mutual influences in parent and adolescent psychological distress. *Developmental Psychology, 31,* 406–419.

Geary, D. C. (2003). Learning disabilities in arithmetic: Problem-solving differences and cognitive deficits. In H. L. Swanson, K. R. Harris, & S. Graham (Eds.), *Handbook of learning disabilities.* New York: Guilford Press.

Geary, D. C. (2004). Mathematics and learning disabilities. *Journal of Learning Disabilities, 37,* 4–15.

Geier, A. B., Foster, G. D., Womble, L. G., McLaughlin, J., Borradaile, K. E., Nachmani, J. et al. (2007). The relationship between relative weight and school attendance among elementary schoolchildren. *Obesity, 15,* 2157–2161.

Geller, B., Craney, J. L., Bolhofner, K., DelBello, M. P., Axelson, D., Luby, J., Williams, M., Zimerman, B., Nickelsburg, M. J., Frazier, J., & Beringer, L. (2003). Phenomenology and longitudinal course of children with prepubertal and early adolescent bipolar disorder phenotype. In B. Geller & M. P. DelBello (Eds.), *Bipolar disorder in childhood and early adolescence.* New York: Guilford Press.

Geller, B., Tillman, R., & Bolhofner, K. (2007). Proposed definitions of Bipolar I Disorder episodes and daily rapid cycling phenomena in preschoolers, school-aged children, adolescents, and adults. *Journal of Child and Adolescent Psychopharmacology, 17,* 217–222.

Geller, B., Zimerman, B., Williams, M., Bulhofner, K., Craney, J. L., DelBello, M. P., & Soutullo, C. (2001). Reliability of the Washington University in St. Louis Kiddie Schedule for Affective Disorders and Schizophrenia (WASH-U-KSADS) mania and rapid cycling sections. *Journal of the American Academy of Child and Adolescent Psychiatry, 40,* 450–455.

Geller, D. A., Biederman, J., Stewart, E., Mullin, B., Farrell, C., Wagner, K. D., Emslie, G., & Carpenter, D. (2003a). Impact of comorbidity on treatment response to paroxetine in pediatric obsessive-compulsive disorder: Is the use of exclusion criteria empirically supported in randomized clinical trials? *Journal of Child and Adolescent Psychopharmacology, 13,* S19–S29.

Geller, D. A., Biederman, J., Stewart, S. E., Mullin, B., Martin, A., Spencer, T., & Faraone, S. V. (2003b). Which SSRI? A meta-analysis of pharmacotherapy trials in pediatric obsessive-compulsive disorder. *American Journal of Psychiatry, 160,* 1919–1928.

Gencöz, T., Voelz, A. R., Gencöz, F., Pettit, J. W., & Joiner, T. E. (2001). Specificity of information processing styles to depressive symptoms in youth psychiatric inpatients. *Journal of Abnormal Child Psychology, 29,* 255–262.

Geoffroy, M.-C., Côté, S. M., Borge, A. I. H., Larouche, F., Séguin, J. R., & Rutter, M. (2007). Association between nonmaternal care in the first year of life and children's receptive language skills prior to school entry: the moderating role of socioeconomic status. *Journal of Child Psychology and Psychiatry, 48,* 490–497.

Georgiades, K., & Boyle, M. H. (2007). Adolescent tobacco and cannabis use: young adult outcomes from the Ontario Child Health Study. *Journal of Child Psychology and Psychiatry, 48,* 724–731.

Georgiades, K., Lewinsohn, P. M., Monroe, S. M., & Seeley, J. R. (2006). Major depressive disorder in adolescence: The role of subthreshold symptoms. *Journal of the American Academy of Child and Adolescent Psychiatry, 45,* 936–944.

Gerard, M. W. (1939). Enuresis: A study in etiology. *American Journal of Orthopsychiatry, 9,* 48–58.

Gerdes, A. C., Hoza, B., & Pelham, W. E. (2003). Attention-deficit hyperactivity disordered boys' relationships with their mothers and fathers: Child, mother, and father perceptions. *Development and Psychopathology, 15,* 363–382.

Gerull, F. C., & Rapee, R. M. (2002). Mother knows best: The effects of maternal modeling on the acquisition of fear and avoidance behaviour in toddlers. *Behaviour Research and Therapy, 40,* 279–287.

Gettinger, M., & Koscik, R. (2001). Psychological services for children with learning disabilities. In J. N. Huges, A. M. La Greca, & J. C. Conoley (Eds.), *Handbook of psychological services for children and adolescents.* New York: Oxford University Press.

Ghaziuddin, M., Thomas, P., Napier, E., Kearney, G., Tsai, L., Welch, K., & Fraser, W. (2000). Brief report: Brief syntactic analysis in Asperger's syndrome: A preliminary study. *Journal of Autism and Developmental Disorders, 30,* 67–70.

Gibbs, J. T. (2003). African American children and adolescents. In J. T. Gibbs, L. N. Huang, and Associates (Eds.), *Children of color: Psychological interventions with culturally diverse youth.* San Francisco: Jossey-Bass.

Gibbs, J. T., Huang, L. N., & Associates. (2003). *Children of color: Psychological interventions with culturally diverse youth.* San Francisco: Jossey-Bass.

Gil, A. G., Wagner, E. F., & Vega, W. A. (2000). Acculturation, familism, and alcohol use among Latino adolescent males: Longitudinal relations. *Journal of Community Psychology, 28,* 443–458.

Gillberg, I. C., Hellgren, L., & Gillberg, C. (1993). Psychotic disorders diagnosed in adolescence. Outcome at age 30 years. *Journal of Child Psychology and Psychiatry, 34,* 1173–1185.

Gilmour, J., Hill, B., Place, M., Skuse, D. H. (2004). Social communication deficits in conduct disorder: a clinical and community survey. *Journal of Child Psychology and Psychiatry, 45,* 967–978.

Ginsburg, G. S., & Silverman, W. K. (1996). Phobic and anxiety disorders in Hispanic and Caucasian youth. *Journal of Anxiety Disorders, 10,* 517–528.

Ginsburg, G. S., & Silverman, W. K. (2000). Gender role orientation and fearfulness in children with anxiety disorders. *Journal of Anxiety Disorders, 14,* 57–67.

Ginsburg, G. S., LaGreca, A. M. & Silverman, W. K. (1998). Social anxiety in children with anxiety disorders: Relation with social and emotional functioning. *Journal of Abnormal Psychology, 26,* 175–185.

Ginsburg, G. S., Riddle, M. A., & Davies, M. (2006). Somatic symptoms in children and adolescents with anxiety disorders. *Journal of the American Academy of Child and Adolescent Psychiatry, 45,* 1179–1187.

Glantz, L. H. (1996). Conducting research with children: Legal and ethical issues. *Journal of the American Academy of Child and Adolescent Psychiatry, 35,* 1283–1291.

Glantz, M. D., & Leshner, A. I. (2000). Drug abuse and developmental psychopathology. *Development and Psychopathology, 12,* 795–814.

Gleason, M. M., Egger, H. L., Emsile, G. J., Greenhill, L. L., Kowatch, R. A., Lieberaman, A. F. et al. (2007). Pharmacological treatment for very young children: Contexts and guideliness. *Journal of the American Academy of Child and Adolescent Psychiatry, 46,* 1532–1572.

Gliner, J. A., Morgan, G. A., & Harmon, R. J. (2000). Single-subject designs. *Journal of the American Academy of Child and Adolescent Psychiatry, 39,* 1327–1329.

Glowinski, A. L., Madden, P. A. F., Bucholz, K. K., Lynskey, M. T., & Heath, A. C. (2003). Genetic epidemiology of self-reported lifetime DSM-IV major depressive disorder in a population-based twin sample of female adolescents. *Journal of Child Psychology and Psychiatry, 44,* 988–996.

Glueck, S., & Glueck, E. T. (1968). *Delinquents and nondelinquents in perspective.* Cambridge, MA: Harvard University Press.

Goddard, H. H. (1912). *The Kallikak family.* New York: Macmillan.

Goeke, J., Kassow, D., May, D., & Kundert, D. (2003). Parental opinions about plastic surgery for individuals with Down syndrome. *Mental Retardation, 41,* 29–34.

Goenjian, A. K., Yehuda, R., Pynoos, R. S., Steinberg, A. M., Tashjian, M., Yang, R. K., Najarian, L. M., Fairbanks, L. A. (1996). Basal cortisol, dexamethasone suppression of cortisol, and MHPG in adolescents after the 1988 earthquake in Armenia. *American Journal of Psychiatry, 153,* 929–934.

Goldberg, W. A., Osann, K., Filipek, P. A., Laulhere, T., Jarvis, K., Modahl, C. et al. (2003). Language and other regression: Assessment and timing. *Journal of Autism and Developmental Disorders, 33,* 607–616.

Goldberg-Arnold, J. S., & Fristad, M. A. (2003). Psychotherapy for children with bipolar disorder. In B. Geller & M. P. DelBello (Eds.), *Bipolar disorder in childhood and early adolescence.* New York: Guilford Press.

Golden, C. J. (1987). *Luria-Nebraska Neuropsychological Battery: Children's revision manual.* Los Angeles: Western Psychological Services.

Goldston, D. B., Walsh, A., Arnold, E. M., Reboussin, B., Daniel, S. S., Erkanli, A. et al. (2007). Reading problems, psychiatric disorders, and functional impairment from mid- to late adolescence. *Journal of the American Academy of Child and Adolescent Psychiatry, 46,* 25–32.

Golombok, S. (2006). New family forms. In A. Clarke-Stewart & J. Dunn (Eds.). *Families count. Effects on child and adolescent development.* New York: Cambridge University Press.

Gomez, R., Gomez, A., DeMello, L, & Tallent, R. (2001). Perceived maternal control and support: Effects on hostile biased social information processing and aggression among clinic-referred children with high aggression. *Journal of Child Psychology and Psychiatry, 42,* 513–522.

Gomez, R., Harvey, J., Quick, C., Scharer, I., & Harris, G. (1999). DSM-IV AD/HD: Confirmatory factor models, prevalence, and gender and age differences based on parent and teacher ratings of Australian primary school children. *Journal of Child Psychology and Psychiatry, 40,* 265–274.

Gooding, D. C., & Iacono, W. G. (1995). Schizophrenia through the lens of a developmental psychopathology perspective. In D. Cicchetti & D. J. Cohen (Eds.), *Developmental Psychology* (Vol. 2). New York: John Wiley Interscience.

Goodlin-Jones, B. L., Burnham, M. M., & Anders, T. F. (2000). Sleep and sleep disturbances: Regulatory processes in infancy. In A. J. Sameroff, M. Lewis, & S. M. Miller (Eds.), *Handbook of developmental psychopathology* (2nd ed.). New York: Kluwer Academic/Plenum Publishers.

Goodman, R., & Stevenson, J. (1989). A twin study of hyperactivity-II. The aetiological role of genes, family relationships and perinatal adversity. *Journal of Child Psychology and Psychiatry, 30,* 691–709.

Goodman, S. H., Schwab-Stone, M., Lahey, B., Shaffer, D., & Jensen, P. (2000). Major depression and dysthymia in children and adolescents: Discriminant validity and differentiated consequences in a community sample. *Journal of the American Academy of Child and Adolescent Psychiatry, 39,* 761–770.

Goodwin, R. D., Fergusson, D. M., & Horwood, L. J. (2004). Early anxious/withdrawn behaviours predict later internalising disorders. *Journal of Child Psychology and Psychiatry, 45,* 874–883.

Goodyer, I. M., & Cooper, P. (1993). A community study of depression in adolescent girls: II. The clinical features of identified disorder. *British Journal of Psychiatry, 163,* 374–380.

Goodyer, I. M., Park, R. J., & Herbert, J. (2001). Psychosocial and endocrine features of chronic first-episode major depression in 8–16 year olds. *Biological Psychiatry, 50,* 351–357.

Gordis, E. B., Granger, D. A., Susman, E. J., & Trickett, P. K. (2006). Asymmetry between salivary cortisol and α-amylase reactivity to stress: Relation to aggressive behavior in adolescents. *Psychoneuroendocrinology, 31,* 976–987.

Gordis, E. B., Margolin, G., & John, R. S. (2001). Parents' hostility in dyadic marital and triadic family settings and children's behavior problems. *Journal of Consulting and Clinical Psychology, 69,* 727–734.

Gordon, J., King, N. J., Bullone, E., Muris, P., & Ollendick, T. H. (2007). Treatment of children's nighttime fears: The need for a modern randomized controlled trial. *Clinical Psychology Review, 27,* 98–113.

Gordon, M., Barkley, R. A., & Lovett, B. J. (2006). Tests and observational measures. In R. A. Barkley (Ed.), *Attention-deficit hyperactivity disorder. A handbook for diagnosis and treatment.* New York: The Guilford Press.

Gordon-Larsen, P., Adair, L. S., & Popkin, B. M. (2002). Ethnic differences in physical activity and inactivity patterns and overweight status. *Obesity Research, 10,* 141–149.

Gortmaker, S. L., & Sappenfield, W. (1984). Chronic childhood disorders: Prevalence and impact. *Pediatric Clinics of North America, 31,* 3–18.

Gottesman, I. I. (1993). Origins of schizophrenia: Past as prologue. In R. Plomin & G. E. McClearn (Eds.), *Nature and nurture & psychology.* Washington, DC: American Psychological Association.

Gottlieb, G. (2003). Probabilistic epigenesis of development. In J. Valsiner & K. J. Connolly (Eds.), *Handbook of developmental psychology.* Thousand Oaks, CA: Sage Publications.

Gould, M. S., Greenberg, T., Velting, D. M., & Shaffer, D. (2003). Youth suicide risk and preventive interventions: A review of the past 10 years. *Journal of the American Academy of Child and Adolescent Psychiatry, 42,* 386–405.

Gowers, S., & Bryant-Waugh, R. (2004). Management of child and adolescent eating disorders: The current evidence base and future directions. *Journal of Child Psychology and Psychiatry, 45,* 63–83.

Graber, J. A., Seeley, J. R., Brooks-Gunn, J., & Lewinsohn, P. M. (2004). Is pubertal timing associated with psychopathology in young adulthood? *Journal of the American Academy of Child and Adolescent Psychiatry, 43,* 718–726.

Grace, W. J., & Graham, D. T. (1952). Relationship of specific attitudes and emotions to certain bodily diseases. *Psychosomatic Medicine, 14,* 243–251.

Graetz, B. W., Sawyer, M. G., Hazell, P. L., Arney, F., & Baghurst, P. (2001). Validity of DSM-IV ADHD subtypes in a nationally representative sample of Australian children and adolescents. *Journal of the American Academy of Child and Adolescent Psychiatry, 40,* 410–417.

Graham, S., & Harris, K. R. (2003). Students with learning disabilities and the process of writing: A meta-analysis of SRSD studies. In H. L. Swanson, K. R. Harris, & S. Graham (Eds.), *Handbook of learning disabilities.* New York: Guilford Press.

Grandin, T. (1997). A personal perspective on autism. In D. J. Cohen & F. R. Volkmar (Eds.), *Handbook of autism and pervasive developmental disorders.* New York: John Wiley.

Grant, K. E., Compas, B. E., Stuhlmacher, A. F., Thurm, A. E., McMahon, S. D., & Halpert, J. A. (2003). Stressors and child and adolescent psychopathology: Moving from markers to mechanisms of risk. *Psychological Bulletin, 129,* 447–466.

Gray, J. A. (1987). *The psychology of fear and stress.* New York: Cambridge University Press.

Greco, L. A., & Morris, T. L. (2004). Assessment. In T. L. Morris & J. S. March (Eds.), *Anxiety disorders in children and adolescents.* New York: Guilford Press.

Greco, P., Pendley, J. S., McDonell, K., & Reeves, G. (2001). A peer group intervention for adolescents with type 1 diabetes and their best friends. *Journal of Pediatric Psychology, 26,* 485–490.

Green, J. (2006). Annotation: The therapeutic alliance—a significant but neglected variable in child mental health treatment studies. *Journal of Child Psychology and Psychiatry, 47,* 425–435.

Green, J., & Goldwyn, R. (2002). Annotation: Attachment disorganization and psychopathology: New findings in attachment research and their potential implications for developmental psychopathology in childhood. *Journal of Child Psychology and Psychiatry, 43,* 835–846.

Green, R. (2004). The evolution of kinship care policy and practice. *The Future of Children, 14,* 131–149.

Green, W. H., Padron-Gayol, M., Hardesty, A. S., & Bassiri, M. (1992). Schizophrenia with childhood onset: A phenomenological study of 38 cases. *Journal of the American Academy of Child and Adolescent Psychiatry, 31,* 968–976.

Greene, R. W. (1995). Students with ADHD in school classrooms: Teacher factors related to compatibility, assessment, and intervention. *School Psychology Review, 24,* 81–93.

Greenhill, L., Kollins, S., Abikoff, H., McCracken, J., Riddle, M., Swanson, J. et al. (2006). Efficacy and safety of immediate-release methylphenidate treatment for preschoolers with ADHD. *Journal of the American Academy of Child and Adolescent Psychiatry, 45,* 1284–1293.

Greenhill, L., Pliszka, S., Dulcan, M. K., & the Work Group on Quality Issues. (2002). Practice parameter for the use of stimulant medications in the treatment of children, adolescents, and adults. *Journal of the American Academy of Child and Adolescent Psychiatry, 41,* Supplement, 26S-49S.

Greenhill, L. L., Jensen, P. S., Abikoff, H., Blumer, J. L., De-Veaugh-Geiss, J., Fisher, C. (2003a). Developing strategies for psychopharmacological studies in preschool children. *Journal of the American Academy of Child and Adolescent Psychiatry, 42,* 406–414.

Greenhill, L. L., Vitiello, B., Riddle, M. A., Fisher, P., Shockey, E., March, J. S. et al. (2003b). Review of safety assessment methods used in pediatric psychopharmacology. *Journal of the American Academy of Child and Adolescent Psychiatry, 42,* 627–633.

Greenspan, S., & Love, P. F. (1997). Social intelligence and developmental disorder: Mental retardation, learning disabilities, and autism. In W. E. MacLean (Ed.), *Ellis' handbook of mental deficiency, psychological theory and research.* Mahwah, NJ: Lawrence Erlbaum.

Greenstein, D., Lerch, J., Shaw, P., Clasen, L., Giedd, J., Gochman, P. et al. (2006). Childhood onset schizophrenia: cortical brain abnormalities as young adults. *Journal of Child Psychology and Psychiatry, 47,* 1003–1012.

Greenwood, C. R. et al. (1992). Out of the laboratory and into the community: 26 years of applied behavior analysis at the Juniper Gardens Children's Project. *American Psychologist, 47,* 1464–1474.

Greenwood, C. R., Hart, B., Walker, D., & Risley, T. (1994). The opportunity to respond and academic performance revisited: A behavioral theory of developmental retardation and its prevention. In R. Gardner et al. (Eds.), *Behavior analysis in education: Focus on measurably superior instruction.* Pacific Grove, CA: Brooks/Cole.

Gregory, A. M., Caspi, A., Eley, T. C., Moffitt, T. E., O'Connor, T. G., & Poulton, R. (2005). Prospective longitudinal associations between persistent sleep problems in childhood and anxiety and depression disorders in adulthood. *Journal of Abnormal Child Psychology, 33,* 157–163.

Gregory, A. M., Eley, T. C., & Plomin, R. (2004). Exploring the association between anxiety and conduct problems in a large sample of twins aged 2–4. *Journal of Abnormal Child Psychology, 32,* 111–122.

Gregory, A. M., Rijsdijk, F. V., & Eley, T. C. (2006). A twin-study of sleep difficulties in school-aged children. *Child Development, 77,* 1668–1679.

Griffiths, L. J., Wolke, D., Page, A. S., & Horwood, J. P. (2006). Obesity and bullying: Different effects for boys and girls. *Archives of Disease in Childhood, 91,* 121–125.

Grigorenko, E. L. (2001). Developmental dyslexia: An update on genes, brains, and environments. *Journal of Child Psychology and Psychiatry, 42,* 91–125.

Grigorenko, E. L., Klin, A., & Volkmar, R. (2003). Annotation: Hyperlexia: Disability or superability? *Journal of Child Psychology and Psychiatry, 44,* 1079–1091.

Grinspoon, S., Thomas, E., Pitts, S., Gross, E., Mickley, D., Miller, K., Herzog, D., & Klibanski, A. (2000). Prevalence and predictive factors for regional osteopenia in women with anorexia nervosa. *Annals of Internal Medicine, 133,* 790–794.

Gross, D., Fogg, L., Webster-Stratton, C., Garvey, C. W., & Grady, J. (2003). Parent training with parents of toddlers in day care in low-income urban communities. *Journal of Consulting and Clinical Psychology, 71,* 261–278.

Grossman, A. W., Churchill, J. D., McKinney, B. C., Kodish, I. M., Otte, S. L., & Greenough, W. T. (2003). Experience effects on brain development: Possible contributions to psychopathology. *Journal of Child Psychology and Psychiatry, 44,* 33–63.

Grossman, H. J. (1983). *Classification in mental retardation.* Washington, DC: American Association on Mental Deficiency.

Grusec, J. E. (1992). Social learning theory and developmental psychology: The legacies of Robert Sears and Albert Bandura. *Developmental Psychology, 28,* 776–786.

Grych, J. H., & Fincham, F. D. (1999). Children of single parents and divorce. In W. K. Silverman & T. H. Ollendick (Eds.), *Developmental issues in the clinical treatment of children.* Boston: Allyn and Bacon.

Gullone, E. (2000). The development of normal fear: A century of research. *Clinical Psychology Review, 20,* 429–451.

Gunnar, M. R., & Vazquez, D. (2006). Stress neurobiology and developmental psychopathology. In D. Cicchetti & D. J. Cohen (Eds.), *Developmental psychopathology. Vol. 2. Developmental neuroscience.* (2nd ed.). Hoboken, NJ: John Wiley & Sons.

Gunnar, M. R., Van Dulmen, M. H. M., and The International Adoption Project Team. (2007). Behavior problems in postinstitutionalized internationally adopted children. *Development and Psychopathology, 19,* 129–148.

Gunther, D., & Diekema, D. (2006). Attenuating growth in children with developmental disability: A new approach to an old dilemma. *Archives of Pediatric and Adolescent Medicine, 160,* 1013–1017.

Gur, R. E., Cowell, P., Turetsky, B. I., Gallacher, F., Cannon, T., Bilker, W., & Gur, R. C. (1998). A follow-up magnetic resonance imaging study of schizophrenia. *Archives of General Psychiatry, 55,* 145–152.

Guralnick, M. J. (1998). Effectiveness of early intervention for vulnerable children: A developmental perspective. *American Journal on Mental Retardation, 102,* 319–345.

Gurwitch, R. H., Kees, M., & Becker, S. M. (2002). In the face of tragedy: Placing children's reactions to trauma in a new context. *Cognitive & Behavioral Practice, 9,* 286–295.

Hafner, A. J., Quast, W., & Shea, M. J. (1975). The adult adjustment of one thousand psychiatric patients: Initial findings from a twenty-five year follow-up. In R. O. Wirt, G. Winokur, & M. Roff (Eds.), *Life history in psychopathology,* Vol. 4, Minneapolis: University of Minnesota Press.

Hallahan, D. P., & Kauffman, J. M. (1978). *Exceptional children: Introduction to special education.* Englewood Cliffs, NJ: Prentice Hall.

Hallahan, D. P., & Mock, D. R. (2003). A brief history of the field of learning disabilities. In H. L. Swanson, K. R. Harris, & S. Graham (Eds.), *Handbook of learning disabilities.* New York: Guilford Press.

Halmi, K. A. (1985). Eating disorders. In H. I. Kaplan & B. J. Sadock (Eds.), *Comprehensive textbook of psychiatry* (4th ed.). Baltimore: Williams & Wilkins.

Hammad, T. A., Laughren, T., & Racoosin, J. (2006). Suicidality in pediatric patients treated with antidepressant drugs. *Archives of General Psychiatry, 63,* 332–339.

Hammen, C. (1992). Cognitive, life stress, and interpersonal approaches to a developmental psychopathology model of depression. *Development and Psychopathology, 4,* 189–206.

Hammen, C., & Brennan, P. A. (2001). Depressed adolescents of depressed and nondepressed mothers: Tests of an interpersonal impairment hypothesis. *Journal of Consulting and Clinical Psychology, 69,* 284–294.

Hammen, C., Burge, D., Burney, E., & Adrian, C. (1990). Longitudinal study of diagnosis in children of women with unipolar and bipolar affective disorders. *Archives of General Psychiatry, 47,* 1112–1117.

Hammen, C., Rudolph, K., Weisz, J., Rao, U., & Burge, D. (1999). The context of depression in clinic-referred youth: Neglected areas in treatment. *Journal of the American Academy of Child and Adolescent Psychiatry, 38,* 64–71.

Hammen, C., & Rudolph, K. D. (2003). Childhood mood disorders. In E. J. Mash & R. A. Barkley (Eds.), *Child psychopathology* (2nd ed.). New York: Guilford Press.

Hammill, D. D. (1993). A brief look at the learning disabilities movement in the United States. *Journal of Learning Disabilities, 26,* 295–310.

Handen, B. L. (1998). Mental retardation. In E. J. Mash & L. G. Terdal (Eds.), *Treatment of childhood disorders.* New York: Guilford Press.

Handen, B. L., & Gilchrist, R. (2006a). Mental retardation. In E. J. Mash & R. A. Barkley (Eds.), *Treatment of childhood disorders.* New York: The Guilford Press.

Handen, B. L., & Gilchrist, R. (2006b). Practitioner review: Psychopharmacology in children and adolescents with mental retardation. *Journal of Child Psychology and Psychiatry, 47,* 871–882.

Hane, A. A., & Fox, N. A. (2006). Ordinary variations in maternal caregiving influence human infants' stress reactivity. *Psychological Science, 17,* 550–556.

Hanish, L. D., & Guerra, N. G. (2002). A longitudinal analysis of patterns of adjustment following peer victimization. *Development and Psychopathology, 14,* 69–89.

Hankin, B. L., Abramson, L. Y., Moffitt, T. E., Silva, P. A., McGee, R., & Angell, K. E. (1998). Development of depression from preadolescence to young adulthood: Emerging gender differences in a 10–year longitudinal study. *Journal of Abnormal Psychology, 107,* 128–140.

Hankin, B. L., Fraley, R. C., Lahey, B. B., & Waldman, I. D. (2005). Is depression best viewed as a continuum or discrete category? A taxometric analysis of childhood and adolescent depression in a population-based sample. *Journal of Abnormal Psychology, 114,* 96–110.

Hanna, K. M., DiMeglio, L. A., & Fortenberry, J. D. (2007). Initial testing of scales measuring parent and adolescent perceptions of adolescents' assumption of diabetes management. *Journal of Pediatric Psychology, 32,* 245–249.

Hannah, M. E., & Midlarsky, E. (2005). Helping in siblings of children with mental retardation. *American Journal on Mental Retardation, 110,* 87–99.

Hansen, C., Weiss, D., & Last, C. G. (1999). ADHD boys in young adulthood: Psychosocial adjustment. *Journal of the American Academy of Child and Adolescent Psychiatry, 38,* 165–171.

Happé, F., Briskman, J., & Frith, U. (2001). Exploring the cognitive phenotype of autism: Weak "central coherence" in parents and siblings of children with autism: I. Experimental tests. *Journal of Child Psychology and Psychiatry, 42,* 299–307.

Happé, F. G. E. (1994). Wechsler IQ profile and theory of mind in autism: A research note. *Journal of Child Psychology and Psychiatry, 35,* 1461–1471.

Harbeck-Weber, C., & Peterson, L. (1996). Health-related disorders. In E. J. Mash & R. A. Barkley (Eds.), *Child psychopathology.* New York: Guilford Press.

Harcourt Assessment. (2003). *The Stanford Achievement Test, Tenth Edition.* San Antonio, TX: Harcourt Assessment.

Harkness, S., & Super, C. M. (2000). Culture and psychopathology. In A. J. Sameroff, M. Lewis, & S. M. Miller (Eds.), *Handbook of developmental psychopathology.* New York: Kluwer/Plenum Publishers.

Harlaar, N., Spinath, F. M., Dale, P. S., & Plomin, R. (2005). Genetic influences on early word recognition abilities and disabilities: a study of 7-year-old twins. *Journal of Child Psychology and Psychiatry, 46,* 373–384.

Harley, J. P., & Matthews, C. G. (1980). Food additives and hyperactivity in children: Experimental investigations. In R. M. Knights and D. J. Bakker (Eds.), *Treatment of hyperactive and learning disordered children.* Baltimore: University Park Press.

Harrington, R. (2001). Adolescent depression: Same or different? *Archives of General Psychiatry, 58,* 21–22.

Harrington, R., Rutter, M., Weissman, M., Fudge, H., Groothues, C., Bredenkamp, D., Pickles, A., Rende, R., & Wickramaratne, P. (1997). Psychiatric disorders in the relatives of depressed probands: I. Comparison of prepubertal, adolescent and early adult onset cases. *Journal of Affective Disorders, 42,* 9–22.

Harris, P. L. (1994). The child's understanding of emotion: Developmental change and the family environment. *Journal of Child Psychology and Psychiatry, 35,* 3–28.

Harris, S. L., & Handleman, J. S. (2000). Age and IQ at intake as predictors of placement for young children with autism: A four-to-six-year follow-up. *Journal of Autism and Developmental Disorders, 30,* 137–142.

Harrison, S. I., & McDermott, J. K. (1972). *Childhood psychopathology.* New York: International University Press.

Hart, B., & Risley, T. R. (1992). American parenting of language-learning children: Persisting differences in family-child interactions observed in natural home environment. *Developmental Psychology, 28,* 1096–1105.

Harter, S. (1985). *Manual for the Self-Perception Profile for Children.* Denver, CO: University of Denver.

Hartman, C. A., Willcutt, E. G., Rhee, S. H., & Pennington, B. F. (2004). The relation between sluggish cognitive tempo and DSM-IV ADHD. *Journal of Abnormal Child Psychology, 32,* 491–503.

Hartung, C. M., & Widiger, T. A. (1998). Gender differences in the diagnosis of mental disorders: Conclusions and controversies of the DSM-IV. *Psychological Bulletin, 123,* 260–278.

Hartup, W. W. (1996). The company they keep: Friendships and their developmental significance. *Child Development, 67,* 1–13.

Haskett, M. E., Nears, K., Ward, C. S., & McPherson, A. V. (2006). Diversity in adjustment of maltreated children: Factors associated with resilient functioning. *Clinical Psychology Review, 26,* 796–812.

Hastings, R. P., Daley, D., Burns, C., & Beck, A. (2006). Maternal distress and expressed emotion: cross-sectional and longitudinal relationships with behavior problems of children with intellectual disabilities. *American Journal on Mental Retardation, 111,* 48–61.

Hastings, R. P., Kovshoff, H., Ward, N. J., degli Espinosa, F., Brown, T., & Remington, B. (2005). Systems analysis of stress and positive perceptions in mothers and fathers of preschool children with autism. *Journal of Autism and Developmental Disorders, 35,* 635–644.

Hatcher, P. J., Hulme, C., Miles, J. N. V., Carroll, J. M., Hatcher, J., Gibbs, S. et al. (2006). Efficacy of small group reading intervention for beginning readers with reading-delay: a randomised controlled trial. *Journal of Child Psychology and Psychiatry, 47,* 820–827.

Hatcher, P. J., Hulme, C., & Snowling, M. J. (2004). Explicit phoneme training combined with phonic reading instruction helps young children at risk of reading failure. *Journal of Child Psychology and Psychiatry, 45,* 338–359.

Hathaway, W. L., Dooling-Litfin, J. K., & Edwards, G. (2006). Integrating the results of an evaluation. In R. A. Barkley (Ed.), *Attention-deficit hyperactivity disorder. A handbook for diagnosis and treatment.* New York: The Guilford Press.

Hawker, D. S. J., & Boulton, M. J. (2000). Twenty years' research on peer victimization and psychosocial maladjustment: A meta-analytic review of cross-sectional studies. *Journal of Child Psychology and Psychiatry, 41,* 441–455.

Hawkins, B. A., Eklund, S. J., James, D. R., & Foose, A. K. (2003). Adaptive behavior and cognitive function of adults with Down syndrome: Modeling change with age. *Mental Retardation, 41,* 7–28.

Hawkins, E. H., Cummins, L. H., & Marlatt, G. A. (2004). Preventing substance abuse in American Indians and Alaska Native youths: Promising strategies for healthier communities. *Psychological Bulletin, 130,* 304–323.

Hay, D. F., Pawlby, S., Sharp, D., Schmucker, G., Mills, A., Allen, H., & Kumar, R. (1999). Parents' judgements about young children's problems: Why mothers and fathers might disagree yet still predict later outcomes. *Journal of Child Psychology and Psychiatry, 40,* 1249–1258.

Hay, D. F., Payne, A., & Chadwick, A. (2004). Peer relations in childhood. *Journal of Child Psychology and Psychiatry, 45,* 84–108.

Hayes, G. J. (2003). Institutional review boards: Balancing conflicting values in research. In W. O'Donohue & K. Ferguson (Eds.), *Handbook of professional ethics for psychologists.* Thousand Oaks, CA: Sage Publications.

Hays, S. C. (1998). Single case experimental design and empirical clinic practice. In A. E. Kazdin (Ed.), *Methodological issues & strategies in clinical research.* Washington, DC: American Psychological Association.

Hayward, C., Wilson, K. A., Lagle, K., Killen, J. D., & Taylor, C. B. (2004). Parent-reported predictors of adolescent panic attacks. *Journal of the American Academy of Child and Adolescent Psychiatry, 43,* 613–620.

Heaton, P., & Wallace, G. L. (2004). Annotation: The savant syndrome. *Journal of Child Psychology and Psychiatry, 45,* 899–911.

Hebben, N., & Milberg, W. (2002). *Essentials of neuropsychlological assessment.* New York: John Wiley & Sons.

Hechtman, L. (1991). Developmental, neurobiological, and psychosocial aspects of hyperactivity, impulsivity, and inattention. In M. Lewis (Ed.), *Child and adolescent psychiatry: A comprehensive textbook.* Baltimore: Williams & Wilkins.

Hechtman, L. (2005). Attention-deficit disorders. In B. J. Sadock & V. A. Sadock (Eds.), *Comprehensive textbook of psychiatry.* Philadelphia: Lippincott Williams and Wilkens.

Hechtman, L., Abikoff, H., Klein, R. G., Weiss, G., Respitz, C., Kouri, J. et al. (2004). Academic achievement and emotional status of children with ADHD treated with long-term methylphenidate and multimodal psychosocial treatment. *Journal of the American Academy of Child and Adolescent Psychiatry, 43,* 812–819.

Heim, S., & Benasich, A. A. (2006). Developmental disorders of language. In D. Cicchetti & D. J. Cohen (Eds.), *Developmental psychopathology: Vol. III. Risk, disorder, and adaptation.* Hoboken, NJ: John Wiley & Sons.

Helgeson, V. S., Janicki, D., Lerner, J., & Barbarin, O. (2003). Adjustment to juvenile rheumatoid arthritis: A family systems perspective. *Journal of Pediatric Psychology, 28,* 347–353.

Helgeson, V. S., Snyder, P. R., Escobar, O., Siminerio, L., & Becker, D. (2007). Comparison of adolescents with and without diabetes on indices of psychosocial functioning for three years. *Journal of Pediatric Psychology, 32,* 794–806.

Hellander, M., Sisson, D. P., & Fristad, M. A. (2003). Internet support for parents of children with early-onset bipolar disorder. In B. Geller & M. P. DelBello (Eds.), *Bipolar disorder in childhood and early adolescence.* New York: Guilford Press.

Heller, K. (1996). Coming of age of prevention science: Comments on the 1994 National Institute of Mental Health–Institute of Medicine prevention reports. *American Psychologist, 51,* 1123–1127.

Hendin, H., & Commission on Adolescent Suicide Prevention. (2005a). Defining youth suicide. In D. L. Evans, E. B. Foa, R. E. Gur, H. Hendin, C. P. O'Brien, M. E. P. Seligman, & B. T. Walsh (Eds.), *Treating and preventing adolescent mental health disorders. What we know and what we don't know: A research agenda for improving mental health of our youth.* New York: Oxford University Press.

Hendin, H., & Commission on Adolescent Suicide Prevention. (2005b). Targeted youth suicide prevention programs. In D. L. Evans, E. B. Foa, R. E. Gur, H. Hendin, C. P. O'Brien, M. E. P. Seligman, & B. T. Walsh (Eds.), *Treating and preventing adolescent mental health disorders. What we know and what we don't know: A research agenda for improving mental health of our youth.* New York: Oxford University Press.

Hendin, H., & Commission on Adolescent Suicide Prevention. (2005c). Universal approaches to youth suicide prevention. In D. L. Evans, E. B. Foa, R. E. Gur, H. Hendin, C. P. O'Brien, M. E. P. Seligman, & B. T. Walsh (Eds.), *Treating and preventing adolescent mental health disorders. What we know and what we don't know: A research agenda for improving mental health of our youth.* New York: Oxford University Press.

Henggeler, S. W., & Lee, T. (2003). Multisystemic treatment of serious clinical problems. In A. E. Kazdin & J. R. Weisz (Eds.), *Evidence-based psychotherapies for children and adolescents.* New York: Guilford Press.

Henggeler, S. W., Melton, G. B., & Smith, L. A. (1992). Family preservation using multisystemic therapy: An effective alternative to incarcerating serious juvenile offenders. *Journal of Consulting and Clinical Psychology, 60,* 953–961.

Henggeler, S. W., Schoenwald, S. K., Borduin, C. M., Rowland, M. D., & Cunningham, P. B. (1998). *Multisystemic treatment of antisocial behavior in children and adolescents.* New York: Guilford Press.

Henin, A., & Kendall, P. C. (1997). Obsessive-compulsive disorder in childhood and adolescence. In T. H. Ollendick & R. J. Prinz (Eds.), *Advances in clinical child psychology* (Vol. 19). New York: Plenum Press.

Herrenkohl, T. I., Hawkins, J. D., Chung, I. J., Hill, K. G., & Battin-Pearson, S. (2001). School and community risk factors and interventions. In R. Loeber & D. P. Farrington (Eds.), *Child delinquents: Development, interventions, and service needs.* Thousand Oaks, CA: Sage.

Hetherington, E. M., Bridges, M., Insabella, G. (1998). What matters? What does not? Five perspectives on the association between marital transitions and children's adjustment. *American Psychologist, 53,* 167–184.

Hetherington, E. M., & Kelly, J. (2002). *For better or worse: Divorce reconsidered.* New York: W. W. Norton & Company.

Hetherington, E. M., & Stanley-Hagan, M. (1999). The adjustment of children with divorced parents: A risk and resiliency perspective. *Journal of Child Psychology and Psychiatry, 40,* 129–140.

Hewitt, J. K., Silberg, J. L., Rutter, M., Simonoff, E., Meyer, J. M., Maes, H., Pickles, A., Neale, M. C., Loeber, R., Erickson, M. T., Kendler, K. S., Heath, A. C., Truett, K. R., Reynolds, C. A., & Eaves, L. J. (1997). Genetics and developmental psychopathology: 1. Phenotypic assessment in the Virginia Twin Study of Adolescent Behavioral Development. *Journal of Child Psychology and Psychiatry, 38,* 943–963.

Hibbs, E. D., & Jensen, P. S. (2005). Analyzing the research: What this book is all about. In E. D. Hibbs, & P. S. Jensen (Eds.), *Psychosocial treatments for child and adolescent disorders.* Washington, DC: American Psychological Association.

Hibbs, E. D., & Jensen, P. S. (2005). *Psychosocial treatments for child and adolescent disorders: Empirically based strategies for clinical practice.* (2nd ed.). Washington, DC: American Psychological Association.

Hicks, C. L., von Baeyer, C. L., Spafford, P. A., van Korlaar, I., & Goodenough, B. (2001). The Faces Pain Scale—Revised: Toward a common metric in pediatric pain measurement. *Pain, 93,* 173–183.

Higgins, E. L., Raskind, M. H., Goldberg, R. J., & Herman, K. L. (2002). Stages of acceptance of a learning disability: The impact of labeling. *Learning Disability Quarterly, 25,* 3–17.

Hilden, J. M., Emanuel, E. J., Fairclough, D. L., Link, M. P., Foley, K. M., Clarridge, B. C. et al. (2001). Attitudes and practices among pediatric oncologists regarding end-of-life care: Results of the 1998 American Society of Clinical Oncology survey. *Journal of Clinical Oncology, 19,* 205–212.

Hill, J. (2002). Biological, psychological, and social processes in the conduct disorders. *Journal of Child Psychology and Psychiatry, 43,* 133–164.

Hinshaw, S. P. (1998). Is ADHD an impairing condition in childhood and adolescence? Chapter prepared for NIH Consensus Development Conference on Attention-Deficit Hyperactivity Disorder (ADHD): Diagnosis and Treatment. Bethesda, MD.

Hinshaw, S. P. (2001, Winter). Is the inattentive type of ADHD a separate disorder? *Clinical Psychology: Science and Practice, 8,* 498–501.

Hinshaw, S. P. (2002a). Prevention/intervention trials and developmental theory: Commentary on the Fast Track special section. *Journal of Abnormal Child Psychology, 30,* 53–60.

Hinshaw, S. P. (2002b). Preadolescent girls with attention-deficit/hyperactivity disorder: I. Background characteristics, comorbidity, cognitive and social functioning, and parenting practices. *Journal of Consulting and Clinical Psychology, 70,* 1086–1098.

Hinshaw, S. P. (2005). The stigmatization of mental illness in children and parents: developmental issues, family concerns, and research needs. *Journal of Child Psychology and Psychiatry, 46,* 714–734.

Hinshaw, S. P., Carte, E. T., Sami, N., Treuting, J. J., & Zupan, B. A. (2002). Preadolescent girls with attention-deficit/hyperactivity disorder: II. Neuropsychological performance in relation to subtypes and individual classification. *Journal of Consulting and Clinical Psychology, 70,* 1099–1111.

Hinshaw, S. P., & Erhardt, D. (1993). Behavioral treatment. In V. B. Van Hasselt & M. Hersen (Ed.), *Handbook of behavior therapy and pharmacotherapy for children: A comparative analysis.* Boston: Allyn and Bacon.

Hinshaw, S. P., Lahey, B. B., & Hart, E. L. (1993). Issues of taxonomy and comorbidity in the development of conduct disorder. *Development and Psychopathology, 5,* 31–49.

Hinshaw, S. P., & Lee, S. S. (2003). Conduct and oppositional defiant disorders. In E. J. Mash & R. A. Barkley (Eds.), *Child psychopathology* (2nd ed.). New York: Guilford Press.

Hinshelwood, J. (1917). *Congenital word-blindness.* London: H. K. Lewis.

Hirschfeld, R. M. A. (2000). History and evolution of the monoamine hypothesis of depression. *Journal of Clinical Psychiatry, 61(Suppl. 6),* 4–12.

Hirshfeld-Becker, D. R., Biederman, J., & Rosenbaum, J. F. (2004). Behavioral inhibition. In T. L. Morris & J. S. March (Eds.), *Anxiety disorders in children and adolescents.* New York: Guilford Press.

Hirsh-Pasek, K., Kochanoff, A., Newcombe, N. S., & de Villiers, J. (2005). Using scientific knowledge to inform preschool assessment: Making the case for "empirical validity." *SRCD Social Policy Report, 19(1).*

Hoagwood, K. (2003). Ethical issues in child and adolescent psychosocial treatment research. In A. E. Kazdin & J. R. Weisz (Eds.), *Evidence-based psychotherapies for children and adolescents.* New York: Guilford Press.

Hoagwood, K. (2005). The research, policy, and practice context for delivery of evidence-based mental health treatments for adolescents: A systems perspective. In D. L. Evans, E. B. Foa, R. E. Gur, H. Hendin, C. P. O'Brien, M. E. P. Seligman, & B. T. Walsh (Eds.), *Treating and preventing adolescent mental health disorders. What we know and what we don't know: A research agenda for improving mental health of our youth.* New York: Oxford University Press.

Hoagwood, K. E. (2005). Family-based services in children's mental health: A research review and synthesis. *Journal of Child Psychology and Psychiatry, 46,* 690–713.

Hoagwood, K. E., Vogel, J. M., Levitt, J. M., D'Amico, P. J., Paisner, W. I., & Kaplan, S. J. (2007). Implementing an evidence-based trauma treatment in a state system after September 11: The CATS Project. *Journal of the American Academy of Child and Adolescent Psychiatry, 46,* 773–779.

Hobbs, T., & Westling, D. L. (1998). Promoting successful inclusion through collaborative problem-solving. *Teaching Exceptional Children, 31,* 12–19.

Hockfield, S., & Lombroso, P. J. (1998). Development of the cerebral cortex: IX. Cortical development and experience: I. *Journal of the American Academy of Child and Adolescent Psychiatry, 37,* 992–993.

Hocutt, A. M. (1996). Effectiveness of special education: Is placement the critical factor? *The Future of Children, 6,* 77–102.

Hodapp, R. M., Burack, J. A., & Zigler, E. (1990). Summing up and going forward: New directions in the developmental approach to mental retardation. In R. M. Hodapp, J. A. Burack, & E. Zigler (Eds.), *Issues in the developmental approach to mental retardation.* New York: Cambridge University Press.

Hodapp, R. M., & Dykens, E. M. (2003). Mental retardation (Intellectual disabilities). In E. J. Mash & R. A. Barkley (Eds.), *Child psychopathology.* New York: Guilford Press.

Hodapp, R. M., Kazemi, E., Rosner, B. A., & Dykens, E. M. (2006). Mental retardation. In D. A. Wolfe & E. J. Mash (Eds.), *Behavioral and emotional disorders in adolescents.* New York: The Guilford Press.

Hodapp, R. M., & Zigler, E. (1997). New issues in the developmental approach to mental retardation. In W. E. MacLean (Ed.), *Ellis' handbook of mental deficiency, psychological theory and research.* Mahwah, NJ: Lawrence Erlbaum.

Hodges, K. (1994). Evaluation of depression in children and adolescents using diagnostic clinical interviews. In W. M. Reynolds and H. F. Johnston (Eds.), *Handbook of depression in children and adolescents.* New York: Plenum Press.

Hogan, D. M. (1998). The psychological development and welfare of children of opiate and cocaine users: Review and research needs. *Journal of Child Psychology and Psychiatry, 39,* 609–620.

Hoge, C. W., & Pavlin, J. A. (2002). Psychological sequelae of September 11. *New England Journal of Medicine, 347,* 443.

Hohnen, B., & Stevenson, J. (1999). The structure of genetic influences on general cognitive, language, phonological, and reading abilities. *Developmental Psychology, 35,* 590–603.

Holden, E. W., Deichmann, M. M., & Levy, J. D. (1999). Empirically supported treatment in pediatric psychology: Recurrent pediatric headache. *Journal of Pediatric Psychology, 24,* 91–109.

Hollenbeck, A. M. (2007). From IDEA to implementation: a discussion of foundational and future responsiveness-to-intervention research. *Learning Disabilities Research & Practice, 22,* 137–146.

Hollis, C. (2000). Adult outcomes of child- and adolescent-onset schizophrenia: Diagnostic stability and predictive validity. *American Journal of Psychiatry, 157,* 1652–1659.

Hollis, C. (2002). Schizophrenia and allied disorders. In M. Rutter & E. Taylor (Eds.), *Child and adolescent psychiatry.* Oxford, UK: Blackwell Publishing.

Holmbeck, G. N., Bruno, E. F., & Jandasek, B. (2006). Longitudinal research in pediatric psychology: An introduction to the special issue. *Journal of Pediatric Psychology, 31,* 995–1001.

Holmes, C. S., Chen, R., Streisand, R., Marschall, D. E., Souter, S., Swift, E. E., & Peterson, C. C. (2006). Predictors of youth diabetes care behaviors and metabolic control: A structural equation modeling approach. *Journal of Pediatric Psychology, 31,* 770–784.

Holtzman, W. H. (1997). Community psychology in full-service schools in different cultures. *American Psychologist, 52,* 381–389.

Honda, H., Shimizu, Y., & Rutter, M. (2005). No effect of MMR withdrawal on the incidence of autism: a total population study. *Journal of Child Psychology and Psychiatry, 46,* 572–579.

Hoover, H. D., Dunbar, S. B., & Frisbie, D. A. (2001). *The Iowa Tests of Basic Skills, Form A.* Itasca, IL: Riverside Publishing.

Hops, H., Andrews, J. A., Duncan, S. C., Duncan, T. E., & Tildesley, E. (2000). Adolescent drug use development: A social interactional and contextual perspective. In A. J. Sameroff, M. Lewis, & S. M. Miller (Eds.), *Handbook of developmental psychopathology* (2nd ed.). New York: Kluwer Academic/Plenum Publishers.

Hops, H., Biglan, A., Sherman, L., Arthur, J., Friedman, L., & Osteen, V. (1987). Home observations of family interactions of depressed women. *Journal of Consulting and Clinical Psychology, 55,* 341–346.

Hops, H., Davis, B., & Longoria, N. (1995). Methodological issues in direct observation: Illustrations with the Living in Familial Environments (LIFE) coding system. *Journal of Clinical Child Psychology, 24,* 193–203.

Horne, J. (1992). Sleep and its disorders in children. *Journal of Child Psychology and Psychiatry, 33,* 473–487.

Horowitz, F. D. (1992). John B. Watson's legacy: Learning and environment. *Developmental Psychology, 28,* 360–367.

Houts, A. C. (2002). Discovery, invention, and the expansion of the modern Diagnostic and Statistical Manual of Mental Disorders. In L. E. Beutler & M. L. Malik (Eds.), *Rethinking the DSM.* Washington, DC: American Psychological Association.

Houts, A. C. (2003). Behavioral treatment of enuresis. In A. E. Kazdin & J. R. Weisz (Eds.), *Evidence-based psychotherapies for children and adolescents.* New York: Guilford Press.

Houts, A. C., Peterson, J. K., & Whelan, J. P. (1986). Prevention of relapse in full-spectrum home training for primary enuresis: A component analysis. *Behavior Therapy, 17,* 462–469.

Howlin, P. (1994). Special education treatment. In M. Rutter, E. Taylor, & L. Hersov (Eds.), *Child and adolescent psychiatry: Modern approaches.* Cambridge, MA: Blackwell Scientific.

Howlin, P., Goode, S., Hutton, J., & Rutter, M. (2004). Adult outcome for children with autism. *Journal of Child Psychology and Psychiatry, 45,* 212–229.

Hoza, B., Gerdes, A. C., Hinshaw, S. P., Arnold, L. E., Pelham, W. E., Molina, B. S. G. et al. (2004). Self-perceptions of confidence in children with ADHD and comparison children. *Journal of Consulting and Clinical Psychology, 72,* 382–391.

Huang, L., Stroul, B., Friedman, R., Mrazek, P., Friesen, B., Pires, S., & Mayberg, S. (2005). Transforming mental health care for children and their families. *American Psychologist, 60,* 615–627.

Huang-Pollock, C. L., Nigg, J. T., & Carr, T. H. (2005). Deficient attention is hard to find: applying the perceptual load model of selective attention to attention deficit hyperactivity disorder. *Journal of Child Psychology and Psychiatry, 46,* 1211–1218.

Hubbard, J., Realmuto, G. M., Northwood, A. K., & Masten, A. S. (1995). Comorbidity of psychiatric diagnosis with posttraumatic stress disorder in survivors of childhood trauma. *Journal of the American Academy of Child and Adolescent Psychiatry, 34,* 1167–1173.

Hudson, J. L., & Rapee, M. (2001). Parent-child interactions and anxiety disorders: An observational study. *Behaviour Research and Therapy, 39,* 1411–1427.

Hudson, J. L., & Rapee, M. (2002). Parent-child interactions in clinically anxious children and their siblings. *Journal of Clinical Child and Adolescent Psychology, 31,* 548–555.

Hudziak, J. J., Heath, A. C., Madden, P. F., Reich, W., Bucholz, K. K., Slutske, W., Bierut, L. J., Neuman, R. J., & Todd, R. D. (1998). Latent class and factor analysis of DSM-IV ADHD: A twin study of female adolescents. *Journal of the American Academy of Child and Adolescent Psychiatry, 37,* 848–857.

Huesmann, L. R., Eron, L. D., Lefkowitz, M. M., & Walder, L. O. (1984). Stability of aggression over time and generations. *Developmental Psychology, 20,* 1120–1134.

Hughes, C. (1999). Identifying critical social interaction behaviors among high school students with and without disabilities. *Behavior Modification, 23,* 41–60.

Humphreys, L., Forehand, R., McMahon, R., & Roberts, M. (1978). Parent behavorial training to modify child noncompliance: Effects on untreated siblings. *Journal of Behavior Therapy and Experimental Psychiatry, 9,* 235–238.

Huntington's Disease Collaborative Research Group. (1993). A novel gene containing a trinucleotide repeat that is expanded and unstable on Huntington's disease chromsomes. *Cell, 72,* 971–983.

Hurley, A. D. (2005). Psychotherapy is an essential tool in the treatment of psychiatric disorders for people with mental retardation. *Mental Retardation, 43,* 445–448.

Hynd, G. W., Marshall, R., & Gonzalez, J. (1991). Learning disabilities and presumed central nervous system dysfunction. *Learning Disability Quarterly, 14,* 283–296.

Hynd, G. W., & Semrud-Clikeman, M. (1989a). Dyslexia and brain morphology. *Psychological Bulletin, 106,* 447–482.

Hynd, G. W., & Semrud-Clikeman, M. (1989b). Dyslexia and neurodevelopmental pathology: Relationships to cognition, intelligence, and reading skill acquisition. *Journal of Learning Disabilities, 22,* 205–218.

Hysing, M., Elgen, I., Gillbert, C., Lie, S. A., & Lundervold, A. J. (2007). Chronic physical illness and mental health in children. Results from a large-scale population study. *Journal of Child Psychology and Psychiatry, 48,* 785–792.

Iannotti, R. J., & Bush, P. J. (1993). Toward a developmental theory of compliance. In N. A. Krasnegor, L. Epstein, S. B. Johnson, & S. Yaffe (Eds.), *Developmental aspects of health compliance behavior.* Hillsdale, NJ: Lawrence Erlbaum Associates.

Ievers, C. E., Brown, R. T., Drotar, D., Caplan, D., Pishevar, B. S., & Lambert, R. G. (1999). Knowledge of physician prescriptions and adherence to treatment among children with cystic fibrosis and their mothers. *Journal of Developmental and Behavioral Pediatrics, 20,* 335–343.

Ingoldsby, E. & Shaw, D. S. (2002). Neighborhood contextual factors and the onset and progression of early-starting antisocial pathways. *Clinical Child and Family Psychology Review, 5,* 21–55.

Institute of Medicine. 2004. *Immunization Safety Review: Vaccines and Autism (2004). A report of the Institute of Medicine.* Washington, DC: National Academies Press.

Ishikawa, S. S., & Raine, A. (2003). Prefrontal deficits and antisocial behavior: A causal model. In B. B. Lahey, T. E. Moffitt, A. Caspi (Eds.), *Causes of conduct disorder and juvenile delinquency.* New York: Guilford Press.

Israel, A. C. (1988). Parental and family influences in the etiology and treatment of childhood obesity. In N. A. Krasnegor, G. D. Grave, & N. Kretchmer (Eds.), *Childhood obesity: A biobehavioral perspective.* Caldwell, NJ: The Telford Press.

Israel, A. C. (1990). Childhood obesity. In A. S. Bellack, M. Hersen, & A. E. Kazdin (Eds.), *International handbook of behavoir modification and therapy.* New York: Plenum.

Israel, A. C. (1999). Commentary: Empirically supported treatments for pediatric obesity: Goals, outcome criteria, and the societal context. *Journal of Pediatric Psychology, 24,* 249–250.

Israel, A. C., Guile, C. A., Baker, J. E., & Silverman, W. K. (1994). An evaluation of enhanced self-regulation training in the treatment of childhood obesity. *Journal of Pediatric Psychology, 19,* 737–749.

Israel, A. C., & Ivanova, M. Y. (2002). Global and dimensional self-esteem in preadolescent and early adolescent children who are overweight: Age and gender differences. *International Journal of Eating Disorders, 31,* 424–429.

Israel, A. C., Pravder, M. D., & Knights, S. (1980). A peer-administered program for changing the classroom behavior of disruptive children. *Behavioural Analysis and Modification, 4,* 224–238.

Israel, A. C., Roderick, H. A., & Ivanova, M. Y. (2002). A measure of the stability of family activities in a family environment. *Journal of Psychopathology and Behavioral Assessment, 24,* 85–95.

Israel, A. C., & Shapiro, L. S. (1985). Behavior problems of obese children enrolling in a weight reduction program. *Journal of Pediatric Psychology, 10,* 449–460.

Israel, A. C., Silverman, W. K., & Solotar, L. C. (1986). An investigation of family influences on initial weight status, attrition, and treatment outcome in a childhood obesity program. *Behavior Therapy, 17,* 131–143.

Israel, A. C., & Solotar, L. C. (1988). Obesity. In M. Hersen & C. G. Last (Eds.), *Child behavior therapy casebook.* New York: Plenum.

Israel, A. C., Stolmaker, L., & Andrian, C. A. G. (1985). The effects of training parents in general child management skills in a behavioral weight loss program for children. *Behavior Therapy, 16,* 169–180.

Israel, A. C., & Zimand, E. (1989). Obesity. In M. Hersen (Ed.), *Innovations in child behavior therapy.* New York: Springer.

Ivanova, M. Y., Achenbach, T. M., Dumenci, L., Rescorla, L. A., Almqvist, F., Weintraub, S. et al. (2007a). Testing the 8-syndrome structure of the CBCL in 30 societies. *Journal of Clinical Child and Adolescent Psychology, 36,* 405–417.

Ivanova, M. Y., Achenbach, T. M., Rescorla, L. A., Dumenci, L. Almqvist, F., Bathiche, M., et al. (2007b). The generalizability of Teacher's Report Form syndromes in 20 cultures. *School Psychology Review 36,* 468–483.

Ivanova, M. Y., & Israel, A. C. (2006). Family stability as a protective factor against psychopathology for urban children receiving psychological services. *Journal of Clinical Child and Adolescent Psychology, 35,* 564–570.

Izard, C. E., Fine, S., Mostow, A., Trentacosta, C., & Campbell, J. (2002). Emotion processes in normal and abnormal development and prevention intervention. *Development and Psychopathology, 14,* 761–787.

Izard, C. E., Youngstrom, E. A., Fine, S. E., & Mostow., A. (2006). Emotions and developmental psychopathology. In D. Cicchetti & D. J. Cohen (Eds.), *Developmental psychopathology, Vol. 1. Theory and method.* Hoboken, NJ: John Wiley & Sons.

Jackson, D. A., & King, A. R. (2004). Gender differences in the effects of oppositional behavior on teacher ratings of ADHD symptoms. *Journal of Abnormal Child Psychology, 32,* 215–224.

Jacob, R. G., & Pelham, W. H. (2000). Behavior therapy. In B. J. Sadock & V. A. Sadock (Eds.), *Kaplan & Sadock's Comprehensive textbook of psychiatry* (Vol. II). Philadelphia: Lippincott Williams & Wilkins.

Jacobi, C., Hayward, C., de Zwaan, M., Kraemer, H. C., & Agras, W. S. (2004). Coming to terms with risk factors for eating disorders: Application of risk terminology and suggestions for a general taxonomy. *Psychological Bulletin, 130,* 19–65.

Jacobsen, L. K., & Rapoport, J. L. (1998). Research update: Childhood-onset schizophrenia: Implications of clinical and neurobiological research. *Journal of Child Psychology and Psychiatry, 39,* 101–113.

Jaffee, P. G., Poisson, S. E., & Cunningham, A. (2001). Domestic violence and high-conflict divorce: Developing a new generation of research for children. In S. A. Graham-Bermann & J. L. Edleson (Eds.), *Domestic violence in the lives of children: The future of research, intervention, and social policy.* Washington, DC: American Psychological Association.

Jaffee, S. R., Caspi, A., Moffitt, T. E., Dodge, K., Rutter, M., Taylor, A. et al. (2005). Nature x nurture: Genetic vulnerabilities interact with physical maltreatment to promote conduct problems. *Development and Psychopathology, 17,* 67–84.

Jaffee, S. R., Caspi, A., Moffitt, T. E., Polo-Tomás, M., & Taylor, A. (2007). Individual, family, and neighborhood factors distinguish resilient from non-resilient maltreated children: A cumulative stressors model. *Child Abuse & Neglect, 31,* 231–253.

Jaffee, S. R., Caspi, A., Moffitt, T. E., & Taylor, A. (2004). Physical maltreatment victim to antisocial child: Evidence of an environmentally mediated process. *Journal of Abnormal Psychology, 113,* 44–55.

Jaffee, S. R., Moffitt, T. E., Caspi, A., & Taylor, A. (2003). Life with (or without) father: The benefits of living with two biological parents depend on the father's antisocial behavior. *Child Development, 74,* 109–126.

James, A. C. D., & Javaloyes, A. M. (2001). The treatment of bipolar disorder in children and adolescents. *Journal of Child Psychology and Psychiatry, 42,* 439–449.

Jarbin, H., Ott, Y., & von Knorring, A-L. (2003). Adult outcome of social function in adolescent-onset schizophrenia and affective psychosis. *Journal of the American Academy of Child and Adolescent Psychiatry, 42,* 176–183.

Jay, S. M. (1988). Invasive medical procedures: Psychological intervention and assessment. In D. K. Routh (Ed.), *Handbook of pediatric psychology*. New York: Guilford.

Jay, S. M., Elliott, C. H., Fitzgibbons, I., Woody, P., & Siegel, S. (1995). A comparative study of cognitive behavioral therapy versus general anesthesia for painful medical procedures in children. *Pain, 62,* 3–9.

Jay, S. M., Elliot, C. H., Katz, E., & Siegel, S. E. (1987). Cognitive behavioral and pharmacologic intervention for children's distress during painful medical procedures. *Journal of Consulting and Clinical Psychology, 55,* 860–865.

Jay, S. M., Elliot, C. H., Ozolins, M., Olson, R., & Pruitt, S. (1985). Behavioral management of children's distress during painful medical procedures. *Behavior Research and Therapy, 23,* 513–520.

Jay, S. M., Elliot, C. H., Woody, P. D., & Siegel, S. (1991). An investigation of cognitive-behavioral therapy combined with oral valium for children undergoing painful medical procedures. *Health Psychology, 10,* 317–322.

Jelalian, E., & Mehlenbeck, R. (2003). Pediatric obesity. In M. C. Roberts (Ed.), *Handbook of pediatric psychology* (3rd ed.). New York: Guilford Press.

Jelalian, E., Wember, Y. M., Bungeroth, H., & Birmaher, V. (2007). Bridging the gap between research and clinical practice in pediatric obesity. *Journal of Child Psychology and Psychiatry, 48,* 115–127.

Jensen, P. S. (2006). Commentary: After TADS, Can we measure up, catch up, and ante up? *Journal of the American Academy of Child and Adolescent Psychiatry, 45,* 1456–1460.

Jensen, P. S., Arnold, L. E., Swanson, J. M., Vitiello, B., Abikoff, H. B., Greenhill, L. L. et al. (2007). 3-year follow-up of the NIMH MTA study. *Journal of the American Academy of Child and Adolescent Psychiatry, 46,* 989–1002.

Jensen, P. S., Martin, B. A., & Cantwell, D. P. (1997). Co-morbidity in ADHD: Implications for research, practice, and DSM-IV. *Journal of the Academy of Child and Adolescent Psychiatry, 36,* 1065–1075.

Jensen, P. S., & Mrazek, D. A. (2006). Research and clinical perspectives in defining and assessing mental disorders in children and adolescents. In P. S. Jensen, P. Knapp, & D. A. Mrazek (Eds.), *Toward a new diagnostic system for child psychopathology*. Moving beyond the DSM. New York: The Guilford Press.

Jensen, P. S., & Shaw, J. (1993). Children as victims of war: Current knowledge and future research needs. *Journal of the American Academy of Child and Adolescent Psychiatry, 32,* 697–708.

Jersild, A. T., & Holmes, F. B. (1935). Children's fears. Child Development Monograph, No. 20.

Jessor, R., & Jessor, S. L. (1977). *Problem behavior and psychosocial development*. New York: Academic Press.

Jockin, V., McGue, M., & Lykken, D. T. (1996). Personality and divorce: A genetic analysis. *Journal of Personality and Social Psychology, 71,* 288–299.

Johnson, C. J., & Beitchman, J. H. (2005a). Expressive language disorder. In B. J. Sadock & V. A. Sadock (Eds.), *Comprehensive textbook of psychiatry*. Philadelphia: Lippincott Williams and Wilkens.

Johnson, C. J., & Beitchman, J. H. (2005b). Mixed receptive-expressive disorder. In B. J. Sadock & V. A. Sadock (Eds.),

Comprehensive textbook of psychiatry (*Vol. II*). Philadelphia: Lippincott Williams and Wilkens.

Johnson, C. J., & Beitchman, J. H. (2005c). Phonological disorder. In B. J. Sadock & V. A. Sadock (Eds.), *Comprehensive textbook of psychiatry*. Philadelphia: Lippincott Williams and Wilkens.

Johnson, C. P., & Myers, S. M, and the Council on Children with Disabilities. (2007). Identification and evaluation of children with autism spectrum disorders. Retrieved October 29, 2007, from http://www.aap.org

Johnson, J. H., Rasbury, W. C., & Siegel, L. J. (1997). *Approaches to child treatment: Introduction to theory, research, and practice* (2nd ed.). Boston: Allyn and Bacon.

Johnson, S. B. (1993). Chronic diseases of childhood: Assessing compliance with complex medical regimens. In N. A. Krasnegor, L. Epstein, S. B. Johnson, & S. Yaffe (Eds.), *Developmental aspects of health compliance behavior*. Hillsdale, NJ: Lawrence Erlbaum Associates.

Johnson, S. B. (1995). Managing insulin-dependent diabetes mellitus in adolescence: A developmental perspective. In J. Wallander & L. Siegel (Eds.), *Adolescent health problems: Behavioral perspectives*. New York: Guilford Press.

Johnson, S. B. (1998). Juvenile diabetes. In T. H. Ollendick & M. Hersen (Eds.), *Handbook of child psychopathology* (3rd ed.). New York: Plenum Press.

Johnson, W., Bouchard, T. J., Krueger, R. F., McGue, M., & Gottesman, I. I. (2004). Just one *g*: Consistent results from three test batteries. *Intelligence, 32,* 95–107.

Johnston, C., & Mash, E. J. (2001). Families of children with attention deficit/hyperactivity disorder: Review and recommendations for future research. *Clinical Child and Family Psychology Review, 4,* 183–207.

Johnston, C., & Ohan, J. L. (1999). Externalizing disorders. In W. K. Silverman & T. H. Ollendick (Eds.), *Developmental issues in the clinical treatment of children*. Boston: Allyn and Bacon.

Johnston, L. D., O'Malley, P. M., Bachman, J. G., & Schulenberg, J. E. (2007). *Monitoring the Future: National results on adolescent drug use: Overview of key findings, 2006*. Bethesda, MD: National Institute on Drug Abuse.

Joiner, T. E. (2000). A test of hopelessness theory of depression in youth psychiatric inpatients. *Journal of Clinical Child Psychology, 29,* 167–176.

Joinson, C., Heron, J., Emond, A., & Butler, R. (2007). Psychological problems in children with bedwetting and combined (day and night) wetting: A UK population-based study. *Journal of Pediatric Psychology, 32,* 605–616.

Jones, M. C. (1924). A laboratory study of fear: The case of Peter. *Pedagogical Seminary, 31,* 308–315.

Jopp, D. A., & Keys, C. B. (2001). Diagnostic overshadowing reviewed and reconsidered. *American Journal on Mental Retardation, 106,* 416–433.

Jordan, N. C., Hanich, L. B., & Kaplan, D. (2003). A longitudinal study of mathematical competencies in children with specific mathematical difficulties versus children with comorbid mathematics and reading difficulties. *Child Development, 74,* 834–850.

Joseph, R. M., Tager-Flüsberg, H., & Lord, C. (2002). Cognitive profiles and social-communicative functioning in children with autism spectrum disorder. *Journal of Child Psychology and Psychiatry, 43,* 807–821.

Jouriles, E. N., Murphy, C. M., & O'Leary, K. D. (1989). Interspousal aggression, marital discord, and child problems. *Journal of Consulting and Clinical Psychology, 57,* 453–455.

Juffer, F., Bakermans-Kranenbug, M. J., & van Ijzendoorn, M. H. (2005). The importance of parenting in the development of disorganized attachment: evidence from a preventive intervention study in adoptive families. *Journal of Child and Adolescent Psychology, 46,* 263–274.

Jureidini, J. N., Doecke, C. J., Mansfield, P. R., Haby, M. M., Menkes, D. B., & Tonkin, A. L. (2004). Efficacy and safety of antidepressants for children and adolescents. *British Medical Journal, 328,* 879–883.

Kagan, J. (1997). Temperament and the reactions to unfamiliarity. *Child Development, 68,* 139–143.

Kagan, J., Reznick, J. S., & Snidman, N. (1990). The temperamental qualities of inhibition and lack of inhibition. In M. Lewis & S. M. Miller (Eds.), *Handbook of developmental psychopathology.* New York: Plenum Press.

Kalff, A. C., de Sonneville, L. M. J., Hurks. P. P. M., Hendriksen, J. G. M., Kroes, M., Feron, F. J. M. et al. (2003). Low- and high-level controlled processing in executive motor control tasks in 5–6-year-old children at risk for ADHD. *Journal of Child Psychology and Psychiatry, 44,* 1049–1057.

Kamin, L. J. (1974). *The science and politics of IQ.* Potomac, MD: Erlbaum.

Kaminsky, L., & Dewey, D. (2002). Psychosocial adjustment in siblings of children with autism. *Journal of Child Psychology and Psychiatry, 43,* 225–232.

Kamon, J., Tolan, P. H., & Gorman-Smith, D. (2006). Interventions for adolescent psychopathology. In D. A. Wolfe & E. J. Mash (Eds.), *Behavioral and emotional disorders in adolescents.* New York: The Guilford Press.

Kamphaus, R. W. (1993). *Clinical assessment of children's intelligence.* Boston: Allyn & Bacon.

Kamphaus, R. W., & Frick, P. J. (1996). *Clinical assessment of child and adolescent personality and behavior.* Boston: Allyn and Bacon.

Kanaya, T., & Ceci, S. J. (2007). Are all IQ scores created equal? The differential costs of IQ cutoff scores for at-risk children. *Child Development Perspectives, 1,* 52–56.

Kanaya, T., Scullin, M. H., & Ceci, S. J. (2003). The Flynn effect and U. S. policies. *American Psychologist, 58,* 778–790.

Kanner, L. (1943). *Autistic disturbances of affective contact, Nervous Child, 2,* 217–250.

Kanner, L. (1973). *Childhood psychoses: Initial studies and new insights.* Washington, DC: V. H. Winston & Sons.

Kanner, L., & Eisenberg, L. (1956). Early infantile autism, 1943–1955. *American Journal of Orthopsychiatry, 26,* 55–65.

Kaplan, R. M. (1985). The controversy related to the use of psychological tests. In B. Wolman (Ed.), *Handbook of intelligence.* New York: Wiley.

Karmiloff-Smith, A., & Thomas, M. (2003). What can developmental disorders tell us about the neurocomputational constraints that shape development? The case of Williams syndrome. *Development and Psychopathology, 15,* 969–990.

Karoly, P., & Bay, R. C. (1990). Diabetes self-care goals and their relation to children's metabolic control. *Journal of Pediatric Psychology, 15,* 83–95.

Kashani, J. H., Daniel, A. E., Dandoy, A. C., & Holcomb, W. R. (1992). Family violence: Impact on children. *Journal of the American Academy of Child and Adolescent Psychiatry, 31,* 181–189.

Kashani, J. H., & Orvaschel, H. (1990). A community study of anxiety in children and adolescents. *American Journal of Psychiatry, 147,* 313–318.

Kaslow, N. J., Adamson, L. B., & Collins, M. H. (2000). A developmental psychopathology perspective on the cognitive components of child and adolescent depression. In A. J. Sameroff, M. Lewis, & S. M. Miller (Eds.), *Handbook of developmental psychopathology* (2nd ed.). New York: Kluwer Academic/ Plenum Publishers.

Kaslow, N. J., Brown, R. T., & Mee, L. (1994). Cognitive and behavioral correlates of childhood depression: A developmental perspective. In W. M. Reynolds and H. F. Johnston (Eds.), *Handbook of depression in children and adolescents.* New York: Plenum Press.

Kaslow, N. J., & Racusin, G. R. (1990). Childhood depression: Current status and future directions. In A. S. Bellack, M. Hersen, & A. E. Kazdin (Eds.), *International handbook of behavior modification and therapy* (2nd ed.). New York: Plenum.

Kataoka, S., Stein, B. D., Nadeem, E., & Wong, M. (2007). Who gets care? Mental health service use following a school-based suicide prevention program. *Journal of the American Academy of Child and Adolescent Psychiatry, 46,* 1341–1348.

Katz, L. J., & Slomka, G. T. (1990). Achievement Testing. In G. Goldstein & M. Hersen (Eds.), *Handbook of psychological assessment* (2nd ed.). New York: Pergamon.

Katzman, D. K. (2005). Medical complications in adolescents with anorexia nervosa: A review of the literature. *International Journal of Eating Disorders, 37 (Suppl.),* 52–59.

Kauffman, J. M., McGee, K., & Brigham, M. (2004). Enabling or disabling? Observations on changes in special education. *Phi Delta Kappan, 85,* 613–620.

Kaufman, A. S., & Kaufman, N. L. (2004). *Administration and scoring material for the Kaufman Assessment Battery for Children, Second Edition* (KABC-II). Circle Pines, MN: American Guidance Service.

Kaufman, J., Blumberg, H., & Young, C. S. (2004). The neurobiology of early-onset mood disorders. In D. S. Charney & E. J. Nestler (Eds.), *Neurobiology of mental illness.* (2nd ed.). New York: Oxford University Press.

Kaufman, J., & Zigler, E. (1987). Do abused children become abusive parents? *American Journal of Orthopsychiatry, 57,* 186–192.

Kaugars, A. S., Klinnert, M. D., & Bender, B. G. (2004). Family influences on pediatric asthma. *Journal of Pediatric Psychology, 29,* 475–491.

Kavale, K. A., & Forness, S. R. (2003). Learning disability as a discipline. In H. L. Swanson, K. R. Harris, & S. Graham (Eds.), *Handbook of learning disabilities.* New York: Guilford Press.

Kaye, W. H., Bulik, C. M., Thornton, L., Barbarich, N., Masters, K., & the Price Foundation Collaborative Group. (2004). Comorbidity of anxiety disorders with anorexia and bulimia nervosa. *American Journal of Psychiatry, 161,* 2215–2221.

Kaye, W. H., Frank, G. K., Bailer, U. F., Henry, S. E., Meltzer, C. C., Price, J. C. et al. (2005). Serotonin alterations in anorexia and bulimia nervosa: New insights from imaging studies. *Physiology and Behavior, 85,* 73–81.

Kazak, A. E. (2002). *Journal of Pediatric Psychology* (JPP), 1998–2002: Editor's vale dictum. *Journal of Pediatric Psychology, 27,* 653–663.

Kazak, A. E. (2005). Evidence-based interventions for survivors of childhood cancer and their families. *Journal of Pediatric Psychology, 30,* 29–39.

Kazdin, A. E. (1985). *Treatment of antisocial behavior in children and adolescents.* Homewood, IL: Dorsey.

Kazdin, A. E. (1989). Identifying depression in children: A comparison of alternative selection criteria. *Journal of Abnormal Child Psychology, 17,* 437–454.

Kazdin, A. E. (1993). Treatment of conduct disorder: Progress and directions in psychotherapy research. *Development and Psychopathology, 5,* 277–310.

Kazdin, A. E. (1994). Informant variability in the assessment of childhood depression. In W. M. Reynolds and H. F. Johnston (Eds.), *Handbook of depression in children and adolescents.* New York: Plenum Press.

Kazdin, A. E. (1997). Practitioner review: Psychosocial treatments for conduct disorder in children. *Journal of Child Psychology and Psychiatry, 38,* 161–178.

Kazdin, A. E. (1998). Drawing valid inferences from case studies. In A. E. Kazdin (Ed.), *Methodological issues and strategies in clinical research.* Washington, DC: American Psychological Association.

Kazdin, A. E. (2003). Problem-solving skills training and parent management training for conduct disorder. In A. E. Kazdin & J. R. Weisz (Eds.), *Evidence-based psychotherapies for children and adolescents.* New York: Guilford Press.

Kazdin, A. E. (2005). Child, parent, and family-based treatment of aggressive and antisocial child behavior. In E. D. Hibbs & P. S. Jensen (Eds.), *Psychosocial treatments for child and adolescent disorders: Empirically based strategies for clinical practice.* (2nd ed.). Washington, DC: American Psychological Association.

Kazdin, A. E., & Kolko, D. J. (1986). Parent psychopathology and family functioning among childhood firesetters. *Journal of Abnormal Child Psychology, 14,* 315–329.

Kazdin, A. E., & Marciano, P. L. (1998). Childhood and adolescent depression. In E. J. Mash & R. A. Barkley (Eds.), *Treatment of childhood disorders* (2nd ed.). New York: Guilford Press.

Kazdin, A. E., Rodgers, A., & Colbus, D. (1986). The Hopelessness Scale for Children: Psychometric characteristics and concurrent validity. *Journal of Consulting and Clinical Psychology, 54,* 241–245.

Kazdin, A. E., & Weisz, J. R. (2003). *Evidence-based psychotherapies for children and adolescents.* New York: Guilford Press.

Kazdin, A. E., Whitley, M., & Marciano, P. L. (2006). Child–therapist and parent–therapist alliance and therapeutic change in the treatment of children referred for oppositional, aggressive, and antisocial behavior. *Journal of Child Psychology and Psychiatry, 47,* 436–445.

Kearney, C. A. (2001). *School refusal behavior in youth: A functional approach to assessment and treatment.* Washington, DC: American Psychological Association.

Kearney, C. A., Albano, A. M., Eisen, A. R., Allan, W. D., & Barlow, D. H. (1997). The phenomenology of panic disorder in youngsters: An empirical study of a clinical sample. *Journal of Anxiety Disorders, 11,* 49–62.

Kearney, C. A., Eisen, A., & Silverman, W. K. (1995). The legend and myth of school phobia. *School Psychology Quarterly, 10,* 65–85.

Kearney, C. A., & Silverman, W. K. (1992). Let's not push the "panic button": A critical analysis of panic and panic disorder in adolescents. *Clinical Psychology Review, 12,* 293–305.

Kearney, C. A., & Silverman, W. K. (1996). The evolution and reconciliation of taxonomic strategies for school refusal behavior. *Clinical Psychology: Science and Practice, 3,* 339–354.

Kearney, C. A., Sims, K. E., Prusell, C. R., & Tillotson, C. A. (2003). Separation anxiety disorder in young children: A longitudinal and family analysis. *Journal of Clinical Child and Adolescent Psychology, 32,* 593–598.

Keel, P. K., & Klump, K. (2003). Are eating disorders culture-bound syndromes? Implications for conceptualizing their etiology. *Psychological Bulletin, 129,* 747–769.

Keller, M. B., Lavori, P. W., Wunder, J., Beardslee, W. R., Schwartz, C. E., & Roth, J. (1992). Chronic course of anxiety disorders in children and adolescents. *Journal of the American Academy of Child and Adolescent Psychiatry, 31,* 595–599.

Keller, P. S., Cummings, E. M., & Davies, P. T. (2005). The role of marital discord and parenting in relations between parental problem drinking and child adjustment. *Journal of Child Psychology and Psychiatry, 46,* 943–951.

Kellerman, J. (1980). Rapid treatment of nocturnal anxiety in children. *Journal of Behavior Therapy and Experimental Psychiatry, 11,* 9–11.

Kelly, J. B. (2000). Children's adjustment in conflicted marriage and divorce: A decade review of research. *Journal of the American Academy of Child and Adolescent Psychiatry, 39,* 963–973.

Kelly, M. L., & Heffer, R. W. (1990). Eating disorders: Food refusal and failure to thrive. In A. M. Gross & R. S. Drabman (Eds.), *Handbook of clinical behavioral pediatrics.* New York: Plenum.

Kempe, C. H., Silverman, F. N., Steele, B. B., Droegemueller, W., & Silver, H. K. (1962). The battered child syndrome. *Journal of the American Medical Association, 181,* 17–24.

Kendall, P. C. (1992). *Coping cat workbook.* Ardmore, PA: Workbook Publishing.

Kendall, P. C. (2006). Guiding theory for therapy with children and adolescents. In P. C. Kendall (Ed.), *Child and adolescent therapy: Cognitive-behavioral procedures.* New York: The Guilford Press.

Kendall, P. C., Aschenbrand, S. G., & Hudson, J. L. (2003). Child-focused treatment of anxiety. In A. E. Kazdin & J. R. Weisz (Eds.), *Evidence-based psychotherapies for children and adolescents.* New York: Guilford Press.

Kendall, P. C., Chu, B. C., Pimentel, S. S., & Choudhury, M. (2000). Treating anxiety disorders in youth. In P. C. Kendall (Ed.), *Child and adolescent therapy: Cognitive-behavioral procedures.* New York: Guilford.

Kendall, P. C., Flannery-Schroeder, E., Panichelli-Mindel, S., Southam-Gerow, M., Henin, A., & Warman, M. (1997a). Therapy for youth with anxiety disorders: A second randomized clinical trial. *Journal of Consulting and Clinical Psychology, 65,* 366–380.

Kendall, P. C., & Hedtke, K. (2006). *Coping Cat workbook (2nd ed.).* Ardmore, PA: Workbook Publishing.

Kendall, P. C., Hedtke, K. A., & Aschenbrand, S. G. (2006). Anxiety disorders. In D. A. Wolfe & E. J. Mash (Eds.), *Behavioral and emotional disorders in adolescents: Nature, assessment, and treatment.* New York: The Guilford Press.

Kendall, P. C., Panichelli-Mindel, S. M., Sugarman, A., & Callahan, S. A. (1997b). Exposure to child anxiety: Theory, research, and practice. *Clinical Psychology: Science and Practice, 4,* 29–39.

Kendall, P. C., Safford, S., Flannery-Schroeder, E., & Webb, A. (2004). Child anxiety treatment: Outcomes in adolescence and impact on substance use and depression at 7.4-year follow-up. *Journal of Consulting and Clinical Psychology, 72,* 276–287.

Kendall, P. C., & Suveg, C. (2006). Treating anxiety disorders in youth. In P. C. Kendall (Ed.), *Child and adolescent therapy: Cognitive-behavioral procedures* (3rd ed.). New York: The Guilford Press.

Kendler, K. S., Neale, M. C., Kessler, R. C., Heath, A. C., & Eaves, L. J. (1992a). A population-based twin study of major depression in women: The impact of varying definitions of illness. *Archives of General Psychiatry, 49,* 257–266.

Kendler, K. S., Neale, M. C., Kessler, R. C., Heath, A. C., & Eaves, L. J. (1992b). The genetic epidemiology of phobias in women: The interrelationship of agoraphobia, social phobia, situational phobia, and simple phobia. *Archives of General Psychiatry, 49,* 273–281.

Kennard, B., Silva, S., Vitiello, B., Curry, J., Kratochvil, C., Simons, A., et al. and the TADS Team. (2006). Remission and residual symptoms after short-term treatment in the Treatment of Adolescents With Depression Study (TADS). *Journal of the American Academy of Child and Adolescent Psychiatry, 45,* 1404–1411.

Kerr, A. (2002). Annotation: Rett syndrome: Recent progress and implications for research and clinical practice. *Journal of Child Psychology and Psychiatry, 43,* 277–287.

Kerwin, M. E., & Berkowitz, R. I. (1996). Feeding and eating disorders: Ingestive problems of infancy, childhood, and adolescence. *School Psychology Review, 25,* 316–328.

Kessler, J. W. (1966, 1988). *Psychopathology of childhood.* Englewood Cliffs, NJ: Prentice Hall.

Kessler, R. C., Avenevoli, S., & Merikangas, K. R. (2001). Mood disorders in children and adolescents: An epidemiologic perspective. *Biological Psychiatry, 49,* 1002–1014.

Kestenbaum, C. J. (2000). How shall we treat children in the 21st century? *Journal of the American Academy of Child and Adolescent Psychiatry, 39,* 1–10.

Kiesler, C. A. (2000). The next wave of change for psychology and mental health services in the health care revolution. *American Psychologist, 55,* 481–487.

Killen, J. D., Hayward, C., Wilson, D. M., Taylor, C. B., Hammer, L. D., Litt, I., Simmonds, B., & Haydel, F. (1994a). Factors associated with eating disorder symptoms in a community sample of 6th and 7th grade girls. *International Journal of Eating Disorders, 15,* 357–367.

Killen, J. D., Taylor, C. B., Hayward, C., Wilson, D. M., Haydel, K. F., Hammer, L. D., Simmonds, B., Robinson, T. N., Litt, I., Varady, A., & Kraemer, H. (1994b). Pursuit of thinness and onset of eating disorder symptoms in a community sample of adolescent girls: A three-year prospective analysis. *International Journal of Eating Disorders, 16,* 227–238.

Kilpatrick, D. G., Acierno, R., Schnurr, P. P., Saunders, B., Resnick, H. S., & Best, C. L. (2000). Risk factors for adolescent substance abuse and dependence: Data from a national sample. *Journal of Consulting and Clinical Psychology, 68,* 19–30.

King, B. H., Hodapp, R. M., & Dykens, E. M. (2000). Mental retardation. In B. J. Sadock & V. A. Sadock (Eds.), *Comprehensive textbook of psychiatry* (Vol. II). Philadelphia: Lippincott Williams & Wilkins.

King, B. H., Hodapp, R. M., & Dykens, E. M. (2005). Mental retardation. In B. J. Sadock & V. A. Sadock (Eds.), *Kaplan and Sadock's comprehensive textbook of psychiatry.* New York: Lippincott Williams & Wilkins.

King, N. J., & Bernstein, G. A. (2001). School refusal in children and adolescents: A review of the past 10 years. *Journal of the American Academy of Child and Adolescent Psychiatry, 40,* 197–205.

King, N. J., Ollendick, T. H., & Gullone, E. (1990). School-related fears of children and adolescents. *Australian Journal of Education, 34,* 99–112.

King, N. J., Ollendick, T. H., Mattis, S. G., Yang, B., & Tonge, B. (1997). Nonclinical panic attacks in adolescents: Prevalence, symptomatology, and associated features. *Behaviour Change, 13,* 171–183.

King, N., Tonge, B. J., Heyne, D., & Ollendick, T. H. (2000). Research on the cognitive-behavioral treatment of school refusal: A review and recommendations. *Clinical Psychology Review, 20,* 495–507.

King, R. A., Pfeffer, C., Gammon, G. D., & Cohen, D. J. (1992). Suicidality of childhood and adolescence: Review of the literature and proposal for establishment of a DSM-IV category. In B. B. Lahey & A. E. Kazdin (Eds.), *Advances in clinical child psychology,* Vol. 14, New York: Plenum.

Kirby, D. (2005). *Evidence of harm.* New York: St Martin's Press.

Kirgin, K. A. (1996). Teaching-Family Model of group home treatment of children with severe behavior problems. In M. C. Roberts (Ed.), *Model programs in child and family mental health.* Mahwah, NJ: Erlbaum.

Kirk, S. A., Gallagher, J. J., & Anastasiow, N. J. (2000). *Educating exceptional children.* Boston: Houghton Mifflin Company.

Kirov, R., Kinkelbur, J., Banaschewski, T., & Rothenberger, A. (2007). Sleep patterns in children with attention-deficit/hyperactivity disorder, tic disorder, and comorbidity. *Journal of Child Psychology and Psychiatry, 48,* 561–570.

Kistner, J. A., David-Ferdon, C. F., Lopez, C. M., & Dunkel, S. B. (2007). Ethnic and sex differences in children's depressive symptoms. *Journal of Clinical Child and Adolescent Psychology, 36,* 171–181.

Kleiger, J. H. (2001). Projective testing with children and adolescents. In C. E. Walker & M. C. Roberts (Eds.), *Handbook of clinical child psychology* (3rd ed.). New York: John Wiley & Sons.

Klein, D. F., Mannuzza, S., Chapman, T., & Fyer, A. (1992). Child panic revised. *Journal of the American Academy of Child and Adolescent Psychiatry, 31,* 112–113.

Klein, D. N., Lewinsohn, P. M., Seeley, J. R., & Rohde, P. (2001). A family study of major depressive disorder in a community sample of adolescents. *Archives of General Psychiatry, 58,* 13–20.

Klein, M. (1932). *The psycho-analysis of children.* London: Hogarth Press.

Klein, N. C., Alexander, J. F., & Parsons, B. V. (1977). Impact of family systems intervention on recidivism and sibling delinquency: A model of primary prevention and program evaluation. *Journal of Consulting and Clinical Psychology, 45,* 469–474.

Klein, R. G., Abikoff, H., Hechtman, L., & Weiss, G. (2004). Design and rationale of controlled study of long-term methylphenidate and multimodal psychosocial treatment in children with ADHD. *Journal of the American Academy of Child and Adolescent Psychiatry, 43,* 792–801.

Klesges, R. C., & Hanson, C. L. (1988). Determining the environmental causes and correlates of childhood obesity: Methodological issues and future research directions. In N. A. Krasnegor, G. D. Grave, & N. Kretchmer (Eds.), *Childhood obesity: A biobehavioral perspective.* Caldwell, NJ: The Telford Press.

Klin, A., & Volkmar, F. R. (1997). Asperger's Syndrome. In D. J. Cohen & F. R. Volkmar (Eds.), *Handbook of autism and pervasive development disorders.* New York: John Wiley.

Klinger, L. G., Dawson, G., & Renner, P. (2003). Autistic disorder. In E. J. Mash & R. A. Barkley (Eds.), *Child psychopathology.* New York: Guilford Press.

Klingner, J. K., & Vaughn, S. (2002). The changing roles and responsibilities of an LD specialist. *Learning Disabilities Quarterly, 25,* 19–31.

Klinnert, M. D., McQuaid, E. L., McCormich, D., Adinoff, A. D., & Bryant, N. E. (2000). A multimethod assessment of behavioral and emotional adjustment in children with asthma. *Journal of Pediatric Psychology, 25,* 35–46.

Klump, K. L., & Gobrogge, K. L. (2005). A review and primer of molecular genetic studies of anorexia nervosa. *International Journal of Eating Disorders, 37 (Suppl.),* 43–48.

Klump, K. L., McGue, M., & Iacono, W. G. (2000). Age differences in genetic and environmental influences on eating attitudes and behaviors in preadolescent and adolescent female twins. *Journal of Abnormal Psychology, 109,* 239–251.

Knapp, P., & Jensen, P. S. (2006). Recommendations for DSM-V. In P. S. Jensen, P. Knapp, & D. A. Mrazek (Eds.), *Toward a new diagnostic system for child psychopathology. Moving beyond the DSM.* New York: The Guilford Press.

Knoff, H. M. (1998). Review of the Children's Apperception Test (1991 Revision). In J. C. Impara & B. S. Plake (Eds.), *The thirteenth mental measurement yearbook.* Lincoln: The University of Nebraska-Lincoln.

Kobak, R., Cassidy, J., Lyons-Ruth, K., & Ziv, Y. (2006). Attachment, stress, and psychopathology. In D. Cicchetti & D. J. Cohen (Eds.). *Developmental psychopathology. Vol. 1. Theory and method.* Hoboken, NJ: John Wiley & Sons.

Koegel, L. K. (2000). Interventions to facilitate communication in autism. *Journal of Autism and Developmental Disorders, 30,* 383–391.

Koegel, R. L., Koegel, L. K., & Brookman, L. I. (2003). Empirically supported pivotal response interventions for children with autism. In A. E. Kazdin & J. R. Weisz (Eds.), *Evidence-based psychotherapies for children and adolescents.* New York: Guilford Press.

Koegel, R. L., Koegel, L. K., & McNerney, E. K. (2001). Pivotal areas in intervention for autism. *Journal of Clinical Child Psychology, 30,* 19–32.

Koegel, R. L., O'Dell, M. C., & Koegel, L. K. (1987). A natural language teaching paradigm for nonverbal autistic children. *Journal of Autism and Developmental Disorders, 17,* 187–200.

Koger, S. M., Schettler, T., & Weiss, B. (2005). Environmental toxicants and development disabilities. *American Psychologist, 60,* 243–255.

Koinis-Mitchell, D., McQuaid, E. L., Seifer, R., Kopel, S. J., Esteban, C., Canino, G., et al. (2007). Multiple urban and asthma-related risks and their association with asthma morbidity in children. *Journal of Pediatric Psychology, 32,* 582–595.

Kolko, D. (1987). Simplified inpatient treatment of nocturnal enuresis in psychiatrically disturbed children. *Behavior Therapy, 18,* 99–112.

Kolko, D. J. (2005). Treatment and education for childhood firesetting: description, outcomes, and implications. In E. D. Hibbs & P. S. Jensen (Eds.), *Psychosocial treatments for child and adolescent disorders: Empirically based strategies for clinical practice* (2nd ed.). Washington, DC: American Psychological Association.

Kolko, D. J., Day, B. T., Bridge, J. A., & Kazdin, A. E. (2001). Two-year prediction of children's firesetting in clinically referred and nonreferred samples. *Journal of Child Psychology and Psychiatry, 42,* 371–380.

Kolvin, I. (1971). Psychoses in childhood—a comparative study. In M. Rutter (Ed.), *Infantile autism: Concepts, characteristics, and treatments.* London: Churchill-Livingstone.

Koocher, G. P. (1980). Pediatric cancer: Psychosocial problems and the high costs of helping. *Journal of Clinical Child Psychology, 9,* 2–5.

Koocher, G. P., & Sallan, S. E. (1978). Pediatric oncology. In P. R. Magrab (Ed.), *Psychological management of pediatric problems,* Vol. 1. Baltimore: University Park Press.

Kopp, C. B. (1994). Trends and directions in studies of developmental risk. In C. A. Nelson (Ed.), *Threats to optimal development: Integrating biological, psychological, and social risk factors: The Minnesota symposium on child psychology. Vol. 27.* Hillsdale, NJ: Erlbaum.

Koppitz, E. M. (1984). *Psychological evaluation of human figure drawings by middle school pupils.* Orlando, FL: Grune & Stratton.

Korbin, J. E., Coulton, C. J., Chard, S., Platt-Houston, C., & Su, M. (1998). Impoverishment and child maltreatment in African American and European American neighborhoods. *Development and Psychopathology, 10,* 215–233.

Kotimaa, A. J., Moilanen, I., Taanila, A., Ebeling, H., Smalley, S. L., McGough, J. J. et al. (2003). Maternal smoking and hyperactivity in 8-year-old children. *Journal of the American Academy of Child and Adolescent Psychiatry, 42,* 826–833.

Kotler, L. A., Cohen, P., Daview, M., Pine, D. S., & Walsh, B. T. (2001). Longitudinal relationships between childhood, adolescent, and adult eating disorders. *Journal of the American Academy of Child and Adolescent Psychiatry, 40,* 1434–1440.

Kovacs, M. (1992, 2003). *Children's Depression Inventory (CDI): Technical manual update.* North Tonawanda, NY: Multi-Health Systems, Inc.

Kovacs, M. (1996). Presentation and course of Major Depressive Disorder during childhood and later years of the life span.

Journal of the American Academy of Child and Adolescent Psychiatry, 35, 705–715.

Kovacs, M. (1997). Depressive disorders in childhood: An impressionistic landscape. *Journal of Child Psychology and Psychiatry, 38,* 287–298.

Kovacs, M., Devlin, B., Pollack, M., Richards, C., & Mukerji, P. (1997). A controlled family history study of childhood-onset depressive disorder. *Archives of General Psychiatry, 54,* 613–623.

Kovacs, M., Goldston, D., & Gatsonis, C. (1993). Suicidal behaviors and childhood-onset depressive disorders: A longitudinal investigation. *Journal of the American Academy of Child and Adolescent Psychiatry, 32,* 8–20.

Kovacs, Y., Haworth, C. M. A., Harlaar, S. A., Petrill, S. A., Dale, P. S., & Plomin, R. (2007). Overlap and specificity of genetic and environmental influences on mathematics and reading disability in 10-year-old twins. *Journal of Child Psychology and Psychiatry, 48,* 914–922.

Kowatch, R. A., & DelBello, M. P. (2006). Pediatric bipolar disorder: Emerging diagnostic and treatment approaches. *Child and Adolescent Psychiatric Clinics of North America, 15,* 73–108.

Kowatch, R. A., Fristad, M., Birmaher, B., Wagner, K. D., Findling, R. L., & Hellander, M. (2005). Treatment guidelines for children and adolescents with bipolar disorder. *Journal of the American Academy of Child and Adolescent Psychiatry, 44,* 213–235.

Kozol, J. (1991). *Savage inequalities: Children in America's schools.* New York: Crown Publishers.

Krahn, G. L., Hohn, M. F., & Kime, C. (1995). Incorporating qualitative approaches into clinical child psychology research. *Journal of Clinical Child Psychology, 24,* 204–213.

Kraijer, D. (2000). Review of adaptive behavior studies in mentally retarded persons with autism/pervasive developmental disorder. *Journal of Autism and Developmental Disorders, 30,* 39–47.

Kratochwill, T. R., & Levin, J. R. (1992). *Single-case research design and analysis.* Hillsdale, NJ: Lawrence Erlbaum.

Krausz, M., & Muller-Thomsen, T. (1993). Schizophrenia with onset in adolescence: An 11-year followup. *Schizophrenia Bulletin, 19,* 831–841.

Kuczynski, L., & Kochanska, G. (1995). Function and contexts of maternal demands: Developmental significance of early demands for competent action. *Child Development, 66,* 616–628.

Kuhn, T. S. (1962). *The structure of scientific revolutions.* Chicago: University of Chicago Press.

Kumpulainen, K., Räsänen, E., & Henttonen, I. (1999). Children involved in bullying: Psychological disturbance and the persistence of the involvement. *Child Abuse and Neglect, 23,* 1253–1262.

Kumra, S., Ashtari, M., Cervellione, K. L., Henderson, I., Kester, H., Roofeh, D. et al. (2005). White matter abnormalities in early-onset schizophrenia: a voxel-based diffusion tensor imaging study. *Journal of the American Academy of Child and Adolescent Psychiatry, 44,* 934–941.

Kumra, S., Bedwell, J., Smith, A. K., Arling, E., Albus, K. et al. (2000). Neuropsychological deficits in pediatric patients with childhood-onset schizophrenia and psychotic disorder not otherwise specified. *Schizophrenia Research, 42,* 135–144.

Kupersmidt, J. B., & Patterson, C. J. (1991). Childhood peer rejection, aggression, withdrawal, and perceived competence as predictors of self-reported behavior problems in preadolescence. *Journal of Abnormal Child Psychology, 19,* 427–449.

Kupfer, D. J., First, M. B., & Regier, D. A. (2002). Introduction. In D. J. Kupfer, M. B. First, & D. A. Regier (Eds.), *A research agenda for DSM-V.* Washington, DC: American Psychiatric Association.

Kupfer, D. J., & Reynolds, C. F. (1992). Sleep and affective disorders. In E. S. Paykel (Ed.), *Handbook of affective disorders* (2nd ed.). New York: Guilford Press.

Kvernmo, S., & Heyerdahl, S. (1998). Influence of ethnic factors on behavior problems in indigenous Sami and majority Norwegian adolescents. *Journal of the American Academy of Child and Adolescent Psychiatry, 37,* 743–751.

Kvernmo, S., & Heyerdahl, S. (2003). Acculturation strategies and ethnic identity as predictors of behavior problems in arctic minority adolescents. *Journal of the American Academy of Child and Adolescent Psychiatry, 42,* 57–65.

Kylliäinen, A., & Hietanen, J. K. (2004). Attention orienting by another's gaze direction in children with autism. *Journal of Child Psychology and Psychiatry, 45,* 435–444.

La Greca, A. M. (1999). *Manual and Instructions for the SASC, SASC-R, SAS-A (Adolescents) and Parent versions of the scales.* Miami, FL: University of Miami.

La Greca, A. M., & Bearman, K. J. (2001). If "an apple a day keeps the doctor away," why is adherence so darn hard? *Journal of Pediatric Psychology, 26,* 279–282.

La Greca, A. M., & Bearman, K. J. (2003). Adherence to pediatric treatment regimens. In M. C. Roberts (Ed.), *Handbook of pediatric psychology* (3rd ed.). New York: Guilford Press.

La Greca, A. M., Silverman, W. K., & Wasserstein, S. B. (1998). Children's predisaster functioning as a predictor of posttraumatic stress following Hurricane Andrew. *Journal of Consulting and Clinical Psychology, 66,* 883–892.

La Greca, A. M., Silverman, W. K., Vernberg, E. M., & Prinstein, M. J. (1996). Symptoms of posttraumatic stress in children after Hurricane Andrew: A prospective study. *Journal of Consulting and Clinical Psychology, 64,* 712–723.

La Greca, A. M., & Stone, W. L. (1993). Social anxiety scale for children-revised: Factor structure and concurrent validity. *Journal of Clinical Child Psychology, 22,* 17–27.

Lachar, D., & Gruber, C. P. (2001). *Personality Inventory for Children-Second Edition.* Los Angeles: Western Psychological Services.

Lackaye, T., Margalit, M., Ziv, O., & Ziman, T. (2006). Comparisons of self-efficacy, mood, effort, and hope between students with learning disabilities and their non-LD-matched peers. *Learning Disability Research & Practice, 21,* 111–121.

Ladd, G. W., & Troop-Gordon, W. (2003). The role of chronic peer difficulties in the development of children's psychological adjustment problems. *Child Development, 74,* 1344–1367.

Laessle, R. G., Uhl, H., & Lindel, B. (2001). Parental influences on eating behavior in obese and nonobese preadolescents. *International Journal of Eating Disorders, 30,* 447–453.

Laessle, R. G., Wurmser, H., & Pirke, K. M. (2000). Restrained eating and leptin levels in overweight preadolescent girls. *Physiology and Behavior, 70,* 45–47.

LaFromboise, T., & Dizon, M. R. (2003). American Indian children and adolescents. In J. T. Gibbs, L. N. Huang and Associates (Eds.), *Children of color: Psychological interventions with culturally diverse youth.* San Francisco: Jossey-Bass.

Lahey, B. B. (2001, Winter). Should the combined and predominantly inattentive types of ADHD be considered distinct and unrelated disorders? *Clinical Psychology: Science and Practice, 8,* 494–497.

Lahey, B. B., Applegate, B., McBurnett, K., Biederman, J., Greenhill, L., Hynd, G. W., Barkley, R. A., Newcorn, J., Jensen, P., Richters, J., Garfinkel, B., Kerdyk, L., Frick, P. J., Ollendick, T., Perez, D., Hart, E. L., Waldman, I., & Shaffer, D. (1994). DSM-IV field trials for attention deficit hyperactivity disorder in children and adolescents. *American Journal of Psychiatry, 151,* 1673–1685.

Lahey, B. B., Hartdagen, S. E., Frick, P. J., McBurnett, K., Conner, R., & Hynd, G. W. (1988). Psychopathology and antisocial behavior in the parents of children with conduct disorder and hyperactivity. *Journal of the American Academy of Child and Adolescent Psychiatry, 29,* 620–626.

Lahey, B. B., Pelham, W. E., Stein, M. A., Loney, J., Trapani, C., Nugent, K., Kipp, H., Schmidt, E., Lee, S., Cale, M., Gold, E., Hartung, C. M., Willcutt, E., & Baumann, B. (1998). Validity of DSM-IV Attention-deficit/Hyperactivity Disorder for younger children. *Journal of the American Academy of Child and Adolescent Psychiatry, 37,* 695–702.

Lahey, B. B., & Waldman, I. D. (2003). A developmental propensity model of the origins of conduct problems during childhood and adolescence. In B. B. Lahey, T. E. Moffitt, A. Caspi (Eds.), *Causes of conduct disorder and juvenile delinquency.* New York: Guilford Press.

Lahey, B. B., Waldman, I. D., & McBurnett, K. (1999). The development of antisocial behavior: An integrative causal model. *Journal of Child Psychology and Psychiatry, 40,* 669–682.

Lahti, J., Räikkönen, K., Kajantie, E., Heinonen, K., Pesonen, A-K., Järvenpää A-L., & Stranberg, T. (2006). Small body size at birth and behavioural symptoms of ADHD in children aged five to six years. *Journal of Child Psychology and Psychiatry, 47,* 1167–1174.

Laing, E., Hulme, C., Grant, J., & Karmiloff-Smith, A. (2001). Learning to read in Williams syndrome: Looking beneath the surface of atypical reading development. *Journal of Child Psychology and Psychiatry, 42,* 729–739.

Laird, R. D., Jordan, K. Y., Dodge, K. A., Petit, G. S., & Bates, J. E. (2001). Peer rejection in childhood, involvement with antisocial peers in early adolescence and the development of externalizing behavior problems. *Development and Psychopathology, 13,* 337–354.

Lakin, K. C., Prouty, R., Polister, B., & Coucouvanis, K. (2003). Selected changes in residential service systems over a quarter century, 1977–2002. *Mental Retardation, 41,* 303–306.

Lambert, N. M. (1988). Adolescent outcomes for hyperactive children: Perspectives on general and specific patterns of childhood risk for adolescent educational, social, and mental health problems. *American Psychologist, 43,* 786–799.

Landry, R., & Bryson, S. E. (2004). Impaired disengagement of attention in young children with autism. *Journal of Child Psychology and Psychiatry, 45,* 1115–1122.

Lang, P. J. (1984). Cognition in emotion: Concept and action. In C. E. Izard, J. Kagan, R. B. Zajonc (Eds.), *Emotions, cognition, and behavior.* New York. Cambridge University Press.

Langer, D. H. (1985). Children's legal rights as research subjects. *Journal of the American Academy of Child Psychiatry, 24,* 653–662.

Lansford, J. E., Chang, L., Dodge, K. A., Malone, P. S., Oburu, P., Palmérus, K. et al. (2005). Physical discipline and children's adjustment: Cultural normativeness as a moderator. *Child Development, 76,* 1234–1246.

Lansford, J. E., Deater-Deckard, K., Dodge., K. A., Bates, J. E., & Pettit, G. S. (2004). Ethnic differences in the link between physical discipline and later adolescent externalizing behaviors. *Journal of Child Psychology and Psychiatry, 45,* 801–812.

Lansford, J. E., Dodge, K. A., Pettit, G. S., Bates, J. E., Crozier, J., & Kaplow, J. (2002). A 12-year prospective study of the long-term effects of early childhood physical maltreatment on psychological, behavioral, and academic problems in adolescence. *Archives of Pediatrics and Adolescent Medicine, 156,* 824–830.

Lapouse, R., & Monk, M. A. (1959). Fears and worries in a representative sample of children. *American Journal of Orthopsychiatry, 29,* 803–818.

Larner, M. B., Zippiroli, L., & Behrman, R. E. (1999). When school is out: Analysis and recommendations. *The Future of Children, 9(2),* 4–20.

Lask, B. & Bryant-Waugh, R. (1992). Early-onset anorexia nervosa and related eating disorders. *Journal of Child Psychology and Psychiatry, 33,* 281–300.

Last, C. G. (1988). Separation anxiety. In M. Hersen & C. G. Last (Eds.), *Child behavior therapy casebook.* New York: Plenum Press.

Last, C. G., Hersen, M., Kazdin, A. E., Orvaschel, H., & Perrin, S. (1991). Anxiety disorders in children and their families. *Archives of General Psychiatry, 48,* 928–934.

Last, C. G., & Perrin, S. (1993). Anxiety disorders in African-American and white children. *Journal of Abnormal Child Psychology, 21,* 153–164.

Last, C. G., Perrin, S., Hersen, M., & Kazdin, A. E. (1992). DSM-III-R anxiety disorders in children: Sociodemographic and clinical characteristics. *Journal of the American Academy of Child and Adolescent Psychiatry, 31,* 1070–1076.

Last, C. G., Perrin, S., Hersen, M., & Kazdin, A. E. (1996). A prospective study of childhood anxiety disorders. *Journal of the American Academy of Child and Adolescent Psychiatry, 35,* 1502–1510.

Last, C. G., & Strauss, C. C. (1989). Panic disorder in children and adolescents. *Journal of Anxiety Disorders, 3,* 87–95.

Last, C. G., & Strauss, C. C. (1990). School refusal in anxiety-disordered children and adolescents. *Journal of the American Academy of Child and Adolescent Psychiatry, 29,* 31–35.

Last, C. G., Strauss, C. C., & Francis, G. (1987). Comorbidity among childhood anxiety disorders. *Journal of Nervous and Mental Disease, 175,* 726–730.

Latner, J. D., & Stunkard, A. J. (2003). Getting worse: The stigmatization of obese children. *Obesity Research, 11,* 452–456.

Lau, A. S., & Weisz, J. R. (2003). Reported maltreatment among clinic-referred children: Implications for presenting problems, treatment attrition, and long-term outcomes. *Journal of the American Academy of Child and Adolescent Psychiatry, 42,* 1327–1334.

Lavigne, J. V., & Faier-Routman, J. (1993). Correlates of psychological adjustment to pediatric physical disorders: A meta-analytic review and comparison with existing models. *Developmental and Behavioral Pediatrics, 14,* 117–123.

Law, J., & Garrett, Z. (2004). Speech and language therapy: Its potential role in CAMHS. *Child and Adolescent Mental Health, 9,* 50–55.

Laws, G., & Gunn, D. (2004). Phonological memory as a predictor of language comprehension in Down syndrome: A five-year follow-up study. *Journal of Child Psychology and Psychiatry, 45,* 326–327.

Lazarus, A., & Abramavitz, A. (1962). The use of emotive imagery in the treatment of children's phobia. *Journal of Mental Science, 108,* 191–192.

Leach, J. M., Scarborough, H. S., & Rescorla, L. (2003). Late-emerging reading disabilities. *Journal of Educational Psychology, 95,* 211–224.

LeBovidge, J. S., Lavigne, J. V., Donenberg, G. R., & Miller, M. L. (2003). Psychological adjustment of children and adolescents with chronic arthritis: A meta-analytic review. *Journal of Pediatric Psychology, 28,* 29–39.

LeBovidge, J. S., Lavigne, J. V., & Miller, M. L. (2005). Adjustment to chronic arthritis of childhood: The roles of illness-related stress and attitude toward illness. *Journal of Pediatric Psychology, 30,* 273–286.

Lee, T. H., Blasey, C. M., Dyer-Friedman, J., Glaser, B., Reiss, A. L. & Eliez, S. (2005). From research to practice: teacher and pediatrician awareness of phenotypic traits in neurogenetic syndromes. *American Journal of Mental Retardation, 110,* 100–106.

Lefkowitz, M., & Burton, N. (1978). Childhood depression: A critique of the concept. *Psychological Bulletin, 85* (4), 716–726.

le Grange, D., Loeb, K. L., Van Orman, S., & Jellar, C. C. (2004). Bulimia nervosa in adolescents: A disorder in evolution? *Archives of Pediatric & Adolescent Medicine, 158,* 478–482.

Leinonen, J. A., Solantaus, T. S., & Punamäki, R-L. (2003). Parental mental health and children's adjustment: The quality of marital interaction and parenting as mediating factors. *Journal of Child Psychology and Psychiatry, 44,* 227–241.

Leitenberg, H., Yost, L. W., & Carroll-Wilson, M. (1986). Negative cognitive errors in children: Questionnaire development, normative data, and comparisons between children with and without self-reported symptoms of depression, low self-esteem, and evaluation anxiety. *Journal of Consulting and Clinical Psychology, 54,* 528–536.

Lemanek, K. L., Kamps, J., & Chung, N. B. (2001). Empirically supported treatments in pediatric psychology: Regimen adherence. *Journal of Pediatric Psychology, 26,* 279–282.

Lemerise, E. A., & Arsenio, W. F. (2000). An integrated model of emotion processes and cognition in social information processing. *Child Development, 71,* 107–118.

Lenhard, W., Breitenbach, E., Ebert, H., Schindelhauer-Deutscher, H. J., Zang, K. D., & Henn, W. (2007). Attitudes of mothers towards their child with Down syndrome before and after the introduction of prenatal diagnosis. *Intellectual and Developmental Disabilities, 45,* 98–102.

Leonard, H. L., Ale, C. M., Freeman, J. B., Garcia, A. M., & Ng, J. S. (2005). Obsessive-compulsive disorder. *Child and Adolescent Psychiatric Clinics of North America, 14,* 727–743.

Leonard, L. B. (1998). *Children with specific language impairment.* Cambridge, MA: The MIT Press.

Leonard, L. B., Camarata, S. M., Pawlowska, M., Brown, B., & Camarata, M. N. (2006). Tense and agreement morphemes in the speech of children with specific language impairment during intervention: Phase 2. *Journal of Speech, Language, and Hearing Research, 49,* 749–770.

Leonard, L. B., Weismer, S. E., Miller, C. A., Francis, D. J., Tomblin, J. B., & Kail, R. V. (2007). Speed of processing, working memory, and language impairment in children. *Journal of Speech, Language, and Hearing Research, 50,* 408–428.

Lerner, R. M., Fisher, C. B., & Weinberg, R. A. (2000). Toward a science for and of the people: Promoting civil society through the application of developmental studies. *Child Development, 71,* 11–20.

Leslie, L. K., Plemmons, D., Monn, A. R., & Palinkas, L. A. (2007). Investigating ADHD treatment trajectories: Listening to families' stories about medication use. *Journal of Developmental and Behavioral Pediatrics, 28,* 179–188.

Leslie, L. K., Weckerly, J., Landsverk, J., Hough, R. L., Hurlbut, M. S., & Wood, P. A. (2003). Racial/ethnic differences in the use of psychotropic medication in high-risk children and adolescents. *Journal of the American Academy of Child and Adolescent Psychiatry, 42,* 1433–1442.

Lester, B. M., Andreozzi, L., & Appiah, L. (2006). Substance use during pregnancy: Research and social policy. In H. E. Fitzgerald, B. M. Lester, & B. Zuckerman (Eds.), *The crisis in youth mental health. Vol. 1.* Westport, CT: Praeger.

Lester, B. M., Bigsby, R., & Miller-Loncar, C. (2004). Infant massage: So where's the rub? *Social Policy Report, 18(1),* 8.

Leve, L. D., Chamberlain, P., & Reid, J. B. (2005). Intervention outcomes for girls referred from juvenile justice: Effects on delinquency. *Journal of Consulting and Clinical Psychology, 73,* 1181–1184.

Leventhal, T., & Brooks-Gunn, J. (2000). The neighborhoods they live in: The effects of neighborhood residence on child and adolescent outcomes. *Psychological Bulletin, 126,* 309–337.

Levi, J., Segal, L. M., & Gadola, E. (2007). *F as in fat: How obesity policies are failing America.* Washington, DC: Trust for America's Health.

Levine, M. P., & Harrison, K. (2004). Media's role in the perpetuation and prevention of negative body image and disordered eating. In J. K. Thompson (Ed.), *Handbook of eating disorders and obesity.* Hoboken, NJ: John Wiley.

Levy, S. R., Jurkovic, G. L., & Spiro, A. (1995). A multisystems analysis of adolescent suicide attempters. *Journal of Abnormal Child Psychology, 23,* 221–234.

Lewin, A. B., Heidgerken, A. D., Geffken, G. R., Williams, L. B., Storch, E. A., Gelfand, K. M., & Silverstein, J. H. (2006). The relationship between family factors and metabolic control: The role of diabetes adherence. *Journal of Pediatric Psychology, 31,* 174–183.

Lewinsohn, P. (1974). A behavioral approach to depression. In R. J. Friedman & M. M. Katz (Eds.), *The psychology of depression: Contemporary theory and research.* Washington, DC: Winston.

Lewinsohn, P. M., Clarke, G. N., Hops, H., & Andrews, J. (1990). Cognitive behavioral treatment for depressed adolescents. *Behavior Therapy, 21,* 385–402.

Lewinsohn, P. M., Clarke, G. N., Seeley, J. R., & Rohde, P. (1994). Major depression in community adolescents: Age at onset, episode duration, and time to recurrence. *Journal of the American Academy of Child and Adolescent Psychiatry, 33,* 809–818.

Lewinsohn, P. M., Hops, H., Roberts, R. E., Seeley, J. R., & Andrews, J. A. (1993a). Adolescent psychopathology: I. Prevalence and incidence of depression and other DSM-III-R disorders in high school students. *Journal of Abnormal Psychology, 102*, 133–144.

Lewinsohn, P. M., Klein, D. N., & Seeley, J. R. (1995a). Bipolar disorders in a community sample of older adolescents: Prevalence, phenomenology, comorbidity, and course. *Journal of the American Academy of Child and Adolescent Psychiatry, 34*, 454–463.

Lewinsohn, P. M., Rohde, P., Klein, D. N., & Seeley, J. R. (1999). Natural course of adolescent Major Depressive Disorder: I. Continuity into young adulthood. *Journal of the American Academy of Child and Adolescent Psychiatry, 38*, 56–63.

Lewinsohn, P. M., Rohde, P., & Seeley, J. R. (1995b). Adolescent psychopathology: III. The clinical consequences of comorbidity. *Journal of the American Academy of Child and Adolescent Psychiatry, 34*, 510–519.

Lewinsohn, P. M., Rohde, P., & Seeley, J. R. (1996). Adolescent suicidal ideation and attempts: Prevalence, risk factors, and clinical implications. *Clinical Psychology: Science and Practice, 3*, 25–46.

Lewinsohn, P. M., Rohde, P., & Seeley, J. R. (1998). Major Depressive Disorder in older adolescents: Prevalence, risk factors, and clinical implications. *Clinical Psychology Review, 18*, 765–794.

Lewinsohn, P. M., Rohde, P., Seeley, J. R., & Fischer, S. A. (1993b). Age-cohort changes in the lifetime occurrence of depression and other mental disorders. *Journal of Abnormal Psychology, 102*, 110–120.

Lewinsohn, P. M., Seeley, J. R., & Klein, D. N. (2003). Bipolar disorder in adolescents: Epidemiology and suicidal behavior. In B. Geller & M. P. DelBello (Eds.), *Bipolar disorder in childhood and early adolescence*. New York: Guilford Press.

Lewinsohn, P. M., Solomon, A., Seeley, J. R., & Zeiss, A. (2000). Clinical implications of "subthreshold" depressive symptoms. *Journal of Abnormal Psychology, 109*, 345–351.

Lewinsohn, P. M., Striegel-Moore, R. H., & Seeley, J. R. (2000). Epidemiology and natural course of eating disorders in young women from adolescence to young adulthood. *Journal of the American Academy of Child and Adolescent Psychiatry, 39*, 1284–1292.

Lewis, S. Y. (2001). Coping over the long haul: Understanding and supporting children and families affected by HIV disease. *Journal of Pediatric Psychology, 26*, 359–361.

Liaw, F., & Brooks-Gunn, J. (1994). Cumulative familial risk and low-birthweight children's cognitive and behavioral development. *Journal of Clinical Child Psychology, 23*, 360–372.

Licht, B. G., & Kistner, J. A. (1986). Motivational problems of learning-disabled children: Individual differences and their implications for treatment. In J. K. Torgesen & B. Y. L. Wong (Eds.), *Psychological and educational perspectives on learning disabilities*. New York: Academic Press.

Lichtenstein, P., & Annas, P. (2000). Heritability and prevalence of specific fears and phobias in childhood. *Journal of Child Psychology and Psychiatry, 41*, 927–937.

Liddell, G. A., & Rasmussen, C. (2005). Memory profile of children with nonverbal learning disabilities. *Learning Disabilities Research & Practice, 20*, 137–141.

Lilienfeld, S. O. (2003). Comorbidity between and within childhood externalizing and internalizing disorders: Reflections and directions. *Journal of Abnormal Child Psychology, 31*, 285–291.

Lilienfeld, S. O., Lynn, S. J., & Lohr, J. M. (2003). *Science and pseudoscience in clinical psychology*. New York: Guilford Press.

Lilienfeld, S. O., Waldman, I. D., & Israel, A. C. (1994). A critical examination of the use of the term and concept of comorbidity in psychopathology research. *Clinical Psychology: Science and Practice, 1*, 71–83.

Lilly, M. S. (1979). Special education. Emerging issues. In M. S. Lilly (Ed.), *Children with exceptional needs*. New York: Holt, Rinehart and Winston.

Limond, J., & Leeke, R. (2005). Practitioner review: cognitive rehabilitation for children with acquired brain injury. *Journal of Child and Adolescent Psychology, 46*, 339–352.

Lin, K. K., Sandler, I. N., Ayers, T. S., Wolchik, S. A., & Luecken, L. J. (2004). Resilience in parentally bereaved children and adolescents seeking preventive services. *Journal of Clinical Child and Adolescent Psychology, 33*, 673–683.

Linares, L. O., Montalto, D., Li, M. M., & Oza, V. S. (2006). A promising parenting intervention in foster care. *Journal of Consulting and Clinical Psychology, 74*, 32–41.

Linnet, K. M., Dalsgaard, S., Obel, C. et al. (2003). Maternal lifestyle factors in pregnancy risk of attention deficit hyperactivity disorder and associated behaviors: Review of the current literature. *American Journal of Psychiatry, 160*, 1028–1040.

Linscheid, T. R., & Rasnake, L. K. (2001). Eating problems in children. In C. E. Walker & M. C. Roberts (Eds.), *Handbook of clinical child psychology* (3rd ed.). New York: John Wiley & Sons.

Lipka, O., Lesaux, N. K., & Siegel, L. S. (2006). Retrospective analyses of the reading development of grade 4 students with reading disabilities. *Journal of Learning Disabilities, 39*, 364–378.

Lipka, O., & Siegel. L. S. (2006). Learning disabilities. In D. A. Wolfe & E. J. Mash (Eds.), *Behavioral and emotional disorders in adolescents. Nature, assessment, and treatment*. New York: The Guilford Press.

Lipschitz, D. S., Rasmusson, A. M., Yehuda, R., Wang, S., Anyan, W., Gueoguieva, R. et al. (2003). Salivary cortisol responses to dexamethasone in adolescents with posttraumatic stress disorder. *Journal of the American Academy of Child and Adolescent Psychiatry, 42*, 1310–1317.

Little, M., & Kobak, R. (2003). Emotional security with teachers and children's stress reactivity: A comparison of special-education and regular-education classrooms. *Journal of Clinical Child and Adolescent Psychology, 32*, 127–138.

Llewellyn, G., Dunn, P., Fante, M., Turnbull, L., & Grace, R. (1999). Family factors influencing out-of-home placement decisions. *Journal of Intellectual Disability Research, 43*, 219–233.

Lobato, D. J., & Kao, B. T. (2005). Family-based group intervention for young siblings of children with chronic illness and developmental disability. *Journal of Pediatric Psychology, 30*, 678–682.

Lochman, J. E., Powell, N. R., Whidby, J. M., & Fitzgerald, D. P. (2006). Aggressive children: Cognitive-behavioral assessment and treatment. In P. C. Kendall (Ed.), *Child and adolescent therapy: Cognitive-behavioral procedures* (3rd ed.). New York: The Guilford Press.

Lochman, J. E., Whidby, J. M., & FitzGerald, D. P. (2000). Cognitive-behavioral assessment and treatment with aggressive children. In P. C. Kendall (Ed.), *Child and adolescent therapy: Cognitive-behavioral procedures* (2nd ed.). New York: Guilford.

Lock, J. (2004). Family approaches for anorexia nervosa and bulimia nervosa. In J. K. Thompson (Ed.), *Handbook of eating disorders and obesity*. Hoboken, NJ: John Wiley.

Lock, J., & le Grange, D. (2005). Family-based treatment of eating disorders. *International Journal of Eating Disorders, 37 (Suppl.),* 64–67.

Loeb, S., Fuller, B., Kagan, S. L., & Carrol, B. (2004). Child care in poor communities: Early learning effects of type, quality, and stability. *Child Development, 75,* 47–65.

Loeber, R. (1988). Natural histories of conduct problems, delinquency, and associated substance use: Evidence for developmental progressions. In B. B. Lahey & A. E. Kazdin (Eds.), *Advances in clinical child psychology,* Vol. 11. New York: Plenum.

Loeber, R., Burke, J. D., Lahey, B. B., Winters, A., & Zera, M. (2000). Oppositional defiant and conduct disorder: A review of the past 10 years, Part I. *Journal of the American Academy of Child and Adolescent Psychiatry, 39,* 1468–1484.

Loeber, R., & Farrington, D. P. (2000). Young children who commit crime: Epidemiology, developmental origins, risk factors, early interventions, and policy implications. *Development and Psychopathology, 12,* 737–762.

Loeber, R., Green, S. M., Keenan, K., & Lahey, B. (1995). Which boys will fare worse? Early predictors of the onset of conduct disorder in a six-year longitudinal study. *Journal of the American Academy of Child and Adolescent Psychiatry, 34,* 499–509.

Loeber, R., & Hay, D. F. (1994). Developmental approaches to aggression and conduct problems. In M. Rutter & D. F. Hay (Eds.), *Development through life: A handbook for clinicians.* Malden, MA: Blackwell Scientific.

Loeber, R., & Keenan, K. (1994). Interaction between conduct disorder and its comorbid conditions: Effects of age and gender. *Clinical Psychology Review, 14,* 497–523.

Loeber, R., & Schmaling, K. B. (1985) Empirical evidence for overt and covert patterns of antisocial conduct problems: A meta-analysis. *Journal of Abnormal Child Psychology, 13,* 337–354.

Loeber, R., & Stouthamer-Loeber, M. (1998). Development of juvenile aggression and violence: Some common misconceptions and controversies. *American Psychologist, 53,* 242–259.

Loeber, R., Wung, P., Keenan, K., Giroux, B., Stouthamer-Loeber, M., Van Kammen, W. B., & Maughan, B. (1993). Developmental pathways in disruptive child behavior. *Development and Psychopathology, 5,* 103–133.

Lofland, K. R., Sturges, J. M., & Payne, T. J. (1999). Headache. In A. J. Goreczny & M. Hersen (Eds.), *Handbook of pediatric and adolescent health psychology.* Boston: Allyn and Bacon.

Logan, D. E., & King, C. A. (2001). Parental facilitation of adolescent mental health service utilization: A conceptual and empirical review. *Clinical Psychology: Science and Practice, 8,* 319–333.

Loney, B. R., Firck, P. J., Clements, C. B., Ellis, M. L., & Kerlin, K. (2003). Callous-unemotional traits, impulsivity, and emotional processing in adolescents with antisocial behavior problems. *Journal of Clinical Child and Adolescent Psychology, 32,* 66–80.

Long, P., Forehand, R., Wierson, M., & Morgan, A. (1994). Does parent training with young noncompliant children have long term effects? *Behaviour Research and Therapy, 32,* 101–107.

Lonigan, C. J., Burgess, S. R., & Anthony, J. L. (2000). Development of emergent literacy and early reading skills in preschool children: Evidence from a latent-variable longitudinal study. *Developmental Psychology, 36,* 596–613.

Lonigan, C. J., Vasey, M. W., Phillips, B. M., & Hazen, R. A. (2004). Temperament, anxiety, and the processing of threat-relevant stimuli. *Journal of Clinical Child and Adolescent Psychology, 33,* 8–20.

Lorch, E. P., Milich, R., Sanchez, R. P., van den Broek, P., Baer, S., Hooks, K. et al. (2000). Comprehension of televised stories in boys with attention deficit/hyperactivity disorder and nonreferred boys. *Journal of Abnormal Psychology, 109,* 321–330.

Lord, C., Risi, S., Lambrecht, L., Cook, E. H., Levanthal, B. L., DiLavore, P. C. et al. (2000). The Autism Diagnostic Observation Schedule-Generic: A standard measure of social and communicative deficits associated with the spectrum of autism. *Journal of Autism and Pervasive Developmental Disorders, 30,* 205–223.

Lord, C., Shulman, C., & DiLavore, P. (2004). Regression and word loss in autistic spectrum disorders. *Journal of Child Psychology and Psychiatry, 45,* 936–955.

Lorian, R. P. (2000). Community, prevention, and wellness. In M. Hersen & R. T. Ammerman (Eds.), *Advanced abnormal child psychology.* Mahwah, NJ: Lawrence Erlbaum Associates.

Losier, B. J., McGrath, P. J., & Klein, R. M. (1996). Error patterns on the continuous performance test in non-medicated and medicated samples of children with and without ADHD: A meta-analytic review. *Journal of Child Psychology and Psychiatry, 37,* 971–987.

Lott, B. (2002). Cognitive and behavioral distancing from the poor. *American Psychologist, 57,* 100–110.

Loughry, M., Ager, A., Flouri, E., Khamis, V., Afana, A. H. et al. (2006). The impact of structured activities among Palestinian children in time of conflict. *Journal of Child Psychology and Psychiatry, 47,* 1211–1218.

Lovaas, O. I. (1987). Behavioral treatment and normal educational and intellectual functioning in young autistic children. *Journal of Consulting and Clinical Psychology, 55,* 3–9.

Lovaas, O. I., & Smith, T. (1988). Intensive behavioral treatment for young autistic children. In B. B. Lahey & A. E. Kazdin (Eds.), *Advances in clinical child psychology,* Vol. 2. New York: Plenum.

Lovaas, O. I., & Smith, T. (2003). Early and intensive behavioral intervention in autism. In A. E. Kazdin & J. R. Weisz (Eds.), *Evidence-based psychotherapies for children and adolescents.* New York: Guilford Press.

Lovaas, O. I., Young, D. B., & Newsom, C. D. (1978). Childhood psychosis: Behavioral treatment. In B. B. Wolman (Ed.), *Handbook of treatment of mental disorders in childhood and adolescence.* Englewood Cliffs, NJ: Prentice Hall.

Lovejoy, M. C., Graczyk, P. A., O'Hare, E., & Newman, G. (2000). Maternal depression and parenting behavior: A meta-analytic review. *Clinical Psychology Review, 20,* 561–592.

Loveland, K. A., & Tunali-Kotoski, B. (1997). The school-age child with autism. In D. J. Cohen, & F. R. Volkmar (Eds.). *Handbook of pervasive and developmental disorders.* New York: John Wiley.

Lucas, A. R., & Holub, M. I. (1995). The incidence of anorexia nervosa in adolescent residents of Rochester, Minnesota, during a 50-year period. In H. C. Steinhausen (Ed.), *Eating disorders in adolescence: Anorexia and bulimia nervosa.* Berlin: Walter de Gruyter.

Luciana, M. (2003). Computerized assessment of neuropsychological function in children: Clinical and research applications of the Cambridge Neuropsychological Testing Automated Battery (CANTAB). *Journal of Child Psychology and Psychiatry, 44,* 649–663.

Luckasson, R. et al. (1992). *Mental retardation: Definition, classification, and systems of supports.* Washington, DC: American Association on Mental Retardation.

Luckasson, R. et al. (2002). *Mental retardation: Definition, classification, and systems of support.* Washington, DC: American Association on Mental Retardation.

Ludwig, J. & Mayer, S. (2006). "Culture" and the intergenerational transmission of poverty: The prevention paradox. *Opportunity in America. Future of Children, 16,* 176–196.

Luman, M., Oosterlaan, J., Hyde, C., van Meel, C. S., Sergeast, J. A. (2007). Heartrate and reinforcement sensitivity in ADHD. *Journal of Child Psychology and Psychiatry, 48,* 890–898.

Lurie, N., & Dubowitz, T. (2007). Health disparities and access to health. *Journal of the American Medical Association, 297,* 1118–1121.

Lustig, S. L., Kia-Keating, M., Knight, W. G., Geltman, P., Ellis, H., Kinzie, J. D. et al. (2004). Review of child and adolescent mental health. *Journal of the American Academy of Child and Adolescent Psychiatry, 43,* 24–36.

Luthar, S. S. (1999). *Poverty and children's adjustment.* Thousand Oaks, CA: Sage.

Luthar, S. S. (2006). Resilience in development: A synthesis of research across five decades. In D. Cicchetti & D. J. Cohen (Eds.), *Developmental psychopathology. Vol. 3. Risk, disorder, and adaptation.* Hoboken, NJ: John Wiley & Sons.

Luthar, S. S., & Cushing, G. (1999). Neighborhood influences and child development: A prospective study of substance abusers' offspring. *Development and Psychopathology, 11,* 763–784.

Luthar, S. S., & D'Avanzo, K. (1999). Contextual factors in substance use: A study of suburban and inner-city adolescents. *Development and Psychopathology, 11,* 845–867.

Luthar, S. S., & Goldstein, A. (2004). Children's exposure to community violence: Implications for understanding risk and resilience. *Journal of Clinical Child and Adolescent Psychology, 33,* 499–505.

Lynch, M., & Cicchetti, D. (1998). An ecological–interactional analysis of children and contexts: The longitudinal interplay among child treatment, community violence, and children's symptomatology. *Development and Psychopathology, 10,* 235–257.

Lynskey, M. T., & Fergusson, D. M. (1995). Childhood conduct problems, attention deficit behaviors, and adolescent alcohol, tobacco, and illicit drug use. *Journal of Abnormal Child Psychology, 23,* 281–302.

Lyon, G. R., & Cutting, L. E. (1998). Learning disabilities. In E. J. Mash & R. A. Barkley (Eds.), *Treatment of childhood disorders.* New York: Guilford Press.

Lyon, G. R., Fletcher, J. M., & Barnes, M. C. (2003). Learning disabilities. In E. J. Mash & R. A. Barkley (Eds.), *Child psychopathology.* New York: Guilford Press.

Lyon, G. R., Fletcher, J. M., Fuchs, L. S., & Chhabra, V. (2006). Learning disabilities. In E. J. Mash & R. A. Barkley (Eds.), *Treatment of childhood disorders.* New York: The Guilford Press.

Lyons-Ruth, K., Zeanah, C. H., & Benoit, D. (2003). Disorder and risk for disorder during infancy and toddlerhood. In E. J. Mash, & R. A. Barkley (Eds.), *Child psychopathology.* New York: Guilford Press.

Maccini, P., & Hughes, C. A. (1997). Mathematics interventions for adolescents with learning disabilities. *Learning Disabilities Research and Practice, 12,* 168–176.

Maccoby, E. E. (1992). The role of parents in the socialization of children: An historic overview. *Developmental Psychology, 28,* 1006–1017.

Maccoby, E. E., & Martin, J. A. (1983). Socialization in the context of the family: Parent-child interaction. In P. H. Mussen (Ed.), *Handbook of child psychology, Vol. IV.* New York: John Wiley.

MacDonald, A. W., Pogue-Geile, M. F., Johnson, M. K., & Carter, C. S. (2003). A specific deficit in context processing in the unaffected siblings of patients with schizophrenia. *Archives of General Psychiatry, 60,* 57–63.

Mace, F. C., Vollmer, T. R., Progar, P. R., & Mace, A. B. (1998). Assessment and treatment of self-injury. In T. S. Watson & F. M. Gresham (Eds.), *Handbook of child behavior therapy.* New York: Plenum Press.

MacFarlane, J. W., Allen, L., & Honzik, M. P. (1954). *A developmental study of the behavior problems of normal children between 21 months and 14 years.* Berkeley: University of California Press.

Machover, K. (1949). *Personality projection in the drawing of the human figure.* Springfield, IL: Chas. C. Thomas.

Macintosh, K. E., & Dissanayake, C. (2004). Annotation: The similarities and differences between autistic disorder and Asperger's disorder: A review of the empirical evidence. *Journal of Child Psychology and Psychiatry, 45,* 421–434.

MacLaren, J. E., & Cohen, L. L. (2005). A comparison of distraction strategies for venipuncture distress in children. *Journal of Pediatric Psychology, 30,* 387–396.

MacLean, K. (2003). The impact of institutionalization on child development. *Development and Psychopathology, 15,* 853–884.

MacMillan, D. L., Keogh, B. K., & Jones, R. L. (1986). Special educational research on mildly handicapped learners. In M. C. Wittrock (Ed.), *Handbook of research on teaching.* New York: Macmillan.

MacMillan, D. L., & Reschly, D. J. (1997). Issues of definition and classification. In W. E. MacLean, Jr. (Ed.), *Ellis' handbook of mental deficiency, psychological theory and research.* Mahwah, NJ: Lawrence Erlbaum.

MacMillan, R., McMorris, B. J., Kruttschnitt, C. (2004). Linked lives: Stability and change in maternal circumstances and trajectories of antisocial behavior in children. *Child Development, 75,* 205–220.

Madsen, K. M., Lauritsen, M. B., Pedersen, C. B., Thorsen, P., Plesner, A-M., Andersen, P. H., & Mortensen, P. B. (2003). Thimerosal and the occurrence of autism: Negative ecological evidence from Danish population-based data. *Pediatrics, 112,* 604–606.

Maguin, E., & Loeber, R. (1996). Academic performance and delinquency. In M. Tonry (Ed.), *Crime and justice* (Vol. 20). Chicago: University of Chicago Press.

Mahone, E. M., Prahme, M. C., Ruble, K., Mostofsky, S. H., & Schwartz, C. L. (2007). Motor and perceptual timing deficits among survivors of childhood leukemia. *Journal of Pediatric Psychology, 32,* 918–925.

Main, M. (1996). Introduction to the special section on attachment and psychopathology: 2. Overview of the field of attachment. *Journal of Consulting and Clinical Psychology, 64,* 237–243.

Major, B., & O'Brien, L. T. (2005). The social psychology of stigma. *Annual Review of Psychology, 56,* 393–421.

Malmquist, C. P. (1977). Childhood depression: A clinical and behavioral prospective. In J. G. Schulterbrandt & A. Raskin (Eds.), *Depression in childhood: Diagnosis, treatment, and conceptual models.* New York: Raven Press.

Malone, R. P., Maislin, G., Choudhury, M. S., Gifford, C., & Delaney, M. A. (2002). Risperidone treatment in children and adolescents with autism: Short- and long-term safety and effectiveness. *Journal of the American Academy of Child and Adolescent Psychiatry, 41,* 140–147.

Manassis, K., Tannock, R., & Barbosa, J. (2000). Dichotic listening and response inhibition in children with comorbid anxiety disorders and ADHD. *Journal of the American Academy of Child and Adolescent Psychiatry, 39,* 1152–1159.

Manicavasagar, V., Silove, D., Curtis, J., & Wagner, R. (2000). Continuities of separation anxiety from early life into adulthood. *Journal of Anxiety Disorders, 14,* 1–18.

Manimala, R., Blount, R. L., & Cohen, L. L. (2000). The effects of parental reassurance versus distraction on child distress and coping during immunizations. *Child Health Care, 29,* 161–177.

Manly, J. T., Kim, J. E., Rogosch, F. A., & Cicchetti, D. (2001). Dimensions of child maltreatment and children's adjustment: Contributions of developmental timing and subtype. *Development and Psychopathology, 13,* 759–782.

Mannuzza, S., Klein, R. G., Bessler, A., Malloy, P., & LaPadula, M. (1993). Adult outcome of hyperactive boys. *Archives of General Psychiatry, 50,* 565–576.

Mannuzza, S., Klein, R. G., Bessler, A., Malloy, P., & LaPadula, M. (1998). Adult psychiatric status of hyperactive boys grown up. *American Journal of Psychiatry, 155,* 493–498.

March, J., Silva, S., Vitiello, B., & the TADS Team. (2006). The Treatment for Adolescents With Depression Study (TADS): Methods and message at 12 weeks. *Journal of the American Academy of Child and Adolescent Psychiatry, 45,* 1393–1403.

March, J. S., & Albano, A. M. (1998). New developments in assessing pediatric anxiety disorders. In T. H. Ollendick & R. J. Prinz (Eds.), *Advances in clinical child psychology* (Vol. 20). New York: Plenum Press.

March, J. S., Franklin, M. E., Leonard, H. L., & Foa, E. B. (2004). Obsessive-compulsive disorder. In T. L. Morris & J. S. March (Eds.), *Anxiety disorders in children and adolescents.* New York: Guilford Press.

March, J. S., Franklin, M., & Foa, E. (2005). Cognitive-behavioral psychotherapy for pediatric obsessive-compulsive disorder. In E. D. Hibbs & P. S. Jensen (Eds.), *Psychosocial treatments for child and adolescent disorders: Empirically based strategies for clinical practice.* (2nd ed.). Washington, DC: American Psychological Association.

March, J. S., & Mulle, K. (1998). *OCD in children and adolescents: A cognitive-behavioral treatment manual.* New York: Guilford Press.

March, J. S., Parker, J. D. A., Sullivan, K., Stallings, P., & Conners, C. K. (1997). The multidimensional anxiety scale for children (MASC): Factor structure, reliability and validity. *Journal of the American Academy of Child and Adolescent Psychiatry 36,* 554–565.

Marchetti, A. G., & Campbell, V. A. (1990). Social skills. In J. L. Matson (Ed.), *Handbook of behavior modification with the mentally retarded.* New York: Plenum.

Marchi, M., & Cohen, P. (1990). Early childhood eating behaviors and adolescent eating disorders. *Journal of the American Academy of Child and Adolescent Psychiatry, 29,* 112–117.

Marenco, S., & Weinberger, D. R. (2000). The neurodevelopmental hypothesis of schizophrenia: Following a trail of evidence from cradle to grave. *Development and Psychopathology, 12,* 501–527.

Margolin, G. (1998). Effects of domestic violence on children. In P. K. Trickett & C. J. Schellenbach (Eds.), *Violence against children in the family and the community.* Washington, DC: American Psychological Association.

Margolin, G., & Gordis, E. B. (2000). The effects of family and community violence on children. *Annual Review of Psychology, 51,* 445–479.

Markson, S., & Fiese, B. H. (2000). Family rituals as a protective factor for children with asthma. *Journal of Pediatric Psychology, 25,* 471–479.

Marsella, A. J. (1998). Toward a "global-community psychology": Meeting the needs of a changing world. *American Psychologist, 53,* 1282–1291.

Martell, M., Nikolas, M., & Nigg, J. T. (2007). Executive function in adolescents with ADHD. *Journal of the American Academy of Child and Adolescent Psychiatry, 46,* 1437–1444.

Martinez, C. R., Jr., & Eddy, J. M. (2005). Effects of culturally adapted parent management training on Latino youth behavioral health outcomes. *Journal of Consulting and Clinical Psychology, 73,* 841–851.

Marton, K., & Schwartz, R. G. (2003). Working memory capacity and language processes in children with specific language impairment. *Journal of Speech, Language, and Hearing Research, 46,* 1138–1153.

Masi, G., Favilla, L., Mucci, M., & Millepiedi, S. (2000). Panic disorder in clinically referred children and adolescents. *Child Psychiatry and Human Development, 31,* 139–151.

Masi, G., Millepiedi, S., Mucci, M., Poli, P., Bertini, N., & Milantoni, L. (2004). Generalized anxiety disorder in referred children and adolescents. *Journal of the American Academy of Child and Adolescent Psychiatry, 43,* 752–760.

Masten, A. S. (2001). Ordinary magic: Resilience processes in development. *American Psychologist, 56,* 227–238.

Masten, A. S., & Coatsworth, J. D. (1998). The development of competence in favorable and unfavorable environments: Lessons from research on successful children. *American Psychologist, 53,* 205–220.

Masten, A. S., & Shaffer, A. (2006). How families matter in child development: Reflections from research on risk and resilience. In A. Clarke-Stewart & J. Dunn (Eds.), *Families count. Effects on child and adolescent development.* New York: Cambridge University Press.

Matarazzo, J. D. (1992). Psychological testing and assessment in the 21st century. *American Psychologist, 47,* 1007–1018.

Matson, J. L., LeBlanc, L. A., & Weinheimer, B. (1999). Reliability of the Matson Evaluation of Social Skills with Severe Retardation (MESSIER). *Behavior Modification, 23,* 647–661.

Mattila, M-L., Kielinen, M., Jussila, K., Linna, S. L., Bloigu, R., Ebeling, H. et al. (2007). An epidemiological and diagnostic study of Asperger syndrome according to four sets of diagnostic criteria. *Journal of the American Academy of Child and Adolescent Psychiatry, 46,* 636–446.

Mattison, R. E. (2000). School consultation: A review of research on issues unique to the school environment. *Journal of the American Academy of Child and Adolescent Psychiatry, 39,* 402–413.

Maughan, B., Rowe, R., Messer, J., Goodman, R., & Meltzer, H. (2004). Conduct disorder and oppositional defiant disorder in a national sample: Developmental epidemiology. *Journal of Child Psychology and Psychiatry, 45,* 609–621.

Maughan, B., & Rutter, M. (1998). Continuities and discontinuities in antisocial behavior from childhood to adult life. In T. H. Ollendick & R. J. Prinz (Eds.), *Advances in clinical child psychology* (Vol. 20). New York: Plenum Press.

Maughan, D. R., Christiansen, E., Jenson, W. R., Olympia, D., & Clark, E. (2005). Behavioral parent training as a treatment for externalizing behaviors and disruptive behavior disorders: A meta-analysis. *School Psychology Review, 34,* 267–286.

Mawhood, L., Howlin, P., & Rutter, M. (2000). Autism and developmental receptive language disorder—a comparative follow-up in early adult life. I: Cognitive and language outcomes. *Journal of Child Psychology and Psychiatry, 41,* 547–559.

Mayes, L. C., & Suchman, N. E. (2006). Developmental pathways to substance abuse. In D. Cicchetti & D. J. Cohen (Eds.), *Developmental psychopathology, Vol. 3: Risk, disorder, and adaptation* (2nd ed.). Hoboken, NJ: John Wiley & Sons.

Mayes, S. D. (1992). Rumination disorder: Diagnosis, complications, mediating variables, and treatment. In B. B. Lahey & A. E. Kazdin (Eds.), *Advances in clinical child psychology,* Vol. 14. New York: Plenum.

McAlpine, C., & Singh, N. N. (1986). Pica in institutionalized mentally retarded persons. *Journal of Mental Deficiency Research, 30,* 171–178.

McArthur, D. S., & Roberts, G. E. (1982). *Roberts Apperception Test for Children: Manual.* Los Angeles: Western Psychological Services.

McArthur, G. M., Hogben, J. H., Edwards, V. T., Heath, S. M., & Mengler, E. D. (2000). On the "specifics" of specific reading disability and specific language impairment. *Journal of Child Psychology and Psychiatry, 41,* 869–874.

McCabe, M. P., & Ricciardelli, L. A. (2004). Weight and shape concerns of boys and men. In J. K. Thompson (Ed.), *Handbook of eating disorders and obesity.* Hoboken, NJ: John Wiley.

McCartney, K. (2006). The family-child-care mesosystem. In A. Clarke-Stewart & J. Dunn (Eds.). *Families count. Effects on child and adolescent development.* NewYork: Cambridge University Press.

McCarton, C. M., Brooks-Gunn, J., Wallace, I. F., & Bauer, C. R. (1997). Results at age 8 years of early intervention for low-birth-weight premature infants: The infant health and development program. *Journal of the American Medical Association, 277,* 126–132.

McCarty, C. A., McMahon, R. J., & Conduct Problems Prevention Research Group. (2005). Domains of risk to the developmental continuity of firesetting. *Behavior Therapy, 36,* 185–195.

McCauley, E., Pavlidis, K., & Kendall, K. (2001). Developmental precursors of depression: The child and the social environment. In I. M. Goodyer (Ed.), *The depressed child and adolescent* (2nd ed.). Cambridge, UK: Cambridge University Press.

McClellan, J., Breiger, D., McCurry, C., & Hlastala, S. A. (2003). Premorbid functioning in early-onset psychotic disorders. *Journal of the American Academy of Child and Adolescent Psychiatry, 42,* 666–672.

McClellan, J. M. (2000). Early-onset schizophrenia. In B. J. Sadock & V. A. Sadock (Eds.), *Comprehensive textbook of psychiatry* (Vol. II). Philadelphia: Lippincott Williams & Wilkins.

McClellan, J. M. (2005). Early-onset schizophrenia. In B. J. Sadock & V. A. Sadock (Eds.). *Comprehensive textbook of psychiatry. Vol. 2.* Philadelphia: Lippincott Williams & Wilkins.

McClellan, J. M., Werry, J. et al. (2001). Practice parameter for the assessment and treatment of children and adolescents with schizophrenia. *Journal of the American Academy of Child and Adolescent Psychiatry, 40:7* Supplement, 4S–23S.

McClellan, J. M., & Werry, J. S. (2000). Research psychiatric diagnostic interviews for children and adolescents. Introduction. *Journal of the American Academy of Child and Adolescent Psychiatry, 39,* 19–27.

McClure, E. B., Connell, A. M., Zucker, M., Griffith, J. R., & Kaslow, N. J. (2005). The Adolescent Depression Empowerment Project (ADEPT): A culturally sensitive family treatment for depressed African American girls. In E. D. Hibbs & P. S. Jensen (Eds.), *Psychosocial treatments for child and adolescent disorders: Empirically based strategies for clinical practice.* (2nd ed.). Washington, DC: American Psychological Association.

McClure, E. B., Kubiszyn, T., & Kaslow, N. J. (2002). Advances in the diagnosis and treatment of childhood disorders. *Professional Psychology: Research and Practice, 33,* 125–134.

McClure, E. B., & Pine, D. S. (2006). Social anxiety and emotion regulation: A model for developmental psychopathology perspectives on anxiety disorders. In D. Cicchetti & D. J. Cohen (Eds.), *Developmental psychopathology* (2nd ed., vol. 3). Hoboken, NJ: John Wiley & Sons.

McConaughy, S. H. (2005). *Clinical interviews for children and adolescents: Assessment to intervention.* New York: The Guilford Press.

McCulloch, R., & Collins, J. J. (2006). Pain in children who have life-limiting conditions. *Child and Adolescent Psychiatric Clinics of North America, 15,* 657–682.

McDowell, K. D., Lonigan, C. J., & Goldstein, H. (2007). Relations among SES, age, and predictors of phonological awareness. *Journal of Speech, Language, and Hearing Research, 50,* 1079–1092.

McEachin, J. J., Smith, T., & Lovaas, O. I. (1993). Long-term outcome for children with autism who received early intensive behavioral treatment. *American Journal on Mental Retardation, 97,* 359–372.

McEvoy, R. E., Rogers, S. J., & Pennington, B. F. (1993). Executive functions and social communication deficits in young autistic children. *Journal of Child Psychology and Psychiatry, 34,* 563–578.

McGee, R., Feehan, M., Williams, S., & Anderson, J. (1992). DSM-III disorders from age 11 to age 15 years. *Journal of the American Academy of Child and Adolescent Psychiatry, 31,* 50–59.

McGee, R., Feehan, M., Williams, S., Partridge, F., Silva, P. A., & Kelly, J. (1990). DSM-III disorders in a large sample of adolescents. *Journal of the American Academy of Child and Adolescent Psychiatry, 29,* 611–619.

McGee, R., Prior, M., Williams, S., Smart, D., & Sanson, A. (2002). The long-term significance of teacher-rated hyperactivity and reading ability in childhood: Finding from two longitudinal studies. *Journal of Child Psychology and Psychiatry, 43,* 1004–1017.

McGee, R., Williams, S., & Poulton, R. (2000). Hallucinations in nonpsychotic children. *Journal of the American Academy of Child and Adolescent Psychiatry, 39,* 12–13.

McGee, R. A., & Wolfe, D. A. (1991). Psychological maltreatment: Toward an operational definition. *Development and Psychopathology, 3,* 3–18.

McGloin, J. M., & Widom, C. S. (2001). Resilience among abused and neglected children grown up. *Development and Psychopathology, 13,* 1021–1038.

McGrath, M. L., Mellon, M. M., & Murphy, L. (2000). Empirically supported treatments in pediatric psychology: Constipation and encopresis. *Journal of Pediatric Psychology, 25,* 225–254.

McGue, M., & Lykken, D. T. (1992). Genetic influence on risk of divorce. *Psychological Science, 6,* 368–373.

McLanahan, S., & Sandefur, G. (1994). *Growing up with a single parent: What hurts, what helps?* Cambridge, MA: Harvard University Press.

McLeer, S. V., & Wills, C. (2000). Psychopharmacological treatment. In M. Hersen & R. T. Ammerman (Eds.), *Advanced abnormal child psychology* (2nd ed.). Mahwah, NJ: Lawrence Erlbaum Associates.

McLeskey, J. Hoppey, D., Williamson, P., & Rentz, T. (2004). Is inclusion an illusion? An examination of national and state trends toward the education of students with learning disabilities in general education classrooms. *Learning Disabilities Research and Practice, 19,* 109–115.

McMahon, R. J., & Estes, A. M. (1997). Conduct problems. In E. J. Mash & L. G. Terdal (Eds.), *Assessment of childhood disorders* (3rd ed.). New York: Guilford Press.

McMahon, R. J., & Forehand, R. L. (2003). *Helping the noncompliant child: Family-based treatment for oppositional behavior* (2nd ed.). New York: The Guilford Press.

McMahon, R. J., & Wells, K. C. (1998). Conduct disorders. In E. J. Mash & R. A. Barkley (Eds.), *Treatment of childhood disorders.* New York: Guilford.

McMahon, R. J., Wells, K. C., & Kotler, J. S. (2006). Conduct problems. In E. J. Mash & R. A. Barkley (Eds.), *Treatment of childhood disorders* (3rd ed.). New York: The Guilford Press.

McNulty, M. A. (2003). Dyslexia and the life course. *Journal of Learning Disabilities, 36,* 363–381.

McQuaid, E. L., Kopel, S. J., Klein, R. B., & Fritz, G. K. (2003). Medication adherence in pediatric asthma: Reasoning, responsibility, and behavior. *Journal of Pediatric Psychology, 28,* 323–333.

McQuaid, E. L., Kopel, S. J., & Nassau, J. H. (2001). Behavioral adjustment in children with asthma: A meta-analysis. *Journal of Developmental and Behavioral Pediatrics, 22,* 430–439.

McQuaid, E. L., Mitchell, D. K., Walders, N., Nassau, J. H., Kopel, S. J., Klein, R. B., et al. (2007). Pediatric asthma morbidity: The importance of symptom perception and family response to symptoms. *Journal of Pediatric Psychology, 32,* 167–177.

McQuaid, E. L., & Walders, N. (2003). Pediatric asthma. In M. C. Roberts (Eds.), *Handbook of pediatric psychology* (3rd ed.). New York: Guilford Press.

McQuaid, E. L., Walders, N., Kopel, S. J., Fritz, G. K., & Klinnert, M. D. (2005). Pediatric asthma management in the family context: The Family Asthma Management System Scale. *Journal of Pediatric Psychology, 30,* 492–502.

McReynolds, P. (1987). Lightner Witmer: Little-known founder of clinical psychology. *American Psychologist, 42,* 849–858.

Measelle, J. R., Stice, E., & Hogansen, J. M. (2006). Developmental trajectories of co-occurring depressive, eating, antisocial, and substance abuse problems in female adolescents. *Journal of Abnormal Psychology, 115,* 524–538.

Mednick, S. A., Machon, R. A., Huttunen, M. O., & Bonnett, D. (1988). Fetal viral infection and adult schizophrenia. *Archives of General Psychiatry, 45,* 189–192.

Meijer, S. A., Sinnema, G., Bijstra, J. O., Mellenbergh, G. J., & Wolters, W. H. G. (2000). Social functioning in children with a chronic illness. *Journal of Child Psychology and Psychiatry, 41,* 309–317.

Meins, E., Fernyhough, C., Fradley, E., & Tuckey, M. (2001). Rethinking maternal sensitivity: Mothers' comments on infants' mental processes predict security of attachment at 12 months. *Journal of Child Psychology and Psychiatry, 42,* 637–648.

Melamed, B. G., & Siegel, L. J. (1975). Reduction of anxiety in children facing hospitalization and surgery by use of filmed modeling. *Journal of Consulting and Clinical Psychology, 43,* 511–521.

Melamed, B. G., & Siegel, L. J. (1980). *Behavioral medicine: Practical applications in health care.* New York: Springer.

Mellon, M. W., & McGrath, M. L. (2000). Empirically supported treatments in pediatric psychology: Nocturnal enuresis. *Journal of Pediatric Psychology, 25,* 193–214.

Melnick, S. M., & Hinshaw, S. P. (1996). What they want and what they get: The social goals of boys with ADHD and comparison boys. *Journal of Abnormal Child Psychology, 24,* 169–185.

Meltzer, H. Y., Alphs, L., Green, A. I., Altamura, C., Anand, R., Bertoldi, A. et al. (2003). Clozapine treatment for suicidality in schizophrenia. *Archives of General Psychiatry, 60,* 82–91.

Meltzer, L., Reddy, R., Pollica, L. S., Roditi, B., Sayer, J., & Theokas, C. (2004). Positive and negative selfperceptions: Is there a cyclical relationship between teachers' and students' perceptions of effort, strategy use, and academic performance? *Learning Disabilities Research & Practice, 19,* 33–44.

Meltzer, L. J., Johnson, S. B., Pappachan, S., & Silverstein, J. (2003). Blood glucose estimation in adolescence with type 1 diabetes: Predictors of accuracy and error. *Journal of Pediatric Psychology, 28,* 203–211.

Menning, C. L. (2002). Absent parents are more than money: The joint effect of activities and financial support on youth's educational attainment. *Journal of Family Issues, 23,* 648–671.

Mental Health: A Report of the Surgeon General. (2001). Surgeongeneral.gov/library/mentalhealth/index.html. Washington, DC: Office of the Surgeon General, Department of Health and Human Services.

Mercer, C. D. (1997). *Students with learning disabilities.* Upper Saddle River, NJ: Prentice Hall.

Mercer, C. D., & Mercer, A. R. (2001). *Teaching students with learning problems.* Upper Saddle River, NJ: Merrill/Prentice Hall.

Merikangas, K. R. (2005). Vulnerability factors for anxiety disorders in children and adolescents. *Child and Adolescent Psychiatric Clinics of North America, 14,* 649–679.

Mertin, P., & Hartwig, S. (2004). Auditory hallucinations in nonpsychotic children: Diagnostic considerations. *Child and Adolescent Mental Health, 9,* 9–14.

Mesibov, G. B. (1992). Letters to the editors. Response to Thompson and McEvoy. *Journal of Autism and Developmental Disorders, 22,* 672–673.

Mesibov, G., B., & Van Bourgondien, M. E. (1992). Autism. In S. R. Hooper, G. W. Hynd, & R. E. Mattison (Eds.), *Developmental disorders.* Diagnostic criteria and clinical assessment. Hillsdale, NJ: Erlbaum.

Mezzich, J. E., & Üstun, T. B. (2005). Epidemiology. In B. J. Sadock & V. A. Sadock (Eds.), *Kaplan and Sadock's comprehensive textbook of psychiatry. Vol. 2.* Philadelphia: Lippincott Williams & Wilkens.

Miceli, P. J., Rowland, J. F., & Whitman, T. L. (1999). Chronic illnesses in childhood. In T. L. Whitman, T. V. Merluzzi, & R. D. White (Eds.), *Life-span perspectives on health and illness.* Mahwah, NJ: Lawrence Erlbaum Associates.

Mick, E., Biederman, J., Faraone, S. V., Sayer, J., & Kleinman, S. (2002). Case-control study of attention-deficit hyperactivity disorder and maternal smoking, alcohol use, and drug use during pregnancy. *Journal of the American Academy of Child and Adolescent Psychiatry, 41,* 378–385.

Middleton, J. A. (2001). Psychological sequelae of head injury in children and adolescents. *Journal of Child Psychology and Psychiatry, 42,* 165–180.

Mikkelsen, E. J. (2001). Enuresis and encopresis: Ten years of progress. *Journal of the American Academy of Child and Adolescent Psychiatry, 40,* 1146–1158.

Milan, S., Pinderhughes, E. E., & the Conduct Problems Prevention Research Group. (2006). Family instability and child maladjustment trajectories during elementary school. *Journal of Abnormal Child Psychology, 34,* 43–56.

Milich, R., Balentine, A. C., & Lynam, D. R. (2001, Winter). ADHD combined type and ADHD predominantly inattentive type are distinct and unrelated disorders. *Clinical Psychology: Science and Practice, 8,* 463–488.

Miller, B. C., Fan, X., Christensen, M., Grotevant, H. D., & van Dulmen, M. (2000). Comparisons of adopted and non-adopted adolescents in a large, nationally representative sample. *Child Development, 71,* 1458–1473.

Miller, J. E. (2000). The effects of race/ethnicity and income on early childhood asthma prevalence and health care use. *American Journal of Public Health, 90,* 428–430.

Miller, J. N., & Ozonoff, S. (2000). The external validity of Asperger's Disorder: Lack of evidence from the domain of neuropsychology. *Journal of Abnormal Psychology, 109,* 227–238.

Miller, L. C., Barrett, C. L., & Hampe, E. (1974). Phobias of childhood in a prescientific era. In A. Davids (Ed.), *Child personality and psychopathology: Current topics,* Vol. 1. New York: John Wiley.

Miller, L. K. (1999). The savant syndrome: Intellectual impairment and exceptional skill. *Psychological Bulletin, 125,* 31–46.

Miller, S. A. (1998). *Developmental research methods.* Upper Saddle River, NJ: Prentice-Hall.

Miller, S. L., & Tallal, P. (1995). A behavioral neuroscience approach to developmental language disorders: Evidence for a rapid temporal processing deficit. In D. Cicchetti & D. J. Cohen (Eds.), *Developmental psychopathology.* Vol. 2. New York: John Wiley.

Millican, F. K., & Lourie, R. S. (1970). The child with pica and his family. In E. J. Anthony and C. Koupernik (Eds.), *The child in his family,* Vol. 1. New York: Wiley-Interscience.

Milner, K. A., Craig, E. E., Thompson, R. J., Veltman, M. W. M., Thomas, N. S., Roberts, S. et al. (2005). Prader-Willi syndrome: intellectual abilities and behavioural features by genetic subtype. *Journal of Child Psychology and Psychiatry, 46,* 1089–1096.

Minde, K., Popiel, K., Leos, N., Falkner, S., Parker, K., & Handley-Derry, M. (1993). The evaluation and treatment of sleep disturbances in young children. *Journal of Child Psychology and Psychiatry, 34,* 521–533.

Mindell, J. A. (1993). Sleep disorders in children. *Health Psychology, 12,* 151–162.

Mindell, J. A. (1999). Empirically supported treatments in pediatric psychology: Bedtime refusal and night wakings in young children. *Journal of Pediatric Psychology, 24,* 465–481.

Mindell, J. A., & Owens, J. A. (2003). *A clinical guide to pediatric sleep: Diagnosis and management of sleep problems.* Philadelphia: Lippincott Williams & Wilkins.

Minshew, N. J., Sweeney, J. A., & Bauman, M. L. (1997). Neurological aspects of autism. In D. J. Cohen & F. R. Volkmar (Eds.), *Handbook of autism and pervasive developmental disorders.* New York: John Wiley.

Minty, B. (1999). Annotation: Outcomes in long-term foster family care. *Journal of Child Psychology and Psychiatry, 40,* 991–999.

Mirkin, M. P. (1990). Eating disorders: A feminist family therapy perspective. In M. P. Mirkin (Ed.), *The social and political contexts of family therapy.* Boston: Allyn & Bacon.

Mishna, F. (2003). Learning disabilities and bullying: Double jeopardy. *Journal of Learning Disabilities, 36,* 336–347.

Mitchell, J. E., Agras, S., & Wonderlich, S. (2007). Treatment of bulimia nervosa: Where are we and where are we going? *International Journal of Eating Disorders, 40,* 95–101.

Mitsis, E. M., McKay, K. E., Schulz, K. P., Newcorn, J. H., & Halperin, J. M. (2000). Parent-teacher concordance for DSM-IV Attention-Deficit/Hyperactivity Disorder in a clinic-referred sample. *Journal of the American Academy of Child and Adolescent Psychiatry, 39,* 308–313.

Moens, E., Braet, C., & Soetens, B. (2007). Observation of family functioning at mealtime: A comparison between families of children with and without overweight. *Journal of Pediatric Psychology, 32,* 52–63.

Moffitt, T. E. (1993a). Adolescence-limited and life-course-persistent antisocial behavior: A developmental taxonomy. *Psychological Review, 100,* 674–701.

Moffitt, T. E. (1993b). The neuropsychology of conduct disorder. *Development and Psychopathology, 5,* 135–152.

Moffitt, T. E. (2006). Life-course-persistent versus adolescence-limited antisocial behavior. In D. Cicchetti & D. J. Cohen (Eds.), *Developmental psychopathology, Vol. 3: Risk, disorder, and adaptation* (2nd ed.). Hoboken, NJ: John Wiley & Sons.

Moffitt, T. E., Caspi, A., Harrington, H., & Milne, B. J. (2002). Males on the life-course-persistent and adolescence-limited antisocial pathways: Follow-up at age 26 years. *Development and Psychopathology, 14,* 179–207.

Moffitt, T. E., Caspi, A., Rutter, M., & Silva, P. (2001). *Sex differences in antisocial behaviour: Conduct disorder, delinquency, and violence in the Dunedin longitudinal study.* Cambridge, UK: Cambridge University Press.

Moldavsky, M., Lev, D., & Lerman-Sagie, T. (2001). Behavioral phenotypes of genetic syndromes: A reference guide for psychiatrists. *Journal of the American Academy of Child and Adolescence Psychiatry, 40,* 749–760.

Molden, D. C., & Dweck, C. S. (2006). Finding "meaning" in psychology. *American Psychologist, 61,* 192–203.

Mollica, R. F., Poole, C., Son, L., Murray, C. C., & Tor, S. (1997). Effects of war trauma on Cambodia refugee adolescents' functional health and mental health status. *Journal of the American Academy of Child and Adolescent Psychiatry, 36,* 1098–1106.

Molloy, C. A., Dietrich, K. N., & Bhattacharya, A. (2003). Postural stability in autism spectrum disorder. *Journal of Autism and Developmental Disorders, 33,* 643–652.

Montague, C. T., Farooqui, I. S., Whitehead, J. P. et al. (1997). Congenital leptin deficiency is associated with severe early-onset obesity in humans. *Nature, 387,* 903–907.

Monti, P. M., Colby, S. M., & O'Leary, T. A. (Eds.) (2001). *Adolescents, alcohol, and substance abuse: Reaching teens through brief interventions.* New York: Guilford.

Moore, B. D. (2005). Neurocognitive outcomes in survivors of childhood cancer. *Journal of Pediatric Psychology, 30,* 51–63.

Moore, D. R., & Arthur, J. L. (1989). Juvenile delinquency. In T. H. Ollendick & M. Hersen (Eds.), *Handbook of child psychopathology, 2nd ed.* New York: Plenum.

Moore, P. S., Whaley, S. E., & Sigman, M. (2004). Interactions between mothers and children: Impacts of maternal and child anxiety. *Journal of Abnormal Psychology, 113,* 471–476.

Moos, B. S., & Moos, R. H. (1994). *Family Envirnoment Scale* (3rd ed.). Menlo, CA: Mind Garden, Inc.

Moreno, C., Laje, G., Blanco, C., Jiang, H., Schmidt, A. B., & Olfson, M. (2007). National trends in the outpatient diagnosis and treatment of bipolar disorder in youth. *Archives of General Psychiatry, 64,* 1032–1039.

Moreno, C., Roche, A. M., & Greenhill, L. L. (2006). Pharmacotherapy of child and adolescent depression. *Child and Adolescent Psychiatric Clinics of North America, 15,* 977–998.

Morgan, D. L., & Morgan, R. K. (2001). Single-participant research design. *American Psychologist, 56,* 119–127.

Morgan, R. K. (1999). *Case studies in child and adolescent psychopathology.* Upper Saddle River, NJ: Prentice-Hall.

Morrison, J., & Anders, T. F. (1999). *Interviewing children and adolescents: Skills and strategies for effective DSM-diagnosis.* New York: The Guilford Press.

Morrison, J. A., Friedman, L. A., & Gray-McGuire, C. (2007). Metabolic syndrome in childhood predicts adult cardiovascular disease 25 years later: The Princeton Lipid Research Clinics follow-up study. *Pediatrics, 120,* 340–345.

Morroco, C. C., Aguilar, C. M., Clay, K., Brigham, N, & Zigmond, N. (2006). Good high schools for students with disabilities. Introduction to the special issue. *Learning Disabilities Research & Practice, 21,* 135–145.

Morrongiello, B. A. (2005). Caregiver supervision and child-injury risk: I. Issues in defining and measuring supervision. Findings and directions for future research. *Journal of Pediatric Psychology, 30,* 536–552.

Morrongiello, B. A., & Matheis, S. (2007a). Assessing the issue of falls off playground equipment: An empirically-based intervention to reduce fall-risk behaviors on playgrounds. *Journal of Pediatric Psychology, 32,* 819–830.

Morrongiello, B. A., & Matheis, S. (2007b). Understanding children's injury-risk behaviors: The independent contributions of cognitions and emotions. *Journal of Pediatric Psychology, 32,* 926–937.

Morrongiello, B. A., Ondejko, L., & Littlejohn, A. (2004b). Understanding toddlers' in-home injuries: II. Examining parental strategies, and their efficacy, for managing child injury risk. *Journal of Pediatric Psychology, 29,* 433–446.

Mortensen, P. B. et al. (1999). Effects of family history and place and season of birth on the risk of schizophrenia. *New England Journal of Medicine, 340,* 603–608.

Mowrer, O. H., & Mowrer, W. M. (1938). Enuresis: A method for its study and treatment. *American Journal of Orthopsychiatry, 8,* 436–459.

MTA Cooperative Group. (1999a). A 14–month randomized clinical trial of treatment strategies for attention-deficit/hyperactivity disorder. *Archives of General Psychiatry, 56,* 1073–1086.

MTA Cooperative Group. (1999b). Moderators and mediators of treatment response for children with attention-deficit/hyperactivity disorder. *Archives of Psychiatry, 56,* 1088–1096.

MTA Cooperative Group. (2004a). National Institute of Mental Health Multimodal Treatment Study of ADHD follow-up: Changes in effectiveness and growth after the end treatment. *Pediatrics, 113,* 762–769.

MTA Cooperative Group. (2004b). National Institute of Mental Health Multimodal Treatment Study of ADHD follow-up: 24–month outcomes of treatment strategies for attention-deficit/hyperactivity disorder. *Pediatrics, 113,* 754–761.

Mufson, L., Pollack Dorta, K., Moreau, D., & Weissman, M. M. (2005). Efficacy to effectiveness: Adaptations of interpersonal psychotherapy for adolescent depression. In E. D. Hibbs & P. S. Jensen (Eds.), *Psychosocial treatments for child and adolescent disorders: Empirically based strategies for clinical practice.* (2nd ed.). Washington, DC: American Psychological Association.

Mufson, L., Pollack Dorta, K., Wickramaratne, P., Nomura, Y., Olfson, M., & Weissman, M. M. (2004). The effectiveness of interpersonal psychotherapy for depressed adolescents. *Archives of General Psychiatry, 45,* 742–747.

Mufson, L., Weissman, M. M., Moreau, D., & Garfindel, R. (1999). Efficacy of interpersonal therapy for depressed adolescents. *Archives of General Psychiatry, 56,* 573–579.

Mulder, E. J., Anderson, G. M., Kema, I. P., De Bildt, A., van Lange, N. D. J., Den Boer, J. A., & Minderaa, R. B. (2004). Platelet serotonin levels in pervasive developmental disorders and mental retardation: Diagnostic group differences, within-group distribution, and behavioral correlates. *Journal of the American Academy of Child and Adolescent Psychiatry, 43,* 491–499.

Mulvaney, S. A., Goodwin, J. L., Morgan, W. J., Rosen, G. R., Quan, S. F., & Kaemingk, K. L. (2006). Behavior problems associated with sleep disordered breathing in school-aged children—The Tucson Children's Assessment of Sleep Study. *Journal of Pediatric Psychology, 31*, 322–330.

Mundy, P. (1993). Normal versus high functioning status in children with autism. *American Journal on Mental Retardation, 97*, 381–384.

Munoz, R. F., Mrazek, P. J., & Haggerty, R. J. (1996). Institute of Medicine report on prevention of mental disorders: Summary and commentary. *American Psychologist 51*, 1116–1122.

Muris, P. (2006). The pathogenesis of childhood anxiety disorders: Considerations from a developmental psychopathology perspective. *International Journal of Behavioral Development, 30*, 5–11.

Muris, P., Merckelbach, H., Ollendick, T. H., King, N. J., & Bogie, N. (2001). Children's nighttime fears: Parent-child ratings of frequency, content, origins, coping behaviors and severity. *Behaviour Research and Therapy, 39*, 13–28.

Murphy, A. (2001). Front-Runner. *Sports Illustrated, 95*(21), 62–66.

Murphy, K. C. (2005). Annotation: Velo-cardio-facial syndrome. *Journal of Child Psychology and Psychiatry, 46*, 563–571.

Murphy, L. M. B., Thompson, R. J., Jr., & Morris, M. A. (1997). Adherence behavior among adolescents with type I insulin-dependent diabetes mellitus: The role of cognitive appraisal processes. *Journal of Pediatric Psychology, 22*, 811–825.

Murphy-Berman, V., & Weisz, V. (1996). U. N. Convention of the Rights of the Child: Current challenges. *American Psychologist, 51*, 1231–1233.

Murray, H. A. (1943). *Thematic Apperception Test.* Bloomington, MN: Pearson Assessments.

Murrie, D. C., Marcus, D. K., Douglas, K. S., Lee, Z., Salekin, R. T., & Vincent, G. (2007). Youth with psychopathy features are not a discrete class: a taxometric analysis. *Journal of Child Psychology and Psychiatry, 48*, 714–723.

Nadder, T. S., Silberg, J. L., Rutter, M., Maes, H. H., & Eaves, L. J. (2001). Comparison of multiple measures of ADHD symptomatology: A multivariate genetic analysis. *Journal of Child Psychology and Psychiatry, 42*, 475–486.

Nader, K., Pynoos, R. S., Fairbanks, L. & Frederick, C. (1991). Childhood PTSD reactions one year after a sniper attack. *American Journal of Psychiatry, 147*, 1526–1530.

Nansel, T. R., Overpeck, M., Pilla, R. S., Ruan, W. J., Simons-Morton, B., & Scheidt, P. (2001). Bullying behaviors among US youth: Prevalence and association with psychosocial adjustment. *Journal of the American Medical Association, 285*, 2094–2100.

Nathan, P. E., & Langenbucher, J. W. (1999). Psychopathology: Description and classification. *Annual Review of Psychology, 50*, 79–107.

Nation, K., Clarke, P., Marshall, K. M., & Durand, M. (2004). Hidden language impairments in children: Parallels between poor reading comprehension and specific language impairment? *Journal of Speech, Language, and Hearing Research, 47*, 199–211.

National Cancer Institute. (2004, June). Annual report to the nation. Retrieved September 2004, from http://nci.nih.gov.

National Center for Health Statistics. (2006). *Health, United States, 2006 with chartbook on trends in the health of Americans.* Hyattsville, MD: National Center for Health Statistics.

National Commission for the Protection of Human Subjects of Biomedical and Behavioral Research. (1979). *The Belmont Report: Ethical principles and guidelines for the protection of human subjects of research.* Washington, DC: U.S. Government Printing Office.

National Insitute of Mental Health. (1977). *Child abuse and neglect programs: Practice and theory.* Washington, DC: U.S. Government Printing Office.

National Institute on Drug Abuse. (2006). *NIDA InfoFacts.* Retrived August 2007 from http://www.drugabuse.gov

National Institutes of Health. (1997). *Highlights of the expert panel Report 2: Guidelines for the diagnosis and management of asthma* (NIH publication No. 97–4051 A). Washington, DC: U.S. Department of Health and Human Services.

Neal, J. A., & Edelmann, R. J. (2003). The etiology of social phobia: Toward a developmental profile. *Clinical Psychology Review, 23*, 761–786.

Neely-Barnes, S., & Marchenko, M. (2004). Predicting impact of childhood disability on families: Results from the 1995 National Health Interview Survey Disability Supplement. *Mental Retardation, 42*, 284–293.

Nelson, C. A., & Bloom, F. E. (1997). Child development and neuroscience. *Child Development, 68*, 970–987.

Neumeister, A., Bain, E., Nugent, A. C., Carson, R. E., Bonne, O., Luckenbaugh, D. A., Eckelman, W., Herscovitch, P., Charney, D. S., & Drevets, W. C. (2004). Reduced serotonin Type 1_A receptor binding in panic disorder. *The Journal of Neuroscience, 24*, 589–591.

New, M. J., Lee, S. S., & Elliott, B. M. (2007). Psychological adjustment in children and families living with HIV. *Journal of Pediatric Psychology, 32*, 123–131.

Newcomb, A. F., Bukowski, W. M., Pattee, L. (1993). Children's peer relations: A meta-analytic review of popular, rejected, neglected, controversial, and average sociometric status. *Psychological Bulletin, 113*, 99–128.

Newman, F. L., & Tejeda, M. J. (1996). The need for research that is designed to support decisions in the delivery of mental health services. *American Psychologist, 51*, 1040–1049.

Newsom, C. (1998). Autistic disorder. In E. J. Mash & R. A. Barkley (Eds.), *Treatment of childhood disorders.* New York: Guilford Press.

Newsom, C., & Hovanitz, C. A. (1997). Autistic disorder. In E. J. Mash & L. G. Terdal (Eds.), *Assessment of childhood disorders.* New York: Guilford Press.

Newsom, C., & Hovanitz, C. A. (2006). Autistic spectrum disorders. In E. J. Mash & R. A. Barkley (Eds.), *Treatment of childhood disorders.* New York: The Guilford Press.

NICHD Early Child Care Research Network. (2003). Does amount of time spent in child care predict socioeconomic adjustment during the transition to kindergarten? *Child Development, 74*, 976–1005.

NICHD Early Child Care Research Network. (2004). Trajectories of physical aggression from toddlerhood to middle childhood: Predictors, correlates, and outcomes. *Monographs of the Society for Research in Child Development, 69* (4, serial no. 278).

NICHD Early Child Care Research Network. (2006). Child-care effect sizes for the NICHD Study of Child Care and Youth Development. *American Psychologist, 61*, 99–116.

Nicholls, D. (2004). Eating problems in childhood. In J. K. Thompson (Ed.), *Handbook of eating disorders and obesity*. Hoboken, NJ: John Wiley.

Nickman, S. L., Rosenfeld, A. A., Fine, P., MacIntrye, J. C., Pilowsky, D. J., Howe, R. A. et al. (2005). Children in adoptive families: overview and update. *Journal of the American Academy of Child and Adolescent Psychiatry, 44*, 987–995.

Nicolson, R., Awad, G., & Sloman, L. (1998). An open trial of risperidone in young autistic children. *Journal of the American Academy of Child and Adolescent Psychiatry, 37*, 372–376.

Nicolson, R., & Rapoport, J. L. (2000). Childhood-onset schizophrenia: What can it teach us? In J. L. Rapoport (Ed.). *Childhood onset of "adult" psychopathology*. Washington, DC: American Psychiatric Press.

Nigg, J. T. (2001). Is ADHD a disinhibitory disorder? *Psychological Bulletin, 127*, 571–598.

Nigg, J. T. (2006a). Attention deficits and hyperactivity-impulsivity in children: A multilevel overview and causes and mechanism. In H. E. Fitzgerald, B. M. Lester, & B. Zuckerman (Eds.), *The crisis in youth mental health. Critical issues and effective programs. Volume 1.* Westport, CT: Praeger Publishers.

Nigg, J. T. (2006b). Temperament and developmental psychopathology. *Journal of Child Psychology and Psychiatry, 47*, 395–422.

Nigg, J. T., Blaskey, L. G., Huang-Pollock, C. L., & Rappley, M. D. (2002). Neuropsychological executive functions and DSM-IV ADHD subtypes. *Journal of the American Academy of Child and Adolescent Psychiatry, 41*, 59–66.

Nigg, J. T., Goldsmith, H. H., & Sachek, J. (2004). Temperament and attention deficit hyperactivity disorder: The development of a multiple pathway model. *Journal of Clinical and Adolescent Psychology, 33*, 42–53.

Nigg, J. T., & Hinshaw, S. P. (1998). Parent personality traits and psychopathology associated with antisocial behaviors in childhood attention-deficit hyperactive disorder. *Journal of Child Psychology and Psychiatry, 39*, 145–159.

Nigg, J. T., Hinshaw, S. P., & Huang-Pollock, C. (2006). Disorders of attention and impulse regulation. In D. Cicchetti & D. J. Cohen (Eds.), *Developmental psychopathology. Vol. III. Risk, disorder, and adaptation.* Hoboken, NJ: John Wiley & Sons.

Nigg, J. T., & Huang-Pollock, C. L. (2003). An early-onset model of the role of executive functions and intelligence in conduct disorder/delinquency. In B. B. Lahey, T. E. Moffitt, A. Caspi (Eds.), *Causes of conduct disorder and juvenile delinquency.* New York: Guilford Press.

Nock, M. K. (2003). Progress review of the psychosocial treatment of child conduct problems. *Clinical Psychology: Science and Practice, 10*, 1–28.

Nock, M. K., Kazdin, A. E., Hiripi, E., & Kessler, R. C. (2007). Lifetime prevalence, correlates, and persistence of oppositional defiant disorder: Results from the National Comorbidity Survey Replication. *Journal of Child Psychology and Psychiatry, 48*, 703–713.

Nolan, E. E., Gadow, K. D., & Sprafkin, J. (2001). Teacher reports of DSM-IV ADHD, ODD, and CD symptoms in schoolchildren. *Journal of the American Academy of Child and Adolescent Psychiatry, 40*, 241–248.

Nolen-Hoeksema, S. N., & Girgus, J. S. (1994). The emergence of gender differences in depression during adolescence. *Psychological Bulletin, 115*, 424–443.

Nolen-Hoeksema, S. N., Mumme, D., Wolfson, A., & Guskin, K. (1995). Helplessness in children of depressed and nondepressed mothers. *Developmental Psychology, 31*, 377–387.

Nottelmann, E. D., & Jensen, P. S. (1995). Comorbidity of disorders in children and adolescents: Developmental perspectives. In T. H. Ollendick & R. J. Prinz (Eds.), *Advances in clinical child psychology* (Vol. 17). New York: Plenum Press.

Novins, D. K., Beals, J., & Mitchell, C. M. (2001). Sequences of substance abuse among American Indian adolescents. *Journal of the American Academy of Child and Adolescent Psychiatry, 40*, 1168–1174.

Novins, D. K., Duclos, C. W., Martin, C., Jewett, C. S., & Manson, S. M. (1999). Utilization of alcohol, drug, and mental health treatment services among American Indian adolescent detainees. *Journal of the American Academy of Child and Adolescent Psychiatry, 38*, 1102–1108.

Nowicki, E. A. (2003). A meta-analysis of the social competence of children with learning disabilities compared to classmates of low and average to high achievement. *Learning Disability Quarterly, 26*, 171–188.

Núñez, J. C., González-Pienda, J. A., González-Pumariega, S., Roces, G., Alvarez, L., & González, P. (2005). Subgroups of attributional profiles in students with learning disabilities and their relation to self-concept and academic goal. *Learning Disabilities Research & Practice, 20*, 86–97.

Nurmi, E. L., Dowd, M., Tadevosyan-Leyfer, O., Haines, J. L., Folstein, S. E., & Sutcliffe, J. S. (2003). Exploratory subsetting of autism families based on savant skills improves evidence of genetic linkage to 15q11-q13. *Journal of the American Academy of Child and Adolescent Psychiatry, 42*, 856–863.

Nyborg, V. M., & Curry, J. F. (2003). The impact of perceived racism: Psychological symptoms among African American boys. *Journal of Clinical Child and Adolescent Psychology, 32*, 258–266.

Oberman, L. M., & Ramachandran, V. S. (2007). The simulating social mind: the role of the mirror neuron system and simulation in the social and communicative deficits of autism spectrum disorders. *Psychological Bulletin, 133*, 310–327.

O'Brien, K. M., & Vincent, N. K. (2003). Psychiatric comorbidity in anorexia and bulimia nervosa: Nature, prevalence, and causal relationships. *Clinical Psychology Review, 23*, 57–74.

O'Brien, M. (1996). Child-rearing difficulties reported by parents of infants and toddlers. *Journal of Pediatric Psychology, 21*, 433–446.

O'Byrne, K. K., Peterson, L., & Saldana, L. (1997). Survey of pediatric hospitals' preparation programs: Evidence of the impact of health psychology research. *Health Psychology, 16*, 147–154.

Ochoa, S. H., & Palmer, D. J. (1995). A meta-analysis of peer rating of sociometric studies with learning disabled students. *Journal of Special Education, 29*, 1–19.

O'Connor, T. G. (2003). Natural experiments to study the effects of early experience: Progress and limitations. *Development and Psychopathology, 15*, 837–852.

O'Connor, T. G., Dunn, J., Jenkins, J. M., & Rasbash, J. (2006). Predictors of between-family and within-family variation in parent-child relationships. *Journal of Child Psychology and Psychiatry, 47*, 498–510.

Ogden, C. L., Carroll, M. D., Curtin, L. R., McDowell, M. A., Tabak, C. J., & Flegal, K. M. (2006). Prevalence of overweight and obesity in the United States, 1999–2004. *Journal of the American Medical Association, 295*, 1549–1555.

Ohman, A., & Hultman, C. M. (1998). Electrodermal activity and obstetric complications in schizophrenia. *Journal of Abnormal Psychology, 107,* 228–237.

Olds, D. L., Sadler, D., & Kitzman, H. (2007). Programs for parents of infants and toddlers: Recent evidence from randomized trials. *Journal of Child Psychology and Psychiatry, 48,* 355–391.

O'Leary, K. D., & Emery, R. E. (1985). Marital discord and child behavior problems. In M. D. Levine & P. Satz (Eds.), *Developmental variation and dysfunction.* New York: Academic Press.

Ollendick, T. H. (1983). Reliability and validity of the Revised Fear Survey Schedule for Children (FSSC-R). *Behaviour Research and Therapy, 21,* 685–692.

Ollendick, T. H., Birmaher, B., & Mattis, S. G. (2004a). Panic disorder. In T. L. Morris & J. S. March (Eds.), *Anxiety disorders in children and adolescents.* New York: Guilford Press.

Ollendick, T. H., Davis, T. E., & Muris, P. (2004). Treatment of specific phobia in children and adolescents. In P. M. Barrett & T. H. Ollendick (Eds.), *Handbook of interventions that work with children and adolescents: Prevention and treatment.* Hoboken, NJ: John Wiley & Sons.

Ollendick, T. H., & King, N. J. (1998). Empirically supported treatments for children with phobic and anxiety disorders: Current status. *Journal of Clinical Child Psychology, 27,* 156–167.

Ollendick, T. H., King, N. J., & Chorpita, B. F. (2006). Empirically supported treatments for children and adolescents. In P. C. Kendall (Ed.), *Child and adolescent therapy: Cognitive-behavioral procedures.* New York: The Guilford Press.

Ollendick, T. H., King, N. L., & Hamilton, D. I. (1991). Origins of childhood fears: An evaluation of Rachman's theory of fear acquisition. *Behaviour Research and Therapy, 29,* 117–123.

Oltjenbruns, K. A. (2001). Developmental context of childhood grief and regrief phenomena. In M. S. Stroebe, R. O. Hansson, W. Stroebe, & H. Schut (Eds.), *Handbook of bereavement research: Consequences, coping, and care.* Washington, DC: American Psychological Association.

Oltmanns, T. F. & Emery, R. E. (2007). *Abnormal psychology.* Upper Saddle River, NJ: Pearson Education, Inc.

Olweus, D. (1993). *Bullying at school: What we know and what we can do.* Cambridge, MA: Blackwell.

Olweus, D. (1994). Bullying at school: Basic facts and effects of a school based intervention program. *Journal of Child Psychology and Psychiatry, 35,* 1171–1190.

Omigbodun, O., Bella, T., Dogra, N., & Simovan, O. (2007). Training health professionals for child and adolescent mental health care in Nigeria: A qualitative analysis. *Child and Adolescent Mental Health, 12,* 132–137.

Ondersma, S. J., & Walker, E. (1998). Elimination disorders. In T. H. Ollendick & M. Hersen (Eds.), *Handbook of child psychopathology* (3rd ed.). New York: Plenum Press.

Oosterlaan, J., Logan, G. D., & Sergeant, J. A. (1998). Response inhibition in AD/HD, CD, comorbid AD/HD+CD, anxious, and control children: A meta-analysis of studies with the Stop task. *Journal of Child Psychology and Psychiatry, 39,* 411–425.

Organista, K. C. (2003). Mexican American children and adolescents. In J. T. Gibbs, L. N. Huang and Associates (Eds.), *Children of color: Psychological interventions with culturally diverse youth.* San Francisco: Jossey-Bass.

Orobio de Castro, B., Slot, N. W., Bosch, J. D., Koops, W., & Weerman, J. W. (2003). Negative feelings exacerbate hostile attributions of intent in highly aggressive boys. *Journal of Clinical Child and Adolescent Psychology, 32,* 56–65.

Orsmond, G. I., & Seltzer, M. M. (2000). Brothers and sisters of adults with mental retardation: Gendered nature of the sibling relationship. *American Journal on Mental Retardation, 105,* 486–508.

Öst, L. (1987). Age of onset in different phobias. *Journal of Abnormal Psychology, 96,* 123–145.

Owens, J. A., Spirito, A., McGuinn, M., & Nobile, C. (2000). Sleep habits and sleep disturbance in elementary school-aged children. *Developmental and Behavioral Pediatrics, 21,* 27–36.

Ozonoff, S. (1997). Casual mechanisms of autism: Unifying perspectives from an information-processing framework. In D. J. Cohen & F. R. Volkmar (Eds.), *Handbook of autism and pervasive developmental disorders.* New York: John Wiley.

Ozonoff, S., & Cathcart, K. (1998). Effectiveness of a home program intervention for young children with autism. *Journal of Autism and Developmental Disorder, 28,* 25–32.

Paardekooper, B., de Jong, J. T. V. M., & Hermanns, J. M. A. (1999). The psychological impact of war and the refugee situation on South Sudanese children in refugee camps in Northern Uganda: An exploratory study. *Journal of Psychology and Psychiatry, 40,* 529–536.

Palmer, D. L., Berg, C. A., Wiebe, D. J., Beveridge, R. M., Korbel, C. D., Upchurch, R. et al. (2004). The role of autonomy and pubertal status in understanding age differences in maternal involvement in diabetes responsibility across adolescence. *Journal of Pediatric Psychology, 29,* 35–46.

Palmer, D. S., Fuller, K., Arora, T., & Nelson, M. (2001). Taking sides: Parent views on inclusion for their children with severe disabilities. *Exceptional Children, 67,* 467–484.

Paniagua, F. A. (2000). Culture-bound syndromes, cultural variations, and psychopathology. In I. Cuéllar & F. A. Paniagua (Eds.), *Handbook of multicultural mental health.* San Diego: Academic Press.

Papolos, D. F. (2003). Bipolar disorder and comorbid disorders: The case for a dimensional nosology. In B. Geller & M. P. Del-Bello (Eds.), *Bipolar disorder in childhood and early adolescence.* New York: Guilford Press.

Pardini, D. A., Lochman, J., & Frick, P. J. (2003). Callous/unemotional traits and social-cognitive processes in adjudicated youths. *Journal of the American Academy of Child and Adolescent Psychiatry, 42,* 364–371.

Parish, S. L. (2006). Juggling and struggling: A preliminary work-life study of mothers with adolescents who have developmental disabilities. *Mental Retardation, 44,* 393–404.

Parker, J. G., & Asher, S. R. (1987). Peer relations and later personal adjustment: Are low-accepted children at risk? *Psychological Bulletin, 102,* 357–389.

Parker, J. G., Rubin, K. H., Erath, S. A., Wojslawowicz, J. C., & Buskirk, A. A. (2006). Peer relationships, child development, and adjustment: A developmental psychopathology perspective. In D. Cicchetti & D. J. Cohen (Eds.), *Developmental psychopathology. Vol. 1. Theory and method.* Hoboken, NJ: John Wiley & Sons.

Paschall, M. J., & Hubbard, M. L. (1998). Effects of neighborhood and family stressors on African American male adolescents' self-worth and propensity for violent behavior. *Journal of Consulting and Clinical Psychology, 66*, 825–831.

Patenaude, A. F., & Kupst, M. J. (2005). Psychosocial functioning in pediatric cancer. *Journal of Pediatric Psychology, 30*, 9–27.

Patja, K., Iivanainen, M., Vesala, H., Oksanen, H., & Ruoppila, I. (2000). Life expectancy of people with intellectual disability: A 35-year follow-up study. *Journal of Intellectual Disability Research, 44*, 591–599.

Patterson, G. R. (1976). The aggressive child: Victim and architect of a coercive system. In L. A. Hamerlynck, L. C. Handy, & E. J. Mash (Eds.), *Behavior modification and families*. New York: Brunner/Mazel.

Patterson, G. R. (1982). *Coercive family process: A social learning approach*, Vol. 3. Eugene, OR: Castalia.

Patterson, G. R., DeBaryshe, B. D., & Ramsey, E. (1989). A developmental perspective on antisocial behavior. *American Psychologist, 44*, 329–335.

Patterson, G. R., DeGarmo, D. S., & Knutson, N. (2000). Hyperactive and antisocial behaviors: Comorbid or two points in the same process? *Development and Psychopathology, 12*, 91–106.

Patterson, G. R., Reid, J. B., & Dishion, T. J. (1992). *Antisocial boys*. Eugene, OR: Castalia Publishing Company.

Patterson, G. R., Reid, J. B., & Eddy, J. M. (2002). A brief history of the Oregon Model. In J. B. Reid, G. R. Patterson, & J. Snyder (Eds.), *Antisocial behavior in children and adolescents: A developmental analysis and model for intervention*. Washington, DC: American Psychological Association.

Patterson, G. R., Reid, J. B., Jones, R. R., & Conger, R. E. (1975). *A social learning approach to family intervention*, Vol. 1. Eugene, OR: Castalia.

Patton, G. C., Carlin, J. B., Shao, Q., Hibbert, M. E., Rosier, M., Selzer, R., & Bowes, G. (1997). Adolescent dieting: Healthy weight control or borderline eating disorder. *Journal of Child Psychology and Psychiatry, 38*, 299–306.

Paulesu, E., Démonet, J.-F., Fazio, F., McCrory, E., Chanoine, V., Brunswick, N. et al. (2001). Dyslexia: Cultural diversity and biological unity. *Science, 291*, 2165–2167.

Pavuluri, M. N., Birmaher, B., & Naylor, M. W. (2005). Pediatric bipolar disorder: A review of the past 10 years. *Journal of the American Academy of Child and Adolescent Psychiatry, 44*, 846–871.

Pavuluri, M. N., Graczyk, P. A., Henry, D. B., Carbray, J. A., Heidenreich, J., & Miklowitz, D. J. (2004). Child- and family-focused cognitive-behavioral therapy for pediatric bipolar disorder: Development and preliminary results. *Journal of the American Academy of Child and Adolescent Psychiatry, 43*, 528–537.

Pavuluri, M. N., Henry, D. B., Devineni, B., Carbray, J. A., & Birmaher, B. (2006). Child Mania Rating Scale: Development, reliability, and validity. *Journal of the American Academy of Child and Adolescent Psychiatry, 45*, 550–560.

Paxton, S. J., Neumark-Sztainer, D., Hannan, P. J., & Eisenberg, M. E. (2006). Body dissatisfaction prospectively predicts depressive mood and low self-esteem in adolescent girls and boys. *Journal of Clinical Child and Adolescent Psychology, 35*, 539–549.

Pearson, D. A., Lane, D. M., Santos, C. W., Casat, C. D., Jerger, S. W., Loveland, K. A. et al. (2004). Effects of methylphenidate treatment in children with mental retardation and ADHD:

Individual variation in medication response. *Journal of the American Academy of Child and Adolescent Psychiatry, 43*, 686–698.

Pederson, S., Vitaro, F. Barker, E. D., & Borge, A. I. H. (2007). The timing of middle-childhood peer rejection and friendship: Linking early behavior to early-adolescent adjustment. *Child Development, 78*, 1037–1051.

Pediatric OCD Treatment Study (POTS) Team. (2004). Cognitive-behavior therapy, sertraline, and their combination for children and adolescents with obsessive-compulsive disorder: The Pediatric OCD Treatment Study (POTS) randomized controlled trial. *Journal of the American Medical Association, 292*, 1969–1976.

Pelham, W. E. (2001, Winter). Are ADHD/I and ADHD/C the same or different? Does it matter? *Clinical Psychology: Science and Practice, 8*, 502–506.

Pelham., W. E., Fabiano, G. A., Gnagy, E. M., Greiner, A. R., & Hoza, B. (2005). The role of summer treatment programs in the context of comprehensive treatment for attention-deficit/hyperactivity disorder. In E. D. Hibbs & P. S. Jensen (Eds.), *Psychosocial treatments for child and adolescent disorders*. Washington, DC: American Psychological Association.

Pelkonen, M., Marttunen, M., Laippala, P., & Lönnqvist, J. (2000). Factors associated with early dropout from adolescent psychiatry outpatient treatment. *Journal of the American Academy of Child and Adolescent Psychiatry, 39*, 329–336.

Pellicano, E., Maybery, M., & Durkin, K. (2005). Central coherence in typically developing preschoolers: does it cohere and does it relate to mindreading and executive functioning? *Journal of Child Psychology and Psychiatry, 46*, 533–547.

Penn, D. L., Judge, A., Jamieson, P., Garczynski, J., Hennessy, M., & Romer, D. (2005). Stigma. In D. L. Evans, E. B. Foa, R. E. Gur, H. Hendin, C. P. O'Brien, M. E. P. Seligman, & B. T. Walsh (Eds.), *Treating and preventing adolescent mental health disorders. What we know and what we don't know: A research agenda for improving mental health of our youth*. New York: Oxford University Press.

Pennington, B. F., & Lefly, D. L. (2001). Early reading development in children at family risk for dyslexia. *Child Development, 74*, 816–833.

Pennington, B. F., & Ozonoff, S. (1996). Executive functions and developmental psychopathology. *Journal of Child Psychology and Psychiatry, 37*, 51–87.

Pennington, B. F., & Welsh, M. (1997). Neuropsychology and developmental psychopathology. In D. Cicchetti & D. J. Cohen (Eds.), *Developmental Psychopathology*. New York: John Wiley.

Pérez-Edgar, K., & Fox, N. A. (2005). Temperament and anxiety disorders. *Child and Adolescent Psychiatric Clinics of North America, 14*, 681–706.

Perlman, M. D., & Kaufman, A. S. (1990). Assessment of Child Intelligence. In G. Goldstein & M. Hersen (Eds.), *Handbook of psychological assessment* (2nd ed.). New York: Pergamon.

Perren, S., & Alsaker, F. D. (2006). Social behavior and peer relationships of victims, bully-victims, and bullies in kindergarten. *Journal of Child Psychology and Psychiatry, 47*, 45–57.

Perrin, S., Smith, P., & Yule, W. (2000). The assessment and treatment of post-traumatic stress disorder in children and adolescents. *Journal of Child Psychology and Psychiatry, 41*, 277–289.

Peshkin, M. M. (1959). Intractable asthma of childhood: Rehabilitation at the institutional level with a follow-up of 150 cases. *International Archives of Allergy, 15*, 91–101.

Peters, R., Petrunka, K., & Arnold, R. (2003). The Better Beginnings, Better Futures Project: A universal, comprehensive, community-based prevention approach for primary school children and their families. *Journal of Child and Adolescent Psychology, 32*, 215–227.

Peterson, B. S. (1995). Neuroimaging in child and adolescent neuropsychiatric disorders. *Journal of the American Academy of Child and Adolescent Psychiatry, 34*, 1560–1576.

Peterson, C. C. (2004). Theory-of-mind development in oral deaf children with cochlear implants or conventional hearing aids. *Journal of Child Psychology and Psychiatry, 45*, 1096–1106.

Peterson, L. (1989). Latchkey children's preparation for self-care: Overestimated, underrehearsed, and unsafe. *Journal of Clinical Child Psychology, 18*, 36–43.

Peterson, L., Farmer, J., Harbeck, C., & Chaney, J. (1990). Preparing children for hospitalization and threatening medical procedures. In A. M. Gross & R. S. Drabman (Eds.), *Handbook of clinical behavioral pediatrics.* New York: Plenum.

Peterson, L., Reach, K., & Grabe, S. (2003). Health-related disorders. In M. C. Roberts (Ed.), *Handbook of pediatric psychology* (3rd ed.). New York: Guilford Press.

Peterson, L., Schultheis, K., Ridley-Johnson, R., Miller, D. J., & Tracy, K. (1984). Comparison of three modeling procedures on the presurgical and postsurgical reactions of children. *Behavior Therapy, 15*, 197–203.

Peterson, L. J., & Mori, L. (1988). Preparation for hospitalization. In D. K. Routh (Ed.), *Handbook of pediatric psychology.* New York: Guilford.

Pettigrew, T. F. (2004). Justice deferred: A half century after *Brown v. Board of Education. American Psychologist, 59*, 521–529.

Pfeffer, C. R. (2000). Suicidal behaviour in children: An emphasis on developmental influences. In K. Hawton & K. van Heeringen (Eds.), *The international handbook of suicide and attempted suicide.* Chichester, UK: John Wiley & Sons, Ltd.

Pfefferbaum, B. (1997). Posttraumatic stress disorder in children: A review of the past 10 years. *Journal of the American Academy of Child and Adolescent Psychiatry, 36*, 1503–1511.

Pfefferbaum, B., Nixon, S., Tivis, R., Doughty, D. E., Pynoos, R. S., Gurwitch, R. H., & Foy, D.W. (2001). Television exposure in children after a terrorist incident. *Psychiatry, 64*, 202–211.

Pfefferbaum, B., Nixon, S. J., Krug, R. S., Tivis, R. D., Moore, V. L., Brown, J. M., Pynoos, R. S., Foy, D., & Gurwitch, R. H. (1999a). Clinical needs assessment of middle and high school students following the 1995 Oklahoma City bombing. *American Journal of Psychiatry, 156*, 1069–1074.

Pfefferbaum, B., Nixon, S. J., Tuckerm, P. M., Tivis, R. D., Moore, V. L., Gurwitch, R. H., Pynoos, R. S., & Geis, H. K. (1999b). Posttraumatic stress responses in bereaved children after the Oklahoma City bombing. *Journal of the American Academy of Child and Adolescent Psychiatry, 38*, 1372–1379.

Pfefferbaum, B., Seale, T., & McDonald, N. (2000). Posttraumatic stress two years after the Oklahoma City bombing in youths geographically distant from the explosion. *Psychiatry, 63*, 358–370.

Pfiffner, L. J., Barkley, R. A., & DuPaul, G. J. (2006). Treatment of ADHD in school settings. In R. A. Barkley (Ed.), *Attention-deficit hyperactivity disorder. A handbook for diagnosis and treatment.* New York: The Guilford Press.

Phelps, L. (2006). *Chronic health-related disorders in children: Collaborative medical and psychoeducational interventions.* Washington, DC: American Psychological Association.

Phillips, E. L. (1968). Achievement Place: Token reinforcement procedures in a home-style rehabilitation setting for 'pre-delinquent' boys. *Journal of Applied Behavior Analysis, 1*, 213–223.

Phipps, S., Dunavant, M., Lensing, S., & Rai, S. N. (2005). Psychosocial predictors of distress in parents of children undergoing stem cell or bone marrow transplantation. *Journal of Pediatric Psychology, 30*, 139–153.

Piacentini, J., Bergman, L., Keller, M., & McCracken, J. (2003). Functional impairment in children and adolescents with obsessive-compulsive disorder. *Journal of Child and Adolescent Psychopharmacology, 13*, S61–S69.

Pianta, R. C. (2006). School, schooling, and developmental psychopathology. In D. Cicchetti & D. J. Cohen (Eds.), *Developmental psychopathology. Vol. 1. Theory and method.* Hoboken, NJ: John Wiley & Sons.

Pickles, A., & Angold, A. (2003). Natural categories or fundamental dimensions: On carving nature at the joints and the rearticulation of psychopathology. *Development and Psychopathology, 15*, 529–551.

Pickles, A., Starr, E., Kazak, S., Bolton, P., Papanikolaou, K., Bailey, A. et al. (2000). Variable expression of the autism broader phenotype: Findings from extended pedigrees. *Journal of Child Psychology and Psychiatry, 41*, 491–502.

Pickren, W. E., & Tomes, H. (2002). The legacy of Kenneth B. Clark to APA. *American Psychologist, 57*, 51–59.

Pina, A. A., & Silverman, W. K. (2004). Clinical phenomenology, somatic symptoms, and distress in Hispanic/Latino and European American youths with anxiety disorders. *Journal of Clinical Child and Adolescent Psychology, 33*, 227–236.

Pine, D. S., Alegria, M., Cook, E. H. Jr., Costello, E. J., Dahl, R. E., Koretz. D. et al. (2002). Advances in developmental science and DSM-V. In D. J. Kupfer, M. B. First, & D. A. Regier (Eds.), *A research agenda for DSM-V.* Washington, DC: American Psychiatric Association.

Pisecco, S., Huzinec, C., & Curtis, D. (2001). The effect of child characteristics on teachers' acceptability of classroom-based behavioral strategies and psychostimulant medication for the treatment of ADHD. *Journal of Clinical Child Psychology, 30*, 413–421.

Piven, J., Harper, J. Palmer, P., & Arndt, S. (1996). Course of behavioral change in autism: a retrospective study of high-IQ adolescents and adults. *Journal of the American Academy of Child and Adolescent Psychiatry, 35*, 523–529.

Piven, J., & Palmer, P. (1997). Cognitive deficits in parents from multiple-incidence autism families. *Journal of Child Psychology and Psychiatry, 38*, 1011–1022.

Plaisted, K., Swettenham, J., & Rees, L. (1999). Children with autism show local precedence in a divided attention task and global precedence in a selective attention task. *Journal of Child Psychology and Psychiatry, 40*, 733–742.

Pliszka, S. (2003). *Neuroscience for the mental health clinician.* New York: The Guilford Press.

Pliszka, S. and the AACAP Work Group on Quality Issues. (2007). Practice parameter for the assessment of children and adolescents with attention-deficit/hyperactivity disorder. *Journal of the Academy of Child and Adolescent Psychiatry, 46,* 894–921.

Plomin, R. (1994a). Genetic research and identification of environmental influences. *Journal of Child Psychology and Psychiatry, 35,* 817–834.

Plomin, R. (1994b). *Genetics and experience. The interplay between nature and nurture.* Thousand Oaks, CA: Sage Publications.

Plomin, R. (2005). Finding genes in child pychology and psychiatry: When we are going to be there? *Journal of Child Psychology and Psychiatry, 46,* 1030–1038.

Plomin, R., & Crabbe, J. (2000). DNA. *Psychological Bulletin, 126,* 806–828.

Plomin, R., DeFries, J. C., & McClearn, G. E. (1990). *Behavioral genetics: A primer* (2nd ed.). New York: W. H. Freeman and Company.

Plomin, R., & McGuffin, P. (2003). Psychopathology in the postgenomic era. *Annual Review of Psychology, 54,* 205–225.

Ploog, B. O., & Kim, N. (2007). Assessment of stimulus overselectivity with tactile compound stimuli in children with autism. *Journal of Autism and Developmental Disabilities, 37,* 1514–1524.

Poling, A., Gadow, K. D., & Cleary, J. (1991). *Drug therapy for behavior disorders: An introduction.* New York: Pergamon.

Pollitt, E., Golub, M., Gorman, K., Grantham-McGregor, S., Levitsky, D., & Schürch, B. et al. (1996). A reconceptualization of the effects of undernutrition on children's biological, psychosocial, and behavioral development. *Social Policy Report, Society for Research in Child Development, X,* 1–22.

Pollock, L. A. (2001). Parent-child relations. In D. I. Kertzer & M. Barbagoli (Eds.), *The history of the European family. Vol. One. Family life in early modern times, 1500–1789.* New Haven, CT: Yale University Press.

Poltorak, D. Y., & Glazer, J. P. (2006). The development of children's understanding of death: Cognitive and psychodynamic considerations. *Child and Adolescent Psychiatric Clinics of North America, 15,* 567–573.

Porrino, L., Rapoport, J. L., Behar, D., Sceery, W., Ismond, D. R., & Bunney, W. E. (1983). A naturalistic assessment of the motor activity of hyperactive boys: I. Comparison with normal controls. *Archives of General Psychiatry, 40,* 681–687.

Posner, J. K., & Vandell, D. L. (1999). After-school activities and the development of low-income urban children: A longitudinal study. *Developmental Psychology, 35,* 868–879.

Potter, H. W. (1972). Mental retardation in historical perspective. In S. I. Harrison & J. F. McDermott (Eds.), *Childhood psychopathology.* New York: International Universities Press.

Pottick, K. J., Kirk, S. A., Hsieh, D. K., & Tian, X. (2007). Judging mental disorder in youths: Effects of client, clinician, and contextual differences. *Journal of Consulting and Clinical Psychology, 75,* 1–8.

Powell, L. M., Szczypka, G., Chaloupka, F. J., & Braunschweig, C. L. (2007). Nutritional content of television food advertisements seen by children and adolescents in the United States. *Pediatrics, 120,* 576–583.

Power, T. J. (2006). Collaborative practices for managing children's chronic health needs. In L. Phelps (Ed.), *Chronic health-related disorders in children: Collaborative medical and psychoeducational interventions.* Washington, DC: American Psychological Association.

Powers, S. W., Blount, R. L., Bachanas, P. J., Cotter, M. W., & Swan, S. C. (1993). Helping preschoolleukemia patients and their parents cope during injections. *Journal of Pediatric Psychology, 18,* 681–695.

Powers, S. W., Jones, J. S., & Jones, B. A. (2005). Behavioral and cognitive-behavioral interventions with pediatric populations. *Clinical Child Psychology and Psychiatry, 10,* 65–77.

Praisner, C. L. (2003). Attitudes of elementary school principals toward the inclusion of students with disabilities. *Exceptional Children, 69,* 135–145.

President's New Freedom Commission on Mental Health. (2003). *Achieving the promise: Transforming mental health care in America. Final report* (U.S. DHHS Pub. No. SMA-03-3832). Rockville, MD: U.S. Department of Health and Human Services.

Price, R. A. (1995). The search for obesity genes. In D. B. Allison & F. X. Pi-Sunyer (Eds.), *Obesity treatment: Establishing goals, improving outcomes, and reviewing the research agenda.* New York: Plenum Press.

Pring, L., Hermelin, B., & Heavey, L. (1995). Savants, segments, art, and autism. *Journal of Child Psychology and Psychiatry, 36,* 1065–1076.

Prinstein, M. J., Boergers, J., & Vernberg, E. M. (2001). Overt and relational aggression in adolescents: Social-psychological adjustment of aggressors and victims. *Journal of Clinical Child Psychology, 30,* 479–491.

Prior, M., Smart, D., Sanson, A., & Oberklaid, F. (1999). Relationship between learning difficulties and psychological problems in preadolescent children from a longitudinal sample. *Journal of the American Academy of Child and Adolescent Psychiatry, 38,* 429–436.

Prior, M., & Werry, J. S. (1986). Autism, schizophrenia, and allied disorders. In H. C. Quay and J. S. Werry (Eds.), *Psychopathological disorders of childhood.* New York: Wiley.

Progress for Children. (2007, Dec.). A World Fit for Children Statistical Review. Retrieved December 10, 2007, from http://www.unicef.org/progressforchildren/2007n6/

Prout, H. T., & Nowak-Drabik, K. M. (2003). Psychotherapy with persons who have mental retardation: An evaluation of effectiveness. *American Journal on Mental Retardation, 108,* 82–93.

Puhl, R. M., & Latner, J. D. (2007). Stigma, obesity, and the health of the nation's children. *Psychological Bulletin, 133,* 557–580.

Pumariega, A. J., & Glover, S. (1998). New developments in service delivery research for children, adolescents, and their families. In T. H. Ollendick & R. J. Prinz (Eds.), *Advances in clinical child psychology* (Vol. 20). New York: Plenum Press.

Puolakanaho, A., Ahonen, T., Aro, M., Eklund, K., Leppänen, P. H. T., Poikkeus, A-M. et al. (2007). Very early phonological and language skills: Estimating individual risk of reading disability. *Journal of Child Psychology and Psychiatry, 48,* 923–931.

Purcell, K., Brady, K., Chai, H., Muser, J., Molk, L., Gordon, N., & Means, J. (1969). The effect on asthma in children of experimental separation from the family. *Psychosomatic Medicine, 31,* 144–164.

Purvis, K. L., & Tannock, R. (2000). Phonological processing not inhibitory control differentiates ADHD and reading disability. *Journal of the American Academy of Child and Adolescent Psychiatry, 39,* 485–494.

Pynoos, R. S., Frederick, C., Nader, K., Arroyo, W., Steinberg, A., Eth, S., Nunez, F., & Fairbanks, L. (1987). Life threat and post-traumatic stress in school-age children. *Archives of General Psychiatry, 44,* 1057–1063.

Quay, H. C. (1993). The psychobiology of undersocialized aggressive conduct disorder: A theoretical perspective. *Development and Psychopathology, 5,* 165–180.

Querido, J. G., Bearss, K., & Eyberg, S. M. (2002). Theory, research, and practice of parent-child interaction therapy. In F. W. Kaslow & T. Patterson (Eds.), *Comprehensive handbook of psychotherapy: Vol. 2. Cognitive/behavioral/ functional approaches.* New York: John Wiley.

Querido, J. G., & Eyberg, S. M. (2005). Parent-child interaction therapy: Maintaining treatment gains of preschoolers with disruptive behavior disorders. In E. D. Hibbs & P. S. Jensen (Eds.), *Psychosocial treatments for child and adolescent disorders: Empirically based strategies for clinical practice* (2nd ed.). Washington, DC: American Psychological Association.

Rabian, B., & Silverman, W. K. (2000). Anxiety disorders. In M. Hersen & R. T. Ammerman (Eds.), *Advanced abnormal child psychology* (2nd ed.). Mahwah, NJ: Lawrence Erlbaum Associates.

Rahman, A., Mubbashar, M., Harrington, R., & Gater, R. (2000). Annotation: Developing child mental health services in developing countries. *Journal of Child Psychology and Psychiatry, 41,* 539–546.

Raine, A., Moffitt, T. E., Caspi, A., Loeber, R., Stouthamer-Loeber, M., & Lynam, D. (2005). Neurocognitive impairments in boys on the life-course persistent antisocial path. *Journal of Abnormal Psychology, 114,* 38–49.

Rait, D. S., Ostroff, J. S., Smith, K., Cella, D. F., Tan, C., & Lesko, L. M. (1992). Lives in a balance—perceived family functioning and the psychosocial adjustment of adolescent cancer survivors. *Family Process, 31,* 383–397.

Raitano, N. A., Pennington, B. F., Tunick, R. A., Boada, R., & Shriberg, L. D. (2004). Pre-literacy skills of subgroups of children with speech sound disorders. *Journal of Child Psychology and Psychiatry, 45,* 821–835.

Ramey, C. T., & Campbell, F. A. (1984). Preventive education for high-risk children: Cognitive consequences of the Carolina Abecedarian Project. *American Journal of Mental Deficiency, 88,* 515–523.

Ramey, C. T., & Ramey, S. L. (1998). Early intervention and early experience. *American Psychologist, 53,* 109–120.

Ramey, S. L. (1999). Head Start and preschool education: Toward continued improvement. *American Psychologist, 54,* 344–346.

Rao, U., Dahl, D., Ryan, N. D., Birmaher, B., Williamson, D. E., Giles, D. E., Rao, R., Kaufman, J., & Nelson, B. (1996). The relationship between longitudinal clinical course and sleep and cortisol changes in adolescent depression. *Biological Psychiatry, 40,* 474–483.

Rapee, R. M., Barrett, P. M., Dadds, M. R., & Evans, L. (1994). Reliability of the DSM-III-R childhood anxiety disorders using structured interview: Interrater and parent-child agreement. *Journal of the American Academy of Child and Adolescent Psychiatry, 33,* 984–992.

Rapee, R. M., Kennedy, S., Ingram, M., Edwards, S., & Sweeney, L. (2005). Prevention and early intervention of anxiety disorders in inhibited preschool children. *Journal of Consulting and Clinical Psychology, 73,* 488–497.

Rapoport, J. L. (1989). The biology of obsessions and compulsions. *Scientific American, 260,* 83–89.

Rapoport, J. L., & Inhoff-Germain, G. (2000). Treatment of obsessive-compulsive disorder in children and adolescents. *Journal of Child Psychology and Psychiatry, 41,* 419–431.

Rapoport, J. L., Inhoff-Germain, G., Weissman, M. M., Greenwald, S., Narrow, W. E., Jensen, P. S., Lahey, B. B., & Canino, G. (2000). Childhood obsessive-compulsive disorder in the NIMH MECA study: Parent versus child identification of cases. *Journal of Anxiety Disorders, 14,* 535–548.

Rapoport, J. L, & Ismond, D. R. (1996). *DSM-IV training guide for diagnosis of childhood disorders.* New York: Brunner/Mazel.

Rapport, M. D. (1993). Attention deficit hyperactivity disorder. In T. H. Ollendick & M. Hersen (Eds.), *Handbook of child and adolescent assessment.* Boston: Allyn and Bacon.

Rapport, M. D., & Chung, K-M. (2000). Attention deficit hyperactivity disorder. In M. Hersen & R. T. Ammerman (Eds.), *Advanced abnormal child psychology.* Mahwah, NJ: Lawrence Erlbaum.

Rapport, M. D., Chung, K-M., Shore, G., & Isaacs, P. (2001). A conceptual model of child psychopathology: Implications for understanding attention deficit hyperactivity disorder and treatment efficacy. *Journal of Clinical Child Psychology, 30,* 48–58.

Raymond-Speden, E., Tripp, G., Lawrence, B., & Holdaway, D. (2000). Intellectual, neuropsychological, and academic functioning in long-term survivors of leukemia. *Journal of Pediatric Psychology, 25,* 59–68.

Rea, P. J., McLaughlin, V. L., & Walther-Thomas, C. (2002). Outcome for students with learning disabilities in inclusive and pullout programs. *Exceptional Children, 68,* 203–222.

Realmuto, G. M., August, G. J., & Hektner, J. M. (2000). Predictive power of peer behavioral assessment for subsequent maladjustment in community samples of disruptive and nondisruptive children. *Journal of Child Psychology and Psychiatry, 41,* 181–190.

Reddy, R., Rhodes, J. E., & Mulhall, P. (2003). The influence of teacher support on student adjustment in the middle school years: A latent growth curve. *Development and Psychopathology, 15,* 119–138.

Regier, D. A., & Burke, J. D. (2000). Epidemiology. In B. J. Sadock & V. A. Sadock (Eds.), *Kaplan & Sadock's comprehensive textbook of psychiatry* (Vol. I). Philadelphia: Lippincott Williams & Wilkins.

Reich, W. (2000). Diagnostic Interview for Children and Adolescents (DICA). *Journal of the American Academy of Child and Adolescent Psychiatry, 39,* 59–66.

Reich, W., Huang, H., & Todd, R. D. (2006). ADHD medication use in a population-based sample of twins. *Journal of the Academy of Child and Adolescent Psychiatry, 45,* 801–807.

Reichenberg, A., & Harvey, P. D. (2007). Neuropsychological impairments in schizophrenia: Integration of performance-based and brain imaging findings. *Psychological Bulletin, 133,* 833–858.

Reid, J. B. (Ed.) (1978). *A social learning approach to family intervention* (Vol. 2: *Observations in home settings*). Eugene, OR: Castalia.

Reid, J. B., Patterson, G. R., & Snyder, J. (Eds.) (2002). *Antisocial behavior in children and adolescents: A developmental analysis and model for intervention.* Washington, DC: American Psychological Association.

Reid, M. J., Webster-Stratton, C., & Baydar, N. (2004). Halting the development of conduct problems in Head Start children: The effects of parent training. *Journal of Clinical Child and Adolescent Psychology, 33,* 279–291.

Reifman, A., Villa, L. C., Amans, J. A., Rethinam, V., & Telesca, T. Y. (2001). Children of divorce in the 1990s: A meta-analysis. *Journal of Divorce and Remarriage, 36,* 27–36.

Reiss, A. L., & Dant, C. C. (2003). The behavioral neurogenetics of fragile X syndrome: Analyzing gene-brain-behavior relationships in child developmental psychopathologies. *Development and Psychopathology, 15,* 927–968.

Reitan, R. M., & Wolfson, D. (1993). *The Halstead-Reitan Neuropsychological Test Battery: Theory and clinical interpretation* (2nd ed.). Tucson: Neuropsychology Press.

Reiter-Purtill, J., Gerhardt, C. A., Vannatta, K., Passo, M. H., & Noll, R. B. (2003). A controlled longitudinal study of the social functioning of children with juvenile rheumatoid arthritis. *Journal of Pediatric Psychology, 28,* 17–28.

Rellini, E., Tortolani, D., Trillo, S., Carbone, S., & Montecchi, F. (2004). Childhood Autism Rating Scale (CARS) and Autism Behavior Checklist (ABC) correspondence and conflicts with DSM-IV criteria in diagnosis of autism. *Journal of Autism and Developmental Disorders, 34,* 703–708.

Rende, R. D., Plomin, R., Reiss, D., & Hetherington, E. M. (1993). Genetic and environmental influences on depressive symptomatology in adolescence: Individual differences and extreme scores. *Journal of Child Psychology and Psychiatry, 34,* 1387–1398.

Renouf, A. G., & Kovacs, M. (1994). Concordance between mothers' reports and children's self-reports of depressive symptoms: A longitudinal study. *Journal of the American Academy of Child & Adolescent Psychiatry, 33,* 208–216.

Reppucci, N. D., Woolard, J. L., & Fried, C. S. (1999). Social, community, and preventive interventions. *Annual Review of Psychology, 50,* 387–418.

Reschly, D. J. (1992). Mental retardation: Conceptual foundations, definitional criteria, and diagnostic operations. In S. R. Hooper, G. W. Hynd, & R. W. Mattison (Eds.), *Assessment and diagnosis of child and adolescent psychiatric disorders, Vol. II. Developmental disorders.* Hillsdale, NJ: Erlbaum.

Rescorla, L. (2002). Language and reading outcomes to age 9 in late-talking toddlers. *Journal of Speech, Language, and Hearing Research, 45,* 360–371.

Rescorla, L., Achenbach, T., Ivanova, M. Y., Dumenci, L., Almqvist, F., Bilenberg, N. et al. (2007). Behavioral and emotional problems reported by parents of children ages 6 to 16 in 31 societies. *Journal of Emotional and Behavioral Disorders, 15,* 130–142.

Rettew, D. C., Swedo, S. E., Leonard, H. L., Lenane, M. C., & Rapoport, J. L. (1992). Obsessions and compulsions across time in 79 children and adolescents with obsessive compulsive disorder. *Journal of the American Academy of Child and Adolescent Psychology, 31,* 1050–1056.

Rey, J. M. (1993). Oppositional defiant disorder. *American Journal of Psychiatry, 150,* 1769–1778.

Reynolds, C. R., & Kamphaus, R. W. (2004). *Behavioral Assessment System for Children, Second Edition (BASC-2).* Bloomington, MN: Pearson Assessments.

Reynolds, C. R., & Richmond, B. O. (1985). *Revised Children's Manifest Anxiety Scales (RCMAS).* Lutz, FL: Psychological Assessment Resources, Inc.

Reynolds, W. M. (1987, 2002). *RADS-2, Reynolds Adolescent Depression Scale: Professional manual.* Lutz, FL: Psychological Resources, Inc.

Reynolds, W. M. (1989). *Reynolds Child Depression Scale.* Lutz, FL: Psychological Assessment Resources, Inc.

Reynolds, W. M. (1994). Assessment of depression in children and adolescents by self-report questionnaires. In W. M. Reynolds and H. F. Johnston (Eds.), *Handbook of depression in children and adolescents.* New York: Plenum Press.

Rhee, S. H., & Waldman, I. D. (2002). Genetic and environmental influences on antisocial behavior: a meta-analysis of twin and adoption studies. *Psychological Bulletin, 128,* 490–529.

Rhee, S. H., & Waldman, I. D. (2003). Testing alternative hypotheses regarding the role of development on genetic and environmental influences underlying antisocial behavior. In B. B. Lahey, T. E. Moffitt, A. Caspi (Eds.), *Causes of conduct disorder and juvenile delinquency.* New York: Guilford Press.

Ricciardelli, L. A., & McCabe, M. P. (2004). A biopsychosocial model of disordered eating and the pursuit of muscularity in adolescent boys. *Psychological Bulletin, 130,* 179–205.

Rice, F., Harold, G., & Thapar, A. (2002). The genetic aetiology of childhood depression: A review. *Journal of Child Psychology and Psychiatry, 43,* 65–79.

Richards, D. F. (2003). The central role of informed consent in ethical treatment and research with children. In W. O'Donohue & K. Ferguson (Eds.), *Handbook of professional ethics for psychologists.* Thousand Oaks, CA: Sage Publications.

Richards, M. H., Larson, R., Miller, B. V., Luo, Z., Sims, B., Parrella, D. P., & McCauley, C. (2004). Risky and protective contexts and exposure to violence in urban African American young adolescents. *Journal of Clinical Child and Adolescent Psychology, 33,* 138–148.

Richler, J., Bishop, S. L., Kleinke, J. R., & Lord, C. (2007). Restricted and repetitive behaviors in young children with autism spectrum disorders. *Journal of Autism and Developmental Disorders, 37,* 73–85.

Richters, J. E., & Cicchetti, D. (1993). Mark Twain meets DSM-IIIR: Conduct disorder, development, and the concept of harmful dysfunction. *Development and Psychopathology, 5,* 5–29.

Riddle, M. A., Kastelic, E. A., & Frosch, E. (2001). Pediatric psychopharmacology. *Journal of Child Psychology and Psychiatry, 42,* 73–90.

Rie, H. E. (1971). Historical perspectives of concepts of child psychopathology. In H. E. Rie (Ed.), *Perspectives in child psychopathology.* New York: Aldine-Atherton.

Riekert, K.A., & Drotar, D. (2000). Adherence to medical treatment in pediatric chronic illness: Critical issues and answered questions. In D. Drotar (Ed.), *Promoting adherence to medical treatment in chronic childhood illness: Concepts, methods, and interventions.* Mahwah, NJ: Lawrence Erlbaum Associates.

Rieppi, R. et al. (2002). Socioeconomic status as a moderator of ADHD treatment outcomes. *Journal of the American Academy of Child and Adolescent Psychiatry, 41,* 269–277.

Ries, L. A. G., Eisner, M. P., Kosary, C. L., Hankey, B. F., Miller, B. A., Clegg, L., & Edwards, B. K. (Eds.) (2001). SEER Cancer Statistics Review, 1973–1998, National Cancer Institute. Bethesda, MD, http://seer.Cancer.gov/Publications/CSR1973 1998/2001.

Ringel, J. S., & Sturm, R. (2001). National estimates of mental health utilization and expenditures for children in 1998. *Journal of Behavioral Health and Research, 28,* 319–333.

Ripple, C. H., & Zigler, E. (2003). Research, policy, and the federal role in prevention initiatives for children. *American Psychologist, 58,* 482–490.

Roberts, M. C., & Wallander, J. L. (1992). Family issues in pediatric psychology: An overview. In M. C. Roberts & J. L. Wallander (Eds.), *Family issues in pediatric psychology.* Hillsdale, NJ: Erlbaum.

Roberts, R. E., Ramsay Roberts, C., & Xing, Y. (2006). Prevalence of youth-reported DSM-IV psychiatric disorders among African, European, and Mexican American adolescents. *Journal of the American Academy of Child and Adolescent Psychiatry, 45,* 1329–1337.

Roberts, R. E., Roberts, C. R., & Xing, Y. (2007). Comorbidity of substance use disorders and other psychiatric disorders among adolescents: Evidence from an epidemiological survey. *Drug and Alcohol Dependence, 88S,* S4–S13.

Robin, A. L. (2003). Behavioral family systems therapy for adolescents with anorexia nervosa. In A. E. Kazdin & J. R. Weisz (Eds.), *Evidence-based psychotherapies for children and adolescents.* New York: Guilford Press.

Robin, A. L. (2006). Training families with adolescents with ADHD. In R. A. Barkley (Ed.), *Attention-deficit hyperactivity disorder. A handbook for diagnosis and treatment.* New York: The Guilford Press.

Robin, A. L., Koepke, T., & Moye, A. (1990). Multidimensional assessment of parent-adolescent relations. *Psychological Assessment, 2,* 451–459.

Robins, D., Fein, D., Barton, M., & Green, J. (2001). The modified checklist for autism in toddlers: An initial study investigating the early detection of autism and pervasive developmental disorders. *Journal of Autism and Developmental Disorders, 31,* 131–144.

Robins, L. N., Murphy, G. E., Woodruff, R. A., Jr., & King, L. J. (1971). The adult psychiatric status of black school boys. *Archives of General Psychiatry, 24,* 338–345.

Robinson, T. N. (1999). Reducing children's television viewing to prevent obesity: A randomized controlled trial. *Journal of the American Medical Association, 282,* 1561–1567.

Robinson, T. N., & Killen, J. D. (2001). Obesity prevention for children and adolescents. In J. K. Thompson & L. Smolak (Eds.), *Body image, eating disorders, and obesity in youth: Assessment, prevention, and treatment.* Washington, DC: American Psychological Association.

Roblek, T., & Piacentini, J. (2005). Cognitive-behavior therapy for childhood anxiety disorders. *Child and Adolescent Psychiatric Clinics of North America, 14,* 863–876.

Rodenburg, R., Stams, G. J., Meijer, A. M., Aldenkamp, A. P., & Dekovic, M. (2005). Psychopathology in children with epilepsy: A meta-analysis. *Journal of Pediatric Psychology, 30,* 453–468.

Rodriguez, A., & Bohlin, G. (2005). Are maternal smoking and stress during pregnancy related to ADHD symptoms in children? *Journal of Child Psychology and Psychiatry, 46,* 246–254.

Rogers, A. G. (2000). When methods matter: Qualitative research issues in psychology. *Harvard Educational Review, 70,* 75–85.

Rogers, S. (1998). Empirically supported comprehensive treatments for young children with autism. *Journal of Clinical Child Psychology, 27,* 168–179.

Rogers, S. J., & Ozonoff, S. (2005). Annotation: what do we know about sensory dysfunction in autism? A critical review of the empirical evidence. *Journal of Child Psychology and Psychiatry, 46,* 1255–1268.

Rogers, S. J., Hepburn, S. L., Stackhouse, T., & Wehner, E. (2004). Imitation performance in toddlers with autism and those with other developmental disorders. *Journal of Child Psychology and Psychiatry, 44,* 763–781.

Rohde, P., Lewinsohn, P. M., Clarke, G. N., Hops, H., & Seeley, J. R. (2005). The Adolescent Coping With Depression Course: A cognitive-behavioral approach to the treatment of adolescent depression. In E. D. Hibbs & P. S. Jensen (Eds.), *Psychosocial treatments for child and adolescent disorders: Empirically based strategies for clinical practice.* (2nd ed.). Washington, DC: American Psychological Association.

Roid, G. H. (2003). *Stanford-Binet Intelligence Scale* (5th ed.). Chicago: Riverside.

Romer, D., & McIntosh, M. (2005). The roles and perspectives of school mental health professionals in promoting adolescent mental health. In D. L. Evans, E. B. Foa, R. E. Gur, H. Hendin, C. P. O'Brien, M. E. P. Seligman, & B. T. Walsh (Eds.), *Treating and preventing adolescent mental health disorders. What we know and what we don't know: A research agenda for improving mental health of our youth.* New York: Oxford University Press.

Ronan, K., Kendall, P. C., & Rowe, M. (1994). Negative affectivity in children: Development and validation of a self-statement questionnaire. *Cognitive Therapy and Research, 18,* 509–528.

Rosenfeld, A. A., Pilowsky, D. J., Fine, P., Thorpe, M., Fein, E., Simms, M. D., Halfon, N., Irwin, M., Alfaro, J., Saletsky, R., & Nickman, S. (1997). Foster care: An update. *Journal of the American Academy of Child and Adolescent Psychiatry, 36,* 448–458.

Ross, A. O. (1972). The clinical child psychologist. In B. J. Wolman (Ed.), *Manual of child psychopathology.* New York: McGraw-Hill.

Ross, C. K., Lavigne, J. V., Hayford, J. R., Berry, S. L., Sinacore, J. M., & Pachman, L. M. (1993). Psychological factors affecting reported pain in juvenile rheumatoid arthritis. *Journal of Pediatric Psychology, 18,* 561–573.

Ross, D. M. (1988). Aversive treatment procedures: The school-age child's view. *Newsletter of the Society of Pediatric Psychology, 12,* 3–6.

Ross, R. G. et al. (1999). Evidence for bilineal inheritance of physiological indicators of risk in childhood-onset schizophrenia. *American Journal of Medical Genetics, 88,* 188–199.

Ross, R. G., Heinlein, S., Zerbe, G. O., & Radant, A. (2005). Saccadic eye movement task identifies cognitive deficits in children with schizophrenia, but not in unaffected child relatives. *Journal of Child Psychology and Psychiatry, 46,* 1354–1362.

Rosselló, J., & Bernal, G. (1999). The efficacy of cognitive-behavioral and interpersonal treatments for depression in Puerto Rican adolescents. *Journal of Consulting and Clinical Psychology, 67,* 734–745.

Rosselló, J., & Bernal, G. (2005). New developments in cognitive-behavioral and interpersonal treatments for depressed Puerto Rican adolescents. In E. D. Hibbs & P. S. Jensen (Eds.), *Psychosocial treatments for child and adolescent disorders: Empirically* based strategies for clinical practice. (2nd ed.). Washington, DC: American Psychological Association.

Rossi, A., Pollice, R., Daneluzzo, E., Marinangeli, M. G., & Stratta, P. (2000). Behavioral neurodevelopment abnormalities and schizophrenic disorder: A retrospective evaluation with the Childhood Behavior Checklist (CBCL). *Schizophrenia Research, 44,* 121–128.

Rothbart, M. K., & Posner, M. I. (2006). Temperament, attention, and developmental psychopathology. In D. Cicchetti & D. J. Cohen (Eds.), *Developmental psychopathology. Vol. 2. Developmental neuroscience.* Hoboken, NJ: John Wiley & Sons.

Rotheram-Borus, M. J., & Duan, N. (2003). Next generation of preventive interventions. *Journal of the American Academy of Child and Adolescent Psychiatry, 42,* 518–530.

Rourke, B. P., & Fuerst, D. R. (1995). Cognitive processing, academic achievement, and psychological functioning: A neurodevelopmental perspective. In D. Cicchetti & D. J. Cohen (Eds.), *Developmental psychopathology.* New York: John Wiley.

Rovet, J., & Fernandes, C. (1999). Insulin-dependent diabetes mellitus. In R. T. Brown (Ed.), *Cognitive aspects of chronic illness in children.* New York: The Guilford Press.

Rowe, R., Simonoff, E., & Silberg, J. L. (2007). Psychopathology, temperament, and unintentional injury: cross-sectional and longitudinal relationships. *Journal of Child Psychology and Psychiatry, 48,* 71–79.

Rubin, K., Bukowski, W., & Parker, J. (2006). Peer interaction and social competence. In W. Damon & R. L. Lerner (Eds.), *Handbook of child psychology. Vol. 3* (6th ed.). New York: John Wiley & Sons.

Rubin, K. H., Burgess, K. B., Kennedy, A. E., & Stewart, S. L. (2003). Social withdrawal in childhood. In E. J. Mash & R. A. Barkley (Eds.), *Child psychopathology* (2nd ed.). New York: Guilford Press.

Rucklidge, J. J., & Tannock, R. (2002). Neuropsychological profiles of adolescents with ADHD: Effects of reading difficulties and gender. *Journal of Child Psychology and Psychiatry, 43,* 988–1003.

Rudolph, K. D., & Asher, S. R. (2000). Adaptation and maladaptation in the peer system: Developmental processes and outcomes. In A. J. Sameroff, M. Lewis, & S. M. Miller (Eds.), *Handbook of developmental psychopathology* (2nd ed.). New York: Kluwer Academic/ Plenum Publishers.

Rudolph, K. D., Hammen, C., & Daley, S. E. (2006). Mood disorders. In D. A. Wolfe & E. J. Mash (Eds.), *Behavioral and emotional disorders in adolescents: Nature, assessment, and treatment.* New York: The Guilford Press.

Rusby, J. C., Estes, A., & Dishion, T. (1991). *The Interpersonal Process Code (IPC).* Unpublished manuscript. Oregon Social Learning Center, Eugene.

Rushton, A., & Dance, C. (2007). The adoption of children from public care: a prospective study of outcome in adolescence. *Journal of the American Academy of Child and Adolescent Psychiatry, 45,* 877–883.

Rushton, A., & Minnis, H. (1997). Transracial family placements. *Journal of Child Psychology and Psychiatry, 38,* 147–159.

Russ, S. W. (1995). Play psychotherapy research: State of the science. In T. H. Ollendick & R. J. Prinz (Eds.), *Advances in clinical child psychology.* Vol. 17. New York: Plenum.

Russell, A. T., Bott, L., & Sammons, C. (1989). The phenomenology of schizophrenia occurring in childhood. *Journal of the American Academy of Child and Adolescent Psychiatry, 28,* 399–407.

Russell, S. T., & Joyner, K. (2001). Adolescent sexual orientation and suicide risk: Evidence from a national study. *American Journal of Public Health, 91,* 1276–1281.

Rutgers, A. H., Bakersman-Kranenburg, M. J., van Ijzendoorn, M. H., & van Berckelaer-Onnes, I. A. (2004). Autism and attachment: A meta-analytic review. *Journal of Child Psychology and Psychiatry, 45,* 1123–1134.

Rutter, M. (1983). School effects on pupils progress: Research findings and policy implications. *Child Development, 54,* 1–29.

Rutter, M. (1987). Psychosocial resilience and protective mechanisms. *American Journal of Orthopsychiatry, 57,* 316–331.

Rutter, M. (1989). Pathways from childhood to adult life. *Journal of Child Psychology and Psychiatry, 30,* 23–51.

Rutter, M. (2000). Psychosocial influences: Critiques, findings, and research needs. *Development and Psychopathology, 12,* 375–405.

Rutter, M. (2002). Nature, nurture, and development: From evangelism through science toward policy and practice. *Child Development, 73,* 1–21.

Rutter, M. (2003). Critical paths from risk indicator to causal mechanisms. In B. B. Lahey, T. E. Moffitt, A. Caspi (Eds.), *Causes of conduct disorder and juvenile delinquency.* New York: Guilford Press.

Rutter, M. (2005). Natural experiments, causal influences, and policy development. In M. Rutter & M. Tienda (Eds.), *Ethnicity and causal mechanisms.* New York: Cambridge University Press.

Rutter, M. (2006). The promotion of resilience in the face of adversity. In A. Clarke-Stewart & J. Dunn (Eds.), *Families count: Effects on child and adolescent development.* New York: Cambridge University Press.

Rutter, M., Caspi, A., & Moffitt, T. E. (2003). Using sex differences in psychopathology to study causal mechanisms: Unifying issues and research strategies. *Journal of Child Psychology and Psychiatry, 44,* 1092–1115.

Rutter, M., Colvert, E., Kreppner, J., Beckett, C., Castle, J., Grootheus, C. et al. (2007). Early adolescent outcomes for institutionally deprived adoptees. I: Disinhibited attachment. *Journal of Child Psychology and Psychiatry, 48,* 17–30.

Rutter, M., Giller, H., & Hagell, A. (1998). *Antisocial behavior by young people.* Cambridge, England: Cambridge University Press.

Rutter, M., Kim-Cohen, J., & Maughan, B. (2006). Continuities and discontinuities in psychopathology between childhood and adult life. *Journal of Child and Adolescent Psychology, 47,* 276–295.

Rutter, M., & Maughan, B. (2002). School effectiveness findings 1979–2002. *Journal of School Psychology, 40,* 451–475.

Rutter, M., Mawhood, L., & Howlin, P. (1992). Language delay and social development. In P. Fletcher & D. Hall (Eds.), *Specific speech and language disorders in children.* San Diego, CA: Singular Publishing Group.

Rutter, M., Moffitt, T. E., & Caspi, A. (2006). Gene-environment interplay and psychopathology: multiple varieties but real effects. *Journal of Child Psychology and Psychiatry, 47,* 226–261.

Rutter, M., & Schopler, E. (1987). Autism and pervasive developmental disorders: Concepts and diagnostic issues. *Journal of Autism and Developmental Disorders, 17*, 159–186.

Rutter, M., & Silberg, J. (2002). Gene-environment interplay in relation to emotional and behavioral disturbance. *Annual Review of Psychology, 54*, 463–490.

Rutter, M., Silberg, J., O'Connor, T., & Simonoff, E. (1999). Genetics and child psychiatry: II Empirical research findings. *Journal of Child Psychology and Psychiatry, 40*, 19–55.

Rutter, M., & Smith, D. J. (1995). *Psychosocial disorders in young people: Time trends and their causes.* New York: Wiley.

Rutter, M., & Sroufe, L. A. (2000). Developmental psychopathology: Concepts and challenges. *Development and Psychopathology, 12*, 265–296.

Ryan, N. D., Puig-Antich, J., Ambrosini, P., Ravinovich, H., Robinson, D., Neilson, B., Iyenhar, S., & Toomey, J. (1987). The clinical picture of major depression in children and adolescents. *Archives of General Psychiatry, 44*, 854–861.

Sadeh, A. (2005). Cognitive-behavioral treatment for childhood sleep disorders. *Clinical Psychology Review, 25*, 612–628.

Sadeh, A., Raviv, A., & Gruber, R. (2000). Sleep patterns and sleep disruptions in school-age children. *Developmental Psychology, 36*, 291–301.

Sahler, O. J., Frager, G., Levetown, M., Cohn, F. G., & Lipson, M. A. (2000). Medical education about end-of-life care in the pediatric setting: Principles, challenges, and opportunities. *Pediatrics, 105*, 575–584.

Saler, L., & Skolnick, N. (1992). Childhood parental death and depression in adulthood: Roles of surviving parent and family environment. *American Journal of Orthopsychiatry, 62*, 504–516.

Sallis, J. F., & Glanz, K. (2006). The role of built environments in physical activity, eating, and obesity in childhood. *The Future of Children, 16*, 89–108.

Salmon, K., & Bryant, R. A. (2002). Posttraumatic stress disorder in children: The influence of developmental factors. *Clinical Psychology Review, 22*, 163–188.

Salmon, K., & Pereira, J. K. (2002). Predicting children's response to an invasive medical investigation: The influence of effortful control and parent behavior. *Journal of Pediatric Psychology, 27*, 227–233.

Salmon, K., McGuigan, F., & Pereira, J. K. (2006). Optimizing children's memory and management of an invasive medical procedure: The influence of procedural narration and distraction. *Journal of Pediatric Psychology, 31*, 522–527.

Salzinger, S., Feldman, R. S., Ng-Mak, D. S., Mojica, E., & Stockhammer, T. F. (2001). The effect of physical abuse on children's social and affective status: A model of cognitive and behavioral processes explaining the association. *Development and Psychopathology, 13*, 805–825.

Sameroff, A. (2006). Identifying risk and protective factors for healthy child development. In A. Clarke-Stewart & J. Dunn (Eds.), *Families count: Effects on child and adolescent development.* New York: Cambridge University Press.

Sameroff, A. J. (1990). Neo-environmental perspectives on developmental theory. In R. M. Hodapp, J. A. Burack, & E. Zigler (Eds.), *Issues in the developmental approach to mental retardation.* New York: Cambridge University Press.

Sandberg, D. E., & Zurenda, L. (2006). Endocrine disorders. In L. Phelps (Ed.), *Chronic health-related disorders in children: Collaborative medical and psychoeducational interventions.* Washington, DC: American Psychological Association.

Sandberg, S., Rutter, M., Pickles, A., McGuinness, D., & Angold, A. (2001). Do high-threat life events really provoke the onset of psychiatric disorder in children? *Journal of Child Psychology and Psychiatry, 42*, 523–532.

Sanson, A., Smart, D., Prior, M., & Oberklaid, F. (1993). Precursors of hyperactivity and aggression. *Journal of the American Academy of Child and Adolescent Psychiatry, 32*, 1207–1216.

Santostefano, S. (1978). A biodevelopmental approach to clinical child psychology. New York: Wiley-Interscience.

Saris, W. J. M. (1995). Metabolic effects of exercise in overweight individuals. In K. D. Brownell & C. G. Fairburn (Eds.), *Eating disorders and obesity: A comprehensive handbook.* New York: Guilford Press.

Sattler, J. M. (1992). *Assessment of children.* (Revised and updated 3rd ed.). San Diego: Jerome M. Sattler, Publisher.

Sattler, J. M. (1998). *Clinical and forensic interviewing of children and families: Guidelines for the mental health, education, pediatric, and child maltreatment fields.* San Diego: Jerome M. Sattler, Publisher, Inc.

Savin, D., Sack, W. H., Clarke, G. N., Meas, N., & Richart, I. (1996). The Khmer Adolescent Project: III. A study of trauma from Thailand's Site II refugee camp. *Journal of the American Academy of Child and Adolescent Psychiatry, 35*, 384–391.

Savin-Williams, R. C. (2001). Suicide attempts among sexual-minority youths: Population and measurement issues. *Journal of Consulting and Clinical Psychology, 69*, 983–991.

Savin-Williams, R. C., & Ream, G. L. (2003). Suicide attempts among sexual-minority male youth. *Journal of Clinical Child and Adolescent Psychology, 32*, 509–522.

Saylor, C. F., Boyce, G. C., & Price, C. (2003). Early predictors of school-age behavior problems and social skills in children with intraventricular hemorrhage (IVH) and/or extremely low birthweight (ELBW). *Child Psychiatry and Human Development, 33*, 175–192.

Saylor, C. F., Cowart, B. L., Lipovsky, J. A., Jackson, C., & Finch, A. J., Jr. (2003). Media exposure to September 11: Elementary school students' experiences and posttraumatic symptoms. *American Behavioral Scientist, 46*, 1622–1642.

Saylor, C. F., Powell, P., & Swenson, C. (1992). Hurricane Hugo blows down the broccoli: Preschoolers' post-disaster play and adjustment. *Child Psychiatry and Human Development, 22*, 139–149.

Scahill, L., Kano, Y., King, R. A., Carlson, A., Peller, A., LeBrun, U. et al. (2003). Influence of age and tic disorders on obsessive-compulsive disorder in a pediatric sample. *Journal of Child and Adolescent Psychopharmacology, 13*, S7–S17.

Scarr, S. (1982). Testing for children: Assessment and the many determinants of intellectual competence. In S. Chess & A. Thomas (Eds.), *Annual progress in child psychiatry and child development 1982.* New York: Brunner/Mazel.

Scarr, S. (1998). American child care today. *American Psychologist, 53*, 95–108.

Schachar, R., & Tannock, R. (2002). Syndromes of hyperactivity and attention deficit. In M. Rutter & E. Taylor (Eds.), *Child and adolescent psychiatry.* Oxford, UK: Blackwell Publishing.

Schaeffer, J. L., & Ross, R. G. (2002). Childhood-onset schizophrenia: Premorbid and prodromal diagnostic and treatment histories. *Journal of the American Academy of Child and Adolescent Psychiatry, 41,* 538–545.

Schalock, R. L., Luckasson, R. A., Shogren, K. A. et al. (2007). The renaming of mental retardation: Understanding the change to the term intellectual disability. *Intellectual and Developmental Disabilities, 45,* 116–124.

Schapman-Williams, A. M., Lock, J., & Couturier, J. (2006). Cognitive-behavioral therapy for adolescents with binge eating syndrome: A case series. *International Journal of Eating Disorders, 39,* 245–251.

Scharff, L., Marcus, D., & Masek, B. J. (2002). A controlled study of minimal-contact thermal biofeedback treatment in children with migraine. *Journal of Pediatric Psychology, 27,* 109–119.

Scheerenberger, R. C. (1983, 1987). *A history of mental retardation.* Baltimore: Brookes Publishing Co.

Scheeringa, M. S., Zeanah, C. H., Myers, L., & Putnam, F. W. (2003). New findings on alternative criteria for PTSD in preschool children. *Journal of the American Academy of Child and Adolescent Psychiatry, 42,* 561–570.

Schetky, D. H. (2000). Ethical issues in child and adolescent psychiatry. In B. J. Sadock & V. A. Sadock (Eds.), *Comprehensive textbook of psychiatry* (Vol. II). Philadelphia: Lippincott Williams & Wilkins.

Schieve, L. A., Blumberg, S. J., Rice, C., Visser, S. N., & Boyle, C. (2007). The relationship between autism and parenting stress. *Pediatrics, 119 Suppl.* S114–121.

Schiff, W. B., Holtz, K. D., Peterson, N., & Rakusan, T. (2001). Effect of an intervention to reduce procedural pain and distress for children with HIV infection. *Journal of Pediatric Psychology, 26,* 417–427.

Schiffman, J., & Daleiden, E. L. (2006). Population and service characteristics of youth with schizophrenia-spectrum diagnoses in the Hawaii system of care. *Journal of Child Psychology and Psychiatry, 47,* 58–62.

Schippell, P. L., Vasey, M. W., Cravens-Brown, L. M., & Bretveld, R. A. (2003). Suppressed attention to rejection, ridicule, and failure cues: A unique correlate of reactive but not proactive aggression. *Journal of Clinical Child and Adolescent Psychology, 32,* 40–55.

Schniering, C. A., Hudson, J. L., & Rapee, R. M. (2000). Issues in the diagnosis and assessment of anxiety disorders in children and adolescents. *Clinical Psychology Review, 20,* 453–478.

Schniering, C. A., & Rapee, R. M. (2002). Development and validation of a measure of children's automatic thoughts: The Children's Automatic Thoughts Scale. *Behaviour Research and Therapy, 40,* 1091–1109.

Schopler, E. (1994). Behavioral priorities for autism and related developmental disorders. In E. Schopler & G. B. Mesibov (Eds.), *Behavioral issues in autism.* New York: Plenum.

Schopler, E. (1997). Implementation of TEACCH philosophy. In D. J. Cohen & F. R. Volkmar (Eds.), *Handbook of autism and pervasive developmental disorders.* New York: John Wiley.

Schopler, E., Reichler, R. J., DeVellis, R. F., & Daly, K. (1980). Toward objective classification of childhood autism: Childhood Autism Rating Scale (CARS). *Journal of Autism and Developmental Disorders, 10,* 91–103.

Schopler, E., Reichler, R. J., & Renner, B. R. (1988). *The Childhood Autism Rating Scale (CARS).* Los Angeles: Western Psychological Services.

Schopler, E., Short, A., & Mesibov, G. (1989). Relation of behavioral treatment to "normal functioning": Comment on Lovaas. *Journal of Consulting and Clinical Psychology, 57,* 162–164.

Schreibman, L. (1997). Theoretical perspectives on behavioral intervention for individuals with autism. In D. J. Cohen & F. R. Volkmar (Eds.), *Handbook of autism and pervasive developmental disorders.* New York: John Wiley.

Schreibman, L. (2000). Intensive behavioral/psychoeducational treatments for autism: Research needs and future directions. *Journal of Autism and Developmental Disorders, 30,* 373–378.

Schroeder, C. S., & Gordon, B. N. (2002). *Assessment and treatment of childhood problems: A clinician's guide* (2nd ed.). New York: Guilford Press.

Schulte-Körne, G. (2001). Annotation: Genetics of reading and spelling disorder. *Journal of Child Psychology and Psychiatry, 42,* 985–997.

Schultz, D., Izard, C. E., Ackerman, B. P., & Youngstrom, E. A. (2001). Emotion knowledge in economically disadvantaged children: Self-regulatory antecedents and relations to social difficulties and withdrawal. *Development and Psychopathology, 13,* 53–67.

Schultz, R. T., & Klin, A. (2002). Genetics of childhood disorders: XLIII. Autism, Part 2: Neural foundations. *Journal of the American Academy of Child and Adolescent Psychiatry, 41,* 1259–1262.

Schumaker, J. B., & Deshler, D. D. (2003). Can students with LD become competent writers? *Learning Disability Quarterly, 26,* 129–141.

Schuster, M. A., Stein, B. D., Jaycox, L. H., Collins, R. L., Marshall, G. N., Elliott, M. N. et al. (2001). A national survey of stress reactions after the September 11, 2001 terrorist attacks. *New England Journal of Medicine, 345,* 1507–1512.

Schwab-Stone, M., Chen, C., Greenberger, E., Silver, D., Lichtman, J., & Voyce, C. (1999). No safe haven II: The effects of violence exposure on urban youth. *Journal of the American Academy of Child and Adolescent Psychiatry, 38,* 359–367.

Schwartz, D., Dodge, K. A., & Coie, J. D. (1993). The emergence of chronic peer victimization in boys' play groups. *Child Development, 64,* 1755–1772.

Schwartz, D., Dodge, K. A., Coie, J. D., Hubbard, J. A., Cillessen, A. H. N., Lemerise, E. A., & Bateman, H. (1998). Social-cognitive and behavioral correlates of aggression and victimization in boys' play groups. *Journal of Abnormal Child Psychology, 26,* 431–440.

Schwartz, D., Dodge, K. A., Pettit, G. S., & Bates, J. E. (1997). The early socialization of aggressive victims of bullying. *Child Development, 68,* 665–675.

Schwartz, J. A. J., Gladstone, T. R. G., & Kaslow, N. J. (1998). Depressive disorders. In T. H. Ollendick & M. Hersen (Eds.), *Handbook of child psychopathology* (3rd ed.). New York: Plenum Press.

Schwartz, J. A. J., Kaslow, N. J., Seeley, J., & Lewinsohn, P. (2000). Psychological, cognitive, and interpersonal correlates of attributional changes in adolescents. *Journal of Clinical Child Psychology, 29,* 188–198.

Schwartz, L., & Drotar, D. (2006). Posttraumatic stress and related impairment in survivors of childhood cancer in early adulthood compared to healthy peers. *Journal of Pediatric Psychology, 31,* 356–366.

Schwebel, D. C., & Gaines, J. (2007). Pediatric unintentional injury: Behavioral risk factors and implications for prevention. *Journal of Developmental & Behavioral Pediatrics, 28,* 245–254.

Schwebel, D. C., Summerlin, A. L., Bounds, M. L., & Morrongiello, B. A. (2006). The Stamp-in-Safety Program: A behavioral intervention to reduce behaviors that can lead to unintentional playground injury in a preschool setting. *Journal of Pediatric Psychology, 31,* 152–162.

Scorgie, K., & Sobsey, D. (2000). Transformational outcomes associated with parenting children who have disabilities. *Mental Retardation, 38,* 195–206.

Scott, S. (1994). Mental retardation. In M. Rutter, E. Taylor, & L. Hersov (Eds.), *Child and adolescent psychiatry. Modern approaches.* Cambridge, MA: Blackwell.

Scourfield, J., Rice, F., Thapar, A., Harold, G. T., Martin, N., & McGuffin, P. (2003). Depressive symptoms in children and adolescents: changing aetiological influences with development. *Journal of Child Psychology and Psychiatry, 44,* 968–976.

Scruggs, T. E., & Mastropieri, M. A. (2002). On babies and bathwater: Addressing the problems of identification of learning disabilities. *Learning Disability Quarterly, 25,* 155–168.

Sears, H. A. (2004). Adolescents in rural communities seeking help: Who reports problems and who sees professionals? *Journal of Child Psychology and Psychiatry, 45,* 396–404.

Sears, R. R. (1975). *Your ancients revisited: A history of child development.* Chicago: University of Chicago Press.

Seiffge-Krenke, I. (1998). The highly structured climate in families of adolescents with diabetes: Functional or dysfunctional for metabolic control? *Journal of Pediatric Psychology, 23,* 313–322.

Seligman, M. P., & Peterson, C. (1986). A learned helplessness perspective on childhood depression: Theory and research. In M. Rutter, C. E. Izard, & P. B. Read (Eds.), *Depression in young people: Developmental and clinical perspectives.* New York: Guilford.

Seltzer, M. M., Greenberg, J. S., Floyd, S. J., Pettee, Y., & Hong, J. (2001). Life course impacts on parenting a child with a disability. *American Journal on Retardation, 106,* 265–286.

Seltzer, M. M., Krauss, M. W., Shattuck, P. T., Orsmond, G., Swe, A., & Lord, C. (2003). The symptoms of autism spectrum disorders in adolescence and adulthood. *Journal of Autism and Developmental Disorders, 33,* 565–581.

Selye, H. (1956). *The stress of life.* New York: McGraw-Hill.

Semrud-Clikeman, M., Steingard, R. J., Filipek, P., Biederman, J., Bekken, K., & Renshaw, P. F. (2000). Using MRI to examine brain-behavior relationships in males with attention deficit disorder with hyperactivity. *Journal of the American Academy of Child and Adolescent Psychiatry, 39,* 477–484.

Serafica, F. C., & Vargas, L. A. (2006). Cultural diversity in the development of child psychopathology. In D. Cicchetti & D. J. Cohen (Eds.), *Developmental psychopathology. Vol. I. Theory and method.* Hoboken, NJ: John Wiley & Sons.

Searafica, F. C., & Vargas, L. A. (2006). Cultural diversity in the development of child psychopathology. In D. Cicchetti & D. J. Cohen (Eds.), *Developmental psychopathology. Vol. 1. Theory and method.* Hoboken, NJ: John Wiley & Sons.

Sergeant, J. (2006). The cognitive-energetic model: An empirical approach to attention-deficit hyperactivity disorder. *Neuroscience and biobehavioral reviews, 24,* 7–12.

Sethi, S., Bhargava, S., & Phil, S. M. (2005). Nocturnal enuresis: A review. *Journal of Pediatric Neurology, 31,* 11–18.

Shadish, W. R., Cook, T. D., & Campbell, D. T. (2002). *Experimental and quasi-experimental designs for generalized causal inference.* Boston: Houghton Mifflin.

Shaffer, D., & Waslick, B. D. (1996). Elimination and sleep disorders. In J. M. Wiener (Ed.), *Diagnosis and psychopharmacology of childhood and adolescent disorders.* New York: John Wiley.

Shah, A., & Frith, U. (1993). Why do autistic individuals show superior performance on the block design task? *Journal of Child Psychology and Psychiatry, 34,* 1351–1364.

Shalev, R. S., Manor, O., Kerem, B., Ayali, M., Badichi, N., Friedlander, Y. et al. (2001). Developmental dyscalculia is a familial learning disability. *Journal of Learning Disabilities, 34,* 59–65.

Shapiro, S., Newcomb, M., & Loeb, T. B. (1997). Fear of fat, disregulated-restrained eating, and body-esteem: Prevalence and gender differences among eight- to ten-year-old children. *Journal of Clinical Psychology, 26,* 358–365.

Shaw, D. S., Lacourse, E., & Nagin, D. S. (2005). Developmental trajectories of conduct problems and hyperactivity from ages 2 to 10. *Journal of Child Psychology and Psychiatry, 46,* 932–942.

Shaw, P., & Rapoport, J. L. (2006). Decision making about children with psychotic symptoms: using the best evidence in choosing a treatment. *Journal of the American Academy of Child and Adolescent Psychiatry, 45,* 1381–1386.

Shaywitz, B. A., Shaywitz, S. E., Blachman, B. A., Pugh, K. R., Fulbright, R. K., Skudlarski, P. et al. (2004). Development of left occipitotemporal systems for skilled reading in children after a phonologically-based intervention. *Biological Psychiatry, 55,* 926–933.

Shaywitz, S. (2003). *Overcoming dyslexia.* New York: Knopf.

Shaywitz, S. E., Fletcher, J. M., & Shaywitz, B. A. (1996). A conceptual model and definition of dyslexia: Findings emerging from the Connecticut Longitudinal Study. In J. H. Beitchman, N. J. Cohen, M. M. Konstantareas, & R. Tannock (Eds.), *Language, learning, and behavior disorders.* New York: Cambridge University Press.

Shaywitz, S. E., & Shaywitz, B. A. (2003). Neurobiological indices of dyslexia. In H. L. Swanson, K. R. Harris, & S. Graham (Eds.), *Handbook of learning disabilities.* New York: The Guilford Press.

Shaywitz, S. E., Shaywitz, B. A., Fulbright, R. K., Skudlarski, P., Mencl, W. E., Constable, R. T. et al. (2003). Neural systems for compensation and persistence: Young adult outcome of childhood reading disability. *Biological Psychiatry, 54,* 25–33.

Shaywitz, S. E., Shaywitz, B. A., Pugh, K. R., Fulbright, R. K., Constable, R. T., Mencl, W. E., Shankweiler, D. P., Liberman, A. M., Skudlarski, P., Fletcher, J. M., Katz, L., Marchione, K. E., Lacadie, C., Gatenby, C., & Gore, J. C. (1998). Functional disruption in the organization of the brain for reading in dyslexia. *Proceedings of the National Academy of Sciences, 95,* 2636–2641.

Sheffield, J. K., Spence, S. H., Rapee, R. M., Kowalenko, N., Wignall, A., Davis, A. et al. (2006). Evaluation of universal, indicated, and combined cognitive-behavioral approaches to the prevention of depression among adolescents. *Journal of Consulting and Clinical Psychology, 74,* 66–79.

Sheinkopf, S. J., Munday, P., Oller, D. K., & Steffens, M. (2000). Vocal atypicalities of preverbal autistic children. *Journal of Autism & Developmental Disorders, 30,* 345–354.

Sicotte, C., & Stemberger, R. M. T. (1999). Do children with PDDNOS have a theory of mind? *Journal of Autism and Developmental Disorders, 29,* 225–233.

Siegel, L. J., & Conte, P. (2001). Hospitalization and medical care of children. In C. E. Walker & M. C. Roberts (Eds.), *Handbook of clinical child psychology* (3rd ed.). New York: John Wiley & Sons, Inc.

Siegel, L. S. (2003). Basic cognitive processes and reading disabilities. In H. L. Swanson, K. R. Harris, & S. Graham (Eds.), *Handbook of learning disabilities.* New York: Guilford Press.

Siegler, R. S. (1992). The other Alfred Binet. *Developmental Psychology, 28,* 179–190.

Sigman, M. (1998). Change and continuity in the development of children with autism. *Journal of Child Psychology and Psychiatry, 39,* 817–828.

Silk, J. S., Nath, S. R., Siegel, L. R., & Kendall, P. (2000). Conceptualizing mental disorders in children: Where have we been going and where are we going? *Development and Psychopathology, 12,* 713–735.

Silva, P. A., Hughes, P., Williams, S., & Faed, J. M. (1988). Blood lead, intelligence, reading attainment, and behaviour in eleven year old children in Dunedin, New Zealand. *Journal of Child Psychology and Psychiatry, 29,* 43–52.

Silverman, W. K., & Albano, A. M. (1996). *The Anxiety Disorders Interview Schedule for Children for DSM-IV: Clinical Manual (Child and Parent Versions).* San Antonio, TX: Psychological Corporation.

Silverman, W. K., & Dick-Niederhauser, A. (2004). Separation anxiety disorder. In T. L. Morris & J. S. March (Eds.), *Anxiety disorders in children and adolescents.* New York: Guilford Press.

Silverman, W. K., & Ginsburg, G. S. (1998). Anxiety disorders. In T. H. Ollendick & M. Hersen (Eds.), *Handbook of child psychopathology* (3rd ed.). New York: Plenum.

Silverman, W. K., & Kurtines, W. M. (2005). Progress in developing an exposure-based transfer-of-control approach to treating internalizing disorders in youth. In E. D. Hibbs & P. S. Jensen (Eds.), *Psychosocial treatments for child and adolescent disorders: Empirically based strategies for clinical practice* (2nd ed.). Washington, DC: American Psychological Association.

Silverman, W. K., Kurtines, W. M., Ginsburg, G. S., Weems, C. F., Lumpkin, P. W., & Carmichael, D. H. (1999). Treating anxiety disorders in children with group cognitive-behavior therapy: A randomized clinical trial. *Journal of Consulting and Clinical Psychology, 67,* 995–1003.

Silverman, W. K., La Greca, A. M., & Wasserstein, S. (1995). What do children worry about? Worries and their relation to anxiety. *Child Development, 66,* 671–686.

Silverman, W. K., & Moreno, J. (2005). Specific phobia. *Child and Adolescent Psychiatric Clinics of North America, 14,* 819–843.

Silverman, W. K., & Ollendick, T. H. (2005). Evidence-based assessment of anxiety and its disorders in children and adolescents. *Journal of Clinical Child and Adolescent Psychology, 34,* 380–411.

Simonoff, E., Bolton, P., & Rutter, M. (1996). Mental retardation: Genetic findings, clinical implications and research agenda. *Journal of Child Psychology and Psychiatry, 37,* 259–280.

Simonton, D. K. (2003). Qualitative and quantitative analysis of historical data. *Annual Review of Psychology, 54,* 617–640.

Simos, P. G., Fletcher, J. M., Bergman, E., Breier, J. I., Foorman, B. R., & Castillo, E. M. et al. (2002). Dyslexia-specific brain activation profile becomes normal following successful remedial training. *Neurology, 58,* 1203–1213.

Simos, P. G., Fletcher, J. M., Sarkari, S., Billingsley-Marshall, R., Denton, C. A., & Papanicolaou, A. C. (2007). Intensive instruction affects brain magnetic activity associated with oral word reading in children with reading disabilities. *Journal of Learning Disabilities, 40,* 37–48.

Singer, L., Arendt, R., Farkas, K., Minnes, S., Huang, J., & Yamashita, T. (1997). Relationship of prenatal cocaine exposure and maternal postpartum psychological distress to child development outcome. *Development and Psychopathology, 9,* 473–489.

Singh, N. N., Oswald, D. P., & Ellis, C. R. (1998). Mental retardation. In T. H. Ollendick & M. Hersen (Eds.), *Handbook of child psychopathology.* New York: Plenum Press.

Siok, W. T., Perfetti, C. A., Jin, Z., & Tan, L. H. (2004). Biological abnormality of impaired reading is constrained by culture. *Nature, 431,* 71–76.

Skinner, B. F. (1948). *Walden two.* London: Macmillan.

Skinner, B. F. (1953). *Science and human behavior.* New York: Macmillan.

Skinner, B. F. (1968). *The technology of teaching.* New York: Appleton-Century-Crofts.

Skovgaard, A. M., Houmann, T., Christiansen, E., Landorph, S., Jørgensen, T., and Copenhagen Child Cohort 2000 Study Team. (2007). The prevalence of mental health problems in children 1½ years of age—the Copenhagen Child Cohort 2000. *Journal of Child Psychology and Psychiatry, 48,* 62–70.

Slomkowski, C., Klein, R., & Mannuzza, S. (1995). Is self-esteem an important outcome in hyperactive children? *Journal of Abnormal Child Psychology, 23,* 303–315.

Sloper, P. (2000). Predictors of distress in parents of children with cancer: A prospective study. *Journal of Pediatric Psychology, 25,* 79–91.

Sloper, P., Knussen, C., Turner, S., & Cunningham, C. (1991). Factors related to stress and satisfaction with life in families of children with Down's syndrome. *Journal of Child Psychology and Psychiatry, 32,* 655–676.

Slusarek, M., Velling, S., Bunk, D., & Eggers, C. (2001). Motivational effects on inhibitory control in children with ADHD. *Journal of the American Academy of Child and Adolescent Psychiatry, 40,* 355–363.

Smith, B. H., Barkley, R. A., & Shapiro, C. J. (2006). Attention-deficit/hyperactivity disorder. In E. J. Mash & R. A. Barkley (Eds.), *Treatment of childhood disorders.* New York: The Guilford Press.

Smith, D. W., & Brodzinsky, D. M. (2002). Coping with birth parent loss in adopted children. *Journal of Child Psychology and Psychiatry, 43,* 213–223.

Smith, G. T., & Goldman, M. S. (1994). Alcohol expectancy theory and the identification of high risk adolescents. *Journal of Research on Adolescence, 4,* 229–248.

Smith, G. T., Goldman, M. S., Greenbaum, P. E., & Christiansen, B. A. (1995). Expectancy for social facilitation from drinking: The divergent paths of high-expectancy and low-expectancy adolescents. *Journal of Abnormal Psychology, 104,* 32–40.

Smith, G. T., Simmons, J. R., Flory, K., Annus, A. M., & Hill, K. K. (2007). Thinness and eating expectancies predict subsequent binge-eating and purging behavior among adolescent girls. *Journal of Abnormal Psychology, 116,* 188–197.

Smith, J. L., Johnstone, S. J., & Barry, R. J. (2003). Aiding diagnosis of attention-deficit/hyperactivity disorder and its subtypes: Discriminant function analysis of event-related potential data. *Journal of Child Psychology and Psychiatry, 44,* 1067–1075.

Smith, P. K., Cowie, H., Olafsson, R. F., & Liefooghe, P. D. (2002). Definitions of bullying: A comparison of terms used, and age and gender differences, in a fourteen country international comparison. *Child Development, 73,* 1119–1133.

Smith, S. D., Pennington, B. F., Boada, R., & Shriberg, L. D. (2005). Linkage of speech sound to reading disability loci. *Journal of Child Psychology and Psychiatry, 46,* 1057–1066.

Smith, T. (1999, Spring). Outcome of early intervention for children with autism. *Clinical Psychology: Science and Practice, 6,* 33–49.

Smith, T., Groen, A., & Wynn, J. W. (2000). Randomized trial of intensive early intervention for children with pervasive developmental disorder. *American Journal on Mental Retardation, 104,* 269–285.

Smith, T. J., & Adams, G. (2006). The effect of comorbid AD/HD and learning disabilities on parent-reported behavioral and academic outcomes of children. *Learning Disabilities Quarterly, 29,* 101–112.

Smolak, L., & Murnen, S. K. (2002). A meta-analytic examination of the relationship between child sexual abuse and eating disorders. *International Journal of Eating Disorders, 31,* 136–150.

Smolak, L., & Murnen, S. K. (2004). A feminist approach to eating disorders. In J. K. Thompson (Ed.), *Handbook of eating disorders and obesity.* Hoboken, NJ: John Wiley.

Smolak, L., Murnen, S. K., & Ruble, A. E. (2000). Female athletes and eating problems: A meta-analysis. *International Journal of Eating Disorders, 27,* 371–380.

Smyke, A. T., Koga, S. F., Johnson, D. E., Fox, N. A., Marshall, P. J., Nelson, C. A. et al. (2007). The caregiving context in institution-reared and family-reared infants and toddlers in Romania. *Journal of Child Psychology and Psychiatry, 48,* 210–218.

Snell, E. K., Adam, E. K., & Duncan, G. J. (2007). Sleep and the body mass index and overweight status of children and adolescents. *Child Development, 78,* 309–323.

Snowling, M., Bishop, D. V. M., & Stothard, S. E. (2000). Is preschool language impairment a risk factor of dyslexia in adolescence? *Journal of Child Psychology and Psychiatry, 41,* 587–600.

Snowling, M. J. (1991). Developmental reading disorders. *Journal of Child Psychology and Psychiatry, 32,* 49–77.

Snowling, M. J. (2000). Language and literacy skills: Who is at risk and why? In D. V. M. Bishop & L. B. Leonard (Eds.), *Speech and language impairments in children: Causes, characteristics, intervention and outcome.* Philadelphia: Taylor & Francis.

Snowling, M. J., Bishop, D. V. M., Stothard, S. E., Chipchase, B., & Kaplan, C. (2006). Psychosocial outcomes at 15 years of children with a preschool history of speech-language impairment. *Journal of Child Psychology and Psychiatry, 47,* 759–765.

Snowling, M. J., Gallagher, A., & Frith, U. (2003). Family risk of dyslexia is continuous: Individual differences in the precursors of reading skill. *Child Development, 74,* 358–373.

Snowling, M. J., Muter, V., & Carroll, J. (2007). Children at family risk of dyslexia: A follow-up in early adolescence. *Journal of Child Psychology and Psychiatry, 48,* 609–618.

Snyder, H. N., & Sickmund, M. (2006). *Juvenile offenders and victims: 2006 national report.* Washington, DC: U.S. Department of Justice, Office of Justice Programs, Office of Juvenile Justice and Delinquency Prevention.

Snyder, J. (2002). Reinforcement and coercion mechanisms in the development of antisocial behavior: Peer relationships. In J. B. Reid, G. R. Patterson, & J. Snyder (Eds.), *Antisocial behavior in children and adolescents: A developmental analysis and model for intervention.* Washington, DC: American Psychological Association.

Sokolov, S., & Kutcher, S. (2001). Adolescent depression: Neuroendocrine aspects. In I. M. Goodyer (Ed.), *The depressed child and adolescent* (2nd ed.). Cambridge, UK: Cambridge University Press.

Soliday, E., Kool, E., & Lande, M. B. (2000). Psychosocial adjustment in children with kidney disease. *Journal of Pediatric Psychology, 25,* 93–103.

Sonuga-Barke, E. J. S. (1994). On dysfunction and function in psychological theories of childhood disorder. *Journal of Child Psychology and Psychiatry, 35,* 801–815.

Sonuga-Barke, E. J. S. (1998). Categorical models of childhood disorder: A conceptual and empirical analysis. *Journal of Child Psychology and Psychiatry, 39,* 115–133.

Sonuga-Barke, E. J. S., Dalen, L., & Remington, B. (2003). Do executive deficits and delay aversion make independent contributions to preschool attention-deficit/hyperactivity disorder? *Journal of the American Academy of Child and Adolescent Psychiatry, 42,* 1335–1342.

Sonuga-Barke, E. J. S., De Houwer, J., De Ruiter, K., Ajzenstzen, M., & Hollands, S. (2004). AD/HD and the capture of attention by briefly exposed delay-related cues: Evidence from a conditioning paradigm. *Journal of Child Psychology and Psychiatry, 45,* 274–283.

Sourander, A., Jensen, P., Davies, M., Niemelä, S., Elonheimo, H., Ristkari, T., et al. (2007). Who is at greatest risk of adverse long-term outcomes? The Finnish From a Boy to a Man Study. *Journal of the American Academy of Child and Adolescent Psychiatry, 46,* 1148–1161.

Sourander, A., Santalahti, P., Haavisto, A., Piha, J., Ikäheimo, K., & Helenius, H. (2004). Have there been changes in children's psychiatric symptoms and mental health service use? A 10-year comparison from Finland. *Journal of the American Academy of Child and Adolescent Psychiatry, 43,* 1134–1145.

Sowell, E. R., Thompson, P. M., Welcome, S. E., Henkenius, A. L., Toga, A, W., & Peterson, B. S. (2003). Cortical abnormalities in children and adolescents with attention-deficit hyperactivity disorder. *The Lancet, 362,* 1699–1707.

Spafford, P. A., von Baeyer, C. L., & Hicks, C. L. (2002). Expected and reported pain in children undergoing ear piercing: A randomized trial of preparation by parents. *Behaviour Research and Therapy, 40,* 37–50.

Sparrow, S. S., & Cicchetti, D. V., & Balla, D. A. (2005). *Vineland Adaptive Behavior Scales-Second Edition (Vineland-II).* Bloomington, MN: American Guidance Service.

Spector, S. G., & Volkmar, F. R. (2006). Autism spectrum disorders. In D. A. Wolfe & E. J. Mash (Eds.), *Behavioral and emotional disorders in adolescents. Nature, assessment, and treatment.* New York: The Guilford Press.

Spence, S. H., Sheffield, J., & Donovan, C. L. (2003). Preventing adolescent depression: An evaluation of the Problem Solving for Life program. *Journal of Consulting and Clinical Psychology, 71,* 3–13.

Spence, S. H., Sheffield, J., & Donovan, C. L. (2005). Long-term outcome of a school-based universal approach to prevention of depression in adolescents. *Journal of Consulting and Clinical Psychology, 73,* 160–167.

Spence, S. H., & Shortt, A. L. (2007). Research review: Can we justify the widespread dissemination of universal, school-based interventions for the prevention of depression among children and adolescents? *Journal of Child Psychology and Psychiatry, 48,* 526–542.

Spencer, M. B., Harpalani, V., Cassidy, E., Jacobs, C. Y., Donde, S., Goss, T. N. et al. (2006). Understanding vulnerability and resilience from a normative developmental perspective: Implications for racially and ethnically diverse youth. In D. Cicchetti & D. J. Cohen (Eds.), *Developmental Psychopathology. Vol. 1. Theory and method.* Hoboken, New York: John Wiley & Sons.

Spessot, A. L., & Peterson, B. S. (2006). Tourette's syndrome: A multifactorial, developmental psychopathology. In D. Cicchetti & D. J. Cohen (Eds.), *Developmental psychopathology. Vol. 3. Risk, disorder, and adaptation* (2nd ed.). Hoboken, NJ: John Wiley & Sons.

Spicer, P. & Sarche, M. C. (2006). Responding to the crisis in American Indian and Alaska Native children's mental health. In H. E. Fitzgerald, B. M. Lester, & B. Zuckerman (Eds.) *The crisis in youth mental health. Childhood disorders. Vol. 1.* Westport, CT: Praeger Publishers.

Spielberger, C. D. (1973). *Manual for the State-Trait Anxiety Inventory for Children.* Lutz, FL: Psychological Assessment Resources, Inc.

Spinath, F. M., Price, T. S., Dale, P. S., & Plomin, R. (2004). The genetic and environmental origins of language disability and ability. *Child Development, 75,* 445–454.

Spirito, A., Stark, L. J., & Tyc, V. L. (1994). Stressors and coping strategies described during hospitalization by chronically ill children. *Journal of Clinical Child Psychology, 23,* 314–322.

Spitz, R. A. (1946). Anaclitic depression. In *The psychoanalytic study of the child,* Vol. 2. New York: International Universities Press.

Spitzer, R. L., Gibbon, M., Skodol, A. E., Williams, J. B. W., & First, M. B. (2000). *DSM-IV-TR case book.* Washington, DC: American Psychiatric Publishing.

Spock, B. M., & Rothenberg, M. (1992). *Dr. Spock's baby and child care.* New York: Pocket Books.

Spring, B., Chiodo, J., & Bowen, D. J. (1987). Carbohydrates, tryptophan, and behavior: A methodological review. *Psychological Bulletin, 102,* 234–256.

Springer, K. W., Sheridan, J., Kuo, D., & Carnes, M. (2007). Long-term physical and mental health consequences of childhood physical abuse: Results from a large population-based sample of men and women. *Child Abuse & Neglect, 31,* 517–530.

Sroufe, L. A. (1997). Psychopathology as an outcome of development. *Development and Psychopathology, 9,* 251–268.

Sroufe, L. A., Duggal, S., Weinfeld, N., & Carlson, E. (2000). Relationships, development, and psychopathology. In A. J. Sameroff, M. Lewis, & S. M. Miller (Eds.), *Handbook of developmental psychopathology* (2nd ed.). New York: Kluwer Academic/Plenum Publishers.

Sroufe, L. A., Egeland, B., Carlson, E. A., & Collins, W. A. (2005). *The development of the person.* New York: The Guilford Press.

Sroufe, L. A., & Rutter, M. (1984). The domain of developmental psychopathology. *Child Development, 55,* 17–29.

St. Pierre, R. G., & Layzer, J. I. (1998). Improving the life chances of children in poverty: Assumptions and what we have learned. Social Policy Report. *Society for Research in Child Development.* Vol. XII (4).

Stahl, A. (1991). Beliefs of Jewish-Oriental mothers regarding children who are mentally retarded. *Education and Training in Mental Retardation, 26,* 361–369.

Standart, S., & Le Couteur, A. (2003). The quiet child: A literature review of selective mutism. *Child and Adolescent Mental Health, 8,* 154–160.

Stanger, C., Achenbach, T. M., & Verhulst, F. C. (1997). Accelerated longitudinal comparisons of aggressive versus delinquent syndromes. *Development and Psychopathology, 9,* 43–58.

Stanger, C., MacDonald, V. V., McConaughy, S. H., & Achenbach, T. M. (1996). Predictors of cross-informant syndromes among children and youths referred for mental health services. *Journal of Abnormal Child Psychology. 24,* 597–614.

Stanovich, K. E. (1989). Learning disabilities in broader context. *Journal of Learning Disabilities, 22,* 287–291, 297.

Stark, K. D., Hargrave, J., Sander, J., Custer, G., Schnoebelen, S., Simpson, J., & Molnar, J. (2006). Treatment of childhood depression: The ACTION treatment program. In P. C. Kendall (Ed.), *Child and adolescent therapy: Cognitive-behavioral procedures.* (3rd ed.). New York: Guilford Press.

Stark, K. D., Rouse, L. W., & Kurowski, C. (1994). Psychological treatment approaches for depression in children. In W. M. Reynolds & H. F. Johnston (Eds.), *Handbook of depression in children and adolescents.* New York: Plenum Press.

Stark, K. D., Sander, J. B., Yancy, M. G., Bronik, M., & Hoke, J. A. (2000). Treatment of depression in childhood and adolescence: Cognitive-behavioral procedures for the individual and family. In P. C. Kendall (Ed.), *Child and adolescent therapy: Cognitive-behavioral procedures* (2nd ed.). New York: The Guilford Press.

Stark, K. D., Schmidt, K. L., & Joiner, T. E. (1996). Cognitive triad: Relationship to depressive symptoms, parents' cognitive triad, and perceived parental messages. *Journal of Abnormal Child Psychology, 24,* 615–631.

State of the World's Children. (2000). UNICEF, United Nations. Online, unicef.org/sowc/stat_tab.htm. March 21, 2002.

State, M. W., King, B. H., & Dykens, B. (1997). Mental retardation: A review of the past 10 years. Part II. *Journal of the American Academy of Child and Adolescent Psychiatry, 36,* 1664–1671.

Staub, D., & Peck, C. A. (January 1994/December 1995). What are the outcomes for nondisabled students? *Educational Leadership, 52,* 36–40.

Steele, C. M. (1997). A threat in the air: How stereotypes shape intellectual identity and performance. *American Psychologist, 52,* 613–629.

Steele, R. G., Nelson, T. D., & Cole, B. P. (2007). Psychosocial functioning of children with AIDS and HIV infection: Review of the literature from a sociological framework. *Journal of Developmental & Behavioral Pediatrics, 28,* 58–69.

Steffenburg, S., Gillberg, C., Hellgren, L., Andersson, L., Gillberg, I. C., Jakobsson, G., & Bohman, M. (1989). A twin study of autism in Denmark, Finland, Iceland, Norway and Sweden. *Journal of Child Psychology and Psychiatry, 30,* 405–416.

Steinberg, A. B., & Phares, V. (2001). Family functioning, body image, and eating disturbances. In J. K. Thompson & L. Smolak (Eds.), *Body image, eating disorders, and obesity in youth: Assessment, prevention, and treatment.* Washington, DC: American Psychological Association.

Steinberg, L., Lamborn, S. D., Darling, N., Mounts, N. S., & Dornbusch, S. M. (1994). Over-time changes in adjustment and competence among adolescents from authoritive, authoritarian, indulgent, and neglectful families. *Child Development, 65,* 754–770.

Steiner-Adair, C., Sjostrom, L., Franko, D. L., Pai, S., Tucker, R., Becker, A.E. et al. (2002). Primary prevention of eating disorders in adolescent girls: Learning from practice. *International Journal of Eating Disorders, 32,* 401–411.

Steinhausen, H. C. (1997). Outcome of anorexia nervosa in the younger patient. *Journal of Child Psychology and Psychiatry, 38,* 271–276.

Sterba, S. K., Prinstein, M. J., & Cox, M. J. (2007). Trajectories of internalizing problems across childhood: Heterogeneity, external validity, and gender differences. *Development and Psychopathology, 19,* 345–366.

Stern, M., Mazzeo, S. E., Gerke, C. K., Porter, J. S., Bean, M. K., & Laver, J. H. (2007). Gender, ethnicity, psychological factors, and quality of life among severely overweight, treatment-seeking adolescents. *Journal of Pediatric Psychology, 32,* 90–94.

Sternberg, R. J., Wagner, R. K., Williams, W. M., & Horvath, J. A. (1995). Testing common sense. *American Psychologist, 50,* 912–927.

Stetson, E. G., & Stetson, R. (2001). Educational assessment. In C. E. Walker & M. C. Roberts (Eds.), *Handbook of clinical child psychology* (3rd ed.). New York: John Wiley & Sons.

Stevens, M. C., Fein, D. A. Dunn, M., Allen, D., Waterhouse, L. H., Feinstein, C., & Rapin, I. (2000). Subgroups of children with autism by cluster analysis: A longitudinal examination. *Journal of the American Academy of Child & Adolescent Psychiatry, 39,* 346–352.

Stevenson, J. (1996). Developmental changes in the mechanisms linking language disabilities and behavior disorders. In J. H. Beitchman, N. J. Cohen, M. M. Konstantareas, & R. Tannock (Eds.), *Language, learning, and behavior disorders.* New York: Cambridge University Press.

Stevenson, J., & Fredman, G. (1990). The social environmental correlates of reading ability. *Journal of Child Psychology and Psychiatry, 31,* 681–698.

Stevenson, J., Langley, K., Pay, H., Payton, A., Worthington, J., Ollier, W. et al. (2005). Attention-deficit hyperactivity disorder with reading disabilities: Preliminary genetic findings on the involvement of the ADRA2A gene. *Journal of Child Psychology and Psychiatry, 46,* 1081–1088.

Stewart, A. J., Steiman, M., Cauce, A. M., Cochran, B. N., Whitbeck, L. B., & Hoyt, D. R. (2004). Victimization and posttraumatic stress disorder among homeless adolescents. *Journal of the American Academy of Child and Adolescent Psychiatry, 43,* 325–331.

Stewart, S. M., Kennard, B. D., Lee, P. W. H., Hughes, C. W., Mayes, T. L., Emslie, G. J., & Lewinsohn, P. M. (2004). A cross-cultural investigation of cognitions and depressive symptoms in adolescents. *Journal of Abnormal Psychology, 113,* 248–257.

Stewart, T. M., & Williamson, D. A. (2004). Assessment of body image disturbances. In J. K. Thompson (Ed.), *Handbook of eating disorders and obesity.* Hoboken, NJ: John Wiley.

Stice, E., & Bearman, S. K. (2001). Body image and eating disturbances prospectively predict increases in depressive symptoms in adolescent girls: A growth curve analysis. *Developmental Psychology, 37,* 1–11.

Stice, E., Shaw, H., & Marti, C. N. (2006). A meta-analytic review of obesity prevention programs for children and adolescents: The skinny on interventions that work. *Psychological Bulletin, 132,* 667–691.

Stiffman, A. R., Alexander-Eitzman, B., Silmere, H., Osborne, V., & Brown, E. (2007). From early to late adolescence: American Indian youths' behavioral trajectories and their major influences. *Journal of the American Academy of Child and Adolescent Psychiatry, 46,* 849–859.

Stinton, M. M., & Birch, L. L. (2005). Weight status and psychosocial factors predict the emergence of dieting in preadolescent girls. *International Journal of Eating Disorders, 38,* 346–354.

Stone, W. L. (1997). Autism in infancy and early childhood. In D. J. Cohen & F. R. Volkmar (Eds.), *Handbook of autism and pervasive developmental disorders.* New York: John Wiley.

Stoneman, Z., & Gavidia-Payne, S. (2006). Marital adjustment in families of young children with disabilities: Associations with daily hassles and problem-focused coping. *American Journal on Mental Retardation, 111,* 1–14.

Storch, E. A., Milsom, V. A., DeBraganza, N., Lewin, A. B., Geffken, G. R., & Silverstein, J. H. (2007). Peer victimization, psychosocial adjustment, and physical activity in overweight and at-risk-for-overweight youth. *Journal of Pediatric Psychology, 32,* 80–89.

Stores, G. (1996). Assessment and treatment of sleep disorders in children and adolescents. *Journal of Child Psychology and Psychiatry, 37,* 907–925.

Stormshak, E. A., Dishion, T. J., Light, J., & Yasui, M. (2005). Implementing family-centered interventions within the public middle school: Linking service delivery to change in problem behavior. *Journal of Abnormal Child Psychology, 33,* 723–733.

Strauss, C. C. (1994). Overanxious disorder. In T. H. Ollendick, N. J. King, & W. Yule (Eds.), *International handbook of phobic and anxiety disorders in children and adolescents.* New York: Plenum Press.

Strauss, C. C., & Last, C. G. (1993). Social and simple phobias in children. *Journal of Anxiety Disorders, 7,* 141–152.

Strauss, C. C., Lease, C. A., Last, C. G., & Francis, G. (1988). Overanxious disorder: An examination of developmental differences. *Journal of Abnormal Child Psychology, 16,* 433–443.

Strein, W., Hoagwood, K., & Cohn, A. (2003). School psychology: A public health perspective I. Prevention, populations, and systems change. *School Psychology, 41,* 23–38.

Streisand, R., & Efron, L. A. (2003). Pediatric sleep disorders. In M. C. Roberts (Ed.), *Handbook of pediatric psychology* (3rd ed.). New York: Guilford Press.

Streissguth, A. P., Bookstein, F. L., Sampson, P. D., & Barr, H. M. (1995). Attention: Prenatal alcohol and continuities of vigilance and attentional problems from 4 through 14 years. *Development and Psychopathology, 7,* 419–446.

Strickland, B. R. (2000). Misassumptions, misadventures, and the misuse of psychology. *American Psychologist, 55,* 331–338.

Striegel-Moore, R. H., & Bulik, C. M. (2007). Risk factors for eating disorders. *American Psychologist, 62,* 181–198.

Stuber, J., Fairbrother, G., Galea, S. Pfefferbaum, B., Wilson-Genderson, M., & Vlahov, D. (2002). Determinants of counseling for children in Manhattan after the September 11 attacks. *Psychiatric Services, 53,* 815–822.

Stuber, M. L., & Shemesh, E. (2006). Post-traumatic stress response to life-threatening illness in children and their parents. *Child and Adolescent Psychiatric Clinics of North America, 15,* 597–609.

Sturmey, P. (2005). Against psychotherapy with people who have mental retardation. *Mental Retardation, 43,* 55–57.

Sue, S. (2003). In defense of cultural competency in psychotherapy and treatment. *American Psychologist, 58,* 964–970.

Sullivan, P. F., Kendler, K. S., & Neale, M. C. (2003). Schizophrenia as a complex trait. *Archives of General Psychiatry, 60,* 1187–1192.

Susman, E. J. (1993). Psychological, contextual, and psychobiological interactions: A developmental perspective on conduct disorder. *Development and Psychopathology, 5,* 181–189.

Sutcliffe, J. S., & Nurmi, E. L. (2003). Genetics of childhood disorders: XLVII. Autism, Part 6: Duplication and inherited susceptibility of chromosome 15q11-q13 genes in autism. *Journal of the American Academy of Child and Adolescent Psychiatry, 42,* 253–256.

Sutton, P. D. (2003). Births, marriages, divorces, and deaths: Provisional data for October–December 2002. *National Vital Statistics Reports* (Vol. 51). Hyattsville, MD: National Center for Health Statistics.

Suveg, C., Aschenbrand, S. G., & Kendall, P. C. (2005). Separation anxiety disorder, panic disorder, and school refusal. *Child and Adolescent Psychiatric Clinics of North America, 14,* 773–795.

Swaab-Barneveld, H., de Sonneville, L., Cohen-Kettenis, P., Gielen, A., Buitelaar, J., & van Engeland, H. (2000). Visual sustained attention in a child psychiatric population. *Journal of the American Academy of Child and Adolescent Psychiatry, 39,* 651–659.

Swain, J. E., Lorberbaum, J. P., Kose, S., & Strathearn, L. (2007). Brain basis of early parent-infant interactions: psychology, physiology, and *in vivo* functional neuroimaging studies. *Journal of Child Psychology and Psychiatry, 48,* 262–287.

Swain, J. E., Scahill, L., Lombroso, P. J., King, R. A., & Leckman, J. F. (2007). Tourette disorder and tic disorders: A decade of progress. *Journal of the American Academy of Child and Adolescent Psychiatry, 46,* 947–968.

Swanson, H. L., & Hoskyn, M. (1998). Experimental intervention research on students with learning disabilities: A meta-analysis of treatment outcomes. *Review of Educational Research, 68,* 277–321.

Swanson, H. L. & Hoskyn, M. (2001). Instructing adolescents with learning disabilities: A component and composite analysis. *Learning Disabilities Research & Practice, 16,* 109–119.

Swanson, J. M., McBurnett, K., Christian, D. L., & Wigal, T. (1995). Stimulant medications and the treatment of children with ADHD. In T. H. Ollendick & R. J. Prinz (Eds.), *Advances in clinical child psychology.* New York: Plenum Press.

Swedo, S. E., Rapoport, J. L., Leonard, H., Lenane, M., & Cheslow, D. (1989c). Obsessive-compulsive disorder in children and adolescents: Clinical phenomenology of 70 consecutive cases. *Archives of General Psychiatry, 46,* 335–341.

Szatmari, P., MacLean, J. E., Jones, M. B., Bryson, S. E., Zwaigenbaum, L., Bartolucci, G. et al. (2000). The familial aggregation of the lesser variant in biological and nonbiological relatives of PDD probands: A family history study. *Journal of Child Psychology and Psychiatry, 41,* 579–586.

Szymanski, L. S., & Crocker, A. C. (1985). Mental retardation. In H. I. Kaplan & B. J. Sadock (Eds.), *Comprehensive textbook of psychiatry/IV.* Baltimore: Williams and Wilkins.

Tager-Flüsberg, H. (1993). What language reveals about the understanding of minds in children with autism. In S. Baron-Cohen, H. Tager-Flüsberg, & D. J. Cohen (Eds.), *Understanding other minds.* New York: Oxford.

Tager-Flüsberg, H. (1997). Perspectives on language and communication in autism. In D. J. Cohen & F. R. Volkmar (Eds.), *Handbook of autism and pervasive developmental disorders.* New York: John Wiley.

Talge, N. M., Neal, C., Glover, V. (2007). Antenatal maternal stress and long-term effects on child neurodevelopment: how and why? *Journal of Child Psychology and Psychiatry, 48,* 245–261.

Tallal, P., & Benasich, A. A. (2002). Developmental language learning impairments. *Development and Psychopathology, 14,* 559–579.

Tanguay, P. E. (2000). Pervasive developmental disorders: A 10-year review. *Journal of the American Academy of Child and Adolescent Psychiatry, 39,* 1079–1095.

Tannock, R. (1998). Attention deficit hyperactivity disorder: Advances in cognitive, neurobiological, and genetic research. *Journal of Child Psychology and Psychiatry, 39,* 65–99.

Tannock, R. (2005a). Disorders of written expression and learning disorders not otherwise specified. In B. J. Sadock & V. A. Sadock (Eds.), *Comprehensive textbook of psychiatry.* Philadelphia: Lippincott Williams and Wilkens.

Tannock, R. (2005b). Mathematics disorder. In B. J. Sadock & V. A. Sadock (Eds.), *Comprehensive textbook of psychiatry.* Philadelphia: Lippincott Williams and Wilkens.

Tannock, R. (2005c). Reading disorder. In B. J. Sadock & V. A. Sadock (Eds.), *Comprehensive textbook of psychiatry.* Philadelphia: Lippincott Williams and Wilkens.

Tantleff-Dunn, S., Gokee-LaRose, J., & Peterson, R. D. (2004). Interpersonal psychotherapy for the treatment of anorexia nervosa, bulimia nervosa, and binge eating disorder. In J. K. Thompson (Ed.), *Handbook of eating disorders and obesity.* Hoboken, NJ: John Wiley.

Taylor, B., Miller, E., Farrington, C. P., Petropoulos, M-C., Favot-Mayaud, I., Li, J., & Waight, P. A. (1999). Autism and measles, mumps and rubella vaccine: No epidemiological evidence for a causal association. *Lancet, 353,* 2026–2029.

Taylor, E. (1994). Syndromes of attention deficit and hyperactivity. In M. Rutter, E. Taylor, & L. Hersov (Eds.), *Child and adolescent psychiatry: Modern approaches.* New York: Blackwell Scientific.

Taylor, E. (1995). Dysfunctions of attention. In D. Cicchetti & D. J. Cohen (Eds.), *Developmental psychopathology.* New York: John Wiley.

Taylor, E., & Rogers, J. W. (2005). Practitioner review: Early adversity and developmental disorders. *Journal of Child Psychology and Psychiatry, 46,* 451–467.

Taylor, H. G. (1988). Learning disabilities. In E. J. Mash & L. G. Terdal (Eds.), *Behavioral assessment of childhood disorders* (2nd ed.). New York: Guilford.

Taylor, H. G. (1989). Learning disabilities. In E. J. Mash & R. A. Barkley (Eds.), *Treatment of childhood disorders.* New York: Guilford.

Taylor, J., Iacono, W. G., & McGue, M. (2000). Evidence for a genetic etiology of early-onset delinquency. *Journal of Abnormal Psychology, 109,* 634–643.

Tennant, C. (1988). Parental loss in childhood: Its effects in adult life. *Archives of General Psychiatry, 45,* 1045–1050.

Tercyak, K. P., Donze, J. R., Prahlad, S., Mosher, R. B., & Shad, A. T. (2006). Identifying, recruiting, and enrolling adolescent survivors of childhood cancer into a randomized controlled trial of health promotion: Preliminary experiences in the Survivor Health and Resilience Education (SHARE) Program. *Journal of Pediatric Psychology, 31,* 252–261.

Terr, L. (1979). Children of Chowchilla. *The Psychoanalytic Study of the Child, 34,* 522–563.

Terr, L. (1983). Chowchilla revisited: The effects of psychic trauma four years after a school-bus kidnapping. *American Journal of Psychiatry, 140,* 1543–1550.

Tesman, J. R., & Hills, A. (1994). Developmental effects of lead exposure in children. *Social Policy Report. Society for Research in Child Development, VIII (3),* 1–16.

Thabet, A. A. M., Abed, Y., & Vostanis, P. (2004). Comorbidity of PTSD and depression among refugee children during war conflict. *Journal of Child Psychology and Psychiatry, 45,* 533–542.

Thapar, A., Gottesman, I. I., Owen, M. J., O'Donovan, M., & McGuffin, P. (1994). The genetics of mental retardation. *British Journal of Psychiatry, 164,* 747–758.

Thase, M. E., Jindal, R., & Howland, R. H. (2002). Biological aspects of depression. In I. H. Gotlib & C. L. Hammen (Eds.), *Handbook of depression.* New York: The Guilford Press.

Thelen, E., & Adolph, K. E. (1992). Arnold L. Gessell: The paradox of nature and nurture. *Developmental Psychology, 28,* 368–380.

Thelen, M. H., Powell, A. L., Lawrence, C., & Kuhnert, M. E. (1992). Eating and body image concerns among children. *Journal of Consulting and Clinical Psychology, 21,* 41–46.

Them, M. A., Israel, A. C., Ivanova, M. Y., & Chalmers, S. M. (2003). *An investigation of the assessment of and of and relationships between various aspects of family stability.* Boston, MA: Association for the Advancement of Behavior Therapy.

Thomas, A. M., Peterson, L., & Goldstein, D. (1997). Problem solving and diabetes regimen adherence by children and adolescents with IDDM in social pressure situations: A reflection on normal development. *Journal of Pediatric Psychology, 22,* 541–561.

Thompson, J. K., & Smolak, L. (2001). Body image, eating disorders, and obesity in youth—The future is now. In J. K. Thompson & L. Smolak (Eds.), *Body image, eating disorders, and obesity in youth: Assessment, prevention, and treatment.* Washington, DC: American Psychological Association.

Thompson, J. R., Bryant, B. R., Campbell, E. M., Craig, E. M., Hughes, C., Rotholz, D. R. et al. (2004). *Supports intensity scale.* Washington, DC: AAIDD.

Thompson, J. R., & McEvoy, M. A. (1992). Letters to the editor. Normalization—still relevant today. *Journal of Autism and Developmental Disorders, 22,* 666–671.

Thompson, R. A. (2000). The legacy of early attachments. *Child Development, 71,* 145–152.

Thomson, G. O. B., Raab, G. M., Hepburn, W. S., Hunter, R., Fulton, M., & Laxen, D. P. H. (1989). Blood-lead levels and children's behaviour—results from the Edinburgh Lead Study. *Journal of Child Psychology and Psychiatry, 30,* 515–528.

Thorell, L. B. (2007). Do delay aversion and executive function deficits make distinct contributions to the functional impact of ADHD symptoms? A study of early academic skill deficits. *Journal of Child Psychology and Psychiatry, 48,* 1061–1070.

Thorndike, E. L. (1905). *The elements of psychology.* New York: Seiler.

Thurber, C. A., & Sigman, M. D. (1998). Preliminary models of risk and protective factors for childhood homesickness: Review and empirical synthesis. *Child Development, 69,* 903–934.

Tienari, P., Lahti, I., Sorri, A., Naarala, M., Moring, J., Kaleva, M., Wahlberg, K-E., & Wynne, L. C. (1990). Adopted-away offspring of schizophrenics and controls: The Finnish adoptive family study of schizophrenia. In L. N. Robins & M. Rutter (Eds.), *Straight and devious pathways from childhood to adulthood.* New York: Cambridge University Press.

Tienari, P., Wynne, L. C., & Wahlberg, K.E. (2006). Genetics and family relationships in schizophrenia and the schizophrenia spectrum disorders. In S. M. Miller, S. H. McDaniel, J. S. Rolland, & S. L. Feetham (Eds.). *Individuals, families, and the new era of genetics.* New York: W. W. Norton & Co.

Tillman, R., Geller, B., Bolhofner, K., Craney, J. L., Williams, M., & Zimerman, B. (2003). Ages of onset and rates of syndromal and subsyndromal comorbid DSM-IV diagnosis in a prepubertal and early adolescent bipolar disorder phenotype. *Journal of the American Academy of Child and Adolescent Psychiatry, 42,* 1486–1493.

Timko, C., Baumgartner, M., Moos, R. H., & Miller, J. III (1993). Parental risk and resistance factors among children with juvenile rheumatic disease: A four-year predictive study. *Journal of Behavioral Medicine, 16,* 571–588.

Todd, R. D., Huang, H., Smalley, S. L., Nelson, S. F., Willcutt, E. G., Pennington, B. F. et al. (2005). Collaborative analysis of DRD4 and DAT genotypes in population-defined ADHD subtypes. *Journal of Child Psychology and Psychiatry, 46,* 1067–1073.

Tolan, P. H., & Dodge, K. A. (2005). Children's mental health as a primary care and concern: A system for comprehensive support and service. *American Psychologist, 60,* 602–614.

Tolan, P. H., & Thomas, P. (1995). The implications of age of onset for delinquency risk II: Longitudinal data. *Journal of Abnormal Child Psychology, 23,* 157–181.

Tolani, N., & Brooks-Gunn, J. (2005). Are there socioeconomic disparities in children's mental health? In H. E. Fitzgerald, B. M. Lester, & B. Zuckerman (Eds.), *The crisis in youth mental health. Vol. 1.* Westport, CT: Praeger.

Tomblin, J. B. (2006). A normativist account of language-based learning disability. *Learning Disabilities Research & Practice, 21,* 8–18.

Tomblin, J. B., Zhang, X., Buckwalter, P., & Catts, H. (2000). The association of reading disability, behavioral disorders, and language impairment among second-grade children. *Journal of Child Psychology and Psychiatry, 41,* 473–482.

Tomblin, J. B., Zhang, X., Buckwalter, P., & O'Brien, M. (2003). The stability of primary language disorder: Four years after kindergarten diagnosis. *Journal of Speech, Language, and Hearing Research, 46,* 1283–1296.

Tomporowski, P. D., & Tinsley, V. (1997). Attention in mentally retarded persons. In W. E. MacLean (Ed.), *Ellis' handbook of mental deficiency, psychological theory and research.* Mahwah, NJ: Lawrence Erlbaum.

Tonge, B. (1994). Separation anxiety disorder. In T. H. Ollendick, N. J. King, & W. Yule (Eds.), *International handbook of phobic and anxiety disorders in children and adolescents.* New York: Plenum Press.

Toppelberg, C. O., Medrano, L., Pena Morgens, L., & Nieto-Castanon, A. (2002). Bilingual children referred for psychiatric services: Associations of language disorders, language skills, and psychopathology. *Journal of the American Academy of Child and Adolescent Psychiatry, 41,* 712–722.

Toppelberg, C. O., & Shapiro, T. (2000). Language disorders: A 10-year research update review. *Journal of the American Academy of Child and Adolescent Psychiatry, 39,* 143–152.

Torbeyns, J., Verschaffel, L., & Ghesquière, P. (2004). Strategy development in children with mathematical disabilities: Insights from the choice/no-choice method and the chronological-age/ability-level-match design. *Journal of Learning Disabilities, 37,* 119–131.

Torgesen, J. K., Alexander, A. W., Wagner, R. K., Rashotte, C. A., Voeller, K. K. S., & Conway, T. (2001). Intensive remedial instruction for children with severe reading disabilities: Immediate and long-term outcomes from two instructional approaches. *Journal of Learning Disabilities, 34,* 33–58, 78.

Toro, P. A., Weissberg, R. P., Guare, J., & Liebenstein, N. L. (1990). A comparison of children with and without learning disabilities on social problem-solving skill, school behavior, and family background. *Journal of Learning Disabilities, 23,* 115–120.

Treatment for Adolescents with Depression Study (TADS) Team. (2004). Fluoxetine, cognitive-behavioral therapy, and their combination for adolescents with depression: Treatment for Adolescents with Depression Study (TADS) randomized controlled trial. *Journal of the American Medical Association, 292,* 807–820.

Treatment for Adolescents with Depression Study (TADS) Team. (2005). The Treatment for Adolescents with Depression Study (TADS): Demographic and clinical characteristics. *Journal of the American Academy of Child & Adolescent Psychiatry, 44,* 28–40.

Treffert, D. A. (1988). The idiot savant: A review of the syndrome. *American Journal of Psychiatry, 145,* 563–572.

Tremblay, G. C., & Israel, A. C. (1998). Children's adjustment to parental death. *Clinical Psychology: Science and Practice, 5,* 424–438.

Tremblay, G. C., & Peterson, L. (1999). Prevention of childhood injury: Clinical and public policy issues. *Clinical Psychology Review, 19,* 415–434.

Tremblay, R. E., Nagin, D. S., Seguin, J. R., Zoccolillo, M., Zelazo, P. D., Boivin, M. et al. (2004). Physical aggression during early childhood: Trajectories and predictors. *Pediatrics, 114,* E43–E50.

Trevarthen, C., & Aitken, K. J. (2001). Infant intersubjectivity: Research, theory, and clinical applications. *Journal of Child Psychology and Psychiary, 42,* 3–48.

Trickett, P. K., Allen, L., Schellenbach, C. J., & Zigler, E. F. (1998). Integrating and advancing the knowledge base about violence against children: Implications for intervention and prevention. In P. K. Trickett & C. J. Schellenbach (Eds.), *Violence against children in the family and the community.* Washington, DC: American Psychological Association.

Tripp, G., & Alsop, B. (2001). Sensitivity to reward delay in children with attention deficit hyperactivity disorder (ADHD). *Journal of Child and Adolescent Psychology, 42,* 691–698.

Trzesniewski, K. H., Moffitt, T. E., Caspi, A., Taylor, A., & Maughan, B. (2006). Revisiting the association between reading achievement and antisocial behavior: New evidence of an environmental explanation from a twin study. *Child Development, 77,* 72–88.

Tully, L. A., Arseneault, L., Caspi, A., Moffit, T. E., & Morgan, J. (2004). Does maternal warmth moderate the effects of birthweight on twins' Attention-Deficit/Hyperactivity Disorder (ADHD) symptoms and low IQ? *Journal of Consulting and Clinical Psychology, 72,* 218–226.

Turnbull, A. P. (2004). President's address 2004: "Wearing two hats": Morphed perspectives on family quality of life. *Mental Retardation, 42,* 383–399.

Turner, L. M., & Stone, W. L. (2007). Variability in outcome for children with ASD diagnosis at age 2. *Journal of Child Psychology and Psychiatry, 48,* 793–802.

Turner, M. (1999). Annotation: Repetitive behaviour in autism: A review of psychological research. *Journal of Child Psychology and Psychiatry, 40,* 839–849.

U.S. Bureau of the Census. (1998). *Statistical Abstract of the United States: 1998* (118th ed.). Washington, DC: U.S. Government Printing Office.

U.S. Bureau of the Census. (2001). *Statistical Abstract of the United States: 2001* (121st ed.). Washington, DC: U.S. Government Printing Office.

U.S. Bureau of the Census. (2003). *Statistical abstract of the United States: 2003* (123rd ed.). Washington, DC: U.S. Government Printing Office.

U.S. Bureau of the Census. (2004). *Statistical Abstract of the United States, 2004. The National Data Book* (124th ed.). Washington, DC: U.S. Government Printing Office.

U.S. Census Bureau. (2003). *Adopted children and stepchildren: 2000.* Retrieved May 2007 from http://www.census.gov.

U.S. Census Bureau. (2005). *Current population survey, annual social and social and economic supplements.* Retrieved May 2007 from http://www.census.gov.

U.S. Department of Education. (2000). *Summary—Twenty-second Annual Report to Congress on the Implementation of the Individuals with Disabilities Education Act.* Retrieved August 16, 2004, from http://www.ed.gov.

U.S. Department of Education. (2007). National Center for Educational Statistics. Digest of Education Statistics. Retrieved November 20, 2007, from http://nces.ed.gov/programs/digest/d06/tables/dt06_048.asp

U.S. Department of Health and Human Services. (2005). *Code of Federal Regulations, Title 45, Public Welfare.* Revised June 23, 2005.

U.S. Department of Health and Human Services, Administration on Children, Youth and Families. (2007). *Child maltreatment 2005.* Washington, DC: Government Printing Office.

U.S. Food and Drug Administration. (2007). *Revisions to product labeling.* Retrieved July 11, 2007, from http://www.fda.gov/cder/drug/antidepressants/antidepressants_label_change_2007.pdf.

U.S. Office of Education. (1977). Definition and criteria for defining students as learning disabled. Federal Register, 42:250, p. 65083. Washington, DC: U.S. Government Printing Office.

Ullmann, L. P., & Krasner, L. (1975). *A psychological approach to abnormal behavior* (2nd ed.). Englewood Cliffs, NJ: Prentice Hall.

Ulloa, R. L. et al. (2000). Psychosis in a pediatric mood and anxiety disorders clinic: Phenomenology and correlates. *Journal of the American Academy of Child and Adolescent Psychiatry, 39,* 337–345.

Valone, K., Goldstein, M. J., & Norton, J. P. (1984). Parental expressed emotion and psychophysiological reactivity in an adolescent sample at risk for schizophrenia spectrum disorder. *Journal of Abnormal Psychology, 93,* 448–457.

Van Acker, R. (1997). Rett's syndrome: A pervasive developmental disorder. In D. J. Cohen & F. R. Volkmar (Eds.), *Handbook of autism and pervasive developmental disorders.* New York: John Wiley.

van Daal, J., Verhoeven, L., & van Balkom, H. (2007). Behaviour problems in children with language impairment. *Journal of Child Psychology and Psychiatry, 48,* 1139–1147.

van Goozen, S. H. M., Fairchild, G., Snoek, H., & Harold, G. T. (2007). The evidence for a neurobiological model of childhood antisocial behavior. *Psychological Bulletin, 133,* 149–182.

Van Hoecke, E., De Fruyt, F., De Clercq, B., Hoebeke, P., & Vande Walle, J. (2006). Internalizing and externalizing problem behavior in children with nocturnal and diurnal enuresis: A five-factor model perspective. *Journal of Pediatric Psychology, 31,* 460–468.

van IJzendoorn, M., & Juffer, F. (2006). The Emanuel Miller Memorial Lecture 2006: Adoption as intervention. Meta-analytic evidence for massive catch-up and plasticity in physical, socio-emotional, and cognitive development. *Journal of Child Psychology and Psychiatry, 47,* 1228–1245.

van IJzendoorn, M. H., Juffer, F., & Poelhuis, C. W. K. (2005). Adoption and cognitive development: a meta-analytic comparison of adopted and nonadopted children's IQ and school performance. *Psychological Bulletin, 131,* 301–316.

van IJzendoorn, M. H., Rutgers, A. H., Bakersman-Kranenburg, M. J., Swinkels, S. H. N., van Daalen, E., Dietz, C. et al. (2007). Parental sensitivity and attachment in children with autism spectrum disorder: comparison with children with mental retardation, with language delays, and with typical development. *Child Development, 78,* 597–608.

van Lier, P., Boivin M., Dionne, G., Vitaro, F., Brendgen, M., Koot, H. et al. (2007a). Kindergarten children's genetic vulnerabilities interact with friends' aggression to promote children's own aggression. *Journal of the American Academy of Child and Adolescent Psychiatry, 46,* 1080–1087.

van Lier, P. A. C., van der Ende, J., Koot, H. M., & Verhulst, F. C. (2007b). Which better predicts conduct problems? The relationship of trajectories of conduct problems with ODD and ADHD symptoms from childhood into adolescence. *Journal of Child Psychology and Psychiatry, 48,* 601–608.

Vandell, D. L., & Shumow, L. (1999). After-school child care programs. *The Future of Children, 9(2),* 64–80.

Vannatta, K., & Gerhardt, C. A. (2003). Pediatric oncology. In M. C. Roberts (Ed.), *Handbook of pediatric psychology* (3rd ed.). New York: Guilford Press.

Varela, R. E., Vernberg, E. M., Sanchez-Sosa, J. J., Riveros, A., Mitchell, M., & Mashunkashey, J. (2004). Anxiety reporting and culturally associated interpretation biases and cognitive schema: A comparison of Mexican, Mexican American, and European American families. *Journal of Clinical Child and Adolescent Psychology, 33,* 237–247.

Varni, J. W., Katz, E. R., & Waldron, S. A. (1993). Cognitive-behavioral treatment interventions in childhood cancer. *The Clinical Psychologist, 46,* 192–197.

Vasey, M. W., & Daleiden, E. L. (1994). Worry in children. In G. C. L. Davey & F. Tallis (Eds.), *Worrying: Perspectives on theory, assessment and treatment.* Chichester, England: Wiley.

Vaughn, S., La Greca, A. M., & Kuttler, A. (1999). The why, who, and how of social skills. In W. N. Bender (Ed.), *Professional issues in learning disabilities.* Austin, TX: PRO-ED.

Veenstra-vanderweele, J., & Cook, E. H. (2003). Genetics of childhood disorders: XLVI. Autism, Part 5: Genetics of autism. *Journal of the American Academy of Child and Adolescent Psychiatry, 42,* 116–118.

Vellutino, F. R. (1979). *Dyslexia. Theory and research.* Cambridge MA: MIT Press.

Vellutino, F. R. (1987). *Dyslexia, Scientific American, 256,* 34–41.

Vellutino, F. R., Fletcher, J. M., Snowling M. J., & Scanlon, D. M. (2004). Specific reading disability (dyslexia): What have we learned in the past four decades? *Journal of Child Psychology and Psychiatry, 45,* 2–40.

Velting, O. N., & Albano, A. M. (2001). Current trends in the understanding and treatment of social phobia in youth. *Journal of Child Psychology and Psychiatry, 42,* 127–140.

Verduin, T. L., & Kendall, P. C. (2003). Differential occurrence of comorbidity within childhood anxiety disorders. *Journal of Clinical Child and Adolescent Psychology, 32,* 290–295.

Verhulst, F. C., & van der Ende, J. (1997). Factors associated with mental health service use in the community. *Journal of the American Academy of Child and Adolescent Psychiatry, 36,* 901–909.

Vernick, J., & Karon, M. (1965). Who's afraid of death on a leukemia ward? *American Journal of Diseases of Children, 109,* 393–397.

Vernon, D. T. A., & Thompson, R. H. (1993). Research on the effects of experimental interventions on children's behavior after hospitalizations: A review and synthesis. *Developmental and Behavioral Pediatrics, 14,* 36–44.

Vickers, B., & Garralda, E. (2000). Hallucinations in nonpsychotic children. *Journal of the Academy of Child and Adolescent Psychiatry, 39,* 1073.

Viding, E., Spinath, F. M., Price, T. S., Bishop, D. V. M., Dale, P. S., & Plomin, R. (2004). Genetic and environmental influences on language impairment in 4-year-old same-sex and opposite-sex twins. *Journal of Child Psychology and Psychiatry, 45,* 315–325.

Villani, S. (2001). Impact of media on children and adolescents: A 10-year review of the research. *Journal of the American Academy of Child and Adolescent Psychiatry, 40,* 392–401.

Visser, J. H., van der Ende, J., Koot, H. M., & Verhulst, F. C. (2003). Predicting change in psychopathology in youth referred to mental health services in childhood or adolescence. *Journal of Child Psychology and Psychiatry, 44,* 509–519.

Vitiello, B. (2006). An update on publicly funded multisite trials in pediatric psychopharmacology. *Child and Adolescent Psychiatric Clinics of North America, 15,* 1–12.

Vitiello, B., Severe, J. B., Greenhill, L. L., Arnold, L. E., Abikoff, H. B., Bukstein, O. G. et al. (2001). Methylphenidate dosage for children with ADHD over time under controlled conditions: Lessons from the MTA. *Journal of the American Academy of Child and Adolescent Psychiatry, 40,* 188–196.

Vitiello, B., & Swedo, S. (2004). Antidepressant medications in children. *New England Journal of Medicine, 350,* 1489–1491.

Vitiello, B., Zuvekas, S. H., & Norquist, G. S. (2006). National estimates of antidepressant medication use among U.S. children, 1997–2002. *Journal of the American Academy of Child and Adolescent Psychiatry, 45,* 271–279.

Volkmar, F. R. (1987). Annotation. Diagnostic issues in the pervasive developmental disorders. *Journal of Child Psychology and Psychiatry, 28,* 365–369.

Volkmar, F. R. (1996a). Autism and the pervasive developmental disorders. In M. Lewis (Ed.), *Child and adolescent psychiatry: A comprehensive textbook.* Baltimore: Williams & Wilkins.

Volkmar, F. R. (1996b). Childhood and adolescent psychosis: A review of the past 10 years. *Journal of the American Academy of Child and Adolescent Psychiatry, 35,* 843–851.

Volkmar, F. R., Becker, D. F., King, R. A., & McGlashan, T. H. (1995). Psychotic processes. In D. Cicchetti & D. J. Cohen (Eds.), *Developmental psychopathology.* New York: John Wiley.

Volkmar, F. R., Carter, A., Grossman, J., & Klin, A. (1997). Social development in autism. In D. J. Cohen & F. R. Volkmar (Eds.), *Handbook of autism and pervasive developmental disorders.* New York: John Wiley.

Volkmar, F. R., & Dykens, E. (2002). Mental retardation. In M. Rutter & E. Taylor (Eds.), *Child and adolescent psychiatry.* Oxford, UK: Blackwell Publishing.

Volkmar, F. R., & Klin, A. (2000). Pervasive developmental disorders. In B. J. Sadock & V. A. Sadock (Eds.), *Comprehensive textbook of psychiatry* (Vol. II). Philadelphia: Lippincott Williams & Wilkins.

Volkmar, F. R., Klin, A., & Schultz, R. T. (2005). Pervasive developmental disorders. In B. J. Sadock & V. A. Sadock (Eds.), *Comprehensive textbook of psychiatry. Vol. 2.* Philadelphia: Lippincott Williams & Wilkins.

Volkmar, F. R., Klin, A., Schultz, R. T., Rubin, E., & Bronen, R. (2000). Asperger's disorder. *American Journal of Psychiatry, 157,* 262–267.

Volkmar, F. R., Lord, C., Bailey, A., Schultz, R. T., & Klin, A. (2004). Autism and developmental pervasive disorders. *Journal of Child Psychology and Psychiatry, 45,* 135–170.

von Gonard, A., Backes, M., Laufersweiler-Plass, C., Wendland, C., Lehmkuhl, G., Zerres, K. et al. (2002). Psychopathology and familial stress—comparison of boys with fragile X syndrome and spinal muscular atrophy. *Journal of Child Psychology and Psychiatry, 43,* 949–957.

Votruba-Drzal, E., Coley, R. L., & Chase-Lansdale, P. L. (2004). Child care and low-income children's development: Direct and moderated effects. *Child Development, 75,* 296–312.

Vuijk, P., van Lier, P. A. C., Huizink, A. C., Verhulst, F. C., & Crijnen, A. A. M. (2006). Prenatal smoking predicts non-responsiveness to an intervention targeting attention-deficit/hyperactivity symptoms in elementary schoolchildren. *Journal of Child Psychology and Psychiatry, 47,* 891–901.

Wachsler-Felder, J. L., & Golden, C. J. (2002). Neuropsychological consequences of HIV in children: A review of current literature. *Clinical Psychology Review, 22,* 441–462.

Wade, S. L., Taylor, G., Yeates, K. O., Drotar, D., Stancin, T., Minich, N. M., & Schluchter, M. (2006). Long-term parental and family adaptation following pediatric brain injury. *Journal of Pediatric Psychology, 31,* 1072–1083.

Wade, T. J., Cairney, J., & Pevalin, D. J. (2002). Emergence of gender differences in depression during adolescence: National panel results from three countries. *Journal of the American Academy of Child and Adolescent Psychiatry, 2002, 41,* 190–198.

Wagner, B. M., Silverman, M. A., & Martin, C. E. (2003). Family factors in youth suicidal behaviors. *American Behavioral Scientist, 46,* 1171–1191.

Wagner, J. L., Chaney, J. M., Hommel, K. A., Page, M. C., Mullins, L. L., White, M. M., & Jarvis, J. N. (2003). The influence of parental distress on child depressive symptoms in juvenile rheumatic diseases: The moderating effect of illness intrusiveness. *Journal of Pediatric Psychology, 28,* 453–462.

Wagner, W. G., Smith, D., & Norris, W. R. (1988). The psychological adjustment of enuretic children: A comparison of two types. *Journal of Pediatric Psychology, 13,* 33–38.

Wahler, R. G., & Dumas, J. E. (1989). Attentional problems in dysfunctional mother-child interactions: An interbehavioral model. *Psychological Bulletin, 105,* 116–130.

Wakefield, A. J. et al. (1998). Ileal-lymphoid-nodular hypoplasia, non-specific colitis, and pervasive developmental disorder in children. *Lancet, 351,* 637–641.

Walco, G. A., Sterling, C. N., Conte, P. M., & Engel, R. G. (1999). Empirically supported treatments in pediatric psychology: Disease-related pain. *Journal of Pediatric Psychology, 24,* 155–167.

Waldman, I. D., Lilienfeld, S. O., & Lahey, B. B. (1995). Toward construct validity in the childhood disruptive behavior disorders: Classification and diagnosis in DSM-IV and beyond. In T. H. Ollendick & R. J. Prinz (Eds.), *Advances in clinical child psychology.* Vol. 17. New York: Plenum Press.

Waldron, N. L., & McLeskey, J. (1998). The effects of an inclusive school program on students with mild and severe learning disabilities. *Exceptional Children, 64,* 395–405.

Walker, C. E. (2003). Elimination disorders: Enuresis and encopresis. In M. C. Roberts (Ed.), *Handbook of pediatric psychology* (3rd ed.). New York: Guilford Press.

Walker, D. R., Thompsom, A., Zwaigenbaum, L., Goldberg, J., Bryson, S. E., Mahoney, W. J. et al. (2004). Specifying PDD-NOS: A comparison of PDD-NOS, Asperger's syndrome, and autism. *Journal of the American Academy of Child and Adolescent Psychiatry, 43,* 172–180.

Wallace, G. L., Schmitt, J. E., Lenroot, R., Viding, E., Ordaz, S., Rosenthal, M. A. et al. (2006). A pediatric twin study of brain morphology. *Journal of Child Psychology and Psychiatry, 47,* 987–993.

Wallander, J. L., Thompson, R. J., Jr., & Alriksson-Schmidt, A. (2003). Psychosocial adjustment of children with chronic physical conditions. In M. C. Roberts (Eds.), *Handbook of pediatric psychology* (3rd ed.). New York: Guilford Press.

Wallander, J. L., & Varni, J. W. (1998). Effects of pediatric chronic physical disorders on child and family adjustment. *Journal of Child Psychology and Psychiatry, 39,* 29–46.

Wallerstein, J. S. (1991). The long-term effects of divorce on children: A review. *Journal of the American Academy of Child and Adolescent Psychiatry, 30,* 349–360.

Walsh, B. T. and the Commission on Adolescent Eating Disorders. (2005a). Defining eating disorders. In D. L. Evans, E. B. Foa, R. E. Gur, H. Hendin, C. P. O'Brien, M. E. P. Seligman, & B. T. Walsh (Eds.), *Treating and preventing adolescent mental health disorders. What we know and what we don't know: A research agenda for improving mental health of our youth.* New York: Oxford University Press.

Walsh, B. T., and the Commission on Adolescent Eating Disorders. (2005b). Prevention of eating disorders. In D. L. Evans, E. B. Foa, R. E. Gur, H. Hendin, C. P. O'Brien, M. E. P. Seligman, & B. T. Walsh (Eds.), *Treating and preventing adolescent mental health disorders. What we know and what we don't know: A research agenda for improving mental health of our youth.* New York: Oxford University Press.

Walsh, B. T. and the Commission on Adolescent Eating Disorders (2005c). Treatment of eating disorders. In D. L. Evans, E. B. Foa, R. E. Gur, H. Hendin, C. P. O'Brien, M. E. P. Seligman, & B. T. Walsh (Eds.), *Treating and preventing adolescent mental health disorders. What we know and what we don't know: A research agenda for improving mental health of our youth.* New York: Oxford University Press.

Warfield, M. E. (2001). Employment, parenting, and well-being among mothers of children with disabilities. *Mental Retardation, 39,* 297–309.

Warren, S. L., Gunnar, M. R., Kagan, J., Anders, T. F., Simmens, S. J., Rones, M., Wease, S., Aron, E., Dahl, R. E., & Sroufe, L. A. (2003). Maternal panic disorder: Infant temperament, neurophysiology, and parenting behaviors. *Journal of the American Academy of Child and Adolescent Psychiatry, 42,* 814–825.

Warren, S. L., Howe, G., Simmens, S. J., & Dahl, R. E. (2006). Maternal depressive symptoms and child sleep: Models of mutual influence over time. *Development and Psychopathology, 18,* 1–16.

Warren, S. L., Huston, L., Egeland, B., & Sroufe, L. A. (1997). Child and adolescent anxiety disorders and early attachment. *Journal of the American Academy of Child and Adolescent Psychiatry, 36,* 637–644.

Waschbusch, D. A. (2002). A meta-analytic examination of comorbid hyperactive-impulsive-attention problems and conduct problems. *Psychological Bulletin, 128,* 118–150.

Waschbusch, D. A., & King, S. (2006). Should sex-specific norms be used to assess attention-deficit/hyperactivity disorder or oppositional defiant disorder? *Journal of Consulting and Clinical Psychology, 74,* 179–185.

Waslick, B. (2006). Psychopharmacology interventions for pediatric anxiety disorders: A research update. *Child and Adolescent Psychiatric Clinics of North America, 15,* 51–71.

Waterhouse, L., & Fein, D. (1997). Perspectives on social impairment. In D. J. Cohen & F. R. Volkmar (Eds.), *Handbook of autism and pervasive developmental disorders.* New York: John Wiley.

Watkins, C. E., Campbell, V. L., Nieberding, R., & Hallmark, R. (1995). Contemporary practice of psychological assessment by clinical psychologists. *Professional Psychology: Research and Practice, 26,* 54–60.

Watkins, J. M., Asarnow, R. F., & Tanguay, P. E. (1988). Symptom development in childhood onset schizophrenia. *Journal of Child Psychology and Psychiatry, 29,* 865–878.

Watson, J. B. (1913). Psychology as the behaviorist views it. *Psychological Review, 20,* 158–177.

Watson, J. B. (1930). *Behaviorism.* New York: Norton.

Watson, J. B., & Rayner, R. (1920). Conditioned emotional reactions. *Journal of Experimental Psychology, 3,* 1–14.

Wazana, A., Bresnahan, M., & Kline, J. (2007). The autism epidemic: Fact or artifact? *Journal of the American Academy of Child and Adolescent Psychiatry, 46,* 721–730.

We the Children: Meeting the Promises of the World Summit for Children. (2001). Report of the U.N. Secretary General Kofi Annan. New York: United Nations.

Webster-Stratton, C. (2005). The incredible years: A training series for the prevention and treatment of conduct problems in young children. In E. D. Hibbs & P. S. Jensen (Eds.), *Psychosocial treatments for child and adolescent disorders: Empirically based strategies for clinical practice* (2nd ed.). Washington, DC: American Psychological Association.

Webster-Stratton, C., & Hancock, L. (1998). Parent training: Content, methods, and process. In E. Schaefer (Ed.), *Handbook of parent training* (2nd ed.). New York: Wiley.

Webster-Stratton, C., & Reid, M. J. (2003). The incredible years parents, teachers, and children training series: A multifaceted treatment approach for young children. In A. E. Kazdin & J. R. Weisz (Eds.), *Evidence-based psychotherapies for children and adolescents.* New York: Guilford Press.

Wechsler, D. (2002). *Wechsler Preschool and Primary Scale of Intelligence—Third Edition (WPPSI-III).* San Antonio, TX: Harcourt Assessment.

Wechsler, D. (2003). *Wechsler Intelligence Scale for Children—Fourth Edition (WISC-IV).* San Antonio, TX: Harcourt Assessment.

Weersing, V. R., & Brent, D. A. (2003). Cognitive-behavioral therapy for adolescent depression: Comparative efficacy, mediation, moderation, and effectiveness. In A. E. Kazdin & J. R. Weisz (Eds.), *Evidence-based psychotherapies for children and adolescents.* New York: Guilford Press.

Wehmeyer, M. L. (2003). Eugenics and sterilization in the heartland. *Mental Retardation, 41,* 57–60.

Weinberger, D. R., & McClure, R. K. (2002). Neurotoxicity, neuroplasticity, and magnetic resonance imaging morphometry. *Archives of General Psychiatry, 59*, 553–558.

Weinrott, M. R., Jones, R. R., & Howard, J. R. (1982). Cost-effectiveness of teaching family programs for delinquents: Results of a national evaualation. *Evaluation Review, 6*, 173–201.

Weiss, B., & Garber, J. (2003). Developmental differences in the phenomenology of depression. *Development and Psychopathology, 15*, 403–430.

Weiss, G., & Hechtman, L. T. (1986). *Hyperactive children grown up.* New York: Guilford.

Weiss, K. B., Gergen, P. J., & Hodgson, T. A. (1992). An economic evaluation of asthma in the United States. *New England Journal of Medicine, 326*, 862–866.

Weissberg, R. P., Kumpfer, K. L., & Seligman, M. E. P. (2003). Prevention that works for children: An introduction. *American Psychologist, 58*, 425–432.

Weissman, M. M., Kidd, K. K., & Prusoff, B. A. (1982). Variability in rates of affective disorders in relatives of depressed and normal probands. *Archives of General Psychiatry, 39*, 1397–1403.

Weissman, M. M., Warner, V., Wickramarante, P., Moreau, D., & Olfson, M. (1997). Offspring of depressed parents: 10 years later. *Archives of General Psychiatry, 54*, 932–940.

Weissman, M. M., Wickramaratne, P., Nomura, Y., Warner, V., Verdeli, H., Pilowsky, D. J., Grillon, C., & Bruder, G. (2005). Families at high and low risk for depression: A 3-generation study. *Archives of General Psychiatry, 62*, 29–36.

Weist, M. D. (1997). Expanded school mental health services: A national movement in progress. In T. H. Ollendick & R. J. Prinz (Eds.), *Advances in clinical child psychology* (Vol. 19). New York: Plenum Press.

Weist, M. D., & Christodulu, K. V. (2000). Expanded school mental health programs: Advancing reform and closing the gap between research and practice. *Journal of School Health, 70*, 195–200.

Weist, M. D., & Cooley-Quille, M. (2001). Advancing efforts to address youth violence involvement. *Journal of Clinical Child Psychology, 30*, 147–151.

Weist, M. D., Finney, J. W., Barnard, M. U., Davis, C. D., & Ollendick, T. H. (1993). Empirical selection of psychosocial treatment targets for children and adolescents with diabetes. *Journal of Pediatric Psychology, 18*, 11–28.

Weisz, J. R., Chaiyasit, W., Weiss, B., Eastman, K. L., & Jackson, E. W. (1995). A multimethod study of problem behavior among Thai and American children in school: Teacher reports versus direct observations. *Child Development, 66*, 402–415.

Weisz, J. R., McCarty, C. A., & Valeri, S. M. (2006). Effects of psychotherapy for depression in children and adolescents: A meta-analysis. *Psychological Bulletin, 132*, 132–149.

Weisz, J. R., Sandler, I. N., Durlak, J. A., & Anton, B. S. (2005). Promoting and protecting youth mental health through evidence-based prevention and treatment. *American Psychologist, 60*, 628–648.

Weisz, J. R., Southam-Gerow, M. A., Gordis, E. B., & Connor-Smith, J. (2003). Primary and secondary control enhancement training for youth depression. In A. E. Kazdin & J. R. Weisz (Eds.), *Evidence-based psychotherapies for children and adolescents.* New York: Guilford Press.

Weisz, J. R., Suwanlet, S., Chaiyasit, W., Weiss, B., Walter, B. R., & Anderson, W. W. (1988). Thai and American perspectives on over- and undercontrolled child behavior problems: Exploring the threshold model among parents, teachers, and psychologists. *Journal of Consulting and Clinical Psychology, 56*, 601–609.

Weisz, J. R., Sweeney, L., Proffitt, V., & Carr, T. (1993b). Control-related beliefs and self-reported depressive symptoms in late childhood. *Journal of Abnormal Psychology, 102*, 411–418.

Weisz, J. R., Thurber, C. A., Sweeney. L., Proffitt, V. D., & LaGagnoux, G. L. (1997). Brief treatment of mild to moderate child depression using primary and secondary control enhancement training. *Journal of Consulting and Clinical Psychology, 65*, 703–707.

Weisz, J. R., Weiss, B., Suwanlert, S., & Chaiyasit, W. (2006). Culture and youth psychopathology: Testing the syndromal sensitivity model in Thai and American adolescents. *Journal of Consulting and Clinical Psychology, 74*, 1098–1107.

Weizman, Z. O., & Snow, C. E. (2001). Lexical input as related to children's vocabulary acquisition: Effects of sophisticated exposure and support for meaning. *Developmental Psychology, 37*, 265–279.

Wekerle, C., Wall, A. M., Leung, E., & Trocmé, N. (2007). Cumulative stress and substantiated maltreatment: The importance of caregiver vulnerability and adult partner violence. *Child Abuse & Neglect, 31*, 427–443.

Wekerle, C., & Wolfe, D. A. (2003). Child maltreatment. In E. J. Mash & R. A. Barkley (Eds.), *Child psychopathology* (2nd ed.). New York: Guilford Press.

Wellman, H. M. (1993). Early understanding of mind: The normal case. In S. Baron-Cohen, H. Tager-Flüsberg, & D. J. Cohen (Eds.), *Understanding other minds.* New York: Oxford Press.

Wells, K. C., Forehand, R., & Griest, D. L. (1980). Generality of treatment effects from treated to untreated behaviors resulting from a parent training program. *Journal of Clinical Child Psychology, 9*, 217–219.

Wender, P. H., Kety, S. S., Rosenthal, D., Schulsinger, F., Ortmann, J., & Lunde, I. (1986). Psychiatric disorders in the biological and adoptive families of adopted individuals with affective disorders. *Archives of General Psychiatry, 43*, 923–929.

Wentz, E., Gillberg, C., Gillberg, I. C., & Rastam, M. (2001). Ten-year follow-up of adolescent-onset anorexia nervosa: Psychiatric disorders and overall functioning scales. *Journal of Child Psychology and Psychiatry, 42*, 613–622.

Werner, E., Dawson, G., Osterling, J., & Dinno, N. (2000). Brief report: Recognition of autism spectrum disorder before one year of age: A retrospective study based on home videotapes. *Journal of Autism and Developmental Disorders, 30*, 157–162.

Werner, E. E., & Smith, R. S. (1982). *Vulnerable but invincible.* New York: McGraw-Hill.

Werry, J. S. (1986). Physical illness, symptoms and allied disorders. In H. C. Quay & J. S. Werry (Eds.), *Psychopathological disorders of childhood*, 3rd ed. New York: Wiley.

Wertheim, E. H., Paxton, S. J., & Blaney, S. (2004). Risks factors for the development of body image disturbances. In J. K. Thompson (Ed.), *Handbook of eating disorders and obesity.* Hoboken, NJ: John Wiley.

Wertlieb, D., Hauser, S. T., & Jacobson, A. M. (1986). Adaptation to diabetes: Behavior symptoms and family context. *Journal of Pediatric Psychology, 11*, 463–479.

West, M. O., & Prinz, R. J. (1987). Parental alcoholism and childhood psychopathology. *Psychological Bulletin, 102*, 204–218.

West, P., & Sweeting, H. (2003). Fifteen, female, and stressed: Changing patterns of psychological stress over time. *Journal of Child Psychology and Psychiatry, 44,* 399–411.

West, S. G., Sandler, I., Pillow, D. R., Baca, L., & Gersten, J. C. (1991). The use of structural equation modeling in generative research: Toward the design of a preventative intervention for bereaved children. *American Journal of Community Psychology, 19,* 459–480.

Westenberg, P. M., Drewes, M. J., Goedhart, A. W., Siebelink, B. M., & Treffers, P. D. A. (2004). A developmental analysis of self-reported fears in late childhood through mid-adolescence: Social-evaluative fears on the rise? *Journal of Child Psychology and Psychiatry, 45,* 481–495.

Western Psychological Services. (2004). *WPS 2004 catalogue.* Los Angeles: Western Psychological Services.

Western Psychological Services. (2006). *Autism Diagnostic Interview, Revised (ADI-R).* Los Angeles: Author.

Wexler, A. (1995). *Mapping fate.* New York: Random House.

Whalen, C. K., & Henker, B. (1998). Attention-deficit/hyperactivity disorders. In T. H. Ollendick & M. Hersen (Eds.), *Handbook of child psychopathology.* New York: Plenum Press.

Whalen, C. K., Henker, B., King, P. S., Jamner, L. D., & Levine, L. (2004). Adolescents react to the events of September 11, 2001: Focused versus ambient impact. *Journal of Abnormal Child Psychology, 32,* 1–11.

Whaley, A. L., & Davis, K. E. (2007). Cultural competence and evidence-based practice in mental health services. *American Psychologist, 62,* 563–574.

Whitaker, A., Johnson, J., Shaffer, D., Rappoport, J., Kalikow, K., Walsh, B. T., Davies, M., Braiman, S., & Dolinsky, A. (1990). Uncommon troubles in young people: Prevalence estimates of selected psychiatric disorders in a nonreferred adolescent population. *Archives of General Psychiatry, 47,* 487–496.

White, H. R., Bates, M. E., & Buyske, S. (2001). Adolescence-limited delinquency: Extending Moffitt's hypothesis into adulthood. *Journal of Abnormal Psychology, 110,* 600–609.

White, K. J., & Kistner, J. (1992). The influence of teacher feedback on young children's peer preferences and perceptions. *Developmental Psychology, 28,* 933–940.

White, S. H. (1992). G. Stanley Hall: From philosophy to developmental psychology. *Developmental Psychology, 28,* 25–34.

White, S. W., Scahill, L., Klin, A., Koenig, K., & Volkmar, F. R. (2007). Educational placements and service use patterns of individuals with autism spectrum disorders. *Journal of Autism and Developmental Disorders, 37,* 1403–1412.

Whitehurst, G. J. (1982). Language development. In B. B. Wolman (Ed.), *Handbook of developmental psychology.* Upper Saddle River, NJ: Prentice Hall.

Whitehurst, G. J., & Fischel, J. E. (1994). Early developmental language delay: What, if anything, should the clinician do about it? *Journal of Child Psychology and Psychiatry, 35,* 613–648.

Whitman, T. L., Hantula, D. A., & Spence, B. H. (1990). Current issues in behavior modification with mentally retarded persons. In J. L. Matson (Ed.), *Handbook of behavior modification with the mentally retarded.* New York: Plenum.

Whitman, T. L., O'Callaghan, M., & Sommer, K. (1997). Emotion and retardation. In W. E. MacLean (Ed.), *Ellis' Handbook of mental deficiency, psychological theory and research.* Mahwah, NJ: Lawrence Erlbaum.

Wicks-Nelson, R., & Israel, A. C. (2006). *Behavior disorders of childhood. Sixth Edition.* Upper Saddle River, NJ: Prentice-Hall.

Widiger, T. A., & Clark, L. A. (2000). Toward DSM-V and the classification of psychopathology. *Psychological Bulletin, 126,* 946–961.

Widiger, T. A., Frances, A. J., Pincus, H. A., Davis, W. W., & First, M. B. (1991). Toward an empirical classification for DSM-IV. *Journal of Abnormal Psychology, 100,* 280–288.

Wiebe, D. J., Alderfer, M. A., Palmer, S. C., Lindsay, R., & Jarrett, L. (1994). Behavioral self-regulation in adolescents with type I diabetes: Negative affectivity and blood glucose symptom perception. *Journal of Consulting and Clinical Psychology, 62,* 1204–1212.

Wiebe, D. J., Berg, C. A., Korbel, C., Palmer, D. L., Beveridge, R. M., Upchurch, R. et al. (2005). Children's appraisals of maternal involvement in coping with diabetes: Enhancing our understanding of adherence, metabolic control, and quality of life across adolescence. *Journal of Pediatric Psychology, 30,* 167–178.

Wiener, J., & Tardif, C. Y. (2004). Social and emotional functioning of children with learning disabilities: Does special education placement make a difference? *Learning Disabilities Research & Practice, 19,* 20–32.

Wiesner, M. (2003). A longitudinal latent variable analysis of reciprocal relations between depressive symptoms and delinquency during adolescence. *Journal of Abnormal Psychology, 112,* 633–645.

Wight, R. G., Sepúlveda, J. E., & Aneshensel, C. S. (2004). Depressive symptoms: How do adolescents compare with adults? *Journal of Adolescent Health, 34,* 314–323.

Wilfley, D. E., Passi, V. A., Cooperberg, J., & Stein, R. I. (2006). Cognitive behavioral therapy for youth with eating disorders and obesity. In P. C. Kendall (Ed.), *Child and adolescent therapy: Cognitive-behavioral procedures.* New York: The Guilford Press.

Wilkinson, G. S., & Robertson, G. J. (2006). *Wide Range Achievement Test 4 (WRAT-4).* Lutz, FL: Psychological Assessment Resources, Inc.

Willcutt, E. G., & Pennington, B. F. (2000). Psychiatric comorbidity in children and adolescents with reading disability. *Journal of Child Psychology and Psychiatry, 41,* 1039–1048.

Willcutt, E. G., Pennington, B. F., Brada, R., Ogline, J. S., Tunick, R. A., Chhabildas, N. A., & Olson, R. K. (2001). A comparison of the cognitive deficits in reading disability and attention deficit/hyperactivity disorder. *Journal of Abnormal Psychology, 110,* 157–172.

Willemsen-Swinkels, S. H. N., Bakermans-Franenburg, M. J., Buitelaar, J. K., van IJzendoorn, M. H., & van Engeland, H. (2000). Insecure and disorganized attachment in children with a pervasive developmental disorder: Relationship with social interaction and heart rate. *Journal of Child Psychology and Psychiatry, 41,* 759–767.

Williams, B., & Pow, J. (2007). Gender differences and mental health: An exploratory study of knowledge and attitudes to mental health among Scottish teenagers. *Child and Adolescent Mental Health, 12,* 6–12.

Williams, S., & McGee, R. (1996). Reading in childhood and mental health in early adulthood. In J. H. Beitchman, N. J. Cohen, M. M. Konstantareas, & R. Tannock (Eds.), *Language learning, and behavior disorders.* New York: Cambridge University Press.

Williamson, D. E., Forbes, E. E., Dahl, R. E., & Ryan, N. D. (2005). A genetic epidemiologic perspective on comorbidity of depression and anxiety. *Child and Adolescent Psychiatric Clinics of North America, 14,* 707–726.

Willoughby, M. T. (2003). Developmental course of ADHD symptomatology during the transition from childhood to adolescence: A review with recommendations. *Journal of Child Psychology and Psychiatry, 44,* 88–106.

Willoughby, M. T., Curran, P. J., Costello, E. J., & Angold, A. (2000). Implications of early versus late onset of attention-deficit/hyperactivity disorder symptoms. *Journal of the American Academy of Child and Adolescent Psychiatry, 39,* 1512–1519.

Wills, T. A., & Dishion, T. J. (2004). Temperament and adolescent substance abuse: A transactional analysis of emerging self-control. *Journal of Clinical and Child and Adolescent Psychology, 33,* 69–81.

Wills, T. A., & Filer, M. (1996). Stress-coping model of adolescent substance use. In T. H. Ollendick & R. J. Prinz (Eds.), *Advances in clinical child psychology* (Vol. 18). New York: Plenum Press.

Wilson, C. C., & Haynes, S. N. (1985). Sleep disorders. In P. H. Bornstein & A. E. Kazdin (Eds.), *Handbook of clinical behavior therapy with children.* Homewood, IL: Dorsey.

Wilson, G. T., Becker, C. B., & Heffernan, K. (2003). Eating disorders. In E. J. Mash & R. A. Barkley (Eds.), *Child psychopathology* (2nd ed.). New York: Guilford Press.

Wilson, G. T., Grilo, C. M., & Vitousek, K. M. (2007). Psychological treatment of eating disorders. *American Psychologist, 62,* 199–216.

Wilson, K. M., & Swanson, H. L. (2001). Are mathematics disabilities due to a domain-general or domain-specific working memory deficit? *Journal of Learning Disabilities, 34,* 237–248.

Wing, L. (1997). Syndromes of autism and atypical development. In D. J. Cohen & F. R. Volkmar (Eds.), *Handbook of autism and pervasive developmental disorders.* New York: John Wiley.

Wiseman, C. V., Sunday, S. R., & Becker, A. E. (2005). Impact of the media on adolescent body image. *Child and Adolescent Psychiatric Clinics of North America, 14,* 453–471.

Wolf, L., Fisman, S., Ellison, D., & Freeman, T. (1998). Effect of sibling perception of differential parental treatment in sibling dyads with one disabled child. *Journal of the American Academy of Child and Adolescent Psychiatry, 37,* 1317–1325.

Wolf, M. M., Braukmann, C. J., & Ramp, K. A. (1987). Serious delinquent behavior as part of a significantly handicapping condition: Cures and supportive environments. *Journal of Applied Behavior Analysis, 20,* 347–359.

Wolfe, D. A., Rawana, J. S., & Chiodo, D. (2006). Abuse and trauma. In D. A. Wolfe & E. J. Mash (Eds.), *Behavioral and emotional disorder in adolescents: Nature, assessment, and treatment.* New York: The Guilford Press.

Wolfe, J., Grier, H. E., Klar, N., Levin, S. B., Ellenbogen, J. M., Salem-Schatz, S. et al. (2000a). Symptoms and suffering at the end of life in children with cancer. *New England Journal of Medicine, 342,* 326–333.

Wolfe, J., Klar, N., Grier, H. E., Duncan, J., Salem-Schatz, S. Emanuel, E. J., & Weeks, J. C. (2000b). Understanding of prognosis among parents of children who died of cancer: Impact on treatment goals and integration of palliative care. *Journal of the American Medical Association, 284,* 2469–2475.

Wolfe, V. V. (2006). Child sexual abuse. In E. J. Mash & R. A. Barkley (Eds.), *Treatment of childhood disorders,* (3rd ed.) New York: The Guilford Press.

Wolfensberger, W. (1980). *The principle of normalization in human services.* Toronto: National Institute on Mental Retardation.

Wolke, D., Woods, S., Bloomfield, L., & Karstadt, L. (2000). The association between direct and relational bullying and behaviour problems among primary school children. *Journal of Child Psychology and Psychiatry, 41,* 989–1002.

Wolraich, M. L. (2003). Annotation: The use of psychotropic medications in children: An American view. *Journal of Child Psychology and Psychiatry, 44,* 159–168.

Wolraich, M., Wilson, D. B., & White, J. W. (1995). The effect of sugar on behavior or cognition in children. *Journal of the American Medical Association, 274,* 1617–1621.

Wonderlich, S., Crosby, R., Mitchell, J., Thompson, K., Redlin, J., Demuth, G., & Smyth, J. (2001). Pathways mediating sexual abuse and eating disturbance in children. *Journal of Eating Disorders, 13,* 25–34.

Wonderlich, S. A., Joiner, T. E., Keel, P. K., Williamson, D. A., & Crosby, R. D. (2007). Eating disorder diagnoses. *American Psychologist, 62,* 167–180.

Wonderlich, S. A., Lilenfeld, L. R., Riso, L. P., Engel, S., & Mitchell, J. E. (2005). Personality and anorexia nervosa. *International Journal of Eating Disorders, 37,* S68–S71.

Wong, B. Y. L., Butler, D. L., Ficzere, S. A., & Kuperis, S. (1997). Teaching adolescents with learning disabilities and low achievers to plan, write, and revise compare-and-contrast essays. *Learning Disabilities Research & Practice, 12,* 2–15.

Wong, B. Y. L., Harris, K. R., Graham, S., & Butler, D. L. (2003). Cognitive strategies instruction research in learning disabilities. In H. L. Swanson, K. R. Harris & S. Graham (Eds.), *Handbook of learning disabilities.* New York: Guilford Press.

Wood, B., Watkins, J. B., Boyle, J. T., Noguiera, J., Aimand, E., & Carrol, L. (1989). The "psychosomatic family" model: An empirical analysis. *Family Process, 28,* 399–417.

Wood, B. L, Cheah, P. A., Lim, J. H., Ritz, T., Miller, B. D., Stern, T., & Ballow, M. (2007a). Reliability and validity of the Asthma Trigger Inventory applied to a pediatric population. *Journal of Pediatric Psychology, 32,* 552–560.

Wood, B. L., Lim, J. H., Miller, B. D., Cheah, P. A., Simmons, S., Stern, T., et al. (2007b). Family emotional climate, depression, emotional triggering of asthma, and disease severity in pediatric asthma: Examination of pathways of effect. *Journal of Pediatric Psychology, 32,* 542–551.

Wood, J. J., McLeod, B. D., Sigman, M., Hwang, W. C., & Chu, B. C. (2003). Parenting and childhood anxiety: theory, empirical findings, and future directions. *Journal of Child Psychology and Psychiatry, 44,* 134–151.

Wood, J. J., Piacentini, J. C., Southam-Gerow, M., Chu, B. C., & Sigman, M. (2006). Family cognitive behavioral therapy for child anxiety disorders. *Journal of American Academy of Child and Adolescent Psychiatry, 45,* 314–321.

Wood, M., & Valdez-Menchaca, M. C. (1996). The effect of a diagnostic label of language delay on adults' perceptions of preschool children. *Journal of Learning Disabilities, 29,* 582–588.

Woodcock, R. W. (1998). *Woodcock Reading Mastery Tests-Revised-Normative Update: Examiner's Manual, Forms G and H.* Circle Pines, MN: American Guidance Service.

Woodward, L. J., & Fergusson, D. M. (2000). Childhood peer relationship problems and later risks of educational underachievement and unemployment. *Journal of Child Psychology and Psychiatry, 41,* 191–201.

Woodward, L. J., Fergusson, D. M., & Horwood, L. J. (2000). Driving outcomes of young people with attentional difficulties in adolescence. *Journal of the American Academy of Child and Adolescent Psychiatry, 39,* 627–634.

World Health Organization. (1992). *International classification of diseases: Tenth revision.* Chapter V. Mental and behavioural disorders. Diagnostic criteria for research. Geneva: Author.

Woznick, L. A., & Goodheart, C. D. (2002). *Living with childhood cancer: A practical guide to help families cope.* Washington, DC: American Psychological Association.

Wren, F. J., Berg, E. A., Heiden, L. A., Kinnamon, C. J., Ohlson, L. A., Bridge, J. A. et al. (2007). Childhood anxiety in a diverse primary care population: Parent-child reports, ethnicity, and SCARED factor structure. *Journal of the American Academy of Child and Adolescent Psychiatry, 46,* 332–340.

Wright, H. F. (1960). Observational child study. In P. H. Mussen (Ed.), *Handbook of research methods in child development.* New York: John Wiley.

Wysocki, T., Greco, P., & Buckloh, L. M. (2003). Childhood diabetes in psychological context. In M. C. Roberts (Ed.), *Handbook of pediatric psychology* (3rd ed.). New York: Guilford Press.

Yates, A. (1989). Current perspectives on the eating disorders: I. History, psychological and biological aspects. *Journal of the American Academy of Child and Adolescent Psychiatry, 28,* 813–828.

Yates, T. M. (2004). The developmental psychopathology of self-injurious behavior: Compensatory regulation in posttraumatic adaptation. *Clinical Psychology Review, 24,* 35–74.

Yeates, K. O., Bigler, E. D., Dennis, M., Gerhardt, C. A., Rubin, K. H., Stancin, T. et al. (2007). Social outcomes in childhood brain disorder: A heuristic integration of social neuroscience and developmental psychology. *Psychological Bulletin, 133,* 535–556.

Yeates-Frederikx, M. H. M., Nijman, H., Logher, E., & Merckelbach, H. L. G. M. (2000). Birth patterns in mentally retarded autistic patients. *Journal of Autism and Developmental Disorders, 30,* 257–262.

Yeatts, K. B., & Shy, C. M. (2001). Prevalence and consequences of asthma and wheezing in African-American and White adolescents. *Journal of Adolescent Health, 29,* 314–319.

Yeganeh, R., Beidel, D. C., Turner, S. M., Pina, A. A., & Silverman, W. K. (2003). Clinical distinctions between selective mutism and social phobia: An investigation of childhood psychopathology. *Journal of the American Academy of Child and Adolescent Psychiatry, 42,* 1069–1075.

Yeh, M., Hough, R. L., McCabe, K., Lau, A., & Garland, A. (2004). Parental beliefs about the cause of child problems: Exploring racial/ethnic patterns. *Journal of the American Academy of Child and Adolescent Psychiatry, 43,* 605–612.

Yeh, M., McCabe, K., Hough, R. L., Lau, A., Fakhry, F., & Garland, A. (2005). Why bother about beliefs? Examining relationships between race/ethnicity, parental beliefs about causes of child problems, and mental health service use. *Journal of Consulting and Clinical Psychology, 73,* 800–807.

Yeo, R. A., Hill, D. E., Campbell, R. A., Vigil, J., Petropoulos, H., Hart, B. et al. (2003). Proton magnetic resonance spectroscopy investigation of the right frontal lobe in children with attention-deficit/hyperactivity disorder. *Journal of the American Academy of Child and Adolescent Psychiatry, 42,* 303–310.

Yerys, B. E., Hepburn, S. L., Pennington, B. F., & Rogers, S. J. (2007). Executive function in preschoolers with autism: evidence consistent with a secondary deficit. *Journal of Autism and Developmental Disorders, 37,* 1068–1079.

Youdin, M. B. H., & Riederer, P. (1997). Understanding Parkinson's disease. *Scientific American, 276,* 52–59.

Young, A. R., Beitchman, J. H., Johnson, C., Douglas, L., Atkinson, L., Escobar, M., & Wilson, B. (2002). Young adult academic outcomes in a longitudinal sample of early identified language impaired and control children. *Journal of Child Psychology and Psychiatry, 43,* 635–645.

Young, K. M., Northern, J. J., Lister, K. M., Drummond, J. A., & O'Brien, W. H. (2007). A meta-analysis of family-behavioral weight-loss treatments for children. *Clinical Psychology Review, 27,* 240–249.

Young, M. H., Brennan, L. C., Baker, R. D., & Baker, S. S. (1996). Functional encopresis. In R. S. Feldman (Ed.), *The psychology of adversity.* Amherst: University of Massachusetts Press.

Young, R. C., Biggs, J. T., Ziegler, V. E., & Meyer, D. A. (1978). A rating scale for mania: Reliability, validity, and sensitivity. *British Journal of Psychiatry, 133,* 429–435.

Youngstrom, E. A., & Duax, J. (2005). Evidence-based assessment of pediatric bipolar disorder, Part I: Base rate and family history. *Journal of the American Academy of Child and Adolescent Psychiatry, 44,* 712–717.

Youngstrom, E. A., Findling, R. L., Danielson, C. K., & Calabrese, J. R. (2001). Discriminative validity of parent report of hypomanic and depressive symptoms in the General Behavior Inventory. *Psychological Assessment, 13,* 267–276.

Youngstrom, E. A., Findling, R. L., & Feeny, N. (2004). Assessment of bipolar spectrum disorders in children and adolescents. In S. L. Johnson & R. L. Leahy (Eds.), *Psychological treatment of bipolar disorder.* New York: Guilford Press.

Yow, V. R. (2005). *Recording oral history.* Walnut Creek, CA: AltaMira Press.

Yule, W. (2000). Emanuel Miller Lecture: From pogroms to "ethnic cleansing": Meeting the needs of war affected children. *Journal of Child Psychology and Psychiatry, 41,* 695–702.

Yule, W., Udwin, O., & Murdoch, K. (1990). The "Jupiter" sinking: Effects on children's fears, depression and anxiety. *Journal of Child Psychology and Psychiatry, 31,* 1051–1061.

Zahn-Waxler, C., Crick, N. R., Shirtcliffe, E. A., & Woods, K. E. (2006). The origins and development of psychopathology in females and males. In D. Cicchetti & D. J. Cohen (Eds.). *Developmental psychopathology. Vol. 1. Theory and method.* Hoboken, NJ: John Wiley & Sons.

Zalecki, C. A., & Hinshaw, S. P. (2004). Overt and relational aggression in girls with attention deficit hyperactivity disorder. *Journal of Clinical Child and Adolescent Psychology, 33,* 125–137.

Zalsman, G., Brent, D. A., & Weersing, V. R. (2006). Depressive disorders in childhood and adolescence: An overview: Epidemiology, clinical manifestation and risk factors. *Child and Adolescent Clinics of North America, 15,* 827–841.

Zalsman, G., Oquendo, M. A., Greenhill, L., Goldberg, P. H., Kamali, M., Martin, A., & Mann, J. J. (2006). Neurobiology of depression in children and adolescents. *Child and Adolescent Psychiatric Clinics of North America, 15,* 843–868.

Zametkin, A. J., & Rapoport, J. L. (1986). The pathophysiology of attention deficit disorder with hyperactivity: A review. In B. B. Lahey & A. E. Kazdin (Eds.), *Advance in clinical child psychology.* Vol. 9. New York: Plenum.

Zametkin, A. J., Zoon, C. K., Klein, H. W., & Munson, S. (2004). Psychiatric aspects of child and adolescent obesity: A review of the past 10 years. *Journal of the American Academy of Child and Adolescent Psychiatry, 43,* 134–150.

Zero to Three/National Center for Infants, Toddlers and Families. (2005). *Diagnostic classification of mental health and de-velopmental disorders of infancy and early childhood, Revised.* Washington, D.C.: Author.

Zigler, E., Balla, D., & Hodapp, R. (1984). On the definition and classification of mental retardation. *American Journal of Mental Deficiency, 89,* 215–230.

Zito, J. M., Safer, D. J., dos Reis, S., Gardner, J. F., Boles, M., & Lynch, F. (2000). Trends in the prescribing of psychotropic medications to preschoolers. *Journal of the American Medical Association, 283,* 1025–1031.

Zucker, R. A. (2006). Alcohol use and the alcohol use disorders: A developmental-biopsychosocial systems formulation covering the life course. In D. Cicchetti & D. J. Cohen (Eds.), *Developmental psychopathology, Vol. 3: Risk, disorder, and adaptation* (2nd ed.). Hoboken, NJ: John Wiley & Sons.

Credits

CHAPTER OPENER PHOTOS

Page 1 Dag Sundberg/CORBIS-NY.

Page 20 Richard Hutchings/Hutchings Photography.

Page 39 Photolibrary.com.

Page 71 David Young-Wolff-PhotoEdit Inc.

Page 92 David Young-Wolff-PhotoEdit Inc.

Page 119 David Mager/Pearson Learning Photo Studio.

Page 156 Silver Burdett Ginn.

Page 190 Shirley Zeiberg/Pearson Education/PH College.

Page 232 Ken Karp/Pearson Education/PH College.

Page 262 Ken Karp/Pearson Education/PH College.

Page 295 Will Faller.

Page 327 Charles Gatewood/Pearson Education/PH College.

Page 361 Richard Hutchings/PhotoEdit Inc.

Page 391 Charles Gatewood/Pearson Education/PH College.

Page 413 Ken Karp/Prentice Hall School Division.

CARTOONS

Page 25 © The New Yorker Collection 2001 Robert Weber from cartoonbank.com. All Rights Reserved.

Page 40 © The New Yorker Collection 2006 Barbara Smaller from cartoonbank.com. All Rights Reserved.

Page 75 © The New Yorker Collection 2003 Michael Shaw from cartoonbank.com. All Rights Reserved.

Page 123 © The New Yorker Collection 2007 Barbara Smaller from cartoonbank.com. All Rights Reserved.

Page 201 © The New Yorker Collection 2006 Danny Shanahan from cartoonbank.com. All Rights Reserved.

Page 237 © The New Yorker Collection 1999 Robert Weber from cartoonbank.com. All Rights Reserved.

Page 366 © The New Yorker Collection 2008 Jack Ziegler from cartoonbank.com. All Rights Reserved.

CHAPTER 1

Page 7 Figure 1–2   From Collishaw, Maughan, Goodman, & Pickles, 2004.

Page 8 Table 1–2   Based in part on Hartung & Widiger, 1998. Gender differences in the diagnosis of mental disorders: conclusions and controversies of the SDN-IV.

Psycological Bulletin 123, pp. 260–278. © 1998 by the American Psychological Association. Reprinted with permission.

Page 9 Figure 1–4   From Bongers, Koot van de Ende, & Verhulst, 2003.

Page 12 Accent "Little Hans" Kessler, 1966.

Page 17 "Aaron: Clinical, Legal, and Ethical Considerations" adapted from Schetky, 2000, p. 2944.

CHAPTER 2

Page 20 "Elizabeth: No Obvious Explanation" adapted from Morgan, 1999, p. 46.

Page 22 Figure 2–1   Adapted from Achenbach, T. M. (1990). Conceptualization of Developmental Psychopathology. In M. Lewis & S. M. Miller (eds.) *Handbook of Developmental Psychopathology.* Reprinted by permission from Springer Science and Business Media.

Page 26 Figure 2–2   Adapted from Compas, Hinden, and Gerhardt (1995). Adolescent Development: Pathways and Processes of Risk and Resilience. Reprinted with permission from the *Annual Review of Psychology,* © 1995, volume 46, pp. 265–293. www.annualreviews.org

Page 27 Table 2–1   Based in part on Coie et al., 1993

Page 28 Figure 2–4   Adapted from Grant et al., 2003.

Page 28 Accent "The Timing of Risky Experiences" Rutter, 1989b

Page 29 Table 2–2   From Masten, A. S. & Coatsworth, J. D. (1998). The Development of Competence in Favorable and Unfavorable Environments: Lessons From Research on Successful Children. *American Psychologist,* 53, pp. 205–220. © 1998 by the American Psychological Association. Reprinted with permission.

Page 29 "Ann and Amy: The "Ordinary Magic" of Resilience" adapted from Cummings et al., 2000, p. 40.

Page 30 Table 2–3   Based on Masten, A. S. & Coatsworth, J. D. (1998) The Development of Competence in Favorable and Unfavorable Environments: Lessons from Research on Successful Children. *American Psychologist* 53, 205–220 and Werner, E. E. & Smith R. S. (2001). Journeys from Childhood to Midlife, Ithaca, NY: Cornell University Press.

Page 33 Table 2–4   Adapted from Lyons-Ruth, Zeanah, Benoit, 2003.

Page 34   "Carl: A Case of 'Goodness-of-Fit'" Chess & Thomas, 1977, pp. 220–221.

Page 35   Table 2–5   From Rothbart, M. K. & Posner, M. I. (2006). Temperant, Attention, and Developmental Psychopathology. In D. Cicchetti & D. J. Cohen (eds.) Developmental Psychopathology, Vol. II Developmental Neuroscience. Copyright 2006. Reprinted by permission of John Wiley & Sons, Inc.

Chapter 3

Page 47   Table 3–1   Adapted from Plomin, 1994b.

Page 52   Figure 3–5   Based in part on Belsky (1980); Bronfenbrenner (1977); and Lynch & Cicchetti (1998).

Page 53   Figure 3–6   Based in part on Maccoby & Martin, 1983.

Page 55   Table 3–3   From English, 1998.

Page 55   Figure 3–7   Adapted from U.S. Department of Health & Human Services, *Child Maltreatment 2005* (Washington, DC, 2007.)

Page 58   Figure 3–8   Adapted from De Bellis, 2001.

Page 59   Figure 3–9   Adapted from U.S. Census Bureau, *Statistical Abstract of the United States: 1998, 2003* (118th and 123rd eds. And Current Population Survey, 2005) Washington, DC, 1996, 2003, 2005.

Page 60   Figure 3–10   From Hetherington, Bridges, and Insabella, 1998.

Page 62   "Delano: A Problematic Friendship" adapted from Hartup, 1996, p. 1.

Page 64   Figure 3–11   DeNavas-Walt, C., Proctor, B. D., & Lee, C. H., U.S. Census Bureau, Current Population Reports, P60–231. *Income, Poverty, and Health Insurance Coverage in the United States: 2005*, U.S. Government Printing Office, Washington, DC, 2006.

Page 65   Figure 3–12   From Evans, 2004.

Page 66   Figure 3–13   Based on Leventhal & Brooks-Gunn, 2000.

Page 67   "Anna: Ugliness in People's Hearts" Kozel, 1991, p. 35.

Chapter 4

Page 79   Figure 4–2   From Ramey, C. T. & Campbell, F. A. (1984). Preventive Education for High-Risk Children: Cognitive Consequences of the Carolina Abecedarian Project. *American Journal of Mental Deficiency,* 88, pp. 515–523.

Page 82   Figure 4–5   From Koegel, O'Dell, and Koegel (1987). A Natural Language Teaching Paradigm for Nonverbal Autistic Children. *Journal of Autism and Developmental Disorders,* 17, pp. 187–200. Reprinted by permission from Springer Science and Business Media.

Page 88   Table 4–4   Summarized from the Report from the Committee for Ethical Conduct in the Children Development Research. SRCD Newsletter (Winter 1990). Society for Research in Child Development, Inc., 2007. http://www.srcd.org.ethicalstandards.html.

Chapter 5

Page 94   Table 5–1   Reprinted with permission from the *Diagnostic and Statistical Manual of Mental Disorders,* Fourth Edition, Text Revision, Copyright 2000 American Psychiatric Association.

Page 94   "Kevin: Seeking a Diagnosis" adapted from Frances & Ross, 2001, pp. 8–11.

Page 95   Table 5–2   Reprinted with permission from the *Diagnostic and Statistical Manual of Mental Disorders,* Fourth Edition, Text Revision, Copyright 2000 American Psychiatric Association.

Page 98   Table 5–3   Adapted from Achenbach, T. M. & Rescorla, L. A. (2001). *Manual for the ASEBA School-Age Forms and Profiles.* Burlington, VT: University of Vermont, Research Center for Children, Youth and Families.

Page 102   "Alicia: An Initial Assessment" adapted from Schroeder & Gordon, 2002, pp. 49–50.

Page 109   Table 5–4   Adapted from Luciana, 2003.

Page 110   Figure 5–3   Adapted from Weisz, Sandler, Durlak, & Anton, 2005.

Chapter 6

Page 121   Table 6–1   Adapted from Achenbach, T. M. & Rescorla, L. A. (2001). *Manual for the ASEBA School-Age Forms and Profiles.* Burlington, VT: University of Vermont, Research Center for Children, Youth and Families.

Page 123   Table 6–2   Reprinted with permission from the *Diagnostic and Statistical Manual of Mental Disorders,* Fourth Edition, Text Revision, Copyright 2000 American Psychiatric Association.

Page 124   "Carlos: A Specific Phobia" adapted from Silverman & Moreno, 2005, pp. 834–835.

Page 125   Table 6–3   Reprinted with permission from the *Diagnostic and Statistical Manual of Mental Disorders,* Fourth Edition, Text Revision, Copyright 2000 American Psychiatric Association.

Page 125   Table 6–4   By permission of author Annette M. La Greca.

Page 127   "Louis: Social Phobia and Its Consequences" adapted from Silverman & Ginsberg, 1998, pp. 260–261.

Page 129   Table 6–5   Reprinted with permission from the *Diagnostic and Statistical Manual of Mental Disorders,* Fourth Edition, Text Revision, Copyright 2000 American Psychiatric Association.

Page 129   "Kenny: Separation Anxiety" adapted from Last, 1988, pp. 12–13.

Page 132   Table 6–6   Reprinted with permission from the *Diagnostic and Statistical Manual of Mental Disorders,* Fourth Edition, Text Revision, Copyright 2000 American Psychiatric Association.

Page 132   "John: Generalized Anxiety Disorder" Anothony, 1981, pp. 163–164.

Page 133   "Frank: Panic Attacks" adapted from Rapaport & Ismond, 1996, pp. 240–241.

Page 134   Table 6–7   Reprinted with permission from the *Diagnostic and Statistical Manual of Mental Disorders,* Fourth Edition, Text Revision, Copyright 2000 American Psychiatric Association.

Page 134 Table 6–8 Reprinted with permission from the *Diagnostic and Statistical Manual of Mental Disorders,* Fourth Edition, Text Revision, Copyright 2000 American Psychiatric Association.

Page 137 Table 6–9 Reprinted with permission from the *Diagnostic and Statistical Manual of Mental Disorders,* Fourth Edition, Text Revision, Copyright 2000 American Psychiatric Association.

Page 138 Figure 6–1 Adapted from De Bellis, "Developmental Traumatology: The Psychobiological Development of Maltreated Children and Its Implications for Research, Treatment and Policy," *Development and Psychopathology,* 13 (2001), pp. 539–564 © 2001. Reprinted with the permission of Cambridge University Press.

Page 139 Table 6–10 Adapted from Fletcher, 2003.

Page 141 Table 6–11 Reprinted with permission from the *Diagnostic and Statistical Manual of Mental Disorders,* Fourth Edition, Text Revision, Copyright 2000 American Psychiatric Association.

Page 141 "Stanley: The Marian Rituals" Rapoport, 1989, p. 84.

Page 141 "Sergei: Impairment in Functioning" Rapoport, 1989, p. 83.

Page 149 Table 6–13 Adapted from Kendall and Suveg, 2006.

Chapter 7

Page 158 Table 7–1 Adapted from Kazdin, A. E. (1989). Identifying Depression in Children: A Comparison of Alternative Selection Criteria. *Journal of Abnormal Child Psychology,* 17, pp. 437–454. Reprinted by permission from Springer Science and Business Media.

Page 159 Table 7–2 Reprinted with permission from the *Diagnostic and Statistical Manual of Mental Disorders,* Fourth Edition, Text Revision, Copyright 2000 American Psychiatric Association.

Page 159 Table 7–3 Reprinted with permission from the *Diagnostic and Statistical Manual of Mental Disorders,* Fourth Edition, Text Revision, Copyright 2000 American Psychiatric Association.

Page 160 "Nick: The Problems of Depression" adapted from Compas, 1997, pp. 197–198.

Page 162 Figure 7–1 From Hankin, Abramson, Moffitt, Silva, McGee, & Angell (1998). Development of Depression from Preadolescence to Young Adulthood: Emerging Gender Differences in a 10-Year Longitudinal Study. *Journal of Abnormal Psychology,* 107, pp. 128–140. © 1998 by the American Psychological Association. Reprinted with permission.

Page 162 Figure 7–2 Journal of Clinical Child and Adolescent Psychology by Kistner et al. Copyright © 2007 by Taylor & Francis Informa UK Ltd. Reproduced with permission of Taylor & Francis Informa UK Ltd.—Journals in the format Textbook via Copyright Clearance Center.

Page 170 "Mary: Family Interactions and Depression" adapted from Cummings, Davies, & Campbell, 2000, pp. 305–306.

Page 171 "Joe and Frank: Difference Outcomes" adapted from Cummings, Davies, & Campbell, 2000, pp. 299–300.

Page 171 Figure 7–4 Adapted from Ivanova & Israel, 2006.

Page 173 Table 7–4 Reprinted with permission from the *Diagnostic and Statistical Manual of Mental Disorders,* Fourth Edition, Text Revision, Copyright 2000 American Psychiatric Association.

Page 175 Figure 7–5 From Weisz, Thurber, Sweeney, Proffitt, & LaGagnoux (1997). Brief Treatment of Mild-to-Moderate Child Depression Using Primary and Secondary Control Enhancement Training. *Journal of Consulting and Clinical Psychology,* 65, pp. 703–707. © 1997 by the American Psychological Association. Reprinted with permission.

Page 177 Figure 7–6 From Rosselló & Bernal, 1999. "The Efficacy of Cognitive-Behavioral and Interpersonal Treatments for Depression in Puerto Rican Adolescents," from the *Journal of Consulting and Clinical Psychology,* 1999, Vol. 67, No. 5 pp. 734–745. © 1999 by the American Psychological Association, Inc.

Page 178 Table 7–5 Reprinted with permission from the *Diagnostic and Statistical Manual of Mental Disorders,* Fourth Edition, Text Revision, Copyright 2000 American Psychiatric Association.

Page 179 Table 7–6 Adapted from Geller et al., 2003.

Page 180 Table 7–7 Adapted from Kowatch, R. A. & DelBello, M. P. (2006). Pediatric Bipolar Disorders: Emerging Diagnostic and Treatment Approaches. Child and Adolescent Psychiatric Clinics of North American, 15, pp. 73–108. © 2006 Elsevier. Reprinted by permission.

Page 181 "Biopolar Disorder: The Need Support for Families" adapted from Hellander, Hisson, & Fristad, 2003, p. 314.

Page 181 "Joseph: Early Biopolar Symptoms" adapted from Egeland, Hostetter, Pauls, & Sussex, 2000, p. 1249.

Page 183 "Patty: A Suicide Attempt" adapted from Pfeffer, 2000, p. 238.

Chapter 8

Page 191 Figure 8–1 Adapted from Dishion, T. J. & Patterson, G. R. (2006). The Development and Ecology of Antisocial Behavior in Children and Adolescents. In D. Cicchetti & D. J. Cohen (eds.). Developmental Psychopathology, Volume Three: Risk, Disorder, and Adaption (2/E). Copyright © 2006. Reprinted by permission of John Wiley & Sons, Inc.

Page 192 "Henry: Preschool Oppositional Behavior" adapted from Schroeder & Gordon, 2002, pp. 374–376.

Page 193 Table 8–1 Reprinted with permission from the *Diagnostic and Statistical Manual of Mental Disorders,* Fourth Edition, Text Revision, Copyright 2000 American Psychiatric Association.

Page 193 "Jeremy: Oppositional Defiant Disorder" adapted from Spitzer et al., 2000, pp. 342–343.

Page 194 Table 8–2 Reprinted with permission from the *Diagnostic and Statistical Manual of Mental Disorders,* Fourth Edition, Text Revision, Copyright 2000 American Psychiatric Association.

Page 195 "Doug: Early Aggressive and Antisocial Behavior" adapted from Kazdin, 1985, pp. 3–4.

Page 195 Table 8–3 Adapted from Achenbach, T. M. & Rescorla, L. A. (2001). *Manual for the ASEBA School-Age Forms and Profiles.* Burlington, VT: University of Vermont, Research Center for Children, Youth and Families.

Page 196 Figure 8–2 Adapted from Stanger, C. et al. (1997). Accelerated Longitudinal Comparisons of Aggressive vs. Delinquent Syndromes. *Development and Psychopathology,* 9, pp. 43–58. Reprinted with the permission of Cambridge University Press.

Page 197 Figure 8–3 From Frick, P. J. (1998b). Conduct Disorders. In T. H. Ollendick & M. Hersen (eds.) *Handbook of Child Psychopathology* (3rd ed.). Reprinted by permission from Springer Science and Business Media.

Page 202 "Henry: A Victim of Bullying" adapted from Olweus, 1993, pp. 49–50.

Page 203 Figure 8–4 Adapted from Maughan et al., 2004.

Page 206 Figure 8–5 Reprinted from Loeber, R., & Hay, D. F. (1994). Interaction Between Conduct Disorder and Its Comorbid Conditions: Effects of Age and Gender. *Clinical Psychology Review,* 14, pp. 497–623 with permission from Elsevier Science.

Page 207 Table 8–4 Adapted from Loeber, R., & Farrington, D. P. (2000). Young Children Who Commit Crime: Epidemiology, Developmental Origins, Risk Factors, Early Interventions, and Policy Implications. *Development and Psychopathology,* 12, pp. 737–762. Copyright 2000. Reprinted by permission of Cambridge University Press.

Page 210 Figure 8–6 From Patterson, Reid, & Dishion, 1992. *Antisocial Boys.* Eugene, OR: Castalia Publishing Co.

Page 212 Figure 8–7 From Capaldi et al., 2002.

Page 216 Figure 8–8 Adapted from van Lier, P., Boivin, M., Dionne, G., Vitara, F., Brendgen, M., Koot, H., Tremblay, R., & Perusse, D. (2007). Kindergarten Children's Genetic Vulnerabilities Interact with Friends' Aggression to Promote Children's Own Aggression. *Journal of the American Academy of Child and Adolescent Psychiatry,* 46, pp. 1080–1087.

Page 217 "Rodney: Alcohol and Nicotine Use" adapted from Morrison & Anders, 1999, pp. 286–287.

Page 220 Figure 8–9 From Mayes, L. C. & Suchman, N. E. (2006). Developmental Pathways to Substance Abuse. In D. Cicchetti & D. J. Cohen (eds.). Developmental Psychopathology, Volume Three: Risk, Disorder, and Adaption (2/E). Copyright © 2006. Reprinted by permission of John Wiley & Sons, Inc.

Page 223 Table 8–5 Adapted from Kazdin, 1997.

Page 224 Table 8–6 Adapted from Querido, Bearss, & Eyberg, 2002.

Page 225 Table 8–7 Adapted from Kazdin, 1997.

Page 227 "Maggie: The Need for Multiple Services" adapted from Henggeler et al., 1998, p. 23.

Page 228 Figure 8–10 Adapted from Henggeler, S. W. et al. (1992). Family Preservation Using Multisystematic Therapy: An Effective Alternative to Incarcerating Serious Juvenile Offenders. *Journal of Consulting and Clinical Psychology,* 60, pp. 953–961. © 1992 by the American Psychological Association. Reprinted with permission.

CHAPTER 9

Page 233 Table 9–1 Reprinted with permission from the *Diagnostic and Statistical Manual of Mental Disorders,* Fourth Edition, Text Revision, Copyright 2000 American Psychiatric Association.

Page 235 Figure 9–1 Adapted from Dane, Schachar, & Tannock, 2000.

Page 239 "Jimmy: Combined Subtype and ADHD" from Hathaway, Dooling-Litfin, & Edwards, 2006, pp. 390–391.

Page 239 "Tim: Predominantly Inattentive Subtype of ADHD" from Hathaway, Dooling-Litfin, & Edwards, 2006, pp. 410–411.

Page 242 Figure 9–2 Adapted from Burke et al., 2005.

Page 244 Figure 9–3 Adapted from Shaw, Lacourse, & Nagin, 2005.

Page 246 Figure 9–4 From Barkley, R. A. (1997). Attention-Deficit/Hyperactivity Disorder. In E. J. Mash & L. G. Terdal (eds.) *Assessment of Childhood Disorders.* New York: Guilford Press. Reprinted with permission.

Page 248 Figure 9–5 Adapted with permission (from an illustration by Carol Donner) from Youdin and Riederer (1997). Understanding Parkinson's Disease. *Scientific American,* 276, pp. 52–59.

Page 251 Table 9–3 From Barkley & Edwards, 2006.

Page 251 Table 9–4 From Connors, 2008.

Page 255 Table 9–6 Adapted from Anastopoulos, Rhoads, & Farley, 2006.

Page 255 Table 9–7 From DuPaul, Guevrement, and Barkley in *The Practice of Child Therapy,* 2e, Kratochwill Morris. Published by Allyn and Bacon, Boston, MA. Copyright © 1991 by Pearson Education. Adapted by permission of the publisher.

Page 259 Figure 9–6 Jensen, P. S., Arnold, L. E., Swanson, J. M., Vitello, B., Abikoff, H. B., Greenhill, L. L. et al. (2007). 3-year Follow-up of the NIMH MTA Study. *Journal of the American Academy of Child and Adolescent Psychiatry,* 46, pp 989–1002. © 2007. Reprinted by permission.

CHAPTER 10

Page 263 "Thomas: So Many Abilities" Hinshelwood, 1917, pp. 46–47.

Page 263 Table 10–1 Based on Hallahan & Mock, 2003.

Page 267 Table 10–3 Based on Bryant 1997; Whitehurst, 1982.

Page 268 Table 10–4 From American Psychiatric Association, 2000.

Page 268 "Ramon: Phonological Disorder" adapted from Johnson & Beitchman, 2005c, p. 3151.

Page 269 "Amy: Problems in Language Expression" adapted from Johnson & Beitchman, 2005a, p. 3138.

Page 269 "Trang: Problems in Language Reception and Expression" adapted from Johnson & Beitchman, 2000b, p. 2642.

Page 270 Figure 10–2 Adapted from Taylor et al., 2002.

Page 272 Table 10–6 From American Psychiatric Association, 2000.

Page 275 Figure 10–1   Adapted from Retrospective Analyses of the Reading Development of Grade 4 Students with Reading Disabilities. By Lipka et al., (2006), pp. 364–378. *Journal of Learning Disabilities, 39.* Copyright 2006 by the Hammill Institute on Disabilities. Reprinted with permission.

Page 275 "C.J.: Writing, Writing, All Day Long" adapted from Tannock, 2005a, pp. 3126–3127.

Page 276 Figure 10–2   Adapted from Taylor, 1988.

Page 277 Figure 10–3   From Wong, Butler, Ficzere, & Kuperis, 1997. Teaching Adolescents with Learning Disabilities and Low Achievers to Plan, Write and Revise Compare-and-Contrast Essays. *Learning Disabilities Research and Practice*, 12, pp. 2–15.

Page 279 "Jenny: A Profilel of NVLD" adapted from Anderson et al., 2001, pp. 425–432.

Page 280 Figure 10–4   From Willcut & Pennington, 2000.

Page 283 Figure 10–6   Adapted from Shaywitz & Shaywitz, 2003.

Page 284 Figure 10–7   Based on Simos et al, 2002. Courtesy of J. M. Fletcher.

Page 287 Figure 10–8   From Taylor, H. G. (1989). Learning Disabilities. In E. J. Mash & R. A. Bankley (eds.) *Treatment of Childhood Disorders.* New York: Guilford Press. Reprinted with permission.

Page 289 Figure 10–9   From Lyon et al., 2006.

Page 291 Figure 10–10   *Students with Learning Disabilities*, 5/E by Cecil D. Mercer © 1997. Reprinted by permission of Pearson Education, Inc. Upper Saddle River, NJ.

CHAPTER 11

Page 296 Figure 11–1   Adapted from Luckasson et al., 2002.

Page 297 Table 11–1   Luckasson et al., 2002.

Page 297 Table 11–2   Reprinted with permission from the *Diagnostic and Statistical Manual of Mental Disorders,* Fourth Edition, Text Revision, Copyright 2000 American Psychiatric Association.

Page 299 Table 11–3   From Kirk, Gallagher, & Anastasiow, 2000.

Page 302 "Annalise: Profound Intellectual Disabilites" adapted from King et al., 2005, pp. 3084–3085.

Page 302 Table 11–4   Based on American Psychiatric Association, 2000; and Singh, Oswald, & Ellis, 1998.

Page 303 Figure 11–3   From Kirk, Gallagher, & Anastasiow, 2000.

Page 305 Table 11–5   Adapted from King, Hodapp, & Dykens, "Mental Retardation" from Kaplan & Saddock's *Comprehensive Textbook of Psychiatry.* © 2000 Lippincott, Williams and Wilkins.

Page 306 "Johnny: Unknown Cause of MR" adapted from King et al., 2000, p. 2599.

Page 306 Table 11–6   Adapted from Hodapp & Dykens, 2003.

Page 308 Table 11–7   From Luckasson et al., 2002.

Page 309 Table 11–8   Based on Aman, Hammer, & Rojahn, 1993; Bailey et al., 2000; Capone, 2001; Hodapp et al., 2006; Karminoff-Smith & Thomas, 2003; King, Hodapp, & Dykens, 2005; Moldavsky et al., 2001;

State, King, & Dykens, 1997; Volkman & Dykens, 2003; Whitman, O'Callaghan, & Sommer, 1997.

Page 310 Figure 11–4   Courtesy of the March of Dimes Birth Defects Foundation.

Page 311 Figure 11–5   American Journal of Mental Retardation by Blasey et al. Copyright 2005 by American Association on Intellectual Developmental Disabilities. Reproduced with permission of American Association on Intellectual Developmental Disabilities in the format Textbook via Copyright Clearance Center.

Page 312 "Robert: An Example of Williams Syndrome" adapted from King et al., 2005, p. 3082.

Page 318 Figure 11–6   Mental Retardation by Polister et al. Copyright 2003 by American Association on Intellectual Developmental Disabilities. Reproduced with permission of American Association on Intellectual Developmental Disabilities in the format Textbook via Copyright Clearance Center.

Page 319 "Brian: Life in the Mainstream" adapted from King et al., 2005, p. 3083–3084.

Page 322 Figure 11–7   Adapted from Newsom, 1998. Autistic Disorder. In E. J. Mash & R. A. Barkley (eds.) *Treatment of Childhood Disorders.* New York: Guilford Press. Reprinted with permission.

Page 324 Figure 11–8   Durand, "Functional Communication Training Using Assistive Devices: Recruiting Natural Communities of Reinforcement," *Journal of Applied Behavior Analysis*, 1999, 32, pp. 247–267, Number 3, Fall 1999.

CHAPTER 12

Page 328 Table 12–1   Reprinted with permission from the *Diagnostic and Statistical Manual of Mental Disorders,* Fourth Edition, Text Revision, Copyright 2000 American Psychiatric Association.

Page 329 Figure 12–1   Adapted from Dissanayake and Crossley, 1996. Proximity and Social Behaviours in Autism: Evidence for Attachment. *Journal of Child Psychology and Psychiatry*, 27, pp. 149–156.

Page 334 Figure 12–2   From Volkmar, F. R., Klin, A., & Schultz, R. T. (2005). Pervasive Developmental Disorders. In B. J. Sadock & V. A. Sadock (Eds.). *Comprehensive Textbook of Psychiatry*, Volume II. Copyright 2005. Reprinted by permission of Wolters Kluwer.

Page 334 "Temple Grandin: A Personal Account" Grandin, 1997, p. 1039.

Page 335 Figure 12–3   Two theory of mind tasks. From Baron-Cohen et al., 1999.

Page 336 Figure 12–4   From Happé, Briskman, & Frith, "Exploring the Cognitive Phenotype of Autism: Weak 'Central Coherence' in Parents and Siblings of Children with Autism: I. Experimental Test" *Journal of Child Psychology and Psychiatry*, Vol. 42, No. 3, pp. 299–307, 2001.

Page 339 Figure 12–5   From Madsen et al., 2003.

Page 340 Figure 12–6   Based on Szatmari et al., 2000.

Page 341 "Robert: Asperger's Disorder" adapted from Volkmar et al., 2000.

Page 342 Table 12–2 From F. R. Volkmar, A. Klin, and R. T. Schultz, "Pervasive Development Disorders" in B. J. Sadock & V. A. Sadock (eds.). Kaplan & Sadock's Comprehensive Textbook of Psychiatry, Vol. II © 2005. Reprinted by permission.

Page 343 "Bob: Childhood Disintegrative Disorder" adapted from Volkmar, 1996a, pp. 496–497.

Page 343 "Leslie: PDD-NOS" adapted from Volkmar et al., 2005, p. 3181.

Page 346 Table 12–3 Based on Koegel, Koegel, & McNerney, 2001.

Page 346 Table 12–4 Adapted from Lovaas & Smith, 2003.

Page 347 Table 12–5 Based on Schloper, 1997. Implementation of TEACCH Philosophy. In D. J. Cohen & F. R. Volkmar (eds.) Handbook of Autism and Pervasive Developmental Disorders. New York: John Wiley and Sons, Inc.

Page 349 Table 12–6 Reprinted with permission from the Diagnostic and Statistical Manual of Mental Disorders, Fourth Edition, Text Revision, Copyright 2000 American Psychiatric Association.

Page 350 Table 12–7 Adapted from Green et al., 1992; Russell et al., 1989; and Volkmar et al., 1991. Schizophrenia with Childhood Onset. A Phenomenological Study of 38 Cases. Journal of American Academy of Child and Adolescent Psychiatry, 31, pp. 968–976; and Russell, A. T., et al. 1989. The Phenomenology of Schizophrenia Occurring in Childhood. Journal of the American Academy of Child and Adolescent Psychiatry, 28, pp. 399–407; and Volkmar, F. R. 1991. Childhood Schizophrenia in M. Lewis (ed.) Child and Adolescent Psychiatry: A Comprehensive Textbook. Baltimore: Williams and Wilkins.

Page 350 Table 12–8 From Russell, Bott, & Sammons, 1989.

Page 352 "Mary: Developmental Course of Childhood Schizophrenia" adapted from Asarnow & Asarnow, 2003, p. 455.

Page 353 Figure 12–7 From Frazier, J. A., McClellan, J., Findling, R. L., Vitello, B., Anderson, R., Zablotsky, B., et al (2007). Treatment of Early-Onset Schizophrenia Spectrum Disorders (TEOSS). Demographic and Clinical Characteristics. Journal of the American Academy of Child and Adolescent Psychiatry, 46, pp. 979-88. © 2007 Reprinted by permission.

Page 354 Figure 12-8 Dr. E. Fuller Torrey and Dr. Weinberger/National Institute of Mental Health.

Page 357 Figure 12–9 From Bearden, C. E., Meyer, S. E., Loewy, R. L., Niendam, T. A., & Cannon, T. D. (2006). The Neurodevelopmental Model of Schizophrenia: updated. In D. Cicchetti & D. J. Cohen (eds.). Developmental Psychopathology, Volume three: Risk, Disorder, and Adaption (2/E). Copyright © 2006. Reprinted by permission of John Wiley & Sons, Inc.

Page 358 Table 12–9 Adapted from Asarnow, Tompson, & McGrath, 2004.

CHAPTER 13

Page 362 "Jay: Enuresis and Its Consequences" adapted from Ondersma & Walker, 1998, pp. 364–365.

Page 364 "Susan: Encopresis and Its Consequences" adapted from Indersma & Walker, 1998, pp. 371–372.

Page 367 Figure 13–2 From Snell, Adam, & Duncan, 2007.

Page 369 "Danielle: Sleepwalking" adapted freom Spitzer et al., 2000, pp. 337–338.

Page 370 Table 13–1 Adapted from Wilson and Haynes, 1985. Sleep Disorders. In P. H. Bornstein & A. E. Kazdin (eds.) Handbook of Clinical Behavior Therapy with Children. Homewood, IL: Dorsey.

Page 371 Figure 13–3 Reprinted from Muris et al., Children's Nighttime Fears: Parent-Child Ratings of Frequency, Content, Origins, Coping Behaviors and Severity, Behaviour Research and Therapy, 39 (2001) pp. 13–28 with permission from Elsevier Science.

Page 371 "Matthew: Recurrent Nightmares" adapted from Schroeder & Gordon, 2002, pp. 214–216.

Page 375 Figure 13–4 Adapted from Centers for Disease Control and Prevention, 2007.

Page 377 "Sean: Obesity and Family Environment" adapted from Israel & Solotar, 1988.

Page 378 Figure 13–5 From Israel, A. C. et al. (1994). An Evaluation of Enhanced Self-Regulation Training in the Treatment of Childhood Obesity. Journal of Pediatric Psychology, 19, pp. 737–749. Reprinted by permission of Oxford University Press.

Page 379 Table 13–2 Reprinted with permission from the Diagnostic and Statistical Manual of Mental Disorders, Fourth Edition, Text Revision, Copyright 2000 American Psychiatric Association.

Page 380 Table 13–3 Reprinted with permission from the Diagnostic and Statistical Manual of Mental Disorders, Fourth Edition, Text Revision, Copyright 2000 American Psychiatric Association.

Page 384 Figure 13–7 Adapted from Collins, 1991. Body Figure Perceptions and Preferences Among Preadolescent Children. International Journal of Eating Disorders, 10, pp. 199–208. This material used by permission of John Wiley and Sons, Inc.

Page 385 "Ida: A Sparrow in a Golden Cage" adapted from Bruch, 1979, pp. 23–24.

Page 387 "Gayle: Interpersonal Role Transitions" adapted from Tantleff-Dunn, Gokee-LaRose, & Peterson, 2004, p. 170.

CHAPTER 14

Page 392 "Loren: Managing Asthma" adapted from Creer, 1998, p. 411.

Page 394 Figure 14–1 Adapted from Wood, Lim, et al., 2007.

Page 396 Figure 14–2 From Wallander and Varni, 1998. Effects of Pediatric Chronic Physical Disorders on Child and Family Adjustment. Journal of Child Psychology and Psychiatry, 39, pp. 29–46.

Page 397 Figure 14–3 Adapted from LeBovidge, Lavigne, & Miller, 2005.

Page 397 "Lisa: Diabetes Management and Family Context" adapted from Johnson, 1998, pp. 428–429.

Page 402   Table 14–1   Adapted from Karoly & Bay, 1990.

Page 404   Figure 14–4   Adapted from Palmer et al., 2004.

Page 404   Table 14–2   Adapted from Thomas, Peterson, & Goldstein, 1997. Problem Solving and Diabetes Regimen Adherence by Children and Adolescents with IDDM in Social Pressure Situations: A Reflection on Normal Development. *Journal of Pediatric Psychology*, 22, pp. 541–561. Reprinted by permission from Springer Science and Business Media.

Page 405   "Cindy: Chronic Headache Pain" adapted from Powers, Jones, & Jones, 2005, p. 72.

Page 408   Table 14–3   Adapted from Dahlquist, 1992. Coping with Aversive Medical Treatments. In A.M. LaGreca, L. J. Siegal, J. L. Walander, & C. E. Walker (eds.) *Stress and Coping in Child Health*. New York: Guilford Press. Reprinted with permission.

CHAPTER 15

Page 415   Figure 15–1   From Geoffroy et al., 2007.

Page 416   Figure 15–2   Urban Institute for Calculations from the 1997 National Survey of America's Families. Capizzano, Tout, & Adams, 2000.

Page 419   Figure 15–3   From Allen & Bissell, 2004.

Page 422   Table 15–1   Adapted from Huang, L., Stroul, B., Friedman, R., Mrazek, P., Firesen, B., Pires, S., & Mayberg, S. (2005). Transforming Mental Health Care for Children and Their Families. *American Psychologist*, 60, pp. 615-627. © 2005 Reprinted by permission of the American Psychological Association, Inc.

Page 423   Figure 15–4   Data from *The State of the World's Children*, 2000, UNICEF, United Nations.

Page 425   Figure 5–5   From Ehntholt & Yule, 2006.

Name Index

Abed, Y., 424
Abela, J. R. Z., 167
Abikoff, H., 257
Ablon, S. L., 113
Abramavitz, A., 408
Abramowitz, J. S., 151
Abrams, D. M., 106
Abramson, L. Y., 162, 167
Abu-Akel, A., 351
Achenbach, T. M., 6, 14, 22, 63, 93, 97, 98, 99, 100, 103, 104, 121, 148, 163, 171, 194, 195, 196, 221
Ackard, D. M., 380
Ackerman, B. P., 279
Acosta, O. M., 200
Adair, L. S., 376
Adam, E. K., 367
Adams, G., 240, 280, 289, 416
Adams, R., 62
Adamson, L. B., 167
Adelman, H. S., 101
Adolph, K. E., 14
Adrien, J. L., 329
Ageton, S. S., 221
Agras, W. S., 387
Ainbinder, J. G., 86
Aitken, K. J., 337
Akshoomoff, N., 337
Alarcon, R. D., 97
Albano, A., 103, 120, 124, 125, 126, 127, 128, 130, 132, 135, 146, 147, 152
Albee, G. W., 112
Alderfer, M. A., 396
Alexander, F., 391
Alexander, J., 226
Algozzinne, B., 101
Allen, M., 419
Allison, D. B., 376
Alloway, T. P., 271
Alloy, L. B., 167
Alriksson-Schmidt, A., 395
Alsaker, F. D., 62
Alsop, B., 246
Altman, H., 357
Aman, M. G., 309
Amato, P. R., 59, 60, 61, 212
Ambrosini, P. J., 103

American Academy of Child and Adolescent Psychiatry (AACAP), 177, 178, 180, 182, 186, 203, 217, 222, 343
American Academy of Pediatrics, 42, 375
American Association on Intellectual and Developmental Disabilities (AAIDD), 313, 320, 322
American Orthopsychiatric Association, 14
American Psychiatric Association (APA), 3, 93, 100, 115, 122, 123, 125, 129, 132, 134, 136, 141, 148, 159, 191, 192, 193, 203, 204, 222, 233, 242, 268, 270, 272, 277, 278, 297, 304, 305, 306, 328, 333, 343, 349, 362, 363, 364, 365, 367, 370, 373, 374, 379, 380, 381, 382, 387, 388
American Psychological Association, 6, 17, 68, 80, 87, 200, 252, 254, 255, 257, 258, 345, 358
American Sleep Disorders Association, 367, 370
Amtmann, D., 275, 277
Anastasi, A., 105, 299
Anastasiow, N. J., 286, 303
Anastopoulos, A. D., 252, 253, 254, 255
Anders, T. F., 218, 366, 367, 372
Anderson, B. J., 403, 404
Anderson, C. A., 67, 208
Anderson, D. A., 279, 378
Anderson, J. C., 132, 161
Anderson, M., 298
Anderson, P. M., 376
Anderson, V., 10, 39, 43
Anderson-Fye, E. P., 383
Andrasik, F., 405
Andreozzi, L., 43
Andrian, C. A. G., 377
Aneshensel, C. S., 162
Angell, K. E., 162
Angold, A. C., 5, 6, 7, 10, 14, 85, 95, 96, 119, 122, 161, 163, 202, 204, 241, 339
Annas, P., 144
Anthony, J. L., 6, 132, 271
Anton, B. S., 109
Antrop, I., 246
Antshel, K. M., 236
Aos, S., 226, 227
Appiah, L., 43
Ariès, P., 10

Armbruster, P., 17
Armstrong, F. D., 401
Armstrong, T. D., 218
Arnold, L. E., 112, 345
Arsenio, W. F., 35, 36
Arthur, J. L., 199
Asarnow, J. R., 174, 351, 352, 353, 354, 355, 356, 358, 359
Asarnow, R. F., 352, 353, 354, 355
Aschenbrand, S. G., 130, 132, 149
Asher, S. R., 172, 213
Asperger, H., 327, 341
Atkinson, L., 314
Attia, E., 388
Attie, I., 383
August, G. J., 63, 233, 254
Austin, A. A., 119–120, 122
Awad, G., 345
Axelson, D., 178, 182
Axline, V., 114
Azar, S. T., 56, 57, 58

Babinski, L. M., 205
Bachanas, P. J., 401
Bagwell, C., 111, 237
Bailey, A., 337, 338
Bailey, D. B., 309, 311, 313
Baird, G., 343, 344
Baker, B. L., 315
Baker, J. E., 378
Baker, L., 270
Bakersmans-Kranenburg, M. J., 33
Balboni, G., 316
Balentine, A. C., 232
Balk, D. E., 411
Balla, D., 307, 316
Banaschewski, T., 108
Bandura, A., 14, 49, 149, 281
Barakat, L. P., 396
Baranek, G. T., 329
Barber, B. L., 59, 60, 61
Barber, J. G., 419
Barbosa, J., 241
Bardone-Cone, A. M., 384
Barenbaum, J., 423, 424
Barkley, R. A., 232, 234, 236, 237, 238, 239, 240, 241, 242, 243, 245, 246, 248, 249, 250, 251, 252, 253, 254, 255

Subject Index